IAN FLEMING

Also by Nicholas Shakespeare

Fiction
The Vision of Elena Silves
The High Flyer
The Dancer Upstairs
Snowleg
Secrets of the Sea
Inheritance
Stories from Other Places
The Sandpit

Non-fiction
Bruce Chatwin
In Tasmania
Priscilla
Six Minutes in May

IAN FLEMING

The Complete Man

NICHOLAS SHAKESPEARE

HARPER

An Imprint of HarperCollinsPublishers

IAN FLEMING. Copyright © 2023 by Nicholas Shakespeare. All rights reserved. Printed in the United States of America. No part of this book may be used or reproduced in any manner whatsoever without written permission except in the case of brief quotations embodied in critical articles and reviews. For information, address HarperCollins Publishers, 195 Broadway, New York, NY 10007.

HarperCollins books may be purchased for educational, business, or sales promotional use. For information, please email the Special Markets Department at SPsales@harpercollins.com.

Originally published in Great Britain in 2023 by Harvill Secker, an imprint of Vintage.

FIRST U.S. EDITION

Library of Congress Cataloging-in-Publication Data has been applied for.

ISBN 978-0-06-301224-0

24 25 26 27 28 LBC 6 5 4 3 2

TO MY FATHER –
JOURNALIST, DIPLOMAT, TRAVELLER

'My name's Bond – James Bond. I write books – adventure stories . . . When I said "stories" I didn't mean fiction. I meant the sort of high-level gossip that's probably pretty near the truth. That sort of thing's worth diamonds to a writer.'

FOR YOUR EYES ONLY

CONTENTS

INTRODUCTION

'Good evening, Mr Bond.'

QUEEN ELIZABETH II

'Mr Fleming,' she said in her deep voice, 'to me you're the epitome of the English cad.'

'Mrs Leiter, you're so right. Let's have a Martini.'

It became common for those who had not met Ian Fleming to take the hostile position of Marion Oatsie Leiter, who, on encountering him for the first time at a party on a warm evening in Jamaica, chastised Fleming for how he had treated her friend in an affair.

His niece Gilly says, 'I was only allowed to meet Uncle Ian when I was past eighteen because he was so dangerous. He'd had lots of women and drank too much, my mother said. She was appalled at his behaviour.'

Just as Graham Greene has been boiled down to 'sex, books and depression', so is Ian Fleming rendered into tabloid fat as a card-playing golfer who hits the road after whipping his wife, roaring home late at night in his Ford Thunderbird from Royal St George's golf course or Boodle's, fortified on a diet of Martinis, Turkish tobacco and scrambled eggs, before tip-toeing, slip-on shoes in hand, up the narrow staircase in Victoria Square, past Ann's smart guests, to his monastic top-floor bedroom, where, after first removing his polka-dotted bow-tie and navy blue Sea Island cotton shirt, he would lie with his blanket over his head listening to over-educated voices on the floor below snigger at his latest book.

This caricature still broadly holds, which is why I was wary when the Fleming Estate wondered if I might consider writing a new biography, with the promise of access to family papers that had not been seen before; in order to guarantee artistic integrity, it would be up to me to find a publisher.

xiii

But was there anything more to learn or say about Ian Fleming that had not been well told already? Furthermore, did I wish to spend four or five years in the company of this 'moody, harsh and withdrawn person, habitually rude and often cruel' – as even one of his best friends portrayed him. Oatsie Leiter groaned in response to yet one more question about what he had been really like, 'Darling, I think I'm about *out* of Ian Fleming.'

Like most baby boomers in Britain, America, Canada and Australia, I had grown up on James Bond. Yet about his creator, I knew no more than titbits picked up when interviewing one or two of his contemporaries.

Before deciding, I conducted a background check. I sought out Fleming's previous biographers. I spoke to his surviving family and friends. I looked out some of the new material that has appeared since the last major biography in 1995. And what I found is what you find when you dive deeper and then deeper. Under the jarring surface of his popular image I could see a different person.

A shining example, literally, of the uneasy contract between the public and private Fleming is the story about him flinging a squid at the novelist Rosamond Lehmann when she was staying at his home in Jamaica. In the version told by the writer Peter Quennell, Fleming did this to frighten Lehmann into leaving early since he was expecting the arrival of another lover. Lehmann's less well-known account sheds a more satisfying light on the story.

Lehmann came across the squid on the kitchen floor; Fleming had speared it, intending to have it for dinner. 'As I looked at it,' she recalled, 'I suddenly caught its eye. It seemed to stare at me, and I felt for some reason that this was a creature every bit as intelligent as we were and that it was suffering terribly. So I persuaded Ian to throw it back in the sea. He grumbled a bit and said, "How typical of a soft old pseudo-liberal like you. You may think nature is beautiful, but it is very cruel, very ruthless. Just you see. As soon as we throw the squid back in the sea, all the other creatures will go for it. Just you see." So we did throw it in, and it was quite extraordinary, for suddenly this odd, grey, inanimate creature began to light up in the water until it was quite phosphorescent. Then it swam away as we watched and Ian was completely speechless. It was an incident that I always meant to write a story about, but never have.'

As with the squid, so with its fisherman. The unsympathetic image I had formed from sideways glimpses of a prickly, self-centred bounder camouflaged another, more luminous person. This Ian Fleming, so far from having an unimportant desk job in the Second World War, had played a singular part in the war that he could never talk about, tantalising bits of which emerged in the novels that he started writing after this adventure was essentially over, but who also lived life to the full and had a wonderful laugh and, in the words of another friend, 'brought colour (and occasional fury) into the lives of countless others'. He broke the taboos of our time but not of his own, carrying on as if it were wartime – which perhaps, for Fleming, his life always was. For all his undeniable shortcomings, he was an unfailingly intriguing character who, as Leiter herself had been swift to recognise, was more than capable of being sympathetic, funny, vital, humane: of glowing. If he was not an unblemished paragon like his father, a war hero, neither was he the unpleasant, frivolous second son I had imagined. As in the story of the squid and the reassessment it begs, the new material – unpublished letters and diaries, declassified files, previously uninterviewed witnesses – sets off Fleming and his life in a new light that leads to new conclusions about the man.

You felt his presence on the page and, what is not so common for a writer, also in the room.

'I can see him walking through the door at Buscot into the tiny sitting room,' says his wife's niece Sara Morrison. 'He stops and puts his elbow on the upright piano on the right and tells us children to go to bed. He had an absolutely hypnotically attractive voice to a child, haunting and never raised, and everyone seemed to shut up when he spoke. I was rather intrigued by grown-ups' reaction to him. We all knew that something big had come into the room, and everyone jumped to.'

'He was rather good-looking to say the least of it,' says Fleming's stepson Raymond. 'In my mother's album there's a photo of him, and underneath she's written "Beautiful Ian".'

His American friend Ernie Cuneo has given us a pen-portrait of Fleming's sad, bony, 'fateful' features: 'a high forehead with a head of thick brown, curlyish hair, parted on the side and neatly combed over to the left. His eyes were piercing blue and he had a good, firm jaw.' The American journalist Dorothy Thompson sighed after meeting the young Ian Fleming in Kitzbühel: 'The moulding of those cheekbones.' His nose had been broken and repaired with a metal plate, giving him the look of a light heavyweight boxer. To Lady Mary Pakenham, the journalist daughter of the Earl of Longford, 'Ian was the best-looking man I have ever seen with a broken nose and a damned soul/fallen angel expression. He was taller than Peter, about five eleven, I imagine. Slightly round-shouldered, but with marvellous legs.' They were the smooth-muscled legs of a runner, 'with rather large calves', observed Cuneo, a former football star.

Then the voice. His stepdaughter Fionn remembers it as curiously light for a man. 'Because of the image of James Bond, you think you're going to get a deep baritone, but it's a lyric tenor.' She says: 'His voice surprised people.'

As did his physicality. 'Ian moved as quickly as a lizard,' said Mary Pakenham. 'If he got up to fetch a book, he would dart across the room in a flash. For older or slower people, it was exhilarating to have him about.'

Ivar Bryce met him first when Fleming was eight, knew him to the end of his life, and was still able to summon his 'magnetic, electrically charged personality' ten years after his death. 'The way he burst into a room, radiating enthusiasm for some never-before-thought-of project, the jollity and warmth of his language, his strikingly good looks even, make him seem so much more alive than most of us.' Bryce wrote in an unpublished account: 'I should not feel surprised, only overjoyed, if he were to come crashing in. "Why should you think I was dead?"'

This vitality was singled out by Noël Coward, whom Fleming chose to be his best man. 'Half of his world was fantasy. That was what made him such an enchanting person to be with. At any moment you would find yourself slap in the middle of this dream world of his and you would be carried along and it would be wonderful, and unlike being with anyone else.'

Lisl Popper first knew Ian Fleming in Austria in the 1920s. 'All the things people said about him later, about his gloom, melancholy, solitariness, frankly amaze me. He was exactly the opposite.'

Clare Blanshard was another dissenter. She had met Fleming in Ceylon in 1944, and went on to work for him at the *Sunday Times* in New York, and was the first to read his books. In one of 'the hilarious sessions we had over his manuscripts', Blanshard admonished him for being damagingly cavalier about his public image. 'I painted horrible pictures of the false "self" he was presenting to the world.'

The 'imbalance', as Blanshard saw it, of his private, generous, funny side, and the rude, brooding Fleming on formal display was captured in one of only two or three portraits of him, painted in 1962 by his friend Amherst Villiers. Fleming had paid £525 for the oil painting, which was used as the frontispiece in a limited edition of *On Her Majesty's Secret Service*, but 'Mr Fleming was of the opinion it was valueless', according to his secretary. Objecting to the 'doom-fraught eyes', he grumbled that it made him look like 'an aged Dracula or a young Somerset Maugham'. Eventually, it was to hang outside the gun room at his home in Wiltshire – with Fleming's face turned to the wall by his widow after his death.

Blanshard offered this tribute when asked to describe Fleming's truer face: 'It was his innocence, geniality, merriment, wonderful sense of humour . . . all that and his zest for extracting what cheer he could from the daily situation, & injecting joie de vivre into companions, that rendered him so attractive to be with. He was privately, almost secretly, generous-minded, and there was nothing petty about him.'

One of his most understanding lovers, Maud Russell, who had paid for Fleming's house in Jamaica, wrote in her diary: 'After being with I[an]. I always feel a more sensible, less petty and more courageous person.'

Old lovers went on loving him. Seven years after his death, Maud still had not forgotten his effect. 'Sometimes I think of Ian – mostly of his personality, his character & his innate kindliness.'

Kindliness is not the first characteristic that James Bond evokes, yet it is telling how often this word or something like it bobs up in connection with his author. Rosamond Lehmann had the briefest fling with Fleming in Jamaica, but essentially she felt the same – 'really he was a very kind person'.

It would be wrong to think this kindliness was directed exclusively at women. 'A ladies' man par excellence', said his wartime associate Peter

Smithers, Fleming was also that rare combination, 'a man's man if ever there was one'. Plenty of Fleming's other male colleagues attest to the generous and loyal stripe in his make-up. They also appreciated his humour, adopting Fleming's maxim: *When hungry in France and looking for a restaurant, always ask a fat policeman.* A feature that distinguishes his male friends is that, barring one or two garish exceptions, they are characters in the upright mould of his banking grandfather Robert Fleming: they are unlikely to have been duped by a cad.

'The inimitable and lovable Ian Fleming,' Denis Hamilton, his editor at the *Sunday Times* called him. Robert Harling, who worked with Fleming for 25 years: 'The most generous, least malicious, most merry yet most melancholy man I ever knew.' His lawyer Matthew Farrer says: 'If he said he'd do something, it would never have occurred to me he wouldn't. I'd trust him absolutely.' Fleming's cousin Lord Wyfold was adamant: 'Whatever you hear, if Ian had his last possession in the world and it was a dollar, and you needed a dollar, he would give it to you.'

Not that Fleming was someone to broadcast his deeds. He agreed with the Australian journalist Richard Hughes, to whom he had done an invisible good turn, that one of the great pleasures in life was 'to do good by stealth and have it discovered by accident'. A small example of his surprising concern for others is recollected by the son of Jock Campbell, chair of the company that bought Fleming's literary estate. Weeks before Fleming died, John Campbell, aged twenty-four, stayed with him in a small flat overlooking the golf course at Sandwich on the Kent coast. 'We were talking about shaving. I told him, "I still wet shave, I don't use electricity." That evening, I found a lovely old badger brush sitting beside my watch which I'd put on my bedside table.'

'Like him?' says the thriller writer Len Deighton, who met Fleming when writing the first of his two Bond screenplays. 'I'd go down on the knees and say prayers for his afterlife. Lord, yes.'

While many would find it easier to praise the exemplary character and all-round achievements of Fleming's outstanding elder brother, the poet John Betjeman felt otherwise: 'I like Peter, but Ian was a much kinder, nicer, more sensitive person.'

*

Kinder, and more important.

Fleming's blatant legacy is the fictional hero he created in his last dozen years, almost as an afterthought. This English secret agent has gone on to have a profound global impact on the culture of the twentieth century and thereafter, with the titles of his adventures and the names of his villains and heroines now in the lexicon. According to the historian Max Hastings, he remains known to peoples throughout the world, from western capitals to desert wildernesses of Arabia and icy wastelands of North America. 'It seems to me that whatever reservations we all have about Ian Fleming and Bond, today it is impossible to overstate their quite extraordinary influence in making something English seem important in the twenty-first-century world. James Bond has a stature to which no modern prime minister, nor royal, nor indeed anything can lay claim.'

The source of Fleming's notoriety was 'the fast-moving, high-living' character who was 'unrivalled in modern publishing history', according to the blurb of *The Man with the Golden Gun*,* the twelfth novel in the series, that was published a year after his death – by which time global sales of Fleming's books surpassed forty million.

This character needs no introduction. Like Paddington Bear or Winnie-the-Pooh, he enjoys universal appeal. Anywhere in the world, the five words 'The name's Bond. James Bond' are guaranteed to ignite a smile.

In the United States alone, James Bond has been invoked as a model by successive presidents, from John F. Kennedy and Ronald Reagan to George Bush, Jr. and Donald Trump, as if they believe he exists. 'James Bond is a man of honour,' said Reagan. 'Maybe it sounds old-fashioned, but I believe he's a symbol of real value to the Free World.'

Bond's ability to create myths and interest is undiminished. His con-tinuing purchase on our imagination astonished Fleming's last publisher at Cape, Tom Maschler. Shortly before his death in 2020, Maschler

* To differentiate between Fleming's novels and the films of the same name, the titles of novels are given in italics and of films in inverted commas.

protested, 'You can't open a newspaper without a reference to James Bond.'*

That no day passes without James Bond making a media appearance is a testament to the enduring power of his brand. But Bond is more than a commercial icon. Few of us appreciate, quite, the reach of his influence.

Like Fleming, who predicted electric cars in the 1950s and decried the environmental harm that petrol engines could do, James Bond was frequently ahead of the game. A champion of modernisation and the latest technology, he has acted as a lightning rod for three generations and their understanding of politics, culture and sex. As much as any president, James Bond helped establish our post-war attitude towards the United States, and our less positive image of Russia, whose present leader is characterised in the British press as 'this Botoxed Bond villain who won't sit at a table with other people. All that's missing is a trapdoor and a pool of sharks'. It is James Bond, discovered by sociologists in the 1960s and 1970s to hold an almost equal attraction for a female audience as for a male one, who was at the wheel of the sexual revolution in London in the Swinging Sixties, and, after that, pretty much everywhere else. He is an avatar for us all, says Dwight Macaulay, president of the Intrepid Society in Winnipeg, which honours the life of Fleming's Canadian spy chief, William Stephenson: 'Let's face it – every man has secretly wanted to be him, and every woman wanted to meet him.'

Not only to foreigners has Bond succeeded in promoting a seductive ideal of what it means to be British. He has done this most effectively to the

---

* A sample of headlines from the time bore this out:
  'The only character to marry James Bond' (*Times* obituary of Diana Rigg, 11 September, 2020)
  'Ian Fleming's family are shaken after vandals target the James Bond writer's grave' (*Daily Mail*, 29 September)
  'No Time to Die: Bond 25 pushed back again to spring 2021' (*Guardian*, 2 October)
  'Bikini worn by Dr. No Bond girl Ursula Andress set to sell for $500K' (*Daily Mail*, 7 October)
  'Subsea speedboat has echoes of 007' (*Times*, 13 October)
  'World's greatest collection of James Bond novels goes up for sale' (*Times*, 19 October)
  'Declassified Files Reveal a Possible Spy in Poland—Named James Bond' (*Wall Street Journal*, 23 October)
  'Jeffrey Epstein behaviour based on Bond pastiche' (*Sunday Times*, 25 October)
  'The legendary actor, 007 Sean Connery, has past [*sic*] on to even greener fairways' (Donald Trump, Twitter, 1 November)

British themselves. When we required an ambassador to represent us at the opening of the 2012 London Olympics, who did we pluck from the heavens to act as the Queen's bodyguard, in a cameo appearance watched by an estimated 1 billion people, but the one other Britisher to have enjoyed Her Majesty's fame (she had attended not a few of his premieres as well). Born fully formed in the year of her coronation and still going strong after her death, Bond is at the heart of the British subconscious, chosen to symbolise Britain not merely over the Cold War period, but into the twenty-first century. 'Who first introduced James Bond?' is Question 12 of 24 in the 2020 test for British citizenship.

In his most tremendous leap, Bond has managed to survive in our contemporary world as an emblem of Britain's vision of itself, despite the tidal shift in our notions of pluralism, diversity and sexual equality. He is an indissoluble force, who is tricksy enough to resist our best intentions, however diligently we work to refine our fantasies. He somehow continues to be 'a product of his era and a reflector of the times', to borrow Paul Gallico's phrase from 1961. However offensive he may appear to us, however much we might tire of him, outgrow him, or grow disenchanted, we find it impossible to escape him. He is a shorthand for something we have not yet fully resolved in ourselves.

Why has Bond endured? Eric Ambler, E. Phillips Oppenheim, Peter Cheyney, Mickey Spillane. Not one of the authors with whom Fleming was compared created a character who has continued to prosper against traditional gambling odds. An easy answer would be that the films were exceptionally popular. Yet could it not also be that they were only so popular because the character Fleming created was so unique and captivating, at once a hero of modernisation and yet a symbol of retrospective power? In this respect, Bond is like the gold Louis that Fleming observed in Monte Carlo: an out-of-date currency unaccountably still in use.

He came into his first burst of popularity in the depressing wake of the Suez Crisis – 'one of the most pitiful bungles in the history of the world, if not the worst', Bond tells Japanese agent Tiger Tanaka. Fleming's contemporaries recall Suez as a painful summation of the slow, grey post-war decade: a grim, unhealthy period characterised by too much smoking/drinking/bad food/currency restriction – no one had travelled, except in the army, for years – and a habitual silence about the Second World War (the historian Antonia Fraser did not know her husband Hugh had fought in the Battle of the Bulge until they were watching a film about it). Peter Fleming explains in *The Sixth Column*, the thriller he dedicated to Ian and published six months before *Casino Royale*: 'Almost any form of exciting fiction provided a welcome antidote to the restrictions and frustrations of life in England at that time.' Britain had lost an empire, yet all at once, through Bond, it discovered a different way of being reunited with the world.

Conceived as a post-war British fantasy, as a balm for a demoralised imperial power on its uppers, James Bond has evolved into an immaculate agent of escapism. The lower the sun has sunk on the empire that Bond was born into, the more radiant his glow.

As the Bond legend has grown, it has carried its own time with it. James Bond is a man of the moment who has made the moment last till now. Seven decades on, after a divided Britain battles to go it alone – again – and the latest Bond movie arrives to rescue the film industry, a new generation continues in a post-pandemic era, with war in Ukraine, to scan our porridge skies for that familiar St George-like figure to parachute in out of the blue. To save and distract us from the dragons that currently threaten; to restore to us an image that is likeable to ourselves and the rest of the world.

The same two questions are always on the mind of Dwight Macaulay when he sits on the edge of his movie seat in Winnipeg. How will Bond avoid annihilation, and who exactly is James Bond? 'Was he purely fictional, or was he based on a real-life individual?'

This last question perennially fascinates Fleming's legions of fans. It has been asked numerous times since 1953 and the publication of *Casino Royale*. How *did* Bond spring into being; what inspired this outrageously successful character?

How much Bond is a legend that has covered for his author is another ongoing controversy. To no trivial extent, Fleming modelled himself on John Buchan's fictitious hero Richard Hannay, whose favourite dictum was, 'If you want to hide something, put it directly under the light.' Bond's flamboyant reputation has long been Fleming's disguise, but it also led to what his first authorised biographer, John Pearson, called his 'terrible nemesis'.

We tend to think of John le Carré before George Smiley. With Fleming, it is the reverse, as if Bond's unstoppable waves of popularity have lapped back over the author, submerging him. More often than not, he is left out of the picture entirely, like the missing comma in the film 'From Russia with Love'.

'There are parasite ants that eat the host,' says Len Deighton. 'Fleming's book writing has been devoured by the films. There's this gigantic mass of interest in the Bond phenomenon and a smaller interest in Ian Fleming.'

Admiral John Godfrey was not the only one of Fleming's wartime colleagues to lament how the man himself had been 'overtaken by Bond' with little more 'than a screen of lampoons and parodies erected around him'; bluntly, 'Ian has disappeared'.

This elimination is all the stranger, and even now it is not possible to explain, because Fleming was a lot more substantial than his fictional character. In the assessment of CIA director Allen Dulles, 'It took a Fleming to create him.' No less a fan than the poet Philip Larkin praised the Bond books for being 'instinct with a personality much more complex, much more intelligent, much more imaginative than Bond's – the personality, in short, of Fleming himself'.

When all this is said, Fleming emerges as significant despite Bond and not wholly because of Bond. He was an influential figure in his own right, someone even world leaders wished to consult, who had a fascinating story to tell, but one that security concerns and a strong stripe of diffidence prevented him from writing. To simplify horribly, there would be no James Bond had Ian Fleming not led the life he did, but if Bond had not existed, Fleming is someone we should still want to know about.

The pre-Bond Fleming was a patriotic Scot who had lived in Austria, Munich and Geneva as Hitler was coming to power. He made a noteworthy contribution to the Second World War – and not only in organising covert operations in Nazi-occupied Europe and North Africa that helped to shorten the conflict. He was also one of a trusted few who were charged with trying to bring the United States into the fight, and worked to set up and then coordinate with the foreign Intelligence department that developed into the CIA. Following the Allied victory of 1945, he continued to play an undercover role in the Cold War from behind his *Sunday Times* desk.

Fleming's talent and business was to know the movers and shakers on close terms. Winston Churchill was a family friend: Fleming kept Churchill's framed obituary of his father on the wall beside his bed, and for the first eight months of the war he listened to the First Lord pace the floor directly above his desk. After the war, Fleming was on first-name terms with another Prime Minister, Anthony Eden, who stayed at his house in Jamaica during Britain's most serious post-war drama at the very moment when Fleming's wife Ann was embarking on an affair with the Leader of the Opposition.

Fleming was part of the tiny circle in the room when important decisions were made. After a visit to Washington in December 1953, he joked to Ernie Cuneo, who had worked in President Roosevelt's White House during the war, 'I spoke severely to the White House before leaving, and I am glad to see that Dulles and the President have acted so promptly on my advice.' Seven years later, Fleming had an intimate supper in Washington with a future American president and gave a bewitched Jack Kennedy the benefit of his wartime experience in suggesting how to deal with Fidel Castro.

Squashed around their dining-room table in London, Ian and Ann Fleming sat up to three times a week between the most influential political, cultural and social figures of the 1940s, 50s and 60s. It is not a stretch to say that Fleming formed the fascia of his class: elusive, at once separating and connecting, and serving a role that most people did not know existed but was fundamental at a time when his nation was engaged first in defending and then in healing itself.

Few better appreciated Fleming's worth than Cuneo, his rumbustious long-term associate, the New York lawyer, journalist, former quarterback for the Brooklyn Dodgers and Intelligence operative, who worked with him during and after the war. Three years older, twenty pounds heavier, 'all belly and bald head' according to John Pearson, Cuneo was Fleming's main source of information on America. Fleming once wrote to him: 'I am already vastly looking forward to some of those perspiring walks along the dusty Vermont lanes while I pick your brains for my books.' For Cuneo, dedicatee of *Thunderball*, research assistant for *Live and Let Die*, *Diamonds are Forever* and *Goldfinger*, and a superb talker with beguilingly brilliant eyes that made you forget his corpulence, 'the books of Ian Fleming plus the actual documentation of Ian Fleming's life add up to a fascinating three-dimensional study, a rare psychological compendium of the mind of the Twentieth Century man.'

Cuneo was unequivocal: Fleming was more than his books and plays a part more central to our understanding of his time than his avatar has allowed. Yet Cuneo was quick to accept that his friend of twenty-three years was also someone who did not like to be fathomed and shot off into other disguises if the attention was narrowed on him. 'Typical of twentieth-century artists, Ian Fleming was many people.'

It is not an exaggeration to say there were even more Ian Flemings than there are actors who have played Bond. Fleming's long-time editor William Plomer did not need to remind his listeners at Fleming's memorial service that he was 'not a man of single aspect', but of multiple, conflicting personalities. 'Thunderbird', 'Byron', 'Faust', 'Sir Tristam', 'Falstaff', 'Walter Mitty', 'Ibsen's Dora', 'B & B' (short for Blue shirt and Bow tie), 'Jocky' (as his father had called him), 'Iarn' (as he was called in America), 'the Colonel' (as Peter sometimes called him and as Ian sometimes called Peter, along with the interchangeable nickname 'Cracker', and an earlier nickname 'Turnip'), '17F' (as Ian was known in the war), 'the Commander' (as he was called in Jamaica), 'Frank Gray' (as he once or twice signed himself, as well as 'Cory Anan' and 'R. Coranville'), 'Fine Lingam' (Ivar Bryce's anagram of him, sketched on a French napkin). Then, as others saw him: 'boy scout', 'broken-nosed pirate', 'Roman emperor', 'Greek god', 'fallen angel', 'a bottlenecked figure with a large bum', 'a Holy Innocent', 'the Devil'. Not to omit how he variously presented himself: athlete, soldier, journalist, banker, stockbroker, book collector, publisher, Intelligence officer, thriller writer, clubman, scuba-diver, bridge-player, golfer.

Ian's last love, Blanche Blackwell, understood that he was 'a very private person because he was so many people'. He was so inward-looking that it was a challenge to know who he was – or thought he was. Ian told Noël Coward that on a visit to Bombay he had gladly autographed a book by him, and then in quick succession books by William Plomer, Stephen Spender and W. H. Auden. Not even then had Fleming begun to cover what Ann called 'the whole gamut of your vast range of Freudian moods'.

Fleming's only child Caspar was bipolar, a disorder now considered 'highly heritable'. Caspar's father was never consistent or predictable in his moods or relationships with people. 'There was a peculiar duality in this too,' said the Jamaican journalist Morris Cargill, who observed that Fleming was 'extremely fond' of the literary critic Cyril Connolly and very proud of his friendship. 'Yet time after time he would go on about, "that terrible shit Connolly".'

He liked to keep friends in separate compartments, perhaps suspecting what Clare Blanshard called their 'interminable ruminations about him'. No friend mulled over the enigma of Ian Fleming with more obstinate curiosity than Mary Pakenham, who complained that whenever you called on him 'you never quite knew what you would find because you never knew what mood he would be in' – on top of that, he was 'never, never the same two days running'. Pakenham wrote in her diary after another frustrating evening spent trying to work him out: 'Ian has *more* characteristics than anyone I know.' She watched with compassion how these characteristics 'warred with each other, and went on warring until the end'.

It means that virtually anything you can say of Ian Fleming, the opposite is true also.

Graham Sutherland: 'He was good on art.'

John Hayward: 'You never heard him mentioning a painting he really liked.'

Roald Dahl: 'Ian adored money.'

Ivar Bryce: 'Money really wasn't important to Ian. All he really wanted were cars, movement, books, cigarettes and a few antiques.'

Ann Fleming: 'He was most emphatically not a snob.'

Sean Connery: 'A real snob.'

Edward Merrett: 'I never saw him lose his temper.'

Peter Quennell: 'When the Commander really became annoyed he would appear like an angry Aztec idol.'

Ralph Arnold: 'He was completely and utterly irresistible to women. He was the only man I have known who really was.'

Mary Pakenham: 'Nine out of ten women couldn't stand him.'

Raymond O'Neill: 'I always saw Bond as Ian.'

John Godfrey: 'Ian hadn't the remotest resemblance to James Bond.'

And so on.

He was lazy yet never stopped working; a playboy puritan who never stopped punishing himself; a deep melancholic who never stopped laughing. ('There's never been anyone could make me laugh quite so much as Ian,' said Noël Coward, 'we just laughed and laughed until it hurt us.') Easily bored, he sought the company of bores. ('Ann,' he used to say, 'but I *love* bores.') He was a life-enhancer at one moment, a killjoy at another. At night, a whip-wielding sadist; by day, according to Joan Saunders, who worked with him at the Admiralty, 'the least violent man I have ever known'. A loner who needed a group. An ultra-conservative who was a non-conformist. A man of iron routine who craved excitement and change to an unnatural degree. And after forty-three years of living and sparring with all these versions of himself and more, a confirmed bachelor who then married his opposite.

He listed himself in *Who's Who* as 'author and publisher', and the first item under his recreations was 'First editions' (followed by spearfishing, cards and golf). Among the myriad things I never knew about him was that in one of his compartmentalised identities he had owned and directed not only the Queen Anne Press, but also the leading bibliographic journal, the *Book Collector*; and long before that, he had himself been a dedicated collector of rare books.

An image that stays is the description by one of Fleming's girlfriends of his grey-painted bachelor studio in Ebury Street before the war: the forbidding volumes, each in its fleece-lined black box embossed in gold with the Fleming coat of arms, but with the pages inside showing no indication of having been touched. She had the sudden insight that he himself was like a rare first edition, yet to be read or understood by its collector.

So is Ian Fleming to us. For all that we feel we know him, this ultimately popular author remains unread in unexpected ways.

Mike VanBlaricum is the founder and president of the Ian Fleming Foundation, and the world's leading collector of 'the writings by and about Ian Fleming and the entire James Bond phenomenon'. After forty years of immersing himself in Fleming and his work, VanBlaricum still considers him an enigma. 'A mystery remains how a single individual, through the life he had led, changed popular culture. After he wrote the books, everyone knows what happened. But what was in his life to 1952, until he started putting that stuff on paper?' Deep in his masonry, in the deepest reaches of the books, articles, theses, symposiums, TV dramatisations, films and headlines that Fleming continues to generate a lifetime after his death, there is a genuine and still unresolved inner puzzle.

Fleming's public reputation is undercut by the testimonies of those closest to him. That said, he never fully revealed himself to anyone, and even with his friends was guarded about his true feelings, motivations and thoughts. 'Ian's basic complication in life was just communicating with people,' said Ann. Few managed to swim near enough to crack that 'puzzling' personality and understand how who he was and how these tensions within him led Fleming to impact popular culture to the degree that he has. Fleming's wartime chief, Admiral Godfrey, who oversaw one of the most effective Intelligence organisations in the world, was astounded by 'how very little I knew about a man with whom I had worked so closely for four years.' Godfrey said, 'he might have known my best friend but he would never have told me.'

His favourite position was to stand at the edge, or to sit alone at a corner table watching others. Whatever he was thinking, he kept it to himself. 'I've never known anyone who gave so little of himself away,' wrote John Pearson.

The mask reveals more than the face. For Cuneo, this aphorism captured 'in the truest and kindest sense, James Bond, Fleming himself, and the different postures he took with his widely varied friends. Ian's masks were not those of deceit: they covered wounds, early wounds, of great depth and pain.'

On the other hand, Fleming's schoolfriend Hilary Bray speculated that he might have solved the answer to life's riddle: 'I sometimes think it strange that ILF with his, at times, distant focus as upon some clue to life that lay beyond the horizon, had within himself and used only for others, the true philosopher's stone. This was the imprisoned splendour.'

The Royal portable on which he started to type out his first Bond story in Jamaica had a meaningful association for Fleming that the typewriters of his fellow novelists Graham Greene and John le Carré did not. They, like Bond, had been minor players in British Intelligence. Fleming was in the inner sanctum of the 'central inaccessible citadel', as Admiral Godfrey called it – and a more significant figure in the history of covert operations than Bond, Greene or le Carré ever were. Ian and his brother Peter formed part of an unbelievably select group who were cleared to know the war's top secrets, the decrypts from the code-cracking centre in Bletchley Park in Buckinghamshire: in April 1940, the list of those with access to this information, known as ULTRA, was restricted to less than thirty.

Ian Fleming's portable Royal resembled nothing so much as the cipher-generating Geheimschreiber typewriter G–292 that Fleming's commandos seized in Algiers in November 1942, assisting cryptanalysts at Bletchley to read Abwehr Enigma traffic passing between North Africa, France and Germany.

As he began typing on that February day in 1952, the words that had been accumulating for a decade clattered out in a rush – two thousand by the end of that morning – his old typewriter taking him back to the shadow world of the 1930s and 1940s in which Fleming had operated as a free agent; a world of secrets that he had helped to decipher but was forbidden to reveal.

In a Borges riddle to which the answer is 'knife', the only word that may not be used is 'knife'. The most basic principle of Enigma – no letter could be encrypted as itself. If you press the letter 'I', it is the one letter that will not light up on the lamp board.

In a hut at Bletchley Park, I type the letters IAN FLEMING on a three-rotor Enigma machine. It scrambles the name into what reads like a shorthand for titles of further novels he might have written had he lived longer. This biography's mission is to unscramble him back, decode him, and maybe solve the enigma of NVP TGLPYUM.

PART ONE

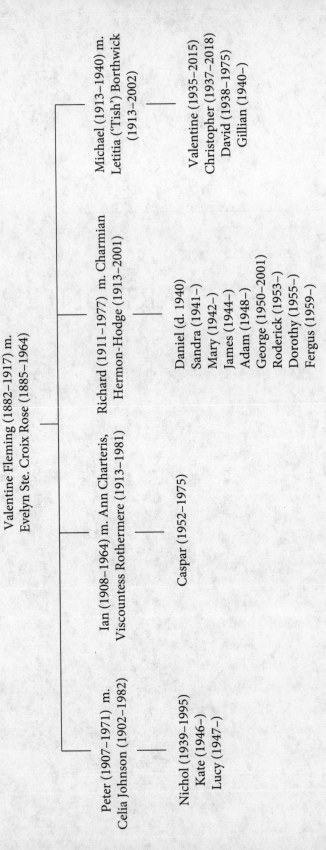

FLEMING FAMILY TREE

Valentine Fleming (1882–1917) m.
Evelyn Ste. Croix Rose (1885–1964)

Peter (1907–1971) m.
Celia Johnson (1902–1982)

Ian (1908–1964) m. Ann Charteris,
Viscountess Rothermere (1913–1981)

Richard (1911–1977) m. Charmian
Hermon-Hodge (1913–2001)

Michael (1913–1940) m.
Letitia ('Tish') Borthwick
(1913–2002)

Nichol (1939–1995)
Kate (1946–)
Lucy (1947–)

Caspar (1952–1975)

Daniel (d. 1940)
Sandra (1941–)
Mary (1942–)
James (1944–)
Adam (1948–)
George (1950–2001)
Roderick (1953–)
Dorothy (1955–)
Fergus (1959–)

Valentine (1935–2015)
Christopher (1937–2018)
David (1938–1975)
Gillian (1940–)

PROLOGUE

'Will you be staying long, Mr Bomb?'

GOLDFINGER

Organised in haste, the service is about to begin.

It is a cool and cloudy Saturday afternoon in August 1964 in the Wiltshire village of Sevenhampton. Inside the dimly lit church of St James', the congregation of less than twenty suggests the funeral of an unremarkable local everyman and not a figure whose name is known worldwide. Most of the pews are empty.

Ann Fleming ought to be seated by now. But she is still escorting her late husband's coffin across the lawn to the lake and up through the chestnut avenue to the church.

News of Ian's death at fifty-six reached his younger brother Richard at the family estate in west Scotland three days earlier. Richard was in the dining room at Glen Etive in his kilt, eating his salted porridge standing up, and preparing to set out with his shotgun on Rannoch Moor in a vast line of dogs and cousins, when the lodge's single telephone rang in the gun room. The black Bakelite phone sat on a worktop in a cold, narrow space smelling of gun oil. After putting down the receiver, Richard announced that he had to return to England and catch the sleeper. 'He didn't say anything about Ian dying,' remembers his daughter Mary. 'He didn't say anything at all.'

It was a Fleming trait to give away little of yourself. Peter was staying for the start of the grouse season 150 miles away in Dumfriesshire with the Keswicks. The call came after breakfast. Without a word, Peter stepped out of the house. He returned minutes later and, not wishing to spoil the shooting, said nothing until evening, then set off south.

3

Hilary Bray made both calls from his home in Kent. Ian's old school-friend lived not far from the golf course in Sandwich where Ian collapsed following a weekend at his cherished Royal St George's club. His famous last words to the ambulance attendants taking him to Canterbury Hospital: 'I'm sorry to trouble you chaps'. He was pronounced dead at 1.20 a.m. the next day. As well as the start of the grouse-shooting season, it was his only child Caspar's twelfth birthday.

After telephoning Richard and Peter in Scotland, Bray assumed responsibility for 'the many details arising on Ian's death'. He gathered up Ian's personal effects – 'none of which comprise anything of exceptional value' – and paid for six copies of his death certificate and the funeral arrangements.

The funeral takes place at Ian's parish church on the boundary of his country home near Swindon; following extensive renovations, he and Ann had moved in the previous summer.

In the chill interior, the gas lights flicker over the sombre faces. Among those seated in the front pew are Ian's twenty-nine-year-old nephew Valentine Fleming, son of Ian's youngest brother Michael who died of his wounds after Dunkirk. Next to him sit Valentine's wife Elizabeth; his sister Gilly and their mother Tish. 'A terribly nice wee church,' Valentine wrote afterwards in his diary, 'with ancient stove in one corner, crumbling roof, and individual gas lights for each pew.'

Where is Ann?

It would hurt her that 'not one of my family offered to come'.

Among other glaring absences are Ian's ostracised last love, Blanche Blackwell; his stepdaughter Fionn, pregnant in Brazil; his son Caspar and Ann's thirteen-year-old nephew, Francis Grey, who have been kept in London.

No photographer captured Ian's marriage to Ann at his Jamaican home twelve years previously. Nor is there anyone to take pictures on this occasion. This is owing to the far-reaching Fleet Street connections of Ian's widow, whose previous husband owned the *Daily Mail*, and of the deceased, who had served fourteen years as Foreign Manager of the *Sunday Times*.

The only press to disregard the family's request for privacy are two local journalists from Swindon, who lurk about the grave 'looking rather like detectives', in Elizabeth's recollection, as they wait outside for the coffin to materialise. The scoop hinted at by one of the reporters is preserved in a single line of the *Wiltshire Gazette and Herald*: 'Mrs Fleming with others walked to St James Church, arriving three minutes late after the service had begun.'

'A sad Service.' Valentine's spare diary entry is typical of the family's restraint about all things personal, but it fails to register the drama that was unfolding right in front of him and has never been recounted.

Even though six decades have passed, Valentine's wife and sister have a searing recollection of the incident that took place moments before Ann Fleming, distraught and on medication, walked in behind the coffin to find the service already under way.

At the appointed time, the local vicar, the Revd Edward Burnley, had raised his eyes to the front pew, and mistaking Valentine's mother Tish for Ann, stood up to perform the ceremony.

'He'd never read a James Bond book' is how Gilly makes sense of it. 'He knew so little about Ian that he couldn't even recognise the widow. He didn't know she wasn't there.'

'I was looking to see where Ann was,' remembers Elizabeth. 'One was so gripped that the service started without her, it was surreal. "We are all gathered together," and we weren't gathered together at all – and then she appeared and came up the aisle, and everyone slightly gasped.

'The vicar then stopped everything, and we regrouped, as one might say, *and the service had to start again.*'

As in life, so in death, a strong woman had played a defining role.

Susan Woolliams once lived in the stables at Sevenhampton Place, where Ann employed Susan's father as a driver. Susan's grandson Corey today works as a groundsman on the estate. 'I saw an otter the other day, only the one,' says Corey. 'I spotted him on a bank and I was walking the dogs and he swam with us and came on down so far and then he swam off.'

After visiting the family plot where Ian, Ann and Caspar are buried, next to the house cleaner Joan Prew, we head back to the house. This is the path that Fleming's mourners would have taken, following the ceremony, for a very English 'cup of tea'. As we walk towards the lake, Susan says: 'You read a lot of things about Ian Fleming, and you don't know what's true and what isn't.'

Nearly sixty years after Fleming's private burial in the aptly named churchyard of St James', there are ample and legitimate reasons to go right back to the beginning; to turn the soil of his personal history and revisit his legacy from a contemporary perspective.

I
'LAIRN TO SAY NO, LADDIE'

'Very strange people the Flemings.'
NOËL COWARD

On a journey through China, Peter discovered that 'Fleming' could be trans-literated into Chinese as *Fu Lei Ming*, meaning 'Learned Engraver on Stone'.

In *State of Excitement*, a short book about Kuwait that the Kuwait Oil Company commissioned Ian to write in 1960 but never published, Ian poked fun at an imaginary British nouveau riche family who, having won the pools, are desperate to etch a name for themselves. 'They become fool-ishly rather ashamed of their lowly origins and decide that, for social reasons, they would like to invest their name and their family firm with some of the trammels of high birth . . . Becoming enthusiastic they visit the College of Arms and pay for further researches into their past, at the same time acquiring a modest coat of Arms.'

This described Ian's great-uncle John Fleming, Lord Provost of Aber-deen, who, in 1900, gazed up at the ceiling of his council chamber 'upon which were emblazoned the arms of many town and county families' and thought he should like his arms among them.

Not to be outshone, in 1921, Ian's grandfather Robert Fleming was pres-sured by his wife Kate for a coat of arms with the head of a goat and the clan motto, *Let the Deed Shaw*. The legend refers to the fourteenth-century Rob-ert Fleming who held up the dripping head of John 'Red' Comyn, whom he had slain in a church. Ian chose the motto for his bookplate.

Ian was more loyal to his Scottish background than snobbish about it. 'Alas, I am very unfilial and lacking in ancestor worship,' he wrote to a woman in Cyprus who claimed kinship. To another enquirer, 'I am no rela-tion of any medical Fleming – not even of Sir Alexander.' He joked to the book collector, Percy Muir: 'We're not Scots. We're Flemings. A lot of nasty old Dutch merchants.'

By Ian's time, the Flemings were understood as posh and rich. Alaric Jacob joined Reuters at the same moment as Ian and recalled visiting Eve Fleming's home in Cheyne Walk, where she lived with her four sons in some opulence. 'To see them all together in their magnificent house in Chelsea was to see a microcosm of what the English ruling class ought to look like but rarely does – epicene yet forceful, well exercised in body and in mind . . . Yet the wonder was – they were all of very humble origin indeed.'

Ian's mother was an exceedingly snobbish woman, who, while claiming Highland ancestry, used to tell her daughter Amaryllis that 'the Flemings were a dreadful lot of lowland Scots'. Mary Pakenham was shocked when a friend ticked her off 'for consorting with someone as common as Peter Fleming'. Peter would not have disagreed. 'My grandfather's upbringing was humble in the extreme.'

On one of their railway trips across America, Ian mused to Ernie Cuneo: 'Men are like elephants. They go home to die. Someday,' waving a hand, 'I guess I'll just go back to Scotland.'

Ian was about to set out on his return journey when he suffered his final heart attack in August 1964. He had told the American ambassador, David Bruce, one of the last people he spoke to, that he planned 'to revisit the scenes of his youth'.

'You can't go back to anything,' Ian said to Cuneo. 'But something calls you to the neighbourhood of your people's place. It's a mystique.'

Dundee was his people's place. He was interested at once in anyone who knew the city – like the CIA's head of Counterintelligence, James Angleton. 'Talking about Dundee was one of the easiest ways of communicating with Fleming.' In New York, Ian would stay with the Bryces, whose head house-maid, an elderly, eccentric Dundonian, May Maxwell, 'coddled him with adulation for his Scottishness – a sentiment that he fully returned.'

'I am Presbyterian and Scotch,' he insisted to Maud Russell. He put 'Scottish' as his nationality when he briefly worked for the League of Nations in Geneva, and later, on his CV: 'Born May 28th 1908 of Scottish parents.'

That northern blood was on his mother's side too: her Rose grandfather had married into a family originally from Bothkennar in Stirlingshire that traced itself back to 1543. When not furiously claiming descent from John of Gaunt, she told her sons, 'Remember you're Scots.' Ian never forgot. Their son Caspar was two when Ann wrote, 'Ian is determined that he should wear some curious tartan that belongs to his mother's clan!'

Scotland was stitched into Ian Fleming's fabric as it was into James Bond's. 'That's where I come from,' says Bond, explaining his reason for turning down an honour in a telegram to 'M': 'EYE AM A SCOTTISH PEASANT AND WILL ALWAYS FEEL AT HOME BEING A SCOTTISH PEASANT OHOHSEVEN.'

Ian Fleming was the son of wealth, but the grandson of poverty. He is proof of how mobile society was then. Robert Fleming's father John never earned more than £1 a week. Still, Robert managed in one generation to be, from nothing, one of the wealthiest men in Europe, with a grand house in Grosvenor Square that was later knocked down to be replaced by the American embassy, a 2,000-acre country estate at Nettlebed near Henley employing twenty-seven gardeners, a huge Scottish shooting and fishing estate in Argyllshire, and a merchant bank named after him. 'By 1928, he was controlling in today's money maybe a trillion pounds,' calculates one of his several descendants to work for Robert Fleming & Company. 'He had a colossal influence.' The great difference between Robert's wealth and that of the landed aristocracy, who were much wealthier on paper, was that *his* was 'ready' money.

In his drawing room in Oxfordshire, beneath a small oil painting of Loch Dochart on Black Mount, his Scottish estate ('my favourite place'), I ask the former chairman, Robert's last surviving grandchild Robin Fleming, and the head of the family, to what extent he and his first cousin Ian had absorbed the founder's ethos and character. He answers with tremendous care: 'One probably did think he left a culture, a way of doing things, that one subconsciously inherited.'

An earlier chairman had been Ian's younger brother, Richard. Sir Claude Hankes was at a meeting where two Americans tried to offer 'some incredible opportunity' to the bank. 'When they finished, he said, "I'm afraid I'm not interested." "But you were writing everything down." "Yes," and he turned the notepad for them to see "NO" twenty times.'

Richard's daughter Mary says: 'I come from rather a clannish Scottish family, from someone who made a lot of money, came south and crashed the class barrier, which is easier to do if you're Scottish and talking in a very Scottish accent, and whose explanation for his success was "Lairn to say No, laddie."' This had been Robert's response to a young thruster wanting to know the secret behind his achievement.

Robert Fleming is of central importance in his grandson's story. Not only for the example he set and for those aspects of his character that Ian inherited, but crucially for what Ian did not inherit. Richard's eldest son James says: 'Ian was much influenced by the wealth that wasn't his.'

The first Flemings came over in 1066 with William the Conqueror from Flanders and migrated north out of Devon. A Theobald the Fleming (*Theobaldus Flamaticus*) appears in Kelso in the twelfth century. Further Flemings emigrated from the Low Countries in the fourteenth century to teach the English and Scots the art of weaving, bringing with them the epigram 'Forgetful of feeling as a Fleming'.

Robert's family emerges from the mists of east Perthshire in the early nineteenth century, as crofters, poachers and whisky smugglers in the village of Glen Shee near Kirkmichael, to which the young Robert would return at weekends. Before Robert's crofter grandfather, who spoke Gaelic when he did not want his children to understand, everything is supposition.

In 1928, Robert Fleming donated a sizeable endowment to Dundee, equivalent to £12 million today, to build accommodation for single women working in the mills. He did not want their children to grow up as he had.

Robert's first home was a two-roomed rented cottage in Liff Road, Lochee, west of Dundee; the other room was rented out to workers from the flax mill below. He was born in 1845 in the wake of tragedy. In 1843, his three siblings, James, Betsy and Annie, died within a fortnight, all under the age of five. Ian's niece Gilly says: 'I saw the children's grave in the churchyard at Kirkmichael. You will cry. Diphtheria.' In 1847, Robert's mother, Ann, had another son, John, and then two more children, James (named for his dead brother) and Jean, who lost their lives during a second epidemic in 1859. Deranged with grief, Ann died the following year. All Robert knew growing up were ghosts and death and heartbreak.

Widowed, John took consolation in God and temperance. In 1868, he published a book on what he had learned about the jute industry: *The Warping Overseer's Assistant, or a short and simple method of finding the length, breadth, weight and quantity of yarn in any chains with tables and practical remarks*. If James Bond has a literary lineage, it can be traced in part to this pamphlet, which ran into five editions.

Of the two of his seven children to survive, John, his namesake, entered the wood trade, selling timber for boats in the herring boom, and then on to become a knight, Lord Provost of Aberdeen and MP for Aberdeen South; Robert, the eldest, left school at thirteen and followed his father into the jute business. Robert scarcely saw his brother John again after they set off on their separate paths. This was a Fleming characteristic: to be clannish but not intimate. Other characteristics include the inherited tone of voice (Peter's wife Celia wrote to him in India after meeting Ian in London, 'The back of his neck is like yours and the way he speaks'). The solitariness.

Robert's next years are hazy. For a man whose motto was *Let the Deed Shaw*, he was reticent to an extraordinary degree. 'If there is one thing I hate above everything, it is to hear that I have been quoted.' His life has to be woven together from glimpses and eavesdroppings.

He could not hide his physical toughness and stamina, also Fleming characteristics. Ian's athletic genes come from him. Robert walked eleven miles on a Monday morning from the family farm at Glen Shee to Blairgowrie to catch the 9 a.m. train to Dundee, on one occasion 'at an average of 11 and half minutes to the mile'. He excelled at rowing, winning the double skulls at the Newport Regatta three years in a row. Inheriting his skill, his two sons Valentine and Philip went on to row in the Eton VIII and for their Oxford colleges, racing at Henley, an achievement crowned by Philip winning a gold medal in the 1912 Stockholm Olympics. 'The emphasis on physical exercise has persisted into my generation,' says James Fleming. 'Keep going till it's done, don't give in. Guests at Glen Etive, where the hills are sheer, were 100 per cent expected to follow suit. It was always said that "the hills were white with the bones of the Flemings' guests."'

Robert was bright. At Brown Street Elementary School, he discovered a talent for arithmetic. James says, 'The real secret to his success is that he had one of those brains that can make instant calculations in the days when there were no machines to do the adding for you.'

Owing to its jute and flax industries, Dundee was thriving. The fabrics came from Scottish-managed plantations near Calcutta. Shipped back to spinning mills and flax factories in and around Dundee, they were turned into sails for ships like HMS *Victory*, and sandbags for the American Civil War. By 1862, 700 tons of jute bagging and linens were leaving Dundee each week for the United States. Dundee merchants such as Cox Brothers and Edward Baxter & Son made enormous profits. But where to invest them?

Robert Fleming found the solution.

By the time he was thirty, Robert was the leading British financier in his field: a tall, lean, upright figure, with a large moustache and an 'oary' Dundee accent that he never shed. 'It was a wonder people could understand him,' says James. Just how he ascended the rungs from Dundee office boy to everyone's favourite investor on both sides of the Atlantic, consorting with the most famous bankers in the world, eluded his biographer Bill Smith; 'throughout his life, he was very sparing with details of his career. In his business affairs he laid great stress on utmost confidentiality.'

In the Netflix drama *Succession*, Logan Roy is a Scottish-American media patriarch who, on a rare pilgrimage back to Dundee, is chauffeured to the modest street where he was born and cannot face climbing out of his limo. There is a little of the dour, closed Logan in Robert.

I travel to Dundee with Robert's great-grandson James to see where the Flemings came from through Fleming eyes. A novelist like his uncle, James owns and edits Ian's antiquarian journal the *Book Collector*. He has never before visited the city of Ian's origins.

But Robert's early traces prove elusive. The gravestone to his mother and two youngest siblings lies on its back in the Western Cemetery, the names not visible. The cottage where he was born in Liff Road no longer exists, nor his home in Ramsay Street, where Robert's mother ran a grocery. The family's next lodging, 3 Lansdowne Place, although renamed and part of an office block, is there still; as is Tighnavon, the large house perched on a slope directly across the Tay, where Robert the young millionaire built a tennis court and Ian's father Valentine was born in 1882. But a moment arrived when Robert wished to get out of Dundee. A similar exodus is still felt today. In the Brown Street school where Robert learned his maths, now a pub called Duke's Corner, James Fleming and I are the sole people having lunch. The barman says, 'Once you've been here quite a while, there's not a lot left.' Aside from Fleming Gardens East, West, North and South on the housing estate that he paid for, there is the Fleming Gym, also funded by Robert, where they now perform autopsies, much called for in Dundee, which has the lowest life expectancy in Western Europe, plus the highest rate of drug deaths. This is the extent of Robert's imprint.

A vestige of the golden age when Dundee was famous for 'journalism, jute and jam' is the head office of D. C. Thomson, publishers of *The Dandy* and *The Beano*. If Dundee admits to a favourite son, it is the comic magazine strongman, Desperate Dan, commemorated by his black statue in the city centre.

Dundee's most ignored prodigy is Winston Churchill, for fourteen years the city's Liberal MP, from 1908 to 1922, who left Dundee in humiliation after polling fourth in the 1922 election. Churchill never forgave the city for its rejection of him. He swore the grass would grow over him before he set foot there again (he never did), recalling how 'the bestial drunkenness of Dundee' was unmatched in Great Britain and how at one of his first break-fasts in the Queen's Hotel, 'I had half eaten a kipper when a huge maggot crept out and flashed his teeth at me!' Yet he also insisted: 'I always retain the strongest regard and respect for the citizens of Dundee.' Few Dundonians were more prominent than Robert Fleming. Dundee was their uncommon denominator.

Churchill was Dundee's MP at the precise moment when Robert was establishing his bank in London and on his way to becoming one of the rich-est Dundonians in history. It explains Churchill's bond with the Fleming family, consolidated by Robert's sons Valentine and Philip joining Church-ill's regiment and training at Blenheim summer camps with Churchill and his brother Jack. Churchill's self-interest in keeping in with a leading and wealthy constituent caused him to beat a regular path to Robert's doors in Grosvenor Square and Nettlebed and to look upon his host's uncouth Lochee accent as if it represented the voice of his majority.

Our taxi driver is from Lochee too. 'Dundee doesn't acknowledge its his-tory. It's like it's ashamed of it. Go to Council and ask about James Bond, the most famous character going, and they wouldn't have a clue he started in Dundee.'

So how did Robert climb to the position which allowed him to leave?

Robert 'got his chance' when he was taken up as a clerk by the Cox family, owners of the Camperdown works, the largest jute factory in Europe, and became interested in the stock market. A catastrophic loss taught Robert his lifetime lesson. In 1865, 'seeing before me illimitable wealth', he invested in the Oriental Commercial Bank, which then collapsed, leaving him owing eighteen months' salary. In the same year, 1866, he left Cox Brothers and joined Edward Baxter & Son, and there discovered how to be an indispensable factotum to an older man. Robert passed on to Ian his ability to charm, convince and stand up to the wealthy.

Still in his early twenties, Robert became confidential 'clerk and bookkeeper' to the seventy-five-year-old Edward Baxter, head of the family and an expert in American securities. The Civil War now over, Baxter alerted his canny assistant to the opportunities springing up in the nineteenth-century equivalent of the Silicon Valley boom: the railways already under construction across the Americas. By Baxter's death in 1871, Robert was dealing in railway stocks from Potomac to Peru on behalf of Baxter and twenty-five other clients. It speaks for Robert's hard work, tenacity and clear-sighted analytical skills that someone from his background was listened to. Two years later, he established himself as a principal underwriter of this New World explosion.

A simple calculation launched Robert Fleming on the path to his wealth. He saw a fortune to be made by borrowing cash in England at three per cent and investing it in the US at seven per cent. In 1873, aged twenty-seven, he set up the Scottish American Trust to collect and invest his clients' capital in the US. By a supreme quirk of history, he took the Foreign and Colonial Government Trust as his model, the first collective trust of its kind. This had been created five years earlier by Sir Philip Rose, an energetic City of London lawyer. Rose was the grandfather of Ian's mother Eve. What Ian's maternal great-grandfather had initiated, his paternal grandfather developed over the next fifty years to a scale beyond recognition.

Robert could see through a company's accounts and at once grasp the true position. He invested not merely in railways but in cattle ranches, electricity, sugar and oil, and not just in North and South America and Cuba: Anglo-Persian Oil, later BP, would be one of these companies.

Sporty, clever, solitary, canny – also lucky. In March 1873, Robert made his first trip to America. He planned to sail on the *Atlantic*, but at the last moment changed his mind and sailed two days later on the *Abyssinia*. The *Atlantic* ran aground in Nova Scotia and sank with the loss of 560.

By 1923, he claimed to have made the crossing 128 times 'to make investments' and pick up good business from the Scottish diaspora in America.

Robert stayed four months on that first visit, meeting bankers like Jacob Schiff and Junius Morgan. He possessed what his brother John called 'the scotch gift of "speirin" questions'. In his thick Dundee accent, he felt no reticence about telling these men what he thought of them. Barely thirty, he wrote a notorious letter to Morgan saying that if he did not conduct his affairs any better, he would withdraw his support. Pivotal in the reconstruction of the Texas and Pacific Railway, he clashed with the railroad speculator Jay Gould, of whom it was said that 'he had not a conception of a moral principle'. Of himself, people would say, 'straight as a die and in every way reliable'. His eldest son Valentine christened him 'The Man of Iron' – like his railroads.

Ian's romance with American railways came from Robert. When travelling across America with Cuneo, Ian hoped that Caspar was 'liking my train postcards!' In *Diamonds are Forever*, Serrafimo Spang drives an 1870 train with a Victorian carriage through Spectreville, a ghost town of the Old West, much as Ian did. After visiting Hollywood, Ian reported in thrilled tones: 'I went in the cabin of the Super Chief & drove it over the Rockies!! & down into the Apache country full of cowboys & purple sage. No foreigner has ever been in the cabin before.'

Ian had greater trouble following Robert's principle of saying No – which Ian termed 'Fleming's theory of the Imperative Negative'. Robert admitted to some difficulty himself. 'It is, I find, one thing having it in your notebook & another thing altogether acting up to it . . . Human nature is so weak that you have to be a veritable iceberg to always escape the effect of Yankee enthusiasm.'

Robert could be that iceberg: monosyllabic, austere, not spending a penny more than he had to. Two of his favourite expressions were: 'money made easily is apt to take flight suddenly' and 'I don't believe it'.

Inevitably, what he acknowledged as his 'hereditary aversion to paying anything more than 20/- in the pound' led to stories of Robert's thriftiness. How he never took a taxi in his life. How he kept his coppers in his left-hand pocket, his silver in the right, explaining to his head messenger that he 'had one day mistakenly handed over half a crown instead of a penny (*both being much the same size*) and from that time on always kept his coppers separate . . .'. That trait resurfaced in the character of Strangways at the start of *Dr. No*, when about to give money to a blind beggar. 'He ran his thumbnail down its edge to make sure it was a florin and not a penny.'

Robert's meanness is the characteristic most associated with the Flemings. His younger son Philip was said to know all the Tube stations where the ticket collector would not be standing at the top of the stairs. 'It gave Uncle Phil a great deal of pleasure', says his niece Sandra, 'to walk from 12 Hyde Park Square to Paddington Station to find if he was passing a shop selling items at cut-price. I remember him fishing from his jacket a tin of Campbell's condensed tomato soup.'

This characteristic passed down through the next generations. 'In terms of day-to-day life, they certainly didn't throw it around,' says a former director of Flemings. 'If going to Heathrow, they all went on the Tube.' He recalls once travelling with one of Robert's great-grandsons to America on business. 'Boston in February is cold, but we bloody well had to walk everywhere and he was unhappy about the bill when we went to a restaurant.'

'We're not mean,' says Ian's niece, Gilly. 'We're just dreadfully, dreadfully careful – very, very "ribby". We turn off lights.'

Set against that 'canniness', as the Flemings prefer to call it, were the sums that Robert consciously handed away – even if Robert's outward behaviour rarely betrayed his 'unostentious benevolence'. After a good night on the town, the novelist Anthony Powell's father brought Robert's son-in-law home, drunk, to Grosvenor Square, and pressed half a crown into the hand of someone he took to be the butler, who put it in his dressing-gown pocket and closed the door. 'Only then I realised I'd put 2/6d into the hand of the richest man in Europe.'

Robert was so purse-lipped that not even his wife had any notion of his fortune. Ian's boyhood friend Amherst Villiers was designing the super-charger for Bentley Motors when he met Robert and Kate at their large country house near Henley, Joyce Grove. Ian's grandmother told him 'how, after being married some twenty years, one day she said, "Robert, you simply can't wear that old hat any longer" – to which he answered, "it is rather shabby for a millionaire" – this was the first time she knew how very well off he was.'

Not till February 1919, when Ian was ten, did his taciturn grandfather break silence in an unrevealing interview with the *New York Tribune*. 'Robert Fleming is not a well-known figure to the American public; but there is not a banker or a railroad man who does not know him.'

He had directed the bulk of British investment in America for more than forty years, putting 'billions of capital into American stocks and bonds,' and was said to know more about American railroads than any man in America, having 'covered probably every foot of the United States'.

'There are international bankers who have their names more talked about (Robert Fleming never gets into the newspapers, and I think this is the first time that he has ever talked for publication), but there are none who carry more weight . . .' What he actually said, though, remains obscure.

Ian knew him as Pap or Papsie and 'often spoke with affection' of him. He would be a hard act to follow.

His small, forceful wife was the socially ambitious one. In 1881, aged thirty-five, Robert invested in 'that most hazardous of all ventures' – marriage. His twenty-three-year-old bride, Kate Hindmarsh, was the daughter of a customs official from Fife. He had met her at the Congregational church in Lindsay Street. On his marriage certificate, she pushed him to elevate his father John, dead for six years, to 'Tea Merchant'.

A friend described Kate as 'kind, very simple and a happy, childish snob'. On their honeymoon in Paris, Kate wrote how 'my dear Robert made me laugh inordinately' by asking an old Frenchman dining next to them, 'if he did not think "the duck was spiffing"'. They saw the *Venus de Milo*. They walked arm in arm through cobbled streets ('Robert was very anxious about the price of butter and eggs'). In Monte Carlo, they visited the Casino and observed the gamblers at the rouge et noir tables 'where only gold is played'.

Kate wrote in her diary: 'one old man we saw win Fr. 3,000 and walk away.' The honeymooners returned twice more to see 'money lost and won'. They resisted the urge to gamble, but the urge was there and it re-emerged in their grandson.

Dynamic, with boundless energy, Kate matched her husband in his worship of exercise. She performed physical jerks every morning, swam before breakfast, and was capable of a twenty-mile walk over the moors of Black Mount at seventy. She still stalked deer at eighty and played golf wherever possible, sometimes bringing Ian, who recounted how the caddies hid in the bushes at Huntercombe when they saw her approaching. She was known for undertipping. Ian saw her hand one caddie a toothbrush.

'Generosity was not her second name,' says her great-granddaughter, Mary. 'My grandfather Lord Wyfold erred by generosity in all things. My mum said the difference was when my Wyfold grandpa had two people to dinner, he would say, "What, Dorothy, only one chicken?" – whereas Kate, when the butler was serving out dinner, would whisper to him "DCSC" = don't cut second chicken.'

In Robert, Kate had married a husband who was driven beyond normal bounds. South was where the money was. London was the hub of the world. He wanted to be part of it.

In 1890, the Flemings relocated from Dundee to 'an old rambling house with wooded surroundings' in Chislehurst, Kent. In keeping with Robert's reputation as 'Scotland's Dick Whittington', they soon exchanged this for a central London mansion in Mayfair, before ending up at 27 Grosvenor Square.

Once she discovered the extent of her husband's wealth, Kate was driven to flaunt it. In 1903, she razed to the ground a pretty William and Mary house near Henley and in its place erected Joyce Grove, a forty-four-bedroomed red-brick monstrosity modelled after one of the French chateaux she had visited on her honeymoon, possibly even the Casino at Monte Carlo which she had considered 'a splendid building with beautiful laid out gardens all round'. 'At great expense,' said Peter's best friend Rupert Hart-Davis, 'the worst stained-glass artists in France were brought over to make enormous windows and huge balustrades.' Ian resurrected it as Goldfinger's ugly turn-of-the-century mansion; massive Rothschildian pieces of Second

Empire furniture, imposing stairway, sombre wood-carved ceilings. 'What a bloody awful deathly place to live in, this rich heavy morgue among the conifers.' Movie directors loved it. The exterior doubled for Bletchley Park in 'The Imitation Game' (2014).

In the dark-panelled rooms, hung with the stuffed heads of animals that she and her daughters had shot, including a rhinoceros, Ian's grandmother entertained royally, namely Queen Mary, and the two of them would go off antique-hunting. Queen Mary was not so popular with the rest of the family. When Ann made one of her flick-knife remarks that Ian in his brand-new Daimler looked 'rather like the late Queen Mary', he returned the car that day. Queen Mary met her equal in Kate Fleming's mingling of economy and extravagance. The regal habit of admiring some possession that had caught the queen's fancy in the frank expectation of the admired object then being offered – in one instance, a French table at Joyce Grove – resulted in Kate presenting her instead with a 'chunk of rock' found on a hill at Black Mount.

'She was a very direct lady,' Ian's brother Richard said of their Granny Kate. During the General Strike of 1926, while Ian was manning the signals at Leighton Buzzard railway station, a hostile crowd assembled outside the Flemings' Grosvenor Square residence, chanting, 'You rich buggers!' Kate went out and berated them in her Scottish accent: 'My husband made his money out of his own hard work and his father was the son of a crofter,' and the crowds dispersed. She could be ferocious in defence of her children. Peter Smithers witnessed a spat between Kate and a naval officer who interjected with 'Much too young, much too young' when he heard Kate boast that her eldest son Valentine had gone into Parliament at the age of twenty-seven. 'This immediately caused an explosion. Grandmother blew up. This was one of the first social rows that I had ever seen in my life. It was quite spectacular.'

No one was allowed to criticise Kate's dead son Val.

Though dour, Robert possessed an unexpected literary talent. Written on the ship to New York and never published, 'Prince Curly' was a fantasy about a boy called Philip who is kidnapped by gypsies, then joins a travelling circus and develops into a young superman. 'On the bare back of any of the horses he could turn somersaults or double somersaults, jump through hoops or anything else that the best performer could do.' Reunited with his family, this mini-Bond goes on to Eton and Oxford 'and became a man of importance in the country'. Philip was named after Robert's second son, yet his superhuman attributes applied in more obvious ways to the elder brother that Philip 'so adored': Ian's father Valentine, known as Val.

'My father didn't talk about Val,' says Philip's son, Robin. 'Rather untouchable, that would sum it.'

Ian barely knew his father except through photographs and stories, and he told Ivar Bryce that he could not remember him. The stories about Val bear out Winston Churchill's signed obituary that Ian kept framed on his bedroom wall and later in his office at Mitre Court, and which said, in effect, 'what a Sir Galahad his father had been'. After the war, Peter Fleming wrote to Churchill asking him to sign his copy: 'We boys hardly knew him but he must have been a wonderful chap.' Peter and Ian's prep-school headmaster had encountered Val only once, and that was enough. 'I have never been more attracted by any man than I was by him when I just met him like that for a few minutes. Over and over again, I've said to my wife, "Oh, he was a *man*."' Amaryllis regarded him in haloed terms 'as if he was a sort of saint'.

To his grandson Fergus, Val is a measure of how the Flemings were purified within one generation. 'Robert came down to London with a splash, and saw his favourite eldest son into Society with a capital S.'

At Eton, Val was elected to the elite body of prefects known as Pop along with Ian's future English teacher, George Lyttelton (who called Val 'one of the best of my Eton friends'); Robert Vansittart (who had dealings with Ian at the Foreign Office); and Churchill's younger brother Jack. Athletic like his father, Val was in the school rowing VIII and winner of his house long jump, high jump and hundred yards. He only failed to get a rowing blue at Oxford, said Peter, 'because he got a boil just before the trials'. He read history at Magdalen, qualified to become a barrister, and in 1904 joined his local Territorial regiment, the Queen's Own Oxfordshire Hussars, where his association with Churchill began. 'Winston was quite a friend,' said Peter. 'Used to come to Joyce Grove and shoot rather badly before the war.' By contrast, Val was an excellent shot, a keen fisherman and 'a good man to hounds'; he hunted hare with bassets, and, at the house that he bought near Joyce Grove in the year of his marriage, he kept a pack of twenty-two, with names like

Striver, Sinbad and Doubtful. Val also had 'sterling qualities as a deerstalker', in the words of his obituary. Out of all the things he enjoying doing, stalking ranked near the very top. At the time of his death, he had just built a lodge, Arnisdale, in Invernessshire.

Val was a paragon of whom no one said a bad word and a credit to his parents in every respect. 'There was absolutely nothing that he couldn't have done if he wanted to,' wrote his sister Dorothy. 'There never has been anybody like him, even as a dear little boy always loved & looked up to.' The only time he seems to have rowed against his family was in his choice of a wife. The Flemings had little in common with 'the lurid bombshell' who in 1906 landed in their midst.

II
EVE

'Character would greatly depend on upbringing, and,
whatever Pavlov and the Behaviourists might say, to a
certain extent on the character of the parents.'
FROM RUSSIA, WITH LOVE

'I've always been inclined to say "No".' James Bond grapples with Robert Fleming's mantra in 'the book of golden words', as Ian called the notebook in which he scribbled down 'thoughts and comments' for his character. 'It's a shorter word than "Yes." And it commits you to less. But it's wrong and a bad way of life. What people call the "full life" is a commitment up to the hilt.'

Ian's mother tugged in the opposite direction. She was a Yes-girl from the tip of her broad-brimmed, ostrich-feathered hats to the hem of her swishing yellow crinolines. Her motto resurfaced in Ian's children's book *Chitty-Chitty-Bang-Bang*: 'Never say "no" to adventures. Always say "yes"; otherwise, you'll lead a very dull life.' Her untempered ache for excitement also informed Peter's theory that 'you must *never* refuse a risk to which you feel attracted even if doesn't seem a very sensible one to take. If you do start refusing risks that you want to take you are sunk & you will be run over by a bus or something silly like that.'

William Stephenson said of Ian: 'You will understand him better if you understand how the crazy genes from his mother were always dancing round the strong, silent Scottish genes from his father.'

Evelyn Sainte Croix* Rose was a dark-haired girl with large striking eyes

---

* Bond's mother was Monique Delacroix, a nod to Eve. But the Sainte Croix in Eve's name had nothing to do with her family. Lucy de Sainte Croix was 'a dear friend' of Eve's grandmother, Margaretta Rose. A childless widow from Guildford, Lucy left her estate to Margaretta. In Lucy's memory, the Roses named Eve's father George Sainte Croix.

who came from the nearby Thameside village of Sonning, now famous for George Clooney and Theresa May. She had attended a French finishing school and played the violin. She was vain, selfish and extremely pretty, remembered Mary Pakenham. 'Her expression was the blank, wide-eyed stare of the professional beauty.' She once wrote to the portrait painter Philip de László: 'I am a good sitter though difficult to do, I believe!' Augustus John painted her sixteen times and never caught her scatter-brained vanity.

Ian's niece Mary met her later in life at the Grosvenor Hotel. 'She gave me a pearl necklace for my twenty-first and I went wearing it to thank her. She was in bed. She wanted to order us a cake for us to eat and for something to occupy the staff, and then she smiled and it was the most beautiful smile I've ever seen, ever, and I could understand how beautiful she must have appeared to others.'

Eve first smiled at her future husband at Henley's Royal Regatta, where her father acted as a steward. Her louche brother Harcourt had rowed with Valentine at Eton and Oxford: in all likelihood, he introduced them. Years later, Ian wrote to her that the ghillie at Black Mount still talked about Eve's fishing prowess. 'He never met anyone who would cast a line so straight into the wind.' Once Eve had hooked her gaze on Robert Fleming's handsome, rich young son, she did not release him, 'and married him almost immediately,' said Ian's half-sister Amaryllis. 'He was the one person in the world who had been able to cope with her.'

Eve Rose's square, sane, country-loving in-laws would always be a bit suspicious of her. 'Robert disapproved of his son marrying Miss Rose from the start,' recalled Ian's tutor, Ernan Forbes Dennis. 'Said she wasn't the real goods.'

A discordant note that she shared with Robert's wife Kate was her obsession with lineage. Eve's brittle insistence on the importance of ancestry explained Ian's second name, Lancaster: after a Mary Lancaster in the eighteenth century, and so back, somehow, to John of Gaunt, first Duke of Lancaster – from whom, as Ian used to point out, 'half England could be descended'. Towards Lancaster, Ian adopted the attitude of Bertie Wooster whose middle name was Wilberforce ('except in moments of great emotion one hushed it up').

Hester Chapman, the daughter of Ian's prep-school headmaster, was so astounded by Eve's social aspirations that she cast her in a novel as 'the Duchess of Lancaster' who was unable to stand at the top of the stairs without a tiara – which in Eve's case resembled 'a glorified jam tart'. Amaryllis recognised how 'Ian's dislike of sociability is probably a revolt against my mother's absurd socialite phase. She was always having ridiculous people to her parties which were quite appalling. People with titles just because they were titles. She had a fantastic regard for position.' Eve's much later lover, the 16th Marquess of Winchester, informed his no less socially ambitious Parsee wife, whom Eve had usurped, that Eve 'descended from a Spanish woman called SANTAQUARA who kept a pub in Portsmouth'.

If not publicans, Eve's family was as upwardly mobile as Val's. The third child of George and Beatrice Rose, she grew up in a middle-class Georgian villa on the Thames, where her father, another keen oarsman, was president of the Sonning regatta. George, a solicitor, was the ninth child of the founding father of asset management, Sir Philip Rose.

A philanthropist responsible for the Royal Brompton Hospital, Eve's grandfather had acquired his baronetcy for services rendered to the British Prime Minister Benjamin Disraeli, later Lord Beaconsfield, with whom he had been at school in Islington and 'learned their simple alphabet together'. Paunchy, bald, with a short white beard, Sir Philip Rose is caricatured by 'Spy' in *Vanity Fair* as 'Lord Beaconsfield's friend'. He was, in addition, Disraeli's executor as well as his legal and financial adviser.* It was Rose's investment trust – the first anywhere – on which Robert Fleming had modelled his Scottish American Trust.

Disraeli threaded Eve's paternal Rose grandfather to her maternal grandfather, the eminent doctor Sir Richard Quain. A matching 'Spy' cartoon shows 'Lord Beaconsfield's Physician' as a beak-nosed man with the same ruminative expression that people later observed in Ian, of one who, in the words of his obituary, 'may be said to have known everyone worth knowing and seen everything worth seeing'.

Peter Fleming inherited his ivory chalice. 'I think whatever brains we have must come from old Quain.'

---

* The mother of Rose's wife, Margaretta Ranking (already a status-conscious name), was Elizabeth Amos, which may explain Ian's cryptic reference to 'the mixture of Scottish and Jewish blood which runs in my veins'.

Richard Quain was Irish, born on the Blackwater River, and apprenticed aged fifteen to a surgeon in Limerick. His medical background explained how he got to know the Roses. In London, Quain became a consultant at Sir Philip Rose's Royal Brompton Hospital and 'the most capable young physician of his day'. He attended Disraeli in his final days, and Queen Victoria as her physician-extraordinary. Among Quain's patients were Thomas Carlyle and his wife, Jane. Ian would have known the story of how Quain allegedly examined Jane Carlyle in late life and was led to expostulate in amazement, 'Why! You're virgo intacta!' Apparently, Jane had then revealed to Quain how on her wedding night she was so hysterically nervous that she had burst out laughing to find that her husband 'in a blue funk was frigging himself' beneath the sheets, whereupon he stormed from the room.

Not to be confused with his cousin – the physician Richard Quain, author of *The Diseases of the Rectum* (1855) – his area of expertise was the heart, from its opening beat to its last. Yet the one ambition of his life remained unfulfilled: to publish a small work on 'the Diseases of the Walls of the Heart' – a likely cause of Ian's death. Instead, Quain threw it aside to concentrate on *Quain's Dictionary of Medicine* (1882), a project that took him eight years, ensured his place in the medical books, and inspired a story by Borges.

A meticulous proofreader, Quain was in the last stage of putting to bed his 2,500-page dictionary when he received news that Benjamin Disraeli was dying, and he was summoned jointly with Ian's other great-grandfather. The *Pall Mall Budget* pictured the scene. 'About five minutes before the breathing ceased Sir Philip Rose and Dr Quain arrived. Then a most placid appearance came over his lordship's face, which deeply moved all in the room . . . thus without suffering, without a struggle, Lord Beaconsfield's life slowly passed away.'

Compared with these two Victorian pillars, Eve's brothers Ivor and Harcourt were 'so disreputable they were kept out of sight'.

Churchill called the Fleming brothers, Ian's father and uncle, 'the Flemingoes'. Eve's brothers gained notoriety as 'the wild Roses'. Both alcoholics, both three times married, both declared bankrupt, they were the gaudy reverse of Valentine and Philip, an example of everything that Robert Fleming had worked each day to avoid. They reminded him of the immoral Jay Gould and other American chancers, and motivated Robert to act to limit their threat so that the fortune he had made for his family did not take sudden flight.

'Harky', or 'Ingle' as Harcourt Rose was known by his stepson, the actor Christopher Lee, blamed his plunge on having been 'brought up in an atmosphere of considerable affluence'. In 1928, the New York bank Speyer & Company appointed him their London representative 'with every reason to believe that he would not earn less in salary and commission than £20,000 a year', approximately £12.5 million today. He overspent this sum by the same amount on 'unjustifiable extravagance in living'. Lee's childhood was a pageant of chauffeur-driven Buicks, silver-fox furs, one country house after another, and shooting parties at which 'Ingle' could be smelt downwind for miles 'because of an evil mixture of creosote and vinegar of his own invention to keep insects off his face'. With the same pungent creativity, he batted away creditors and ex-wives. Lee recalled a short, energetic, prodigiously strong man of 'sheer animal verve' who could bend a poker round his neck and excelled at word games. He was a friend of Rasputin's assassins, claimed to know a lot about drink – he had forty bottles of Tokay from Franz Josef's cellars in Vienna – and remained 'a very free spender'. By 1936, it was all gone. Harcourt told the Bankruptcy Court that his 'only asset was a ring which had realised £1.15s'.

Lee was able to draw on Harcourt's characteristics when he played the three-nippled assassin Scaramanga in the film of Ian's last novel, *The Man with the Golden Gun*.

Harcourt's only recorded sighting after that was when a stranger knocked one night on Amaryllis's door and said he was her Uncle Harky, come to see what she looked like, and produced a large chicken. 'This is all they seem to have in Norfolk,' he added, and disappeared.

Ivor was Eve's elder brother. Christopher Lee wrote that 'we never met Ivor, seemingly because he'd married an Eskimo'. But Ivor's third wife was not Innu: she was the daughter of Richard White, an expert on the Innu who ran a network of trading posts in Labrador. In the late 1930s, when several hundred Innu were dying of starvation, he led a party on dog-sleighs to save them. His reckless son-in-law never saved anyone. After leaving Eton to fight in the Boer War, Ivor was wounded in the First World War. He then squandered his inheritance on yachting holidays and expensive cars, making his daughter paint the radiator badges vermilion 'to enable people to see how fast he was coming'. He contested one of a blizzard of speeding fines saying he could not have been driving so fast because his wife was sitting on his knee. He ended his debt-ridden days in a coachman's cottage.

Eve ensured that neither Ivor nor Harcourt came anywhere near her children. Ian, in particular, might have found their whimsical appetites to his taste. Ivor's one subsequent reappearance occurred shortly after Ian joined White's Club in St James's when an older member introduced himself as 'Your Uncle Ivor' and offered Ian a selection of pornographic postcards.

'A fortune once acquired should never be endangered' was another maxim in Robert Fleming's notebook. Upon Val's marriage in February 1906, Robert gave him a one-off settlement of £250,000 (£36 million in today's money). The behaviour of the 'wild Roses', who were indeed to come knocking on their sister's door for cash, may have persuaded Val to accept his father's advice on safeguarding this inheritance when he made his will. The measures and clauses that Val put in place on the eve of his going to war were to have a tremendous impact on his children.

III
A STORMY CHILDHOOD

*'He was a complex creature but all the complications derived from his
home & schooldays – as most complications do.'*

ROBERT HARLING

'The four madmen to whom I gave birth,' as Eve called them, appeared in
quick succession. Peter was born on 31 May 1907; and Ian, another Gemini,
one year later, on 28 May 1908, at 27 Green Street, the house his parents
leased off Park Lane. Three years separated Ian from Richard, born in 1911.
Michael, the youngest, was born in 1913.

About his early years, Ian talked as sparingly as James Bond. In an
unpublished essay on 'Bondsmanship', Stephen Potter observed that there
was 'no patter of little feet in Bond Street'. Bond never says to his companion, 'This is where I first learned to ride a bicycle.' Like the stamps and
cigarette cards Ian collected as a boy, the story of his childhood has to be
assembled from disparate sources.

It was a privileged upbringing, overprivileged even. Quite how
unhappy is revealed in the Blitz when Ian's lover Maud Russell telephoned
him, distraught. Her son Raymond had been found unconscious in a gutter in Cambridge, having taken half a bottle of Adalin pills. 'He said he
sometimes thought of putting his head in a gas oven,' Maud wrote in
her diary. 'Poor I[an]. had a very troubled youth himself and understands
this dreadful tangle better than anyone I know and better than I do . . .
He groaned as I told him. His heart is so good.' Ian's advice for Maud
boiled down to doing what he wished his own mother had done for him:
*'Go on, make more sacrifices. You won't forgive yourself unless you do,
unless you do your utmost. If you can, be emotional. Cry if you can.'* Maud

28

followed his advice because she knew Ian had had 'such a stormy child-hood himself'.

But why so stormy? Ian's tutor in Kitzbühel, Ernan Forbes Dennis, after-wards became a professional analyst, and was mystified by Fleming's attitude towards his early years – 'the sense of deprivation . . . which lasted all through his life'. This puzzled Fleming's schoolfriend Gerald Coke. 'He had everything he could have wanted – looks, money, brains, position . . . but he behaved as if he was permanently deprived.'

His unhappiness is present from early on. He has been left at home with Peter and his new baby brother, Richard, when their nanny writes to Eve from Brazier's Park, the Flemings' country house near Henley. This is the first glimpse we have of Ian Fleming – as a constipated three-year-old:

'Now Master Ian, he was so cross on the morning you left we did not know what to do with him. I gave him one of his Powders Squares. It kept him going all the Tuesday. I was very sorry for him. They had not done that before so I made him a cup of arrowroot [for diarrhoea] for his supper. He was very pleased and came the next night to see if I had another. On Thurs-day I gave him gravy and toast as he will not eat potatoes for his dinner and he has had good dinners each day since and he is quite good about the bacon fat if he has a tiny bit of fat on each finger of bread.'

Peter said: 'He always made his feelings very clear about bad food even as a boy. At Joyce Grove, when he was very young, he used to object to his porridge and used to throw it on top of the wardrobe, where of course it soon produced a fine growth of fungus.'

Ann observed the same cross, fussy appetite at play, the desire for that extra bit of fat. 'He always acted as if someone hadn't given him the lion's share. He had a sort of hunger for things. Whenever he was in France I used to hear him ordering breakfast in the morning and the words "un double" kept recurring. Double orange juice, double eggs, double coffee. Double everything.' Rarely was his hunger satisfied, since it had little to do with food. 'Ian was a melancholic, and needed much solitude. I have a photo-graph of him with his three brothers . . . In the picture, three boys are smiling at the camera and there's one looking saturnine. This was Ian. He was differ-ent. I don't think he was a very easy child.'

He is in tears in the next glimpse. On 3 September 1911, Val writes from Loch Choire Lodge near Helmsdale to 'Master Ian Fleming'. He is three and a half.

'My dear Baba, I hope you are quite well & have been a good boy & that you eat your food without crying, 'cos it is stupid to cry & little boys who cry get laughed at when they go to school.

'Dada would like to come & see you and play with you on the sands, and build big sand castles to keep the sea back.

'Dada sends you a picture of himself shooting a big stag.

'Look after your Mumma, if you lose her Dada will be angry 'cos she is a unique specimen,

'Your loving DADA'

His father with a stag at his feet was a formative image. Val, pipe in mouth, was another. Ian knew him as 'Mokie', after the clouds of tobacco smoke in which his eyebrow moustache and prematurely balding head appeared to be permanently enveloped. Val called Ian variously 'Baba', 'Johnny', and 'Jocky' out of the same blurred focus.

That summer of 1911, Robert Fleming, a grandchild of crofters and poachers, rented the deer-stalking on the Loch Choire estate in the northern High-lands of Scotland from the Duke of Sutherland, who demanded references. One referee wrote back that in case His Grace did not know it, Robert Fleming was one of the wealthiest men in Britain. Robert had a telephone cable run from the lodge to hear what was going on in the world. The game bag of 130 stags and 1,814 grouse broke all records.

Robert spent every August and September in a Scottish deer forest; taking sporting estates at Rannoch Lodge in Perthshire, and then, for six seasons, Glenborrodale, 'a dotty red sandstone castle' on the Ardnamurchan peninsula. From 1924 on, he leased from the Marquess of Breadalbane a 110,000-acre slab of land on Loch Tulla in north-east Argyllshire called Black Mount. In the 1930s, during the agricultural depression, the family bought the estate, and since then, Black Mount has been 'the tribal centre' of the Flemings. 'We'd go north in August and September like migrating birds,' says Richard's daughter Mary, 'and then when the geese went over you knew it was time to come south.'

All three of Ian's brothers inherited Val's reverence 'for sporting holidays marked by a degree of bloodthirstiness and physical exhaustion rarely seen out of wartime'. Days were spent wading through icy burns and trudging across savage moors. A family poem celebrated Robert's spartan ethos that he had carried since boyhood:

> If you can crawl or worm upon your belly
> If you can fall on rocks and never squeal
> Although your limbs are battered to a jelly
> And there's a normous blister on your heel . . .
> In short if you are strong enough to bear creation
> If you can smile when frozen in a wave
> You will have earned the Flemings' approbation,
> Or else – they'll write 'Hic Jacet' on your grave!

Ian's brothers were addicted to this ardent regime. 'Peter is flying north for three more days of grouse shooting,' Rupert Hart-Davis wrote to George Lyttelton in September 1959. 'Shooting is like a religion to him – something solemn and ritual, which can scarcely be joked about.'

Their strenuous outdoor exercise made Val's sons uniformly fit. Dressed in plus-fours in Black Mount green and brown tweed designed by Robert's daughter Dorothy, they looked 'curiously muscle-bound' to one observer from south of the border, 'so that, during a meal, when one of them turned to speak he moved not merely his head or his head and shoulders alone, but his whole tweed-coated torso'. Peter Quennell noticed the same rigidity about Ian, 'which grew more pronounced should his temper have been aroused or his spirits happen to be low.'

Nothing lowered Ian's spirits more than the prospect of joining his family in Argyllshire. 'He used to get very sullen towards Christmas,' said Ann. 'Apparently, as a boy, he had always hated going to Black Mount for the traditional deer-hunting thing with the Flemings. Felt claustrophobia in the family circle.' His reply when asked what he wanted to do after the paucity of the previous day's sport passed into Fleming lore. 'Well, if it's all the same to you I'd rather catch no salmon than shoot no grouse.'

Ian's aversion to following a stag or trampling the moors with a shotgun was inexplicable to his brother Richard. 'Don't ask me why he didn't. Never really understood. I took to these things almost by instinct.'

Richard, the most Scottish of the brothers, who would twirl through Cheyne Walk in a kilt, had an obsession with hunting. Once, when his daughter Sandra suggested that 'there are other things to do in life other than get on a horse and hunt', his wife replied: 'What, dear? Life is hunting.'

'I don't like hunting or shooting,' Ian wrote to Ann. He was 'not greatly interested in horses' either. He had regarded them as 'dangerous at both ends and uncomfortable in the middle' ever since, aged twelve, he was sent off, complaining, to a nearby meet in Oxfordshire from which he was ordered home 'until you can learn to ride'.

Hunting on foot held no more allure, after one of Val's beagles went for Ian when he was six. 'He never liked dogs after that,' said Peter. Putting up a rod had less appeal still. On a list that Ian compiled of 'the empty hours of my life' – up there with being in hospital, on watch at sea, listening to bad opera, and hawk hunting in Kuwait – he counted 'fishing Scottish lochs in the rain'.

Ian characterised Scotland as 'wet rhododendrons' and 'dripping evergreens'. At Glenborrodale Castle, 'I spent some of the unhappiest years of my youth.' Black Mount made him no happier. As another family poem put it:

> *Here we are, Black Mount again:*
> *Same old smells, same old rain*

He once warned Hilary Bray and his wife against living in Scotland. 'For God's sake, don't or you'll both end up growing hair on your cheeks and huddled up in a tartan rug round a peat fire.'

'We were all wild creatures at Black Mount,' says Richard's daughter Sandra. 'We were "put out" after breakfast and expected not to appear until lunch time.' Some guests barricaded themselves in their rooms rather than face their hosts' idea of fun. Prominent among the recalcitrants were Eve and Ian. Eve was nicknamed 'Mie' ('mumm-mee') or 'Yer' ('She's *yer* aunt,' the cousins would say). She liked to go off and practise on her violin in the stag larder, a green corrugated shed outside. 'Her nephews and nieces used to wait until she was inside,' says Mary, 'and then run up and scrape their nails down the corrugated iron.' Ian followed his mother's lead in opting to stay behind and listen to music. 'To the exasperation of my family, I had a weakness for the Hawaiian guitar, and I played records of the Royal Hawaiian Serenaders when I should have been out of doors killing something.'

Indoors, Robert Fleming's frugality set the tone. You were not allowed sugar on your porridge, it had to be salt. Robert disapproved of alcohol and would not employ anyone who was not 'absolutely free from any tendency in that direction'. Success had not lightened his dourness. Rupert Hart-Davis recalled 'a pathetic, dithery, little old man with a red face' who was apt to let slip a bit of food now and then on his moustache, whereupon Kate would say '*Essuyez*, Robert! Something clings!' – an expression that became part of the family's parlance when someone had food around their mouth. His wife resented the fact that he was getting old. In London, a policeman would stop the traffic to let him pass. He enjoyed no such dispensation from her. 'Robert, hold your hands up!' she shouted at bridge. 'Your cards are shaking,' and kick him under the table when he seemed slow in answering a question. 'Make conversation, Robert, dear! It helps to keep the larynx clear.' His grave reply: 'Kate, Ah'm naw entir–r–e–l–y deaf!'

This was the ethos and regime that shaped Ian and his brothers, says James Fleming. 'Rain was better for one than sun, little good would ever come from something that could be done easily, smoking was disgusting . . . more than a glass of sherry and one was leading to perdition.'

It was a regime that tolerated no crying, and no hugging, says Richard's daughter Mary. 'We were absolutely not physically demonstrative, except in sport, and would run a mile at the thought of being touched. If mum had said to me she loved me, I'd have been sick. Love was meant to be Launcelot and Guinevere, and had nothing to do with parents.'

If the next generation of Flemings loved you, they teased you, observes Peter's daughter Kate. 'When Fleming meets Fleming their first instinct may not be to hug, but it will be to make the other laugh.'

*

Putting Val's stalking glass to the eye, there is a tempting explanation for Ian's stormy childhood. What he had been starved of, what had fed his melancholy, his saturnine expression, his fussy 'hunger for things', was Eve's undivided love at a time when Ian needed it most.

His elder brother's illness had dictated Ian's first years and robbed him of the most important early attachment that he could share with his mother. At the moment Ian was born, weighing just short of nine pounds, Eve's focus was wrenched from him when Peter contracted colitis. Peter said: 'It wasn't recognised in those days and I was more or less despaired of.' He suffered unbearable stomach pains, on one occasion vomiting for fourteen hours. A stammer wore off, but Peter was left with no sense of taste or smell ('I once saw him put pepper on peaches,' said a friend). He also grew up shorter than his brothers. In a state of permanent concern, the Flemings travelled to Lausanne over four successive years for Peter to undergo a month-long treatment under the supervision of a Swiss specialist.

All this attention on his delicate brother proved too much for Ian, who, aged five, made a great scene 'and had to be carried screaming and kicking from the Beau Rivage Hotel'.

Back home, Peter's stomach pains continued. Eve wrote in her diary in July 1914: 'We were going to Scotland to Glenelg Hotel to watch the building of Arnisdale but Peter had one of his attacks and a temperature of 104.'

Ian's screaming and kicking did not subside either.

'Of course, we fought like cat and dog for most of our boyhood,' said Peter. 'We were so close together. It often happens like that. Ever seen two fox cubs? It was like that with us.'

Ian nicknamed Peter 'Pudding', after a medicinal dessert that he had to eat at prep school. Peter lashed back with 'Turnip'.

A governess in whalebone stays called 'Mivvy' had prepared them for their prep school. In September 1916, in the second year of the war, the two brothers were sent away together to Durnford House, close to the Dorset coast.

IV
VAL

'There is a tragedy under every roof.'
IAN FLEMING'S 'BOOK OF GOLDEN WORDS'

Durnford House was a converted eighteenth-century manor house in Langton Matravers, set back three miles from the sea on six acres of grounds.

Ian had the surrounding countryside in mind when hunting for his final home. 'The only areas of my childhood for which I have affection are Dorset and the West Coast of Scotland,' he wrote to Ann in 1957, somewhat contradicting his earlier claims. 'The Purbeck Hills are thrilling and covered with snakes and orchids and the Dorset houses are lovely.' Nearby was the Moigne Combe estate belonging to the Bond family, descendants of the Elizabethan spy John Bond, whose motto, *Non Sufficit Orbis*, 'the world is not enough', was pillaged by a later Bond.

This landscape of wooded valleys and stone-walled pastures formed the backdrop of Ian's first romance. A love poem he wrote on leaving Durnford aged thirteen included these lines:

> *Sunlight over the Purbeck hills,*
> *Flooding the dreamy Dorset street*
> *Bathing its cobbles in sudden gold*
> *Treading the world with gilded feet.*

Established in 1893 by Tom Pellatt and his wife Nell, Durnford House was a private school for sixty boys, with a reputation for being 'unusual' in that it operated, said their daughter, on 'the completely novel idea for those days that boys should be happy at school'.

Pellatt, or 'T.P.' as the boys called him, was a pot-bellied playwright with a thick moustache. Peter considered him a teacher of 'character, genius', and 'a most original man'.

With fees that were the highest in the UK at £90 per term (approximately £10,500 today), Durnford was a feeder for Eton, where Ian's father and three uncles had gone. Pellatt sent three-quarters of his boys there, including the children of two Eton headmasters, Cyril Alington, who would be Ian's headmaster, and Claude Elliott, whose son Nicholas worked with Ian in Intelligence; Ian's admission may even have owed something to Pellatt's position as a lay member of the Admiralty board which interviewed prospective naval officers.

Eve dropped off her two sons on the first day of the autumn term. Val was away at the front.

The person who kitted out Peter and Ian with their school cap was the inspiration for Ian's poem, the Pellatts' seventeen-year-old daughter Hester. She wrote how one boy 'had to be torn, shrieking, from his mother's arms as she collapsed into the station fly. Twenty minutes later, he was playing touch-last in the orchard.'

'Dear Mokie, I like school rather – some things are nice. I hope the war will soon be over lots of love & xxx fr Ian'. These are Ian Fleming's earliest words to survive, penned to his father, then in Ypres. Val had sent him a postcard showing the ruined city centre.

Already, the outlines of Ian's character are present in a letter to his nanny, Miss Perticher, on 10 October 1916. 'The first day I went swimming. I am some body's slave. I am in a hury.'

A letter to his mother ten days later is more plaintive. 'It is the longest time I have had away from you, and it is not at all nice.' There was no telephone. Eve would be kept at arm's length until half-term. Then, in his next communication: 'My dear Mum I dont like school half so much now. Thanks for the knife. Here is a map that I drew at lessons. Some of the boys are beastly. We have 8 hours lissons. Some of the boys say that we are beasts. Peter is a great help to me. We are aloud knives Lots of love and lots of xxxxxxxxxxxx'. The term does not improve. 'I am afraid that I do not like school very much I do not know what form im in im in so mony. I am afraid I have not made any friends, they are so dirty and unreverent.'

Herbert Laurie was a schoolfriend who witnessed Ian's early mood swings. 'For some days, he would be sweet as summer and the most delightful of companions. Then abruptly, he would withdraw into a slough of moroseness and to approach him at such periods would be to court a snub. At length the surly phase would end and he would once more be the soul of amiable gentility.'

Another Durnford contemporary was the engraver Reynolds Stone, who went on to provide the illustrations for Ian's edition of Evelyn Waugh's *The Holy Places* and the royal arms on the *Times* masthead and British passports. Abnormally shy, Stone avoided being teased by fantasising that he was a unicorn. He is unlikely to have been one of Ian's dirty bullies; in any event, Ian seems to have returned like for like.

Peter said: 'Ian was basically a naughty boy.' The precise form of his naughtiness is unclear, but 'T.P.' singled him out early on as someone who needed monitoring. 'Ian will be a first-rate little boy after a bit, only he is of course a difficult child in some ways.'

To lift his son's spirits, Val pencilled Ian a longer letter from his miserable forward position in northern France. It was October 1916. He had been away two years.

'My Dear Jocky,
'I hope you are enjoying school fairly well, and getting used to it. I
expect you found it a bit funny at first being among a lot of strange
boys. And I expect their ways seemed funny to you, but you will
soon see that everyone has ways of their own and may be quite all
right though they are different from your ways. So you try and get
into what Peter and you and Mr Pellatt think are the right ways and
if other boys seem different just leave them alone and don't say
anything about it. To them or anyone else. You will have plenty to
do looking after yourself without bothering about other boys. I hear
you have kicked four goals at football. That is very good . . . I
suppose you have stopped bathing at [Dancing Ledge]. It must be a
topping bathing place at Durnfords. Do you sleep in a separate
room with Peter or in a dormitory? Do they give you nice things to
eat? Tell Peter I am going to write to him tomorrow. I hope you can

read this letter. I have not got any pens or ink here. I am sitting in a hut I made of old shell boxes. Its nice but the rain and wind come in. Best love, Mokie.'

He was writing from an 'awfully cold and wet' dugout even as a 'big German howitzer' shelled his camp.

Named in the endless rolls of those killed or wounded, the school lost fifty-one old boys in this 'stupendous cataclysm', as Pellatt called the 1914–18 war. Among those to meet their muddy death in battle was the ebullient music master Mr Nowell, who had led the boys in hymns at the upright piano on Sunday nights. The Pellatts' daughter Hester recalled how 'the casualty lists were a real source of terror to us, and we got quite used to breaking this sort of news to the boys'.

Pellatt wrote to Val's father: 'One dreads the post & the coming of telegrams.' Robert Fleming sat every day in his office hoping not to hear news from the front where his two 'good swank lads' were fighting side by side in the same regiment. He confided his worries to a banker in New York. 'It is indeed a time of times in which we live, in which the very foundations of our world's social structures are being shaken, and out of which no man can say what will emerge . . .'

Val had joined his father's bank as a partner on its formation in 1909. The following year, he stood for Parliament. On 15 January 1910, the son of a man brought up in a Dundee slum was elected Conservative and Unionist MP for Boris Johnson's former constituency of Henley, displacing the Liberal incumbent, the husband of Lady Ottoline Morrell – who, according to Peter, was so indignant when the polls were declared, 'she had slapped Mother's face'. Val was twenty-seven. On his election, he decided he must have 'a proper London house'. In October 1913, the family moved to Wildwoods on Hampstead Heath, a grey, twelve-bedroomed house with a billiard room, two tennis courts and a four-acre garden overspilling with rhododendrons. Val renamed it Pitt House, after a previous owner, Prime Minister William Pitt, who had secluded himself in a small room on the third floor. Peter said: 'My mother's bedroom had been Pitt's room and still had two serving hatches so that when Pitt shut himself in there with gout, he could be given his food without seeing anyone.' Eve was not so retiring. She at once built for herself 'the most original music room, the walls of which are covered with moonlight blue glass', according to *Vogue*. Here she practised her violin while her husband played at being a constituency MP.

Val was 'absolutely a non-politician', said Peter. 'He went into Parliament because it was what was expected of him. It was a duty he had to perform. But he regarded it as a chore.' His friend Churchill observed that 'the fierce tumults' that swayed political life were not for Val. The one time he took flight was in a speech on the Territorial Army. 'I believe if we heard a little less about the rights and a little more about the duties of citizens of this country we should be a great deal better off.' On 1 November 1913, he asked his last question, on 'the lack of accommodation in existing sanatoria'.

Eight months later, the country went to war.

On 4 August 1914, Eve wrote in her diary. 'War was declared early this morning. I had a cold shiver down my spine . . .' Mobilisation orders arrived the following day. Val took with him his white cairn terrier Cluanie, named after a deer forest, plus the telescope he used for stalking. Eve was determined not to weep until he was gone.

Less than a week after Val left for Dunkirk, she was invited to visit him at the instigation of Winston Churchill: as First Lord of the Admiralty, he was making an incognito visit to Belgium. Eve accompanied Jack Churchill's wife Gwendoline on the ferry from Dover. Jack was in Val's regiment.

In the Hussars' stables at Dunkirk, Val showed Eve the greys he had transported from Joyce Grove. 'It seemed so funny to see them there drawing the ammunition wagon instead of the brake from Henley.' The high point of her visit was a dinner with Winston Churchill, who arrived out of the blue, having 'come straight from the battle of the Aisne and had been to the trenches!!' Eve sat opposite him 'and listened with all my ears'.

Churchill's account of the battlefield revealed the fast-changing face of war. 'W says swords are useless and that all the cavalry now have bayonets . . . W said that once the French and Germans were so near, and they had to throw away their rifles and fight hand to hand, and the French bit off the German noses!!'

She went up afterwards and thanked Churchill for letting her come – 'it was he who suggested it to Val'. She promised not to tell anyone about him being at the front.

Val's was the first territorial unit to see action. He and Philip, who served as his second-in-command, would be in France on and off for three years.

On 14 November 1914, Eve wrote in her diary following the first battle of Ypres: 'I hear on all sides of his bravery.' She had learned from an officer in his regiment how 'Val crawled to their trench to see if they were all right after a shell had exploded near them', and how 'he saw the Germans bringing up a gun out of sight of the French who were next to them . . . No one but a stalker would have seen them.' Still viewing the war in deer-hunting terms, Val reported to Eve how he had climbed the church tower, and 'pulling out my stalking glass' had seen Germans 'all in grey uniforms looking fat'. He had 'crawled back to headquarters who telephoned to the French & they got the guns on to the Germans at dusk'.

Eve told her children, 'he wrote to me every single day of the war.' He called her 'my sweet of sweets'. She missed him intensely. 'I hear women who can speak French are wanted out there & I would love to go if it wasn't for the children.'

It is unlikely that Val would have welcomed her presence. Four days previously, he had written a sober assessment of 'this astounding conflict' to Churchill. One of the earliest and most graphic descriptions of the First World War, Val's letter is all the more poignant for anticipating his fate. Talk of nose-biting has ceased; his glossy grey horses and sword are history.

'Imagine a broad belt, ten miles or so in width, stretching from the Channel to the German frontier near Basle, which is positively littered with the bodies of men and scarified with their rude graves; in which farms, villages, and cottages are shapeless heaps of blackened masonry; in which fields, roads and trees are pitted and torn and twisted by shells and disfigured by dead horses, cattle, sheep and goats, scattered in every attitude of repulsive distortion and dismemberment. Day and night in this area are made hideous by the incessant crash and whistle and roar of every sort of projectile, by sinister columns of smoke and flame and by the cries of wounded men, by the piteous calls of animals of all sorts, abandoned, starved, perhaps wounded.'

Val's letter to Churchill is a condemnation of war's destructiveness. Yet it was also a defiant hymn to the British Empire and its modern weaponry. With a relish for the latest technology, Val marvelled at how 'all the appliances of 20th-century civilisation can be brought to work and the result is good'. Fluttering above these 'invisible, irresistible machines' were the banners of an alliance that had the glamour of a modern crusade. He ends his letter with an unforgettable scene.

'One night last week, beautifully starlit, I was riding up the reverse slope of a wooded hill round which were encamped the most extraordinary medley of troops you could imagine, French Cuirassiers with their glistening breastplates and lances, a detachment of the London Scottish, an English howitzer battery, a battalion of Sikhs, a squadron of African Spahis with long robes and turbans, all sitting round their camp fire, chattering, singing, smoking, the very apotheosis of picturesque and theatrical warfare with their variety of uniforms, saddlery equipment and arms. Very striking it was to see the remnants of an English line battalion marching back from the trenches through these merry warriors, a limping column of bearded muddy, torn figures, slouching with fatigue, with wool caps instead of helmets, sombre looking in their khaki, but able to stand the cold, the strain, the awful losses, the inevitable inability to reply to the shell fire, which is what other nations *can't* do.'

The lineaments of his son's fictional hero stare out from those sombre English faces. Valour. Duty. A stoical obedience to a noble cause. A taste for the most up-to-date gadgets. The same taste in food even. 'A dish of scrambled eggs and bacon, two cups of lovely coffee and a good whack of scones and Oxford marmalade and butter would be the most acceptable present anyone could make me just when it begins to get light.'

Then these Bond characteristics. Val single-handedly put out the flames on a lorry loaded with ammunition exploding in all directions. Twice mentioned in despatches, his code was *Leave No Man Behind*. When one of his men was badly shot in the shoulder, Val crawled out in broad daylight and had him bandaged. Then, wrote Philip, even though 'they were quite exposed to the Germans', his brother 'carried the man back to the place where the doctor was behind the line'.

In April 1915, Val was again in Ypres, helping Major W. G. Shakespeare, who was in charge of the hospital there. 'You never saw such an exodus,' Val wrote. 'The RAMC people and we got out 359 stretcher cases in all and carried them to a field $\frac{1}{5}$ of a mile in the rear.' Both men breathed in the same 'great cloud of green gas'. Shakespeare wrote: 'Two of the officers were violently sick and had to be taken off in a motor and I escaped with an hour's difficult breathing and an ensuing mild bronchitis.' Val escaped lightly too. 'Luckily we only got the fringe of it, but it made me cough and spit like anything ... some were choked on the spot ... It was the most appalling, inhuman savage sight I have ever seen.' This chlorine attack marked a sea-change in Val's attitude. 'Up to now I have not really felt bitter against the Germans, but now!!! I cannot find words to express my loathing'.

The shelling was incessant, one big shell every two minutes. 'It's absolutely like nothing on earth,' Shakespeare wrote, 'and must be very like Hell', and he described 'the swish of the shell through the air, coming louder and louder every second; the noise is very like the sound of a golf club in the air before it hits the ball.'

Val was extraordinarily lucky. 'A shell burst on top of my dug-out not thirty seconds after I had got out of it, blew my fur coat and both my woollies to fragments, broke my pipe and my stick etc, but not a splinter in my fat form!'

On 20 May 1917, his luck ran out.

He had been back in London two weeks earlier to attend a secret debate in Parliament. Ian was at Durnford for the start of the summer term; for his next birthday, on 28 May, Val would leave behind for him Rudyard Kipling's *France at War*, the last present Ian ever received from his father. Peter was recuperating in Pitt House, having had his tonsils out. 'I remember screaming for joy to see him when he came into my room and hurting my throat.'

It was their final exchange. On 13 May, Val returned to France.

His brother Philip was with him shortly before it happened. 'I remember suggesting to Val to sit down and rest a bit. Not he, though. He hadn't cleaned his teeth that morn so I remember him doing that, then changing his boots and socks, then getting busy writing his various orders for that evening. Well, it was getting late and I had to get back to Roisel, so I said goodbye to them all and went off ... That was the last time I saw dear old Val – in that cellar there at Lempire sitting writing his orders.'

Val had gone with his squadron to take over Gillemont Farm, a forward post opposite the Hindenburg Line north of St Quentin. At two thirty in the morning a heavy bombardment started up. Val was making his way to the right hand sector of the line when 'he was hit in the back by a big piece of shell', according to the regimental chaplain. 'The doctor who saw him after-wards tells me his death must have been instantaneous and that his face had an extraordinarily peaceful expression. We laid him to rest in a quiet little spit among the trees behind the line.'

His friend and fellow officer Arthur Villiers arrived on the scene moments later. 'It is almost impossible to describe the grief of his men,' he wrote to Eve. 'There has never been a braver man than Val.'

Philip wrote to console their parents, his congestion evident. 'What held that position against the Germans, who tried to attack after, was Val's abso-lutely extraordinary example of sticking to duty. It was outstanding and held the men – this influence of Val's. It was a hero's death he died. Dear Mum and Papsie, help yourselves by knowing that Val could not have died a more noble death.'

Peter had arrived home, on his way back to school after convalescing in Joyce Grove for ten days, and was walking in delicate steps through the hall at Pitt House with his mother when her younger sister Kathleen came 'as though from an ambush, out of the dining room on our right. She had a paper in her hand. "Eve," she said. "A telegram has come about Val." Some-body grabbed me and bustled me away upstairs. Behind me in the hall were the terrible sounds of grief. I knew that my father had been killed.' Weeks later, a dazed Peter was still saying, 'How awful, how awful, how could they do such an awful thing.'

Abandoned on a sofa upstairs, Peter heard from somewhere the sound of his grandfather crying. For Robert Fleming, who showed emotion so infre-quently, the words on the telegram tore open the pent-up grief of his early years and the death of his five siblings. He had overcome and achieved so much. Now this. 'It was a sort of bellowing noise', wrote Peter in a memoir that he abandoned. A pitch of sobbing that would haunt him and reverber-ate through their childhood.

A colleague of Robert's saw him later that day. 'Poor fellow, he could hardly speak . . . his anxiety about his sons has always seemed to me to be almost beyond his control.' Robert wrote to Philip in France: 'I cannot speak of Val without breaking down.'

It was Robert's idea to ask Churchill to write the tribute. 'I thought of him at once.' Years later, Arthur Villiers told Peter how pleased Churchill had been when he had finished it, especially the last sentence: 'It is a very good sentence.' The obituary appeared in *The Times* on 25 May. 'As the war lengthens and intensifies and the extending lists appear, it seems as if one watched at night a well-loved city whose lights, which burn so bright, which burn so true, are extinguished in the distance in the darkness one by one.'

Soon after, Churchill went to see Val's grave, at Sainte-Émilie, three miles behind the line. 'It is in a ruined garden,' he wrote to Eve, 'where many beautiful flowers and bushes still survive the havoc wrought by the enemy. He lies in good and gallant company. I picked some branches of great round white flowers and laid them on his grave as a tribute to the memory of a dear friend and a dauntless gentleman.'

At Durnford, Tom Pellatt read about Val's death in the paper. Hester never forgot 'how upset my mother was when she had to tell Ian about it'.

Like Churchill's framed obituary above his bed, the phantom of his dead father loomed over Ian for the remainder of his life. 'In his four sons you will find your only comfort,' Churchill had written to Eve, '& they will find in his life the inspiration and standard of their loss.' Just how significant was Val's influence can be read in this letter that Ian wrote to Peter a year before his own death. 'In my next opus James Bond's obituary appears in *The Times* – "M writes etc" – and I would very much like to put above it *The Times* masthead in the form they use it for copies of obituaries such as the one on Mokie.'

With Bond, and ultimately only with Bond, the son of a Scotsman from the Highlands, would the eight-year-old Ian Fleming be able one day to join his father at the front.

V
DURNFORD

'Don't *be downhearted about the boys having to grow up
without a father.*'
TOM PELLATT to Eve, May 1917

Eve's 'expressive grief' would cause her to paint every room black in the new
lodge at Arnisdale, even the lavatory.

The day after learning of Val's death, while 'waiting to see dear old Peter
off to school', Robert appealed to his devastated daughter-in-law: 'If Val
could speak to you now I am sure he would say "If you love me as I know
you do, think of these tender pledges. Continue to devote your care &
thought on making them men even as I was."' Quite shocking to a modern
audience but less surprising for that era is how Peter was sent back to Durnford within hours of hearing that his father had been killed.

Tom Pellatt contacted Eve on Peter's return. 'My wife is reading your letter to the boys. It was heartbreaking to read what you wrote. Don't say you
wish to die. He would not have wished it. Don't say it, try to live for the
children . . . I cannot look at the two, your two, without tears.'

'T.P.' was more upbeat three weeks later. 'Ian brought me a photograph of
his father.' Pellatt co-wrote plays that were performed on the London stage
under the pseudonym of Wilfred T. Coleby. His letter to Eve ended with the
theatrical assurance that 'not for one in a million has this opportunity been
given of going out of this world as your husband did, in a manner so noble,
for a reason so splendid that ever hereafter so long as the world continues
his name stands there written in deathless letters of fame to abide when we
are long long forgotten.'

This was Val's image that Eve strained to preserve. She seized on Pellatt's words and Robert's as her guiding rule – to bring up 'those four young fellows to be like him' – and elevated her dead husband from an absent, pipe-smoking, deer-stalker to an iconic figure in the clouds with whom she alone enjoyed privileged communication. ' "The height holds peace". That is what I put on Mokie's cross, and I would have you keep that before you all your lives.' She had sent Val's photograph for Ian to give to the Pellatts and taught him to say in his prayers 'and make me like Mokie'. It alarmed Rupert Hart-Davis to see how Eve used 'any sort of blackmail to get her way with the boys. "Your father's spirit has spoken to me," she'd say when particularly keen on getting them to do something they didn't want to.'

The impact of Val's death on his sons cannot be overstated. The need to prove themselves like him consumed them. As well as to escape Eve, it motivated Peter to go exploring through the Amazon and Siberian wildernesses. Christopher Isherwood, travelling with W. H. Auden, met him in China, and after observing the risks Peter took described how 'Auden and I recited passages from an imaginary travel book called *With Fleming to the Front*.' When Michael died from his wounds at Dunkirk, a fellow officer wrote to his widow: 'At least he fulfilled his great ambition, he was worthy of his father.'

The pain of Val's death was intensified by the reading of his will, which Val had signed on 7 August 1914. Robert's letter to Philip about Eve's expectations more than hinted at his involvement with its terms. 'She will, of course, be very comfortable. Val leaves the whole income from his capital which as you know is not small.' On Val's death, his third share in Robert Fleming & Company appears to have devolved to his two partners, Robert and Phil. Eve inherited Pitt House, but there was a condition she cannot have anticipated: the bulk of Val's estate, worth approximately £27 million in today's money, remained in a trust fund to which she had access only if she remained a widow. It would pass to their children were she to remarry, drastically limiting her income to no more than £3,000 per year (some £310,000 today), which would have left her still astoundingly well off. It never incentivised Eve to unshackle this golden leg-iron. On the other hand, it freed her to chafe bitterly about 'a bad will', which did not endear 'Mrs Val' to the other Flemings, and drove her to exploit another clause, giving Eve the power to distribute Val's money among their sons as she saw fit, even to disinherit them. For Ian, the canniness that his grandfather had honed in Dundee had consequences that Robert could not have foreseen.

Already cast as the difficult one, Ian took the blow of Val's death hard. It was not merely that he had to live up to his father's and grandfather's standards. Ian was at the martyred mercy of his histrionic thirty-two-year-old widowed mother: her blackmails, insecurities and extravagant, often punitive whims. Adrian House came to know Ian in Kitzbühel in the 1930s and recognised how 'he was enormously affected by the death of his father. This was one of the original sources of his melancholy.' On top of everything, it threw out of kilter his fox-cub relationship with Peter – who had been told by Eve on the station platform, 'You're responsible now.'

No father. Eve in control, holding the purse strings. Peter second-in-command. If there was a moment when the mould set, it was May 1917. Like Peter Pan, part of Ian remained frozen at the age of eight.

Dada would like to come & see you and play with you on the sands, and build big sand castles to keep the sea back.

During that summer of 1917 on the beach at Bude, Ian met the person who became his lifelong friend, a bronzed boy with bright blue eyes, a wide mouth, and a limp from a tobogganing accident which made one leg three inches shorter than the other. 'He was a polished hazelnut colour all over,' says Marina Warner, who knew him in old age, 'except his lips which were full and purplish – like his feet, where the veins bulged.'

Ivar Bryce was the son of an Anglo-Peruvian father who had made a fortune from guano and then disappeared in the war after his regiment wandered by mistake into Holland. There he was interned, fell in love with a Dutch lady and never came back. Bryce's mother would remarry in 1923 and write detective stories after being effectively thrown out of his childhood home: Moyns Park, a Jacobean manor house on the Essex and Suffolk border, which Bryce was to buy back in 1950 and where he contrived to recapture and preserve 'part of the old England which was engraved in his heart'.

When he met Ian, weeks after Val was killed, Bryce's nanny Miss Horniblow was trying to take the young boy's mind off the news that his father was missing. 'Let's go to the beach.'

Under Granny Kate's eye, the four Fleming boys were building a moated fortress in the sand with what Bryce described as frenzied energy. 'The leaders were Ian and Peter, and I gladly carried out their exact and exacting orders.' Bryce's first impression of Ian was of 'a most egotistical little boy. There was no question of other architects for his sandcastles. As a child, no matter who the people were, he always wanted his own way.' They did not meet again for another four years.

It may have been on this Cornish holiday that Ian went looking for amethyst in a cave near St Ives, found a two-pound lump of thick, grey, odourless paste, and decided it was ambergris (a secretion from a sperm whale's intestines, and used in perfume manufacture), worth the equivalent today of £70,000 an ounce. 'There would be no scolding or punishments ever again,' Ian fantasised. 'I would not have to go back to my private school or indeed to any more work at all. I had found the shortcut out of all my childish woes.' The waiter at the Tregenna Castle Hotel, to which he scampered back, dropping it on the carpet, explained that Ian's treasure was rancid New Zealand butter from a torpedoed supply ship that had congealed in the salt water. For the remainder of his life, Ian never ceased to view the world in its most exotic colours. All his butter would be ambergris; all his bottle tops, Spanish doubloons – an attitude that was bound to set him up for repeated disappointment. Practically the only memory the young Bond retains of childhood is 'the painful grit of wet sand between young toes when the time came for him to put his shoes and socks back on' and 'the precious little pile of sea shells and interesting wrack on the sill of the bedroom window' accompanied by the shake of a female head. 'No, we'll have to leave that behind, darling, it'll dirty up your trunk.'

After one of his wartime missions to America, Ian told Maud Russell that coming back to England 'was as depressing as those dread days in little boys' lives when the holidays end and the good times, and they have to go back to drab, drear school.'

Ian was at English boarding schools for almost as long as he spent writing novels. Forty years after he left Durnford, he received a letter from his first teacher, Basil Maine. The sight of 'the writing which used to sternly mark my childish papers' undammed a reservoir of memories, starting with another teacher, Arthur Worsley, a bachelor and former county cricketer 'who used to pull my hair out in handfuls'.

Among the faces that streamed back were Ian's first love Hester, and her parents, Tom and Nell Pellatt.

In a temper, 'T.P.' could bellow like a bull, his anger taking on 'the colour and appearance of a lacquered mask of a Chinese war demon', wrote another Durnfordian, 'his features contorted, his full moustache a-bristle, his teeth bared and gnashed in menacing grimace'. Hester witnessed one of these ignitions after Eve sent him a letter. '*Dear Mr Pellatt, Will you make sure Ian cleans his teeth. They were quite green when he returned home from school last term* . . . I remember this threw my father into a towering rage. "Pack the boy's trunk," he shouted. "I won't be written to like this by any boy's mother." It took us all a long time to calm him down.'

Ian claimed: 'I was bullied at school'. He told Ann that he was belted on his first day. When he had asked why, he was told, 'for arriving'. Peter questioned the extent of this. 'I wouldn't say that Ian came in for more than anyone else.' Generally speaking, Ian's 'scoldings' were for misbehaviour. 'I had to write out hundreds of lines of Virgil as punishment,' Ian was reminded in 1957 when visiting the cave near Naples where Aeneas approached the Styx.

Three years into the war, Durnford was a spartan school, if not an infernal one. 'It was very uncomfortable,' said Peter. 'And the food was terrible. Ian always objected to that. I remember his horror when an entire head of a rabbit turned up in some stew.'

The lavatories were reached across a courtyard, and consisted of a long row of earth closets in the open air, and a urinal known as 'Vespasian', which resembled 'a loft for gigantic pigeons'. The wall of Vespasian overlooked the cricket fields. Boys competed in trying to relieve themselves over it by drinking water to build up the pressure.

The dormitories were unheated. Every morning at 7 a.m. Peter and Ian raced in the nude along cold passages and up staircases lit by oil lamps, to jump into the indoor plunge pool on the first floor. In Peter's story of a dying explorer in the frost-bound Kum La pass, the hero recalls Durnford's sub-zero temperatures and the big fireplace at the end of a schoolroom, 'before which little boys warmed the shiny seats of their trousers and those who had colds dried their dirty handkerchiefs, from which the steam rose thinly'. The colds could be terrible. Peter rarely admitted to hardship, but he revealed that 'a boy died while we were there'. The boy had reported sick with whooping cough 'and the matron just refused to take any notice'. Ian exemplified the school policy in a letter to Eve. 'My coff has grown the whoping coff now, please don't tell Mister Pellat, cause just this morning he said that nun of us had got coffs.'

Beyond the cricket field, a wooded path led to a stone summer house known as The Fort, which became a centre for the games devised by Pellatt. One team was designated to build 'houses' in the woods, the other to dam the stream. 'Ian always chose the stream,' said Hester. 'I can still see him as a very small boy standing up to his armpits in the river in the pouring rain.' In her Durnford novel, *Ever Thine,* she described how spending 'an afternoon in the woods gave one the ardent melancholic intensely receptive sensation that comes when we dream that we can do anything – write a wonderful poem, ride a winged horse, swim an ocean, stir up and lead a crowd of staring face-less people.'

As central to Ian's school universe as The Fort and the woods was what Val had called 'a topping bathing place': Dancing Ledge.

In the mountain of lost Fleming material is black-and-white footage of Peter and Ian leaping naked into the sea. The film was taken on a very hot half-holiday in 1918 by a man in a Guards tie and a leather overcoat. He directed Peter and Ian plus sixty of their fellow pupils to jump, 'registering pleasure', into the clear waters of the Channel from the edge of a rock-pool that 'T.P.' had blasted out of the cliffs. Peter wrote, 'I can well remember the chagrin and resentment with which we learned that this scene would have to be cut, owing to our not having worn bathing dresses.'

The skinny dip was a Durnford ritual. Each afternoon of the summer term, between midday and 1.45 p.m., a crocodile line of white-flannelled boys set off on a forty-five-minute walk to the sea. Smugglers had made the cart track to the ledge. It led between steep bramble-covered mounds con-cealing Iron Age fortresses, down crumbling limestone steps to the quarried rock shelf. The pool was thirty feet by ten, refreshed at high tide. Every new boy had to swim a length under Pellatt's eccentric tutelage. Dressed in a pan-ama hat, and slung in a canvas noose suspended from a bamboo pole, 'T.P.' cried: 'Kick, now – kick – in, out!'

His daughter assisted in teaching the boys how to swim. Hester took them round to smugglers' caves where sea-birds nested. She led them out to sea, to turn on their backs and look up 'at the burial ground of the men of the Iron Age'. In her mermaid company, Ian was shown where to find sea anemones and feed them with crumbs. 'There's no bathing like this in the world. None,' she wrote. Ian's challenge was to find another place like it.

A significant event of the summer term was the Great Picnic, with diving competitions and 'flying jumps' from the dunes. The artist and set designer Laurence Irving found Peter and Ian in charge when he returned to his old school on a visit. 'Now the school appeared to be captained efficiently by the Fleming brothers; Peter, as later I might have guessed, had appropriated the transport, goading a donkey with its load of sandwiches, garibaldi biscuits and lemonade to the farm where it was off-loaded to boy-bearers for the last precipitous lap of the picnic path.'

Down on Dancing Ledge, Hester had no sense of time. 'I have only to shut my eyes to see again the group round the tea basket, the stacked heaps of food, the captain of the school and two of his subordinates preparing vast jugs of lemonade, the curious greedy gulls wheeling in and hovering over us, the enamel mugs, the scattered shoes and socks, the china-smooth reds and pinks of the boys' faces above their cream-coloured blazers . . .'

The high point of Ian's school week was Nell's Sunday night reading of an adventure story. This took place in the hall, a large room two storeys high, with an oak staircase to a gallery that led to the Pellatts' private quarters. Perched together in chairs, on window seats, on the stairs, the whole school assembled to hear Hester's mother read aloud from *Treasure Island*, *Moonfleet*, *The Prisoner of Zenda*, *The Mystery of Dr Fu-Manchu* – and in Ian's final year, *Bulldog Drummond* by Sapper (the pen-name of H. C. McNeile). Dressed in an elegant tea gown, Nell lay on the long sofa with her silk-stockinged feet up over the laps of two boys who were required to tickle them. 'Considerable prestige was conferred by this honour,' recalled Nicholas Elliott. 'Boys competed to be the lucky pair.'

Ian sat enthralled, listening to Nell change her voice for each character. On sweltering evenings, she read aloud under the chestnut trees on the lawn. Tales of pirates and buried treasure and galleons stranded in the Sargasso Sea. Her 'special' voices became a part of the children's lives, wrote Hester. 'I remember a rich, bubbling voice for Mr Bultitude; a creepy dark one for Long John Silver . . .'

The effect of this Sunday ritual on Ian, his first real taste of story-telling, is worth stressing. Elliott wrote: 'Not one of Nell's successive audiences would read again those books she brought to life without recalling the tone and inflexion of her voice, the thrill of her delivery of the last line that precluded a week's suspense.'

Out on the playing field, Ian was starting to emulate the athletic skills of Robert and Val. 'I am in an awfully good bait about the sports because I have won the hurdles.' Not only the hurdles but the long and triple jump. 'What I am in the best bate about is that I beat the whole school by 1 foot 3 inches & I jumped 18 foot 10 inches.' With any luck, he would get a cup, he wrote to Eve – 'because I do want to repay you by getting a little Renown at any rate at sports & I would be so glad if only to repay you for always being so naughty.'

To be renowned at sports gave Ian the hope of blunting her disapproval. Illustrated with a drawing of 'me long jumping', Ian made a list of resolutions to pacify his mother:

1 I promise not to be naughty at all
2 tell lies
3 be rude
4 not to say nasty things to you
5 I promise to be very good always
6 to help you
7 work at school
8 not to be greedy
9 not to worry you
10 not to be disobedient

He was unable to keep even one of these promises.

By contrast, Pellat had identified Ian's older brother as 'a brilliantly clever child' whose précis of Balzac's *La Peau de chagrin* Pellatt kept as a model. 'When Peter was with me, I felt "in my bones" that he would distinguish himself quite early in life.'

In 1920, after his 'effortless assumption of responsibility as head boy', Peter went on to Eton, failing to gain his expected scholarship because at exam time he was in bed with measles caught at a circus. It was all very last minute. Eve suddenly discovered that Val had not put their names down at birth 'and there was something of a panic to get us in'.

Aged twelve, Ian now enjoyed his first Peter-free year. His behaviour improved. Hester said: 'It was difficult to go on being naughty at a school where you could really do what you liked.' He won a shelf of sporting trophies, including a couple of prizes for golf on the course that 'T.P.' had laid out between the playing fields and woods. Deep in the woods, Ian swapped damming the stream for house-building; his playhouse in the trees was an early prototype of the one he erected three decades later in Jamaica. He assured his mother: 'My house is getting on alright. My spots have nearly gone and I am so glad.'

The last meaningful ceremony at Durnford took place on the final evening of the summer term in July 1921. This was 'T.P.'s pi-jaw'. Ian was summoned to the headmaster's room adjoining the hall, and there in the dim lamplight he was initiated by 'T.P.' into the mysteries of sex. 'You have no sister. If you had, you would see that where you have something dangling down in front, she has a hole. If you want to have a baby, you put what you have dangling down into her hole and you relieve yourself into it. Goodbye and good luck . . .'

The irony here is that the person who aroused these mysteries in Ian was Hester. 'He had a passion for the Headmaster's daughter,' said Mary Pakenham, to whom Ian later confided that Hester was 'the only woman I have ever really been in love with'.

With Hester, Ian had built a house in the woods. They had dived together off Dancing Ledge, explored caves, discovered the secrets of the sea. He had held Hester's waist in dance classes, wearing a white shirt with a number stitched in red. He told her long afterwards that 'his number Twenty-six had become a symbol of good fortune and that he constantly and successfully betted on it during his visits to Monte Carlo'.

> *A breathless kiss in the dim half-light*
> *The last soft touch of a lingering hand*
> *Dreams which we shared with a careless love*
> *Schemes for the future, minutely planned.*

Ian was in his final term when he composed his poem to Hester. Another thirty years would go by before he again experienced such emotions. 'So you see, my sweet, I am lost and gone and sold down the river,' he wrote to Ann Rothermere in 1946, 'and I haven't felt like this since the headmaster's daughter when I was twelve and lying in a field of mustard with the sun in my eyes eating a piece of plum cake which she had stolen for me.' Hester had afterwards married a man who had then run away with a gym teacher from Bournemouth.

On Ian's last night, after they sang 'Lead us, heavenly Father, lead us,' accompanied on the upright piano beneath the staircase, 'T.P.' turned to address the leavers, a group that included Ian, Reynolds Stone and five other boys headed for Eton.

'I've only this to say – try in the best sense, to *enjoy* as much of your lives as you can . . . try to be alive to everything that comes your way, and to get something out of it, and then nothing you do – nothing you feel – will be wasted. Whatever you are now, whatever you become, is your responsibility.' Pellatt hoped they would grow up 'to take the place in some measure of the beloved "special" ones we have lost in the war'.

Four years had passed since Ian had presented Val's photograph to 'T.P.' The pressure for him to be more like Mokie had not lessened as he prepared to join Peter at Eton.

VI
ETON

'English public schools are supposed to grow people up
very quickly and teach them how to behave.'
THE SPY WHO LOVED ME

Eton College, founded in 1440 by Henry VI on the edge of Windsor, principally for the education of seventy poor boys, had a view of the royal castle
across the Thames. When Ian arrived, the 1,118 pupils, all male, were distributed among twenty-nine boarding houses. The fees were £230 a year
(approximately £12,200 today), and boys generally stayed for five years. In
many cases, they were marked, as Ian was, for life.

The novelist Phyllis Bottome taught Ian in Kitzbühel immediately after
he left Eton and was Ian's 'first contact with a "famous writer"'. In her 1946
novel *The Lifeline,* she based the character of Mark on Ian, after observing
how much of his identity came from being an Etonian. 'You said the word
"Eton", and instantly, Mark thought, the Castle walls were there, the Park,
the silver gleam, the Castle itself, moving silently into the mind with the
stateliness of a swan rounding the curve of a river. You could turn your back
on them – as many boys did – oblivious, contemptuous, self-absorbed; but
long years afterwards – all over the world in the strangest places, if someone
said that word again, up the picture sprang, and there was an emotion at the
bottom of the heart to match it – so that for ever and wherever you were, you
felt fundamentally linked to that unspoken symbol.'

Hilary Bray, whose name Bond uses as an alias in *On Her Majesty's Secret
Service,* once returned to Eton with Ian, who, on inhaling the scents of
cricket pads, urine and cabbage, claimed that he was instantly carried back
to adolescence. '"Ah yes, it even smells the same." But it didn't. And all the

things he remembered were totally wrong. You see, he had a great gift for plunging back into the past, but in an inaccurate way.'

When Ian took the American novelist Paul Gallico to his old room in The Timbralls, Gallico thought Ian was going to be sick. 'I was desperately unhappy,' Ian told another friend. 'Away from the hours I spent on the playing field, I hated the place. Yet if ever I had a son, his name would go down on the Eton waiting lists within three days of his birth. It just shows what a conventional so-and-so I am at heart.'

Ian's emotional connection to the school ran deep. He not only put Caspar down for Eton. He sported an Old Etonian tie all his life, deflecting when asked why, 'Oh, the colours are really quite unobjectionable.' Almost his first act on leaving the school was to join the Old Etonian cricket club, the Ramblers; he also liked to wear their tie. In October 1961, Ann wrote to Evelyn Waugh on the 150th Anniversary of the Eton Society, the formal name for the school's self-elected prefects: 'At this moment Thunderbird is roistering at the Dorchester with 700 members of the Eton institution called "Pop".' The following summer, in contrast to Peter's legacy – 'The Peter Fleming Owl', for the best-written item in the *Eton College Chronicle* – Ian donated a silver chamber pot to the Old Etonian Golfing Society – 'The James Bond All Purposes Grand Challenge Vase'.

An ex-pupil who claimed to have hated the place, Ian kept in lifelong touch. 'When the chips were down,' said Ernie Cuneo, 'he was as certainly Etonian as a West Pointer is a West Pointer.'

Cuneo attributed Ian's 'effortless superiority' to his Eton education. But this surface self-possession came at a well-camouflaged cost. Phyllis Bottome detected in both Fleming brothers 'Eton's strange faults and absurdities; its isolationism; its defensive arrogance; its inconsiderate insolence, and its deep unconscious selfishness.' Eton engraved itself on Ian in other ways: his arrested schoolboy humour, his taste for pranks, and his 'mobbing' language – 'Lights out, Miss Potterton,' he tormented Caspar's nanny at Goldeneye. Then those hours in College Chapel. 'You can't grow up in the English school system without it having an effect on you,' he told Clare Blanshard after falling ill in New York and asking her to light a candle for him in St Patrick's Cathedral.

The school's most observable legacy was the company he kept in this life. Eton introduced Ian to the narrow group of people who ran his world; an exclusive club like Pop that had an impact, out of all proportion to its numbers, on every aspect of British society, forming networks 'as deep and pervasive as Japanese knotweed'.

In a remarkable paragraph in his memoirs, Gladwyn Jebb, who had dealings with Ian when he ran SOE [Special Operations Executive], drew attention to 'the extent to which the entire Government machine on the foreign side, outside No 10, was at the beginning of the war dominated by Old Etonians' – Eden, Halifax, Cadogan, Vansittart, Harold Macmillan, Duff Cooper. 'So were the two Ministers successively responsible for SOE, Dalton and Selborne, together with the Heads of the two Secret Services, Stewart Menzies and (after myself) Charlie Hambro.' Jebb did not say this was necessarily a good thing, but 'the fact that they had all had the same start did do something to facilitate relationships and thus promote efficiency.'

Etonians did not stop at running Whitehall. Before setting off to the Amazon, and believing that 'an Old Boy is worth two young men', Peter Fleming hailed an Eton contemporary sauntering down Gower Street – 'Roger, come to Brazil.' Peter spent much of the 1930s going around the world with Etonians or staying with them in consular and mercantile outposts. Wherever he travelled, Peter carried with him like a uniform 'le sangfroid d'ancien élève d'Eton'. In Brazil, he put on his old school tie to meet the Interventor of Goyaz ('We hoped devoutly that the Interventor would know an Old Etonian tie when he saw one'). In China, Peter taught a music teacher from Ulan Bator how to sing the Eton Boating Song, 'the only song I have ever sung more than once'. ('I often think of him,' Peter wrote, 'a distant gesticulating figure, teaching the Eton Boating Song to the inhabitants of Outer Mongolia.') At Harbin, Peter bathed at the Yacht Club with 'One-Arm' Sutton, 'the only Old Etonian claiming to hold the rank of General in the Chinese Army', who had been in Pop with Val. In Shanghai, he hunted down Gerald Yorke, a former Captain of the Oppidans like Peter, now living with no money in a temple with a bandit. When plotting his journey across China, he had stayed at the British Legation in Peking with the future British ambassador to Washington and Provost of Eton, Harold Caccia, who had been in The Timbralls with Peter and Ian. Eton's clump-forming perennials were to be discovered everywhere, from China to Guatemala.

It repays to list Ian's Eton connections, those boys with whom he was to be, in Cyril Connolly's phrase, 'shaken about like stones in a tin' for one tenth of his life. It was a spy network already in the making, a class of English men raised to rule the Empire, who formed a sort of fraternity because they were all known to one another from boyhood, and did indeed form most of the connections Ian needed in later life.

The range of characters was extraordinary. As well as with kings, dukes, and maharajas, Ian walked every morning across the cobbles of School Yard into College Chapel with future writers, publishers, secret agents and artists; all dressed in tailcoats and top hats, or, if in Pop, flamboyant silk waistcoats; all passing by G. F. Watts' painting of Sir Galahad (and St George, who had been up in the Choir Screen slaying a rather pathetic dragon since about 1500); all jammed together in creaking oak pews for seven hours a week.

They included: Cyril Connolly (who commissioned for *Horizon* Ian's first serious piece of writing and then was employed by Ian at *The Sunday Times*), Peter Watson (sponsor of *Horizon*), George Orwell (the first to use the phrase 'Cold War'), John Lehmann (brother of Rosamond), Anthony Powell, Robert Byron, Henry Yorke, Harold Acton, Brian Howard, James Lees-Milne, A. J. Ayer, Oliver Messel, Wilfred Thesiger; Randolph Churchill, whose father Winston had been Valentine's friend; Alec Douglas-Home, who became another Prime Minister; and, from January 1924 to February 1925, the future traitor Guy Burgess.

Burgess would wear an Old Etonian tie in Moscow to meet Ian's foreign correspondent Richard Hughes for his world scoop. In cold exile, surrounded by photos of himself at Eton, Burgess was dominated by impressions of school, which Connolly formulated in his Theory of Permanent Adolescence. 'The plopping of gas mantels in the class-rooms, the refrain of psalm tunes, the smell of plaster on the stairs, the walk through the fields to the bathing places . . . the rattle of tea things, the poking of fires'.

Some pupils resurfaced years afterwards in Ian's life, as in a Powell novel. Dunstan Curtis, who led Ian's intelligence-gathering commando unit, 30AU. David Herbert, employed by Ian to ferry agents to France. Alan Pryce-Jones, who lived in the same building off Piccadilly when both worked in Intelligence. Christopher Chancellor, who was with Ian in Reuters and later headed the news agency. John Carter, who became an editorial director of

Ian's antiquarian quarterly the *Book Collector*. Rupert Hart-Davis, who worked for Peter and Ian's publisher, Jonathan Cape, and leased a house on the Nettlebed estate. George Newman, who rented Goldeneye in the months when Ian was not in Jamaica. Robin Darwin, great-grandson of Charles and principal of the Royal College of Art, who appointed Ian a Fellow. John Foster, also in Ian's house, who acted as one of Ian's lawyers in his 1963 plagiarism trial. Jock Campbell, who bought the James Bond franchise when chair of the sugar company Booker Brothers McConnell. Not to forget Shane O'Neill, whose wife ran off with Ian and later married him.

A feature that distinguishes Eton from its more ancient and academic model, Winchester, is the degree to which Etonians stick together afterwards. John Buchan's hero Sandy Arbuthnot made his lifelong friends at the school. This was the case for Ian, another younger son. Those he trusted, whom he chose to spend time with at the bridge table or on the golf course, to whom he showed a loyalty blind and unconditional, had shrunk by the end of his life to a tiny group. They included 'Boofy' Gore, later the Earl of Arran, who described his friends like this: 'I recognise that I have five, or possibly six . . . I would cut off my right arm for them. When I talk of friends I mean people who will stick by one regardless. People who when I am unmasked as the stoat in the Great Train Robbery will say, Tut-tut. Naughty fellow. He shouldn't have done it, but all the same . . .' Ian's tight loyal circle numbered in addition: Ivar Bryce, Hilary Bray, John Fox-Strangways, Gerald Coke and Philip Brownrigg – all of whom he had encountered at Eton and who would end up in his books.

As well, Eton furnished Ian with names for his fiction. Two further sets of brothers were the Chittys – A. M. Chitty and J. T. Chitty, sons of the college chaplain; and G. A. Scaramanga, *ma.* (major) and T. A. Scaramanga, *mi.* (minor). Somewhat to his irritation, 'Boofy' Gore found himself recast as a minor Bond villain, 'Boofy Kidd'. Mr Big's battered black top hat has suspicious Etonian contours, as does Oddjob's lethal bowler: boys wore bowlers at puppy shows for the school's beagles. With a nod to the Wall Game, Goldfinger is described as having a 'great brown and orange football of a head'. Probably the most famous Etonian reincarnation is the head of the criminal syndicate SPECTRE. Thomas Robert Blofeld had been taken away from Eton with mastoids two years before Ian's arrival, but Ian, on meeting his son Henry at

Boodle's in 1960, explained how he had needed an evil name and could not think of one. Henry says: 'One morning he went to Boodle's, sank into a leather chair and grabbed the Club membership list and got to "B" and, gobsmacked by three Blofelds, slammed the book shut, gave a yelp of delight, and ordered a pewter mug of champagne and never looked back.'

Ian arrived at Eton a year after Peter, in September 1921, aged thirteen. He would leave a term before him, in April 1926. His only triumph over his brother, said Mary Pakenham, was his height. Peter, being under the required height of five foot four inches, still had to wear a 'bumfreezer' jacket; Ian wore tailcoats from the start.

Because of the muddle of not being assigned a housemaster by joining a 'list' at birth, Peter said, The Timbralls was the only house they could get into. 'For at that time it was the most unpopular house in the school.'

The architect of The Timbralls was Henry Woodyer, who designed hostels for Fallen Women. Built in 1860 in the style of Keble College, Oxford, and named after Eton's timber hall which housed the wooden scaffolding for College Chapel, The Timbralls was an imposing house of wine-red brick on the Slough Road, the first building as you came into Eton, and looking out over School Field. Ian entered from New Schools Yard, stopping to read the notices or collect his books from the 'Slab'. Old names on blackened wood up the oak staircase led to his bedroom-cum-study on the first floor: open coal fire (there was no central heating), curtained-off narrow folding bed, a washstand (there was no running water), a padlocked ottoman (for cricket gear and so on, in which Ian probably concealed his cigarettes and hair oil), an easy chair, a bookshelf, and his 'burry' – a three-drawer bureau with a fold-out writing surface. On the walls, he hung Eve's watercolours of Ireland, where Eve travelled with Augustus John ('Do draw & paint me some pictures of the places you go through, they would be so topping for my room'). In this narrow space, Ian slept and studied, and with one or two others made a daily high tea along the passage, scrambled eggs and sausages, or a pheasant or partridge from Joyce Grove. 'The transfer from Durnford to Eton,' wrote Nicholas Elliott, 'was like moving from a doss house into Claridge's. I shall never forget the joy and privacy of a room of my own.'

The one fly in this ointment was Ian's housemaster, Edward Vere Slater, whom the broadcaster Ludovic Kennedy recalled as 'a large, bald man with large horn-rimmed spectacles and a purple nose', and 'one of the few remaining housemasters who beat boys with a cane on the bare bottom.' In a story reminiscent of Ian being belted at Durnford, Ann heard how on Ian's first night at Eton, after her Rolls-Royce had pulled away, his housemaster, or 'm'tutor', as boys referred to him, came in and said, 'I'm going to break you, Fleming.' True or not, it captures a relationship that striped Ian's time at Eton. 'Ian hated his House Master,' said Hilary Bray. 'A tyrant and a bully.' Influenced by what Ian had told her, Phyllis Bottome brought a Slater-like figure into her novel *Danger Signal*. 'Ronnie considered that he had been irretrievably harmed by this medieval brute; had his housemaster been capable of understanding him what difference to Ronnie's whole subsequent career this understanding would have made.'

A mountain-climbing bachelor known to other masters as 'Sam', Slater was 'Bumface' to the forty boys in his house. 'Rather an inferior man,' was George Lyttelton's opinion, recalling how a friend who had dined with Slater reported that 'there should have been some sort of warning as a guest might have a weak heart'. One of Slater's successors as housemaster says: 'He had a thing about VD and on occasion would get boys to answer the roll-call known as "Absence" naked, and thus attired parade past him for inspection. No wonder the boys didn't exactly love him.' In a history of Eton, Slater is described as a 'sadist' with not much to his credit. 'For at least one member of his House, the day he heard that Slater had been killed mountaineering was the happiest of his boyhood.'

On a Swiss peak in the Engadine with three Eton masters, Slater plummeted to his death in August 1933. The guide who discovered him, in his 'unique pair of twill trousers', said that he had fallen head first: 'All were in a terrible condition, their necks broken, and their bodies covered with wounds. The rope with which they were tied together was twisted about their necks.' An axe was found with Sam Slater's name on it. Fourth on the rope, it had been Slater 'who drove his ice-axe to the hilt with his last strong gesture'.

Slater's dramatic end was in circumstances identical to the deaths of James Bond's parents in the Aiguilles Rouges above Chamonix when Bond was eleven. How Harold Caccia interpreted Slater's dislike for the young

Fleming is revealing: 'Slater would have looked at Ian and seen Bond in miniscule [*sic*].'

An early source of friction was the Trumper's hair oil that Ian liked to rub on – until Slater banned the practice. Ian assured his mother: 'I am trying my best to get unselfish, and m'tutor has stopped me brushing my hair back although now it looks sloppy and beastly.'

The die was cast, even so. Years later, another boy in The Timbralls recalled the brouhaha caused by what even Peter conceded to be Ian's 'slightly flash' behaviour. 'That hair oil is important. You see he was really Bond already, and it was the Bond in him that old Sam objected to.'

A large number of boys had no father. Of the 5,703 Etonians who had served in the war, 1,157 were killed. Val's name was inscribed in the colonnade under Upper School along with 324 Etonians who had died in the Ypres Salient. For the next four years, Peter tried to fill Val's role – 'I did feel rather over-responsible for the family' – but he was able to exert less and less control over Ian. Connolly said, 'Peter became the father figure, but also something far more. Something very fierce. A competitor more than an ordinary father.' Connolly likened their rivalry to 'the situation of Cain and Abel'.

The Fleming Room in The Timbralls is a tribute to this fraternal struggle and the topsy-turvydom of fame. Today, boys in the house associate the Fleming name exclusively with the author on the framed book jackets of *From Russia, with Love* and *You Only Live Twice* that hang alongside posters of three Bond films on the grey-painted walls of what was once Slater's schoolroom. The name of Ian's elder brother draws a blank. Yet had you mentioned the name Fleming in this room at any time between the 1920s and the 1950s, the talked-about author would have been Peter. 'He was,' says Mark Amory, one of Peter's successors as literary editor of the *Spectator* and the editor of Ann Fleming's letters, 'one of the most famous Etonians there's ever been.'

In his Eton memoir, *Enemies of Promise*, Cyril Connolly noted, 'Boys do not grow up gradually. They move forward in spurts like the hands of clocks in railway stations.' If not in height, then in every other respect Peter had developed since leaving Durnford. He was 'a great swell in the school', wrote

Rupert Hart-Davis, who came across Peter first as a 'neat, black-haired little boy in a large white collar who seemed to know all the answers'. Caccia recalled that 'even to his contemporaries, Peter Fleming was completely outstanding. It wasn't just what he did, but the style in which he did it.' In a phrase of Antony, Viscount Knebworth, who proposed Connolly for Pop, Peter was one of 'the great almighty tremendous ones'.

Peter won the Duke of Newcastle's Spanish and the King's French prizes. He became house captain, then Captain of the Oppidans, representing the majority of boys who were not in College. He acted in 'The Devil's Disciple' and most memorably in 'Androcles'. He was no mean sportsman either, making the Oppidan Wall, one of the two teams in the Wall Game, a kind of football that had originated at the school. He also edited the school magazine, the *Eton College Chronicle*. In short, he was 'the King of Eton really' – as Ann Fleming's brother, Hugo Charteris, described him. Charteris disliked Ian intensely and did not bother to disguise Peter's name in his novel, *The Coat*. 'Peter' was 'a hero, a boy, as the dean said, to whom much had been given and from whom much would be required.' In sorry contrast was Peter's younger brother Tim. In one scene, Tim 'stole a look at his elder brother: but the dazzle was too much'.

Outclassed and outdistanced, Ian struggled to define himself. Tall for his age, good-looking, although still unsmiling in photographs, he took dandyish care over his appearance, wearing his hair long, and sporting silk handkerchiefs and a black hat. Yet he cut a withdrawn figure among his peer group.

He was more popular with older boys. One of those he took up with was the boy with a limp last encountered on a Cornish beach.

Ivar Bryce was eighteen months Ian's senior. He was now living with his mother, his older sister Amaryllis and his new stepfather on the Sussex coast. For reasons never established, he was known as 'Burglar' Bryce – in one version because his cheque had bounced at Eton and in a later one because he stole other men's wives and daughters.

'Bryce was his friend because he made him laugh,' said a future girlfriend of Ian. But the two boys were bound by more than a sense of humour and the coincidence of shortly afterwards having sisters with the exotic name of Amaryllis. Bryce filled the part of a non-competitive elder sibling, while

Bryce found in Ian the brother he needed. Many years later, Robert Harling looked back on their relationship and similar philosophy. 'I decided that the closest Fleming had ever come or would ever come to authentic compatibility had been with Ivar Bryce.'

'Burglar' Bryce recalled that Ian was not 'a terribly good mixer. He kept himself very much to himself. Started the habit there of requiring time for himself. Used to sit in his study on his own.'

Ian's brother Richard joined The Timbralls in 1924 and he could see straight away that Ian was not using this '¾ hour of solitude a day' to study. 'At Eton, Ian was fairly difficult. He was exceedingly idle and very erratic. He went through school with a combination of triumph and disrepute.'

However much Ian admitted to 'hero-worshipping' his brother, it crushed him to be an adolescent in Peter's accomplished academic and dramatic shadow. Ian looked like a black sheep, whatever he did. His solution was to find an identity that emphasised their differences. As Mary Pakenham saw it, 'the gooder Peter became, the naughtier Ian would have to become.' If the impeccable Peter was an embodiment of the finest Fleming and Etonian virtues, then the persona Ian adopted took after Eve's renegade brothers, those dissolute fantasists Harcourt and Ivor.

It was not merely his long slick hair. Ian received many 'White Tickets' for bad work. 'I'm afraid I wasn't terribly good at my books.' When asked if he has had some education, James Bond laughs. 'Mostly in Latin and Greek. All about Caesar and Balbus and so on. Absolutely no help in ordering a cup of coffee in Rome or Athens after I'd left school.'

On top of his undistinguished academic achievement, another concern of Eve's was Ian's frivolous extracurricular life.

Hilary Bray remembered how the word 'apolaustic' was used by masters like Hugh Macnaghten – 'an ogre for the purple patch' – to describe the self-indulgent. Hart-Davis first observed Ian's 'apolaustic' leanings when he watched him stroll each morning with his friend Lord Ancaster 'for a black coffee and buttered eggs at a place called the Red House near the river'. In his third year at Eton, Ian discovered an appetite for West End theatre. Eve was with Augustus John in Dublin when she received Ian's letter expressing contrition for many 'lapses', among them for having spent every afternoon of half-term seeing plays in London. 'I know I shouldn't have gone to any of those theatres, but I was so bored by myself.'

His feelings towards his housemaster had become more hostile. 'He's so awfully offensive & he gets frightfully on my nerves,' Ian complained. 'If, for every night for the past year or so you'd had ¼ hours jaw, about the same thing every night, I think you'd probably be pretty bored. Then he thinks that I think I'm such a frightfully good chap, well I don't think that's so frightfully true, because I've proved myself a rotter in so many ways.'

A rotter in so many ways. Ian was writing to Eve following a disciplinary incident. According to Richard, Ian had been 'walloped for taking a crib into an exam'. Either Slater or the headmaster, Cyril Alington, had felt it necessary to inform Eve.

Once again, Ian found himself having to mollify his mother for his bad behaviour. 'I am awfully sorry for my terrible lapse the other day, just after I'd promised to be good. I minded that much more than the punishment.' Ian vowed not to repeat his offence. 'I am afraid I'm not absolutely straight yet, but I really will try now that I know it matters a lot.' Thirty years later, he wrote to Ann about their three-year-old son: 'Try & teach him about promises & truth or he'll have an awful time at school.'

Ian did have one piece of news to cheer his mother. 'I am up to [being taught by] an absolutely ripping "lush" this half [term] called Lyttelton, he's extraordinarily nice, & the whole div: [class] adores him because he understands you so well & you feel that you want to do your best up to him.' Appealing to a connection guaranteed to resonate, he told his mother that Lyttelton 'was in the XI while Mokie was in the VIII'. As for the unspecified reason behind Ian's punishment, Lyttelton had been 'awfully decent about it & saw that it was a question of necessity for me to get it done and that's the sort of thing that makes you want him to think you a better chap. Diff: from m'tutor who merely saw that I'd "cribbed" & nothing else.'

Ian was fortunate to be 'up to' the Hon. George Lyttelton. A teacher with an infectious passion for literature who liked to get his class to define the difference, say, between pride and vanity, Lyttelton was editor of *An Eton Poetry Book*, published in Ian's penultimate year. One of the more outstanding English schoolmasters of his generation (and father of the trumpeter Humphrey), he later singled out those 'Extra Studies chaps' he was proud to have taught: Aldous Huxley, Jack Haldane, John Lehmann, George Orwell, Cyril Connolly, Alan Pryce-Jones and Peter Fleming. He made this list in the late 1950s, in a letter to another former pupil, Rupert Hart-Davis. Significant is the name he leaves out. In the same correspondence, Lyttelton writes how he is reading Ian Fleming's *Moonraker* on Hart-Davis's recommendation. 'It thrilled me, IF must be a devilishly clever fellow . . . I must get hold of his other novels. I wonder why I never came across him at Eton.' Fleming *mi.* had made no impression on his favourite teacher.

Not until his third year did Ian attract the attention of his contemporaries. As at Durnford, he found a milieu in athletics. Already in football he had demonstrated 'an exceptionally long kick for his age'. After he won his House Colours for the Field Game (another, more widely played Etonian variety of football), his for once approving housemaster noted how 'on some days he plays very badly indeed; but on others, and these are – dieu merci – in the majority, he plays with a calmness, fortitude and even genius quite out of proportion to his years.'

Ian's breakthrough came in the spring of 1924, with a string of startling athletics victories. His placatory letter to Eve is largely an account of these.

First, the School Mile on 21 February. Ian won it by half a yard in a time of 4 minutes and 54 seconds.

Ian wrote, desperate to impress his reproachful mother: 'I managed to win the whole thing in only 3 secs: more than the quickest Jnr: time ever done, I meant to send you a telegram: but then I thought I'd wait. The Steeplechase came off on Wednesday, 150 competitors and I managed to win that too, by some fluke, by 60 yrds: the course is two miles long. Thus procuring in all two challenge cups for m'tutor's and an order for £2 at the school stores. Not worth it considering the amount of training I had to do, but still I was awfully pleased, & on last Sat: I saw myself on the Cinema, a terrible face, covered with sweat, with mouth wide open, such is fame!'

Filmed by Pathé, the story behind the 1924 college steeplechase has passed into Fleming's mythology. He had won this following his walloping, according to Richard. In a more lurid version, Ian told Paul Gallico how he petitioned the headmaster to 'swish' him early in time to compete, which Ian did with 'his shanks and running shorts stained by his own gore'.

There is no mention of this in his letter to Eve, written a day or so after his punishment. 'I'm going in for all the rest of the Jnr school events & Tatham, an International runner, is training me, a frightful bore but worth it. I hope your pleased. I am, frightfully.'

Wilfrid Tatham, who had run for Eton and Cambridge, was the world record holder in the two-mile relay and that year's British 440-yard hurdles champion. A modest and 'very sardonic man', he was back at Eton as a teacher. Tatham coached Ian along the lines of his own training for that summer's Paris Olympics, the games that featured in 'Chariots of Fire'. Tatham would also go on to represent Britain in the 1928 Olympics. His tutelage made all the difference and was to leave an imprint more enduring than any swishing.

Days later, the *Chronicle* recorded that Ian had won five out of the six events, including the junior hurdles, the junior mile, the junior half-mile, and the junior long jump. 'The achievement of Fleming *mi.* was the most remarkable thing in the School sports. He won all the junior races and scored the greatest number of points in the Victor Ludorum Cup, though he was disqualified as a junior.'

His victory in the long jump had a special sweetness. Ian's winning distance of 17 feet 11 inches beat his father's best jump in March 1900 by 5 inches. John Pearson described a photograph of Ian's leap. 'The strain over that teenage face has to be seen to be believed. It really is painful and already you feel this is a man who's going to push himself to the limit and he was only 15.'

Ian continued to admire anyone who excelled in games of endurance. Jacques Cousteau, the diver. Peter Thomson, the golfer. The mountaineer, Heinrich Harrer. Above all, the breaker of the four-minute mile. 'The only man since Michaelangelo to have been both artist and scientist is Roger Bannister. I know. I used to run the mile myself, but I ran to prove something to myself: he ran to prove both a belief in himself and to prove a theory to the world.'

Disqualified for being too young in 1924, Ian then won the Victor Ludorum in 1925 and 1926. His sporting achievement became an essential ingredient of his legend. Cuneo, a champion footballer himself, wrote that 'Ian was part of a select group whose reputations as great athletes would be enjoyed for the rest of his life,' and even beyond it. 'Ian Fleming was born in 1908 and educated at Eton where he excelled at athletics,' began the blurb on his posthumous novel *The Man with the Golden Gun*. James Bond's supreme fitness is the result of his following the strict regime prescribed by Ian's Eton coach.

On a par with his uncle Philip's Olympic gold, Ian winning a race at Eton is one of the episodes in the Fleming family saga in Lawrence Toynbee's frieze in the conservatory at Peter's house, Merrimoles. Yet the bigger picture is less exceptional than Ian made out and was an early illustration of his flair for self-promotion. He lamented to Mary Pakenham that 'by bad luck he was at the one house at Eton where athletics didn't count'. In truth, the indifference to athletics extended to pretty well the entire school, which regarded them, according to Tim Card's history of Eton, as on a par with fencing: 'Etonians fairly contently lost at either'. To Ian's contemporary Esmond Warner, 'the Victor Ludorum thing didn't really count for very much at Eton.' Indeed, for Cyril Connolly, 'being Victor Ludorum was rather a hollow crown. Nothing much mattered except getting into the [cricket] Eleven.'

Even Ian's family downplayed his victory, teasing Granny Kate that he had been made Victor Ludendorff, and reciting:

> *Dear Ian won a steeplechase;*
> *He won it third – three in the race.*

For the Flemings, field sports were the thing. They were much more impressed when Ian shot his first stag at Black Mount on 9 September 1924.

Shortly after his seventeenth birthday, Ian published his first story. This was a further attempt to differentiate himself from Peter, who had yet to try his hand at fiction.

In 1924, Ivar Bryce had co-edited a one-off magazine, *Snapdragon*, whose leading feature was a ghost story by the school's Provost, M. R. James. He sold it at the St Andrew's Day Wall Game, making a profit of £90 (approximately £6,400 today), mainly from advertising. 'Burglar' Bryce used his share to buy a Douglas motorbike that he kept at a yard in Peascod Street in Windsor and on the back of which, together with Ian, 'we became involved in many, often illicit activities'.

Ian was constantly short of money at Eton. 'Do you think you could possibly send me my £3 because I have not had any money this half?' he wrote to Eve. 'PS Can I buy a new pair of flannel trousers. I've had these for 1½ years & they are too small.' Attracted by the 'rich proceeds' that 'Burglar' had made from local tradesmen, Ian was emboldened to copy his friend's formula. The following June, days after King George V and Granny Kate's friend Queen Mary attended morning service in Lower Chapel, Ian published the *Wyvern*, a thirty-two-page magazine which he sold at the Eton and Winchester match at Lords.

Ian had relied on Eve's smart friends for most of its contents. Unpublished drawings by Augustus John and Edwin Lutyens, a poem by Vita Sackville-West. He also conjured a contribution out of his Durnford teacher, Basil Maine.

The most intriguing addition to 'this galaxy of talent' as the Eton *Chronicle*, edited by Peter, described the *Wyvern*, was a short story, 'The Ordeal of Caryl St George', signed 'I. L. F.'

Sandwiched between adverts for the *Tatler* ('which, like Eton passes an unbreakable chain round the entire world') and Aertex underwear, Ian's first piece of fiction is a melodrama about an adulterous couple who are craftily exposed by the cuckolded husband. Ian later dismissed it as 'a shameless crib of Michael Arlen!' Yet the story is interesting for the template it sets: both for the setting – a building overlooking Admiralty Arch – and for the situation: a young bachelor debating whether to run off with an 'absolutely ravishing' married woman.

In the character of Michael Tanqueray, the friend of a wealthy man whom he is betraying, Ian anticipated the kind of *ménage à trois* to which he himself became no stranger when working at the Admiralty. He even looked like Ian. 'Michael, tall, slim and handsome in a slightly effeminate way, sat opposite her and wished that her husband was dead, for, as he so often told his friends, it was about time he settled down with some rich and pretty woman as his wife. He believed that he had found his ideal in Mrs St George.' Michael is leaning down to kiss his lover when a shot rings out from the room below. It appears at a quick glance that Caryl's husband has killed himself with a battered service revolver, presenting Michael with what only a moment before he had coveted. Instead of gathering Caryl in his arms, Michael runs blindly from the house. But Paul, the contemptuous husband, is not dead. The gunshot was a ploy designed to reveal Michael for the shabby fellow he is. 'He was always such a coward, so I put him to the test,' Paul tells his wife before she faints.

In his first foray as an editor, Ian claimed to have made the same sum out of the *Wyvern* as Bryce had the year before, with 'a record sale'. Not without bias, the magazine was praised by Peter in the *Chronicle* as 'both original and good'. One item that Peter singled out was the drawing by Augustus John, 'whose name must surely convey something even to the most confirmed Philistines'.

What neither brother knew at the time was that their mother was several months pregnant by John.

In 1923, Eve sold Pitt House and moved to 118 Cheyne Walk, knocking together three buildings, one of them J. M. W. Turner's studio, to create a comfortable base in Chelsea. Here she worked industriously to establish a salon to rival that of Emerald Cunard. Among the composers, politicians, architects, writers, artists and minor royalty she attracted to Turner's House was Augustus John, a regular at the pub next door, who, though he was to paint Eve numerous times (as well as draw Ian, who named Caspar partly after John's son), was of the settled opinion that Eve 'couldn't tell a drawing from a cowpat'. John, who needed a stiffening drink before attending Eve's lunch parties, much later confessed to Amaryllis, the daughter he was to have with Eve, that their affair started only because he found her so unutterably boring there was nothing to do but take her to bed. Soon, there was 'reprehensible gossip' about the couple. Eve's housemaid Joan Regent told Richard's son Adam: 'Oh, Addie, they locked the door. We all knew what was going on.'

Eve was used to getting her own way. 'Mrs Val had a sort of power complex,' noticed Phyllis Bottome's husband, Ernan Forbes Dennis. 'Everything had to go exactly as she wanted it to go.' The moment arrived when Eve resolved to have a child with John.

Ian was in his first year at Eton when one of John's teenage models gave birth to a daughter called Zoe. Eve at once offered to adopt the baby, and kidnapped Zoe for a time to North Wales, dressing the girl in clothes with Fleming name-tapes. Zoe was returned to her frantic mother, but in the spring of 1925 Eve travelled with Augustus John to Germany. In Berlin, they stayed with the British ambassador, Lord d'Abernon. Amaryllis was conceived under his diplomatic roof.

Round about the time Ian was distributing the *Wyvern* at Lords with Augustus John's contribution, Eve summoned Joan Regent and the staff at Turner's House, and confected a narrative to compete with 'The Ordeal of Caryl St George'. She explained that she was going on a cruise and closing Turner's House, but Joan would be re-employed on her return. She then stepped into the mist.

Eve was absent from her sons' lives for the next few months, a break they may have welcomed. 'She had no sense at all of what would embarrass the boys,' recalled Rupert Hart-Davis. 'She came once in bright yellow and the boys wrote, "Dear Mum. Please do not come in yellow again."' When she reappeared, she was holding a red-headed baby called Amaryllis, born on 10 December 1925, which Eve claimed to have adopted, despite having her features. 'It seems quite a humorous brat,' Peter reported to Hart-Davis. Nearly forty years on, Hart-Davis wrote to Lyttelton: 'I remember the appearance of this baby when P and I were at Eton, and even then in my innocence I thought Mrs F's account of how she adopted this child ... rather unnecessarily protracted.' Eve's Hungarian violin teacher remarked that no adoption on earth could have made a woman's breasts swell so dramatically, while Lord Wyfold, whose son had married Val's sister Dorothy, lay back and 'laughed for a week'. Until Amaryllis confronted her, Eve steadfastly and aggressively denied that she was the mother and Augustus John the father. John later told Amaryllis: 'Oh, she put the fear of God into me! I can't remember what she said she'd do if I ever told you, but whatever it was I thought I'd better not risk it.'

Simultaneously with Eve's disappearance, Ian was elected to the Eton Society, or Pop.

Even today, the room of the Eton Society remains out of bounds to masters, its six windows covered by thick crimson curtains, permanently drawn to deter inspection. The dark ground floor room at the rear of Hodgson's House overlooks a courtyard off the High Street. For a bastion of unquestioned authority, it is not a prepossessing place. Inside: three scuffed leather chesterfields; framed lists of ancient honoured members; four shelves of books, including Churchill's history of the Second World War; and a plush, throne-like chair up two red-velveted steps where the president sits beneath a chipped yellow bust of the founder, Charles Fox Townshend. The place reeks of stale tobacco.

In Fleming's time, this is where Pop's two dozen members ceremonially 'pop-tanned' with bamboo canes boys who had committed a range of offences, from not knowing the names of boys in Pop, to speaking first to a boy in a year above, or for being 'generally uppish'; George Orwell got beaten 'for being late for prayers'.

Founded in 1811 as a debating and history society, Pop had developed into 'an autonomous self-perpetuating elite', with 'dandiacal privilege', whose 'responsibilities have never been defined with precision', as Peter wrote in *The Times* on the occasion of Pop's 150th anniversary dinner that he had attended with Ian. Most Etonians aspired to be members. Connolly recorded the moment of his election as one of his life's accomplishments. 'The door burst open and about twenty Pops, many of whom had never spoken to me before, with bright coloured waistcoats, rolled umbrellas, buttonholes, braid, and "spongebag" trousers, came reeling in, like the college of cardinals arriving to congratulate some pious old freak whom fate had elevated to the throne of St Peter.' Such was the prestige, Connolly wrote, that some boys who failed to get in never recovered. Antony Knebworth's excitement was not untypical. 'I can't tell you how divine it is being in Pop or how happy I am . . . We are incredibly officious, fearfully bumptious, and entirely selfish, absolutely screaming with joy all the time.'

In December 1925, 'after 1 hr 37 minutes of extremely boring electioning', Ian was elected at the second attempt as the Society's twenty-fourth member. He had joined Val and Peter, plus his uncle Harcourt, in what Harcourt's stepson Christopher Lee called 'the most privileged society imaginable . . . It was England at its zenith, hampers and endorsing textbooks compounded with the delicious smells of Linseed oil and athletes' hair cream.'

Ian's time in Pop was curtailed to two terms. He tried many times afterwards to replicate a comparable self-elected elite; in the 1930s with a group of Old Etonians known as the 'Cercle'; during the war at the Admiralty; after the war, at the *Sunday Times*, the Portland Club, Royal St George's. 'Having been in Pop at Eton,' wrote Alaric Jacob who came to know Ian six years later, 'he had decided that it would be a pleasant contrivance if one remained in Pop for the rest of one's life. And he succeeded – oh definitely, he succeeded . . .'

No information has emerged of the silk waistcoat Fleming *mi.* wore; his nickname, if he had one (Connolly was called 'Ugly'); or who he pop-tanned. Fleming *ma.*, on the other hand, is recorded as having delivered '7 successive cuts, all in the same place' to five boys from the Rugger XV after they showed too much 'joie de vivre at Rowlands the sock [tuck] shop'. On a separate occasion, Peter beat boys who were receiving pornographic mail from France; 'they got what they deserved.'

'My dear boy,' says Bond's punisher in *Casino Royale*, fingering his carpet-beater and sounding like Sam Slater. 'You have stumbled by mischance into a game for grown-ups.'

Le Chiffre, the first of Fleming's villains, found his non-fictional counterpart in *Enemies of Promise*. 'The beatings were torture,' wrote Cyril Connolly. 'We knelt on the chair bottoms outwards and gripped the bottom bar with our hands, stretching towards it over the back. Looking round under the chair we could see a monster rushing towards us with a cane in hand, his face upside down and distorted . . . The pain was acute.'*

Transfixed by Le Chiffre, Raymond Chandler was similarly captivated by Connolly's account of 'the silken barbarity of Eton'. Denys King-Farlow, by then an oil executive working in Tulsa, wrote to Connolly to say that the beatings he witnessed at Eton had left him with a loathing for the whole business, which later 'came out in the form of a mild delight in the flagellation of young women'. When Paul Gallico reflected on Ian's account of being walloped before the steeplechase, he wondered whether that incident might

---

* David Herbert remembered, 'You nearly fainted from the pain because at the end of each lash the headmaster gave the birch a flick, and off came a piece of your skin . . . The irony was that when your report was sent to your parents at the end of each term, at the end was written: "School Medicine 10/6d." (The price of a new birch.)'

have formed 'part of the strange sadism thing' which Ian exhibited in his books and relationships.

Eve's hands were not so full with her new baby that she was prepared to leave Ian alone.

In Michaelmas Term 1925, Ian was in the Fifth Form Upper Division B Second Remove and not heading for Oxford like Peter. Earlier in the year, Eve had decided that Ian should consider a career in the Army, in the footsteps of Mokie and her renegade brother Ivor. In February, she had arranged through Queen Mary to have Ian's name put down for the King's Royal Rifle Corps, a well-trodden route for Etonians who wished to avoid the Foot Guards. While in Berlin with Augustus John, she had also canvassed Major General Arthur Wauchope of the Black Watch, who hoped 'one day to see your son wearing the Black Watch tartan. He must be a fine fellow.' But Ian showed little enthusiasm to join a Highland regiment. His housemaster was on his side for once. 'Since m'tutor won't let me go into Army Class, I don't think I shall have anything of a colossal chance of doing well at Sandhurst, because you must have some preparation for it.'

Eve's unrealistic aspirations prevailed, nonetheless. In the 1926 Lent Term, Ian was shifted into a class with seven prospective candidates, some of them a year younger, for the Sandhurst exams in June. Hilary Bray considered the idea absurd. 'The Army Class at Eton was the bottom of the entire school, the waster-paper basket.'

The arrival of an unexpected new sister, coupled with his removal from classes specialising in science, history and maths to 'a low general standard course', only unsettled Ian further. In addition, his athletics career was in the doldrums, following a head-on collision on the soccer pitch with Henry Douglas-Home, brother of Alec, which required a broken-nosed Ian to have a metal plate inserted in his septum. The operation left Ian with his signature piratical look and had repercussions on his health. Ann ascribed his melancholy to 'the most terrible migraines' he suffered from. 'Inside a hot room, the brass used to expand and cause the headaches.'

Ian was on a collision course also with his brother. Probably, he would not have been elected to Pop without Peter's support. He then seems to have needed Peter's intercession to stay on at the school. Ernan Forbes Dennis's first recollection of Ian shortly afterwards was of hearing that 'several times he was on the point of being asked to go, and several times it was Peter who had to intervene to save him'. Inevitably, this tested the brothers' relationship. Peter regretted that 'towards the end at Eton we became curiously non-close.'

The end, when it came, was abrupt. Ian's peremptory departure was a decision taken by his mother, not by Eton. Peter could have done nothing to stop it.

The ostensible reason was a girl Ian had met on one of his out-of-bounds excursions with Bryce. 'Burglar' later commemorated these 'escapades' on the back of his motorbike in a handwritten draft of his memoirs, saying they were 'not forgotten and reference to which were used in clear code between us a third of century after'. The only clue to this particular escapade is the marginal addition by Bryce: 'motor bike letters'.

Quite how involved Ian became with Pearl Sim of 116 Kings Road, Reading, is open to speculation that Ian did nothing to discourage. 'His career at Eton was brief and undistinguished,' reads *The Times*'s obituary of James Bond in *You Only Live Twice*. 'As a result of some alleged trouble with one of the boys' maids, his aunt was requested to remove him.' Hugo Charteris was possibly drawing on inside information when he wrote in *The Coat* of 'a boy called Fraser at Fison's who had been found in the bedroom of the Austrian cook. Both had been naked, and both been sacked.' Yet Ian gave little away. 'I was bullied at school and lost my virginity like so many of us used to do in the old days,' was one of his rare pronouncements on the subject. Only in conversation with friends like Robert Harling did he suggest that the circumstances of 'where and how he first made love to a woman' may have prefigured the embarrassing experience of Derek in *The Spy Who Loved Me*.

In his last year at Eton, Derek meets Vivienne. After a quick courtship – portable gramophone on 'an electric canoe', scrambled eggs and coffee in The Thatched House – he takes her to a box at the Royalty Kinema on Farquhar Street in Windsor, where they begin to make love on the wooden floor when the furious manager bursts in. 'What the hell do you think you're doing in my cinema? Get up, you filthy little swine.'

As so often with Ian, the taller the story, the tighter it sticks. But how true is it? Or, come to that, Card's assertion in his history of Eton that Ian left the school 'after some trouble with girls'?

Ian denied the venue to his editor at Cape. 'There is no Royalty Kinema in Windsor and no street with a name anything like Farquhar Street.' The extent of his sexual experience needs to be questioned as well. In his review of David Benedictus's 1962 Eton novel, *The Fourth of June*, a copy of which Guy Burgess kept on his Moscow shelf next to a picture of himself at Eton, Ian felt that the author's ripe portrait of 'sexuality (hetero-, homo-, and auto-)' had 'outstripped the bounds of truth'. The same can be said about the rumours surrounding Ian's premature departure from Eton.

'Burglar' Bryce recalled how 'enormously sheltered' they both were about sex, 'not only innocent but totally ignorant by modern standards. I believe, for instance, that neither Ian nor I had the slightest notion of the world of girls which was soon to become so important to us and many of our friends, until our twentieth birthdays were behind us.' Ian's friend Loelia, Duchess of Westminster echoed how 'absurdly innocent' in sexual matters those boys and girls in her circle were. 'Hard though it is to believe, most of us knew nothing at all about the "facts of life" even though we were fifteen or sixteen years of age.'

When it came to learning the facts of life at Eton, wrote 'Boofy' Gore, 'in the end we had to go to the medical dictionary [edited by Ian's great-grandfather] and the juicier books of the Old Testament.' Rebuked for having visited the Folies Bergère in his holidays – 'not the sort of place where Etonians go' – Cyril Connolly left Eton without having masturbated, having no idea how intercourse was performed, or how babies were born. Yet in a revealing line in a draft of *Enemies of Promise*, he wrote how boys caught having sexual intercourse with each other were expelled on the spot, and even to be suspected could be fatal. Ann later came to detest Ian's friendship with Ivar Bryce and 'occasionally intimated that their union was of doubtful origin'; if so, the evidence has not survived, or that Ian formed any such relationship with another boy – unlike say Eric Blair, better known later as George Orwell ('I am afraid I am gone on East-wood' – to which Connolly's response was 'Naughty Eric'). All we have to go on is a relatively tame note that Ian wrote from The Timbralls to 'Miss

Pearl Sim' before half-term on 14 March 1926. It is Ian's first recorded love letter:

> My darling
> I was awfully disappointed not to find you in when I went to
> Reading to look for you. I was afraid you wouldn't write to me any
> more. I'm afraid I shant be able to see you till a few days after Easter.
> [He ends:] Be an angel and send me a photograph. I do want one
> awfully badly. Please darling.
>
> Write again soon. Love Ian.

On the envelope, Peter has written: 'The letter which led to ILF being asked to leave Eton.'

How then to make sense of the following rebuttal from Eton's headmaster, Cyril Alington, to Eve, written a year later when Ian was at Sandhurst? 'It is entirely false to say that Ian was sent away from Eton for spending the night with a girl at Reading. No such charge was ever brought against him or have I ever heard it even suggested – nor was he sent away from Eton. I am delighted, but not surprised, to hear that he is doing so well. You are quite at liberty to make any use you wish of this letter which will I hope dispose of the slander once for all.'

The only breach of school rules suggested by Ian's letter to Pearl Sim is that he went illegally on Bryce's Douglas to deliver this or another letter like it personally to Pearl in Reading. One possible reading is that Sam Slater intercepted Ian's 'motor bike letter' and before any action was taken or contemplated Eve decided to remove Ian at the end of term, as Ann Fleming, forty years on, pre-emptively removed Caspar after a gun was discovered in his room. Whether she wished to avoid him having a relationship with Pearl or was cross with the school for him getting into trouble about it, the result was a school career that was cut short suddenly.

Ian returned from half-term to compete in his final sports day on 3 April 1926. Because of his nose operation, he was not allowed to enter the mile or steeple-chase, but he came first in the 120-yard hurdles, second in the long jump and third in throwing the cricket ball. He left Eton four days later and four terms early, having been crowned Victor Ludorum for the second time and clasping the traditional gift from the headmaster, *Poems* by Thomas Gray.*

On his first night as an Old Etonian, Cyril Connolly cried himself to sleep. Antony Knebworth was affected in the same way. 'I've never come across anyone yet who said they wished they'd left Eton sooner.' This was not Ian's experience. His immediate attitude towards his old school resembled that of his future rival on the *Observer*, David Astor. 'I didn't learn much from Eton but I did learn that –', putting four fingers in his mouth to summon a taxi in Whitehall.

Eton had entrenched the contradictions in Ian's nature; his extravagant Fleming conformity, and his extravagant 'wild Rose' eccentricity. To keep them in harness would always be his challenge. As solitary as Ian was, he needed to be within a conventional circle before he felt bold enough to be unconventional.

Only over time did Ian come to appreciate how Eton had taught him to think and act for himself. He was too junior to have spoken to Connolly at school without being caned, but when they met up again in Kitzbühel in 1938 and later during the war, Ian burbled with career advice. Connolly said: 'His view of life was that it was a rugger scrum and that you would never get on unless you went hard for the ball. It was the Eton Wall Game all over again. Not going hard was the worst crime of all.'

The ball did not fall into Ian's hands until 1939 when everything he had learned at school came into its own. In Toronto during the war, Ian joined a sabotage course that required him to place an imaginary bomb in a heavily guarded power station. The story goes that he alone triumphed by hiding in full view, flaunting who he was, explaining 'in his best British accent and Etonian manner that he was a visiting expert from the UK' – and was at once ushered through the gates on a formal tour. Ian's Etonian manner

* Ian claimed to Paul Gallico that his winning of the Victor Ludorum two years in succession was 'a feat unique in Eton's history'. Twelve others have had back-to-back wins since Fleming in 1925 and 1926; the most recent holder in that category was 2007 and 2008.

opened many locked gates until the day arrived when he could look back on his schooldays through a fond lens. With characteristic contrariness, he altered a phrase in Paul Gallico's article on him, that he had 'an implacable distaste' for Eton which had lasted to that day, to 'a mysterious affection'.

Whatever his conflicted feelings towards Eton, there is no disputing that Ian's time there was hugely formative, and not simply for the contacts he had made and was to pick up again. Phyllis Bottome observed how after their 'secret initiation' at Eton, Ian and Peter 'seemed to know effortlessly how to behave to everybody, and how to meet without apparent flurry, all the emergencies of life'.

Bottome had only one reservation about the character she had based on Ian. 'He could tackle every difficulty he had yet met, except one – that of falling in love – adequately.' This difficulty was not merely Ian's, says his niece Kate. 'No father, four brothers, all male boarding schools from the age of eight, difficult mother – in different ways, the brothers had no clue about women.'

VII
SANDHURST

'He has the sort of "stuff" in him that makes the best sort of soldier.'
TOM PELLATT

Lathbury Park was a Georgian country house set in fifty acres of wooded grounds on the River Ouse. To prepare Ian for the Sandhurst examinations in June, Eve enrolled him for one term at this army crammer near Newport Pagnell, owned and run by the seventy-year-old Major William Trevor. Pupils had to dress for dinner and could not leave the premises without permission. The atmosphere was not so different from The Timbralls. Ian arrived with four blankets, two pairs of sheets, and three towels – all conspicuously sewn with his name.

Familiar among the new faces was another second son from Eton. Like Ian, David Herbert, son of the Earl of Pembroke, was 'the despair of serious people and the delight of countless well-wishers'. Herbert, who had grown up at Wilton House, had few illusions about Lathbury Park. 'We can neither of us have been particularly bright, or we would not have been sent to such a place by our respective parents!'

Ian worked hard enough to impress Major Trevor, who wrote to Eve on 12 July, commending her son as 'exceptionally nice . . . manly and sensible beyond his years. Here he is quite "a Triton among minnows"'. Trevor's note is famous for flagging up Ian's Achilles heel. 'He ought to make an excellent soldier, provided always that the Ladies don't ruin him.' Ian passed eleventh out of that year's Sandhurst intake of nearly 200, winning a Prize Cadetship and further praise from Trevor. 'He is far above the average army Candidate in literary ability.' How pleased Eve must have been: Mokie's obituarist Winston Churchill had not got in until his third attempt.

A measure of Eve's continuing concern was the working holiday she arranged for Ian to take before he entered Sandhurst. Eve had learned from a friend, Lord Ellesmere, of an unusual couple who had opened up their house in the Austrian Tyrol to coach a small number of English and American adolescent boys in French and German. This childless pair were gaining a reputation for knowing how to handle 'delinquent' children, inspired by the latest educational theories coming out of Vienna. Ernan Forbes Dennis, a former Intelligence officer, and his half-American novelist wife, Phyllis Bottome, had looked after Lord Ellesmere's nephew Cyril, who had been at Eton with Ian, plus two teenage brothers, cousins of the Roosevelts. Eve decided that Ian would make a splendid addition. In August 1926, she paid £17 for his return train ticket to Kitzbühel.

Ian's first summer in Kitzbühel was not a success. 'He was really quite impossible when he first came to us,' Ernan Forbes Dennis said. 'Terribly rude and inconsiderate.'

Ian was afterwards candid about his appalling behaviour, writing to Ernan: 'I shirked my work when I could, and I thought fit to be rude to Mrs Forbes Dennis when she was kindest to me.' Phyllis's mother had died in August and Phyllis was unable to focus on Ian, who treated her with the 'self-preserving insolence' typical of Etonians.

Ian groaned to his mother that Ernan was 'working him too hard' and making him read André Maurois's *Ariel* in French. Preferable was climbing the Kitzbühler Horn, diving into the lake, or sitting in the Café Reisch under the flowering chestnut trees, where he could pick up 'the local Heidis and Lenis and Trudis'.

When at the end of August, Ian waved goodbye to the Forbes Dennises and their German shepherd dog Luchs, he never expected to see the couple again. But they and Kitbzühel were to play a critical part in his life, and he would be back within a year, his insolent Etonian tail between his legs.

Ian arrived at the Royal Military College in Camberley, thirty miles south of London, on 3 September, one of 186 new recruits. He expected to be commissioned after completing the eighteen-month course. Eve had shifted her sights for him to join the Scottish infantry battalion, the Black Watch; its tartan uniform was in keeping with Mokie.

Ian went into No. 5 Company whose commander was Major Ronald

Fellowes, 2nd Baron Ailwyn. The company were housed in Old Building, a Greek Revival mansion where Ian attended lectures, ate and slept. His room looked out over the Assistant Commandant's garden and the stables.

From day one, Prize Cadet Fleming was subjected to a discipline that grated after the freedoms of Kitzbühel. Reveille was at 7 a.m. He was out drilling on Old Building Square for the first six weeks. His uniform was then inspected. Breakfast was at 8 a.m., lunch at 12.45 p.m., with lectures in between, which he attended in a red-and-white striped blazer, white flannels, and a red-and-white pillbox hat worn over his right eye. His life was organised down to the last minute; he often only had five minutes to change in and out of various uniforms, from his lecture kit into his gym kit to his 'Blue Patrols' for formal dinners. He played games four afternoons a week, with matches on Saturday. He dined at 8 p.m. and went to his room at 8.45, when 'rooms were called'. He stood outside his door with his rifle while a senior officer cadet inspected his kit. A speck of fluff or a missed roll-call could mean 'losing one's name' and being 'awarded restriction of privileges' (known as 'Strickers'), or his drill boots being hurled from the window. After that, he was expected to remain in his room. Lights went out at 10 p.m.

It would be hard to contrive a more uncongenial setting for the eighteen-year-old Ian Fleming. 'Sandhurst wasn't his place,' said Ivar Bryce, then up at Christ Church* with Peter and enjoying 'all the splendid freedom there, whereas poor old Ian found himself in another school with even more ridiculous rules and restrictions than at Eton.'

Social life was primarily confined to the military college itself, sherry with company officers. The only free time was Saturday evening and Sunday afternoon after tea. In his second term, emphasis was on riding, which Ian disliked.

He lasted one further term, completing one year out of the eighteen-month course, by the end of which he had sunk to 141st place. His only distinction was on the athletics track. In May 1927, he came second in a 120-yard hurdle race against Cranwell and Woolwich. This seems to have been his last competitive race (although thirty years later, he played wing-back with

* After Ian died, Ivar Bryce donated money for an Ian Fleming Room at Christ Church: staircase four, room five in Blue Boar Quad.

Ernie Cuneo in the Beverly Hills Hotel against some professional footballers in the lounge after dinner, 'and they never got past us,' said Cuneo). He also claimed to the *New Yorker* to have shot for Sandhurst against West Point.

Because Ian left prematurely, he did not have a position in the final order of merit and although his name appears in his company photograph for September, his face does not. Yet remnants of his Sandhurst year engrained themselves. He learned to dress neatly and quickly, organise his time and be punctual. He also gained knowledge of weapons and military history. One thing he failed to learn was what his chief in Naval Intelligence called 'senior officer veneration'.

Ian told a colleague at the Admiralty how he hated taking orders at Sandhurst. 'There are only two people you should ever call Sir, your Commanding Officer and God.' The conclusion of his CO, Major the Lord Ailwyn, in Ian's only report in July 1927 was: 'Capable & could do very well if he wished' – but Ian would do well only if he made 'the best of what is, to him, a bad job and settle down . . .'

Ian performed the opposite manoeuvre. It is hard to piece together the unravelling – the second within a year. Forbes Dennis, who saw Ian immediately before and after he went to Sandhurst, blamed Ian's abrupt departure on 'general idleness and antagonism to the whole place'. That, and 'trouble over the ladies'.

The lady this time was Peggy Bainbridge, the daughter of an Indian Army colonel, who had been introduced to Ian by Hester Pellatt's sister. Cyril Connolly was later involved with Peggy, and described her as a blonde, violet-eyed girl 'tall in her smallness, with a very neat erect figure', whose company was enjoyed best before midnight, after which 'the glass fills and refills'. According to Connolly, Peggy came to watch Ian compete in Sandhurst's annual sports day; then, much to Ian's disappointment, she went off with another suitor to an Oxford Commem ball. 'Ian said that if she did, he would go to London and have a tart. He did and caught gonorrhoea.'

Days later, Ian was staying with his mother in Turner's House when the result of his revels at the 43 Club could no longer be ignored. These were the days before penicillin. Treatment, with the help of silver nitrate, was likely to be drawn out.

The full force of Eve's fury descended on her errant second son – and not only Eve's fury. 'Uncle Phil used to give him a dressing down from time to time on behalf of the family,' said Ralph Arnold, who met Ian in Kitzbühel shortly after. 'He hated that.'

In a flash, Eve saw her social reputation compromised in the royal circles that she had courted to launch Ian on his military career. According to one of Ian's biographers, Andrew Lycett, she organised for Ian to be treated at a clinic in Beaumont Street and then sought Sandhurst's permission for her son to take a term off to recuperate. Her request was granted, yet Ian's 'sickness', as Sandhurst recorded it, was not merely venereal. His mental health was so agitated, Mary Pakenham heard, that 'Ian tried to shoot himself'.

At this precise moment, Peter was staying with the Forbes Dennises in Kitzbühel, on Eve's orders, to brush up his German following his first year at Christ Church. 'What a brain he had,' marvelled Forbes Dennis. 'Enormously disciplined, and he went through German like a razor through butter.'

Forbes Dennis was now in a position to compare the brothers. 'The contrast was enormous.' He perceived Ian as 'a vastly discouraged second son. Who would not have been discouraged by the pre-eminence of such an eldest son as Peter Fleming, who swept everything before him at Eton and Oxford? Where could Ian possibly make good? . . . He saw all roads to glory closed.' Here was a young man whose father was a saint, his grandfather one of the richest men in Great Britain, his elder brother a success in all he attempted, who was floundering in life, looking at himself and seeing only failure.

By August 1927, Eve's lofty ambitions for her self-destructive son were in the same discouraged state as Ian. Two years earlier, she had contemplated an unspecified future for him in the Cape, probably following in Ivor's footsteps ('I think that's an awfully good idea about S. Africa,' Ian had responded). Now, said Forbes Dennis, she was 'so far at her wit's end that she was on the point of sending him off to Australia with a shilling'. Meanwhile, Ian was in no condition to return to Sandhurst. At the direction of Eve, who had made him write to Peggy calling off their affair, Ian wrote to the Commandant, Major General Charles Corkran, to say he would not be coming back.

The episode was so painful that to the end of his life Ian could not admit the truth. At Reuters, he would learn 'to be sure of his facts' – but his facts when explaining his last days at Sandhurst were wispy in the extreme. 'He left Sandhurst of his own accord,' Lord Ailywn confirmed on 1 December 1927, without going into detail. Ian never mentioned gonorrhoea as an issue. He told Ann 'that he had hammer toes, & that they had scotched his career at Sandhurst'. He told Ralph Arnold, one of Forbes Dennis's new intake, how he had been confined to barracks for arriving late from a visit to London nightclubs, and had 'sent the commandant a p.c. saying he wouldn't be coming back'; Arnold, a cousin of General Ironside, the prototype of Buchan's Richard Hannay, was unpersuaded. Ian gave yet one more reason on his CV. He had resigned because he did not want to be a 'glorified garage hand', since he had heard 'a terrible rumour' that the army was about to be mechanised. He lamented – in his last interview – 'that the great days of polo and the cavalry' were going to end forever; 'no more pigsticking and that sort of thing'. This was hogwash. Not only was Ian never headed for the cavalry – he hated horses anyway and would much have preferred a tank – but according to the Sandhurst historian Anthony Morton, 'the British Army did not begin to mechanise seriously until 1934, and in the 1920s was little more than a colonial policing force.' Even Peter was forced into Ian's charade. 'All that happened was that he hurt his back at Sandhurst, couldn't go on the appropriate manoeuvres, and so rather than be put back a year, decided to chuck it in.'

In Kitzbühel, Forbes Dennis received a letter from Eve 'saying that she had been asked to take Ian away from Sandhurst and was terribly worried about him. She wanted her sons to be a credit to herself and the family, or not have anything to do with them at all.' A few months before, Forbes Dennis might have left it at that; neither he nor Phyllis had enjoyed having Ian to stay the previous August. But since then, their theories on teaching troubled second sons had undergone a small revolution. After getting to know Peter that summer, and having had further dealings with his domineering mother, Forbes Dennis felt confident about dealing with Ian. 'I said, "Why not send him out to us for the winter, and I'll see what we can do. Then you can decide."'

Eve seized on Forbes Dennis's offer. Ian said, 'My infuriated mother decided that I must do *something*, something respectable.' He had not followed Mokie and Peter to Oxford. He had fallen at the first hurdle to becoming a soldier. But over the next months a third future took shape. Eve's son would be a diplomat like her friend Lord d'Abernon, Ambassador in Berlin, whose photograph she kept by her bed. He would follow the dream career of Ian's Eton contemporary Antony Knebworth. 'I go into the Diplomatic Service. I become the greatest Englishman in Europe, sworn by in 5 capitals, deified by the Hindoos while Viceroy, and eventually Foreign Minister . . . then perhaps PM.'

VIII
KITZBÜHEL

'I thought we might spend the honeymoon in Kitzbühel.
I love that place.'
on her majesty's secret service

'There came to me a time not very long after I left school when I found myself as lonely as it is possible to be . . . I found myself with no friend, no passion, no anchor whatever.'

Turbott Wolfe was a first novel by William Plomer, a twenty-two-year-old South African living in Japan. In his last term at Eton, Ian wrote the unknown author an appreciative letter, 'already using his valuable gift,' Plomer remembered in his memorial address, 'of recognising, and, therefore encouraging, other men's abilities'.

Ian faced the predicament of Plomer's fictional character as he steeled himself to return to Austria. Kitzbühel was to save Ian, though. It provided him with friends, passion and an anchor. Not only that, it was where he learned about writing.

He stayed under the Forbes Dennises' roof and in their orbit for the next three years while they sorted him out. He would return to Kitzbühel throughout the 1930s with three important women in his life, whom he had met there – Lisl Jokl (later Popper), Edith Morpurgo and Muriel Wright; and then after the war with his wife Ann and his last lover, Blanche Black-well. Significantly, it is to Kitzbühel that James Bond is motoring for his honeymoon with the only woman he ever marries when Blofeld drives up and shoots her.

Kitzbühel was more than Ian's sanatorium and university. It came to assume a mythical status, a symbol of lost love and happiness, as it had for Cyril Connolly, whom Ian re-encountered there in 1938 with his old flame

Peggy Bainbridge. Connolly was struck by how glowingly the Alpine resort had lodged in Ian's mind when, at their last meeting, days before Ian's death, 'he talked mostly of Kitzbühel' and 'that golden time when the sun always shone'. A still-grateful Connolly gave him as a parting gift a copy of *The Unquiet Grave*, writing in it: 'Ian with love from Cyril – see p66 for Kitzbühel where our friendship ripened which led to me getting my job on the *Sunday Times* and so solvency'.

The passage can only have tightened Ian's heart-strings. 'The body remembers past pleasures and being made aware of them, floods the mind with sweetness. Thus the smell of sun-warmed pine-needles and the bloom on the ripe whortle-berries reopen the file marked Kitzbühel and bring back the lake with its warm muddy water, its raft conversations and pink water-lilies; the drives over white Alpine roads through the black fir-woods or the walks over meadows where runnels of water sing in wooden troughs beside the chalets. Remembering all these communicates several varieties of pleasure'.

Ian had been too self-absorbed on his first visit to take notice of his hosts. Ernan Forbes Dennis and Phyllis Bottome are not well known today, but they were famous enough to stay in the White House with the Roosevelts and have their names in the newspapers when they crossed the Atlantic.

Ernan's niece, Frederica Freer, looked after him following Phyllis's death in 1963. 'They were such a distinguished-looking couple, had tremendous "presence", you couldn't fail to wonder who they were'. She describes Ernan as 'handsome, well dressed, and terribly polite to doormen – although his tip was too small as he didn't realise things had gone up. I once asked, "What did you do when you were young?" He looked vague and rather pained and seemed to be thinking about it and didn't tell me anything'. It shocked her after he died to discover that Ernan had been a spy.

The grandson of a general from Aberdeenshire, Ernan was an autodidact like his wife. Hauled out of school at thirteen to run the family estate following the suicide of his father, Ernan had suffered a breakdown at nineteen and travelled to St Moritz to mend himself. There he met Phyllis Bottome, a novelist, two years older, who was recovering from tuberculosis. Tall, flamboyant, with a taste for bright clothes and 'a face like a melancholy eagle', Phyllis was the daughter of an impoverished American clergyman and a possessive English mother who rivalled Eve in her stifling snobbery. Phyllis's bright eye fell on Ernan, and following a prolonged courtship, they married in 1917.

Phyllis worked for John Buchan in London for the next two years at the Department of Information, where Buchan ran the foreign propaganda section. Her observations on how Buchan gathered political information in different countries found their way into novels like *Private Worlds*, made into a film with Claudette Colbert, and *The Mortal Storm*, starring James Stewart, which premiered on the day Hitler's troops entered Paris.

In March 1918, Ernan was wounded at Arras in northern France as he ran across open ground, a wound so deep that 'the surgeon could get his large hand into it'. While convalescing, he joined the Intelligence Corps. He was posted to Marseille, where Phyllis joined him, and then to Vienna, as Passport Control Officer to Austria, Hungary and Yugoslavia, providing cover and resources for British agents, and recruiting them.

When Ernan gave up his posting to look after Phyllis, whose tuberculosis had returned, his Foreign Office connections made it a natural next step to open a language school: in Ian's words, 'he took a few boys and taught them German for the diplomatic'. In 1927, Ernan remained vice consul for the Tyrol, maintaining his links with Military Intelligence and in a position to provide a reference for pupils he considered Foreign Office material. There is no evidence that Phyllis was an agent, but she knew his role.

Ernan had needed a good climate for his wife's lungs. They settled on Kitzbühel, an unspoiled, cobble-stoned town 3,000 feet up a windless valley dotted with medieval churches and castles, and almost unknown except to a few skiers. One of these was Cecil Roberts, a prolific journalist who visited Kitzbühel when Ian was in residence and set two novels there, both featuring him. 'The town, red and grey roofed, with cream and white walls,' Roberts wrote fondly, 'was like a toy taken out of an ark and set in the sunshine.'

In their second winter, Ernan rented an old farmhouse in an apple orchard, Villa Tennerhof, built in 1679 on the south slope of the Kitzbühler Horn, 2,000 feet above. Written into his lease was Ernan's duty to fly a white sheet from his roof when a thunderstorm approached. The handful of upper-class English and American boys – 'these young cabbages' one visitor derogatorily called them – each had his own room. There was a large dining room with a ping-pong table and a gramophone, and a Bechstein grand piano which Ernan, who also gave music lessons, needed little encouragement to play. Upstairs was Phyllis's workroom, where the boys played cards and read.

Ernan taught German and French pronunciation and grammar in the mornings, and a local teacher worked on their conversation while Phyllis, still suffering bouts of TB, stayed in bed and wrote. The primary breadwinner now, she appeared in Cecil Roberts's fiction as the histrionic American novelist Madame Baker, a self-described 'Great Genius', who has published twenty-two novels and conducts her interviews in bed. 'She did not lie in bed; she sat enthroned. Two large lace pillows at her back . . .'

In the afternoons, Ernan took the boys skiing or on mountain hikes with the dog Luchs. In summer, they swam in the Schwartzsee, a dark brown, pine-fringed lake on the east side of the valley, with dressing huts, a wooden platform on which bathers could enjoy the sun and exchange gossip, and a high diving board. On the opposite bank were mud baths much like those Ian would find after the war in Saratoga, whose radioactivity was considered miraculous for rheumatism. In June, the place became 'the Valley of the Tummies', with elderly German men and women 'wallowing in mud like hippopotami'. The young Englishman who reappeared that autumn of 1927, behind the wheel of a two-seater khaki Standard Tourer with an enamelled Union Jack on its bonnet, was in need of a miracle cure as well.

'When Ian turned up at the Tennerhof he was in appalling disgrace,' said Ralph Arnold, another who was cramming for the Foreign Office. 'Everyone in the family, and his mother especially, seemed to think that he had behaved abominably. He used to admit it all, say he had been banished, and get us all to regard him as a sort of romantic exile . . . he saw himself striding round Kitzbühel, and people pointing at him and whispering, "That's the man who sent the postcard to his commandant and was then banished from England."'

In his pose as a disgraced remittance man, Ian treated orders as challenges to be disobeyed. Phyllis recorded an incident when Ian 'shouted on a soft snow slope against a warning from a guide' – and a small avalanche then buried him 'in a salutary way up to his chin'. His insubordination was one of several issues that needed addressing.

It excited Ian to set off small avalanches. He reminded Ernan of Byron, at times of Faust. 'There was a lot of conflict in him. He wanted to get happiness out of excitement, danger, fast cars, good food, but of course was never satisfied by them.' One night, Ernan received a call that Ian had crashed his car on the way back from Munich. Ian was quite shaken up, although not hurt. 'With his impatience, speed was terribly important to him.'

Ian prized his athletic image with the same tense energy. The exercise regime he had begun at Eton was one of the few disciplines he adhered to. Ernie Cuneo climbed with him thirty years later in the hills above Ivar Bryce's farm in Vermont, and he witnessed how Ian's observation of his ritual had something about it that was puritan and self-punishing, religious even: 'the long dull inconvenient pounding, the sweat and the pain and then: Hallelulah! the hot shower, the great cleansing & the glorious ease of earned tiredness.'

'He was immensely athletic,' Connolly remembered, 'restless, dressed in white shorts, and always telling us that he had just climbed a particular mountain. I remember a particularly anguished look he always seemed to have, like an athlete at the very peak of his effort.' A favourite route led him to the white summit above the Tennerhof. Ernan said: 'He used to climb up the Kitzbühler Horn and then have coffee and scrambled eggs at the little café at the foot of the mountain. "Ah, scrambled eggs and coffee," he would sigh to me. "The only two things in the world which never let you down."' Ernan got the boys to read Ibsen's play *A Doll's House*. Ian was like Nora, 'that beautiful, unhappy girl always waiting for something *wunderbar* to happen and always disappointed because it never quite did.'

Impatient for risk-taking excitement, Ian involved the Tennerhof's students in his pranks. He was 'endlessly inventing the most bizarre situations,' said Ralph Arnold. Ian once entered Arnold into the Kitzbühel tennis tournament without his knowledge. A reluctant Arnold, who was no tennis player, was drawn against a recently widowed Czech playboy who styled himself Graf Schlick, yet Ian was reassuring. 'Anyone who knows how to hold a racquet could beat him.' On arriving at the courts, Arnold discovered not only 'the biggest crowd I have ever seen in Kitzbühel', but that his opponent, in addition to being a well-known racing driver, 'was the Tyrolean champion or something, and to get the crowds to come Ian had passed word round that I was Southern Counties champion. I got a terrible licking, but somehow afterwards Ian was so charming and amusing about it that he made it all right. This was a strange quality he had. He could be very cruel, but he always seemed to make it alright.'

On another occasion, Ian targeted an English student who was teetotal. Irritated to see him drinking water at the Café Reisch, Ian arranged for his glass of water to be switched for a glass of colourless gentian schnapps. Then Ian stood up and proposed a toast for the King's birthday. 'The eyes of the rest of Kitzbühel are upon us. All Englishmen drink a birthday toast to His Majesty, even if it has to be in water.' The young man stood up with the rest and downed the entire glass, said Arnold. 'We had to put him to bed later that night completely drunk.'

Ian's tipple was sex. 'What Austria had for him was chiefly girls at this time,' said the bookseller Percy Muir, who stayed with him in Kitzbühel, for some reason in a room over a ski-maker's shop where Ian was living in 'indescribable squalor'. Ian had made the revitalising discovery that Austrian women had 'a powerful weakness for young Englishmen'. Plus, they were intrepid in acting on their desires. At the Tennerhof, Phyllis noted the 'premarital laxity' of her cooks and maids, who considered it 'quite normal' to have a child before marriage.

One of the first Austrian women to meet Ian on his initial visit in 1926 was 'a plain-looking Jewish girl', twenty-six-year-old Lisl Jokl, who remained a loyal friend and was left £500 in his will, and was described by Ann, who thought she was a spy as well as a lesbian, as the first of Ian's 'intelligent Jewesses who kept influence by flattery'. Lisl was with a female friend in the Café Reisch when she saw 'this extraordinarily good-looking young man sitting on his own, wearing a dark-blue shirt. In those days no one had seen a dark-blue shirt on a man before. So I told my friend that if she was really interested in him, she should go and pretend to fall over his legs. She did.'

She was not the only girl to trip into Ian's arms. Thirty years later, Ann accompanied Ian back to the Café Reisch and observed how 'he clings to youth and dreams of days when he was the Kitzbühel Casanova'. Alan

Pryce-Jones joined them for two days and Ian gave him a tour. 'He pointed out the spots where he had gone with various women, and it always seemed to be the anniversary of the night he first met X or slept with Y.' Lisl Jokl said, possibly from experience: 'He was quite ruthless about women. Or rather absent-minded. He would sleep with someone and then honestly forget that he had done it.'

Intrigued by the gossip, Cecil Roberts dashed off two pot-boilers with this 'confident Adonis' at their centre. In the second, Ian grows up to be 'a famous novelist', with the last volume of his great saga of English life, *Time's Journey* 'to be seen in the window of almost every bookshop in Europe'.

Roberts joined Ian in the twice-weekly confetti battles between apple-cheeked girls and grinning youths in tight-fitting deerskin shorts and jackets, 'cut away over the hips like a boy's Eton suit'. On her 1958 visit, Ann Fleming watched how 'the confetti is thrown with great violence, the English nanny of some German Jewish acquaintances lost an eye last Saturday.' Incomprehensible to Ann, 'these confetti orgies have great significance for Ian; he spent his nineteenth and twentieth years here being coached for the Foreign Office, they remind him of his youth.'

Choked with confetti, Roberts afterwards brushed down with Ian in the Café Reisch, where Ian's presence – like the member of a Tyrolean Pop, in a red waistcoat and chrome yellow leather shorts, slashed and laced at the sides – 'fluttered the Austrian girls'. Roberts took notes: 'he ran like a prairie fire through the girls of Kitzbühel. He had announced that "technique in bed is important", something he had discovered at twenty!'

'The flame of life burned lustily in him.' In Roberts's 1930 novel *Spears Against Us*, the nineteen-year-old Ian is thinly disguised as a tall, dark General's son who comes to Kitzbühel to study for the Foreign Office. Roberts transfers the irresistible young Fleming from café to page with barely an alteration: he even calls him Ian. Just like Ian Fleming, his athletic doppelgänger shows off at the muddy lake, jack-knifing from the diving board to draw envious glances. 'Ian's a regular bull!' says another young Englishman. 'I wish I'd his build.' When Ian tries to seduce a servant girl in the hay, she slaps him. 'You're no longer a boy, Herr Ian – no, I won't!' He has better luck with the daughter of the local count, Paula. Caught in a storm up the Königspitz, the couple take shelter in a mountain hut. 'He could dimly see the outline of her shoulders, the wet bodice moulding her breasts, her hair beaten down over her gleaming wind-reddened face.' Paula succumbs soon afterwards. But immediately Ian suffers remorse. 'He wanted to run away, to leave his own self here on the mountainside, to find the Ian he had lived with so long in the valley. For there were two Ians now. At the moment they denied relationship.'

Not everyone was so forgiving of Fleming's womanising or split person-alities. Conrad O'Brien-ffrench was a British Intelligence officer based in Kitzbühel, running a network of agents under cover of a travel agency, Tyro-lese Tours. His verdict, a common one: 'He was something between a wolf and a rake'.

Ernan and Phyllis regarded Ian 'as having sex on the brain, and an unstoppable desire to make conquests of women'. The cause of Ian's prob-lems had clarified for them shortly before his second time back at the Tennerhof in the autumn of 1927. Nothing they observed about his subse-quent behaviour – in Kitzbühel, Munich, Geneva, London and Jamaica, where they were also to run a school – persuaded the Forbes Dennises to alter their original diagnosis. 'The intense sibling rivalry he experienced with his brother Peter seemed to be replayed in his endless cuckolding of men he regarded as his friends.'

As at Eton and Sandhurst, trouble over the ladies brought matters to a head. Soon after his return, Ian made such a nuisance of himself that both Ernan and Phyllis decided to be shot of him. It was the equivalent to Ernan's white sheet that he shook as a thunderstorm warning.

According to Phyllis's biographer, 'Ian got one of the maids at the Ten-nerhof pregnant'. The claim is impossible to verify, but it is plausible that this or something like it led to the bitter confrontation with Phyllis in which his insolence was so hurtful that Ernan threatened to expel Ian and send him back to Eve. The spectre of a trebly disappointed mother was not an alluring one. Ian's only chance of staying in Austria lay in convincing his hosts that he fully recognised what 'a rotter' he was – not only that, but he was capable, with their help, of reform.

Ian needed to hone a new depth of self-awareness in the letter he wrote to save himself: 'I see now, Ernan, that everything good that I have done, everything that I thought good, that I have thought generous has been a sham.' Ian continued in this abject vein: 'Intelligence I may have, but what was its use when it went to perfecting this sham – what is its use now when it makes me realise my rottenness? God knows, I hope it will one day produce something which I can show you and make me more worthy to ask for forgiveness.'

His letter was a turning point. Persuaded of his contrition, Ernan gave him one last chance on condition that he apologise to Phyllis in person. Following 'a tearful repentance scene', Ian was permitted to stay. Now the challenge for all three was how to convert 'the blasted spectacular sham which I chose to call my character' into something worthier. The unlikely vehicle was a tubby little man from Vienna.

Soon after setting up the Tennerhof, Ernan had learned of a former member of Freud's inner circle, Alfred Adler, who was turning Viennese education 'upside down', according to Phyllis, 'by teaching the teachers how to produce a good human being'. It followed a series of lectures Adler had given on 'The Difficult Child'. This was Forbes Dennis territory. Ernan decided to visit him in Vienna.

The man who received Ernan in his old stomping ground was a small, stout, sallow-faced fifty-four-year-old with a sweet tooth and memorable eyes who sat in a high straight-backed chair, feet swinging off the floor.

Ernan told him there were several things he wanted help on for his pupils, 'including Ian of course'.

Adler offered Ernan a cigarette. Then, pointing up at his shelves, he told him to read his books and come back. When Ernan returned, they had five long conversations, laying the foundations for a relationship that lasted until Adler's death. It resulted in Ernan becoming an analyst himself and in Phyllis writing Adler's biography.

The books that Ernan had read in German were a revelation. Adler's theories made him realise that 'complete retraining' was needed in order to deal with someone like Ian Fleming.

Adler had parted company with Freud over the origins of neurosis. For Adler, the causes lay in feelings of inferiority towards a sibling. Birth order was significant. Sibling rivalry could turn toxic. The second child often became 'a rebel if he is strong or a dreamer if he is weak'.

A model elder brother had made Adler's childhood unhappy. The combination of a mother he resented and the urge never to lag behind his brother gave Adler his 'inferiority feeling'. But the flip side of this was a superiority complex. Adler recognised that 'every neurosis can be understood as an attempt to free oneself from a feeling of inferiority in order to gain a feeling of superiority.'

Ernan was mesmerised. Not only did Adler's sibling relationship mirror Ernan's with his elder brother Fred, a lieutenant colonel who had died a hero in the war. Closer to home, it reflected what Ernan had observed of Ian's relationship with Peter. On the one occasion Ernan spoke to his niece about the Fleming brothers, he described Peter 'as a glossy racehorse out in front, Ian struggling to keep up with him'.

Ian betrayed every symptom of Adler's 'inferiority complex'. As Phyllis summarised it, children often chose a *Gegenspieler*, 'a person to compete with at all costs in an endless neurotic duel'. Most often, it was a brother or sister 'by whom the child has felt dethroned or otherwise out-distanced'.

Once acquired, the complex was easily transferred. The danger in almost any intimate relationship that followed was that 'the child as he develops into the man will build up the same perpetual antagonism between himself and *any* loved person'. Phyllis saw Ian falling into this turbulent trap. Ian had found his niche as the disgraced younger brother and become neurotically addicted to this role.

As it happened, Adler had visited the Tennerhof when Peter was there. Phyllis and her half dozen 'cabbages' fell under the spell of this rotund cake-lover. 'Our boys, one and all, delighted in him.' Even Luchs went up and rested his snout in Adler's lap.

'I knew that what I was looking at, and listening to, was a great man.' Phyllis's encounter with Adler in 1927 upended her 'strange hot-house world,' as Ralph Arnold described the Tennerhof. Phyllis's biographer likened it to a religious conversion. At the age of forty-three, Phyllis decided that not only was Alfred Adler, in her words, 'the greatest child educator of our day', but 'one of the greatest liberators of human personality that the world has ever known', the foundation of whose work was 'the discovery of a human being's power to turn a minus into a plus'. She made it her mission to effect this transformation on the delinquent in their midst.

Ian ticked all the boxes to be a perfect specimen to work with. And, like a drunk going along with the programme if it meant he did not have go back to Eve, Ian submitted to their regime. It was a wonderful position for an opportunist, as his mother had forced him to become, to be full of potential and believed in. 'Ian played up to all this like nobody's business,' said Arnold, who then watched how the Tennerhof evolved into 'a sort of Adlerian menagerie' on the side of the mountain. 'Ian walked into this imaginary world of old Phyllis's like a gift from God.' Once it was decided that Ian could stay on, he became their first subject for Adlerian research and improvement. 'He was their prize exhibit.'

In Munich in the last months of 1932, Phyllis found herself with a group of Adler's students sitting in the Café Heck opposite 'a little pasty-faced, brown-suited fellow with Charlie Chaplin's look and moustache; but none of his genius or his laughter.' Adolf Hitler came alone to this café in the winter before he seized power, occupying the same reserved table, his back to the wall – while a few yards from him sat Phyllis's group, who had come 'fresh from our problem-children's clinic, eager with delight at the startling changes worked in these children by the use of Adlerian training'.

A student at Phyllis's table was thirty-one-year-old Joshua Bierer, who one Sunday in 1928 had been 'sent up' urgently by Adler 'as tutor' to Ian during his worst excesses. Half a century later, Bierer, by then a prominent psychiatrist in London, made this arresting claim: 'Ian Fleming had the type of personality which, if he had not found a role in which to excel, would have led to the gutter, a mental hospital or prison.' In Bierer's professional opinion, it was Ian's Adlerian training that had stopped him from being 'a psychopath' like the brown-suited man in the Café Heck who that January became chancellor.

Ian acknowledged the startling changes wrought on him by Adler's teachings, and afterwards pressed his work on friends like Noël Coward, who declared himself cured of several breakdowns by reading one of Adler's books, and put at his disposal a box at the theatre so Adler could see *The Astonished Heart*, which Coward had written as a result. Percy Muir met Ian at this vital period. 'I remember he became terribly impressed by Adler, as he did about people. Thought he was greater than Freud. Greater than anyone.' Ian told Mary Pakenham of his conviction 'that Adler had got at the truth about character & that it would help other poor devils to avoid the miseries he had gone through'. He gave £100 ('which I could ill afford') to Adler's clinic (approximately £8,300 today), and in May 1937 was treasurer on the committee that brought Adler to Britain for a series of lectures – Adler would die of a heart attack in Aberdeen on the last leg of the tour. Two years later, in the spring of 1939, Ian begged Loelia Westminster, then in New York: 'Please do this for me! I want two books which I can't get here. "The Man Who Killed Hitler"* and "Organ Inferiority" by Alfred Adler, translated from the German & published in US some years ago. It isn't pornography! Will you be an angel & bring them back for me. The last will be very difficult I'm afraid. PLEASE.' Adler even makes an appearance in *The Man with the Golden Gun*. 'Passing to the wider implications of gun ownership, we enter the realms of the Adlerian power urge as compensation for the inferiority complex . . .'

Back in 1928, Phyllis's prescription for Ian's inferiority complex had been not the gun, but the pen.

Eve wrote to Ernan to ask how Ian was faring. On 27 February 1928, following their blow-out, Ernan felt able to reply. It was one of his earliest stabs at Adlerian analysis.

'Ian's qualities are considerable. His general intelligence is above the average; he has imagination and originality, with the power of self-expression.

'He has excellent taste; a love of books, and a definite desire both for truth and knowledge. He is virile and ambitious, generous and kind-hearted.

'But he is 19, and going through the most difficult period of his development. With unusual physical and intellectual maturity he has not yet acquired mental discipline or a working philosophy.

'He therefore lacks stability and direction. His ambitions are considerable but vague. He has not yet learned to enjoy work or to subordinate his impulses to his permanent aims, nor has he yet grown out of the schoolboy's fear of authority and the mental dishonesty which such fear often produces.

* By a California trio, Dean S. Jennings, Ruth Landshoff, and David Malcolmson, but listed as Anonymous.

This coupled with the strength of his desires, often makes him fall below his theoretically high standard of conduct.

'These facts should not cause dismay. He requires time in order that he may learn to handle a complex nature.

'Since 1926 it has been possible to watch his qualities taking the field against his defects. He is now more balanced, less of a rebel, and not only more aware of his own defects, but more anxious to mend them.'

Encouraged, Eve arranged through Lord d'Abernon for Ian to meet the Foreign Office selection board. On 1 May 1928, Ian was interviewed at 6 Burlington Gardens by the First Civil Service Commissioner Sir Roderick Meiklejohn. The outcome was positive. No short cut was offered, but Ian was recommended to continue his studies, with the goal of sitting the highly competitive entrance examination in the autumn of 1931.

The regime that the Forbes Dennises created for Ian had the curative effect of the mud baths in the Schwartzsee. Ernan's priority was to give Ian a fresh goal that would challenge him, 'but for someone with Ian's extreme ambition it had to be an important aim or nothing'.

Eve's choice of the Foreign Office was an obvious one. Few teachers possessed Ernan's qualifications to coach Ian for exams in which he would have to compete with top students from Oxford and Cambridge – students like Peter. Ian, by contrast, did not even have his school certificate. It made the stakes in Kitzbühel that much higher.

Ernan drew up a syllabus. He centred Ian's reading 'on the idea of the struggles of the human being throughout the ages to improve himself'. The core theme was reflected in the books Ian began collecting at this time, eventually to blossom into the Fleming Collection. Ian recalled studying – 'thanks to the encouragement of the Forbes Dennises' – the works not only of Adler and Freud, but Kafka, Musil, Zweig, Schnitzler, Werfel, Rilke, von Hofmannstal, and buying first editions illustrated by Kokoschka and Kubin. When Peter asked Ian what he wanted for his twenty-first birthday, Ian replied: 'if you'd really like to know, I should love the paintings of D. H. Lawrence obtainable at some fabulous sum at Dulau's in Bond Street, which is the first publication of the Mandrake Press. They cost £10, so if Mama would add her tithe and Richard & Michael, it would cause a very gay smile to flit furtively across my disillusioned face as I open my "shumppe" (German) on the fateful day.'

It was at Dulau's bookshop shortly after Ian's twenty-first birthday dinner at Turner's House when he caught sight of Percy Muir's freshly written notice in the window: 'The new D. H. Lawrence'. The notice was for *Pansies*, Lawrence's last volume of poetry.

Ian came in – and met Muir for the first time.

Broad shoulders, wide-set grey eyes, with a sonorous and measured diction from his days as a music-hall entertainer, Muir was fourteen years older and hoping to be a partner of the bookshop, something he achieved with Ian's assistance. Muir wrote: 'We spent the whole morning talking and eventually lunched together. He was engaged for dinner, but we met again later in the evening and talked until the early hours of the morning.' As well as texts for Ernan's syllabus, Ian commissioned Muir to send him new books that he thought Ian might like to read, and he interceded when Muir was required to raise £1,500 (approximately £115,000 today) for his partnership. Muir could only manage half that sum. It seems that Ian in due course offered 'to advance £750 to invest in Dulau's if the bank would advance the remainder; and his was such a very distinguished name in the banking world that at the sight of his cheque the bank immediately agreed to the proposal.' Muir's lifelong gratitude and friendship was secured. He asked Ian to be godfather to his daughter Helen; they holidayed together in Austria; and Muir often played bridge with Ian at his club, White's.

Barely two years before, Ian had been consigned to the Army Class at Eton. Now in Kitzbühel, he was reborn as a European highbrow. In letters 'full of youthful didacticism', Ian wrote to his boyhood friend Selby Armitage, the son of the vicar in Nettlebed and regarded by Ian as 'my early hero', telling him of his disciplined work schedule and trying to get Selby into 'Ronald Firbank, James Joyce and Mann'.

The Foreign Office exam required candidates to speak two languages fluently, and one partially. Ernan arranged for Ian to stay first in Munich in the autumn of 1928, while Ernan was away in San Francisco; then at a language school in France in the spring of 1929; and from the autumn of 1929 in Geneva, after Ernan gave up his four-year lease on the Tennerhof that June.

Ian was most fluent in German. At Ernan's suggestion, he translated Klaus

Mann's play, *Anja und Esther*, which Ian presented to Eve, who had it bound. A second work he came near to translating might have nudged his life along a different path. Ian wrote to Peter in April 1929: 'I've read *Im Westen nichts Neues* [*All Quiet on the Western Front*] in German and just missed the job of translating it about 6 months ago – a phenomenal success, & really better than the average destruction war book.' He had been reading *Tom Jones* and Sylvia Townsend Warner's *True Heart*, '& I've just ordered *The Mountain Tavern* by O'Flaherty – otherwise I've been devouring huge tomes such as Spengler's *Decline of the West*, and dozens of German philosophers and French attempts to prove their literature won't die with Romain Rolland.' He was writing to Peter from La Babinière, a crammer like the Tennerhof near Tours, where he had driven in a second-hand Buick sports saloon with a battered radiator that he had nicknamed 'Zoroastra', in order to brush up his second language. 'I'm learning a good deal of French here, but there are a fairly devastating collection of people all with the hurried look of people who have left their respective houses of correction none too soon.'

Ian needed a third language for the Diplomatic Service 'which in my case was Russian'. Ernan found for him in Kitzbühel a small, stout, blonde tutor, the Russian widow of a czarist ambassador who had lost her estates in the Revolution and was earning money to keep her son at Eton by giving lessons. He paid 'Madame C.' four schillings an hour. She later took an overdose of sleeping pills in London when staying at the Ritz, having come to the end of her money. Largely thanks to her, Ian maintained that he had 'fairly fluent Russian', although Sefton Delmer, on a trip to Moscow with him in 1939, recalls Ian speaking to the concierge on their floor 'in bad Russian'. The only two words Delmer remembered were 'Paklava istoria' meaning 'a fine kettle of fish'.

While Ernan groomed Ian for the Foreign Office exams, Phyllis re-directed his imagination to writing.

In the summer after leaving Eton, Ian had planned a follow-up ephemeral to the *Wyvern* called *Medley*. He drafted a letter to potential advertisers, signing himself R. Coranville, and sketched out a contents page that anticipated his Atticus column on the *Sunday Times* devoted to 'People & Things'. 'Interviews with great men', 'Hints on dress', 'Advice to the Lovelorn', 'Limericks',

'Court Circular', and a 'Medical column'. The project was abandoned. He had promised that 'several well-known writers' would be contributing, but Ian's notebook contains potential submissions written solely by himself under another pseudonym 'Cory Anan', including this one:

There was a young lady named Brenda
who mislaid her right leg suspender
She lasted for days
on a lace from her stays
and some wire from the drawing room fender

Under Phyllis's influence, he turned his back on such juvenilia. At the Tennerhof, Ian lived under the roof of a professional author who wrote in bed till lunchtime and in the evenings read *Wuthering Heights* aloud to him beside 'the best of stoves'. Ian absorbed her work methods and her novels, writing to Phyllis shortly before her death: 'I was delighted to be reminded of what really beautiful English you write. It is quite brilliantly good and clear and true.'

Phyllis's conversation was reminiscent of Nell Pellatt. Normally joining them for dinner, she urged the gauche teenagers to reflect, untether their imaginations. Ernan said, 'At the Tennerhof we had a sort of imaginary dining club which Ian entered into with great glee. "The quails are just being flown in from Italy," sort of thing.'

Eager, ardent, with unruly white hair and dark brows, Phyllis spurred on the would-be diplomats to shape and exaggerate their fantasies, and not only about food. She would start off a ghost story and encourage them to continue. Characters in the valley supplied building blocks.

Ian's imagination seized on the Czech playboy, tennis champion and racing-driver Franz Schlick and his late aristocratic wife, Paula von Lamberg, a pioneer ski-jumper known as 'the flying countess' after her twenty-four-metre jump 'in a long skirt and impeccable posture' on the nearby Schattbergschanze. Ian's return to Kitzbühel had coincided with Paula's sensational death during a sidecar race in Salzberg in September 1927 when she was spun out from a car driven by Schlick. Her widower was the talk of the valley, having since inherited her castle. Ian never shed his suspicions. In his last conversation with Cyril Connolly, nearly forty years later, he recalled Graf Schlick as 'the Bluebeard of a horrifying saga'.

Ian outlined his literary ambitions in a series of lost letters to Selby Armitage. 'He was always saying how he was going to write novels himself, the form they were to take and so forth.' Ernan was more than aware of his craving: 'He wanted to write a serious novel later on.' A notebook from this period contains mainly verse fragments, some of which he showed to Lisl. 'In those days Ian wrote marvellous poetry. Descriptions of places. Very lyrical.' Ian came to feel that his poems 'aped Rupert Brooke' in their adolescent maunderings on melancholy ('I find a certain beauty in my sadness') and lost love ('I could not live & remember/And so I love & forget'). A short poem called 'Bravado' gives the flavour.

> *If the wages of sin are Death*
> *I am willing to pay*
> *I have had my short spasm of life*
> *now let death take its sway.*

It is hard to know how much of this verse went into what has become the holy grail for Fleming collectors: a self-published book of Ian's poetry entitled *The Black Daffodil*, which he had bound up in black like his translation of Klaus Mann. The only person who recorded having seen this 'slim, dark volume' was Ivar Bryce, in London in 1928, on the banquette at Boulestin's. 'He read me several poems the beauty of which moved me deeply.' Yet Ian was suddenly profoundly embarrassed. 'He took every copy that had been printed and consigned the whole edition pitilessly to the flames.'

At the Tennerhof, Phyllis hothoused two other future writers, Ralph Arnold and Ernan's sixteen-year-old nephew Nigel Dennis. Ian wrote to her in 1962: 'Looking back, I am sure that your influence had a great deal to do with the fact that, at any rate, three of us later became successful authors, and I remember clearly writing a rather bizarre short story for you which you criticized and which was in fact the first thing I ever wrote.'

Actually Ian's second story, 'A Poor Man Escapes', is set in the snowbound Vienna of Alfred Adler. Its main character is an impoverished newspaper vendor, Henrik Akst, whose wife dies on Christmas Day. Distraught, Henrik pawns their belongings, and then blows the money on cakes, coffee and vermouth in the warm surroundings of the Café Budapest. 'How lovely it had all been while it had lasted.' Unable to pay the bill and facing eviction, he swallows his wife's bottle of Lysol and dies at the table. The last line reads: 'But Henrik had paid and was rich for the first time in his life.'

Ernan said that Phyllis had found Ian's story 'very promising'. A measure of how far Ian had developed is that she later wrote a short story on a similar theme, set in a similar café.

'Both Winston Churchill and I were black sheep once,' Ian wrote thirty years later. '. . . it isn't a bad way of life up to and around the age of 21, which is approximately when my own shade of black dwindled to its present elephant's breath grey.' This metamorphosis took place at the Tennerhof. 'We helped him by having confidence in him,' said Ernan. 'We showed him he had a worthwhile self hidden.'

Ian would always be grateful to the Forbes Dennises. 'I learned far more about life from Ernan than from all my schooling put together.' Ernan with his Scottish upper-middle-class background and his brave war record came to stand in for Mokie. In one of Ian's last stories, *Octopussy*, Ernan serves as the model for the guide Oberhauser, who had looked after the teenage James Bond and taught him to ski. 'He was a wonderful man. He was something of a father to me at a time when I needed one.' Phyllis was a nurturing alternative to Eve, commemorated in Bond's obituary as the aunt-like figure who brings him up, following his parents' death, in the Kent village of Pett Bottom. 'She was such a *dear* person,' Ian wrote to Ernan after Phyllis's death, 'and between you, you spread an extraordinary warmth and light and sympathy wherever you went. You were father and mother to me when I needed them most and I have always treasured the memory of those days at Kitzbühel.'

Ian had badly missed a university training, but from his base at the Tennerhof he gained a European education and found direction. 'Kitzbühel was part of his cure, as far as it went,' said Ernan, 'because, apart from anything else, it simplified his life.' Under the self-educated wings of the Forbes Dennises, Ian became unrecognisable from the melancholy loner who had left England in disgrace in 1927. Lisl Jokl said, 'To all of us who knew him in

Kitzbühel he was exactly the opposite – gay, carefree, terribly happy, the most exciting and vital sort of person. Not like an Englishman at all.'

Ian reciprocated these feelings. He described himself as 'a devoted lover of the Tyrolese'. 'I have been back to the Tyrol countless times since those early days and I am confirmed in the opinion that they are my favourite people in the world.'

IX
MUNICH

'Sixty-five million people in search of a soul.'
ALFRED ADLER

Early on in the war, Ian invited a captured U-boat captain from Munich to lunch at Scott's. To persuade him to open up, Ian talked in German about the city 'where I had spent some of my early youth'.

In September 1928, at the age of twenty, with neither a high school certificate nor a university degree, Ian had moved to Munich to improve his German and Russian in preparation for the Foreign Office exam in three years' time, and to undergo Adlerian analysis. With Ernan away still in America, Ian lodged with Countess Marita Mirbach's family in Habsburgerstrasse, close to the museums and the Technical University. The countess reported to Eve that we 'all like Ian very much and find him responsible and serious for his age'. Ian spoke 'exceptionally well and with a pronunciation one rarely finds with foreigners'. Percy Muir, too, was impressed by Ian's grasp of French and German. 'His command of these languages was extensive and his pronunciation impeccable which was the more remarkable in that he had no ear for music.'

Even so, Ian's claim that he attended 'Munich and Geneva Universities (5 years)' has escaped the record: in neither university does his name feature on the lists of external students. Loelia Ponsonby (soon to be Westminster) visited Munich at this time and she recalled how the city 'was full of English boys and girls who were staying with impoverished Grafins learning a smattering of German, going to the opera in the cheap seats, drinking beer in cafés and altogether having a very harmless, free and easy time.' Hers is a more convincing picture of Ian's 'university' experience.

Eve had left Ian alone in Kitzbühel, but in November 1928 she decided to leave three-year-old Amaryllis behind and visit him in Munich. 'She was most energetic here,' Ian reported to Lady Sackville at Knole, 'and rushed from gallery to gallery flourishing her ten words of German with an intrepidity and unselfconsciousness which put my inborn fear of foreigners to shame.' She had kept Ian on a strict allowance of £30 a month (approximately £2,200 today) – Cecil Roberts noted that 'the only time Ian telephones home is when he wants money!' In contrast, Eve denied herself nothing. She 'spent the whole time running out of money, until I had to be quite firm about further expenditure – she tips everybody colossally, waiters, servants, & everyone, and I'm sure the whole of Munich was sorry she went.'

Not Phyllis, though. She had stayed behind at the Tennerhof while Ernan was in San Franciso, and now met Eve for the first time. Their charged encounter had repercussions. Eve was a terrifying replica of Phyllis's own impossible mother and of Ernan's 'Mamma', whose vampiric 'clutches' meant that Mamma lived 'not only *for* Ernan but *on* him'. On the back of everything Adler had taught her, Phyllis wrote a case study based on a fickle dominating widow like Eve and her destructive ambitions for her son. 'The boy had to become a blend of David and Goliath; George Washington, Abraham Lincoln, Stalin, Hitler, and she seemed inclined to think it possible to throw in Galahad and St Francis of Assisi as well.' Apparent to all was that the poor boy 'was basing his whole life on *a mistaken aim*. He wanted to get ahead – at whatever cost to other people, and this is what his mother wanted for him. He had to be a stunt hero, for his own glory and hers.' Phyllis predicted that if Ian continued on this path according to Eve's 'prestige thinking', he would end as a complete mental wreck.

Adler was away. Ernan always regretted that Ian never met him at this time. 'He should have had a treatment, and it is a great pity.' Ian's earlier analyst Joshua Bierer was teaching in Berlin, so Ernan had arranged for Ian to be seen by another Adler disciple, Dr Leonard Seif, a blunt Swabian. The consultation took place during Eve's visit and was a disaster. Ernan was told that Ian had sat opposite Seif 'but he wouldn't say a word. He just sat there and refused to speak to him'. All became clear, as it had for Phyllis, when Seif met Eve. 'Sief told me afterwards that there just wasn't a hope with a woman like that.'

Ian's friends were united in their verdict of his beautiful but overpowering mother. 'Mrs Val was terrible. Quite ghastly,' was the considered opinion of Rupert Hart-Davis, who travelled the following summer to Corsica with Peter, Ian and Eve. She filled Selby Armitage, who knew her in Nettlebed, with dread. 'His mother was really terrible. A ruthless, cold, dominating person who just didn't give a damn for anyone except herself.' Sandy Glen was one more reluctant visitor to Joyce Grove. 'I was terrified of his Mother, because she used to swoop on you, usually after lunch, and really tear one to pieces as a totally hopeless young man. So much so that I know on one or two occasions as lunch finished I got up quick and hid in the woods.'

Eve had redeeming qualities but she was also imperious, melodramatic, entitled, and a narcissist who dealt acidly with dissent. Her housemaid Joan Regent said: 'With Mrs Fleming, you were either in or you were out.' As a young girl, Eve had pelted her sister Kathleen with potatoes while chasing her down the street. Motherhood had not curbed her harassing behaviour. She would return a day or two in advance to take her sons by surprise and get her maids to spy on them. Her extravagance was unflagging. 'Mrs Fleming would put on a pair of shoes to walk to her car,' remembered Joan Regent, 'and never use them again.' Augustus John never forgot her knickers, hand-made by a French seamstress in gold thread and lined with pink crêpe de chine. They were the clothes of a flighty femme fatale, which was chiefly how Hilary Bray remembered her. 'One of those eating-up mothers who manage to make all their own rules to live by, but who insist that everyone else should live in strictest propriety.' Richard's wife said about Eve and her sons, 'They respected her, but they never loved her.' Amaryllis was more severe. 'I think Ian positively hated my mother. Because he was the one who was least sure of himself and she chose to misunderstand him.' Her most common damning remark to Ian: 'But darling, it's so *stupid*.'

Not for the last time, Eve's 'prestige thinking' caused an unpleasant clash with her son. Soon after his twenty-first birthday, Ian travelled with her to Nice where Peter and Rupert Hart-Davis joined them. Peter had come down from Christ Church that summer, having gained a First in English. His heart was set on a literary career. At Oxford, he had written plays and acted – on one occasion playing Bulldog Drummond on stage at Newport Pagnell. Yet under family pressure from Eve and Robert Fleming, he now reluctantly consented to go to New York to intern in a firm of stockbrokers as a preliminary step to working in the family bank. Ian was sympathetic. 'The City sounds definitely bad, but you will make some money and rise above the infinite pea, which is always something. Writing plays & acting are much more exciting and personal, but it would mean one continual squabble with managers or getting introductions to people you despise . . . and presumably you wouldn't want to spend your time pandering to the tastes of a country like England where 39 million people out of 40 possess all the faculties except that of thinking.'

Ian's months in Austria had exposed him to new theories. He was starting to interrogate his upbringing and culture.

The brothers' holiday with Eve on Corsica's north coast brought family tensions to the boil. Blazing arguments took place between Ian and his mother.

Ian's most explicit statement about his relationship with Eve is the letter he wrote to his 'darling Mama' on his return to the Tennerhof for the last time, before he drove to Geneva to continue his studies there.

'I hope you'll forget the fortnight in Corsica. My rudeness etc was largely due to my disappointment, & the fact that I had no friend with whom I could do things.'

Left by Peter and Rupert to fend for himself with his mother, Ian and Eve had sparred over money and the direction his European education threatened to take him. 'I am sorry that you are taking my "modern" ideas so seriously. You really needn't be so dismayed, for actually I have as good an idea of right & wrong as anyone, & possibly a stronger conscience – to which I admit I often pay little attention. These theories are merely phases like my long hair, my silk handkerchiefs, & my black hat, which I must go through only to find out for myself how stupid they are, "*on est idiot lorsqu'on est jeune pour raconteur lorsqu'on est veillard*" [We are stupid when we are young in order to be able to tell stories when we are old]. I don't think you need attach too much importance to them & if you ignored them instead of denying them they would disappear. I have grown up with an unfortunate idea, fostered by a belief that it is impossible to live up to such a pattern family, that I am of little or no worth in the world. A conception which has become almost a conviction after all the mistakes and false starts I have made. What I always longed for is recognition from you, & I have never done anything to deserve it, and yet have still expected it. My rudeness which I fully admit, &

my attempt to be "different", are only overcompensations for my feelings of inferiority, & will disappear once I have done something of which I myself am proud.'

Adler could hardly have improved on this self-analysis. Ian's bold declaration of self-determination is vital to understanding him. In his desire to make his own mistakes and choose a path for himself, he was outlining the kind of expedition that he was now impatient to embark on – and that Peter would later make through Russia, China and Brazil – in a car, moreover, that Ian had nicknamed after a philosopher who embraced the individual's right to create their own moral code. The iconoclast was taking form in opposition to the conformity demanded by the mother, to whom Ian was insisting on the one thing he had resented: that she ignore him, even as he admitted that all he ever wanted was her recognition.

Ian had needed his mother most in early childhood. By the time she actually focused on him he was a young man ready to make his own decisions.

He ended: 'My troubles will disappear when I have achieved enough confidence in myself to do without the continual assurances I want from the world that I am as good a human being as I want to be.' Eve was shortly to leave for New York to settle Peter into his new job. Ian wrote: 'I hope when you come back I shall be nearer the Diplomatic & to a better conception both of myself & of the world.'

X
GENEVA

'In Switzerland you can cover up all your sins.'

IAN FLEMING NOTEBOOK

Ian left Kitzbühel in the late summer of 1929, driving his black Buick 'Zoro-astra' over the Arlberg pass from 'happy-go-lucky Austria' and down into 'holier than thou' Switzerland. Ernan had drawn up a syllabus 'in preparation for a Foreign Office career' that included anthropology. 'It was because there was a good course in this at Geneva that I suggested Ian should go there'.

In his first weeks, Ian relied on Ernan's Adlerian contacts. Ernan had arranged for him to stay with the daughter of a Russian philosopher who had influenced Nietzsche. She ran the 'acme of pensions' in the rue de Lausanne – 'but Ian couldn't stand it for long'. Ian bracketed his landlady with those determined to keep 'the banner of Calvin flying behind the lace curtains in their fortresses'. Calvin's spirit still brooded 'like a thunderous conscience over the inhabitants'. The conscience of the twenty-one-year-old Ian had more in common with Pechorin in Lermontov's novel *A Hero of Our Time* which Ian studied in Geneva – and is the favourite book of the Soviet agent Tatiana in *From Russia, with Love*, reminding her of Bond. 'This hero chap liked gam-bling and spent his whole time getting in and out of scraps.'

By November, Ian had moved digs to rue Rudolphe Toepffer. His new landlady, Tina Keller-Jenny, was a psychotherapist and close to Carl Jung. From her Ian learned that Jung had delivered a speech that summer on the sixteenth-century Swiss physician Paracelsus. Encouraged by Ernan and with his landlady's assistance, Ian sought Jung's permission to translate the lecture. On 29 November, Jung replied to 'J. Fleming', authorising him. 'I'm glad you made the acquaintance of Mrs Keller. She is indeed quite capable of giving you a fair idea of my work.' Back in London, Ian's translation came as proof to Eve that her son was on the right path, and made a surprise reappearance after the war when it served as his unlikely passport into Edith Sitwell's good books; the pair hatched a plan to co-write a monograph on Paracelsus.

Ernan oversaw Ian's studies from Munich, where he and Phyllis had relocated. Ian later boasted, 'I studied Social Anthropology of all subjects under the famous Professor Pittard.' What Eugène Pittard, founder of Geneva University's Museum of Ethnography, made of his external student remains a mystery. As at Munich University, it is unclear if Ian attended formal lectures at all. A twenty-three-year-old Irish economist, Martin Hill, was employed in the Economic and Finance Section at the League of Nations, of which Pittard was project manager. Hill soon made friends with Ian and observed how 'he read voraciously but was not terribly interested in studies. I doubt whether he even bothered to go to the university.'

Mainly, Ian used his time in Geneva to improve his languages. He read Lermontov and Turgenev in the original with a devoted White Russian, Pyotr Maslov, who nicknamed Ian 'Ivan Valentinovitch' and gets himself mentioned in *Thunderball*. As well, Ian discovered the Austrian novelist Leo Perutz, recipient of his second fan letter, after he came upon Perutz's 1928 novel *Little Apple*. Ian's letter to William Plomer has not survived, but his one to Perutz, handwritten in German, has:

'I have over the last five years read the best and the lowest levels in modern English, German, French and Russian literature, mostly untranslated, and not once have I felt the desire to write to the author.' Such letters, Ian added, normally served more 'to overcompensate the inferiority complex of the writer' than to praise the author. However, 'last Saturday, I took *Wohin rollst du, Äpfelchen* with me on a journey from Munich to London . . . This morning I have finished the book and I have to admit that I am very much moved by it.

'I could write extensively about the book – the psychology, the continuity, and the Edgar Poe-ish humanity of it all – but my German is insufficient . . . so I shall only say that I admire your style, your language and your art down to the minutest details. The word "genius" has long since been devalued through misuse, otherwise I would have called the book simply ingenious.'

Ian lived for nearly two years in Geneva. He told his future chief at Reuters that he had gained 'a Swiss "certificat" in Anthropology' – which would have represented his only official academic qualification – but he spent more time in cafés than in classrooms. Prone to drifting off 'into a pleasant day-dream', he took his Perutz or his Lermontov or the latest issue of *Transition*, a new avant-garde magazine Percy Muir had sent him, and sat and watched the Jet d'Eau in the lake.

In Geneva, Ian found an 'atmosphere of still-water-running-deep' that appealed. Something in its symmetry chimed like its clocks. He admired the Swiss for being clean and orderly. He was relieved not to have to lock 'Zoro-astra' when he left it on the street. He responded to the nation's 'Georges Simenon quality that makes a thriller writer want to take a tin opener and find out what goes on behind the façade'. Returning in 1963 to interview Simenon, Ian pondered the same questions he asked himself each time he visited Geneva: 'How many secrets are safe here? How many refugees hide behind the bland Swiss concierge? Jung, Schweitzer, Joyce – these great non-conformists come to live in the conformist country with its rich leaven of underground fermentation, and how the Swiss ferment.'

In 1929, Ian, too, was fermenting. What he came to realise was that Swit-zerland's solidity was based on an elaborate conspiracy to keep chaos at bay, and when the Swiss were thwarted they went into meltdown. 'Saturday nights in Switzerland the top blows off the well-sealed pressure cooker & the Swiss libido bursts out with smoke & flame & sulphur.' This psychosis affected Ian: 'the reaction of the symmetrist to chaos'. When the placid Swiss erupted, they were like their Jet d'Eau, 'the highest fountain in the world'.

Months after his arrival, Ian experienced such an eruption.

He had broken loose from Ernan's staid circle to join Martin Hill and his jazz-loving colleagues from the Palais Wilson, 'the curious long-haired people that one meets in the corridors', as Basil Thomson describes League of Nations officials in *The Milliner's Hat Mystery*. Ian moved out of Tina Keller-Jenny's lodgings into the Hotel du Lac. For the first time, he felt free. With Peter in New York, there was no elder brother to measure himself inadequately against. On weekends, he went skiing, rock-climbing and golf-ing. In the evenings, he drank port aperitifs at the Brasserie Bavaria. He was invited to private balls. 'We were all far too wild and frivolous for such a serious place,' said Hill. 'But Ian especially seemed the epitome of the *jeu-nesse dorée*' with 'his habit of kidding anyone who seemed stuffy or pompous or to be taking themselves too seriously.' The bookish German baroness, Gisela von Stolzenberg, a research assistant at the League of Nations Secretariat, with whom Ian used to discuss Joyce, said that Ian's 'complete lack of seriousness' was one of his 'saving graces'.

Immersion in one of the world's most conformist institutions set the scene for Ian's eruption. His temporary job at the League of Nations was undertaken to add a further arrow to his diplomatic quiver and reassure Eve that he deserved the allowance she had agreed to pay. He told Percy Muir: 'If there's one subject we have more argument about than sex, it's money.' It was through Hill that Ian was recruited in July 1930 to the Intellectual Cooperation and International Bureaux Section. He replaced an Austrian member of the section who had died in June while preparing the League's *Handbook of International Organisations*.

He went to work at 8.30 a.m., walking around an old dog that lay on the steps at the entrance. In an office with a view over magnolia trees to Lake Geneva, a hundred yards away, and beyond to the Alps and Mont Blanc, Ian earned 850 francs per month putting together and updating chapters on religion, arts and sciences, medicine and hygiene, press, feminism, sport and tourism. The work was notorious for its nit-picking. 'The jokes about the Intellectual Section were unfair,' wrote Frank Moorhouse in his novel *Grand Days*, set in the League of Nations at this period. '. . . the section's accounting was meticulous and they were good about returning files.'

Still, for all the humdrum nature of Ian's job, Intellectual Cooperation was known to have the 'greatest bag of celebrities' on its committee – Henri Bergson, Marie Curie and Albert Einstein. Ian reported to Ernan how 'very bucked' he was to have met Einstein, who talked in an 'extraordinary soft way'; Ian would be one of those invited to a private lunch for him in Earl's Court in September 1933, after Einstein's exile from Germany.

A major event of the League in September 1930 was the first session of the Commission of Enquiry for European Union. Ian was recruited as a useful pair of hands to cover a surge in the workload leading up to this meeting. The Commission's Secretary was the League's founding Secretary-General, Sir Eric Drummond, whose corner office was situated below Ian on the first floor.

They would have recognised each other's old school tie on the broad staircase. Pinstripe trousers, dark jacket, blue shirt, Ian dressed in a fashion identical

114

to Sir Eric, a reserved, pipe-smoking, Scottish Old Etonian who, like Ian, had not been to university, and played golf or fished whenever he felt the weight of the world; large trout were sometimes found flopping out of his wash-basin. Sir Eric must be mentioned here because of his alias during the First World War.

As personal assistant to the Foreign Secretary, Drummond had acted as a contact point between the Foreign Office and the British Secret Service representative in New York, Sir William Wiseman. Later at the Admiralty, and also in New York and Jamaica, Ian dealt with Wiseman and so would have had access to the hundred or more ancient code names for people like President Wilson ('Collier') and Churchill ('Surface'). Drummond's code name was 'Bond'. It was to 'Bond', for instance, that Wiseman ('Cliff') cabled the message in October 1918, 'Lockhart & his party safely out of Russia', after the British diplomat Robert Bruce Lockhart failed in his attempt to spark a coup against the Bolshevik regime.

Intriguingly, James Bond may not have been Ian Fleming's first choice for the name of his agent. 'Mine's Secretan. James Secretan' is how he introduces himself at one point in the original typescript of *Casino Royale*. Ian then crosses out 'Secretan' and replaces it with a handwritten 'Bond'. (Charles Secrétan was a nineteenth-century Swiss philosopher whom Ian was supposed to be studying as part of Ernan's syllabus.)

In 1960, a reader urged Ian to set a Bond novel in Geneva. Ian replied: 'I have just come back from Switzerland and I daresay one of these days "M" will send James Bond there in the course of his duties.' Bond does make several visits to the land of his Swiss mother's birth. In *Goldfinger*, he goes into the Brasserie Bavaria across the lake, and reflects on how this restaurant used to be frequented by diplomats, journalists and international civil servants during the time of the League of Nations. Flying over Lake Geneva in *From Russia, with Love*, Bond closes one of the few books he is ever caught reading, to remember early skiing holidays. He looks down at the glaciers 'and saw himself again, a young man in his teens, with the leading end of the rope round his waist, bracing himself against the top of a rock-chimney on the Aiguilles Rouges as his two companions from the University of Geneva inched up the smooth rock towards him'. He then muses in the philosophical way of Borges, who lived in Geneva in the early 1920s and, like Ian, had climbed the Salève: 'If that young James Bond came up to him in the street and talked to him, would he recognise the clean, eager youth . . .? And what would that youth think of him, the secret agent, the older James Bond?'

Ten weeks in the Intellectual Section was enough, though.

According to his file, Ian resigned a fortnight early, on 30 September 1930, 'as he has to return to London to take up his studies'. He afterwards maintained that his experience made him allergic to almost every form of international agency, conference or committee. 'Having worked briefly in the League of Nations . . . I believe that all international bodies waste a great deal of money, turn out far too much expensively printed paper, and achieve very little indeed.' He waited till 1950 to sum up what a futile exercise it had been when he set a competition in the *Spectator* and prefaced it with this story: how after Sir Eric Drummond held the first General Assembly of the League of Nations in January 1920, the proof of the minutes went to the chief printer who pencilled at the foot of the galleys '(alas! how appropriately!) Alfred de Musset's second verse':

> *La vie est vaine*
> *Un peu d'espoir*
> *Un peu de haine*
> *Et puis, Bonsoir*
> *[Life is vain*
> *A little hope,*
> *A little hate,*
> *And then, Goodnight.]*

'Unluckily the scribble was somehow set up in print by an absent-minded compositor . . . and the shameful document is today on view in the League of Nations section of the Rockefeller Library at Geneva.'*

It was 1930, and he had a new lover. 'I was once engaged to a Swiss girl.'

He had had girlfriends in Kitzbühel and London. After Peggy Bainbridge, Ian became close to Rupert Hart-Davis's sister Deirdre, who inspired

---

* The verse is by Léon Montenaeken, despite Ian's insistence to the contrary.

several Rupert Brooke-ish poems, and Daphne Finch-Hatton, who sewed him a sampler which he hung on his wall; '*Elle a passé comme une ombre charmante dans ma vie*' (She has passed through my life like a charming shadow). But Eve stamped on any blossoming romance, as she had with Peggy. A vigilant overseer of her sons' allowances, holidays, choices of profession, and love lives, Eve had simultaneously nipped in its bud a relationship that Peter had started with Sybil Mayor.

Ian used his Swiss freedom to fall in love for the first time as an adult. Mary Pakenham explained it like this: 'One must consider the ideals of the Twenties. One of them was "living life to the full". Another feature was Grande Passion . . . One should be swept off one's feet. If one wasn't, one was a worm. *Wuthering Heights* was rated tremendously high.'

Stoked by Phyllis Bottome's reading of Emily Brontë's novel around the Tennerhof stove, Ian, at twenty-two, was ready to have his spirit liberated by a headstrong Swiss girl 'of considerable character'.

They met at a private ball one sulphurous Swiss Saturday night. Martin Hill introduced them. Monique Panchaud de Bottens was nineteen and came from Vich, a village twenty miles from Geneva. 'She was slim, dark-haired, with blue eyes and a strong sense of humour, not shy, a lady of culture who read many books and bought paintings, and was very difficult to live with,' says her only child, Charles de Mestral, who still lives on the family estate. Monique's father Lucien had inherited the 1870s white stone chalet and vineyards – which continue to produce the white Chasselas that Ian would have drunk. Lucien was a gentle, distinguished man who had lost a lot of money in a shipment of pigs from Marseille to Buenos Aires 'after the animals died on board' and had no real job other than to serve for forty years as mayor of Vich. Monique's mother Simone was an auburn-haired sculptress and tortoise lover – she kept ten as pets – who got Ian to sit for her in the glassed-in patio so that she could make a bust of his head; Ian subsequently borrowed Simone for the real name of 'Solitaire', the tarot-card reader in *Live and Let Die* who 'looked rather French and very beautiful'.

Monique spoke French and fluent English. When she met Ian, she already had her driving licence and thought little of taking off to Geneva in her father's beige Hillman. 'She was always strong-willed,' says Charles. 'One day, she decided she was going to work. She enrolled as a saleslady for an interior decorator shop in Rolle. She went off at 8 a.m. and was back at noon, totally unable to get along with the staff or clients. She didn't even last a full day.'

Monique swept Ian off his feet. They were engaged for three years, for half of which time Ian was working at Reuters. In winter, they went skiing in Leysin. Monique took a photograph of Ian on their hotel balcony. He stares at her with an intense expression, black-lensed ski-goggles strapped over his tanned forehead. In summer, he moved to be closer to her, into an apartment ten miles from Vich, in an elegant old house next to the château de Coppet. Like Bond with Vesper Lynd in *Casino Royale*, Ian was 'excited by her beauty and intrigued by her composure'. The feelings were 'mutually sincere', says her son.

In September 1931, Ian wrenched himself back to London to sit the Foreign Office exams over ten days in Burlington Gardens. He had spent three years in preparation. Peter had set off to Siberia, but he appreciated how much rode on the outcome. 'I'm longing to hear the news about Ian. I don't see why he may not have passed.' From Hanchow, Peter wrote again to Eve: 'Best love to Ian. O I do hope he has got through. It would be good.'

Yet Forbes Dennis's syllabus of anthropologists and philosophers, Ian's translations of Jung and Mann, his knowledge of German, French and Russian, and his work experience at the League of Nations, were not sufficient. On 24 September, Ian opened *The Times* to read the names of the successful candidates, but his name was not there. Ian had come twenty-fifth out of sixty-two, with only the top two candidates being accepted, and he scored his lowest mark for his English essay – twenty out of a hundred.* As with his departure from Sandhurst, he was unable to process the failure; twenty years later, he was still telling Somerset Maugham, 'I would have you know

---

* Had Ian passed the Foreign Office exam, he might have ended his days as a senior but forgotten diplomat in South America. The two successful candidates were John Ward, who finished his career with a knighthood as ambassador to Argentina and Italy; and Ian Wilson-Young, who was posted to Rio in the war and then to Lisbon, where Ian would have had dealings with him. In 1948, Wilson-Young dropped dead from a heart attack in Buenos Aires, aged forty, when serving at the embassy as counsellor.

that I took English Literature for the Foreign Office exam and achieved high marks therein as a result of my brilliant examination of "Fielding the Novelist".' At twenty-three, he was still unclear about who he was, still disappointing his mother, still flailing.

But he did still have Monique. Immediately on learning that he had failed in his mother's project for him to become a diplomat, Ian invited Monique to England for Christmas. It was time to introduce his fiancée. He must have known that her forthright temperament was unlikely to find favour with Eve.

Martin Hill chaperoned her from Geneva to Dover. Ian was on the dock-side, Monique so excited to see him that she had forgotten her suitcase on the ferry.

He drove her to Joyce Grove to meet his grandparents. She admired the stuffed rhinoceros head and the watercolour of Granny Kate with the three stags she had shot on her seventieth birthday. They walked in the grounds. To the end of her life, Monique kept a small blurred photograph that she had taken of the house as Ian pointed out where he and his brothers used to clamber round the front on the windowsills and arches, not touching the ground; the bet was to climb past their grandfather's window without Robert seeing them.

In London, they stayed at Turner's House, where there was no escaping Eve's eye. She was even more beastly to Monique than Ian had feared. Charles de Mestral says, 'They were already formally engaged in Switzerland. But the simple fact that he got engaged without Eve Fleming having met my mother was enough to gain the hostility of Eve.' Ian had confirmed their engagement with what Eve witheringly dismissed as 'the usual diamond bracelet'.

Ian's mother blamed Monique for his failure to get into the Foreign Office. She made life as degrading as possible for the girl. 'Mrs Val insulted her in every way,' said Mary Pakenham.

One morning, Monique was served caviar at breakfast.

'Caviar! How exciting, I've never had caviar.'

'No, I don't suppose you would.'

Turner's House was icy that winter, but Eve instructed her maids not to light a fire in Monique's bedroom. 'My mother was very susceptible to the cold,' says Charles. 'She covered herself with blankets.' In Coppet, to get warm, she always snuggled up with Ian.

One of Eve's housemaids was Hilda Gee. 'The reason he left Monique, I'll tell you. Mrs Val found her in Mr Ian's bed, and after that she was sent packing.'

Monique said: 'She did her best to try and separate us. When I dared to go into Ian's room, she threw a fit. "My dear," she said haughtily, "we don't do things like that in England." She was simply jealous.'

Her son says it was Monique who took the decision to go. 'She felt very strongly she was not welcome by the Fleming family, and in particular by Eve, and as a result of that attitude she left.'

Over the next eighteen months, Eve was unrelenting in her pressure on Ian to abandon the idea of marrying Monique. He was too young. She was not the right person, not grand enough. Eve hectored Bernard Rickatson-Hatt, Ian's new boss at Reuters, where she had secured her son a job, to intervene. Rickatson-Hatt told her that if he 'so much as raised the matter with Ian he would be perfectly entitled to tell me to go to hell'.

Ian was self-willed. He had broken free to live abroad for three years. He was not yet prepared to relinquish the first woman he had wanted to marry. Whenever a foreign assignment gave him the chance, he went again to stay with Monique in Switzerland. They wrote to each other. 'Mister Ian, he had letters from that girl in his desk stacked up like that,' Hilda Gee remembered, opening her arms accordion-wide.

But Eve was a mistress of attrition. This was the most serious conflict with her son to date. She issued an ultimatum. As reported to Lisl Jokl, it boiled down to money. 'It was a straight choice, the girl or his allowance.'

Finally, in October 1933, Ian 'flung his hand in'.

For Mary Pakenham, Ian's 'Grande Passion' had foundered on the spectre of himself hurtling back towards Robert Fleming's origins. 'It ended with Ian thinking in his head he could not face love in a cottage.'

Each family tells a conflicting account of Monique's reaction. In the Fleming version, her father demanded £2,000 (approximately £165,000 today) for breach of promise. Martin Hill said, 'This was an unheard of thing in Geneva, where you could divorce and fornicate and commit adultery but never jilt. Monique's family considered it an enormous affront to their honour and insisted on the settlement.' Under a German law abolished only in 1998, *Kranzgeld* ('wreath money') was awarded to compensate a woman of 'immaculate reputation' if a man broke off his engagement after having slept with her, 'the loss of virginity lowering the value of a young female in the eyes of a patriarchal society'. Although Monique's father Lucien was mayor of a village where the official language was French, it is possible that he threatened legal action through a German Swiss court. Ian told Mary Pakenham that he paid up 'and admired her for asking for it.'

Yet this is not how Monique's son understands what happened. 'The "theory" around here is that Monique is the one who broke the engagement, as opposed to Ian, following the attitude displayed by Eve Fleming during the trip to London. I suppose we will never know for sure, but it can be said that Monique was perfectly capable of doing so. When she got to observe the fireplace and was not able to have a fire, she was capable of turning round and leaving the same day, on the spot.' Charles de Mestral struggles to believe that Monique's father Lucien would have sued on her behalf, all the more so if Monique was the one who had called the whole thing off. 'If that had happened, I would have known one way or another. My mother with the money would have bought a painting. But it would not be in my grandfather's type to seek money. He never sued anyone else in Switzerland. It's just not like him to do that.'

Like Hemingway with his American nurse Agnes von Kurowsky, Ian never forgot his Swiss fiancée. Their break-up caused pain that lasted on both sides. Going back to Switzerland after the war, Ian allowed himself to entertain a pastoral fantasy of the life he and Monique might have led in their cottage. He wrote in his notebook: 'Over the tiny valleys with the spilled teeth of houses. How fine to live there & share a village life.' Monique is there in his promise to Ann at the rekindling of their affair in 1946: 'One day I shall write my first love letter since I was 22.' When Ian visited Switzerland in 1958 and 1963, Monique was the person he wanted to see again. 'When you break up like that and time goes by,' says her son, 'you only see the good memories, and thirty years later, if your marriage is not a success, you think of the other girl whom you idealise.'

He never sent her his novels. Her son says, 'We bought the Bond books in a book store, none came from him. How Fleming addressed the relationship was by having her become the mother of James Bond.' Bond's Swiss mother, Monique Delacroix, combines the names of Ian's fiancée with a nod to Eve's borrowed Huguenot name, Sainte Croix. Other touches spring from Ian's idyllic summer beside Lake Geneva. Bond catches up with Auric Goldfinger's yellow Rolls-Royce shortly before Ian's lodgings in Coppet. The small manoir where Goldfinger removes the gold from his car is on the site of Monique's family home, where Ian had sipped Lucien's Chasselas on the patio, with a view down three steps over the circular lawn and vineyards to Mont Blanc, while Simone sculpted his head. Bond finds it an attractive house. 'In his mind's eye, he could see the white painted panelling inside.'

Unlike so many of his affairs, Ian never regarded Monique as a dodged bullet. Alaric Jacob, a colleague at Reuters, voiced the disappointment of Ian's friends. 'The feeling was that he should have married the girl and damned his mother. But he didn't.' Mary Pakenham never doubted that his failure to stand up to Eve left him feeling like a worm.

Certainly, Ian found it hard to forgive Eve. He 'often referred to it as some disaster', recalled Didi Hill, whose husband had introduced Monique to Ian. Martin Hill had a similar feeling. 'The breaking off with Monique ended the chance for him of a normal life.' Ian's final lover, Blanche Blackwell, believed it had been 'one of the causes that made him never really trust another woman again because I think he was genuinely in love then'.

Ian's first adult love would always be a taboo. Not even with Lisl Jokl did he discuss it. 'The business over Monique was the one affair of his Ian would never refer to.' To Ernie Cuneo, it explained why Ian might have given up writing poetry. 'I always had the feeling that he had received, somewhere along the line, an emotional beating which bruised him so deeply that the poet in him would not or could not risk taking another beating like it.' He asked Ian, 'but I couldn't bring it out of him'. Over the course of their long friendship – 'I knew him better than most' – Cuneo tried to divine what lay at the root.

'I sensed there was some lissome, ivory-skinned girl with blue-black hair – for this is what he considered to be the ultimate type of beauty – off in some fir-clad hills in the idyllic Alpine snowlands who was the cause of his deep wound.' The break-up with that girl had bound Ian to the hero of his books, was Cuneo's conclusion. 'It seems to me that James Bond embodies Ian's revenge for the terrible hurt; Bond tumbles them into bed, leaves them with the memory of a savage ravishment which, ye gods, leaves them pining for Bond and forever bereft without him.'

XI
REUTERS

'Some of my happiest years were spent in Reuters.'

IAN FLEMING

'YOUR COPY TARDY ETINADEQUATE STOP RECTIFY'

'YOUR SERVICE SLOW COLOURLESS THIN STOP'

'OPPOSITION TRIUMPHANT'

'WELL DONE'

The room on the first floor of the ugly red building off the Embankment was used by the chief editor to wing brickbats and bouquets to his far-flung correspondents. On the afternoon of 7 October 1931, he interrupted work to interrogate a young man who had written asking for a job. He scanned the brief CV, registered the names of the three referees, and studied the applicant.

Ian had left Eton four terms early. He had abandoned Sandhurst. Back in London following four years of study abroad, he had failed at the Diplomatic Service. His confidence had taken 'a bad knock,' said Alaric Jacob, the new Reuters diplomatic correspondent. 'He really didn't know what he wanted to do.'

One thing Ian resolved not to do was follow his siblings into the family banking business. It was 'no life for a gentleman, and in my opinion a pretty poor one for a dung-beetle,' Peter had written to their youngest brother, Michael, who shortly afterwards joined Richard at Robert Fleming & Company. After a miserable stint in New York, Peter was working for the *Spectator* and had taken a four-month leave of absence to travel across Russia to China on the Trans-Siberian Railway.

Uncertain of his next move, with no source of income and nowhere to stay, Ian fell back on his mother for support and lodging. She gave him his own latchkey, but he had to be in early, and she kept him on a tight leash. There were perks to living at home, including free meals and fuel for his car. What he could not do was determine his future.

Eve's next choice for his career was 'rather a comedown' after her ambition 'to turn him into an Ambassador' had failed, but it served for the moment. With his head bowed, Ian went along with her plan.

Ian's family connections gave him entry into a place he otherwise would not have reached. On 1 October 1931, seven days after learning that he had not got into the Foreign Office, Ian composed a letter at Eve's instruction to her friend Sir Roderick Jones, owner and managing director of Reuters news agency. After reminding Jones of their previous meeting at one of Eve's parties, Ian said that he was 'really longing to start regular work as soon as possible', and would be 'gratefull' if Jones considered him for Reuters. Between the polite lines, Ian was calling in a favour.

Thirteen years earlier, Jones had been a settled bachelor of forty-two with 'no intention at all of marrying' when Eve Fleming sat him next to 'a girl obscured by a rich, short-waisted fur coat', the author Enid Bagnold, at a lunch party at Pitt House. 'She's a darling,' Jones later told Eve's friend Lady Sackville over coffee in the Flemings' sitting room. 'I mean to marry her.' Shortly after, he did so.

Alaric Jacob described Sir Roderick Jones as 'a terribly smart businessman cum country squire figure with a long nose, sleeked-back hair, dominated by his far more successful, statuesque, socially conscious wife'. If Jones was unable to recollect meeting Ian, the author of *National Velvet* certainly could. 'All I remember of him as a young man is his looks – his splendid appearance . . . and his impatience & fun.'

Jones was well placed to repay his debt to the woman who had introduced him to his wife. Disregarding Ian's spelling, he arranged for Ian to see his editor-in-chief.

The following Wednesday, Ian turned up at Reuters' headquarters in Carmelite Street for an interview that shaped the course of his life.

*

'I never spent a dull moment in his company,' Sir Roderick Jones said of the man Ian met that afternoon. Bernard Rickatson-Hatt was a fit, thirty-three-year-old, ex-Guards officer of medium height, dressed in clothes that recalled the dark blue and red colours of his regiment. 'He always called in at the Guards' Club on his way to work and back,' says his stepson. 'He was obsessed by the Brigade of Guards and embarrassed by the fact he had not been to public school, and this replaced it.' To complete the meticulous effect, he had a military moustache and wore an eyeglass through which he scrutinised Ian.

Jones had recruited Rickatson-Hatt as his personal assistant in 1925 on the recommendation of none other than Phyllis Bottome's wartime employer, John Buchan. Then deputy chairman of Reuters, Buchan was a neighbour of the Rickatson-Hatts in Elsfield outside Oxford, where the family had a farm. The author of *Greenmantle* vouched for Bernard's character and military record.

Rickatson-Hatt had left school at seventeen to join the Coldstream Guards. He was badly gassed in the First World War, and this affected his eyesight – which was why he needed the monocle, resurrected in *Moonraker* as 'the rimless eyeglass that M. seemed only to use to read menus'. Like Ernan Forbes Dennis, one of Ian's three referees (the others being Lord d'Abernon and Robert Fleming), Rickatson-Hatt had joined the Intelligence Service after the war, and was posted to Constantinople, where he became provost marshal when still only twenty-three, in charge of the British Military Police. His stepson believed that he maintained his links with SIS throughout his Reuters years. 'My mother was certain he was connected to the Secret Service. He was the type, no doubt about it, rather inscrutable. And Reuters would be ideal cover.' If true, this also helps explain the enigma of Ian's recruitment in 1939.

While in the Middle East, Rickatson-Hatt discovered a passion for Greek and Roman literature. He never lost an opportunity to insert classical allusions into his Reuters reports from America, where Jones sent him as chief correspondent. He was known to give free Classics lessons to a black elevator operator, and at a heavyweight prize-fight he described the boxer Gene Tunney as 'a man with the body of a Spartan athlete and with the mind of the Athenian of the days of Pericles'.* He spoke in Latin to his best friend Ernest Simpson (husband of Wallis) when dining at the Guards' Club, and spent a fortune on Greek and Roman books as well as on a collection of pornography said to be one of the finest in private hands, which he put at Ian's disposal. Golf was another shared obsession.

Married three times, Rickatson-Hatt was a better parent to a fatherless young correspondent than to any of his children. He had one son whom he rarely saw, to whom he offered two bits of advice. The first: 'Never tell an Englishman that you don't like cricket.' The second, supplied at the same meal: 'The only thing that ever matters is that you remain nice.'

Under the spur of American competition, Jones had recently recalled Rickatson-Hatt to London and promoted him to chief editor – 'to lead his cohorts in this great battle'. At the time of his interview with Ian, he was working 'to make Reuters product a little more snappy', said Robin Kinkead, a young American reporter whom Rickatson-Hatt had sent to Moscow the year before.

Ian felt the poker-faced gaze of 'the bemonocled ex-guards' officer' evaluating him as he chatted on about Phyllis and Ernan and Geneva and golf. Appealing to the soldier in him, Ian converted his dismal period as a Prize Cadet into an experience that had ended on a rewarding note rather than with a dose of the clap.

Briskly, Rickatson-Hatt decided that Fleming would make a suitable cohort, writing to Jones: 'I was much impressed by him. He is quite the right type and seems most intelligent. He is 23 and unmarried. After leaving Eton, he went to Sandhurst. He will therefore know the value and importance of discipline.' He suggested Ian come in for a month's probationary trial without pay.

Much relieved, Sir Roderick replied in his signature red pencil. 'Go ahead, by all means – I know the family; they are good stock & fine boys.' He initialled the memo with his customary 'C' for 'Chairman'.

---

* He covered several Tunney fights and was invited once by Al Capone as guest of honour to a boxing match Capone was sponsoring, being singled out by the referee. 'In the left corner is Green, in the right corner is Red, and over there is a limey wearing a barnacle.'

Eve was delighted. 'I *am* so glad to hear that you are giving Ian a trial,' she wrote to Jones. 'He has great character & is supposed to be very intelligent, though I ought not to say so.'

At 10 a.m. on 19 October, Ian started work in the editorial department, one of a dozen young men who sat at a long table on the first floor and rewrote copy, and were supposed to be ready to leave on special assignments at any time. Two days later, Rickatson-Hatt reported to Jones that the boy had made 'an excellent impression' so far. 'His languages are sound. His appearance is good, and his manners are agreeable. He suffers, perhaps, from a slight Foreign Office "bump" but I think you can depend on us to put some pep into him before many days have gone by.'

'Wonderful!' was how Ian summed up his time at Reuters. 'My God, it was fun!' He had endured five years of back-to-back disappointment. He now savoured every one of his twenty-seven months in Carmelite Street. He looked back at this period as 'the most exciting time of my life, because in those days news agency work was like a gigantic football match . . . We had some superb battles in Germany and Russia, and so on, and it was all highly enjoyable.'

Initiative was rewarded, 'pep and punch' demanded. In contrast to his work at the League of Nations, Ian delivered news to a world that actively waited on his despatches. He was read and talked about at the highest levels. Few professions were more glamorous to a young man in his early twenties, wrote Alaric Jacob. 'The itinerant reporter rivalled the film star in the attraction of his life.'

Ian's wide brief played to his interests. He covered sport, motor-racing, business, obituaries, and politics, reducing mounds of material into bullet points that could be held in the palm. 'To simplify without distortion is a very great art, and one at which, in particular, foreign correspondents need to be adept,' he later wrote. Scrumpled into the waste-paper basket went his literary pretensions; Leo Perutz and Thomas Mann were no use when he needed to wire the results of a boxing match or an athletics meet. Like Ernest Hemingway on the *Toronto Star* or Graham Greene on *The Times*, Ian was required to hone a style on his Royal portable that 'damned well *had* to be neat and correct and concise and vivid'. Even Vivienne Michel in *The Spy*

Who Loved Me picks up 'a lot about writing' when working on her weekly parish magazine, 'tricks like hooking the reader with your lead paragraph, using short sentences, avoiding "okay" English, and, above all, writing about *people*.' These were tricks Ian learned. 'That Reuters' training was much more valuable to me than all the reading in English literature I did at Eton or in Geneva or wherever . . . It was that career in Reuters that taught me to write fast and above all be accurate because in Reuters if you weren't accurate you were fired and that was the end of it.' Two of the journalists on trial with Ian were soon let go because in Rickatson-Hatt's words they were 'too slow and sleepy for the rush of modern newspaper work'.

Ian was neither slow nor sleepy. For the next two years, he thrived. In an interview published posthumously, he said that if he were twenty-five again and had any choice of career, he would 'go back to newspaper work', but with a camera, and become a TV news journalist.

He sat in the barn-sized newsroom and took the despatches straight off the wire, in French from Havas, in German from Wolff's Telegraphisches Bureau, subbed them, and sent them on again. He did this for a month. 'My previous good opinion of him is confirmed,' Rickatson-Hatt reported to Jones. On 2 December, the Reuters doctor passed Ian as physically fit, and he was formally offered a position at a salary of £150 a year (approximately £12,000 today).

From his first day, Ian sought to make himself indispensable. He used his City connections to mend relations between Reuters and the stockbroking firm Saint Phalle, in a way that 'will help us along considerably', the commercial editor gratefully informed him.

In April, the editor of the *Financial News* wrote Rickatson-Hatt an appreciative note: 'I understand from our night staff that Mr Fleming of your office was extremely helpful Friday night in getting for us back figures on German and French foreign trade and that he went to much trouble to assist us.' Rickatson-Hatt forwarded the note to Ian. 'This is excellent work on your part and shows the right spirit.'

In July, Rickatson-Hatt found further grounds for praise. 'Dear Fleming, The Acting Sports editor writes to me: "I should just like to let you know that Fleming was been exceedingly good in the way he has helped us out here with Mail Sports Reviews during the absence of Blackmore and while we were shorthanded." I was very glad to hear this. Needless to say, this is the way to get on in Reuters.'

That month, he rewarded Ian with his first foreign assignment.

The week-long International Alpine Trials in July followed a 1,614-mile course from Munich to San Remo and was considered the most demanding motoring event in Europe. In 1932, there were more British entries than ever: 43 out of the 107 cars. Ian was to travel as navigator to Donald Healey, driving a British-made 4.5-litre Invicta in which Healey had won the Monte Carlo rally the year before.

Healey was a modest, five-foot Cornishman later responsible for the Austin-Healey. Like his rival car designer, Walter Bentley, Healey's first love was aviation. Deaf in one ear after his Sopwith was downed by friendly fire, he sat all the way beside Ian wearing his First World War pilot's flying jacket to keep him 'toasty warm' in the high passes. A gentle character who never needed sleep, Healey hid a pistol in the glove pocket 'for wolves or bandits'. He instructed Ian to light a candle when the windscreen misted up, and for windscreen-wipers he had to rub the glass with potato halves – the starch would soon disperse the water.

In 1928, Ian had once travelled at 100 m.p.h. in a three-litre Bugatti along the Fair Mile at Henley, but this was a gruelling six days in a vehicle with a low chassis, heavy clutch, and a back half that drifted from side to side as they zigzagged up from Italy into Switzerland. Healey recalled Ian as 'a very nice man who was very happy to get out at the end of it'.

They had set off in heavy rain from Munich at 4 a.m. on 28 July. The start could hardly have been more dramatic. As they roared out of the disused police barracks where the cars had been locked away for the night, Ian witnessed German police with batons charge a gang who had broken in 'for some purpose which has not yet been discovered'. Moments later, one of the rally's two Aston Martins skidded with a resounding crash into a taxi cab and had to abandon the race after a mile.

The second day was less eventful, save for the alarming spectacle of one of the Alvis drivers who experienced trouble with his petrol feed. Ian tele-grammed that evening from Merano: 'His only remedy was to perch himself perilously on the wing and pour petrol direct into the carburettor while his reserve passenger driver steered the car.' Healey never called upon Ian to steer, merely to map-read.

The high point of the rally – in every sense – was the crossing of the Stelvio Pass from Italy into Switzerland. At 9,045 feet, the Stelvio was the highest mountain road in Europe 'and in the climb of 17 miles 50 hairpin bends have to be negotiated'. It was a punishing ascent at an average speed of 20 m.p.h., with a danger of overheating. Healey had to go into reverse at least eight times to bring the Invicta up in a record-breaking climb of 23 minutes 43.5 seconds. The descent put a premium on the drum brakes, down passes where the Swiss postal buses had right of way. Healey was obliged to veer over to the outside of the road when he heard their powerful high-pitched horns. There was only a flimsy barrier between Ian and a fall of thousands of feet.

Ian was shaken up by the ride, Healey could tell. 'He spent the whole time being scared, thundering around at high speed.' At the same time, his enthusiasm had been stirred. Ian never got over the narcotic thrill of sitting beside Healey as he opened the Invicta's throttle to outpace another car. It made an exhilarating change from writing sports reports and obituaries. Healey wrote: 'On many subsequent occasions when I used to cross the Atlantic three or four times a year in the *Queens* [the liners *Elizabeth* and *Mary*] we would meet and recall our rally together.'

On the evening of their descent, Healey drove down into St Moritz and parked his Invicta on the tennis court of the Grand Hotel. Once he had wired the record-winning time, Ian, basking in their achievement, mingled at dinner with the other drivers. Healey afterwards wondered if they had seeded some future characters for Fleming.

Among the competitors was the leading female racing driver, the twenty-three-year-old Scottish-Canadian Margaret Allan, exotic, independent, one year younger than Ian, who had zipped past 'with a broken spare wheel bracket on her Wolseley Hornet'. She won a Coupe des Glaciers, like Healey, and the Coupe des Dames – and later worked at Bletchley Park. 'If there was one thing that sent Bond really moving in life, with the exception of gunplay, it was being passed at speed by a pretty girl screaming round S bends.' Overtaken by a young woman driving a Lancia on the three-mile stretch separating Royale-les-Eaux from Le Touquet, Bond notches 125 m.p.h. in his supercharged Bentley, determined to catch her up, 'and by God, it had been fun!'

Another driver was A. H. Pass, English owner of the rally's sole Rolls-Royce entry, a 1932 Phantom II Continental; Pass had caught up with the other cars after missing the start because of 'business interests'. When 007 tracks Goldfinger's Rolls in the foothills of the Jura and has to negotiate the bends of the N84, 'Bond went at them as if he was competing in the Alpine trials.'

In *You Only Live Twice*, Bond escapes the castle of Ernst Blofeld by jumping onto a helium balloon. A free flight in the Graf Zeppelin was one of the awards for Healey's Coupe des Glaciers. Healey drove Ian to the airship's base near Friedrichshafen for a 4 a.m. start. While in flight Ian was able to buy postcards illustrating the Zeppelin, already stamped and franked with its own special postmark. He dropped them in a mail bag over the post office in Bregenz, in Austria.

A terse letter from Rickatson-Hatt, demanding 'an adequate reply *by return*', interrupted the holiday in Vich that Ian had snatched to be with Monique, who was officially still his fiancée. Enclosed was a complaint from the managing editor of the *Daily Telegraph* who had objected to the exaggeration and 'self-complacency' in Ian's reports.

Stung, Ian composed a detailed rebuff, emphasising that the Alpine Trials were not a race. 'They were a test against a "bogey" as in golf.' Ian directed his defiant explanation at the golfing fanatic in Rickatson-Hatt, who declared himself satisfied. 'I want you to regard a letter of that sort not so much as a complaint as a most useful criticism for your future guidance. We learn much more from criticism than from facile praise.' He did not rap his protégé's knuckles for a more serious inaccuracy: in the opening line of his report on 29 July, Ian had described the Trials as a '10,000 mile run from Munich to San Remo', exaggerating the length of the course by a factor of six to one. On the contrary, Rickatson-Hatt commended Ian to Jones. 'He is accurate, painstaking, and methodical. He also has a good *business instinct* – doubtless a family trait.'

Ian had been at Reuters a year when he wrote a private letter to Sir Roderick Jones – 'the superbly trim figure in the gleaming Rolls Royce who controlled our destinies' – asking for more money. 'I do feel that I am either worth £300 a year to the firm or else, in my opinion, nothing at all.'

His request had the assured tones of a young man who had discovered his worth. He brandished the figure of his grandfather: Robert Fleming, apparently, had head-hunted Ian for the family bank. 'This step would not be at all in accordance with my preferences or my ambition.' Indeed, Ian hoped he had convinced Sir Roderick of how delighted he was with his work at Reuters. 'But this is a materialistic age, and the day is past when a career was merely a hobby . . . If I am not considered to represent an asset of this value to the firm, I owe it to the very excellent education I have received to find a situation where my potential services are considered of this value.' Ian asked for Jones's reply as soon as possible.

Jones did not underestimate the value of Ian's kinship to 'one of the most able, best known & highly respected men of business in the City of London' – as one of Ian's referees had praised his grandfather. Because of Robert Fleming, Ian could draw on a formidable network of contacts, ranging from America through Cuba to the Middle East. This was one reason Jones had taken Ian on.

Ian never doubted his grandfather's value to him. 'The name of my family firm in the City, Robert Fleming & Company, has magical properties.' Ian's City connections had already worked their effect in the case of Sainte Phalle. They proved advantageous again.

An outstanding example was Ian's confidential memo to Rickatson-Hatt in February 1933, 'RE THE ANGLO-PERSIAN OIL COMPANY AND FALSE NEWS OUT OF JERUSALEM'. At stake was the reputation of Reuters in the part of the world where Rickatson-Hatt had made his name.

Robert Fleming's bank had underwritten the Anglo-Persian Oil Company. The press officer there had secretly let Ian see the company's files. 'I am at the moment in a position to get certain favours from the AP which might be of use to us in future, and I was shown these private files in the very strictest confidence.' What Ian had read was alarming – 'material evidence which undoubtedly casts serious reflections on our Services, especially from Jerusalem'.

Ian bowed to Rickatson-Hatt's knowledge of the Middle East, where he had held sway in blue and white armbands as head of the Military Police. 'I am quite sure you will confirm, from personal experience, that Jerusalem is the clearing house for every sort of Near East eye-wash.' The chief editor would not be pleased, therefore, to learn of Reuters' part in dispensing this eye-wash. Since last July, six Reuters news stories from Jerusalem were shown to be 'without foundation'. Then this sting. 'Having regard to the growing influence of the Anglo-Persian in this important Reuters territory, I felt that it would be best to let you know that they consider Reuters material the worst out of Palestine.'

Rickatson-Hatt was shrewd enough to suspect Anglo-Persian of exploiting Ian, which was why 'I am inclined to think ILF's report is a little "windy"'. Yet he was still horrified. At once, he directed his editors in Jerusalem, Constantinople, Teheran, Beirut, Cairo, Alexandria, Baghdad and Basra 'to exercise very great care in the handling of any despatches relating to APOC'. Ian's memo had resulted in the sharpening of Reuters' coverage of the region and the protection his grandfather's assets.

This sort of insider information was what Sir Roderick Jones had in mind when he consented to Ian's demand for a pay rise. One indication of the value Jones placed Ian's 'excellent work' was his instruction to the chief accountant 'not to *mention* this to *anybody* not even the editor-in-chief . . . as a *definite exception* is being made for him because of the special circumstances of his case.' Not even Rickatson-Hatt was involved in the decision to double Ian's salary. 'He is a great favourite,' Jones wrote to Eve.

By October 1932, Ian had been back in London for twelve months. He started his second year at Reuters more confident in himself. When he learned that the novelist Willam Plomer, whom he had written to six years before, had returned from Japan, he invited him to one of Eve's parties at Turner's House.

Plomer has left a portrait of Ian, 'wearing a well-cut dark blue suit and with very good manners, easy, cheerful and welcoming . . . He seemed to me to have good luck on his side and youth, health, strength, money, general eligibility, a social status taken for granted, work that interested him and a consciousness of his powers. At that first encounter, he struck me as no mere conventional young English man-of-the-world of his generation: he showed more character, a much quicker brain, and a promise of something dashing or daring. Like a mettlesome horse, he seemed to show the whites of his eyes and to smell some battle from afar.'

One friend sad to see less of Ian was 'Burglar' Bryce. 'He was busy and not readily available, Reuters had been a big success, and had invested him with a reputation as a *débrouillard*, a good man in a tight spot, a chap with brains, and as much at home with intellectuals as with men of action.'

As in Kitzbühel, something about Ian, some strange rub of energies, made others want to turn him into a fictional character. He had been Ian Crawley in Cecil Roberts's *Spears Against Us*. He was the amoral Max von Ulm in Phyllis Bottome's *Wind in His Fists*. Now Alaric Jacob brought him into his autobiographical novel *Scenes from a Bourgeois Life* as Hugo Dropmore. 'As a character in a novel, he would have been incredible; as a real person I found him a most satisfying work of fiction.'

Jacob considered Ian an excellent friend. 'I was extremely fond of him, and he gave me good reason to be for he would take immense trouble to do little things at awkward times for people who depended on him.' They sat at adjacent tables in Carmelite Street. Together, they visited the International Sports Club in Upper Grosvenor Street, where Ian gave him tickets for the swimming pool; while Jacob swam, Ian went off to play bridge at the St James's Club. On 3 October 1932, Jacob lunched with Ian in a cabman's shelter 'where he'd discovered the eggs and bacon were good'. At the end of March, Jacob introduced Ian to a childhood friend who had been turned down by Reuters, Kim Philby (as a result 'he knew him quite well,' said Jacob);* both Philby and Jacob had suffered from stutters as boys, which Jacob had cured by singing in chapel. Ian displayed no such inarticulacy. To Jacob, he had the appearance of being the glossiest, wittiest, charmingest young man in all of London. 'He looked like a young actor who has never toured but started right in the West End. He was fair of face, deceptively modest in demeanour. He seemed to know everything about everything; but if a subject arose on which he was not informed he would own it at once ... Thomas Mann was his speciality. He would declaim whole passages from *The Magic Mountain* in German.'

* Fleming later gives him a small part in *Goldfinger*. Miss Philby is secretary of the Bank of England women's hockey team.

As one of Sir Roderick Jones's favoured young men at Reuters, Ian was invited for weekends to his house in Rottingdean. On one occasion, Ian made a powerful impression on Lady Sackville's son-in-law, Harold Nicolson – formerly Sir Eric Drummond's secretary at the League of Nations – who reportedly said that Ian Fleming was 'a striking young man who might one day be PM'. He now inserted him into the only novel he wrote. In his thriller *Public Faces*, Nicolson made Ian the indispensable right-hand man of a character based on Jones and gave him a function that illustrated how favoured, how much of an exception he was. To complete his flattering image, Nicolson named the character Fleming.

Public Faces has, in retrospect, a Bondian theme: the race to build an 'atomic bomb' from a new alloy called Livingston – 'an engine of destruction more powerful, more lethal, than any known in the whole history of man'. A single Livingston bomb no bigger than an inkstand 'could by the discharge of its electrons destroy New York'. When a British aeroplane carrying a Livingston bomb explodes 300 miles off the Carolina coast, causing a tidal wave that overwhelms Charleston, the responsibility falls to 'young Fleming' at Reuters, the man 'in charge at the office', to release the news of the atomic explosion. On the basis of Fleming's Reuters cable – 'a masterpiece' – negotiations open with the United States and France, and 'the twentieth century was saved from disaster unparalleled'.

Public Faces came out in 1932. Less than a year later, Ian was given a corresponding opportunity to have a story 'published in the press of the whole world'. The dateline: Stalin's Moscow.

XII
MOSCOW

'His voice was sarcastic. "James Bond."
[He pronounced it "Shems".] . . .'

FROM RUSSIA, WITH LOVE

Before his death in a climbing accident near Mont Blanc, James Bond's Scottish father Andrew worked as an overseas representative for Metropolitan-Vickers.

The British company, known for manufacturing steam turbines, was the one firm operating in the Soviet Union. 'It supplies electrical machinery and equipment made in England, installs it, maintains it and teaches the Russians to make similar stuff,' Britain's consul general in Moscow, Reader Bullard, wrote in his diary. Until March 1933, the firm had enjoyed 'most cordial' relations with the Soviet government.

Bullard's diary shines light on a notorious show trial in Moscow when, that spring, six senior overseas representatives of Metropolitan-Vickers were arrested and charged with sabotaging machinery the company had itself sold to the Russians. It was as a reporter sent to cover their trial that Ian first made a name for himself; and it was Andrew Bond's real-life colleagues who were in the dock.

Reader Bullard, 'a tough Briton', in Churchill's opinion, 'with no illusions', understood why Stalin had acted. Bullard had learned from the manager of Metropolitan-Vickers of colossal blunders made by the Russians in their industrialisation programme. 'He reckons there are twelve 24,000 horsepower turbines lying about unused: they have been completed and shipped but never erected.' On top of that, the Soviet government owed Metropolitan-Vickers the equivalent today of approximately £80 million. 'The government is simply desperate for money and is holding out in the hope of getting better terms.' The existing trade agreement between Britain and Russia expired on 17 April. Stalin needed a bargaining chip.

With no less urgency, the Soviet leader was anxious to divert focus from a catastrophic man-made famine, today recognised as a genocide, that, in March 1933, the *Manchester Guardian* had brought to international attention and laid at Stalin's door. In a classic 'dead cat strategy', Stalin gave the go-ahead for the arrest of six senior Metropolitan-Vickers staff.

On the evening of Saturday 11 March, armed men barged into the log cabin where the British company's foreign staff were eating dinner in their compound outside Moscow, and led them away. Four Russian employees were also arrested, including the company's efficient dark-haired secretary, Anna Kutuzova. The charges were not revealed, but Bullard feared their summary execution: thirty-five agricultural workers rounded up at the same moment had been shot in secret, accused of manipulating figures for the grain harvest. 'This sort of thing always happens when times are bad. Lest people should blame the Government, a few scapegoats are selected.'

On 14 March, the British ambassador visited two of the prisoners in Moscow's Lubyanka prison. Allan Monkhouse, the company's chief engineer, a good-looking New Zealander, had been interrogated for eighteen hours without a break. Leslie Thornton, in charge of building the turbines, was too terrified to say much in case his relationship with Kutuzova reached the ears of his invalid wife in England; his drawn expression gave the ambassador the impression that Thornton, too, had been 'put through it'.

Neither man had been informed of the reason for their arrest.

Not until three days later were the charges disclosed. The foreign staff and their Russian accomplices – now increased to forty-two – had been caught red-handed 'wrecking' power stations at Moscow, Chelyabinsk, Zugres and Zlatoust, as part of a wider plan to discredit communists everywhere. Under article 58, the charges carried a maximum sentence of 'death by shooting'.

In London and in Parliament, there was a furore. Sir Robert Vansittart, permanent under-secretary at the Foreign Office, summoned the Soviet ambassador to impress on him the widespread revulsion at the grotesque allegations. To cheers in the House of Commons, Ramsay MacDonald's National Government secured powers to impose a trade embargo.

At this point, Ian realised he had a fabulous contact: his Eton friend Gerald Coke worked as a salesman for Industrial Steels, a small company owned by Metropolitan-Vickers. In the course of a 'friendly conversation', Coke revealed that the company's engineers were involved in building the Dneprostroi Dam where the Soviets alleged that the blades of the giant turbines had been corroded with 'malicious intent'. Coke told Ian, 'the charges were fantastic . . . but not mechanically impossible'. Ian later regretted that 'the "fantastic" angle was not sufficiently emphasised in my story', but he worked Coke's details – the first specific information he had – into a paragraph that he wrote up for Rickatson-Hatt on March 16. 'Since the blades were made of rustless steel of the very finest quality, sand or acid must have been poured into the turbines in order to bring about the alleged corrosion.' The inference could be drawn that this had occurred.

The BBC got hold of Ian's report and broadcast it. A senior representative of Metropolitan-Vickers issued a heated denial to *The Times*. The sense in Reuters was that Fleming had 'slipped up', but Ian reassured Rickatson-Hatt that 'our facts were substantially correct and the alleged corrosion was by no means the impossible phenomenon alleged in their denial by Metropolitan-Vickers.'

The company remained determined to downplay the gravity of the situation. But when the Soviet authorities announced the date of the upcoming trial, the British government sprang into action. On 22 March, the Foreign Secretary, Sir John Simon, intervened with Sir Roderick Jones and asked that Reuters report news of the trial in full.

The Soviets had arranged the trial to conclude before 17 April, when the trade agreement terminated. Reuters' local correspondents would have to deal robustly with the case, which would be hard for them. At least two senior American newsmen in Moscow were threatened at the end of March with having their press credentials removed unless they repudiated the *Guardian's* allegations about the famine: shamefully, they did so. Bullard wrote in his diary, 'no foreign journalist can tell the truth about the SU if he wishes to remain in it.' Nor could British Intelligence put anyone in, because they would be arrested immediately and flagged in *Pravda* as an evil British spy. Rickatson-Hatt had to pick a fresh reporter, unsullied by Intelligence connections, but with good contacts, who spoke Russian and could be relied on to pass messages to the embassy. He cabled Robin Kinkead, his new bureau chief in Moscow: I AM SENDING YOU IAN FLEMING ONE OF OUR ABLEST YOUNG MEN TO HELP COVERAGE OF THE TRIAL.

On 5 April, Rickatson-Hatt wrote to Jones, 'I spent about an hour this afternoon with Fleming discussing our Moscow coverage in all its details. I gave him a copy of the letter of instructions we sent to Kinkead, and I sent round to his house this evening a copy of the Editorial Order that has been issued about the trial.'

The order stressed the 'supreme importance' of the story to Reuters. 'Everything depends on getting in first.' Rickatson-Hatt advised Ian to see people at the embassy like Bullard 'and also to give the Court-room the once-over and let us have a really bright and interesting dispatch so that Fleet Street will know that our staff man has arrived and is already on the job'.

Early next morning, Ian flew from Croydon to Berlin, and at 6 p.m. he boarded the train to Warsaw and Moscow. He had packed his typewriter and a Turgenev novel and wore a loud bookie's black-and-white check suit like the one Evelyn Waugh favoured when travelling abroad as a foreign correspondent. 'I thought I might get away with it out here,' Ian told Kinkead in Moscow.

In the late 1960s, the screenwriter Jack Whittingham, who had collaborated on the writing of *Thunderball*, started to write a screenplay based on the life of Ian Fleming. Whittingham's daughter Sylvan says: 'He had Fleming as a Reuters correspondent travelling on that train across Russia. Fleming was sitting in a compartment, and this alter ego like a ghost came out of him, and this whole adventure took place. That was how Dad played it – that Fleming had this other life that was Bond.'

The project was aborted, yet it reveals something of Whittingham's perception of Bond that he saw his origins in Ian's first important foreign assignment. During his fortnight in Moscow, Ian confronted a system that crystallised in his twenty-four-year-old mind the kind of enemy Bond would take on in the 1950s and 60s.

Ian had been forewarned from reading Leo Perutz that 'Russia is ruled by an army of executioners' with the Lubyanka as 'the headquarters of death'. He understood the truth behind these remarks as he sat for six days in the packed Moscow courtroom and observed from a few feet away 'the implacable working of the soulless machinery of Soviet Justice'.

In July 1956, after delivering *From Russia, with Love*, Ian told his editor how it was based on what he had witnessed personally, 'a picture of rather drab grimness, which is what Russia is like', and a portrait of state intimidation on a scale that he could never have imagined in Carmelite Street.

During his time in Moscow, Ian formed a hostile picture of the Soviet state that, twenty years later in the context of the Cold War, the rest of the world was ready to gobble up. A system built on fear, routine arrests, the terrorising of innocent men and women in a show trial dominated by a pitiless Stalinist prosecutor, who, in his appetite to break and dehumanise the accused, compared them to 'stinking carrion' and 'mad dogs'.

At 9.45 a.m. on 8 April 1933, Ian's ornate Victorian-style carriage pulled into Belorussky station. On the platform on this cool morning in late spring was Robin Kinkead. The twenty-seven-year-old Stanford graduate had booked them both into the National and he brought Ian up to speed on their drive to the hotel.

The streets they raced through were in grey contrast to Kinkead's rented Lincoln. The unpainted and weather-stained houses reminded Ian of the Gorbals neighbourhood in Glasgow. He agreed with one of the British journalists whom he met for lunch at the National, Arthur Cummings, that Moscow was 'as depressing as a pauper's funeral', with long queues outside the bakeries 'as if the unemployed of half a dozen industrial towns in the north of England had been dumped here and ordered to keep moving'. The faces of the people had the pinched, dead look that came from the malnutrition that had already claimed an estimated five million lives and was provoking tales of cannibalism out in the grain belts. There was nothing in the shops, only busts of Stalin and what Kinkead told Ian were perpetual signs: 'No Lamps', 'No Bulbs', 'No Shoes', 'No Dresses', 'No Cigarettes', 'No Vodka'.

The National was situated near the Trades Union Hall, which the Soviet government had chosen as the venue for the trial. Several seasoned hands were among those journalists downing sixteen-rouble Martinis at the hotel's American bar. In addition to Cummings, political editor of the *News*

Chronicle, there was Walter Duranty, the one-legged Pulitzer winner from the *New York Times* who had denied the famine; A. T. Cholerton of the *Daily Telegraph*; Linton Wells of the International News Service; and Kinkead's secretary-interpreter, Zachariah Mikhailov, 'a dapper little man of fifty odd' with a cane and a grey hat, who had a temporary job with Reuters' rival agency, Central News of London.

Ian was the baby of the pack, the least experienced, yet here he was covering a trial that Cummings told him might prove to be 'the most spectacular event of its kind in recent years – if not since the trial of Dreyfus'.

The Times did not have a man in Moscow, nor the *Manchester Guardian* (Malcolm Muggeridge had left a few days before, 'in a frenzy of frustration'). This meant that a large part of the world was relying on its Russian news from one young man of twenty-four.

The pressure on Ian to come first with the story was exhilarating. He was back on the athletics track. Twelve years later, when Ian became responsible for news from Russia for the *Sunday Times*, he privileged 'the man from headquarters' over the local bureau chief. 'The clear eye and perspective of the special correspondent from London can translate the foreign scene in sharper, simpler colours than the man-on-the-spot who by long residence and experience has become part of that scene.'

The 'so-called "trial"', as *The Times*, relying on Ian's cables, put it, opened at noon on Wednesday 12 April in a building with Greek-style columns that had once been a gentleman's club like White's. Ian had done a recce on Rickatson-Hatt's advice. He set the scene in a paragraph cabled the night before that *The Times* reprinted. 'As the famous clock in the Kremlin Tower strikes twelve, the six Metropolitan-Vickers English employees will enter a room which has been daubed with blue in the Trades Union Hall and thronged with silent multitudes in order to hear an impassive Russian voice read for 4 or 5 hours the massive indictment which may mean death or exile.'

Militia patrolled the streets outside to prevent crowds. Two soldiers with bayonets inspected Ian's press pass. A short flight of red-carpeted steps led him into a high-ceilinged chamber 'hung with crystal chandeliers, expensive damask and all the trappings of Czarist days'. The massive electric chandeliers lit up the platform with the prosecutor's small scarlet-draped table and the boxed-in, low wooden dock with chairs for the seventeen prisoners. The place had a queer, fusty, charnel smell, thought Arthur Cummings, squeezed in beside Ian on the press bench. Next to Ian sat his translator. Ian was fortunate to rely on Aleksei Brobinsky, son of a former count, with a big nose and curly hair, who had learned his English from an Irish governess. Cummings, by contrast, had 'a most perfidious policewoman as interpreter who whispered in his ear what she thought best.'

Bullard wrote in his diary: 'England is humming with sympathy for the imprisoned engineers.' In London, two hours behind Moscow, the morning had begun with the BBC offering prayers for the six British prisoners. Ian watched five of them enter in single file – the technicians who had been released on bail. Minutes later, the sixth and last, a club-footed engineer called William MacDonald, limped to his seat in the front row. His fingers twitched over the dark goatee beard he had grown in the Lubyanka, where he had been in solitary confinement for four weeks. MacDonald's deposition formed the bulk of the Soviet Government's case against the British company.

MacDonald was joined in the dock by eleven of the Russians accused, including Anna Kutuzova, Thornton's secretary and his whispered mistress.

Peter Fleming, passing through Moscow two years earlier, had reported to his brother on the 'startling and universal ugliness of the women'. Yet the abiding memory of Hilary Bray, who had grown up in Russia, 'was of girls with bright smiling eyes looking at him out of enormous furs'. According to Alaric Jacob, Ian picked up a Jewish woman from Odessa, 'and then discovered that she was supposed to be keeping tabs on him'. Rickatson-Hatt formed the idea that 'he got preferential treatment by flirting with the secretary of the chief interpreter.' If so, the evidence has not survived. The only Russian woman Ian wrote about was Anna Kutuzova. She sat directly opposite him for six days, attractive, lively, strong-minded. In her impossible predicament can be glimpsed the first outline of Tatiana in *From Russia, with Love*.

She took her place between MacDonald and Thornton and gazed around at the columned walls, the elaborate cornices, with what Cummings described as a look of birdlike intelligence. 'She wore a dainty black costume with a broad and spotless white collar, and elegant shoes and stockings and her glossy hair was beautifully waved.' Kutuzova was the prosecution's star witness.

Andrei Vyshinsky, the thickset state prosecutor, emerged briskly through a low curtained doorway. Pince-nez, blond moustache, tight-lipped, fifty years old, wearing a blue suit and tie. In 1908, he shared a cell with Stalin, and in 1917 he ordered the arrest of Lenin. His catchphrase: 'Give me the man and I will find the crime.' After the Second World War, Vyshinsky would gain fame as a prosecutor in the Nuremberg Trials and then as Russia's Foreign Minister. In April 1933, his name was synonymous with Stalin's show trials.

A clerk in a droning voice read out into a microphone the seventy-seven pages of charges.

Ian reported two bombshells on the opening day. The first occurred at 3 p.m. when MacDonald was asked if he pleaded guilty. A sensation was caused by his haggard reply. 'Yes, I do.'

The audience gasped.

'To all the charges?'

These included disabling motors by chucking bolts and stones into them, and paying Russian employees to gather military information for British Intelligence.

MacDonald muttered, 'Yes.'

Vyshinsky rubbed his hands.

The court was adjourned. Ian dashed out to write his report in the press room on the floor below. It needed to be submitted to one of the three Soviet censors in a room upstairs and signed and red-stamped before Ian could take it to the central telegraph office two blocks away. He picked up on the general feeling that MacDonald's confession had been 'extracted by OGPU methods', and was 'not entirely unexpected: he had been in prison longer than the others'.

Even so, Bullard wrote in his diary, 'MacD's "confession" was a terrible blow, not merely to the British government but to all of us who believe that British engineers of that type would not commit sabotage . . . it was saddening to think that any pressure could make a man perjure himself so grossly.' The case was 'pure fake'.

'I wish to repudiate this document entirely.' The second bombshell occurred in the evening session when Leslie Thornton retracted his confession. In a clear voice, he added, 'I always built and never destroyed.' When the judge asked him why then he had signed the deposition, he fumbled angrily with his copy of the indictment: 'Because I was nervous. I lost my courage.'

'When did your courage return?'

Thornton replied firmly. On 4 April at 6 p.m., the hour he was released from prison. Duranty was a veteran reporter of these trials. 'This created the greatest sensation the writer has ever seen in a Soviet courtroom.'

The second day exceeded the first for unexpected drama. The court opened at 10 a.m. when Ian witnessed a further 'astonishing development'. Having pleaded guilty the afternoon before, William MacDonald rose stiffly to his feet and said in a loud voice that he was changing his plea. 'I am not really guilty of these crimes. I declare this emphatically.'

Ian wrote: 'Standing upright despite a lame left leg, MacDonald denounced in cold and calculated tones the statements contained both in the indictment and the written statement.' His depositions against himself, against Thornton, 'were a tissue of lies, signed "under the pressure of circumstances" on the premises of the OGPU'. This 'sudden turning of the tables' produced 'the profoundest sensation . . . in the midst of which the microphones "broke down"'.

The court was adjourned and MacDonald escorted away by uniformed OGPU guards. When he reappeared for the evening session, pinched and hollow-eyed, Ian was shocked by his 'remarkably changed demeanour'. Instead of defiantly maintaining his innocence, MacDonald spoke in a low, almost inaudible voice and admitted to further charges, answering 'yes' to every question put to him about wrecking activities.

What could have happened to him in the interval? Ian listened to the press room speculation. Torture was one theory, hypnotism another – the OGPU had possibly resorted to drugs prepared by Tibetans from herbs and administered in the prisoners' food to place them in the psychic power of their gaolers.

The view of the British embassy in Moscow, wrote Bullard, 'was that MacDonald made his "confession" to save the families of various Russian friends.' Ian reported that Anna Kutuzova had been broken like this, 'by the usual threats in regard to her relatives'. But the censors would never have let him cable the actual details: how she had been kidnapped for twenty-four hours and come home battered; how the OGPU had sat her down back-to-back with Thornton; how the chief interrogator had then said to Thornton, 'If you deny what she asserts we will believe you, but citizeness Kutuzova will be shot for perjury.' Thornton had crumpled.

After that, the trial followed a predictable course. Thornton's statement that there was not a word of truth in his deposition was supported by his boss, Allan Monkhouse, who was then forced to listen to Anna Kutuzova repeating to Thornton, her lover, after an initial hesitation, 'mechanically, in an unnatural voice, as if by heart', how she remembered Thornton explaining to her that 'if a piece of metal were thrown into a turbine, a turbine would fly into bits through the ceiling.' In her weary sing-song tone, she made the claim, which sounded improbable even to the many Russians in the hall, that her lover had plotted in her presence. She said the Moscow embassy had provided 50,000 roubles to hire wreckers.

One after another, the Russian prisoners in the dock stood up to testify in the same nervous manner: yes, they had received bribes to throw iron into the machinery, also a fur coat, and in two instances, a bottle of eau de cologne and a pair of trousers.

To all this, the state prosecutor listened with grim detachment, playing noughts and crosses with a stubby pencil, and sipping from glasses of hot tea.

Vyshinsky's winding-up took place over two days, lasted six and a half hours, and resembled, in its exorbitant length, bombastic tone and trumpeting of his world-beating system, not merely the tirades of Sam Slater, Uncle Phil and Eve putting young master Ian in his place, but the speech of virtually every James Bond villain. Ian wrote in *You Only Live Twice*: 'It was pleasant, reassuring to the executioner, to deliver his apologia – purge the sin he was about to commit.'

He began speaking in a tone of unutterable disdain. He did not rave or shout. He spoke with precision, clarity, vigour, and complete control. The trial had been 'a five-day battle of two worlds'. British courts, said Vyshinsky, reading from bulky notes, were 'models of judicial falsehood and corruption'. There was one law for the rich, another for the poor. The USSR, on the other hand, was unique as an administrator of real justice. 'We have the only true justice in the world,' he announced, turning to the prisoners and singling out Thornton as 'a coward and a traitor' and 'the most despicable of all'. 'Perhaps you will be used as manure for our Socialist fields somewhere.'

Out in the streets, Moscow schoolchildren chanted hymns of victory over this sneered-at British capitalist. Thornton sat motionless, except for a finger tapping the dock, his face a dull red, eyes glazed, 'showing signs of the terrible strain'.

Vyshinsky then addressed Thornton's secretary Anna Kutuzova, his lover for the last four years, who had concluded her deposition in a blaze of anger – not towards Thornton, but towards Vyshinsky. 'There is one thing on which I do not congratulate myself, although the Public Prosecutor congratulates me on it – my confession.' Vyshinsky ignored the implication. He told her: 'You sold yourself for money.' Kutuzova had sacrificed her Soviet dignity by pawning her soul for French perfumes and face cream, for dances, evening parties, and joy-riding between Moscow and the Metropolitan-Vickers compound in English motor cars. She was, Vyshinsky said with some malice, 'the most detestable among the hated types of our enemies'.

The state prosecutor stared hard over his pince-nez at the prisoners. In his voice and contemptuous expression were the features of Bond's past and future tormentors. 'Listen, saboteurs,' he said. 'You have seen your attempts are futile. You are the last abject group of the old, hostile technical intelligentsia.' The men and woman in the dock represented the routed and shattered class enemy. Their purpose had been the destruction of electrification in the USSR. But all in vain! They could not restrain 'the tempestuous growth of Soviet construction'.

The judges withdrew at 3.30 p.m. to consider their verdict. Ian paced, ready to rush in when the electric bell rang. The embassy was in direct communication with the Foreign Office, where the Foreign Secretary and 'a number of high officials' stayed throughout the night to receive Ian's cable. *The Times* reported how 'the evening papers which ordinarily close down at 6 p.m. are remaining open awaiting the Reuters flash of the verdict and Fleet Street is lined with vans waiting to dash special editions all over London'. Ian would have to wait another twenty years before his written words were anticipated like this again.

Five hours later, no decision. Ian went to the buffet and consumed a caviar sandwich he later blamed for infecting him with an intestinal tape-worm. He played cards in the press room with the American journalists, and the dice game 'craps'. Even as Ian threw the dice, he concealed from his col-leagues the extent of his ambition to scoop them. Kinkead wrote: 'Fleming had ripped the cords loose on other phones so that our opposition couldn't phone from the Hall.'

That was not all. In Cummings's account, Ian 'hatched a subtle conspir-acy for the discomfiture of a dangerous rival'. The rival in question was the dapper Zachariah Mikhailov, who 'possessed a news sense, knew all the ropes, and could wangle just about everything within reason'.

Mindful of Rickatson-Hatt's order to 'get in first', Ian had arranged for his translator's young brother-in-law to drop news of the verdict 'in an envelope from a window in the Press Room into the grasp of a colleague standing in the street below with one finger on the self-starter of a high-powered motor-car'.

The bell rang in the early hours of Wednesday morning. The judges reas-sembled. Shortly after 5 a.m., the whole court rose. There was a deathlike silence, Ian wrote. 'The prisoners stood with bated breath.' The judgment was then recited in a high rasping voice.

Unfortunately, Cummings reported, when Ian's fourteen-year-old mes-senger sped madly from the courtroom and across to the press room, 'he found the window screwed tightly down.' Ian was trounced by Mikhailov, who happened to be on the telephone to his news desk in London. 'The Cen-tral News editor hadn't heard from him in some time and was merely phoning to find if he were still on the job.'

The sentences were milder than Ian had predicted. Thornton, eight years in prison; MacDonald two; Kutuzova eighteen months; immediate expul-sion for Monkhouse.

Still, this was electrifying news, with repercussions reaching the highest level. In Whitehall, the Foreign Secretary received Ian's cable and flashed the contents by wireless to Ramsay MacDonald who was on board ship on his way to America to meet President Roosevelt. Within an hour of the verdict, it was announced that the Privy Council was to convene on Wednesday morning at Windsor Castle. The fifteen-minute meeting, in the presence of the King, authorised a ban on the import of Russian goods.

At the end of June, Moscow backed down, the prisoners were released and expelled by train to Berlin, and in July, the embargoes removed. Meanwhile, Ian had played a part in opening sane eyes to Stalin's regime. Bullard wrote: 'One good thing has come out of this dreadful trial: at last some of the horrors of life in Russia are set forth officially by the British Government.' Rickatson-Hatt's verdict: 'Moscow was a considerable coup for Reuters, and for Ian too for that matter.' He reported to Jones: 'he is now just beginning to be *really useful*.'

Not that this had prevented the chief editor from sending Ian one of his 'harsh service messages'. It interrupted Ian's celebrations with Kinkead in his hotel room at the National. CENTRAL NEWS BEAT YOU WITH VERDICT BY TWENTY MINUTES STOP REQUEST EXPLANATION IMMEDIATELY.

Ian left it to his new friends in the Moscow press room to do the explaining, in a cablegram that Linton Wells sent to Sir Roderick Jones on 24 April. EYE SHOULD LIKE YOU TO KNOW THAT WE FELLOW JOURNALISTS OF IAN FLEMING WHOM NONE OF US HAD EVER MET BEFORE HIS APPEARANCE HERE COVER METVICKERS TRIAL NOT ONLY CONSIDER HIM PUKHA CHAP PERSONALLY BUT HAVE AN EXTREMELY HIGH OPINION OF HIS JOURNALISTIC ABILITY STOP HE HAS GIVEN ALL OF US A RUN FOR OUR MONEY.

Jones's proud reply: 'We here at Reuters are sensible of Mr Fleming's admirable qualities.'

Ian came out of Russia with a crucifix to hang above his bed next to Churchill's obituary of Mokie, and a short letter from Stalin, badly typed and signed in red ink, refusing Ian's request for an interview.*

The impact of Ian's first visit to Russia was long-lasting. State terror. An attractive, independent-willed woman trapped between rival powers. Wild charges of espionage. The experience of covering the Metropolitan-Vickers trial blooded him. Bryce said, 'he liked the idea of spies, and this was like being one. The next best thing.'

Back in London, Ian was apparently debriefed by Sir Robert Vansittart, Val's Pop contemporary, who arranged for him to report his impressions of

---

* Ian gave a copy of Stalin's letter to his elder brother when Peter travelled back to Moscow in June. On several occasions, Peter tried to use the document 'as a super-visa to bluff his way out of an awkward situation, but never with success'.

Russia 'to a number of anonymous gentlemen in a room at the Foreign Office'. According to Alaric Jacob, 'Such good judges as Harold Nicolson and Robert Vansittart predicted great things for Ian Fleming. With his strong facial resemblance to Vansittart, Ian was then an *ambassadeur manqué . .* ' The connections established marked Ian's first adult brush with the Intelligence Service. It is not insignificant that this is how nineteen-year-old Bond starts out: 'with the help of an old Vickers colleague of his father, he entered a branch of what would subsequently be called the Ministry of Defence.'

XIII
BERLIN

'It's a beastly idea giving up all the fun of life for money.'
IAN FLEMING to Bernard Rickatson-Hatt

They still remembered Ian in Moscow, Peter wrote to Eve that summer on his return to Russia. 'Everyone adored Ian, and all the journalists wish he would come back.' Yet Ian continued to work at Reuters for only a few more months. This time, his grandfather really was behind his leaving, if not for reasons Ian might have predicted.

On 31 July 1933, aged eighty-eight, Robert Fleming died at Black Mount, leaving an estate of £2 million (approximately £165 million today). Peter learnt of his death in China. 'It means I suppose that I am now head of the family, technically speaking, and I shall be expected to become more solid and less fitful. It is funny how anxious I am that he has not left me anything to speak of.'

Something of Peter's anxiety took hold of Ian, who attended Robert's memorial service at St Michael's, Cornhill, on 3 August. Encouraged by Eve, and, like her, failing to recognise that his share in the family bank had died with his father, Ian had anticipated receiving a slice of what had grown since 1917 into a trillion-pound business. Yet when Robert's will was read, Eve's four 'fine boys' had been left not a penny. The entire fortune was to go to his widow Kate and then in trust to Robert's three remaining children, Philip, Kathleen and Dorothy. Still on his travels around the world, Peter's initial disappointment gave way to relief: the money would have made him 'even more unreal'. He cabled Eve, this time from Quebec. QUITE HONESTLY REGARD WILL AS BEST FAMILY JOKE SINCE LOVELETTERS OF A VIOLINIST* DON'T YOU WORRY IM ONLY TOO DELIGHTED.

---

* *Love Letters of a Violinist and Other Poems*, by Eric Mackay (1893). It may just have been that they all laughed at how bad it was.

151

But Eve took it to heart. She blamed the omission on Robert's senility and hated Kate for it. Like a figure in a Sargent painting, hand on forehead, she composed a long and emotional letter to her sons. She had done all she could for them. It was time they made their way in the world, as she now had to make hers. There had been no shortage of marriage offers. She was thinking of accepting one. (No names, but Joan Regent said that Eve 'liked older men', and that the politician Wilfrid Ashley, who was raised to the peerage as Lord Mount Temple in 1932, was often to be seen at Turner's House.) Eve went on: 'I am very ambitious for you because you are Mokie's sons, and that you should ever allow yourself to slide into mediocrity would distress me terribly.'

His mother's histrionic behaviour alarmed Ian. 'You are still passing sleepless nights because of this will,' he wrote. 'You will only get overtired and then one day at Joyce Grove you will forget yourself and throw a bun at Dorothy or call them all cads or something and we shall never be on speaking terms again.'

A portion of Eve's concern was for Ian. Never far from her thoughts was the prodigal example of her bankrupt brothers. The publication that August of Peter's travel book *Brazilian Adventure* brought him overnight fame 'not seen since Byron'; for the time being, Eve could stop fretting about Peter's career, although his romantic life continued to be as much a source of annoyance to her as Ian's. Richard and Michael, who had not featured much in their elder brother's life, were financially insulated in secure, well-remunerated jobs at Robert Fleming & Company. By contrast, Ian worked in a precarious, poorly paid profession on a salary of £300 (approximately £25,000 today). He had complained to Alaric Jacob that 'he wasn't getting enough money'.

Ian does not seem to have been personally avaricious. There is a telling line in *On Her Majesty's Secret Service* when Bond refuses a £1 million dowry from Marc-Ange Draco, saying, 'That is the only kind of money to have – not quite enough.' Even so, his career choices were dictated by financial concerns. 'The financial prospects in Reuters were very meagre,' he wrote.

Meanwhile, Reuters had ambitious plans for Ian. Before his Moscow assignment, the agency had sent him to Germany to report on Hitler's final election speech from Königsberg on 4 March. Ian seized the opportunity to stay again in Vich with Monique. This was to be their last time together.

Then in mid October, Rickatson-Hatt despatched Ian a second time to

Nazi Germany 'to reinforce the Berlin bureau', on what turned out to be a five-week assignment to cover the November parliamentary elections, the first since Hitler seized power.

On the eve of Ian's departure, Sir Roderick Jones summoned him to see if he would like to be posted on promotion afterwards to Shanghai, as assistant to Christopher Chancellor. When Chancellor had been asked if he would go to China, his answer was simple. 'Two words. Yes. When?' Ian's response was more hesitant, according to Jones's memo to Rickatson-Hatt: 'No salary mentioned – Emphasised he have to work *very* hard, & for year be learning. Begin small – advised him to take the long view. Said his marriage off. Asked for week to consider. I agreed.'

Ian claimed that he was poised to say Yes. But then, he explained to Jones, 'just a week after our conversation, when I was about to write and accept the post you offered me, a businessman with whom I am only slightly acquainted asked me to see him and offered me what at first sight appeared to be quite an exceptional post in his firm of merchant bankers. The gist of the offer was that he himself intended shortly to retire and that he offered me his partnership in the firm after two years of learning the business.'

The businessman was Gilbert Russell, a banker friend of the Churchills – Winston was a client and his brother Jack worked for him – although it was his forty-two-year-old wife Maud whom Ian knew better, the daughter of a wealthy German-Jewish stockbroker and racehorse owner who had helped Gilbert set up the merchant bank Cull & Company. Ian had met the Russells with Granny Kate at a charity matinee in December 1931. Years later, Maud wrote in her diary: 'I knew him first when he was 23, a clerk at Reuters and starting out – or dashing out – into the world, a life.' Ian had begun to see Maud regularly since then. Her diaries give little more information, but the two of them dined at L'Escargot, and on one occasion when Maud was in Paris Ian joined her for a couple of days. From this time on, she acted as a discreet guiding presence in his life. It was on her recommendation that Gilbert Russell, a warm-hearted, witty asthmatic sixteen years older than her, made his offer.

Eve urged Ian to seize it with both hands. She considered Reuters 'stupid and undignified', even though she had engineered his job there. The prospect of a lucrative partnership in Cull & Company was consistent with her original plans; it would provide Ian with capital and serve as a stepping stone to Robert Fleming & Company. After taking Ian out to lunch, Rickatson-Hatt left Sir Roderick Jones in no doubt that Eve had convinced Ian he would be letting his family down by not ultimately going into the family business. 'Fleming confirmed that his Mother was principally responsible for persuading him to accept the offer in the City.'

From Berlin, where he arrived on 16 October, Ian had written to let both men know of his decision. His letter to Rickatson-Hatt reflects how conflicted Ian was, and how much a father figure the chief editor had become. 'The idea of having to go and sit on an office stool for the rest of my life is all the worse compared with the marvellous time you have given me with Reuters. But however much I hate the idea, I really can't afford to miss this amazing offer which will mean the hell of a lot of money very soon.' After making his fortune, he planned to come back to Reuters, possibly in a managerial role.

Days later, Ian wrote to Eve, reiterating his wish to 'make enough money by the age of 30 to take some shares in Reuters and help to direct it from the other end'.

In the meantime, he intended to go out on a high note. In Moscow, he had failed to secure an interview with Stalin, but he was on the verge of netting a fish even bigger in Germany. 'I have got official permission to go with Hitler in his plane to Munich next week and hear him make his election speeches there, which will be enormous fun and a fit end to the sowing of my journalistic oats.'

Sir Roderick had told Ian to pay his respects to the new British ambassador. Ian's calling on Sir Eric Phipps in the residence where Amaryllis was conceived led to Ian staying with Gerry Young, Third Secretary at the embassy, 'who is very nice and seems not to mind having me indefinitely'.

Because of Ian's coverage of the Moscow trial, Young knew that he would be interested in meeting a Canadian couple who in April had gone off their own bat to the station to meet four of the Metropolitan-Vickers engineers expelled from Russia, and then driven them around Berlin. Harold Hemming was a financier for J. G. White & Municipal and General Securities; his pregnant wife, Alice, a journalist from Vancouver.

Jointly with Young, the Hemmings acted as Ian's hosts in Berlin. They took him to parties and introduced him to international journalists. No longer engaged to Monique, Ian was witnessed sowing more than his journalistic oats. He appeared at the Hemmings' apartment in Tiergartenstrasse in the company of an American girl, Katherine Janeway, who was 'very smitten with Fleming,' Alice wrote in her diary, although 'we find her a bit too prim'.

'This is rather a nuisance.' Rickatson-Hatt's first instinct on receiving Ian's letter was to recall him, but Victor Bodker, the stressed Reuters Berlin correspondent, begged for Ian to stay on a little longer, arguing that there was 'plenty of work for Fleming to do'. Rickatson-Hatt gave his consent. 'He has done first rate work, and one never knows when a situation will blow up when, of course, he would be invaluable.' He decided to keep Ian in Berlin 'until after the elections (Nov 12) which will be a big story.'

Ian was in Berlin at a turning point in Germany's history. Back in April, he had witnessed the cynical operation of Soviet Communism. He now saw how a totalitarian regime behaved in the days before it consolidated power.

A topic at Ian's dinner with the Hemmings on 22 October was Hitler's decision to remove Germany from Ian's former employers, the League of Nations. Harold had fought in the First World War. Hitler's withdrawal from Geneva made him fear that another war was likely. He had watched the events of that year with revulsion: the burning of the Reichstag, and of books; the pink boycott signs stuck on Jewish shop windows. He told Ian how one night in August, a group of Nazis had raided their apartment, demanding to see a postcard that the Hemmings' Jewish nanny had received from the Soviet Union. ('She popped upstairs and tossed the offending card out of the window.') With opposition parties banned, the Nazi Party's victory in the forthcoming election was a foregone conclusion. The Hemmings' landlady, Frau Zwilgmeyer, truly believed that Hitler was 'sent by God'.

On 12 November, Frau Zwilgmeyer joined the long queue outside the polling booth, afterwards flaunting a round metal badge in her collar bearing the word 'Ja'. When the results were declared, Hitler had won 92.3% of the vote. 'Even the unfortunate inmates of the concentration camps', wrote the *Times* correspondent, 'thought it prudent to vote almost solid for their oppressor.'

Fleming left no evidence that he flew with Hitler to Munich and none of the cables he filed from Berlin appear to have survived. His swansong seems to have been a talk that he gave on the BBC, now lost, in which, following Rickatson-Hatt's firm instructions, Ian was 'strictly objective and non-controversial' but 'made mention of the fact that he was Reuters' Chief Correspondent in Berlin so that we got a good advertisement out of it'.

On 13 November, the day on which Hitler claimed 'incomparable victory', Ian invited Gerry Young and the Hemmings to a party thrown by Victor Bodker, the Reuters bureau chief. They ate steak-and-kidney pie and danced. 'Fleming v. funny,' wrote Alice.

He was smiling, but he was sick inside. This was his final foreign assignment. He was leaving Reuters 'very reluctantly', Jones explained to Christopher Chancellor, and was abandoning a vocation 'in which he was destined, I feel, to make a brilliant success', to transfer himself 'to a career the fascination of which certainly has not yet cast its spell upon him'. Ian had been abject in his letter to Rickatson-Hatt. 'I was pretty well pushed into it from all sides. I was assured it was the right thing to do for the sake of the family.' In the same way, he had given up the woman he loved, again out of fealty to his family and Eve. 'However much he hated her,' said Mary Pakenham, 'he could never really escape from her or write her off.' At any rate, something manic and unresolved in Ian found a target in his host on that so-called victory night in Berlin.

Ian's last act as a Reuters journalist was to bring home a candid assessment of Victor Bodker, who had pleaded for Fleming to stay on in Germany. Rickatson-Hatt relayed the information to Jones after lunching with Ian on 27 November. 'The fact is, Fleming said, "people don't respect him". Fleming's words were: "He has absolutely gone to seed. He is the kind of man who will end up as a beachcomber on an island in the Pacific."' Spin forward thirty years, and visitors to Goldeneye were saying the same about Ian Fleming.

Fleming left Reuters on 18 December. Rickatson-Hatt wrote to Jones: 'He came to see me this morning to say goodbye. I think in his heart of hearts, he is rather sorry he is going.' Jones ringed the last sentence in red pencil and scribbled: 'I am sure he is, C.'

One indication of Ian's mixed thoughts is a note he wrote in 1959 for the character of James Bond. 'Everyone has the revolver of resignation in his pocket. This shoots twice. With one barrel, it makes a small hole in his boss. With the other, it makes a hole in himself. The size of the hole varies with the circumstances. But with each shot, there is an element of murder and an element of suicide. It is seldom courage which pulls the trigger. Resignation is more often from weakness than from strength.'

XIV
GLAMOUR BOY

'They had leisure to think of other things besides their work.
Indeed, they had so much leisure that it is a wonder they
thought of their work at all.'
P. G. WODEHOUSE, *Psmith in the City*

The standard portrait that emerges of Ian in the 1930s is of a young man marvellous to meet, who bowls you over and uses you for whatever he wants, and then is off to the next person, and neither thinks nor cares about anyone but himself.

At first glance, Ian did not appear to develop in the six years he spent in the City – seventeen months as a merchant banker with Cull & Company; four years as a stockbroker with Rowe & Pitman. His younger brother Richard, who in 1936 was made a director of Robert Fleming & Company, along with their youngest brother Michael, spoke for the majority. 'When Ian was in the City, he was the very worst stockbroker in the world. He never really believed in any of it.'

If anything, Ian seemed to regress. Encountering him in Brook Street wearing an Eton Ramblers club tie, Cyril Connolly was reminded of an elegant bored animal playing the part of a playboy businessman. 'In those days, he seemed like the hero of a Wodehouse novel.'

For the first time, Ian was no longer short of money – unlike Connolly. 'He seemed wealthy (more so than after the war). Went where he liked. His job in the City never interfered with his skiing.' He was not making the fortune of his grandfather, or Uncle Philip or his brothers, but he enjoyed a salary never less than £2,000 (approximately £170,000 today), and a good life, with a new car (a Lagonda, followed by a supercharged Graham-Paige convertible coupé), and a place of his own (a converted Baptist chapel near

Victoria station). 'A City man with time for interesting hobbies,' Ivar Bryce called him.

From 1933 to 1939 Ian lapsed back into the role he had assumed at Eton, in the shadow of his brilliant elder brother. Peter wrote of this period, 'I kept on popping off into the shark-infested jungle, coming back & writing books about it & popping off again.' In reaction to Peter's success, Ian put on hold his literary pretensions. He became, said Gerry Coke, 'a thorough material-ist and lived entirely in the present'.

In the company of Coke and a circle of primarily Old Etonian clubland chums, like a diluted Pop, plus a stream of compliant girlfriends, Ian lived the brittle, flippant life of a bachelor-about-town whose sole entanglement was with himself. 'London has got its claws into me,' he admitted to Ernan Forbes Dennis on the latter's visit to arrange, with Ian's help, a lecture tour for Alfred Adler.

Although never analysed by Adler, Ian was submitted to sustained examination by Lady Mary Pakenham. After spending three years shut-tling between fascination and revulsion, she concluded: 'He was merely an attractive black sheep, and no one could have guessed that he would become world famous.'

It is easy to construe Ian's behaviour as unfeelingness, his weekends in Dieppe and Sandwich as betraying a lack of ambition. But this is not the whole picture. Ian's Tennerhof contemporary Ralph Arnold observed that 'he was very complex. Took great trouble to hide his intentions.'

In his mid to late twenties, Ian planted miscellaneous seeds which would come to fruition in wartime conditions at a particular moment. To his knowledge of languages and journalism, he added banking and book-collecting, and struck up friendships with press lords like Rothermere, Kemsley and Beaverbrook, as well as cultivating contacts in London's financial and Intelligence communities. He would have to wait until May 1939 before his career and interests aligned. Until then, said Ann Fleming, who met him at this time as Lady O'Neill, Ian was known as 'Glamour Boy' and regarded both by men and women in that light. 'Everyone felt that he was just a rich, rather bored, rather aloof young man,' said Alaric Jacob.

*

On her honeymoon in Paris in 1881, Ian's grandmother Kate had called in to the Bourse. 'We saw hundreds of men violently gesticulating and shouting to each other. I could never imagine much business was done in that way, but my husband tells me there is even method in the confusion.'

Neither Ian nor Peter inherited their grandfather's business methods or ended up working in his bank. On Wall Street, Peter had sat in a room and stared glumly at the slide rule that Eve had given him. 'You can have no idea how boring the work is . . . Short of carving one's name on the desk, there is nothing to do to fill up the time. I have met no one connected with finance who seems to me worthy of liking or admiration!' Peter understood as much about the stock market as he did about the zodiac. When Wall Street crashed, a pale-faced man burst into his office and announced in tones of horror: 'Anaconda's right down the drain!' Peter had a picture of two sanitary inspectors angling for a boa constrictor with a lump of meat.

Like Peter, Ian was not naturally suited for the City, any more than was his future downstairs neighbour, T. S. Eliot, who worked eight years at Lloyd's Bank. Ian wrote: 'I could never work out what a sixty-fourth of a point was. We used to spend our whole time throwing telephones at each other. I'm afraid we ragged far too much.'

Cull & Company was based at 11 Throgmorton Avenue, near the offices of Robert Fleming & Company. The only financial insight Peter brought back from New York was that 'so much of the Fleming business depends on personal relationships'. Carefully dressed in his blue pin-striped suit and old school tie, and clutching his soft homburg hat, Ian strolled over to 8 Crosby Square to seek assistance and commissions from Richard, the least visible of his brothers, but always calm, discreet, understanding. ('He was the quiet one,' wrote his son James, 'the man behind the scenes, the man to whom everyone goes for advice'.) He picked up again with Gerry Coke at Industrial Steel. He lunched with Harold Hemming at the St James's Club.

Hemming had come from Berlin with Alice, having started a new job with the stockbrokers Nathan & Roselli. On his arrival in London, Ian took him to hear Peter's lecture on China. Hemming stayed at Joyce Grove, dined with Eve at Turner's House, and spent Christmas in Scotland, shooting badly with Ian on Christmas Eve. In London, according to Hemming's diaries, they played poker and bridge in the evenings ('Win as usual'), went to movies ('To foul French film "La Rue Sans Nom". Low and dirty'), and met up during the week to talk business.

On 4 February 1935, Hemming wrote: 'Work on Canadian bonds. Lunch with Ian Fleming.' One topic dominated their discussion: the ingenious swindle that had overshadowed Ian's first year in the City. The story never lost its power to fascinate. His fellow golfers at Royal St George recalled Ian returning to the subject towards the end of his life, sitting in his usual leather-backed wing chair.

The scandal that preoccupied Ian involved a naturalised Armenian client, Garabed Bishirgian, a short, thick-set Surrey pig farmer known as 'The Pepper King', who, after attempting to corner the markets in caviar, tin and shellac, had formed a pool of investors to buy up all the white pepper in the world, and used Ian's merchant bank to underwrite the purchase. In September 1934, Cull & Company had raised £425,000 (approximately £36 million today). Although it specified that the funds should not be used for speculation, Bishirgian had not honoured this, instead paying for 21,000 tons of pepper at a price which promptly plummeted by forty-five per cent. Three days after Ian's lunch with Hemming, Bishirgian's company went into liquidation, with Bishirgian himself facing two years in prison under the Larceny Act. Soon after, Cull & Company, as the issuing house, became a limited liability.

Ian had expected to take over Gilbert Russell's partnership when Gilbert retired on 1 June: this was what had lured him away from Reuters. But in the wake of the Bishirgian scandal, Gilbert was asked to stay on. Bored, with his prospects thwarted and the reputation of Cull & Company suddenly 'ill-regarded in the City', Ian began looking for a partnership elsewhere.

On 17 June 1935, the stockbrokers Rowe & Pitman of 43 Bishopsgate announced: 'We have admitted Mr Ian Lancaster Fleming a partner in our firm.'

Ian's first sustained piece of prose non-fiction, now lost, was a corporate history of Rowe & Pitman. The senior partner, Lancy Hugh Smith, had asked Ian to write this to make better use of his talents, which were not for stockbroking.

Rowe & Pitman was a leading City broker. Its clients ranged from Agatha

Christie to Ford Motors, and included the dukes of Marlborough and West-minster, Harry Oppenheimer of the Anglo American Corporation, Hambro's bank (Olaf Hambro was a cousin of Lancy's), and Lord Beaverbrook, who counted on Lancy's firm to build his stakes in newspaper companies.

Relevant to Ian's wartime employment, Rowe & Pitman had long-standing connections with Naval Intelligence. The firm's unpublished official history, replacing Ian's rejected draft, speculated that Lancy might have been 'a long-term talent spotter for British Intelligence'. This revelation would have come as no shock. Lancy had worked for the Admiralty during the First World War. His brother Aubrey was the wartime deputy Director of Naval Intelligence. Not only that, but Claude Serocold, a cousin of Lancy's earlier employed at Rowe & Pitman, and now 'the doyen of stockbrokers', had served as the DNI's personal assistant.

Lancy was a wealthy old bachelor and a colossal snob who prized his royal contacts. Another partner was Jock Bowes-Lyon, whose sister was mar-ried to the future King George VI. Ian's unassailable qualification was his grandfather. Lancy boasted: 'I always felt that if they keep their heads up and their overheads down, a firm containing three members of great City families must succeed.' He meant Smith, Baring and Fleming. He had taken Ian on 'with an eye to his connections with Robert Fleming,' said Hilary Bray.

Ian's successful pulling of Fleming strings threaded him into an incred-ibly tight-knit group of people. He adored his new employers as much as he had hated Cull & Company, according to Percy Muir. 'He loved everyone there and was loved in return.' Hilary Bray took over Ian's partnership ten years later. He recalled how good Ian was to have around. 'Everyone appre-ciated him because he was an amusing companion, a breath of fresh air in the squirrel's cage of the city, the man who had actually been to Moscow.' Conrad O'Brien-ffrench was not surprised. 'This after all was the milieu he felt at ease in. Latent in his character, deep in his subconscious, was the billycock hat and an umbrella of city life.'

If Ian was popular at Rowe & Pitman, this was because he could get on so well with Hugo Pitman, a senior partner to whom he was attached as an apprentice. According to Ian's first authorised biographer, John Pearson, they soon struck up 'a father/long lost son sort of relationship'. Pitman was a fellow Scot who had won a silver medal for rowing at the 1912 Stockholm

Olympics. Tall, dark brown hair, moustache, conservative dress, the forty-three-year-old Pitman was 'someone you took notice of,' says his daughter Jemima, except that he had a considerable handicap: he was deaf in one ear following an injury in the war. Pitman struggled with groups, preferring the one-on-one conversations that Ian was adept at conducting. 'He was tremendously fond of Ian,' says Jemima. 'I can see Ian might have regarded him as a father figure.'

Pitman, who had no sons, became Ian's new mentor.

A nephew of the firm's founder, and married to the niece of the American painter John Singer Sargent, Pitman was a collector of modern art and financial adviser to Augustus John. It was Pitman who broke the news to Ian of his sister's paternity, after first informing Amaryllis. Jemima says: 'She came to my father and asked him about the truth of the matter, and he felt he couldn't lie.' Ian immediately afterwards greeted Mary Pakenham at lunch: 'What do you think? Hugo Pitman's just told me that Amaryllis is really Mama's daughter!!!!' It had never occurred to him before. 'He was shocked and at the same time delighted to catch his mother tripping.'

Pitman's parents lived on the tee-off at Muirfield. Ian played golf there with Hugo, and bridge. They travelled together abroad. In October 1937, Pitman took Ian with him on the *Europa* to New York – when Ian seized the chance to visit Alaric Jacob, now posted to Washington. On this, his first visit to America, Ian also met J. P. Morgan Jr, who had known Robert Fleming. Yet not even the force of that connection snapped Ian into line, says Jemima. 'At one dinner with Morgan and other distinguished businessmen, my father said, "You've got to behave." In the middle of dinner, Ian announced he had the most terrible headache and had to go – and left. When my father returned to the hotel later, he found Ian together with some lady. He was quite difficult to handle. The same thing happened on a business trip to France.'

Ian's attitude to stockbroking was that of Viscount Castlerosse, employed by Rowe & Pitman at Beaverbrook's request, who, Lancy complained, 'would not cross the road to do a day's work'. Ian's routine was to talk to his clients knowledgeably about the strategy of investments, then take them out to a good lunch at the Savoy or the St James's Club (from which he resigned following an argument with the hairdresser) or White's (which he joined in

163

1936 but resigned from 'because he couldn't stand the shits at the bar'), and afterwards turn them over to the client investment section. He was known in the office to have only one regular client, according to Andrew Lycett in his history of Rowe & Pitman.

A rare surviving example of Ian's business method involved British Intelligence and Reuters, and provides the earliest evidence of his fascination with ciphers. In November 1936, Ian wrote in strict confidence to his former employer Sir Roderick Jones, offering him first refusal on a matchless opportunity to invest in a mysterious new transatlantic cable company 'in process of formation which will have a very marked effect on cable rates, in the first instance between London and New York, and subsequently throughout the world'.

On 14 December, Ian and a 'Foreign Office gentleman', who went under Ian's favoured name of 'Mr Secretan', met with the shrewd head of Reuters' commercial services to discuss 'Mr Ian Fleming's Coding Agency'. The company that Ian represented proposed to cut existing cable rates of 5.5 pence per word to 3.6 pence, 'by condensing the telegrams by means of Mr Secretan's code'.

The Commercial Editor reported back to Jones two reservations.

First: the elusive coder's identity. 'I found it impossible to extract any information on the matter of Mr Secretan's connexion with the Foreign Office.' Inquiries revealed no one of that name worked there.

Second: the service that Fleming and Secretan proposed contravened Clause 51 para 3 of the Telegraph Regulations Act, which, if enforced, would put the proposed company out of business. 'They studied this clause with some astonishment and said that they were afraid I had dealt them a real body blow. They couldn't understand how this point had never cropped up during the three years in which the company had been in preparation.'

Jones scrawled his verdict in red capital letters. 'A KNOCK-OUT, I'D THINK.'

After Lancy rejected Ian's history of the firm, allegedly for going on too much about the Pitmans, Ian was asked to write the monthly investment circular. He showed this to Mary Pakenham. 'It was fearfully pretentious, foamy and frothy and somewhat a departure from the norm. He brought in the word "masochistic" and one of the partners objected to it as indecent, mistaking it for "masturbation".'

Securities for Investment, the company newsletter in which Ian liked to recommend 'risky stocks in out of the way places', accounted for most of his literary output in the 1930s. Peter's ascendance as a travel writer discouraged Ian from pursuing his aspiration, admitted earlier to Selby Armitage and Ernan, to attempt a serious novel. 'My brother Peter's the writer in the family and he's really terribly good at it.'

As at Eton, Peter's literary success thrust Ian back into the shade; only now, Peter's shadow stretched in pretty well every direction.

For the next twenty years, Ian had to steel himself to be called 'the brother of writer Peter Fleming', as a decade before Evelyn Waugh had been 'the brother of Alec Waugh', after Alec's controversial, best-selling novel *The Loom of Youth* (1917), written when he was still a schoolboy, had 'sent shudders of horror down many respectable British spines'.

Like Ian, Evelyn had grown up in the slipstream of a successful elder brother. Then in the 1950s both Alec and Peter were to experience a dramatic reversal.

By the time of Ian's death in August 1964, it would be Evelyn Waugh and not Alec who had grounds to be considered England's most eminent living writer – and Ian Fleming and not Peter, England's most popular. In a symmetrical twist that would have escaped neither author, a rapidly deteriorating Evelyn Waugh was to sit for the last months of his life enthroned in Ian Fleming's invalid chair, which Ian, or more likely Ann, had left him.

When Evelyn died nineteen months after Ian, Graham Greene said, 'I felt my commanding officer was dead.' Ian was famous for lacking 'senior officer veneration', but to the end he had felt a similar connection. If there was a writer Ian wished he could have been, Evelyn Waugh was high up in the pantheon. Ian published Waugh's *Holy Places* as the first title of the Queen Anne Press, and he was always talking at the *Sunday Times* conference about 'throwing a fly' over Waugh to see if he might write for the paper.

Their kinship was not merely literary. Sibling rivalry had been a vital motivating factor in each of their make-ups. 'Envy has its ugly sides,' Ian wrote, 'but if I, as a second son amongst four, had not been envious of my elder brother and his achievements I would not have wished all my life to try and emulate him.' As with the brothers Waugh, the story of Peter and Ian Fleming is ultimately the fable of how the rebellious and overlooked second son rose, after various vicissitudes, to overtake and even obliterate the first-born pedestal child.

'The thing which upset Ian,' said Robert Harling, 'was the fantastic success of his brother's life. There Peter was, an international figure in the literary world, and his adventures, great treks across Asia and so forth, and Ian was envious. I think his brother was always in the background.'

The prolific author and BBC broadcaster S. P. B. Mais, who had taught Alec Waugh at Sherborne and was responsible for getting *The Loom of Youth* published, was not alone in perceiving Ian's elder brother in the guise of a Bond prototype. 'Peter Fleming goes to the end of the earth, undergoing the most hideous privations, and running his neck into nooses from which there would appear to be no escape, and seems to find it all rather boring.'

In 1936, 'the offhandedly amazing Peter Fleming', as *The Times* called him, followed up *Brazilian Adventure* and *One's Company* with *News from Tartary*. By now, Peter's many admirers included Vita Sackville-West, who baptised him 'a modern Elizabethan', Harold Nicolson, J. B. Priestley, and Ian's favourite teacher at Eton, George Lyttelton. 'Surely all who care about the art of writing must recognise how good he is.' In 1939, as Peter approached the height of his fame, it amused him to make a joke of it. Possibly hatched at a dinner of the Literary Society, of which Peter and Rupert Hart-Davis were keen members, a story circulated that an obscure French scholar, Comte Henri de Turotz, had won a prize for his book, *Peter Fleming: sa place dans la littérature anglaise*.

Meanwhile, Peter's primary ambition, he told Hart-Davis, was to write 'a Buchanish novel'.

Ian declined to compete with his brother on the page. His literary interest found an outlet not in writing books but buying them. What turned out to be his sharpest investment of his time as a stockbroker was the collection that he started in June 1935 with Percy Muir, and funded for the next three years – 'an investment out of which more amusement and kudos were obtainable than share certificates.'

XV
THE COLLECTOR

'He's got some sort of establishment in Ebury Street . . .
some sort of hideout of his. Keeps it very quiet.
Probably takes his women there.'

MOONRAKER

On the day after he was made a junior partner at Rowe & Pitman in the summer of 1935, Ian celebrated by giving Percy Muir £250 (approximately £21,000 today) to purchase the first thirty of what would amount to 'around two thousand volumes or items'.

Muir had moved from Dulau's to the bookseller Elkin Mathews. Ian made his proposal in the elegant double-fronted shop in Conduit Street. It threw a lifeline to Muir at a difficult time for the firm and provided both men with intellectual stimulation. The result, said Muir, was 'one of the proudest achievements of my life' and guaranteed his readiness always to forgive and defend Ian.

Ian told different versions of how he conceived the idea for his collection of 'the first book, broadsheet, pamphlet or paper on a particular subject'. In an unpublished interview, he located the Eureka moment to his reading of Hervey Allen's 1933 novel *Anthony Adverse* in Divonne-les-Bains near Vich when 'recovering from some disease or other', possibly in March 1933 during his last stay with Monique.

'It was just about that time when the first edition market crashed, and all my costly purchases became almost valueless. I was buying first editions of D. H. Lawrence and Aldous Huxley and A. E. Coppard and Powys and many of the leading writers of the time, and I suddenly realised I had been wasting my money and my energy in buying these things, and I thought what a good book this is . . .

'So I sat and thought and wondered what books really were important and would hold their value in the world forever, and I came to the conclusion that any book which signalised a right-angle in the thought on that particular subject, that book would undoubtedly have a permanent value in the history of the world.

'I then began to think through every human activity, from art to sport physics, and with the help of a great friend of mine who is still my bookseller, we got out a tremendous list of the great books of the world. We limited ourselves to the 19th century and after, let's say starting in 1800, and we set about collecting them.'

What Ian himself called books that had 'started something' and Percy Muir 'milestones of progress', built on Ernan's original theme – the struggles of mankind to improve itself. Muir explained the rules they settled on. The books had to be first editions in the language of their original publication, 'anything that had affected human outlook and habits, from the atomic theory to the zip fastener and from lawn tennis to Mendelian hypothesis'.

Most of Ian's books were bought for a few pounds or less, often from endangered bookdealers in Berlin and Munich, for whom 'first editions were largely out-of-date text-books to be thrown away'. Muir, who spoke excellent German, enjoyed the spadework; Ian 'was not prepared to do any research'. This suited them both, said Muir. 'He could be, as I often told him, the most exasperating, pig-headed creature in existence. He called me a short-sighted, small-minded puritan. Our long friendship was strong and deep enough to withstand the worst we could say of each other, and it would be hard to say better of it than that.'

The thirty-three items in Muir's first sales invoice for £62 4s 1d ranged from 4s 6d for *The Experimental Chemotherapy of Spirilloses* by Paul Erlich and S. Hata, to a first edition of T. S. Eliot's *The Waste Land* for £4 10s, and £8 10s for Marie Curie's *Theses*. By the end of 1935, the collection had grown to 230 titles. The most expensive item would cost £94: Karl Marx's *Manifest der Kommunistischen Partei*. Others titles were Adolf Hitler's *Mein Kampf*, Friedrich Nietzsche's *Also sprach Zarathustra*, Henry Allan's 1869 'Prize Essay on Kleptomania', Ely Cuthbertson's *Contract Bridge*, and the earliest treatises on cricket and golf.

'The books themselves sound a rum lot,' said John Hayward, who after the war edited the *Book Collector* under Ian's ownership, 'but reflect his particular ingenuity that made him such an excellent journalist. A sort of eye to the main chance, practicality, call it what you like. A canniness of where power, money, influence really lay.' The bibliophile Nicolas Barker, who succeeded Hayward as editor, says Ian and Percy played complementary parts. 'I think the choice of Ignaz Semmelweiss's *Die Aetiologie* 1861 as the key work on antisepsis is a good example of IF's and PHM's joint originality.'

Ian's youthful passion for book-collecting, which in 1936 led to him becoming a non-executive director of Elkin Matthews, was a proxy for what he truly wanted to do. Meanwhile, he spent around a quarter of his total investment encasing each of his books in buckram boxes lined with thin white strips of fleece 'so that no impious moth or deadly beetle will ever get at them'. The expensive black boxes, costing £2 10s each, bore the Fleming crest and motto *Let the Deed Shaw* in gilt, and had colour-coded spines – yellow for science, green for literature, brown for religion. It annoyed Percy Muir how frequently 'the cases cost more than the books'.

It made for an impressive display, though. Ann's nephew by marriage, the television presenter Bamber Gascoigne, recalled his boyhood wonderment when he saw Ian's fancy pillared bookcases. 'I couldn't believe there were bookshelves in which each book had its own separate box it lived in, and thinking this was the most glamorous library I'd ever seen.'

At the same time, the collection remained voraciously unread. Muir once invoiced him for seven books, only for Ian to write, 'Could you please let me know why these particular seven books are so desirable.' Muir's astringent reply: 'if you will open each book you will find a typed description inside.' Muir believed that Ian never looked at a book again, once it was put in a case. This was Mary Pakenham's impression, too. 'I never saw him reading a book in spite of being surrounded by them.'

The ingredients which make Bond enduring have their origins in Ian's bachelor days. The characteristics that Ian shares with Bond's enemies are less obvious. Not lost on Ian's friends was the fact that his villain's nerve centre in *Moonraker* – which concealed Hugo Drax's homing device to bring down an atomic rocket 'to destroy London' – was the site of Ian's pre-war Pimlico address.

In October 1936, Ian took over the lease of 22b Ebury Street from Harold Nicolson's former boss, Oswald Mosley, who had used the Baptist meeting hall for gatherings of the British Union of Fascists. Tucked away round the corner from Buckingham Palace and Victoria station, it was 'far enough away from Fitzrovia, close enough to Bohemia and within reasonable distance of the City'. A regimental coat of arms formed the knocker on the front door. A giggly Irish maid called May came down to let you in. The murky little entrance led into a large high-ceilinged room like the hall of Ian's prep school.

Lisl Jokl was an early visitor. She had escaped Austria with the assistance of Percy Muir and a gay dress designer, Harry Popper, whom she married, although they did not live together; with Harry's help, she became a knitwear designer for Aquascutum. Ian's ill-lit interior reminded her of ugly apartments in Berlin. 'The Ebury Street house was the first house of his own Ian had had, and typically he knew exactly how he wanted it. He built a gallery at one end to provide himself with a bedroom. He put the lavatory where the altar had been, and had it decorated in a style I called Berlin Jewish. He had the book collection all round the walls.'

The Berlin Jewish touch was provided by an interior designer, Rosie Reiss, another refugee helped by Muir, who painted the windowless walls grey and found the furniture. Light fell through a blue-tinted skylight onto upright leather armchairs, one upholstered 'in blue gent's suiting'; an oversized black couch without a back; and an open grate with a fire that blazed even in summer.

'Ebury Street was not a beautiful place at all,' said Gerry Coke, 'but it was formed around Ian's somewhat bizarre standards of comfort.' Sefton Delmer was amused by 'a great business of Ian looking for a cane seat for his WC. He found it in Brighton.' Ian's 'mechanical ingenuity', as Coke saw it, was reflected in the gadgets. Next to the cane seat in the renovated altar space was a liquid soap machine as found in trains or hotels. From Eve's bedroom in Pitt House, Ian copied the idea of a serving hatch so that, like Pitt when suffering from gout, Ian could be given his food without seeing anyone.

Mary Pakenham said: 'Somewhere also there was a lodger called Preston whom I never saw and whose flat was a complete mystery to me.' The upstairs gallery was large enough to fit a small dining table. 'Through a door in the gallery was Ian's bedroom – bare-ish, but with a double bed with a very grand counterpane given him by some female friends.'

Among the possessions on display were his father's framed obituary, his athletics cups from Eton, the crucifix from Moscow, Mussolini's discontinued passport, a small black bust of Nelson, another of Napoleon, prints of the Viennese riding school ('a sure sign of a disciplinarian', said Lucian Freud), and a selection of pornographic books, several on loan from Rickatson-Hatt, that from time to time Ian took out and pressed on Mary Pakenham or on Percy Muir's wife Barbara, who would 'be offered the run of his collection of erotica to keep me quiet while he and Percy chatted'.

Ian's stepson Raymond recalls that many were from the Obelisk Press in the rue de Rivoli, Paris. 'One I remember, a marvellous book, in English, *The Horn Book*, a girl's guide to the sixty-three Positions. I passed it round to one or two of my friends.'

Ian's converted Baptist/Fascist meeting hall was his centre of operations. An unremarkable stockbroker by day, he came home from Bishopsgate to enjoy himself at night. From 1936 until the war, 22b Ebury Street was where Ian entertained a group of card- and golf-playing male friends.

These dozen or so 'Yes-men', as Mary Pakenham called them, formed a loose club that Ian promoted in Woosterish terms as 'Le Cercle gastronomique et des jeux de hazard' to underline the importance of food and cards to their gatherings, although the former rarely reached the level of haute cuisine, let alone the imaginary feasts Ian had conjured at the Tennerhof. 'He could crack up the food,' Mary said, 'as Ian cracked up everything, but it was never terribly good. Usually coffee and kedgeree or a bit of smoked haddock.'

The Cercle's 'members' numbered Percy Muir and Gerry Coke, who, thanks to Muir, now started an important collection parallel to Ian's, of musical manuscripts by Handel and his circle; the Muirs travelled each year to Berlin, with Barbara smuggling out precious pamphlets under her girdle. There was also Greville Worthington, the third partner of the Elkin Matthews bookshop with Muir and Ian, a six-foot-five, bushy-moustached, overgrown schoolboy; George Duff-Sutherland Dunbar, a bachelor barrister with a passion for draughts, bridge and Wedgwood china, who was 'adept at cutting me down to size'; John Fox-Strangways, the very fat second son of the Earl of Ilchester; Ivar Bryce, when in England; and Jack Beal, an Old Harrovian GP who became Ian's doctor.

An occasional member and the oldest was the forty-seven-year-old Robert Gordon-Canning, best man at Oswald Mosley's wedding to Diana Guinness in 1936 – which had been the reason for Mosley relinquishing the lease. Later interned in the war, 'Bobbie' represented a reminder of the previous use of the premises. Whether he served as a reliable indicator of the Cercle's political leanings is harder to establish.

Ian's statement in March 1939 that he had 'no political prejudices whatsoever' seemed consistent with his assertion to Ann after the war that 'I am not interested in English politics let alone American' and his insistence in the *Spectator* in 1959, 'I am a totally non-political animal.' At the *Sunday Times*, it was observed that 'Fleming treated politics with amused boredom'. Yet this had not been his position as a young man.

An article on 'Fascism in Britain' by one of his school contemporaries in the *Wyvern*, the magazine Ian edited in 1925, argued that Fascism could be 'summed up in the one word – REALITY' and said it was 'of the utmost importance that centres should be started in the Universities and in our Public Schools' to counteract the 'ever-growing tendency towards Revolution', and even commending Cambridge for giving 'a magnificent lead in this respect'. Ian's friends in the 1930s included Harold Nicolson, who had worked for Mosley and briefly held a torch for Mosley's prospects. It is not hard to believe that someone who owned Mussolini's passport enjoyed nationalist sympathies. Except for the leftish Muir, who was known to have 'Marxist leanings', the Cercle's members were unapologetically Conservative. Even so, by the mid 1930s their outward behaviour was less in step with the British Union of Fascists and more raggedly reminiscent of Ian's proposal for Operation RUTHLESS in 1940, involving 'a group of young hotheads who thought the war was too tame and wanted to have a go at the Germans'.

At weekends, the hotheads took off to the links at Gleneagles or Sandwich. Sometimes joined by 'Burglar' Bryce, they discovered the casinos of Le Touquet, Deauville and Dieppe, 'with their intoxicating atmosphere of freedom from the real world of facts and figures'. On the deck of HMS *Fernie* off Dieppe in 1942, Ian would look back at a break in the smoke, and, seeing the casino in ruins, remember 'painful pre-war visits to French tables' and a pleasure resort with well-kept gardens, tidy hotels and cafés where he had tasted delicious 'filets de sole Dieppoise'.

Huntercombe golf course was another destination. Granny Kate was getting doddery, but she allowed her outsized country house to be run as a free family hotel to which all members came at weekends, bringing guests. Mary Pakenham remembered Coke and Dunbar playing bridge with Ian in a little French drawing room to themselves while Peter and his friends sat on leather armchairs in the Green Room, and Richard in another room, while in another wing of the house Michael entertained his City friends with their girlfriends. 'At meals we gathered round an immense long table where quantities of very heavy, not very nice food were served. The conversation was entirely badinage exchanged between the Fleming brothers . . . A particular game was for Peter to imitate Ian. He was very good at it. Got his "exploding" voice marvellously. Used to call him "the Colonel". Then after dinner Ian would go off with his three men friends to play bridge. Golf was played on Sunday morning.'

Alaric Jacob noticed how little of the Cercle's time was spent on women. 'Pleasant creatures though they were, one couldn't really fit them into the world of Pop.' But women there were.

'Ian's great attraction, the thing that got under one's skin, was super cosiness,' said Mary Pakenham. 'You felt you had at last met a soul mate, a twin stolen from the cradle, someone with whom you could relax, be natural, tell all.'

Ian was fastidious in separating his male from his female friends, like the buckram boxes on his shelves. On non-Cercle evenings, his beaming Irish maid opened the door to a collection of keen-eyed women who took their place on the backless couch beside the ever-burning fire for a cosy conversation with the elegant young man who sat there resembling the caddish dilettante in Ian's first story, 'The Ordeal of Caryl St George'.

Ian never talked of his girlfriends. Others told stories which flared in the retelling. John Hayward heard rumours that Ian had 'a great reputation as a ravisher of virgins in taxis'. Roald Dahl explained Ian's discretion otherwise, having shared one of his post-war partners in Washington. 'This was because they were almost always married.'

Shortly after entertaining Ian's prim American girlfriend in Berlin, Alice Hemming joined Harold in London. On 28 February 1934, she wrote in her diary: 'Dinner with Ian Fleming and painted girl at Fleming's Chelsea home.' The girl's identity is unknown, but a procession of single and married women moved to occupy the vacancy left by Ian's Swiss fiancée Monique.

Mary Pakenham once tried to list his conquests and gave up. Even so, her partial tally gives the flavour. A deb called Olivia (possibly Olivia Campbell, who became his biographer's mother-in-law: 'I discovered he impregnated her,' says John Pearson, 'and it had to be dealt with'); an American girl who 'acceded to his lust' in Mrs Val's Rolls-Royce parked in the Turner's House garage – 'after which he never bothered with her again'; a marquess's chubby daughter known as the 'galloping bedstead'; the wife of the monocled Austrian tenor Richard Tauber, whom he picked up on a train and seduced in her wagon-lit; a mink-coated American girl called Phyllis, whom he drove with Bryce to Kitzbühel and then dumped on the way; a bubble dancer named Storm; a divorcée in Capri, who disgusted him after she ducked behind a rock to change her tampon. Yet another married woman was the Irish wife of his Geneva friend Martin Hill, who had invited Ian to be best man at their wedding. He was a good lover, she said, though selfish. 'He had no compunction. If he saw someone, he thought he must have her. I don't flatter myself: he wanted somebody and it happened to be me.'

There is no hiding the nasty taste this behaviour leaves. Pakenham understood Ian's cut-and-run conduct as his ugly response to Eve Fleming and the brutal way she had made him renounce Monique. Subscribers to this view included Ernie Cuneo, Robert Harling, Joan Bright, Sandy Glen, Blanche Blackwell, Ralph Arnold and Morris Cargill. 'He was always looking for his mother in women,' said Cargill, 'and then hating them when they gave in.'

Robert Harling typed out a paragraph to show Ian, copied from Peter Quennell's book on Byron's years of fame, which, Harling said, could well describe Fleming (and may even have been inspired by him). Ian was furious. 'Myself and Byron! You must be mad! That semi-cripple, semi-poofter.' He then read the cutting. '*Byron hated women because he had hated and perhaps resented his mother: he pursued them because affection and admiration never come amiss and because he himself was sufficiently feminine to find in their society – much as he despised it – a strange influence that he could not account for. Among men, his social facilities were keyed up, he was at his best.*

He listened with empathy to your shattered past, then took you to bed and forgot you. Mary Pakenham had heard the stories. 'He was known as a great Don Juan. And his looks made it worse, you know. That hollow-cheeked, saturnine look of his. He really seemed a bad Lord Byron sort of figure.'

Byron was one parallel, Ernest Hemingway another. Fleming was a 'fanatical admirer' of Hemingway, said Norman Lewis. 'He told me that he had read all his books several times, and believed he had come to absorb Hemingway's distinctive style in such a way that he frequently wrote passages agreed among his friends to be indistinguishable from the work of the master.' It was not merely the simple prose style they shared, leading to Cyril Connolly's nickname of 'Flemingway'; or that both writers were ultimately devoured by their own myth when they proved unable to live up to it. An over-controlling mother loomed behind their destructive engagement with the opposite sex.

Women were not put off by his image as a lady-killer. Plenty were drawn to it. Len Deighton says, 'If I can quote something I wrote in one of my books: womanisers are the rocks against which reckless women dash themselves.' Frequently, Ian's male friends seemed more aggrieved by his behaviour than were the parties involved. As Mary Pakenham could attest, Ian retained the affection of many old girfriends he had disappointed, remaining friends with them till he died. 'His forte was entangling women emotionally, quite apart from bed, so that they were fond of him for 20–30 years.' Following Ian's death, Rebecca West wrote to his secretary, Beryl Griffie-Williams, to say that her husband had a new secretary from Jamaica, whose sister-in-law, Blanche Blackwell, 'believes herself to be the one woman Ian Fleming ever loved! There must be enough of them to fill the Albert Hall bless his heart!'

Back in his late twenties, with 22b Ebury Street as his base, Ian went after women in the alternately determined and careless manner with which he collected first editions: the hunt, the acquisition, the shelving. 'Ingenious excitement during the pursuit, naughty triumph and then contempt and repulsion,' is how Mary Pakenham defined the pattern. Ian told Robert

Harling it was because he didn't want to be involved. 'Apart from a favoured two or three, most of my friendships with women have been exclusively sexual, superficial and short-lived. I'm apt to find that when sex is over, everything's over.'

According to Ivar Bryce, another unrepentant womaniser, Ian would always say to his girlfriends: 'You must treat our love as a glass of champagne.' He treated his girlfriends more like the kedgeree that Eve's cook had taught May how to make. Lisl Popper said: 'Ian really knew nothing about women. For him, they were just another sort of fish-cake.'

Before they married, he told Ann that she was the only woman he had ever stayed in bed with all night long. Whether this statement was true, there was enough truth in it. 'If he had stayed longer, the emotions would have started to get out of hand, and he would have been landed in that boring complicated world he was so anxious to avoid.' Whenever intimacy threatened, Ian was like the octopus in his Jamaican reef that 'launched itself sideways with streamlined compactness and shot into the deeps.'

Behind all these young women shimmered the memory of Monique Panchaud de Bottens.

> '*She was like you.*'
> '*Let me take her place, Tommy,*' the girl said very quietly.

One book Ian did read from start to finish was Hugh Edwards's 1933 novel *All Night at Mrs Stanyhurst's*, which Ian persuaded Cape to reprint shortly before he died. Published in the year when he broke off his engagement with Monique, it features a woman like Eve, 'my sainted and peculiarly detestable mother,' and a plot redolent of Ian's situation: the story of a young man who confuses a woman with the dead girl he had loved. This was the narrative of Ian's relationships in the mid 1930s with Edith Morpurgo and Muriel Wright.

He had met both girlfriends in Kitzbühel. Perfectly obvious to Mary Pakenham, who looked on him 'as a sort of Kitzbühel skiing boy', was that 'mittel Europe remained his centre of romance'.

Dr Helmut Morpurgo is a retired engineer living in Vienna. In 1985, he was talking in his garden with his great-aunt Edith, 'a humorous, self-confident lady, who dressed always in black and lived rather poorly but very optimistically; to earn a little money, she had worked for the Swedish firm Electrolux in an office opposite St Stephen's Cathedral.'

Edith revealed that she had once been in love with an Englishman who was 'the only one she ever loved,' and that only recently had it astonished her to discover that he had become a writer of 'robbery books', something she never could have envisaged when she met him in Kitzbühel in 1934 aged thirty.

She had stood out from her group of rich friends. Four years older than Ian, with dark wavy hair and a candid gaze, Edith Morpurgo had been divorced eight years and had reverted to her maiden name. Ian knew nothing of her marriage to Rico Thonet, who had worked with Walter Gropius and designed chairs and tables for the cafés where Edith and Ian began their relationship.

'His mistress was a Rumanian baroness,' wrote Alaric Jacob – who had lent Ian keys to his spare studio in Marylebone Lane, where, unknown to Jacob, Ian then continued his affair. Actually descended from Austrian-Jewish bankers, Edith was a baroness only until 1919, when it was forbidden in Austria to use the title. Her father, Robert Morpurgo, was an aristocratic gadfly and architect. In 1904 he was involved in a scandal over an office development near Vienna's Konzerthaus. Robert fled with the one-year-old Edith and her mother, a Polish film actress, to America, where he worked as an illegal consulting engineer, before returning to Vienna to face the music and a brief spell in jail. Edith adored him and was eventually buried in the same grave. She spoke English with a Chicago accent, and represented one of the forthright young women Ian found hard to resist. When asked years later to describe his ideal woman, he had Edith in mind: 'thirtyish, Jewish, a companion who wouldn't need education in the arts of love. She would aim to please, have firm flesh and kind eyes.'

They skied. They climbed mountains. They talked about buying a castle. Their affair was serious enough for Edith to move to London at the end of 1934 where Ian put her up in Jacob's studio. 'I called it his fucking studio,' said Lisl. Handwritten in German, and sounding more playful in that language, Ian's letters – including one furiously torn up and Sellotaped back together – are among the few records from this period. They illustrate the gamut of passions he provoked.

'Esteemed baroness', Ian begins one letter, on which he has pasted an advertisement for woollen underpants. In another, he sketches her without clothes on and writes '*Wo ich Dich küssen will*' – 'where I want to kiss you' – marking crosses on her lips, breasts, and between her legs. 'I kiss you where you wouldn't allow me.' In a longer letter, Ian reveals more risqué sexual preferences. 'If I were to say "I love you" you would only quarrel with me, and then I would have to spank you, and you would cry and that I don't want. I only want you to be happy, but I also want to hurt you because you deserve it and to tame you like a little wild animal.'

These outpourings on Cull & Company stationery established a formula Ian repeated in letters to future girlfiends like Loelia Westminster and Ann O'Neill: the teasing tone, the treasure map of buried kisses, the house-masterly threat of corporal punishment, the aggrieved denouement.

By April 1935, the affair had guttered out. 'I have found myself feeling like a child in front of its malicious governess. At the end, I could do no right, and everything was a personal injury to you . . . If you wanted to hurt me, you have done so, and you can be glad that you have brought our friend-ship to a hideous end.'

Edith's great-nephew says: 'She told me she was always quarrelling with him. He wanted to marry her and live in London, and she didn't want to. He was very jealous. He didn't like that she wanted to be in contact with her Viennese friends, and didn't want to be fixed down. It's a love story without a solution.'

Months later in Kitzbühel, in the summer of 1935, Ian started a new affair with a striking-looking Englishwoman.

Her name was Muriel Wright. Ian knew her as 'Moo' or 'Honeytop' after her mop of blonde curly hair. She was twenty-six years old, a competitive polo player, and worked as a fashion model in Knightsbridge. 'She was very good-looking. Long thin neck and attractive,' said Joan Bright, who lived across the road from her, 'and she would toss her head as she went by.'

Someone who observed their relationship unfold was seven-year-old Adrian House, future managing director of the publishers William Collins. His parents had fallen in love with Kitzbühel, and the family met up as a group over the next three summers with Muriel and Ian. 'He was slightly larger than life and quite jokey, with a lack of formality I associate with Ian at that time.' It was their well-connected young English friend Muriel whom Ian was 'very keen about'.

The holiday romance developed into one of the most enduring relationships in Ian's life, despite his infidelities and wretched treatment of her.

Merry, beguiling, dotty, with a commanding deadpan manner, Moo was a rebellious aristocrat from Derbyshire. She was the seventh of eight children, and grew up at Yeldersley Hall, near Ashbourne, on a farm and a lake, with a succession of ungovernable Dutch barge dogs and chows. 'Her nieces looked up to her in spite of her wayward ways!' wrote one of them. Hand in hand with her love of nature and animals strode the independent streak that had characterised Monique and Edith.

Muriel's family were related through her mother's side to Mary, Queen of Scots, whose escapes from castles provided an imperious role model. 'Aunt Moo was brilliant at climbing out of windows down a sheet,' says her niece Tamara. 'Once with her sisters and cousins, she commandeered every grey horse in the area and one black horse, and dressed up as ghosts, with her as the devil, and they rode up a track near Dugdale, and waited until the bus was nearby, and then they all rode across the road and the bus bolted.' This kind of exploit was manna to Ian.

She had had a stormy upbringing at Yeldersley, finding her parents too strict. Her half-German father had been an MP, then chairman of the family firm of Butterley Steel, which had built St Pancras station and once upon a time employed Mellors, the gamekeeper in D. H. Lawrence's novel *Lady Chatterley's Lover* ('I was a clerk in Butterley offices, thin, white-faced fellow, fuming with all the things I read'). Muriel's religious mother was related to the dukes of Buccleuch and as proud of her ties to the aristocracy as she was pious. The household assembled in the big hall for prayers each morning before breakfast, with the housemaids sitting in rows. On Sunday, they filed through the wild flowers to Osmaston church across the fields. The Wrights had missionaries in the family. Muriel was expected to marry a vicar or a cousin. To marry someone out of 'one's galère', as her mother called it, like Ian Fleming, would have been utterly extraordinary.

She could not wait to leave home. Her strongest ally was her elder brother Stephen, who had gone to Jamaica to manage the Castle Wemyss banana plantation east of Montego Bay. Stephen provided Ian with his earliest impressions of the island. 'Within a couple of years there was only one banana, and he was the champion amateur jockey,' says his son Nigel. 'He was having a lovely time, but was no good at money.'

Muriel chose London for her escape route. 'She broke away from her family completely,' says her niece Cathryn. But rumours of what she was getting up to in the big smoke, such as that she had a latchkey to 22b Ebury Street, trickled back to Yeldersley. Cathryn says: 'I was aware Aunt Moo was a black sheep in my grandmother's eyes. She disapproved of her living with Ian.' Muriel's parents perceived Ian in the same dubious stripes as Lady Chatterley's gamekeeper. 'I don't think they felt he was at all a suitable person,' says Cathryn. 'We had the image of rather a nasty man, frightfully selfish and cruel. He used to ring her up and say "I've run out of cigarettes, go and get me some," at all hours.'

At one point the family was so upset, says Tamara, that Muriel's eldest brother Fitzherbert turned up at 22b Ebury Street to impress their collective displeasure on Ian with a riding crop. 'Fitz was sent by grandpapa and grandma to horse-whip him.' Ian was out at the time.

Ian's reluctance to commit defined his private life.

Once again, his mother was the stumbling block. She watched him dance with Muriel at one of her parties, and was overheard lamenting that it only remained for Ian to marry a barmaid. She directed Amaryllis to steer clear. 'Until Mother put a stop to it, I was going to stay with Muriel Wright in London when I was studying.' Late in the war, after his relationship with Muriel had been going on for nine years, Ian did eventually steel himself to propose. But he had plucked up his courage too late.

What had sapped him was the traumatic memory of Eve's reaction to Peter's choice of wife a decade earlier.

Mary Pakenham had been involved in Peter's arrangements and she witnessed the debacle at close quarters. 'His mother had already put a stop to one engagement to a girl called Sybil, and he feared her as a powerful witch who could put a spell on anything.' It was a family joke that Eve thought the only person in England Peter could marry was the Princess Royal. When in December 1935 he decided to marry the actress Celia Johnson, the daughter of 'a nice, quiet doctor in Richmond, extremely intelligent, unselfish, reserved and with very little feminine nonsense', Peter did not tell his mother – or Ian – until a week before, and he took along Mary for support.

They first went to Joyce Grove to break the news to Granny Kate, who thought Mary was a rejected flame of Peter's brought down for consolation. 'She took a mad passion for me and kept telling me how much she would prefer me to Celia.'

Then they drove two miles to Greys Court, a Tudor house which Eve afterwards claimed only to have bought with Peter in mind. She had spent the year at great expense doing up the Cromwellian stables for his studio, and when they arrived, she was beating the mullions with chains to make them look old. In a story which became family lore, Mrs Val had put champagne on ice because she thought Peter was announcing his engagement to Lady Mary. The champagne was sent back to the kitchen when he told her he was getting married to Celia. Mary recalled how Eve then showed them the painted orange attic where her sons were to sleep, as if they were children who would never leave home. ' "And this is Ian's room," she said, "and this is Peter's room," just as though the marriage didn't exist. With difficulty, just as we were leaving, Peter forced her to discuss it. She stared up with big, wondering eyes as though she were being made to talk about higher mathematics.'

Eve wrote to Rupert Hart-Davis, 'I am miserable about this wedding.' Nevertheless, it went ahead on 2 December. After the reception, Eve told her chauffeur driving the couple to the station in her Rolls-Royce 'not to be too long as Amaryllis had a music lesson'.

Even then, Eve did not give up. She insisted that her savage disappointment with Peter's choice of bride was shared by the rest of the Fleming family. Not merely Granny Kate was opposed to Celia – she had seen her act and 'thought George Robey better'. There was, apparently, one other person of influence who was vehemently hostile to 'the Crackwit', as Peter called his wife. An unnamed male testator on Kate's side of the family had allegedly threatened to cut Peter out of any future inheritance if he married Celia, fearing that he would get 'mixed up in the theatre'.

Eve's unbelievable claim provoked Ian into an unstinting defence of his elder brother. Late one night at Turner's House he crept downstairs to write a letter to his mother. It was the closest Ian came to describing what Peter meant to him.

'Now listen – what ever you may think, I feel that we must all back Peter up in this – and if some testator has cut him out you must go round at once and say you've thought it over and feel after all it's for the best. *You* must not side with the rest of the family and leave Peter all by himself . . . We must not go over to "Granny's Camp". We must manage OUR affairs & put a brave face on our tribulations by ourselves. It is so unthinkable that Peter should feel a hostile faction in his own camp . . . He *is* a law unto himself – a genius and an admirable, truthful, good man. We have all benefited by him and his particular personality in some way and I think we must expect – especially you – to put up with the particularities which have made him without question one of the 2 or 3 most brilliant men of his generation. We mustn't get into the way of having a perfection complex about him. The outstanding is always a little inhuman – & always must be, in order to be outstanding, and, darling Maman, we, & ultimately the whole of England, have a lot to be grateful for in Peter's existence. He really *is* setting a standard of sanity & truthfulness for a whole generation – he alone, a lot of people think . . . I feel disappointed myself and yet glad at the same time that he is married. I *should* feel annoyed about not being told & not being best man & one thing & another, but I really don't mind him treating me as a minor criminal and as utterly untrustworthy because he does know best in so many other things that one can't expect him to be tolerant and *humane* in all others.'

He begged his mother: 'You MUST go to this testator and make him change his mind.'

There is no evidence that Eve confronted the anonymous testator – and huge suspicion that the testator was Eve herself.

As she had with Monique, Eve continued to be foul to Celia and treat her as though she did not exist. Mary Pakenham wrote: 'Even when she paid a state visit to their flat with me as the only extra person, she ignored Celia.'

Ian was determined to avoid his brother's fate.

XVI
A CHARACTER SKETCH

'His reputation was so bad that I did not want
my name connected with his.'
MARY PAKENHAM

One girl who did not sleep with Ian was Mary Pakenham, the twenty-eight-year-old daughter of the late Earl of Longford and a gossip columnist on 'Londoner's Diary'.

The night before Peter's wedding in December 1935, Mary had dinner in front of the fire at Turner's House, where Ian was still living. This was their first recorded meeting. 'To my amusement I noted that he was conscious of me and was ready for a gallop and I felt the mild pleasure one feels when ogled by an Italian soldier or gondolier.'

Definitely attracted, Mary contemplated 'a walk out', even though 'it was obvious that he would never be in love with me, and if I got hurt it would be my own affair.'

After Ian moved into Ebury Street months later, 'I expressed a wish to see it and got asked to tea . . . but the moment I got inside, I realised that there was no cause for alarm and that I should never, never, never, find myself in a jam – and indeed throughout our acquaintance, sex never did rear its ugly head. I returned feeling like Christian when the burden rolled from his back.'

Her freedom allowed Mary to observe Ian with detachment. 'I was absolutely fascinated by him and for six months was very devoted.' They went to the cinema and art galleries, and dined *à deux* once a week. Ian told her how he wanted to start a magazine like the short-lived *Night and Day*, to which she was a contributor; and of his ambition to be 'the Renaissance ideal, the Complete Man'; 'and then he had appendicitis and went to Capri to recuperate. I went too and was terribly bored and we returned only just on speakers.'

Their holiday in Capri with Ivar Bryce made Mary realise they had no tastes in common. Having initially thought Ian to be Byronic, she decided he was a figure more like Falstaff – 'fascinating, but also ridiculous'.

Before her marriage in December 1939, Mary tore out the photographs of their ill-fated trip from her album. The same fury stopped her from dedicating her first book, which he had proofread, to Ian. But what has somehow survived is a five-page handwritten document.

Mary was provoked enough by Ian's behaviour into pinning him down in her lined notebook. As she recorded their maddening encounters and tried to work him out, she inadvertently became an unwitting Fleming specialist. She knew his family. She enjoyed a privileged vantage point into his private life – on one occasion short of further detail, hiding in his bedroom while Ann O'Neill and her husband Shane came in to listen to the announcement of war on the wireless. In the process of trying to explore the source of her infuriation, Mary produced, however imperfect, a surprisingly three-dimensional character analysis. Her pen portrait is the most integrated picture of Ian in his late twenties by a contemporary commentator who was also a good observer and witness:

If the creatures in the moon wanted to see a sample of human nature, I should send them to Ian. In one man, they would then have the treat of seeing all the most characteristic characteristics of homo sapiens, such as trying to have your cake & eat it, getting more out of a jug than you put into it, calling the kettle black & so on.

Ian was born enthusiastic & excitable, with a somewhat feminine temperament. Unfortunately, he was stuck in the middle of a very solid, foursquare family, which considered him too peculiar for words & were always trying to get him into line with the rest of them. This was very painful for everyone concerned and, in his efforts to escape from their suffocating rule, he did everything he could think of that they didn't do . . .

Having scrapped his family's gods and being in need of something to put in their place, he set up his own whims instead, which had the advantage of being clear & easy to follow, but changed so often they did not get him anywhere.

This worried him slightly in that he had imbibed enough of his family's tradi-
tions to feel that one ought to be getting somewhere, but it did not worry him
very much, as whenever he did begin to get anywhere, he disliked the look of
the place. This whim worship also made it very tricky for his friends, but those
who complained about it were told that they needn't play if they didn't want to.
As the poet says: He cast off his friends as a huntsman his pack/As he knew
when he chose he could whistle them back.

A great many people, both men & women, found him very attractive &
were prepared to pay for the pleasure of his company by putting up with a lot
of rot that they would not have stood from anyone else. I sometimes try &
imagine what his life would have been like if he had not been attractive, but
beyond knowing that it would have been very different, I cannot picture it.

It should, however, be said that Ian very sweetly never seemed to have
noticed the attraction he had for people. He never tried deliberately to cash in
on it or exploit it in a calculated way. In fact, he always seemed surprised every
time he got away with a new bit of pretentiousness or a woman came to pieces
in his hand.

Talking of women, I have not much to say on this subject except that his
lamentable habit it was to take them up thoughtlessly and then, after a short
inspection, let them drop with a crash (a few, however, who shall be nameless,
clung on with their teeth, which were fortunately strong). His general taste,
roughly speaking, was for tarts who looked like nice girls.

Sooner or later, he was bored & disappointed by all women. I never quite
made out where he thought they failed him. Perhaps he just hoped to fall in
love with them, but he never could . . .

Well, as someone said of him, 'You can't do with him, he's so selfish.' And
equally, as someone else said of him, 'You can't help liking him, he's so alive.'

This was Mary Pakenham's first of several attempts to pinpoint his elusive
personality. 'With Ian, before the war, one never came to the end of his con-
tortions,' she told John Pearson. 'One was endlessly fascinated by what he
would do next, and one just never knew. The only impossible thing in those
days seemed to be that he could ever turn respectable.'

XVII
'M'

'*"He said you were his comfort during the war."*
I answered rather awkwardly: "I hope I was."'

MAUD RUSSELL

Granny Kate died in February 1937 as she was about to set off for a golfing holiday in South Africa. She had failed to make a will or alter her husband's will. Since she died intestate, her estate passed to her surviving three children, Philip, Dorothy and Kathleen, leaving nothing to Ian and his brothers.

It had not been unreasonable for Eve to have expected that part of Robert's share of the bank would come to the children of his favourite son. There could have been a moment when the will might have been adjusted to meet this expectation. The fact that Robert's estate was not divvied up into four equable slices led to decades of grumbling. But Philip may have had little choice other than to be guided by the lawyers. Plus, Eve was so unpopular; her illegitimate child by a notorious womaniser had gone down poorly with the puritanical Flemings. As for her four sons: Peter was given the Nettlebed estate, while Richard and Michael were directors of the bank anyway, with Richard standing to inherit some of Robert's money, since he had married his first cousin, Dorothy's daughter.

It was Ian alone who lost out. Surrounded on all sides by real money, he did not have money of his own and, although absurdly well off by the standards of the day, he would never be sustained by Philip's generosity, being regarded by his reserved and 'ribby' uncle as a chip off Eve's rickety block and a poor reflection of Philip's adored brother Val.

*

By 1938, Ian's career was in the doldrums. Richard voiced what both Fleming 'camps' felt about Ian's five years in the City. 'If his life had ended with the war, everyone would have said it was rather wasted.' An unexceptional stockbroker with one known client, he was like Wodehouse's character, who, after considerable reflection, came to the conclusion that his talents lay elsewhere. 'At lugging ledgers I am among the also-rans – a mere cipher.'

But where did Ian's talents lie? Given his playboy reputation, a question remains: how was Ian Fleming considered for the job which hurtled him from the periphery to the centre?

Someone in a position to answer was another girlfriend – the petite heiress who had secured Ian his position with Cull & Company and makes a peeping appearance in *For Your Eyes Only* as Mary Ann Russell.

Maud Russell had kept in the background, monitoring his relationships and job changes from a distance. Ian's Eton friend Alan Pryce-Jones was one of a tiny group to suspect her importance for Ian. 'If he did not marry until middle age it was partly because a long love-affair held him back. His love was older than he and spent much time in a ravishing country house filled at weekends with mutual friends, most of whom were quite unaware of the love affair.'

Ian called her 'M'. Mary Pakenham knew her real identity. 'His maitresse en titre (his own words) was Mrs Gilbert Russell, a little Jewess who was a lot older than him.' Although Maud Russell was not yet, as Ian wrote later to Ann, 'the age you think I like – about 55!', she was seventeen years his senior and in her mid forties when their affair began. 'I've an idea he used to sleep with her on and off for years,' said Ann, who never shed her jealousy. 'I used to tell Bryce, in the days when I spoke to him, not to bother to let me know what Ian was up to until he saw him near a middle-aged Jewess.'

Maud Russell was an astute and loyal mentor and confidante for more than a decade. On 21 June 1945 she wrote in her diary of Ian: 'he is my oldest friend, a strong link with my past life and the one person I could say anything to – and often do.' Her forthrightness was what had attracted Gilbert. She possessed, said her husband, 'the most direct nature I've ever seen. No humbug or snobbery or social ambition.'

If Maud lacked social ambition, it was perhaps because she was at the centre of Society. She had been painted by John Sargent and William Nichol-son, and twice in charcoal by Henri Matisse, whom she found boring. She was not at first glance remarkable: quiet country clothes, immaculate dark hair, and in the words of John Julius Norwich, 'a soft, gentle, slightly breath-less voice, with a tendency to repeat what you had just said before answering'. Ann's first choice to write Ian's life, the biographer James Pope-Hennessy, was a friend. 'Her strange mewing manner is very disarming; she is so well read, so original and funny.' In Maud's low, gurgling laugh, Frances Par-tridge detected 'something a little Oriental in her appearance and her movements' – that 'Byzantine look' which Matisse had managed to capture.

In 1934, Maud and Gilbert bought Mottisfont Abbey in the Test valley in Hampshire, a thirteenth-century Augustinian priory set in two thousand acres. They transformed it into what Norwich called 'the most desirable country house in England'. Maud commissioned Rex Whistler to fresco the long gothic drawing-room, and she packed the house at weekends with leading politicians, writers, and artists. 'I like the house to be full & the lawns dotted with figures.'

Maud's weekend guests were heady company for a bachelor in his mid twenties. Ian argued with Randolph Churchill, 'like some fair gorilla'. He dis-cussed art with Cecil Beaton, who was 'dumb with envy and rage' at Rex Whistler's fresco. He shot with Joseph Ball, the secretive head of the Conserva-tive Research Department. Other regulars were Norwich's parents, Duff Cooper, then First Lord of the Admiralty, and his wife Diana; Maud's child-hood friend Robert Vansittart or 'Van', chief diplomatic adviser to the government, who had kept an eye on Ian since his trip to Moscow; Harold Nicolson, ditto; and the ornithologist Richard Meinertzhagen, a banker's son like Ian, whose family had owned Mottisfont, and whose imaginative military exploits in the First World War both Ian and Peter were to copy in the next war.

On arrival at Mottisfont, Ian's grey suitcase was taken by a footman to his room and unpacked by a maid, who turned down his bed after lunch so that he might enjoy an hour's siesta. Afternoon tea on the lawn, watching the Test flow by, involved a silver pot with a burner underneath, cucumber sandwiches, and chocolate cake with jam. Croquet, mushroom-picking, golf and shooting were among the activities. Ian dressed for dinner.

Maud was as curiously secretive as Ian. She abhorred 'snooooping' as she pronounced it. None of the guests were allowed in her bedroom. John Julius Norwich had a headache once and went to see if she had some aspirin. She opened her door a crack and squeezed her hand out to give it to him. Maud's granddaughter Emily, editor of her diaries, believes it likely that Ian and Maud became lovers in the 1930s, and the affair continued intermittently after Gilbert's death in 1942. The clues: a small envelope containing a lock of black hair, with 'I.'s' in pencil on the envelope; a report of Maud's lady's maid Adele once finding them in bed together; and a reference in Maud's diary to Ian seeing 'my bedroom'. Emily says: 'He was surely there.'

Ian was in Ceylon in January 1945 when a Sinhalese man told his fortune. Maud's diary reveals what he said. 'Ian asked if there were any women in his (I.'s) life who had influenced it very much. The fortune teller said yes, two. His mother and another woman, a widow. He couldn't tell in what relationship she stood to him; he couldn't see it clearly. She'd given him (I.) money, for what purpose the soothsayer didn't understand.' One year later, Maud gave Ian the money to buy and build Goldeneye.

Emily says: 'A side of me questions whether he was using her, mining a rich Jew. But she normally spotted that, and the fact she wasn't suspicious of Ian speaks well of him.' From the early 1930s to the mid 1940s, Ian was the person Maud saw most outside her family circle and she used her important contacts to help him.

In Maud's accepting company, Ian could be his least tangled, whimsical self. He concealed nothing from her – his other affairs, ambitions, concerns. She knew him better than his male friends in the Cercle, better than any of his girlfriends, with the exception of Mary Pakenham. He turned to Maud for the guidance that his mother had never provided. He trusted her judgment, even when he did not act on it. She was unpossessive, sympathetic, an insightful older woman who uncomplicatedly loved him, understood him, and saw and appreciated his good points, in spite of his often complicated behaviour. In 1938, he gave her *Breviary of Love*, Jeanne Grivolin's intense private journal about an impossible romance. Maud gave him a gold cigarette case which later on he had oxidized to appear like gunmetal. It was a regret to both of them they were not the same age. 'He is a lonely man. I am always afraid that when he is attracted by some girl he looks for not only youth and attractiveness, but many of my virtues, vices and oddness, and these he can never hope to find in anyone young, and quite likely in no one else but me.'

An example of the girl Maud had in mind was the thirty-six-year-old Loelia, Duchess of Westminster, not long separated from her first husband 'Bendor', and on the hunt for another.

Quite severe-looking under one of her immense hats, Loelia (pronounced Leelia) was from the same family as Lady Caroline Lamb who had a notorious affair with Byron before branding him 'mad, bad, and dangerous to know'. Ian exerted the same spell on Loelia, after she met him at a party of Lord Rothermere's. 'Really I. F. is dangerously attractive,' she wrote in a diary until recently thought destroyed. Her entry for 25 August 1938 picks up the thread. 'Interesting letter from Ian.' He was inviting her to join him in Le Touquet on Friday evening and hoping, he wrote, that she 'might indulge in a little *deboulonnage* [bolting] with me, because I would come and meet you with a car & you could take a few days out of your life & then forget about them . . . PS This is a love letter!' Soon they were dining together two or three times a week, and playing foursomes of bridge with Loelia's young friends, Lord and Lady O'Neill.

On 28 December 1938, Maud lunched with Ian at Boulestin's 'and he told me about his dallying flirtation with Loelia Westminster and again about Muriel and from there onto odder topics,' by which Maud may have meant her own relationship with Ian.

XVIII
MR SECRETAN

'No doubt his name was mentioned in quiet conversations
in hallowed clubs and jotted down in little notebooks by small
gold pencils belonging to people who count.'

IVAR BRYCE

Maud Russell was not only privy to Ian's love life as well as a continuing part of it; she was involved intimately in his career. Six years after facilitating his passage from Reuters to her husband's merchant bank, she and Gilbert manoeuvred Ian from his dead-end stockbroker's job into Naval Intelligence.

Many have found it singularly odd that someone with Ian's reputation and no naval background should have been recruited to such a delicate position. Seen from another angle, it would have been odd if Ian had not been considered for what he called 'nefarious activities'. Since prep school, he had moved among talent spotters for British Intelligence who were familiar with his flaws as well as his potential.

The full circumstances remain opaque. The SIS file on Ian Fleming is classified, if one exists. This makes it hard to unpack overlapping claims about when he started working for the Intelligence services, if not on 1 June 1939, as his Naval Intelligence Division (NID) record states. James Bond had joined SIS in 1938, but any account of Ian's entry has to rely on uncorroborated sources like the journalist Sefton Delmer, who told John Pearson: 'Balls. Of course, Ian had been doing work before.'

Although Ian had failed to get into the Foreign Office, he had kept up his connections there. Since his 1933 Moscow assignment and his debriefing by Vansittart's men, Ian maintained contact with diplomats like Michael Wright, Philip Nichols and Maurice Peterson, later Ambassador to Moscow. Whatever the actual identity of 'Mr Secretan of the Foreign Office', it was known to Adrian House that Ian 'was already in the mid-thirties supplying the Foreign Office in London with information about the rise of the Nazis'. Not only the Nazis. Alaric Jacob recalled Ian's visits to Washington in 1937 and 1938, 'ostensibly for his stockbroking firm, but in fact all the questions he was asking me seemed political and military'.

Ian revealed a tail-fin of his ambition in four pieces that he wrote for *The Times* in the late 1930s: a letter in September 1938 about Germany's aggressive intentions, and three reports in March 1939 from Moscow, which Ian visited as a special correspondent weeks before the Molotov–Ribbentrop Pact. It cannot have hindered Ian's chances of publishing these pieces that Peter had begun working for the newspaper, not merely as a protégé of the editor Geoffrey Dawson, who put him to writing witty fourth leaders, but spoken of as Dawson's likeliest successor.

The shadow of Maud Russell's excitable childhood friend 'Van' flitted behind Ian's four contributions to *The Times*. Vansittart helped Maud secure visas for her German-Jewish cousins in Berlin. In Ian's case, the former permanent under-secretary unlocked Foreign Office doors. What went on behind these doors is unknown, but a lunch Maud arranged during the war specifically 'for Ian and Van to meet' lasted three hours and caused Ian to miss his daily directive meeting. 'They talked about many curious things . . .'

A violent anti-appeaser, Vansittart must be considered a source for Ian's long letter to *The Times* on 28 September 1938, four days before the Munich debate in the House of Commons. An 'extremely rare' circular had come into Ian's possession – 'I know of only one other copy, in the Nazi archives at the Brown House'. This alarming document detailed the Nazi Party's original programme of February 1920, most policies of which had now been executed. Ian cited it to make a patriotic clarion call for crystal clarity not only about Germany's aims but Chamberlain's response. 'We must state what we would fight for and why.' Unless Hitler agreed to a binding disarmament pact in exchange for his remaining demands, Ian accepted that 'it will be time to organise this country on a wartime basis'. Meanwhile, he still hoped that 'the dangerous counsels of the slaughter-house brigade' could be ignored, and also 'the bemused vaporings' of those who wished England 'out of the fight for ever.' Ian hated both fates. It would not be long before he found the third way: Intelligence work, the secret war that could save lives.

According to his biographer Ian Colvin, Vansittart was 'master now of a curious patchwork of special intelligence about Europe'. His tiller hand can be detected behind Ian's otherwise inexplicable second visit to Moscow on a one-off foreign assignment for *The Times*.

On 18 March 1939, Ian took a sudden leave of absence from Rowe & Pitman to accompany the Overseas Trade Minister, Robert Hudson, on a five-day mission to Russia ostensibly to improve trade relations. On the eve of Ian's departure, Vansittart summoned the Soviet ambassador, Ivan Maisky, and 'spoke heatedly and at length about the importance of making Hudson's visit a success'. Vansittart's peroration achieved nothing. The Soviet Foreign Minister, Maksim Litvinov, afterwards reported that 'the visit had no political or economic repercussion whatsoever'. But trade had not been Vansittart's sole objective. While in Moscow, Ian was directed to keep his eyes peeled for signs of Russia's military build-up.

As far as *Times* readers could make out, the visit seemed devoted mainly to tourism. Ian joined the British delegation to watch a bowdlerised version of Glinka's opera *A Life for the Tsar*. The next morning, he drove with Hudson into the Kremlin through the armour-plated medieval gate. They were shown the crown jewels and then led out in single file 'through a sliding bombproof doorway' to the Lenin mausoleum in Red Square, to admire the embalmed features of the creator of the Soviet Union.

Ian's actual purpose was suspected by Sefton Delmer of the *Daily Express*. A large man with an unusually soft voice, Delmer accompanied Ian on the train from Warsaw, and in Moscow they shared a hotel room. Delmer noticed how Ian made a great display of typing, and later called London, saying 'Is that enough now?' Delmer took it for granted that Ian meant, *Is that enough copy for you to give me the cover I need?* 'For, of course, he was there doing a job for the Secret Service. No question about it.' According to Delmer, who had his own links with SIS, they tramped to see Maksim Litvinov's flat without any luck. They also picked up a couple of women. 'Ian knew enough about Moscow to leave the International Hotel to go for his girls to the Metropole. Ian paid his girl with the bottom of his pair of silk pyjamas.' Chief among Delmer's recollections was Ian's purchase of local condoms. 'It was a very useful way of discovering something about the Russian synthetic rubber industry.' Their Moscow adventures bound them together for life. Delmer became 'a particularly close friend of mine', said Ian, who called him 'Jimkin' and later employed Delmer at the Admiralty and was godfather to his son.

Ian lunched with Maud at Boulestin's on his return. He declared himself to be 'wholly and completely anti-Bolshevik', but had enjoyed himself, as he revealed in a letter to Loelia Westminster, at that moment visiting America. 'It was enormous fun – no Tchekov & lilac, just plain "nostalgie de la boue" – and I wrote a world-beating memorandum on the Russian Army when I got back. The chancelleries are still quaking from it & I expect it will start a war.'

Entitled 'Russia's strength. Some cautionary notes', Ian's confidential memorandum reads like a job application for SIS as much as a punchy assessment of the Soviet armed forces. He prefaced it with a bold declaration: 'N.B. The writer returned from Soviet Russia last week. He has no political prejudices whatsoever.'

Ian estimated Russia's war strength at 11 million, with 5,000 aircraft and 150 submarines. To parade his credentials, he cited Polish, Russian, French and German sources. His earlier brush with Stalin's favourite prosecutor gave him the confidence to put on record that 'no world war could have caused the same ravages to the ranks of the Russian High Command as did the activities of the GPU in 1937 and 1938'. Ian lacked his habitual prescience only when suggesting that 'not too much weight should be attached to the possibility of a Russo-German alliance at the moment.'

Nearer the mark was Ian's prediction of the danger posed by Russia. The dark hand of the USSR became a central theme of his thrillers. 'The threat of a territorial world war should not blind us to the ideological struggle which will have to come one day. The possibility of her descending, carrion-like, on the stricken battlefield of Europe after the war, should not be left out of account. War begat Bolshevism, and war will be its spawning-ground.'

In May, Maud Russell had a drink with Ian 'in his big room' at 22b Ebury Street to hear his plans. 'I think he would like to do secret service work, or journalism or both. He wrote a report about Russia and another about Germany after he'd been there this spring to show to his friends. G[ilbert] read one of them and had the idea of introducing him to M[ilitary] I[intelligence], which he did.'

*

The timing was perfect. 'Suddenly, I heard this grinding of machinery in the background and funny little questions being asked, friends would tell me that so-and-so had been asking about me, where had I been, what did I know, and this was a quiet casing of me for a job in Naval Intelligence.'

Ian had put out feelers right at the moment when the new Director of Naval Intelligence was casting about for a personal assistant. Rear Admiral John Godfrey had taken over his department in February. He found to his alarm a solid two decades of neglect under predecessors including Admiral Sir Barry Domville, who was to be interned during the war for his pro-Hitler sympathies. 'One sat down with a clean sheet of paper and had to produce something out of nothing.'

From the outset, Godfrey had welcomed the guidance of Admiral Sir Reginald 'Blinker' Hall. At sixty-eight, the former Director of Naval Intelligence (DNI) from the First World War was still a revitalising force, known for 'blinking and churning his false teeth' while quoting Goethe: '*It is personality on which everything depends.*' Hall loaned Godfrey his flat at 36 Curzon Street and advised him as a priority to recruit a personal assistant with 'a corkscrew mind' in the mould of his wartime PA, Sir Claude Serocold, the stockbroker who had taken charge of the unorthodox duties that the First World War had produced. 'It had worked brilliantly, and I decided to do the same,' said Godfrey. 'My PA had to have contacts in the City, be a bit of a man of the world, get on with people and have imagination.'

To find a civilian capable of thinking and operating outside the naval box, Hall told Godfrey to consult Montagu Norman, governor of the Bank of England, who, like Robert Vansittart and Joseph Ball, kept his own mini-Intelligence service.

Admiral Godfrey had never met Norman when they spoke on the telephone. 'He said he would come round to see me. He did. The next morning. Called me "Sir". Said my time was much more valuable than his, which I thought was a pretty rum thing for a Governor of the Bank of England to say.'

This crucial meeting took place on Friday 12 May 1939. Norman wrote in his diary: '10.45 Adm Godfrey at Admiralty, succr to Sir R Hall: as to collecting "intelligence" now & in war. I will consult Serocold.'

Norman summoned Claude Serocold three days later, on Monday 15 May at 11 a.m. The main item on the agenda was Godfrey's requirement for a younger clone of Serocold – slim, well groomed, innovative. Serocold was to ask around.

Five days later, Norman invited Godfrey to his home in Kent and said that he was in a position to recommend someone. He gave Godfrey one name: a thirty-one-year-old stockbroker at Serocold's old firm. 'I think we've found the man you need. Young fellow called Fleming. Everyone speaks most highly of him.'

Apparently, Ian was the unanimous choice of the 'high City authorities' whose brains Norman and Serocold had picked, prominent among them Sir Edward Peacock of Baring Brothers and Olaf Hambro, chairman of Hambros Bank. It would have been a strange dereliction if Norman had not also spoken to Ian's present and former bosses: Bernard Rickatson-Hatt, who in 1941 became Norman's adviser on press relations; and also Lancy Hugh Smith, who had earlier employed Serocold. Both men regarded Ian in a fond light.

On 24 May, Godfrey invited Ian to lunch at the Carlton Grill near the Admiralty, together, Ian recalled, with 'a couple of other very quiet characters in plain clothes'. One was Lancy's white-bearded brother, Sir Aubrey Hugh Smith, who had been deputy DNI under Hall. The other was an Irish businessman doing Intelligence work for Godfrey in Copenhagen. Godfrey said: 'I didn't really tell Ian what was in store for him at this point. Wanted to have a good look at the fellow.'

Ian's lunch with Godfrey ranks alongside his dinner with John F. Kennedy twenty-one years later as a turning point. Whatever Ian suspected about his invitation, he was aware that he had to shine. And as Ann knew from watching him with Lord Kemsley, when Ian set out to shine 'he was really formidable'.

Godfrey later felt that he had been lucky to survive the lunch: 'no doubt he was wondering if I was worth "taking up". I and not he was being interviewed.'

Ian's host was a divisive figure. For all those who respected Rear Admiral John Godfrey, others never warmed to him, like his future chief of personnel in Delhi. 'The dome of a prelate, the eyes of a devil and the mouth of a petulant child.' With unwavering pale blue eyes, tall, his large head and broad shoulders tapering to 'the legs of a dancing master', Godfrey was known to be an advocate of the unvarnished truth and a perfectionist. He had the manner of a relentless advocate, wrote Robert Harling, who also worked for Godfrey, and he would assume 'the demonical relenting smile at the end of a grilling that could make a strong man wet in the palms'. When he sat down opposite Ian, he was looking for someone with people skills, widespread interests and contacts, who spoke languages, knew the City, had military training, knew how to take orders but also the initiative, would stand up to senior officers, who was bookish (Godfrey, who was widely read, singled out Ian's qualification as 'a collector of books on original thought'), with Intelligence experience and a journalistic background.

Near the top of Godfrey's shopping list was someone to establish good relations with the press. The Press Section was part of the Naval Intelligence Division. Already, Godfrey had 'cased' Ian's bridge partners Lords Kemsley and Rothermere, as well as Ian's previous employer, Sir Roderick Jones, who placed Reuters entirely at Godfrey's disposal. These were not the only journalistic references Godfrey relied on. Jones's general manager Christopher Chancellor had become Godfrey's best friend in Shanghai after the Japanese invasion of 1937. It was Godfrey who had made Chancellor's career 'by helping him get the news out before anyone else, through the Navy'. Ian is unlikely to have let slip an opportunity to tell Godfrey how close he had come to working for Chancellor.

Instead of sailing to China, Ian had gone into the City – another essential Godfrey requirement. A neglected dimension of Intelligence was the mobilisation of banks to shift large funds around the world to finance covert operations. Ian's banking connections in London and New York were an attractive asset.

Add to that a host of sentimental and nepotistic motives. Augustus John was a personal friend of Godfrey – he would sketch his portrait during the war, and Ian's too. By the time of their lunch, Godfrey had in addition sought the advice of Vansittart, as well as Vansittart's successor at the Foreign Office, Sir Alexander Cadogan, whose daughter was engaged to marry one of Ian's close friends, Gerry Coke; Ian was to be best man.

There were naval and Intelligence links, too. Ian's uncle Lord Wyfold, married to Dorothy Fleming, had a brother, Claude Hermon-Hodge, who was deputy DNI until 1938. By May 1939, Peter Fleming had begun working for Military Intelligence, in a role parallel to the position that Godfrey sought to fill in Naval Intelligence.

Perversely, Ian's brother may have been a clinching reason for the unusual kinship that Godfrey felt for Ian. He understood the hardship of being an overshadowed second son. 'Having had a very clever older brother,' Godfrey wrote of his brother Charlie, 'I know what the tyranny of clever men feels like – and dreaded it.' His knowledge of what Ian underwent cemented his sympathy for the playboy stockbroker. In his unpublished memoir, Godfrey wrote: 'I quickly made up my mind that here was the man for the job.'

To friends at the time like Cyril Connolly, Ian Fleming might have appeared as something out of P. G. Wodehouse, but to the Director of Naval Intelligence he was the one person who fitted the bill. 'With literally the manpower of Great Britain to choose from, I had to pick the sort of man who could give me the service I needed. I chose Ian Fleming and was never to be disappointed.'

Ian's mother had wanted him to pursue an obvious public profession as a soldier, diplomat, or banker. Yet it was his less obvious qualities that most commended her son to the man under whose command he would germinate. Ian's untidy, unsatisfactory career had been a preparation for this moment.

Ian was one of twenty civilians whom Godfrey asked to hold themselves in readiness for 'when the balloon went up'. Then he would be commissioned as a lieutenant in the Royal Naval Volunteer Reserve (Special Branch). Ian was still a stockbroker, but Godfrey suggested that he came in 'for three or four half days a week to familiarise himself with the section's work'. The two met socially. Godfrey's appointments' diary for 20 July, following a rained-off royal garden party at Buckingham Palace, records 'Dinner HRH Elizabeth, Ian Fleming, Betty Byrne.'

The spring in Ian's step was instantaneous. After beginning work at the Admiralty on 1 June, he was transformed, engaged, purposeful, and writing a breezy letter to Loelia in New York about the situation in London. 'I spend much time at the War Office on various nefarious pretexts, though remaining firmly convinced there will be no war. I'm tired of saying so . . . Winston refuses to join the Cabinet except on his own terms – the Cabinet is terrified at the idea of letting the fox in among the chickens.'

On the domestic front, Ian remained unfazed by the affair that two of his bridge partners, Ann O'Neill and Esmond Rothermere, were enjoying. 'Annie gets on and off Esmond as if he were a bus & Shane [Ann's husband] continues to explore the avenues of "complaisance" with unruffled mien.'

In his next letter, Ian stuck to his guns that there would be no conflict. 'The "Situation" is following the "Fleming Plan" and being all for the best. It has done everyone a lot of good and the only snag is that it has made a lot of people grow moustaches. Everyone is still playing Red Indians hard and will be very disappointed when it is all over. I get wiser every day, which is very nice but a bore for my friends. Now that is enough – except for one gastronomic hint for you. If you ever buy a ham, always stipulate the LEFT ham, because pigs scratch with the right leg only, so the right ham gets tough! Isn't that remarkable!' His last six years had thickened Ian's skin too.

Still not hearing from Loelia, Ian hoped that she was not enjoying herself too much: 'Were you honeymooning in the Grand Canyon?' Loelia was, in fact, being chased by a glamorous associate of President Roosevelt, Colonel William Donovan, a wealthy Republican lawyer whose path was soon to cross with Ian's. Quiet Irish voice, blue piercing eyes, and a limp like Ivar Bryce – from a German machine gun after he refused to leave his men – Donovan was a much-decorated war hero whose exploits in the New York's 69th Infantry Regiment were about to be screened in a forthcoming Warner Brothers movie as 'the epitome of our national courage'.

'Wild Bill' was also a ladies' man. He agreed with General Patton that what mattered most in life was 'sex and combat', in that order. Once his 'dallying raised eyebrows' had been lifted by the flirtatious Loelia, Donovan refused to leave her alone. 'He is going to lend me his car & his chauffeur to motor to San Francisco. Too good to be true!' His ardent pursuit over the next two years was characterised by Loelia's diary entry: 'Pouncing with Bill Donovan.'

Throughout that last lazy summer of peace, Ian continued to juggle Muriel, Maud and Loelia. Harling described the last as 'a sexy-seeming effervescent woman of the world, clearly accustomed to getting her own ways and ways', who would effusively encompass Ian in 'an affectionate half nelson'. Quite how long Ian stayed in her grip is hard to gauge.

Exactly as Maud had predicted, Ian blew hot and cold over Loelia, in one moment considering her a 'Mayfair jezebel', a tactless gossip and mischief-maker; in the next, a reserved, efficient, and loyal friend. He later lent her maiden name Loelia Ponsonby to Bond's faithful though unsuccumbing secretary.

World events faced competition from Loelia's daily rituals of fasting, shopping and sorting out her hair. ('April 13, 1944: Had my hair permed in preparation for the second front!'). Her one sustained occupation was needlepoint. She embroidered her own designs, 'mingling beads with silk and wools in the Early Victorian manner'. From now until his death, she stitched Ian into the pattern of her pampered, slightly disappointed existence. Her diaries in the months leading up to the war are studded with references to cosy dinners with Ian, their foursomes of bridge and golf with the likes of Esmond Rothermere and Shane and Ann O'Neill, their ongoing flirtations ('Pleasant interlude with Ian . . . wore my USA sharkskin').

In early July 1939, Loelia's celebrated American suitor materialised on her London doorstep. 'Bill Donovan suddenly appeared off the Clipper & I had a cocktail with him. V. gloomy about Germany and the war.'

Gloomier still was Maud, who had been caring for her German-Jewish aunts and cousins from Berlin. Their stories appalled her.

In the same month, the Duke of Marlborough, a client of Rowe & Pitman, held a coming-out dance for his seventeen-year-old daughter Sarah. 'Now listen,' Ian wrote to Loelia. 'Bert M[arlborough] wants me to "entertain" for the Blenheim Ball.' Ian's house party would be one of the last occasions when he was able to invite friends to Joyce Grove, which Uncle Phil had gifted as a convalescent home to Saint Mary's hospital, Paddington after Peter said he did not want it. 'Shane & Annie are staying with me . . . Will you come too? I shan't get any more girls, I expect. They are too much nuisance. The house is the ugliest in the Southern Counties, and the cooking is "plain Scotch", but there are certain rude comforts, and I would love you to come even though you are a Duchess, which will frighten the staff out of its wits.'

The dance at Blenheim was spectacular. The powerful coloured lights, trained on Vanburgh's baroque stone façade and the lake below, could be seen from miles around. Ambrose's Jazz Band played in a pavilion on the lawn as footmen in powdered wigs poured champagne for more than seven hundred guests. These included three future world leaders whose lives were to intersect with Ian's: Winston Churchill, who had been born at Blenheim, Anthony Eden, who was seen chatting and smoking with Churchill on the terrace, and the young John F. Kennedy ('never had a better time') who spent the night pursuing the Duchess of Kent.

As dawn lit the skies, the last dancers finished off the party with coffee and hotdogs. 'Chips' Channon was stumped for comparisons. 'I have seen much, travelled far and am accustomed to splendour, but there has never been anything like tonight . . . It was gay, young, brilliant and perfection . . . The whole world was there.' It was, he decided afterwards, 'the happiest night of my life'.

Maud Russell was another guest. Ian had come with his house party, but he abandoned Loelia and the O'Neills to be with her. 'Blenheim was a wonderful sight,' she wrote in her diary, 'a sort of landmark of beauty, something lovely to store in one's memory. The floodlit front was staggering . . . Ian saw me as I arrived and took me at once to see the garden. The cedars, obelisk and lake were floodlit and the scene was magically beautiful. I am glad I saw it with Ian, who is so starred with romance and whose romantic needs are so seldom satisfied.'

The Blenheim dance drew down the curtain on what Lisl Popper called Ian's 'social period'. At the end of July, Ian was summoned full-time to the Admiralty. Apart from 'a surprising dalliance' in early August with Loelia in Deauville, sailing there as guests of Lord Kemsley on his yacht *Princess*, he worked at his desk in Room 39.

From Loelia's diary. '22 Aug. A bombshell in the way of Germany announcing she has made a pact with Russia. I feel we may be at war any moment . . . finished another square.'

From Maud's diary. 'London, Friday August 25. I lunched with I[an] at the Carlton yesterday. It was crowded with uniforms, and I thought of the last war when, too, it was full and crowded with uniforms.'

'Mottisfont, Saturday, September 2. We do little else but listen in, go away and do some small job and then hurry back to the wireless.'

On that Saturday morning, Ian was at Percy Muir's new house in Takeley, near Bishop's Stortford, where, at the last moment, Ian had decided to move his book collection for safekeeping. He had earlier helped Muir pack the buckram boxes into tea chests. 'Ian had already been at his Admiralty post for some weeks, informing those who came to ask when the war would break out to look out of the window onto the Horse Guards Parade to see whether the balloon had gone up.' Tethered to the parade ground like a miniature Zeppelin at dock, the barrage balloon waited to be released, trailing long cables to obstruct German bombers.

Then in late August, Ian gave Muir the promised quiet tip that it would be advisable to move before the railways became congested. Ian and Muir drove to Takeley with the more precious items.

The removal of his book collection accounted for Ian's failure to turn up for Gerry Coke's wedding on 2 September at St James's, Piccadilly, where he was expected to be best man. 'The wedding was originally planned for 19 September,' says Coke's son David. 'However, my mother's father, Sir Alec Cadogan, knew that war was coming, so advised them to marry quickly. They had apparently got to the church and found that Ian Fleming was absent, so they went out onto Piccadilly, and there was Gerald Palmer, an old friend, just ambling past, so they grabbed him.'

By the time Ian returned to the Admiralty, a great silver elephant of a barrage balloon was floating in the evening sky above Horse Guards Parade.

XIX
ROOM 39

*'And with one little gesture Vittorin wiped his life's slate clean of two
years that had cast him in the role of adventurer, murderer, hero,
coalheaver, gambler, pimp, and vagrant.'*
LEO PERUTZ, *Little Apple*

'All through his youth, he had been in disgrace for one thing or another,' said
Mary Pakenham, 'so walking down the street in the uniform of a naval commander must have been absolute bliss.'

Ian arrived at 6.30 a.m. He entered the smoke-grimed Admiralty building from a door at the start of the Mall, stepping into a small Georgian
hallway with a statue of Nelson in a niche and a one-armed doorman in a
frock coat who, though pleased to see him, was adamant about inspecting
his pass.

A long white corridor and a stone floor of coloured mosaic led to the
lobby outside Ian's office on the ground floor. Messengers, tea-ladies, and
chars with mops and pails huddled round the coal fire. 'Let old 'itler try and
drop a bomb on me,' threatened Mrs Smith. 'Let 'im try.' Mingled in with the
bravado was an undercurrent of apprehension. There was a joke that the tea
trolley which clanked its way round the third floor was the only serviceable
tank in the British Army.

Opposite, the black door with '39' painted in white opened into a noisy
room, hazy with tobacco smoke and bustling with men and women telephoning, arguing, writing, typing. By the end of 1942, there were twenty-four
people in this never-empty 'cave', as Admiral Godfrey called it. The discordant clatter earned Room 39 its nickname of 'the Zoo'. Sefton Delmer, brought
here by Ian that first autumn, likened the atmosphere to an Arab bank. Donald McLachlan was a bony, sandy-haired Scotsman who came to work with

Delmer in the Propaganda section as one of Ian's 'pupils': to McLachlan, the cream-painted office, with its angular mouldings on the ceiling, black marble coal fireplace and central table, more resembled a club smoking room or the newsroom of the *Sunday Telegraph* that he went on to edit. For Ian, the working conditions were familiar to those he had known at Reuters.

Ian felt 'a round peg in a round hole' from the moment he sat down at his desk in the left-hand corner, next to a tall oak-framed window that overlooked Horse Guards Parade and the back entrance to No. 10 Downing Street. Maud Russell dined with him two days after war was declared. 'I[an] was in a sub-lieutenant uniform and looked as if he'd always worn those clothes.' Three weeks on, Maud reported that 'he loves his NID better than anything he has ever done, I think, except skiing.'

John Godfrey slept on a camp bed in the adjoining smaller office in those early days. He complained to his wife: 'The Admiralty is a noisy place at night & I haven't mastered the technique of sleeping with the telephone bell ringing next door.' The noise in the day was unbearable. 'Everyone had a telephone of their own; some had two or three; they used them incessantly and relentlessly – almost savagely.' Godfrey wrote in his unpublished memoirs: 'It got so bad that I had a green baize door installed between Room 39 and my room.'

Ian sat on the opposite side, guarding it, in a state of alertness for 'the one, two, three or four strokes' of Godfrey's bell to summon him.

Ian's last duty in Room 39, following VJ Day, was to sign a pledge never to reveal what he had done there. All his wartime colleagues in Naval Intelligence took these ordinances seriously. William Plomer said: 'Even I, in my unimportant niche, was asked to sign a statement that I wouldn't later talk or write about NID, so I've kept my trap shut & shall keep it shut.'

Because, like Buchan and Somerset Maugham before him, Ian was never allowed to write the truth about his war work, facts about his life are hard to see clearly through the aura cast by the success of James Bond. Ian's six years in Naval Intelligence gave him the secret material that he drew on to write his novels. Yet a clear and reliable picture of his duties and the depth and range of his knowledge and responsibilities does exist, and has remained unacknowledged.

It was the custom for many years to deride Ian as a 'chocolate sailor', after a Hershey's advertisement in the late 1930s, suggesting he was little more than a desk-bound pen-pusher who had enjoyed, so contemporaries like Ian Gilmour believed, 'a competent but safe war in naval intelligence at the Admiralty', yet was too wedded to his comforts and smart uniform to risk going into action himself – with the result that 'all he commanded was in-trays, out-trays and ashtrays'. Given his track record of dabbling interestingly but without success in several different fields, such people wondered with something of a sneer whether he could have done anything really useful during the war.

A simultaneous idea has grown up that Ian Fleming boasted about his work. Quite the opposite is true. After dining with him early in the war, Ann O'Neill wrote in her diary how she had wanted to hear the result of 'a secret trip to Dover where he was doing a hush-hush job for the Admiralty. He was an oyster.' In the grim days following Dunkirk when he learned that his youngest brother Michael was missing, Maud Russell, who had never seen someone's face turn white before, watched Ian's 'lovely face' turn white when a drunken man started talking stupidly at a nearby table. 'I[an] got up quickly and stopped him.' His stepdaughter Fionn never once heard Ian lowering his guard to talk about what he had done. 'I can't imagine him breaking his silence to impress.'

If there was one rule Ian absorbed and that suited his character, it was the imperative for sealed lips and leaving behind no traces. In a booklet that Ian prepared in August 1944 for his force of intelligence-gathering commandos, he emphasised that 'great care must therefore be taken to burn all waste paper, documents and carbons relative to such a force when no longer required.'

One indiscretion about Enigma could result in years of work being thrown away – 'it would have taken only a very small change to the machine to make the ciphers unreadable throughout the war, with the loss of all the Ultra intelligence,' says Michael Smith, an authority on Bletchley Park – while details about a successful operation could jeopardise its future reuse against a fresh enemy. In his recommendation to William Donovan for an American Intelligence agency loosely based on the Admiralty model, Ian strongly advised Donovan to 'make an example of someone at an early date for indiscretion, and continue to act ruthlessly where lack of security is concerned.' Ian had his own example.

In July 1941, Paul Lewis Claire, a French naval officer working for the British but suspected of passing secrets about SIS in Spain to Vichy, was drugged in the British embassy in Madrid and transported by car to Gibraltar. After he revived from the morphine and began shouting for help, he was hit on the head with a revolver and subsequently died. SIS sought Ian's help in countering German and Vichy claims that Claire had been kidnapped. Ian informed the Red Cross that Claire was 'missing, believed drowned' on SS *Empire Hurst*, which had been sunk by enemy aircraft three weeks later. There is no record of Ian speaking about this. Even to his close ally and friend Ernie Cuneo, 'Fleming never uttered a word on his operational assignments.'

This ruthless concern for security continued after the war, not merely covering what Ian felt still unauthorised to divulge, but affecting those who had been his commanding officers. In 1947, Godfrey was invited to edit a secret history of NID, but he was neither permitted to take papers home nor work on them in the Admiralty when their custodian was out of the office. Meanwhile, 'C', the head of SIS, insisted that 'we should all remain as secret in peacetime about what we had been doing at Bletchley Park as we had in wartime.'

The clampdown became more stringent as the Cold War continued. Twenty years later, Peter Fleming was asked to write the official history of strategic deception, but the Cabinet Office refused him access even to his own reports. When, after appealing to friends in high places, he was permitted to look at files in the War Office, it was on condition 'you will not acknowledge in your book that access to the records has been permitted'.

While a great amount of material was saved, a lot was deliberately destroyed, even as the war progressed. In an operation that involved Ian, Churchill wrote to Roosevelt: 'I shall be grateful if you will handle this matter entirely to yourself and, if possible, burn the letter when you have read it. The whole subject is secret to a degree which affects the safety of both our countries. The fewest possible people should know.'

The wholesale destruction of records began in earnest when peace was in sight. On 3 May 1945, Maud Russell, whom Ian had employed in the Propaganda section, went to her room at the Admiralty. 'My work there is over, and I started tearing up papers.' She was back a week later. 'I went to the Admiralty and tore up more of my papers.'

The acrid smell of charred records floated everywhere that summer. 'They had these weeding parties at weekends,' says Richard Dearlove, a former head of MI6, 'and used working or former SIS staff, and literally destroyed tons and tons of paper.' Weeding of material is standard – to thin the vast volumes of material to a manageable volume – and not always sinister: it is estimated that barely one per cent of pre-1914 Admiralty records survive. At Bletchley Park, where she worked for four years and remembered Ian visiting, Admiral Burrough's daughter Pauline says everything no longer needed at the site and the outstations was destroyed, including the Polish Intelligence archives, which had come to Britain at the start of the war. 'We burned a lot,' she says. Ian's golfing friend Jack Beevor, a member of Royal St George's and head of SOE in Lisbon, recalled how, after SOE was formally liquidated in January 1946, 'the bulk of its records were then destroyed'. The same with William Stephenson's archives of the British Security Co-ordination in New York, which mapped the alliance between the British and the nascent American Intelligence agencies. Stephenson had 'everything burned'.

It was not only the Intelligence services that destroyed its paperwork. Just like the copies of Ian's poetry collection *The Black Daffodil*, the precious records of Ian's friends were fed to the flames. Rupert Hart-Davis built a pyre to which he consigned all but one letter of his correspondence with George Lyttelton*. Many of Ian Fleming's letters were burned after his death. His last secretary, Beryl Griffie-Williams, told John Pearson, 'I have spent a lot of time destroying a great deal of private correspondence which would cause individuals nothing but pain if it came to light.' Prominent among the incinerated bundles were Ian's letters to Selby Armitage from the 1920s and Peter Fleming's 'nitpicker letters', which he sent to Ian after reading every Bond manuscript.

Then those papers too damaged to decipher, like the archives of the London Cage, where German prisoners were interrogated by Ian's 'pupils' – 'contaminated by asbestos and destroyed by flood water'. Or simply lost, like Ian's letters to Ivar Bryce and from Peter Smithers; or Peter Fleming's Greek

* The author arrived the next day, having pleaded with RH-D to save one letter for the BBC to film.

action journal, which went down with the *Kalanthe* in April 1941, after Messerschmitts bombed his boat and before Peter's dramatic rescue by an SIS officer named Bond.

Loss of records can equally be exaggerated. A vast amount does survive, just not necessarily filed where it is supposed to be. And there are those tantalising glimpses of papers that may still be out there. Early in my research, I bought a second-hand copy of the SIS agent Conrad O'Brien-ffrench's memoirs. Out of it tumbled a handwritten letter from O'Brien-ffrench to one 'Lalla' dated 19 March 1980 and containing this riveting information: 'You know I have not touched the totality of my resources – I have 66 diaries, many of them extremely detailed & ample which yet have to be exploited.'

'In the absence of documents, the most romantic version of intelligence history is irresistible,' wrote Timothy Naftali in a study of William Stephenson. Extraordinary growths sprout from cracks in the story, and some stick like burrs in the public mind – for example, the exotic notion that Ian was responsible for luring Hitler's deputy Rudolf Hess to Britain in May 1941.*

What does survive of the documentary record is haphazard, random, and frequently given a spin it rarely deserves. Plus a document can be wrong or downright misleading. The final entry for Peter Fleming's Bletchley Park clearance card for ULTRA reads '1947, 29.4 A03/87 F. appointed Director, Joint Intelligence Bureau, Melbourne.' I knew that in 1950 Peter had been considered for Menzies's replacement as 'C', and I began to envisage a whole new unsuspected post-war life for Peter as he directed Australian intelligence operations from his Nettlebed estate, when I discovered that this was an error and referred to the Australian infantry officer Colonel A. P. Fleming. It underlined William Stephenson's belief that 'nothing deceives like a document'.

---

* In his 1997 book *Op. JB*, former British Intelligence agent Christopher Creighton argued that Fleming was personally involved in capturing Martin Bormann from Hitler's bunker in Berlin. Taken with the story, Peter Fleming's biographer Duff Hart-Davis agreed to ghost-write Creighton's account. 'I think (for me) the final straw came when Creighton [who also claimed to be the godson of Churchill's Intelligence expert, Desmond Morton] claimed that Fleming had brought Hitler, as well as Bormann, out of the bunker, and that on their way to the Weidendamm bridge Hitler's head had been blown off by an incoming shell.'

There are other considerations. Simply because Ian is not listed in the minutes of a high-level meeting does not mean he was not there in the room. Godfrey's 'super Attaché' in Spain, Alan Hillgarth, after meeting with Churchill and the Chiefs of Staff to tell them what he was doing in Madrid under Ian's instructions, was vastly relieved to find no record in the minutes had been made of his presence. President Roosevelt discouraged any records being kept of sensitive matters. So did Churchill. Regarding the raid on Dieppe in August 1942, which included the first outing by Ian's force of intelligence-gathering commandos, General Ismay wrote to Churchill: 'in the vital interests of secrecy, nothing was put on paper.' Peter Smithers said, 'as a matter of principle, I NEVER kept notes.'

These are merely some of the obstacles that make it impossible to render a complete account of Ian's war and life. After assembling all possible material from the available sources, Ian's first authorised biographer John Pearson was confronted by one further hurdle: the censorship imposed by Ian's widow. On 2 February 1966, Ann Fleming wrote to Clarissa Eden: 'I am pestered by the unsophisticated young man who is writing Ian's life, the MSS arrived with the influenza and produced unsuspected suicidal wishes, luckily followed by rage. I summoned him to the bedside and he appeared to accept alterations and eliminations without rancour; at the moment I cannot obliterate your visit to Jamaica which he had made much of, including "The Prime Minister and Ian Fleming were on Christian names terms." Oh the vulgarity.'

The hazards of writing about the years 1939 to 1945 throw up no more revelatory example than John Godfrey's own frustrated attempts to do so. Even as Pearson was busy researching his Fleming biography, Godfrey struggled to put his memoirs on paper. What added to the knottiness of his endeavour was that the person he had earlier approached to help him was none other than Ian Fleming. While recovering from a heart attack in 1961, Ian reported: 'Am receiving the most extraordinary selection of advices from various genii'. These included: 'Be more spiritual' (Noël Coward); 'Be sucked off gently every day' (Evelyn Waugh); 'Write the story of Admiral Godfrey' (Admiral Godfrey).

Reading Godfrey's seven volumes of unpublished memoirs, it soon becomes obvious why he sought his former PA's assistance. In the words of his eventual biographer, Godfrey seems 'to have got up each morning, oblivious of what he had written on the day before, and said to himself, "Now what shall I put down today?"' Godfrey's private papers are more illuminating. These not only track a fascinating behind-the-scenes campaign to thwart Pearson but, wrapped up in the argument advanced for not co-operating with him, they offer the first tangible evidence of the scope and significance of Ian's war work.

By January 1965, Godfrey was in a bind. On the one hand, he was peeved that others had published their accounts, like Duff Cooper, H. Montgomery Hyde, and Ewen Montagu. On the other hand, he was impatient to straighten his own record, after he was peremptorily removed as DNI in 1942 and, uniquely, not given an honour. Although sensible of Compton Mackenzie's prosecution in 1932 after the Scottish writer and Intelligence officer published *Aegean Memories*, Godfrey initially was prepared to 'evade or gatecrash the security barrier' and support Pearson in his project, largely at the behest of William Plomer, who reminded Godfrey: 'You are the only person who really knows about Ian during the war.' After first setting out to Pearson one or two conditions (e.g. not to contact 'Biffy' Dunderdale, SIS station head in Paris in 1940), Godfrey made a list of people for him to interview. These included Alan Hillgarth, Norman Denning, Donald McLachlan and Lisl Popper.

Yet shortly afterwards, Godfrey screeches into reverse gear. In a startling letter to McLachlan written on 30 March, he cautions him not to co-operate with Pearson after all. 'Ian would have wished (indeed insisted) that a veil should be drawn over these years.'

Suddenly in Godfrey's about-turn, Ian Fleming is glimpsed as a more considerable player, who knew everything, but was himself unknowable, even to men like Godfrey, who had sat beside him, and to Plomer, who went on to edit his books; but who was also a figure more complex, sophisticated and central to the action that was taking place – sometimes in operations which Fleming had instigated – than his fictional Agent 007 ever would be. This was what Pearson had started to suspect yet, maddeningly, could not prove. 'Ian was so much more exciting than Bond – a totally unique individual,' he wrote in a mollifying letter to Godfrey, 'and there seems to have been scarcely a thing he touched where his originality and wit didn't show.'

Privately, Godfrey agreed, but he still would not give Pearson the proof. Only behind the veil, to Norman Denning, his successor as DNI, did Godfrey acknowledge Ian's value. 'I made a point of keeping Ian in touch with *all* aspects of NID work. He was the only officer who had a finger in practically every pie. I shared *all* secrets with him so that if I got knocked out, someone else would, we hoped, be left to pick up the bits and achieve some sort of continuity.' In that 'practically all Ian's work was "on the edge"' and 'for the most part, highly secret and intimately linked with mine', giving details of it 'would be tantamount to revealing the inner workings of the NID'.

Downplaying all this, Godfrey wrote to Pearson: 'The best way to tackle the problem is to accept that Ian's 6 years war time work must remain a mystery, and build up your story round this central inaccessible citadel.' He stressed: 'The nearer you approach the citadel, the more inaccessible it will become – it is in fact surrounded by a security moat, and a maze and a fog.'

Still, Godfrey seemed aware of the impact his withholding co-operation would have, writing to another colleague: 'Poor Pearson is like a famished man gazing, his mouth watering, into the butcher's and confectionary shop windows and having to be content with a stale turnip (or swede) from the greengrocer.'

Inevitably, forced to make do with stale turnips and fog, accounts of Ian's Fleming's war have watered down his contribution. 'It has taken time to realise how central Ian Fleming is,' says the Intelligence historian Michael Smith.

Christopher Moran is a professor of US National Security who specialises in Fleming's Secret Service work. He says, 'It's impossible to cling to the orthodoxy that Ian Fleming was a nobody. He was unique, there is nobody to compare him with. He was invested in and aware of the whole cycle of intelligence, which is remarkable when you think of the compartmentalised world – "the need to know" – of intelligence. Fleming transcended that world. He was not a desk officer, he was *the* desk officer. He knew it all, as a spy chief should, operating as a proxy spy chief for three to four years. He was the glue that glued these bits and pieces.'

Any idea that Ian Fleming preferred to sit out the war at his desk does not represent the truth. He took part in operations in Paris and Bordeaux even as France was falling apart. He volunteered to crash-land a Heinkel bomber into the Channel. In another scheme, Ian proposed that he 'and an equally intrepid wireless operator' be dropped by submarine on the Frisian island of Borkum to monitor U-boat movements. 'He is beginning to want a more active life than he gets at DNI,' Maud Russell wrote in November 1941. 'He wanted to know what I thought about him resigning and going to King Alfred training ship and getting a MTB [motor torpedo boat].'

Godfrey vetoed all these plans. It would have meant breaking one of the basic rules: no one on the ULTRA list should risk falling into enemy hands. There was never any reluctance on Ian's part. 'Ian always wanted missions. But he was always too valuable to be spared.'

Peter Smithers had repeated experience of watching Ian champing to follow in Val and Peter Fleming's footsteps. 'This he could never do because he was the repository of so much exceedingly secret information. Some of it so secret that even the Director of Naval Intelligence himself would probably not have discussed it.'

Not James Bond, not the Joint Intelligence Committee Chair, not even Churchill's confidential adviser on Intelligence, Desmond Morton, were in the 'charmed circle' that had ULTRA clearance. Ian was initiated from the beginning. His name features as one of only twenty-four on a 'Most Secret' list dated 8 April 1940 of those 'having access to Huts 1 and 6 GCCS [Government Code and Cipher School] or to whom the source of the reports is known'. A memo to 'C' in February 1943 confirms there was little classified material Ian was not privy to. 'Any ordinary CX [MI6] report of especial Secrecy to be addressed "Commander Fleming – Personal."'

The fact that he was only a commander is misleading. Because of the nature of his relationship with Godfrey, said Smithers, 'Ian, in spite of his modest rank, was at the very centre of the British Intelligence machine.' He was involved across all three services at the highest level, and on a daily basis was the focus within NID and probably the naval staff as a whole for all policy issues touching on naval SIGINT [Signals Intelligence]. He operated as the DNI's confidential liaison with the cryptographers at Bletchley Park, but also with SIS and SOE, MI5, the Inter-Service Topographical Department in

Oxford (ISTD), the London Cage, the Radio Security and Auxiliary Units, the War Office, the Political Warfare Executive (PWE), the Ministry of Economic Warfare (MEW), the Joint Intelligence Committee (JIC), and the American Co-Ordination of Strategic Information (COI) and Organisation of Strategic Services (OSS), and was one of an exclusive handful who had knowledge of some of Britain and America's most closely guarded wartime secrets. He had remarkable hiring and firing powers. He represented the DNI at three important wartime summit conferences – Trident, Quadrant and Sextant, and as the war drew to a close, he chaired JIC meetings and was involved in drafting recommendations for the top-secret Bland Report on the future of British Intelligence. It was not merely Godfrey's opinion that Ian acted to all intents as DNI and after Godfrey's departure 'kept the torch burning'.

'If you thought he was sitting at a desk in the Admiralty – no,' says the Bletchley Park historian David Kenyon, in a room at Bletchley Park which the coder Mavis Batey claimed that Ian visited once a fortnight. 'And what he was doing touched on so much of the war.'

All this helps to explain Admiral Godfrey's famous yet fuzzy description of Ian as 'a war-*winner*' and why Godfrey wrote to Ann after Ian's death to say that 'the country and the Allies owe him one of those great debts that can never be repaid.'

XX
UNCLE JOHN

'A man who cannot tell a good story is a dull dog.'
ADMIRAL JOHN GODFREY

Four hours after Neville Chamberlain's broadcast on Sunday 3 September 1939, Admiral Godfrey scribbled a note to his wife. ' "Going to war" has been quite eclipsed by the announcement that Winston is coming here as First Lord . . . Just met the great man in the passage. The first person he asked for on arrival was the DNI!'

Upon reoccupying his old room on the first floor, Churchill released the accumulated energy of his years in the wilderness. Geoffrey Shakespeare, Churchill's 'indefatigable second in command', was to be his Parliamentary and Financial Secretary for the next six months, and it was to him he gave his first order on that Sunday evening – asking for a bottle of whisky. Shakespeare wrote: 'How firmly Churchill has his finger on the Admiralty's pulse.'

A successful journalist before he was a politician, Churchill regarded himself as the Empire's most effective publicist. He took an excessive interest in broadcasting the Royal Navy's triumphs and in having any setbacks explained to him personally. Dictated the last thing at night, a torrent of memoranda descended on the Admiralty, usually starting with the words 'Pray inform me' or 'Pray, what are we doing about the German ships interned in Vigo?' These memos added to the strain of Godfrey's first months. 'The wording was insistent, frequently harsh, and an answer was usually demanded by a certain time, say 5 p.m.'

The return of his father's 'dear friend' to the office upstairs was Ian's chance to prove his mettle. Godfrey put the former Reuters correspondent onto answering Churchill's 'Prayers'. 'It was now that I began to appreciate the qualities of my personal assistant,' Godfrey wrote. 'Usually by lunchtime he had got to the heart of the matter.' A draft produced on half a sheet of paper, because that was all Churchill was known to read, would be on God-frey's desk with the boldly scrawled initial 17F, or just F, written in simple and vigorous language – what McLachlan called 'news agency gusto'. Approved, and then typed out by Godfrey's secretary, it would be sent up to Churchill before he rose from his siesta.

A self-confessed hero-worshipper, Ian regarded the First Lord in the same glow as his father and elder brother. ' "*Pray*, could you find out . . ." is a Churchillianism much used by Ian,' remembered Clare Blanshard. Another habit he mimicked was wearing polka-dot bow-ties, which Ian tied 'with Churchillian looseness'. Like Bond's Scottish housekeeper, Ian affected to 'call no man "Sir" except . . . English Kings and Winston Churchill'. One of three surviving letters to 'Churchill the Immortal', as Ian called him, accom-panied a copy of *Live and Let Die* that he signed simply 'The Author'. 'I hope you will accept it and forgive my theft of a hundred words of your wonderful prose.' The passage lifted from *Thoughts and Adventures* hid in plain sight the kind of covert shenanigans that Ian was soon entrusted with overseeing. 'In the higher ranges of Secret Service work, the actual facts in many cases were in every respect equal to the most fantastic inventions of romance and melodrama. Tangle within tangle, plot and counter-plot, ruse and treachery, cross and double-cross, true agent, false agent, double agent, gold and steel, the bomb, the dagger and the firing party, were interwoven in many a tex-ture so intricate as to be incredible and yet true. The Chief and High Officers of the Secret Service revelled in these subterranean labyrinths, and pursued their task with cold and silent passion.'

Val Fleming and their journalistic background aside, Fleming and Churchill shared a schoolboy delight in gadgetry; also in advancing out-landish schemes to outfox the enemy, these inspired by favourite adventure stories. Churchill's instruction that 'all kinds of Munchausen tales can be spread about to confuse and baffle the truth' gave Ian a green light. Too often, Ian had had to put a bridle on what the SIS aerial photographer Sid-ney Cotton recognized as Ian's 'strange sort of imagination'. Ian was now goaded to give this imagination full rein, encouraged not only by the mad-cap example of his overlord upstairs but by Godfrey, who proposed a section in the Admiralty 'to which ideas might be submitted, even while immature, under absolute pledge that neither their immaturity nor their seeming departure from the officer's proper sphere would be held against him'. Godfrey's order to Sam Bassett, a Royal Marine colonel tasked with setting up a Topographical section, was music to Ian's otherwise unmusical ears: 'You've simply got to *act* big and *think* big!' Geoffrey Pyke's proposals to freeze clouds and put guns on them or build aircraft carriers from ice were aligned with Godfrey's method of thinking. Ian fitted into this sort of atmosphere perfectly. Years later, he would tell his wife's niece Sara: 'Don't be afraid to think.'

An early memorandum Ian prepared for Godfrey was the notorious 'Trout Memo' circulated to service Intelligence chiefs on 29 September 1939, containing suggestions for 'introducing ideas into the heads of the Germans'. Many of these ideas bore Ian's stamp. Ben Macintyre noted in his history of Operation MINCEMEAT how they ranged from the possible to the wacky and included 'dropping footballs painted with luminous paint to attract submarines; distributing messages cursing Hitler's Reich in bottles from a fictitious U-boat captain; a fake "treasure ship" packed with commandos; or sending out false information through bogus copies of *The Times* ("an unimpeachable and immaculate medium").'

Idea Number 28 was based on a 1937 novel in Ian's library, *The Milliner Hat Mystery*, written by an Old Etonian spy-catcher who had recently died. 'The following suggestion is used in a book by Basil Thomson: a corpse dressed as an airman, with despatches in his pockets, could be dropped on the coast, supposedly from a parachute that had failed. I understand there is no difficulty in obtaining corpses at the Naval Hospital, but, of course, it would have to be a fresh one.' The despatches could include 'bogus future convoy rendezvous'.

This idea formed the kernel for Operation MINCEMEAT, which Ewen Montagu and Alan Hillgarth helped to organise off the coast of Spain in April 1943, with the posthumous re-creation of a Welsh tramp Glyndwr Michael into Major William Martin of the Royal Marines, whose body was washed ashore near Cadiz with apparent top-level plans designed to disguise the Allies' invasion of Sicily.

Ian's success at drafting memos like this and in placating Churchill 'fully and convincingly and not in a way that would provoke a comeback' encouraged Godfrey to expand Ian's lines of duty and throw on him 'full power and responsibility'.

Generally understood as the model for Bond's boss 'M', Godfrey had the nickname of 'Uncle John' or 'UJ', which Peter Smithers reckoned 'somehow suited him exactly – a wicked but kindly uncle who regarded his "boys" with a personal and proprietary affection'. If it was Ian who indeed came up with 'Uncle John', then this disguised a relationship that in Ian's case verged more on the filial. According to another NID colleague, Godfrey looked at his talented PA 'almost as the son he never had'.

To the surprise of many, but not to Smithers who witnessed how well they operated together in Washington, Ian took Godfrey's multiplying demands in his hurdler's stride. 'Godfrey needed somebody who would supply those elements which he did not have. This accounts for their extraordinary partnership in which Ian became almost a part of Uncle John.' Under the DNI's tutelage, the warring characters who had been Ian Fleming coalesced into a substantial and coherent young man, who brought out the best in his boss, having learned after years of work how to handle his difficult mother.

Ian had the 'corkscrew mind' that Godfrey needed but did not possess, while Godfrey's forensic pragmatism ('the right place for intuition is the sullage bin') acted as a brake on Ian's crazier schemes. Described as having the impatience of a sports car driver in a traffic jam, Godfrey depended on Ian's 'benevolent presence' to smooth out the dents caused by his abrupt accelerations. 'He was quite a formidable character,' says his daughter Eleanor. 'He could have a real temper if he felt like it.'

A brilliant but choleric perfectionist, Godfrey behaved no less eruptively in the office, where his reputation for hurling ink bottles at those he considered impertinent oafs made him enemies, including Churchill, who eventually accepted his removal. In recalling Godfrey's upbraidings, his sleepier successor, Commodore Edmund Rushbrooke, admitted that nobody would have called Godfrey 'matey'. 'He was the world's prize shit, but a genius,' wrote Ewen Montagu, head of the Special Intelligence section NID 17M, whom Godfrey once reduced to tears. 'I had enormous admiration for him as an intelligence brain and organiser – the more sincere as I loathed him as a man.'

Ian, though, saw Godfrey's kinder, more humorous sides, being skilful at navigating his master's 'brilliant, unconventional and labyrinthine mind'. Kind but ruthless, open-minded but dogmatic, a superb technician but no salesman, least of all of himself . . . After discarding other descriptions, Ian decided that the DNI possessed 'the mind & character of a Bohemian mathematician'. In the same letter to Smithers, Ian described Godfrey in language identical to how Godfrey posthumously summarised Ian. 'He is a real war-winner, though many people don't realise it & are put off by his whimsy.'

After learning of Godfrey's attempts to prod Ian to write his life, it tickled Cyril Connolly to make their relationship more intimate still. In *Bond Strikes Camp*, a lampoon Connolly wrote a year before Ian died, 'M' sends for Bond and orders him to disguise himself as a woman to trap a visiting KGB general who 'likes drag'. The general turns out to be 'M' in disguise.

'I'm sorry, James. It was the only way I could get you. Don't you think I haven't fought against it.'

Connolly's widow Deirdre remembers Ann and Ian coming for lunch, and Cyril reading it aloud to the four of them. 'Cyril was terribly nervous in case Ian didn't like it. Ian loved it,' she says.

'All his life,' said Ann, 'Ian succeeded because elderly gentlemen fell in love with him.'

Once Admiral Godfrey placed his trust in his personal assistant, Ian had exceptional autonomy. 'It was really much more than the words P.A. imply,' said Godfrey. 'I told Ian everything.'

Godfrey installed a direct line from his flat in Curzon Street to Ian's desk, empowering him to speak to admirals and field marshals on his behalf. 'Admiral Godfrey feels very strongly about this,' Ian was overheard telling General Dallas Brooks, director of the Political Warfare Executive. With perfect composure, he addressed on even terms Admiral Pound, First Sea Lord; Lord Louis Mountbatten, Chief of Combined Operations; Stewart Menzies ('C'); Brigadier Colin Gubbins, head of SOE; and Bill Cavendish-Bentinck, the JIC Chair.

'They treated him as his own man,' Peter Smithers said, 'and, of course, he spoke with the authority of Uncle John, and his standing with Uncle John was such he was so much Uncle John's other half that he really was the Director of Naval Intelligence when he spoke.'

Ian's sway over his subordinates was 'something very special too,' said Sandy Glen, whose first impression on meeting Ian at the Admiralty was shared by others in Room 39. 'I use one word: "excitement". Ian gave us a zip to things, an enthusiasm.'

All this made for a very recognisable *esprit de corps*. 'If we wanted to make any move,' said Smithers, 'the central point at which we would make contact first would probably be Ian.' In an informal way, Ian would explain in 'a no-nonsense manner' what something was about. 'If you suggested something which he thought didn't make sense, you would know quickly. You would get "My dear old boy, for crying out loud what is all that?" In addition to this, we knew that if we got into trouble, Ian would go to bat for us back home. He was an extremely good defender of the interests of all his friends.'

Godfrey was determined to rebuild what was a very run-down, financially starved department, and gave Ian free rein to bring in more staff. Smithers, an Oxford First, was recruited on one of Ian's telephones (black, extension line 991; green; extension line 22). Someone in Room 39 asked if there might be an opening for a naval friend about to be discharged from Haslar hospital. Ian called the hospital. 'Hold Lieutenant Smithers. The Director of Naval Intelligence wants him immediately.' But for that call, Smithers would have joined a minesweeper that was subsequently sunk. Instead, he was dispatched to Paris 'as naval member of MI6' and then to Washington as Assistant Naval Attaché specifically charged with the exchange of intelligence. 'Such are the chances which alter the entire course of life.'

With such wide powers of patronage, Ian was able to employ one of his earliest literary heroes William Plomer, then working as chief literary adviser at Jonathan Cape, to edit the secret *Weekly Intelligence Report*; Robert Harling, a skilled young typographer Ian had met before the war, to compile a registry of experts, in response to Godfrey's belief that 'somewhere in or near London can be found *the* great authority on *any* subject, the problem is to find him'; David Herbert, his Eton and army crammer contemporary, whom Ian sent off in a boat to Brittany to mix with the French fishing fleet and ferry back information and spies; Ivar Bryce, whom Ian installed in William Stephenson's office in New York, where 'Burglar' drew on family connections in Brazil and Peru to create fake maps of Nazi intentions to take control of South America; and Muriel Wright, who, bored with modelling dresses, was taken on as an Admiralty despatch rider and swiftly became the department's 'enchanting and beloved mascot'.

Evelyn Waugh had no such luck. 'Went to Admiralty where everything was shipshape,' he wrote in his diary on 17 October 1939. 'Saw Fleming, who told me there was no immediate chance of employment, but that my name was "on his list".' Ian arranged for Percy Muir to be interviewed by MI6, although nothing came of it.

David Astor's experience was the least happy; hired by Ian to work in the Propaganda section, Ian's future rival on *The Observer* was let go after two days, a brush-off Astor never forgot.

One result of Ian's hiring and firing was 'a new kind of Naval Intelligence', as Smithers called it. Following the lead he had given Harling, Ian mastered the art of finding out who the expert was in their field and going to them. He then proved adept at placing his own nominees in jobs at the centre. This meant, said Smithers, that everywhere you looked, from Washington to Spain to Stockholm, 'the situation was covered by somebody who had been installed by Ian, and who worked through Ian, corresponded with Ian, who generated ideas with Ian'. Ian later replicated such a network on the *Sunday Times* with his foreign correspondents.

Perversely, Ian's existing service profile has failed to reflect his influence. Yet he *was* influential, says Andrew Boyd, author of a definitive history of Naval Intelligence in the twentieth century. 'He was Godfrey's right-hand man, in the background, but a constant, fertile source of ideas, a supreme fixer, a brilliant draftsman and a master bureaucrat, very quick to work out how the system worked and place himself at the centre of, effectively, a spider's web. He knew instinctively which buzzers to press, who had power, who didn't, how they could be manipulated, and then how to put the right things on paper, taking complex ideas and writing them down succinctly.'

'Fleming's work and mine were inextricably intermingled.' Ian not only represented Godfrey at interdepartmental meetings and conferences and on the JIC. He drafted Godfrey's memos. He decided what papers the DNI should read; 'a paper specially addressed to the Director would be intercepted by him', observed Donald McLachlan, 'and come back with the remark "Absolutely of no consequence 17F".' Above all, he gave Godfrey the reassurance to know that there was someone guarding his flanks who spoke with his mind. 'Oddly enough both Fleming and I have come to the same conclusions without collaborating,' Godfrey wrote in July 1942, arguing for someone's promotion.

When Maud Russell came to work for NID in 1943, she had little conception of Ian's role. 'He has various jobs and is an important person.' It took her a year to realise how important. 'Among other things he is the head of the Naval Secret Service – agents, their names, jobs etc.' Peter Smithers worked for Ian for five years, and never doubted the weight of his position. 'It was of very great importance.'

Most compellingly, Ian's centrality was recognised by his boss. 'I once said that Ian should have been DNI and I his naval adviser.' Nor was Admiral Godfrey the only Intelligence chief who believed this. 'Really, it was Ian who was the DNI through most of the war,' said William Stephenson, Britain's spymaster in New York. 'In all those conferences I saw them at in America, it was Ian who could have been the Admiral. It was evident that he was more the DNI than DNI himself.'

Godfrey was not the sole model for 'M'.

'The expression "phoney" war had no meaning in the Admiralty,' Godfrey wrote. On 3 September 1939, Ian's first evening in Room 39, a U-boat torpedoed the British passenger liner SS *Athenia* off the Irish coast. He was continuously engaged from then on, 'so absorbed in and fascinated by his work,' Maud Russell wrote in her diary, 'that he can barely detach his mind from it.'

One of Ian's earliest initiatives in 'the string-and-stickfast days' that followed was to commission Sidney Cotton to take aerial photographs. Cotton – 'this remarkable man', as Ian called him – was an Australian colour photographer who had been picked up by Godfrey to make illicit flights under SIS cover to photograph Ireland's southern coastline in case the Germans had U-boat bases there (they did not). As Aerial Photographic Reconnaissance developed, Ian was deeply involved with policy issues and establishing the structures to make it work for the Royal Navy. Although his early freelance moves caused friction with the Air Ministry, Ian persuaded Cotton in his specially adapted duck-egg green Spitfire to photograph unusual shipping at Emden and Wilhelmshaven, which revealed the vessels to be invasion barges.

On 27 September 1939, concerned to discover how the German navy avoided Allied minefields in the Skagerrak, Ian took two captured German U-boat officers to lunch at Scott's. Ian told Maud Russell what happened. 'There was only one exit, and that was watched. They could not be made to give anything away. Food and wine made no difference.' Despite his fluent German, Ian failed to direct conversation away from pre-war Munich.

The immediate outcome was a slap on the wrist from Godfrey after a suspicious waiter reported Ian to Scotland Yard. Still, Godfrey then authorised a trial on a NID volunteer with the truth drug Evipan which, combined with hypnosis, 'might have considerable military value' in making a prisoner unable to resist interrogation. Godfrey accepted the compelling arguments against proceeding but he made intelligence-gathering from POWs an early priority.

In search of prisoners to interrogate, Churchill, after becoming Prime Minister, directed the Admiralty to target the French tunny fishing fleet that David Herbert was monitoring under Ian's supervision. Ian described this fleet off Ushant as 'the most important link for "C"'s activities as they are given permits for several days absence from port which gives this opportunity of coming to England.'

One high point was a collision at sea.

In a memo he drafted for Godfrey, Ian explained how 'rather a sticky and urgent problem' arose when shortly after midnight on 23 September 1940, 'in order to obtain prisoners as instructed by the Admiralty at the request of the Prime Minister', a Polish destroyer hailed the sixty-ton vessel *Erquy* and, after taking the seven fisherman on board, rammed and sank their ship. The crew had since been interrogated at Cannon Row Police station, 'and on 25th further in presence of MI6', but meanwhile Ian was requesting £550 (approximately £42,000 today) from Treasury funds 'to compensate these men for the loss of their boat, and send them back as soon as possible' before their absence aroused suspicion.

An indication of how deeply Ian penetrated the inner sanctum is his presence at a '*MOST SECRET*' meeting with 'C' on 31 December 1941 'to consider General de Gaulle's demands for closer collaboration with the SIS and SOE as regards activities in France'.

The meeting was held in the light of reports that Germans were trying to plant agents into Britain disguised as Free French volunteers 'who would offer to return to France and act as bogus agents'. Among the 14 present were Menzies ('C'), Gubbins and Hambro (both future heads of the SOE), Cavendish-Bentinck (chair of the JIC), and Morton ('Prime Minister's Office').

'Commander I. Fleming R.N.V.R.' heads the list.

The demands on Room 39 were never more intense than during Ian's first weeks, when Churchill was still First Lord. 'I am told that Winston is already driving the Admiralty to distraction by his interference and energy,' wrote 'Chips' Channon on 14 September 1939. Godfrey groused that Churchill 'needed a diet consisting of the carcases of abortive and wild cat operations'. Among a stream of 'unsound enterprises' which Ian had to field was the stillborn Operation CATHERINE, which envisaged sending superannuated R-class battleships fortified with extra armour into the Baltic.

Another pet project was to stop the export of Swedish ore from the Norwegian port of Narvik. Churchill also pressed NID, part of whose brief then was sabotage, to explore methods of preventing the Axis powers from exploiting the Danube.

In a chance meeting at the Admiralty, Ian talked with Merlin Minshall, who had spent a year sailing his fifteen-ton yacht *Hawke* down the Danube in the company of a woman who turned out to be a German Intelligence agent. Minshall told Ian of his plan to block the river at 'the one and only spot' which could stop all navigation between the Romanian oil wells and Germany. In January 1940, Ian sent Minshall on an abortive mission to Bucharest with a suitcase containing five pounds of plastic high explosive in small pieces packed in Mackintosh's toffee wrappers. Minshall wrote: 'I was, though I didn't know it at the time, sowing the seeds of the future James Bond.'

Minshall's memoir *Guilt-Edged* joins a crowded field of books that tend to focus on exciting operations that Ian was involved with and yet, in most cases, were never put into action. Although many of Ian's ideas were brilliant, others, said Norman Denning, then running the Operational Intelligence Centre in the Citadel, were 'just plain crazy'. In giving too much prominence to the ideas at the madder end of the spectrum, says Andrew Boyd, these books neglect areas of Ian's work that were more practical 'and ignore the rather grinding reality of keeping this thing on the road day by day. The Bond image has much to answer for here since it is inevitably projected back to imply that Fleming spent his entire time planning and even participating in operations more characteristic of SOE than NID. They fail to convey NID's role and responsibilities and how it linked with the wider intelligence community, the last being an area where Fleming was hugely important.'

A lesser-known deception plan that was more strategically effective drew on Ian's City experience and contacts. This occupied Ian from his third week in Room 39 until late in 1941. It also introduced him to the most vicious character he had come across since Stalin's state prosecutor in Moscow.

XXI
'THE MOST UNSCRUPULOUS
MAN IN SPAIN'

'I don't keep books.'
JUAN MARCH

On 23 September 1939, an ageing, bald Spaniard with a birdlike, extremely pale face, smoking a cigar and squinting through thick glasses, came in with an interpreter to see Admiral Godfrey. The son of a Mallorcan pig farmer, and in one legend illiterate till he was forty, he spoke no English. He walked towards Ian's desk with bent crooked steps that he attributed to his seventeen months in a Madrid prison, charged with the bribery of government officials. Juan March was the richest and allegedly 'the most unscrupulous man in Spain'. The reason for his unusually cordial reception was that he had been sent here by the author of that epithet: Godfrey's trusted new Naval Attaché in Madrid, Alan Hillgarth.

Godfrey had known Hillgarth since 1938 when Hillgarth, then vice consul in Mallorca's capital, Palma, had secured a guarantee of safe passage for Godfrey's battlecruiser *Repulse* to evacuate five hundred British subjects trapped by the Spanish Civil War.

'Hillgarth is pretty good.' The First Lord was another figure to put his faith in the 'strange and brilliant' Naval Attaché, a veteran of the Dardanelles who had prospected for gold in Bolivia before he settled in Mallorca. Churchill had met Hillgarth in Palma as well. What was to be the start of their long and confidential friendship seeded when Hillgarth put the Churchills up for two nights after Clementine complained about the overpowering drains in their hotel.

There were many in Spain for whom Juan March exuded the same stench, including the deputy who shouted from the bench in the Spanish

Congress: 'Mr March should have been hanged by the Republic in the Puerta del Sol – and I would have pulled on his feet!'

Inevitably in Mallorca, Hillgarth had crossed paths with March, then a notorious tobacco smuggler. March had since become better known for bankrolling General Francisco Franco's rise to power. By his own calculation, the irresistibly wicked March was the world's seventh richest man. In one week alone in September 1936, he deposited for his own benefit 121 metric tons of gold in the Bank of Italy, greater than most national gold reserves. With a separate loan of £942,000 (approximately £73 million today) from Kleinwort's Bank in London, he had paid for a British de Havilland Dragon Rapide, chartered in Croydon, to pilot Franco from the Canary Islands to Spanish Morocco to ignite the counter-revolution.

'Franco can refuse me nothing,' March boasted to Hillgarth. March's claim that Franco knew and approved his audacious idea compelled Hillgarth to study it with special attention.

Days after Hitler's invasion of Poland, and the Royal Navy's retaliatory blockade of European ports, March had approached Hillgarth with an extraordinarily interesting proposition. Hillgarth, in his report to London, regarded March's plan as 'feasible and very useful to Great Britain', with certain reservations. 'It would be a mistake to trust him an inch. But as long as that is kept in mind, it need not in itself prevent the scheme going through.' It was to discuss this plan that March had come to see Godfrey.

Short and physically unprepossessing, March was not, on Ian's initial inspection, an obvious or appetising ally. One woman who sat next to him at dinner said he had no conversation at all, and none was expected. The *New Yorker* writer John Brooks investigated March over a period and came gradually to think of him 'as some strange mutant – a disembodied mind detached from all emotions but acquisitiveness'. His greatest talent was the ability 'to exploit conflicting forces to his personal double advantage'. In June 1916, Basil Thomson, the wartime head of Special Branch and author of *The Milliner's Hat Mystery*, wrote in his diary: 'The Germans offered him money, and he replied that they might as well offer him an elephant.' With his 'prodigious political adaptability', March had used his extensive network in the Mediterranean to supply the British with information on German shipping movements; at the same time, he fed the Germans with information on

Allied ships loaded with gasoline. The fifty-eight-year-old March continued to employ the same methods of corruption, bribery and coercion. He was 'a scoundrel of the deepest dye', according to an intelligence profile that Ian had read.

For the next two years, Ian studied him with fascination. 'There's absolutely no doubt that Juan March indeed impressed himself on Ian Fleming very strongly,' says the historian David Stafford.

Already, March's scheme had attracted the close interest of Churchill. 'I should like to see Señor Marche [sic] this afternoon at five o'clock if possible.' Churchill was exceptionally anxious for Godfrey to listen to what March had to say. 'This man is most important and may be able to render the greatest service in bringing about friendly relations with Spain.' Churchill's priority was to keep the Axis-leaning Franco out of the war – and the Germans out of the Iberian Peninsula. Godfrey's friend Admiral Tom Phillips, Vice Chief of the Naval Staff, flagged up the danger. 'If the Atlantic ports of the Peninsula and with them the coast of northwest Africa go over to the enemy, I do not know how we shall carry on.'

Hence Churchill's receptiveness to March's proposal.

Far from being put off by Juan March's brigandish reputation, Churchill seems to have been beguiled by it. Like Roosevelt, he was attracted by mavericks and people who could get things done and cut through bureaucracy. Taking his cue from Hillgarth, Churchill decided that March did indeed speak in the capacity of Franco's representative. 'On the whole, I am inclined to favour the transaction proposed.'

March's proposal, outlined to Godfrey by his interpreter while March chewed on his uncommonly thick cigar, was this: fifty-nine German ships lay tied up in Spanish ports because of the British blockade. If Britain advanced the funds, March would buy these ships, which the British could then use.

Further, March offered to place his impressive Intelligence network at Godfrey's disposal. Since he claimed to control oil supplies in Morocco, the Canary Islands and most of Spain, he would do all in his power to help Godfrey prevent German U-boats from taking aboard fuel and food in Spanish waters. 'The advantages of his organisation', Hillgarth wrote, 'are that it is entirely Spanish, that it is entirely in his hands, that I deal with no one but himself, that it costs us nothing, that he is perfectly ruthless when necessary. He has already had two German agents shot in Ibiza.'

Those murders were not a one-off. In 1916, March was thought to have paid for the assassination of Rafael Garau, his business partner's son, on the camino del Grao in Valencia. 'I have been killed by bad friends!' Garau gasped before he died. Twelve years later, in an episode that anticipated the fate of Auric Goldfinger, the Belgian financier Alfred Loewenstein, at one point the controlling shareholder of March's principal company Barcelona Traction, died in what *The Times* called 'one of the strangest fatalities in the history of commercial aviation', when, crossing from Croydon to Brussels in his private plane, Loewenstein apparently fell out, 'unnoticed by his pilot, his mechanic, two stenographers, and a valet, all of whom were aboard'.

March's proposal foreshadowed Britain's Lend-Lease Agreement with America the following year. He would pay the Germans for their fifty-nine ships by instalments in pesetas deposited in Spanish banks, earning five per cent interest till the end of the war.

'An account of his remarkable and very secret interview was given limited circulation in the Admiralty and Foreign Office', wrote Godfrey's biographer Patrick Beesly, a colleague of Ian in Naval Intelligence. A very strong presumption follows that this account was penned by Ian, who was instructed to work with his City and SIS contacts to buy up a Spanish shipping company and advance March the funds. Yet even as Ian attempted 'to get briefs from the City', March appears to have dragged his heels, reverting to type as the 'traitorous and miserly Majorcan', as one of March's innumerable critics described him.

In February, a frustrated Ian wrote to Godfrey: 'I think we should quickly get the matter out of the docket stage and see if it will fly. Otherwise let it die. It is already half throttled with paper.'

It was then that Ian discovered the existence of March's eye-watering debt to a British bank. The banker who alerted him, to whom March owed the money, was one of the financiers who had recommended Ian's name to Godfrey five months earlier: Sir Edward Peacock, managing director of Baring Brothers. Juan March's £942,000 loan from Kleinwort's, used to finance Franco's ascent, had been called in when war was declared, compelling March to seek a similar loan from Peacock.

All at once, Ian had leverage. 'A vague hint that it might be called again,' Ian wrote, 'would certainly bring M to his senses and get him to come back to brass tacks ... we must bind him body and (if any) soul to the Allied Cause before we can go ahead with any of our main plans.'

Ian's scheme worked. Secret funds were released to buy up the German ships through a shipping company purchased by the British government; and although most vessels remained in German hands and the British never got to use any of them, March received a gold deposit in the Bank of England in the name of a Swiss company he owned for 236,686.39 ounces (worth approximately £305 million today).

Was all the time and money spent on March worthwhile, or did he take everyone for a ride? These were questions Ian never fully resolved. And this was merely the first of his dealings with this 'hideous old chap' as one British businessman described him.

Churchill strained to keep neutral Spain and Portugal out of the conflict in Europe, even as he plotted to pull neutral America into it. At his corner desk in Room 39, Ian operated as one of his shadow warriors in both arenas.

One person Ian relied on to keep him informed was David Eccles, who worked as economic adviser at the Lisbon embassy. A self-confident family friend known as 'Smartyboots', Eccles collaborated with Ian to achieve Churchill's agenda in Lisbon and Washington.

In June 1940, Eccles's boss in London, Hugh Dalton, Minister of Economic Warfare, was given the task of organising all forms of resistance to the enemy on the Continent and 'setting Europe ablaze'. This became the Special Operations Executive (SOE). In Lisbon, Eccles found himself close to the flames. 'Dalton wanted to believe that Franco was in Hitler's pocket and that these two villains would, sooner rather than later, combine to attack Gibraltar and close the entrance to the Mediterranean.'

To prevent that calamity, Churchill's personal security adviser, Desmond Morton, to whom Ian had been sending daily intercepted shipping signals, urged SOE to adopt 'bribery, corruption, murder'. Ian's work exposed him to these activities, bribery specifically. 'We couldn't fight for Gibraltar,' said Eccles. 'So we bribed.'

Once again, the middleman for this clandestine operation – and 'never one to miss a chance to fish in troubled waters' – was Juan March.

His newest proposal was delivered in person by Alan Hillgarth to Churchill in June 1940, one month after he became Prime Minister. The fall of France had increased the stakes in Spain considerably. The situation as Eccles saw it from Lisbon was perilous. 'The Quislings could so easily turn Franco out and set up a puppet Axis government.'

Magnificently simple, March's plan was for the British to pay a handful of prominent Spanish officers in General Franco's government to restrain Franco from siding with the Axis powers. The sum recommended was $10 million (approximately £300 million today). March would distribute it through Spanish banks and businesses, receiving a commission. Churchill agreed on the spot.

As before, Godfrey deputed Ian to liaise with March and Hillgarth. Ian's job was to work his banking connections in London and New York and to unlock and shift these massive funds into Spain through Lisbon, which became March's wartime base. 'In general, much of this was kept verbal,' says David Stafford, who has done most to bring this story to light. 'Fleming often writes to Godfrey in elliptical terms saying things like, "I shall explain to you verbally." But there's enough written down to get a good sense of what's happening.'

Released by the Treasury and deposited with the Swiss Bank Corporation in New York, the money was siphoned into the pockets of the 'right people', as Hillgarth called them, including General Antonio Aranda Mata and General Luis Orgaz Yoldi. By the spring of 1941, the scheme was thought to be working well, and a further $3 million was injected. Dalton wrote in his diary, 'the Cavalry of St George have been charging,' referring to the gold sovereigns, stamped with St George slaying the dragon, that were being used to undermine the pro-Nazi ambitions of the Falange government, evidence of which seemed to come when Spain's fanatic Foreign Minister, Ramón Serrano Suñer, fell out with Franco over Spain's policy towards Germany.

Ian's fingerprints are all over these transactions – although 'it would never be found on the books of the Treasury,' said Peter Smithers. 'He operated this system, which was purely informal, with the most conspicuous success.'

On Ian's behalf, another NID officer, Paul Furse, shuttled between Lisbon and Madrid and was able to verify how successful. 'It was fantastic how quickly the situation changed for the better, and how well our plans worked out. So much so that Spain refused to help Germany and would have resisted by force if the Germans had tried to enter Spain in force.'

Godfrey afterwards confirmed that he knew personally from Juan March 'that the Germans would *not* invade Spain. We took precautions nonetheless. If attacked, Spain would fight. Portugal would have let us into Lisbon.' These precautions were enshrined in Operations GOLDENEYE and TRACER, which Ian would put into motion in late 1940. As to whether the results of those better-known operations remotely matched the time, effort and money expended, Andrew Boyd says, 'I am very doubtful.' Both operations would later be shelved 'with the tide of war now running in our favour', but that was three years off.

XXII
'COMPLETELY OUTWITTED'

'I gathered he sometimes goes on dangerous jobs
though he gave no details.'
MAUD RUSSELL

The Phoney War ended in the early hours of 9 April 1940. News that the German navy had invaded Norway revealed to a stunned Admiral Godfrey the extent of his department's twenty years of shocking neglect.

Gladwyn Jebb was holidaying at Godfrey's house near Sevenoaks. 'It was totally unexpected by the Admiralty and everybody else,' wrote Jebb, who took executive charge of SOE twelve weeks later. 'Where was the Navy?'

How the Germans had taken Norway from under the teeth of the British Navy was the mystery. 'The Navy is here!' had been Churchill's war cry. In Lisbon, David Eccles lamented to his wife, 'Norway was like the first stroke on a funeral bell.'

Anchored to his desk in Room 39, where he had had to deal with everything from the *Altmark* affair, when Royal Navy destroyers liberated 299 British prisoners from a German tanker off the Norwegian coast, to cumulative warning pointers on German intentions, to bitter disputes about overall U-boat numbers, Ian watched Peter volunteer for action with a mingling of pride and envy. The opportunity to shine like their father had arrived. From the Norway invasion onwards, Ian possessed an abnormal awareness of what Peter was up to.

Three days later, Peter walked out 'imperturbably' from his office at Military Intelligence Research. Under the codename of 'Flea', Peter had orders to lead a small party of six 'to conceal and facilitate the landing of an Allied Expeditionary Force'. Together with 'Louse', his fellow officer Martin Lindsay, the man who *would* one day marry Loelia Westminster, they touched down by flying boat in the Namsen Fjord near the small village of Bangsund at 3.30 p.m. on 14 April.

In a secret report for the War Office, Peter recorded his belief that 'we were the first British troops to land in Norway' – which would have made him the first British officer to set foot on Continental soil since the war began.

'We have been completely outwitted,' Churchill admitted in private after the German invasion of Norway. With his zest for taking charge, the First Lord became a source of muddle and chaos.

'Admiralty in a state of jitters from top to bottom,' Sir John Reith, the Minister for Information, wrote in his diary on 14 April. On the same day, Ian was spreading stories to baffle the truth, speaking on the BBC's German Service Programme about the Royal Navy's successful counterattack off the Narvik coast. Sefton Delmer recalled how 'introduced with a flourish of trumpets, Ian was responsible for helping to hot up the propaganda.'

'I listened to Ian broadcasting to the Germans in German,' Maud Russell wrote in her diary. 'He wasn't bad. His voice is higher than I thought. I had never noticed the pitch of Ian's voice before. He says the stuff given to him to broadcast is dreadful, dull stuff, and he tries to improve it.'

Ian had heard no recent news of Peter when, on 26 April, he received a shattering rumour out of Sweden. Beneath a picture of his brother captioned 'Peter Fleming reported slain', a Stockholm newspaper quoted Norwegian refugees as having said that 'the brilliant young journalist and explorer had been killed in an air raid in Norway.' The report was picked up by Lord Kemsley's *Daily Sketch*, which headlined the story 'Author killed in Norway'.

Their mother afterwards wrote to Geoffrey Dawson at *The Times* that Ian 'had a ghastly time till he found it was not true'. Two days later, Dawson was telephoned with 'the joyful certainty that Peter was not only alive, but actually at Nettlebed'.

On the morning his death was announced, Peter flew back to Scotland under instructions from his commanding officer, Major General Adrian Carton de Wiart, to ascertain from the War Office what was happening. Atrocious weather meant that he arrived twenty-four hours late in Inverness, receiving 'many congratulations at the Station Hotel as I had been reported killed the night before'. Peter had missed the night train, but his secret mission was of such state importance that with Bond-like panache he pulled strings to order 'a special train' with an enormous railway engine and a special sleeping car 'panelled with exotic timbers from different parts of the Empire'.

After seeing Churchill ('in silk combinations & cigar') and then Ian at the Admiralty on 28 April, and rushing on to Nettlebed to stay the night with Celia at Merrimoles, Peter flew back to Namsos for the wretched last phase of 'the fiasco of Norway', which ended after sixteen days with the evacuation of the Allied Expeditionary Force. Peter carried a brown paper parcel full of time fuses to blow up bridges and petrol dumps. Whatever guerrilla activities he and Martin Lindsay got up to during these humiliating last hours, 'Flea' and 'Louse' formed the template for Colonel Gubbins's 'Independent Companies', which were left behind to cause havoc and out of which there developed that summer, under Gladwyn Jebb's auspices, the fighting force known as the Commandos.

Immediately on his return to London, Peter briefed Geoffrey Dawson on the campaign's shortcomings in advance of a procedural motion on the Whitsun adjournment, which the opposition would use to move a no-confidence vote in the government; *The Times*'s coverage was more critical as a result.

The details scarcely need to be recapitulated here. Known subsequently as the Norway Debate, the two-day parliamentary drama unseated Chamberlain and in a 'splendid upheaval' installed in his place the man from the room above Ian.

On 10 May, Loelia Westminster wrote in her diary: 'Hitler invaded Holland & Belgium. Bombed Brussels also many towns in France. Spent my time playing tennis at Selfridges.' After Germany's overrunning of the Low Countries, invasion seemed imminent. Overjoyed to see Peter alive, Ian spent that Whitsun weekend with him on the east coast, chauffeured in the back of a camouflaged staff car to Southend to investigate an anonymous letter apparently written by a German agent. According to this, enemy paratroopers were expected to descend at 1 a.m. on Sunday 12th.

Southend was enjoying its Bank holiday, with the beaches and cinemas packed, and the band in their hotel's blacked-out ballroom playing 'South of the Border'. Peter wrote that 'when, soon after one o'clock, a report came in that there was no unusual air activity anywhere, the Official Eye-Witnesses sought out their car, put the elderly driver, who was dead drunk, in the back seat, and made for London.'

Ian steered his brother through the darkness. The return journey was slow. The signposts had all been removed and the dimmed headlights made it hard to see further than a few yards in front.

Later that week, Maud Russell dined with Ian at the Ivy. 'We were very gloomy and depressed and filled with forebodings about north France and Flanders.' Ian's brother Michael was fighting there.

Ernie Cuneo told Ian that the only time he saw his friend Damon Runyon cry was when Runyon talked about the war. 'War reads a hell of a lot better than it lives.'

Ian nodded grimly. 'A hell of a lot better. God,' and shook his head as if warding off a blow.

Cuneo said, 'Fleming was regarded by many as sombre. It is a wonder he was able to smile at all.'

Ian had lost his father in the First World War. An early fatality in the Second was his cousin Anthony Rose, Harcourt's son, killed in a flying accident on a night training flight on 11 September 1939.

Another needless death, in March 1942, was that of Greville Worthington, his partner at Elkin Matthews, who, on hearing that Ian had been made a commander, remarked with a wicked grin: 'Well, I always said he was a fixer.' In charge of security at the port of Dover, Worthington was testing his men's alertness when he was challenged by a panicked sentry and shot. Ian gave Percy Muir the sad news and arranged for permits for Muir to attend his burial at sea off the coast at Dover.

Then the deaths of school friends like Shane O'Neill in Italy, and Anthony Winn, killed at the Second Battle of El Alamein; men in NID like Commander Ned Coghan, shot down by a Focke-Wulf on his way to Gibraltar 'to do snap interrogation of U-boat crew'; men in Ian's commando unit like Peter 'Red' Huntington-Whiteley, killed by surrendering German troops at Le Havre; friends like Rex Whistler, decapitated by a shell after climbing out of his tank; the sons of friends like Colin Gubbins and Lord Kemsley . . .

'Ian was sitting more or less safely at Whitehall,' says Ian's stepson Raymond O'Neill, 'whilst so many sons, fathers, brothers were out in the field being shot at.'

In this grim roll-call, two deaths affected Ian more than any others. The second, towards the end of the war, was the death of the woman he had decided to marry. The first, in the opening months, was the death of his youngest brother Michael, aged twenty-seven.

His battalion had gone missing after Dunkirk. Peter tried to reassure Michael's wife Tish: 'A whole battalion cannot just vanish into thin air.' Michael had seen his baby daughter Gilly on leave in January and then departed for France as adjutant of the 4th battalion of Oxfordshire and Buckinghamshire Light Infantry.

Michael had distinguished himself at the battle of Cassel, buying time for troops to be evacuated from Dunkirk. The battalion war diary for 28 May recorded that he was mentioned three times in despatches. 'Throughout the whole battle, the men, though very tired and hungry, kept extremely cheerful and were greatly helped by Captain Fleming, who, completely unmoved by any form of fire, came riding on his motorcycle over the rubble of demolished houses looking as though he were out for a Sunday afternoon ride and distributing cigarettes or other luxuries which he had discovered.'

On 29 May, his battalion was ordered to break out and head for Dunkirk. Only six men made it. Michael was shot in the left thigh, possibly from a Panzer tank, outside the village of Watou.

Left behind, Michael was captured and sent as a prisoner to Lille. 'He has a fracture just below the hip,' David Eccles reported to his wife on 2 October, having heard from Tish. 'News takes ages – her last postcard from him is dated 15 July.' His daughter Gilly says: 'He died in Lille hospital after he refused to let them remove his legs because of gangrene. "That you will not do" – because he couldn't bear the idea of not fishing or stalking, and that killed him.'

He had died on 1 October, but the news did not reach the family for another two months. Dick Troughton, an officer in the same battalion, wrote to Tish, 'This war has taken the best of us, and it is a tragic business. There will never be anyone quite like him again. At least he fulfilled his great ambition, he was worthy of his father.'

Eve wrote to Lord Esher on 8 December: 'Peter, poor Peter, came and told me. It is the second time in his life that he has been with me in my sorrow. If he had been killed outright, it would not be so hard to bear, but for anyone with any imagination the thought of those months of suffering alone and dying alone without hands to hold are too pitiful to contemplate. If only I could have got to him! I feel that with my strength and healing in my hands I could have saved him.'

He had left four children under the age of five, who came to live with Peter's family at Merrimoles. Gilly was the youngest. 'I only saw my father once,' she says. 'I had his driving gloves, sheepskin with big cuffs, and a bed-side clock and a whistle. My mother never talked about him again.'

Maud Russell was to dine with Ian on 13 June, 'but had a message in the morning to say he'd gone to France. I don't know what his job is . . . News disastrous all the time. France collapsing.'

The speed of the German advance had disrupted communications. Cut off from the embassy, Godfrey took the uncharacteristic risk of ordering his personal assistant to Paris. 'It was essential to keep in touch with [Captain Ned] Pleydell-Bouverie, our Naval Attaché in Paris, as the French government and our Embassy fell back towards Bordeaux.' Quite why Godfrey might have broken his rule to send Ian is a mystery. Clearly, other factors were in play.

On top of tracking down Ned Pleydell-Bouverie, Ian was given the responsibility of restoring links with Admiral François Darlan, the French Navy's commander-in-chief, who had moved his headquarters to Tours, 150 miles south. It was a matter of urgency to find out what Darlan intended to do with the 270 warships of the Marine nationale, in particular its two new fast battleships *Richelieu* and *Jean Bart*.

Godfrey had met Darlan in January, and, despite Darlan's reputation as a prickly opportunist, remained convinced that 'he meant to be a good ally'. But as the Panzers thundered towards the French capital, the need for Darlan to demonstrate his intentions became pressing: if Germany obtained these ships, the balance of nautical power would tilt in Hitler's favour.

In Paris, the Germans were expected at dawn on 14 June. Peter Smithers, seconded to the SIS office in avenue Charles Floquet, had evacuated the MI6 records in a French Army truck. In rapid succession, Ian emptied 'a very substantial sum of money' from the safe in the Rolls-Royce company office where SIS kept its funds, 'acquired a wireless set and operator', and went round to the embassy where he found Pleydell-Bouverie's stepdaughter Elizabeth Montagu burning files. 'The elegant fireplace was far from suited to the task without enough matches or lighter fuel,' she wrote, 'but with streaming eyes and much spluttering we eventually managed to reduce the documents to a pulpy, black mess.' Not till 9 p.m. was everyone ready to leave. The front door was closed firmly and locked. 'The embassy was now empty and silent and the Union Jack no longer fluttered from the flagpole.'

It was a hot evening. In the Faubourg Saint-Honoré, they tumbled into their cars. The streets were choked with slow traffic streaming out of the city, and the exhaust fumes made everyone sleepy.

Ian took all the next day to reach Tours. Admiral Godfrey retained 'a very vivid recollection' of conversations he had with Ian, who 'was able to communicate with me by teleprinter at intervals en route'. Ian was replicating Peter's experience in Norway, when Peter had had to rely on a Marconi H/6a wireless to communicate with the Royal Navy as Stuka dive-bombers screamed down.

He left no record of what he found in Tours, where the French government had temporarily fled. Elizabeth Montagu recalled the throng in the Hôtel de L'Univers, with confused elderly senators pushing their way through; 'some of them were accompanied by ladies in skirts too tight, heels too high and hair too blonde – they were surely not their legal wedded wives.'

Not till the following day, through Commander Pierre Barjot, 'a close colleague', did Ian establish contact with Darlan.

Events were moving rapidly. One week earlier, Darlan had met General François d'Astier, who had assumed charge of the French air force, at the château d'Artigny and assured him that whatever happened, the French fleet would continue to fight, 'even if it does so under the British flag'.

Churchill now gave the go-ahead for civil servants to draft a 'Declaration of Union' based on an idea of Vansittart and Morton to make Great Britain and France 'one nation while retaining their separate political organisations'.

It was in this context, with plans altering by the moment, that Ian pursued an idea he had discussed at the embassy: to designate the Isle of Wight as a French enclave to which Darlan could bring his fleet. But Darlan would have none of it. Ian transmitted back the Frenchman's defiant message that the British were being far too pessimistic.

With the collapse of Reynaud's government twenty-four hours later, Ian was instructed to impress on Darlan the position of Churchill, that France could negotiate peace only after the French fleet came over to the British. But Darlan jumped ship – accepting Marshal Pétain's invitation to join his new administration as Minister of Marine, in effect becoming a collaborator with the Nazis. General d'Astier could not believe his ears when he met Darlan in Bordeaux on 17 June and reminded him of their promise to continue fighting. 'But Admiral, just yesterday you were telling me . . .' Darlan cut him off: 'Yesterday, yes. Today, I am a Minister.'

Pétain's resolution to sign an armistice agreement with Germany concentrated minds in Downing Street. Earlier, Darlan had given Churchill his personal assurance that he would not let the Germans seize the French fleet. On a last-ditch mission to prevent this, Churchill ordered to Bordeaux his two most senior Naval representatives: his 'heavy, fat and fair' successor as First Lord, A. V. Alexander, and Admiral Dudley Pound, the First Sea Lord.

Godfrey was at his desk in Room 38 when he heard the tap of Pound's iron ferrule on the steps leading down to the private Admiralty entrance under his office, and realised that Pound was on his way to France. Godfrey at once rushed out to caution him. He informed the disbelieving Pound that he had just returned from a meeting with a former ambassador to France, Lord Tyrell, who had asked Godfrey 'to come and see him urgently'. Tyrell had warned from his invalid chair that Admiral Darlan was likely to be 'a twister'.

In France meanwhile, Ian was battling to bring over to the British side the head of French signals Intelligence, urging Colonel Gustave Bertrand and his colleagues and members of the Polish Cipher Bureau, who had escaped from Poland and were working with the French, to join them in England. Ian had met Bertrand the previous August when, together with 'Biffy' Dunderdale, SIS station chief in Paris, Bertrand had smuggled the

Polish copy of a German Enigma machine to London under diplomatic seal.*

The only surviving SIGINT report to mention Ian during these turbulent days is a message from Bletchley Park to Bertrand on 23 June. '*Vous et les officiers de votre etat major ainsi que vos collegues polonais seront beinvenus chez nous: s'addresser ou au Lieutenant FLEMING ou a WHINNIE [Patrick Whinney, Assistant Naval Attaché] a Bayonne et y embarquez.*' (You and the officers on your staff as well as your Polish colleagues will be welcome with us: contact either Lieutenant Fleming or Whinney in Bayonne and embark there.) The offer was not taken up.

Patrick Beesly was then a Naval Intelligence officer specialising in France. Ian afterwards maintained to Beesly – who conducted Ian's conversations with Godfrey from the Admiralty's underground war room – that if he had managed to contact Bertrand and make arrangements to ensure that both navies could communicate in secret, then the Royal Navy's tragic sinking of the French fleet at Mers-el-Kébir ten days later might have been averted.

The drama of these intense hours worked its way into Ian's fiction. He gives the terrorist group SPECTRE its HQ in 'some large and well-guarded chateau in Normandy'. He sits Lieutenant Hugo von der Drache, before he became Drax, in one of the Panzer tanks that fatally wounded Michael Fleming as they 'ran through the British Army in France like a knife through butter'. He promotes Captain Ned Pleydell-Bouverie, the Naval Attaché whom Godfrey had ordered Ian to liaise with, to Colonial Secretary Pleydell-Smith.

At the British consulate in Bordeaux, Ian caught up with Pleydell-Bouverie, who had only just escaped the port of Nantes as the Germans arrived. Usually immaculate, Ned looked frayed. Wearily, he reported that it was 'all up' with the French. *Sauve qui peut* was the motto of the 600,000 refugees who flooded into Bordeaux. His stepdaughter Elizabeth recalled the city as 'a vast ant heap: the wide boulevards and streets being impassable

---

* Marina Weir, whose father had known Dunderdale as a boy in Odessa, heard the story from 'Biffy' himself. 'He told me, sitting at his dining room table, that he was the messenger, he was literally handed it in Paris, and he took it with Bertrand to London and dropped it off under the clock tower at Victoria station with someone from Intelligence.' Dressed in black tie, Stewart Menzies, then deputy head of SIS, gathered up the machine from the two men on his way to a reception.

with people, livestock and vehicles, all crowding together in a swarming mass. The chaos was indescribable, and one saw fear and despair on nearly every face.'

More confusion surrounds Ian's next movements. In another snatched conversation, Godfrey directed him to load crates containing 'new aircraft parts' onto a ship in the estuary; recent research hints that this cargo may have included French atomic secrets and scientists.

Much has been written about the arrival on the jetty at Saint-Jean-de-Luz of two army trucks containing King Zog of Albania and his over-perfumed daughters, plus a number of long green metal coffins, 'one of which nearly fell into the water' as it was manhandled from a swaying sardine boat onto SS *Ettrick*. Packed in these metal boxes was Albania's gold reserve. Less attention has been given to a shipment that linked Ian Fleming and Ned Pleydell-Bouverie with 198 tons of Belgian gold.

The unit name for 30AU contains the chemical symbol for gold – *Au*. Auric Goldfinger reflects Ian's life-long obsession with this precious metal. 'I love its colour, its brilliance, its divine heaviness . . . But above all, Mr Bond, I love the power that gold alone gives to its owner.' The war had brought Ian into contact with colossal amounts of the stuff. His bullion dealings involved not merely Juan March, but the Belgian Finance Minister, Camille Gutt.

Days earlier, Gutt had organised for his country's gold reserves to be removed from Brussels and transported in 4,944 sealed boxes to Bordeaux. Many of these boxes were loaded onto the French cruiser *Victor Schoelcher*. In the classified in-house history of SIS's Section D, responsible for 'sabotage and other clandestine operations', much pride is expressed in 'overseeing the embarkation at Bordeaux of £84,000,000 [approximately £6,525 million today] in gold bars.' The boxes eventually arrived in Dakar on the West African coast on 28 June. The prospect of retrieving this gold from the Vichy French port in Senegal was a factor behind British support for Operation MENACE, which was spearheaded by de Gaulle's Free French Forces, to capture Dakar in September.

Ian had a City friend now in SOE, a Belgian banker named Louis Franck, who was on that ill-fated and abortive Dakar expedition (along with Hilary Bray and Evelyn Waugh). Franck, a partner of the merchant bank Samuel Montagu & Company and one of Ian's contacts for his operations with Juan

March, was charged by the Treasury with '*discovering where the gold, about which you have had conversations with the Treasury, is located.*' Although Franck never managed to step ashore in Dakar, he remained aware that not all of Belgium's gold reserves had ended up in Vichy and German hands, and that 'part of the gold bullion' removed from Brussels and kept in the Banque de France's vaults in Bordeaux had gone missing.

What had happened to it?

A chance meeting in 2019 at the Harvard Boat Club unpicked one strand of the mystery. Few are alive who are able to give a first-hand account of the evacuation from Bordeaux. At ninety-six, Francis de Marneffe was one of the last. 'I have very detailed memories of the whole adventure of 1940, as if it was yesterday.' The astonishing story that this retired Belgian doctor tells beside the Charles River in Massachusetts touches on Ian and his activities during those June days and provides a possible explanation of why Godfrey sent Ian to France.

Before the war, Marneffe, a passionate rower, had been a double sculler with Gutt's son Étienne, who was his best friend. When the Germans invaded Belgium, the sixteen-year-old Marneffe had bicycled ahead to Poitiers where he was thrilled to encounter Gutt *père*, the Finance Minister, also heading south in a convoy of trucks that included the president of the Belgian National Bank. Gutt promised to help Marneffe obtain a visa for England. They drove to Bordeaux where, on 17 June, they joined a dozen members of the Belgian Cabinet for dinner at the Chapon Fin; Ian was to dine there the following night.

The next morning, the Belgian government met in executive session amid packing cases on which some of them sat, in a second-floor room on rue Blanc Dutrouilh, to decide whether to continue the war and go on to England or not. Gutt asked Marneffe to run to the British consulate nearby and let him know the instant the British ambassador arrived. Upon Marneffe coming back to tell him that a distinguished-looking gentleman had turned up, Gutt excused himself and spent an hour in private with Sir Ronald Campbell, at the end of which Marneffe overheard Campbell say: 'Monsieur Gutt, I cannot tell you how grateful we are for what you have done, and is there anything we can do for you?'

Gutt pointed at Marneffe and said he was his 'nephew' and could Campbell provide him with a British visa?

Exactly why Campbell was ready to grant this visa was explained afterwards to Marneffe. 'We learned that Gutt had been engaged in a very crucial transaction with the Ambassador, hence the latter's gratitude. Monsieur Gutt had lent the whole of the Belgian gold reserve to the British government for the duration of the war. Ninety per cent of the gold we were told had been travelling in 14 trucks from Belgium to Bordeaux.'

The role played by Ian and Ned in evacuating either all or a section of this treasure out of Bordeaux is suggested in a Bank of England receipt in the possession of Ned's son. This relates to a consignment of gold that was transported first to French Equatorial Africa and then, by Ned himself, two years later to the bank's headquarters in Threadneedle Street.

RECEIVED FROM
Captain The Hon Edward PLEYDELL-BOUVERIE MVO
442 (Four hundred and forty-two boxes) boxes numbered:
S. 922 to 1022
T. 1 to 330
WITH SEALS AND BANDS INTACT AND SAID TO CONTAIN
356, 024.61 (Three hundred and fifty-six thousand and twenty-four, decimal six one) OUNCES OF FINE GOLD.
For the Bank of England. J. Paddon. DATE: 29 June 1942.

This would be worth £462 million at today's prices. Were these boxes why Admiral Godfrey despatched Ian to France and why the DNI felt it 'essential' for his personal assistant to keep in touch with Ned Pleydell-Bouverie? Certainly, if both Ian and the gold arrived coincidentally in Bordeaux, it would have made sense for Ian to assist in exfiltration, which might have required naval resources.

If someone was boring him, Ian never felt shy about telling them the story of a Fleet Street crasher from his Reuters days who once tried to attract the attention of a well-known columnist at the bar by saying to him loudly, 'Tomorrow, I'm going to Bordeaux.'

'Who,' asked the columnist, turning, 'is Deaux?'

Yet Bordeaux was the setting for some of Ian's most memorable adventures.

Another Godfrey instruction was to help Peter Smithers evacuate the British ambassador, plus MI6 personnel and files, on board HMS *Arethusa*.

The cruiser was anchored in the mouth of the Gironde, sixty miles north of Bordeaux, along with seven or eight merchant ships. 'Ian thought that the first priority was to get a transport of some sort to take our people out,' said Smithers. Dressed in their smart white caps and naval uniforms, they went to ask the harbourmaster for the use of his small ferry. The Frenchman made a windy speech about Pétain, now in charge of his country's destiny, until Ian delved into his pocket and produced from the wad that he had taken from the SIS safe 'a very large denomination French note . . . and with a suitable interval and a little bit of talk we had the ferry'.

By this time, a swelling number of refugees had parked their cars along the dockside – 'Rolls Royces, Delages, all sorts,' said Smithers, who told his stepson how he and Ian afterwards drove the abandoned vehicles into the sea. ('They put them in gear and ran them off the pier.') There were too many passengers for the *Arethusa* to take on board, so Ian and Smithers did a round of the other ships to ask if they would agree to transport refugees to England.

In Bordeaux that morning, Francis de Marneffe and his patron, the Belgian Finance Minister, had spoken to one of the captains, who claimed 'he didn't have enough fuel to do that' and he was scared that his ship might be sunk – there was a rumour of two Italian submarines in the estuary. When Marneffe finally made it on to the ferry boat that Ian had hired and was taken out to the SS *Nariva*, 'we were denied permission to come on board.'

Smithers witnessed how Ian then changed the minds of reluctant captains. 'He said, "Well, you were bombed by the Germans in the anchorage last night. If you don't take these people, you will probably be bombed by the RAF tomorrow night." One or two needed a bit of persuasion, but in the end they all went.'

Keen to embark as many as possible, Smithers and Ian told each passenger they could take only what they could carry. 'We looked at their passports, about which we didn't really know very much, and little by little, they filtered out to the boats, and at a very moving moment Ian and I stood at the top of the stairs after they took off, and I remember them waving to us. In the end I suppose that a couple of hundred people got aboard and sailed for Britain.'

It was owing to Ian Fleming that Marneffe was taken aboard the SS *Madura* instead, although he never knew this at the time. 'Boarding this British ship was an incredible relief. Somebody was in charge who knew what to do, and I felt I was in good hands.'

Among the 1,350 passengers crammed onto the *Madura*'s decks were some familiar figures: Sefton Delmer, Marie Curie's daughter Eve, and the gravel-voiced American correspondent Virginia Cowles; Ian had seen Virginia three weeks previously at Greenwich Court with Loelia, when trying to get her then lover Basil, Marquess of Dufferin 'off his drunk charge'.*

Smithers was still only halfway through his 'extraordinary 48 hours' in Bordeaux. He spent that night on the *Arethusa*, but the captain sent for him the next morning. 'Commander Fleming says that you are to report to the First Lord of the Admiralty, who is in Bordeaux negotiating for the French Fleet.'

Alexander was due to land with Pound at 1 p.m. to meet Darlan. Before that, Smithers joined Ian at the British consulate. The building was open but deserted. 'We found a lot of documents which we amused ourselves by burning there and then in the fireplaces.' Ian took the key and they called on the American consul, who refused to accept it, protesting that his country was neutral and he had no instructions. 'Ian simply stuffed it into his pocket and we walked away.'

Later that afternoon, Smithers accompanied Alexander as his French-speaking Flag Officer to the Hôtel Métropole for discussions with a nervy Darlan. 'It was quite clear that he was not going to do anything at this juncture which would help the British. It was simply a dead refusal.' The final act took place at a dinner that evening in the Chapon Fin. Smithers and Ian attended, together with Alexander and what remained of the British and French General Staffs. 'It was a depressing affair. The proprietor had gone into his cellar and had opened the wines of the century rather than wait for

* Only by chance was Loelia not on board the *Madura*. She had told Ian that she was 'thinking of going out to France' with Cowles.

the Germans to drink them. But nobody was in a state of mind to enjoy them. The French were bitterly ashamed. The British bitterly disappointed, and the outlook poor. German aircraft were in the air overhead from time to time and it was a very sad situation.'

Throughout these chaotic hours, Ian was totally self-composed, said Smithers. 'He might have been talking in a London club. Nothing ruffled him in the slightest. When we parted, he was going to leave for Portugal. He had work to do for NID in Lisbon.'

Ian maintained his composure all the way to Spain, where, following discussions with David Eccles and others at the Lisbon embassy, Ian needed to fly to meet Alan Hillgarth. A Lufthansa official in Lisbon refused to sell him a ticket, and only the German airline operated civilian flights to Madrid. Smithers heard the story from a NID colleague who witnessed it. 'Lufthansa looked at him rather strangely and said, "But, sir, you are a British Naval Officer. Are you not aware that there is a war going on between our countries?" Ian replied with the greatest coolness, "I know that there is a war going on between our countries, but you are a common carrier. This is a neutral country and you are obliged by law to take me," and they took him, and so Lufthansa flew Ian from one neutral country to another neutral country.'

XXIII
LITTLE BILL

*'I did more to further the cementing of good working
Anglo-American relations in the war years than any
other individual then involved.'*

WILLIAM STEPHENSON

For Britain to survive, Spain and Portugal had to be kept out of the war. Victory depended on another neutral country coming in.

On 18 May 1940, as France collapsed, Randolph Churchill interrupted his father shaving. Churchill told him: 'I think I see my way through.' He finished patting his face, then turned and said, 'I shall drag the United States in.' Simultaneously to setting Europe ablaze, Churchill determined to put a fire under his mother's country. During the fateful eighteen months between Dunkirk and Pearl Harbor, Ian served as one of his match-lighters in the dry stubble of US Intelligence.

At a time when Hitler's armies had overrun Europe from Narvik to the Pyrenees, and threatened to gain control of North Africa, the Mediterranean and potentially the Middle East, Ian was part of the small advance guard that laid the ground for what the historian David Stafford has described as 'the greatest intelligence alliance in history'.

Myths persist, and a narrative to which a host of vested interests have accrued on either side has to be unpicked with care. Ian claimed that he wrote two timely memorandums, the first being the original charter of the Organisation of Strategic Services, the second, on how to create an American Secret Service. Ian's contributions were memorialised in the Northern Ireland number plate of Ann's blue Rover, beginning 'CIA', and in William Donovan's better-known though oddly untraceable gift to Ian of a .38 Police Positive Special pistol with the engraving 'for special services'.

How special were Ian's services? John Pearson was warned off when he tried to pry an answer out of Admiral Godfrey. 'The suggestions that an obscure Commander RNVR created, or had anything to do with the creation of the OSS, would not help Anglo-American relations.' Denning likewise batted Pearson away, writing to Godfrey in February 1965: 'I had him out to lunch the other day and explained to him what must never be revealed, such as sources of intelligence, co-operation with other intelligence agencies and anything of a nature which could lead to political embarrassment or controversy.'

While the precise nature of Ian's involvement leaves many questions unanswered, it has become harder to dispute that he was a valuable presence at a vital moment, and deserves his place among the select few responsible for the word 'special' becoming associated with what was foremost an Intelligence relationship. Ray Cline, a future deputy director and historian of the CIA, was not alone in believing that the OSS 'might never have come into being if it had not been urged upon the US by the British and fashioned after the British intelligence system'.

Ian was one of the three main spearheads.

The creation of an American foreign Intelligence service and its fusion on so many levels with the British SIS was encouraged by Churchill and Roosevelt; but their unofficial personal representatives must also take credit, in particular the two millionaires known as 'Big Bill' and 'Little Bill', with whom Ian worked closely. All three were kindred spirits with shared interests and goals who operated outside the system, with an authority not recognised by bureaucracies, and a flexibility that enabled them to get things done.

Even as Lufthansa flew Ian to Madrid, a short, unobtrusive forty-three-year-old Canadian businessman was arriving in New York on an undercover mission for the chief of SIS, Brigadier Stewart Menzies, to open an SIS station and establish a liaison with the director of the FBI, J. Edgar Hoover.

Menzies hoped that, once successfully established, the Canadian could exploit Intelligence relationships to encourage American military aid. He could also help counter the 'all is lost' defeatism of Americans, including the ambassador in London, Joseph Kennedy. An American isolationist told David Eccles in Lisbon: 'We should abandon England – "Why not? It's only a museum and a cabbage patch."' An overwhelming proportion of the American population agreed. A Gallup poll in July 1940 revealed that a mere 7.7 per cent favoured getting embroiled in a new European conflict, which Britain was bound to lose.

If the Canadian's immediate task was to improve British Intelligence operations in the Americas and the Caribbean, this would eventually expand to a brief to 'do all that was not being done, and could not be done by overt means . . . eventually to bring America into the war'.

Who was this abnormally private, prairie-born Winnipegger who planned to shift American public opinion while operating under the hat of a British 'Passport Control Officer'? Two of Ian's circle had trouble spelling his name: William Stephenson. Harold Hemming had known him since their Berlin days, yet he often referred to him in his diary as 'Stevenson'. Loelia Westminster, too. '17 October 1939. Fascinating Mr Stevenson came in for a cocktail.'

No one would be more fascinated by William Stephenson than Ian. The five-foot-two Canadian was to become a huge figure in Ian's life, with an influence that survived the war and stretched beyond espionage. He advised Ian on his post-war career, and where to live in the 1940s and 50s, offered financial guidance, and assisted Ian in getting his Bond novels filmed. To what level Stephenson's own life and example informed those novels has been the subject of much conjecture.

It was Ian who first alluded to the importance that Stephenson held for him. 'People often ask me how closely the "hero" of my thrillers, James Bond, resembles a true, live secret agent.' If there had to be one candidate, he teased, it was this man of few words with a magnetic personality who possessed 'the quality of making anyone ready to follow him to the ends of the earth'. In 1946, Ian had followed Stephenson to the north shore of Jamaica.

Ian had first come across him as the business associate of Hemming, who had helped Stephenson with the finance to build the Earl's Court exhibition hall, then the world's largest indoor stadium. But Hemming's relationship was closer than business.

Stephenson was an important freelance spymaster behind the screen of his multiple portfolios, which included Sound City (later Shepperton

Studios). In the mid 1930s, he had set up a private organisation, the British Industrial Secret Service, which gathered information on German rearmament and steel production. Hemming supplied him with facts and figures about what he had seen after each of his trips to Germany. Stephenson then passed the information on to Desmond Morton, who shared the material with Churchill.

The wealthy Winnipegger was also godfather to the Hemmings' three-year-old son John, whom he had rescued from drowning, plunging fully clothed into Stephenson's water-lily pond near Marlow – and so living up to fellow boxer Gene Tunney's description of him as 'quick as a dash of lightning'.

'Men of super qualities *can* exist,' wrote Ian. 'Such a man is "The Quiet Canadian".'

Stephenson had been famous since childhood for his boxing skills, but also for his photographic memory. In Winnipeg, his great-nephew Irvin Stefansson says: 'He used to play the memory game. He'd leave the room, and someone would move an object around, and he'd come back in and say what it was. His memory was unimpeachable. He'd remember five years earlier meeting you, the time of day.'

Yet Stephenson's prodigious recall had gaps. Once he left Winnipeg, he conspicuously failed to remember his Manitoba upbringing. Like Stephenson, Hemming's wife Alice had come from poverty in Canada. However, not even with Alice did he discuss his background. 'He would talk about anything without hesitation,' said a Canadian friend. 'Not Winnipeg.'

Entitled 'Intrepid', Ian's fulsome portrait became the foreword to Stephenson's first published biography, *The Quiet Canadian* (1962), by H. Montgomery Hyde. Ian had by then known his subject for more than twenty years. He called him 'the real thing', and positioned him 'high up' on his list of heroes, in a cohort that included Peter, Churchill and the Queen. 'It would be a foolish person who argued his credentials.' But sixteen years after Ian's death, only a foolish person could have trusted them. Following the publication of a widely publicised further biography, *A Man Called Intrepid* (1978), by the confusingly named author (and no relation) William Stevenson, it was discovered that Stephenson had not been called 'Intrepid' – this was the cable address for his wartime office in New York: his code was 48000 or 'G'. He was not even called Stephenson.

My Icelandic-Canadian father-in-law, Dr George Johnson, a former Minister of Health and Education for the Manitoba provincial government, is credited with disclosing his real name and background. In 1980, William Stephenson returned on a private visit to Winnipeg for the first time in six decades in the company of Dr Johnson's old friend and colleague Derek Bedson, a New York acquaintance of Stephenson's since the 1950s. Bedson drove him from the Fort Garry Hotel to 175 Syndicate Street where Stephenson had grown up, but Stephenson did not call on any of his relations. 'Nobody told us till after he left,' says Irvin Stefansson. At this point, Dr Johnson filled out the story to Bedson, explaining who Stephenson's relations were – and why the man called Intrepid had not dared step foot in his hometown since 1922.

Stephenson's close-knit Icelandic family were Dr Johnson's patients and relatives. From all that they had told him, the quiet Canadian had sound reasons for his silence.

Almost every detail in Ian's portrait of 'Intrepid's first twenty years was incorrect. He had been born William Samuel Clouston Stanger on 23 January 1897 (not on 11 January 1896). His father was not the son of a pioneering Scottish lumber-mill owner 'of independent means' who died in the Boer War, but an impoverished labourer from the local flour mill, who died of muscular dystrophy when William was four. Unable to cope with three small children, his mother Sarah Johnson, a first-generation Icelandic immigrant, persuaded an Icelandic couple on the next street to take care of her son. She then abandoned Winnipeg, allegedly for Chicago. William never saw his mother or his sisters again.

William Stanger grew up at 175 Syndicate Street in the house of Vigfús and Kristin Stefánsson, whose surname he adopted and anglicised. His only education was at Argyle Elementary School (not Exeter College, Oxford). He left school at twelve to become a telegram delivery boy. His formidable memory was noticed when he identified a fugitive bank robber while delivering on a bicycle: John Krafchenko was later hanged as a result. Among Krafchenko's possessions was a fountain pen filled with explosive nitroglycerine. Stephenson, who loved gadgets, later gave Ian a similar pen.

In 1916, he lied about his age to enlist in the Winnipeg Light Infantry. Standing only five foot two, he 'passed as bugler'. He learned to blow his own trumpet away from Winnipeg, claiming to have shot down twenty enemy aircraft after retraining as a pilot and to have won the world amateur light-weight championship at the Inter-Allied Games, where he had sparred with Gene Tunney. No record survives of his boxing triumph, possibly because he was a POW, after French gunners mistakenly shot down his Sopwith on 28 July 1918.

In 1919, he returned to Canada with another gadget. His great-nephew says, 'he came back with a can-opener he had stolen from the Germans, which he patented to sell in Winnipeg.' His nickel-plated 'Kleen Kut' can-opener, 'liberated' from a store-room at Holzminden POW camp, was advertised as 'a Canadian invention made in Canada . . . It cuts the top off the tin and binds down the cut edge, leaving it smooth.'

The Winnipeg General Strike erupted in May 1919, paralysing the city. The febrile mood ought to have warned Stephenson that this was a bad time to start a new business. Nevertheless, he formed a company to sell his can-opener, raising the capital from the Icelandic community. One of the largest investors was his foster-father, Vigfús. Another was Irvin Stefansson's father. 'My dad lent him a bunch of money and he never paid it back.' My father-in-law's patients were among the further ninety-five creditors who 'lost their shirts' when, on 13 August 1922, William filed for bankruptcy. By then, he had been living four months in London, having left town 'in the dark of the night', according to the daughter of another swindled creditor. He had not returned to Winnipeg since – 'because he thought that there might be a war-rant out for his arrest'.

Inexplicable, although never in dispute, was his astonishing reinvention into what Ian called 'one of the great secret agents of the last war'. Within two years of arriving in London as a bankrupt, William Stephenson was described by the *Daily Mail* as 'a brilliant scientist' and 'a leader of industry'. He had married a Tennessee tobacco heiress he had met on the crossing, who financed his start-ups. Stephenson's most impressive achievement, smoothing his remaining edges and making him a millionaire by the time he was thirty, was to patent a process to transmit photographic images by wireless 'suitable for newspaper reproduction'. His process was adopted by newspapers worldwide and it was in wireless terms that he defined his relationship with Churchill. 'There was instant communication,' he wrote of their first meeting in early 1938. 'Winston and I found ourselves to be on the same wavelength sometimes of ultrahigh frequency . . . Thereafter we met at every opportunity' – culminating in their most significant encounter, during the fall of France, when Churchill allegedly asked Stephenson to go as his personal representative to America.

Stephenson told several versions. The conversation took place at the Admiralty; at Beaverbrook's house; on 10 May; on 12 May. At any rate, 'It was a fine evening, with the washed-out blue skies that come in late May or early June.' According to Ian, Churchill looked him straight in the face. 'Your duty lies there. You must go.' The problem for historians is that there is not one documented confirmation of this exchange, or that Stephenson ever met Churchill in his life. Everything is verbal.

'Blinker' Hall and Stewart Menzies developed delusions of grandeur in retirement. Stephenson too, says John le Carré. 'He became a boastful old fabricator of his own image, and a pain in MI6's arse, shooting off his mouth from Bermuda,' to where Stephenson had moved from Jamaica.

That the modest, tight-lipped Canadian should have turned into an embarrassing blabbermouth has been ascribed to his two strokes and his alcohol intake – Ian wrote that he used to mix 'the most powerful Martinis in America and serve them in quart glasses'.

Unfortunately for his reputation, when Stephenson decided to open up about his achievements he removed the lid on too many worms. His contradictory accounts have led to the rest of his narrative being questioned. 'Much has been written on Stephenson,' decided the Foreign Office historian Gill Bennett, 'but none of the accounts is reliable.'

The same accusations have been levelled against Ian, whose own Intelligence record can appear either over-inflated or undervalued. As Ian discovered, just because you reinvent yourself, it does not mean all your lives are untrue. Countering Stephenson's impressive absence from the record is the argument that it was the essence of his work to be secret. If certain of his claims need to be taken 'with huge heaps of salt', as David Stafford has cautioned, then Stafford also accepts that Stephenson's uncontested achievements are nonetheless remarkable.

Set against the inventions of his first and last twenty years is the public recognition of Stephenson by Britain, America and Canada for his wartime service. Add to this the fierce loyalty and admiration he inspired in a roll-call of noteworthy figures who worked for him. 'Everyone did!' said Joan Bright. 'I'm certain that one day an Aboriginal will walk out from the far reaches of the outback, and he'll say, "Oh yes, I was working for Sir William."'

Roald Dahl was one of Stephenson's wartime recruits in New York. He recalled 'Bill's many chaps floating around rather like wasps, you never realised they were working for him'. The swarm included many friends of Ian: Ivar Bryce, Ernie Cuneo, Peter Smithers, Noël Coward, David Niven, Louis Franck. Not to mention Alexander Korda, Cary Grant, David Ogilvy (the 'Father of Advertising'), Peter Wilson (later head of Sotheby's), Paul Dehn (screenwriter of *Goldfinger* and *The Spy Who Came in from the Cold*) and H. Montgomery Hyde.

Mountbatten and Gubbins praised 'Little Bill' unreservedly. So did David Bruce, later American ambassador to London (and one more who had worked for him). 'Had it not been for Sir William's achievements it seems to me highly possible that the Second World War would have followed a different and perhaps fatal course.' J. Edgar Hoover of the FBI proved to be yet another surprising admirer. 'When the full story can be told I am quite certain that your contribution will be among the foremost in having brought victory finally to the United Nations' cause.'

Stephenson lived long enough to be welcomed by 750 OSS veterans on the eponymous aircraft carrier USS *Intrepid* where, on 22 September 1983, he was presented with the William J. Donovan medal and a letter from President Reagan: 'All those who love freedom owe you a debt of gratitude; but we as Americans are particularly grateful to you.'

It was a medal that the former fugitive bankrupt William Stanger could put alongside his knighthood in 1945 from King George VI ('This is dear to my heart,' Churchill is supposed to have written when recommending it), his Companion of the Order of Canada, his bronze statuette in the CIA HQ at Langley, his statue in downtown Winnipeg etc., etc.

Yet no honour had meant more to him than the Presidential Medal for Merit awarded by President Truman in 1946 for 'valuable assistance to

America in the fields of intelligence and special operations', and pinned to his chest by none other than 'Big Bill', William J. Donovan himself, who admitted: 'Bill Stephenson taught us all we ever knew about foreign intelligence.'

'Big Bill' was the third prong in this trident.

XXIV
BIG BILL

'We aren't as wild as you, Bill!'

INFANTRYMAN OF THE FIGHTING 69TH TO

COLONEL DONOVAN, FRANCE, 1916

In July 1940, days after 'Little Bill' slipped unnoticed into New York, 'Big Bill' flew in the opposite direction on a much-fanfared visit to London. His brief: to find out if Britain was a fighter that stood a chance and was worth supporting – or if the British were in danger of 'falling on their faces', as Joseph Kennedy maintained. Ian was one of those hand-picked to impress on William Donovan that Kennedy was wrong.

The public profile of Loelia Westminster's fifty-seven-year-old 'Sugar Daddy', as she called Donovan, stood in tall contrast to that of the diminutive and secretive Stephenson. 'Anybody can start a fight . . . but here are the guys who can finish it.' *The Fighting 69th* had played in cinemas since January, with George Brent acting the part of America's wartime hero: 'Wild Bill' – as the world continued to know Colonel Donovan – who had led his regiment into battle in a steel helmet, was four times wounded and repeatedly cited for courage. 'He has every decoration which the American government can bestow for bravery under fire,' the new Secretary of the Navy, Frank Knox, said of his old friend. Despite having built up a successful international law practice on Wall Street, Donovan had been a frontline hero in search of a role ever since. Another friend said: 'Donovan was like a fire horse waiting for the bell to ring.'

In June 1940, President Roosevelt, who was at Columbia Law School with Donovan, and cautiously trusted his 'old friend' for his integrity and independence, raised Donovan's hopes that he might be made Secretary of War, but at the last moment he reappointed a former War Secretary, Henry

Stimson. To cloud matters, Donovan's personal life was in turmoil. On the same rainy afternoon the Germans invaded Norway, his twenty-three-year-old daughter Patricia had crashed into a tree after her car skidded in a patch of water. She died that evening. Donovan's light brown hair turned white overnight.

Roosevelt approved of Frank Knox's idea to send Donovan to London on a fact-finding mission to take his mind off his daughter and as compensation for not giving him a government post. France had capitulated. Britain stood alone. America was divided. Should the United States help or keep away? 'Wild Bill' was the man to find out.

The visit was informal and vague, to assess 'certain aspects of the British defense situation', but Stephenson cleverly oversold it to Menzies, saying that Donovan was travelling as a personal emissary on behalf of both Roosevelt and Hoover and was 'presently the *strongest* friend . . . we have'. As a result, Menzies arranged access to 'all leading Government officials and ministers', which in turn handed Donovan the material that promoted him in Roosevelt's eyes to a position, one year later, where Donovan could name his ticket.

Over seventeen days in July 1940, Donovan was shown Britain's newest military secrets, including radar. He met everyone from the Prime Minister to the King and Queen and the heads of the Intelligence services, making friendships that would have deep-reaching implications for American Intelligence later on. On 23 July, he even had time to squeeze in a visit to Loelia. 'Sugar Daddy Donovan came to see me and was up to his old tricks. Unsuccessful!'

His three meetings with Admiral Godfrey, with whom Donovan 'got along famously', were more fruitful. Godfrey convinced him that Britain, although beleaguered, would not be invaded – but only if America provided the necessary destroyers and military equipment. Donovan spent his last night at Godfrey's house near Sevenoaks, staying up till 2 a.m. to talk about what materiel Britain required. After returning home to spread the message, Donovan wrote to thank Godfrey: 'Certainly you aided me in getting a perspective that I could not have had otherwise.' The Director of Naval Intelligence knew who to thank when Stephenson cabled that Roosevelt had authorised the go-ahead to exchange fifty First World War destroyers for rights to operate military bases in Canada and the Caribbean. 'It was

Donovan who was responsible for getting us the destroyers, the bombsight and other urgent requirements,' Godfrey wrote. 'There is no doubt that we can achieve more through Donovan than any other individual.'

This was Stephenson's assessment too, and Churchill's. 'Give yourself fifty pats on the back sometime,' Churchill congratulated Menzies, who as 'C' was in charge of Stephenson's covert operation in New York. 'Without Colonel D, it could not possibly have happened at this time.'

Military aid was the first step. The second was persuading America to create a counterpart to SIS with whom the British could work as soon as possible. Both Knox and Stimson concurred: 'our intelligence services are pretty bum.'

In 1940, the US Secret Service was a bodyguard for the President. There was no foreign Intelligence agency. Stimson, then Secretary of State, had disbanded its closest equivalent, 'the Black Chamber', eleven years earlier because 'gentlemen should not read each other's mail'. As for Army Intelligence (G2), US Chief of Staff General George Marshall wrote that G2 comprised 'little more than what a military attaché could learn at dinner, more or less, over the coffee cups.'

By now, Godfrey and Stephenson had identified Donovan as the key to reforming an Intelligence apparatus not fit for purpose, and creating a Secret Service based on the British model. But for that to happen, 'Big Bill' needed to be inducted into this model so he would be tempted to champion and copy it. Ian became a central figure in this project.

In December 1940, 'Little Bill' accompanied Donovan back to London on a second unofficial fact-finding mission to the Balkans, the Iberian Peninsula, North Africa and the Mediterranean. Stephenson claimed to have drafted the signal issued from Admiral Godfrey's office – a function ordinarily fulfilled by Ian – which proclaimed that Donovan was 'the most important emissary that any of our high commanders in the field was ever likely to encounter in this world'. Once again, he cleverly overplayed Donovan's informal association with the President as something more substantial, even promoting him, three years early, to 'Major-General'. The British would pay for the two-month trip.

In England, Donovan was given unprecedented access to Godfrey's

Intelligence network. Colonel Vivian Dykes was assigned to accompany him. Known as 'damn-me-Dykes' for 'the transports of violent and profane language that he used', he noticed how unusually focused the American was. 'The one genuinely secret aspect of a surprisingly public mission was Donovan's voracious interest in British intelligence organisation.'

Under the pseudonym of 'Mr Smith', Donovan visited the Topographical Department in Oxford, established by Godfrey after the farce of Norway. Donovan was so impressed that he later sent fifty US servicewomen to sort out and catalogue the locations of the 60,000 holiday snaps that the public had sent in, following requests on the BBC for photographs of French and German beaches, ports, bridges and other potential targets ('a Fleming move', according to Robert Harling, who worked for the unit). Donovan was educated in Sefton Delmer's fake German radio stations for black propaganda activities that Ian had helped set up, and 'sat in on our morning conference'. Stuck in Plymouth for four days, Donovan was excited to watch a newly formed commando unit go through its training, and to hear details of Peter Fleming's XII Corps Observation Unit: a guerrilla cell of saboteurs, copied from the Wehrmacht's use of stay-behind bands.

Peter had, in utmost secrecy, trained a resistance army of three thousand men, many of them gamekeepers and foresters who knew every inch of their land. In the event of a German invasion, they were to conceal themselves in underground shelters, emerging at night to harass the enemy. Ian's Tennerhof contemporary, Ralph Arnold, visited one of Peter's lairs. His guide casually kicked a tree stump. 'It fell back on a hinge to reveal a hole with a rope ladder dangling into a cavern that had been enlarged from a badger's sett.' Sitting on kegs of explosives were soldiers from Richard Fleming's regiment, the Lovat Scouts. Known as Auxiliary Units, and one of the nine British Secret Services of the Second World War, this was the kind of clandestine organisation, so secret that its existence was not admitted till 1955, which it inspired Donovan to go home and replicate.

Packed though Donovan's schedule was, he sneaked a moment before embarking on his prolonged tour of the Mediterranean to visit Loelia Westminster at Send Grove, her weekend retreat near Woking. '20 December 1940. Bill Donovan came down for the night – in his usual old form! He thinks the Germans will invade Italy before coming here.' 'Big

Bill' was less sanguine when he visited her again at the end of his tour on 9 March 1941. 'He says the next six months are going to be very tough for us indeed.'

It would have been strange if their conversations had not touched on Ian Fleming, with whom Donovan had spent an intense ten days.

'He could persuade you with logic, charm and presence, but always persuade you,' a colleague said of Donovan. Ian's task was to persuade 'Big Bill' to make Britain's fight America's fight too.

Godfrey had enlisted the 'driving force' of his personal assistant to help achieve Godfrey's aspiration for the 'complete fusion of the British and American intelligence services'.

Ian had met Donovan when he toured the Admiralty the previous July, and before that with Loelia. He considered him 'a splendid American'. On Godfrey's orders, Ian had flown to meet Donovan in Gibraltar on 24 February 'on a secret mission', as he told his mother (who then told Augustus John, who wrote to a friend, who told her daughter: 'As he doesn't know Spain or Spanish it will necessarily be very secret.'). Ian also let slip to Maud Russell how he had spent a week in Gibraltar, Spain and Portugal 'attached to the American observer, Colonel Donovan'.

In Gibraltar, Ian discussed with 'Big Bill' his ideas for GOLDENEYE and TRACER. Intelligence that Germany intended to seize Gibraltar in early 1941 to choke off the Western Mediterranean was the catalyst. Both operations evolved out of networks Ian and Hillgarth had built up with Juan March's assistance to track Spanish vessels reportedly supplying U-boats with fuel oil and provisions.

Ian had hatched TRACER with Godfrey, drawing on the example of Peter's network of resistance hideouts in Kent. This was a larger version. A cave on Gibraltar's southern ridge, cork-tiled to reduce the noise, was to be fitted out with ten thousand gallons of water, a bicycle to recharge the wireless and an eighteen-foot aerial on which to report ship movements, with six men trained to hole up there in the event of Germany invading Spain. Donovan was impressed.

TRACER came under the superstructure of GOLDENEYE, which was less concrete and best described by Godfrey: 'The plan to help the Spaniards if the Germans invaded Spain. On lines of the Wellington campaigns in Peninsular War.' Not a single operation, GOLDENEYE was the confusing umbrella-name for ideas designed to meet two wildly different contingencies: SPRINKLER was a plan to help the Spanish resist the Nazi threat, using the Royal Navy to escort Spanish ships out of German hands to British ports in West Africa; while if General Franco capitulated or collaborated with the Nazis, this would activate SCONCE, a plan for guerrilla and sabotage activity on mainland Spain and Portugal. After taking leave of Donovan, Ian wrote a pencil note about 'the whole GOLDENEYE position', to be delivered by hand only. 'The work has been done & now it is only a question of sorting out personalities.'

From Gibraltar, Ian drove with Donovan to Madrid in the company of Alan Hillgarth and Vivian Dykes, whose account of the journey is short on enlightening detail, save for one image: Dykes's snapshot of a tipsy Ian. 'He is a brother of Peter Fleming and was on the Reuters staff before the war. He told me some interesting experiences as a Reuters' man and was a bit inclined to knock it back too much.' This is the first mention of Ian's drinking. The extraordinary composure he had displayed on his last visit to Madrid eight months before was cracking.

Donovan was teetotal, but Ian's alcohol intake at this time was a match for Stephenson's. 'They did drink, these chaps,' says Ivar Bryce's cousin, Lady (Janet) Milford Haven. 'They thought that the end was nigh. And looking into what happened, it shook them.' Maud Russell sat and watched Ian drink 'a prodigious amount' during an evening with Nancy Mitford. 'I[an] was rather drunk, noisy, nonsensical and provocative. He was enjoying himself which I love seeing as he leads such a serious life now, lives with so many mysteries and carries so many burdens.'

In Room 39, Ian was known not to expose his emotions. 'I wondered what was going on inside him,' said Edward Merrett, the jolly, snuff-taking, former solicitor who sat opposite. 'I grew used, as others did, to that smiling, well-mannered way he had of rebuff.' Merrett called it 'the wall'. Yet in the third year of the war, Ian's wall showed signs of crumbling. He had been shaken by the news that Peter might have been killed in Norway and then by their youngest brother's death. In the tense period following D-Day, when

Ian was panicking about his men's whereabouts, Robert Harling witnessed him erupt in 'the most explosive brainstorm I have witnessed'. He never forgot Ian's face, veins protruding, 'distorted as if in apoplexy, inflamed as if doused in red pepper, eyes ablaze with homicidal fury'.

Ian's drinking was responsible for an embarrassing incident five months after he parted company with Donovan in Lisbon. Flying from Lisbon again, Ian went on the town in Tangier with a British businessman whom Ian had asked to head a new NID office there should Gibraltar tumble. Denny Marris, who had flown into Tangier at the same moment, was a witness to Ian's riotous antics.

In Washington only days before, Ian had been staying with Marris, 'a remarkable chap' in Ian's opinion, who worked for the Ministry of Economic Warfare. In Tangier, he and Ian were again billeted together. Marris told his daughter how Ian had 'woken the town at an appalling hour. There was the noise of police cars and people shouting, and then a careworn figure climbed over the wall. Ian Fleming had got into the bull-ring and written something offensive and guaranteed to get the British community in Tangier in trouble. He'd done it with something very tiresome and difficult to remove.'

Whatever Ian had painted – in his version, 'a 20 foot V' – he hastened to apologise to Eccles in Lisbon, who had arranged his visit, for what Ian called 'Operation Catastrophe'. 'I was extremely contrite at the time,' he wrote to Smithers, 'but as the incident created nothing but mirth with all but the Consul General, no harm seems to have been done.'

Ian was living up to his brother's act of commandeering a train when he chartered a plane to fly him back to Lisbon, and charged the Admiralty £110 (approximately £7,300 today). Meanwhile, Peter Fleming had nearly died in a genuine catastrophe. It may have been this that coloured Ian's wild behaviour. Neither liked to talk about it, but what happened to Peter on 24 April 1941 had a lasting impact on both of them.

XXV
RODNEY BOND

'He set a very fine example to all ranks.'
Citation for Lt Rodney Bond's MC,
for action near Moeuvres, 27 September 1918

The story of how Peter Fleming nearly lost his life in a remote bay in Greece deserves retelling. First, it conveys the desperate military situation that lay behind Ian's mission to Washington in May 1941. Second, it sowed a name in Ian's mind.

'I have total memory. We were all hiding in a cave while bombs were falling on our boat in the harbour below.' Clarissa Caccia lost her uncle Oliver in the same German air attack, and witnessed 'his instant departure to nothingness on a bright sunny evening in the Aegean'. Peter might have perished too but for an English Intelligence officer who came to their rescue. This man was to give Ian the surname for his secret agent, says Clarissa.

What Peter Fleming was doing in the Aegean can also be traced back to Donovan. In February 1941, five days before Donovan met Ian in Gibraltar, 'Big Bill' had been in Cairo urging General Archibald Wavell, Commander-in-Chief Middle East, to go to the aid of Greece which had not yet been invaded by Germany. 'It is best to leap in now when the going is good.' On 19 February, Vivian Dykes observed Wavell dine alone with Donovan. 'I think his judgment has been considerably influenced by Donovan's advocacy, as it was a very finely balanced question to decide.'

The decision to withdraw Wavell's forces from Libya and send fifty thousand troops to Salonika handed an opportunity to Peter, who was kicking his heels in Cairo. On Hugh Dalton's orders, Peter had raised a small band of commandos known as the YAK Mission, to undertake SOE activities in Italy with the aim of toppling Mussolini. His idea was to land with a division of anti-fascist Italian POWs recruited from camps outside Cairo. Unfortunately, Peter could not persuade a single Italian prisoner to volunteer. 'Fleming's Foot are at present in a state of stagnation,' he wrote to Celia.

Through the 'sheer force of his own personality', Peter had established with the one-eyed, taciturn Wavell the kind of filial relationship Ian enjoyed with Godfrey. He now persuaded Wavell to let him take his YAK Mission to northern Greece, and, exactly as he had attempted in Norway a year before, 'do what I could to organise, train and equip local personnel for post-occupational resistance and sabotage in areas likely to be overrun by the enemy'.

Recruited from friends, Peter's four fellow officers included Oliver Barstow – whose sister Nancy was married to Peter's Eton contemporary Harold Caccia, then based at the embassy in Athens. On 25 March, Peter and Oliver stayed the night with the Caccias, and the next morning drove with the YAK Mission to Greece's frontier with Yugoslavia. They had hardly pitched camp when 'the enemy in considerable strength crossed the Yugoslav frontier'. To delay the unstoppable German advance, Peter's men booby-trapped a bus on a bridge crossing the Aliakmon, demolished a road north of Corinth, and drove an ammunition train out of Larissa. When German bombers attacked, 'we engaged the aircraft ineffectively with a Tommy gun.'

In his overcrowded room at the Admiralty, Ian's mind flashed back a year as he read the cables from Athens. Maud wrote: 'He is afraid we may be going to have a second Norway fiasco in Greece.' Ian warned her over lunch at the Carlton Grill on 9 April: 'be prepared for bad news.' When three weeks later, Ian appeared for dinner at Mottisfont, he looked 'thin and rather worn. G[ilbert] who hadn't seen him for two years says he looks like a man of 40.' Ian told them the latest. 'Athens has been taken by the Germans and Greece lost.' He had not heard from his brother.

Peter, Oliver and the rest of the YAK Mission had made it back to Athens three days earlier. At 8 p.m. on 23 April, Peter had joined the Caccias, their two small children, Clarissa and David, plus seventy or so others from the British embassy, on a one-funnelled steamboat, *Kalanthe*. 'The Yaks threw a lot of their equipment on board,' wrote Nancy in a long letter to her parents, '& as darkness fell we steamed quietly out.'

They were sailing under cover of night to Crete, where they hoped to join the Fleet. As the sun rose, they dropped anchor off the coast of 'an uninhabited island, just south of Kimolos called Poliegos (many goated) but in many maps it is not marked'.

Nancy took her children and their nanny ashore. It was very hot and she went off to bathe. 'I undressed in a secluded corner, & using my pants as a bathing cap crept in. The sea was breathtakingly cold at first, but was delicious when one's skin got accustomed. I swam & waded over to a little island with a few goats on it and sat & sunned hoping the distance would conceal my nudity.'

In the afternoon, Nancy found shade for her family inside a cave. Peter and Oliver remained guarding the *Kalanthe*.

Clarissa remembers: 'We were going to sail at night because the Germans commanded the air.'

Clarissa's mother was about to pack up when she heard planes coming in low and saw the smoke of bombs. She ran outside to grab her daughter.

A plane flew with guns firing low over the *Kalanthe* and hit the bridge where Peter and Nancy's brother Oliver were manning the Lewis guns. Three explosions followed. Nancy said 'Oliver' and ran out. 'Nanny shrieked at me to remember the children or something & I ran & ran but my legs were wobbly like a dream. The boat was drifting & on fire, & the sea all round full of black wreckage.'

Then Peter appeared, 'also pitch black & streaming with blood, but giving orders & sitting up looking skinny & shivering'. Nancy tore off her blouse and sluiced sea water over him to wash the black oil out of his wounds. He was bleeding profusely from his leg and shoulder, and from a two-inch gash in his forehead.

'I tell her about Oliver,' Peter wrote, 'but I think she knows already.' Nancy was lugging Peter over the prickly low scrub when the *Kalanthe* blew up.

Clarissa says: 'We were fetched by fishermen from Kimolos who came over to see what the bombing had done, and moved into their school. Peter and Dad from there sent a Morse message to Crete to see if anyone was prepared to come back into enemy-occupied territory and get us.'

The message was picked up by an SIS colleague of Caccia's from the

British embassy in Athens. His name was Bond. Rodney Clarence Mortimer Bond.

Lieutenant Bond had escaped Athens in a small, slow caique, *'being attacked by enemy aircraft on the way'* – according to the citation for the MBE that he was awarded for his subsequent action. He had only just reached Crete when he received Peter's SOS. Bond volunteered at once to return to rescue the marooned party.

'He risked his own safety,' says Clarissa.

Disregarding the German threat from the sky, Bond set sail in broad daylight, bringing with him two other Intelligence officers and a doctor, and 'masses of food & 250 blankets'. *'By their gallantry and self-sacrifice these officers were responsible for saving the Legation party who would otherwise ultimately have been captured. Some were badly wounded and probably owe their lives to the arrival of the rescuers.'* At 10.30 a.m. on Saturday 26 April, Bond stepped ashore on Kimolos.

Clarissa says: 'We clambered aboard with the wounded.' Badly injured YAK Mission men, children and others, with Bond at the helm. 'We all slept on deck under the sky. Rodney Bond only had the stars and a child's atlas of the Mediterranean to navigate with, but the next day, as the sun rose, Santorini appeared on the skyline.'

Harold Caccia lived to become ambassador to JFK's Washington and Provost of Eton. Not until the end of his life did he reveal to Clarissa their rescuer's identity. 'You do know, don't you, darling, we only survived because of a chap called Rodney Bond.'

Like Poliegos, Lieutenant Rodney Bond appears in few records. A forty-four-year-old war hero, he had been born in Penzance but brought up in Constantinople, where his father was a marine engineer. He won his Military Cross in France in September 1918 near where Val Fleming was killed. Following the First World War, Bond disappears into the Intelligence Corps, emerging briefly in 1941 in Athens to perform the same function of 'Passport Control Officer' as William Stephenson in New York. In 1944, operating out of Constantinople under the codename 'Hatzis', he arranged the escape of the future Greek Prime Minister Georgios Papandreou – receiving him on a beach near Smyrna and flying him to Cairo. He rose to become a lieutenant colonel and, in one mention, died in 1953 in New York, the year of the first James Bond book. By coincidence, his eldest child was called James.

In the same conversation as Caccia revealed to Clarissa the name of their saviour, he told her how after the war, Peter Fleming was having breakfast at his family home in Oxfordshire while reading the newspapers when his brother Ian came in and said: 'Peter, I've written a bloody good thriller, but I can't get a name for my hero.' Without lowering his newspaper, Peter replied: 'Try Bond.'

Peter recovered from his wounds, but the episode was a turning point. Great things had been prophesied before the war. He would become editor of *The Times* or Viceroy of India. 'If I were dictator, I might try someone like Peter Fleming,' wrote Lord Halifax, the former Viceroy and now Britain's ambassador in Washington, who had been expected to succeed Chamberlain as Prime Minister. Peter was indeed sent to India months later. 'Once my brother Peter gets out there,' Ian promised Smithers, 'doubtless the Japanese will pack up and return home. He is going out on Wavell's staff and is, of course, delighted.' Based in Delhi, Peter's job in strategic deception mirrored Ian's work at the Admiralty, but it was in a distant arena on the sidelines and marked the end of his ascendancy over Ian. As he wrote to Celia, 'It's no place to be in for a war.'

From this moment on, Peter was Halifax to Ian's Churchill.

XXVI
'SPECIAL SERVICES'

'He founded the CIA. Did you know that?'
BLANCHE BLACKWELL

A Rodney Bond was needed to save Britain in that spring of 1941. Germany had invaded Greece and Yugoslavia; Rommel had forced Wavell back in Cyrenaica; U-boats had sunk 194 Allied ships since December, with the Enigma code for the German navy not yet being broken in 'real time'. 'The war has come to the point of absolute crisis,' David Eccles reported on 21 April from Washington. 'We can't win if the US doesn't come in.'

Ian's mission to Washington proved how much one individual on the spot could achieve. The initiative was Admiral Godfrey's.

Fortified by Godfrey, 'Big Bill' had returned from his European tour convinced that America needed a new co-ordinated foreign Intelligence agency. This was the case that Donovan put to Roosevelt in a powerful memorandum on 26 April. Godfrey and Stephenson did not doubt that 'Big Bill' was the person to run this agency.

There was one snag. Fired up by what he had seen of the British commandos and special operations such as Peter's Auxiliary Units and YAK Mission, Donovan hankered to be a fighting soldier again, in the mould of his recent on-screen image; even to command a regiment like the 69th. To be appointed a behind-the-scenes Intelligence chief like 'Little Bill' held less appeal.

Donovan's wobbles had to be steadied at once. It was one reason why Godfrey left London at this moment: to make a personal assessment and plea. He wanted Ian with him as an 'intermediary for the most daring but informal approaches' – a wise decision, he later acknowledged. 'The unfamiliar work on which I was engaged in the US was made much easier by the presence and help of Ian. He got on well with Americans; operating on a slightly different plane to mine, he was able to discover how the land lay and to warn me of pitfalls. His command of English ensured that everything I wrote was to the point, was devoid of ambiguity and worded in a way that appealed to Americans.'

'Big Bill' was Godfrey's principal target. Stephenson said, 'Donovan would always say to anyone he got on with or was impressed by, "Well, let's have it in writing then."' With Ian at the DNI's side, and, when necessary, speaking or writing for him, it was Godfrey's triple purpose to promote Donovan's candidacy for the new US agency he had in mind, persuade a foot-dragging Donovan to accept its leadership, and assist Donovan in outlining a framework for how it might operate. Together with Godfrey and Stephenson, Ian played an important part in levering Donovan into the position of 'Co-ordinator'.

They flew by Clipper, dressed in civilian clothes. The flying boat's windows were covered with brown paper to conceal their passage. Stopping over in Lisbon, they had a meeting with the Naval Intelligence team who were to work on Operation GOLDENEYE, and they saw the new ambassador, Sir Ronald Campbell, last encountered in Bordeaux, whom Godfrey painted as 'tired & never the same after leaving Paris'; his 'son is a prisoner of war'.

Lisbon was a cornucopia for anyone accustomed to rations in the blackout. 'Am eating far too much & enjoying the hot sun,' Godfrey wrote in a postcard home. And in another: 'I find one just goes on eating. Everything is so good & lots of it. Lovely oranges, tangerines, butter, cream & fish.'

The same abundance was on display in the espionage community, according to Paul Furse, the eccentric Assistant Naval Attaché and botanist soon to be transferred by Ian to Washington. 'Lisbon was a cockpit of intrigue, and the scene of every trickery.' Whenever you went into a hotel or bar, you could expect to find at least four people who would confide in you that 'I am the Head of the British Secret Service in Portugal.' You had to put up with your luggage being searched every day. 'The hotels always had men available, whom the other side would tip for a soap impression of the key.'

Jack Beevor ran SOE in Lisbon. He warned Ian about the Abwehr-controlled brothels; girls were briefed to target British seamen ashore and hand out invitations – 'Madame A. cordially invites you to her home on . . . at . . . p.m. to have a jolly good time and dancing too.'

Ian had booked himself and Godfrey into the Palacio Hotel in Estoril along the coast. Ian had many friends at the embassy – not only Furse and Beevor, but 'Boofy' Gore, David Eccles, and Sandy Glen. They tipped him off that the resort in Estoril was especially 'crawling with German secret agents' who gambled every night at the casino. Ian immediately suggested to Godfrey that they should go along to the casino and have a look at these people. 'We went, and there were three men whose descriptions we had, playing at the high Chemin de Fer table. The DNI didn't know the game. I explained it to him, and then the feverish idea came to me that I would sit down and gamble against these men and defeat them, thereby reducing the funds of the German Secret Service.' Ian had some £50 in travel money. 'I bancoed and lost. I suivied and lost again, and suivied a third time and was cleaned out.'

Much has been made of this episode, which Ian recast in *Casino Royale* as 'the kernel of James Bond's great gamble against Le Chiffre', but when John Pearson asked Godfrey about it, 'he said that they weren't German, F[leming]. wasn't playing for high stakes, and that it was only *afterwards*, rather casually, that F. had said, "Suppose they had been German secret service men and suppose we had cleaned them out." In fact, of course, he lost.'

From Lisbon, they flew to Bermuda, where Godfrey introduced Ian to what would become his post-war passion. 'Bermuda is renowned for the beauty of its underwater coral flora and fauna and I took the precaution of including a pair of underwater goggles in my luggage.' After collecting 2,224 pounds of mail, it was a short leg to New York. Godfrey grumbled of his personal assistant, 'Instead of sitting next to me he disappeared and sat next to the prettiest girl on the plane.'

Also on the Dixie Clipper was the fashion designer Elsa Schiaparelli, dressed in 'a navy blue travelling suit with wine-coloured waist and matching turban', and full of the privations of Occupied Paris that seemed a foretaste of Occupied London. Instead of a suitcase, she carried a wicker basket – 'this is what we use for luggage, we have no more leather.' Caught in the blaze of flash-bulbs that greeted her at La Guardia, Ian appears over Schiaparelli's right shoulder as an anonymous blur in a hat. 'Our mission was supposed to be highly secret,' Godfrey wrote, 'as the US was still neutral.'

In New York, Stephenson showed them around his 'highly mechanised eyrie' in Rockefeller Center that operated as British Security Co-ordination's office behind a door marked 'Rough Diamonds, Ltd.' Roald Dahl, who came to work there, told his mother that the lifts to the thirty-sixth floor 'go up and down faster than I've ever dived in an aeroplane'. No previous British Passport Control Officer had enjoyed such premises, but Stephenson was a millionaire; having declined to take a salary, he was at liberty to channel his money into advancing Churchill's agenda. 'How much I admire the wonderful set-up you have achieved in New York,' Godfrey afterwards thanked him. 'As the prototype of what such an organisation should be, I consider it beyond praise.' The corridors were sheeted with black marble, and a secret annexe led into a room with the very latest teleprinters and decoding machines 'to handle up to one million messages a day', staffed by Canadian secretaries who had been recruited 'TO WORK FOR BRITAIN', according to the job advertisement in the *Toronto Telegram*. 'There were dozens of them, each lovelier than the last,' recalled the screenwriter Benn Levy, one of eight hundred spies and decoders eventually employed by Stephenson.

These young women from Toronto and Winnipeg were not unresponsive to the bachelor allure of a visiting Naval commander. When Fleming walked into the office, one Canadian secretary remembered how 'just like dominoes the girls would go down – whoosh like that'. As if only now it had dawned on him, Godfrey observed how his personal assistant was 'an amazingly quick worker with the ladies. I took him to some friends on Long Island. The hostess was a very smart New York socialite, and ten minutes after Ian arrived, he suggested they should go up to bed together. He must have had any number of rebuffs, but they never seemed to worry him.'

Meanwhile, getting into bed with the Americans was the priority. The sinking of HMS *Hood* in Denmark Strait on 24 May with 1,415 dead had made their mission even more vital.

Godfrey and Ian hit nothing but brick walls over the next fortnight.

Stephenson had organised for them to meet the FBI director, J. Edgar Hoover, whom Stephenson had come to know through their mutual boxing friend, Gene Tunney. Ian described Hoover as a 'chunky enigmatic man with slow eyes and a trap for a mouth', who 'received us graciously' for sixteen minutes, but was 'politely uninterested in our mission'.

It took less time still with the irascible US Navy chief, Admiral Ernest King, to pick up that he hated the British, but not as much as he hated the US Army. Godfrey knew that the relations between the US Army and Navy were bad, but he did not realise how bad until he and Ian tried to get them to see eye to eye and collaborate with the State Department. 'These three departments showed the utmost goodwill towards me and Ian Fleming, but very little towards each other.' They behaved like serpents in the 'rather creepy crawly film' that Godfrey watched with the composer Irving Berlin at the White House on 10 June. 'Collaboration hardly existed.'

Stephenson advised Godfrey that 'the only person who could and would handle this question with any hope of success' was President Roosevelt himself. Eleanor Roosevelt was persuaded by Stephenson's predecessor, Sir William Wiseman, to invite Godfrey to dinner and ensure that he had an hour afterwards with 'Flywheel', as Godfrey referred to the President in cables to London. Following the film, about snake worship in Laos, Godfrey, dressed in black tie, was invited into the Oval Office where he sat in Lincoln's chair while Roosevelt talked for seventy-five minutes from his wheelchair. 'At last I got a word in edgeways. I said it a second time, and a third time – one intelligence security boss, not three or four.'

Roosevelt did not ask who Godfrey had in mind. Nor did Godfrey consider it wise to say. Both men knew that Donovan had submitted a further memorandum to 'Flywheel' earlier in the day. This memorandum, wrote David Eccles, who was in on the secret, advised Roosevelt 'to set up a co-ordinator of strategic information, responsible directly to himself as Commander-in-Chief.'

Donovan had worked on the proposal for days, with 'considerable' input from Godfrey, Stephenson, Ian, and, in 'the pre-natal stages', Eccles, whom the Ministry of Economic Warfare had sent from Lisbon with the same end: 'to get the USA somewhere and as soon as possible into the war'. Eccles had been in Washington since April, advising Donovan. At Donovan's invitation, he had moved to Donovan's house in Georgetown, 'and there on the porch at the back we worked on the memoranda for the President'.

Eight days after Godfrey's meeting in the Oval Office, on 18 June 1941, Roosevelt summoned Donovan and asked him to be the Co-ordinator. At first, Donovan baulked. 'I told the President that I did not want to do it.' 'Big Bill' still harboured 'Wild Bill's' military ambitions to be in uniform and 'handle troops'. He consented only after Roosevelt gave a verbal promise that Donovan could have his guerrilla outfit.

That night, Stephenson cabled London on receiving from Ian the news of Donovan's acceptance. 'Donovan saw President today and after long discussion wherein all points were agreed, he accepted appointment. He will be co-ordinator of all forms [of] intelligence including offensive operations equivalent SO2 [part of SOE]. He will hold the rank of Major-General and will be responsible only to the President. Donovan accuses me of having "intrigued and driven" him into appointment. You can imagine how relieved I am after three months of battle and jockeying for position in Washington that our man is in a position of such importance to our efforts.'

In New York the next day, Eccles caught up with Donovan, who told him how Roosevelt had asked him to hammer out the details for what was blandly to be called the Co-ordination of Strategic Information (COI), explaining how it might work. Eccles wrote to his wife, 'He offered me any job I liked in his organisation.' Eccles then went for a long walk up Fifth Avenue, wondering whether to accept. When he decided not to, it was Ian who slipped smartly into Eccles's boots – and sheets. 'In order not to break the continuity of collaboration between us and Bill on this subject, I have installed Ian Fleming in my bed at Bill's house. He knows much more about the details of intelligence work than I do.'

2920 R Street NW in the Washington district of Georgetown was a detached, cream-coloured house, with a grey slate roof like a small chateau, set back across a lawn overshadowed by a large conifer. Donovan's wife Ruth was still shattered by their daughter's death. Patricia's room was as she had left it a year before, with bookshelves of modern poetry, and her photographs everywhere. Possibly out of respect for her grief-stricken parents, Ian spread his two months in Washington shuttling between Donovan, Denny Marris on 3125 O Street, and Peter Smithers on 28th Street NW.

Cobbled streets, red-brick pavements, black lamp-posts with globe lights. No war had come to this genteel backwater since 1814. Georgetown was a place of tree-lined calm in which to plot the defence of the free world.

Here is where to examine Ian's bold claim that 'I spent some time with [Donovan] in his home writing the original charter of the OSS' (as the COI became eleven months later). Ian wrote this to Colonel Rex Appleyard in 1957. Five years later, he spoke to the writer and historian Cornelius Ryan about 'my memorandum to Bill on how to create an American Secret Service'.

How to make sense of these assertions? It does seem odd that Donovan would offer a Brit a job in US Intelligence, especially when Godfrey and Fleming were never entirely clear themselves about the organisation they were pressing on the Americans.

Further confusion arises from the assumption that Ian was talking about two memoranda, when there appear to have been at least three, or even four: Donovan's initial memo of 26 April; his wide-ranging, but general, paper to Roosevelt of 10 June, to which Ian, Eccles, Stephenson and Godfrey contributed; and apparently two more detailed memoranda (one of which is missing) that Ian wrote on his own for Donovan to finesse ideas for the President on what a future Secret Service might look like. To Bryce alone did Ian relate the improbable story that he had been whisked off to a room in the embassy, 'locked in it with a pen and paper and the necessities of life, and had written under armed guard around the clock, a document of some seventy pages covering every aspect of a giant secret intelligence and secret operational organisation'.

A reliable assessment of Ian's claim was stymied by Stephenson's burning the British Security Co-ordination papers in 1945. So much had to be kept covert because of the Neutrality Act which made it dangerous for the US, before Pearl Harbor in December 1941, to take a strong pro-British stance. Gagged by the blanket of neutrality, Roosevelt risked being impeached if anything of his complicity with British Intelligence on US soil was revealed. Still, Roosevelt signalled his active connivance when he appointed the Anglophile Donovan as his new Intelligence chief and confidential assistant.

'You are my legs,' he told Donovan. From now on, Donovan communicated directly with Roosevelt over a portable Zenith radio in his Buick, and Roosevelt's son James was deputed to work for him.

Ian already had this sort of relation with 'Uncle John'. When Godfrey needed to fly back to London in June, he left Ian alone with full authority to represent him. 'This arrangement bore immediate fruit,' confirmed an American Intelligence report. Ian had carried with him to Washington 'a brochure on NID organisation specially prepared for the occasion'. He gave this to Donovan.

Hitler's invasion of Russia on 22 June 1941 reinforced the relief of all parties that the appointment of 'Big Bill' had come not a moment too soon. With Ian's help, Donovan hammered out the details that Roosevelt had requested. According to Bryce, 'The information was then passed on through Donovan to FDR himself.'

Many of Ian's meetings were held in Smithers's small drawing room. 'I always made a point of being absent when he was going to be there,' said Smithers, 'because if I were Donovan I would want the fewer people listening in the better. He got on very well with Donovan and it seems to have been a successful relationship.'

Charm is hard to convey outside its influence. Ian was always more than 'an obscure lieutenant commander RNVR'. He was a seductive and persuasive force who, because of his presence and personal magnetism, could achieve things not always recorded on paper. 'One thing that staggered me,' says Michael Goodman, official historian of the Joint Intelligence Committee, 'was the role of personalities, the huge difference that one individual could make, and how they could progress through the system.'

Godfrey wrote that Ian's position 'had no frontiers'. With no defined role, Ian was able to write his own job description and break through boundaries quickly by establishing an instant rapport with the architects and future leaders of what became the CIA.

Ernie Cuneo was Donovan's personal liaison between Stephenson, the Department of Justice and the State Department. 'I was a part of a very small White House group called the Palace Guard' – with 'immediate access' to the White House and Donovan. 'It was apparent to me,' wrote Cuneo, on first meeting Ian in Stephenson's penthouse apartment at the Dorset Hotel, 'that

Fleming carried a great weight beyond his Lieutenant Commander rank.' Robert Harling came to Washington on Ian's recommendation to advise Donovan on how to set up a contacts registry. 'One of the leading American Intelligence people called Fleming "The Head of the Naval Intelligence Division", and he was,' said Harling. 'He was an absolutely, you know, gold piece for them.'

Ian's role in American Intelligence has earned him and his fictional hero an exhibition room at the International Spy Museum in Washington. Anna Slafer, a senior curator there, says, 'You're not looking at hundreds of people who are setting up OSS in the first place, you're looking at two or three.'

Charisma aside, Ian was one of very few in Washington at the time with the experience and the ability, as Smithers was there to witness, 'to impart to "Wild Bill" Donovan some of the specialist knowledge which went into the OSS.' Ian had spent two years going the rounds of British Intelligence with the blessing of Godfrey. Like his grandfather who put Scottish capital into the American West, Ian invested Britain's Intelligence capital to establish the joint Secret Service machinery.

Ian did not have the experience to advise on the creation of an offensive Human Intelligence gathering service, but this would not stop him from trying. 'We were not afraid to try things that had not been tried before,' said Donovan. Ever since their briefings in Gibraltar, it was apparent they shared a similar Churchillian approach. Godfrey had praised Donovan's 'energy and drive', words that he applied to his personal assistant, while Donovan's assistant David Bruce described 'Big Bill' in ways that could have applied to Ian. 'His imagination was unlimited. Ideas were his plaything. Excitement made him snort like a racehorse.' Certain of Donovan's ideas, like explosive dung, might have been plucked from Ian's missing NID brochure. 'For painful weeks under his command,' Bruce recalled, 'I tested the possibility of using bats – they were to carry delayed action incendiary bombs – taken from concentrations in Western caves, to destroy Tokyo.' Ian's recommendations came out of the same basket, 'a remarkable mix of wishful thinking, imperial arrogance and common sense', in the view of one recent US Intelligence historian.

At Smithers's little frame house in Georgetown, which Ian baptised 'Chateau Smithers', Ian passed on to Donovan the most guarded details about the 'dirty-tricks department'; psychological warfare and fake radio broadcasts;

how to grade intelligence, A to E for source and 1 to 5 for contents; prisoner of war interrogation techniques; the Joint Intelligence Committee–Joint Intelligence Staff 'set up'.

He suggested personnel: NID's Eddie Hastings as director of communications; Dorothy Thompson, the American columnist who had admired Ian's looks in Kitzbühel; and for Donovan's man in London, Junius Morgan Jr., then looking after Hugo Pitman's daughter Jemima in New York ('Ian came over and visited us there two or three times, in naval uniform, to take news of us back to my parents') – Ian later writing to commend Donovan 'for having chosen such an outstanding officer to work with us'.

As well, Ian recommended to Stephenson his part-Peruvian best friend Ivar Bryce, who had spent that summer sketching a map of fictitious Nazi ambitions for South America, along the lines of the Zimmermann telegram, that had swayed the United States into declaring war on Germany in 1917. Hopes were raised for a similar outcome when a supposedly indignant Roosevelt decried Bryce's map as a bona fide Nazi blueprint in a dramatic broadcast to the nation on 27 October 1941. The map, 'slightly travel stained with use', had been forged in a hilltop mansion in Toronto by another of Stephenson's agents, the songwriter Eric Maschwitz, and placed in Roosevelt's hands with Donovan's connivance.

Ian's one surviving memorandum dated 27 June 1941, with the tell-tale words 'See my previous memo', urged Donovan to act on his recommendations with speed 'in order that your organisation can be set up in time to meet war before Christmas'. Ian was urgent for a reason. On 19 July, a week after Donovan was confirmed in his post, Ian sent Godfrey a 'MOST SECRET' cable. 'President is very enthusiastic and Donovan has his full support but rumour that Donovan is British nominee and hireling of British SIS is spreading and should be carefully watched.'

The snake-pit was hissing. Paul Furse, summoned to Washington to act as a link between Ian, Donovan and Stephenson, had found 'horrifying competition and jealousy between the US Military intelligence "G2" and the Naval "ONI" everywhere we went: they were still in the schoolboy throat-cutting stage ...'. The one thing uniting the US Navy, Army and State Department was hostility towards Donovan's new COI, which General Sherman Miles branded 'calamitous'.

Ian stressed to Godfrey: 'Value of this organisation to British intelligence will depend entirely on Mr Stephenson.'

More than twenty years later, Ian abandoned a storyline featuring an anonymous all-seeing director based on 'Little Bill'. In May 1963, he assigned the rights to MGM for £1. The following year, it became the hugely popular television series 'The Man from U.N.C.L.E.' and was borrowed afterwards as a device for 'Charlie's Angels'.* Ian sketched out his idea on a sheaf of Western Union telegrams: about a best-selling thirty-six-year-old author, Napoleon Solo, who each week 'will solve a problem of international import-ance' after first reporting to a 'very modern office – radio concealed, padded door with light above, where "He" the anonymous chief has his office. "He" is frequently referred to. "He" says to go: etc. etc.' Ian was drawing on Wil-liam Stephenson's control room and invisible methods, and from all he had learned that summer.

The deeper Stephenson took Ian into his confidence, the more Ian shared Godfrey's conviction that 'Little Bill' was pivotal to the success of Churchill's plan to involve America.

Ian witnessed Stephenson's burgling of codes from the safe of the Japa-nese consulate on the floor adjacent to the BSC offices. 'One night,' said Stephenson, 'with the help of the janitor, we got into their office and pinched their ciphers to copy. Ian was there at the time, and was particularly bucked because he could go back and report to Uncle John.' Bond's first 'oo' assas-sination is in that Rockefeller Center office.

Not only was Ian in on the secret operation to film the German minister meeting his mistress in a Manhattan hotel. He was privy to Stephenson's discussions with Donovan about receiving British censorship material from Bermuda; about BSC's fake news operations, like Bryce's false Nazi map, and the incriminating card that the isolationist politician Hamilton Fish was photographed holding, 'Der Führer thanks you for your loyalty', thrust into his hand by one of Stephenson's agents; about the sabotage operation organ-ised by Furse in the balsa wood forests of Ecuador – 'Someone incited a discontented Indian to drive a spike into a trunk, so the teeth were stripped

* In the 2019 movie, 'Charlie's Angels', the villain is Peter Fleming, 'a short-sighted greedy traitor'.

off the circular saw (in a German-owned sawmill!)'; and about setting up a training camp in Canada, where Donovan's men could be instructed in SOE guerrilla techniques along the lines of Peter's commandos.

Godfrey wrote, 'As far as I was concerned we had no secrets.'

Not surprisingly, American historians downplay the role of Stephenson, Godfrey and Fleming in helping to establish America's first foreign Intelligence service, rather as British historians exaggerate their contribution. The truth lies in between. COI, under British tutelage, became an undoubted success – even if, in practice, 'coordination' in line with the Godfrey–Fleming vision never really happened, with the existing agencies sceptical at best, hostile at worst, and zealously guarding their roles.

Ian's value at this vulnerable moment was to have stiffened Donovan's resolve, provided him with an outline, and acted as the conduit between 'Little Bill', 'Big Bill' and the DNI, to make certain Donovan had the information that he required to build up the COI and a year later the OSS. Donovan's name appeared thirty-six times in lists for meetings and calls between August and September 1941. He and Stephenson 'practically lived together,' Stephenson said. 'We were known on all fronts as "the Two Bills" because we were always together.' The effectiveness of their joint campaign to shift American public opinion was reflected in a Gallup survey that November, with eighty-five per cent now thinking that the US would go to war with Germany.

Desmond Morton disclosed the hidden fruit of that Washington summer: a 'most secret fact of which the PM is aware . . . is that to all intents and purposes US Security is being run for them at the President's request by the British'.

Notwithstanding his subsequent exaggerated claims, Stephenson's casting of the relationship in mentor–pupil terms was something Donovan never challenged. In a draft proposal he wrote in 1945 for a post-war agency, Donovan argued for a service that would allow the US to free itself from 'our present national dependence upon British intelligence'.

On 9 August 1941, Roosevelt and Churchill met at Placentia Bay off Newfoundland on the deck of the *Prince of Wales*, and sang 'For those in peril on the sea' alongside ranks of British and American sailors. Churchill's principal private secretary was among them. 'You would have been pretty hard-boiled not to be moved by it all – hundreds of men from both fleets all mingled together, one rough British sailor sharing his hymn sheet with one American.'

One week later, Ian called on Ann O'Neill in London. 'He was reticent about America,' she recorded in her diary, 'but seems to have had a beautiful time.'

*'For such a novel enterprise, it is essential an officer with
drive and imagination of the highest order is supervising
matters at headquarters.'*

ADMIRAL JOHN GODFREY to JIC, 25 June 1942

'Big Bill' was the mover behind a secret training camp on Lake Ontario:
'Camp X'.

In Washington, Donovan had picked Ian's brains on how to create an
American guerrilla force, with teaching facilities like the SOE schools that
Ian's brother had been involved with. Until he went to run strategic deception in India in 1942, Peter ran the School of Street Fighting in the
bombed-out ruins of Battersea; before that, he was involved with the Special
Training Centre at Inverailort in the west Highlands where his radio set
from Norway was used to teach Morse code.

Donovan envisaged something similar. Back in 1915, he had recruited a
regiment to fight Mexican revolutionaries on the Texas border. In the late
summer of 1941, he sought Stephenson's co-operation to prepare an American guerrilla outfit for the war he foresaw coming. He was willing to fund it. A
list compiled for Donovan by Barty Pleydell-Bouverie, Ned's cousin, then running the SOE office in Washington under Stephenson's direction, itemised 'the
quantities of special devices which we shall be glad if your organisation will
undertake to manufacture and deliver to us'. The devices included 1.5 million
pencil fuses, one thousand fighting knives, five thousand Type 6 limpet mines,
and ten thousand K tablets (to render someone unconscious).

Supervised by 'Little Bill' in the autumn of 1941, 280 acres of orchard
were purchased across the US border at Oshawa, east of Toronto, for the
joint instruction of SOE and COI/OSS operatives 'who were later dropped

into occupied territory', said Stephenson. Up to a hundred students at a time were taught by a staff of thirty British experts in 'sabotage, the conduct of agents in the field and the gathering of information'. The SOE officer who controlled the training was Ian's colleague from his Juan March operations, the Belgian banker Louis Franck.

Stephenson said in his dotage that Ian had come top of the agent course. This involved clamping limpet mines to a submerged hull in Lake Ontario, breaching Toronto's main power station, and being prepared to shoot a supposed enemy agent in cold blood. The story was rejected as pure invention by David Stafford, who questioned whether Ian ever set foot in Oshawa. On the other hand, Ian admitted in an interview with Canadian television that he went to Canada 'two or three times on naval intelligence work'. Peter Smithers was certainly under the impression that Ian had stayed at 'Camp X' and participated in training exercises. 'When I was in Washington, he took ten days to go to a special course in dirty tricks in Canada.' Afterwards, Ian presented Smithers with a 7½-inch 'Commando dagger' with 'FS' engraved on it. Ian joked that the letters stood for 'Fleming-Smithers'. In fact, they represented 'Fairbairn-Sykes', after one of the instructors at 'Camp X', Captain William Fairbairn from the Shanghai police, who had taught close-quarter pistol shooting at Inverailort.*

Whatever Ian's performance level, it counted for less than the idea he came back with, to create a similar outfit under his command. Stephenson alleged that 'Ian took extensive notes at the time and used a lot of what he learned there when he was setting up his own 30AU.'

On a visit to Ian's small flat in Athenaeum Court, where he had been forced to move during the Blitz, Maud Russell noticed 'new uniforms and equipment lying about. He has a private army of 300 men.' The uniforms had special shoulder flashes with the figure '30' in light blue on dark blue. 'His men, his "army", are marine-commandos.'

'Have you ever heard of 30AU?' Ian asked Robert Harling, on Harling's return from a job for the Topographical Department in Alexandria.

---

* Ian told Smithers he had learned 'how to kill a man in close combat by biting him in the back of the neck if you got the chance to do that'.

'Never.'

'Well, it's short for Number Thirty Assault Unit . . . basically, the unit's job is to seize enemy equipment, ciphers, scientific know-how before such material can be destroyed.' He wanted Harling to join.

Ian's covert intelligence-gathering unit would grow from twenty-four men in 1942, to fifty in 1943, to 150 in 1944, to 450 in 1945. At the same time, its name changed, from 30 Commando, with the cover name of Special Engineering Unit, to 30 Assault Unit (on 31 December 1943), and finally to 30 Advance Unit in March 1945. Ian referred to the men as his 'Red Indians'. They were otherwise known as 'Fleming's private Navy', 'sailors in jeeps', 'a bunch of armed Limey gangsters' (General Patton), and 'No. 30 Indecent Assault Unit' (the First Sea Lord). They included the grandson of one Prime Minister (Stanley Baldwin), the grandfather and father-in-law of another (Boris Johnson), and a burglar who was the only man to escape twice from Peterhead prison.

The '30' signified Room 30 at the Admiralty where Ian's secretary worked. 30AU served in France, Germany, the Mediterranean and North Africa, the Greek islands, Norway, Pantelleria, Sicily, Italy and Corsica, and a section was posted to Lebanon, but what the latter did remains secret. It is still diffi-cult to tell their full story.

The unit was always hedged by secrecy. One of 30AU's last survivors, Bill Marshall, aged ninety-four, says: 'A did not know B, and B did not know X. No one knew. Afterwards . . . when I put my number into the government website, up came *This person does not exist*. The Admiralty said my records won't be released till 2050, some of them.'

The handbook that Ian prepared for Bill's operations – meticulously planned and directed by Ian from the small, smoke-filled room in the Admiralty building known as the Citadel – instructed that no one was to talk about what they did, even to senior officers. 'Mention of the existence of such a Force and discussion of its activities outside official circles even after it has been disbanded may well jeopardise the success of any future opera-tions and therefore must be avoided at all costs.'

Furthermore, the unit was chopped up into small mobile groups of six to eight men who moved at speed across a battleground where the front line was in flux. Commander Jan Aylen, one of Ian's officers whom Bill Marshall chauffeured into Kiel, wrote that 30AU's activities were so 'widely spread that just about no one except those on a particular job in hand knew what was happening. It took a man like Ian Fleming, the creator of James Bond, to mastermind this extraordinary outfit.'

After the war, NID, and 30AU especially, served as Ian's bullion, to be cut into slices in his books. This is why the Bond books endure, says Nicholas Rankin, author of the best history of the unit. 'They work because he's a storyteller. They are firmly rooted in convincing details,' and they were details his men had risked their lives over. 'What we see as inventiveness is part of his naval knowledge.'

30AU evolved in the wake of Ian's aborted initiative for a commando raid in Spain in March 1942. As part of his planning for Operation GOLDENEYE, he had played 'a leading role' in pressing for direct SOE action to blow up a network of infra-red bolometers, or 'Bodden beams', that German agents had installed on both sides of the straits, to keep a 'detailed and deadly watch' on Allied shipping.

Godfrey had supported Ian, but Britain's ambassador in Madrid, Samuel Hoare, or 'the pink rat' as Eccles called him, urged a diplomatic solution, obliging Ian to fall back on mere propaganda, a course of inaction that he was resolved not to follow.

Two months earlier, on 27 January 1942, Ian had instructed Smithers in Washington to spread false rumours through his Swedish contacts 'that the Straits of Gibraltar are now mined by an ingenious new method and that you think this has something to do with atomic mines invented by the Americans. This is a useful line in connection with the German U-boats in the Mediterranean against which we have had notable success lately . . .'

But Ian's optimism had been short-lived. Four days later, on 1 February 1942, the German Navy introduced a new four-rotor Enigma machine. This was much harder to break. During the ensuing SIGINT blackout, U-boats sank 615,000 metric tons of shipping in February and 723,000 tons in March – twice the level of 1941 losses. No amount of Smithers's propaganda looked likely to reduce the threat. The pressing need for a breakthrough in cracking German Naval Enigma traffic triggered the formation of 30AU.

Like James Bond in *From Russia, with Love*, one of Ian's priorities was to obtain the German equivalent of 'the brand new Spektor machine. The thing we'd give our eyes to have . . . the machine that would allow [us] to decipher the Top Secret traffic of all.' Unlike Bond, Ian had been closely involved from the start of the war with the cryptographers at Bletchley Park. His main contacts were in Hut 4 Naval Section, notably Frank Birch and Harry Hinsley. Pauline Burrough served in the ground floor office of Bletchley's Naval deputy director, Commander Bradshaw, and she confirms Ian's presence at Bletchley. She remembers meeting Admiral Godfrey for drinks. 'He was a bit brusque, a little bit scary. You needed to know exactly what you were saying. Ian Fleming was there.'

The codebreaker Alan Turing was among Ian's contacts in Hut 8. An example of Ian's fertile energy and approach was his response to a crisis that involved Turing and German Naval Intelligence, initially believed to be 'unbreakable'. Godfrey had written to Birch, head of the German Naval Section, 'I think the solution will be found in a combined committee of talent in your department and mine who can think up cunning schemes.'

One of the more cunning schemes was Ian's.

On 10 September 1940, Hut 4 reported on Germany's fast new air-sea rescue craft propelled by an unfamiliar new fuel and operating from Dutch harbours. The *Schnellboote* were likely to carry the latest Enigma settings, but how to get hold of one of these speedboats? Ian's brainwave: instead of trying to go after the enemy, why not let the enemy come to you? Two days later, he wrote his proposal for Operation RUTHLESS.

Ian envisaged a leading role for himself and Peter Smithers. 'The idea was this,' said Smithers. 'He and I, and about three other people, would fly out in a captured German aircraft wearing German uniforms, come down in the water and be rescued by the Germans. We would simply knock the Germans on the head, throw them into the sea and drive the boat back with the Naval Codes which the rescue boat would be containing.' An admirer since Durnford of the Caribbean buccaneer Sir Henry Morgan, Ian referred to these codes as 'booty' and 'loot'. A namesake of the pirate's, the novelist Charles Morgan, recorded details of Ian's proposal in his history of NID. The pilot was to be 'tough', a 'bachelor, able to swim', a German speaker, 'and was further earmarked, with a touch of autobiographical genius, as "Fleming".'

Godfrey vetoed Ian's participation because of the 'risk of his falling into enemy hands.' Otherwise all for Ian's scheme, Godfrey pulled strings with Beaverbrook, the new Minister of Aircraft Production, to adapt a restored Heinkel 111 bomber. This would pretend to get into difficulties as it tagged after German bombers returning from a raid, and come down in the Channel close to German guns on the opposite coast. Charles Fraser Smith, perhaps Ian's model for 'Q', was introduced at an early stage. 'My task was to provide German uniforms for the commandos to wear on the raid. Fleming, ever a dramatist at heart, insisted that the Trojan Horse's bomber crew should be dressed correctly.' Fraser Smith located a firm in Staffordshire to make the Luftwaffe cap badges. Smithers said, 'I myself went to Cardington to collect the German uniforms.' Ian showed his uniform 'with all the insignia of a German pilot' to Peter Fleming at his HQ in Kent, where Peter was marshalling his Auxiliary Units. 'He told me he was going to capture a German rescue launch. He had a German rubber dinghy with him in his car.'

Operation RUTHLESS was cancelled on 16 October after no *Schnellboote* were detected in the Channel. Ian wrote soon after to Smithers: 'Our little operation with the uniform has not yet come off, but I think you may find that they have been baptised by the time I see you again. We have played various other practical jokes along the same lines.' This referred to a 'pinch' on 4 March 1941 when the Enigma settings for February were taken from the German armed trawler *Krebs* during a commando raid on Lofoten in northern Norway. Codebreakers at Bletchley made two hundred decrypts from this 'booty'. But the breakthrough was relatively small.

A land-based 'pinch' was an obvious next step, seizing codes and machines from shore stations which transmitted to all naval units. Hot on the heels of the German Navy introducing its impenetrable new rotor, Ian proposed a fresh radical scheme: a specialist commando unit trained and staffed by Naval Intelligence to 'capture Intelligence material in the course of raids on the enemy coast-line.'

Ian wrote to Admiral Denning after the war: 'It was in fact I who invented this R.N. unit based on similar units employed by the Germans.' Peter had played a seeding role. He had escaped Greece in April 1941 with reports of a super-efficient, self-contained Abwehr unit which rode on motorbikes into the Athens Naval HQ and seized valuable British Intelligence material. Further inspiration was supplied by a former accountant, Jim 'Sancho' Glanville, a swarthy SOE agent doubling as vice consul in Zagreb. On his return to London, he told Ian about this Abwehr unit's operations in Yugoslavia, suggesting that NID copy them. Glanville went on to write the NID unit's internal history.

Modelled on the German Navy's Marine-Einsatz-Kommando, 30AU was a chance to put into practice the ideas for a guerrilla force that Ian had developed with Donovan in Georgetown and Camp X. 'It was one of those little private shows that Ian *would* want to run,' said Selby Armitage, who, unlike Harling, turned down Ian's invitation to join.

While 30AU owed much to Peter's Auxiliary and YAK units, in another way, says Nicholas Rankin, it emulated the clan system of Ian's Fleming forebears. '30AU is referred to by him as "Red Indians", but they were more like Border raiders going to steal English cattle from Scottish bases.' Val Fleming had been a stalker. The Lovat Scouts, in which Ian's brother Richard served, and members of which were sent to train Peter's operatives, had started in the Boer War, recruiting a very small and tight mafia of lairds and their gamekeepers with the skills to walk across country and take on the Boers. 'These groups are personal,' says Rankin. 'Ian Fleming is acting like a Scottish laird, like Lovat and Gubbins. They all go off to estates in the north to do training, and down to White's to recruit people.'

The officers that Ian selected for his Intelligence assault unit were a remarkable bunch. 'Sancho' Glanville was a butterfly collector who, after landing at Juno beach in June 1944, pointed with his walking stick – 'Look! a Black-veined White. You don't see many of those at home.' Patrick Dalzel-Job was a veteran of the Norway campaign and a bagpipe player, who admitted to being 'one of the more "difficult" members in your private army'. A fellow officer, Tony Hugill, caricatured Job as always wandering about 'with a cannon strapped to his crutch, another under his arm and knives stuck into every portion of his clothing'. Ralph Izzard was an ex-*Daily Mail* Berlin correspondent, six foot four, with a quiet Oxbridge accent that delighted Americans. 'We would call him up, with nothing on our minds, merely to be able to hear him answer the phone by saying, "Izz-a-a-d he-a-ar."' Quentin Riley was a beaky-nosed Arctic explorer, small, dapper, vigorous, who knew that such groups had to live by their wits 'just as a Polar party must do'. The eventual action head of 30AU was Ian's decorated Eton contemporary, Dunstan Curtis, DSC, a lawyer and linguist who in March 1942 had captained the lead boat into St Nazaire in Operation CHARIOT. His father died when he was five and his mother had worked as a 'dame' (matron) at Eton before starting her own boarding school. Curtis was an ardent sailor. With his trimmed pointed orange beard, privateer's moustache and peaked dark blue hat that lent Curtis the appearance of a Drake or Raleigh, there was, Hugill wrote, 'something truly Elizabethan about him'.

The most popular 'Gentleman Pirate' had been with 30AU from the start: a young man, in Hugill's opinion, of 'extraordinary charm of manner, and diffidence combined with confidence.' Herbert Oliver 'Peter' Huntington-Whiteley, affectionately known in the unit as 'Red' for his fiery head of hair, was another tall, thin, languid Etonian, a relative of Kipling, a grandson of Stanley Baldwin, a fine cricketer and banjo player, and known for his aversion to swearing. On 30AU's disastrous trial run in August 1942, a young marine waiting to land asked him, 'For Christ's sake, sir, where the fucking hell are we?' Huntington-Whiteley gestured at the black smoke billowing from the ruined casino. 'That is Dieppe – and I want to see you in my office tomorrow morning for using improper language.'

'Red' was Ian's favourite. At a parade held in Littlehampton to receive Ian as the original architect of 30AU, Marine Jim Burns watched how Fleming, 'disdaining protocol, walked straight from his car to Red, took his hand and shouted something like, "Whiteley, my boy, how are you, how's father and the family?"'

Aged twenty-two, 'Red' was put in charge of the first unofficial rehearsal of Ian's embryonic unit – as part of Operation JUBILEE.

The Anglo-Canadian raid on Dieppe on 17 August 1942 intended to repeat in magnified form the successful Lofoten raid of the year before – except that it was a rout. Only 2,210 of the 4,963 Canadian soldiers made it back.

Among the 1,043 dead was Roger Pettiward, who had accompanied Peter Fleming to the Amazon.

'Red' was more fortunate. He was burnt when the landing craft carrying his section was shelled as it tried to breach the mole, but he managed to swim away. 'I am right as rain now except for a peeling face, a couple of outsized lips and two redbrick legs,' he wrote from Brighton Hospital.

Dieppe is a source of continuing debate, most understandably among William Stephenson's fellow Canadians. The thesis of the Canadian historian, David O'Keefe, is that the whole *raison d'être* of the raid was to seize the new four-rotor Enigma encrypting machine from a quayside hotel that NID had mistakenly identified as the Kriegsmarine HQ. Ian's 'pinch' operation was not a subsidiary objective but the central goal. Andrew Boyd is more cautious. 'Was Fleming exploiting an opportunity, a raid that would happen anyway, or did SIGINT requirements at least influence the target choice?' Boyd, like Rankin, regards the capture of cipher material as merely one important strand and not the sole priority. 'You've got to be very sure what you want is going to be there. Dieppe is not a U-boat base. It's not my first choice.'

The question of Ian's influence on 'pinch' policy, and how far he directed the shift from 'pinch by opportunity' to 'pinch by design', or whether it was all more evolutionary, finds no answer in the record. It is worth stressing, however, Ian's second protocol in his 30AU pamphlet for intelligence gathering: 'No raid should be laid on for Sigint purposes only.'

Not even 'Red' was informed of the broader reason for his mission. He had received 'a careful and detailed briefing from NID in certain particular requirements which were of extreme urgency at the time in question' and 'the importance of which is sufficient to justify the mounting of special operations and the incurring of heavy casualties' – but he was not told the real significance. 'Red' was simply instructed by his commanding officer Robert Ryder to take his detachment to the Hôtel Moderne at 21 rue Vauquelin and look for documents that might be cribs for codes and files with covers bearing the emerald cross, denoting 'Chefsache' or top secret material.

He was also to pick up 'if possible, a new German respirator' – something which resembled a typewriter. That was it. Ian emphasised that officers who had not been ULTRA-cleared were not 'to have any knowledge of progress made in breaking enemy cyphers or of the methods and machinery used in British crypto-analytic procedure.' This imperative for secrecy about ULTRA and Enigma was maintained until 1974.*

Ian watched the raid from the deck of the Hunt-class destroyer HMS *Fernie*, seven hundred yards offshore. Thick smoke obscured his view, but he could hear everything. His vivid account for Plomer's *Weekly Intelligence Report* catalogued the 'extraordinary medley of sounds' during the battle. 'The volume of the naval 4-inch predominated with their usual whip-lash crack; then there was the continual undertone of machine gun fire with the heavier unctuation of Oerlikon-type guns, the hasty bark of pom-poms, and the soft stutter of fighter cannon far above, occasionally overshadowed by the deep whine of a Junkers going into a steep dive to let go his bombs. But the noise which I remember best was the deliberate wooden, knock, knock, knock of (I think) German anti-tank guns.'

In one horrifying moment, a shell whooshed out of the smoke, killed a man standing next to the funnel and wounded four others.

Dieppe yielded nothing. Ian had waited in vain for a special motor launch to bring him the captured cipher material, 'with instructions to return to the nearest British port with any booty obtained by the IAU'.

The code word for this booty was 'Bullion'. 'Any RM officer or NCO giving the codeword *Bullion* is to be given priority passage in any R-Boat from Rutter harbour.' But the Hôtel Moderne was never reached, and the code-word never used. What Ian valiantly called 'a bloody gallant affair' had been an out-and-out disaster. 'It was a scene of utter desolation and destruction which one was glad to leave, though with a heavy heart.'

Nevertheless, he brought back a series of 'useful' recommendations to Lord Mountbatten, Chief of Combined Operations, which Mountbatten curtly 'noted for future operations'. The design of special heavily armoured HQ ships, 'to all intents and purposes Floating Fortresses'. Large quantities of Bovril to be issued to all ships, 'with fatigue-preventing tablets of a Benzedrine nature'. And security to be further tightened. Ian had been unique

---

* National security was a fetish with Godfrey, whose daughter Kathleen worked at Bletchley. He once had her to lunch at the Admiralty. 'What are you up to?' He was thrilled at her reply, 'I'm afraid I can't tell you.'

among the *Fernie*'s passengers, who included two senior American officers, to obey orders not to carry personal papers and passes on board. These were collected and placed in an empty sandbag in the captain's cabin. 'The salvage of this haul by the enemy had the ship been sunk would have been an interesting prize.'

Flippantly, Ian described his participation in a celebrity golf tournament in 1957 as 'the most dreadful experience since the Dieppe raid'. On his return, he had had lunch with David Eccles and Celia, after which Celia wrote to Peter: 'Even Ian who in Fleming fashion understates nicely seemed not exactly staggered but as if he had his breath taken away once or twice. To me it sounded like blank stupefying chaos.'

Maud Russell recognised how the experience had shaken Ian when he asked her to get him an identity disc bracelet, to be worn in case of capture, serious injury or death. 'I got a plain silver one and put my initial on it, as he wanted.' Ian told her the raid had been 'thrilling and pretty dangerous. The attack failed at most points except Lord Lovat's section. But I think I thought it'd been useful.'

In the *Weekly Intelligence Report*, he wrote, 'Dieppe was an essential preliminary for operations ahead.'

'Red' Huntington-Whiteley's detachment had embarked for Dieppe 'while the question of the formation unit was still under consideration'. Godfrey's support was crucial to making 30AU happen. He had backed Ian's proposal to the Joint Intelligence Committee. He now fought with success to keep 'this interesting and unique unit' under Ian's control and out of anyone else's clutches.

Within a week of the Chiefs of Staff giving their approval, Ian's 'driving force' had 'ensured rapid transit through the departments with the minimum of red tape'.

He had envisaged a special inter-service unit of twenty men, including officers 'who should have detailed knowledge of the intelligence work of all services'. He made it a requirement that these officers speak German and one other language: when Patrick Martin-Smith captured an Italian admiral and his wife on Capri in July 1943, the admiral's wife kept referring to Martin-Smith as 'this charming young Rhinelander' under the impression that a German officer was removing her. The officers would have specialist knowledge, be given specific targets, and were to be protected by Royal Marines assigned to the unit.

Ian was engaged in recruiting, training, and operational planning, and in defending the unit against the irritated bafflement of other services. When Commodore Rushbooke replaced Godfrey in November 1942, the new DNI felt it necessary to remind 'C' of 30AU's in-built fragility, in a memo drafted by Ian: how 'for security reasons it is impossible to explain its purpose to all the authorities with whom it is forced to come in contact' and how 'a lucky burst of machine gun fire might easily reduce its strength by a quarter during the course of any one operation.'

Ian's dedication to protecting and nurturing his unit impressed the future DNI, Admiral Denning. 'I myself know how carefully [Fleming] fathered its development and activities.'

He had thought out a lot of the training for Dieppe and then for Operation TORCH in November 1942. 'Red' was in charge during instruction and most of the initial recruiting and interviewing. The men were enrolled at Peter Fleming's old street-fighting school in Battersea. Later, they took courses at Amersham, Littlehampton, Guildford, RAF Ringway, and at Achnacarry near Inverailort.

Bill Marshall says, 'I was taught how to throttle and use a knife and was trained in explosives.' Plus, how to blow open safes, handle mortars, mines and booby-traps; and to recognise enemy uniforms. There was even a course to inspect a captured German submarine, U-570, boarding at night to find a way into the cipher room.

One of Ian's unorthodox requirements was that the men 'should be encouraged to read novels and books on Intelligence work'. He took Cyril Connolly to lunch at the Étoile and asked him 'to make out lists of books for sailors to read at the North Pole, and so forth'. If Ian could not crash-land a German bomber in the Channel, or lead his commandos ashore at Dieppe or Algiers, he could stride in his strange imagination at their head.

Dunstan Curtis was put in charge of the unit for TORCH. In time, the two locked horns. Curtis regarded Ian as 'that boorish bully' who caused 'ceaseless lunatic bureaucratic interference' from 'the Fleming dungeon' in the Citadel. Ian considered Curtis 'a vain, romantic egotist . . . straight out of some farcical paperback.' Yet on 30AU's first official testing as part of the Anglo-American landings in North Africa, Curtis doffed his peaked blue cap to Ian, acknowledging his grip on the whole naval intelligence scene. 'I was astonished at how much he knew about Algiers, how extremely detailed his intelligence was, and how much thought he had given to our whole show. He had organised air pictures, models, and given us an exact account of what we were to look for once we got to the enemy HQ.'

Curtis and his 30 Commando landed in the dunes twelve miles west of Algiers after coming under shellfire from the Vichy Navy. Sergeant Paul McGrath was one of the Royal Marines in the unit who were there to safeguard Curtis and the material he found. 'The memories of the German cannon fire we had endured at Dieppe tautened our nerves.'

Ian had supplied Curtis with 'a very detailed shopping list – the best catch was for ciphers, anything marked *Geheim* [secret], magnetic mines, the latest torpedo and so on' – and, if that twister Admiral Darlan was available, nab him too.

In a hilltop villa, Curtis discovered an Italian codebook in the pocket of an abandoned greatcoat. His most precious find was a modified Enigma machine. Unknowingly captured by the Americans in the Hôtel Aletti, recently occupied by the German Armistice Commission, the cipher machine 'complete with drums' had been tossed in the back of an American vehicle and was considered unimportant. Recognising at once what it was, Curtis promptly removed it for safekeeping. On 13 November, he arranged for it to be flown as a priority 'by special plane' to Gibraltar. Rushed back to Bletchley, the 'KK rewired turnover Abwehr machine' allowed Dilly Knox, Margaret Rock and Mavis Batey to break six weeks of unread Abwehr traffic.

This pinch alone, in Nicholas Rankin's assessment, 'completely vindicated the IAU's existence'. By December, the four-rotor Enigma was broken. A paragraph that Ian deleted from *From Russia, with Love* hints at the crown jewels the coders at Bletchley hoped for. 'All the accumulated traffic that they had intercepted since the war, millions of words of it, that was at present unreadable and useless, would now yield its fabulous secrets. In a matter of weeks, they would know all the High Policy of past years, State Secrets of every description, the innermost workings of the MGB and GRU, naval military and air strengths and orders of battle – everything that Russia had wanted to hide from the West. It was fantastic, incredible. A defeat it would take Russia decades to recover from, and that might almost mean the destruction of Communist power if the propaganda value of the secrets was put to good use.'

For 'Russia', read 'Nazi Germany'.

Curtis was back in North Africa in January 1943 with 'Red', now a captain. The two officers earned a reputation for their unit as 'mad bastards'. They rode up to their targets on the back of the lead vehicle, or on motorcycles. At Sfax, Curtis went so far ahead of the British troops that he was fired on by German tanks and wounded in the leg. When he next came under fire, he leapt from his Jeep into the nearest cover, shouting to 'Red', 'Your show, Peter!' Yet their methods were not so mad. At the Italian HQ in Sfax, 'Red' found an up-to-date chart marked with the minefields on the Sicilian coast. This proved invaluable to planning staff for Operation HUSKY, the Sicily landings in July.

30AU was embedded in HUSKY, splashing ashore on a rutted limestone plain near Capo Passero. On this occasion with 'Sancho' Glanville, 'Red' raced in a Bedford lorry to the Port Augusta naval base, where he found 'a slightly damaged but not destroyed' Enigma machine with a plug board.

The 'booty' which 'Red' shipped back to the Admiralty via Malta helped to accelerate the Allied victory on the Italian mainland. It was fitting that the voice to broadcast the news should be Ian's.

At 6 p.m. on 9 September, Maud tuned in to the BBC German Naval Programme and 'heard first the announcement of the armistice with Italy in German to the German seamen, and then Ian's talk to them. It was very well done.' Ian had matured since his broadcast at the time of the Norway fiasco. 'His voice is excellent – firm, vigorous and dignified. I was pleased with the performance and told him so later when he came to dinner ... I. was exhausted with the week's excitement. He was satisfied but not a bit exuberant.'

XXVIII
'WHAT A NUISANCE SEX IS!'

*'Sometimes the most important kind of work is concealing
how much you do know.'*

ERNIE CUNEO

Outside Room 39, Ian played the part expected of a Chocolate Sailor. He impressed Loelia Westminster as a bit of a fantasist who liked to make out he was a secret agent. 'Of course, he wasn't. He just liked people to think he was.' At a more junior level, John le Carré experienced the same frisson. 'I relished the notion of appearing to be someone dull, while all the time I was someone terribly exciting.'

To Loelia, he was much the same Ian, who played a lot of bridge and golf, was keen on first editions, occasionally tried to sleep with her, and succeeded with some of her friends like Ann O'Neill – although not till the end of the war did Ian admit to Maud Russell that 'he'd slept with her a few times', after always denying it.

In Lisbon, 'Smartyboots' Eccles observed the promiscuity among his circle. 'Everyone sleeping with everyone else and being catty about the others. What a nuisance sex is! Why can't we mind less?'

The biographer Victoria Glendinning's normally discreet mother Eve was a member, like Ian, of the Lansdowne Club. 'She told me that when Freddy, our father, was away at the war she came out of the club and met the eye of a passing American officer. He stopped and, wordless, they went off together – whether back to her room at the Lansdowne or somewhere else I do not know. She did not seem at all ashamed or guilty, more that she just wanted someone to know that she had such adventures.'

Len Deighton remembers the sexual humidity. 'Trysts were based on the fact there would be no consequence. You said "Goodbye" to someone and you didn't want the last word exchanged to be abrasive or insensitive. Though I don't remember anyone being frightened, the general feeling was that our lives wouldn't be extended beyond the war.'

The war had burnished Ian's appeal. On a visit to the Muirs in the Essex village of Takeley, following his escape from Bordeaux, Ian, in his naval commander's uniform, impressed Percy's wife Barbara as slim and debonair. 'Uniform suited his sardonic good looks. I had never thought him handsome; his face was too bony, with its high cheekbones, deep-set eyes and sharp lines running from bumpy nose to full-lipped mouth. There was a suggestion of arrogance which made it attractive to women'. He had arrived not on any romantic assignment but to discuss his book collection that Percy was looking after.

Ian had been the second biggest lender after John Maynard Keynes to an exhibition at Cambridge in May 1940 to commemorate the quincentenary of Gutenberg's invention of the printing press. 'With my twenty-six soldiers of lead I have conquered the world', was the last line of the catalogue. Ian's twenty-four items included the first printed references to calculus, cricket, anaesthetics, and macadamised roads, as well as Lenin's *What is to be Done?* and Hitler's *Mein Kampf*. But the exhibition in the Fitzwilliam Museum had closed early 'owing to the new danger of damage from air raids'.

Loelia was at Send Grove, a house full of fragile rococo white china, when the Blitz began on 7 September 1940. 'A terrific air raid developed while we were dining & I heard my first bombs, including one screamer. I can't say I liked it! German planes are still pouring over the house as I write & all the lights are out.' Days later, she went with Ian to inspect a deep crater nearby.

For the next five years, the urging drone of the German bombers overhead – 'like the enlarged sound of a wasp' in Elizabeth Bowen's phrase – was the equivalent of Wagner's music in 'Apocalypse Now': the presage to a nightly conflagration.

From Takeley, Percy Muir enquired anxiously after Ian. 'I hear that they very nearly got the Admiralty building the other morning, and Ebury [Street] can be no haven of rest with that glass roof and general lack of protection – nevertheless, I trust that your name has not been on any of the bombs so far delivered.' Muir had heard of casualties in the book trade. 'I am glad I got the old firm's stuff down here when I did.' The very next day, a bomb fell on Dulau's, destroying the building and killing his former employer, Leslie Chaundy.

Anxious for his books not to go up in flames, Ian transferred the collection to Eve's house in Oxfordshire. Soon afterwards, he moved from Ebury Street into the Carlton Hotel with 'a gang' from the Admiralty.

The bombs fell closer and closer. 'London was flooded with them,' says Bill Marshall, then training as a Marine in Chatham. 'They were dropping on top of the barracks. We were sent up to put out fire bombs with buckets of sand.'

On 27 September, Ian arrived to the usual orchestra of anti-aircraft guns at Le Coq d'Or, 'his favourite for the moment', and told Maud how the house he had been in at Dover 'was blown up and everyone killed soon after he'd left it'.

For those who survived it, the bombing had the stopped-clock effect of contracting time and suspending the present. 'I liked the air-raids,' Ann O'Neill told Mary Pakenham, being the only London hostess who continued to give parties – from her rooms at the Dorchester, which had become Ann's wartime refuge. 'They seemed like something happening.'

The following month, a bomb blast suspended Fleming as he dined with Sefton Delmer and a select group in Delmer's top-floor flat at Lincoln's Inn. The building received a direct hit, obliterating Ian's little Opel parked outside, and leaving Ian and his friends marooned on the third floor.

'We were left high in the air,' Ian told Maud, 'just hoping that the floor wouldn't finally give way, and drinking the rest of the champagne, partly to keep our courage up and partly not to waste it.' Eventually there was a tap on the window, a fireman's head appeared. 'I order you to cease your disgusting orgy, and come down immediately; the building is about to collapse.'

Maud wrote: 'The story was told as if there hadn't been any danger.'

Two police detectives later called on Delmer at the Savoy where he had taken refuge. Someone had informed them that his guests had been speaking foreign languages and signalling to the raiders with electric torches. 'Could I please say what had happened, and give them a list of my guests? Snob that I am, I did so with relish.' The other guests were Prince Bernhard of the Netherlands; the daughter of the Belgian Prime Minister; the banker Leonard Ingrams; and Commander Ian Fleming.

A month later, on 14 November, Ian's digs were targeted. He pencilled a note to Eve. 'Darling Mama, Just a line to tell you that the Carlton is no more but that I am completely unscathed. An astonishing miracle, which I'm sure I've not earned. I am letting you know because you might have heard from elsewhere & been worried. Not sure where I shall move to now, but will let you know. Just off to pick some relics from the ruins of my room . . . Will tell you details later.'

He had been sleeping on the third floor when the bomb hit, Maud wrote in her diary. 'The place swayed, masonry started falling, the wall to the passage disappeared and I. was covered with cement, plaster and bricks, but miraculously not hurt. Heard cries and moans. Rescued a waiter and a maid pinned down by debris. Finished the night in the hotel grill-room where other people were sleeping.' It was in this room, one year before, that Admiral Godfrey had recruited him to Naval Intelligence. Ian was woken by an old man urinating on the carpet, a bishop with a bladder problem.

Ian moved into a small flat on Piccadilly in 'a large block of concrete monstrosities' where he was to live 'a ratlike existence' to the end of the war. In the months up to VE Day, Maud brought Ian his weekly rations here: the room reminded her of a dormitory that she had seen in a reconstructed German POW camp. His neighbours in the building included Alan Pryce-Jones, after an incendiary bomb burned down his house, and the Hungarian astrologer Louis de Wohl, 'a right swindler' who was employed successively by SOE, Stephenson and Delmer to write Hitler's horoscope on the women's pages and have the superstitious Führer's sudden death predicted in the stars. 'It will haunt him,' de Wohl guaranteed.

Athenaeum Court lacked the luxuries that Ian had sampled in Georgetown chez Smithers. 'If you can lay your hands on two large tubes of Kolynos toothpaste, I would be very grateful as our toothpaste manufacturers have run out of glycerine and the stuff either pours out of the tube on to the floor or turns into a sort of white asphalt! I would also like a pair of sensible American braces of the finest technologically efficient design.' And in a PS to Smithers: 'If there is any way of sending me Chesterfield cigarettes, please do so to any amount. I will repay!' Wartime rationing presented obstacles to Ian's generous alcohol requirements. 'When I tell you that the Savoy Hotel are now mixing martinis out of bath-tub gin and sherry, you will know that we are rapidly progressing back to swamp life, and the transitional period is distasteful . . . I flit uneasily from one to another of the Soho restaurants in the evening.'

At least Ian could afford to eat out. He was still a partner at Rowe & Pitman, continuing at Hugo Pitman's insistence to draw his partner's cut; from time to time, he came in for lunch wearing his naval commander uniform. Nor did every evening end in broken glass and brick dust.

'The ordinary social life went on, in between the work and the bombs.' Joan Bright was General Ismay's assistant who helped run his Special Information Centre.* She had got to know Ian through Peter, and then at the high-level conferences held by the Allied leaders, which she had a hand in organising: Trident (Washington) in May 1943, Quadrant (Quebec) in August 1943, and Sextant (Cairo) in November 1943. 'The one thing you could do was to go to a movie, and Ian was a tremendous movie fan. So we often used to go, then have supper and then go home.' Peter Fleming would join them on his rare visits from Delhi.

One November night, Loelia Westminster met Ian's boss at a dinner party. 'Sat next to Admiral Godfrey & talked about Ian.' What they discussed goes unrecorded. It was Godfrey's rule that 'private lives were not my concern unless they interfered with people's work.' A notable exception was someone Ian had recruited to NID: the recipient of his first fan letter, William Plomer.

Early in 1943, Plomer was reported to the police by a sailor he had approached at Paddington station. There followed what John Lehmann, a friend of Ian and Plomer, called 'a mess with the naval authorities'. Homosexuality was a criminal offence. Plomer risked losing his job. He persuaded Ian to intervene on his behalf. The charge was dropped after Godfrey provided a reference that Plomer in his work for Naval Intelligence 'has conducted himself to my entire satisfaction'. Plomer repaid this debt when he read Ian's first novel a decade later and recommended *Casino Royale* for publication, after that editing each of Ian's books.

Foremost among those who wondered whether Ian might himself be bisexual was the woman who later married him. After observing the

---

* 'Pug Ismay is alleged to be infatuated with her,' wrote 'Chips' Channon. 'A metallic brilliant girl . . . I suspect that she is an intriguer.'

horseplay between Ian and Sefton Delmer, Ann O'Neill wrote in her diary: '[Delmer] is a clever interesting man and rouses all Ian's brain mania plus his sublimated homosexualism.'

Ann dined at the White Tower one evening with Ian and his Eton contemporary Nigel Birch. 'Nigel is in love with Ian and always at his best with him.'

Not every man was so enamoured as Delmer or Birch or the Olympic fencer Ian Campbell-Gray, who found Ian 'dazzling'. Ann greeted 1940 with a New Year's Eve party at the Dorchester that included the Duff Coopers, Esmond Rothermere, the Churchillian MP Brendan Bracken, the new War Minister David Margesson, and Loelia. 'As midnight drew near, we all imbibed Punch and Ian Fleming as the darkest man present came over the threshold and embraced one and all. This was popular with all save Duff, who refused to start a New Year by kissing a man.'

As some of his bisexual or gay friends might have asserted, Ian was more camp than gay. The homosexual poet James Kirkup met Ian at a pub in the Blitz. 'There was only one other person seated at the bar, and I could tell at once that he was not "gay".'

'Gay?' says Ian's stepdaughter Fionn. 'Not in a million years. People always think people sleep together when they probably didn't.'

Fionn had heard rumours involving Ian and George Duff-Sutherland Dunbar, but these were fuelled by her uncle Hugo Charteris, Ann's brother, who detested Ian as 'a subtle bitch and in fact married to no one but himself', and wrote him off to another sister as a friendless loner. 'His one friend, his only friend, [George] Patrick Duff Dunbar is a sweet and gentle soul – and has quite sublimated into humour and fantasy the sadism and buggery which originally linked him with Ian as a young man.'

Maud Russell had a more nuanced understanding of Ian's male friendships after observing him with Oliver Lyttelton (later Lord Chandos and President of the Board of Trade). 'I. and Oliver are always funny together. They like each other, laugh at each other, banter and wrangle and behave like two very young men who, attracted and half in love with each other (perfectly chastely as young men are) can't leave each other alone and are always teasing and tearing each other about like puppies. They first met staying with us at Stanway [which Maud then rented off the Charteris family] and the fun started straightaway. They wrangled away up to bed and into Ian's room. Gilbert when he came to mine, said: "Oliver and Ian have fallen in love with each other." Oliver is 16 or 17 years older.'

Rosamond Lehmann was one of Ian's girlfriends to be struck by his female side. 'There was a peculiar femininity about him – I felt it might almost have been the ghost of his mother, something very feminine which always seemed to be curiously at odds with his masculinity.' Mary Pakenham sensed this too. 'I once said to him, "You're just like your mother without her violin".'

To Peter Quennell, Ian's tantrums were 'just like the tantrums of a beautiful woman. Noël [Coward] always treated him like a very beautiful woman. "Ian, darling. You're just a beautiful bitch".' Coward never disguised his feelings for Ian. 'I loved him and he loved me. There was nothing physical about it. I'm not saying a little boozle or two wouldn't have done Ian the world of good. I always felt that he was almost suspiciously over-emphatic about sex. Of course, he loved fucking women. It was as simple as that and he was quite unscrupulous about it.'

Convincing evidence has yet to appear of Ian having had a male 'boozle', least of all with Coward. Once in Jamaica, Coward called on Ian, who had bronchitis. Ann reported to Evelyn Waugh: 'Noël has always found T-B [Thunderbird] fearfully attractive and jumped at the opportunity to handle him. While Noel fetched ice cubes from the frigidaire T-B's language was something horrible, he blamed me for exposing himself to homosexual approach.'

Fionn witnessed Ian explode in his first and last winter at Sevenhampton Place, the home near Swindon where he and Ann moved in 1963, when her Charteris grandfather exchanged schoolboy experiences with Peter Quennell. Ian grew red in the face and stalked from the room. 'I will not have buggery discussed at Christmas.' His homophobia was in line with the prevailing attitudes of the time. On a visit to Morocco, Ian was reunited with David Herbert, known locally as the Queen Mother of Tangier. 'He's been very sweet to me, but I'm fed up with buggers. They all do absolutely nothing all day long but complain about each other and arrange flowers, which I must say are quite wonderful here. I even went so far as to buy three dozen roses for myself!'

Ian transferred his sexual identity into the character of Bond, who regards homosexuals as 'a herd of unhappy sexual misfits – barren and full of frustration'. In a letter to the *Guardian*, Ian wrote that 'perhaps Bond's blatant heterosexuality is a subconscious protest against the current fashion for sexual confusion.' This is disingenuous, too. Stephen Potter in his analysis of 'Bondsmanship' seemed more on the nail: he perceived that 'Bond's greatest success is with men, particularly with businessmen of the more introvert and intellectual type.' In Ian's posthumous last novel *The Man with the Golden Gun*, Bond looks at the manager of Scaramanga's hotel 'with the recognition that exists between crooks, between homosexuals, between secret agents. It is the look common to men bound by secrecy – by common trouble'.

Ian's bachelor status was an advantage at work. Bond reflected in *Moonraker* that for men in the Secret Service 'marriage and children and a home were out of the question if they were to be of any use "in the field".' Bond was married to 'M' as Ian was wedded to Godfrey. Still, it did not mean he was correspondingly faithful in his private life. If Ian never did 'sleep with a problem', as one colleague alleged, this was because he was otherwise engaged.

Muriel Wright and Maud Russell owed their Admiralty jobs to Ian while they continued to be his lovers. Muriel was especially devoted, Selby Armitage noticed. 'Rather a deadpan, disorganised, beatnik sort of girl. Used to arrive for a weekend without any nightclothes and forget her toothbrush.'

Maud was older, more cerebral, more experienced, and recently widowed. 'I was pleased when he said he felt comfortable with me,' she wrote in her diary. 'Lots of people don't.' Another entry: 'Ian dined and talked till midnight. He is always anxious about me, my health, my sleeping, my happiness.' Then this: 'He talked about marrying me. I had qualities he wants to find. I said, "No, our ages make it impossible." He said, "If I was five years older." "No," I said, "If you were at least 10 years older." For he is sixteen and a half years younger than me. If he were 10 years older I would marry him, but it's no use a woman of 52 trying to keep pace with a man of 36 . . . He is very good to me.' He brought her presents from America: hairpins, nail varnish, hot-water bottles, zip fasteners, and on one occasion, 'a packet of

Bromo', a brand of loo paper. He advised Maud about the mental difficulties that her second son Raymond was going through. At weekends, he came to Mottisfont to unwind. On 18 April 1943, Maud met Ian off the train. 'He is very tired and in need of rest. Played records after dinner – *Lac des Cygnes* and *Francesca da Rimini*. Today I. went out fishing.'

What preyed on him was a recorded talk between German POWs in a camp near London. This spoke of secret launching sites in northern France for huge fifteen-ton V-weapons that could fly ten miles or more into the stratosphere. 'Rocket bombs or their more modern successors will destroy us in a few hours. He talked as if he believed in this horrible prediction. He wears himself out.' Ian returned again and again to the subject.

In November 1943, in what was a very significant task, Ian chaired the JIC's BODYLINE subcommittee, looking at the German development of rockets, pilotless aircraft and glider bombs. Its reports highlighted the 'imminence of a threat against this country' – especially from the V-2 rocket codenamed BIG BEN – and concluded that an attack 'equivalent to a 2,000-ton bomb raid could be launched from 100 ski sites in under 24 hours. It might be 4 or 5 times as great.'

Ann's sister Laura had heard the horror stories. She told Ann brightly, 'Don't just hold your eyes in, press them hard, the blast sucks them out from simply miles away.'

On another occasion, Ian talked again to Maud 'about the German new "secret" weapon: the rocket . . . and if it started I was to get out *at once*. I was to keep a bag packed and leave London immediately without warning the Admiralty or anyone . . . He said it would be a relief for people to know other people were safe.'

Like his admirer Philip Larkin, who ran three lovers at once, Ian then began sleeping with Ann O'Neill. Her daughter Fionn says, 'If I had to choose a date, I'd say she started sleeping with Ian in 1943 when her diary stopped, because life became too complicated. The O'Neills, descended from four generations of clergymen, were already horrified by her behaviour, living openly with Esmond, and thought she'd behaved appallingly to my father.'

Ann's very public affair with Esmond Rothermere – 'Chips' Channon called them 'the great inseparables' – had become more so since Shane was away fighting in North Africa. Fionn's brother Raymond says, 'My father went off to the war in 1940 and never came back, and during the war when I had a day out we'd often go to one of Esmond's houses, and later Ian came along; he was the third party. Ian, Esmond and my father all played golf at Sandwich; this was why they all knew each other so well.' Ian was a guest at each of the three wartime properties rented by Esmond Rothermere: a house near Ascot; South Wraxall Manor in Wiltshire; and a cottage at Buscot in the upper Thames valley.

Near the end of the war, Ian invited his stylish Admiralty colleague Robert Harling to Buscot. 'A young man with the laughing, big-eared, long-nosed face of a medieval court jester and the shrewd appraising eyes of a physician' is how Harling impressed Sefton Delmer, who worked with him in NID. Clare Blanshard was later employed by Harling on Ian's recommendation. 'Ian must have thanked God (yes, he knew him) that he had someone as rivetingly alive & independent & original & resourceful & stimulating as Robert for all those years in uniform.'

Harling recalled, 'We were friends from the word go.' There were two subjects about which he and Ian never tired of talking. The first was typography. In *The Spy Who Loved Me*, Vivienne Michel works for a parish magazine made up each week by 'a man called Harling who was quite a dab at getting the most out of the old-fashioned typefaces'. The second subject was women. Harling's attitude may be gauged from his advice to his secretary, when he was editor of *House & Garden*, who said she had a cold coming on and wanted a day off. 'My dear, there's nothing in life which can't be solved by a good fuck or a gargle.' His recollections of Ann O'Neill at Buscot can be seen in this light.

The hostess who greeted Harling was in her early thirties, 'slim, dark-haired, fine-featured, with a mildly imperious profile and presence. She was clearly a woman possessed of looks, vivacity, wit, vitality, charm – and brains.'

She had been born Ann Charteris, a granddaughter of the Earl of Wemyss. She had grown up at Stanway, a beautiful country house in the Cotswolds. Her father was eccentric and remote; her mother had died young.

Harling had heard rumours that Ann was Esmond Rothermere's mistress, but sharing a bed and cottage with Ian Fleming. Rothermere remained apparently unaware of the situation.

Ann asked Harling, 'Has Ian put you in the picture?'

'Not this particular picture.'

'He rarely does. He tells me you're one of the few people in the Admiralty who talks his language.'

'The language of carefreedom,' Harling claimed was his reply.

Like a coral that soon drains of colour when detached from its reef, Ann needed to be encountered in her own setting and times, her own chosen company, to appear in her best light. 'She was very funny and vital, with piercing brown eyes,' recalls Antonia Fraser, 'but her true interest was herself.' Among the many whom she intimidated was one of Ian's nieces. 'I was terrified of her thin eyebrows and thin lips. She was snide, uncosy to a degree, rather like Wallis Simpson.'

Ann's niece Sara, though, understands her aunt's allure for Ian. 'She was a sort of light bulb in a fairly dingy room. What she never did was steal anybody's thunder; she tried to magnify it. She had one of the most infectious and flattering laughs I've ever heard. Wow, did people hang on her words, which were not particularly intelligent, and frequently half-witted, but her voice and demeanour were encouraging to a degree. Anyone she talked to thought they were the most interesting person in the world. In that sense, she was contagious, and Ian was always slightly standing to one side laughing at this.'

On a walk across the Buscot meadows with Harling, Ann displayed her talent for transforming a listener into a confidant. She told him how she had been infatuated with Ian from the moment she set eyes on him in a Le Touquet hotel in 1937. The arrogant hero figure entering the foyer had totally ignored his teenage admirer. She more or less swooned, but she had sworn 'that at some point in the not too-distant-future she must and would have him'.

Now Ann found herself caught between her two lovers.

In 1941, she had persuaded Esmond they must marry or part, and had gone through 'the rigmarole' of giving evidence to a solicitor in Bournemouth in order to get a divorce from O'Neill first. This coincided with one of Ian's forty-eight-hour leaves. Ian persuaded Ann and Esmond to drive him to Cornwall for a day's golf. 'Ian met us at Bournemouth, and we motored (press lords had plenty of petrol). I was being sick every twenty minutes from nerves and guilt. Ian told Esmond I was not to be indulged. We were to stop at no more inns and I could damn well be sick in the hedge. This had a curative effect! When we arrived, I went to bed. Ian came to my room, told me I was behaving very badly and must return to Shane. I burst into tears.'

Two months later, Esmond reneged on his promise, refused to be cited as a co-respondent in a divorce petition, and urged a three-year plan, 'the desertion ticket'. Ann told Harling, 'Esmond's fear of scandal is fully equalled by Ian's fear of marriage.'

Ian's dread deepened following the death of Muriel Wright in March 1944, in a bomb attack. Ann recognised the power of her phantom rival to haunt him. 'I'm not sure he'll ever get Muriel out of his memory. It may sound a trifle cynical, but I think he had more or less got her out of his mind while she was alive, but cannot now she's dead.'

Ann was not the only one of Ian's friends who thought that Muriel had been 'the tragedy of his life'. This was Harling's phrase and belief. 'Like so many other lovers in this sad world he had only recognised the rare qualities of his beloved too late – after her death.'

Ann's niece Sara says, 'We'd been brought up to believe that his heart was broken in the war when his fiancée was killed in a raid. We were always told that by Nanny Sillick.'

Muriel was thirty-four when she died, thirteen years past the average age for marriage in 1944. She had held a torch for Ian since 1935. 'She was dotty about him,' said Harling, 'and, in order to be near him, she became a dispatch rider and he managed to get her attached to the Admiralty.'

For three years, Muriel zigzagged through the ruined streets, carrying urgent decrypts to Bletchley, to Woburn, from the Topographical Department in Oxford. Admiral Godfrey had relied on Muriel to collect the wallet of papers which kept him busy during the hour-and-a-half weekly drive to Oxford. She collected these in the evening 'and brought another batch which I worked on next morning during the drive up to London'.

Following Godfrey's sudden transfer to India in 1943, Muriel was one of his former staff that Ian supplied him with news about. 'Dispatch riders – a Muriel – are flourishing.'

'I remember her in dispatch-rider clothes,' says her niece Tamara. 'She just looked right in it.'

Adrian House was crossing Piccadilly with his parents when the traffic thinned for a moment. 'A large glossy motorbike with an extremely attractive, slim lady wearing goggles pulled in and came to standstill, and she touched my father on the leg – "Darling!" Both my parents threw up their hands and screamed in joy. The conversation was about the lovely times we'd had in Austria and Kitzbühel.'

Within NID, Muriel had scratched the heart of Sefton Delmer, who described her as 'the dream vision of a James Bond fetishist' – 'From under a crash helmet peeped corn-coloured curls. Her slender waist was tightly strapped in a leather corset. There she stood awaiting my command, her cheeks flushed by the icy before-dawn air, her crimson lips slightly parted.'

Harling was one more wistful admirer. 'Once her helmet was doffed and those chestnut tresses gaily shaken out she was revealed as what she truly was: a fey, sly enchantress.' Harling, too, understood her as a model for the Bond girls, outdoorsy, no make-up, no nail varnish, very simple dress, like Vesper Lynd in *Casino Royale* who had transferred 'to Head of S's office' from the WRNS. When Allen Dulles asked Ian, 'What is your ideal woman?' he replied, 'I very much like the WRN type of woman. I like the fact that they seem to want to please, to make one happy.' For Harling, this was Muriel. 'Along with every other officer in the unit I failed to understand why she had not become Mrs Fleming . . . She was a woman in 10,000 . . . we all adored her. Simple. Anybody would – any man. And he treated her badly.'

Ted Merrett thought that Muriel was the bravest person he knew, and he resented Ian's behaviour. 'She demanded nothing of him except love, and I think he gave it. It was an affair unlike anything he'd had before, a very simple love affair. I don't think violence came into it as it had into most of his other affairs. But at the same time he treated her very, very badly. She'd do any chore for him.' When Ian wanted his Morland Specials collected, the handmade Turkish cigarettes with three gold bands round them to represent the braid on his lieutenant commander's sleeve, Muriel would speed off on her motorbike to Ian's tobacconist at 83 Grosvenor Street. 'Also sexually, of course, she was absolutely available for him. She was a very sweet girl, she was compliant, she was motherly, she was kind, she was good. And this wasn't really what Ian wanted, or part of Ian wanted. He found it very difficult to love consistently anybody, he was so bound up in himself and in his own conundrums and problems and difficulties.'

Ian's ambivalence to settling down was expressed in a PS he wrote to Smithers. 'JOKE ACHTUNG. When dispatch rider swerved to avoid a child & fell off the sofa. F.' At the same time, Ian was prepared to be seen in public with Muriel, as a couple. On 12 March 1943, they stayed with Gerry Coke in his three-bedroomed cottage at Bentley in Hampshire, writing their names in his visitors' book.

Muriel's life can be glimpsed in letters to her brother Stephen, a POW in Colditz in 1944. Her small house at 9 Eaton Terrace Mews. Her large dog kennel for her out-of-control chow Pushkin, 'which of course he never goes in!' Her motorbike. 'Have not fallen off recently. Makes a difference.' Her bumping into Ivar Bryce with Ian. 'He met you in Jamaica. Dark, film star looking man who is lame. I don't like him much. He is married to a rich American woman.' Her up-and-down relationship with Ian. 'IF working very hard & we have even more rows but get on very well in between.' She had Ian's photograph by her bed. One month before she died, her younger sister Judith saw her in London – 'looking absolutely *lovely* & v happy. She was with IF at the time.'

Anecdotal evidence suggests her radiance had a reason.

Marriage had been much on Ian's mind during these weeks, according to Maud Russell. 'He is worn out every time I see him and wants to talk about cottages, seashores, Tahiti, long naked holidays on coral islands and marriage.' Maud had encouraged him. 'I said he would be happier married and shouldn't leave it too long.'

Ian had taken all this while to forget Monique, but in the spring of 1944, he decided to travel up to Yeldersley to ask Henry Wright's permission to marry his daughter.

Muriel's niece Tamara picks up the story. 'We always came down after tea from the schoolroom upstairs, and played horse-racing games on the floor in the corner, throwing a dice with our Elwes cousins. One afternoon, we heard the grown-ups talking. One of the aunts said, "You know Ian's going to see Father to ask for her hand in marriage?" My mother Margaret said, "Oh, no. I hope Father says No. He's too conceited and selfish to make her a good husband. He'll never make her happy." She died the next week. We were horrified at her death. We were told she and Ian were going out to dinner and he'd come to fetch her and they were talking in the sitting room, and an air raid started and she ran out onto the landing because her horrible dog might have been frightened, and a bit of metal killed her instantly. That's what we were told.'

Maud Russell recorded that evening in her diary. 'A very noisy raid started after dinner and for once I felt anxious and very nervous. I don't know why this should have been but this morning I heard that Muriel Wright, I.'s girl, had been killed. Strange things happen. I heard in my room at the Admiralty that she'd been killed by debris flung up from a crater in the road coming through her roof and falling on her in bed. Most of the room was untouched. Appalled for I. and found it difficult to concentrate. I know he will be overcome with remorse and blame himself for not marrying her and for a thousand other things none of which he is to blame for.'

At Yeldersley, Muriel's parents received Ian's handwritten letter.

Dear Captain & Mrs Wright,

I'm afraid I cannot put into words all that I feel about Muriel nor how much I share in your tragic loss. This is just to tell you of my very profound sorrow at the death of one whom I have loved very dearly for many years and who was my dearest friend and companion.

I have written at some length to your son Fitz and I will not repeat here what I have said to him. I can only tell you that she was entirely happy and carefree on the night she died and she leaves not a shadow on her memory. She never did any evil thing and had no enemy in the world. She was admired and loved by all who knew her in London and her war record amongst the WRNS in the Admiralty was second to none.

She leaves a gap in my own life which can never be filled, but there it is. At any rate she is out of reach of suffering & misfortune and there is much to be grateful for in the way she died . . .

Certainly she will continue to live in my heart for ever and I am grateful to you for all that she has been to me for so many years. Please forgive my inability to say anything more to comfort you.

Yours sincerely Ian Fleming.

He was skilled at hiding what he felt, even from himself, and it is easy to get him wrong – as Julie Cohen of Morland's can be forgiven for having done when Ian turned up at his tobacconist to collect two hundred cigarettes. 'But your girl took them last night.' 'Oh,' Ian said. 'She's dead. I'd better have some more.' Joan Bright, Muriel's neighbour, believed that 'Ian was absolutely shattered.'

The following week, Ian went to dinner with Maud, 'first time since Muriel Wright's cruel death. We didn't talk about her at all. I left it to him if he wanted to, but he said nothing and I didn't probe. But he talked about his health and that his fingers trembled. We talked about things like that – hair, health, skin, twitching, fingers trembling. He's going to Scotland for a week's getaway.'

He did not say he was going to Muriel's funeral.

She was buried in the crypt at Osmaston, one mile from Yeldersley. Ian did not stay around after the service. Muriel's sister Margaret watched him leave and walk away through the crocuses. The plaque inside the church reads: 'Killed by enemy action 14th March 1944 in city of Westminster, three years a dispatch rider in the WRNS. Fearless and free.'

XXIX
BILL

'We owe our freedom and security to your dedication,
because you were ready to risk your life.'
PRESIDENT EMMANUEL MACRON to William Marshall, 19 June 2019

Ian buried his grief in work. It is hard to form a consistent picture of his wartime activities because his duties took him to many parts of the country and sometimes abroad. His base in the months following Muriel Wright's death was a bomb-proof bunker in the Admiralty where his main focus was concentrated on driving the Nazis from Occupied France.

30AU had returned from Italy to prepare for the Normandy landings. The unit had been reorganised and expanded following criticism by the Chiefs of Staff and the US Army. With D-Day less than three months away, Ian needed to discipline his intelligence-gatherers for the task ahead.

The American writer John Steinbeck was a war correspondent for the *New York Herald Tribune* when he came across five of Ian's commandos on Capri. 'They were small, tired-looking men who might have been waiters or porters at a railway station. Their backs were slightly bent and their knees knobbly and they walked with a shuffling gait . . . Their leader looked like a weary and petulant mouse.' Steinbeck described them as shambling 'monsters'.

'Red' Huntington-Whiteley was among the naval officers reprimanded for the unit's behaviour. Trained to kill, the tough Royal Marines who were part of the unit and there to guard the officers were, in the view of one 30AU naval officer, 'hugely disinclined to take no for an answer from foe or *fraulein*'. Their habit of departing from regulations, wrote 'Sancho' Glanville, had merely emphasised the impression of a 'purely private army' which was engaged in removing intelligence material 'for its own nefarious purposes'.

There were charges of looting, misconduct, eccentricities of dress. There was too much 'party spirit'.

Ian told Glanville: 'You can't behave like Red Indians any more. You have to learn to be a respected and disciplined unit.' Ian had come in for criticism for uneven briefings and lack of communication.

In response, Ian set up a command centre in the Citadel to signal daily situation reports. He staffed this smoky, windowless basement room with Glanville, who was entrusted with drafting a dossier of naval targets in north-west Europe. They were assisted by Margaret Bax, a bluestocking history don from Leeds, who later typed out Glanville's internal Admiralty history of 30AU. After accepting Ian's invitation to join, Robert Harling took charge of handling topographical material.

Harling's first 30AU task was 'to list enemy equipment and data which divisional heads in the Admiralty and elsewhere wished the unit to acquire and deliver ASAP'. This list, known as the 'Black Book', proved invaluable in the war's last months. Lieutenant-Commander Jan Aylen led one of 30AU's field teams after D-Day – a team that included Bill Marshall. The first British soldier to cross the Rhine, Aylen drove around carrying in his battle-dress trousers a neat booklet of abstracts from Ian's 'Black Book' – which Aylen praised as 'a stupendous tabloid listing the exact position and importance of hundreds of targets (and often key people). This had been compiled largely from POW interrogation and every source available to DNI, and was uncannily helpful in leading, if not directly to a target then to a secondary source, which perhaps led to further unlisted targets of opportunity.'

Ian had a key role in deciding targets for British and American T-Forces, the joint mission to secure German scientific and industrial secrets before they could be destroyed, as a member of both the Combined Intelligence Priority Committee (CIPC) and Combined Intelligence Objectives Sub-Committee (CIOS). Dunstan Curtis recalled how Ian 'had worked out a great map of Western Europe with exactly what to go for everywhere. Thanks to this skill at intelligence 30AU did accomplish a great deal.'

That was not the end of his responsibilities. In March 1944, Ian presided over a secret committee to organise the flow of cryptographic material from Bletchley to the Allied force commanders for the vast operation ahead.

*

There was a tremendous wind on 5 June 1944. When Ian arrived for dinner at Maud's flat in Upper Grosvenor Street, he looked unusually worn and tired to her. 'As I came into the room, he said, "Does this wind worry you?" I thought it was an odd question, and I answered, "Well, yes, I've had a headache for three days." He said, "I mean all this rustling and whistling and shushing . . ."'

His speech was blurred as if he had drunk a fair number of cocktails. 'I said, "You've got something on your mind." He said, "It's this invasion." He told me he might be rung up during the evening and had given my number.' There had been reports that London might be bombed by long-range rockets when it started. 'I didn't guess though.'

The first Maud knew was the following morning when the woman massaging her neck said the invasion had begun at 8.00.

Only much later did Ian tell Maud what a narrow squeak it had been. The campaign of German V-1 'doodlebugs' started about 13 June. 'If there had been no Normandy landing by that date, all the V-1 sites in that region would have come into action against London and the south coast, as well as those that actually did, and the destruction would have been immense.'

Ian was more relaxed when he saw Maud five days later, on 11 June. 'We had a great evening talking and laughing. He is satisfied about the progress. Weather conditions have been bad all the time and we are a bit behind schedule, but casualties have been much lighter than was ever dreamed of.'

So impatient am I to meet the last surviving member of 30AU, who was part of that D-Day landing, that I arrive a Wednesday early. The windows are dark in his bungalow near Milton Keynes. The bell does not work. I knock. Silence. Then a shadow shimmers behind the glass-panelled door.

A gruff voice, 'Who is it?'

Presently, some keys are fetched, the door opens, a hand appears.

'I was expecting you next week,' says a tall, thin man with a white moustache, long narrow face, and glasses.

Later, I am glad I got the date wrong. Bill Marshall will be hospitalised five days after our conversation. Had I come at the right time, I would never have heard what he tells me.

'I'm ninety-four.'

'How old do you feel?'

'A hundred and four.'

He digs out some black-and-white photographs. The Villa Rothschild in the Bois de Boulogne: the former German Naval HQ, where Bill spent part of August and September 1944 during the Liberation of Paris. 'Oh la la!' is scribbled on the back. The twenty-year-old Bill in a white vest, standing in a trench in a wood near Eckernförde with a spade. 'Chap who built the rockets, I took all his stuff out of the hole.' Bill has since lost the hair ribbons that he scooped from Dr Hellmuth Walter's house, which Bill's daughter wore for years. Also, the tin of black shoe polish that was made, Bill was told, 'from the grease of burned bodies from the crematorium', and the aconite suicide pills sewn into each of his sleeves, in case he was captured – 'the Commandos were on Hitler's wanted list'. But he has retained some war spoils. An ashtray from Paris 'of a little boy hiding his winkie – when you put ash in it, he pees.' A silver cigarette case presented to him by the Mayor of Kiel in gratitude for saving the port. The faded silk map of France – 'in case I got lost' – which he spreads out and then scrunches up into the size of a brass button. And his prize possession, which he slides respectfully out of its leather sheath, his stainless steel commando knife –'good for opening canned beef'. The Fairbairn-Sykes stiletto with 'the special knob for quick and easy withdrawal' had distinguished Bill from regular soldiers at the front.

The most recent item is a white-and-green medal. This arrived days before – the Légion d'Honneur, accompanied by a letter from the French President. 'We must never forget the heroes like you who came from Britain and the Commonwealth to begin the liberation of Europe by liberating France.'

Bill's life in 30AU provides a unique lightning rod back into Ian's unit. He was one of the Royal Marines who protected and chauffeured the Admiralty 'boffins' and coders. He accompanied Ian's naval officers on their hunt for secret German intelligence, equipment and personnel. He helped fight for, capture, guard, and transport the booty. 'The muscle that protected the brain,' says Nicholas Rankin.

His father was a railwayman in charge of the cleaning sheds at Selhurst, and his mother a laundry lady. Aged seventeen, Bill enlisted with the Marines at Chatham. He was a champion boxer and crack shot, winning the

Bisley Cup with a shot at 1,001 yards. 'I told Sergeant McGrath, "I could shoot you through your buckle." "McGrath said to me, "You don't go behind me, Marshall." '

One day in the barracks, Regimental Sergeant Major Jarvis told Bill to go downstairs and look at a sign in his office window. *'Two marines wanted for hazardous duties.'* The following night Bill was sent to Budleigh Salterton and taken into a big marquee where a Royal Marine officer with a green beret was sitting on his own. 'Can you drive a steam engine?' This was Bill's introduction to 'one of finest officers I ever met', Captain Peter 'Red' Huntington-Whiteley. 'He went to the same school as the chap you're writing about. The day he got killed was the end of the news for me. I had nothing else to live for.'

'Red' took Bill for training at Achnacarry; to the London School of Tactics; to Salisbury Plain for glider training; and to RAF Ringway near Manchester, where he was taught how to parachute.

'In ten days, I did eight jumps.'

'Frightened?'

'Of course I was. Had to jump out of balloons, since there were no more aeroplanes of the type they wanted us to get into.'

'Red' kept secret that Bill's training was for an operation to seize the Villa Rothschild in Paris. Among Bill's papers is a reference to 'Exercise Ruman'. This was Fleming's plan, as Ian described it, 'for an airborne drop by my little party, 30 Assault Unit, on the German Naval Headquarters. The drop never came off because the Unit went in with the first wave of the French Army.'

Before D-Day, Bill had observed a wooden crate arrive under armed guard at 30AU's HQ in Littlehampton. Inside, provided by NID's Topographical Department, was a sand-tray model of the Villa Meurice, the German Naval HQ in Cherbourg. Bill's mission was to gather what intelligence it contained and place beehive explosives on top of the ventilation shafts.

Bill insists that he was camping in the wood at Sainte-Mère-Église on the night *before* D-Day. 'I first knew it was happening when we see a bloke hanging by the neck off the bell tower. He's alive, hanging from a parachute. I knew D-Day had started.'

I took this to be a mistaken memory, like my getting the date wrong for our interview, or else Bill remembering something that he had read or watched in films like 'The Longest Day', and absorbing it into his account, as can often happen. But then how trustworthy were his Marine records, which recorded that he was part of 'X' Troop that was detached on 5 June 'to special duties' and 'embarked [from] UK 8.6.44' – which would have him arriving on D-Day +2? I discovered an unpublished interview with Alan Schneider, who worked alongside Ian in US Naval Intelligence, based in Totnes. 'We were sending over groups of three to work with the underground. And Ian and I would work with these groups. We would brief them on what we wanted to know. We knew where the landings were going to be, and we were interested in what sort of fortifications were there, and how many troops were there, and what was the morale of the Germans. Ian had this group which were nicknamed Ian's Red Indians, and he would use those.'

Captain Geoff Pike was in charge of 30AU's X Force which landed at Saint-Aubin-sur-Mer. 'Before we landed, the beach had been reconnoitred by the Special Service people, who had been going over for weeks beforehand, and even months beforehand, to take samples of what the beach was like . . . and whether it was negotiable for the tanks.' The Intelligence historian Michael Smith says it is credible that Bill Marshall could have been among the fifteen 'Sussex teams' that were parachuted into France the night before D-Day. The British penchant for official secrecy can be exaggerated, but he would be forbidden to talk about it.

Bill has little difficulty speaking of the American glider shot down hours later. 'We saw it go down into the wood. Me and Jack Watson went to help, and they were all dead, necks broken. We pinched a Canadian Ford Jeep out of the glider, and we kept her for four months.'

He was with the advance guard into Cherbourg. The Germans had blown up the U-boat pens where 30AU had hoped to find one of the *Schnellboote* that Ian had been looking for since 1940. 'There was nothing for us to take,' says Bill. 'I'd never seen anything like it.' One of Bill's officers, Tony Hugill, described the scene in his diary and in a novel he published in 1946, *The Hazard Mesh*. Dense, smarting smoke filled the air. 'Irregular lumps of concrete 100 cubic feet in volume had been blown 100 yards. Enormous girders were lying twisted and torn like paper.'

On 26 June, Bill was south-west of Octeville. He has never talked in public about the incident that took place there. It is unlikely that Ian, a micromanager of his unit, would not have learned the details.

Bill speaks slower, preparing the scene. 'I had no clothes, only what I'd put on, no sleeping bag. The government had decided we were not military. We were a private army, mercenaries. *Attain by surprise* was the motto. You had to fend for yourself. I had a licence to kill because anything was fair game, nothing was off limits.'

To set his next action in context, he quotes what he heard 'Red' Huntington-Whiteley say about two German soldiers captured near Cherbourg. '*Take them back to the POW camp up the road. Anyone who takes them back can have their blankets.*' Five minutes later, says Bill, there were two shots and two men came back with extra blankets.

Then on 26 June, Bill watched as German snipers fired from the windows of a hotel, killing one medical orderly and shooting another through the knee as they attended wounded American soldiers in the street. It was raining when the German riflemen surrendered. Another witness told Nicholas Rankin how not long afterwards he had seen their blood flowing in the rainwater.

Bill grows quiet, withdrawn. 'I shot four Germans in cold blood.'

'What did you feel?'

'Nothing. How do you feel seeing two men trying to attend being shot?'

What happened next, whether he was reprimanded or Returned to Unit, he does not say. He has said enough. I think of another character who inherited Bill's licence to kill. This was the compost out of which James Bond emerged.

'Have you read Ian Fleming?'

'No.'

'Have you seen the films?'

'No.'

But Bill Marshall did meet Ian Fleming not long after. When the unit regrouped to Carteret – to a villa on a cliff top overlooking Jersey, living on US rations and sleeping in a classroom – 'the chap you're writing about, he came to visit us and break up 30AU in France. He gave us all a talk in the school on a field above a cliff.'

This was the first time Ian had set foot in France since June 1940. He arrived on 7 July 1944 with the DNI, Edmund Rushbrooke, to inspect and enthuse, but also to inject discipline into his unit, which Admiral Andrew Cunningham, the First Sea Lord, had suggested, 'after some rather illicit exploit in Cherbourg', should be renamed as '30 Indecent Assault Unit'. The reason was not Bill's summary execution of the surrendered German snipers. According to an American officer whom Ian trusted, the 30AU Marine wing 'has made itself highly objectionable through its lack of discipline (drunkenness, dis-orderliness, flouting of MPs [Military Police], etc.) and through demands for food and transportation'.

Demands were also being made of the local population. Weeks later, a 30AU Marine informed his officer, 'I've 'ad three fucks – if you'll pardon the word, sir – since we got 'ere. And NOT A FRANC TO PAY.'

'They must have been very low women.'

'Not at all, sir. One of them even 'ad a boudoir.'

Ian was incensed that his unit had lost a disproportionate amount of men, having been used on the front line for fighting purposes instead of intelligence gathering. Eight had been killed and twenty-one wounded, including the commander, Colonel Woolley. Not only that, but Ian's men were fighting among themselves. 'We had a fight the night before in the mess room,' says Bill. 'A Scotsman was playing cards and cheating, and got stabbed in the hand.' He remembers Ian telling them, '*You were not designed for combat.*' Bill understood that Ian had come 'to break the Unit up because they were not doing what they were supposed to do – look for paperwork'.

Bill was not impressed by Ian in his smart blue uniform with three gold rings. 'I thought him an "old queer", his feminine ways. I was so different in responsibilities.' Bill's reservations were shared by officers who had endured a month of attrition. They found it hard to stomach an Admiralty pundit who had not seen, as had Dalzel-Job, his men lacerated by a 'butterfly' bomb in a vicious shower of splinters, or the inside of a man's head vanish 'like the inside of a finished breakfast egg'. Dalzel-Job viewed Ian as an egotistical opportunist – 'somewhat cold and austere, very "Pusser" and on his dignity so far as the unit was concerned.'

'Sancho' Glanville called Ian 'the egregious Fleming, who always claimed to know everything', and considered his arrogance the armour for an unhappy soul.

Robert Fleming, Ian's canny grandfather. Born in a Dundee slum, he became one of the richest men in Europe after founding the bank Robert Fleming & Company. His recipe for success: 'Lairn to say No, laddie.'

Kate Fleming, Ian's grandmother, 'a happy, childish snob', taught him to play golf on the Huntercombe course near Nettlebed. She walked twenty miles a day, shot three stags on her seventieth birthday, and was captain of the Oxfordshire Ladies County Golf committee. She once tipped her caddie with a toothbrush.

Valentine Fleming, Ian's war-hero father, known as 'Mokie'. 'There was absolutely nothing that he couldn't have done if he wanted to.' He was killed in France when Ian was eight. Ian kept Churchill's obituary of him framed on his wall.

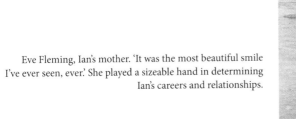

Eve Fleming, Ian's mother. 'It was the most beautiful smile I've ever seen, ever.' She played a sizeable hand in determining Ian's careers and relationships.

In mourning for Val. One of Augustus John's sixteen portraits of Eve, with whom he had a daughter, Amaryllis. 'I am a good sitter though difficult to do, I believe!'

Peter with Ian on the beach. 'We fought like cat and dog for most of our boyhood.'

Eve with 'the four madmen to whom I gave birth'. On one side are Michael, Richard and Peter. Ian sits apart on the left, 'looking saturnine'. Ann said, 'He was different. I don't think he was a very easy child.'

Ian was 'not greatly interested in horses', regarding them as 'dangerous at both ends and uncomfortable in the middle'.

Among 'the empty hours of my life', Ian counted 'fishing Scottish lochs in the rain'.

The four Fleming brothers: Michael and Richard (standing) became directors of the family bank; after the war, Richard became chairman. Peter (seated left) thought that banking was 'no life for a gentleman, and in my opinion a pretty poor one for a dung-beetle'. Ian (seated right) agreed whole-heartedly. 'Writing plays & acting are much more exciting and personal.'

Ian (top) and Peter (bottom) in their 1925 house team for the Eton Wall Game. Peter was 'one of the most famous Etonians there's ever been'. By contrast, Ian, who hero-worshipped his elder brother, was 'a rotter in so many ways'.

At Eton, Ian excelled as an athlete, twice winning the Victor Ludorum Cup, and in 1924 winning the Junior Mile by half a yard and '3 secs: more than the quickest Jnr: time ever done'.

Ian competing for Sandhurst in May 1927. He came second in the 120-yard hurdles. It was his last competitive race.

Ian at the Swiss ski resort of Leysin in 1931, photographed by his Swiss fiancée Monique.

Ian in Tyrolean dress at the Café Reisch in Kitzbühel, chatting to 'the local Heidis and Lenis and Trudis', 1928. He was always 'a devoted lover of the Tyrolese'.

In Geneva, Ian's 'complete lack of seriousness' was one of his 'saving graces'. He read Russian and German novels beside the lake, and worked briefly for the League of Nations under Sir Eric Drummond, whose codename in the First World War was 'Bond'.

The 'Glamour Boy' stockbroker, posing outside Joyce Grove, his grandparents' country estate near Nettlebed. 'Everyone felt that he was just a rich, rather bored, rather aloof young man.'

Ian, Mary Pakenham, and Ian's best friend Ivar Bryce in Capri, 1938. 'We returned only just on speakers,' said Mary. Having initially thought Ian to be Byronic, she decided he was a figure more like Falstaff – 'fascinating, but also ridiculous'.

Ian's first adult love, Monique Panchaud de Bottens, the 'lissome, ivory-skinned girl with blue-black hair' from Vaud. They were engaged for three years, until Eve forced him to break it off.

Muriel Wright or 'Moo'. She became a dispatch rider at the Admiralty. Ian's friend Robert Harling said, 'Along with every other officer in the unit I failed to understand why she had not become Mrs Fleming . . . She was a woman in 10,000 . . . we all adored her.'

Ian had decided to propose when Muriel was killed by a bomb in March 1944. 'She leaves a gap in my own life which can never be filled.'

Maud Russell, Ian's 'maitresse en titre', with her husband Gilbert. She understood Ian better than anyone, helped him get a job in the City, then in Naval Intelligence, and paid for him to buy Goldeneye. Long after his death, Maud wrote in her diary, 'Sometimes I think of Ian – mostly of his personality, his character & his innate kindliness.'

Blanche Blackwell, Ian's last love, at her home in Jamaica. 'Jamaica and me: we could have kept him alive.'

Commander Ian Fleming RNVR (Special Branch). 'All through his youth, he had been in disgrace for one thing or another, so walking down the street in the uniform of a naval commander must have been absolute bliss.'

Ian was described as 'a war-*winner*' by his boss, Admiral Godfrey. 'The country and the Allies owe him one of those great debts that can never be repaid.'

A rare portrait of Ian in Room 39, drawn by Robert Bartlett, 1943. 'If you thought he was sitting at a desk in the Admiralty – no. And what he was doing touched on so much of the war.'

'We none of us liked him very much.' Tony Hugill was another who had little time for Ian. After 'a pleasant talk with the Herr Geheimrat Ian Fleming', Hugill drove him to see Crossbow sites from which 'the new 15-ton horror' V-2 rockets were to be fired. Hugill was angered by Ian's drawling dismissal of some captured cognac. '*But my dear feller, this stuff's undrink-able.*' 'When he belly-ached about the brandy (I admit it was only Three Star), I became very angry and abusive and had to be shushed down.' Hugill's resentment deepened after Ian 'also interfered with us on a high level'. Hugill vented in his diary: 'Blast Fleming. He's brought some hot news of a mine store near Carentan & I've got to go flogging off tomorrow with only a vague idea that it's south of Carentan.' He had to break off writing his entry. 'News has just come in of an allied pilot who's fallen in the sea off the point so I must stop and organise a spot of Air Sea Rescue with Dunstan.'

By now, the person who liked Ian least was the head of the section, Dunstan Curtis. When one of his marines reported that he had seen 'a chap descend by parachute' and land in the sea, Curtis had leaped up to help.

Hugill wrote in his diary: 'Fleming rather annoyed us all by saying "It's no part of your duties to go buggering about doing air/sea rescue work." As Dunstan replied, he (Fleming) ought to try being by himself in the drink one day and see what it's like.'

Back in London, Ian told Maud about his week in Normandy. 'As usual he didn't make much of it, saying: "It was just like what you've seen in the papers, nothing happened. There was a football match and I had to tell my people they *must not* win by more than a couple of goals!" There was a presentation to the members of a fishing boat who had put out in bad weather to try and find an airman who had baled out over the sea. After a long search they found him.'

Bill Marshall had been in the rescue party. 'It was below the field where Fleming came. We saw a light bobbing in the water off the coast. We found a boat with no oars, pushed it out, two of us, with our hands. An RAF pilot on his last legs. We got him home, gave him a uniform. He stayed with us two days.'

*

30AU had landed in France in three troops. The unit was now split into eight or more smaller sections. Bill Marshall's section headed for the Channel ports.

'I went to Le Havre with Huntington-Whiteley.'

He chauffeured 'Red' there in the Canadian Jeep. En route, 'Red' made Bill drive into Dieppe, his six-foot-three figure towering over the windscreen. Several in the troop had taken part in the 1942 raid. They visited the beach. In a cave at the foot of the cliffs, they found the six-pounder gun that had shelled 'Red' in his landing craft and burned him.

Ian tracked their progress on his map. Harling wrote down a typical Fleming instruction. 'In pursuance of orders received from ANCXF you are to proceed by road to Tarbes and subsequently to Bayonne for the purpose of carrying out certain investigations on behalf of the Royal Navy, the French Navy and the US Navy. You are not in any circumstances to deviate from this given route.'

Dunstan Curtis was in Besançon when he received Ian's signal asking him to look out for liquid air and heavy water. 'I sent back, "What are they? Old men's diseases?"' Ralph Izzard was near Liège when the message arrived to pick up a French professor who specialised in liquid oxygen, and who turned out to be 'a very beautiful, very scared, lady Professor'. One of Ian's standing orders was to blow open every enemy safe. Several times, the Germans had left a can of petrol inside or a rude note. Glanville and Harling had abandoned the Citadel to join in the hunt for the targets they had spent the last months collating. On 31 August, Glanville received an 'Immediate and Top Secret' message from Ian to head to Fécamp, west of Dieppe, to capture intact a 'Midget under-water craft'. Reaching Étretat on 2 September, Glanville discovered that eight of these rumoured mini-submarines had left two days before by road, eight metres long with pointed noses, under canvas canopies. Children told him of large lorries having difficulty turning the corner. Then, near the Albert–Bapaume road, he found one, the 'X-craft' that Bond refers to in *Moonraker*, on a burnt-out trailer, plus two twenty-one-inch torpedoes.

In a railway yard outside Le Havre, Bill and Huntington-Whiteley came upon a Red Cross carriage twice the length of an ordinary rail carriage. 'It had been held up by the train being bombed,' says Bill. 'This was the only part left.' He parked the Jeep. Together they walked along the side of the carriage, until a hole attracted Huntington-Whiteley's attention. Bill says, 'I put my hand into it and it shook. The side of the train was all plastic.' They clambered up. At the end of the carriage was a cubby-hole with a trap door. Bill fetched a screwdriver. 'There was an instrument inside, just as it was. "Red" said, "Leave me here and take it to the docks as soon as you can." We both carried it to the Jeep. I took it down and it was put on a special ship. It was the nose cone of a rocket. It's now in the Imperial War Museum,' says Bill.

The last time Bill saw 'Red' was in a vineyard. 'His grandfather Stanley Baldwin used to stay at this farm. We showed up in the Jeep and the owner shows us where he had kept the champagne during the war, in a false wall in the farmyard. There were thousands of bottles. He got a bottle out for "Red" to take to London to give to Baldwin. We had champagne. A couple of days later he was dead.'

Bill had not accompanied 'Red' on 12 September, the day that 'Red' went into Le Havre to accept the surrender of the German garrison. 'A jack handle of a lorry had turned back on my arm. I was left behind to do dinner.'

'Red' had been assured that all resistance had ceased, but the same thing had happened at Tailleville: a white flag was raised from the German HQ, yet when the Canadians slowly advanced to receive the surrender, the Germans had shot at them.

Fresher in 'Red''s mind as he drove into Le Havre was the capture by Tony Hugill and eight men of the radar station at Saint-Pabu, along with 282 Germans, after Hugill bluffed them 'into believing I was an emissary from a larger force'.

'Red' had arrived at the square on the seafront in a scout car. German machine-gunners emerged with a white flag and started talking to him. The diffident 'Red', 'the best of the Troop Commanders,' in Hugill's estimation, 'was feeling rather out of things and was trying to capture something really good in order to "justify himself" as he put it.' Suddenly, a different Schmeisser section appeared. The gunners opened fire on 'Red', as well as on their own comrades.

It was a Major from the 51st Highland Division who told Bill. 'You 30 Commando? Don't you pick up your dead?'

Bill borrowed an American truck to collect his body. 'He was laid out on the quay. He'd been shot through the chest. I felt very awful about it. I did. I carried him. All I did was pick him up and chuck him in the back of the lorry. I drove to the US cemetery and left him out on a field.'

News of the death of 'Red' devastated 30AU. 'It was like a blow in the face,' wrote Hugill. Peter 'Red' Huntington-Whiteley had been with the unit from the first day, part of Ian's founding core. Marine Jim Burns called him 'a man so beloved of his troops that they were never the same after his death'. Even the normally bombastic Dalzel-Job felt his loss. 'In my memory, Peter sits on the edge of a camp bed plucking a banjo gently and singing one of Edward Lear's nonsense rhymes quietly to himself.' He was only twenty-four.

Bill takes off his glasses to wipe each eye, and repeats, 'The kindest man I ever met. Every year, I pay £7 for a cross for him in Westminster Abbey on November 11.'

XXX
GLOBETROTTER

'In Ian, I had a sense of courage, endurance, patience.'
CLARE BLANSHARD

30AU had been Ian's baby but he was no longer its parent. So Glanville implied in his *History of 30 Commando*. 'Since the unit had always been something of a problem child in Combined Operations, CCO [Chief of Combined Operations, Major General Robert Laycock] was anxious now to be rid of it.'

Ian lost direct control over the unit when Allied Naval Command moved to France in October 1944. In November, a Royal Marine colonel, Humphrey Quill, assumed nominal command. Stuck in Room 39 working for Godfrey's uninspiring successor, Ian fretted to get away.

Only to Maud Russell, who by now had been working at the Admiralty for eighteen months, did Ian hint how his position had altered with his new boss, Rushbrooke: how 'bored to death' he was under 'Rush-Admiral Rearbrooke'; how 'he regrets the old DNI every moment of the day'; how 'his old boss suited him admirably. This one doesn't at all. He is conventional and doesn't have an idea. And he doesn't like fighting battles.'

'Poor I. the wolves are after him,' Maud wrote on 7 November. 'He told me he was off abroad at the end of the week, this time to the Mediterranean and all around it. He expects to be away a month but is so sick of the Admiralty, the dullness and stupidity choking it, that he hopes he will be away much longer.'

There are few sightings after that. On 7 December, he was spotted in Cairo at Shepheard's Hotel, meeting Britain's ambassador to Moscow, Archie Clark Kerr – who was posted shortly after to Washington. Alaric Jacob, now the *Express* correspondent in Moscow, joined Clark Kerr for 'drinks with

Fleming, with whom argue on Russia'. On 18 December, Jacob again had drinks with Ian, 'en route to Colombo & then round world by Pearl Harbor.'

He was gone four months, on a tour that took him to Ceylon, India, Australia, Honolulu and America. His ostensible mission was to advise the DNI on how best to organise Naval Intelligence for the new British Pacific Fleet and, according to his only Bletchley file card to survive the furnace, 'enquire into command, org, & admin.' of the naval 'Y' station on the Anderson golf course near Colombo.

Beyond his official duties, Ian's journey assumed a personal significance that emerged only after he had become an author. What was a round-the-world trip for himself provided a potent last glimpse of an empire which then ruled a quarter of the world, having eclipsed its colonial rivals, France, Holland and Germany. Within fifteen years, Britain's empire would go the same way: by 1960, its colonies had fractured into sixty-four independent nations, starting with India, Pakistan, Burma and Ceylon. How much did Ian's global trip inform his view of Britain's diminishment? Quite a lot, reckons the British author Simon Winder in *The Man Who Saved Britain: A Personal Journey into the World of James Bond*. After the war, Ian harked back to this vanished empire with a 'bitter wistfulness' which would 'ultimately create Fleming's own enormous fan base'. Winder makes the case that Ian's nostalgic memory of these months shook him into resurrecting an image of 'the Britain which Bond did so much to buoy up'.

In Ceylon, Ian was reunited with his energetic NID colleague from Madrid, Alan Hillgarth, now Chief of British Naval Intelligence, Eastern Theatre. On 23 December 1944, Hillgarth wrote to his girlfriend about Ian. 'He takes up masses of my spare time . . . But it is nice seeing him because he brings a breath of the big world.'

Rushbrooke wanted Ian to review the Intelligence structure Hillgarth had set up. Andrew Boyd senses a bigger story behind Ian's mission. 'What could he do that Hillgarth and others could not? If he remained indispensable to Rushbrooke, why would the latter let him go for four months? I don't have answers.' Was Ian perhaps thinking of himself for the position when he recommended in his report that 'the Head of ANDERSON' should be 'first and foremost an able administrator, who has spent some time at G. C. & C. S. before taking up his command'?

Ian's two reports were typed out by Hillgarth's personal assistant, 2nd Officer Clare Blanshard, a WRN described by Hillgarth as a woman whose loyalty was indestructible, with an ordered mind, unusual stamina, and 'a supreme discretion, for she knew almost all the secrets of the Higher Command'. Ian's introduction to Blanshard was the best thing that happened to him on his world tour. Ernie Cuneo worked alongside her later with Ian in New York. 'Clare Blanshard was what Ian would call "a square-heeled solid English type", firm as a Wren Lieutenant, deeply religious, warm, unbounded in energy and loyalty.' In time, she became the custodian of Ian's secrets, a dependable editor and friend.

Blanshard recorded Ian's impact in a letter to her brother. 'A beauteous being has swum into my ken – on an official visit – and I like him very, very, very much indeed (but unfortunately that's the whole story, there's no more to tell).' They had worked and played together 'quite a lot' but she had kept her feelings in check. 'Well, as the Wrens say, whose letters I censor so monotonously, he's absolutely *It*. It doesn't make any difference that I don't mean anything to him as he's so awfully nice . . . Next time I write, he'll have gone forever and ever & practically won't have existed. But believe me, he's the right shape, size, height, has the right sort of hair, the right sort of laugh, is 36 & beautiful.'

One night, Ian invited her to a party at the Galle Face Hotel in Colombo. She was relieved to find him 'a chuggish dancer': she disliked men who danced well. Ian would be recuperating from a heart attack seventeen years later when his mind shuffled back to that night. He had watched her from behind a palm tree, 'clearing the floor in the centre' in a long, white silk dress threaded with glinting silver.

Nearly forty years on, Clare still recalled Ian's month-long visit, interrupted by a four-day detour to Delhi. 'We went to the cinema practically every evening in Ceylon! (bamboo boxes & "Please to bring own drink").' Then on to a nightclub called the Silver Faun 'which he nicknamed the Septic Prawn'. She escorted him on excursions through the jungle to the hill station at Kandy, and to the beach at Mount Lavinia, where a Sinhalese came up to tell Ian's fortune.

Already, Ian was focusing ahead. 'He used to stare out to 180° sunsets over the sea, I'm sure fashioning his adventure tales even then.' His time in

Ceylon was important for one further reason. 'This was where he decided to have a house in the tropics. He loved it. "Now I see how people live in the sun," he said.' He never wanted to spend winter in England again.

Ian described Clare as neither conceited nor a bluestocking. He dubbed her 'my ayah', 'the angel Clare', and 'the Flying Midwife', after she accompanied him with Hillgarth in an unheated flying boat, buried under rugs, to Melbourne. He saved her from drowning 'in the breakers of Moonga', but plucking her from the Australian surf was the extent of his hand-holding. As with Mary Pakenham and Joan Bright, their relationship endured because there was no more to tell.

Earlier on, in Colombo, Ian had met up with Maud Russell's eldest son Martin, who worked as a cipher clerk. Together with Clare Blanshard, they all went to see a documentary film, 'Two Ancient Abbeys'. It dumbfounded Ian to discover that one of these abbeys was Mottisfont. When he saw Maud's bedroom on screen, 'he felt as if he were the object of sorcery'.

After spending Christmas in Colombo and before setting off for Australia, Ian flew up to Delhi on 31 December 1944 to see in the New Year with his brother.

'Ian appeared here on New Year's Eve looking fat & being very funny & sensible as usual. I put him in my room & slept in a tent on the lawn & we had many hearty laughs & lots of curry & fishcakes.'

The brothers' reunion in Delhi reflected the tilt in their relationship. They had last met in Washington eighteen months before, at Trident. A plan to watch Cole Porter's Broadway musical 'Something for the Boys' was thwarted when Ian disappeared after they got to New York, leaving Peter to squire Joan Bright, who had helped to organise the conference. 'It was always good to see his square face with its wide smile,' she wrote of Peter, 'and to straighten out one's own fevers and uncertainties against his calm acceptance of events and tolerance of human frailty.'

By contrast, Joan felt that Ian 'had more apparent and vocal concern towards the people he liked, wanting them to do what he thought would be to their advantage; but he could also detach himself from them and temporarily but summarily dismiss them from his thoughts'.

Washington had been the scene of Ian's NID triumph two years earlier, when he worked in concert with Donovan to set up what was now the OSS. For Peter, though, Washington stood for the failure of Anglo-American coordination in the Far East. He had arrived in May 1943 for ten days of discussion about who would control deception in Asia. But his charm offensive for a British-designed Intelligence body ran into trouble. Peter's remit, which ran from India through Burma and Malaya to Sumatra, represented for Roosevelt all those colonies which America wished to see liberated after the war.

The man who might have been Viceroy, had Britain's ambassador to Washington been given a say, was now a lieutenant colonel in charge of strategic deception for South East Asia Command (SEAC, which the Americans quipped stood for 'Save England's Asian Colonies'). In Delhi, Peter felt a Blimpish exile. 'SEAC continues to make no sense at all,' he wrote to Celia in Nettlebed.

Burma had imploded, like Norway, like Greece. 'Burma was the third withdrawal I have been in and they all smelt the same.' Unlike Room 39, with its view onto No. 10, Peter's ground-floor office in Lutyens's red sandstone government building had windows high up on the walls, protected by bars. 'You can't see anything out of them except another row of barred windows.' The lack of a view framed his frustration.

Peter's new boss, who had previously been in overall charge of 30AU, was the man who had evacuated him from Norway. In September 1943, Mountbatten had been promoted to Supreme Allied Commander South East Asia.

On the surface, Peter's work mimicked Ian's. He created his own unit. He planned sabotage operations. He ran agents. He organised fake broadcasts, such as Plan HICCOUGHS, in which Peter tried to suggest a fantasy network of non-existent agents by reading out from *King Lear*, emphasising key words. This gobbledygook was repeated on All India Radio twice daily for three years 'to create alarm and apprehension in Japan as to the existence of an allied spy ring in Japan'. But *King Lear* sailed over the enemy's heads. In January 1943, Peter wrote: 'No indication has in fact been received that the Japanese are paying the slightest attention to HICCOUGHS.'

An example of the different outcomes for the two brothers was Operation FATHEAD, D. Division's version of Operation MINCEMEAT. In the early hours of 17 November 1943, the stinking corpse of a supposed Bengali

Hindu agent was parachuted into Burma, with codes and a radio set, on the Japanese lines of communication. After the corpse's parachute failed to open, D. Division's Control station in Calcutta listened for six months on FATHEAD's frequencies without hearing a bleep.

MINCEMEAT, 'the man who never was', had achieved an important deceit of the enemy. 'Not so our man in Burma,' wrote Squadron Leader Terence O'Brien. 'In the hierarchy of nonentity our man was far superior. He not only never was, he also never did.'

Peter felt the same way after he was grounded. This followed his free-lance foray on an abortive mission to Burma in March 1944 when, flying into enemy territory east of the Chindwin, his glider crash-landed into a gully and 'all hell broke loose', according to Peter's second-in-command, Major Peter Thorne. 'No one could raise the matter of the risk to ULTRA because some of those present were not aware of its existence.' This was the situation Admiral Godfrey had feared when banning Ian from crashing a Heinkel into the Channel. Peter brought his party safely back through the jungle – 'at its best it was like an intensely exciting stalk,' he wrote to Celia – but he was forbidden to volunteer for further operations.

'I am bored, but have no right to be, with Delhi.' Peter's letters home are redolent of his grounding. 'I play chess in the lunch hour, squash in the evening, & have had a few very good days shooting.' He itched to get away. 'It really is a *dreadful* place.'

In February 1943, after taking the entire Wavell family to watch Celia in the film *In Which We Serve*, written and directed by Noël Coward, Peter had written to his mother, 'it's about the nearest most of them will have got to the war.'

The chasm between the Peter Fleming who had started the war stepping ashore at Namsos, and the Peter Fleming who ended it leading 'this routine suburban life', was brought home in July 1945, when, clearing his desk, Peter confronted 'the rubbish I've been wrestling with for the last 3½ years'.

While, as he wrote to Celia, 'I think you can take it that the first phase of your Conquest of Asia is complete', Peter himself had stagnated in 'the rather childish atmosphere of this sub-continent'. With downcast heart, he read through 'the old controversies, complaints, attempts-to-get-a-move-on, insincerities, eyewash, long analyses about pay, about the telephone, about correspondence going astray, nonsense about security precautions, requests for an electric fan, raspberries, reconciliations ... more complaints about pay, about aeroplanes, about the lavatory, about the American General Staff, about topees and travel allowance and time-saving – you never *saw* so much bumf ... I feel I've just woken up from a particularly horrible and arbitrary nightmare. I am glad it is all over.'

In the Delhi heat, Ian visited Admiral Godfrey, now in charge of the Royal Indian Navy, in his official bungalow at No. 12 King George's Avenue.

Here, Ian's former boss lived with fifteen servants, 'a partridge, two hares, a hoopoe, a mongoose and a handsome green parrot'. He had recovered from a six-week bout of jaundice, and, despite the temperature of 102 degrees Fahrenheit outside and the grave shortage of experienced officers, was able to tell Ian during his 'short visit to Delhi' that he was 'no longer sorry' to have left NID.

Upon his unexpected appearance in India in March 1943, Godfrey had seized on Peter as an Ian substitute. 'Peter Fleming I've seen a lot of,' he wrote to his wife. Peter reported back to Eve: 'Admiral Godfrey has arrived here and is full of praise for Ian, whom he obviously misses very much.'

Ian reciprocated, even if the record is pretty silent on what he thought of Godfrey's sacking.* Ian had a ringside seat, must have had strong views on what happened, and, given the closeness of their relationship, must have been upset.

Ian wrote to assure Godfrey, 'You are much missed by the Division and particularly by those who know what you did for the Navy & and the war in those early months – & most, I suspect, by Your affectionate Ian.'

In February 1944, Ian had written again to Godfrey. 'You will be amused

---

* Godfrey's biographer Patrick Beesly remained mystified by Godfrey's sacking and subsequent lack of recognition. That said, Beesly's papers contain allegations that Godfrey might have had a German mistress in Dolphin Square, the discovery of which astounded Beesly, who wrote to his informant, Group Captain F. W. Winterbotham: 'I am well aware that, to put it mildly, he had "an eye for the ladies" but that the Director of Naval Intelligence from January 1939 to November 1942 should have had a *German* mistress and this fact was known to people such as yourself without anything being done about it, seems to me quite frankly incredible. Unless it was in fact the reason behind his dismissal ...' Winterbotham – the first to reveal the existence of ULTRA in his 1974 book, *The Ultra Secret* – knew Godfrey privately. He replied: 'John was a clever operator.'

to hear that I gave a lecture to the new Naval Staff Course at Greenwich on Monday with the title "Espionage and Intelligence" in which I made free use of your name and dicta.'

Security made it 'extremely difficult to write anything but banalities without overstepping certain proprieties.' Nonetheless, Ian did compose 'a few headlines' about Godfrey's ex-colleagues, before ending his letter: 'Please read & eat!'

'Big Bill went to [Operation] Husky. His stars are OK but no dividends yet.'

'Little Bill nearly Stellenbosched but rescued by PM & us and now a green bay tree.'

'TRACER doing final exercise then being blocked.'

'All JIC the same. Bill B. still in situ (recalls you ruefully!)'

The last referred to Bill Cavendish-Bentinck, described by Ian as 'a first-rate companion and a close friend of mine' and by Godfrey as 'a very agile and subtle mind', who, for all his ruefulness, had played a role in Godfrey's mysterious banishment to Delhi, a landlocked backwater from where Godfrey wrestled to control the Indian Navy's 117 ships and 20,000 personnel.

'It's rather a long story,' Godfrey explained to Hillgarth twenty years later. 'I seemed to have lacked the political instinct of self-preservation which warns people that danger is near.' Godfrey recognised that his disagreements had not added to the tranquillity of the JIC meetings, smoothly chaired by the aristocratic Cavendish-Bentinck. Godfrey was always too much his own abrasive master for his fellow Intelligence and service chiefs, who had not wished him to be renewed as DNI, complaining of his 'somewhat overbearing attitude towards them and the fact he was not temperamentally a "team-worker"'.

Looking back, Godfrey admitted to Alan Hillgarth: 'I really asked for it . . . However, my going didn't matter so much in the end as the momentum of the NID carried it along for another couple of years plus IAN, who kept the torch burning. There were only two more development projects to carry through – (Intelligence commandos & technical Intelligence) both of which Ian coped with triumphantly.'

XXXI
DRAX'S SECRETS

*'It is no exaggeration to say that the information obtained by
30AU was both a material contribution towards winning the war,
and also helped us to get well ahead into the lead with the various
technical and scientific advances which all navies must have nowadays.'*

DIRECTOR OF TORPEDOES AND MINES, 1946

After stopping off in Sydney (Pretty's Hotel, cheap oysters, 'slick' nightclubs, a weekend at Whale Beach beachcombing for electric blue sponges) and Pearl Harbor ('a mass of unsalvaged wrecks'), Ian was back at his desk in late February 1945. His new responsibility was to decide on the targets for 30AU's final push into Germany.

In January, in what Ralph Izzard saw as 'a typical Ian touch', the unit had set up its HQ near the battlefield of Waterloo, at Genappe, east of Brussels. Before joining Bill Marshall in his signals truck, Douglas Stott, a specialist coder, found an antique flintlock pistol from the 1815 battle in the cellar of a ruined farm building.

The focus of Ian's intelligence-gathering operation had shifted following the Liberation of Paris. A priority for the battle ahead, as it became clear that the Allies were going to win the war, was to get hold of German scientists and their technology before the Russians did. Ian was party to the top-level panic that the Germans had succeeded in developing the atomic bomb. 'We didn't know where Germany was with the atom,' he later wrote to Ann, but it was imperative to find out. When one Admiralty scientist embedded in 30AU was asked what his expertise was, he answered in hushed tones, 'Atomic science!'

'They were hectic times,' remembered Marine 'Bon' Royle, 'chasing about over pretty much the whole of northern Germany, arranging for security personnel to put adequate guards on whatever looked good, and for transport to move it back to our own sectors.' The enemy was not the only hazard, said Royle. 'Tommy Atkins was quite likely to light a top secret file to boil the tea on.'

Douglas Stott was one of the technical experts who knew what German developments to look for. Over the winter, Bill Marshall had driven Stott and another RN signals officer in a US wireless truck with a Mark V transmitter. At night, Bill had to find a safe place to park for Stott to communicate with Ian.

'It was a very dangerous job,' Bill says. 'The Germans were always tuning in to find out where the unit was signalling to the RN.' To receive a signal, Bill needed to tie a hundred-foot length of wire to the highest available point. He was not allowed to sleep in the truck. 'Even in a foot of snow, I had to sleep outside. They'd be working in it all night, all back to Bletchley. I'm told nothing.'

Where in France did Bill drive to?

'I don't know. The officer told me where to go.'

Before he died, Stott revealed that Bill Marshall had driven their signals van from Paris to Cassis; then from Marseille through Digne-les-Bains to Besançon, where Bill ended up in hospital with scabies. 'I hadn't washed in five months.'

Stott never forgot seeing – at a death camp – a lampshade fashioned from tattooed human skin. It made the whole D-Day enterprise seem absolutely worthwhile and essential.

From February to June 1945, Bill was part of a 30AU field team under Colonel Humphrey Quill's command, working with T-Force, which searched for German rocket scientists and equipment in a race against the Russians.

A top target on Ian's 'Black List' was the *Walterboot*, an underwater twin of the *Schnellboote*. Since 1943, Ian had read reports of a new German submarine capable of the exceptional speed of 28 knots. This U-boat was named after its inventor Dr Hellmuth Walter who had designed it in the eponymous Walterwerke on the outskirts of Kiel.

Walter's secret fuel was hydrogen peroxide, carried in external leather bags and codenamed INGOLIN. Most people knew the diluted version as the bleach that makes 'peroxide blondes', but it could be used as a propellant in higher concentrations. In 1939, a Walter engine powered the first ever rocket-fuelled flight of an aircraft, the Heinkel He 176. Since then, Walter had developed rocket-assisted aircraft, torpedoes, and launching systems for Ian's dreaded V-1 and V-2. These had caused 5,475 deaths, most of them near London. Both rockets relied for their primary boost and pumping power on Walter's peroxide.

On 1 May, Loelia wrote in her diary: 'Hitler is dead. Dies in Berlin, Donitz has taken over & is continuing to fight. It seems an anti climax. Left early & had my hair done.'

On a jetty in Hamburg on 3 May, Jan Aylen found the first evidence of a *Walterboot*, a 1,600-ton vessel that resembled a 'huge fish'. Three of these Type XVIIB submarines had apparently passed down the Kiel Canal hours earlier.

Kiel now became 30AU's main objective.

Shortly before six in the evening on 4 May, the Australian war correspondent Alan Moorehead gathered with other correspondents in a tent at Field Marshal Montgomery's headquarters on a wild hill-top on Lüneburg Heath. At a trestle table covered with a plain army blanket, the supreme commander-in-chief of the German Navy, Admiral Hans-Georg von Friedeburg, and five high-ranking German delegates prepared to sign the surrender of all land, air and sea forces in north-west Germany on behalf of the new Reich President, Admiral Karl Dönitz. Moorehead listened to Montgomery, 'spectacles on nose', read out the terms 'slowly, precisely and deliberately in English. The Germans, who hardly spoke a syllable of English, sat there without a word, for the most part staring at the grey army blanket.' The ceasefire was to start at 8.00 the following morning, Saturday 5 May. Germany's final surrender would not come into force until one minute after midnight on 7 May. Until that moment, the situation remained clouded and tense, with anxiety on all sides about the path of the Red advance.

At 10.05 a.m. on 5 May a 30AU field team led by Dunstan Curtis in three Jeeps flying white ensigns sped into Kiel with T-Force, ahead of the First Army, and captured the Walterwerke on the south bank of the Kiel Canal.

Ten minutes later, Curtis arrested Dr Walter, who was living next to his factory – a series of neat red-brick buildings, with extensive concrete underground testing cells, laboratories, workshops, drawing offices, and a handsome panelled boardroom which Curtis took over as 30AU's Mess.

Hellmuth Walter's precious hydrogen peroxide was stored in two thick-walled bunkers each holding ten twenty-ton aluminium tanks. The INGOLIN was highly flammable. Walter told Aylen how one of his factory hands had eaten far too many onions before cleaning one of the tanks. 'Unfortunately, his gases they escaped, you understand, and he was blown – poof – through the manhole of the tank.'

Dr Walter was a prolix, flabby-cheeked, dark-haired man of forty-four who spoke good English and was married with five children. It was from one of his daughters' beds that Bill Marshall confiscated a fistful of hair ribbons. 'Walter was there in a fur hat.'

To the intense frustration of Aylen, Walter was reluctant to reveal more about his INGOLIN. A Nazi Party member since 1932, he felt bound by his oath of secrecy to his mentor, Dönitz. After accepting Aylen's offers of tea and coffee, Walter disclosed that he and his staff had spent the previous two days burning 'all secret papers and drawings'.

The situation was acute. The Russians were only forty miles away beyond Lübeck. Intercepts from the Japanese embassy in Stockholm indicated that the USSR was planning to break the Yalta agreement, seize Denmark and control the Baltic. Everyone's jitteriness was exposed when a burly North Country sergeant was shown into Aylen's office, vigorously saluted, and announced that not only had he brought the Russians, but he had locked them in the next room; 'it was with much relief that we discovered he was talking about *rations* not Russians.' However, a Russian officer did wander in as Aylen began dismantling the Walterwerke.

To break Walter's code of silence, Curtis revisited Rear Admiral Joachim von Gerlach in his bunker at the German Naval HQ in Kiel. Here the day before, Curtis had accepted Gerlach's surrender, surrounded by 25,000 downcast, edgy German troops. Curtis now persuaded Gerlach to telephone Dönitz at his HQ in Flensburg, forty-five miles north-west of Kiel on the Danish border – the provisional seat of the new German government. Dönitz was still walking free in this unconquered enclave. A fortnight later, following his arrest by a Royal Marine from 30AU, John Brereton, 'with instructions to prevent him swallowing a cyanide tablet', Dönitz would be found wearing eight pairs of underpants in case his weak bladder humiliated him in front of the enemy. But before his capture, in one of his relatively few instructions as Head of State, Dönitz ordered that 'all secret documents and material whether already placed in secret hiding or not' were to be shared with the unit commanded by Colonel Quill ('Herr Oberst Quel'). Dönitz sent a Naval captain to tell Walter personally 'that nothing whatever was to be withheld'.

From 10 May, Walter gave the British a full account of his work, later arranging demonstrations to the countless investigators who turned up.

Walter's important papers were missing, but under a coal heap in the cellar a collection of microfilms was discovered, which were at once copied to London and Washington. The hoard included a 16-millimetre film of new secret weapons shown to Hitler in his bunker before his death. A forerunner of Polaris was a submarine that could rest on the seabed and fire a rocket. Aylen watched footage of the Messerschmitt Me 163 interceptor fighter, one of the first aircraft to be powered by jet. 'A film showing a take-off and climb to six miles almost vertically in two minutes was as breathtaking to an audience of 1945 as was the first moon rocket film many years later.' In the field of jet engines and torpedoes 'some staggering technical advances had been made.' Other projects in the early stage of development were a jet-driven hydrofoil, a silent steam cannon, zigzagging torpedoes, and 'plans for more destructive depth charges' that resurfaced in *Thunderball* ('the latest German pressure mines charged with the new Hexogen explosive').

The average rate of finding new weapons for the first fortnight was about two per day. 'All in all,' Aylen wrote, 'Walter and his team produced a very formidable armoury, perhaps of the sort which might have looked well in a catalogue of weapons thirty years later designed to appeal to certain Middle Eastern gentlemen.'

Or to a former Panzer tank-driver like Sir Hugo Drax.

Ian imbibed everything that Aylen reported back and he re-used details for the thrillers that he set in the Cold War. In *Moonraker*, Drax relies on a German scientist 'Dr Walter' and his team to build an atomic rocket inside the white cliffs of Dover. Drax shares both the self-esteem of the original Walter – who was induced to work on submarines for the British at

Barrow-in-Furness – as well as his capacity for making the eyes of his aco-
lytes glaze over with stupefied admiration. One of Walter's staff told Aylen
that his master's name would go down in history like Dr Diesel. Walter
agreed. When asked on VJ Day what he thought of the atom bombs dropped
on Japan, Walter replied that he considered atomic energy was 'only one
stage ahead of his own work'.

An estimated 12,000 important intelligence documents were gathered
by 30AU. In the second week of May, Bill Marshall was present at the discovery of one of the more impressive troves. Not only that, he dug it up.

While Curtis and Aylen examined the Kiel targets, another team, led by
Lieutenant Commander Guy Postlethwaite and including Marshall, crossed
the Kiel Canal to a research station in Eckernförde, where the German Navy
had conducted its principle torpedo trials.

The German Director of Torpedoes swore that nothing had been withheld, but the next morning he suggested that Postlethwaite obtain a spade, a
truck and two strong men, and he led the way to a nearby wood.

Bill Marshall was one of the men.

'*Bring two shovels, Marshall, and have a look.*' Seventy-five years on, Bill
stares at the photograph of himself standing in a vest in a trench. 'A Royal
Navy officer took me into the woods. We had to dig this hole, which was full
of metal boxes, rocket material, rocket plans, all sealed with aluminium. We
loaded them into a lorry.'

Aylen was told that the director's deputy, an unrepentant Nazi, had committed suicide 'because of the disgrace brought on his superior by this
action'.

How many boxes? Bill waves at his bookcase that covers one wall to
indicate the size of the haul.

'The Americans and English took it.'

Like Ian, Dunstan Curtis never opened up about his work for 30AU, not
even to his son Christopher.

'The one thing he did tell me was that he took Admiral Dönitz's surrender.' This was Dönitz's order to Gerlach to surrender the naval base at Kiel
on 5 May, disarm all German naval forces and freeze shipping. 'My father

drove in a Jeep ahead of T–Force, and on the way to Gerlach's HQ in Kiel he passed a hotel and saw a Rolls-Royce parked outside. He told one of his guys to go inside and find out who owned it and ask if he could borrow this Rolls for a few hours, thinking it more appropriate than his dirty Jeep. He returned it afterwards in good order to its owner.'

XXXII
TAMBACH

'We made a brief inspection of the contents which
proved quite breathtaking.'
'SANCHO' GLANVILLE, *The Official History of 30AU*

To accept the formal surrender of the German Navy in Kiel was not quite the last coup of Ian's unit, satisfying though this must have been. Days earlier in Paris, Ian had climbed into a staff car with an Admiralty chauffeur, 'plus two marines in a naval patrol car as bodyguards,' and was driven at top speed on a 400-mile journey across France deep into southern Germany.

Even as General Eisenhower was setting the terms for Dönitz's nationwide surrender on 7 May, Ian's small convoy pulled into the courtyard of a converted monastery in Lower Bavaria owned by a Hungarian countess, who still occupied one wing. Ian told Harling on his return that 'he had arranged for himself to be directed by the DNI to visit the *schloss*'. Additional strings had to be pulled with various American Army Groups for Ian to reach Tambach Castle ahead of the Russians. 'A bas les Russes' (Down with the Russians), he wrote to his OSS host in Paris, Charles Grey, one of the US Intelligence officers who facilitated his mission.

'*tatty lot heinie admirals xxx incl archives german adm xxx 1870 to present.*'

This signal from 'Sancho' Glanville had arrived on Ian's desk on 27 April after Glanville and a small 30AU field team had taken possession of Tambach. Decoded, the words referred not simply to the three admirals, Walther Gladisch, Arno Spindler and, germanely, Kurt Assmann: *heinie* was slang for buttocks as well as the derogatory term for German soldiers. Hugely more important, the signal denoted the seizure, intact, of nothing less than 'the most closely guarded secrets of the German navy'. Glanville's prize catch included, as he wrote in his *Official History of 30AU*, 'logs of U-boats and surface vessels, documents relating to naval planning and high command orders, minutes of naval and political discussions and studies of problems in naval warfare by German naval historians and operational research workers, several of whom, incidentally, were included in the capture.' Never one to seek concealment beneath a bushel, Glanville judged this capture, which took place under his command, as 'probably the most successful operation ever undertaken by 30AU'.

Not long after sending his initial signal to Ian, Glanville composed another, more urgent, emphasising the need to move quickly to avoid the possibility of the archive falling into Russian hands. This was why Ian had risked driving into the heart of the battle-zone.

Back in London by 11 May, Ian told Maud Russell 'all about his journey to Schloss Tambach, near Coburg, from Paris . . . how kind and excellent the Americans were without exception, how cold it was, how they raced along and finally how they arrived at the Schloss and seized the complete German Naval Docs and Records – complete up to January 1945 when the documents were evacuated there in charge of a couple of admirals.' Ian had described the extraordinary situation in the Schloss and the outbuildings, the owners politely allowed to stay in their own rooms by the Americans, who doubled up rather uncomfortably themselves. 'Every building was packed and stuffed with people: escaped prisoners, displaced persons, foreign workers, Americans, Russian women. The whole thing was chaotic. However the documents were there safe and sound and constitute a great prize.'

'Rarely if ever can any country have captured so much of another country's past,' was Nicholas Rankin's assessment in *Ian Fleming's Commandos*.

If Hellmuth Walter embodied the hardware of the future, Tambach was the software of history. It was, in Ian's estimation, 'one of the most significant and rewarding historical archive hauls of the war'. The snapping up of this unique archive, which made it possible to find out how much the enemy had discovered about our secrets, had its origins in Ian's library of technical breakthroughs. Ian admitted to Harling that 'his book collector's instincts had been aroused by the thought of such a killing'.

The summit of Ian's war career was a prime example of the cooperation that Ian had envisaged back in 1941 with William Donovan, and the outcome of Ian's unusually close relationship since then with US Intelligence – something Peter Fleming had not benefited from in Delhi. Tambach has been claimed as primarily a 30AU success story. However, the seizure was a combined effort in an area assigned to American forces. Even though it happened mostly by accident, Tambach represents for US Naval historians like David Kohnen 'one of the greatest triumphs of Anglo-American collaboration during the Second World War'.

In London, Ian shared his 'Black Book' – the secret Admiralty publication compiled by Glanville and Harling – with his US counterpart, Captain Tully Shelley. No coloured pin defined Tambach as a target. Although there had been vague reports of lorry-loads of documents arriving at the Schloss for several months, the priority was locating Nazi scientists like Hellmuth Walter and his weapons technology.

Out in the field, Glanville had been assisted by two US Navy lieutenants who had received SOE training in Scotland. Claims that they inspired the character of Felix Leiter have been made for both officers: Hubert Potter Earle, a Harvard-educated lawyer nicknamed 'Saucy' after his initials (those of Britain's popular brown HP sauce), and John Lambie, a forty-three-year-old Rugby and Stanford-educated linguist who had been shot in the face as he guided a 30AU team into the bunker at Cherbourg. Earle and Lambie were part of the US Navy Forward Intelligence Unit, and regarded by 30AU as comrades-in-arms. It was Earle who put Ian on the path to Tambach; Lambie, who assisted with the granting of clearances for 'Detachment Glanville' to get there and evacuate the material, and who consistently rendezvoused with Earle and Glanville during the push into Germany. As Glanville started towards Tambach, he carried a document with Eisenhower's signature in blue ink: 'THE BEARER OF THIS CARD WILL NOT BE INTERFERED WITH IN THE PERFORMANCE OF HIS DUTY BY MILITARY POLICE OR ANY OTHER MILITARY ORGANIZATION.'

The first sign that the German Admiralty had left Berlin with its archives came in April. Earle was 30AU's US liaison officer, based in Paris. On 12 April, he alerted Ian to an intercepted call sign 'believed to belong to German Naval Intelligence with a fix at Bad Sulza, near Weimar.' Ian passed this on to Humphrey Quill, 30AU's CO in Genappe, who briefed Glanville. The next morning, Glanville left with a small party to search for the German Admiralty records which, Quill impressed on him, 'were to be captured at all costs'.

Earle accompanied 'Detachment Glanville' to Bad Sulza, in the Soviet sector near Naumberg. On the way, they paused at Buchenwald. Glanville could never erase the moment he saw the heaps of corpses, with songbirds in their cages beside the carefully tended gallows.

They reached Bad Sulza on 17 April. In a boarded-up cellar in the high school, a 30AU Marine picked up the blackened remains of the carbon copy of a letter. 'It was badly charred but still legible and consisted of confirmation to the High Command that, in accordance with orders, all classified material had been transferred to 2 SLK/KA at Tambach.'

Tambach was a common name in Bavaria. A study of the map showed at least three Tambachs.

Earle was ordered back to London, with twenty-five cases of 'interesting documents', which he transported in a special Dakota. He told Ian on his arrival at the Admiralty that Glanville was proceeding with his men to the village of Tambach near Ingolstadt, 150 miles south.

This was discovered to be the wrong Tambach, a mere staging post for U-boat crews. The next most likely candidate was a former baroque abbey 100 miles north, owned by the counts of Ortenburg.

Glanville about-turned his four vehicles and off they set again. His eleven men were crammed into a Jeep with fixed Lewis guns, an armoured Chevrolet scout car, a 15 cwt Bedford truck for stores and ammunition, and a three-ton truck to transport captured material. The main highways were dangerous, thronged with refugees and deserters. Glanville used local roads. Speed was vital. Angus Thuermer was another American FIU officer who worked alongside Glanville. 'The targets had to be reached in that knife-edge period before defenders sabotaged them, or our troops ignored/looted/let them be destroyed during the melee of surrender.'

At sunset on 25 April, Glanville arrived at the imposing H-shaped former monastery. He walked towards the west wing and, peering through the ground floor windows, saw bookcases that snatched his breath away. 'There were shelves and shelves of files with the magic purple covers bearing the emerald cross, denoting "Chefsache" or top secret material. Such files had been one of the "Grails" for which our unit had been searching ever since it was formed.'

Glanville tried various doors in the courtyard until he found one that opened. Inside, a surprised German naval rating raised his hands. Then three admirals appeared, led by Walther Gladisch, much relieved to see British and not Russian troops. American soldiers had appeared twice already, on 11 and 13 April, but they had departed without suspecting the existence of an archive.

The admirals had since been abandoned by their subordinates; only a few ratings remained, a secretary, and a number of female staff, the German equivalent of WRNs. But the atmosphere was fraught. Even as the admirals dedicated themselves to preserving the archive, the women of the Kriegsmarine Hilferinnen were hell-bent on its destruction. Gladisch told Ian days later that 'one or two of the more fervently patriotic women working there had set about burning the records as they received them.' Gladisch had stopped this 'pronto', but the sixty-three-year-old Admiral remained in considerable fear of the women's leader, Fräulein Andröde, described by Lieutenant Jim Besant as a 'formidable character' in the mould of Rosa Klebb. 'Built as anything but a sylph-like figure, I wondered while eyeing her quietly why she had not been drafted to Ravensbruck as the Wardress in Charge!'

Arson was not the admirals' sole anxiety. Gladisch was dismayed to think what would happen if Andröde and her henchwomen appealed to one of the SS detachments roaming the woods outside. This was still a fortnight before Germany's official surrender. Gladisch told Glanville that should the women make contact with the Waffen SS, 'there would be no doubt that the loyal personnel would be shot and the archives destroyed.'

A similar risk related to the post-occupational resistance forces – ' "Werewolves", Hitler Jugend et al' – and marauding bands of Polish and Russian deserters. The latter especially were dreaded, wrote Glanville. 'These people some of whom, with their pointed heads, hooked noses, tufted eyebrows and long arms reaching nearly to their knees looked scarcely human.'

Such was Glanville's dilemma that night.

He posted armed sentries at strategic points to protect the material. But his small force could not sustain their vigil for long. The premises were huge and the 'vast' mass of documents were distributed throughout the castle 'in all rooms, and in farm buildings with sheep, cows and pigs'.

At 6.30 the next morning, Glanville went in a Jeep to find General Patton's HQ in order to obtain an adequate guard until the archives could be removed and to inform Ian of the capture. Glanville's signal to the Admiralty was sent as a special concession, in the name of the American GOC. A company from the Third Army was promised.

On his return to Tambach, bearing American cigarettes and coffee, Glanville learned that Andröde had lit another fire in the library, but this had been stamped out.

With the arrival of a guard of US armoured troops, Glanville felt emboldened to press on in search of other 'Black Book' targets. By the time he drove back to Tambach, three days later, Earle had turned up with Ralph Izzard and they were manifestly not in control.

The GIs remained outside, lolling by their tanks, smoking, drinking coffee, under orders not to fraternise. Meanwhile, the countess moved freely through the castle, 'an extremely vivacious middle-aged woman of Hungarian origin', according to Izzard. 'She had an extraordinary taut-buttocked walk. On one occasion when the Grafin trotted across the courtyard to feed her horses, one of [the GIs] made us laugh by commenting: "She looks as if she's got a deck of cards stacked between the cheeks of her butt and she's trying to shuffle out the joker!"'

All this time, important files were leaking out under the noses of the American troops. Earle witnessed a German using 'a cart and oxen to take documents into the forest.' One large cache was later found buried in the woods; another, under the doorstep of the Royal Naval occupational HQ at Plön. General Patton himself had appeared one day and left with 'a crateful of stuff'. Two inexperienced desk men sent out by Ian from NID to collect the archives had proved to be useless and 'failed to keep physical control of the documents in their charge'. One of them never made it beyond Genappe, and the other was too terrified by reports of werewolves to stay long.

It was against this chaotic background that Glanville had sent his second signal, which brought Ian to Tambach in the first week of May.

Ian was familiar with the Tambach area from his student days in Munich. Mountain background. Forest clearing. Lake. He described the unheatable castle to Harling. 'Cold. Dismal. Comfortless. Ghastly. Count Dracula stuff.'

In German, he discussed the collection with Admiral Gladisch as he might have chatted about scientific first editions with Percy Muir. The 'old boy' had been 'shattered when we arrived, but he soon became quite helpful'. Dönitz had visited Tambach once, Admiral Canaris twice. They had specifically charged Gladisch with safeguarding the archive and keeping it shipshape 'to show posterity a well-documented clean bill of wartime behaviour by Germany's glorious navy'. The possibility of the destruction of those priceless naval records had caused Gladisch 'quite a few sleepless nights'.

Ian made a recce of the castle and its grounds. He met the forty-nine-year-old chatelaine, Ilona von Ortenburg, known as 'Ily'. She was a good-looking, unconventional widow who spoke English and chastised Glanville's men: 'But, gentlemen, when a lady enters the room you have to get up.' A horse-breeder who made a daily outing in a carriage drawn by two Lipizzaners from her stud farm, she had lived since December 1943 in 'a kind of uneasy coexistence' with the German admirals and their staff of twenty-three, forbidding them to fly a Nazi flag from the building, but only the red-and-white family crest. Until now, she had enjoyed the protection of an admirer who was head of the Bamberger Reiter cavalry regiment nearby, but the regiment had surrendered, and the Russian zone cut through the estate less than a mile away.

The sound of the motors of Russian IS tanks in the woods never left Ian. The background noise was menacing, conceivably permanent, and reminiscent of the 'swift rattling roar' that Bond hears thundering from the German lines in the Ardennes. Hence the message to Charles Grey, 'A bas les Russes'. Ian had warned six years earlier about Russia 'descending, carrion-like, on the stricken battlefield of Europe after the war'. The ongoing Soviet threat would underpin his fiction.

Immediately on his return to London, Ian summoned Glanville, 'profoundly disturbed by what he had seen'. Ian was worried about the security of the castle 'in case its contents, and particularly the admirals, should fall into Russian hands'. He tasked Glanville to go back with a suitable force and extract the archive.

Glanville's strange story of Ian telling him to 'eliminate' the three admirals, who, Ian apparently said, were 'solely concerned with plotting and planning the next war', does not tally with Ian's accounts to Harling and Maud, or with the good impression that Gladisch had made on 30AU's Lieutenant Besant as a person with a 'warmth of temperament'. It squares more with Dunstan Curtis's assessment of 'Sancho' Glanville. 'Alongside all his virtues, he packed a pigheaded and arrogant certainty of his own rightness. His judgment never seemed to me to be particularly good, and for that reason I personally never took him very much into my confidence.'

Nonetheless, Glanville can take credit for organising the transportation of the archive back to London in a convoy of armed three-ton lorries. Once again, Glanville worked successfully with Earle, his American counterpart at Third Army HQ, who supervised the convoy's passage to Herzogenaurach airfield, seventy miles south. From there, Earle chartered the aircraft that flew an estimated 1,084 cases weighing sixteen tons to the Admiralty. Ian also commissioned a 2,000-ton fishery vessel to ferry a consignment from Hamburg. This likely included heavier gear like rocket engines, torpedoes, infra-red devices and U-boat technology from the Walterwerke. Tabulating all the shipments, analysts at first estimated the 'weight of the total collection to be forty-eight (48) tons'. But according to Colonel Robert Storey, in charge of gathering documents for Nuremberg, at which the Tambach files would form vital evidence for the prosecution, the weight of documents may have exceeded 485 tons.

About what to do with this mammoth trove, the arguments were only beginning. 'The situation in respect of the Tambach archives is almost farcical,' wrote the head of Naval Section 6 at Bletchley weeks later. Heading a list of seven interested parties was the name of 'Cdr. Fleming who has been given liberty to do as he pleases . . .'

By 17 May, 30AU's operations in Europe had ended. Ian played down this final phase to Clare Blanshard. 'Apart from stealing the archives of the Germany Navy on the Czechoslovak border & flogging a few German WRNS, I have had no devilry for too long . . . Work has increased since we beat the Germans. It's mostly worrying the carrion of the German navy & squabbling for the wish-bones.'

The Joint Intelligence Committee met weekly in the JIC Secretary's room in Great George Street on Whitehall. 30AU's capture of Dr Hellmuth Walter and the German Naval archives were major coups that the DNI or his representative were bound to have reported.

Created in 1936, the JIC was charged with coordinating Intelligence from all sources and 'to some extent controlling the British intelligence organisation throughout the world'. The daily summaries of most of its 391 wartime meetings were not preserved, and none of its Weekly Surveys of Intelligence have been released. Ian did, however, chair meetings of the JIC when Bill Cavendish-Bentinck was unavailable, as well as the BODYLINE and CROSSBOW subcommittees on German rocket developments. He was also involved in chairing meetings on the future of SIS and had a key role in establishing the new post-war Joint Intelligence Bureau (JIB).

The ideas that the two Fleming brothers submitted for the post-war strategy of British Intelligence suggest their high standing in this close-knit community. In June 1942, Peter wrote a paper on 'Total Intelligence' which he circulated to Gubbins, Wavell, and his former Military Intelligence boss, Major General Paddy Beaumont-Nesbitt. Two years later, in April 1944, Ian drafted a Top Secret letter to Cavendish-Bentinck as part of Sir Nevile Bland's report on 'Future Organisation of the S.I.S.' From their separate spheres in Delhi and London, both brothers reached the same conclusion: Intelligence would be as important in peacetime as it had been in war.

The Official Secrets Act, plus the classification and destruction of key documents, has made it easy to ignore Ian's contribution. Not even the former head of MI6, Richard Dearlove, was aware of his work for the JIC. 'It's pretty significant if he drew up bits of the Bland report,' says Dearlove. 'A lot was going on, trying to figure out what the Intelligence community was going to look like after the conflict ended. That was a key document in the determinant.'

Ian's Top Secret letter focused on the tasks and the countries on which 'the S.I.S. should concentrate after the war'. He had written to Rushbrooke from Melbourne: 'what DNI requires and what will be of great value to future DNIs will not be a detailed history of "how I won the war" variety, but some notes on major mistakes and failures with suggestions as to how to avoid them in the next war.'

He offered these suggestions, beginning with a nod to modern-drones:

'We shall require high grade technical intelligence on weapons development by the major powers. This will particularly apply to Radar, new explosives and fuels, the use of magnetic, acoustic and other principles for the directing and firing of underwater weapons, and remote control flight of aircraft or missiles, submarine, torpedo, and mine development in all its branches.'

He predicted a need for 'Topographical and beach information in protected areas, including any clues as to the establishing of new naval bases, aerodromes and arsenals.'

He listed as future trouble spots: 'Spanish Morocco, the Dardanelles, the Suez Canal, the Middle East oilfields, and the Gulf of Maracaibo in Venezuela.'

He disputed that China was a priority. 'China is not a naval power or likely to become one.'

In a crossed-out paragraph, he envisaged cyber conflicts. 'I urge that highly trained agents for this field of enquiry should be selected and strategically disposed as soon as possible after the war.'

By VE Day, Ian had spent six years at the centre of this spider's web. 'Both centrally, and in the field,' said Smithers, 'he acquired an extraordinary knowledge of the operation of the whole system.' Tambach was an opportunity to expand Ian's varied knowledge still further. He instructed Izzard: 'Get the top twelve German Admirals and order them to write 10,000 words each on "How the Germans lost the war at sea".' Initiatives like this had provided Ian with a perspective on the service's future requirements that not many could rival.

Ian's recommendations contributed to a substantial restructuring. Not only did he help Cavendish-Bentinck create the JIB. Beginning work in August 1945, Ian chaired a further committee 'to turn the concept into reality'. He drew on his discussions with Donovan back in 1941 to advance the committee's proposals for an inter-service 'Central Intelligence Bureau'. According to Andrew Boyd in *British Naval Intelligence in the Twentieth*

Century, these proposals resulted in 'the full integration of the armed service intelligence agencies twenty years later'.

He still smoked seventy cigarettes a day. The night duty officer in NID's Room 30 left a note complaining about the amount of cigarette ash on the floor – Margaret Bax swept it all into a tiny hole each night before going home. But throughout his time at the Admiralty, Ian had commanded a great deal more than in-trays, out-trays and ashtrays.

XXXIII
THE COMPLETE MAN

'My job in naval intelligence got me right into the inside of everything.'

IAN FLEMING

Ian had clipped her bracelet to his key ring. He thought of her every time he opened his door or started his car. He was not over Muriel Wright's death when he lost another friend, his golfing and bridge partner Shane O'Neill. Ian had known Shane since Eton.

In October 1944, in action in Italy, Ann's husband had climbed a church tower in Mercato to reconnoitre, and was shot by a sniper. 'The saddest news,' Loelia wrote in her diary. 'That's the last of the good people I personally wanted to get through this war.'

Shane's son Raymond was eleven at the time. 'I was at prep school at Ludgrove when the headmaster asked me to come in and see him and told me a telegram had been received.' Ann was staying at Lovel Dene House near Ascot with Esmond, who at once telephoned Loelia to come over. 'Found Ian there,' Loelia wrote. 'We had a lot to drink & played crazy bridge, which was the best way of dealing with the evening.'

Also present was Shane's eight-year-old daughter Fionn. She had made up a treasure hunt with rhyming clues on that day and was disappointed when it went to waste. Fionn says, 'I didn't know my father, not at all. The fuss I made was slightly histrionic. My mother was desperate for me to be in her bed that night, but I didn't want to. I did, of course. She wasn't particularly a huggy mother. It was very unusual.'

The Times printed a tribute from a brother officer who had been in Mercato. 'Shane took the fineness his country had to offer and gave his finest back. Of men like this, brave men, kind men, just men, who die on the field of battle, one speaks with humility; the debt is too large to be repaid.' Years later, Ann told her daughter, 'If your father had lived, we'd have got back together again.' Fionn says, 'I regarded that with a tremendous pinch of salt.'

Shane's death left Ann free to marry the forty-seven-year-old Esmond.

Maud's diary suggests that Ian did not cease to torment himself over Muriel. 'April 5 45 I. proposed himself to dinner. Had been spending a week's leave with Esmond Rothermere and Ann O'Neill, who have taken Lord Moyne's house at Littlehampton, and was so fed up, bored and aggravated by the atmosphere, the frivolity and the chatter that he packed up and left four days before his leave ended.'

Fionn was witness to Ian's excruciating position. He was still viewed as a Chocolate Sailor while forbidden to disclose the nature of his job. 'Chaps used to come in,' said Harling, 'and would refer to him as "Sailor of the Strand" or "Sailor of Piccadilly".' Fionn says, 'My mother and her friends were mobbing him up and not taking him seriously. I was very aware of them teasing him. Teasing Ian would be something that you did. However fond I was of him, I would not have thought of him as an impressive figure in those days, and I think my mother made a terrible mistake.'

Only to Maud could Ian unburden himself. 'He complained about that crowd and said why had I let him see such people, why hadn't I said what I thought about them? To which I answered: I didn't want to run down people he liked seeing, and that many who worked hard and seriously all day long often needed the relaxation of gay, light chatter, and that Duff and Mr Asquith, and countless other men have found that sort of society a great rest . . . I. said, "That is the wrong world for me. I can't imagine why I ever see them. I am Presbyterian and Scotch."'

Meanwhile, he had not stopped thinking about marriage. Maud was the person he felt secure enough to confide in. Ian had written to her from Colombo, 'You're the one reason I want to see London again. I have missed you very much.' Whenever they met, he continued to talk about 'the sort of person he should marry'.

In a strange display of match-making, Ann threw herself into seeking a safe mate for Ian. Only days before she married Esmond, Ann brought Ian together at dinner with Elizabeth Leveson-Gower, a rich, twenty-year-old orphan who stood to inherit the earldom of Sutherland. Maud was present.

'I thought her quite pleasant and obviously she would be a good marriage for him. Ann had rung him up a few days after the dinner and urged him to ask the girl to dine with him. He had done so . . . he was taking her out to lunch on Saturday and motoring down to the country with her. All this he told me, a bit excited, unsettled. I said it sounded very suitable. And so I'm sure it is. But I felt sad . . .'

Days later, Maud learned that the meeting had been 'a failure and he never went to the country with her after all. He talked about Ann O'Neill who has just married Esmond Rothermere.'

Another candidate for Ian's hand, whom the thirty-two-year-old Ann had considered up to the last moment, was herself. 'The night before I married Esmond [28 June 1945] I dined with Ian, and we walked and talked in the park. He said several times, "I want to leave some kind of mark on you"; if he had suggested marriage, I would have accepted.' But Robert Harling was not so convinced. He once asked Ann why she had not married Ian. '"I suppose because I wanted to be Lady Rothermere," was the simple but undoubtedly authentic answer.' Harling believed that her 'sole reason' for marrying Esmond was to do with 'her yearning for wealth'.

In an atmosphere of similar anticlimax, the war trudged to its end. On 5 July, having torn up her classified papers, Maud relinquished the secret identity that she had forged under same roof as Ian. 'I went down to the Admiralty and handed in my two passes, signing a declaration to the effect that I would never divulge in any form what I had learned during my work there – neither openly nor covertly in the guise of a play, a novel etc. I felt a pang, as I love working there. Went to Room 39 for the last time and I saw I. for a moment. A year ago, V-1s were roaring overhead, life was very different, duty was clear, and life sharp and valuable.'

'Little Bill' was knighted, 'Big Bill' awarded the Distinguished Service Medal, and even James Bond went on to be made a Companion of the Order of St Michael and St George. But there was no honour or public commendation for Admiral Godfrey or Commander Ian Fleming, who wrote breezily to his former chief: 'their lordships' sole contribution of my admittedly trifling contribution was to reduce me in rank to a lieutenant on demobilisation!'

It was part of his job description, as those in the Secret Services have always known. Even so, it rankled: what Harling called 'the extraordinary non-recognition of Fleming's role in the founding and direction of No 30AU, all that, apart from his many other services for Naval Intelligence.'

As compensation for not having received an Order of the British Empire like Peter or a Military Cross like Richard, for 'devotion to duty of the highest order' at the Battle of the Triangle on 18 July 1944, Ian grabbed three mementos from the Admiralty: a quill pen, a black cloth pin-cushion, and the typed signal announcing VE Day to all Divisions. Maud wrote: 'He had extracted it from the board it was on or the folder it was in, and decided he'd worked hard enough to deserve it: it reads "*Immediate*. Splice the main brace."' He asked her to get it framed for him.

On VJ Day, 15 August 1945, she took it to his flat as newspaper sellers were chalking up on blackboards JAPAN ACCEPTS SURRENDER TERMS. 'There was a general feeling the war was at an end though there were no crowds in the street and no excitement. I bought some small flags and placed one behind the little black bust of Nelson in Ian's room. And I fetched the Admiralty signal on VE Day "Splice the Main Brace" from the shop where I had framed it; and there it is in I.'s room in its red frame and the Union Jack and the bust of Napoleon.'

The Ian Fleming who walked out of Room 39 after six years at the Admiralty had gained tremendously in stature. In the same way, the war had transformed 'the ordinary man', wrote the war correspondent Alan Moorehead, after following armies round the world through ten campaigns. 'You could almost watch him grow from month to month in the early days. He was suddenly projected out of a shallow and materialist world into an atmosphere where there really were possibilities of touching the heights, and here and there a man found greatness in himself ... And at those moments, there was a surpassing satisfaction, a sense of exactly and entirely fulfilling one's life, a sense even of purity, the confused adolescent dream of greatness come true.'

This had been Ian's experience. He had felt that what he was doing was a clear and definite good, the best he could do. As in Moorehead's description,

'He was, for a moment of time, a complete man, and he had this sublimity in him.'

Ian never lived at such an intense level again. He would spend the rest of his life in peacetime, trying to recapture moments of time like these. The way he did that was by writing the books which have become the reason we are still reading about him today.

PART TWO

XXXIV
A PUDDLE OF MUD

'What did peace offer that was half as exciting as no-man's
land on a dark night in wartime?'
RICHARD USBORNE

An enormous melancholy pervaded Britain after the war. The tone was set
by the general election on 5 July 1945. Because of the time it took to gather
in votes from British troops like Peter still serving abroad, the outcome was
not known until the middle of the Potsdam Conference to determine the
post-war reconstruction of Europe, on 26 July.

Ann was less than a month into her marriage to Esmond when she threw
an election party at the Dorchester at which the results were to flash up on a
lighted screen. Ian invited Maud to join him. 'It was the first time I. and I
had been anywhere together for many years.'

They were not the only couple there that night also to have danced at the
Blenheim Ball before the war. Ann's ninety guests included the Duff Coopers, Virginia Cowles and Peter Quennell. Most expected Churchill to emerge
triumphant. To Ian's 'withering scorn', Loelia was the one person in his circle
who thought otherwise. He made a wager with her after visiting Conservative Central Office 'to confer with top brass'. Ian reckoned he was betting on
a certainty when he suggested a pound for each Labour majority.

Esmond had provided enough champagne 'to celebrate the Second Coming', wrote Quennell. The guests needed it to quench their disappointment.
Maud reported: 'I couldn't resist laughing a good deal at the results and some
of the long, foolish faces.' As Tory strongholds fell one after another, Ann's
hot-tempered brother-in-law, Lord Dudley, strode through the stunned
crowd prophesying revolution. Meanwhile, Esmond muttered that they were
'all finished'. Labour had achieved a majority of over two hundred.

'Disastrously unexpected,' rejoiced Loelia. 'I have won £250 off the unfortunate Ian Fleming!' He owed her the equivalent today of £13,200.

In Potsdam, the conference was interrupted for two days until the results were announced. Joan Bright was organising the British delegation and had to hurry Mary Churchill's things out of the bedroom when Clement Attlee replaced Winston Churchill as Britain's representative. 'Churchill never came back, and no wonder Stalin was surprised. He couldn't understand it. I think they probably thought we had bumped him off.'

Evelyn Waugh captured the foreboding that overtook Ian on Clement Attlee's election. 'All that seeming-solid, patiently built, gorgeously ornamented structure of Western life was to melt overnight like an ice castle, leaving only a puddle of mud.'

It was not merely Churchill's shock defeat. There was the disappointing aftertaste of victory. In New York, Ernie Cuneo marked VE Day by going with William Stephenson to the 21 Club. 'We almost suffered emotional "bends" the day the war ended. Tension went out like a power line turned off . . . Aside from its horrors you miss the frightful challenge of war. I think Fleming missed it as much as most; he seemed both grumpy and disconsolate.'

Ann's daughter Fionn registered his altered state. 'The war took it out on people. It really changed Ian. The glamorous boy at the end was looking tired and strained.' He hankered for what he had shared with Maud in Room 39, 'tension, excitement, hammering energy'.

The Allies may have won the war yet what followed Potsdam was no settled peace. In August, the explosion of two atom bombs in Japan provoked this 'strange thought' in Maud: 'one day a madman may touch one off over the earth and the verse of the poets will whirl away into space and their bones become liquid gas.'

Ian had no doubt this madman's face was Russian.

Overnight, Stalin, during wartime a beaming ally, was the bogeyman. Joan Bright said, 'In 1945, none of us would have been surprised if we had got to go to war against Russia.'

One night, Ian dined with Maud, 'very tired and tormented with worries about the new world we are hoping to build. The Russians seem to be playing a most unscrupulous double-dealing game of power politics.' After giving her a gold locket, he blurted out his concerns: 'he thinks we shall sink back into slothfulness, indifference and become ostriches again just as we did after the last war.'

Astonishingly, Peter was the person who came to exemplify Ian's apprehensions. If the war had changed Ian and his circumstances, and revealed new aspects and talents, it had not worked the same transformative effect on his brother.

In the first post-Potsdam garden party at Buckingham Palace, Mary Pakenham's brother Frank noticed a male figure by the lake wearing waders and field glasses. His top hat, containing a notebook, lay on the bank. 'It was Peter Fleming . . . checking up on the surviving varieties of rare royal duck.' Like most of his generation, Peter wrote and talked little of what he had done in the war. In the opinion of his biographer and friend Duff Hart-Davis, this was also 'perhaps because of his own disappointments with what he had been able to achieve'. Max Hastings says, 'I'm always rather moved by the essential failure of Peter Fleming's life, after that precocious series of pre-war triumphs. I met him in old age and was bewildered by the huge melancholy. The war was Peter Fleming's undoing, although he chummed up with Wavell etc., he came out of it definitely not a hero. His deception activities were pathetic.'

Peter returned from Delhi in July 1945, having not seen Celia for a year. Cyril Connolly's infamous spectre of domestic life awaited him. At Merrimoles, Celia had been looking after eight children, including Michael's. 'There is a doll's pram in the hall, spilling over with dolls . . .'

Meanwhile, in the assessment of the film magazine *Picturegoer*, Celia had bloomed in Peter's absence into 'just about the most talented actress on the British screen today'. When Noël Coward's adaptation of *Brief Encounter* opened in November, and Celia was nominated for an Oscar, Peter chose to step from the limelight. While in Delhi, he had written to Celia, 'I *have* made various discoveries about myself,' one of which was that 'Nature never intended me to be a pillar of *The Times*.' On his return, Peter ruled himself out of the editorship and refused the offer of his father's safe seat in the House of Commons, opting to manage the Nettlebed estate. On 13 October 1945, after six years working in the inner sanctums of Intelligence, he was 'signed off ULTRA list' according to his Bletchley file card.

As for his writing, 'I don't think I shall ever write anything good and I rather doubt I shall try to.' Nothing that he published afterwards matched the success of his pre-war travel books. Although he would be sporadically 'smitten with the desire to write again', and wrote several excellent non-fiction works, Peter's literary ambition yielded to his self-image as a reclusive landowner in the middle of a 2,000-acre beech wood. Here, surrounded by his black Labradors and a fox he played with, Peter became known as 'Colonel Fleming', the pre-war sobriquet he had mockingly bestowed on Ian. If not shooting something, Peter's happiest occupation was to pen humorous columns for the *Spectator* under the pseudonym of 'Strix'.

Ian had no estate or capital to fall back on, only sporadic, humiliating hand-outs from Eve, plus his 'very meagre portfolio'. Yet there was always something absurd in his profession of poverty, which was only in comparison to his mother and two brothers and some of his incredibly wealthy friends. Ian had quite enough to live well. His cigarettes were custom-made. His suits were tailored. He could afford to dine out, garage his car, play golf and travel. Still a partner at Rowe & Pitman, Ian 'thought at one time of going back into the City to try to make a lot of money'. A return to journalism was another option. Gomer Kemsley's elder brother Lord Camrose, who owned the *Telegraph*, appeared keen to use Ian's services. Ian mulled over the options with Maud, 'whether to take a newspaper job with the *Daily Telegraph* and go hustling and bustling all his life, or whether to live in a cottage, take off his collar and tie, and write a novel or two'.

Ian allegedly broached the latter plan with his mother. Eve met Patrick Dalzel-Job on the train to Oxford in the autumn of 1945, and told Job, who later reported their conversation to Ian, 'that you would make a worldwide success for yourself as an author after the war' – although Ian denied he had then held any such ambition.

A third possibility, reseeded in Ceylon, was to leave England and live on a desert island in the sun. He had written to Edith Morpurgo a decade before, 'I would like to go to bed with you and not do anything to you, only to embrace and hold you tight and to find you there when I wake up. But it has to be sunny. Where will we find sun in the sad grey land?'

In 1940, one of Ian's literary heroes, Ernest Hemingway, had decided to settle in Havana with his new wife, Martha Gellhorn. But Cuba was bound up in Ian's mind with Robert Fleming. Ian wanted a place he could regard 'as his own special pigeon, his own private bachelor paradise.' His first choice, debated with Maud in September 1943, was Hawaii, land of the Royal Hawaiian Serenaders whose guitar music Ian had played at Black Mount. Weeks later, Hawaii ceded to 'Tahiti – or any escape island'.

Then on 6 February 1944, Tahiti gave way to another candidate. 'Ian came to dinner, looking well and busy with a dream, the dream being a house and 10 acres on a mountain slope in Jamaica after the war.' He had doodled designs of 'the kind of cliff-edge hideout I want' on his Admiralty blotter to take his mind off the V-1s and V-2s.

For the immediate present, Ian's future lay in the Intelligence world. In mid July 1945, as he was helping to create the Joint Intelligence Bureau, Ian told Maud that he was 'likely to be offered a new job he thinks he won't be able to refuse. It would carry with it the rank of Commander if he cared to remain in uniform. Goodbye then to Jamaica . . . and the dreams that have sustained him during the hard work of these last years. I felt a pang for him.'

It relieved Maud to report Ian's change of heart. 'He has refused the new job. He feels he must break away. So Jamaica is on again.'

Ian found his solution soon afterwards. He had been offered 'a handsome job on a newspaper', he told Maud cautiously on 14 August, not mentioning which one. But he was negotiating his terms. 'That life will be best for him provided he can have four months to himself in Jamaica or elsewhere every winter. He said apropos of Jamaica, "Why don't you take a house there too?"'

XXXV
SHAMELADY HALL

'This really is Flemingland.'
JOHN PEARSON, *Ian Fleming: The Notes*

Passengers during the war disembarking at Kingston's Palisadoes airport were offered a glass of rum punch. Ian never forgot this first taste of Jamaica as he stepped out, wearing his thick blue serge uniform, into the heat.

It was October 1942, at the end of his second visit to America with Admiral Godfrey. Ian had travelled to Kingston with 'Burglar' Bryce.

Ian had arranged for 'Little Bill' to release Bryce from his liaison duties with Donovan's OSS, and accompany Ian to an Anglo-American naval conference at Kingston's Myrtle Bank Hotel. 'There was a big wave of U-boat sinkings in the Caribbean,' said Bryce. The five-day conference in the badly air-conditioned hotel had been called to decide what to do.*

Bryce was enthusiastic to go. Sheila, his attractive but frail American wife of three years, owned 'a great house' in the hills above Kingston called Bellevue. Bryce had not been there since the war started, but he promised Ian that the eighteenth-century stone mansion possessed 'the world's most beautiful, and I say it advisedly, view' and he painted an enticing picture. 'We took the train down to Miami, ate stone crabs there, and then flew on to Kingston.'

It was Ian's first time in the tropics. The luscious scents ambushed him as they would anyone who carried in their nostrils the 'mean little stink' of domestic gas escaping from the bombed-out houses of the Blitz. After the grey smog and drizzle, with flowers struggling to bloom between the devastated brickwork, and a soul-destroying diet of 'toad-in-the-hole, powdered

---

* Blanche was always clear that another purpose of Ian's visit was to sack a problematic agent.

egg omelettes, spam fritters, soya bean sausages,' Jamaica was an explosion of fresh fruit, fresh fish, fresh coffee, of intoxicating colour and warmth.

For Bond as for Ian, Jamaica represented 'one of the oldest and most romantic of former British possessions'. The island had lain suggestively in the background since Eton. Ian's English teacher, George Lyttelton, had talked of a great-great-grandfather who was governor. In 1925, after leaving Oxford, Cyril Connolly spent six months on an estate near Kingston, as tutor to Charlie d'Costa, a pampered son of the plantocracy. Connolly had conveyed the island's beguiling atmosphere, 'nothing but hills and greenery, endless flowers and palms, scenery like Chinese poems or more often like Christmas carols on a Hawaiian guitar'. In the 1930s, Eve's former lover Augustus John had sailed to Jamaica, attracted by images of rum, treacle, white devilry and black magic. Ian had heard further stories from Muriel's horse-mad brother, Stephen.

Another neglected influence was Evelyn Waugh's elder brother Alec, who later took credit for passing on to Ian his strict writing regime. Waugh had first visited Jamaica in 1929. The ten days he had spent in Montego Bay on the north coast, where Ian would settle, were 'as good as any ten days that I have ever spent, sunbathing and swimming and gossiping and dancing'. In his travel books, Waugh popularised the Caribbean as a sun-drenched Eden. This idyllic image had carried Waugh through the Blitz, and his work for Military Intelligence in Baghdad and Cairo. 'How often during the war when evenings fell upon bomb-scarred London or on the brown burnt wastes of the Syrian desert have I not dreamed myself back on to a long verandah, looking on to the row of palms that flanks a broad, green savannah.'

This dream of warm seas and heavy scents, the drumbeat of rain on banana trees, had taken root in Ian's mind following his wartime visit with Ivar Bryce.

It was the middle of the rainy season, so damp that tiny toadstools sprouted on his leather shoes in the night. On their first evening of the conference, they borrowed an official car, packed Ian's cardboard suitcase into the back, and zigzagged up a rough mountain track with hairpin bends that could 'only be negotiated by reversing'. He could have been climbing the Stelvio Pass.

A note that Ian wrote for Bond in 1957 describes such a journey. 'The evening was very still. On the horizon, there was a sideways flickering and the growl of half-hearted thunder, as if someone was trying out thunder flashes in the wings. Then a deep experimental growl came out of the skies, and at the same time, drops of water the size of a shilling began to fall heavily, straight down from the skies.'

Bellevue House lay at the top of the track, 1,500 feet above sea level. Bryce led Ian through the downpour, up stone steps, to a flat lawn, and hammered on a locked door. They were not expected. 'Elizabeth!'

Presently, Elizabeth appeared, the old black lady who was the caretaker. Wrapped in sacking against the rain, she pottered about lighting lamps, opening the rooms.

Over time, Ian came to appreciate what Bryce had billed as Bellevue's 'unique view' – down to a broad plain dotted with mango trees and what Bryce described as 'the distant mirage of a city which was Kingston, and further still, the harbour, fourth largest in the world, then across the site of old Port Royal (that den of iniquity and stronghold of the pirates that slipped into the sea during the devastating earthquake of 1692), the endless blue azure of the Caribbean sea . . .'

Six years later, in January 1948, Loelia Westminster was working for Robert Harling on *House & Garden* when she came with Ian to Bellevue – 'really one of the most fascinating houses I have ever seen & done up in great taste,' she wrote in her diary. 'The garden is lovely too.' But not on this theatrically stormy evening.

Originally a coffee plantation, Bellevue had survived several slave rebellions, and changed hands twelve times before Bryce's wife bought and restored it. The central feature was a high, square inner room with walls two feet thick. 'This was the hurricane room, strong enough to withstand a tempest' – although purportedly permeable to spirits 'from some other world'. A woman had been murdered by her husband in the corner of the dining room, and Ian's friend 'Lady Molly' Huggins, the Governor's sociable wife, once reported seeing the ghost of the victim as she was eating steak-and-kidney pie. 'She had on the tight-waisted dress of the Edwardians, full puffed sleeves and long skirts . . . I was about to say "hello" when she disappeared.'

Another figure known to have sat out on the verandah was a childhood icon of Ian's. For an unspecified period in 1780, Horatio Nelson was lent Bellevue to convalesce from yellow fever. Bryce believed that 'he spent some pleasant weeks there being cosseted and nursed back to strength.'

Nelson was not the only significant person to have stayed here. A compelling factor in Ian's decision to choose Jamaica for his desert island was Bellevue's association with two contemporary heroes, both of whom were to buy properties on the north coast. The first was Bryce's boss, William Stephenson, who had borrowed Bellevue during the war. The second was the most famous agent that Stephenson recruited. Three months after Ian's visit, 'Little Bill' organised for Bryce to send an 'exhausted and almost voiceless' Noël Coward to stay at Bellevue for a fourteen-day rest cure. Coward was instantly entranced.

> *Jamaica's an island surrounded by sea*
> *(Like Corsica, Guam and Tasmania).*
> *The tourist does not need to wear a topee*
> *or other macabre miscellanea.*

'The spell was cast, and I knew I should come back,' wrote Coward.

In the event, Ian beat him to it.

While Elizabeth cooked up a meal of stringy chicken and yams, Bryce found a bottle of grenadine, a pink syrup for cocktails, and diluted it with water in two long glasses. Ian went out on the verandah and found an old iron chair 'which he reversed so as to lean forward on its back'. There Ian sat in his contrary pose, brooding over his non-alcoholic drink. 'He edged as near the falling curtain of rain as possible, and stared out into the streaming darkness, lost in thought.'

After the conference ended, they flew to Key West. Ian was absorbed in his files. Then, just before they landed, he snapped his brief-box shut. 'You know, Ivar, I've made a great decision. When we have won this blasted war, I am going to live in Jamaica. Just live in Jamaica and lap it up, and swim in the sea and write books.'

The 'lush green beauty of Jamaica' stayed with him and was on Ian's mind when he bumped into Ralph Arnold in Ceylon early in 1945. 'He said he was going to abandon everything when the war was over and do nothing except live in Jamaica, spending half his time on land and half in the sea.'

The war over, the Bryces returned to Bellevue. Ivar looked forward to indulging his 'violent addiction to being left undisturbed'. But his peace was soon broken. In the autumn of 1945, he was dabbling at reorganising his wife's plantation, when he was contacted by Ian, who sought help in buying some land. 'Ten acres or so, away from towns and on the coast.'

Bryce wrote to an old planter and agent, Reggie Acquart, who replied soon after. 'I think I have found the right place for your friend the Commander. Would he go up to two thousand pounds?' (Approximately £105,000 today.) It was a fourteen-acre strip near the run-down little port of Oracabessa, where the banana boats called in, on an old donkey racetrack between the coast road and the sea: 400 yards long, 300 yards wide, above a forty-foot cliff and a tiny rectangle of yellow sand the size and shape of a cricket pitch. Bryce believed he had struck 'the bull's eye' and cabled Ian. The answer came next day, peremptory as a Churchill memo. 'PRAY PAUSE NOT IAN'. Although Bryce promised to advance Acquart the money, the Scotsman in Ian seems to have avoided completing the purchase until he had first inspected this and other plots.

In December, Ian used his Intelligence contacts to get a passage to New York on the American aircraft carrier USS *Enterprise*, and on 20 January 1946 he flew to Kingston. He divided his next six weeks between the Bryces at Bellevue, and Hillowton, the Stephensons' new property above Montego Bay.

'He used to take the Jeep we had and go off for days on end, exploring the island.' Stephenson was all for Ian finding a place nearby. He had successfully lured to Montego Bay Sir William Wiseman, his predecessor as Britain's Intelligence chief in the US; also his fellow Canadian, Max Beaverbrook, who built a house called Cromarty. Stephenson hoped Ian might be another neighbour. 'Then one day he came to us and said, "I've found the place I want."' Bryce had driven Ian to see the donkey track near Oracabessa.

It reminded him of the walk to Dancing Ledge. The two picked their way through rough grass scattered with silk cotton trees and covered with a plant that curled up when Ian brushed the leaves, until they stood on the edge of a cliff above a small beach.

Bond recaptures the moment in *Casino Royale*. 'How many times in his life would he have given anything to have turned off a main road to find a lost corner like this where he could let the world go by and live in the sea from dawn to dusk?'

The woman who had taught Ian to write experienced the same frisson. Phyllis Bottome and Ernan Forbes Dennis were among Ian's first guests. They ended up also living on the island and writing about it. In *Under the Skin*, her 1950 novel about Jamaica, Bottome's heroine follows a grass path through an impassable thicket to a strip of lint-white sand. 'This *must* be paradise!' she cried, looking into the warm, clear water and out over a deep turquoise sea edged with foam. 'You'd think not even Robinson Crusoe had landed here.'

Small, square-tailed birds were flying in and out of a hole in the cliff. Bryce said, 'We went down to that wonderful little bay, and as we looked down there was a dusky, unclothed girl swimming in the sea. "Look," I said. "It's got everything."'

Five thousand miles and a seventeen-hour flight away, Robert Harling asked: 'Why Jamaica?'

'Because it seems to have everything for someone hopeful of finding a place for the occasional self-indulgent break.'

The Riviera was no longer a candidate, any more than Le Touquet or Deauville. In the rubble of post-war France, it was hard to find fresh, let alone instant, coffee. With no rubber for car tyres and a petrol shortage, the most aristocratic families went about in a horse and trap.

England was in hardly better shape. One of Ian's notes for Bond read: 'For the moment, England is not herself. Her certainty has left her.' In the aftermath of Potsdam, Ian's entitled circle felt endangered, like those playing cricket on Goodwin Sands before the tide came in. A mutiny in the Indian Navy under Admiral Godfrey in February 1946 portended the post-war reality. In 1945, Molly Huggins had visited England on leave from Jamaica. The Governor's wife was shattered by the devastation of London, the queues, the lack of vitality. 'Everything looked so terribly shabby, and the people so tired, and of course, everybody still had ration cards.' Not only was rationing in force, but life was tougher in some respects than in wartime, thanks to wheat shortages and a failed potato crop. In that bitterly cold first winter, the oak panelling in the London Cage at Kensington Park Gardens, where Ian's men had interrogated German POWs, was torn down and burnt in the fireplace. The dismantling of the Empire felt like this. When a polio outbreak in the hot summer that followed infected his friend Christopher Courtauld, Ian offered his new Jamaican retreat as the perfect place to convalesce in.

Jamaica never lacked provisions. In London, bread was scarce; in Montego Bay, the lobster and the rum punch tasted superlatively good. Ian had enjoyed Bond's daily breakfast of 'paw paw with a slice of green lime, a dish piled with red bananas, purple star-apples and tangerines, scrambled eggs and bacon, Blue Mountain coffee – the most delicious in the world – Jamaican marmalade, almost black, and guava jelly.'

The behaviour of visitors, Blanche Blackwell noticed, was 'completely different when they got into the tropics. They let go.' It was not simply the sun, the food and the terrain he loved. Ian saw in Jamaicans a people whose contradictions dovetailed with his. 'He would obviously live a very white life there,' says his niece, Kate Fleming, 'but he was more interested in Jamaican life than many of the expats.'

Ruins of great houses, hurricanes, riots. The undertow of violence and melancholy. Something about Jamaica reassured. It was a home for misfits and remittance men, for second and third sons like Muriel's brother Stephen. Here, Ian could be a rebel yet enjoy the benefits and certainties of empire – even as that empire crumbled.

Like the Tasmanian-born film star Errol Flynn, who arrived on the island in the same year, Ian could parade as a self-absorbed piratical squire in his tropical Black Mount, where he was free to wander about naked, attended by a housekeeper (Violet), a cook (Daisy), a gardener (Holmes), an old maid (Ann), a houseboy (Hall), and a pack of mongrels called Fox, Charles, Himmler and Satan. 'I never expected to own a dog. All sorts of new things are happening to me,' he wrote to Ann.

High on Jamaica's list of attractions was its status as a Fleming-free zone. There were few outposts that Ian's elder brother had not colonised in his travel writing. Yet apart from a stopover in 1930 on his way to Guatemala, Peter had left Jamaica alone, and he never visited Ian. On the unique occasion when Eve stayed with Amaryllis, Ian was not at home; his mother and sister found the place so uncomfortable, they moved into a hotel.

Then the bay. 'We never wear any clothes when we bathe; and it is just a question of walking out of bed and down to the steps into the warm sea.' As Ian floated with nothing on, caressed by seagrass and vivid shoals of angel fish, he differentiated himself from his brother.

Above ground, Peter had the edge: on Scottish moors and river banks, stalking, blasting away at grouse, riding through his woods. Submerged off his Jamaican beach, Ian became lord of the marine universe that he peered at through his goggles. 'The Commander' – in a strange parallel to Nettlebed, where Peter was 'the Colonel'.

It amazed Bryce how soon Ian knew the entire underwater geography, every fish and every hole and what was in it. 'He would spend hours and hours by himself with his mask and his snorkel, just watching the fish in the reef. His conversation was all about the fish – a shark he'd seen, a giant grouper, and always it was his own sort of talk – very Flemingy.'

Ian was pleased to credit Admiral Godfrey for introducing him to underwater swimming. When the DNI had lent him his goggles in Bermuda, Godfrey had 'added a new dimension to my view of the world'. Ian now became obsessed with exploring it. Days after taking possession of his Jamaican house, Ian put on his green rubber flippers and picked up his new Espadon Tarzan Beuchat spear gun. The shallow reef was less than a hundred yards from shore, and Ian had to walk out quite a way before he could swim. On the left-hand side of the beach was a deep hole full of very colourful parrot fish which brought the reef alive with what Peter Quennell likened to the colour scheme of a Holbein state portrait.

'I spent the whole of this morning shooting fish,' Ian wrote to Ann. 'You will be surprised to hear that my apparatus works very well and is the envy of all. So SUCKS. This morning we shot four big parrot fish, which are delicious and all colours of the rainbow – weighing in eleven pounds! So you see. Finally, we had to stop because there were too many big barracuda about and they have the nasty habit of biting off one's balls. They are really horrid looking – long and grey and very quiet with great underslung jaws and THREE rows of teeth.'

He was re-enacting his wartime exploits when he spotted two 'Hunt class barracudas' and christened them 'Bicester' and 'Beaufort'. A remora sucking fish attached to a shark was 'like a small fighter plane beneath a bomber'. 'And if you were lucky,' said Blanche Blackwell, who came to know the bay better even than Ian, 'you saw a moray eel in time before you stepped on it because it lived in the reef . . .'

Months after Ian's death, Blanche showed John Pearson where she used to swim with Ian. His biographer emerged from the sea with a richer under-standing of his subject than Godfrey had been willing to provide. The main lesson Pearson understood from swimming in Ian's waters: 'At last he was in the real world of effortless superiority – an introvert's heaven.'

Jamaica was more than a Peterless haven. On the island, an empire nos-talgist could lie back and think of Nelson when Jamaica was the prized heart of the British Empire and the Royal Navy was based here; or pretend to be a bachelor buccaneer like Henry Morgan, free to roam and dream unchal-lenged. 'They had neither wives nor children,' wrote Alec Waugh, who had likewise grown up on 'those serial stories of buried treasure and galleons stranded in the Sargasso Sea with which our boyhoods were entranced'.

Jamaica became the displaced centre where Ian updated those stories of treasure and pirates; where he could be himself most naturally; where he finally got married; where he was more at ease, wrote Harling, 'than in any other setting in which I had seen him, with the possible exception of Boodle's'.

'How much I owe it to you!' Ian wrote to 'Burglar' Bryce years later. 'I wouldn't be here and I doubt if I would have written the books without you. Odd.'

Aside from Peter, one important person in his life never visited Ian in his Jamaican bolt-hole: the woman who had paid for it.

In March 1946, shortly before Ian returned to England, having sorted out his architects and builders, Maud received a long letter from him 'saying he had bought the propriété in Jamaica for £2,000 & proposed creat-ing a house costing £5,000 according to the rough plans he had shown me. He described the spot as a paradise in a letter vigorous, characteristic &

evocative, & he has called it Shamelady Hall because the Sensitive Plant which grows in profusion in these parts is called locally *Shamelady*.'

That Maud paid for it is clear from her entry of 31 March headlined 'My budget' and itemizing all expenditures. The ninth item on her list: 'Shamelady Hall, £5,000' (approximately £255,000 today).

XXXVI
THE FOREIGN MANAGER

'Only three things are needed for a successful career in journalism.
Rat-like cunning, a plausible manner and a little literary ability.'
NICK TOMALIN to John Pearson

With arrangements in place to start building Shamelady Hall, Ian sailed back home on the *Queen Mary* in March 1946. His fellow passengers included Loelia Westminster, Joan Bright, who may have been hoping for a shipboard romance, and Winston Churchill, fresh from delivering his 'Iron Curtain' speech at Fulton, Missouri. This referred for the first time to Britain's 'special relationship' with the United States. Few had worked harder to make it so than Ian.

On 26 March, Loelia went to see Winston and his wife Clemmie in their cabin. 'Then Ian came and discoursed on Jamaica!'

Ian's reunion with his hero was an anticlimax. Joan Bright noticed how Churchill 'made it clear that he would rather it had been Peter Fleming'.

Afterwards, Ian told Joan he would no longer socialise with those he knew during the war – 'I am not going to see anybody' – and disappeared into his cabin.

They docked in Southampton the following day, arriving two hours late through a thick fog.

Ian had not been at his new desk for four months. He had resigned in early November 1945 as a partner at Rowe & Pitman, freeing Hilary Bray to take over his partnership. Then, on 24 November, Lord Kemsley announced a surprise appointment: 'Commander Ian L. Fleming RNVR' to be 'the Foreign Manager of Kemsley Newspapers', a post previously unheard of.

Five days later, Ian had appeared before 120 senior staff at a company banquet in the Dorchester, seated beside Lord Kemsley's voluptuous second wife, and resembling, to jealous journalists like Leonard Russell wondering who this Ian L. Fleming might be, 'the bust of a slightly embarrassed and disenchanted Roman emperor of a very good epoch'.

Ann's election night party had set the atmosphere for the post-war period. This second gathering in the same room determined Ian's next fifteen years. It launched Ian back into his old profession, in a position which allowed him to write his books.

Out of all the options rehearsed with Maud, Ian had plumped for his first love, journalism. In 1933, pleading poverty, he had resigned from Reuters, stating his intention one day to come back as a manager, editor or owner. When Reuters was sold in October 1941, Ian's 'latent tycoon instincts' were aroused as he watched his bridge partners Esmond Rothermere and Gomer Kemsley divvy up Ian's former agency between them. In 1951, Kemsley eventually became chairman.

Ian's ambition to be a player at this table was recognised by Denis Hamilton, Ian's future editor and protector at the *Sunday Times,* who always perceived him as 'a newspaper proprietor manqué'. 'He loved then and later, all the big talk about circulations, advertisement rates, developments in this or that group. Ideas would flow from him for starting new papers or transforming old ones, most of them crazy, some of them brilliant. All of them unconventional.'

In the last months of the war, Kemsley had pressed Ian to join the Kemsley Newspapers group, which owned the *Sunday Times*, *Sunday Graphic* and *Daily Sketch*. After some tough negotiating, Ian had signed a contract. The dinner at the Dorchester was Ian's introduction to his new colleagues.

It unnerved Kemsley's guests as they tucked into their *volaille du Surrey rôtie à la brioche* to observe the thirty-seven-year-old former Naval commander at Lady Kemsley's side displaying an unnatural familiarity with his hosts. Ian called her 'Edith' in the same intimate tone that he addressed her stiff, autocratic husband by his Welsh Christian name 'Gomer'; no one else outside Kemsley's family did such a thing.

To most of his 4,500 staff, Kemsley was a remote being, like Churchill at the Admiralty, whose existence Ian's young assistant (and future biographer) John Pearson had to take on trust. 'I never knowingly caught sight of the old boy throughout the eight years I laboured in his vineyard. I was no more than 14 feet beneath/away from him. Throughout this time, he remained a name, and I knew him only by His Lordship's elephantine tread lumbering across the floor above, which was reached by a separate lift the rest of us ordinary mortals were banned from using.'

Not even Ian's secretary, Una Trueblood, met Kemsley, although she received a telephone call one Friday. 'I'm a huge tennis fan and used to have the commentary on the radio,' she says. 'The message was to turn it down a bit. Lord Kemsley was "doing something".'

Godfrey Smith was Kemsley's personal assistant. One of his tasks was to keep the key to Kemsley's private lavatory. Smith first met Ian when he came round the door of Smith's tiny office on the executive floor and asked 'with a conspiratorial grin' if he could borrow the key. 'That was no problem, then or countless times later, because I knew about the mysterious role he played in Kemsley's life. Robert Harling, our design consultant, who'd served with Ian in Naval Intelligence during the war, used to say Kemsley had six real sons (of whom one was killed in the war and another, Oswald, would die soon from drink), one technical son in C. D. Hamilton (later Sir Denis, editor-in-chief of this newspaper), and one emotional son in Ian.'

The new Foreign Manager held more than the key to Kemsley's toilet. It was explained to John Pearson 'that because Lord Kemsley supposedly regarded Ian as the son he wished he'd had (in preference to those which fate had given him) and Lady Kemsley was in love with him, he granted him privileges to distinguish himself still further from the hoi polloi who put the *Sunday Times* to bed. Every Thursday evening Ian would apparently turn up at the Portland Club at six-thirty to play bridge with Lord Kemsley.'

Ian had known the bridge-obsessed Kemsleys since the late 1930s; their love of card games losing them 'more money, thanks to their poor play than will ever be known', in the calculation of Denis Hamilton, who joined the *Sunday Times* a year after Ian. Unduly impressed by the discovery that Fleming belonged to the merchant banking family of that name, Kemsley had invited Ian to 'lots of bridge' at Chandos House, his London home in Queen Anne Street, and to Dropmore, Kemsley's country retreat in Buckinghamshire.

The ambitious press lord was keen to inject into his newspaper chain the flair for reorganisation and zip Ian was rumoured to have brought to

Room 39. As Ivar Bryce saw it, 'Kemsley believed, and with good reason, that the man who had presided over the ubiquitous news providers of British Naval Intelligence could put together the greatest foreign news service in existence.'

Gomer Kemsley was a further example of the fascination that Ian could exert over an older man. 'He twisted old Kemsley round his little finger,' said Ann. Like Admiral Godfrey before him, Kemsley had a role in the genesis of Bond.

XXXVII
'K'

'Lady Ower and I would be very glad if you would come down to the
Towers tomorrow evening and spend the night.'
'The Shameful Dream'

Born Gomer Berry, Ian's new employer had been elevated in 1945 to the first Viscount Kemsley of Dropmore.

His staff knew him as 'K', which was how he initialled his memos. Although not a man to tell a joke, he was nicknamed 'Groucho' because he resembled the comic Marx brother, with his square moustache and large nose that was said to grow longer with his ambitions. Kemsley considered himself the spitting image of the Duke of Wellington. More brutally, Alaric Jacob caricatured the sixty-two-year-old Kemsley as Viscount Narsteigh, vulgarest of the paper lords, 'whose very privies had to be contrived by professional decorators'.

A case in point was Dropmore, whose library Lady Kemsley had furnished with 'unopened books from a wholesale warehouse', according to Robert Robinson, who ran the *Sunday Times*'s Atticus column after Ian.

Ian was a frequent weekend guest at this white-stuccoed Georgian pile near Farnham Royal that was encircled by oppressive dark conifers and 'as big as, and rather resembling, the Admiralty'. Ann O'Neill was often in the same house party. On a visit in 1941, Ann shuddered at the 'tasteless luxury' of her hosts and their 'penchant for ostentation'. Male guests were expected to dress in white tie and the women to wear tiaras.

Kemsley's seven children inherited his tastes. Six of his family were directors of Kemsley Newspapers, including his youngest son, whom he put in charge of the *Sunday Chronicle*. 'He'd do anything he was told,' grumbled a sub-editor, 'including bringing out the paper in Urdu and decorated with arseholes, if only his father would let him have a Bentley instead of a Jag'.

Ann regarded Kemsley as a narrow-minded, good-hearted, jumped-up idiot. 'The vulgarity of the Kemsleys is quite amazing: Lord K is arch, coy and common. He talked incessantly about the power of the press which in his case I trust is nil.'

For Ian, the brashest trait 'K' displayed was his conception of himself as an all-powerful magnate. Kemsley stamped 'A Kemsley Newspaper' on the masthead of his titles. He styled himself editor-in-chief of the *Sunday Times*, his flagship newspaper. But he had no feeling for journalism. His true comfort zones were the circulation and advertising departments, where he had started.

Like his fellow proprietor, bridge partner and friend, Esmond Rothermere, Kemsley remains an ungraspable figure, with his high-bodied black Rolls-Royces and censorious second wife, his ambitions and pieties. Frank Giles, Ian's successor as Foreign Manager, considered him 'at once pompous, self-satisfied, ignorant, snobbish and obstinate'. Like Rothermere, he has left no paper trail, not even a record of his ludicrous trip to parley with Hitler in July 1939. In his 1940 novella, *The Flying Visit*, Peter Fleming lampooned Kemsley as Hitler's friend, Magnus, Lord Scunner of Hymper Hall, the son of a manufacturer of collapsible greenhouses. Kemsley's lack of judgement could be near incredible. He assured the Führer in his hour-long interview that the one British politician he need not worry about was Churchill. He held fast to that position when he invited Ian and Loelia Westminster to join him a week later on his yacht to Deauville, and on 10 September when Loelia went to lunch at Dropmore. 'Lord K talked his usual b-s.' A year on, he remained puffed up with the belief that 'if it had been left to him he could have managed Hitler and he could have stopped the War.'

Gomer Kemsley's overtures to Ian had started in earnest in March 1945 as the war was winding down. Immediately on returning from his round-the-world trip, Ian was invited to Dropmore. 'No place for a hedonist & a heliotrope,' he wrote glumly to Clare Blanshard as he surveyed the conifers. 'I am staying a day with a press lord hence this great craw on the back of the envelope.'

The Kemsley coat of arms with its 'griffin sejant collared and chained' and motto *persevera et vince* (persevere and conquer) was a further example of Kemsley's addiction to personal aggrandisement, which had caused him to upgrade the name of his previous country house from Farnham Chase to Farnham Park. In *On Her Majesty's Secret Service*, it entertained Ian to ennoble Lord Kemsley as Lord Bentley, who wished to style himself Lord Bentley Royal, after the village in Essex, only to be advised that this prerogative was reserved for the reigning royal family – might he consider Lord Bentley Common instead?

In 'The Shameful Dream', an unfinished story about Gomer that he wrote in 1951, Ian cast Kemsley as Lord Ower, who was hungry to rise higher still in the peerage. At the time of Ian's arrival as Foreign Manager, Kemsley was hoping for an earldom. Whatever journalistic ambitions Kemsley pretended to Ian, this interventionist High Tory would never allow anyone to interfere with his 'half-promised' advancement, not even the former Naval officer soon to be dubbed the 'Crown Prince of Kemsley House'.

It is easy to see why they got on initially. Kemsley was a Welsh version of Ian's grandfather, catapulted to the House of Lords from humble origins in the mining valleys, after leaving school at fourteen. Gomer never alluded to his first job – as a floor walker in the haberdashery section of Merthyr Tydfil's largest department store. Gomer's father had been an estate agent in Merthyr Tydfil. His older brother, Seymour, died young from a fall off his horse. Little is remembered of him, except the local joke that the good folk of Merthyr were collecting for a memorial, to the horse. But the £100 that Seymour lent his more dazzling middle sibling William, later Lord Camrose, financed the Berry brothers' first title, *Advertising World*.

Summoned by William to London to work on the magazine, Gomer sold advertising space from their third-floor flat off the Strand, where he and William took turns frying sausages in a second-hand pan. *Boxing World* was their next title. Then in 1915, for £80,000 (approximately £1.1 million today), they purchased the *Sunday Times*, 95 years old, circulation 30,000, which Gomer raised to 270,000 in the Second World War. They expanded fast, buying the *Financial Times* in 1919, *Bystander* in 1920, and in 1927 the *Daily Telegraph*. Gomer was knighted the following year, and in 1936 became Baron Kemsley. Hungry for more titles, the brothers spread into the provinces, acquiring a chain of eighteen newspapers in Cardiff, Glasgow, Sheffield, Newcastle and Middlesborough. By 1937, when the brothers decided to divide their company, Allied Newspapers was the largest newspaper group in Britain. William held on to the *Daily Telegraph*. Edith, who had married Gomer in 1931 following the death of his first wife, advised her cautious husband to keep the

Sunday Times or else he would have no position in Society. As usual, Gomer did what she said. She expected the same compliance from Ian.

Edith was a divorced French-Mauritian with a 'Rubens appearance and bosoms', in 'Chips' Channon's phrase. Gomer was very much in love with her, and she drove his political, social and financial aspirations. 'Everyone said that she was the one who spent the money', Ian wrote in 'The Shameful Dream', casting her as Bell Ower, 'a fine, lower-middle-class woman from Guernsey . . . with social ambitions that could only be described as atomic . . . her most kindly sobriquet was "The Bellyful".' Her obsession – like Ann's – was to entertain. In the Kemsleys' Adam dining room at Chandos House, nothing satisfied Edith more than to sit down to *crêpe Newburg* with thirty princesses and cabinet ministers. 'I have the best cook in London and the best wine', her husband boasted; 'they all come.'

As Ian soon discovered from his Dropmore weekends, the Kemsleys were as priggish as they were ostentatious. Gomer – and therefore Ian – took his editorial cues from Edith. She sat in the library on Saturday afternoons, scanning the proofs of the Sunday editions in case the word 'sex' had slipped past the sub-editors, who had standing orders to replace it with the word 'glamour'. If anything on Edith's proscribed list slipped through, she called her husband, who would then report glumly to Ian, 'I'm in trouble with Lady Kemsley.'

Uncharacteristically, Ian had to be on permanent good behaviour with Edith. She could see sexual implications around the sharpest corners, wrote Hamilton. When the *Daily Graphic* ran a front-page picture of a bull – the Smithfield winner, 'whose organs hung down like bagpipes' – the equipment that the champion beast had used to raise the standard of dairy farming had to be hand-painted out after the first edition.

Gomer's euphemism for 'pornographic' was 'off-colour'. Another off-colour story featured *Memorable Balls*, a book about parties like the one Ian had attended at Blenheim. Copies were on prominent display at a *Sunday Times* Book Exhibition until it was learned that Lord Kemsley was going to tour the exhibition with Queen Mary. Ian's future publisher Tom Maschler was told to remove every volume of *Memorable Balls* from the publisher's stand. 'Lady Kemsley's in a roaring state!' But one copy was overlooked – which Queen Mary pounced on. 'What an intriguing title!'

Happy in his married life, Kemsley believed all true Kemsley men should be married with children, a conviction that would have severe repercussions for Ian seven years later. Even before then, it resulted in Ian having to sack one of his early appointments, Eric Siepmann, after Siepmann's first marriage exploded in public.

Shocked to learn that his theatre critic, James Agate, was homosexual, Kemsley wanted him sacked too. Lady Kemsley thought Cyril Connolly was another homosexual on overhearing him call a man 'dear'. After Kemsley at the Tuesday editorial conference relayed her opinion that Connolly should not occupy Desmond Mortimer's slot as lead book reviewer when Mortimer was on holiday, Ian unexpectedly threw back his head with laughter, ridiculing Kemsley's judgement of literary form. Instead of then sacking his Foreign Manager, as he was known in the end to sack everyone, Kemsley's reply, in a voice with a faint trace of Welsh in it, only added to Ian's reputation as a gilded insider. 'Now don't be so ve-hement, I-arn.'

Despite his paternal fondness for Ian, Gomer Kemsley was an unenlightened dictator whose strict Merthyr Tydfil morals stood at right angles to Ian's worldview. After the Newcastle *Sunday Chronicle* bought rights to Nicholas Monsarrat's *The Cruel Sea*, Kemsley instructed that all passages be removed in which men on the ship's bridge speculated about what they would do to the missus when they got home. 'THOSE ARE MY ORDERS.' When the day came that a stunned Lord Kemsley was made aware of what Ian Fleming was doing with another newspaper proprietor's missus, and in Kemsley's own home to boot, he did not shrink to act.

'He has deeply felt principles and will not swerve from them,' Ann wrote of Kemsley early on in her marriage to Esmond, in her unpublished account of the press barons. 'He stands for the Empire, family life and the Conservative Party.' But she issued this harsh prediction: 'Lord Kemsley will not make journalistic history.' Determined to prove his critics wrong, Kemsley had recruited Ian, in puritanical ignorance of his relationship with Ann, to steer Kemsley Newspapers into the future.

An immediate challenge was the low quality of the group's journalism. In Robert Robinson's opinion, 'nothing in the Kemsley's frowzy empire looked capable of anything but lining a cat litter.'

At a Kemsley dinner in February 1942, Ann wrote how 'Randolph

[Churchill] reduced Groucho to tears of anguish and rage by stating loudly and long that *Daily Sketch* was read solely by children and ranked with *Tiger Tim's Weekly*.' Her most damaging charge concerned Kemsley's flagship title, the *Sunday Times*. 'Its feature page is ruined by blimpish views drearily expressed and articles by eminent gentlemen approaching their centenary.'

David Astor was Ian's opposite number on the *Sunday Times*'s principal competitor, the *Observer*. Sacked by Ian from Room 39, Astor showed no restraint in ridiculing Ian's boss for being outdated, autocratic and 'shut off from everything of significance in post-war Britain'. Kemsley 'orders his politics from Central Office as if it were a commodity like newsprint'.

When, largely for these reasons, Ian declined Kemsley's first offer of the post of Foreign Editor, Kemsley was taken aback. Ian then raised the game. He would accept only if Kemsley upgraded his standards of journalism: more candour, more controversy, and more vigorous blame of public figures to remove 'the pall of genteel discretion' suffocating Kemsley Newspapers, which, Ian told him, were 'weighed down with redundant rewrite men and Fleet Street ex-beachcombers' and had 'become incapable of telling a straight story'. Extraordinarily, Lord Kemsley convinced Ian that this was his ambition too.

On top of that, Kemsley appears to have dangled over Ian the prospect of him taking over the *Sunday Times* editorship from the complacently insular William Hadley. This was not an absurd goal. Before Frank Giles took Ian's job sixteen years later, he asked Ian whether it was realistic to think of becoming editor one day. Giles wrote, 'In his debonair way, he replied to the effect that such a prospect was indeed entirely likely.' Giles went on to become editor.

A further carrot was a seat on the board. This was Ivar Bryce's surmise: Ian had 'secretly hoped that he would also have been offered a directorship'.

Kemsley's clinching offer, directed at Ian's ambition expressed twelve years earlier to Rickatson-Hatt, was for Ian to start a foreign news service 'as a rival to Reuters' to be shared by all his papers. Ian fought for the specially created title of Foreign Manager.

Ian set out his other conditions. No editorial interference – whatever he penned for the paper must go in untouched. Money: his salary of £4,500 and £500 expenses (a combined total of approximately £255,000 today) placed him on a rung above other departmental heads. And an 'iron-clad' annual holiday: two months' paid leave so he could winter in Jamaica.

Kemsley was not accustomed to conditional acceptance when offering an important post, wrote Bryce, but 'after some exasperated comments, duly agreed'.

Fifteen years later, 'K' made an unexpected sale of the *Sunday Times*. Robert Harling, one of Ian's first hirings, met Kemsley shortly afterwards and observed how his former editor-in-chief derived 'a curious latter day pride from recalling the eccentric contract he had granted Fleming with those curious holiday arrangements. That those spells in Jamaica ultimately contributed substantially to the emergence of Bond was undoubtedly true.'

This was Ian's conviction. 'Would these books have been born if I had not been living in the gorgeous vacuum of a Jamaican holiday? I doubt it.'

XXXVIII
MERCURY

'Wasn't it just acting like the chief (and Bond had known many of them who would fit the picture) of some super-secret project during the war who had reinforced official security with his own private spy system?'

MOONRAKER

It was a shock to come back from Jamaica.

Brown lino, bacon-coloured carpets, passages lined with white lavatory tiles. Kemsley House was a tumbledown red-brick office block between Clerkenwell and King's Cross. To Robert Robinson, it had 'the dejected air of a building site where the money had run out and the owners had decided to let the building project go to hell and make do with the Portakabins.'

Emerging on the second floor, Ian walked in his 'lean loping gait' into a rookery of temporary cubicles with frosted glass partitions which were constantly being re-partitioned. Ian had another partition erected to create 'an outer office like a waiting room,' says Una Trueblood. She had arrived at Kemsley House in 1948 from Wimbledon Secretarial College and worked as Ian's PA; she later typed out his novels and screenplays, and witnessed his book contracts. 'Mrs Trueblood will handle anything,' Ian assured his publisher.

She says, 'There was a big oblong table with magazines and he did like them laid out in a certain order. In his office, he liked his desk in a certain way, very tidy, a big blotter, a black telephone, ashtray, silver cigarette box, in-tray, and a file marked "famous people" which contained their contact details. My chair and desk were also in the same room. There was a hatch to the outer office. You pushed or pulled post or stuff though it.'

He hung up a print of Montego Bay to remind him of Jamaica.

'He would arrive in the office at 10, take a longish lunch, usually at

383

White's every day, and go home at six,' remembers the woman Ian praised as 'my invaluable secretary'.

Seventy years on, Trueblood recalls her boss as a kind, smartly dressed man – 'always a navy bow tie and short sleeves, which were unusual then' – who smoked a lot through a long Dunhill holder. 'He had sciatica, so he had to dictate standing up, on bad days walking round the room. When he started writing his novels, he sent his own typed manuscript with corrections, and I would type it out.'

One day, she found herself typing out her name. '*Trueblood opened her mouth to scream. The man smiled broadly. Slowly, lovingly, he lifted the gun and shot her three times in and around the left breast. The girl slumped sideways off her chair.*'

She opens her copy of *Dr. No* at Ian's inscription. 'To Una, with apologies for the sudden death!'

Did she know she was going to be killed?

'I found out pretty soon when I was typing.'

Until then, most of what Trueblood typed had to do with foreign news. She sent messages through the hatch to Ian's correspondents around the world, and collected their KEMNEWS cables from a machine in the cable room. 'I remember it churning out, and I'd have to bring them to Mr Fleming.'

They were written in cable-ese.

Did she read them?

'No.'

A tan from six weeks of Caribbean sun on his face, Ian threw himself into setting up the Kemsley Imperial and Foreign Service, known as 'Mercury' after the Greek messenger of the gods.

While in Jamaica, he had outlined his ideas to Stephenson. Ian had thought that Mercury 'would be useful for gathering information if the need arose. By then, he was fascinated by the whole thing of Intelligence and I think couldn't bear to let it go.'

Ian was not unique in his fascination. On returning from Europe to work in his old law firm, Allen Dulles found it 'an appalling thing to come back, after heading a spy network, to handling corporate indentures.' Dulles wrote to his former colleagues in the OSS: 'Most of my time is spent reliving those exciting days.' The same was true of many of Ian's intelligence friends who sought to revive their wartime networks in some form; Alan Hillgarth went to work for Juan March and kept open his private channel with Churchill, sending reports on defence and visiting him at Chartwell to inform him on Soviet aims in Europe.

Only when John Pearson met these ex-spooks in 1965 did he understand 'how Secret Service work really does put a mark on a man for life. Even a hard-headed old millionaire like Stephenson never escaped from it. He is still quite barmy over all this.'

Ian kept in touch with Stephenson throughout the post-war period. From his Jamaican base, still using the cable address Intrepid, Stephenson recreated the World Commerce Corporation in the image of his pre-war commercial Intelligence outfit, with former OSS or MI6 officers in forty-seven countries, 'continually on the alert in every part of the world'. Crucially, Stephenson's shareholders were agents he had worked with: William Donovan; William Wiseman; David Ogilvy, who had penetrated the Gallup organisation for Stephenson; David Niven, Ian's sometime choice for the role of Bond (who would play Stephenson in a TV miniseries). Their enemy now was Russia, whose threat intensified by the day.

Just as Stephenson had warned about German re-armament, in the Cold War he alerted London and Washington to the dangers of communist aggression. Previously discreet to the point of invisibility, Stephenson inflated himself as a player 'preoccupied with the fate of the whole Western world'. After Jamaica gained independence in 1962, Stephenson took his preoccupation with him to Room 3603 on the sixth floor of the Princess Hotel in Bermuda. A journalist who came to interview him recorded how 'to this day his Telex machine chatters busily with messages from around the world, from people too loyal to the spirit and time of Intrepid to see his informal information network dissolve.'

Stephenson was visited in his pink-painted Bermuda eyrie by Mountbatten and Gubbins, and by the CIA's Thomas Troy, whom Stephenson wanted to involve in an Intelligence network called 'Olds', to monitor the movement of 'Black Power' activists between the Caribbean and Washington.

David Cornwell, already writing under the pseudonym of John le Carré, was another agent with a peripheral view of 'Little Bill'. 'I nearly visited Stephenson, but the blarney in Stevenson's biography of him held me back. Sir Dick White, the then head of MI6, told me that, if I did see him, I should urge him to return the Office files he had taken with him to Bermuda.'

The television series 'The Man from U.N.C.L.E.' had been running for a year when Pearson met Stephenson in his penthouse suite in Bermuda in June 1965, after Ian's acknowledged hero had suffered two heart attacks and could barely walk. 'I went up in a lift to a weird place at the top of the hotel. It sticks in the memory. There were plate-glass windows overlooking the sea and something strange in the men on phones there, five or six chaps, as if on reconnaissance – clearly some sort of operation Bill was still running.'

It is tempting to see Ian in the same barmy light, back in this Biggles world, playing the Great Game from a wheelchair, still imagining he had ''fluence'. 'Stephenson and Fleming between them were substantial fantasists,' was Cornwell's conclusion. Tom Stacey joined the *Sunday Times* as a foreign reporter in 1960, the year after Ian relinquished Mercury, and he used to meet Ian at White's, where Stacey's father was chairman. 'Ian was mildly smiled at as being a self-invented secret service star, a bit of laughter in the next room. He purported to have a whole network of useful contacts. These were old duffers he'd met at some point in his life and completely no use.'

This was the dismissive view also of Frank Giles, who in 1961 took over Ian's desk at the *Sunday Times*. As a much younger journalist, Giles had first met Ian in his office in the summer of 1946. The Foreign Manager sat in front of a canary yellow map of the world, like the map he had studied before D-Day, with tiny flashing bulbs to pinpoint the distribution of his correspondents. Giles thought this Stephenson-inspired gadgetry 'a fair old load of bullshit'.

The precise nature of the Intelligence relationship between journalists and MI6 is known to those involved and few others. Pearson worked closely with Ian on Atticus for seven years. Could Fleming have been running spies under Mercury's wings? He says, 'It's very much the sort of thing Ian Fleming would do and enjoy doing . . . It's quite possible.'

*

Like Ian, Donald McLachlan had returned to journalism. While writing his history of Room 39, McLachlan gave a talk to senior Intelligence officers about 'the parallels between intelligence and newspaper work'. Ian's Mercury organisation was an outstanding example – an association Ian pays tribute to in one of his last stories. In 'The Property of a Lady', he writes of a Sotheby's sale of Russian Fabergé eggs, with batteries of TV cameras – 'amongst them the MI5 cameraman with a press pass from the *Sunday Times*'.

This coveted pass had a pedigree. Before the war, SIS was quite tiny, pared down to the bone in the 1920s and 1930s. One of the ways it maintained its existence was through an extensive network of journalists and businessmen who reported back. Newspapers and news agencies provided traditional camouflage for intelligence gatherers.

At the start of the war, Roderick Jones had given Admiral Godfrey access to all Reuters' traffic. In Lisbon in 1940, Ian was in touch with two SOE officers, M. D. Shaw and J. Barnes, who spread anti-German propaganda under journalistic cover. Over in America, Ian was privy to William Stephenson's impressive muck-raking media operation against isolationists. Ian saw at first hand how Stephenson used Cuneo, his personal liaison with Donovan and the OSS, to steer the broadcaster Walter Winchell and the leading columnist Drew Pearson into a pro-British line with stories that Stephenson supplied. 'When Walter finished broadcasting on Sunday night,' said Cuneo, 'he had reached 89 out of 100 adults in the U.S.' Cuneo calculated that 'between us, Winchell, Pearson and myself, we had 50 million daily circulation and would saturate the country.' Few suspected the part played by Cuneo, who went on to marry one of Stephenson's Canadian secretaries from the Rockefeller Center and whose son Jonathan became Stephenson's godson. 'My father wrote 100% of Walter Winchell's political items. That's what Herman Klurfeld [Winchell's ghostwriter] has told me.'

Inevitably, Ian's flashing yellow map has invited speculation. Was Kemsley's Foreign Manager simultaneously operating as a Cold War spymaster in the tradition of Stephenson, Godfrey and Donovan? Or was he just 'playing Red Indians'?

There is no doubt that Mercury would have presented Ian with a personal mini-Intelligence network – like the 'Intelligence Corps' that Vansittart controlled before the war. Tellingly, Ian had pushed for journalists to occupy a key position in a future American intelligence organisation. Donovan was said to run OSS 'like a country editor'. Was this the kind of editorship Ian had in mind?

There is evidence even before VE Day that Ian was on manoeuvres in respect of some kind of future intelligence gathering. He wrote to Peter Smithers on behalf of 'Biffy' Dunderdale: 'he and his party have definite designs on you after the war, and I agree that you should bear this possibility in mind; even if you combine nefarious activities with being a Professor at Harvard, you can probably put in some useful work in your spare time.' In January 1944, Ian informed Smithers about John Foster, Fleming's Timbralls contemporary and their colleague at the Washington embassy: 'I have started machinations to put him into occupational and post-war spheres where he will be more useful to me and others.' Soon afterwards, Foster, promoted to brigadier, became chief of the legal section for Eisenhower's Supreme Headquarters Allied Expeditionary Force (SHAEF).

Ian treated his correspondents overseas as he had treated Naval Attachés like Smithers, adopting Admiral Godfrey's 'technique' of taking subordinates into his confidence and then throwing full power and responsibility on them. 'From what I have since heard,' wrote Godfrey, 'Ian believed in and practised similar methods during his fifteen years tenure of office as head of the Kemsley press foreign department.'

Ian was not shy to invite the parallels. He defined his working life at Mercury as 'an old-age pensioner's version of Room 39'. The *Sunday Times*'s literary editor, Leonard Russell, noticed how Ian brought with him 'something of the jargon and a great deal of the organisation technique of the wartime Admiralty . . . a briefing message was a "signal" and a rebuke to a correspondent a "Mark I bottle".' Ian instructed his correspondents to write 'sitreps' – after the wartime daily situation reports that gathered background intelligence from abroad – and kept a copy of *Bentley's Complete Phrase Code* in his office. His own code was 'wyput', with the cipher 29421.

He employed not merely the language and practices of Naval Intelligence, but its staff. Robert Harling was brought in as the Kemsley group's designer. Clare Blanshard was sent to run the New York office; Stephen Coulter to Paris; Donald McCormick, Tangier. Lieutenant Commander

William Todd, former manager of Thomas Cook, assumed charge of travel arrangements.

Ian did not limit himself to former DNI personnel, wrote Anthony Cavendish in *Inside Intelligence*. 'Indeed, the Kemsley Press allowed many of their foreign correspondents to cooperate with MI6 and even took on MI6 operatives as foreign correspondents.' Other Mercury correspondents had SIS connections. Ian posted Eric Siepmann, Antony Terry and Ian Colvin to Berlin; the Czech-born Henry Brandon (formerly Brandeis) to Washington; Richard Hughes to Tokyo.

'I remember the map,' Una Trueblood says. 'Some of the stringers I had dealings with, I knew they'd been spies. They came over and were treated like old friends.'

'Could they have been spying for him?'

'Only on reflection.'

One clue that Ian perceived his ninety-odd correspondents as agents lies in the reference book he wrote for them. In this, Ian defined 'the ideal foreign correspondent' in terms that he had used previously to describe suitable candidates for COI/OSS and 30AU: 'he must be a credit to his country and his newspaper abroad; he should either be a bachelor or a solidly married man . . . his person must be such that our Ambassador will be pleased to see him when occasion demands. He must know something of protocol and yet enjoy having a drink with the meanest spy or the most wastrelly spiv. He must be completely at home in one foreign language and have another one to fall back on. He must be grounded in the history and culture of the territory in which he is serving; he must be intellectually inquisitive and have some knowledge of most sports. He must be able to keep a secret; he must be physically strong and not addicted to drink . . . and able to drive a car.'

The Intelligence historian Christopher Moran reflects of Mercury: 'it looks like a spying operation, it smells likes a spying operation, ergo I think it is a spying operation.'

The historian Alistair Horne let slip to Ian's niece Kate how in the early 1950s he filed stories for the *Daily Telegraph* from Berlin while supervising three agents for MI6, a task that required him to ferry secret documents in a false-bottomed suitcase. 'He told me they were all at it.'

Asked to speculate on the case of Ian Fleming were Ian to have continued operating as an agent, a former head of MI6 says, 'If Fleming was following the process, he would have been recruited as a UA, a head agent, and he would have been collecting material from sub-sources. This would have been reported in CX reports. It was all symbolised, so no name would appear. His ciphers, if following regulations, would have ended in "Z". His report would be written up and handed over to a case officer. Menzies might say, "Let's have lunch, but I'd like your case officer to do your formal reporting." No one reading Fleming's reports would know who the source or sub-source was.'

David Cornwell very nearly came to work for Ian in the 1950s when still at Oxford. He was interviewed by Denis Hamilton – before Cornwell's MI5 handlers rowed back on their original idea for him to masquerade as a secret communist intellectual under *Sunday Times* cover. Later, Cornwell was posted to Germany in the guise of a junior diplomat and he had dealings with the press. 'When I was a spook in Berlin, there was still a cluster of British journos, and all I can tell you is that a very high percentage of our lot were "symbolised", as we say. You are known to us by NS JR342 so people didn't know you.'

Cornwell divided his journalistic contacts into 'casual' or 'unconscious sources', and 'conscious sources'.

'An unconscious source is loose-tongued or believes he is telling it to someone else. A conscious person knows he is talking to a member of SIS.'

'What would he get in return?'

'A jolly good lunch,' says Cornwell. 'The clubland stuff was absolutely real, and I believe to quite an extent it is still. That off-the-record, club-code.'

Ian's succession of clubs – the St James's, Lansdowne, White's, Boodle's, the Portland – were comforting venues, with a silent vetting process for admission sufficiently reliable for members to turn up knowing they were among friends. At the Portland, Ian sat at one long table. A member would come up to him, or vice versa, and say before dinner, 'I've kept you a seat, there's something I want to talk to you about.' The steward would turn over two chairs, tipped forward onto the table, to reserve two places.

It is easy to forget that the way people communicated then was more limited. London clubs, and restaurants like Wilton's and Scott's, were popular with those who wished to exchange classified information sotto voce with someone from the 'old firm', as Graham Greene called it. Cornwell says he could easily imagine how Greene, another novelist with an Intelligence background, might have travelled to Havana to report to SIS on Fidel Castro's revolution. 'Dick White, who was then "C", would have rung him and said, "Let's have lunch," and over lunch tell him, "We would love you to write a novel in Cuba." Graham would probably not have been paid beyond expenses.' In 1940, Noël Coward was not paid by Stephenson for his Intelligence work, preferring the arrangement to remain casual; Greene was a lot stingier and may have demanded some SIS play money, as he had in Vietnam in the early 1950s when Ian published his reports about the last days of Indo-China. Cornwell says, 'Before Graham left for Cuba, he'd have gone to have a briefing from Dick, and when he came back, he would pass on what he knew. His motive? Patriotism. *It's us and them, old boy.* And the pleasure of feeling like an insider, a spy. As well, it tightens you up to have an ideal, an agenda.'

One of the first Mercury correspondents Ian sent to Berlin, during the airlift in February 1949, was Eric Siepmann, who had been recommended by Malcolm Muggeridge, a veteran like Greene of SIS Section V. Siepmann wrote to his lover, the future novelist Mary Wesley, after meeting Ian: 'They are most excellent employers, on what Fleming calls an "adult" basis of doing things.' Siepmann's first action was to call on his brother Harry, a director of the Bank of England, which continued to maintain channels with SIS. 'They are providing me with important contacts, on the understanding that I provide them with intelligence.' Ian directed Siepmann to drive into the Soviet sector as soon as the blockade was lifted, but Ian was immediately forced to suspend his new correspondent after Mary joined her lover in Berlin.

Siepmann's determination to 'do nothing which might bother Kemsley, say nothing about my private affairs and generally lie low' was blown out of the water when his aggrieved wife Phyllis aggressively burst into Ian's office to tell him that her husband was 'a violent, adulterous, alcoholic, wife-beating child molester' and said that 'no little boy in Cairo had been safe there during the war'.

Not prepared to antagonise 'K', Ian at once replaced Siepmann with Antony Terry, who became 'a good friend and one of the finest foreign correspondents I have ever known.'

One of Ian's four star appointments, with Henry Brandon, Donald McCormick and Richard Hughes, Antony Imbert-Terry was the illegitimate son of a captain in the 7th Hussars and a suffragette schoolteacher. A journalist in pre-war Berlin, where his father was attached to the embassy in the Enemy Debts Office, Terry's first wife Rachel described him as a slight, bespectacled man with colourless hair and a taste for nondescript dark suits that allowed him to blend into crowds.

Terry had entered the war as an Intelligence officer, but was captured at Saint-Nazaire in March 1942 on Dunstan Curtis's commando raid. Upon his release in 1945, he became a senior interrogator of German POWs, and worked on war crimes investigations in the highly secret London Cage at 6 Kensington Palace Gardens, where Ian's men had questioned prisoners. One day, Terry came face to face with the Gestapo officer who had mistreated him when he was a POW. In a re-enactment, a swagger cane was thrust down the German's back, his hair yanked, his ears bawled into, and he was ordered to do three days toilet cleaning; Terry was alleged in one report to have beaten him with a hide whip.

Terry's reputation for extracting information earned him a reputation among prisoners as 'the shit with the glasses'.

Released from his interrogation duties in June 1947, Terry was recruited by MI6 to go to Vienna, posing as Ian's Mercury correspondent there. He was vetted at Simpson's and the Carlton Club with Rachel, his then girlfiend, the daughter of an Islington shoe-salesman. Ian arranged their cover as a husband and wife working for the *Sunday Times*.

After they moved to Berlin, Terry admitted to Rachel, now Mrs Terry, that 'his double life and double profession continued'. Rachel became a novelist, whom Ian once tried half-heartedly to seduce – but he reminded her too much of her husband. She perceived how Terry 'had been expert in using his promiscuity to cover his espionage, moving easily between the two kinds of intrigue'. She had no doubt that Ian was in the picture.

How Ian exploited his Foreign Manager's position is illustrated by an early instruction for Terry to look up a certain von Mouillard in Hamburg, 'who has been well recommended to me as being particularly well-informed, especially regarding Russian manoeuvres in Germany, and I think that from time to time you may get useful material from him.' Terry used Rachel to deliver a parcel containing a pistol and to take some papers from von Mouillard, carbon copies of lists, closely typed, of things unobtainable in East Germany or Russia. These Terry had to fly to London 'to put into the Chief's own hand.'

Ian demanded that Terry, along with all his other flashing lights, submit sitreps. Sefton Delmer had filed this sort of 'eyes only' material from pre-war Berlin. 'While my reports for the *Express* were read by about twelve million people before being used to light a fire,' those Delmer delivered to his case officer in MI6 'were distributed to several hundred persons, read by no one, and then incinerated as secret waste.'

Donald McCormick, a Naval Intelligence officer in wartime Algiers, was another Mercury correspondent. Before he came to work at Kemsley House, McCormick was Ian's stringer in Tangier's international zone, with a brief to monitor communist activities in North Africa. 'Tangier will be in the news,' Ian predicted, 'because Russians will put it there.' In his dealings with McCormick, Ian acted like the taciturn head of the picture desk at the Jamaican *Gleaner* who was James Bond's controller in *Casino Royale* – sending Bond off on 'simple operations requiring nothing but absolute discretion, speed and accuracy. For these occasional services he received twenty pounds a month.' Ian paid this sum to McCormick, whom he commended for his sitreps. 'Your service continues to be excellent, and your private memoranda most helpful and workmanlike.' McCormick could never be sure whether a request from Ian 'to meet an amiable rogue named Don Gómez-Beare in the El Minzah Hotel Tangier tomorrow at 1800 hours' was 'intended to produce a story for publication, an answer to an Intelligence problem or information solely for Fleming'. But 'some of the material obtained from sitreps was undoubtedly passed on to branches of Intelligence'.

With the Cold War hotting up, Soviet Russia was the 'top priority' for the *Sunday Times* to cover. This was Mercury's Achilles heel. 'We are at the moment weak behind the Iron Curtain,' Ian acknowledged. 'Countless applications for visas in Moscow have been refused or ignored.'

Ian's struggle to insert a Mercury man in Russia offers the most convincing example of how he operated Mercury for the twin benefit of his newspapers and the security services.

In October 1946, Derek Selby, Mercury's correspondent in Warsaw, was asked to leave Poland and his interpreter-driver was sentenced to eight years in prison for helping Selby to establish contacts with the Polish underground. Ian moved to plug the gap with Nicholas Carroll, who had covered the Nuremberg war crimes trials. 'CYPHER CABLE FOLLOWS IMMEDIATELY', Ian telegrammed Carroll. 'We badly need representation in Moscow,' he explained, and that 'if ever opportunity offers, you should make a trip to Moscow'. He suggested how to achieve this. 'You might start some Russian hare in Polish territory and follow it back to its lair. If a Russian dramatic company arrives in Warsaw, this might provide you with a sudden feverish desire to see more Soviet drama. The same applies to Soviet art and Soviet medicine. The Russians are still most anxious to have their so-called "culture" admired abroad, and these suggestions may lead you to the soft under-belly.'

Only once Carroll's visa looked like being granted did Ian outline the sort of reporting he expected. His demands point to an Intelligence angle. Apart from a weekly 1,200 word 'Letter from Moscow', 'I would also greatly appreciate occasional confidential letters not for publication in which you would give us your interpretation (with the gloves off) of events.'

Carroll was to airmail these 'background letters as often as possible' via the diplomatic bag, a safe conduit that would have required the ambassador's knowledge and sanction. 'I fear all codes are useless, and most of them are blown wide open in any case.' The diplomatic bag was a more secure secret alternative outlet for Carroll's sitreps. 'I am sure that if you ever wanted to get anything confidential to us in a hurry you could so do through the Ambassador [Sir Maurice Peterson], who is a close personal friend of mine.'

Ian's last piece of advice was for the 'young and sturdy' Carroll to hold fast to his patriotism. 'I expect you will find writing for a Conservative Group of newspapers from Russia will be a trying experience since you will be subject to every form of propaganda which may gradually seep into your copy . . . You can only correct this possible tendency by bearing constantly in mind our own great social achievements and evolution and our vast contributions to the health and sanity of the world. I strongly recommend that you take with you Trevelyan's *History of England* and his *History of English Culture* and a few similar books and read a chapter or two whenever you have felt particularly inspired by a fine performance at the Moscow Ballet or a visit to a show hospital.'

Caroll's visa was declined.

'The way you go on playing Red Indians. It's so – so selfish.' Tracy's outburst to Bond in *On Her Majesty's Secret Service* could suggest that Mercury was nothing more than the nostalgic fantasy of a superannuated Naval Intelligence officer.

'I used to dabble in that kind of thing,' Bond tells Goldfinger. 'Hangover from the war. One still thought it was fun playing Red Indians. But there's no future to it in peacetime.'

Why, then, seven years of peace before Bond?

John Pearson ascribes part of the reason Ian put off writing his books to his streak of diffidence. 'He had little self-confidence and great fear of ridicule.' In this scenario, unwilling to compete with Peter in case he was shown up, Ian created Mercury, which evolved after five years into a well-compensated escape route from routine and boredom; at Kemsley's expense, Ian legitimately could fly round the world calling on his foreign correspondents, and spend two months every New Year snorkelling in Jamaica.

But Oliver Buckton offers an alternative interpretation in his 2021 biography, suggesting that Ian could have been using Bond to brush over his tracks. 'Perhaps Fleming didn't need to create a fictional spy immediately following the war because he was still recruiting and running real ones.'

Ian never escaped the Intelligence world. When Norman Lewis met him at a Jonathan Cape party in 1957, it was 'quite clear in the course of the conversation that followed that despite his current occupation with a newspaper, his links with Intelligence had not been severed'. Before Ian tasked Lewis with going to Cuba for the *Sunday Times*, 'it was evident that he had been able to come by the full details of my highly undistinguished army career in

Field Security at the bottom of the Intelligence pyramid.' Equally obvious to Lewis's wife Lesley is that neither did Norman break his connections with SIS. 'When Norman was in Tunisia with me in 1962, he crossed over one night, all cloak and dagger, dressed up in Chinese boots, to meet the FLN in Algiers. "My code name is BISMUTH."'*

Ian betrayed his continuing involvement with SIS in his correspondence about the refreshment course that he went on each summer with the RNVR Special Branch: he was obliged to do this in order to keep his naval commission. Five years after the war, he wrote to Ted Merrett, 'I am leaving on Monday for Invergordon to do my fortnight RNVR sea-time in an elderly submarine called Alderney.' However, by July 1951 Ian felt that his annual experience underwater was 'of no immediate value' and he sought an exemption from Captain Vladimir Wolfson, whom he had known during the war when Wolfson was Assistant Naval Attaché in Istanbul. Ian took pains to remind Wolfson that 'I am still involved to a minor extent in my previous activities.' He hoped that 'my rather special position' would induce the DNI 'to accept my special activities as an adequate substitute for two weeks training in a naval ship or establishment'. Ian looked forward to discussing his request at a secure venue. 'Perhaps when we meet at the 36 Club cocktail party, we can talk about my fortnight's naval training.'

Ian failed to get his exemption, but a follow-up letter on 9 November 1951 contains this blatant statement: 'As Foreign Manager of the *Sunday Times* and Kemsley newpapers, I am engaged throughout the year in running a world-wide intelligence organisation, and there could not be better training for the duties I would have to carry out for the DNI in the event of war. As you know, I also carry out a number of tasks on behalf of a department in the Foreign Office.'

To a minor extent. Special position. A number of tasks. How much was Ian downplaying his role, or else exaggerating routine fact-gathering and report-writing for the Foreign Office on places he knew about? In Kemsley House,

---

* In July 1960, two years after Norman Lewis filed his reports on Castro for Ian, a former SIS agent in Basel with apparent unbroken Intelligence connections contacted Lewis to ask if he would go on 'another trip to those parts'. 'Do you think the *Sunday Times* would be sufficiently interested to engage themselves financially?' he asked.

he adopted the same security measures as in Room 39. Philip Brownrigg recalled his habit of quoting a phrase from Homer. 'When imparting some desperately secret intelligence about the imminent firing of an editor, he would always say *Herkos odónton* – keep it behind "the barrier of your teeth".'

The 36 Club at which Ian had wanted to talk to Wolfson provides the most persuasive evidence of Ian's ongoing SIS activities. This was a 'Secret Society' of Naval Intelligence officers that met four times a year at the Junior Carlton or the Army and Navy. Admiral Godfrey had based it on Buchan's 'The Runagates Club', with a membership comprised mainly of those who had served under him from 1939 to 1942, and named for his wartime address at 36 Curzon Street.

This paragraph Ian drafted for his Atticus column gives a picture. 'Guests at these reunions rarely include anyone less hush-hush than the Chief of the Secret Service or the Head of MI5, and Atticus would give much to have his microphone under the table. It would be indiscreet to reveal the identity of 80 or so members. Yes, Commander James Bond CMG, RNVR (S) is of course a member.'

Yet look at how disparagingly Bond regards these 'Old Boys' when he sits down to dinner with them in *The Man with the Golden Gun*. His table-companions resemble nothing so much as P. G. Wodehouse's Drones: 'the fraternity of ex-secret service men that went under the name of "The Twin Snakes Club" – a grisly reunion held in the banqueting hall at Blades that gave enormous pleasure to a lot of people who had been brave and resourceful in their day but now had old men's and old women's diseases and talked about dusty triumphs and tragedies which since they would never be recorded in the history books must be told again that night over the Cockburn '12.'

That was in 1964. But back in the 1950s, the reunions had a more strategic 'function', to use Godfrey's word: 'the Cold War was very much "on".' Further, it is possible to read Bond's decrepit portrayal in the light of Ian's humorous 1958 *Sunday Times* review of *Our Man in Havana*, which Greene's biographer Richard Greene believes may have been an attempt to protect Graham Greene from MI5. 'By emphasising that it was "Wodehousian" and unlike reality, Fleming may have been trying to fend off the trouble that eventually came to Greene for giving too precise a picture of what was going on in the field.'

Following Ian's death, Godfrey wrote to Ann singling out the 36 Club and saying how its 'functions he attended so regularly . . . lacked warmth on the rare occasions that he was absent.' For Ian, they were not merely convivial gatherings, but invaluable meetings with Britain's senior spymasters.

In October 1951, Ian dined with Stewart Menzies, still head of MI6, whom he referred to as 'S', and received advance warning of the new Secret Service chief such as could only have been given to a trusted source. Ian wrote to Stephenson, 'S is finally going to retire and be succeeded by his deputy – Sinbad [John Sinclair, MI6].'*

Ian excused himself to Ann on another occasion. 'HAVE to dine with DNI on Thursday 17th. Please forgive. I really can't dodge it.' Nothing would keep him away from the 36 Club. There he was certain of meeting not only Godfrey, 'C' and the DNI, but Peter Smithers, Sandy Glen, Donald McLachlan, Ewen Montagu, Sam Bassett, Norman Denning – and Nicholas Elliott, who was latterly Ian's main link with SIS.

Like Ian, Elliott was a product of Durnford and Eton. 'In those days SIS kept in touch with useful persons. And Ian was quite useful: he had important contacts in certain places, and every now and then he got hold of a useful piece of information. I would ask him if I needed someone in the City and, very occasionally, if I needed someone out in the field.'

It is not impossible that Ian went out in the field under Mercury cover. He was once spotted by the Conservative MP Jakie Astor, flying first class and wearing a light Burberry, 'and looked like a Graham Greene character who was clearly a secret agent'. Dressed like this in November 1960, Ian landed in Beirut to visit Elliott, who had been posted there as station chief.

Before he left on his Middle East tour, to write a book about Kuwait, Ian had volunteered his services to Norman Denning. The DNI appeared keen to use them, but seemingly to no avail, as Ian apologised on his return. 'I am afraid the frontier with Iraq was closed to me and I was unable to get to

* Pearson makes reference in his notes to a 1953 letter from Ian to Bryce, now lost, which suggested 'there was a chance that Ian might have gone back into MI6. But this fell through. (Because of opposition of Sinclair whom Ian disliked and almost certainly vice-versa.)'

Basra. But I met one of our good friends in Beirut and told him of your requirements in Basra and he promised to look after it, so I hope you got what you wanted.'

Ian's mission had been nebulous in its results, rather like all Mercury's links with SIS.

XXXIX
THE MISSING DIPLOMATS

*'For this was yet one more of those Committees of Inquiry dealing with
the delicate intricacies of the Burgess and Maclean case.'*
FROM RUSSIA, WITH LOVE

Ian's post-war relationship with SIS remains a blur seen through frosted partitions. The closest he came to breaking Intelligence cover was in his portrait of James Bond's 'good friend' in Japan: the hard-drinking Station J Chief, Dikko Henderson.

Ian based Henderson on the journalist Richard Hughes, 'a giant Australian with a European mind and a quixotic view of the world', who had covered the 1942 Casablanca landings and later charmed his way into le Carré's fiction as 'Old Craw', doyen of the Hong Kong Correspondents' Club. ('Some people, once met,' said le Carré, 'simply elbow themselves into a novel.') Ian dedicated his penultimate novel, *You Only Live Twice*, to him.

Hughes was not a model for Bond but he was a source for Bond. He was the chief reporter of Ian's Mercury network in the Far East who worked as a double agent. An extra attraction was his personal experience of three characters who fascinated Ian: Richard Sorge, Guy Burgess and Donald Maclean.

The son of a ventriloquist from Melbourne, Richard Hughes had left school early, like Robert Fleming and Gomer Kemsley, to work as boy shunter on the Victorian railways. He joined the *Victorian Railways Magazine* as a sub-editor, rising to be a war correspondent in Japan, North Africa and Korea – which was when his association with Ian began. 'He always called me Dikko. And a very good friend he was. I was very much in his debt. If it hadn't been for Fleming I would have been killed.'

Hughes was a beneficiary of the prescience that Ian's friends often attributed to him and that the Australian credited for twice saving his life. The first occasion was in August 1950. Hughes had planned to curtail his month's leave in Tokyo to go back and report on the Korean War with two colleagues who had been with him covering the Eighth Army's war. 'I got a cable from Ian Fleming saying, "No, Richard, you're staying there and can serve your two weeks and join your friends when your two weeks leave have passed."' Hughes would have been with them on their first trek when their Jeep detonated a mine and they were 'just blown to pieces'.

Ian saved him a second time in Hong Kong. Hughes was about to fly to a film exhibition in Taipei. At the last minute, Ian ordered Hughes on 'some absurd China watching job'; the plane on which he would have travelled was destroyed coming back. 'It had a forced landing and everyone on board was killed.'

Hughes was Ian's favourite Mercury correspondent. He acted as his guide and 'excellent companion' in Hong Kong and Japan when Ian was researching *You Only Live Twice* and his round-the-world travel book, *Thrilling Cities*. Hughes said, 'He named me as "Dikko" Henderson, head of Australian security in Japan. I wrote to him threatening libel and he said, "Dear Dikko, go ahead as you like, but if you make any case that stands up, then I'll write the truth about you."'

Much of that truth was conveyed in the enigmatic smile which accompanied an ironic statement by Ian Lang, the *Sunday Times*'s Foreign Editor. Donald McCormick was deputing for Fleming while he was in America, when Lang came in to see him. 'I have been into Fleming's office and taken the whole of his file on Dick Hughes. I think the Chairman will be somewhat displeased with the news that Dick is being used for other purposes.'

Hughes had been approached to work for Russian Intelligence; he reported this to Ian who, after consulting SIS, wrote back: 'Demand that they double whatever pay they offer you. They will be impressed by this professional, if avaricious approach and it will establish your bona fides.' Ian organised for SIS in Bangkok to provide Hughes with false information to feed Russian diplomats in Japan. In an operation that duplicated Ian's work in Naval Intelligence, he seized on Hughes as a double agent to run against the communist enemy. Late in the game, he was repaying the Russians with a dose of their own poison.

Russia's most notorious spy, awarded the supreme decoration of 'Hero of the Soviet Union', was a German journalist, Richard Sorge, who had been hanged by the Japanese in 1944. 'He is the first Russian hero of the secret war,' wrote le Carré. 'He is of the same vintage, and perhaps the same stamp, as Donald MacLean.'

When Ian discovered that Hughes had known Sorge in Tokyo, he wanted to know every detail, like Sorge's habit of crumbling empty match boxes and chewing toothpicks. Albeit from the distance of London, Ian had been a seasoned Sorge-watcher, describing him with laconic envy as 'the brilliant luxury-loving German who worked for Russia in Tokyo' and 'the man whom I regard as the most formidable spy in history'. For Ian, he represented the Soviet threat in its most dangerous guise. Stalin and Vyshinsky were the ugly face of Russia – Anna Kutuzova and Richard Sorge the most seductive.

He was a man who could have charmed the whiskers off Blofeld's cat, the only person in history to have been simultaneously a member of the Nazi and Soviet Communist parties. Ian and the craggy-faced German press attaché, although enemies, were not so dissimilar. Sorge's first wife – one of a legion of women that he immediately seduced with one look ('It was as if a stroke of lightning ran through me') and then abandoned – complained that 'no one, ever, could violate the inner solitude, it was this which gave him his complete independence'. A later foreign correspondent, Murray Sayle, viewed Sorge as the 'psychic twin' of Kim Philby, hiding recklessly in plain sight, and a textbook example of that 'rare species we might call *Homo undercoverus*', to which Ian Fleming also belonged. 'Ostentation is a kind of camouflage.'

Hughes saw Sorge in the same romantic tints, having gone out drinking with him ('If you are drinking with us, Mister Hughes, please be reasonable'), including an occasion when Sorge saved him from a punch-up in a Nazi bar in Tokyo. 'He was a man I had great admiration for. He was number one head of the Sorge spy ring, the greatest spy ring that ever existed.'

Fiction would free Ian to recast Sorge's spy ring as part of a global Soviet network that had infiltrated SIS. As Ian reveals in *From Russia, with Love*, Sorge's Moscow controller is General Vozdvishensky – a deliberate nod to Stalin's state prosecutor, Andrei Vyshinsky – who has not merely handled and trained Sorge, but has 'been on the inside of the Burgess and Maclean operation'.

Guy Burgess and his partner in espionage crime, Donald Maclean, were the double agents who perturbed Ian even more than Richard Sorge. These two fellow countrymen, with whom Ian had so many things in common, had operated to destroy the strength of the British, which, according to their Russian handlers in Ian's thriller, 'lies in the myth – the myth of Scotland Yard, of Holmes, of the Secret Service'. A strong motivation when Ian created James Bond was to repair the damage they had done.

Burgess and Maclean were the two Foreign Office officials who disappeared in May 1951, leaving everyone in dread that they had defected to Russia. It is hard to re-imagine the impact of their treachery, but the chaos they left behind is important for understanding the context of Ian Fleming's fiction. Anguish at the loss of British prestige; a need to restore both this and the reputation of SIS; a vacuum of hard information about their fate. Bond was born out of turmoil at a moment when the end of the Burgess and Maclean story was still unresolved.

The news of their disappearance was a seismic event for Ian, who had overlapped for a year at Eton with Burgess. Cyril Connolly had known both men reasonably well – Maclean sometimes stayed in his house – and he struggled to explain their behaviour. They were 'members of the governing class, of the high bureaucracy, the "they" who rule the "we" . . .' To John Lehmann, another school contemporary, their likely defection 'acted like a small but violent earthquake in the fairly close-knit intellectual world of our generation'.

Maclean had access to atomic secrets; Burgess was an agent runner for MI6. On discovering how the pair had burrowed into the badger setts of British and American Intelligence, 'Fleming was speechless', said Ernie Cuneo. The idea that two of Britain's 'top Intelligence Chiefs were Communist Moles' was a 'heart-splitter'. It was as if two of its members had placed in jeopardy all that the 36 Club stood for.

Following the couple's vanishing act, 15,000 policemen from Italy to Malta had failed to locate them, with the FBI reporting that the renegade pair had fled to Buenos Aires disguised as women. 'A myth is slowly transfiguring them,' Connolly wrote.

*

'Who is your best friend?' asks the man in drag who James Bond believes to be General Apraxin, head of KGB security (but who is in fact the DNI).

'Guy Burgess,' replies Bond, dressed in a chestnut wig and 'slinky black lace panties', and lowers his eyes. 'He was my lover.'

'One can see that by the way you walk.'

A send-up of Ian's close relationship with Godfrey, *Bond Strikes Camp* was Cyril Connolly's second excursion into Burgess and Maclean territory. His pamphlet *The Missing Diplomats* had been one of the first publications of the Queen Anne Press in 1952. Ian commissioned this a year after their disappearance, Connolly basing it on a pair of articles that had appeared in the *Sunday Times* in late September.

Ian had skin in this game as much as Connolly, whose telephone was tapped by MI5 in the belief he had privileged information. Not only had Ian and Connolly been at Eton with the homosexual Burgess, but they moved in the same social group of journalists, writers and painters. Then this jarring coincidence. On 29 May 1951, in the very week he vanished, Ian and Ann were invited with Burgess to a dinner party thrown by Kemsley's nephew and his wife, Michael and Pamela Berry. One guest was the art historian Anthony Blunt, later to be uncovered as the Soviet ring's Fourth Man after Philby. (Connolly had written in Ian's copy of *The Missing Diplomats*: 'Inside every third man is a fourth man – and more to come.') Another guest was Ian's schoolfriend Alan Pryce-Jones, now editor of Ian's favourite periodical, the *Times Literary Supplement*.

Pryce-Jones recalled how they waited some forty minutes for an absent guest, until Ann asked Pamela Berry who they were waiting for. '"Guy Burgess," said she ...'. Burgess was apparently hoping that Michael, who had once unsuccessfully proposed Burgess for Pop, might give him a job as motoring or diplomatic correspondent on the *Daily Telegraph*, owned by Michael's father.

'The talk was cut short by Blunt saying that Burgess either came on time or not at all: we had no reason to wait any longer.' If Blunt sounded peremptory, this was because he had spent the afternoon removing evidence from Burgess's flat in New Bond Street; he knew that Burgess would not be turning up for dinner, having fled England with Maclean on the midnight ferry to St Malo four days earlier.

News of their sudden disappearance broke shortly after the Berrys' dinner party. 'The story hit Ian Fleming's social circle like a freight train,' wrote the American screenwriter and Bond historian John Cork. Eric Ambler called their vanishing act 'one of the most baffling mysteries of modern times . . . since the disappearance of Adolf Hitler'.

For months after, it became the only topic, like the flight of Rudolf Hess to Scotland in 1941, wrote Connolly, 'a mystery which cannot be solved while so many facts remain unknown'. On 22 September, Ian took Cyril Connolly to see Coward 'and we all discussed Maclean and Burgess'. Were they helpless victims, or high-minded but incompetent traitors? Had they left like Verlaine and Rimbaud to start a new life together? Had they been recalled before they could give away others who were more secret and more important? Had they been imprisoned or liquidated? For Connolly, every theory bristled with difficulties. But Ian was sure of the answer. Connolly said, 'He always believed they had defected to Russia.'

Since that moment, five more years had passed. Still no one knew where they were or why they had departed abruptly.

Then late on Saturday 11 February 1956, dateline Moscow, the Kemsley Imperial and Foreign Service broke what would be the biggest news story in its fifteen-year existence. This was Richard Hughes's world-exclusive interview with Donald Maclean and Guy Burgess, the latter wearing an Eton bow-tie for the occasion. 'It was a hot story because nobody had heard from them,' Richard Hughes said of his scoop, for which Kemsley would pay him a £1,000 bonus (approximately £31,000 today) and receive him back in London 'like royalty'.

Ian's antennae for a story had prepared the way. Four years after they vanished, in September 1955, he returned to the subject of the missing diplomats in his Atticus column. 'Many first-class minds outside our intelligence Services have continued to brood over the Burgess and Maclean case as one might brood over an unfinished detective story.'

The following week, on 29 September, Ann and Ian had tea at Chequers with Anthony Eden, who had taken over as Prime Minister in April. Eden's wife Clarissa, a friend of Burgess during the Blitz, flew out of the garden door and muttered in a stage whisper, 'Please don't mention Burgess or Maclean.'

Inside, under a rug, Eden was gloomily reading bulletins on a chaise longue. He was reeling from the belated publication of a disastrously received White Paper 'on the Disappearance of the Two Former Foreign Office Officials', which had revived the scandal. Henry Fairlie in the *Spectator* reflected the public fury at the cover-up. From beneath his Jaeger rug, Eden read Fairlie's stinging new phrase for Britain's elite, 'The Establishment'. Ian Fleming was on the fringes of this elite. Even so, his response to the Burgess–Maclean story proved to Denis Hamilton that Ian was 'an Etonian radical of journalism, striving all the time to see that the whole truth was told'.

Richard Hughes happened to visit Ian in Kemsley House soon after. He was preparing to return to the Far East after spending his leave in London. Himself about to depart for Jamaica, Ian suggested that Hughes fly back via Moscow. 'I think Khrushchev is ready for an exclusive interview. Try and get it, and, of course, home in on the Burgess-Maclean thing.' Ian requested him 'in a filial cable to "assure my mother that I was in adjectival health" – the adjective to reflect in degree my realistic evaluation of the contact'.

Ian related the lead-up to Ann. 'I told him to hell with interviews with Bulganin and to keep after the diplos and nothing else.'

The Soviet leaders Nikolai Bulganin and Nikita Khrushchev were due shortly on an official visit to London, but they declined Hughes's requests to meet first. After being repeatedly fobbed off to the ballet, Hughes was called back to London having signalled the impasse with the adjective 'buoyant'. Ian cabled: 'Your coverage appreciated, but Chairman decided you should unfailingly return.'

Then, a week before Hughes's departure for London, Vyacheslav Molotov, the Foreign Minister, agreed to meet him in what turned out to be Molotov's final press interview. Hughes drank 'a cup of vodka' and wrote a last-ditch joint memorandum to Khrushchev and Bulganin and handed it to Molotov. 'If you persist in this monotonous nonsense of not saying anything about Burgess and Maclean, you'll make a joke out of your trip to England. You're going to be asked this question perpetually at press conferences. You'll be the subject of the most deplorable and contemptuous cartoons, and if you have got any sense you will produce them just before you go – and to me.' Hughes said, 'I gave this to Molotov and said, "Would you please read this?" so he stood up and polished his glasses and leaned against the desk, and his handsome and voluble secretary began translating and read it to him.'

Hughes heard nothing further until his last night as he was packing. 'On that Saturday, it was 7 o'clock, and I was in Room 123. It was a wintry evening, a snowy evening, and I got a call. "Oh Mr Hoojis, would you please come to room 101?"'

By coincidence, this was the same room at the National Hotel in which Ian had stayed in Moscow twenty-three years before when covering the Metropolitan-Vickers trial. 'I thought, *This is the manager who wants me to say goodbye to him*, so I went around and there was a man who got up, a tall, sad-looking man, and said, "I am Donald Maclean." Another man got up grinning, and said, "And I'm Guy Burgess." I asked a couple of questions and they said, "No, we're not making any more comment. That's enough." Burgess said with a grin, "Look, I've been in the trade too, and I know what a story I've given you tonight, so don't ask any more questions." I got out running hard and I went without galoshes out into the street and fell down twice and got the story off in time. It was run in the Russian papers and Reuters had it later. The story was, I'd seen Burgess and Maclean.'

Ann had arrived in Chantilly to stay with the Duff Coopers when the story broke. 'Summoned to phone,' she wrote to Ian, to whom she had now been married for four years. 'Boofy to tell me the *Sunday T* had scooped with Burgess and Maclean. I hope Gomer is grateful to you for building his foreign prestige.'

XL
'THE SHAMEFUL DREAM'

'The essential leadership, which must come from you, is lacking.'
Ian Fleming to Lord Kemsley, 1951

Ian had been the privileged pet of 'K' when he joined Kemsley House in 1945. He addressed his chief as Gomer. He played bridge with him at the Portland Club, he was invited to Dropmore.

At the Tuesday morning conferences, Ian alone wore a bow-tie, short-sleeve shirt and moccasins; the other directors and department heads followed Kemsley's dress code of stiff white collar, dark grey suit and tie. Ian's holiday arrangements did nothing to sweeten their resentment. 'For the first fortnight after my return to Grays Inn Road,' he told Percy Muir, 'I spend all my time plucking assegais from my back and hurling them back along the corridor.'

The journalist Hunter Davies met him briefly when Ian was Foreign Manager. 'Mainly, he sloped off early on Friday – yeh, on a Sunday paper, disgusting, we all thought – to play golf at Sandwich.'

Ian was revered by his own team, though. He took his lead from Denis Hamilton, who felt that running the *Sunday Times* was like being in battle again: 'I *did* care intensely for every one of my team, just as I had done in the Army.' Ian had never forgotten a letter from a sergeant in his father's regiment, saluting Val 'for his great leadership and fine care and consideration of his men.'

Philip Brownrigg praised 'the superb way' Ian protected his staff. 'Although I think he was not naturally patient, he was always ready to listen with compassion and apparent patience to one's trouble, so much so that he invented "the Fleming absorbent shoulder pad" to mop up the tears that were being perpetually shed on his shoulder.'

Donald McCormick had worked for Ian in Naval Intelligence, and as a journalist in the field and in the London office. After Ian's death, he felt it necessary to challenge 'the superficial, snide and often purely fanciful comments about him which have been both said and written'. McCormick was an elaborate fantasist not all of whose statements can be trusted – such as his claim that Ian masterminded Hess's flight to Scotland. Still, his corrective portrait is a reminder of what an effective Foreign Manager, administrator and delegator 'this Richard Hannay of a newspaper executive' could be. 'Fleming has been portrayed as a playboy who liked to fantasise and a snob who kept his staff at a distance. This is not a true portrayal. He was unique in the way in which he cared for and looked after his staff, especially those overseas.' For McCormick, Ian's 'real forte was in leadership, for he had to an exceptional degree the qualities which inspire and bring out the best in people . . . nobody had greater talent for passing on the most difficult of assignments while at the same time convincing one that "you alone, dear boy, have the inimitable qualities for carrying this out". It was not, as so many lesser minds thought, the gift of blarney, but that of passing on his own confidence and trust.'

The fact that Henry Brandon put down Ian Fleming as his next of kin confirmed 'how Fleming was some kind of father to us all.'

Not all his recruits were ex-spooks. Susan Cooper, 'an unsophisticated pony-tailed 21-year-old fresh from Oxford', came to work for him in 1957 after submitting a colour piece on the National Rose Show at the Royal Horticultural Hall in Westminster. 'I heard an old lady asking a question, at the next nurseryman's booth. "How far apart should I keep my Passions?" "Eighteen inches is a safe distance, Madam," the nurseryman said. It was perfect. I had my intro.' At the weekly editorial conference, it caught the eye of Ian Fleming, who took her on as a reporter. 'He was the remote Foreign Manager who'd also recently taken over the column "Atticus" – tall, self-possessed, good-looking, well-dressed, the embodiment of sophistication. He gave me a lift once in his black Ford Thunderbird convertible, and I don't think I uttered a word all the way, except thank you.'

Get it First, but FIRST get it RIGHT. It had excited Ian to be the 'new wine' Kemsley claimed to want. Ian borrowed his mantra from Rickatson-Hatt. He wrote to Ann early in 1946, 'The mighty Kemsley foreign service is thrusting out deep and enduring roots into the lush soil.' After five years, he had raised the number of words his reporters published annually from 2.4 million to just under 4 million. He had enlarged to eighty-eight 'our small army round the world': twenty-four of whom were staff, seven were women 'and very good too', sixty-eight per cent were university educated and spoke an average of 3.1 languages, with an average age of thirty-eight. He was pleased how international coverage had improved under his watch.

At the same time, Ian faced pressure from 'the saboteurs' in the floor above, where Mercury was regarded as a 'fantastically expensive toy'. In 1949, the pound devalued and the price of newsprint soared. 'My department is melting like snow in sunshine,' he moaned to Ann. Restricted to eight pages, the *Sunday Times* had less space for foreign news. A scoop from Tangier, for which Ian commended McCormick, appeared in ten lines on the back of the *Manchester Evening Chronicle*. Foreign news masqueraded as local news. Concern about the spread of communism, the overriding interest of SIS, had to yield to an interview with a Scottish golf professional who worked for the pasha of Marrakesh.

Ian's disaffection is evident in his demands to Antony Terry over the summer of 1950 to slash Mercury's Berlin expenses. 'It is only by the most prudent housekeeping that I have so far been able to avoid the axe . . . By hook or by crook, you must cut the Berlin overheads down to £100 a month.' The biggest single item was the bill for the telephone, without which Terry could not reasonably function. 'It must be halved.' Such demands dampened initiative. A request for Terry to interview Hitler's sister Paula had to be dropped, Terry explained, after it had 'already cost us a lot of money in telephone calls to Bavaria'.

Ian was capable of cutting costs. 'My Scottish blood and other factors make me economically minded.' What depressed him was the 'lack of vitality and intelligence' in Kemsley Newspapers. Ian revealed his disillusion in a brutal letter to the owner. 'I have now been with you nearly four years, and I confess that this summer I feel stale and disheartened.' Ian had consented to join the company only after receiving Kemsley's assurances that he shared Ian's 'fine ideal' of 'intelligent journalism'. However, Ian went on, 'I have seen no signs of a scheme to improve the content of our papers.' Ian's Foreign

Department 'scarcely ever receives praise or blame and works, so to speak, in a vacuum'. The adventurous spirit that Ian hoped to inject had been repressed by 'K''s undimmed reverence for family, respectability and the pursuit of his next aristocratic title.

'I felt rather like a press lord!' Ian had written to Ann early on in his employment with Kemsley. He had begun in such high hopes, with an attempt, which nearly came off, to buy the *Tangier Gazette* off the Marquess of Bute, and to 'run it as the *Mediterranean Times*', covering the entire region. But since then it had become clearer to Ian that his original ambition to be another Kemsley – or a Jones or a Rothermere – was stuck fast in his second-floor cubicle.

Inexplicably, the prospect of a directorship had receded, causing 'a small hurt to his pride', in Bryce's opinion, 'as if he had been blackballed from the Turf'. Nor was an editorship in view. In 1950, William Hadley retired after eighteen years as editor of the *Sunday Times*. He was succeeded by his assistant editor, Harold Hodson, a slim, silver-haired Fellow of All Souls. Ian's fantasy of one day becoming a newspaper proprietor seemed suddenly equally unrealistic: after Kemsley offered to sell him the *Sunday Chronicle* for £1 million, it dwindled into Ian's taking over responsibility for ailing and uncommercial publishing ventures that no longer held Kemsley's interest, namely the Dropmore Press and the *Book Handbook*. In 1951, Ian was given leave to rename the former the Queen Anne Press, after Kemsley's London address, with Ian's friends Percy Muir and John Hayward as directors; as a further sop, Ian was permitted to re-launch the *Book Handbook* as the *Book Collector* with the same three in charge and Robert Harling as the design consultant. Ian eventually bought both the Queen Anne Press and the *Book Collector* off Kemsley. Still, this was hardly a newspaper empire.

Ian ploughed his frustration into 'The Shameful Dream'. The villain of this unfinished story is a ruthless and amoral press baron who never wants his newspapers to offend the Establishment. Its unhappy hero is manifestly based on Ian, but in his creation of Caffery Bone there is the tension of a dynamic alter ego pacing to break out of his partition.

Bone is literary editor of *Our World*, a newspaper with a circulation of

400,000 that is aimed 'at the new educated classes catered for at the weekend by the *Sunday Times* and *Observer*' but in reality 'designed to bring power and social advancement' to its shrewd owner, Lord Ower, a proprietor with the 'skin of an armadillo' who has come far since his days on the Charing Cross Road when he peddled pornographic titles like *Our Old Men*.

Like Ian, Bone has been at Ower House for five years and is 'now the most sought after literary editor in London and certainly the best paid'. He has risen to his position largely because of his understanding of Ower's thirst for prestige. Bone knows to put a blue pencil through 'anal-eroticism' in his critic's review of the new Angus Wilson. Bone takes it on the chin when Ower sacks his poetry reviewer after he is spotted wearing only black tie at a ball attended by minor royalty. Bone spends a disproportionate amount of office time 'inserting at the cost of many friendships and much self-respect, slavish reference to Lord Ower or his interests'. In a passage worthy of Wodehouse, Bone grapples with a Frith (i.e. Connolly) lead review of a new life of Shelley that seems to offer no loophole for any reference laudatory or otherwise to Lord Ower. Bone inserts at the last moment, after the poet's death at thirty-three: 'Curiously enough, this is just a year short of half the age of that great contemporary patron of literature, Lord Ower, thanks to whose wisdom and generosity so much space on this page is devoted to the consideration of poets and poetry'. Kemsley was then sixty-eight.

Bone has been at Ower House the longest and that alone makes him vulnerable. 'For Lord Ower sacked everyone sooner or later.' One day, Bone receives an invitation on a 'stiff sheet of Basildon Bond'. A summons to The Towers, Lord Ower's huge house in Hampshire, is 'like the summons to the Last Supper, that dread meal to which senior men were always invited just before they were fired . . . before leaving to take up a modest post on the *Nigerian Echo*.'

A butler leads Bone into a long room where forty feet away at a large desk, Lord Ower is absorbed in his papers.

'Ah, my dear Bone. Take a seat. Take a seat. I will join you in one moment.'

There the story ends, the fate of Bone, the subservient literary editor, in the balance. Yet within a year, Ian was writing fiction again. This time,

Bone would step back out into the world not as jobbing journalist to Lagos, but as Bond, the impregnable action man whose oyster was the world.

Why was Ian passed over? Pearson located the answer in Kemsley's Victorian priggishness, the same attitude that had compelled Ian to suspend Eric Siepmann. 'Gradually, it dawned on him that there was a reason – a private reason – for this absence of recognition. In one respect, he was made to feel, he had failed to preserve the high moral tone of Kemsley House: it was the delicate matter of his friendship with a married woman.'

Kemsley had set out his journalistic philosophy in his 1950 introduction to *The Kemsley Manual of Journalism*. 'I have always taken the view that . . . the dignity of a journalist is reduced if he is asked to intrude into the private affairs and in particular the private grief of others.' Just when he might have bestowed on Ian the laurel of a directorship, Kemsley had been asked by another press lord, his friend and bridge partner Esmond Rothermere, to intrude into his protégé's private life.

Ever since his arrival at Kemsley House in 1947, Denis Hamilton had battled to prevent news of Ian's love life reaching the third floor. 'As his close friend, I had to keep from Lord Kemsley the fact that Fleming was consorting with the wife of Kemsley's fellow newspaper proprietor Lord Rothermere, indeed was sleeping with Anne Rothermere under Kemsley's own roof.' On being told this by Rothermere, Kemsley's reaction was that of Lord Ower: 'deep distress and disgust' as if 'something sacred' had been betrayed. In Kemsley's abruptly opened Welsh chapel-going eyes, Ian L. Fleming could no longer be considered Crown Prince material. He was inexcusably 'off-colour'.

The likeliest source was Loelia Westminster. On 13 January 1949, Loelia wrote in her diary: 'Lunched with Esmond. We discussed the whole A & I situation most frankly. I am most worried it is all going the way of the Peek marriage.[*] Dined Kemsley & again had a heart to heart about A & I. Consider it is all most serious.'

---

* Sir Francis Peek had left his wife for Marilyn Kerr whom he married in November 1949; she later married Peter Quennell as his fifth wife.

'Chips' Channon observed that Loelia was 'tactless, a gaffeur, and awkward but well-intentioned'. What she had not known or revealed in her discussions with Rothermere and Kemsley was that Ann had been pregnant with Ian's baby. A child, furthermore, that Esmond Rothermere, believing himself to be the father, had wanted to make the heir of his considerable newspaper business.

XLI
DROOPY

'Droopy would never suspect anyone of anything.
He lives in a world of his own.'
NOËL COWARD, *Pomp and Circumstance*

Esmond Rothermere never came to terms with Ian's betrayal. He eventually married again and had another son, also called Esmond, who grew up in a home where the names of Ian and Ann were not to be mentioned.

'They were two absolutely forbidden subjects. My father loved spy novels, but there were no Ian Fleming books. We had a cinema at Daylesford [Rothermere's Gloucestershire estate], and he'd get the first run of films, but it was never possible to have James Bond. I was quickly told by my nanny Mrs Hardy – who had been nanny to families in the mafia – never to bring it up.' Esmond is recalled as a kind, laid-back parent, well-dressed, a twinkle in his eye, fond of pranks, but with an intimidating streak. 'Once in Palm Beach, my mother thought he was flirting with someone, and he was glacial. The dining room had a thick white pile carpet, and he suddenly picked up a bottle of red wine and poured it over the carpet and returned it to the table, and she burst into tears and ran from the room. I was in the house at the time and remember seeing the stain.'

Ann had been the love of Esmond's life, but also its blight. In the late 1940s, his daughter Esmé moved to a farm in Kent where her father joined her, 'deeply wounded by his collapsing marriage, for his wife had run off with Ian, a character who had been around for some years, and who always seemed to me to be very far from the dashing person so often and mistakenly portrayed.'

Esmond viewed Ian's behaviour as no less treacherous than Kim Philby's when he went off with Maclean's wife in Moscow. He had known Ian since the mid 1930s. They were bridge and golf partners who had spent weekends and Christmases together; in the Dorchester during the war, in Buscot and Ascot, where Ian took his leaves; at Bailiff's Court, the country house at Littlehampton that Esmond rented near 30AU's HQ; at South Wraxall Manor that he rented near Bradford-on-Avon. Ian was part of an extended family that included Loelia, 'Boofy' Gore, Ali Forbes, Clarissa Churchill (later Eden) and Peter Quennell.

On 7 June 1946, one year after Esmond married Ann, Loelia wrote in her diary: 'Wraxall. Peter Q, Ian F & Ali – in fact, the gang.'

Then a year later, on 19 September 1947: 'Wraxall. Just A & Ian here.'

One afternoon, Ann's sister-in-law Virginia Charteris surprised the couple in Ann's bedroom at Warwick House, Esmond's mansion overlooking Green Park. 'There was an atmosphere you could cut with a knife. Ian said apologetically, "I'm just going." They'd just had the mother and father of all rows. Clearly, they thrived on it. They liked hurting each other.'

How they hurt Esmond has been ignored.

Esmond's failure to leave an account has allowed his successor's narrative to prevail. His grandson Vivian Baring says, 'The image that has come down is of a buffoon who was cuckolded and made to look like an idiot. That doesn't marry with my recollections of him.'

Ann's second husband was a tall, tongue-tied man, six foot four, who had the tic of overcoming his shyness by stressing certain words. *Well,* really*! I* must *say. I saw it* all. For a long while, no one thought he knew what was going on under his various roofs.

Noël Coward based the character of Droopy on Esmond in his only novel *Pomp and Circumstance*, which was partially inspired by the post-war bachelor Fleming. 'He had thinning fair hair which was turning grey, his deep-set eyes were blue and looked vulnerable and his figure was impeccable. His weakest feature was his chin, which although not actually receding, looked as thought it might begin to at any minute.'

Ten years older than Ian, with birthdays one day apart, Esmond could be 'as remote as the north pole' in Ann's damning phrase, and in the next moment awkwardly gregarious. 'If a joke suddenly caught his fancy,' remembered Quennell, 'he would emit a loud reverberating laugh.' For most of the time, he was a 'monosyllabic giant' in the phrase of one of his editors – and not merely with his staff. 'He is getting v remote,' wrote Loelia, after another weekend with the gang.

Channon had known Ann since childhood. He became her confidant at the height of her wartime romance with Esmond while her first husband Shane was fighting in Italy. 'She loves Esmond but complains of his cold temperament; that he is clumsy and too [illegible] in bed.' According to Ian's confidante, Mary Pakenham, Ann used to tell Ian 'about her sex life with Rothermere – they copulated in an empty swimming bath and she got a black eye – and ditto with Shane. On her wedding night, she said "Good night" and went firmly to sleep. "I like her because she is such a bitch," Ian said.'

The same expression, which Ian applied also to Eve, formed on the tip of many a tongue. Ann recorded how her brother-in-law Eric Dudley lost his temper with her at a dinner with the Kemsleys 'and said "I always knew you were a – a – a" but fortunately did not say "bitch!"'

It was Esmond's misfortune to be attracted to difficult women who withheld affection. His unstable and flighty mother, Lilian, overshadowed his 'tempestuous childhood'. She had an affair with his father Harold's younger brother, St John, who owned Perrier bottled water. Rumour was that St John might have been Esmond's real father.

Harold Rothermere, founder of the *Daily Mail*, was an 'overwhelming' parent who interfered with his 'excitable and worried' third son at every level. Not long after Esmond married his first wife Peggy Redhead, Harold went on to have an affair with Peggy's younger sister.

The sisters came from Kent. Bubbly and beautiful Peggy was 'a tiresome, common woman,' wrote Channon, 'very "FP" – "front parlour" – who later took to dissipation.' Following his father's lead, Esmond was prolifically unfaithful with her friends: Peggy cited two dozen correspondents and was infuriated into having lovers of her own, including the Aga Khan, after decamping to Claridge's with her three children, leaving Esmond to question their paternity.

Esmond's two gifted elder brothers had been killed in the war. Having himself been given leave not to join up, he was left with tremendous guilt.

What salvaged Esmond's self-esteem was his success with the opposite sex. Esmond once calculated that he had been involved with upwards of a thousand women. 'He was a playboy more than anything else,' says his grandson, Vivian Baring. 'I lived in Warwick House when I was eight with two Irish housemaids, and even at eight I thought they were a little more than housemaids. He collected ladies very easily.'

Fionn says, 'My mother when asked would say Esmond was a much better lover than Ian.'

The youngest MP in the House at twenty-one, Esmond had worked as Lloyd George's ADC at the Versailles Conference. His statue in Budapest records the strange moment in 1928 when he was offered the crown of Hungary after Rothermere's campaigning for Hungary to regain the land it had lost in the Treaty of Trianon. Esmond declined – a grass court suited him better. 'Tennis in Monte Carlo is his most expensive activity,' Ann wrote in her notes on the press barons. 'He plays the game with professional skill.' Esmond's affair with Ann was in its fourth year when his father died and he inherited the *Daily Mail*. That was in November 1940.

Ann found the newspaper world quite as involving as did Lady Kemsley. 'It is a new form of power and an intensely exciting one, more exciting than the divine right of kings or feudal barons.' She loved the access, the influence it gave for Ann to emulate her aunt, Margot Asquith, and her grandmother, Mary Charteris, who had been central figures in that small, turn-of-the-century intellectual clique, the Souls. With Esmond, Ann was summoned by Churchill to Ditchley Park during the fall of Greece. She went riding with Max Beaverbrook at Cherkley Court ('he has a goblin face which reveals an unlimited capacity for mischief'). She threw parties at the Dorchester to which even the Labour politician Herbert Morrison came, and following her marriage to Esmond, she was able to give jobs to her gang, who became known as 'the Dorchester Commandos'. Her brother Hugo Charteris was installed as a correspondent in Paris; 'Boofy' Gore rewarded with a gossip column, Ali Forbes made political correspondent on the *Sunday Dispatch*, and Peter Quennell, with whom she had once slept in the Blitz, though never again, appointed on a generous stipend as the *Mail*'s chief book reviewer.

Her interest in the future of the *Daily Mail* was 'extremely vigorous,' Quennell recorded. After Ann manoeuvred a dashing Welshman, Frank

Owen, into the editorship, she gloated over the editor she had replaced: 'I had been scheming for his liquidation for months.'

'The *Daily Mail* was very heady to her,' says her niece Sara. Ann wrote to Duff Cooper in 1948 during a newspaper strike, 'If the strike gets worse, I shall have all the fun of driving the newspaper vans. I enjoy a good crisis far more than sunbathing.' Plus, it was fun to compete with Ian, the man she would have married had he asked.

Ann said of her husbands that she liked them until she married them, but something seemed to go wrong at the altar. This became true of Esmond with his 'penchant for solitude' – 'He is alone in Sussex with tennis pro,' was soon a normal complaint.

XLII
BUNNY

'I've known him on and off for years. We often play
backgammon together at White's.'
NOËL COWARD, *Pomp and Circumstance*

Ian could only act when he had lost her. In January 1946, seven months into her second marriage, the man she had mocked as a Glamour Boy and Chocolate Sailor wrote to tell Ann that he loved her. Up till that moment, she had denied her feelings. 'I never showed Ian I was in love with him. I knew instinctively it would be fatal, but I didn't know he was becoming more and more dependent on me. He said that I had the heart of a drum majorette which offset his melancholy.'

In December 1945, Ian had composed an earlier love letter, or 'L.L.' while travelling to New York on the USS *Enterprise*, but 'I threw it out of the aircraft carrier into the Atlantic.'

Before flying down to Jamaica on 20 January, he tried again – typing on a broken typewriter his first 'L.L.' to Ann to have survived.

What stirred Ian to declare himself was an unsatisfactory romance he had started in America with a daunting former girlfriend of Roald Dahl: the 'Standard Oil Heiress', Millicent Rogers.

Ian had met Millicent on his wartime missions to Washington. When their affair began in December 1945, he was anxious to give Ann the impression that he had been the one pounced on – 'I have been corralled'. Yet Ian had created the circumstances. Earlier, Millicent had written to her mother about plans for Christmas: 'If Fleming turns up from England, I presume he can stay with us.'

Six years older than Ian and three times divorced, Millicent Rogers was a friend of Marion Oatsie Leiter and Junius Morgan Jr.: she and Ian were guests over the Christmas holiday at the Morgans' Long Island residence, a gloomy Scottish-baronial castle that reminded Ian of his unhappy childhood. Millicent was the owner of Long Island's largest property, arrestingly named The Port of Missing Men. Set on 1,800 acres, this was a colonial-style hunting lodge with beamed ceilings and, as Dahl recalled, 'miles of corridors' that led to the country's biggest private indoor swimming pool and bedrooms with names like The Room of the Ruined Roman Virgins. The 'Port' was merely one of Millicent's homes.

Ian spent that Christmas with Millicent at Claremont Manor, her three-hundred-acre, eighteenth-century estate on the James River in Surry County, Virginia, where she lived with sixteen dachshunds and a Great Dane, and designed distinctive clunky necklaces on legal pads at a desk once owned by Friedrich Schiller.

He also stayed with her in Washington. In her bedroom, Dahl had cast eyes on 'the finest and largest Renoir of red roses that you've ever seen, also a Picasso, a Sisley and a Burne-Jones'. After the austerity of England, the scale of her wealth was staggering.

Millicent never bothered to hide it. She flourished a gold toothpick at meals, ordered couturier blouses by the dozen, and when Ian first knew her drove round wartime New York – where petrol rationing made it impossible to have a car – in a yellow cab that she had upholstered in tiger-skins, with a cab-driver she hired full time on a ticking meter. Fashion editors and gossip columnists fetishised her. But Millicent's inquisitive mind had more depth than her image as a colossally rich Bohemian playgirl suggested.

With typical exaggeration, Dahl had nicknamed her 'Curvature', because of her stooped posture, the result of scoliosis. Her life had been shaped by illness. Flawlessly groomed, with dramatically plucked eyebrows and big gold bracelets on her wrists, she could afford to look fabulous, rather than someone who had never been expected to survive beyond the age of ten. Her fragile health had bolstered her intellectual confidence. As a girl, she learned to translate Rilke and to read Latin and Greek – speaking to her brother in Latin to keep their conversations secret from their parents. In common with Ian, she liked life on her own terms, clever people, serious conversation about books, and pleasure in the moment. She had lived before the war in Austria – Ian may have met her in Kitzbühel. By the time of their affair, she had developed an interest in Native American art. On a famous occasion, she turned up to a party in Montego Bay with two Navajos. 'Yes, I'm fucking them both.' She once had sex with a lover while her then-husband lay asleep in the same room. According to her son, Ian rated Millicent as 'the most sexually insatiable woman he had ever experienced'. To Ann's irritation, she provided him with his Jamaican garden furniture.

Millicent is the likeliest candidate for Ian's complaint that 'right after I had finished kissing her, she insisted on gargling with TCP in case she'd caught something.' Their affair had no sooner taken off than Millicent came down with a cold. They went to a New Year party in Washington, but her cold developed into bronchial pneumonia, and she had to stay in bed for ten days. Ian was 'sweet, helpful and concerned', she wrote to her mother. 'The more I see him, the more I like him. It is a curious shyness that makes him brusque on the outside and when that wears off comes a nice sensitive side and his good commonsense brain to back it with.'

At the end of January 1946, she joined him in Jamaica after he flew down to inspect the plot near Oracabessa that 'Burglar' Bryce had reserved for him. They planned a return by road to New York. 'Ian wants to see something of the country, so we thought we would motor up.' In Ian's company, Millicent was so taken with Jamaica that she bought herself 'a dreamy little house' in Montego Bay.

No further details are known of their romance, which seems to have followed the same abrupt trajectory of his fling two years later with Rosamond Lehmann. Celebrated for her remark that Ian got off with women because he couldn't get on with them, Lehmann revisited their Jamaican affair in her last novel, *A Sea-Grape Tree*. 'She watched him thrusting through the water with powerful strokes, his great shoulders looming as he came abreast of her and passed her without a word or glance. Then suddenly, he turned, swam back, swept her into his arms, gave her a kiss. Not smiling. Saying nothing. A cold, salt kiss. Cheek pressed to cheek they remained, then broke apart . . . "I'm Scotch, you know, I'm close. I like value for my money."'

When, after taking leave of Millicent, Ian returned to England, the American gossip columnist 'Charles' reported that 'the tall, slim, and glamorous Standard Oil heiress had said yes (or at least maybe) to Captain Ian Fleming.' Closer to the truth was a column in the Hearst newspaper chain.

On 25 July 1946, 'Cholly Knickerbocker' revealed that Millicent had been expected to fly to England to marry Ian Fleming, but had gone instead to meet Clark Gable in Los Angeles.

'i have been in the wrong hand all the time.' In his clunkily typed letter to Ann, Ian compared his 'botched affair' to a card game like the 'three-hander bridge' he played with Ann and Esmond, 'where everything starts wrong and getting wronger'.

Even so, he absolved Millicent. 'it really isn't all one persons fault but just that both our sets of rules are wrong – like baseball and rounders, which is really what happens between most English and American people . . . one day I will tell you all the affairs I have ever got into and you will tell me what I have done wrong and why they have been such mazes . . .'

Then he all but revealed himself. He had taken the *Mail*'s American columnist Don Iddon out to lunch and suggested that Iddon write a world diary – 'so if the idea comes home you will know that i never cease to cosset my competitors particularly when i love their wives.'

He signed off as in his letters to Edith Morpurgo and Loelia Westminster with the sketch of a heart pierced by an arrow, bleeding, and the arrow pointing to the single word 'Blood'.

As an illustration of Ian's gift for prophecy, the drawing is hard to beat.

Ian's letter came at 'a damned inconvenient moment' for Ann. It took her no time to reciprocate, though.

On 22 October 1946, Ann landed with Esmond in New York on the *Queen Elizabeth*'s maiden trip. Among other passengers on the rough voyage out were the Soviet Foreign Minister, Vyacheslav Molotov, and his deputy, none other than Andrei Vyshinsky, prosecutor of the Metropolitan-Vickers engineers. Ian arrived the same day by air, having got 'old Gomer to send me over' on Mercury business.

Esmond gave a mildly surprising interview about Russia to the *New York Times* before he departed for Canada 'to see about obtaining newsprint'. He attributed Russia's reticence in talking about what was going on behind the Iron Curtain to internal troubles of which 'I believe they've got a great deal more than we have.'

Ann recalled how as soon as Esmond left, 'Ian arrived at our suite in the

Plaza Hotel with a small briefcase, and said, "I'm moving in." I was appalled. Said I was now so rich and grand that a lady's maid arrived each morning. "Get rid of the bitch," said Ian. So I did though I was alarmed and frightened of running such extreme risks. But in the end I *nearly* always gave in to Ian. So we enjoyed four unforgettable days and nights in New York.'

Once the lovers had declared themselves, they were infatuated.

Ian, from Jamaica: 'You write sweet sweet letters which nearly make me sick with wanting you and wanting to squeeze you until you pant. They make me want to pull your hair and kiss the corners of your mouth and lick your breasts and bite you and lick you and beat you and kiss you all over. I don't miss you any less than in New York and really it is too stupid.'

Ann, after they had spent a week together at Shane's Castle in Ireland: 'They were the nicest days of my life. I love cooking for you and sleeping beside you and being whipped by you and I don't think I have ever loved like this before.'

Ian, from the Dorset Hotel, New York, with his pockets full of match books: 'They say "The Dorset" and "Pen & Pencil". I am going to get some made which say, "I love Ann like Hell" & leave them all over the world.' He told her, 'We are both the first people we have loved with our eyes open.'

He called her 'precious monkey', 'pig', 'black bitch', 'banshee', 'angel'. 'Please write to me often and it doesn't matter about the spelling.'

She took wild gambles in writing and calling.

From South Wraxall Manor. 'Darling, the misery of telephoning ... either Esmond walks into the room or else the children walk in the window.'

From Paris: 'Esmond goes out at 11 and in at 5.30 so it has been impossible to telephone.'

From Portofino: 'I would have telephoned you but there is no privacy and someone always around. Es goes to villa to collect telegrams for him (no doubt DM troubles) and the post which I hope he wont read in case there is something from you.'

Ian was more petrified than Ann of exposure. He pleaded for her to stop 'treating my letters like cracker mottoes' and carelessly leaving them around 'among your brassieres or your pants'; he wanted her to lock them in a box or burn them. 'Please, please, baby it would be too bloody stupid & ugly & untidy. You simply must handle this like a big girl & not as if it was a sort of

Mayfair waffle or else I shall be unhappy. As it is I don't say half the things I want to say . . . So please write & say cross your heart that you have taken our love in both hands & that you will care for it & not let it become a tin can kicked along in the street. Baby, please, please, please & this is only because it makes me sick in my heart to think that it might end tomorrow with a telegram. Do you see my, love. Please see.'

He even made sure not to reveal her first name when he booked Ann into a double berth on a train from Paris. 'I have said it is Amaryllis! Please bring a heavy veil.'

To Maud Russell alone did Ian reveal that he had picked up again with Ann. Maud's reaction is important to quote in full. Before he returned to Jamaica in January 1947 to take possession of the house she had paid for, he told Maud how 'his light-hearted spasmodic affair with Ann Rothermere began to change its character last summer & then into something with much more feeling in it. Ann now pretends to I. that she was always in love with him. I. himself is afraid, I see, of finding himself thoroughly in love with her. I did not say so to him but I think he is so already. But he is half afraid of her chattering confidences, carelessness, devil-take-it behaviour & egotistical recklessness & he doesn't want scandals which she is longing for as she likes scenes, rows & dangers with their attendant excitements. He says she laughs at him for his reserves & "Presbyterian" outlook & tries to provoke him into follies. I said, "would you like to marry her?" to which he answered vehemently: "God forbid." I think he is madly hooked. He called her a "sweet little thing". Poor I.! He knows he is in great danger & that they will both end in a hideous mess if he isn't careful. He said to me: "You never tell me the truth about myself. You never give me enough good advice." To which I said in warning & sepulchral tones, "I will this time; *Listen* & *remember*. Whatever you do, don't marry. It would be a squalid, a hopeless, a disastrous affair." '

Maud understood Ian too well.

To read their correspondence is heart-rending. They begin as honeymooners, obsessive and poetic, unable to keep their hands – or whips – off each other. Then slowly, they descend through nagging and jealousy and piranha shoals of recrimination, until the relationship is stripped of its flesh. They

love each other fiercely, but their characters are too similar and, in obstruct-
ive ways, too opposite to make a working compromise possible. In one 'tiny
L.L.' Ian writes: 'We both belong on our different merry-go-rounds with the
coloured lights & the calliope.' They should have stayed on their separate
merry-go-rounds, but then there would have been no Bond. He sprang out
of Ian's need to step off their carousels, once these had become entangled. To
unbind himself.

Their happiest period was the five years before they married, while Ian
was setting up Mercury. Ann called each one of their greedily snatched
trysts a 'holiday honeymoon'. Ian regarded their illicit time together in the
same pulsing light. He was always wanting something '*wunderbar*' to happen. Invariably, in her company, it did.

Jamaica was an enchanted isle, like Prospero's, and the scene of their
most memorable assignations. Molly Huggins's daughter Ruth was eight
when Ian brought Ann to a big gala at the Governor's residence, King's
House. 'I remember seeing him at the top of this very grand staircase, watching, debonair, and then walking down the two flights of stairs with Ann, and
thinking, "What a glamorous couple."'

He wrote to Ann after her first visit to Jamaica, 'This has been the most
wonderful and unspoilt honeymoon anyone has ever had and I love you still
more than before it began. You are right inside me like a lobster under a
rock.' He passed on what Robert Harling had said. 'He finds us a deeply
romantic couple and the greatest passion of the age.'

At the same moment he fell for Ann, Ian took possession of Goldeneye, as
he decided to rename Shamelady Hall.

His wartime operation in Spain. A play on the local town, Oracabessa,
which in Spanish meant 'golden head'. A novel by Carson McCullers ('I had
happened to be just reading *Reflections in a Golden Eye*'). All these, he
offered as an explanation. 'I was in on the naming of Goldeneye,' said Clare
Blanshard. 'We went through an awful lot of names – most of them with a
Regency flavour . . . Juniper Point was one.' Ann learned on her first visit
that 'Alastair Forbes suggested "Rum Cove", a totally appropriate description
of the owner.' Noël Coward, owner of Goldenhurst in Kent, and the first

person to rent Goldeneye – for an eye-watering sum – immortalised it as 'the nearest ear, nose and throat clinic on the right'.

'Ian's functional house', as Loelia sniffily dismissed it, after she accompanied Ann there in January 1948 to supply 'a sort of "cover" from the social point of view', was an adult realisation of his play-house in the woods at Durnford. Ian boasted to Harling that he had designed every square inch, and to Coward, 'I thought of Goldeneye as something akin to a Caribbean Bauhaus.' Coward replied, 'I prefer Caribbean Cowhouse!' and teased him: 'All you Flemings revel in discomfort. Peter lived for months on cowdung in Tibet and loved it.'

The cuisine at Goldeneye operated under a similar aesthetic. When Ian's housekeeper Violet Cummings, with much smiling, served up her signature curried goat, 'all tasting of armpits', or akee, a fruit that was a deadly poison if not eaten at the right time, Coward made a display of crossing himself before each dreaded morsel.

Ian had admitted to Ann, 'the house is nearly lovely but very barren.' That austerity remained a chief feature. His prose had this simplicity and hardness. There was no glass, so that birds could fly in and out.

Instead of windows, Ernie Cuneo noted, there were 'just open spaces over which shutters can be closed at will; the house is of essentials, sun, sea, and air. Floor of blue polished cement was made from cement mixed with blue dye and then polished by six village women with cut oranges. The chairs are simply cushioned with navy blue drill, a touch of blue printed white here and there. The main window holds an almost postcard sea view.'

Coward complained that the window sill was too high – 'up to one's eyebrows' – and angled to deny the view through two almond trees, which Patrick Leigh Fermor, an early visitor, breathlessly called 'an overhanging fresco of which one could never tire'. Ian hated anyone to block it, especially Peter Quennell.

The large, low-ceilinged living room was sparsely furnished – shelves for sea shells, prints of fish and Viennese horses, a fishing lantern shade of jippa jappa. The kitchen led off it. Ian's bedroom, with blue towels and bedding, led off the other side, with two other bedrooms. When the wind blew in from the sea, it barrelled through the house, banging shutters.

'It was incredibly primitive,' says Ian's stepson Raymond. 'I mean, the plumbing didn't work terribly well.' When Loelia grumbled about the lack of hot water, in keeping with one of his family's Scottish lodges where the bath-tub was in the hall, Ian said, 'but what's wrong with the sea?'

Then the spiders that fell from the roof. On her first night as Ann's chap-erone, Loelia 'slept nervously expecting a bug to land on my face all the time . . . every insect known to man seemed to pour in from the darkness outside.' Jemima Pitman came several times with her father. 'Ian said to me very firmly, "They're all God's creatures," so I never complained again about what was creeping around.' Guests put their bed legs in plates of water against the ants.

The furniture consisted of a few beds – which Clarissa Eden said were uncomfortably hard when she stayed for three weeks with her husband in his last days as Prime Minister – a desk, and planters' wheel-backed chairs like at Ivar's house, Bellevue. They were made to Ian's own design by a local carpenter out of red bulletwood and mahoe.

Coward described crouching gloomily at the end of the vast living room as if he were in a cinema. The dramas played out there would be screen-worthy, certainly.

The whole point of the house was the sea. The builders had cemented forty concrete steps down the cliff to the small private beach. After his first visit, Ian offered Goldeneye to Phyllis and Ernan Forbes Dennis. They con-sidered it magical, 'fantastically beautiful, open only to stars and sea, sharks and pelican'. They descended to the semi-circle of white sand with Ian's fox-terrier Charles and floated in the warm, clear water, threading through forests of coral, and gazing at the coloured fish through glass-bottomed buckets.

Getting into Ian's rubber dinghy at night was the highlight of Loelia's visit. 'We went out on the reef in the moonlight. Lovely.' Ann described another evening in her holiday diary: 'After dinner, it is a ritual that we lean over the cliff railing and as our eyes grow accustomed to the dark watch the spray of the reef or the high bright stars of that region. The air is so clear of dirt or dust there is an illusion of vast universe and the sea horizon is very round. Ian remains longer than us, smoking and wallowing in the melancholy.'

She wrote, 'Only Ian could devise this manner of life.'

It is hard to separate Goldeneye from its mythical dimension and to remove the filters that Ian's visitors have superimposed. The most trustworthy description was written by Ian himself in a letter to the banker Olaf Hambro, one of the Intelligence scouts who had recommended Ian to Admiral Godfrey, and now after the war an associate of Stephenson's World Commerce Corporation. When Hambro rented Goldeneye in 1951, Ian spelt out exactly what to expect. Little would have changed by the time the Edens visited five years later.

There is no telephone except in the village post-office, so anything important should reach you by telegram . . .

There are three double bedrooms, two with shower baths and one with a bath. The latter produces hot water rather reluctantly, and you should tell Violet, my angelic housekeeper, when you would like a bath prepared . . .

There will be three servants and a house-boy to fetch telegrams and run messages, and an excellent gardener who cleans the beach every day, puts out the garden furniture, etc.

You will not be able to wear much more than a shirt and shorts during the day, but it gets cool about six o'clock when the sun sets and then you will need trousers and a sweater of some sort.

I hope neither you nor your sister minds moths and crickets, and such like. They are quite harmless, but they come to the lights in the evening and you should therefore not read in bed with the lights on. Personally, by about 10 o'clock I am quite unable to keep my eyes open.

. . . you should wear gym shoes for bathing as the coral is extremely sharp and the sea urchins, particularly those with long black spines, extremely painful . . . Otherwise the bathing is shallow and absolutely safe.

There are masks and glass-bottomed boxes and I advise you to use at any rate the latter to admire the denizens.

Violet is an excellent cook, but should be firmly dissuaded from giving you such things as boiled mutton, which she considers very genteel!

. . . The laundry is done in the house, and there is a first-class seamstress called Martha, who lives nearby, who will make your sister an excellent evening dress in 24 hours . . .

'The Daily Gleaner' is a splendid newspaper and Violet will get it for you every day . . .

If you want to go out to lunch or dinner, I should choose the Shaw Park Hotel or the Jamaica Inn, both at Ocho Rios about half an hour away.

Hambro was one of a multitude of foreign visitors whom Ian attracted to Goldeneye. 'Couples have spent their honeymoons here. Stricken friends have regained their health, painters and writers . . . have stayed here and worked here.' In Ian's strangely uncomfortable bungalow Peter Quennell finished his book on Shakespeare, Truman Capote wrote part of *The Muses Are Heard*, Errol Flynn part of his autobiography, Rosamond Lehmann part of a novel, a short story, and a poem inspired by her fling with Ian. Lucian Freud did two paintings of bananas. Graham Greene stayed with Catherine Walston – who listed as one of her five all-time memorable scenes with Greene, 'teaching me to swim underwater at Ian's Fleming's house'.

Among other names to descend those Buchanish steps to the beach armed with goggles, glass-bottomed buckets and snorkels: Evelyn Waugh, Stephen Spender, Cecil Beaton, David Niven, Claudette Colbert, Alan Ross, Tom Maschler.

Today, Goldeneye is a luxury boutique resort owned by Chris Blackwell, the son of Ian's last love. The simple house for which Maud Russell paid £5,000 rents for approximately $8,000 a night.

On seeing how the builders had realised his plans, Ian wrote to Ann in January 1947: 'My darling, you would really love this place. The house is a wild success . . . All I can tell you is that I love it all and every bit – except that I want you and miss you all the time. I do hope and hope that you'll come over here one day and nest here a little.'

Ann became pregnant with Ian's child during her first visit a year later in January 1948. She was thirty-four but still had nonsensical ideas about conception. 'My darling,' she would tell Fionn, 'if you sleep with someone a lot, you don't get pregnant.'

In February, she returned on the *Queen Mary*. The first signs came at sea. 'Suddenly nausea over came me and I am back in my cabin.'

A month later, she was writing to her sister-in-law Virginia Charteris, also pregnant, 'I hope your situation is as interesting as mine.' Only the previous year, Ann had informed Duff Cooper about 'a lovely Easter party' she had hosted at South Wraxall Manor, 'everyone with a child or children except for Ian who as far as I know hasn't any'.

Ian's reaction is not recorded, but the news that he was to be a father at the age of forty coincided with recurrent pains in his chest, neck and shoulder. He had first complained of these when he stayed with Ivar Bryce in New York eighteen months before. Ann was sympathetic when Ian said he was now going to see a Harley Street specialist after he had 'an attack of rapid pulse' during a golfing weekend at Royal St George's, which he had joined that year. 'I am sure you got very overtired at Sandwich, the reaction on the Tuesday night showed it had been a nervous and physical strain and I think your curse days are always started by something like that.'

At the end of April, Ann attended George VI's Silver Wedding ball at Buckingham Palace in the dress made for her by Ian's seamstress. Diana Cooper wrote to her son, 'She is big with child but not very big, and dressed in Jamaican muslin and *fichu*, looked like an attractive creole. She should have had a pretty handkerchief tied round her black curls: instead she had a bit of a tiara.'

From South Wraxall Manor, Ann reported to Ian that she had 'rubbed oil all over my obscenely shaped body so as it retains its unblemished perfection after the event.' But she had concerns. 'Would Maud let me come and talk to her, or is that silly? She knows and loves you and may be able to tell me what is going on in your head and if you are changing about me and if you are well, my darling.'

In the event, Ian sought out Maud.

On 25 April 1948, Ian turned up at Mottisfont, his first visit in two years. What he revealed to Maud as they walked out along the river stunned her. 'He had an immense amount to tell me about Jamaica, Annie & his love affair with her. And that she is going to have a baby by him in Oct. And how secret this must be kept. That it was important Esmond shouldn't suspect – or not so much Esmond, oddly enough – but Harmsworth [Esmond's family name] relations as if the child is a boy Esmond is going to make a will leaving the *Daily Mail* to *him*. I said: "But why not to his eldest boy, his son & heir?" And I. said: "Because he believes him to be someone else's son." I must confess the dishonesty & fraud shocked me. This is an absolutely typical Anne fraud. I tried to find words to say I was horrified but could not find them. Love, a baby, the *Daily Mail* – ugh. The sad thing is that I. is weak & easily influenced. He saw it as an awkward situation but not as a very immoral one – I am thinking, when I say immoral, of Anne's anxiety that the relations shouldn't hear of the scandal & spoil the chance of the baby getting the *Daily Mail*. But in fact the whole business seems to me dishonest. I can understand her wanting the baby but she should either make a clean breast of it to Esmond & say: "I am going to have a baby & it isn't yours" (he is very fond of her and would probably forgive) or else she ought to disappear & have it (difficult perhaps) or else take steps to get rid of it. I. is caught up in a dirty sort of world.'

So much may be understood from this astonishing revelation – the tension of the following weeks, Esmond's anguish afterwards, the enmity with his eldest son. Esmond believed that Ann was having his baby. If a boy, the baby would inherit the *Daily Mail*. But the baby was Ian's. It would be the closest Ian came to owning a newspaper empire.

Ian sought out Maud again on 19 August. She wrote, 'Talked about Anne. Said he wanted my support & sympathy . . . he said, "I feel I am going to do something stupid." I said: "How? In what way?" I.: "I don't know." I said: "Don't. When the moment comes, remember, & don't." Christopher Sykes once said: "All the Flemings are mad." '

Two days later, Ian joined Esmond, his pregnant wife, her two children and Loelia Westminster at Gleneagles Hotel in Scotland for a golfing holiday.

Loelia has left a bleak record of those 'disastrous' ten days. They were playing bridge on Ian's first evening when 'poor Annie had a haemorrhage'. The doctors came and wanted to move her to a nursing home. After 'fighting every inch of the way', Ann was taken by ambulance to Edinburgh. 'It has left us all most dismal.'

In driving rain, Esmond motored the next morning to the maternity clinic in Randolph Crescent, from where he telephoned. 'Annie may have to have a caesarean which doesn't sound so good.' Loelia suggested that they join Esmond for lunch the following day. Ian refused. 'I just felt I couldn't.' Shut out from Ann, with Esmond being treated as the father, it added to Ian's suffering that he and Loelia were getting on each other's nerves. He struggled to explain his situation in a letter that failed to reach Ann in time. 'There is no one for me to talk to about you, least of all Loelia who does nothing but frighten one – knowing nothing about it. I just think of you & wait to see you & pray for you & wish I had been better so that my prayers would count more.'

Their child was born on the Friday. This is Loelia's entry: 'Aug 27. Es telephoned to say Annie had had the casearean & he had had a little girl, & that both were alright. But tonight he rang up again to say the baby was dead. It is just so sad its unbearable.'

The baby had defective lungs. 'I held my baby's hand for one minute and was amazed at how long the torture lasted,' Ann wrote afterwards to her sister-in-law. 'It is screaming physical animal pain to lose a child.' It was 'the greatest sorrow' that 'can come to any woman and one can only think of strange things like God chastens those whom he loves'.

In a quick note, Ian addressed Ann as if she were the child they had lost. 'Darling Baby, I hear from Sister & Esmond that you are away from the shadows. Dear love, you must never go near them again.'

For days, she was not well enough to see anyone. 'More horrors pile up for poor Ann,' Loelia wrote. 'She has had to have a stomach pump tonight & again tomorrow as she can't keep anything down. Vile day. Had my hair done.'

Once she came round, Ann wrote to Ian on a temperature chart, the only paper in reach. 'There was morphia and pain and then you were here and now you've gone and there's nothing except the grim realisation of what happened in the last ten days.'

A decision had been made to call the baby Mary, Ann's middle name. Her cousin David, Earl of Wemyss and March, had arranged the burial near the Charteris family seat on the coast east of Edinburgh. Ann was too fragile to attend. 'They christened her after me and put her next to my mother in the family churchyard at the edge of the sea at Aberlady – Esmond, Laura [Ann's sister], my hated grandmother [Anne Tennant], while I was lying in

433

a haze of morphia and you were playing golf – oh my darling, I must grow up soon, but I do love you; please help me over this. I am muddled and distressed and in danger of losing all sense of proportion about it. I feel full of remorse towards Esmond, and yet my grief and loss is entirely bound up with you, and both are too feminine for you to understand; the loss of a baby of 8 hours' age cannot be a grief to a father, so I mustn't get ideas about Esmond's feeling, or get hysterical about it all . . .'

Ann wrote the next morning to say she would have done anything to get that letter back. What she had wanted to convey was 'the hope that one day we may be completely together if it can ever be without too much hurt to others. You are the closest physical and mental relationship I have ever had.'

She later explained to her sister-in-law, 'my deep love for Ian is based on his understanding of [my] mental condition at that time.'

It was during this grim period that Ian made a promise he would find impossible to break, to shield her from another experience like this: 'it mustn't happen again ever . . .'

'What does Esmond feel about it all, we ask ourselves?' Fionn voices the question no one has been able to answer. Hoping for a son and heir, Esmond had found himself burying a dead daughter who was not even his. Did he know? 'It seems extraordinary if he did not,' says Fionn. 'But then Loelia didn't know. It's possible that it was not clear to him that it definitely wasn't his.'

On their odd trip from Bournemouth in 1941 Ian had told Ann how she must return to Shane. Esmond may have understood Ian's expressions of sympathy as coming from the same reflex. Ian wrote to Ann from Gleneagles, 'I feel I shouldn't abandon him.' He could not help but feel a supportive connection. 'The trouble is that Esmond is an adolescent. There is no excuse to hurt him – there is no evil in him, and neither of us wishes him harm. He needs protection and if he *gave* a little more he would deserve it. Anyway he needs it.'

If Esmond had remained in the dark until now, then he was almost on his own. Noël Coward joked that there were only one or two widows left in Worthing who didn't know of the affair. In Jamaica, everyone knew.

Eighteen months previously, in January 1947, before Ann set foot in Jamaica, Ian had attended the opening of Sunset Lodge at Montego Bay, when a woman with 'a hard central European eye' approached him beside a huge bonfire on the beach and said disingenuously, 'I was trying to remember which paper you were mixed up with. I was certain your boss was a woman, but the only woman who seemed possible was Lady Rothermere, which was impossible, of course. Silly, wasn't it.'

Ian at once suspected Max Beaverbrook of being behind her 'clever crack'. From then on, he had lived in fear of Gomer Kemsley finding out.

Immediately after Ann's first visit to Goldeneye in 1948, Ian wrote to her after learning that his name had again appeared in the Hearst chain's gossip column: 'Bad news from New York. The office has cabled that Knickerbocker has had something to say. I don't know what but fear the worst.' After previously reporting on Ian's affair with Millicent Rogers in Jamaica, Cholly Knickerbocker now reintroduced 'Captain Fleming' to his twenty million readers as 'a sort of Beau Brummell of the island'. Ian felt colossal relief on discovering that Knickerbocker 'had got hold of the wrong girl!' – in assuming Loelia Westminster was Millicent's replacement as Ian's 'hottest romance'.

Ann replied, 'I think C Knickerbocker must love me . . . How lucky he gets his facts so wrong.'

Ian was not so sanguine. 'I fear that in due course the new name will be given.' He warned, 'We shall have to keep away from NY for a bit.'

But London was no safer. Ann was still in New York when she met Nancy Hare fresh off the *Queen Elizabeth*, who 'tells me it is all over London that E is not going to tolerate us any longer'. All nonsense, Ann assured Ian. But 'I wish, wish, wish you and I could sit on your Jamaican beach for a month without having to bother about scandals and chaperones.'

Already, she was thinking ahead to her next visit. 'It would be such anguish not to come with you and HOW can I do it without wrecking you with Gomer.' However, any promise to be discreet was likely to be undermined by Ann's insuppressible compulsion to give Knickerbocker a run for his money, as in the gossip column she had suggested penning for the *Mail*, 'Things we want to know' ('most of the news comes from me'). As Randolph Churchill put it: 'If you want anything done, telegraph, telephone, tell Annie.'

Noël Coward had watched their relationship develop – both in Jamaica, where he had bought a property near Goldeneye, and in St Margaret's Bay near Dover, where in the summer of 1949 he offered Ian and Ann the lease of one of the coastguard cottages attached to his house at White Cliffs, as an escape 'nest'.

In Coward's 1960 novel *Pomp and Circumstance*, Ian is Bunny, the unscrupulous, egocentric, perennial bachelor, and Ann is Droopy's wife Eloise, an ex-duchess who possesses 'that particular chemical attraction which brought out what is known as "the beast" in men', and whose spiritual home was the Oliver Messel suite at the Dorchester. 'He was mad about her and she was mad about him and the whole of London was aware of it with the exception of the unfortunate Droopy.'

Then out of the blue, Coward invests Droopy with the dignity to put this canard to rest, after Droopy discloses, 'I've known about the Bunny Colville business for a long time, ever since it began really . . .' Droopy had been friends with Bunny for years. 'I decided it would be better to wait and see how things turned out. It's no use arguing with somebody when they've worked themselves up into a "thing" about somebody else, is it? I mean it only leads to scenes and I loathe scenes.' This, Coward implied, had been Esmond's position. He had pretended discretion with apparent composure, until faced with the embarrassing truth that everybody 'in all quarters of the globe' was discussing his wife's romance.

Her baby's death had not terminated Ann's 'muddly affair', as Maud was sorry to call it. 'It is public property. Anne chatters about it right & left.' Ann's brother updated their sister Mary: 'the status quo is continuing – bed with Fleming, business with Rothermere.'

Once again, Loelia took it upon herself to bring matters to a head. 'I fear the situation is volcanic.' With her capacity for 'sheer mischief making', as Ann perceived it, Loelia had already discussed Ann's affair candidly with both Esmond and Gomer. Since then she had learned who had fathered Esmond's dead child. Then on 25 March 1949: 'Saw Esmond & told him a few observations . . . he is playing his cards understandably badly while that wretched old commander hasn't put a foot wrong.'

Loelia's revelation devastated Esmond. 'He had no idea,' says his grandson. 'Whether he did know and didn't want to admit, he was very hurt.' Just like Droopy, Esmond's odd compliance abruptly gave way to 'an inner ferment of outraged pride, jealousy and an implacable desire to avenge his honour at any cost'.

That July, the aggrieved husband of Graham Greene's lover Catherine Walston, now finding Greene a pest and threat, told Greene that he must not speak to his wife any more. Esmond issued a similar ultimatum to Ann, even convincing her that private detectives were spying on her movements. It was only when this threat had no effect that Esmond had played his trump card and complained, over Denis Hamilton's head, to Lord Kemsley about his Foreign Manager's well-established adultery with a fellow proprietor's wife. This was not behaviour commensurate with the inviolable Kemsley code of 'the Empire, the family and the Conservative Party', and absolutely not conduct becoming of a would-be director or editor. Kemsley regarded this 'poor affair', in Harling's words, 'as akin to a guerrilla raid by an outsider on another newspaper tycoon's private property'.

The upshot was that Kemsley summoned Ian – as the fictitious literary editor Caffery Bone was summoned in Ian's unfinished story – and gave him a carpeting that put on hold Ian's aspiration of ascending by separate lift to a third-floor office in Kemsley House. Kemsley told Ian he could not continue to countenance 'such an embarrassing situation'. Either Ian must marry Ann and 'regularise their position'; or resign from his job.

On returning from her second visit to Goldeneye with Loelia, Ann was in for a shock – the 'telegram' from Esmond that Ian had long feared.

'My Precious, things could not be worse,' she wrote to Ian. 'I don't know if Loelia is a knave or fool, but if she had calmed Esmond, EVERYTHING would be different.'

Loelia was still doing her needlepoint. Not for no reason in *From Russia, with Love* would Ian link the villainous Rosa Klebb to a 'tricoteuse' and in *You Only Live Twice* scornfully send Irma Bunt 'back to her petit point'.

Ann then made this confession: 'I have had to say that I will try and give you up completely. I was met at Southampton by letter saying he would not return to Warwick House until I said I would try.'

From Paris, Ann sent a further disconsolate message: '. . . do you think we ought to try for a bit, my sweetest.'

At the age of forty-two, Ian had reached a crisis point. Should he give

Ann up? Or sacrifice his bachelor existence and 'work out a sensible life of some sort without hurting anyone unnecessarily'?

There was one further consideration. Where would he find an outlet for his journalistic ambitions – now Gomer had made clear that his rung on the Kemsley House ladder was as high as Commander Ian L. Fleming RNVR was likely to climb?

XLIII
'QUITE A STEP'

*'Kissy wondered what moment to choose to tell Bond that
she was going to have a baby and whether he
would then propose marriage to her.'*
YOU ONLY LIVE TWICE

Six months after Ian Fleming's death, John Goodwin, founder of the James
Bond Club in Oxford, took Ian's secretary to lunch at Claridge's. 'Learned all
sorts of interesting secrets about his life,' Goodwin wrote in his diary. 'Wife
blackmailed him into marriage.'

This was the view not merely of Beryl Griffie-Williams, but of Amaryllis,
Mary Pakenham, Denis Hamilton, Hugo Pitman and others. Ann had deliberately become pregnant a second time so he would marry her. Pakenham
said, 'Caspar was born four months after the divorce. As Annie had a dicky
inside, she could easily have got the baby removed, but she (I think so at
least) was determined to GET Ian.'

It is important to stress that Ann was not pregnant when she left Esmond
in October 1951. Nonetheless, says Fionn, her falling pregnant so soon afterwards did ensure that Ian 'would have to marry for my mother to give birth to
a child everyone knew was Ian's'. He had promised Ann that she would never
have to experience again the horror of the Victorian maternity clinic in Edinburgh. It was part of his uprightness, his orthodox side, the side of the clubland
hero and Robert Fleming, that this time he had to do the honest thing.

Ian suffered misgivings to the last. He confided to Robert Harling how
scared he was that if he did marry Ann 'his supposedly carefree life might
come to an end'. He had only to look at the disparities in their characters and
circumstances for his neck-hairs to rise.

He loved Jamaica; Ann loved Mayfair ('Jamaica is no alternative to London,' he wrote to her, 'I never feel well in London'). Ann loved Society ('a wife who inclines to company,' she had described herself), in which Ian admitted to feeling 'hopeless and like a caged beast'. Ann hated being alone ('The idea of the key in the lock and walking in to emptiness,' she warned her niece Sara, 'that is something you must never let yourself endure'); Ian loved solitude ('He liked nothing better than to sit in a café,' said Ann, 'watching the people and brooding in his melancholy sort of way'). She loved chaos and noise; he loved silence and symmetry. ('I am going round smoothing out the dents in the chair covers and sheets and sweeping the cigarette ash off the carpets, cleaning the blood off the sofa cushions and the lipstick off the antimacassars. It's nice to have everything tidy again, or isn't it? Darling banshee.') At every turn, she reflected the contradictions in his make-up.

Their incompatibility, which until now had acted almost as its own narcotic, prevented them from settling even on where to live: 'I wanted a home,' said Ann, 'he wanted to travel.'

Ian pointed out that Ann had 'a lot of people' who depended on her – two children, Raymond, aged eighteen, and Fionn, aged fifteen, who 'shouldn't be shaken up again'; Esmond, who still loved her; her smart friends; plus the weight of her public life at the *Daily Mail*. 'No one depends on me. I give up nothing except my cherished freedom.'

Then his financial position. He had his bachelor pad and salary and stock portfolio, but this was not enough to keep Ann in her opulent lifestyle – liveried servants, chauffeured Rolls-Royces, parkside and weekend mansions. 'It would be a real crime for me to drag you out of a basically happy life into one that would be far more difficult in a thousand ways.'

Ian had seen the effects of marriage on his two closest male companions. It filled him with anguish. He had felt 'rather like a man from Mars' after a weekend with Peter and Celia at Merrimoles. 'A great deal of shooting and galloping horses and barking dogs and crying babies and talk about the BBC and plays and crossword puzzles, which are a passion of Celia's.' His weekend aroused no paternal instinct. Ian had frequently told his loyal friend Lisl Popper 'there was no reason for him to get married because he never had the urge to reproduce. "Peter has a son," he used to say. "The name of the Flemings will not die out. So why should I marry?"'

A matrimonial model still more hair-raising was that of Ivar Bryce, then in the process of divorcing his second wife, Sheila (according to one source, 'because she found him in bed with her daughter, the final straw!'). Ian wrote to Ann from Goldeneye, 'Dinner yesterday was awful, and I'm afraid I shouted at Sheila. I apologised to Ivar at breakfast this morning, and he said he had to face the same sort of thing twice a day. I suppose that's what it's like being married to a shrew!' Ian had grazed a nerve, to judge from Ann's sharp response. 'There seems some mental comparison going on in your nasty mind between a possible marriage of ours and their sad relationship.'

It paralysed Ian, not knowing how to make a sensible move forward 'out of this dear blind life we have been living together'. His letters to Ann circle in on themselves. They go everywhere and nowhere. 'I'm afraid I shall never settle down until I settle into the earth!'

Identical vows made years earlier to Monique and Muriel were ignored as Ian promised Ann 'I would love to nest with you for ever and ever and you are absolutely the only person I have ever contemplated saying that to.' Yet in the next breath – 'I want this to be a sensible balance sheet, but it keeps on trying to be prose, and it keeps on painting the picture too black.'

His indecision tormented him. He looked older, less handsome, Maud noted in her diary. 'I don't believe his romance is going so well anymore.'

Meanwhile, Ann had her own misgivings. She liked hosting 'semi-royal' parties at Warwick House. She liked interfering at the *Daily Mail* (where as *Time* magazine reported, 'it has long been common knowledge in Fleet Street that the real boss wears a petticoat'). She understood Ian's mixed response to getting married. 'It is quite a step for Ian after 43 years of chosen solitude.' She confessed to her brother Hugo her 'lack of courage to leap from the Merry-go-round'.

On the anniversary of her first encounter with Ian in Le Touquet before the war, Ann was staying with friends in France. 'Oh! God, oh! Montreal. Twelve years ago we met over a Norman pig . . . what am I to do?' She had no solution. 'I wish a fairy would arrive with a wand and make everything alright: give Esmond a perfect wife and put me in your bed with a rawhide whip in my hand so I can keep you well-behaved for forty years.'

She left the decision to Ian.

Ian needed less a fairy to conjure him out of his prevarication than a nuclear explosion – to blow them both to Goldeneye, where they could 'carry on the human race' in peace and quiet. 'It's no good unless the atom bomb falls.'

Maud Russell nudged Ian out of his 'cream-puff fog'. Earlier, she had urged him not to marry Ann, foreseeing 'quite clearly' the danger he was in: how Ann 'would enjoy destroying the wise instincts in him & his safeguards & the controls he has imposed on his restless difficult nature'. But Maud had changed her mind, up to a point. 'He never will unless he is pushed into it. I am sure it won't work but he might have 3 or 4 years of rows, excitements, love & reconciliation. And 2 children. Otherwise his life may become barren & bleak.'

She had previously characterised Ann as dishonest. Maud now resolved she might suit him. 'I cannot imagine anyone who would do half as well. Whether she will be able to stand his moroseness, his considerable selfishness & his rather crusty habits forever, I can't pretend to guess. But he has a warm & generous heart, great attraction, great good nature au fond & he adores her.'

Ian acted on Maud's advice. Part of him was tiring of life as it was. 'I had finished organising a Foreign Service for Kemsley Newspapers, and that side of my life was free-wheeling.' Ann had kept him on his mettle for six years. 'He used to say that one of the reasons he married Annie was because she could save the day,' said John Pearson. 'She could destroy the boredom which was beginning to afflict him.' In *Pomp and Circumstance*, Bunny abruptly declares, 'I know I've bashed about a good bit hitherto, but this is the real thing.' Once upon a time, Ian had told Mary Pakenham of his ambition to be the Renaissance ideal. To settle down with a wife and child – did this not represent the last building block in the edifice of Ian Fleming, the Complete Man? As Tiffany Case says in *Diamonds Are Forever*, 'You can't be complete by yourself.'

The decision taken, the next step was to extract Ann from her marriage. In Loelia's experience, 'divorce was such a stigma that even if husbands did have suspicions they generally turned a blind eye with a philosophical calm that would never have been permitted them by a novelist.' But Esmond was no longer able to cloud his gaze and he put up little resistance. Ian told Maud that 'when Ann had gone to ask Esmond for a divorce he had consented "with alacrity"!' He agreed to a settlement of £100,000 (approximately £4 million today).

News that Ann was expecting had decided matters. Although Ian was apparently 'horrified at the prospect of paternity', he consented to announce the divorce once he and Ann were in Jamaica and marry her there. According to Percy Muir, it was Kemsley, with whom Ian and Ann dined on the eve of their departure, who had made him take that particular plunge. 'He cabled Ian – "Come back married or not at all." '

Ann alerted Hugo to her divorce: 'I decided that the easiest way would be that it should take place while I was in Jamaica. I might have told you sooner but it was supposed to be a secret and, mysteriously, it has been easier for me to discuss it with no one until it was a fait accompli. There are no hearts to break, and my only anxiety is the children.'

As for Ann herself, 'my bonnet is over the windmill,' she wrote to Noël Coward. 'Longing to see you in Jamaica and hope you will arrive in time to be a bridesmaid.' Then this PS: 'Bad taste letter, but no one has been hurt, thank God, so there is nothing but rejoicing; Fionn has "always wanted Ian for a father". Had I realised this amazing fact, I would not have had a sleepless night before telling her!'

Fionn recalls the moment. 'We were returning from Ireland by boat and sitting in the train from Stranraer to Euston. She said, "Oh darlings, I've decided to divorce Esmond." I can see Raymond opposite, his finger tips together. "Is that wise, Mother?" – Ian had no money. I can remember how pleased I was.'

In tones more subdued, Ian wrote to warn his *Sunday Times* colleague Denis Hamilton of the forthcoming divorce and marriage – which 'will cause something of a Fleet St. sensation, I fear . . . So please calm down excitement at levels other than K[emsley], who knows & accepts with an apparent good grace.' He promised to tell Hamilton more on his return to Kemsley House in March.

Of the couple's friends, only the Catholic convert Evelyn Waugh expressed pleasure, believing that her marriage would restore Ann to a state of grace. Hugo Pitman's dismay was characteristic of the general reaction. 'Father was not very keen on her,' says Pitman's daughter, Jemima. 'He thought the marriage a mistake, he told me. Ian wasn't the marrying sort.'

In *Pomp and Circumstance*, Coward's female narrator tells Bunny exactly what the author thinks. 'It is my considered opinion that you are making a cracking ass of yourself. Eloise may be beautiful as the day and enchanting in bed, but she isn't your cup of tea really, and never could be, and for you seriously to consider spending the rest of your life with her is sheer idiocy.' The cards were assuredly stacked against a happy Bunny marriage; 'the moment the hullabaloo over the divorce had died down and the first fine raptures were over, he would find himself caught up in an over-social married life for which he was temperamentally unsuited and probably be utterly miserable.'

Alan Pryce-Jones was another of Ian's friends to shake his head. 'He made a mistake in marrying an extrovert, reckless wife with a genius for energising her friends, sometimes to the point of terror. She loved dilemmas, verbal clashes, irresistible forces meeting immovable posts. She was all glitter and paradox – a wonderful friend not to have an affair with.'

'Oh, it was a crazy marriage on both their parts,' said Sandy Glen. 'A lunatic one.'

Phyllis Bottome had looked after Ian more than anyone. She had stayed at Goldeneye. She knew his circumstances, his character. On 19 February 1952, she wrote in regretful tones to her nephew: 'Perhaps you will have seen that our poor Ian, who must now be forty-five [he was forty-three] and has never stopped having love affairs which were all catastrophic, has now at last got himself – in the direction in which they were all pointed – well into the Divorce Court. He is cited as a correspondent in the Rothermere case. * He introduced us to Lady R once, and I thought her as hard as nails; so I very much doubt – even if he wanted to marry her – whether such a marriage would not be the end of him.'

Such a premonition preyed on Ian. His wedding was set for 24 March in the town hall at Port Maria. The thought of dutifully tying the knot was 'a prospect which filled me with terror and mental fidget'.

---

* On 7 February 1952, the Divorce Court granted Esmond a decree nisi 'on the ground that his wife Viscountess Ann Geraldine Mary Rothermere had committed adultery with Mr Ian Lancaster Fleming'.

XLIV
WRITING BOND

*'For a moment he thought nostalgically and unreasonably of the
excitement and turmoil of the hot war, compared with his own
underground skirmishings since the war had turned cold.'*

FROM RUSSIA, WITH LOVE

The idea for Bond came to him as he swam in his bay in Jamaica.

His mid-life crisis had occurred at a decisive moment. In the same month
that Ann left Esmond, Winston Churchill was re-elected Prime Minister,
following six years of Clement Attlee's Labour government. Then, on
6 February 1952, days after Ian and Ann arrived at Goldeneye, George VI
unexpectedly died.

A new Elizabethan age was how Kemsley Newspapers heralded the
young Queen's reign. For Ian, the announcement of a period of royal mourning could not have been more timely. 'My mental hands were empty, and I
was just about to get married, which is a terrible step to take at the age of 43.'

Suddenly, as he floated over the reef, above barracuda he had named after
battleships, Ian saw an exhilarating path back to bachelorhood – by creating a
contemporary naval hero in the tradition of Drake, Morgan and Nelson, loyal
to the Crown, who would reaffirm England as a world power, wipe out the
shame of the Burgess–Maclean defection, and re-establish SIS as 'the most dangerous' Secret Service in Russian eyes. And he would be a bachelor. 'If he were
to marry and settle down he would be of little value to the Secret Service.'

Ian's Cold War offspring emerged from his decision to reach back, not
forward, and explore the path he might have taken. Consciously moulding
his hero in opposition to marriage, Ian set about to retrieve the epoch in
which he had thrived, young, single and free.

In July 1945, Ian had come close to accepting the offer of a senior

Intelligence position in the overhauled SIS that he had had a hand in reshaping. 'He would have made an admirable head of the British Secret Service,' believed Donald McCormick, who considered that 'in reality he was much more like the character "M" than Bond.' Ian had declined, although keeping up his Intelligence contacts through the 36 Club.

His fictional agent, on the other hand, would take the job.

He would work for the new Ministry, the product of the Bland Report, in which he would rise 'to the rank of Principal Officer in the Civil Service'.

Simultaneously, under the renewed direction of England's victorious wartime Prime Minister, Ian's modern buccaneer would do battle with a fresh enemy, whose tanks Ian had heard in the woods at Tambach. He would execute in modern form those plans which Ian had conceived against the Nazis. In wartime, Ian had put these ideas into life; in uneasy peace, he would put them into fiction.

At an early 36 Club dinner, Ian had 'imaginatively pictured' to Admiral Denning 'the adventures he might have had in the last war, given complete freedom and unlimited money'. In his books, Ian became the player that his supervisory role in Room 39 had denied him. From his 'M'-like desk in Jamaica, he sent his agent on missions like the ones Godfrey had forbidden Ian to take part in.

He would not act alone. To assist him in defeating the global menace of Soviet Communism, Ian revived his wartime 'special relationship' with William Donovan. His American counterpart Felix Leiter, although now working for the CIA, would resuscitate the Anglocentric relationship Ian had enjoyed with 'Big Bill', when British Naval Intelligence was indeed 'running the show'.

A perception of Ian's novels that he did much to popularise is that they were a series of sensational fantasies based on 'the most hopeless sounding plots'. This was not the case. They were grounded in reality and a truth that Ian could not reveal but had intensely experienced. He wrote what he knew. By converting his lived experience into fiction, and updating it, he released the burden of that knowledge. Iva Patcevitch, New York chairman of Condé Nast, visited Ian during this period. 'I think he wrote the books primarily because he had a great deal of knowledge of things like this within him, and he had to get it out.'

*

Ian was a fiction writer during the last fifth of his life, but he had nursed literary ambitions since Eton. His aspiration to write a serious novel – confessed to Selby Armitage in 1928 – had been coloured by his reading of William Plomer, Alfred Adler, Leo Perutz, Thomas Mann, James Joyce. None of these influences were noted in reviews of the Bond books. 'Ian Fleming is a gifted storyteller and a man of high intelligence and ability,' remarked one critic. 'Fortunately for us, he has never tried to imitate Joyce.' This was not true.

Only a scrap of his high-brow literary ambition exists, written in the late 1920s or early 1930s on Joyce Grove writing paper. It features a melancholic and philosophical author, Claude Anthony, who is nearing completion of his magnum opus. *'On the floor by his chair was a large volume of quotations in different languages which he interspersed freely in his dialogues & monologues. His great work was drawing to a close, he had written all his discourse & was just finishing his last description – a description of going to sleep.'*

Since leaving Reuters, Ian had had to sedate his literary ambitions in reaction to Peter's success. He had a stock remark about writing – 'Of course, my brother Peter's rather brilliant as a writer, but I wouldn't know how you set about writing a book myself.' Ian had diverted his energies into collecting books and promoting other authors.

In 1937, Ian was a minority shareholder of the short-lived magazine *Night and Day*. He never contributed himself, but he discussed with Cyril Connolly, who had, the idea of starting a magazine like the *New Yorker*. When Connolly founded *Horizon* in 1939, Ian was an early subscriber.

Their friendship had rekindled the year before in Kitzbühel. From this moment on, Connolly became Ian's preferred contact in the literary world. He sought Connolly's recommendations for a reading list for 30AU officers. In 1942, he wrote to Smithers, after sending him to Mexico, to ask for 'some pen pictures' of expatriate English writers who Ian had heard about living in Central America. 'I would pass these on to Cyril Connolly for "Horizon" if it would amuse you, as the life of these peculiar nationals has given rise to much curiosity.'

Connolly seemed grateful for Ian's promotion of his influential monthly literary magazine. 'When I met Ian during the war, he always used to be with someone pretty important – an Admiral, a Brigadier or something – and one would feel rather like a delicate monkey being put through one's tricks.

"Look, General – or Admiral," – he'd say, "This is Connolly who publishes a perfectly ghastly magazine full of subversive rubbish written by a lot of long-haired, drivelling conchies. Of course, all of them will soon be inside for seven years, so perhaps you'd better subscribe to the thing now while you've got a chance, just to see the sort of outrageous things that can get by in a country like this during wartime." And grudgingly, laughingly, the man would be pushed into taking out a subscription.'

In December 1947, Connolly's 'ghastly magazine' published Ian's first substantial piece of non-fiction, 'Where Shall John Go?' – a pen-picture of Jamaica and the peculiar English nationals who had settled there.

After Ian joined Kemsley Newspapers, he hired Connolly as the *Sunday Times*'s lead reviewer. Generally, he still abstained from any writing himself. Donald McCormick recalled one of Ian's foreign correspondents in 1948 coming to London and saying to him over lunch, 'Of course, he can't write a line can he? Probably never will.' Following his *Horizon* article, Ian wrote a short reference book for his Mercury correspondents and, in 1950, a chapter on Foreign News for *The Kemsley Manual of Journalism*. Mainly, he read. Lisl Popper considered his tastes still quite European. 'His favourite writer at this time was [Jacques] Perret, who wrote *Le Caporal Epinglé*.'

However, the itch to write was there. Ian's proposal to Edith Sitwell for a joint translation of Paracelsus came to nothing, but it suggested a desire to be involved with literary figures, and in the case of Sitwell's friend Rosamond Lehmann go to bed with them.

Norman Lewis would chat to Ian at publishing parties thrown by Jonathan Cape in a room that smelled of carbonised Irish stew. 'When I first knew Fleming, he said, "Do you belong to a literary society?" "No." "Do you know any?" Quite obvious to me, he wanted to associate with poets and people he thought wrote well.'

Ian was reticent on the subject of his own writing. Ann said, 'About the time he wrote *Casino Royale*, he was very lacking in confidence. Very much so.' She later much regretted that 'I didn't notice how little confidence Ian had.'

In 1948, he had begun toying again with a novel, at the encouragement of Lehmann, who was staying at Goldeneye when 'Where Shall John Go?' was published. Although Lehmann never read any of his novels, 'he always said I was partly responsible for them because I urged him to take to the pen, after reading a piece he wrote in *Horizon*!'

Ann watched him wrestle with this novel over the next four years. Believing that Ian had picked up his long-abandoned manuscript about Claude Anthony, she kept faith that whatever he was working on might fit on a shelf alongside titles by her literary friends, Connolly, Waugh, Leigh Fermor and Quennell – many of whom Ian was to go on and publish with the Queen Anne Press in the 1950s.

Early on in their affair, Ann had compared Ian's project to her first pregnancy by him. 'You beast,' she wrote to Ian in 1948 from Gleneagles Hotel, 'you must write your book, even if I have to sit in an upright chair knitting beside you, which was how Mrs Galsworthy made Mr Galsworthy give birth to the Forsyte Saga.' She thought it an appropriate *quid pro quo* 'after all the aid you have given me in creation'. In another letter, she looked forward to seeing Ian the following Tuesday. 'You might write another page of your novel before then.' And then this reference: 'This is your hour for buckets of martini and oblivion or else tomato juice, and the third page of the magnum opus.' In her intellectually and socially ambitious mind, Ian's opus would be more Spengler than Sapper, even if it did appear to have stalled several times. '*Claude Anthony was sad. The corners of his mouth drooped as he slept . . .*'

So how did Ian's highbrow European novel turn into *Casino Royale*?

Ann claimed that Ian had confided to 'about five of my best friends and three of his that he intended to write the greatest spy story in the world. But he never mentioned it to me.' Robert Harling almost choked on his K-rations when Ian announced on his visit to France after D-Day: 'In due course I am proposing to write the spy story to end all spy stories!' Ian told William Plomer the same. 'With a diffidence that came surprisingly from so buoyant a man, he said that he had a wish to write a thriller . . . he had in mind some exciting story of espionage and sudden death.'

Ian outlined one story to Peter Quennell when driving back very fast from staying with the Rothermeres at South Wraxall Manor in 1946. 'There would be a murder but no sign of the weapon. The detective and various suspects would be asked to dinner and would sit down to an excellently cooked leg of mutton. Later, it would turn out that the mutton would have been the weapon, deep-frozen in the Frigidaire.' Ian repeated the story to

Roald Dahl, who ran off with it, possibly as payback for how Dahl felt Ian had treated his ex-girlfriend Millicent Rogers – the two men had had words over it. 'Ian was the only person who has ever suggested a plot to me which I have then used.'

By 1952, Ian was hemmed in on all sides by novelists who had used him or his material for their fiction. When she stayed at Goldeneye in 1947, Phyllis Bottome had given him her new spy thriller *The Lifeline*, with its Old Etonian protagonist modelled on Ian. In 1949, Alaric Jacob published his fictionalised memoir *Scenes from a Bourgeois Life*, featuring Ian as Hugo Dropmore. It annoyed Ian to witness the reception of Duff Cooper's *Operation Heartbreak* (1950), a fictionalised account of Operation MINCEMEAT that had originated in an idea of Ian's. In 1951, Cape published *Ever Thine*, a novel about Durnford by Ian's first love Hester Chapman. By the time of Ian's return with Ann to Goldeneye in January 1952, Phyllis Bottome had published another novel, this time set in Jamaica; Robert Harling had finished two more, *The Paper Palace* and *The Dark Saviour*. Moreover, Ian had heard that 30AU's first commander at Dieppe, Robert Ryder, VC, was writing a novel based on his wartime experience, *Coverplan*.

The tinder was there. His parched grasses awaited only the spark.

His elder brother provided it, says Ian's niece Gilly. 'Peter and Ian had a bet. Did you not know about the bet? Peter was writing away. He took himself very seriously, listened to himself on the radio, thought he sounded a stupid man, poured scorn on himself, wanting people to cheer him up and say, "You're wonderful." Ian said, "Oh, for God's sake, write a best-seller, why don't you?" Peter: "It's not that easy." Ian: "I bet you a hundred pounds I could do it." And the bet was honoured. Ian got paid by Peter a hundred pounds. I've always known that story. All Flemings have to win.'

What basis there is to this legend, who can say? Little of the brothers' correspondence has survived. Yet it would be foolish to dismiss the impact of Peter's attempt at a best-seller.

Up to this moment, Ian had suffered 'quite a lot', said the woman who became his New York literary agent, Naomi Burton. 'Ian was always known as Peter Fleming's little brother, and I think that had a sort of effect on him. He didn't want to attempt something serious and fall flat on his face.'

That was until Ian read *The Sixth Column*.

Dedicated to Ian, Peter's thriller was the Buchanesque novel he had promised Rupert Hart-Davis before the war. In August 1950, Peter had sent him 40,000 words of his 'non-thrilling thriller', acknowledging that 'nothing happens' and 'the characters scarcely exist'. The published text confirmed Harold Nicolson's previously held opinion that Peter possessed 'every gift, literary and intellectual, yet he is muscle-bound in the region of the head'.

What is most interesting about Peter's plot is not how it exposes the author as a middle-aged man still living a fantasy life through the works of Sapper, but the uncanny way it foreshadows Ian's career as a novelist. The hero Archie Strume, known as 'the Colonel', Peter's pre-war nickname for Ian, is a former Intelligence officer convalescing in an Indian hill station when he writes 'as an antidote against boredom, what he regarded as a preposterously melo-dramatic thriller'. It is read by an elderly RNVR officer about to return to his peacetime profession of publishing, who 'much to the surprise of the author, insisted on publishing it, and even got Archie to start on a sequel'. This was William Plomer's response to Ian's manuscript one year later.

Archie Strume's debut *Hackforth of the Commandos* 'made an instant and, as it seemed, enduring appeal to a nation', although leaving critics indif-ferent. Regarding his subsequent thrillers, Archie displays Fleming-like self-deprecation: 'They're twaddle really. That sort of thing just doesn't hap-pen. Beside, Hackforth's the most awful bounder.'

Completed around the time of Burgess and Maclean's defection, *The Sixth Column*, like *Casino Royale*, has betrayal as its theme. Peter's story contained elements that Ian also later ransacked for *On Her Majesty's Secret Service* (biological warfare) and *Moonraker* (converting the world's largest airliner into a suicide bomber). As well, Ian borrowed the name of one of Peter's characters, Moneypenny.

Emphatically, what Peter's thriller did not offer Ian was the trumpeted narrative excitement of the two best-selling authors at its centre: Archie, and a left-wing novelist, Paul Osney, who is revealed to be a traitor like Burgess. Alongside his treachery, Osney possessed a deadly characteristic, fatally absent in Peter's narrative, but that Ian was months away from discovering. 'His secret was "readability" . . . he had that rare and indefinable gift for arranging words and the sentence which they formed in such a way that they held your attention, that you simply had to go on reading what he had written.'

On finishing *The Sixth Column*, Ian knew he could do better. He had trespassed on Peter's territory in his travel article for *Horizon*. A further encroachment was Ian's burgeoning friendship with Noël Coward, who had worked with Celia on 'Brief Encounter'. Ian's decision to compete with Peter in writing a best-seller pushed him a stride beyond. When asked why Ian wrote his books, his New York editor Al Hart replied: 'He wrote because he got tired of being Peter Fleming's younger brother. He was determined that Peter Fleming should be known as Ian Fleming's elder brother. And by God he is.'

The literary spirit presiding over *The Sixth Column* with strangulating effect was Sapper's Bulldog Drummond, whom Peter had liked to play on stage and in his badinage with Ian. 'Pity,' he would say with maximum understatement after some calamity; or '*Exactly*' when he meant 'Shut up'; or in his slow dismissive drawl after someone had told a joke that bored: 'And then?' On Ian's post-war visits to Nettlebed, the brothers reverted to this kind of knockabout public-school language. But not in Ian's books.

'No Bulldog Drummond stuff to get you out of this one.'

Donovan Grant's oft-quoted words to Bond in *From Russia, with Love* point the way to Ian's success. For his attempt at a thriller, Ian turned his back on Sapper's character in favour of harder-boiled American counterparts. 'I don't believe in the heroic Bulldog Drummond types. I felt these types could no longer exist in literature. I wanted my characters to more or less follow the pattern of Raymond Chandler and Dashiel Hammett's heroes, who are believable people, believable heroes.'

Ian told Una Trueblood that he wrote *Casino Royale* after reading Mickey Spillane's *My Gun is Quick* on the flight to Jamaica and 'thought he could do better himself'. This may have been the case. But Ian filched a lot from Spillane's Mike Hammer and other fictional American gumshoes. As Umberto Eco has observed, he took their violent behaviour and exhausted attitudes and enlisted them 'with more literary venom than Spillane possesses' into the kind of British Empire-saving adventure that had been the staple of Sapper, Buchan and Peter Fleming. The Bulldog Drummond feature that Ian retained: it still demanded a Briton to do the job.

As for that British hero, Ian remembered the advice of Phyllis Bottome.

'If a writer is true to his characters they will give him his plot.' One reason his first book sprang 'practically whole-panoplied from his brain' was that the character who provided Ian with his story was chiefly himself, the unassailable bachelor he had been to this moment.

Ann's fragment is undated. 'This morning Ian started to type a book. Very good thing. He says he cannot be idle while I screw up my face trying to draw fish.' She liked collecting fish out of a net, bringing them on shore, and painting them. While she painted, Ian put on goggles and flippers and went swimming. On or around 17 February 1952, he sat down at his red bullet-wood desk.

'I had finished killing fish. I knew the sand and rocks of the underwater terrain like my own garden. Only sharks or barracuda, or something just as nasty, were targets for the spear-gun now. So I decided that it was now I should start killing a few humans – on paper, anyway.'

He rolled a sheet of foolscap into his 'battered Royal portable typewriter' that had seen him through Reuters and Room 39, cast his mind back to the French coastal resort where he had met Ann, and began tapping out what she believed was the 'magnum opus' that she had been badgering him to get on with for four years. On his return to England, Ian explained to Maud: 'I was in a terrible state & appalled at the thought of getting married. I sat down at the typewriter & typed 2000 words every day till I'd finished. I didn't reread or correct it & I didn't show it to Ann. When I got back, I told William Plomer what I'd done & he asked to see it.'

When the most famous secret agent in literature introduced himself on the page in Ian's first draft as 'Secretan, James Secretan', Ian was paying tribute to the Scottish side of his family – Robert Fleming's two brothers, both called James, who had died of diphtheria in 1843 and 1859. But Secretan settled less easily. When deciding what to call his child, Ian told Harling that 'a simple first-rate test is: could you shout the name along a crowded beach?'

In the anecdote Peter's diplomat friend Harold Caccia had told his daughter, Peter is supposed to have suggested the surname that Ian ultimately decided on – after Rodney Bond, the Intelligence officer who had saved

Peter's life in Greece. James Bond would rescue Britain and show that SIS was still to be trusted.

Bond was not so large a leap from Ian's fictional protagonist Bone, in his story about Lord Kemsley. Bond also harked back to the First World War codeword used by Ian's chief at the League of Nations, Sir Eric Drummond. Ian may have read Agatha Christie's 1926 short story 'The Rajah's Emerald', featuring one James Bond, educated like Ian's Bond at Fettes, who discovers a precious stone in his pocket when he puts on someone else's trousers. Ian had come across one more Bond when staying with Maud at Mottisfont. On 19 November 1944, Maud watched from the morning room 'the M[edical] O[fficer], Major Bond, scything the lawn (for pleasure) and two Italian P/Ws sweeping up behind him in a very leisurely manner'. It is possible that Ian was aware of James Charles Bond, a Swansea metalworker who served with SOE. The surname was common enough, given to a smart London street and Lord Kemsley's brand of writing paper, and although 'brief, unromantic and yet very masculine', with an Anglo-Saxon sound, it was not exclusive to England. One year before he died, Ian sent a newspaper clipping to Hilary Bray. '*Bond is a huge, quiet-spoken man with a coal-black face and grey curls. He was born in the cottonfields in the poorest part of West Tennessee, and scraped his higher education by being wanted for a university football team.*' Ian joked, 'For pity's sake, don't breathe a word of this!'

Most likely out of all these possible progenitors was another American James Bond, a pipe-smoking Old Harrovian ornithologist based in Philadelphia, whose white-jacketed 1936 book, *Birds of the West Indies,* was "one of my bibles" when in Jamaica. 'I thought, "James Bond, that's a pretty quiet name", and so I simply stole it and used it.'

It is instructive that Ian began writing Bond after going diving. 'What would you really do as the absolute ideal of all things to do?' Ernie Cuneo pressed Ian for his answer following a visit to Goldeneye. Both men had always done pretty much what they wanted. What would Ian do?

Cuneo did not forget his friend's reply. 'He just took off for the upper ether on Cousteau, the French underwater explorer, and the work he was doing especially on the reefs. It was as enthusiastic as I ever saw Fleming.'

Ian revered the French diver almost as much as he had admired William

Stephenson. A highlight of Ian's life was diving with Jacques Cousteau the following April for a sunken Greek galley off Marseille. Ian skipped the launch of *Casino Royale* to descend to the ocean bed, 'aiming to be *the* journalist of the underwater world'. It had been Cousteau, he wrote, 'who taught the common man to look under the sea as he swam' – with his wartime invention of the aqualung. 'Suddenly, swimming became interesting. Interest and curiosity, the act of focusing one's eyes and mind, have results you do not expect.'

A glimpse into how Ian approached thriller-writing is his advice to *Sunday Times* readers on how to emulate Cousteau. 'On holiday this summer, round the shores of England, it will be worth going to the local carpenter and getting him to putty a pane of glass into the bottom of a two-foot square box, about one foot deep, make the whole thing watertight and cut a couple of hand holes near the top of two sides. Then all that is necessary is to walk into the sea, within your depth, and put the box on the surface of the sea and look through it. There, waiting for you, is a new world crammed with treasure and beauty and excitement. From that first moment to goggles and aqualungs and sunken galleys is just turning the pages of the most exciting book that has been given to us since we learnt to fly – the book of the sea.'

This was the excitement Ian felt as he started writing – 'there are times when I can hardly wait to write the next page' – and that many were to experience reading him.

'All writers possessed of any energy annex some corner of the world to themselves,' wrote Kingsley Amis, 'and the pelagic jungle roamed by ray and barracuda is Mr Fleming's.' Ian's thriller was the square box he constructed 'to admire the denizens'. To convert his knowledge of dark secrets that he could not disclose, and bring these to the surface in a simple, exciting shape accessible to millions.

As Cousteau made alive and relevant again an Ancient Greek crew who had sunk two thousand years before, so Ian salvaged the British Secret Service – and by extension, the Establishment and Empire – after it had been holed below the water line.

'We all, when we're reading a book with a particular hero, see ourselves in that hero's shoes,' Ian told Plomer.

Cousteau had democratised the sea. Ian made the Secret Service available to all. His James Bond was a professional agent shorn of personal details who served as a modern, aspirational Everyman. Ian gave his readers licence to imagine themselves in Bond's shoes, in his car, in his bed, navigating the post-war world and its challenges with the aplomb of one of the elite. Not until the eleventh book in the series is it revealed he went to Eton.

Some readers identified with Ian's hero so closely they fancied themselves to have been his model. Four months after Ian's death, Ann wrote to Evelyn Waugh: 'Nothing on the breakfast tray but people who think they are James Bond or want to be James Bond.'

Ian was skilful at fanning speculation. 'To Pat, who was the model. The Author.' This inscription in *Casino Royale* was to Iva Patcevitch, who had stayed at Goldeneye. 'He said that he thought James Bond was meant to look like me.' Then again, Ian said the same thing to another visitor, Ann's friend Lucian Freud, whom he detested. 'You're just like my hero' – which surprised Freud for not being sarcastic, for once.

It was Ernie Cuneo's unswerving belief that Ivar Bryce 'served as a model for James Bond'. Roald Dahl was of this opinion too. 'A good fifty per cent of the Bond thing – the luxury, the atmosphere – came directly from Bryce.'

However, 'Burglar' Bryce – whose grey Bentley Continental Bond likes to drive – was by no means the only candidate. 'It's another nut who says he's James Bond,' grumbles a girl at the switchboard in *The Man with the Golden Gun*. The number of those who have been identified with varying degrees of credibility as Fleming's inspiration would have officered Ian's commando unit.*

* They include, in no special order: William Stephenson, Richard Sorge, 'Biffy' Dunderdale, Peter Smithers, Robert Harling, Sandy Glen, Sidney Cotton, Patrick Dalzel-Job, Merlin Minshall, Fitzroy Maclean, Duško Popov, Edward Scott, Richard Meinertzhagen, Michael Mason, Tony Hugill, Dunstan Curtis, Alan Hillgarth, Patrick Leigh Fermor, Conrad O'Brien-ffrench, David Niven, Antony Terry and Richard Hughes. In *Ian Fleming and SOE's Operation Postmaster,* Brian Lett adds to the mix. 'My personal view is that James Bond was an amalgam of dashing but fiery [Gus] March-Phillipps, cool and controlled Geoffrey Appleyard, the aquatic Graham Hayes, and the expert hunter and ladies' man Anders Lassen. Perhaps a dash of the spy Richard Lippett was also thrown into the equation.' Bond's '007' has several putative prototypes as well – from Elizabeth I's agent, John Dee, who allegedly signed himself '007', to Rudyard Kipling's 1898 story '.007' about a steam locomotive. Top Secret Dockets filed in Room 39 containing Special Intelligence decodes from Bletchley Park were prefixed oo. It was also the number on the door of the ladies' lavatory at the Commonwealth Relations Office. McCormick claimed to have been told by Ian that he took it from the Georgetown zip code in Washington (20007), even though zip codes were not introduced till 1963.

This is the Bond effect. He is a suave vacuum who invites us all to put ourselves in his position and say, *That is how I want to live.* 'Almost everyone has an element of Bond in them – or a would-be Bond,' said Pearson. 'He reaches so many areas of contradiction in a great mass of humanity – most people feel they've failed, most people feel bored, all the things that Bond suffers from – but Bond does actually have the power to go out and do something about it – he goes off and he fights Blofeld or Goldfinger, all the demons, he goes and fights and he wins.'

Looking for a model for Bond can be like looking for the elusive hubarra that Ian and his guide went searching for in his unpublished book on Kuwait: 'a large brownish bustard, white on wings, shy and so perfectly camouflaged in the desert that Said said he had once seen a hawk actually perch on the back of a hubarra without knowing it was there.'

How Ian Fleming elides with James Bond illustrates the relationship that any novelist has with their hero-protagonist. John Buchan's son believed that Richard Hannay was derived from 'two or three people, put together to create one character of fiction, very often undergoing the adventures that happened to several other real-life figures'. David Cornwell had a sensible riposte for readers curious about George Smiley's original. 'All fictional characters are amalgams. All spring from much deeper wells than their apparent counterparts in real life. All in the end, like the poor suspects in my files, are remoulded in the writer's imagination until they are probably closer to his own nature than to anyone else's.' Cornwell deliberately created John le Carré as his avatar. 'In the end, you have to give people bits of yourself so that you can understand them.' This was Raymond Chandler's position when Ian asked if he was Philip Marlowe. 'Well, yes, one puts a certain amount of oneself into one's hero because one knew more about him than anyone else' – but Chandler said that he also put his unattractive traits into his gangsters. Ian did so as well – giving his birthday to Blofeld, his golf handicap to Goldfinger, his habits to Le Chiffre: 'Mostly expensive but discreet. Large sexual appetites. Flagellant. Expert driver of fast cars.'

Was there an original? The ceaseless search illustrates how we never seem satisfied to take people at their word and need to go elsewhere for an explanation. Ian never made any secret that Bond was a fictional compound of the agents and commando types he had met during the Second World

War, a medley of himself and what he had asked others to do or heard they had done. 'It's my experience in Naval Intelligence and what I learned about secret operations of one sort or another, that finally led me to write about them – in a highly bowdlerised way – with James Bond as the central figure.' He had reached out and gathered in all those he had known, all the 'shenanigans' they were involved in, some of which he personally had 'got mixed up in', and reconfigured them into a single protagonist who had contours like Ian's in his bachelor heyday, when he was at the centre of things and not, as he now felt, on the margin.

More than anything, Bond was the solution to Ian's quandary. Ian wrote his thriller to overcome a cluster of frustrations – with Kemsley, Mercury, the state of England, SIS, and the loss of his personal freedom after Ann looked set – like a Wallis Simpson – to remove him from his bachelor's throne.

Add to that the lesion of Ian's unacknowledged war record. As Robert Harling said, 'I think he was a little piqued that he got no decoration at the end of it.'

One of the stranger things about Ian was that if you were allowed past the confidence that in turn became the hallmark of his writing, you encountered a quite startling insecurity. Ian was a very self-contained person, always in control of himself, who never gave himself away. It was easy, wrote Pearson, to overlook 'his chronic sense of failure and dissatisfaction'.

His mother was one of remarkably few who were sensitive to Ian's acute sense of failure. 'Is the following true?' Eve had recently contacted Churchill, ostensibly to congratulate him 'on your saving England again'. Really, her letter was a hurt complaint about Ian's lack of recognition and betrayed her own desire for status. She had been to a party and 'talked for a long time with Admiral Godfrey (late DNI), who told me how & why he had chosen my second son Ian out of all the men in England to be his secretary at the Admiralty, of how well he had done, & of how sorry he was that Ian did not receive any decoration etc etc.'

Meanwhile, she had re-read Churchill's tribute to Val '& I only wish that Val were here to give you his affection, admiration and support in your great work'.

A reply by telegram failed to resolve the mystery. 'THANK YOU SO MUCH FOR YOUR LETTER WINSTON CHURCHILL'.

Val's impossible example was never far from Ian's mind, or his pillow. For his fortieth birthday present to himself three years earlier, Ian had written to Churchill with a request. 'My brother Peter tells me that you were kind enough to autograph a copy of the tribute which you wrote in the *Times* when my father died. I would be grateful if you would be kind enough also to autograph my copy which I enclose. This would make it an even more treasured possession.' He had always wanted to be like his father. It says much that he took Churchill's signed obituary with the *Times* masthead and used it as the model for the obituary of the character who allowed him to be so.

Harling worked more closely with Ian that almost anyone – in Room 39, 30AU, at the *Sunday Times*, the Queen Anne Press and on the *Book Collector*. 'The truth, of course, was (and is) that Bond was a Fleming alter ego, rescued from the dream world of his boyhood and early manhood.'

Ian's models were made early on. Val's heroism in the First World War contributed as much to Bond's make-up as did Peter's record in the Second, which, like Ian's, was strangely unsung. If there was anyone who set the bar for understated courage, a commando before commandos were formed, it was Ian's brother.

Naturally, Ian's readers had other ideas. In an extended interview with Ian for *Playboy* published after his death, Ken Purdy asked him: 'Do you often feel that you are Bond and Bond is Fleming?'

In what were to be his last words on the subject, Ian still struggled for a coherent answer. 'Some of the quirks and characteristics that I give Bond are ones that I know about. When I make him smoke certain cigarettes or drink a certain bourbon, it's because I do so myself, and I know what it tastes like. But, of course, James Bond is a highly romanticised version of anybody, let alone myself, and I certainly couldn't keep up with him, I couldn't even at his age, which is and always has been in the middle thirties.'

One of Ian's golfing friends, Jock Campbell, whose Booker company bought the franchise for the books, called it 'the Fleming/James Bond

ballyhoo'. It has raged ever since publication of *Casino Royale*. The problem is clear, much clearer than any of his attempts to answer it. Ian wished
it both ways, as he had throughout his life. Without giving himself away,
he denied comparisons as deftly as he then invited them, writing to Ivar
Bryce in 1957, 'the next volume of my autobiography . . . should be with
you by now'.

Just how autobiographical were his 'collected works' Ian suggested in an
interview with Canadian television at Goldeneye six months before his
death. Asked to calculate the percentage of himself in the Bond books, Ian
drew on his cigarette. The answer came out with the smoke. 'I can say ninety
per cent personal experience really.'

As William Stephenson said, 'he couldn't write about things he had never
seen.'

'Is Bond Fleming?' asks another golfing friend, Stephen Potter, in his
humorous essay 'Bondmanship'. 'See Who's Who,' is the unpublished reply.

Potter's question divided even those who thought they knew Ian. On the
one hand, they saw reflected in Bond many Fleming qualities; his warm, dry
handclasp; his self-control, his contradictions, his passion for the Navy, his
dislike of lounging, his affection for fish and birds; his blend of decadence
and puritanism; his inability to stay anywhere for long; his Scottish melancholy, his cavalier treatment of women – which carried the sexual climate of
the Blitz into the austerity of the Cold War, and was less modern perhaps
than it was later cracked up to be.

For the film producer 'Cubby' Broccoli, Ian's 'whole persona, the way he
held his cigarette, his laid-back style, that certain arrogance, was pure James
Bond'.

Admiral Godfrey, on the other hand, felt impelled 'to counterbalance the
belief of a misguided and wishful public that Ian was a sort of James Bond
person, which he most certainly never was'.

Ted Merrett certainly resisted attempts to conflate the two. 'He wasn't
James Bond, of course. Just wasn't, old boy. No connection at all . . . he was
a pen pusher, like me.'

Peter Quennell watched Ian writing three Bond books at Goldeneye. 'I
could not take to James Bond. But Ian himself I liked.' Clear to him was that
'James Bond is not a portrait of the artist, but the kind of *alter ego* we

sometimes evoke in an euphoric daydream to make the bold speeches and execute the brave deeds that lie beyond our waking reach.'

At Goldeneye, in the frustrations of 'peace', Ian found a late outlet for his wartime experiences and ambitions. Bond allowed him to do the things he had wanted to do but was prevented by security concerns, and maybe something in his character; the voyeur who liked to experience at one remove. In the thriller he began writing in February 1952, Ian took the cards he had been dealt and slipped them to Bond. Then re-arranged them to play a winning hand.

Ian absolved Bond of his own tortuous complications. He later claimed he had 'no particular interest in his leading character, James Bond, but wanted him to be an anonymous blunt instrument doing the best he could for his chief'. Bond was simply a cipher working for Britain.

In *Casino Royale*, Bond's French counterpart René Mathis viewed Bond as 'a wonderful machine' – not unlike one of the Enigma machines in Hut 6 which Mary Seymour, one of Bletchley's last survivors, used to operate. 'Sometimes it came out in squiggles,' she says, 'sometimes as nothing, and sometimes it came out in German and you knew it was the code of the day.'

The secret that Ian discovered through Bond was how to unscramble the code for narrative. 'There is only one recipe for a best seller and it is a very simple one. You have to get the reader to turn over the page.'

'How *do* you do it?' Plomer wanted to know. 'I believe you could create extreme anxiety out of a cake-judging competition at a Women's Institute.'

Ian had no simple answer. The most obvious thing to say was that it involved a lot more grind than met the eye. 'Novels are very hard work, like all writing is.' Alec Waugh had told Ian that the only way to write in a workmanlike way was simply to be a workman and to keep to a routine from which nothing must be allowed to deter you. This regime had been impressed on Waugh by his English master at Sherborne, the prolific author S. P. B. Mais. Waugh had passed on Mais's inflexible law to Eric Siepmann. 'Interesting statistics,' Eric Siepmann wrote to Mary Wesley in 1948. 'Alec Waugh works 5 hrs a day and writes 2000 words.'

In Jamaica, Ian followed a timetable as strict as Bond's training exercises. Nobody could interrupt it. 'I work about three hours in the morning and one hour in the evening, and I find unless I stick to a routine, if I just wait for genius to arrive from the skies, it just doesn't arrive.' He emphasised to Bryce, when urging him to write the story of his 'extraordinary life': 'don't let anything to interfere with your routine.'

It is difficult to be simple. Style is also a projection of personality. Ian's prose mirrored the corner bedroom in which he sat every morning from 9.30 to 12.30 at his typewriter, blank wall in front, behind closed wooden jalousies to keep out the view and the metallic clamour of kling-kling birds.

Efficient, spare, masculine, austere. His plain writing had been influenced by his training with Reuters, 'where you damned well had to be neat and correct and concise and vivid' – short sentences, no unnecessary adverbs, fast and journalistic like Hemingway, which had made memorandum-drafting at the Admiralty no chore.

In Room 39, Ian had drafted a memo to members of NID setting out certain rules. 'A report should aim at three virtues. First, it should have impact; the reader must be made to know at once what it is about; the opening sentence is therefore of great importance. Second, it should be unambiguous; it must leave no room for doubt or ignorance other than the doubt or ignorance which the writer has himself expressed. Third, it should have the brevity which comes only from clear intention; the writer must know what he wishes to say before he begins to say it; otherwise he will hedge and be verbose. He should imagine himself in the position of one who will have to act, and act quickly, on the information which his report contains.'

Ian wrote his novels in this manner. He had no patience for elaborate writing – 'It holds up the action.' He agreed with Georges Simenon that it was important 'not to be too literary' and he never read a book while engaged on one himself. He repeatedly cited Ann's novelist brother Hugo Charteris as a warning. 'I mustn't write like Hugo might!' . . . 'I'm beginning to write like Hugo, it's an obsession' . . . 'To me, epigrams are danger signals! That way Hugo lies.'

Ian's ideal reader was the crewman in the raid on Dieppe. In the middle of battle, shells exploding overheard, Ian had been fascinated to observe him sitting on a crate of ammunition engrossed in a paperback called *A*

Fortnight's Folly. The cover showed a near-naked young woman being surprised behind a rock where she is sunbathing, by a man in a blue blazer. 'The reader's eyes were popping out of his head with excitement as he greedily turned over the pages.'

This was the absorption that Ian aimed for in his thriller. To generate 'an almost intolerable excitement' so that you forget the world bursting into flames around you.

To achieve this level of 'total stimulation', Ian tossed away his literary models and leapfrogged back to his childhood reading, to those writers who 'used to frighten me most' – Stevenson, Poe, Buchan, M. R. James – and one or two modern examples like Simenon, Maugham, Greene and Ambler, who 'can still raise the fur on my back when they want to'.

Of these writers, Eric Ambler had the sharpest impact.

'Maestro Ambler', Ian called him. 'There are not many authors one can automatically buy sight unseen.' He named Ambler, in a review headlined 'Forever Ambler', as one of few novelists to have caught 'the squalor and greyness of the Secret Service'. When in 1949 Ian had taken over Ambler's sea-front cottage at St Margaret's Bay on which Noël Coward had the lease, Ambler had 'a distinct feeling that Noël said to himself, "Ah well, Eric has failed there. Perhaps Ian will come through."'

Years later, when 'the gusher' had burst and he had come through, Ian took Ambler to lunch at Scott's. Over plaice and a glass of Guinness at the window seat, they discussed how much Ian had profited 'from all the fatherly advice you have been kind enough to give me on a hundred subjects', including recommending Ambler's literary agent Peter Janson-Smith, who would became Ian's.

A more oblique debt to Ambler foreshadows le Carré's determination to make George Smiley an embodiment of everything James Bond was not – cuckolded, ugly, old, unsporty, cerebral, morally torn. Ian had wished his secret agent to have a name that was 'the very reverse of the kind of "Peregrine Carruthers" whom one meets in this type of fiction'.*

* The name Carruthers had first appeared as the British hero-narrator of Erskine Childers' *The Riddle of the Sands* (1903), a book that Ian had pillaged for a potential wartime operation.

'Carruthers of the Secret Service' had featured in Ambler's debut thriller, *The Dark Frontier* (1936). This Carruthers is consequential because of how closely he anticipates Ian Fleming's relationship with James Bond. He encapsulates what every reader is doing when they read Bond – and what Ian was doing when he created him.

Carruthers is a fictional agent within a fiction, like Peter Fleming's Hackforth. We first meet him on the front cover of a detective novel as 'a lantern-jawed man with a blue jowl and an automatic pistol'. He not only looks like Bond, he behaves like him – 'impervious to ordinary human feelings, a man of steel, cold, unemotional', with a 'physical prowess which would have done credit to an Olympian athlete of twenty-five'. Yet Carruthers is not Ambler's actual hero. Shortly after reading about Carruthers's far-fetched adventures, the novel's real protagonist, Henry Barstow, a mild-mannered forty-year-old physicist, has a head injury following a car accident, and wakes up in the Royal Crown Hotel on Dartmoor, believing that *he*, Barstow, is Carruthers. 'Behind that high, clear-cut forehead reposed state secrets of awe-inspiring portent.'

In Carruthers's skin, as it were, 'a grim smile on his thin lips, a steely glint in his eye', Barstow then embarks on an exciting adventure to Zvgorod, capital of Ixania, to save the world from an atomic threat. 'The character that he had so curiously borrowed was but a highly stylised mask; a motley that was significant only against its special background.'

Barstow puts on the persona of Carruthers in the way that Ian at his desk in Jamaica, and later when travelling through the world to research his sequels, donned the mask of Bond. Ambler writes of Barstow: 'His daydreaming had always been of statesmanship behind the scenes with himself as the presiding genius . . . Queer, too, how dreams of that sort stayed with you. One half of your brain became an inspired reasoning machine, while the other wandered over dark frontiers into strange countries where adventure, romance and sudden death lay in wait for the traveller.'

In an episode that Fleming/Bond copied, Barstow/Carruthers races across Europe in a train with a sidekick from America's embryonic foreign Intelligence service who masquerades as a journalist. 'And so,' murmurs Carruthers, 'we are to save civilisation.' Even the subject was the same.

*

Above all, what Ian rated in writers like Ambler was their pace. 'When one chapter is done, we reach out for the next. Each chapter is a wave to be jumped as we race with exhilaration behind the hero like a water-skier behind a fast motor boat.'

To obtain his narrative speed, Ian wrote fast, discursively, not pausing to choose the right word, to verify spelling or fact. 'I went into writing like a blind man. After I had finished a page, I used to hide it away under the others.' Perutz and Perret were forgotten. 'I had decided that to suddenly deposit the reader on a soft, woolly pile of nice thoughts and words was bad enough to destroy the thing altogether, so I let it zip on. In just the same way as Bond went about his life. Very fast.'

In this hectic state, Ian savagely hammered out a page, turned it over, never looked back. If he did, he was sunk. He closed his mind to self-mockery, what his friends and Ann's would say. 'How could I have written this bilge? What a fool the hero is . . . And the writing! Six "formidables" on one page.' 'If you interrupt the writing of fast narrative with too much intro-spection and self-criticism, you will be lucky if you write 500 words a day, and you will be disgusted with them into the bargain.'

Ian expanded on 'my formula' in advice to friends. He had told Charlie Drake in Room 39 that 'the great thing is to get something down, get it started'. When Stephenson contemplated a memoir, Ian recommended he 'start from the beginning and don't forget to describe the weather and the smells and the scenery and really how it felt'. When Bryce was laid up in Vermont with a shattered hip, Ian wrote him two long letters to kick-start his autobiography – which was to end up being a memoir of Ian. 'Never mind about the brilliant phrase or the golden word. Once the typescript is there you can fiddle, correct and embellish as much as you please.' Apart from obstinately sticking to his pre-arranged schedule to do his daily stint, Bryce was to 'pile in every kind of contemporary detail' and 'jot down ten or twenty chapter headings and, during the boring period of lying on your back, think what you are going to put into each and remember all the details of how it was. Think, to begin with, most carefully about chapter 1. because when you have got that finished you will find yourself in a groove and inci-dents and conversations and brilliant reflections will come flooding back.'

The opening sentence is therefore of great importance. Once Ian began, it raced along, because most of the plot was there, coiled up inside him, like a contained Bond, waiting to be released. He did not have to invent from scratch. He was someone who needed to have seen and smelled what he wrote about, the places, the people who sparked his characters that emerged fully formed; to have involved himself in their situations. Plus he had a deadline.

'*The scent and smoke and sweat of a casino are nauseating at three in the morning.*'

He was back in the French town where he first met Ann, in the casino where he had gambled with Loelia in the last month before the war ('won some money at the Casino,' she wrote in her diary, 'was completely deserted by Ian'). He was Bond, playing the high-stakes game that he had floated in Estoril to Admiral Godfrey ('M'). His mission: to eliminate the Opposition's chief agent in France by cleaning him out at baccarat. His accomplices: the CIA, in the shape of Felix Leiter (a blend of Ivar Bryce, Oatsie's husband Tommy, 'Saucy' Earle and John Lambie), René Mathis from the Deuxième Bureau (Colonel Bertrand and Commander Barjot) and a fetching ex-WRN, Vesper Lynd – named after a Jamaican cocktail once served to Ian, and woven from women Ian had loved, Monique, Edith, Ann, and most obviously Muriel, who had cheated him by her death – who would turn out to be a Soviet double agent like Richard Sorge and Guy Burgess. Vesper's controller was the SMERSH card-sharper Le Chiffre, a combination of his sadistic Eton housemaster Sam Slater and unscrupulous figures like Andrei Vyshinsky and Juan March, whose characteristics Ian continued to draw on for Bond's future nemeses. Ian's Jamaican reef had a further hand in shaping Le Chiffre, a denizen of the deep who possessed the 'silence and economy of movement of a big fish' and watched Bond 'like an octopus under a rock'. A clue as to how Bond enabled Ian to unlock his narrative was in the name he gave Le Chiffre: the cipher.

Ian finished writing his 'stark little melodrama' on 18 March. He married Ann a week later.

XLV
A WEDDING

'Precious Annie, who is this extraordinary man you have married?'
W. SOMERSET MAUGHAM

The person who might have stopped Ian from marrying was distracted by her own protracted nuptials. On Ian's advice, his sixty-seven-year-old mother had moved to the Bahamas for tax purposes, taking eight of her portraits by Augustus John and her tiny 1914 Browning automatic pistol. She asked Ian on his first visit to bring a box of cartridges. 'You could put them in your pocket without difficulty. The great thing is to let the blacks know I *have* a pistol.'

Emerald Wave, Eve's seaside house, was not far from the golf course on Cable Beach and close to the Bryces, who were asked to keep an eye on her; Ivar had divorced Sheila, and now lived part of each year in Nassau with his new American wife, the A&P grocery-chain heiress Jo Hartford. They owned Balcony House, the oldest standing residence in Nassau, and a luxurious beach pavilion half an hour's drive away called Xanadu.

In a reverse of the conventional order, although part and parcel with the topsy-turvy life they were leading, Ian had taken Ann to Nassau weeks before their marriage, on 'a marvellous honeymoon among the humming-birds and the barracudas'. On the way out to Goldeneye in January 1952, they had stayed with Ivar, who greeted the prospective newlyweds with wreathes of bougainvillaea. 'Ian didn't appreciate the spikes in the flowers, but I told him they were symbolic.'

Ann was unimpressed by the Bryces, by 'wicked Mrs Fleming', and by the Bahamas. 'It is a hideous island, 50 miles of golden sand polluted by rich villas, pasteboard invitation cards, conversation on money and entertainment high poker.' Neither was Loelia seduced when she followed in their footsteps. 'Went to see Mrs Fleming & all her fabulous Johns. We dined at Xanadu for the Bryces' party. Deadly dull but for some erotic negro dancers.'

It remains a mystery what the two most powerful women in Ian's life thought of each other. Eve had thrown so many spokes in Ian's wheels, but she fell strangely silent now that he was getting married to an intelligent, tough, striking woman like her. She had wanted Ian to have a family. He wrote to her two years before, 'I will bear in mind your injunction that I should settle down and get married. Who do you suggest, and can they sew and cook?' Ann could do neither. She said of Eve, 'I thought that she might disapprove of me, but I think she had no idea at all who I was.'

Eve's grandson James has not heard anyone in the family say a word about their relationship. 'It was a stand-off. They declared a truce immediately.' Robert Harling thought that Ian was drawn to Ann precisely because she belonged to a tougher breed of woman, 'someone along the lines of his dominant frosty mother'.

One other factor explained Eve's truce. Once Eve was established in Nassau, Ann observed that she 'seemed to lose interest in Ian mainly thanks to the Marquess of Winchester'.

Even as Ann prepared to give up her title to marry Ian, his mother had trounced him by announcing that she was to become a marchioness – by 'marrying an old rip called the Marquis of Winchester,' Ian informed Stephenson, 'who, besides being premier Marquis of England, is 89 and went bankrupt for £400,000 [approximately £300 million today].'

Eve had coveted a title ever since Val's death, convinced he would have been knighted had he survived the war. Originally, she had vowed not to remarry until her youngest son Michael came of age. That would have been in 1934. After she met Monty Winchester sixteen years later and he asked her to become his third wife, she grabbed the chance to end her long widowhood. When she gave Monty the size of her finger for a ring, her fiancé was ecstatic. 'The flutter of your kiss on my lips is the token of the affection of our relationship.'

Eve later admitted in court: 'We were informally engaged, and I felt it was the very least I could allow.'

Counsel: 'You were fond of him?'

Eve: 'I was not in love with him in the least.'

After Val the paragon, Eve had chosen to marry an indigent old aristocrat who spoke about the Crimean War with a twinkle in his eye. 'Old Winchester is and always was a horrible man,' George Lyttelton wrote to Rupert Hart-Davis, 'though anyone remotely "enticeable" at ninety must compel some respect.' If his lineage as England's premier marquess, a title created in 1551, satisfied Eve's snobbery, not so seductive was his 'chronic impecuniosity'. Monty had traded on his title on the Riviera since 1930, after he departed England as a certified bankrupt following the crash of the Hatry Group in which he was a major investor. Eve admitted, 'he is rather apt to think anyone will lend him money.' The judge told the High Court, where her relationship with Monty inevitably wound up: 'No one could consider a loan to him a good risk.' The judge expressed fewer illusions still about Eve, who claimed that her actions sprang from a charitable instinct to nurse an old man. 'She is not the type which naturally seeks fulfilment in good works.'

But this was five years in the future.

Meanwhile, Augustus John sent a message to Amaryllis. 'How pleased you must be to hear that Mama is about to join the aristocracy.' Ian was reasonably relaxed about the affair. 'I think, in fact, there is no harm in him,' he confided to Stephenson, 'and he will, at any rate, be someone for Mama to look after. He is now on his way to Nassau to press his suit.'

To welcome the doddery, impoverished Monty to Emerald Wave, Eve had a special swimming pool built, six inches deep, for him to loll in. But she then developed cold feet at the prospect of renouncing Val's wealth, even for such a noble title.

'We are still unspliced,' she wrote to Augustus John in June 1952, 'and I have given up all idea of it although my young man insists on it taking place.'

This was merely the first round in a picaresque legal dispute that for tabloid drama would compete in the High Court with a law case of Ian's.

In the meantime, Eve's second son had got married.

Ian's letter to Ann's brother on the eve of their marriage is often taken as a portrait of it. 'We are, of course, totally unsuited – both Gemini. I'm a non-communicator, a symmetrist, of a bilious and melancholic temperament, only interested in tomorrow. Ann is a sanguine anarchist/traditionalist.

'So china will fly, and there will be rage and tears.

'But I think we will survive as there is no bitterness in either of us, and we are both optimists – and I shall never hurt her except with a slipper.'

They woke on their wedding morning to a new bird making a terrible noise. Ann said, 'I've never heard it again and I don't know what it was. Ian kept saying, "Go out and stop that awful bird, I can't stand hearing that bird again, go out and stop it."'

The whole village had been given a half-holiday on Ann's first wedding in Ireland to Shane. In Jamaica, she spent the morning 'as usual', and was married in the early afternoon with a special licence from the Governor at the decaying Town Hall on Hodgson Street, Port Maria, beneath an enormous framed photograph of Churchill, 'surly, glowering and disapproving of the whole proceeding,' in the view of Noël Coward's secretary, Cole Lesley, who, with Coward, comprised the two witnesses. Coward, Ian's best man, had warned Violet, 'I shall wear long elbow gloves and give the bride away. I may even cry a little at the sheer beauty of it all.' In the event, he and Cole had put on formal white suits and arrived early for the simple ceremony, having filled their pockets with rice.

On his arrival in Jamaica on 16 February, almost exactly the time Ian started writing, Coward had dined with the couple. 'I sensed that Annie was not entirely happy.' He had watched them interact at Goldeneye and in St Margaret's Bay, and he was one more friend who had 'doubts about their happiness if she and Ian were to be married. I think they would both miss many things they enjoy now.'

There are no photographs of the groom dressed in a blue linen shirt and belted blue trousers. He wrote to Plomer nine years later, possibly recalling his own experience, 'Good misprint in *Gleaner* about wedding. "Not to be sartorially outdone, the bridegroom wore an orchid in his bottomhole."' Ann wore a straw hat and a curious pale blue cotton dress made up by Martha at twenty-four hours' notice to cover her pregnancy. 'She shook so much that it fluttered,' said Coward. Both bride and groom were 'surprisingly timorous . . . And the registrar had such terrible breath that when he asked them whether they took each other for man and wife, they both turned their heads away and said weakly, "I do. I do."'

Married at last, Ian caught his best man's eye. They began to giggle and then 'lost our heads entirely' – so much so that when they went outside to their cars, both having hired the same make, Coward mistook his bumper for that of the newlyweds and tied on it the old shoe that he had brought for the purpose, and later drove off trailing it behind, after throwing 'handfuls of musty rice over them'.

The two cars headed first for Coward's house, Blue Harbour, for what Ian called 'le vin d'honneur' but was in fact a fortifying dry martini, then back to Goldeneye for a wedding supper prepared by Violet.

Ian had woken early to catch his first turtle especially for the meal, even if Coward felt that he was chewing an old Dunlop tyre 'on that excruciating banquette'. Violet had also cooked black crab, which 'tasted just like eating cigarette ash out of a pink tin'. But her *pièce de résistance* was a large, slimy wedding cake of unidentifiable ingredients and 'covered with viscous pale green icing' that Coward compared to bird lime. 'Ian was sitting in full view of the door with all the black servants peering through, and had to swallow a bit. The rest of it we had to take quietly out and bury when nobody was looking.'

It was impossible for Coward not to see in that buried green cake anything other than a portent. A calypso that he afterwards sent to Ann's sister Laura included this verse.

> *Mongoose dig about sunken garden,*
> *Mongoose murmur, Oh my – oh my!*
> *No more frig about – beg your pardon,*
> *Things are changing at Goldeneye!*

To round off the evening, Coward recited a wedding anthem called *Don't For My Darlings* that he had composed a month earlier. Ann included the last verse in a letter to Clarissa Churchill. 'I have suffered considerably from his reading it aloud in front of strangers.'

> *Don't either of you, I implore you*
> *Forget that one truth must be faced:*
> *However you measure*
> *Repentance at leisure,*
> *You haven't been married in haste!*

Ann thanked Clarissa for her letter congratulating them, which had come with a cable from Lord Kemsley giving Ian an extra fortnight's holiday. 'We need some encouragement,' Ann admitted, 'as it must be an unpopular union both on temporal and spiritual grounds,' but they had no cause for remorse. 'I only hope that one day you will achieve what you want.'

Clarissa was Ann's ideal confidante, to whom 'I am devoted'. She became Caspar's godmother, astounding her friends on the morning he was born by announcing that she was getting married to Anthony Eden, Churchill's Foreign Secretary and Deputy Prime Minister – which she did two days later.

Clarissa's chilling memory of waking up beside a husband who was a complete stranger was something that Ann could empathise with. Clarissa confided to Duff Cooper: 'I looked at my wedding ring & thought this is too nightmarish to last – & I can never take this thing off my finger as long as I live. Surprising it is that in spite of having seen so much of each other the last six months we both became suddenly ourselves only the day after the marriage. I am alarmed by his shortness of temper & general spoiltness . . . He [is] alarmed & rattled by my downrightness & kind of humour and inability to flatter.'

This was startlingly like Ann's experience with Ian. 'I thought I had married the foreign editor of the *Sunday Times*.' She was wrong.

XLVI
'TELL ME THAT STORY AGAIN'

'James and Tracy Bond! Commander and Mrs Bond!
How utterly, utterly extraordinary!'
ON HER MAJESTY'S SECRET SERVICE

It was 5 February 1964. Ian and Ann had been married nearly twelve years when a couple dropped in on them 'just on the chance'. The American visitors expected to find their entry barred by 'No Trespassing' signs, but the white iron gates were wide open. They drove up a grassy drive between pineapple-topped, pink-plastered posts with 'Goldeneye' painted in crumbling letters. Clothes were drying on bushes. Presently, a Jamaican woman appeared. After they introduced themselves, she rushed off.

Ian was sitting sideways on the big window sill, cigarette in hand, with powerful film lights on him, being interviewed by a Canadian television crew, when Violet interrupted.

The Commander had a visitor, she exclaimed. 'Mister James Bond.'

Taking this for a bad joke, Ian threw off the mike and went outside. His forehead started to bead as he shook hands. Jim – in his sixties, six foot four, a pipe-smoking, bespectacled naturalist – and his wife Mary, a published poet.

On seeing Ian's perspiring face, Jim reflected, 'Poor fellow! I think he was scared.'

Guarded, Ian said, 'So you're not following up on a libel case?'

It was common knowledge that Ian Fleming had recently endured a savage plagiarism trial in London. Mary realised that 'he feared Jim had stormed the citadel to make demands!'

Ian altered on discovering his visitor's identity – Dr James Bond, the Harrow and Cambridge-educated author of *Birds of the West Indies* and curator of the Academy of Natural Sciences in Philadelphia, who had given his

473

name as well to seven birds, a stink bug, a grasshopper and a subspecies of barn owl. Ian flung out his arms and yelled to the television crew in relief. 'This is a bonanza for the CBC! The *real* James Bond! I never saw him before in my life, but here he is – stepped right into the picture!'

The Canadian Broadcasting Company's out-takes of Ian with the Bonds no longer exist, only Mary Bond's diary for that day. Even so, her entry provides a rare and revealing snapshot of Ian's 'last Goldeneye' four months before his death. It also shows the radical change in his life and health since he had married and started writing Bond.

Re-energised, Ian led the couple through a maze of wires and sound equipment, out into the sunken garden, to the rail overlooking the beach.

Below, Ann lay floating in the translucent turquoise water, snorkelling. Seated on a chair in the sand was Ian's friend from school, Hilary Bray, 'a spare handsome man of religious habits and literary tastes', who had taken over Ian's partnership at Rowe & Pitman; and Hilary's 'darling' wife Jenny. Beside Jenny was an open copy of Jim's bird book – 'as if it were a prop,' wrote Mary. 'We all laughed!'

The Brays were among the handful of Ian's acquaintances tolerated by Ann. They possessed, she wrote to them, 'a magic catalyst, making happiness with us, for us, and between us – we are usually cleft in twain by friends or acquaintii!' Famous and lionised throughout the world, Ian now wanted to keep in touch only with friends he had made before he was well known. He needed people around him, he stressed, who 'may even be bores' but they had to be '*douce*'.

For Mary Bond, 'the lovely Hilary Brays were the ingredients which kept up gentlemanly amenities.'

Ian called down, 'Come on up. Mr & Mrs James Bond are here!' – and turned to Jim. 'I'm terribly sorry about all this bother I've made for you!'

Three years earlier, Mary had written to tell Ian how she had found out, after being sent a paperback of *Dr. No*, 'that you had brazenly taken the name of a real human being for your rascal!' Since then, Jim's life had been textured by jokes, winks, and nudges. Back home in Philadelphia, Mary would later have to fend off young women telephoning at night to ask if Bond was there, and her reply, 'Yes, Bond's here, but this is Pussy Galore and he's busy now.'

Facing Ian was the man he claimed to have named Bond after.

To take someone's name belongs less in the category of literary theft, against which Ian had had to defend himself in the High Court, than in superstition. The ornithologist was protected by his utter lack of interest, a protagonist so indifferent to his doppelgänger that he had not even paid him the respect of reading about his adventures.

Jim confessed he had not looked at Ian's books.

'I don't blame you,' Ian smiled, with a combination of embarrassment and relief. He recognised that the eminent naturalist swam in a different sea. Seeing him in the flesh, in the place where he had written his thrillers, was important because it somehow absolved Ian. All at once, it was a meeting with no strings attached.

Ian insisted that the Bonds have a swim and stay for lunch, before excusing himself. 'This wretched interview . . .' The cameraman had been hopping about in the shrubbery, filming them.

The CBC crew that had flown from Toronto to interview Ian about his forthcoming eleventh Bond novel, *You Only Live Twice*, was merely the latest example of what Ann called the 'hysterical success of Bond', resulting in her latest nickname for Ian, 'Beatle Bond'. She had not been able to sleep because a new petrol station near the gate had an 'infernal sound system' that from 9 p.m. to 3 a.m. pumped out the 1963 Island Records hit 'Three Blind Mice', the melody that had been used in the film soundtrack of 'Dr. No'.

Ann's unfriendly reaction to the Bonds after she swam ashore came from her wish to protect Ian from prying journalists like the pushy British investigative broadcaster Alan Whicker, who had proposed bringing a television crew to Jamaica to make Ian the subject of a fifty-minute episode of 'Whicker's World'. According to Ian, Ann had whined afterwards, 'When am I going to stop having to see lower class people?' Ann felt Ian was being unfair. 'Trying to preserve an ill man from the press, the film and television worlds was a nightmare experience. To them, Ian was a property promising golden dividends, while I wished above all to prolong his life.'

Dr James Bond's unexpected appearance was one further intrusion.

Standing with a towel around her and a mop of wet hair, Ann impressed Mary Bond as 'aloof, polite, but scarcely enthusiastic . . . I think Ann Fleming was bored to death with the whole James Bond story.' Yet this story involved Mary and Jim too, not to forget Hilary Bray, whose name Bond had borrowed as a cover in *On Her Majesty's Secret Service*, published the previous year. Bray was as devoted a reader of the series as Mary had become: his search for the line that represented the quintessence of the Bond stories came up with 'He smelled of cordite and sweat. It was delicious. I reached up and kissed him.' (*The Spy Who Loved Me.*)

Unlike Ann, Mary *was* officially married to James Bond and had been since 1953, when the first Bond was published. A writer herself, she was not going to pass up the opportunity to study Bond's creator. Three years earlier, Ian had offered her husband 'unlimited use of the name Ian Fleming for any purposes he may think fit. Perhaps one day he will discover some particularly horrible species of bird which he would like to christen in an insulting fashion that might be a way of getting his own back.' Yielding to a taxonomic, wife-of-a-naturalist impulse, she tried to describe and name the species in front of her.

Hilary Bray took them into his bedroom, with its bust of Noël Coward, to change. Bray asked Jim the name of the chestnut birds in the cliff, little thinking 'when tentatively marking one of the two copies which Ian had at Goldeneye, that the real James Bond would become magically available to be consulted in the flesh.'

Ian wrote an excited letter to Ivar Bryce in whose company he had first sighted the square-tailed bids: 'He duly identified our swallows as cave swallows.'

They walked down the steps, over the tangled roots of the shady beach walk. The sand was scattered with bits of a wrecked ship that had drifted in from Cuba after a hurricane. These storms were fairly regular; they had shipwrecked Bryce here during his honeymoon with Jo. Another storm blew up a day after the Brays left and 'smashed to atoms' a boat with six American tourists, part of 'the international riff-raff' Ian had been instrumental in attracting to Jamaica's north shore.*

---

* Ian was building a cairn from the wreckage with Denis Hamilton – his next and final houseguest – when Noël Coward sauntered down and, looking at Ian over his cigarette holder, uttered the words, 'Fleming's last erection'.

After the Bonds had swum, they went up to lunch. 'Alas, it was mine enemy ackee again!' wrote Mary. 'I said it didn't agree with me.' Violet's akee would, Ian promised. 'She's been with me 18 years.' Ann's attitude remained frosty as she told Mary that 'England had been superb & she'd hated leaving it last Sunday', and only with extreme reluctance had she joined Ian in Jamaica – after Ian had called on the recently installed telephone line to the Flemings' new home at Sevenhampton to say he missed Ann and she was his 'solace'.

Mary chatted away with Ian about her husband's birdwatching adventures. Not lost on Ian was that 'birdwatcher' was slang for 'spy'. Bond had used birdwatching as a cover, if not a particularly effective one. When Bond claims to be an ornithologist, one of Dr No's henchwomen asks, 'Could you please spell that?'

It revitalised Ian to learn that Jim – 'JB authenticus' as Mary called him – had made nearly a hundred expeditions to the West Indies. One of Jim's proudest achievements was discovering an invisible marine barrier across Hispaniola, the island comprising Haiti and the Dominican Republic. This explained why the animals differed from one side to the other. Ian was fascinated. Mary wrote, 'He really *did* understand and appreciate Jim.'

Mary told Ian how she questioned her husband after each expedition – where did he sleep, what did he eat, what were the guides like? Ian suggested that next time she must use a tape recorder, '& I said, "I get it". I say, "Tell me that story again", & Ian and Jim both said almost simultaneously, "What a good title for a book!"'

Ian disappeared after lunch and returned with the guest book, which he asked Jim to sign in big letters, and a copy of his new novel, the last to be published while he was alive, due out in seven weeks. The inscription in *You Only Live Twice* read: 'To the REAL James Bond, from the thief of his identity, Ian Fleming, Feb 5 – 1964 (A GREAT DAY!).'*

Bray wrote to Mary afterwards that it had been indeed 'a red letter day for Ian, as for everyone else. He used to reflect on it happily. And when he got to England, he used to relate it – as the story of the year, Goldeneye 1964.'

That night in the Hotel Maria, Mary hurried to pencil down details. Ian's perspiring forehead, showing the 'heavy pressure' he was under. His

---

* In 2008, it would be sold for $72,000.

concern over the court case. His health. The hostile jealousy of Ann. 'And certain remarks which keep on standing out as increasingly significant? "I was a bachelor a long time," says Jim. "And still are!" says Ian – as if to add, "And so am I." This added to Mrs F's remark when I said, "We're both married to bachelors, & it's OK, isn't it?" "I'm not so sure," says she.'

Writing to Ian three years before, Mary had pleaded: 'Just *don't let* JBBA [James Bond British Agent] marry. Certainly not until he's at least fifty-five!' The famous author with whom she had spent the day was now that age. If there was a named species to which he belonged, it was definitely that of a confirmed English bachelor: 'tall, sunburned, his hair slightly too long, British style at the back & sides of his head, wearing a loose dark blue jumper of sorts . . .

'So *I* see – novelistically speaking – a helluva plot – a woman in a triangle with 2 men, her husband, & the man he's created, absorbing more of his time than *she* is able to command.'

It was a helluva plot.

The story of Ian's last years is the sad, strange drama that Mary Bond divined: how James Bond gained ascendancy over his creator, and how living as James Bond became the death of Ian Fleming.

Ian's best disguise was himself. Worldwide fame came to him when the character he moulded from his secrets and fantasies chimed with the daydreams of his millions of readers. Once he returned to London in April 1952 with his heavily pregnant wife and his manuscript, Ian's independent days were over. About to turn forty-four, Ian knew all he needed to be an author of spy thrillers. His final career consumed him in struggling to feed what Philip Larkin called 'the staggeringly gigantic reputation, amounting almost to folk myth' that grew out of the novels.

It was Larkin who first made the point that Ian's war years provided the bullion he drew upon to produce these books. In a review of Ian's posthumous collection, *Octopussy*, 'the last hardcover splutterings of his remarkable talent', Larkin singled out the title story as the key to understanding Fleming's life and work.

'Octopussy' returns to the chaotic final days of the war with victorious Allied troops looting what they could from the Nazis. The pillagers included 30AU commandos. Bill Marshall had driven a lorry overspilling with 'stuff we had pinched' with one of his mates. 'We unloaded all our purchases into a field, all that we had kept from the beginning of D-Day, and buried it in a hole.' His mate had since been back twice, looking for the field. Glumly, he reported to Bill, 'They've built houses over it.'

In 1939, Juan March had sparked Ian's fascination for gold. Whatever Ian and Ned Pleydell-Bouverie had got up to a year later in Bordeaux with Belgium's bullion reserves only fanned Ian's interest. The idea for 'Octopussy' originated in a letter that Ian received from Antony Terry in 1960 about Nazi treasure hidden in the mountains near Kitzbühel. 'I cannot help feeling that the story of these last sinister days of the war in the Alpine valleys of the Salz-kammergut, with scores of SS and quisling government and Gestapo officials from Berlin . . . wandering about with their cases of gold bars melted down from the gold teeth and jewellery of the Jews gassed in the concentration camps and looking for somewhere to bury them so that no one else knew, and all suspecting each other, with the end drawing in and the Americans only a few miles away, should make a grisly and macabre framework for the story of the now-forbidden search.' Terry provided a further germinating detail. A British agent had been dropped into the area at the end of the war. 'He describes the murder of a thousand concentration camp inmates in the area at Ebensee a few hours before the Americans arrived, to stop them talking.'

Ian's British agent also murders someone for their silence to keep his gold.

'Octopussy' begins at the time of von Gerlach's surrender to 30AU when Ian had been at Schloss Tambach. Its main character is a resourceful British commando officer with a history of easy sexual conquests and the Smithers-like name Dexter Smythe.

In an operation reminiscent of 30AU, Smythe is ordered to track down Nazi records in the peaks above Kitzbühel. He relies on an experienced local ski guide, Hannes Oberhauser, partly based on Hannes Schneider, an Austrian friend who had died in 1955, but also on Ernan Forbes Dennis. The grey-haired, limping Oberhauser had been a father figure to the young Bond – as Ernan was to Ian.

Oberhauser leads Smythe to an ammunition box of Nazi gold, buried beneath a cairn, whereupon Smythe shoots him dead and drops his body into a crevasse. 'Major Smythe gave a groan of joy.' He sits down on a rock and imagines how he will spend this loot: on a lifestyle that became associated with Bond.

Smythe takes his wife Mary to post-war Jamaica, and buys Wavelets, a north shore house with stairs to the beach. Here he lives in comfort off two gold bars, twenty-four kilos each, paring them down to sell to local Chinese gold traders. The Foo brothers fund Smythe's retirement in a paradise of sunshine, unlimited food and cheap drink, a wonderful haven from the spam-munching gloom of Attlee's Britain and 'the worst winter weather for thirty years'. But there is self-revulsion in Ian's portrait of this balding, pot-bellied alcoholic, a golfer like Ian who has had two coronary thromboses and whose bickering wife Mary has become a sleeping-pill addict like Ann (whose middle name was Mary). When Bond turns up at Wavelets to avenge Oberhauser's death after his mentor's body is uncovered in the melting glacier, Smythe, a passionate snorkeller, surrenders himself into the arms of the octopus that lurks in his reef. 'The tentacles snaked upwards and pulled more relentlessly. Too late, Major Smythe scrabbled away the mask.'

Rip off the mask of Bond, and Ian/Smythe is revealed as no more than a wheezing expat kept afloat on wartime memories. In his review, Larkin wrote: 'How easy . . . to see in the career of Major Smythe an allegory of the life of Fleming himself. The two Reichsbank gold bars that the major smuggles out of the army on his discharge from the Miscellaneous Objectives Bureau are Fleming's wartime knowledge and expertise: he emigrates to Jamaica and lives on them – selling a slice every so often through the brothers Foo (presumably his publishers) and securing everything his heart desires: Bentleys, caviar, Henry Cotton golf clubs.'

This was the draining exchange. Once Ian gave birth to Bond, he relied heavily on the hard-earned secret capital of the war. Each book was a different slice of stolen gold until the material ran out.

When Jim and Mary Bond met Ian at Goldeneye in February 1964, the well had run dry.

'Now he stay in bed till eight,' said Violet.

XLVII
TWO BIRTHS

'I wrote "Author" instead of journalist in a new passport.'
IAN FLEMING

On their return to London in March 1952, the Flemings took up residence in a tall-ceilinged Victorian flat overlooking the Thames at Chelsea that Ian had leased for £410 p.a. with financial assistance from Eve.

T. S. Eliot lived two floors below with the invalid bibliophile John Hayward, who spent his day in a maroon dressing gown, watching the Thames and editing. Ian at once recruited Hayward to edit the *Book Collector*.

Into Ian's flat in Carlyle Mansions, which Lisl Popper had decorated to look like White's, Ann brought her two children from Warwick House, plus Jackie – a parrot in a brass regency cage whose repertoire consisted of 'Hello darling' and 'Old buzzard'. Ann wrote to her brother: 'Ian's martyrdom is imminent with the intrusion of talking parrot, saxophone, Raymond, Fionn and self to his perfectly run bachelor establishment and, as the beautiful Austrian maid is in love with him, the immediate future looks rather chaotic.'

Among the first friends to greet them were the Connollys. In early April, Cyril and his new wife Barbara visited the Flemings at their weekend retreat in St Margaret's Bay, where Ian had taken over the lease of Noël Coward's house, White Cliffs. Barbara wrote in her diary: 'Ian Fleming, tanned, fretful and thinner. Ann, greyer, older, happier and obviously pregnant . . . they are both so vitalised and pleasant that it is a successful visit. They were more lovebirdy than ever and kept putting their heads together to inspect the holes in their carpet, and then nesting chirrupy noises would follow as to whether it should be sent to be repaired now or when they were next in Jamaica.'

The newlyweds were still making contented noises when Mary Paken-ham came to tea. 'Ian was excited and amused and very engaging – bubbling over with talk about the situation, and we all three had a good laugh over the various complications. He said he liked having so many difficulties as it made it more interesting. I said he had only one difficulty, which was how to live on his income, with which he agreed.'

Over lunch at the Étoile, Ian confided to Harling that his wife's 'inextin-guishable extravagances' were a worry. She spent money 'like a dozen matelots ashore in Gib on a day-long jaunt'. The future Labour Party leader, Hugh Gaitskell, was told at a christening in 1951, where he was first intro-duced to Ann, that she spent £1,000 a year on flowers alone (approximately £40,000 today).

Previously, Esmond had paid the bills. That burden fell now on Ian. But he carried a potential solution in his briefcase. He disclosed to Robert Har-ling that during his recent spell at Goldeneye, 'he had at last put pen to paper, and completed a first draft of a first novel, tentatively entitled *Casino Royale*.

'I applauded, "At last! The spy story to end all spy stories."

'He grinned and said time would soon show.'

Ian had sent the typescript to William Plomer, now back working as lit-erary adviser to Peter's publisher Jonathan Cape. He was awaiting Plomer's response.

His earlier lunch with Plomer at the Ivy, on 15 May, had completed a cir-cle that began in 1926. Plomer, the recipient of Ian's first fan letter, whom Ian had recruited to Naval Intelligence, whose job he had saved after Plomer was arrested for soliciting, was now in a position to repay him.

'William, if you get smoke inside a woman how do you get it out of her?' 'Exhaled' was a stupid word but so was 'dribbled it out'.

Plomer looked at him and said, 'You've written a book,' and requested to see it.

'Well, not exactly a book; it's a sort of thriller thing.' Besides, it was still 'a dog's breakfast'. Plus, Plomer was known for his uncompromising judgement – he had not been in favour of Malcolm Lowry's *Under the Volcano* and had criticised a popular author for writing novels 'so light that you have to hold them down'.

Ian prevaricated because he lacked confidence. Ann had not asked to read what he had written, having 'reached the stage of permanent discomfort' in her pregnancy, but Clare Blanshard had read it in New York and begged him to put it away or publish under another name. 'He wrote such trenchant, succinct Intelligence reports that I was somewhat scandalised by *Casino Royale* under his own name – but of course I had other deeper reasons. I felt – & told him – that Bond would be a millstone round his neck for the rest of his life.' Whether or not it was after-the-fact wisdom, Lisl Popper's reaction had been the same. 'I went on my knees before him and said, "Ian, do me a favour. Forget it. Don't publish it for God's sake. Everyone will laugh at you."' Even Loelia voiced concern. 'I came to a slightly indelicate sexy passage and I reminded him that Lord Kemsley was very straitlaced and he might well lose his job on Kemsley Newspapers.'

The way you got Ian to do something was to tell him it could not, or better, should not be done. He worked further on the manuscript and gave it to Plomer in July, afterwards protesting that Plomer had 'extracted it from me by force'.

In his eulogy to Ian, Plomer described his response. 'I read, I applauded, he conquered.'

Plomer pressed Ian's manuscript on Cape's 'eagle-eyed' editor Daniel George, who replied on 25 July. 'I sat up till 1.20 last night. *Casino Royale* made me sit up. It was so exciting that I could persuade myself I was back at the old baccarat, and the vodka and caviar were so delicious that I tolerated the abominable condition of the typescript. The author has evidently had great fun in a *genre* of which he is a connoisseur. Whether his characters have any counterparts in real life, I do not know ... It needs, of course, extensive revision ... Anyhow, it has given me very great pleasure, and I hope to be given more by the author's next excursion into fiction. *He knows all the tricks.*'

Ian never lost his talent for keeping a reader up with what Larkin called his 'mesmeric readability'. In March 1962, David Bruce, a former head of OSS in London, who had worked in wartime Intelligence with Ian, was back in England as America's ambassador when he went into a bookshop in Cambridge. 'I bought six of Ian Fleming's adventure stories. They bid fair to ruin my health, for three nights running, I have read until three in the morning.

Ian is fertile in imagination, and his stories move quickly through scenes of almost uninterrupted violence.'

This violence all but scuppered Ian before he had even begun, after Daniel George passed on his manuscript to Jonathan Cape. Ian had never warmed to Peter's publisher, regarding him as 'hard & tightfisted & vain – an Edwardian relic. I have never heard anything *attractive* said about him by anyone.' He did not read thrillers, suspected that Ian was a dilettante, and, as Cape wrote to tell him, was 'against any form of gambling. It goes entirely against my Quaker origins.' It cannot have enthused him that the central scene in *Casino Royale* takes place at a card-table.

Cape shared his reservations with his editorial director Michael Howard, who disliked the book intensely. 'I thought its cynical brutality, unrelieved by humour, revealed a sadistic fantasy that was deeply shocking.' Howard confessed sleepless nights at the idea of being associated with its publication.

A deciding factor was the firm's longstanding connection with Peter Fleming. Cape told Mary Pakenham's brother Frank, 'I suppose we'll have to take it because he's Peter's brother.'

Cape's reluctant acceptance came on the day he heard that Ian had had a son. Once 'you have done a thorough job of revising the MS,' Cape wrote on 13 August, 'I look forward to you having as much success as a novelist as it would seem you are likely to have as a parent.'

Loelia was expecting the Flemings for the weekend of 9 August when Ian telephoned 'to say Annie had started the baby so they weren't coming'. He took Ann to the Lindo wing of St Mary's Hospital, Paddington. Caspar's birth on 12 August was more difficult even than their daughter Mary's had been in Edinburgh, but this time Ian was present.

'I didn't want anyone except Ian.' For weeks afterwards, Ann had 'nightmares about long red rubber tubes'. To start with 'Ian coped with everything because the doctor assured him that much to everyone's surprise my pulse never wavered so there was no need to sound alarms.'

When Ann later developed complications, Ian was not so composed. The ballerina Moira Shearer, wife of the journalist Ludovic Kennedy, had delivered a daughter the previous evening, and was resting in an adjacent room. She looked up to see a stranger at the foot of her bed, sobbing. He came round, knelt down, buried his face in her lap and continued to weep uncontrollably. Moira held his hand and stroked his hair, only realising that it was Ian Fleming, who had been in her husband's house at school, when he said, 'Please forgive me, but my wife is having a terrible time next door.' Suddenly, he got up, took her hand, kissed it and said, 'You've been such a help.'

Hours later, Caspar was born. Ann wrote, 'They decided to do another caesarean because the baby's head was very large and my last operation in some mysterious way meant that a normal birth might rupture and split me open like an old pea pod.'

That night, Loelia wrote in her diary, 'Ann has had a 9lbs son! Ian came to celebrate & we had triumphant canasta.'

Four days later, Ian sat down and typed his wife a letter to celebrate Caspar's arrival. 'He is the most heavenly child and I know he will grow up to be something wonderful because you have paid for him with so much pain.' These words stood out for having been typed on gold keys.

In April, Ian had asked Clare Blanshard in New York to order a gold-plated Royal Deluxe portable typewriter to celebrate the first draft of *Casino Royale*. Peter Smithers's wife Dojean had bought one in 1949, and used it to the day she died. Ian had seen this in the Smithers's house in Wilton Crescent, and he coveted one for himself – 'I deserved an extra wedding present'. The machine had cost $174 (approximately £1,700 today) and the Bryces smuggled it back to England on the *Queen Elizabeth*, wrapped up in Jo's fur coat and hat, to avoid customs duty. Ian received it a day or two after Caspar's birth.

'This is only a tiny letter to try out my new typewriter to see if it will write golden words since it is made of gold . . . My love, please get well soon. I need you so much for the rest of my life. Come home with Kaspar as soon as you can, and I will make you both happy and see that neither of you gets hurt by anything.'*

Thirty people sent flowers, including Max Beaverbrook, the Flemings' north shore neighbour in Jamaica. Ann wrote 'in a coma of morphia & pain'

---

* The words were doubly precious for being among the relatively few composed by Ian on his new Royal Deluxe typewriter. 'Mr F says the type is too small for him to see!' His secretary Beryl Griffie-Williams hated using it. 'Actually, it is a beastly machine and quite inadequate for the work I have to do on it.'

to thank him. 'The baby is splendid, he looks very like you.' Esmond Rother-mere sent many roses and a note – 'Dearest Ann, best wishes to you and your son.' Ann wrote to her brother, 'Oh what a strange character, in sixteen years that one line showed more feeling than when he took my body and vitality utterly for granted.' Esmond later told her, 'I pray that your son will make everything worthwhile.'

What to call him? Ian had written to Ann, 'I think Adam would be a good name.' In the event, the baby was christened Caspar Robert at Chelsea Old Church on 30 October: Caspar after Augustus John's son Caspar, an admiral, and Robert after Ian's grandfather. Until then, he was variously Kaspar, Kasper, and Kasbah. The godparents were the newly married Clar-issa Eden ('the child is remarkably nice – & Ann adores it'), Cecil Beaton (who speculated to Greta Garbo, 'I wonder what the child will grow up to be?'), Noël Coward (who, Ann wrote, 'considers himself responsible for the whole thing'), the 'stout golf player' Duff Dunbar, and Peter Fleming – 'a splendid range of sex and celebrity if not wealth'.

One sadness that Ann confided to her brother: 'The doctors have advised no more babies.'

Soon after receiving Jonathan Cape's offer, Ian bumped into Mary Paken-ham, who recalled that he was 'very excited over getting his book taken, charmingly naïve. "Heady" was the word he used.' He told Maud Russell that Cape had 'paid him well, and want his next one'.

A decade earlier, William Plomer had warned Ian, 'it's no good writing just *one*. With that sort of book, you must become regular in your habit. You must hit the nail again and again with the same hammer until it's driven into the head of your potential public.'

On the back of Plomer's trust in him to deliver a novel every year, Ian saw a path out of what he proclaimed were his financial straits. He could afford to write novels, but it was a badge of honour to say that he would make his fortune by writing; no one else in his family said that. His earlier diffidence gave way to what Norman Lewis observed as an 'extreme self-confidence and determination to involve himself in every aspect of his book's production'. Ian instructed Ivar Bryce, when asking him to find an American publisher: 'What I want is not a publisher but a factory.'

That autumn, months before his first novel was published, Ian bought a defunct theatrical company, Glidrose Productions, to shield any profits that might come out of *Casino Royale*. On the same day, he had lunch with Ralph Arnold, who told him, 'you'll be lucky if you get 200 pounds out of it.'

'Not at all,' Ian replied. 'I shall make a hell of a lot of money.'

When Ian met Cape on 17 September to negotiate his contract, he made it clear that 'I am only actuated by the motives of

a) making as much money for myself and my publishers as possible out of the book and
b) getting as much fun as I personally can out of the project.

His attitude was that of his aunt Dorothy, regarding copies of her father Robert Fleming's story about Curly and the gypsies. 'Print them and sell them and get money and buy me a goat.'

Ian had a financial background. He was a publisher himself. He knew the margins. He treated the publishing of James Bond like an arm of his Mercury empire; as if Cape's editorial staff were working for the *Book Collector*, the first issue of which had appeared in August with a print run of 2,000; or the Queen Anne Press, the inaugural board meeting of which took place a fortnight later, on 8 October, to discuss Cyril Connolly's forthcoming *The Missing Diplomats*, Patrick Leigh Fermor's *A Time to Keep Silence*, and Evelyn Waugh's *The Holy Places*.

When Ian sat down with Jonathan Cape, he brought to their negotiations a knowledge of design, serial rights, royalties, blurbs, distribution and promotion that few first-time authors possessed. Norman Lewis was weirdly engrossed to observe how Ian was able 'to bulldoze Cape into letting him supervise the production of his own books', to the point where Cape wished to have as few dealings with Ian as possible.

In his opening skirmish of what became a 'remorseless and hair-splitting tussle', Ian argued with Cape, the inveterate anti-gambler, for a print run of 10,000 with ten per cent royalties, and additional complimentary author copies to be decided on the flip of a coin ('I toss your secretary double or quits').

Ian consulted Harling over the typeface, Fry's Ornamented, which Harling had used for the Queen Anne Press colophon, and he called on the

Sunday Times' designer Kenneth Lewis for advice on the cover. Ian later told Georges Simenon, 'I think jackets are very important for books.' Hugh Edwards, author of *All Night at Mrs Stanyhurst's*, had designed the cover for his regimental magazine and he inspired Ian to copy his example. 'I have designed a jacket of exquisite symmetry and absolute chastity,' Ian assured Cape, who ended up using it. 'I bet your other authors don't work as hard for you as I do.'

As publication date approached, Ian proved himself to be an absolute networker, a one-man band who employed every device to sell his book. In the judgement of Oliver Buckton, he was 'one of the first modern writers to recognise that aggressive promotion and publicity were crucially important to establishing his reputation and – especially – generating high sales'.

Even so, Ian's ambition at this stage had to remain relatively modest, as he reminded his Pan paperback publisher Aubrey Forshaw eleven years later, on receiving a gold-plated statuette of Pan for one million copies sold of *Casino Royale* – 'a far cry from when you and Cape gingerly handled CR with a pair of tongs and gaze averted!'

In 1953, Ian's loftiest aim was to compete with the pulp fiction crime writer Peter Cheyney, whom Ian brandished to Cape as his yardstick. 'This thriller business is a fly-by-night affair – a light-weight read with a probable ceiling of around 10,000 copies, unless it can be pushed into the Cheyney class . . .'. In Ian's unflagging efforts to push his books into that class, Norman Lewis wrote, 'the foundations of what is now called "hype" were laid.'

Ian contacted Dick Troughton, head of the booksellers W. H. Smith, to ensure that his chain ordered copies and reviewed it in their newsletter. He urged Cape to write to French booksellers in Deauville and Le Touquet. He wrote to Clare Blanshard: 'I am bludgeoning friends and members of my staff into buying it.' He sent out early copies to Kemsley Newspaper editors, and solicited puffs from authors like Paul Gallico ('The book is a knockout'), and Somerset Maugham, who refused to supply a quote – 'I would not do it not even for the author of Genesis' – although Maugham did admit to sharing Daniel George's page-turning enthusiasm: 'I started it last night in bed & at half-past-one, when I was about halfway through, I said to myself: I really must get to sleep; though what I really wanted to do was to read on till the end. I finished it an hour ago. It goes with a swing from the first page to the last & is really thrilling all through . . .'

One hiccup was the dedication. Ian wanted to dedicate his first novel to Ann, who had badgered him to write it and now badgered Beaverbrook to get it noticed: 'Can I count on you to give Ian's book the reviews it deserves – by this, I mean banned by the *Daily Express*, serialised in the *Sunday Express*, praised or damned alternate nights in the *Standard*! It is not so highbrow as much of the literature you read, but contains sufficient beautiful women and vintage champagne to please you. So I am hoping you will bang the drums on the sunny side of the street, as I expect a strange silence from the *Mail*. We have sent P Quennell a copy, and I propose to telephone my old protégé on April Fool's day and ask him how many paragraphs he will devote to it.'

Peter Quennell dedicated two books to Ann, Angus Wilson another. Ian once rebuked her that she kissed anyone with a classical education. John Pearson believed that Ian was keen to produce a book because he wanted to appear in Ann's eyes as their equal. But when Ann got round to reading Ian's thriller, she thought it sadistic and 'didn't care for it at all'. Like Clare Blanshard, Lisl Popper and Loelia Westminster, 'I was rather against him publishing it. He asked if I would like it dedicated to me, and I said, surely one doesn't dedicate books of this sort to people.'

'My mother was capable of violence,' says Fionn. 'I find it very shocking to not have *Casino Royale* dedicated to her. It's unbelievable to me she didn't. There she is, extolling other writers, but she seems to have had no idea what it was to sustain this. She jolly well should, and it must have been very hurtful.'

Ann loved the company of writers, yet at a crucial level she did not understand them. A letter written in his cups from Goldeneye in January 1956 revealed how vulnerable Ian was to his wife's unrealised expectations. 'My love, How different my writing looks from the others you get – from Peter & Evelyn & Hugo. That is the sort of thing one thinks about after 3 gins & tonics & 3 thousand miles of thinking about you.' In another bruised letter, he begged: 'Please be optimistic & encouraging & remember that I can only write as I can . . . My critical standards are just as high as yours. The only difference between us is that I am not ashamed of not attaining them.'

To see the blank dedication page is to stare into the glare of Ian and Ann's marriage. One of Ian's earliest biographers, Leslie Thomas, wrote that their marriage 'was happy from the first day to the last', but that sentence was for the birds and the cameras. Barbara Connolly painted a more sobering picture when she and Cyril visited the Flemings at White Cliffs in May 1953. On a previous visit, Ian had asked her aggressively, 'Had any rows lately?' This time they thrashed out the subject of happiness. 'For how long was it possible to remain in a state of happiness? Ann thought it was not possible for longer than a fortnight . . . "I thrive on tension," said Ann, "but it's so exhausting. One needs a lot of vitality" . . . Ann once stated that all she cared about was power and that she would like to be fabulously rich in order to wield as much power as possible. When she enters a roomful of people, she immediately has to squat in their midst on the floor, she likes to be the core.'

On New Year's Day, 1953, Millicent Rogers had died in New Mexico. She had kept a marble bust of Ian in Claremont Manor. Ian's reaction when he heard of her heart attack, aged fifty, did nothing to make a vulnerable new mother feel secure.

A month before *Casino Royale*'s publication, on 11 March 1953, Loelia wrote in her diary that Ann 'came to lunch & poured out her matrimonial troubles'. It was not merely that Ian was physically put off by the scars left by the two births. The Flemings had woken up like the Edens on the morning after their marriage as two different people.

Ian was a superstitious Scot. It was not a good sign when he opened two bottles of Oestricher Doosberg Riesling that Beaverbook had given as a wedding present, and, serving them to Kemsley at dinner, discovered 'by a piece of ill-fortune they were both corked'.

The Fleming marriage was also losing its taste. Their fundamental incompatibility, so piquant initially, did not blend itself to domesticity. The unsociable Ian was finding it hard adjusting to his company-craving wife. Ann said, 'the fact was that Ian hated all social life.'

A month after Caspar's birth, Ian bared his heart to Maud. 'He said they were surrounded with people. Every week-end there were 4 or 5. [Ann] said to I. she must have people to stay: it was her life. She insists on him giving up the lovely flat & she wants a house. It must not be as far as Hampstead,

Mayfair if possible, so as "to be able to have MPs to lunch: they would never come as far as Hampstead." '

Caspar became their excuse to move out of Carlyle Mansions. 'Childhood should be spent in a house, not a flat,' Ian told Harling, in one of those definitive statements that were his trademark.

Harling had heard of a period house in Victoria Square, one of the smallest squares in London, midway between Buckingham Palace and Victoria station, belonging to 'a fashion tycoon specialising in upstage corsetry'. Ian signed the lease that week and kept the house for the rest of his life.

One of the most famous debuts in literary history was published on 15 April 1953. Ian had suggested the date to Cape, six weeks before Queen Elizabeth II's coronation. 'The "Royale" in the title may help pick up extra sales over the coronation period.'

The sales were respectable for a first novel, although not remarkable. At the last minute, Cape halved the first print run to 4,750 hardback copies, selling for 10s 6d. (Today, says Jon Gilbert, the leading specialist in Ian's novels, 'a truly fine copy in a jacket would be priced around £65,000.'). By late May, Cape had sold out the first run, earning £218 19s 7d, and had reprinted 2,500. 'My profits from *Casino* will just about keep Anne in asparagus over Coronation week,' Ian grumbled to Jonathan Cape. The publisher George Weidenfeld told Mary Pakenham's undergraduate nephew Thomas, 'My dear Thomas, you and I know about the book, but no one outside London has heard of it. It's what we call in the trade "a West End sale".' In America, three leading publishers, Doubleday, Norton and Knopf, turned it down.

The reviews were positive, as they should have been, considering Ian's manipulations. The *Observer* hit the spot that Ian was aiming at, calling him 'Peter Cheyney de luxe'. John Betjeman pleased him the most. 'Ian Fleming has discovered the secret of narrative art. The reader *has* to go on reading.' Ian was responsible for the heaviest log roll. Kemsley had asked who he would like to review it in the *Sunday Times*. Ian selected and then briefed Cyril Ray, whom he had managed to send to Moscow as the Mercury correspondent. Under the pseudonym Christopher Pym, Ray suggested that Ian was on the road to becoming 'the best new thriller writer since Ambler'.

Ian took 'these astonishingly handsome reviews' to his wary publisher. He used them both to argue that Cape should spend £200 on advertising 'if I am to progress into the Cheyney class, which is presumably our ambition', and to improve royalty terms on his next contract. 'Since you are the best publisher in England and I am said to be the best thriller writer since Eric Ambler, I feel it would be very unadventurous if we did not agree to set our sights high! We certainly seem to have got off to a good start – I seem to have hit on a formula which attracts the critics, and you have produced a handsome book and have marketed it superbly. There is a vacuum to be filled and I really do not see why we should not fill it. I shall be giving my next to William Plomer next Tuesday, and I have the plot for a third in my head.'

On 15 May, a wincing Jonathan Cape was persuaded to offer Ian a three-book deal. His editors had read Ian's second James Bond adventure, which Ian had researched with Ivar Bryce and Ernie Cuneo in Brooklyn. Ian had followed the advice of Michael Arlen: write your second book before you see the reviews of the first. On getting to the end of *Live and Let Die*, Plomer had at once written to Ian, 'the new book held this reader like a limpet mine & the denouement was shattering . . . if I'm any judge, this is *just the stuff* – sexy, violent, ingenious – most ingenious – & full of well-collected details of all kinds.' Ian lost no opportunity to rub it in to Cape that 'Daniel George and William think it better than the first.'

XLVIII
THE BOND FORMULA

'What I endeavour to aim at is a certain disciplined exoticism.'

IAN FLEMING

When Captain Robert Ryder VC, MP, told Ian in November 1953 that he had written a novel based on 30AU, Ian congratulated him. 'You must write one every year, and then suddenly you will find that you have hit the jackpot.' It took Ian longer than is generally supposed to hit the jackpot. None of his first five novels sold more than 12,000 copies in hardback. Ian was close to killing off Bond when Bond took off. That was not until 1957.

The Bond novels that followed *Casino Royale* owed their existence to the way Ian's life and career as a writer interlocked. They depended on a tightly patterned routine that was as formulaic as his plots.

He flew to Jamaica every January. (Ann hated flying.) For their son's first four years, Caspar stayed behind in Kent or London with Nanny Sillick, described by Ann's niece Sara as 'a bosomy spinster with short grey hair, very plain, who cooked an utterly disgusting stuffed marrow'.

To keep her company while he wrote, Ann invited friends like Lucian Freud and Peter Quennell to Goldeneye, where Ian was more likely to grit his teeth and grab his flippers than spend time entertaining them. Quennell pictured the scene. 'Palms wave – waves ripple – tarantulas crawl – barracudas undulate... The Commander groans quietly under the horror of his unwanted guests.' No guest was less welcome than Lucian Freud. 'The first night I was sitting on a chair reading, about eight-thirty, nine, and Ian said, "One goes to bed rather early in this part of the world and gets up at four," and left the room and turned the light out with me reading. I got up and put it on, and he looked at my book, "Kafka's diaries: no wonder you're in such a state."'

On coming ashore from his early-morning swim, Ian retreated to his room to hammer out his latest story behind closed shutters. Here in his 'hurricane room', he typed his manuscript from early morning to noon, and secured it in a 'pinch-in' folder. 'If it got lost, it was gone for good: he said he'd just write another book,' recalled Clare Blanshard. 'The whole thing was completely uninhibited writing, and he wouldn't have read the whole thing through until he reached New York.'

Invariably, the first person to read his typescript was Blanshard, in New York, on Ian's way back from Jamaica. 'Ian must have had lots of other Readers (official). But geographically, I was the first.'

Blanshard, this tall, 'slightly angular' Catholic spinster appointed by Ian to run the Kemsley News Service in America, referred to herself as 'the keeper of Ian's conscience'. After Ian gave her his manuscript, 'I'd go to mass at St Patrick, as I usually did in the morning on the way into the office, with this terrible document under my arm.' She never feared to tell Ian that his books made him appear like a pervert and a sadist. 'The only explanation I have is that he wrote uninhibitedly and that the forces of evil, whatever you call them – I'm a Catholic so I call them that. Perhaps you would prefer the spirit of the age – came through them as water comes through a tap.'

Blanshard wrote an account of their editing process. 'I read it (them) at one sitting, marking passages. Next day, we would go through the lot, I, at his urging, excruciatingly blunt (after all he hadn't read them, it was sort of psychiatrist couch stuff) & from this we derived even more entertainment.'

She had made her pencil marks on the blank back of the preceding page. Ian took notes on another sheet. 'Sometimes he altered then & there, sometimes he or I cut, whichever of us had momentary possession.' She compared their editing to 'two dogs with one bone'. 'His innocence was unbelievable. At one stage of our mutual blue-pencilling, Bond plus girl were either down a gun barrel or within a torpedo tube . . . & I said "No, No, you really cannot write this next bit." Querulously, he said, "Why not – Graham Greene does!" We then had a mini-tutorial on English Literature.'

Ian placed Greene on the same high pedestal as Waugh and Ambler, reading everything by him. He rented Goldeneye to Greene, praised him in reviews, cited him as a friend who had recommended Viking when Ian wanted to move US publisher, and was elated when he believed (mistakenly) that Greene had agreed to write an introduction to an American omnibus of Bond. In 1958, Ian swallowed a newspaper report that Greene had dedicated *Our Man in Havana* to him, writing hungrily to Michael Howard at Cape: 'Would you please check and send me the wording?' There was an element here of Ian's hero worship for Peter. But as ever, a contradictory impulse was at work. Blanshard agreed with Ian's American agent that Ian was 'afraid to write anything that would be considered of higher literary value, mainly because of the social circles he & his wife travelled in. In other words, he was afraid they would laugh at him, and he wrote James Bond just so he could be able to laugh with them.'

Blanshard was a self-confessed non-writer. Nonetheless, Ian valued her candid response. She wrote, 'I didn't care to do more than voice my reactions, but he would cry, "Cut it, cut it," & so we would blue pencil with the greatest ease. He had no "side". I once asked him if anyone else reacted, felt as I did – & cared sufficiently to let him know – and he said yes (and that would be Lisl Popper). Those of us who knew him knew him "individually".'

If Ian required additional information, he cabled her from London. She said, 'I did all the research on barracuda teeth in NYC Library. Very interesting. They're set into the roof of the mouth like tiles on a roof, only upstanding like toast in a rack. The fish then GRIND their victims ROUND & ROUND. Ian loved that.' As well, she gave him plot ideas. 'I told him about the small boy who was covered with gold and died. He filed that away and used it in *Goldfinger*.'

In March, Ian returned to Kemsley House with a corrected manuscript that Una Trueblood typed out. He sent this to William Plomer 'to give it a piercing glance'. Ian wrote to him: 'From you, I need no placebos. Only the true verdict will do.'

Plomer made his criticisms in green ink; altering Manet to Monet for the artist that Ian had painting beach scenes in Brittany; asking 'why write "we repaired" when you mean "we went"'; initialling 'LGF' (for Low Grade Fiction) beside Ian's more clichéd expressions. 'M speaks "drily" too often. I think you should be careful about letting your characters grunt, bark, and snarl too freely.'

Other readers were Daniel George and Michael Howard, who, together with Howard's father Wren, the co-chairman, and Cape's son David, formed the Capians or Bedfordians, 'the equivalent of a small boot factory'. Ian received extra input from New York – from Al Hart of Macmillan, Tom Guinzberg of Viking, Truman Talley and E. L. Doctorow of the New

American Library ('Fleming is constitutionally unable to write a dull sentence'), and Naomi Burton at Curtis Brown.

The novels appeared every spring. Ian promoted them even as he corrected his new manuscript. Over the summer, he researched the background for his next book, reading at the British Museum, contacting experts, and travelling on the back of his *Sunday Times* job to gather material in Marseille, the Pyrenees, Vienna, Germany, Turkey, the Seychelles, the Caribbean, America. At certain moments, he had to juggle three Bond books: the one he had proof-corrected, the one he had just written and was rewriting, and the one he was preparing to write in Jamaica.

'What's that humourless bore James Bond going to do this year!' Duff Dunbar once asked, before Ian flew to Goldeneye in January to type out his latest 'opusculum'. Ian's reply: 'What is the continued point of chopping down the tree when the fruit is consistently good.'

Ian promised his first American publisher Al Hart that he would write the 'same book over and over again'. Like Ian's games of bridge at the Portland or his golf rounds at Sandwich or the unvarying habit of his clothes and food, the Bond stories relied for their satisfaction and effect – what Umberto Eco called 'a clever montage of *déjà vu*' – on sticking to the same rules.

His characters and components are present in that first novel: Bond, 'M', Moneypenny, Leiter, the villain and the girl and the fast car that he whips through the night; the gambling, the tobacco, the sun-saturated foreign location that advertised the life he was living in Jamaica for the two months he was writing. When Lord Beaverbrook thanked Ian for 'the thrilling story about the good secret service bloke and the bad bastard', it could have been for any book in the series. Judge William Mars-Jones, who presided over the *Thunderball* plagiarism trial, described Bond to the High Court as well as anyone. 'He is a tough, hard-drinking, amoral man, who saves the citizens of this country, and indeed the whole free world, from the most incredible disasters.' His nationality was indispensable. 'Bond must be an Englishman,' Ian insisted to Ivar Bryce when discussing which actor might play the part.

Bond stands in a line of buccaneering but patriotic Englishmen: Drake, Raleigh, Morgan, Nelson, Hannay, Drummond, who 'killed their men on behalf of Government or governmental authority'. As Richard Usborne saw it in *Clubland Heroes*, his classic survey of British fictional heroes between the wars, 'They gave us our blood-letting, and we enjoyed it vicariously. We liked to identify ourselves with such brave power and such straight shooting: we who could not fight our way out of a paper bag.'

Even though Bond shifts from fighting the Cold War and its associated villains to fighting international crooks and megalomaniacs, his job description never changes. As suggested in *Diamonds are Forever* and *You Only Live Twice*, Bond's role is to protect 'the security of the British Empire' and restore 'the moral fibre of the British, a quality the world so much admired'. He achieves this on his own. 'It is one of the most exciting of all human adventure stories,' Ian wrote about the (real-life) downed American U-2 pilot Gary Powers after his capture by the Russians, 'the single man, in the darkness, facing death alone for the sake of the great mass of his own countrymen'. When Goldfinger threatens the natural order, 'there was only one man in the whole world who could stop it. But how?'

Ian's English teacher George Lyttelton once analysed the Bond formula. 'IF's recipe is cards, wines and dishes (as costly as possible), torture, a seasoning of breasts and thighs, and a series of ludicrous strokes of luck and escapes by that very unattractive Bond from impasses in which the chief, who may have eyes of chilled steel and jaw of ditto, but certainly has a brain of cotton wool, is always landing him.' Bond did not appeal to Lyttelton. 'But I cannot help reading on and there are rich satisfactions eg when Mr Big is crunched by a shark. Very good about food; he always gets details what any meal consists of. The young women are rather oppressively and monotonously bedworthy, but then, of course, he isn't writing for septuagenarians.'

Peter Pan with a gun. Biggles with a cock. 'D'Artagnan and Don Juan combined in a single individual, believably and recognisably modernised' (Richard Maibaum). A twentieth-century St George or Pilgrim. Every reader had their take.

One thing Bond was not was an intellectual. He took his cue from Sapper's Ronald Standish.

> *'But don't you think . . .?' began Marsford.*
> *'I think nothing,' snapped Standish.*

For John Pearson, the Bond stories owed much to the *Odyssey*. 'A lot of Ian is a bit like Ulysses. Ulysses was very tough on women. He shot all the hand-maids of the suitors when he came back to claim his inheritance.' The difference in Bond's case – his bachelordom is what is inviolable. Each tale throws up a new candidate for his hand, to be tested in bed.

A man of cultivated and urbane tastes like his creator, Bond's tongue only leaves his cheek to kiss a girl hard on the lips, long and cruelly. 'He is the first hero in fiction to combine clean living with pretty dirty nights,' wrote Stephen Potter in 'Bondsmanship'. 'He shows that he can make love with all the sophisticated discrimination, the tender awareness of feminine reserve, which we associate with a bull rhino in rut.'

But there is more to Bond than old-style chauvinism. A recurring theme, in the books as in the life, is how Bond is drawn to complicated, messed-up women, ones he can rescue. 'He had come from nowhere, like the prince in the fairy tale, and saved me from the dragon,' as Vivienne puts it in *The Spy Who Loved Me*. The strongest heroines in the novels – something which the movies airbrush out – are in some way damaged or orphaned. Honeychile Ryder with her broken nose, Tiffany Case, who has been gang-raped. Tracy, who has lost a child. Less often commented on, these women are almost always tough and independent. It as if Bond/Fleming is forced to raise his game, emotionally and as a communicator, and relishes the challenge. He is bored with the 'normal' sexual game, as described in *Casino Royale*: 'The conventional parabola – sentiment, touch of the hand, the kiss, the passionate kiss, the feel of the body, the climax in the bed, then more bed, then less bed, then the boredom, the tears and the final bitterness – was to him shameful and hypocritical.'

Bond also touched an exposed nerve that had nothing to do with sex. Each new Bond book excited something in others, often something they did not expect. With V. S. Naipaul, it was the facts of Ian's success. 'I recognise in myself something of Fleming's own romantic attitude to the very successful and very rich.'

Ian's success and wealth derived from sharing his secret fantasies and tastes. It amused him to show anonymous readers like Naipaul, consuming *Diamonds are Forever* in a small flat in Kilburn, 'what pleases and stimulates *me* . . . what my favourite objects are, and my favourite foods and liquors and scents and so on.'

Detail was all, and the illusion of technical accuracy. Part of Ian's technique to anchor Naipaul in what seemed an unbelievable story was to choose something within Naipaul's easy grasp – a steering wheel – and describe it with such gusto that Naipaul identified with the character who steered a Bentley or luxurious motor launch.

'Detail fascinated him,' observed Ernie Cuneo. 'If he ran across a trick of the trade, a nuance, a fillip, he would pursue it like a ferret, for example how cowboys on the range made a barbecue sauce with sugar, ketchup and Worcestershire sauce . . . The temperature and appearance of the fire, kind of wood burned, the size of the pan – all of these things he'd scribble down with the avidity of an explorer taking notes on the opening of Tutankhamun's tomb.'

In the same journalistic spirit, Ian mugged up on Bond's new car, 'a cross between a Continental Bentley and a Ford Thunderbird', writing to Whitney Straight, deputy chairman of Rolls-Royce and married to Ian's old girlfriend Daphne Finch-Hatton: 'I wonder if someone could dig out brief specifications covering type and thickness of armour-plating and glass, extra strength of springs to carry the body, stronger breaks, and so on.'

Ian's stepson inherited his love of fast cars and was a frequent passenger in his Riley 2.5-litre saloon and Ford Thunderbird. Raymond says, 'I don't think he knew very much about the mechanics.' But then neither did Ian know much about guns or diamonds or gold or the criminal underground in Harlem. Or even about wine. 'He was monumentally ignorant about wines,' said Cuneo. What Ian did know, John Pearson discovered, was 'who to go to and how to use what they provided him with. The same with almost all the expertise'. It was as though Ian were re-enacting Admiral Godfrey's memoranda on wartime 'intelligence, security and other matters': '*the true basis is research, and the best results are usually obtained from the continuous study of insignificant details, which though singly of little value, are collectively of great importance.*'

Except that in Naipaul's case, the technique did not work: 'I clearly missed the point.' What compelled Naipaul was 'the triviality of the life', as he saw it, the story of success through fantasy that was 'as grotesque as any cautionary tale', and not the triviality of the books. For Ian's books, Naipaul had no time at all.

Even so, the carefully chosen small details and exact names, what Larkin called Fleming's 'adroit blend of realism and extravagance', seduced and reassured plenty.

Take Bond's levée: Bond picks his teeth with a Steradent toothpick, brushes them with Maclean's toothpaste, splashes Floris into his bathtub, washes his hair with Pinaud Elixir, 'that prince among shampoos', and shaves with a Hoffritz safety razor ('Felix Leiter bought him one in New York to prove they were the best'). He has Cooper's Vintage Oxford marmalade for breakfast, Norwegian heather honey from Fortnum's, coffee poured from a Queen Anne pot, a dark brown egg from a Maran hen boiled for three minutes and fifty-five seconds by his stop-watch (according to *Bond Strikes Camp*) and eaten from a Minton china dark blue and gold eggcup. And that is before he opens the front door of his regency first-floor flat in his plane-tree-filled small square in Chelsea (Wellington Square, according to William Boyd), and eases into his 4.5-litre Bentley with an Amherst Villiers super-charger ('please note the solid exactitude'), to face his day.

Once out in the world, Bond brings the specific knowledge of his bathroom cabinet to Intelligence. When he goes into 'M''s office, he steps across the carpet exuding the crackle of an indoctrinated insider. Further, he knows a few savvy secrets in other departments. Each book is an education in something. Gold, diamonds, jet engines, canasta, sharks, bridge, guano, karate, golf. This knowingness is central to his allure. 'I know the place . . .' he nods, at the mention of 'Old Russia' on Fifth Avenue. It is the nod of Buchan's hero Sandy Arbuthnot when whistling at the botanical ignorance of his villain. 'Not very clever,' says Sandy. '*Ustulata* is impossible on this soil.'

A gourmet for brands and esoteric details, Bond flatters and impresses the reader with abstruse nose-tapping knowledge, not merely about the Latin name for the scorpion fish and that poisonous fish's relation to *rascasse*, the foundation of *bouillabaisse*, but about sex, foreign countries, clothing, drink. When Ian ordered a martini, observed Cuneo, 'he explained each step to the guy who was going to mix it as if it was a delicate brain operation'.

This is how Bond plays with our minds, writes Sam Leith in his 2012 introduction to *Octopussy*. 'Bond is a connoisseur. Sophistication is knowledge, knowledge is power, and Bond is a spy: knowing things is his business. That defines his way of being in the world.'

If Bond recommends 'the Edwardian Room at the Plaza, a corner table', the reader may rest confident that Bond has sat there and for a pleasurable instant is able to imagine sitting in the same seat. Via Bond, Ian's readers gain entry to a club that feels exclusive, of which they can be temporary members. A Blades open to all.

'For the rest,' wrote Umberto Eco, 'so far as the unlikely is concerned, a few pages and an implicit wink of the eye suffice. No one has to believe them.'

Ian's fantasies coincided with the fantasies of millions. More than that, they built on the collective visceral fear that kept his readers awake. Ian's vision of a vulpine Russia feasting on the bones of Europe had proved prophetic. The Soviet tanks that he had heard revving in May 1945 were the vanguard of forces massing now in Korea, Cuba, America even. The 'smashing success of Russia's sputniks' had showed up America's 'scientific know how' and revived the terrifying spectre of V-1 and V-2 rockets that had caused him sleepness nights in wartime London. On 1 January 1953, Ian cabled Clare Blanshard in New York about the 'atom spies' Julius and Ethel Rosenberg, sentenced to death for betraying nuclear secrets to the Russians – 'IF POSSIBLE GET INTERVIEW WITH THEM'.

Ian was writing his Bond books when the threat of a nuclear-armed Soviet Union was as potent as Russia's invasion of Ukraine has made it seem again today, in 2023. 'The great nightmare of the Cold War,' writes the *Times* correspondent Roger Boyes, anticipating Putin's next move, 'was that giant Russian tank armies would not only crush their immediate neighbours but also sweep across the north German plains, hug western cities like Hamburg and hold them hostage.' Umberto Eco emphasised how the dragon that Bond is sent out to fight singlehandedly by his omniscient chief 'M' 'usually works to help Russia'.* Ian wrote about these enemies of Bond with particular exactitude, as if the double agents whom Ian had kept permanently in his cross hairs, Sorge, Maclean, Burgess, were also his villains' handlers.

After 1939, Ian never returned to Russia. His request to join the British Military Mission in September 1941, as Naval representative at the First Moscow Protocol, was vetoed, to his 'great disappointment'. The closest Ian came was in October 1959. 'I spent last weekend fratting with the Russians

---

* The one exception: Jack and Serrafimo Spang in *Diamonds are Forever*.

in East Berlin,' he wrote to Stephenson. 'They all seemed very chilled in their cheap, thin blue trousers and how very small they all are. Still, even pygmies can fire a sub machine gun.'

Ian had brought his secret world to the surface after a long period of hesitation, only to discover that it corresponded to the fantasies and fears of many others, and they wanted more.

So back again he dived, over the reefs, corals and denizens of his previous life.

In *Casino Royale*, Ian had had a free pass. Bond may have begun as bland and featureless, like the scrambled eggs that were his and Ian's favourite dish. But then one of Cape's readers pointed out that Bond would become a security risk if he ate scrambled eggs all the time, since his movements from restaurant to restaurant would easily be traced. 'So I had to give him a more varied diet. This was another step away from the anonymous character I had planned.'

As the appetite grew for his adventures, Bond needed fresh details. Ian had no other source for information about his hero but his own life. In order to make Bond less of a cardboard booby he would have to scrape additional bits of Ian Fleming into his creation.

This posed a challenge. The more popular Bond became, the more attention was riveted on his personal details – and on Ian's inevitable errors, given the speed at which he wrote the books. How he made the sun rise on the wrong side of Jamaica (Morris Cargill), muddled up the Bosphorus and the Golden Horn (Eric Ambler), served Pol Roger in half bottles (Patrick Leigh Fermor), had Goldfinger not know 'that Piesporter Goldtropfchen is a Mosel and not a Hock' (Anthony Berry), gave the porter at the Royal College of Arms brass buttons instead of silver, and the Steradent that Bond picks his teeth with should have been Inter-dens (Tom Driberg: 'Steradent is something for washing false teeth in').

Any inconsistency resulted in 'a sheaf of acid complaints'. A reader from Toronto wanted to know why the light above 'M''s door was blue in *Casino Royale*, green in *Live and Let Die*, and red in *From Russia, with Love*, and why 'M''s office was on the eighth floor and then on the ninth.

'People picked holes in Bond quicker than he shot them in opponents,' wrote Leslie Thomas. Nothing wounded Ian more than a query about Bond's authenticity, as if this was an assault on the author. He defended himself to one reader: 'I pride myself on being a stickler on all matters of factual detail.'

To save himself from howlers, like stalking stags out of season, Ian sent his manuscripts to Peter. Lucy Fleming remembers the packages arriving in the breakfast post, wrapped in brown paper with a string. ' "Oh look, here's Ian's book," and my father would take it straight upstairs to read.'

Peter appointed himself 'Dr Knittpik'. 'He got a number of his facts wrong. Talks at one point about Bond hiding in the new corn in May. Of course, the corn wouldn't hide a rabbit in May, let alone Bond.'

For someone who cared about accuracy, it is surprising how often he slipped up. Noël Coward slapped Ian's wrist for getting his time-differences wrong between Jamaica and England. 'This kind of carelessness makes my eyes steel slits of blue.' On another occasion, Coward had to correct Bond's play in chemin de fer. 'I hate to have to point out these little errors to you, but you are getting a big boy now and in writing about the gaudy pleasures of the Upper Set, which I have adorned so triumphantly for more years than you, you must *try* to get things straight.'

Notoriously, Ian put hydraulic instead of vacuum brakes on the Orient Express, and the wrong perfume on a woman, Vent Vert by Dior rather than Balmain. 'I suppose until I go to my grave sharp-eyed sweet-scented women will continue to rap my bruised knuckles for this mistake and I can only say that I rather enjoy the process!'

He felt a responsibility towards his readers, who corresponded to him from as far away as Bulawayo and New South Wales, and he took special care to address their complaints.

Ian wrote a penitent apology to Mr R. L. Sjostrom in Florida. 'I am afraid you will find that I make mistakes in all my books and I can only plead that Shakespeare was equally remiss' – he had clocks chiming in ancient Rome, for instance – 'and that Jane Austen once had cherry trees flowering in September!'

Jane Austen was not an obvious reference point for James Bond to readers in Ann's circle.

XLIX
'BLOODY INTELLECTUALS'

'The higher one moves in the social scale the more
malicious people become.'
'CHIPS' CHANNON

Integral to the Fleming myth is the story of the stand-off between Ian and his wife's friends. One evening, Ian returns from wherever he has gone to avoid one of Ann's 'gabfests'. He climbs the stairs past the drawing room on the first floor and hears Colin Tennant – or Cyril Connolly, or perhaps another of his wife's 'boobies' or 'fuddy-duddies', as Evelyn Waugh described Ann's circle – read aloud a steamy passage from *Casino Royale* to hysterical mirth. In this story, for which there is no satisfactory source, his audience falls silent when they realise that Ian is standing there.

'Ian said he wrote his first novel to escape from marriage,' says Raymond. 'There is some tincture of truth in that. After they were married, they increasingly led separate lives, and she had her group of intellectuals which he didn't like very much. He was playing bridge at Boodle's, and he'd come back and try and get up the back stairs without being seen.'

Ian was as allergic to his wife's salon as she was to his Bond. It was one reason he travelled. His visit with Ernie Cuneo to Las Vegas in the autumn of 1954 was, said Ian, 'a happy escape from Victoria Square which is frequently being festooned with effeminate intellectuals'. In one of their bitterer spats, he chastised Ann: 'the way to stay married is to compromise and this is a word that just hasn't come in to any of your letters any more than it has into your London life not one fraction of which has ever been designed for my pleasure.' Thomas Pakenham was still at Oxford when Fionn invited him to Victoria Square. 'I have an abiding memory of feeling sorry for Ian, aged twenty. They were very far apart in some ways. Ann was very dominant, a totally different character. She may have liked being whipped, but she was far from being submissive. She treated him like a rather irritating younger brother, and I felt a strong feeling of solidarity with Ian – she was squashing him. I felt he was a man who had failed.'

Ann explained her position to her brother. 'I naturally turn towards happiness and am able to escape from gloom through people.' She wrote to Waugh when Ian was away in October 1954, 'Ian's in America visiting Alcatraz, Nevada, Las Vegas and Los Angeles to collect material for a new plot, so I had his least favourite people to stay – Pope-Hennessy, Quennell and the Freuds.'

Of Ann's friends, Ian was most scathing about the artist Lucian Freud, who reciprocated ('he was a cunt,' Freud said of Ian, 'ghastly, phoney, depressing, snobbish'). Even so, the *Listener*'s art critic could not refrain from pointing out their essential similarity, describing Freud as 'a kind of Sunday Fleming who gripped the world in bright fragments'. Ann had joked to her brother Hugo on the eve of their marriage, 'Ian sends his love and says to tell you he is marrying me so as to have dinner with Lucian Freud every night!' Yet this is what happened. On 24 August 1954, Ian was compelled to sit down to lunch at Victoria Square with Freud ('smoked trout, horseradish sauce/liver, bacon, onions, spinach, pommes puree, sweet corn/petit Suisse'), and the very next evening to a dinner party with Freud at the same table ('game soup/boiled beef, boiled bacon, vegetables/crème brulée'). Once, at Warwick House, Freud had absent-mindedly munched 'a bouquet of expensive purple orchids'.

Ian's wife had come from one of the largest private homes in London, where she hosted parties for 400 and had a uniformed staff, to a small regency house which could fit eight around the dining table in comfort, and twelve at a squeeze. The after-dinner gatherings upstairs were so crowded that Raymond Carr was once pushed onto Princess Margaret's lap.

At 16 Victoria Square, the only permanent staff were the cook and housekeeper, Mary Crickmere, a dark Welsh woman, and her husband Edgar, who flitted between valet, driver and waiter. Ann continued to be a lion-hunter within this confined space, said John Hayward, her former downstairs neighbour at 24 Carlyle Mansions. 'I remember the cook at Victoria Square telling me one day that during that year they had already had 180 luncheon parties and 210 dinners.'

Ann left the menus up to Mrs Crickmere, who served her signature coconut soup to the nation's leading cultural and political figures. Artists were put beside poets, foreign ministers beside leaders of the opposition. So many of Ann's guests came from House of Commons sittings that Ian suggested they install a division bell. Political preferences did not enter into it. What sparked Ann was argument across the spectrum.

'The noise in there!' said Mrs Crickmere. 'They all talked, nobody listened . . . but she was a good listener.'

Ann sat there, taking it all in, with what Robert Harling called her flash-point eyes and imperious air, addressing those she had corralled around her table with the voice of the chestnut-bellied cuckoo at Goldeneye – a 'mixture of chuckle & squawk', Ian described it.

Susanna Johnston, the daughter of Christopher Chancellor, and her architect husband Nicholas were among a carefully chosen group whom Ann later entertained in both town and country. 'I don't think Ann minded what people were like, and didn't mind if she didn't like them. She definitely liked people to be put into awkward situations. It enlivened things up. She had rather big nostrils. Once we drove her to London and she said, "I can't wait for some new blood."'

Nothing gave Ann more pleasure than to be in at the kill. She had once written in ecstasy to Duff Cooper about her eccentric father: 'I am covered with blood and fleas from a nature amble with Papa. He shot all birds and beasts, tore out their intestines for the dogs and flung the bleeding carcases for me to carry.' She aimed for this effect in her dinner parties.

The influential *Washington Post* columnist, Joe Alsop, shuddered to recall the evening when 'Annie Fleming gave a dinner for me, which I suspect was an intended tease – I know Nancy Mitford was expected, and if she had come, sheer physical revulsion would have come close to forcing me to leave at once.' Another time, Alsop found himself sitting opposite the Chancellor of the Exchequer. 'We started on sex with the first course and never left the subject for more than about five minutes. Furthermore, I heard things . . . that made even my limp, thinning and normally non-erectile hair stand straight up on end.'

Ann's friends united in agreement with Cecil Beaton that 'her parties are more amusing than they were at Warwick House'. In September 1953, Beaton attended a fiftieth-birthday celebration that she had thrown for Cyril Connolly. 'Ann was enjoying the success of the party so much that she wanted her beloved husband Ian to savour every nuance of it. She was disappointed that, at two in the morning, he had disappeared to bed.'

What had worried her, Ann wrote to Leigh Fermor, was Ian's 'sitting beside Mary Campbell who bores him, with the result that I became intoxicated'.

Margaret Anne Stuart once sat beside Ian. She says, 'I was wagging my tail like a dachshund. I turned round and tried to talk and he said, "My wife loves these parties, because she gets to sit next to statesmen and academics" – Ann was sitting next to George Brown – "and I get to sit next to their boring wives and girlfriends." Not terribly polite.'

John Hayward found it 'most strange to see Ian at the head of the table – good-looking Ian, among all these intellectual friends of his wife's and not a word to say to any of them. At these dinners, Ian would sit, amiable, smiling, but very bored.' It was Bond's boredom in *You Only Live Twice*. 'The geisha party had been going on for two hours and Bond's jaws aching with the unending smiles and polite repartee.'

Ian had to listen to his *bête noire* Lucian Freud talking about David Cecil 'masturbating his second and third finger with his thumb'. To Evelyn Waugh lecturing him on God, 'First of all, he's not a man.' Sometimes he could not restrain himself. Ian told a table of Ann's 'harem', as he called them, that the craftsmen responsible for his brass pictures on the wall would provide better company 'than all you lot'.

It was as if Ann had recreated Eve's salon, that Ian hated so much, and he was Augustus John who had to fortify himself with a drink. 'Annie is always surrounding herself with bloody intellectuals,' Ian told Morris Cargill, 'and intellectuals always make me feel inferior. I always felt inferior with my brother because he was an intellectual, and I simply detest having to relive the same pattern with my wife.' He would rather, he said, watch two half-naked German women wrestle in the mud in a Hamburg strip joint that he once visited (where the drummer in the jazz band reminded him of 'a young

& equally indignant Evelyn Waugh') than listen to the conversation of Ann's dinner guests. 'I can't stand her parties. Less still the sight of that melon-faced Connolly holding forth.'

Malcolm Muggeridge found it more congenial to leave the 'dismal conversational free-for-all which surged endlessly around Annie' and join Ian upstairs in 'a sort of private apartment at the top of the house where he kept his golf clubs, pipes, and other masculine bric-a-brac. We would sit up there together sipping a highball, like climbers taking a breather above a mountain torrent whose roar could still faintly be heard in the ravine below.'

In a scene witnessed by Caspar and never forgotten, Ann was holding court below, and Ian was upstairs in his bedroom with his blanket over his head.

Whoever it was Ian had overheard reading aloud one of his passages to mocking laughter, it touched a sore spot. Admiral Godfrey once ragged him about his books. 'He suddenly became very angry and said "John, you're denigrating my work."'

More and more, he chose to be out when Ann entertained.

'We had dinner with Ann Fleming.' Rescued in Greece by Rodney Bond, Clarissa Caccia had grown up to marry Alan Pryce-Jones's son David. 'Ian came home and walked straight past the drawing room and up to bed. David and I were in our twenties. We eyed each other. It left a weird feeling. You felt you were being put in same bag as Ann. She said, "There goes Mr Bond."'

L
THE FAST CAR LIFE

'In the books, of course, Ian becomes a little boy.'
WILLIAM STEPHENSON

Ian's fantasy life had to expand if he was to continue plopping onto Plomer's desk his 'great annual cowpat'. Bond incentivised him to go out and observe the world through a new pair of eyes. 'As they happily embarked on their joint adventures,' said John Pearson, 'he could escape from Ann, from the mockery of her writer friends, as he lived out those plots of the early books.'

In the *Sunday Times* office, Pearson bore witness to Ian's transformation. 'Suddenly, he was no longer jaded; he was no longer bored. Everything was exciting again for him as it had been when he was a small boy looking at things.'

Ian's notebooks show how impatiently he eased into Bond's skin. Within moments of stepping onto a plane for Athens, he was liberated into his other persona. 'The darkness outside looked terribly dark – the stars & the moon invisible through his own reflection in the Perspex . . . 34,000 ft. Minus 50 Celsius. Why should anyone wish to know? It all amounted to hysteria, the hysteria of speed – of wanting to be there first, quickest. Well. Wasn't that what he, B, wanted to do?'

Bond represented for Ian and his readers a model of independence, unconstrained by marriage and family and Connolly's 'pram in the hall'. Ian took off from London a hen-pecked husband, father, and office-bound Foreign Manager of the *Sunday Times*. He landed in Athens on a deadly mission. 'B thought, I could break this airport easily – transit to Hong Kong, for instance – they take your passports but not looking – give them a cover & keep your own & then go out & into the town & set up the d[eal], arms, women, smuggling.' Ian's escape route – 'his custom-made drug', Raymond Benson called it – would become a conduit for millions like him.

The purchase of 'an expensive sports car' was an example of Ian's approach. He justified the Ford Thunderbird in a draft letter to his accountant. Ian needed 'this sort of car' to write credibly about his subject matter. His books were 'Secret Service Thrillers in which the hero and other characters make frequent use of fast cars and live in what might be described as "the fast car life".' In regard to 'all Mr Fleming's literary work', Ian went on, 'accurate reportage of things seen and experienced is the quintessence of their success.'

Ann attested to how travel revived him. 'I think Ian was happiest when he, me, and the Thunderbird flew from Lydd to Le Touquet. After the customs officer released the machine, he would park it outside the airport restaurant, and we would eat omelette 'très baveuse' (he always insisted on *très baveuse*) and plan our journey south. We were usually in a hurry.'

The Thunderbird had replaced Ian's 2.5-litre black Riley. It was always a great moment when the car was through customs, and he was free to go, 'the kilometres clicking by like the leaves of a book', in Pearson's image. Ian had never forgotten Gilbert Russell's description of his concept of heaven, outlined at a dinner at Mottisfont: 'Heaven is a place where I shall be forever driving in an open Rolls Royce along a beautiful highway lined with cheering crowds.'

Ian was ruthless in using the *Sunday Times* to subsidise his foreign trips. The assignments he gave himself provided background material for his novels and two books of non-fiction, *The Diamond Smugglers* and *Thrilling Cities*. For the latter, the *Sunday Times* bought him a round-the-world ticket for £803 19s 2d to fly to what he considered 'the most enthralling places on earth'.

Like the travel writer Bruce Chatwin, whose contradictions and restlessness he shared, Ian needed to visit somewhere before he dared to describe it. 'I never write about places I have not seen,' he declared in his blurb for *Live and Let Die*: 'all the settings are based on personal experience.'

In April 1953, he had missed the launch of *Casino Royale* to spend a fortnight scuba-diving in Marseille, the first of Ian's three underwater excursions with Jacques Cousteau. In August, he went pot-holing in the cave of La

Pierre Saint Martin in the Pyrenees. In 1956, he drove Ann on a continental trip through Germany to the Interpol conference in Vienna. He pressed Antony Terry to find an excuse for him to come to Berlin. 'Please see what you can suggest, and we will go off and have a bit of adventure together.' In the meantime, 'I have adventures more or less mapped out – a real treasure hunt in the Seychelles, the great Cave of Niah in North Borneo, gold-smuggling in Macao and so forth.'

'You must realise,' Ann told John Pearson, 'Ian was entirely egocentric. His aim as long as I knew him was to avoid the dull, the humdrum, the everyday demands of life that afflict ordinary people. He stood for working out a way of life that was not boring, and he went where this led him. It ended with Bond, very frightening.'

In May 1958, Ian sailed from Bombay to the Seychelles to look for booty supposedly buried on one of the islands by the French privateer Levasseur. A telegram that arrived for him at Government House from Alan Lennox-Boyd, Colonial Secretary at the Foreign Office, showed how Ian and his creation had merged: '*To*: James Bond Agent. With compliments.'

As his marriage disintegrated, Ian travelled further and further afield: Tangier, Turkey, Kuwait, until he was globetrotting to the Far East in a reca-pitulation of his 1944–5 world tour.

On top of that, from 1954 onwards, Ian spent part of each August with Ivar Bryce and Ernie Cuneo, his two chief guides in the US and Ann's least favourite of his friends, at Black Hole Hollow Farm in Vermont.

Thirty miles from Saratoga Springs, Jo Bryce's 3,000-acre stud farm was less than a mile from Cuneo's country place. Cuneo had grown to be a very close friend of the Bryces as well as their lawyer and neighbour. His son Jonathan says, 'My parents never thought of not going to Black Hole Hollow for din-ner, and they would leave me at home alone. I met Fleming once. He sat on my bed when I was seven and told me a ghost story with great affection, but it scared the bejesus out of me. It was so terrifying, I went downstairs and got a gun and put it by my bed.'

Ian had the Yellow Room at the Bryces' farm, a long, low eighteenth-century stone house above a pond. His only chair was a rocking chair, he wrote to Ann. 'The furniture is waxed pine & there is a cottage rug on the wooden floor which says "Be guided by love". The ceiling is rough-cast cement & the doors have latches with wooden pegs on string. All the lamps are old oil lamps with bulbs in them & the old Vermont 4-poster is surrounded by a canopy of white string. Outside there is a high grey sky & no birds sing as Bond sits in the rocking chair & licks his ballpoint.'

On his first visit, Ian was bitten by a snake. On his fourth summer there, he explained to Ann what drew him back: 'I see deer wherever I walk in the mountains. I'm afraid you would really love it – except for the B[ryce]s. Personally, I find it immensely peaceful with Scottish undertones, which I suppose ring some ancestral chord.' It was Black Mount without the Flemings and the stalking and the midges. He wrote in the guest book, 'Lived here like a king – an uninvited one – in fragrant and luxurious solitude.'

Bryce said that Ian used to tramp alone for hours among the five hundred acres of pine-covered hills and return relaxed and brooding on some embryo new plot, three of which he set nearby. 'He would always wander about the mountains, play golf, often bare-foot, sit by the dam gazing at nothing for hours on end, and then come back and tell us he'd seen a pair of horned owls, or some other bird. In the evenings, we usually played canasta.'

The pivotal part of the farm was the bar, which had a hat stand in the shape of a six-foot carved bear that Tommy Leiter, Oatsie's alcoholic husband, had presented to Jo. Guests dressed for dinner. A regular was Loelia Westminster, who had rented out Send Grove, her country house near Woking, to the Bryces, and in 1958 she spent Christmas with them in Vermont ('an orgy of present giving. The ladies receiving over 50 each, & were too tired to open!'). 'She did wonderful needlepoint,' remembered Jo's daughter Nuala. 'She was always at the farm. And she was, I always thought, rather a sad soul.'

Other guests included Roald Dahl, who had married Patricia Neal from the Bryces' New York house*; and the banking heir William Woodward Jr. and his showgirl wife Ann, who was noted as one of the most beautiful women in the world at the time, and provoked a national scandal, and then a novel by Truman Capote, after she shot dead 'in very grisly circumstances' her husband. (He had once sought marital advice from Ian. 'Divorce her, old boy. Divorce her.') The stories Ian later heard about Woodward and his

* Ivar became godfather to Dahl's son Theo.

drunken treatment of Ann inspired Ian's story 'The Hildebrand Rarity', which raised the question of whether the abused wife brutally killed her husband in cold blood, or was entirely innocent.

Woodward had owned horses and, said Nuala, was a great help to Ian 'in filling him in on the way things worked in the racing world', driving Ian at 110 m.p.h. to the Saratoga racetrack in the summer of 1954 in his bespoke 'Studillac' – a Studebaker with a Cadillac engine. This was the 'fast car life' to which Ann objected, which 'Burglar' Bryce embodied, and about which even Loelia, a duchess, admitted reservations. 'Rich friends are well known to be a demoralising influence.'

Ivar was the consummate host, 'slender, always very tanned, very relaxed', says Jonathan Cuneo. 'He had these leopard skin pants, the first man I've ever met with a duck tail' – in marked contrast to Jonathan's short, bald, rotund father Ernie. Nuala considered Ivar 'the best looking man I ever saw in my entire life . . . and he was extremely bright. He wasn't given credit for being as bright as he was.'

In one of his few descriptions of Bryce, Ian called him 'a bizarre but most attractive Old Etonian who is one of my oldest friends, and who has married the sixth richest woman in the world'. Ian brings him into *Thunderball* as Count Lippe, an extremely handsome, dark-bronzed woman-killer dressed in a vicuna sweater whose features suggested South American blood. 'Bond summed him up as a good-looking bastard who got all the women he wanted and probably lived on them – and lived well.'

But Lippe was a decoy, in Ernie Cuneo's opinion. The sleazy gigolo deflected attention from the character whom Ian manifestly *had* based, in part, on Bryce.

Cuneo once wrote to Bryce: 'No one else has been so much Ian's brother as you have.' Cuneo had got to know the two in wartime New York. He was now, ten years on, the third member of their triumvirate. They dedicated themselves to having 'some riotously enjoyable times together' and sharing 'that fine frankness that always prevailed between us'. Cuneo acted as Ian's interpreter and guide in America and was more than a mentor to Bryce, as Ian once pointed out to him. 'He wrote to me as such, saying I was a father figure to Ivar.'

In the 1950s, the sandcastles that two fatherless boys had patted into shape on a Cornish beach in 1917 became suddenly outrageously real.

Cuneo watched their youthful fantasies materialise. Ivar's marriage to not the sixth richest but perhaps 'the world's richest woman after Barbara Hutton' (according to Roald Dahl) was soon followed by the unprecedented worldwide success of Ian's thrillers. Cuneo wrote: 'Everything Ian Fleming dreamed of became true – in the exploits and adventures of James Bond, who in many ways was in the guise of Ivar Bryce.' Ian's hero suggests the same when he uses Bryce's name in *Live and Let Die*, the thriller that is dedicated to Ivar (whose real name John Bryce had the same initials JB, and whose middle name, Felix, was given to Bond's CIA associate, Leiter). ' "Bryce," said Bond. "John Bryce." '

That is not the only occasion when 007 masquerades as 'Burglar'. In *Dr. No*, Sister Rose asks Bond, 'Your name please Mister – er . . .'

'Bryce, John Bryce.'

Twenty years after Ian's death, Cuneo imagined Ian appearing to him in a dream and saying: 'To the degree that Bond is a reflection of that enigma I have always found myself, any reflection of me is incomplete without the reflection of me as Ivar Bryce saw me. He was both my mirror in which I could from time to time catch glimpses of my fleeting self, and my sounding board, my faithful friend in a world where I found damn few . . .'

Not all of Ian's friends saw Ivar Bryce in this reflective halo. Ann in particular was blind to his charms. She regarded 'Burglar' simply as Count Lippe and it never occurred to her to join Ian in Vermont for his get-togethers. 'It's a pity Ian's so fond of crooks,' she wrote waspishly to Lord Beaverbrook about Bryce, 'particularly as Bryce is an unsuccessful one.' Ann's prejudice stirred Beaverbrook to point Ivar out to his granddaughter, Lady Jean Campbell, as 'the wickedest man in Europe'.

After a few drinks, Ian once wrote to Ann: 'I *love* Ivar. I can't help it. He *needs* me (4 gins & tonics!).' Ann did not doubt this, although Janet Milford Haven has no time for Ann's retrospective suspicion that Ian and Ivar may have had a relationship. 'Ivar and Ian were keen on women. They could be murderers, but they certainly weren't gay, oh no.'

For Ann, Bryce was Ian's 'evil genius', who with his oppressive American coterie formed 'the Scylla and Charybdis of Bryce and New York' – she felt equal hostility for Cuneo, who in turn viewed Ann as 'some kind of a nut'.

She considered 'Burglar' every bit as fake as his wartime maps of South America, writing to Ian during one of his August sojourns in Vermont: 'Come home quickly with a flaming wreath and Ivar's scalp.'

When Ann looked back to what had gone wrong between them, she attributed Ian's decline to his involvement in a scheme of Bryce's that had sucked Ian into the whirlpools of the American super-rich.

Ivar Bryce's sharp-eyed first cousin witnessed the collapse of the venture. Janet Milford Haven is the daughter of Bryce's much older uncle Frank who had died in 1951 when Janet was thirteen. Bryce had no children. From the early 1950s, he acted as Janet's surrogate father, inviting her to spend her holidays at his new wife's various properties in England, America and the Bahamas.

Janet once accompanied the Bryces on the *Queen Elizabeth*. She says, 'They used to take their staff to the Bahamas, black lady cook, butler, white footmen. Ivar had his own valet, Mundon. Jo always travelled with a personal lady's maid. You've never seen anything like Jo's jewellery. I think of it today, a huge 90-carat diamond, called "the Afghanistan", the biggest in the world. You could wear it as a brooch.' Ian used it in the cover design for *Diamonds are Forever*.

Until Ivar's marriage to Jo in 1950, Ian's wealthiest friend had been Roald Dahl's old girlfriend and his, Millicent Rogers. Yet even the Standard Oil Heiress had to take a bow to Jo Bryce, said Dahl. 'For wealth on the Bryce level doesn't really exist in England any longer. Rothermere, Kemsley just aren't in this league. The Bryces are the very rich. Take my word for it – you'd have to go a very long way to find a richer household these days than the Bryces.'

Bryce reintroduced Ian to the extreme wealth of Robert Fleming. Ivar's third wife, Jo Hartford, was the heiress of the largest retailer in the world, the Great Atlantic & Pacific Tea Company, a chain of 16,000 grocery stores built up by her grandfather, a taciturn clerk like Ian's grandfather, with its New York headquarters on the site of what would become the World Trade Center.

By 1934, Jo and her younger brother Huntington had an income of over a million dollars a year (approximately $22 million today). A Lehman Brothers banker described Huntington as 'among the most reckless spenders there ever were'.

Jo avoided the limelight as assiduously as Huntington courted it: he bought Paradise Island in the Bahamas, where 'Thunderball' was later filmed, and founded the Handwriting Institute in Manhattan, fixated by how a person crossed a 't'; he believed that those who crossed halfway were procrastinators. Four times married like his sister, he dedicated his rant against the abstract expressionists, *Art or Anarchy*, to his third wife, who had treated his writing as Ann regarded Ian's Bond books: 'To Diane, who refuses to read it.'

Yet behind the scenes, Jo gave Huntington a run for his money. She wintered with Ivar in New York and the Bahamas, and spent spring and summer in England at Moyns Park, Ivar's childhood home in Essex, which she had repurchased for him as a wedding present. ('I had tried to restore to my husband the things that I thought rightfully belonged to him. He had been disinherited by his mother.') August was Vermont, where Jo arranged her life around her racehorse stables at Black Hole Hollow farm. 'At one point she had 50 horses in training, both in US and UK,' says her son Columbus. Her racing colours, orange and red, were inspired by the Shell petrol sign. Janet Milford Haven says, 'None of us ever bet on her horses when they were running. They never won. Everyone took her for a ride. If ever she won a race, we all fainted.'

Columbus acknowledges Jo's maternal shortcomings. 'I wouldn't say she was a very good mother, not affectionate at all. She should be a model at Harvard Business School: how to run down a company in three generations and lose a fortune through horses, houses and husbands, in that order. I was aware we were very well off. In 1958, she was worth $158m (approximately $1.5 billion today). But she didn't believe in inherited wealth. At a dinner in Vermont, she said, "My ambition is to get rid of it all before I die."'

Ivar would assist her in this project. So too, by close association, would Ian.

His relationship with Ivar's new wife was no better than it had been with the previous two. Jo had 'acted as chaperone' to Ann before the Flemings' marriage, like her friend Loelia Westminster. She hosted Ian in her house on East 74th Street, where her Scottish housekeeper clucked over him; at Moyns, where the aviaries were shrill with lime-green and sky-blue budgerigars and Ian could order devilled kidneys for breakfast from a microphone by his bed; in Xanadu, the Bryces' beach house in Nassau, where he slept in a four-poster decorated with two narwhal tusks; and in the Yellow Room at Vermont. Jo could not fail to observe how Ian was 'slightly enchanted with my way of life and my friends'. He buzzed back again and again to her fabulous households where, said Dahl, the food was 'rather greater than you would get in a first-class restaurant' and his sheets were pressed every night. But he never warmed to Jo – considering her a hypo-chondriac, 'practically taking penicillin shots when she smells a stilton cheese' – or found her attractive, with her 'mustard tweed made so tight by Dior that she looked like a huge turd!'

Jo later admitted to John Pearson: 'Ian consistently influenced Ivar against Americans in general and to some extent against me – this I believe to have had no small part in our probable eventual separation. As Ian was Ivar's best friend, I naturally accepted him as part of my life and was happy to offer him whatever heiresses do – in the way of houses, comfort, gaiety to lighten his gloomy Scottish temperament.' But she found his presence a strain, 'as I knew each time the atmosphere would become charged with back-biting English remarks which, needless to say, goaded me beyond belief.'

A pretext for Ian's 'usual August visit' to Vermont was another business that Jo had financed. Bryce at once got Ian involved. Ian saw it as his chance to realise, finally, the ambition that he had nurtured since 1933.

Jo had given Ivar as a second wedding present after Moyns a major share of the stock in a 'nearly defunct and useless' news agency, North American Newspaper Alliance (NANA) which in its heyday had sent Hemingway to Spain and serialised General John Pershing's memoirs. Although modest compared with Reuters, of which Lord Kemsley had very recently become chairman, this 'wire service and syndicator of features' held out to Bryce the promise of 'an interesting life'.

Ian had striven to replicate Reuters with Mercury. Increasingly thwarted by Kemsley, he now seized on this American agency as his last prospect of becoming a newspaper tycoon. Ann said, 'Ian was by then bored with the *Sunday Times,* and when Ivar Bryce offered to let him come in on NANA, I think Ian saw possibilities of money and travel.'

In a further example of ex-spooks finding a way to recreate their wartime community, Bryce bought the agency with Cuneo, who took on the role of president. In September 1952, Ian was appointed European vice president and 'Foreign Affairs consultant' at a salary of £1,500 p.a. – after he convinced Lord Kemsley how the arrangement was bound to benefit Kemsley Newspapers. Seeing a way to further economise on Mercury, Kemsley agreed to 'a tie-up', sharing costs in exchange for office space in New York on West 41st Street, with NANA enjoying a reciprocal billet in the *Sunday Times* building in London.

The three musketeers started with mountain-walking feet. In the first flurry, Ian employed Harling to design the NANA logo – 'Robert is heaven here & a vast relief', he wrote to Ann. He commissioned Paul Gallico to write about the Coronation, and Donald McCormick to provide a weekly feature, 'International Inside Information'. He next tried to interest Beaverbrook's nephew Bill Aitken in buying NANA outright for $1 million. But the deal with the *Express* fell through.

Gradually, their pace slackened. 'I found it was a lot of fun,' said Bryce. 'But, of course, there was not a chance of making a lot of money out of it.'

Bryce's lackadaisical approach began to annoy Ian. 'He spends all of his time sitting on his ass amid surroundings carefully selected for their agreeability.' Ian referred to their absentee boss in frustrated letters to Cuneo. 'Apparently, he considers that "Ivar Bryce. The World" is a sufficient address.' Bryce was at a fancy dress ball in Biarritz when he should have been acquiring the serialisation rights to Alan Moorehead's *Gallipoli*.

William Stephenson took delight in stirring the pot. 'Both he and Ernie profess to be working very hard on NANA, and I should think that "21" and the Stork Club benefit considerably thereby.'

In his glassed-in cubicle at Kemsley House, Ian was not amused by the photograph of Ivar and Jo dressed as a sultan and sultana. 'Take a letter please, Miss Trueblood.' He dictated a furious message to Ivar. 'While you were sucking your handkerchiefs and picking your noses and recovering from hangovers, "The Saturday Evening Post" stepped in last week and bought the American rights and intend to devote half of one of the issues to the first of five extracts.'

Concerned about Ivar's 'wallowing and waffling' and its demoralising effect on Mercury's American coverage, Ian dictated another directive to Clare Blanshard to keep her sensible eye on things. 'I want an adult machine in NY as soon as possible, and it's up to you to create one. I don't like the thought of this atmosphere existing within the walls of NANA.'

But the pace failed to pick up – and Ivar to show up. Ian laid out the situation to Ann. 'Ernie is fed up with Ivar being always away while he works . . . Ivar is bored & exhausted & incredibly lethargic to the point where he can't even "find time" to get money from the bank or his hair cut.'

That spring, Ian decided to sever 'the mutual exchange of services' with Kemsley Newspapers. Shortly after, Bryce sold his share in NANA to Cuneo. 'I was able to write it off as a tax loss.'

In the same year, 1956, Ian started to think of writing off Agent 007.

LI
'THAT ASS BOND'

'My source material is running rather dry.'
IAN FLEMING to Wren Howard

'He was getting a bit sick of Bond before the Big Breeze Blew,' remembered Cuneo. 'He was contemplating killing him off in a final book.'

By 1955, Ian had published three Bond novels. His second, *Live and Let Die'* had sold 7,500 in hardback. In total, he had earned less than £2,000 (approximately £65,000 today). His royalty statement from Pan, which had started publishing him in paperback in 1954, was for £26 9s 9d. Meanwhile, he needed to raise the rent to £50 per week if he was to keep Goldeneye. No fortune was expected from America where Macmillan had barely sold 4,000 copies of *Casino Royale*. When Lawrence Hughes, publisher of his early paperbacks in the US, suggested he would have to Americanise his third novel *Moonraker* for the American market under the title *Too Hot to Handle*, Ian said, 'Call it what you like. I've written off the American market for my books.'

In Britain, Ian's hope of entering the Peter Cheyney class remained a day-dream, despite the pressure he applied to his editors. In September 1955, Ian flaunted Mark Bonham Carter, a director of Cape's rival publisher William Collins, as a threat. 'He has been trying to prise me loose from you for the last three years,' Ian wrote to Michael Howard. Bonham Carter had claimed that he was about to print 125,000 copies of Alistair MacLean's first novel *HMS Ulysses*. 'He said that if my fourth book was as good as the others he would guarantee to print a first edition of 20,000 . . . I told him that I thought that my readership was confined to the A-class of reader and he said that that was completely disproved by the Pan Book sales of CASINO', which had sold 41,000.

Bonham Carter also made the point that 'unless we made a great push to get through the sound barrier of 10,000 copies I would be permanently stuck there. He said there were moments when a publisher had to beat the big drum about an author . . . I wonder if we really shouldn't have a go with DIAMONDS ARE FOREVER and do a real operation on it.'

Three weeks later, Ian returned to the theme. 'I think we are both agreed that shock tactics of some sort are necessary to get through the sound barrier of 8,000 copies.' His letter suggested that even this reduced threshold had not yet been crossed.

Meanwhile, Ian concentrated on drumming up endorsements. He had failed with Somerset Maugham, as he would with Graham Greene, but in the spring of 1955 he achieved success.

Ian was introduced to Raymond Chandler at lunch with the poet Stephen Spender, who was nursing him after he slipped into alcoholic depression following the death of his wife. Chandler was stranded without her company. Not long after meeting Ian, he telephoned Una Trueblood, looking for a date or more. Chandler 'wanted to take me out to lunch,' she says. 'Looking back, I was very green. Mr Fleming dealt with the situation very tactfully.'

He admired the grief-stricken Chandler as much as he grew to like him. They had a bounty of things to talk about. Like Phyllis Bottome, Chandler was the product of a British mother and an American Quaker father, a railway engineer and epic drinker who abandoned the family when Chandler was a boy. Educated at Dulwich College seven years after P. G. Wodehouse, Chandler had followed William Stephenson into the Canadian army and the Royal Flying Corps, and then operated at a senior level in the oil industry on the west coast of America.

Ian was adroit in exploiting their relationship, having wished Bond 'to more or less follow the pattern of Raymond Chandler'. Pearson said, 'Ian detected very much an ally, a fellow spirit, in Chandler who, as he was trying to do with Bond, had created something out of the ordinary with his character of Philip Marlowe. And this was literature, it wasn't just thriller writing. This was very much what Ian wanted. It was a great moment to get Chandler on his side. As a result of the support of Chandler, he was able to turn *From Russia, With Love* into the most important of the Bond books.'

Ian's newspaper had boosted Chandler's corroded self-esteem with a positive notice of *The Long Goodbye* the previous year – 'for the first time in my life I was reviewed as a Novelist in the London *Sunday Times*.' This was a particularly important moment, says Chandler's biographer Tom Williams. 'His great frustration had been that critics saw him as *just* a crime writer whereas he aspired to something more. Getting this recognition was important, and the fact it was the British who picked up on it meant something to him too.' When, at Ann's urging, Ian invited him to a 'gabfest' at Victoria Square, Chandler felt obliged to accept.

Ann described the lunch in one word. 'Disaster. Raymond Chandler was either drunk or so permanently drunk that the difference was difficult to say. Ian said he must never bring any of his friends here again.'

Ian's wife fell into Chandler's category of 'the St John's Wood–Chelsea literary artistic crowd' and those 'bitchy women who are all darling, darling, darling when they met you, but have an assortment of little knives for your back'. He had worked out a glossary. 'I simply adore her' = 'I'd stick a knife in her back if she had a back.' 'I rather care for that' = 'Give it to me quick.'

Ian moved fast to solicit a quote to promote *Moonraker*, his new Bond novel. 'A word from you which I could pass on to my publishers would make me the fortune which has so far eluded me.' Chandler replied with a sentence that Ian shared with Cape: 'you are probably the most forceful and driving writer, of what I suppose still must be called "thrillers" in England.'

One consequence of these 'gold' words was that the following year, probably at Ian's instigation, Leonard Russell, literary editor of the *Sunday Times*, asked Chandler to review *Diamonds are Forever*.

Chandler was no patsy. It was the first review he had written since his early twenties, and he was acute in diagnosing Ian's problem. He had experienced it himself. 'It is the curse of the "series character" that he always has to go back to where he began . . . let me plead with Mr Fleming not to allow himself to become a stunt writer, or he will end up no better than the rest of us.' He cautioned Ian in a separate letter, written in his 'gusty script': 'I think you will have to make up your mind what kind of writer you are going to be. You could be almost anything except that I think you are a bit of a sadist!'

Ian affected to take Chandler's criticism on the chin. His reply has become Ian Fleming's most quoted defence of his work. 'Probably the fault about my books is that I don't take them seriously enough and meekly accept having my head ragged off about them in the family circle. If one has a grain of intelligence, it is difficult to go on being serious about a character like James Bond. You, after all, write "novels of suspense" – if not straight socio-logical studies – whereas my books are straight pillow fantasies of the bang-bang, kiss-kiss variety'. Ian's talents were extended 'to their absolute limits' in writing books like *Diamonds are Forever*.

But Chandler was not having this. 'Anyone who writes as dashingly as you do, ought, I think, to try for a little higher grade. I have just re-read *Casino Royale*, and it seems to me that you have disimproved with each book.'

His steady degeneration depressed Ian too: he admitted to Chandler, 'my own muse is in a bad way'. But the decline was not merely in his writing. He had booked himself into Enton Hall, a health clinic in Surrey, after feeling palpitations and an increased heartbeat. His doctor, Jack Beal, prescribed new drugs. Then, in July 1956 in New York, Ian had an attack of kidney stones, his second in months, and he was rushed to the Presbyterian Hos-pital. He passed out of 'the Stone Age' as he called it, after Clare Blanshard lit a candle for him, but weeks later he wrote to Godfrey: 'I am still in the grips of sciatica, and find it almost impossible to sit through a lunch.'

The prospect of hammering out another novel in the Jamaican heat over-whelmed him. By the time he had finished writing *From Russia, with Love*, his fifth Bond, putting into it all he had learned from Chandler, Ian was find-ing it an exercise as excruciating as 'La Dame Sciatica' to keep his hero 'spinning through his paces'. In a low moment, he wrote to Ann: 'I have got so desperately tired of that ass Bond.'

With so many other pulls on his time – the *Sunday Times*, the *Book Col-lector*, the Queen Anne Press, NANA, and his young son coming, finally, to Goldeneye for the 1957 season – Ian's solution was to put his character out of action. Stabbed in a Paris hotel room by a poisoned steel blade in Rosa Klebb's boot, 'Bond pivoted slowly on his heel and crashed headlong to the wine-red floor.'

On 28 December 1956, even as he braced to fly to Goldeneye, Ian alerted Cape's co-founder Wren Howard to the strong likelihood that the Bond ser-ies was now at an end. 'I seriously doubt if I shall be able to complete a book in Jamaica this year.'

LII
'THE GREATEST FIASCO OF ALL TIME'

'He was much affected by the demise of the British Empire.'
ERNIE CUNEO

What saved Bond was the Suez Crisis. In the autumn of 1956, without telling the Americans, Anthony Eden joined with the French and Israelis in sending a task force to retake the Canal which Egypt's President had nationalised in July. Over three intense weeks, all attention was fixed on an invalid British Prime Minister, who escaped in the catastrophic aftermath to convalesce in the place where Ian Fleming had conceived James Bond four years earlier.

The point of Eden's going to Goldeneye was to recuperate. But instead of taking his rest, he insisted on continuing to run the country from the two white telephones and teleprinter that Jamaica's governor Sir Hugh Foot had hurriedly installed for the 'very urgent work required to be undertaken by the Prime Minister'.

From 24 November to 13 December, Ian's primitive Caribbean home was the hub of a global operation, with a sick leader sending secret telegrams to London, Washington, Paris, Tel Aviv, Moscow, Ottowa, Sydney, Wellington and Cairo. Eden's announcement of Britain's unconditional withdrawal from the Canal Zone, decided in the gazebo at Goldeneye, had repercussions as devastating as any paranoid order issued from Drax's hideaway in Ebury Street in *Moonraker*.

'They say Eden is literally mad,' Loelia wrote in her diary. 'Chips' Channon went a step further. 'Diana Cooper says that Anthony Eden has the evil eye.' High on amphetamines, Eden presided over the dying convulsion of British Imperialism from Ian's modest lookout, in an echo of how William Pitt had shut himself from communication with the outside world at Ian's childhood home.

'It has been the greatest fiasco of all time,' wrote Channon. Eden's 'tactless' escape to Goldeneye was a cardinal error universally criticised as a political and public relations disaster – as Phyllis Bottome observed, who, like Eden, had also once borrowed Ian's house to recuperate. 'He's attempted to cling on to an outdated version of the world, unable to accept that "Great Britain" is a small island off the coast of Europe!'

Without America's support, the invasion was a D-Day gone wrong. Ian wrote to his wartime chief William Stephenson, 'In the whole of modern history, I can't think of a comparable shambles created by any single country.' Burgess and Maclean's defection seemed insignificant when compared to the humiliating ceasefire that Eden agreed to as British troops were still landing, after President Eisenhower threatened to crash the pound by selling off US government-owned British bonds.

The damage to British prestige and the nation's self-worth cannot be understated. Eden had taken over the premiership from Churchill in April 1955, when Britain was still considered one of the three post-war powers. By the time he returned to London, his actions had reduced that number to two.

Strangely, the effect on Ian would be the opposite. It brought him more publicity than he had known since he wired from Moscow the result of the Metropolitan-Vickers trial. Like Kuwait striking oil in 1952, or the fictitious Smith family winning the pools in Ian's abortive book about that country, it was 'a monumental stroke of good fortune' which inflated Ian's profile and whetted the interest of thousands of new readers in his forthcoming thriller, that he had earlier warned Cape might be his last.

Even as Eden's legacy sank beneath him at Goldeneye, Bond rose from the same waters in a dramatic rebirth.

Ian was part of a circle of non-admirers who knew Anthony Eden as 'Jerk'. The Prime Minister had never impressed him, any more than 'Anthony's toothy smiles and winning manner' had conquered Ann – although she was determinedly loyal to Eden's second wife and Caspar's godmother, Clarissa.

'Chips' Channon was among the insiders pushing Ian's line that 'Jerk is a bad prime minister'. Channon had long considered 'the fatuous Eden' as 'one of the most unaware, ill-informed people I have ever known'. A great many shared this view. In December 1940, a junior lieutenant back from the

Middle East was dining at Pratt's when Eden began holding forth on the Mediterranean situation. The young man turned to a friend, 'I do not know who that man is, but he is talking awful balls.'

Ann had been staying with Churchill in April 1941 when the bad news came from Athens that Peter Fleming was missing. The blame for sending Wavell's expeditionary force to Greece was laid by Churchill on Eden, for whom Churchill was to develop a 'cold hatred' after the war, despite his marrying his niece. Channon wrote of the Greek debacle: 'The whole affair was an unthought-out whim of Anthony Eden's.' Churchill had felt the project should be abandoned, but 'Eden said go-ahead.'

Fifteen years on, history looked to have repeated itself in Egypt.

Eden had only met General Gamal Abdel Nasser once, with Clarissa, at a dinner at the British embassy in Cairo. Still, he had formed a personal loathing of Egypt's President, casting him as another evil brigand like Hitler or Mussolini. On 26 July 1956, Nasser decided to nationalise the Suez Canal Company, telling a crowd in Alexandria, 'Tonight our Egyptian canal will be run by Egyptians. *Egyptians!*'

The Prime Minister received the news at a state dinner for King Faisal of Iraq. In an extraordinary scene, he summoned the Chiefs of Staff, including Mountbatten, now First Lord of the Admiralty, to the Cabinet room – they were in full evening dress, with Eden still in knee breeches – and instructed them to prepare an assessment of the military options. Tetchy and skittish even at ordinary times, Eden contemplated Nasser's assassination.

Ian had predicted in April 1944 that the Canal would be a flashpoint. From his dealings with Darlan, he knew Vice Admiral Pierre Barjot, the French deputy commander of the joint invasion force steaming towards Port Said, on whom he had partly based René Mathis in *Casino Royale*. Nor had Ian found sympathy for the anti-British nationalists who, in 1952, destroyed the bookshop in Cairo belonging to his schoolfriend Esmond Warner and set fire to Shepheard's Hotel, where Ian had had drinks with Alaric Jacob. On 11 September 1956, he wrote to Admiral Godfrey, 'I find only one comfort in all this Suez business, and that is that we are not arguing over some very questionable *casus belli*, such as the Polish Corridor or the Saar, but over an international utility which affects all the maritime nations of the world. For this reason, if for no other, I believe our case and the case of the 18 nations is a good one, and I do hope we obstinately stand firm on it.'

Ian still envisaged a global role for Britain. However, not all who came to Victoria Square shared his view. Suez divided the nation like Munich, and more recently Brexit – events prompting strong emotion rather than rational discussion. One party that broke up in acrimony was hosted, to her intense delight, by Ann.

On 19 November 1956, hours before an important vote in Parliament to refer General Nasser to the International Court at The Hague, tempers flew at a dinner to which Ann had invited her latest admirer, just back from Paris. This was the new Leader of the Opposition, Hugh Gaitskell, who had earlier criticised the invasion as 'an act of disastrous folly whose tragic consequences we shall regret for years'.

Also present on that incendiary evening was the dissident Tory MP, Bob Boothby. Another guest, James Pope-Hennessy, told Maud Russell the details.

In Ian's upstairs drawing room, Boothby produced the draft of a letter to Eden signed by 'a few other Con MPs protesting against the Suez action & announcing they would vote against the Govt. Wrangling talk filled the air, Ann and Ian being pro-Suez, the others, of course, against. To add to the confusion, that loathsome Lucian Freud got drunk & insulted everyone in turn so that the dinner broke up & everyone had left by 10.20. Ann then rang Clarissa and told her about the letter, with the result, so James said, that many MPs rallied to Eden who might otherwise have voted against him. During the wrangle, Ian constantly accused the anti-Suez group of having a Welsh chapel outlook & repeated this phrase too often, far too often. Ann fancies herself as a political hostess & if there is a scandal or row, she thinks the evening has been a success & says so.'

By this measure, Maud felt the dinner must have ranked high in the pantheon of Ann's triumphs. 'She is in many ways a stupid woman, but she chatters in a sparkling way & amuses men. Derek [Hill, the artist] once said of her to me: "How dull, boring & irritating Anne Fleming is. And mischievous too. She is maddening & *very* tiresome." '

This was the woman Ian had been married to for four years. Suez concealed the fault-lines between them. Only a few days before this dinner party, Ann had begun a love affair with Gaitskell that lasted until his death.

The Suez Crisis was all-pervading. No one talked of anything else for the next three months. President Eisenhower made plain his refusal to support Eden in his military action, which struck him as a throwback to 'the Victorian period'. Yet according to Cuneo, 'it was not the US but Canada who threw in the monkey wrench. The High Commissioner told me that [Prime Minister Louis] St Laurent picked up the telephone and told Eden that unless he got out of Suez, Canada would get out of the Commonwealth of Nations. Eden went to Goldeneye broken in health.'

Eden had first collapsed on 5 October. He had visited Clarissa in University College Hospital, where she had gone for a dental operation, and was suddenly admitted himself, with a temperature of 105, the result of ongoing complications from a 1953 gall bladder operation. He was 'in constant need of drugs' after that. Ann's first cousin Martin Charteris was the Queen's Assistant Private Secretary. 'I think the Queen believed Eden was quite mad.'

In New York, Noël Coward dined with William Stephenson. 'He is of the opinion that Anthony Eden has gone round the bend.'

'Anthony very depressed,' Clarissa wrote in her diary after the debate in Parliament, and then in her unrevealing memoir: 'The doctors at this point insisted Anthony should get away.'

At 8 a.m. on 20 November, Channon heard on the wireless 'that the PM is indisposed and suffering from severe nervous strain: in fact, a partial breakdown . . . largely occasioned by Gaitskell's caddish attacks. He is to go away for a rest; but where?'

Leonard Russell learnt the news of Eden's destination in Kemsley House. 'When the sanctuary for the invalid was announced, a faint breath of glory struck the cheeks of the *Sunday Times*, amazingly to anyone who had been there.' The Foreign Manager had 'talked romantically to his friends about it, and a myth had formed round it, now here it was, the centre of the nation's interest and a retreat for Suez's walking wounded.'

Goldeneye was Clarissa's idea. She had heard Ian extolling his modest bungalow over tea in Victoria Square and formed a certain image of

'Fleming's luxurious residence' as *Time* magazine called it. 'Ian was a bit naughty really,' reckoned Denis Hamilton. Goldeneye was 'a shack-like house without any mod cons, without even a telephone. Yet he went around pretending to everyone that he had this great palace in Jamaica, a miniature Ritz. I think it was partly to keep his end up with Ann.'

Noël Coward rolled his eyes. 'Considering the fuss Ian made about Goldeneye, you'd have thought it was Knole, and I suppose Anthony and Clarissa came expecting that it was.'

The official request came through 'Chips' Channon's 'beloved brother-in-law' and long-term lover, Alan Lennox-Boyd, who, as Colonial Secretary, had responsibility for Jamaica, and positively 'encouraged' the choice. He telephoned Ann, asking to borrow Goldeneye for himself, and swearing her to secrecy – 'so naturally I did not tell anyone, or rather naturally I did not tell anyone because it was such a dull secret'.

Then on 17 November, Alan saw Ian 'and disclosed that dear old Golden-eye was considered an appropriate place for the Prime Minister to lick his wounds'.

Ian was delighted. He had been busily trying to lure affluent American tenants like the actress Claudette Colbert. He told Ann, 'it will put up the value of the property, and would I keep my trap shut.' Ian trusted Una True-blood to make arrangements. She says, 'It was all terribly hush-hush, and he wasn't allowed to tell me who was going; I had to keep cabling Violet to expect "special visitors", but he in no way mentioned who it was till Eden got there.'

Ann was not to be told, but she was – and promptly alerted Clarissa forty-eight hours before their departure. 'I warned her . . . that the reef abounded with scorpion fish, barracuda and urchins. I forgot to tell her that if [Anthony] is impregnated with spines he should pee on them . . . The plumbing is not good at the moment, after plugs are pulled noises of hunting horns are heard for at least twenty minutes – so they will have little privacy; I think Torquay and a sun-ray lamp would have been more peaceful and patriotic.'

She exulted in reporting to Evelyn Waugh what happened when Ian went to see Clarissa the night before the Edens left. 'He found her practising with an underwater mask in her drawing room, no doubt part of the delusion that the Suez Canal is flowing through it.'

At Government House in Kingston, the news was received with dismay. When Churchill had visited Jamaica as Prime Minister in January 1953, the road to Prospect, the hilltop plantation where he stayed, had been resurfaced, and a telephone installed in every room. Goldeneye had no telephone – only a watchdog, an Alsatian called Max, as Ann gleefully told the *Daily Express*. For Rab Butler, deputising for Eden, 'the major decisions had to be checked with Anthony in Jamaica, and the only method of communication was by telegraph to the Governor who then had to send a messenger on poor roads all the long distance to Ian Fleming's house.'

That was not the only shortcoming. Colonel Tony Davies worked in the military section in Kingston and he had stayed at Goldeneye. 'It was very, very uncomfortable and the swimming wasn't all that good. I wouldn't recommend it.' Plus, the grounds were choked with weeds.

Sir Hugh Foot decided that the Edens needed to be the guests of the Government of Jamaica rather than the absent Flemings. A working bee was set up, consisting of Blanche Blackwell, a local plantation owner who Ian had met earlier in the year; the Governor's wife Sylvia, and his private secretary, Cora St Aubyn. They moved at a military pace to get Goldeneye into more gracious shape, filling the deep-freeze with lamb chops, and, as Ian imagined it, 'punching up my faded cushions and putting cut-glass vases of flowers beside the detectives' beds' – while taking care not to step on the toes of Violet, who, when Lady Foot suggested that she move aside for one of her staff, rejoined, 'No, I obey the Commander.' Violet had received Una Trueblood's telegram with the identity of Ian's important friend and a warning to brace herself 'for considerable publicity'. 'I must be calm. Because although he is Prime Minister, he is just the next man.'

Concerned about the impact of Violet's curried goat on a broken-down premier, Noël Coward rushed to a charcuterie in Port Maria. 'Violet's divine, but she's no Boulestin, so I bought them a big basket of caviar and foie gras and champagne – anything to mitigate the horrors I knew the poor dears would suffer.' But Coward was barred entry when he came to deliver. Ann reported to Waugh: 'He gossiped with the detectives, and they told him they hated Clarissa and that Sir Anthony suffered from nightmares and frequently screamed in the night. It must be true, for the neighbourhood is full of tales of his night wailing.'

Coward was quick to attribute 'the fairly well authenticated rumours' of Eden's nocturnal screaming to 'the acute discomfort of Ian's bed and the coloured prints of snakes and octopuses that festoon the peeling walls'. Ian gave an alternative reason for his guest's insomnia: bush rats knocking over his shell collection in the drawing room. 'They made such a racket, scurrying about, and a number of them had to be shot by his private detective, which I didn't like.'

By calm contrast, Clarissa presented to Ann a picture of rosy inertia after a week on the beach at Goldeneye, sunbathing and lying in the garden reading detective stories. 'We are blissfully happy & it is everything we had hoped for but far more beautiful. We haven't been outside the gates so far ...' An enormous Cadillac lent by the Premier stood idly in the drive. The press reports of everything the Edens were allegedly doing at Goldeneye had 'made them decide that they should see no one'. Mrs St Aubyn came in every day to do letters and shopping. They had yet to thaw the lamb chops. Anthony was enjoying the local fruit, especially soursop, and they had learned to ask for Irish potatoes when they wanted potatoes, or else they were served yams. 'We have finally got a line on langouste from Oracabessa. We have bought heavily from Mr Antonio of Falmouth – Anthony wears a charming willow pattern shirt, & some fancy-pants run up by a local lady. I have slight trouble at night with all those squeaks & whizzings & then that liver-attack of fireflies in the room whenever one opens one's eyes. We can't get the dawn bathe straight – we never seem to wake up before 9 am which is a great waste.'

When the Edens did descend to the beach, it was 'as nice as one could find', even if 'the woods overlooking the little cave are full of black policemen & there is a police boat going up & down in the open sea'.

Under the protective eye of these policemen, who had carved 'WEL-COME SIR ANTHONY' on the cedar trees, Clarissa spent long hours in the bay. 'I am obsessed by the fishes, & now swim about with a wet towel tied to my back on account of bad sunburn .... I submerge & wander aimlessly up & down the corridors.'

As for her husband: 'After one claustrophobic splash Anthony has absolutely refused to put his head under water, so he swims up & down in the deep bit, occasionally crashing himself into a reef of coral.'

When not swimming, Eden had taken to paddling about in Ian's inflatable

Pak-Boat, until this developed a leak. Ian reported how 'that old rubber boat of mine at Goldeneye is now so out of action that it even sank beneath the Prime Minister of England.'

Eden wrote to Ian afterwards: 'I do not think that there is any other place anywhere that could have given me the rest I had to have. The bathing, the beach, the seclusion, the size of the grounds were all just perfect to enjoy and be concealed.'

But outside the pineapple-topped gates of Goldeneye, the world saw matters in a less generous light, as Ann admitted to Clarissa. 'The immediate reaction to Jamaica was bad.' Another of Ann's dinner guests, Randolph Churchill, wrote that 'even Hitler did not winter in Jamaica'.

Also on the island at the same time, in a luxury hotel in Montego Bay, was the winner of a Paradise Island competition run by the *Daily Mirror* on 'how best to solve the Suez crisis'. Susanna Chancellor was the twenty-one-year-old daughter of Ian's former colleague Christopher Chancellor, now head of Reuters. When her winning entry, recommending 'an entirely new government to take over', was selected from 7,000, she says, 'my father became very pompous, accusing me of spoiling his son's chances of ever entering the foreign service. The *Mirror* had on the front-page, "Susanna Sees Eden Off". They smuggled me onto the tarmac as Eden was about to leave and I was snapped with him exchanging intimate smiles with no one else in frame, and I asked "Will you comment on rumours that you are going to resign?"'

That day was not far off. On 3 January, Eden chaired a Cabinet meeting. A senior official present said, 'I saw in his eyes a man pursued by every demon. I have never seen a look like it in any man's eyes, and I hope I never do again.'

On 9 January, Loelia wrote in her diary: 'Anthony Eden has resigned! Ill health he says, but I wonder.' Eden wrote to Churchill on the same day, 'The benefit of Jamaica is not significant.'

For Ian, the benefit of Eden's visit to Goldeneye was incalculable. What instantly made it so was Beaverbrook's offer to serialise the new Bond novel in the *Express* and capitalise on the publicity that linked the Prime Minister and Ian Fleming to the island where Beaverbrook himself had a home. Months later, the *Express* began also carrying a strip cartoon of James Bond.

This double exposure served as the 'shock tactics' that Ian had sought from Cape. It added considerably to Ian's sales among lower middle-class readers, who had been at the heart of popular support for Eden's invasion. Four months before Ian's death, Beaverbrook wrote to him, 'We sold an estimated twelve to fifteen thousand extra copies of the paper carrying one of your serials! This year the figure is estimated at fifty thousand extra!' He reminded Ian, 'You have already made a great deal of money from the *Express*. That is why we are so poor – having to pay such immense sums for serialisation and strips . . . I am sure you earn more money than I do. I look upon you as a very rich man and I suggest you make a contribution to the Art Gallery in Fredericton.'

Confirmation that the *Express* was to serialise *From Russia, with Love* reached Ian on the eve of his flight to Jamaica. On 2 January 1957, he was in a different mood when he wrote to Wren Howard at Cape: 'I am quite certain that you will sell 20,000 copies if only because, thanks to World Books [an English book club which had reprinted *Live and Let Die*] and *Express* serialisation etc, my name is much better known.'

For the first time since he started writing, and right at the moment when he had been tempted to do away with Bond, Ian looked like breaking through 'the sound barrier' that had eluded him in his previous four novels. When he arrived at Goldeneye on 11 January, all he needed was a new plot.

LIII
LEADERKINS

*'I suppose I shall have to go dancing next Friday
with Hugh Gaitskell to explode his pathetic belief in equality'*
ANN FLEMING to Lord Beaverbrook

Three days after Eden's resignation, Ann landed in Jamaica by boat with Caspar, Raymond and Nanny Sillick.

The crossing had been stormy. Ann wrote to Waugh: 'Owing to my unhinged mind, I was immediately in floods of tears.' Clarissa had posted her some 'very very small photographs of Anthony on the Goldeneye beach'. What Ann omitted to say was that even as the Prime Minister's profile shrank, her affair with the fifty-year-old leader of the Labour Party, Hugh Gaitskell, was blooming. By the time Ann sailed back to London, the relationship had become common knowledge within her circle. 'Apparently Annie & Gaitskell is a romance,' Loelia confirmed to her diary.

The Flemings moved in a narrow world where everyone knew each other. The Suez Crisis swept them up into the unfolding action. This was the defining drama of Britain's post-war history, when Ian and Ann enjoyed unusually intimate relations with two of the principal players.

Isaiah Berlin, a mutual friend, described Gaitskell as 'a v. nice & honest & clear headed, but not a vy resolute man'. Gaitskell was clear-headed enough to understand the source of his allure for Ann: his sudden rise to prominence at this tempestuous moment. The excitement surrounding Suez and Eden's subsequent collapse escalated their flirtation. At the very moment when Ian had been making secret arrangements for the Prime Minister to stay in his bedroom in Jamaica, Ann was in bed with the Leader of the Opposition in a Paris hotel.

At the start of her romance with Ian ten years earlier, Ann had promised him 'it would be impossible for me to be unfaithful to you.' She had teased Ian over her flirtations with Evelyn Waugh and Peter Quennell. '*This familiar face is not accustomed to neglect/and still has the capacity to make other men erect.*'

That became less the case for Ian after Caspar was born. In a heartbreaking letter to her husband, Ann wondered whether if 'had you put half the effort into home relations, it might have been a happier home. I beg you to cease saying I do not like sex, surely you remember our past? I find it easier to understand that after the birth of Caspar and the smell in the hospital bedroom, I should become distasteful to you, and in any case, I think double-bed love is not your kind. Reading your letter, you mention "bad old bachelor days". The only person you stopped sleeping with when they ceased was me!'

The greatest passion of the age had been speared by marriage. Ann explained her affair with Gaitskell as a consequence of Ian's neglect.

Ann and Gaitskell had first met in 1951 as joint godparents at the christening of Virginia Cowles's son, Randall. In political terms they were opposites. Gaitskell's solicitor, Arnold Goodman, was one of many who positioned Ann 'slightly to the right of Attila the Hun'. Ann disliked 'proletarians', preferred 'oligarchs', and would not have disagreed with Raymond Carr that her views were 'outrageously politically incorrect'. One summer when Ian was away in America, Ann wrote to Clarissa Eden that she had been left alone with Caspar 'and August holiday crowds that I would kill if I had a machine gun. If anyone started a fascist movement in this country, I would immediately join it.'

But Gaitskell appealed to the contrariness in her nature and her more or less unquenchable appetite, that she shared with Ian, for something to happen. 'If we have to have a Labour Party,' she told Gaitskell, 'it is as well you should lead it.'

'Leaderkins', as she called him, was a live wire compared to the skittish and effeminate 'Jerk' Eden, who, according to Ann, was rumoured to have 'reading aloud parties, the readers are all male, the play is *Antony and Cleopatra*, and Anthony's favourite part is Cleopatra.' Gaitskell loved poetry, jazz (especially Nat King Cole), dancing. Frank Giles got to know him well and recalled Gaitskell rolling back the carpet at his house in Hampstead, putting pre-war dance music on the record player 'and swooping, chasseé-ing and reversing his way round and round the room until his succession of lady partners pleaded for mercy'. Ann was one of those ladies.

The next time they met, in January 1956, was at a dinner in Victoria Square with Maurice Bowra, Gaitskell's mentor at Oxford, who was in on the secret in the first days of the affair. On the way to dinner, Gaitskell bumped into a band of street musicians and asked them to come round later to the house, where they played jazz on the staircase. Gaitskell recalled how Ian arrived home, paid off the musicians and went to bed. But when the other guests had left, in the small bow-windowed sitting room, with Ian overhead, Hugh kissed Ann. She said it was very nice. He kissed her again.

Unlike Ann, Gaitskell was a Bond devotee. He wrote to thank Ian for a signed copy of the latest Bond: 'As you know, I am a confirmed Fleming fan – or should it be addict? The combination of sex, violence, alcohol and – at intervals – good food and nice clothes is, to one who leads such a circumscribed life as I do, irresistible.' Ann provided Gaitskell's passport into that world.

Leaderkins was soon also a besotted devotee of Ann – who also called him 'Heavenly' or 'Old King Cole', after his taste in jazz. She once showed Harling 'a 30-page letter full of passionate devotion' and said that Gaitskell sent her a worshipful letter almost daily. Harling wrote: 'She was far from enraptured on her own account: "It's difficult to be bowled over by his passion when I compare his looks with those of my husbands, three of the most handsome men in England. Wouldn't you agree?"'

In October 1956, Gaitskell was dining in London with Gladwyn Jebb, now Britain's ambassador to Paris, and drank quite a lot. At 11 p.m., he drove to Victoria Square where Ann was entertaining Lucian Freud, Francis Bacon and Cecil Beaton. They said they were going to a nightclub, the Milroy. Gaitskell gave them a lift, and then, after paying for champagne, invited Ann onto the floor. The more they danced, the more enchanted he became. He had no feeling of being socially seduced, only of being dazzled. He dreamt, were he free, of marrying her.

'He is a changed man,' Ann wrote to Beaverbrook, 'all he wants is wine, women and song.'*

In mid November, Gaitskell was in Paris as a delegate at a NATO conference. Ann joined him later. They danced in Montmartre and went back to the Hôtel Beaujolais. There was one thing he had to tell her. The married Gaitskell was not an experienced seducer. Yet neither was he disgusted by her scars.

Afterwards, he recited some D. H. Lawrence poems. She said that she was not accustomed in such circumstances to have poetry read to her.

From Paris, Ann took Gaitskell on the train to Chantilly to stay with Diana Cooper. Ann reported to Waugh, with the corrosive mockery that for so long prevented Ann from accepting her true feelings: 'He had never seen cocktails with mint in them or seen a magnum of pink champagne, he was very happy. I lied and told him that all the upper class were beautiful and intelligent and he must not allow his vermin to destroy them.'

After Paris, Gaitskell found a place where they could discreetly meet: the Bolton Street flat of his best friend, the Labour politician Tony Crosland. Ann soon became friends with Crosland, telling her niece Sara: 'On Tuesday afternoons when I slept with Hugh Gaitskell, I tried to pretend it was Tony Crosland because he's so much more attractive.'

Gaitskell became mildly jealous, but overcame it. One day when they were all three together he told them that these had been the happiest days of his life.

Ann was slower to acknowledge what the 'gentle and loving' Gaitskell meant to her. 'I fear it is a middle-aged divertissement for me,' she insisted to her socialist friend Frances Donaldson, another who provided cover. Ann never realised 'how much one counted on Hugh's love, gravitas and walks in Battersea Park in the spring while I watched the mating ducks and he waffled on politics, me occasionally saying "Will you repeat the very secret

---

* Her affair had a precedent. In 1887, four years into her marriage, Ann's neglected grandmother Mary Wyndham had transferred her emotional affections from her philandering husband to the Conservative politician and later Prime Minister, Arthur Balfour; references in her letters to 'a good smacking', and hints at the 'liberal education' of a 'poor young girl' that left 'no regions of her little body unexplored' suggested to some a physical, even sadomasochistic relationship. Whatever its nature, it lasted forty years, against Ann's six with Gaitskell.

bits?" ' Fionn says, 'For many years she hid, even from herself, what she felt for Hugh.'

Before the end, though, Ann had begun loving Gaitskell. When she received a cable to say 'dangerously ill and no improvement', Ann confided to her brother how totally stunned she was. 'For six years, he has given me a great bonus of love and support, and, over time, my love for him has become very considerable indeed; a good man and an even more honourable politician than people supposed—in fact, totally . . . honourable.'

After Gaitskell died, on 18 January 1963, following a kidney operation, Ann wrote to Diana Cooper, 'I am profoundly unhappy, but Thank God he knew I loved him.'

How did Ian feel? A dedication in a Bond novel puzzled Gaitskell. 'The ambiguity of your inscription to me adds, suitably enough, a touch of mystery: will James Bond solve it?'

In public, at least, Ian affected not take the Gaitskell 'crush' on Ann too seriously. 'Annie was much lowered by Hugh's death,' he wrote to Harling. 'I was too. I like all my wife's lovers and, indeed, husbands . . . He was quite a chap in the eccentric tradition.'

Never to be forgotten was a humiliating and much publicised episode in January 1960 when Gaiskell mimicked Eden and flew to Jamaica to visit Ann, ostensibly on a fact-finding tour of the West Indies. Hounded by a Beaverbrook reporter, Gaitskell panicked. He fled on foot from Oracabessa and hid 'behind a cactus bush' until Ann rescued him, and delivered Gaitskell to Goldeneye, where a 'horribly amused' Ian welcomed the Leader of Her Majesty's Opposition to a late lunch of what Noël Coward called 'that ghastly grey curry that looked like chinchilla'.

Only in one of the agonising letters that chart Ian's unhappiness and Ann's is Gaitskell mentioned. ('Violet Cripps is going round the island saying you have left me for Hugh, the old bitch.') Yet jealousy never answers to logic. Fionn says, 'I think Ian probably minded more than one might think. He probably didn't know the extent of it. He probably found it quite hard to believe – Gaitskell was not a physically attractive person compared with Tony Crosland. He probably put it to the back of mind, and on a good day recognised he was in no position to take a judgmental line.'

Ian could be dismissive about Gaitskell, unable to see him as a Lothario, more as a figure of fun, but there are signs that Ann's affair hurt. He would not allow Gaitskell's name to be mentioned in the office. Shortly before Gaitkell's death, Ian attended a dinner to welcome David Bruce, America's new ambassador. Bruce's wife Evangeline overheard Ian tell the Frenchwoman next to him who had asked about the man at the head of the table, 'That's my wife's lover. His name's Hugh Gaitskell.' Ian's tone indicated how far his feelings for Ann had deteriorated.

Ernie Cuneo remembered: 'His laughter about his marriage was a bit bloodcurdling. It had the overtones of Roderick Dhu, badly wounded and prisoner in the dark dungeons of Stirling Castle, laughing the Scottish laughter of hopeless defiance.'

Meanwhile, three months after Ann started sleeping with Gaitskell, Ian had begun a parallel relationship with a neighbour in Jamaica. Ann became so jealous, said John Pearson, that she prevented him from writing about it in his biography. 'I had to cut quite a lot of it back.'

LIV
'IAN'S BLACK WIFE'

'Don't be tarred by that brush, and I hope not
by Blanche Blackwell's bush – who seems to look
blanchly or blackly in your letters.'
ANN FLEMING to Ian

Ann was the one more prone to jealousy, even before their marriage. 'I do hope the remoteness of Goldeneye won't force you to collect some sordid female to replace me.' When Ian assured her he had 'little temptation to stick my umbrella into anything except the sea', he was not telling the truth, writing in the next line, 'Rosamond Lehmann is coming to stay tomorrow night'.

His flings with Lehmann and Millicent Rogers consolidated Ian's reputation in the eyes of 'Chips' Channon as 'a gay *sabreur* [swordsman], but a semi-cad' – an image that was underlined by an anonymous note in Ian's papers written in a feminine hand. This was attached to a photograph of Ian with Ivar Bryce's millionaire friend, 'Honeychile' Hohenlohe, taken at Schloss Mittersill, her sporting club near Kitzbühel: 'Writes terrible books. Handsome in an "old shoe" kind of way. Very forward with the ladies. Loves black lingerie, they say . . . PS Fleming is a great "Schuhplattler".'

The Schuhplattler was a traditional Tyrolean dance in which the male dancer rhythmically slapped on his lederhosen-covered bottom, thighs and shoes.

Half a century on, the journalist Christopher Hitchens promoted the scornful opinion that Ian Fleming was 'a heavy sadist and narcissist and all-round pervert' with a particular penchant for the human bottom. Plainly, Ian's appetite for spanking was apparent to Jo Bryce's daughter Nuala at a comic scene in Vermont. 'I brought up a friend of mine, and I remember him chasing her around the dining room table – with a whip. He came up to

540

her and told her that he wanted to beat her. I remember she literally was running round and round the dining room table at the farm. And Ian was chasing her.' The image of Ian, whip in hand, featured in his fantasy of what he said he would like to do to an Englishwoman he met in Tangier – and her reaction. 'Ian, you know, I don't think I'd like that. It all sounds terribly uncomfortable.'

With Ann, Ian had found a willing accomplice, someone he could treat as Bond treats Vesper Lynd. 'He wanted her cold and arrogant body. He wanted to see tears and desire in her remote blue eyes and to take the ropes of black hair in his hands and bend her long body back under his.'

Paul Gallico wondered if being beaten at Eton lay behind this punitive stripe, and Fergus Fleming if Ian's whip may have been the cane he kept from his days in Pop. But Eton was not the *onlie begetter*. In *Casino Royale*, Bond's sensual preferences have roots in his knowledge of torture during the war, 'a sexual twilight where pain turned to pleasure and where hatred and fear of the torturers turned to a masochistic infatuation'.

Certainly, the war produced less inhibition. In November 1940, Maud Russell had lunch with a friend. 'We talked of the sect of flagellants in south Russia and from that to the act of intimacy between man and woman.'

In London, Ian knew one or two sexual flagellants. Prominent among them was his Reuters boss, Bernard Rickatson-Hatt. Once, when working at the Bank of England, Rickatson-Hatt showed his son his cupboard of whips in the office. 'Reputedly, he used these on his secretary Ingrid, who became his third wife. He would turn the red light on outside the door when he was busy with her, spanking.' His older stepson says, 'There was a cruel side. I was beaten, for nothing. Pure sadism. And the culmination came when I was fourteen or fifteen, at Sandy Lodge golf club. At the end of a morning round, we went into the locker room and he told me to pull down my trousers and asked a friend to come and watch and I left screaming and ran up to my mother, who was in the bar as usual, and she told him never to beat me again.'

'*"Oh, men like cruelty," Lucy said lightly; "and so do some girls."*'

In one of Ian's favourite novels, *All Night at Mr Stanyhurst's*, Stanyhurst sees a handsome girl stare up at the rich window of his club. 'A little baggage whom it would be a pleasure to whip' – a Fleming-like response that Cyril Connolly would parody in *Bond Strikes Camp*. Under General Apraxin's pillow is found 'a shoe-horn with a long cane handle' and a piece of paper with 'NO ONE IS THE WORSE FOR A GOOD BEATING' printed in heavy capitals.

Ian joked about Una Trueblood, 'She is writing her memoirs entitled "I Was Secretary to A Sadist".' Ann's circle seemed aware of his predilections. Debo Devonshire wrote to Patrick Leigh Fermor: 'We've had to put a new door with false book-backs in the Library at Chatsworth, and we've got to think of 28 titles . . . Mrs Ham suggested *Bondage* by Ann Fleming.'

Ian's language contains many references to bondage, beating, and whipping, but these should not be taken any more literally than when he writes to Ann 'I do hope . . . that you're not letting people eat bits of you.' In the first paragraph of Ian's story, 'A Poor Man Escapes', a sharp wind 'whipped the surface snow into a blizzard' – rather as 007, in Ian's first Bond book, practising a quick draw on the bed, 'whipped the action to and fro several times'. These words were part of his lexicon.

'My love and a hundred lashes to Barbara,' Ian wrote to Connolly. Casually, he dispensed chastisement even to his mother. 'I must whip that bitch too!' he wrote to Ann, after returning home without his keys – 'I had to get in through Mama & make the fire . . .' And to Lord Beaverbrook, about Ann: 'I have absolutely no authority over her. Have you got a big stick you could loan me?' This was banter, like his protest to William Plomer regarding the delivery of Ian's annual Bond book, 'I have lived with this joke, under your lash!' – and Plomer's response, 'Whacko!'

In the same spirit Bond says to Moneypenny, 'I'll give you such a spanking you'll have to do your typing off a block of "dunlopillo".' Or tells Honeychile in *Dr. No*, 'Honey, get into that bath before I spank you!' In *Goldfinger*, even Lady Luck is threatened with a sound walloping on the golf course. 'Come on Calamity Jane! This one has got to go dead or I'll put you across my knee.'

One recipient of Ian's schoolboy repartee was the young Antonia Fraser, who recalls sitting next to him at a Victoria Square dinner. 'He stopped smoking and looked at me, trying to include me: "You and I both know the love that hangs behind the bathroom door." I didn't know then what he meant, and I don't know now. I prefer the idea of Fleming's wicked whip hanging there, ever at the ready for those who either sought it or deserved it.'

In northern France after D-Day with US Naval Intelligence officer Alan Schneider. Ian was incensed that his unit had been used for fighting purposes instead of intelligence gathering. One of his officers wrote, 'Fleming rather annoyed us all by saying "It's no part of your duties to go buggering about doing air/sea rescue work."'

William Donovan, 'Big Bill', founder and head of America's first foreign Intelligence service, pinning the Presidential Merit in 1946 to the chest of 'Little Bill', William Stephenson, who 'taught us all we ever knew about foreign intelligence'. If there had to be one candidate for the model of Bond, Ian teased, it was this Canadian of few words who possessed 'the quality of making anyone ready to follow him to the ends of the earth'. In 1946, Ian followed Stephenson to the north shore of Jamaica.

'The hole'. Marines excavating valuable enemy documents from where they had been buried.

'*Bring two shovels, Marshall, and have a look.*' Royal Marine Bill Marshall was one of the last survivors of 30AU. He had a licence to kill, and after D-Day was among the first troops into Kiel, searching for German rocket scientists and equipment in a race against the Russians. 'We had to dig this hole, which was full of metal boxes, rocket material, rocket plans, all sealed with aluminium.'

Ian's tutors in Kitzbühel, former Intelligence officer Ernan Forbes Dennis and his novelist wife Phyllis Bottome, who taught Ian to write. 'You were father and mother to me when I needed them most.'

Bernard Rickatson-Hatt, the monocled ex-Guards officer who was Ian's chief editor at Reuters. A passionate classicist, he spoke in Latin to his best friend Ernest Simpson (husband of Wallis) and amassed a fine collection of pornography, which he loaned to Ian.

The writer and editor William Plomer, recipient of the eighteen-year-old Ian Fleming's first fan letter, and later editor of his books. 'I read, I applauded, he conquered.'

Rear-Admiral John Godfrey, Director of Naval Intelligence, Ian's brilliant wartime chief for four years, had 'the mind & character of a Bohemian mathematician'. Ian flourished under his command. Godfrey wrote: 'He was the only officer who had a finger in practically every pie. I shared *all* secrets with him.'

Ernie Cuneo, dedicatee of *Thunderball*. He was Ian's main source of information about America and 'knew him better than most'.

Two of Ann's 'fuddy-duddies' comparing texts. The critic and editor Cyril Connolly (left) commissioned Ian's first serious piece of writing for *Horizon*. The biographer Peter Quennell (right) watched Ian write three Bond novels at Goldeneye. 'I could not take to James Bond. But Ian himself I liked.'

Viscount Kemsley of Dropmore and his second wife Edith. The priggish press lord lured Ian to the *Sunday Times* in 1945 to start a foreign news service 'as a rival to Reuters'. The contract he granted Ian, with two months' annual holiday so he could winter in Jamaica, contributed to the emergence of Bond.

'Take a letter please, Miss Trueblood.' One day, the Foreign Manager's 'invaluable secretary' Una Trueblood found herself typing out her own name. 'Trueblood opened her mouth to scream . . .'

At the *Sunday Times*, Ian Fleming set up the Mercury network as an intelligence-gathering unit in the Cold War, modelling it on Naval Intelligence. The locations of his eighty-eight foreign correspondents, many of them former agents, were marked with flashing lights on a yellow map. His successor Frank Giles considered the gadgetry 'a fair old load of bullshit'.

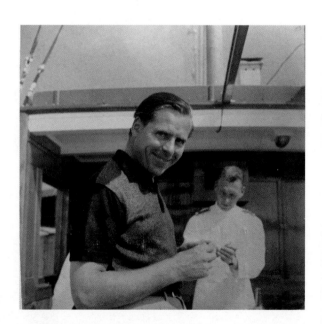

When a BBC Radio 5 film critic asked listeners to name their favourite Bond villain, one person nominated Kevin McClory. The Irish film producer was 'Ian Fleming's nemesis', believed Len Deighton. 'Ian was battered by Kevin's insensitivity while Kevin was chilled by Ian's disdain.'

'Cubby' Broccoli, Ian, Sean Connery and Harry Saltzman in 1961 signing the contract for 'Dr. No', the first Bond film. Since then, according to Broccoli, 'More than half the world's population has seen a James Bond film.'

On set at Pinewood, 1962. Ian was unsure about the choice of the 'fairly unknown' Scottish actor Sean Connery. 'He's not my idea of Bond at all, I just want an elegant man, not this roughneck.' But after viewing 'Dr. No', Ian was convinced, and put some Scottish blood into Bond in his next novel.

Ian with a pregnant Ann Rothermere in Bermuda, weeks before their marriage in Jamaica on 24 March 1952. Ivar Bryce greeted the prospective newlyweds with wreaths of bougainvillaea. 'Ian didn't appreciate the spikes in the flowers, but I told him they were symbolic.'

The Flemings at 16 Victoria Square. 'I did love being with him when he would allow. He was a solitary, melancholic, and not illusioned by his strange success.'

Caspar Fleming, aged six. Clear to Ernie Cuneo was 'that Ian "loved" his son Caspar deeply, more deeply possibly than most fathers'.

Black Mount, Robert Fleming's 110,000-acre property in north-east Argyllshire. In the 1930s, during the agricultural depression, the family bought the estate. Since then, it has been 'the tribal centre' of the Flemings.

Joyce Grove, Robert Fleming's forty-four-bedroomed estate near Henley. Ian wrote to Loelia Westminster, 'The house is the ugliest in the Southern Counties, and the cooking is "plain Scotch", but there are certain rude comforts.' He resurrected it as Goldfinger's turn-of-the-century mansion.

In 1946, for £2,000, Maud Russell bought Goldeneye on the north coast of Jamaica for Ian. In this small, simple bungalow on a former donkey racetrack, he wrote all his Bond books.

In 1963, the Flemings moved to Sevenhampton Place near Swindon but far from the sea and a golf course. Ian took to calling it 'the Towers', while to neighbours it was 'Oh-Oh-Seven-hampton'. Harling placed Ian's move there as 'one of the more gruesome essays in sado-masochism I've encountered in this far-from cosy world'.

Fifty-year-old Ian Fleming at Shane's Castle, County Antrim, 1958.

Ian's monastic top-floor bedroom at 16 Victoria Square. Caspar once found him with a blanket over his head listening to Ann's friends on the floor below snigger at his latest book.

Ian's last ambition was to be captain of the Royal St George's Golf Club at Sandwich. He seemed 'to attach more importance to this than to the success of his books'.

Peter Fleming's shrine to his brother at Merrimoles. 'He was a splendid chap who got more than most people out of life & put more than most people into it . . .'

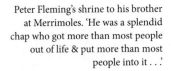

Evidently, regarding Ivar Bryce's second marriage to Sheila, Ian held to the belief that it 'would be much happier if he had given her a bit of roughage!' Blanche Blackwell hinted that this 'roughage' might have spiced her relationship with Ian and explains his inscription in her copy of *Dr. No*, 'In Exchange for much slave-time!' That Ian might not have lost any of his taste for Schuhplattler, Blanche confirmed to a French friend, Jean-Noël Liaut. He says, 'I remember a conversation about sexuality and, as you know, Fleming liked to be whipped. Blanche, who didn't really appreciate this practice, was very concrete, very pragmatic, and she said to me: "You understand, if the man you love asks you, you have to do it, even if you don't like it. I did it as often as he wanted, and I can tell you that he was begging for mercy!"' Whether or not Ann introduced Ian to spanking, as Joan Bright believed, she did admit to sharing the submissiveness of Bond girls like Vivienne in *The Spy Who Loved Me*, who voiced the toxic idea that 'all women love semi-rape.' After Ian died, a lover of Ann's was the philosophy professor Marcus Dick. Rachel Toynbee, a girlfriend of Caspar's, remembers how 'Ann would talk about going to bed with him. "I only like it if it's almost rape."'

Ian had told Ann on the eve of her marriage to Esmond: 'I want to leave some kind of mark on you.' It worked both ways, to judge from their letters. Ian: 'You have made bruises on my arms and shoulders' – the 'bruisings' apparently administered by a hairbrush or sometimes a 'raw cowhide'. Ann: 'I must be perverse and masochistic to want you to whip me and contradict me, particularly as you are always wrong about everything and I shall go on saying so for ever and ever.' Ian, threatening twenty strokes after Ann flirted with an Old Dunfordian in New York: '10 on each buttock because I am the chosen instrument of the Holy Man to whip some of the devil out of you and I must do my duty however much pain it causes me.'

Fionn admits, 'It's terribly difficult for a daughter to imagine that she was someone who wanted someone to hit her, but if you are ebullient and dominant, you want to be dominated. I took a long time to accept it.'*

For Ann, to be amusing and amused trumped all. She dismissed

---

* Fionn believes that a story of Somerset Maugham's secretary complaining about the excessive number of towels used by the Flemings when they stayed at the Villa Mauresque, allegedly 'to alleviate the smart where Ian Fleming whipped his wife', is more indicative of her mother having a period.

bourgeois values as middle class – to be mocked and despised. When trying to make sense of 'the spanky bit', her niece Sara says: 'If it really existed in a way which made a great difference to either, it was most likely a casual and even laughingly shared experimental sort of thing. Her attitude was to take one step back and laugh at life, but with a bottomless curiosity that could have led her into all sorts of cul de sacs, including whipping.'

Having promised her brother that he would only hurt her with a slipper, Ian wrote to Ann: 'Unfortunately, I couldn't hurt you anywhere except in the corners which like being hurt.'

His independence, secrecy and pre-marital history make it easy to cartoon Ian as an unrepentant womaniser. 'It remains an unknown,' says Fionn, 'but I don't think anything happened until Blanche.'

Ian mirrored Ann's romantic passion in the first months of their affair when he said that he could not envisage loving another. 'I see no prospect of liking anyone else, or kissing them, or sleeping with them,' he wrote to her in 1947. 'Waking up in the morning with anyone is quite out of the question.'

Evidence is still thin for Ian waking up beside anyone but Ann after they married. If he was sometimes successful, it is not recorded. 'He really had very square ideas about marriage,' said Mary Pakenham, 'and that one should be faithful and so forth.' In the summer of 1956, he took Beaverbrook's granddaughter Jean Campbell to the cinema in New York. In May 1960, over dinner in Berlin, he suggested to Antony Terry's estranged wife Rachel, 'in a drowsy disengaged manner', that they went to bed together. She declined. At a sixth-floor dance hall in Macao with Richard Hughes, Ian was pampered by a hostess called Garbo ('same like film star'), but allegedly too drunk to take her to bed; and in Tokyo by a thirty-year-old geisha called Masami, who ended up 'seizing my hand and saying I might kiss her, which I did'. These are far cries from the elaborate antics of Ian the Glamour Boy. Plus, his once dashing looks were not what they were, as Cyril Connolly's wife Barbara Skelton was merciless in pointing out.

The affair he began in Jamaica in 1957, however, had a different sort of heat.

*

544

'She must have been virtually the last of them,' wrote John Pearson after he interviewed Blanche Blackwell in the London Ritz, 'the final girlfriend in a regiment of girlfriends'. Pearson described a 'smart and rather sexy' petite lady, with a precise, sing-song lilt to her voice, and good legs that she was slightly vain of. 'She wore a soft, brown tweed suit. She smelt wealthy.' She told Pearson, 'I have left a Fabergé bell push in the ladies' lavatory of the Berkeley Hotel.' Ten minutes later, she was back with it, wrapped in tissue paper.

Thirty years after his death, Blanche was still treating Ian's memory as something precious. 'His last words to me were he would keep in touch & he does all the time in unexpected ways by 007 appearing at my bank in NY, on aeroplanes & on the side of lorries. I know that sounds mad, but it happens the whole time.' She wrote to Robert Harling in 1996 following their lunch: 'It was wonderful talking about Ian & comforting to know that he did love me. I certainly adored him.' She was then eighty-four and liked to eat two dozen oysters and take her pink-uniformed Jamaican maids Novellette One and her daughter Novelette Two to Brixton to play on the fruit machines. She was over a hundred when she told Matthew Parker, author of *Goldeneye*, 'I'm very strange! I'm a wild animal, you know!'

'A very rich widow with a toothy smile and Joyce Grenfell's voice', was how Blanche struck John Gielgud. Ian had met her at the end of his previous visit to Jamaica, in February 1956. The occasion was a dinner in Kingston given by Cyril Connolly's former pupil, Charlie D'Costa. Ian was about to join Ivar Bryce on an expedition to Inagua – 'an island between the Bahamas and Cuba,' he wrote to Ann, 'which has nothing on it but salt and flamingoes. They haven't been visited since 1916.'

Blanche had known Bryce since the 1930s. From Ann's perspective, that was already a strike against her.

It was the first time since his marriage that Ian had been in Jamaica without Ann, who had stayed in England to take a health treatment for an addiction to barbiturates. 'Don't use up your health and take to pills again too soon,' he begged. A letter from him following one of her subsequent visits to Enton Hall, or 'orange-juice land', betrayed his concern. 'I pray that Enton's prison walls have mended your darling heart and somehow got you off this tragic switchback of pills which I implore you to stop . . . You've no idea how they change you – first the febrile, almost hysterical gaiety and then those terrible snores that seem to come from the tomb!'

It was inevitable that Ian and Blanche would meet. Her account has the flavour of Ian's first encounter with Oatsie Leiter a decade earlier. 'He came up to me and said, "Why haven't I seen you before?" I said, "Well, because I've been in England. I've only just come back to Jamaica." And he said, "Oh, where do you live then?" I said, "On the north coast." He said, "Oh good God, I hope you're not a lesbian." And sadly I roared with laughter instead of being cross, and that was that. I gather he liked doing that to shock people, but being unfortunately the sort of person I am, it didn't shock me. And then he sent a telegram to say, "I'm alone, where are you?" So I sent an answer back, "Come and have dinner." I had two people to dinner. I said, "Now listen to me, do not leave this house till Ian Fleming leaves it." And they waited and waited and waited. Eventually, they had to go. I had a wonderful little dog who adored me and if I picked up the dog nobody could come near me. So I picked up the dog who growled at him, and he got the message and left roaring with laughter.'

It was her laughter 'like the sound of water tinkling over a waterfall' that had captivated Errol Flynn, who proposed to Blanche immediately: she rejected him, against her mother's wishes, because of his drinking. Ivar Bryce was another who was entranced. 'Her peals of laughter can banish any despondent thought.' This was her attraction for Ian, she felt. 'He was so desperately depressed, and I felt that really my principal friendship for him was to make him laugh or to forget anything that made him so sad.'

Blanche Blackwell was forty-four, a well-connected local divorcee whose family, the Lindos, originally Sephardic Jews from Spain, owned banana, sugar and coffee plantations, as well as the main rum manufacturers, Appleton Estate and J. Wray & Nephew, not to mention a string of champion racehorses. She had recently come back to Jamaica with her asthmatic eighteen-year-old son Chris after ten years in England. She had a house in Kingston, and was constructing another on a hill midway between Goldeneye and Noël Coward's two properties; her brother Roy had sold both plots.

Coward was to become a genuine friend of 'dear Blanchie' whom he recreated as Adela, a dignified, steady widow, with a heart 'lively as a cricket'. Even as he watched her relationship with Ian unfold in relative innocence, he saw the germ of a fizzier drama. He conceived it as a naughty twin for his chaste play in the film of which Peter's wife Celia had made her name – only this time, knowing Ian and knowing Ann, there would be adultery. 'The idea dropped complete into the mind and I wrote it with very little trouble and a great deal of pleasure . . . It is called *Volcano* . . . it is fairly unlike anything I've done before. *Brief E.* is the nearest, I suppose, but the situations are stronger.'

Days after their dinner, Ian stayed with Blanche in Kingston, writing blandly afterwards to Ann: 'she v helpful over my shopping, and I got a scooter and a wonderful big Japanese train for Caspar to have here next year. She's building a great new house at Bolt and will be quite a pleasant neighbour.'

Blanche had known Goldeneye since childhood. Her father raced horses on the course which had crossed Ian's land and her brother Roy had squeezed into the cave in the cliff to bet on illegal cock-fights. Since her return to the island, her riding haunts had been fenced off by incomers like Ian and Noël. 'It was all built up. So that's why I took to the sea.'

Her new passion was diving. 'She is a fine swimmer,' Ivar wrote, 'and can plunge into the depths in search of triggerfish and octopuses with skill of a high degree.'

Her house, Bolt, had no access to the sea; Ian's was the closest beach. He gave her permission 'to go and swim there every morning and to just keep an eye on the garden and see that things were in order'. She says, 'I used to come down to swim at twelve o'clock when he had more or less finished writing, and that's when we would go on the reef.'

She found a local Jamaican to teach her diving, Barrington Roper, a fisherman and swimming champion, then a lifeguard at the Tower Isle Hotel. 'He took me into real deep water for the first time in my life. And I was swimming in something like 40 or 50 feet of water. And he said to me, "Do you see that down there? It's a shark." And he dived down and prodded it in the ribs. So it swam off. He taught me not to swim away but to swim towards the shark.' She approached Ian with the same boldness.

After she introduced Roper to Ian, it was Roper more than anyone else except Blanche who taught him 'the ways of the reef'.

Asked when Ian was happiest, Blanche gave a long pause before answering. 'I suppose when we were out swimming when he was snorkelling. He seemed to enjoy that.' She remembered a fantastic reef at Pedro Cays off the south coast, a very strong current. 'I had to hold onto his feet so that the tide didn't take him away. And then it was my turn, he held onto my feet. That's the sort of thing that he really loved to do.'

The Governor's niece was with them on the night they realised they were attracted to each other. Twenty-one-year-old Christina Herridge was staying with her aunt at Government House when she befriended Blanche. Christina says, 'She imported me to Bolt. She was allowed to go to the beach on Goldeneye whenever she wanted. We went to swim, Blanche and I, and Ian came down with his snorkel. Blanche said to him as we went up the steps, "I'm taking Christina out to watch a cabaret, could you join us?" "I'd rather a truck ran over my head. What time will you pick me up?" I know people thought he was terrible. I found him particularly charming, also sweet to me and very protective.'

The cabaret was at the Shaw Park Hotel in Ocho Rios. 'A calypso singer came to their table singing a very dirty song. *It was a bed bug that found its way into Marcia's frame.* Ian nearly had a fit. "No, go away, you're not to sing that in front of this girl." He and Blanche sparked off each other a bit. On the beach, there had been no feeling between them. I'd had too much champagne. Blanche had rented a car. We got in the back, Ian in front. I had no shoes. I put my feet out, twiddling his hair and tickling his ears with my toes. "Go on doing that." We dropped him off at Goldeneye, and we went on to Bolt. Afterwards, Blanche told me that night was the beginning of everything.'

Not that Ann was likely to suspect this from Ian's account. 'No other excitements except a beach picnic at Shaw Park with Blanche Blackwell, Roy Lindo's sister, and a very young Foot girl. You should have seen my manners and my gay sparkle.'

It was Coward, then in the middle of writing *Volcano*, who jumped the gun. The gossip from his house, Firefly, up the slope from Bolt, was that Blanche and Ian were lovers, as in Coward's scenario. Blanche was adamant they were not. 'We didn't become more than friends for a year because he was another woman's husband, and I don't go in for other women's husbands.' One night, she got on her horse and rode over to Firefly. 'I said, Noel, I know what you think, and it isn't true.'

There matters rested until the Edens' visit in November, when Blanche offered to help Lady Foot spruce up Goldeneye. Ann, who took so much pride in being a hostess, was put out to learn from Clarissa on her return to Downing Street how wonderfully helpful 'someone called Blanche Blackwell had been', once even rushing to provide the Edens with their lunch when Violet messed up, and acting as a chatelaine in Ann's absence. 'I can tell you,' the Governor wrote to Ian, 'if it had not been for Blanche who lent her own cook from time to time, and throughout the Prime Minister's stay was constantly called upon for help of various kinds, the operation could not have been successful.'

In March 1957, in turmoil over the affair she had started with Gaitskell, Ann returned on the *Carinthia* to England with Raymond several weeks before Ian, to organise Fionn's twenty-first party on 20 March. She left Ian and Nanny Sillick in charge of four-year-old Caspar.

It was their son's first time at Goldeneye. Ann wrote to tell Clarissa that her godson Caspar had taken to 'wearing a hibiscus not behind but in his ear, I thought it charming, but it worried Ian as much as Caspar's constant wish to be called Mary.' This had been his dead sister's name.

Ian moved to reassure Ann that Caspar was settling down without her. He gave a vivid picture of their son taking a black crab for a walk at the end of a string. Caspar's favourite bedtime story, which Ian had made up for him, involved a family who drove a long-abandoned racing car, 'really a member of the family too', that had been rebuilt by an inventor, Commander Caractacus Pott, and on an outing to the Kent coast, revealed that it could fly and swim – like Caspar.

Blanche had helped him to swim with his orange jacket on. 'I must say B is an angel.'

Ian was teaching Caspar the names of the sea.

Blanche said, 'What was wonderful was he didn't give Caspar the common name, he gave Caspar the true name of the fish and the different kinds of reef.'

The opportunity of finding 'stacks of shells for C' was Ian's excuse to make a sudden excursion. 'Treachery! Went to Grand Cayman last weekend with Blanche and Ann Carr [Ann's cousin]. Very chaste and proper though we did have to spend the first night in one room! Blanche jabbers and the other is v dull and cold. Wish you didn't mind aeroplanes. We miss so many adventures . . . It would have made all the difference if you'd been there.'

He dreaded returning to the *Sunday Times*. 'Really, if I could stay away from Kemsley House for another month, I would gladly.' He was more than ever in love with Goldeneye. 'This place really is terribly good for all of us. It charges all our batteries. I wish you'd get reconciled and I miss you so terribly when you're not here. These last two weeks with C have been such a waste without you to play too . . . I only love you two in the world.'

Importantly, he was working well. 'One more chapter to go in the book.'

LV
A HIDEOUS ISLAND

'I'm an Englishman. I'm interested in birds.'

DR. NO

After stalling, undecided between leaving Bond for dead or reviving him, Ian was immersed in a new novel – galvanised by the forthcoming *Express* serialisation and the worldwide publicity provoked by Eden's visit to Goldeneye. Ian had written to the Governor: 'It will amuse you to know that Hugh Gaitskell, who is also, oddly enough, a friend of ours, has caught the fever and is now talking airily about the idea that Goldeneye should become a Caribbean "Chequers".'

For his plot, Ian returned to a rejected treatment he had written for a CBS television series. This drew on his trip with Bryce the previous March.

Ivar had sent a telegram. ESSENTIAL YOU ACCOMPANY FIRST SCIENTIFIC VISIT SINCE 1916 TO FLAMINGO COLONY INAGUA. He signed off, FAIL NOT BRYCE.

According to Cuneo, it was Bryce who persuaded Ian to keep Bond alive and tirelessly encouraged him to plug on when Ian wanted 'to put him out of his misery'. In May 1984, Cuneo wrote to Bryce: 'I well remember in the late fifties, before the lightning struck, of how Ian, discouraged, seriously considered killing him off, and how you vehemently got Bond a stay of execution and thus kept open the way for all of the spectacular things which followed. This, I hasten to add, was no clairvoyance on your part, but a determined faith in Bond, far more than Ian could marshal at the time, and be it noted, the willingness to back it with your own money when no one else would – including Ian.'

The expedition to Inagua that Ivar had financed in March 1956 offered

Bond's route back. Bryce pressed Ian to plunder their field trip for his new novel. 'Ivar is the "sine qua non",' Cuneo believed, 'without which Bond would have died by the wayside.'

The two others in the party were Robert Murphy, Curator of Birds at the American Natural History Museum, 'one of the greatest ornithologists who has ever lived', according to Ian in the account he wrote for the *Sunday Times*; and Arthur Vernay, president of the Bahamian Society for the Protection of the Flamingo.

Vernay had founded his society prompted by the disappearance of these birds from their traditional habitat in the Bahamas; on Andros, the flamingo population had shrunk since 1940 from 10,000 to just ten. On Inagua, Vernay had appointed two Audubon Wardens to shoot the wild hogs, police the bird-egg stealers ('flamingo tongues are considered a delicacy'), and prevent low-flying aircraft from disturbing the nests. He had organised this expedition to check the effectiveness of the society's measures in the largest flamingo colony in the world.

Ian was up for this ornithological adventure. Churchill had known his father and Uncle Phil as 'the Flemingoes'. Over the last seven years, Ann and her father Guy Charteris had educated Ian about birds. 'We must teach C[aspar] something about them. I was forty before I discovered them and most of that was because of you.'

On 13 March 1956, Ian landed in Nassau, staying two nights in Balcony House, the Bryces' palatial residence, where he met up with Eve, now living again with Monty Winchester. On 15 March, Ian and Ivar flew 400 miles to Inagua, the most southerly of the Bahamas. As soon as Ian stepped out of the Cessna into 'the rotten-egg smell of marsh gas in which we lived for two days', he breathed in a potential new novel.

Despite its status as a British possession, the true 'Lords of Inagua' were three American brothers, Bill, Jim and Douglas Erickson, all Harvard graduates, who had arrived in 1936 to develop the salt works. They employed 600 of the island's 800 inhabitants, 'and the last thing they want is the coming of tourists or of any other "civilising" influence.' This attitude was shared by Dr. No, the villain whom Ian placed in command of his fictional island.

There was little anyway to attract the tourist. Ian's group were put up in

Matthew Town, a scatter of shacks in desolate thorny scrub, with heavy machinery lying about, and a general store 'where virtually anything may be bought,' wrote Murphy, 'except what one happens to want.'

The 'worst deficiency' was a marsh buggy. There was just one old patched-up Land Rover with a corroded chassis mounted on four huge tyres, in which the two wardens made the rounds of Lake Windsor, driving through it when the water was low. This, Bryce later recalled, was 'the original flame-throwing dragon with which the dreadful Doctor kept the natives on his island in terrified subjugation.'

'It is a hideous island,' Ian wrote, 'and nobody in their senses ever goes near the place.' All around were the rectangular salt pan areas: 300-acre tracts of bulldozed flat land and burned vegetation, with pools of reddish water and expanses of brine, white and crusty, drying in the heat. When the salt crystallised, it was piled by steam shovels and cranes into enormous heaps waiting to be shipped.

At 5 a.m. the next day, Ian, Ivar and the others were seated in garden chairs on the top of the wardens' truck. They had missed the mosquito season – with swarms so thick they were known to kill wild donkeys. But though the dawn air was calm, Ian was advised to put on sunglasses as partial protection against the tiny flies like grains of sand which 'would burn like fire' if they struck his eyes.

They drove on over the causeways of salt pans to Lake Windsor, one hundred square miles of brackish water which occupied the centre. 'This dreadful lake . . . the colour of a corpse,' wrote Ian, was only two or three feet deep. Dense tangled mangroves covered the shore. Stranded mariners and grounded airmen had died of thirst here. In amongst the mangroves was a poisonous tree with a bark that burned the skin on contact.

The sun rose as they took to a flat-bottomed boat and were pushed for ten miles by the wardens, who wore sneakers against the lacerating limestone ridges. On the bottom of the lake they could see the blurred footprints of flamingoes. The place was hellish. 'And yet it was also wonderful,' Ian wrote. The great mirrored expanse of water, the mirages, the silence, the sense of being on Mars. 'And then the birds. Flamingoes? Every horizon was shocking pink with them, hundreds of them, thousands of them, reflected double in the blue-green glass of the lake.'

The birds flew honking over the trees in small groups. That day they counted 3,500. Murphy estimated a total population of 15,000.

Ian took a swim in the soupy water while Ivar presided by the fire, serving slices of Dundee cake from a tin. They turned in at 6.30 p.m. Ivar and Ian started to sleep outside, but a combination of the wind and the heehawing of a wild donkey moved them into the tent. In the morning, Murphy made scrambled eggs with sweetened Nestlé's condensed milk.

On their last afternoon, it rained. The moisture produced the most memorable image, described by Murphy. 'The rain had brought the wonderfully grotesque land crabs out of the ground along the slopes of the limestone ridge. The narrow road was swarming with them, all standing up pugnaciously to give battle to the car. We did our best to avoid them, but now and then one would explode with a *plop* under our wheel.' Each time this happened, one of the wardens groaned, 'Oh dear!'

The march of the yellow and black crabs stayed with Ian, along with the pervasive smell of hydrogen sulphide, the huge salt mounds, the marsh buggy, the toxic shrubbery, and the impression of an all-powerful employer keeping at bay the outside world. These were the images that were in Ian's mind as he decided to bring Bond, poisoned off in *From Russia, with Love*, back. He wrote to reassure a reader, one of hundreds begging to know what had happened to Bond, that all was fine, he was merely temporarily *hors de combat* – after succumbing to an illness quite as exotic as the fungus of the bamboo rat that later infected Bruce Chatwin. 'It has been confirmed that 007 was suffering from severe Fugu poisoning (a particularly virulent member of the curare group obtained from the sex glands of Japanese Globe fish).' Following a successful course of treatment at St Mary's Hospital, the owners of Joyce Grove and the place where Caspar was born, 'I think we can take it that James Bond will in due course be reporting fit for duty.'

Even as Ann sailed away on the *Carinthia*, her replacement entered the novel that Ian was writing, in the guise of an old guano tanker. But the *Blanche* was a smokescreen for Honeychile Rider, the girl whom Bond first spies on the beach with her back to him, naked but for a green diving mask and a broad leather belt with a knife at her right hip. 'The belt made her nakedness extraordinarily erotic.'

554

Blanche described their first night together to Jean-Noël Liaut. 'Ian was a little nervous undressing and then he spilled some coins from his trouser pocket onto the floor. "Why do you want to pay before you've tasted the merchandise?" she asked him. He burst out laughing, relaxed, and everything went wonderfully well. In memory, she picked up the coins and made them into a bracelet.'

'Honeychile I regard as your Rima,' Plomer wrote to him, referring to the bird-singing jungle girl in W. H. Hudson's South American novel, *Green Mansions*, '& the most attractive of your leading ladies so far.'

Blanche's gift to Ian was her quiet, unmocking companionship. She was undemanding as Ann was disruptive, leaving him free to enjoy the space around him. 'If we were going anywhere and had to wait for public transport, Ian could wait forever. He just sat quietly down and would take everything in. You could see him observing everything, everybody that passed him.'

Ann's friends sought to downplay Blanche's importance; Peter Quennell suggested it was a case of Ian being in need 'of the classical "little woman" whose big eyes reflect only trust and love and admiration'. Morris Cargill regarded Blanche as the mother Ian never had. 'Of course, there was much of the adolescent in Ian, and Blanche simply mothered him much of the time.' It is telling that both of Ann's children became very fond of Blanche. 'There was something winning about her,' says Fionn. 'She wasn't remotely intellectual, she was gutsy for life. Mama could be quite spiky. Blanche was calming and soothing. I know exactly what he saw. She was comfort food, she was absolutely comfort food. What Blanche tried to do was to keep Ian happy when his health and his marriage were in decline.'

Yet to see Blanche as a maternal substitute like Kissy Suzuki in *You Only Live Twice* is also to miscast her, says her son Chris. 'My mother was like a tomboy.'

Her father had brought her up like a son. He taught her cricket – she was a good fielder – and he would wake Blanche at 4 a.m. to take her to one of his estates at the other end of the island. She said, 'I was treated like a man, really. An isolated life, but I didn't mind it.'

She cherished her independence as much as Ian. 'I was driving him back in the evening because in those days the aeroplanes arrived in Montego Bay late at night. And he suddenly said, "Stop the car." I stopped the car and I was kissed rather passionately and asked if I had been faithful and I said, "No, I haven't." With which a lot of biblical words came forward, and all I said was, "I'm sorry I've given you the right to speak to me like that." And that was the end of it.'

Robert Harling saw in Blanche the sweetness of Muriel Wright. 'Fleming had undoubtedly discovered in Blanche Blackwell much of the warmth and delight in his company that he had known with Muriel and what he had experienced so rarely in his life with Ann. Probably more. This time round he was more appreciative. I saw this on my first meeting with Blanche, a chance encounter in the Pere de Nico restaurant, then in Chelsea, where Ian was lunching her. She was, as I had expected, attractive, gentle, lively, responsive, worldly wise. In her company, Fleming seemed far more relaxed than I had known him at any time.'

Christina Herridge had watched the affair begin. She knew Blanche to the end of her life. 'It was a romance. They loved fishing, swimming, going to crappy shacks on the beach and eating lobster. They wouldn't like to hear me say this, but it was comfortable. It's what you want when all the fuss is over. When he was very lost, he would ring, and wherever she was she would go to him, and she was rich enough to do so. "I know how to treat men," she said. "You treat them as children. Make a fuss of them and love them, and they'll be with you for ever."'

Ann was an unforgiving rival, though: as Noel Annan put it in his eulogy at her memorial service in 1981, 'she was implacably dedicated to the discomfiture of enemies.' Malcolm Muggeridge detected an early sign of trouble at Fionn's twenty-first party in March 1957. 'Ann rather quarrelsome with Ian . . . complained that Ian had been bitten by one of his girlfriends. All a kind of elaborate show, legendary set for a long run.'

The next act took place at Victoria Square. Blanche came to England every summer with her mother. That summer of 1957, she was invited for lunch with Patrick Leigh Fermor and Peter Quennell. Ann rolled her hallmark 'apple of discord' into the gathering by introducing Blanche as 'Ian's mistress'.

An awkward silence followed. Blanche broke it with quiet dignity. 'Ann, that's an unfair attack.'

In her jealousy, Ann proceeded to cast Blanche as 'Ian's black wife', turning her name into a somewhat racist joke – even though Blanche was from an upper-class white community (as a child, she said, 'If I went to Kingston I had to wear gloves and a hat'), and did not move among black Jamaicans ('I just wasn't allowed to know any'). Ann refused to see her on a subsequent visit to Jamaica. She pointed out Bolt, Blanche's house, as she drove back from Port Maria with a friend. 'You may look. I cannot.'

Ian had asked Blanche to tend the garden at Goldeneye in his absence. 'All your news about the hedge and the flowers is very exciting,' he wrote to her in October 1961. 'You are an angel to have taken so much trouble and I am longing to see it all.' In her most violent response to Blanche, Ann ripped out the new shrubs she had planted, and hurled them over the cliff.

Blanche was Ann's first experience of acute physical jealousy, and she was tormented, says Fionn. 'There's no doubt about that. It hurt a lot.' Fionn once found her mother in tears at the Old Palace in Bekesbourne, the house near Canterbury where the Flemings spent their weekends after moving out of White Cliffs in 1957. 'She was in her bedroom. People of that generation went on after the war having breakfast in bed – even though servants were thin on the ground, we had temporary cooks. Of course, I could see she was in tears. "Oh don't worry, darling," brushing them away, "don't worry." She was trying to hide the fact that she had been crying about Blanche. Ian was going out to Jamaica and he would inevitably see her.'

LVI
'CAVIAR FOR THE GENERAL'

'I had a wonderful review in the Herald Tribune – *he compared me with Shakespeare.'*

IAN FLEMING to Denise Simenon, 1963

The Prime Minister's escape to Goldeneye in the middle of the Suez Crisis did more than increase the property's rental value. It started what John Pearson called the 'celebrification' of Ian Fleming. 'Everything changed as Ian emerged at last from his literary closet and was suddenly engulfed in fame like the aurora borealis.'

Published four months later, in April 1957, *From Russia, with Love* pushed Ian into the best-seller category in Britain, although not yet in the US, and was regarded by his American publisher Al Hart as 'far and away your best'. Encouraged by Chandler to believe he could write something worthier of his talents, Ian had succeeded. 'A real wowser, a lulu, a dilly and a smasheroo,' Hart went on. 'It is also a clever and above all *sustained* piece of legitimate craftsmanship.'

The sophisticated cover by Richard Chopping, showing a *trompe l'oeil* of a pistol resting on a red rose, inspired by the cover of Chandler's *The Simple Art of Murder* (1950), gave Ian added grounds to believe that he had climbed into a higher category. After waiting so long for recognition, he was impatient to capitalise on it. Overnight, Peter Cheyney was no longer an out-of-reach lodestar but a superannuated model to be stepped over with nostrils pinched.

Ian's first reaction when the *Express* proposed a James Bond strip cartoon in May 1957 was to express severe doubts. 'There is a danger that if stripped we shall descend into the Peter Cheyney class.' In the same month, Lyttelton wrote to Hart Davis, 'I. F. is too good a man to risk reminding one of Peter Cheyney.' As his Pan paperback sales rose from 58,000 in 1956 to 237,000 by 1959, a new lodestar flickered into view.

Ian liked to provoke his novelist brother-in-law Hugo Charteris by saying that his artistic purpose was far, far higher than Ian's. 'He was engaged in the Shakespeare Stakes. The target of his books was the head and to some extent, at least, the heart. The target of my books, I said, lay somewhere between the solar plexus and, well, the upper thigh.'

Nonetheless, it amused Ian to exaggerate his similarities with the Bard for humorous effect. He wrote to Admiral Godfrey, 'I have had to engage in a certain amount of literary dramatics in order to make what, in fact, is a rather dull story come to some sort of life. However, I dare say Shakespeare had to do much the same.' When the *Spectator* rejected Ian's piece on Chandler, 'I dare say Shakespeare used to run into this sort of trouble.' And Shakespeare: 'when he became famous and "got into the money", so to speak, he blew it all on . . . buying the biggest house in where was it now, Stratford on Avon.' This is what Ann had Ian do in Sevenhampton when he became wealthy and famous.

Which class then, if not in the Cheyney or Shakespeare Stakes? Ernie Cuneo was an unstinting admirer of Ian's craftsmanship. 'I think some of Fleming's paragraphs are all but Keatsian, and a good deal of his writing will survive James Bond.' Fleming was not so sure. Cuneo 'not infrequently had to stop Ian from criticising his work, a protective measure far deeper than I had suspected and, I believe, most cruelly exploited by Ann.'

Back in the 1940s, when working on his original 'magnum opus', Ian wrote on his broken typewriter to Ann, 'i am the only person in the world who knows whether what i do is good or not.' He was reticent about his work and discussed it little. 'He never confused his talent with the "greats"', wrote Bryce, 'but simply wrote the very best he could and left it there.' Ian told Simenon, 'I regard my *oeuvres* in a very humble fashion.' He claimed not to re-read them and described himself as 'a spare-time writer of thrillers'.

At the *Sunday Times*, Ian never mentioned his novels and it was a while before John Pearson discovered that his boss was a writer. When Pearson said how much he had enjoyed *Live and Let Die*, Ian replied with characteristic ambiguity, as if he considered it in the low seam of literature but also too high-brow for a commercial readership. 'My dear fellow. Let us not exaggerate. Caviar for the general. That's all my books will ever be. Caviar for the general' – meaning, as Pearson also understood, that they were 'too high fallutin' to appeal to general populace'.

Even after Bond took off, Ian did not deceive himself. He wrote to Beryl Griffie-Williams as he was battling to complete his final Bond, 'Book still going wellish but is terrible nonsense.'

The self-criticism was genuine. To Eric Ambler, it replaced his true worth. 'Critics rarely remark how well-written the Bond stories are.' Ian 'was always such an apologetic man, but I think he was much underrated as a writer. If I were running a course on Eng. Lit. at a university, I would include some of his stuff. The start of *Thunderball*, *From Russia, With Love . . .*' Ian was flattered when his writing was included in a 1958 textbook on the use of English for advanced students. Umberto Eco rated his novels seriously, as did Kingsley Amis, who ranked him alongside the 'demigiants' of an earlier age, Verne, Haggard, Conan Doyle. The verdict that most pleased Ian was John Betjeman's comparison of Bond to an international Sherlock Holmes. 'I think the only other person to have invented a world in our time is Wodehouse. This is real art. I look up to you, old boy, rather as I look up to Uncle Tom Eliot and Wodehouse and H[enry] Moore and, I suppose, Evelyn.'

Authors who admired him included Raymond Chandler, Kingsley Amis, Umberto Eco, Philip Larkin, Somerset Maugham ('I have always had a thing about [Bond]'), Elizabeth Bowen ('here's magnificent writing'), Roald Dahl ('As a writer, he is a man who doesn't miss a trick'), Jan Morris ('as P. G. Wodehouse is to the comic novel, perhaps Ian Fleming is to the thriller'), and Anthony Burgess, who included *Goldfinger* in his book, *99 Novels: The Best in English since 1939* ('I think it is safe to say that James Bond has the stuff of immortality in him.'). For them, Fleming at his best was capable of descriptive writing which Buchan, Conan Doyle, Ambler, were too prosaic to match.

Those who regarded him not so highly numbered V. S. Naipaul ('Bond was Fleming's fantasy self-portrait'), Martha Gellhorn (Fleming's writing was 'so embarrassing it was never *mentioned*, but Ian didn't have any notion of anything else'); Norman Lewis ('it would be fair to say that there were few writers who had more completely escaped the touch of the muse than Fleming'); Mordecai Richler (an 'appalling writer'); Truman Capote, who had spent five days with Ian at Goldeneye engaged on his own book ('I'm quite fond of a number of really terrible writers – Agatha Christie, Fleming etc, but it is important to be aware of the fact that they are bad'); and John le Carré, Fleming's most obvious successor. ('Bond is very two-dimensional,' he insisted in his last public conversation, his opinion unaltered since writing more than half a century before, 'Bond on his magic carpet takes us away from moral doubt, banishes perplexity with action, morality with duty.')

Pervasive among supporters like Noël Coward was the sense that Ian had not achieved his potential. 'I am sure he could have written something other and better than Bond.' Naomi Burton, Ian's New York agent, believed he could have been 'an extraordinary, marvellous writer' if he had written with the passion and soul of which she knew he was capable.

Ian's sole attempt to break out of the thriller straitjacket, *The Spy Who Loved Me*, was catastrophic for his sales and critical reputation, as *The Naïve and Sentimental Lover* would be for le Carré when he made an equivalent move to escape the genre in which he had built up his reader-ship. 'Oh Dear, Oh Dear, Oh Dear,' ran the *Daily Telegraph* headline. 'I have just finished *The Spy Who Loved Me*,' wrote one hitherto loyal reader. 'Really, Mr Fleming, in the sacred name of *Casino Royale* and *From Russia, With Love*, you hadn't oughta have done it.' It was 'a unique experiment', Ian quickly decided afterwards. With Bond, he knew what he was up to. Never again would he write from a woman's point of view or delay Bond's entry until halfway through.

Ann definitely considered that Ian sold himself short. 'He could have written other books – *good* books. I tried to encourage him to branch out.' But as Ian wrote to Clare Blanshard about Burton's ambitions for him, 'I refuse to write a "good" book. One writes what one can & what one has time for. I have the mind of a sexy boy scout & that's the stuff she'll have to peddle.'

Even so, Ian would like to have written 'a good book', believed Donald McCormick, who saw Fleming, like Cuneo did, as a frustrated romantic.

'One felt that deep down he would probably have secretly wanted to write the perfect contemporary love story.'

Ian admitted in his interview with *Playboy*: 'If I really settled down and decided to write *War and Peace* as a thriller, if I shut myself up and decided to do this and nothing else, I daresay I might conceivably bring it off . . . but I'm afraid I shouldn't be able to write it with the sort of depth that would make it into a classic because I'm very interested in surface things and I'm also interested in pace, in writing speed, and I'm afraid I shouldn't have the patience to delve into the psychological reasons and the historical background for such a book in sufficient depth to make it stand up as a classic.'

It says something for Ian's wit and impatience that the copy of *War and Peace* which the assassin Donovan pretends to read in *From Russia, with Love* conceals a gun.

Still, Ian chose *War and Peace* in the German edition as his Desert Island Book. In his boldest admission, he said: 'I would like to leave behind me one classic in this genre – a mixture of Tolstoy, Simenon, Ambler and Koestler, with a pinch of ground Fleming. Unfortunately, I have become the slave of a serial character.'

Denis Hamilton intuited that Ian's aspiration to write a classic never left him. 'He read widely in several languages and secretly regretted that he was not an Evelyn Waugh or a Cyril Connolly.' A credible measure of his standing was Leonard Russell's offer in June 1962 of 'wine or cigars or whatnot to the value of 25 guineas' for Ian's choice of short stories. 'The idea is that we get Evelyn Waugh, Graham Greene, Cyril Connolly, yourself and one or two others to name some short story that has remained in your mind over the years.' Russell then took the puff out of Ian's sails. 'It is possible, I suppose, that your nomination might be less literary than those of the others – though naturally I am not trying to influence you to make it so.'

Ian's choice was Poe, 'The Pit and the Pendulum'; Hemingway, 'The Killers', or 'P & O' by Maugham.

Like Maugham, Ian accepted his position in the second row. 'He knew his place,' says Nicolas Barker, who edited the *Book Collector* after John Hayward. 'The George V in Paris rather than the Ritz.'

In December 1962, he stuck a newspaper cutting on a postcard to Plomer.

'Mr Ian Fleming won the Lord Strathcona and Mount Royal Challenge Trophy for the best collection of vegetables in the amateur class' – adding, 'So please treat me with more respect in 1963!'

'The most disgusting thing I've ever seen in print.' It was inevitable that exposure brought greater controversy. Ann, Lisl, Clare and Loelia were not the only horrified voices. Hugo Charteris wrote to his sister Mary Rose after reading *Casino Royale*, 'I always knew he was neurotic and tangled.'

Ian's younger brother Richard fell into the shocked camp, says James Fleming. 'It is believed, among us children, that our father threw *The Spy Who Loved Me* into the fire on account of its "lewdness". What is certain is that when he flew to America, he had *From Russia, with Love* re-jacketed in brown paper so no one could see he was reading a Bond book.'

'Peter. Read and Burn!' was Ian's self-deprecating inscription in *Casino Royale*; in *Diamonds are Forever*, 'To Peter with the usual apologies'; and in *You Only Live Twice*, 'To Celestial Fleming-san from Terrestrial Fleming-san'.

'What does P. F. think of I. F.'s books?' George Lyttelton itched to know. Rupert Hart-Davis lived on the Nettlebed estate, but he had no answer. 'Peter is the soul of fraternal loyalty in these matters.' However, when Mary Pakenham asked Celia what he thought about *Casino Royale*, Peter's wife replied: 'You must not mention it to him. He minds so dreadfully.' Peter had invented the word 'chumish' – registering the complete dismissal of a book patently ridiculous and impossible. For all his efforts to improve them, the only passing reference Peter makes to John Pearson about Ian's Bond books, 'which frankly I don't all that much care for', suggests that however much Peter admired Ian for what he had achieved, he might have placed them in this category.

In a self-mocking letter to his niece Mary, Peter acknowledged how far his own star had tumbled since the bright days of *Brazilian Adventure*. '"In the twilight of his career" (I quote from the authorised biography) "it is clear that Fleming, for all his outward insouciance, was almost morbidly sensitive to the steady decline of his literary reputation. The sales of his books fell off, & of those who bought them only a minority had the stamina to persevere as far as the end of those increasingly turgid narratives."'

For Hart-Davis and Lyttelton, this described Ian's decline as well. Early Bond devotees, they reflected a sizeable consensus that round about Bond novel six or seven, he lost his grip. In Lyttelton's opinion, Ian Fleming had 'really gone off the rails in the matter of murders and beatings, and tortures, and impossibility and lust. Bond, I thought, was becoming a bore in the last book, and must have made it by now.'

Reading a proof of *Thunderball*, Hart-Davis felt positively let down. 'The new Ian Fleming is disappointingly a feeble parody of the earlier ones.'

Bond was not the only one parodying himself. Cyril Connolly found him a ripe subject for pastiche in *Bond Strikes Camp*. In 1962, the *Harvard Lampoon* published an entire spoof novel, *Alligator*. 'There are some not bad jokes in it,' Ian responded, 'but I think it could still have been funnier.'

The first spoof and the funniest had appeared in the 1955 Christmas issue of *The Spectator*, and purported to be an extract from a new Bond novel suppressed by the Home Office, but rescued out of a wastepaper basket by the *Sunday Times*'s art critic, John Russell.

It begins with Bond ordering a meal from a beautiful woman on a screen.

'The usual, Commander?' Her nostrils showed the admiration she felt, in spite of herself, for the slim trim man with the pressurized waistcoat and the ankles of a gambler.

'Hippo steaks,' said Bond, 'with a double portion of Mobiloil dressing. Those mussels you get for me from Danzig, with some chopped rhinostones. No béarnaise, of course, but some very fresh okapi trotters, boiled in Jordan water, and a carton of old Halstaad crackers.'

The simple meal was nearly finished when the blood-red telephone went galloo-galloo.

'B,' said the familiar voice, and Bond leant forward on his malleable inscuffated drabba-tested gros-point cuffs.

'Would you know Blotkin-Blotkin if you saw him?'

'The YCMA chief?' said Bond. 'The hunchbacked seven foot negro with the long red beard and nine fingers to his right hand? I don't think I'd mistake him.'

'He's in Surrey again. I told the PM he could count on you.'

All tiredness forgotten . . .

*

It further helped fan publicity when Bond was banned in Ireland and South Africa, where the Dean of Cape Town led the charge. 'James Bond is sub-human and his activities worthy of a sharp journey to the waste-paper basket.'

One anonymous reader wrote to Ian: 'Somebody once said of Albert Schweitzer words to the effect that, in our poor world, there (meaning AS) went a truly great man. A man who has added something to the sum of love, dignity and beauty among us. Having read a few pages of your revolting (and boring) writing, I see you as the exact antithesis of – for instance – a man like S. You are doing your bit to make the world a beastlier place . . . I must also add that if I myself ever had the chance . . . I think I should try and kill you.'

A violent assault, albeit only in print, did take place in April 1958. Lyt-telton excitedly wrote to Hart-Davis: 'Did you read the analysis of *Dr No* in last week's *New Statesman* by Paul Johnson?'

In a much-quoted review, Johnson described the sixth Bond novel as 'the nastiest book I have ever read'. He listed Fleming's three base literary ingredients: 'the sadism of a school-boy bully, the mechanical two-dimension sex-longings of a frustrated adolescent, and the crude, snob cravings of a suburban adult'. He continued on in this vein to link 'the Fleming phenomenon' to the torture of prisoners in Cyprus and Algiers. In an unpublished extract from his posthumous *Playboy* interview, Ian went to his death defending himself against Johnson's charges. 'I hear it said that I invent fiendish cruelties and tortures to which Bond is subjected. But no one who knows, as I know, the things that were done to captured secret agents in the last war says this. No one says it who knows what went on in Algeria. As for sex . . . again we live in a violent age. The direct flat approach is not the exception. It is the standard. James Bond is a healthy, violent, non-cerebral man in his middle thirties and a creature of his era.'

For ironists, there are few revelations more satisfying than to learn, years later, that Johnson himself was an aficionado of the self-same behaviour – including being spanked by a compliant young mistress ('this was a big feature of our relationship') – that he deplored in Bond as vulgar, licentious and immoral.

Johnson was in a vocal minority. Plomer wrote to Ann how 'Ian's fans *raven* like something under the sea for his writings, & they seem to be extremely various which is a good thing – old men & maidens, young men & children, & that's not all.'

And Ian had gained another fan, who had started to devour James Bond while convalescing from a back injury: a young American senator.

LVII
A DINNER

'Ian had everything that Kennedy liked.'
OATSIE LEITER

The moment that locked Ian Fleming inescapably to his legend occurred at
a dinner party in Washington in March 1960. The person who organised for
him to be there was none other than the woman who had told Ian that she
resented all the things she had heard about him: (Marion) Oatsie Leiter.

'What a mysterious glamour girl!' Loelia Westminster wrote in her diary
after meeting the dark-haired, brown-eyed Oatsie, an acerbic wit who could
forgive just about anybody if they were interesting. Ian's reaction was no different. Once the two of them had drunk to him being a cad, 'we never looked
back,' said Oatsie; 'he was a charming, charming human being' – although
'he once told me he could never make love to me because of my eyes.'

They knew the same people. Oatsie's house overlooking Montego Bay
was near to where William Stephenson had retired after the war. In 1949,
she had witnessed the shipboard romance on RMS *Queen Elizabeth* between
Ivar Bryce and one of her own best friends, Jo Hartford; they were married
at Oatsie's home in South Carolina. She was also connected to the political
hubs in London and Washington.

Another close friend was John F. Kennedy, who in 1960 announced himself as a Democratic presidential candidate. The Massachusetts senator now
lived round the corner from her in Washington, at Oatsie's old address. The
detached red-brick house on N Street was the venue for the defining dinner
party.

The bones of the story are well known. On the weekend of 11 and 12
March 1960, as the Kennedy election campaign gathered pace, Ian came to
stay with his newspaper's Washington correspondent, Henry Brandon. It

was a routine visit, and Kennedy was an obvious person for him to want to meet. Oatsie was having dinner with the Kennedys and rang up to ask if she could bring Ian along. When she telephoned the Kennedy number, it was out of order.

The following morning, Oatsie remembered, 'Ian called me up and said he'd like to see Georgetown – so I said I'd come and fetch him.'

In her white Chrysler, Oatsie went to collect Ian from Brandon's O Street address. 'We were driving down the street in Georgetown, Ian and I, and suddenly there were Jack and Jackie walking across the street, so of course, I stopped, and we hailed one another.'

She said: 'Jack, I've been trying to get you on the phone all morning. There's someone I want to bring to dinner this evening. And as a matter of fact, he's sitting here now.'

'Who?' asked Kennedy.

'Ian Fleming.'

Oatsie described Kennedy's response in two versions, confirming how entangled Fleming and his creation had become.

In the first version, eyes sparkling: 'James Bond?'

In the second, 'Jack put his head in the window and said, "You don't mean THE Ian Fleming?" and I said, "Yes". Jack said, "Jackie – have him for dinner tonight" – so we went.'

It was Oatsie who had introduced JFK to James Bond. In the mid 1950s, Kennedy was recovering from back surgery. 'He rang up and said "Oats, do you have any books – there's not a book in this house I want to read" . . . and so I said, "Yes, do you like spy stories?" and he said, "Yes, I do," and I said, "I've got something that will interest you," so I sent over three books – one of which was *Casino Royale*.' Oatsie said: 'He enjoyed it tremendously and did I have any more like it, and that's why I would send him my first editions as they arrived.'

Bond was the sort Kennedy admired, a sexy public servant protected by the state and yet sanctioned to do unstatesmanlike things in the line of duty. The Second World War, in which Kennedy had served, was a period when the fate of nations hinged on unconventional individuals. Ian's protagonist was the epitome of the unbound hero. In the words of his premature

Times obituary, Bond dramatised how the 'valorous efforts of this one man' could assure 'the Safety of the Realm' and make a difference in the global world of power politics that Jack was on the verge of entering.

In the 1950s, the idea of individual agency was not yet so strong. It took off two months after Ian's dinner with JFK, with the shooting down on 1 May 1960 of a top-secret U-2 surveillance plane over Soviet territory. On parachuting free, the American pilot, Gary Powers, was captured by the Russians, forcing President Eisenhower to admit what had occurred. As soon as it was revealed that spies really existed, the fantasy of James Bond became more real to American readers.

'It was never said publicly before.' Alexis Albion is the lead curator at the International Spy Museum in Washington, where the main exhibit in the entrance hall is a replica of Bond's silver Aston Martin from the film of 'Goldfinger'. It was from writers like Ian Fleming, Albion says, that you derived your information in the 1950s and 1960s. The downing of the U-2 spy plane swivelled a searchlight onto the world of Ian's thrillers. 'For the first time, the man in the street gets to chime in and has strong ideas that Gary Powers should have done this or that, as if they have some kind of knowledge. Everyone knows how spies are supposed to behave from movies and books.'

Ian was in Jamaica when his opinion and expertise were sought on Powers – to Ann's bemusement. 'An American television company is sending a man all the way from New Y to record Ian's view on the U2 pilot, very rum.'

'Ian Fleming gets interviewed,' says Albion, 'yet fact and fiction is fluid. He's a former Intelligence officer, but he's interviewed as the author of Bond. JFK plays to that – the idea that one man can go and change the world and kick the heads of the Commies.'

At the Blenheim ball, Ian had seen Kennedy and his sisters only at a distance, but he had written in Atticus four years earlier, in July 1956, 'en masse the Kennedys are probably the handsomest family in America.' Ian probably knew from Oatsie that a senator friend of hers was a fan, considering how focused Ian was on getting his books to influential readers, but he could hardly have imagined that Bond would soon become accepted, in John Pearson's description, as 'the resident superman of the New Frontier' and a shorthand for a new vision of masculinity which Jack Kennedy epitomised.

'Undoubtedly, Bond became identified with Kennedy, and the smartness, sexiness, dash, of Bondworld chimed in with the similar qualities being emphasised by Kennedy and his cronies.'

Jack was not the only Bond-smitten Kennedy. His wife Jackie read *From Russia, with Love* and pressed it on Allen Dulles, head of the CIA. 'Here is a book *you* should have, Mr Director.' Dulles was so interested that he bought 'the next two or three' and, with Jack, 'we often talked about James Bond, and we both of us kept up our interest in it'.

Another admirer was Jack's brother Bobby, who, along with Dulles, played an important part in the CIA's Bay of Pigs operation the following year. For Bobby, as for Jack, Bond represented a role model for what the Kennedy brothers could accomplish in their foreign policy. 'He is obsessed by Ian's books,' Ann wrote after sitting next to Bobby at a dinner in London. Earlier, Bobby had sent a handwritten note to Ian: 'As you know, you have many Kennedy fans. We can hardly wait for your next contribution to our leisure hours.' The family's obsession was further confirmed by Henry Brandon after he sat beside Kennedy's sister – 'the entire Kennedy family is crazy about James Bond.'

No Kennedy was a crazier Bond fan, though, nor more curious about his author, than Jack.

Sibilla Tomacelli was married to Ivar Bryce's stepson Columbus and she remembers meeting Kennedy at the Newport home of Jackie's parents in the summer of 1961 after his election. She says, 'It was a late afternoon buffet, about twelve people. He'd just become President. He came up to me and said, "I believe you know Ian Fleming. I love his books. They relax me."' Out of all the weighty matters they could have talked about – the Bay of Pigs, LBJ, Khrushchev – out of all the ice-breakers and trivial chit-chat, the President of the United States wanted to talk about Ian Fleming. One month before his death, Kennedy confirmed that he had read 'all of the Ian Fleming books'.

Oatsie said: 'I think Jack had a bit of James Bond in him. I think he rather liked the idea of being James Bond in his imagination.'

At 7.30 p.m., Oatsie, wearing a black and red Givenchy dress and pearl necklace, turned up with Ian at her old address on 3307 N Street and pressed the bell.

Six others were present that evening. Jack and Jackie; the expressionist painter Bill Walton and his wife; John Bross, a former OSS officer and now Senior Planner at the CIA (and another Bond fan); and the influential *Washington Post* columnist, Joe Alsop, who championed Jack Kennedy to his twenty-five million readers as 'the perfect candidate' with 'real Rooseveltian possibilities' in the upcoming November election.

This was the top table. For Ian, it was a far cry from his wife's London version of Camelot. With his eye for the main chance, he knew this was his moment to seize. His wartime colleague Roald Dahl had gained access to presidential circles through his books: Eleanor Roosevelt had read *The Gremlins* to her grandchildren and asked to meet the author. Like Dahl on his 1943 visits to Roosevelt's country retreat, Ian prepared to put his considerable charisma to work.

At fifty-one, Ian Fleming was in many ways an older version of his forty-two-year-old host, even if he had not aged well. The fall of his looks had been accelerated by overexposure to the sun, his smoking and drinking. That, and sciatica and his underlying heart disease made him appear more like a man in his sixties.

But although he had lost the sharp contours of his former athletic self, he still cut something of his former dash. 'There would be a sort of red glow when he entered the room,' remembered Dahl. To Ian's schoolfriend Hilary Bray, it was more than a glow: 'people changed when he arrived.'

In 1948, Maud Russell had written in her diary: 'I's personality is always stunning to newcomers & nobody could speak if he was talking. I have seen it happen a 100 times.'

This evening in Washington was no exception.

'The rapport was instantaneous,' said Oatsie. 'Jack was mesmerised by Ian. Like a child. From the moment he met him he couldn't have been more thrilled if he had met a top Hollywood star.'

Ivar Bryce felt that the Fleming family 'must have been rather like the Kennedys. There was the same family pride and tightness. The same feeling that they had to rely on each other against the world. The same feeling that they had to make their way in the world to take the place of the chosen head of the family who had died' – Jack's elder brother, Joseph Kennedy, had died in 1944 when his bomber was shot down over the English Channel.

A second son like Ian Fleming, Jack Kennedy had likewise found it a trial to grow up in a brilliant shadow. A pyschologist who analysed Jack assessed that 'a good deal of his trouble is due to comparison with an older brother' – a reading that made sense to Jack's Stanford friend, Henry James. 'All that macho stuff,' James believed, 'all that chasing after women', was 'compensation for something that he hadn't got, which his brother Joe had. Joe was truly macho, truly a man's man. Jack was not. Jack was a woman's man and a man's man.' Seymour Hersh, author of *The Dark Side of Camelot*, says of Jack, 'men adored him, just adored him, fainted in his presence – and Fleming had that image. Both were showing off to each other, strumpeting like peacocks.'

Other connections. They had friends in common from before the war, when Jack lived in London during his father's ambassadorship. The American embassy in Grosvenor Square was on the site of the house of Ian's grandfather Robert Fleming, which Ian had treated like 'a sort of family hotel'.

Both men liked to have access to the top. Both concealed their bad health. Both were golfers, both had a similar snobbery, with similar tastes for English history and literature (five of Kennedy's ten favourite books, as listed in *Life* magazine in March 1961, were English, including, at No. 9, *From Russia, with Love*); and a habit of switching suddenly from the serious to the ridiculous.

Then the women. Seymour Hersh says: 'Kennedy was always interested in someone who had had a lot of women. One noses out the other. Women were such an obsession.'

Fifteen months earlier, Ian had written a name and address in his Bond notebook: 'Durie Chevlin [*sic*], 1102 North Ocean, Palm Beach Florida'. It is not clear whether Ian met Durie Shevlin, but a story later doing the rounds was that Kennedy had married this young Californian socialite after a drunken party in 1947. The marriage was supposed to have been expunged from the record by Kennedy's friend Chuck Spalding, whose girlfriend Kennedy would also sleep with – 'in Spalding's apartment when President, with Spalding remaining at the table while he took her into the bedroom,' says Kennedy's biographer Nigel Hamilton.

On top of everything, both men had served in Naval Intelligence and shared a fascination for spying and 'the agency'. Kennedy's experience was marginal – he had left the Office of Naval Intelligence in disgrace after the FBI gathered 'a large file of explicit tape recordings' of himself and a Danish journalist who had interviewed Hitler. Ian, however, had been there from the start, and, very briefly, at the centre.

In ways that would have been known to Kennedy, Ian was an embodiment of the Anglo-American alliance that had resulted in D-Day and continued to flourish in the Cold War.

Further, Ian had had a hand in launching the CIA's director on his career. Following the Bay of Pigs Invasion, the Soviet newspaper *Izvestia* would refer to Allen Dulles as Fleming's 'best friend'.

Dulles's biographer credited Fleming as 'the man unwittingly responsible two decades earlier for arranging Allen's entry into the profession of espionage'. In the second memorandum that Ian composed while staying in William Donovan's house round the corner, he had recommended that a man of 'absolute discretion, sobriety, devotion to duty, languages and wide experience' was needed to manage Intelligence collection from a New York office. Dulles, Donovan's lawyer and tennis partner – grey tweed, trimmed moustache, gold-rimmed spectacles, pipe – answered to this description.

Dulles had now been head of the CIA for eight years. He would shortly be briefed on the Kennedy dinner by one of the other guests, John Bross.

Ian was implicated not only in Dulles's Intelligence history but also in the undercover work of the CIA's Senior Planner. In the summer of 1942, Bross had taken a four-week course at Camp X, the covert training facility that Stephenson had set up on Lake Ontario at Donovan's suggestion. Bross had then served in London as the OSS's liaison officer with SOE, where he might have known Ian. Many of Bross's subsequent operations in Europe and, later, Central America can be traced back to his Camp X indoctrination and the SOE training syllabus, with its remit of setting Nazi-occupied Europe ablaze.

At the time of the Kennedy dinner, both Bross and Dulles had a new target: Cuba.

*

About that March evening on N Street, Ian was discreet in remembering that 'the Kennedys did say they were excited about James Bond', but 'we really didn't talk much about books, mostly about world affairs.'

Meal over, they filed into the drawing room, where, said Oatsie, the discussion returned to the vexing topic of Fidel Castro. 'Cuba was just becoming one of the subjects everyone in Washington was beginning to worry about, and there had been a certain amount of what's-to-be-done talk over dinner.' Fifteen months after Castro's takeover in January 1959, Cuba had signed a trade agreement with Russia, exchanging part of the island's sugar crop for $80 million worth of Soviet goods.

Jack looked at Ian as if he might know the answer. 'What would Bond do?' he asked.

It was not such a silly question if it is understood that Jack was talking not to James Bond but to Ian Fleming, an experienced Intelligence person and a journalist with insider information. Ian's house on Jamaica's north shore was a little over a hundred miles from Cuba. Both his father and grandfather had had important business interests there – Robert Fleming financed the Cuban Telephone Company, the Havana Electric Company, the Havana Central Railway and the Cuban American Sugar Company. In April 1915, Val Fleming had written to his father, 'I wonder when a German submarine will come and shell Havana.' Soviet submarines now posed the threat.

In addition, Ian had maintained Secret Service links with the island.

One among his many reasons for choosing a Caribbean home was the example of Ernest Hemingway, who in 1940 had settled in Cuba. In 1957, Ian had sent the Spanish-speaking English writer Norman Lewis to Havana, ostensibly to interview Hemingway for the *Sunday Times*, but actually to report on the uprising of Castro and his bearded revolutionaries, *los barbudos*. Ian was convinced that 'trouble was brewing'.

Lewis's assignment to check up on Hemingway was one of his first jobs in journalism. But it did not halt at mere reportage. Lewis had worked in the Intelligence Corps in the war and he had reason to suspect that the information he gathered for Ian in Cuba was passed on, in Ian's other hat, to SIS. 'Ian had some loose connection with MI6,' Lewis told me in 1991.

What would Bond do? The question from the man who would be President sanctioned Ian to indulge in the fantasy he once admitted to Cuneo, 'to be the absolute ruler of a country where everyone was crazy about me. Imagine yourself waking up in the White House . . .'

At his wife's dinner parties in London, 'Ann's friends did not listen to him,' said Loelia Westminster. On this evening in Washington, the other guests would hang on Ian's every word.

Oatsie watched as Fleming 'took over'. She said: 'Ian began talking in that wonderfully casual, slightly bored voice of his.

' "I really don't see what all the fuss is about. Why is this fellow Castro such a problem? You're just making an international figure out of him, by the very importance you seem to attach to him. Instead of which it could be all so simple.'

' "How, Ian?" asked Kennedy. "What do you mean?"

' "Well, there's one weapon you should use but which none of you seem to have thought of."

' "What?"

' "Ridicule. Instead of making him look important to the Cubans, set out to make him look ridiculous."

'And for the next twenty minutes Ian did an impromptu monologue on the Fleming three-point plan for ridiculing Castro.'

Ian had plenty of experience of authorising a 'dirty tricks' campaign. At the Admiralty, he had helped set up a black propaganda unit to use rumours or 'sibs' as a weapon to sap German morale at a time when England expected to be invaded. Special radio stations broadcast news items in German, like this one in October 1941: 'There have been 200 reported cases during the last week of German soldiers' genitals having to be amputated because of frostbite.'

In 1942, Ian had visited Camp X, where British instructors were training OSS officers like Bross in similar dark arts. Donovan's Office of Scientific Research and Development went on to concoct exploding lumps of coal ('Black Joe') for the North African campaign; explosive powder which could be kneaded into a deadly dough and sent to Asia ('Aunt Jemima'), and female sex hormones to be injected into Hitler's vegetables to make his moustache moult and his voice turn soprano.

Ian knew about his elder brother's sabotage work in the Far East, where

Peter was in charge of deception operations against the Japanese. Operation GRENVILLE was inspired by an idea of Ian's, suggesting that a simple way 'to attack Nazi currency and enrage the Germans' would be to produce counterfeit German banknotes. Peter printed and distributed forged Japanese military currency after first ageing the banknotes in a barrel of oil. One of Peter's better-known 'sibs' was a widely circulated story that the Emperor of Japan and his family 'have short furry tails of which they are very proud'.

Ian's suggestions for how to deal with the cigar-smoking, long-bearded, snorkelling Castro carried this schoolboy flavour. They owed not a little to both brothers' childhood fondness for Buchan, Sapper and Le Queux – who in his 1905 novel *The Czar's Spy* had disposed of a Russian minister with an exploding cigar.

There would be nothing new in Ian's resurrection of old ideas for Cuba – he had done the same when he proposed what became Operation MINCEMEAT. His creativity was to update and put a modern spin on them.

His journalist's training had taught Ian the importance of rendering a complex idea so it could be held in your palm. He told Kennedy that the three things Cubans loved most were money, religion and sex. He proposed the following:

1. A high-altitude aircraft to shower forged Cuban pesos over Havana as a goodwill gesture. This would destabilise the currency.

2. The projection of a gigantic cross into the night sky from America's base in Guantanamo. This would force Cubans to look skyward and make them believe the Second Coming was at hand.

3. An aircraft to drop pamphlets purportedly 'from a Swiss sex institute', with photographs of bearded Cubans, plus information that fallout from US nuclear tests in the area had proved that radioactivity settled for the longest periods in men's facial hair – 'and they will become impotent'. The *barbudos* would shave off their beards, and the revolution would be over.

*

'Everyone roared with laughter,' said Oatsie, 'and Jack ended up almost with tears in his eyes. It was a tour de force of brilliance and wit and very, very funny.'

Ian's proposals were actually close to ideas developed by the CIA. This should not surprise, given his Intelligence background. Missing from the record is whether Ian also mooted an assassination attempt on Castro. He would have heard from Alan Lennox-Boyd of the time during the 1956 Suez fiasco – the British equivalent of the Bay of Pigs – when the Prime Minister, 'Jerk' Eden, had screamed down the telephone to the Foreign Office Minister, Anthony Nutting: 'I want him murdered, can't you understand?'

'Assassination may be the only means left of overthrowing a modern tyrant,' Allen Dulles, CIA director at the time of Suez, had told the New York Bar Association on 20 June 1947. More recently, he had spoken along these lines with Britain's ambassador to Washington, the Fleming brothers' old schoolfriend Sir Harold Caccia. Less than three months before the Kennedy dinner party, Dulles told Caccia that he expected Castro 'might get shot at any time'.

About who would shoot Castro, there has long been controversy.

Dulles was no less susceptible to the Bond model as an operative fantasy than the Kennedy brothers. John Pearson noticed how under Dulles's directorship the idea of a Bond-style undercover operator with a licence to kill became very much the American style. 'Just as Ian set up, or sketched out a plan, a memorandum on which the CIA was built, so Bond provided something of a prototype for the sort of man of action that the Americans tried to follow in their secret agents.' When promoting his 1963 book *The Craft of Intelligence*, Dulles let slip that the CIA needed 'half a dozen James Bonds'. Delighted to hear 'that my Agent 008 spoke out so staunchly on my behalf', Ian returned the compliment. In his last novel, *The Man with the Golden Gun*, Bond relaxes in a towel after killing Cuba's former top assassin Scaramanga, by picking up Dulles's *The Craft of Intelligence* – one of few books that Bond is discovered reading, a noteworthy other exception being Kennedy's *Profiles in Courage*. Elsewhere that author, too, gets name-checked. 'We need some more Jack Kennedys,' says Bond.

Weeks before Oatsie took Ian to dinner with Kennedy, Dulles dined with

Ian at the London offices of MI6, having asked Admiral Denning to introduce them. 'We had quite a night of it. Fleming was a brilliant talker, with ideas on everything. Before we got through, we had pretty well torn orthodox Intelligence to pieces. We talked of new tools that would have to be invented for the new era.'

Dulles turned out to be as gadget-minded as Fleming: *Izvestia* reported how, following their dinner, Dulles 'even attempted (but unsuccessfully) to try out in the CIA laboratories the methods recommended by Fleming in his books', including a 'spring-tipped, poison-tipped dagger shoe' and a car-tracking device like the modern Sat Nav or Apple AirTags. The CIA chief had found the author even more impressive in the flesh than in his books. 'Ever since that night, I kept in constant touch with him.'

And now, just when 'Celestial Dulles-San', as Ian called him, could do with an insider's unorthodox input, Ian Fleming had, apparently, according to Oatsie, some 'very interesting ideas' on how to deal with Castro.

Within hours of the dinner party breaking up, Bross had percolated Ian's suggestions to Dulles who at 8.30 next morning rang Oatsie. But Ian had left already for New York with the manuscript of his ninth Bond novel, *Thunderball*. Where he was staying, Oatsie had no idea. She said: 'Allen wanted very much to meet Ian to discuss Cuba.'

It is not known if Dulles reached Ian or not. But the timing was impeccable. Dulles that morning was about to chair a Special Group meeting to discuss a 'Program of Covert Action against the Castro Regime': President Eisenhower greenlit this three days later with a thirteen-million-dollar budget. Since most of the 'Cuba Project' records were destroyed in 1967, it is impossible to connect Ian's ideas and Dulles's subsequent CIA operations by anything more than suggestion. Yet a sign of Ian's uninterrupted involvement with US Intelligence was a second mission to Cuba undertaken by Norman Lewis.

One month after the Kennedy dinner party, on 15 April 1960, through Ian's intercession and at MI6's instigation, Lewis was again on his way to Havana, via Washington, after being briefed by Ian's connections in both the State Department and the CIA, to meet Castro's deputy, Che Guevara. At a moment when no contact existed between the USA and Cuba, Lewis was to convey that 'the US's sole concern was to obtain fair treatment for dispossessed nationals'. But after he arrived in Havana from Panama, 'unexpected developments' prevented Lewis from speaking with anyone more senior than the young new Minister of Communications. Lewis later believed that the *barbudos* had learned about preparations for the Bay of Pigs invasion.

On 28 January 1961, a week after his inauguration, Kennedy reviewed Dulles's plans and authorised two attempts to assassinate Castro. The 'Executive Action Capability', later code-named ZR/RIFLE, was not far removed from Agent 007's licence to kill and makes it hard to disagree with the argument advanced by the American espionage fiction scholar Skip Willman that 'JFK's fixation on covert action to oust Castro was constituted though an underlying fantasy shaped in part by the work of Fleming.'

Willman says, 'Fleming's pillow-book fantasy undergirds the self-conception of the CIA and is what gave the CIA its identity. In dreams, that's how they saw themselves.'

When the 1975 Senate Select Committee studied the Bay of Pigs operation as part of an investigation into US Intelligence abuses, they discovered that several of the CIA's ideas overlapped with Ian's. A box of cigars laced with a depilatory to cause Castro's beard and body hair to fall out. An airdrop of lavatory paper printed with Castro's face to make him look ridiculous. Then this idea put forward by General Edward Lansdale, the overall commander of Operation MONGOOSE, as the campaign of subversion against Castro was known: to flood Cuba on All Souls' Day with rumours of Castro's death and the imminent Second Coming, culminating with the surfacing of a US submarine that would 'fill the sky with starbursts'.

Another proposal was to kill Castro with shellfish poison – one of the themes in Ian's most revelatory story, 'Octopussy'. Or to neutralise him when he was swimming underwater; like Ian, Castro was known to be a passionate diver who collected seashells. Then these CIA experiments listed by British historian, Alex von Tunzelmann: 'There was a poison diving suit, impregnated with fungus spores that would cause a skin disorder. There was a poison aqualung, with the mouthpiece of its breathing apparatus rerouted to release tuberculosis bacilli into his mouth.' Desmond Fitzgerald, head of the CIA's Cuban task force, even wondered if they could make an exploding seashell for Castro to pick up.

The connections remain tenuous. Even so, it is not too much to say that Jack Kennedy's whole Cuban policy was framed in terms of Ian Fleming's fictional world. When Kennedy met William Harvey, the overweight commander of Task Force W, the CIA team that carried out the Bay of Pigs landing, the President eyed him dubiously: 'So you're our James Bond?'

Exasperated by Harvey's failure, Bobby Kennedy later complained, 'Why can't you get things cooking like 007?'

Nor was it merely the President, his brother, the CIA director and John Bross who were entrenched in a Bondian fantasy. Tracy Barnes, the CIA's Assistant Deputy Director for Plans, apparently 'loved James Bond' so much that at Thanksgiving in 1960, he 'laughingly' distributed copies of Ian's novels to his family.

On a porch in the Bahía de Cochinos two locals remember the disastrous invasion. They set each other off, rocking back in their chairs, eyes shining in the evening sun. Suddenly, they are twenty-one again, bombs are dropping from planes with false Cuban markings, and 1,200 men are leaping ashore from aluminium boats – 'and 65 hours later, all POWs'. The flight to the hills, the dead bodies of children. They laugh at their own good fortune, and they don't feel like talking anymore.

Castro said of the attempted invasion: 'It was one of the most ridiculous things that has ever occurred in the history of the US. And they have only themselves to blame.'

The Kennedy brothers had wanted 'boom and bang' on the island. Bobby's morose reaction let slip their plan. 'Why couldn't this have happened to James Bond?'

The 'dirty tricks' had seemed more like the actions of a Bond villain than something Bond himself would do, and had ended up being just as unsuccessful.

It was not merely John F. Kennedy who was overly influenced by Ian Fleming's novels and engaged in secret plots. Another Bond fan was the emotionally disturbed young man who killed him.

At 9 p.m. on Thursday 21 November 1963, a private screening of 'From Russia with Love' was held for fifty guests in the White House projection room. Afterwards, Kennedy's close adviser Ted Sorensen predicted that the President would enjoy it. In the same room one year before, Kennedy had watched the first James Bond film, 'Dr. No'. But on this night, he was in Fort Worth, on his way to Dallas. The novel on which the new film was based featured a top KGB assassin whom Ian, tongue-in-cheek, had named Donovan after his much-decorated friend.

One week after the White House screening, the *Sunday Times*'s New York bureau chief, Evelyn Irons, wrote to Ian from the Hotel Adolphus in Dallas. 'Yesterday, I heard a television announcer describing the library books taken out in New Orleans by Lee Oswald. The absolute end, in his opinion, was that Mr O read Iarn [*sic*] Fleming – the prime exponent of blood and violence. No mention of the fact that poor JFK got so much fun and pleasure out of reading you. Ah, well.'

Kennedy's *Life* magazine choice of *From Russia, with Love* as one of his favourite books had been, said Oatsie, 'like a bomb exploding'. Ian wrote to a friend: 'It's terrifying how Americans of all ages seem to be taking to my books. Surely this is a powerful criticism of the state of American education!' The novel was one of four Fleming titles which Lee Oswald had borrowed from the New Orleans Public Library that summer.

An unsociable, teetotal, non-smoker, Oswald was a twenty-four-year-old ex-marine private with clerical experience of 'adding and some typing michine [*sic*] and filing system', as he wrote in a warehouse job application. In October 1963 he started work as a shipping clerk in Dallas, after coming back from a trip to Mexico. On the bus to Mexico City on 26 September, he had chatted to an English surgeon from Liverpool and his wife. Their son says, 'he spoke a lot to my mother. He seemed a bit ratty and a very, very inconsequential person.' Oswald had plans to distinguish himself, though. In his rooming house at 1026 North Beckley Avenue, detectives found two paperbacks of *Live and Let Die* and *The Spy Who Loved Me,* as well as a copy of Kennedy's *Profiles in Courage*. Oswald's reading, reckoned Skip Willman, 'could be seen as some form of preparation for the assassination'.

Since August, Oswald had used the pseudonym 'Alik James Hidell'. The middle name 'may have been taken from James Bond,' according to his biographer, Priscilla Johnson McMillan, who had interviewed Oswald in Moscow after his defection in October 1959.

Like Ian's fictional Donovan, who defected to the Soviet Union with classified documents, Oswald is suspected of having offered secret radar information on the U-2 spy plane to the Soviets. Gary Powers even blamed his capture on Oswald. 'He worked as a radar operator in our base in Japan. He had access to all our radar equipment. He also knew the altitudes we flew at, how long we stayed out on any mission or training flight, and which direction we went.' Yet instead of being rewarded and decorated as Donovan was in Ian's novel, Oswald – 'a failure at everything he had done' in the judgment of Dulles – was assigned to a menial lathe-operator's job in a radio and television factory in Minsk.

It is not unreasonable to suppose that once Oswald returned to America in June 1962, tail between his legs, and learned of the President's widely publicised reading habits, the fictional career of Donovan as 'the chief executioner' of SMERSH offered Oswald an alternative vision of how his defection was supposed to have played out. Kennedy saw himself as Bond, and Oswald, in a warped version, as an example of Bond's would-be assassin, Donovan Grant – only successful, like the sniper in the window of Ian's story, 'The Living Daylights'. 'He was a reader of James Bond,' explained a behavioural science professor from Mississippi in a memorandum that was sent in January 1964 to the FBI director, J. Edgar Hoover. '. . . it was inevitable that something more than target practise would be needed to consume his need to prove that he was of heroic stature. The presidential parade in Dallas presented a unique and overwhelming stimulus. In magnitude and improbability, the assassination of President Kennedy had all of the characteristics of a James Bond escapade.'

Ian Fleming heard of Kennedy's death at the High Court in London where he was experiencing a symbolic assassination of his own. He was embroiled in litigation over the novel that he had with him in Washington when he met Kennedy at dinner. Ian, at the pinnacle of his success, was being accused of plagiarising his latest plot.

LVIII
THE DARK FRONTIER

'I hate Bond. I think he killed Ian.'
AMARYLLIS FLEMING

The question of how much Ian Fleming copied himself to create James Bond, and how much James Bond then turned on him and 'murdered Ian Fleming' – as Fleming's biographer, widow, sister, and close friends came to believe – is at the centre of what follows.

The 'helluva plot' turned out to be a true one that the ornithologist's wife Mary Bond envisaged on her visit to Goldeneye – 'a woman in a triangle with 2 men, her husband, & the man he's created'.

'In my memory,' said Ann, 'there isn't an exact day, or month, or even year when I became aware that James Bond was taking over our lives. It happened over a dozen years, imperceptibly at first; then, when the paperback presses really began to pour, and the films appeared, it gathered the destructive speed of an avalanche.'

Ian had a spidery sense, after he resuscitated 'that ass Bond', that his fictional character had taken on a sinister spirit of his own. He wrote in a note: 'Gamblers just before they die are often given a great golden streak of luck. They get gay and young and rich and then, when they have been sufficiently fattened by the Fates, they are struck down.'

Somerset Maugham was an author whose life had been distorted by fame. He also had a shrewd understanding of Ian after working with him on serialising Maugham's favourite novels for the *Sunday Times*. He warned Ann: 'He'll never be able to rest now because the public won't let him, and he won't really want not to satisfy his public.'

The Ian Fleming who had finally found his audience – and seemed determined to hang on to it – was the schoolboy winner of the Victor Ludorum, making further and further demands on himself by sheer force of will. It was not all Bond's fault. Ian did not have to carry on, there was no unbreakable contract. He was bound by his own sense of what he had to do.

Ann implored Ian to stop writing when he became ill. 'Other writers don't feel driven to publish a book *every* year. But with publishers, film-makers, the press and the public all seemingly insatiable, the writing of the next Bond fantasy, and then the next, became a compulsion. Bond was his Frankenstein's monster.'

John Pearson could only agree. As Ian's 'leg man' on Atticus, he had sat in the office next to him at the *Sunday Times*. 'It was one of the spookiest things I've ever witnessed,' Pearson wrote in notes for an article he never published, to be called *The Curse of Bond*. 'It always reminded me of how Dr Frankenstein in Mary Shelley's scary novel suddenly realised that the monster he'd created had become too powerful, and his creator was no longer able to control or destroy him by simply ceasing to write books about him.'

Immediately on publication of Pearson's biography in 1966, the journalist Malcolm Muggeridge dashed off a praising letter – which Pearson lost. Not until the end of his life did he find it.

'I've just finished reading your Bond book with the greatest possible interest . . . My opinion that Ian's life was one of the most squalid, unillumined ever lived was confirmed even though you duly convey all the crap about Renaissance Man etc etc. The theme of Bond gradually destroying Ian is magnificently worked out; you haven't told the truth about Ann – how could you? In any case she probably outwitted you as she did Esmond, Ian, Gaitskell & everyone else . . . It's a fascinating story & one, like Hemingway's suicide, to be drawn on constantly by way of illustration.'

Then this: 'Only one word of warning from one who likes you & admires your writing – don't you get destroyed by Bond's ghost as Ian did by his creation. Remember, he's the Devil.'

Muggeridge was one of the earliest to articulate the idea that there is no free lunch with Bond. The hero has hidden costs and he extracts a price from anyone with whom he does any kind of business.

Evelyn Waugh also perceived Ian's hero in the colours of an assassin.

Waugh's real friend was Ann, but he had come to know Ian reasonably well as a guest of the Flemings at St Margaret's Bay, Goldeneye, Victoria Square and Sevenhampton Place. In September 1964, Waugh acted out what Pearson called 'the strange sick saga of James Bond'.

It was the custom in the Waugh household to play charades on the last night of the school holidays. Participants were presented with a word or title to mimic in front of others, who had to guess it. Days after Ian's funeral, Waugh was asked to perform the word 'bondsman'.

Long beyond their return to school, his children were to recall Waugh's charade in the morning room at Combe Florey. His son James watched his father. 'He starts as Ian Fleming praying to Ann, how he had a wonderful idea and would make millions. Then he collapses, mouthing terrible things, and dies screaming, as if to say: "I'm not responsible for my life, it's been taken over by the character of Bond, I've been made a Bondsman."'

Waugh's youngest son Septimus remembers the final act. 'He did a fantastic death rattle on the carpet, and rolled over on the ground, holding his neck.'

James says, 'It was very well acted. The best role of that evening quite comfortably. He didn't like Ian Fleming, partly because Fleming had a better war than he did.'

Ernie Cuneo was one more who saw Bond in a bad light. A former White House lawyer, Cuneo could not but note how those most closely associated with Bond ended up in litigation.* In the most publicised court cases, Ian was sued twice – in 1961 and 1963.

The curse of Bond extended beyond the film world. Cuneo had this to say about the character's malign influence on a British Prime Minister and an American President: 'Whatever his literary existence, James Bond appears as an evil talisman in the very real lives of people in his periphery. Eden's illness and his fleeing to Fleming's place, Goldeneye, has an overtone of "Appointment in Samarra". Jack Kennedy, professing his preference for James Bond, certainly imitated him to a degree no President had even

* Cubby Broccoli with Harry Saltzman; Sean Connery with Cubby Broccoli; the Fleming Estate with Broccoli's company, Danjaq; Monty Norman with the *Sunday Times*.

remotely approached before. President Kennedy's death-duel with Cuba's Castro has James Bond overtones.'

It struck Cuneo that Bond was an agent of forces darker than SMERSH and SPECTRE, and that the person who had suffered most at his hands, as well as 'his son Caspar and eventually Ann', was the author. 'To answer whether or not the greatest tragedy of Ian Fleming was his creation of James Bond . . . that question remains an enigma.'

There are signs that Ian himself came to see Bond in a demonic light. 'I have created a monster,' he told Geoffrey Jenkins in the summer of 1961 at the Caprice. 'I have written every permutation of sex and sadism, and still the public wants more? What shall I write about?'

Cyril Connolly coined the term 'Flemingway' to describe the parallels he perceived between Ian and the American author. 'Like Hemingway, he became a victim of the world he had helped create out of his own private vision. Like Hemingway, he was urged on by a mixture of courage and dissatisfaction to sacrifice himself.'

To feed this monster, Ian had to keep ahead of Bond. As his fear of drying up increased, Ian using his experiences as fast as he gathered them, Bond caught up with him.

In the hurdles competition against Lancing, after Ian broke his nose, the Eton *Chronicle* reported, 'Fleming fell when leading easily'. The moment arrived when Bond started to pull ahead.

One night in Monte Carlo, Ian took the artist Graham Sutherland to the Casino. Sutherland's wife Kathleen was with them. 'He pushed us into the roulette room and said, "Now, children, you amuse yourselves there while I go off and win our supper."' When Ian then lost at baccarat, he put a good face on it, and treated the Sutherlands to a splendid dinner. 'Then, afterwards, he became very James Bond and said, "Are you ready for some real gambling?" We said, "No, Ian, we're older than you. We must get back to bed. We just can't go on to 3 a.m. like you." So he shrugged his shoulders and went off to the main *Salle des Jeux*. But as we drove away, I glanced back, and who should I see, slipping out of the back door of the Casino and into his own car, but Ian. You see, he just wasn't up to being Bond, however much he tried.'

In February 1960, Ian wrote to Plomer: 'Am terribly stuck with JB. What was easy at 40 is v. difficult at 50. I used to believe – sufficiently – in Bonds & Blonds & Bombs. How the keys creak as I type & I fear the zest may have gone. Part of the trouble is having a wife & a child. They knock the ruthlessness out of one. I shall definitely kill off Bond with my next book – better a poor bang than a rich whimper!'

But Bond was as impervious to death as was Dracula, played by Ian's cousin Christopher Lee in the 1958 film. Ian had conceived *The Spy Who Loved Me* as his chance to free himself of Bond by making a woman the protagonist. The plan failed. Every time Ian tried to do away with his character ('I am feeling horribly lethargic about him and very inclined to leave him hanging on his cliff in Vladivostok'), Bond swung back.

It seemed more than symbolic, then, when Ian's diving mask began to slip. After Clare Blanshard sent him a pair of Richards face-snorkelling goggles from New York, he wrote to complain: 'Mask is a flop' – the bottom end blocked his nose and, like Major Smythe in 'Octopussy', he couldn't breathe. Even by the time of *From Russia, with Love*, the bullion of Ian's wartime experiences was running out. The fear that he had not much left in the vault increased each January when he landed in Jamaica with his Royal portable and two hundred blank pages of foolscap. 'My mind is completely empty of any plots for JB,' Ian wrote in an anguished memo to his New York agent.

As he became iller, his inventiveness more exhausted, and in need of more material, he plundered another treatment, this time with calamitous consequences for himself – although not for Bond; in fact, the reverse.

Once again, the facilitator was Ann's *bête noire*, Ivar Bryce. At a loose end after selling NANA, 'Burglar' was looking for a new project. An adult adventure together, like the escapades they had enjoyed at Eton on the back of his motorbike, was what Bryce had in mind when he introduced Ian to the Irish film producer Kevin McClory in the autumn of 1958, with the idea of bringing Bond to the cinema. 'I said he would make a film hero to cap all film heroes.'

Ian's bitter fall-out with McClory contributed to his first heart attack. Not only that, it set in train half a century of 'lawsuits, court cases, injunctions, betrayals, deaths and broken lives'. But it paved the way for the screen Bond that Ian had wanted all along.

LIX
'MINK-COATED INCUBUS'

*'It does seem to me that there is a nasty delayed action
bomb ticking away beneath my chair as far as future film
and television rights in "James Bond" are concerned.'*
IAN FLEMING to Wren Howard

When a BBC Radio 5 film critic asked listeners to name their favourite Bond villain, one person nominated Kevin McClory.

'That caller must have known that Kevin was Ian Fleming's nemesis.'

The thriller writer Len Deighton wrote two Bond scripts, one commissioned by Harry Saltzman (a discarded draft of 'From Russia with Love'). The other was for McClory ('Warhead'). 'Harry Saltzman and Kevin McClory were two of the richest men I ever met,' says Deighton. 'Both made a lot of money, and both died in what I call not penniless circumstances, but damn nearly. A crude analysis as to why – just about all of that money went into lawyers.'

McClory went on suing Ian's estate until his death in 2006. Deighton watched it unravel – a 'legalistic brew that eventually poisoned a thousand relationships from the bacon sandwich teams at Pinewood Film Studios to the Polo Lounge in Beverly Hills'.

Ian had spent six years 'dickering' with the film industry by the time he met Kevin McClory in a private viewing theatre at 146 Piccadilly, to watch a film that Ivar Bryce had financed and McClory directed. Until that moment, Ian had found the movie business incomprehensible.

'Will you please sign the attached gobbledygook and return to me?' Ian wrote to Peter, who was a trustee of the account that Ian had opened in Caspar's name to receive income from his films. Peter was equally flummoxed.

'Gentlemen, I return herewith the documents you sent me. It would be idle to pretend that I fully understand their significance.'

This lack of understanding was only part of the problem.

'Everyone knows what an unscrupulous lot these magnates are.' After coming down from Oxford, Peter had spent a dispiriting week in Paramount Studios on Long Island watching Claudette Colbert retake 'my, you're looking fine' with unabated conviction to a red-faced actor. Colbert was later among the stars Ian courted, urging her to contact his agent if Hollywood decided to film one of his books – 'You would be the perfect heroine for any of them.' Peter's brush with the movie world inspired a short story, 'Sherry', featuring a film assistant who so resents the lead actor that he decides to replace the sherry which the actor is directed to drink with vitriol. Ian came to feel the same sustained hatred for Kevin McClory.

To begin with, though, Ian was beguiled by the charming Irishman with a stammer like Somerset Maugham; whose mother, a missionary, lived, like Ian's mother and McClory himself, in the Bahamas; whose beautiful, rich fiancée 'Bobo' Sigrist had been at school with Ann's daughter Fionn; whose passion for underwater swimming matched Ian's; and whose debut film – the one Ivar was producing – was chosen to open the Venice Film Festival. 'This is a feather in your cap as tall as the Eiffel Tower!' Ian wrote to McClory. '*The Boy and the Bridge* is a small masterpiece for which you can be said to be solely responsible.'

After his failure to penetrate the industry – 'this mink-coated incubus', as he called it – Ian seized on McClory as a potential guarantor of safe passage through this 'dangerous and slippery world'. It soon transpired that McClory embodied every inherent danger and slipperiness in it. He was a villain in the mould of Sam Slater, Andrei Vyshinsky, Juan March and Guy Burgess, and the one who would damage Ian Fleming the most.

Fired up three years earlier by Chandler's quote for *Diamonds are Forever*, Ian had written to his agent in New York: 'I have an idea that one of these days the film and tv rights of James Bond and his adventures may be worth quite a lot of money.'

From early on, Ian was determined to get his novels filmed. This would free him from the *Sunday Times*. Once in Hollywood with Ernie Cuneo, seeing agents, Ian wrote to Ann: 'It's fun making money & I would really like to make some & get it into the bank so that I can be independent of K[emsley].' Eric Ambler was now living in Los Angeles as a screenwriter. 'For films, Ian wanted to sell the whole lot at one go and make a killing.'

Even before Ian signed his first book contract for *Casino Royale*, he had wired the Mercury correspondent in Hollywood, J. M. Ruddy: 'What sums do studio pay for not yet established writer?' He made sure to let Cape know when Paul Gallico 'borrowed duplicate typescript with Hollywood in mind'. Gallico replied a week later, offering to tell the Hollywood agent 'Swanee' Swanson that 'here is a rip-snorter which would make a marvellous movie.'

The upshot was that a Hollywood producer, Gregory Ratoff, a poker-playing White Russian émigré, paid $600 (approximately $6,600 today) for an option on a feature film of *Casino Royale*. Less than a week later, Curtis Brown sold television rights to CBS for $1,000, for a one-hour adaptation in the *Climax!* series. This aired on 7 October 1954, with Bond cast as the fair-haired American, 'Card Sense' Jimmy Bond, played by Barry Nelson.

The following March, Ratoff bought the film rights outright for $6,000. To celebrate, Ian ordered a black Ford Thunderbird to compete with the 'Studillac' of Ivar's soon-to-be-murdered friend, William Woodward. 'Isn't it wonderful having a new car,' Ian enthused to Leonard Russell, 'even better than having a new mistress.' From then on, his Hollywood aspirations accelerated downhill.

Next off the blocks was Alexander Korda, who had served under Stephenson in British Intelligence and subsequently bought his film studio in London. Most likely, it was Stephenson who alerted Korda to Ian's second novel, *Live and Let Die*. 'Your book is one of the most exciting I have ever read,' Korda wrote to Ian after receiving a proof. Unfortunately, the novel would not make 'a good Secret Service Film', but had Ian considered writing for film? Ian replied that his next novel *Moonraker* might be more to Korda's liking – 'I originally thought of this book as a film' – but he had never written a film synopsis. Korda wrote back with the seductive simplicity of the seasoned magnate. 'A film synopsis is just a description of the plot in ten, twenty, thirty pages – as many as you need to tell the tale.' Ian would channel months of his life into writing synopses and scripts for mercurial producers like Korda that were never filmed.

In September 1956, Ian delivered a screenplay of *Moonraker* to Rank, which had bought the film rights for £5,000 (approximately £155,000 today). Una Trueblood had typed this out, Ian borrowing her skills for Miss Brand, the undercover Special Branch officer who is investigating, with Bond, the wealthy philanthropist, card-cheat and former Nazi Werewolf, Sir Hugo Drax. 'I can type on an average 70 words per minute, which means 4,200 words per hour.'

Recently re-discovered, Ian's 120-page screenplay opens with Drax being bullied at his English private school. 'It was, I think, at an English school I first learned to *hate*.' Bond makes his appearance leaning over the open bonnet of his 4.5-litre Bentley – '*A dark-haired man of rather savage good looks who is wearing a grey flannel suit and an expression of rapt wonder*.' The stage directions provide new details. '*James Bond's Bentley is parked outside a small house which has been turned into three flats.* BOND *lives on the first floor*.'

Drax says that before he can take over the world, England has to be destroyed. His instrument is an atomic rocket powered, no less, by Dr Hellmuth Walter's secret INGOLIN fuel, '400lbs of hydrogen peroxide'. But the rocket – described by Drax in Bond-like terms – needs to have the right name to catch the minds of the decadent British: 'something almost flashy, piratical, romantic – so that in their imagination they can picture the thing sweeping up through the night sky – ruthless – all set to conquer continents and planets, principalities of stars, archipelagoes of Milky Ways in a perfect fever of Empire building, the Union Jack waving through the Heavens until great areas of the sky-maps have to be shaded red, roping it all in. (Breaking off and standing perfectly still) "the Moonraker!"' Swirling his brandy glass, Drax toasts the power latent in the Moonraker – 'the power that can help to give *me* – *me*, mark you – world control, world domination.'

Another fresh detail emerges when Bond and Miss Brand go swimming beneath the White Cliffs of Dover.

JAMES *steps from behind the rock. He has taken off all his clothes except his underpants. These are well cut and undeniably blue.*

Ian delivered his screenplay to Rank on 10 September and heard no more. Not making headway, he was confused about which way to go with the Bond rights – film or television. He twice called into Douglas Fairbanks, Jr.'s office in Piccadilly, having known Fairbanks in the navy, to ask advice.

After 'Moonraker', Ian sketched out several 'pilot film outlines' for the NBC television producer, Henry Morgenthau III – introduced to Ian by Jean Campbell. Morgenthau wanted an adventure series of half-hour episodes to be set in Jamaica and based around a naval commander, 'James Gunn – Secret Agent'. Ian 'verbally agreed' to a fee of $1,000 for his initial work.

When Morgenthau decided to shelve the series, Ian diverted the material into *Dr. No*. He needed a plot and Morgenthau had yet to pay him, as Ian's accountant explained to the tax authorities. 'Unfortunately, Mr Fleming has no written contract on which to pursue the matter.' Ian's casual reliance on a verbal agreement would be at the heart of his dispute with McClory.

Two years later, 'James Gunn' was revived, this time by CBS. Ian flew to New York with a proposal for thirteen episodes, believing he stood 'on edge of a vast television deal'. The deal went the way of another CBS project, to make a film with Aristotle Onassis about the Casino at Monte Carlo, adding to the salt mound of simultaneous negotiations that came to nothing, 'innumerable legalistic formalities', arguments over shared commission, who owned what, a gobbledygook of agents, sub-agents, production companies, film producers, freelance television producers, actors, lawyers, 'and other fly-by-nights' – until finally, on 2 July 1959, worn down and 'pestiferated by conflicting interests and bids', Ian decided with 'a great relief' to place 'all my film, television and dramatic rights' in the hands of the Music Corporation of America (MCA) and a single agent there, Laurence Evans.

Despite much interest expressed in adapting James Bond, there had been no breakthrough. When Ian first met Kevin McClory with Ivar Bryce in November 1958, the sum to date of Ian's combined efforts to get his books on air comprised a radio adaptation of *Moonraker* that was broadcast in South Africa from the Durban Repertory Theatre with a quiz show host as James Bond; and the one-hour CBS television episode of 'Casino Royale' in 1954, in which Ian's hero had become an American who only drank water. That was it. Simon Winder puts the situation succinctly. 'Everything about *Casino Royale* implies a dreadful alternative path to Bond – where he could have disappeared into the vast but ephemeral maw of fifties television, never to re-emerge.'

Thanks to Kevin McClory, this never happened.

LX
McCLORY

*'Ian was battered by Kevin's insensitivity while Kevin
was chilled by Ian's disdain.'*
LEN DEIGHTON

The Fleming–McClory saga deserves particular attention in order to understand how the cinematic Bond emerged from the book Bond.

McClory was a flamboyant chancer whose stammer drew you in and whose dyslexia was an excuse to ignore paperwork. Noël Coward portrayed him as 'Ginger' Macleary, son of an Irish seaman and a Samoan prostitute, who achieved 'a certain affluence by pimping for visiting sailors and, as a lucrative sideline, peddling dope'. Another of Ian's neighbours in Jamaica, Jeremy Vaughan, was dubious to what extent McClory could really 'see and write visually for films', as he claimed. 'Really he wanted the glamour. He wanted to be amongst the people he thought he should be amongst . . . I don't think he gave a damn who he walked over and what he did in order to get there.'

Despite his talkative nature, McClory rarely spoke about the wartime experience that had left him with a stutter. This must be taken into account when weighing up his behaviour towards Ian. In February 1943, when he was eighteen, his merchant ship, the oil tanker *Stigstad*, was torpedoed in the North Atlantic. McClory drifted for fourteen freezing days in an open lifeboat. During a voyage of seven hundred miles, eight of his shipmates died, including the Norwegian skipper. McClory could not prise the captain's hand from the tiller and had to cut off the tiller with the hand still attached to it. By the time McClory was picked up off the Irish coast, he had lost the power of speech. He was nine months in hospital before he recovered his voice.

His parents had been actors in Dublin. Prevented by his stammer from pursuing a stage career, McClory found employment at Korda's Shepperton studio as a boom operator. When he met Ivar Bryce in the Bahamas in March 1958, he had worked with John Huston and Mike Todd on three successful films: 'The African Queen', 'Around the World in 80 Days', and 'Moby Dick'. He had made a name for himself on the set of 'Moby Dick' when he rescued the huge metal model of the whale after a cable snapped. McClory jumped into the ocean to tether the valuable prop as the waves pummelled down. Huston wrote how his action had 'saved the whale, saved the picture, saved me'. McClory clung to Bond with the same tenacity.

Excited to direct an underwater movie, McClory had arrived in Nassau to recce a project involving John Steinbeck, about modern treasure hunters in the Bahamas. It never happened. But one night in a bar on Bay Street he started chatting to an employee of Bryce, Pat Broome, who brought McClory back to Balcony House for cocktails.

Bryce was initially taken in by McClory. 'He is of the bragging type and I, innocent of all knowledge of what is laughingly known as "the industry" by film-makers, swallowed his stories about himself without suspicion. It appeared that he was a rising celebrity, an up-and-coming Director, on the threshold of fame and fortune.'

McClory showed Bryce photographs of himself performing various mechanical operations on the set of 'Around the World in 80 Days'. 'He had been responsible for the balloon and for David Niven leaning out of it while crossing the Alps to scoop up snow for the ice bucket of his champagne.'

Weeks later in New York, McClory called in on Bryce with a project for a small-budget film about a boy who ran away from home and lived with a seagull on Tower Bridge. 'In a hurry, as we were going out to dinner, and accepting McClory's word that the expense would be modest, I agreed to become a sleeping partner in the venture.' Together, they formed Xanadu Productions, named for the Bryces' beachside pavilion near Nassau. Paid for by Ivar's wife Jo, the film was shot that August.

A degree of caution must be exercised when piecing together what happened next. Even now, it is not easy to test the authenticity of the accounts of the main players. Everything about Bond, and Ian too, is fast, but in this case it is necessary to slow down.

After Ian and Bryce viewed 'The Boy and the Bridge' in Piccadilly in November, Bryce appeared more than willing to continue his partnership with McClory. How otherwise to explain Bryce's invitation six months later for McClory to meet Ian on 7 May 1959 at Claridge's, where, according to Janet Milford Haven, Bryce 'practically had a flat' and outside which was parked one of Bryce's three chauffeur-driven cars – a grey Bentley Continental, a green Rolls-Royce or a burgundy red Daimler – 'waiting for you every place you went'. Bryce said of this meeting, 'I thought that between us we could get Bond into the big time and have a lot of fun while [Ian] could probably make some money.'

McClory wrote to Ian following their lunch to confirm the plan for Xanadu Productions 'to make a full-length motion picture based on the character created by you, James Bond'. Ian replied the next day in words that doubled back to haunt him. He had visited the set and was 'impressed with the efficient way with which McClory appeared to handle the production unit'. 'After seeing your work on "The Boy and the Bridge", there is no one who I would prefer to produce James Bond for the screen.'

In their impatience to get Bond filmed, neither Ian nor Bryce had read McClory correctly. Too late, Bryce was to discover that McClory had a reputation indeed, 'but not of the kind he himself described. It was for drunken irresponsibility that he had been fired from any position of the slightest consequence which he ever held.'

For Deighton, the relationship was doomed from the outset. The thirty-four-year-old Irishman was a noisy IRA supporter, who never had a drink 'without raising his right elbow sky high, intoning the words "Up the Irish Republic!"' He had nothing in common with the fifty-year-old Scottish Old Etonian and Empire nostalgist. 'While Ian was most at home in dark suits, club ties and polished Oxford shoes, Kevin's light coloured clothes and unbuttoned silk shirts were in a constantly dishevelled state . . . While Ian had the punctuality that is the mark of the professional writer, Kevin was invariably late; sometimes very late. Sometimes he didn't turn up at all.'

For all his wealth, McClory's lifestyle was invariably enjoyed at another's expense. He told Deighton that his motto, given to him as a young man by Mike Todd, was 'Always travel first class', and he had 'subsequently treated it as a golden rule in his life of unbridled extravagance.' Ian's British agent

Peter Janson-Smith met him in the Dorchester, where McClory had hired a suite. 'The meeting was interrupted by a waiter coming in with the drinks, and he said, "Thank you, thank you, thank you," and the chap said, "No, sir, no," so he said, "What's the matter? What's the matter?" and the waiter said, "I'm sorry, sir, I was told to ask for cash." Presumably, he must have defaulted on an earlier bill.' This was Deighton's experience. 'He owed me $27,000 for screenplay writing which I never received.'

Days after their Claridge's lunch, Ernie Cuneo flew in from America for a pow-wow at Moyns Park. For Bryce, this was a second opportunity to reconstitute the three wartime musketeers. He also needed Cuneo's 'erudite' legal brain. For their film to qualify for a subsidy under Britain's Eady Plan, three-quarters of the cast and crew had to be British and the location in the Commonwealth. The Bahamas were ideal.

The discussions took place mostly at Moyns, Xanadu and at Balcony House. Ivar's cousin Janet frequently listened in. 'Ivar and Ian were like brothers and I was like a daughter,' she says. 'I could tell a chancer – the only gift I've got, except in my day I had a lot of looks. I used to sit and watch everyone. I was young, no one paid any attention to me. I was furious that they could be taken in by Kevin McClory. I knew exactly what he was up to. He was full of himself, and he wanted to make a film that Ivar would fund. I don't know how Ivar could have been so stupid, but that's how he was.'

Even more alluring to McClory than Bond was Jo Bryce's fortune, says the Bond historian John Cork. 'Fleming's packet is not what Kevin is after. He's after Bryce's packet. Jo is one of the richest women in the world.'

The first matter to address was which of Ian's seven novels to adapt. Not a reader – 'I have never read any of those books' – McClory had now read three at Ivar's urging. His verdict: not particularly visual and 'steeped in sadism'. Like Korda, he preferred to come up with a new scenario.

'Kevin had his passions,' says Deighton. 'One of them was underwater scuba-diving. If you got him started, he'd tell you how every film with an underwater sequence got its money back. His interest in "Thunderball", his initial main motive, was to make a film underwater. He was an underwater freak.'

McClory suggested they make an original underwater film in the Bahamas using a wide-screen camera lens, Todd-AO, pioneered by Mike Todd.

One name for their project was 'Bond in the Bahamas'. Ian was up for it. He loved diving. He hero-worshipped Cousteau, whose 1956 documentary 'The Silent World' had won the Palme D'Or at Cannes. McClory's connection with Steinbeck, who had reported on 30AU in Italy for the US Defense Department, impressed him.

It remained only to decide on the storyline.

Deighton says, 'Everyone knows screenplays are not written; they are rewritten.' The ideas tossed around in the library at Moyns, and at conferences in London, Le Touquet, Nassau and New York, became the material for two High Court actions, several lawsuits, and a book. Six decades on, the question of who actually invented the story of *Thunderball* remains unresolved. 'A lot of these meetings which were held went on for hours,' said Janson-Smith, 'and they'd probably had several drinks. I can very well understand that the next morning it was very difficult for each one of them to decide who thought of what. And Ian probably never made any notes' – something Beryl Griffie-Williams confirmed. 'He never used to keep anything. That was the trouble over the McClory business.'

This is how Cuneo recalled events: '*Thunderball* I originally wrote the plot for at a weekend at Moyns. It began when I said to Ian, "If you are serious about wanting to make a film, what you must do is to write for somewhere that will qualify for Eady money and yet be exempt from British or American taxation." Where could that be? The Bahamas. So after dinner I wrote out a plot of an atom bomber which gets stolen to hold the world to ransom.'

On his return to America, Cuneo sent his notes to Bryce. Cuneo worked further on the story in the Bahamas and flew with McClory to scout for locations. Xanadu was chosen for Palmyra, the Nassau beach house rented by Largo as a secret base from which to launch his schemes. Jo Bryce, Cuneo's hostess at Moyns, Xanadu and Balcony House, was emphatic about his input: 'Ernest Cuneo wrote the original script of *Thunderball* while with me in Nassau.'

All this explained Ian's dedication, *To Ernest Cuneo – muse*. Ian even proposed Cuneo for the part of a Mafia capo. 'He has a more fabulous gangster face than has ever been seen in the films.'

Ian was now impatient to make a start. More American film companies were nibbling. He urged Ivar to hurry up and make a definite offer 'since

James Bond is my entire stock-in-trade and I have not got the energy to create a new character'. When Ivar responded with a firm bid, it was on 'the "Old Boy" wave', as Ian later characterised it, to which Ian agreed by return in a letter – 'which should be quite enough between us' – that made 'the rather airy suggestion' that Ian should be remunerated in the form of $50,000 worth of shares in Xanadu Productions. If not a newspaper magnate, then why not a movie mogul?

Only now did Ian think to inform Laurence Evans, his newly appointed agent at MCA, of what he had done. 'This is an awkward business due to the friendship element', he acknowledged in a clumsy letter. 'Much will hang on the degree of success of "The Boy and the Bridge".' Princess Margaret was to attend its premiere at the Curzon on 21 July. Ian kept Stephenson in the loop. 'Ivar's film will certainly be a great prestige success, but nobody has any idea whether it will earn money or not.'

McClory's film was panned for its sentimentality and Irish whimsy, and was soon playing to empty cinemas. When it failed to find a distributor in America, Ian wrote emolliently to Bryce: 'The frost-bitten right toe, which I suffered at my delicious Thanksgiving weekend, is pulsating that you may have gone a bit cold on the whole business. If so, I shall perfectly understand.'

By now, Bryce was getting exceedingly chill feet. Not only had he discovered McClory's reputation as 'a contemptible individual not worth taking seriously', in the words of a celebrated Washington lawyer who had thrown McClory out of his office, but McClory refused to release box office figures or his accounts. Instead, he had chartered the luxury yacht *Natalie* to launch the film at the Venice Festival in August where he talked, at the parties he had held for 'the riff-raff', about a budget of $3m (approximately $33 million today) for his new 'James Bond' project.

After watching $400,000 of his wife's fortune 'stream through Kevin's fingers for 18 months', Bryce's patience was running out. He wrote to Ian, 'I am driven mad by the impossibility of getting any facts out of Kevin. Would that Kevin was more reliable and businesslike . . . I simply sit here 3000 miles away and grind my teeth.' He had received for his total investment 'approximately £12,000 from the whole world'.

By the autumn of 1959, Ian had lost all admiration for McClory. He wrote to Bryce: 'I don't particularly like him personally, because I have never liked Irish blarney.' McClory had proved to be no different to every other merchant of hope. 'Showbiz is a ghastly biz,' Ian concluded. 'Am hoping we can get rid of him altogether & join up with a proper company.'

Ian wanted a director like Anthony Asquith or 'best of all' Alfred Hitchcock, whom he had met at Montego Bay airport where they exchanged pleasantries. He wrote to Ambler, whose wife now worked for Hitchcock, enlisting his help. 'I know Hitchcock slightly. And he has always been interested in the Bond saga.'

Hitchcock passed on the offer. He made 'Psycho' instead. Meanwhile, Ian's battle to get Bond on screen turned into its own horror story. In a passage excised from his memoirs, Bryce wrote: 'Then Atropos, the dread Fury with the accursed shears, took vengeance on a life more fortunate than I deserved.'

A portent came when McClory, now on a salary of $1,250 a week, rented at Bryce's expense a house in Victoria Square and an office nearby in 7 Belgrave Place. Not only were they to be neighbours, but McClory had brought with him an American car identical to Ian's. Ann wrote to a friend in October, 'Bobo Sigrist and McClory have taken the house opposite to us – beastly for me, and the McClory Fleming Thunderbirds fight for parking space.'

'Thunderbird', as Evelyn Waugh could not now resist mocking Ian, was determined to shake off McClory, not wanting 'the first James Bond film to be botched' like 'The Boy and the Bridge'. Bryce, though, could not avoid bumping into his production partner in Nassau where McClory had bought a house. 'Burglar' gave McClory six months to find a backer. He had until 15 February. Then Bryce really was pulling out.

In January 1960, Ian arrived in Jamaica after an exhausting five-week round-the-world tour for the *Sunday Times* to Hong Kong, Tokyo, Los Angeles and Las Vegas. His immediate task was to write a new Bond book. He took for his plot the storyline he had worked on with Cuneo, Bryce and McClory, and for which he had submitted two treatments.

Back in the summer, Ian had informed his agent, 'I am now doing the script'. Then in September, McClory had introduced him to an English screenwriter, Jack Whittingham, and it was agreed after an 'excellent meeting' that Whittingham should take over. In December, Whittingham was contracted to write a 'First Draft Continuity Treatment' using Ian's treatments as a basis – as Whittingham acknowledged on the title page: 'Story by Ian Fleming.'

Crucial to what followed was Ian's insistence that McClory rang him at the *Sunday Times* to ask if he would write a novel based on his two treatments and their discussions, which might then be used to promote Whittingham's screenplay. 'He urged me to write the book to help the film.' Bryce supported Ian's claim ('It was McClory who asked Ian to write a book on Thunderball for the sake of the film'), as did a prospective backer, Sir Francis Peek, who testified that McClory had told him Ian was writing a novel based on the script, and furthermore McClory 'was excited by it'. This was also Cuneo's recollection. 'There isn't the slightest doubt in my mind that McClory looked on the novel as a good thing and very helpful to the enterprise.'

'All writers are pickpockets,' Bruce Chatwin used to say. Ian sat down at his desk in Jamaica with a mixture of exhaustion, naivety, entitlement, and carelessness. Light-fingered though he could be, it is highly improbable that he saw himself engaged in an act of deliberate theft. He had published one novel, *Dr. No*, which owed its material to an aborted film treatment; and a story collection, *For Your Eyes Only*, which borrowed on Ian's abandoned pilots for CBS. He approached *Thunderball* in this spirit. As the espionage author Jeremy Duns puts it, 'writing a novel is no easy business, and why waste a plot you have already worked out?' And didn't Shakespeare steal his plots? Ian had freely handed to Roald Dahl the idea for his 1954 story, 'Lamb to the Slaughter'. In John Pearson's eyes, Ian treated McClory 'with the same sort of easy-going exchanging of ideas for books which he had done with Dahl' – besides, he 'always got his way without too much concern for the feelings of people with whom he didn't get on'. It would later be McClory's damaging implication that Ian was as cavalier about copyright as he was about women. However, John Cork refutes this. 'All the McClory/Whittingham scripts use the Mafia, not SPECTRE. With the book, Ian went mostly back to his treatments. But even the small ideas he may have included were not vital. To make a Hollywood comparison, lots of actors improvise lines. They do not get writing credit for those!'

Ian never lacked the confidence to sweet-talk his way out of a mess. Soon after leaving Goldeneye that March, he charmed a glamorous friend of William Stephenson, a 'rich, middle-aged, attractive, blonde, widow, TV semi-tycoon' called Ann Marlow, to whom Stephenson had sent *From Russia, with Love*; 'in a bemused moment' over lunch at Sardi's in New York, on the heels of a rebuff from his American agency, MCA, Ian consigned his television rights to Marlow in the hope she would do for Ian what she had achieved for Somerset Maugham, whose stories had become a successful American television series. 'I need something in writing,' she said. So Ian took out an envelope from his pocket and wrote on it, 'To MCA – I would like Ann Marlow to be my exclusive television and radio representative – worldwide.' One year on, Marlow was extraordinarily generous in returning to Ian this 'scrap of paper' with his signature on it. Had she kept him to his written word, she said, 'the films wouldn't have got made'.

But nor would Bond have reached the screen in quite the way he did had it not been for Ian's sensational falling out with Kevin McClory.

He had nearly finished writing *Thunderball* when McClory flew to Goldeneye in early March 1960 to discuss the script that Whittingham had completed. Ivar had couriered this to Ian on 19 February. During a heated meeting, Ian told McClory he had not yet read it. Ian contended that '99 per cent of the conversation never took place' in which, as McClory afterwards reported, Ian had patronised him over his lack of sufficient experience to make the first Bond film. 'Well, what have you done, old boy?'

Ian had an altogether different recollection of McClory's visit. 'He came out here to see me and show me the script. I told him the book was finished and its title, which he borrowed for the film. If he had any objection to a book being written on the subject, it was then or in the following months that he should have threatened or brought an injunction to restrain me. My own mind is quite clear on the subject.'

What is odd, even so, is Ian's failure to acknowledge in the smallest way Kevin McClory and Jack Whittingham in the novel that he not long afterwards packed into his briefcase and took with him to Washington where he dined with the Massachusetts senator and Bond fan who nine months later would be elected the thirty-fifth President of the United States. Ian's omission proved fatal.

When next morning the CIA director Allen Dulles was looking for Ian to tap his ideas on how to deal with Castro,* Ian was on his way to meet Jules Stein, co-founder and chairman of MCA, to seek his help in making a feature film of James Bond for the American market.

McClory's February deadline having passed, it was Ian's understanding that he and Bryce were now free to peddle the property elsewhere. What Bryce had failed to inform Ian until a month later was that he had 'buckled at the knees' after a hangdog McClory came to see him following his unhappy trip to Goldeneye. With the same 'wallowing and waffling' that Bryce had displayed when he was supposed to be running NANA, he could not find it in himself to prise McClory's hand from the project. Bryce would cable to a stunned Ian on 23 March: 'Have given Kevin six months to waste capital and get show going, otherwise everything reverts to us.'

Meanwhile, even were Bond to have been a free property, Jules Stein was 'clearly not very excited' by a movie based on his 'very British' adventures.

Immediately following Stein's lukewarm reaction, Ian had his smoked-salmon-and-scrambled-egg lunch with Ann Marlow at Sardi's East. After all his efforts, he was back to square one, which explained his impetuous arrangement with her.

Six months passed, with Marlow failing to excite the interest of television companies. ('They'd say, who's James Bond?') Bryce claimed to have heard 'nothing from Kevin for months'. McClory had still not signed off on the accounts for 'The Boy and the Bridge', 'thus making enormous tax losses to Jo (Mrs Bryce) and me'. As the October deadline approached, it pained Bryce to realise that McClory was unlikely ever to place Bond with a film studio.

Meanwhile, the penny had at last dropped that Ian and Bryce were bent on easing him out. It upset McClory to read in the press that Gregory Ratoff had interested Twentieth Century–Fox in making a film of *Casino Royale*; Ian had neglected to tell McClory that Ratoff had bought the rights five years earlier. When an acrimonious McClory did finally get in touch with Bryce, it was to complain that this previous deal compromised McClory's efforts to

---

* In another version, Dulles was anxious to keep Ian from writing about the evening because one of his ideas (about the beards) was too close to the CIA's own plot.

convince interested parties that he possessed the sole option to make the first Bond film, and that 'unfair and unjust things have been said behind my back'. Concerned, Bryce passed on to Ian that Cuneo's legalistic mind sensed a looming threat. 'Ernie thinks that Kevin may claim authorship of *Thunderball*, when you publish it!'

On 30 October the deadline for McClory's extension passed. In assuming that all film rights to Bond at once reverted to Ian and Ivar, Ian's disdain for McClory overrode his better judgement. By this stage, Ian was quite aware of 'this copyright problem' – as he wrote to Robert Fenn at MCA; also the possibility that 'we shall be faced with injunctions by McClory'. Yet Ian went ahead on 19 December 1960 to sign a contract with Cape stating that the novel was his sole exclusive work. He was emboldened to do this by Cuneo, who reminded Bryce: 'you have been robbed by Kevin McClory more than plenty.' The atmosphere needed to be cleared of 'the greasy smog of inaccuracies, half-truths, blarney, optimistic euphoria and incredible self-hypnosis'. Were Cuneo standing in Ian's shoes, he would refuse to let his name and his work 'be used as bait for possible suckers'.

One of the fish on Ian's reef was a remora – 'about a foot long with a flat head that clung to the belly of a shark,' Blanche described it. 'And this was a terrible fish to meet. Sometimes the shark would swim in and scrape him off and then he would be looking for something else to stick onto, and he'd find you and stick onto you.'

Contractually still a partner of Xanadu Productions, McClory maintained that he owned an equal share of Bryce's company, and therefore of Bond. The stammering Irishman who had clamped himself to John Huston's whale in a pitching sea was never going to let go.

Cuneo had earlier sold his rights in the 'Thunderball' story to Bryce for $1. When Ian allegedly offered McClory £2,000 in cash (approximately £54,000 today) in the big hall at Moyns in December 1960, McClory turned him down flat. Deighton recalls how mobile and florid McClory's face became when angry: 'it was the face of a fairground barker.' Not long after, McClory called on Ian's office accompanied by a lawyer and announced he would accept £75,000 as compensation. 'Ian and I were dumbfounded at his action,' wrote Bryce. 'We cut all connections and Ian proceeded with publication.'

Only now did the awful realisation dawn on Ian that he would be unable to charm his way out of this imbroglio. Weeks later, an abject Bryce wrote to Ian at Goldeneye to say that he was 'in a state of collapse over this unspeakable Kevin business and worry incessantly at having been the cause of so much trouble for you'.

The trouble was about to get worse. On 10 March 1961, McClory was allegedly 'shocked' to read an advance copy of *Thunderball*, which he maintained had used large parts of Whittingham's film script without acknowledging Whittingham or McClory.

Ian was on his way back from Goldeneye. He took off from New York, reading in the 17 March issue of *Life* magazine, in an article headlined 'The President's Voracious Reading Habits' (and subtitled 'He eats up news, books at 1,200 words a minute'), that Kennedy had chosen *From Russia, with Love* as one of his ten favourite books. Ian landed in London to learn that McClory intended to charge him with plagiarism. Griffie-Williams was waiting. 'I had the terrible job of being up all night, typing out stuff for the case, and then meeting him at eight in the morning at London airport to tell him that McClory was going to sue.' McClory had applied to the High Court for an injunction to prevent the imminent publication of *Thunderball*. The case had been fast-tracked to be heard on Friday 24 March – three days before publication.

'It could only happen to Ian,' said Pearson. 'You get the mud and the cream. He got the Presidential credentials, and he also got an attack from McClory. And the two things tended to go together for him so much in life.'

LXI
THE BLACK CLOUD

'There has never been any person on earth like that dreadful person.'
MARGUERITE WENNER-GREN to Eve Fleming

It was Ian's second time in the High Court.

Four years earlier, in November 1957, he had had to sit and watch his seventy-three-year-old mother face accusations of lying, after Eve was sued by Bapsybanoo ('Bapsy') Pavry, the fifty-four-year-old Marchioness of Winchester, for 'enticement' of Bapsy's husband Monty, the ninety-three-year-old marquess. Having waited all her life to find a replacement for Val, Eve had chosen to leave Nassau and live with the decrepit old profligate in No. 66 and 67 suites of the Hôtel Mirabeau in Monte Carlo. 'Everybody calls her the twining leech,' said Bapsy.

Eve issued a three-line whip to her sons to improve her credibility in the witness-box. Not only did she demand their presence in court, but she had Peter and Ian photographed arm-in-arm with her as 'a trio for the tabloids', in what Ian admitted was the most demeaning photographic session he had ever taken part in.

'How silly can people be?' wrote Rupert Hart-Davis, after hearing from Peter about 'his mother's humiliating litigation'. He had known Eve since she came to Eton in her yellow dress. She had not changed. Ann wrote to Waugh, 'she inclines to dress like Lady Ottoline Morrell or the Casati, so every morning Peter, Ian and Richard go to her hotel and force her into hospital matron clothes.'

This bizarre, much-publicised trial was debilitating for Ian, who was so upright and private in many ways. Here on display for the world to snigger at was 'the woman of steel', as Harling dubbed her, who still had dominion over his life. For two stressful weeks, Ian was reminded of his mother's controlling character in eye-popping detail.

Eve had broken off her engagement to Monty back in June 1952, in London, on her doctor's advice 'that Lord Winchester was too old for her to take care of him'. The next day, Monty, then eighty-nine, had tea with Bapsybanoo Pavry, the socially ambitious daughter of a Zoroastrian high priest from Bombay, with large estates in Baroda; Monty had last seen Bapsy at a reception twenty-three years before.

While walking with Bapsy to his hotel, Monty proposed. He wanted a son and heir to his title – his present heir was a relative who 'lived in County Wexford and never answered his letters'. Although she was then forty-nine and quite old to be having a baby, Bapsy allowed him to think that she was 'a virgin' of wealth and standing. Like Eve, she had been painted by Augustus John, her portrait hanging in the stairwell of the Royal Academy restaurant – 'pale and red-lipped, her eyes almost on the verge of tears', as Bapsy's biographer Duncan Fallowell described her pose.

At 6 p.m. the following afternoon, Bapsy accepted Monty's proposal, even though he was old enough to be her grandfather. In her desire to become and then firmly remain the premier marchioness of England (and the first Indian woman to hold such a title), Bapsy was to rival Eve for snobbery and McClory for tenacity. Ian called her 'the Black Cloud'.

Fallowell paints a portrait of Bapsy in *How to Disappear: A Memoir for Misfits* as a risible hanger-on. 'Bapsy's breathtaking resilience, her social crudeness, her absolute refusal ever to pick up a dropped hint' was the product of 'a zealous and lifelong campaign to put herself on the world map and become a great figure'. Born in Bombay, and presented at court in 1928 after completing her MA at Columbia, she had, before reuniting with Monty for tea at the Mayfair Hotel, been the pushy guest of most of the crowned heads of Europe, Asia and Africa, as well as of Mussolini (1934), Hitler (1937), President Calvin Coolidge, Neville Chamberlain and Pope Pius XI (1926). To leaf through their signed photographs, wrote Fallowell, was to conclude that 'she never really did anything except social climb'. She and Eve had a lot in common.

Monty proposed on the Friday. They were married on the Wednesday, with no family or friends present, at Caxton Hall, in what 'Chips' Channon called a 'Coronation Marriage', owing to Bapsy's desperation to secure a place at the coronation the following June. Bapsy at once contacted experts at the Royal College of Arms over what to wear ('it would be quite in order for you to wear a Sari under your Kirtle and train,' wrote Chester Herald). On 1 January 1953, Bluemantle Pursuivant of Arms felt obliged to remind Bapsy that her coronet had to be put on only after Queen was crowned, and without the aid of a mirror. 'I hope you will not mind my pointing this out to you, but you might find some difficulty in doing this if the Sari is draped over your head.'

In the event, when Monty claimed he would not attend the coronation because he was too old to stand for hours on end, this was just an excuse. As a certified bankrupt, he had not been invited. To her bitter disappointment, the Earl Marshal denied Bapsy permission to attend.

Their marriage was consummated on 9 July 1952, with Monty claiming to make the discovery that she 'was not a chaste woman'. Soon after, they moved to Monte Carlo. Their first base: the Hôtel Métropole.

To celebrate her fiftieth birthday on Boxing Day, Bapsy arranged for the hotel secretary to type out an article, 'Profile of a great and gracious lady', which Bapsy wired to the *Evening Standard*. This stated that on her notable marriage congratulations were sent by Queen Mary, the Mountbattens and General Eisenhower, and that she was 'recognised for her beauty and grace' and her 'wealth and fabulous jewels', and 'long hailed in Britain as India's unofficial ambassador'.

Eve's barrister looked at the judge. 'That was sheer nonsense.'

The High Court was told that this article was only one of 'a series of annoyances' which led to the rift between Bapsy and her husband, who, in response to Bapsy's description of herself as an ambassador, was reported to have remarked, 'That's how we lost India.' The marquess had become disappointed in marriage, had found no substance in the story of his wife's riches, and was being forced by her to live on one meal a day.

Meanwhile, Eve was circling again.

'Mrs. Fleming was rather upset by this extraordinary and odd marriage. She then heard rumours that Lord Winchester was alone at Monte Carlo and ill-fed and wrote offering him the cottage in the grounds of her home at Nassau.' A letter from Eve contained the line: 'The garden is so lovely, the Garden of Eden without Adam.'

Bapsy insisted that up until that moment, her marriage was 'as happy as the marriage bells . . . He used to worship the ground I walked on,' and she cited a letter from Monty: 'My darling Bapsy . . . I am the luckiest man in the world to have the most wonderful wife in the world.' Yet days later, he departed for the Bahamas wrapped in a blanket after undergoing a dramatic and mysterious change of heart.

In Nassau, Monty met Eve at her seaside home, where their relationship was restored to 'all its former warmth'. A greater mystery to Fallowell was why Eve should have wanted to keep her hand in with him. 'It can't have been his love-making prowess unless Monty was an utterly different man when his clothes were off, which seems unlikely.'

Monty's conclusion that his marriage had been an 'awful mistake' was confirmed by Bapsy's letters demanding him back and attacking Eve in the most vituperative terms – 'your mistress Fleming whom you call crooked-minded . . . you call her bitch.'

Ian listened to Eve's barrister read out further examples of Bapsy's invective to Monty. 'Your title is Mud, as so very many well-known and highly-placed people in England say . . . May a viper's fangs be for ever around your throat, and may you sizzle in the pit in your own juice.'

Counsel: 'Do you think that a husband receiving that sort of letter would be anxious to return to live with you?'

Bapsy: 'Yes. I do.'

She mentioned Ian in several letters that excoriated Eve. 'Everyone says that to cover up her sins she used names of her sons. Here is inserted a press cutting which reads as follows: "Mrs Valentine Fleming of Cable Beach is the mother of Peter Fleming, the well known English author. Another son, Ian, has recently published his first novel *Casino Royale*, a bestseller in America. A second thriller is due for publication early in the New Year." There is no such bestseller in US, and it is a travesty of the truth.'

Bapsy had addressed a telegram directly to Ian, the son most responsible for his mother settling in Nassau. 'The world will be shocked by her immorality and the deamonlike [*sic*] brutalities she has perpetrated on a devoted wife.'

In February 1954, Bapsy turned up in Nassau and cornered a flustered Monty in a car park. He told Bapsy that Eve had asked him not to see her and mentioned Eve's ancient Browning pistol. 'He said that Mrs. Fleming would shoot him. She would shoot him dead. She had got a gun.'

Ivar Bryce supplied this indelible image of Bapsy outside Emerald Wave, Eve's property on Cable Beach: 'an overweight Indian lady clad in a dingy sari, pacing the main road ... but occasionally pausing to raise and shake her fist towards the house.'

Bapsy cut much the same histrionic figure in the High Court. Unable to stem her emotional commentary, she was asked on one occasion to leave the witness box. The judge told her that if she did not shut up, 'I shall send you to spend a night in Brixton prison.'

However, Eve was not a convincing defendant either. Ian squirmed as the prosecution made the case that 'her overmastering desire throughout was to become Lady Winchester.' She had carefully avoided every question she was asked in the witness box, and there were fourteen instances where her evidence was inconsistent. Peter passed a note to Richard: '*Elle ment et le juge le sait*' (She's lying and the judge knows it.)

Peter's fears were well founded. 'Was Mrs Fleming telling the truth?' the judge asked in his summing up. 'I have come to the conclusion that she was not.' He awarded Bapsy costs, estimated at £12,000 (approximately £340,000 today). Eve's barrister said of his client, 'The Judge had, in effect, found her guilty of cold and calculated perjury.'

The judgment was reversed the following July when the Court of Appeal decided that Bapsy had failed to prove her case. Eve was given custody of the marquess, although she never inherited Bapsy's title. With defiance, but also loyalty, she sold Emerald Wave and withdrew with Monty to 'that small cell in the Mirabeau', as Ian described their hotel quarters. Monty had a suite at the end of the ground floor corridor, to which Eve carried him bowls of soup. 'She enters his bedroom, pats the pillow, and turns it down at night,' said a visitor. The marquess could move around only with the aid of sticks.

When Peter's son Nichol visited his grandmother in 1961, he walked with the marquess at what Nichol called 'low cruising speed', in tiny steps, and everyone turned to see. Eve was scarcely more agile. She kept a black Rolls-Royce and a chauffeur called Vivaldi on permanent stand-by, and was said never to walk 'as much as a hundred yards'.

Monty died on 28 June 1962 in the Princess Grace Clinic in Monte Carlo.

He was ninety-nine, and the oldest member of the House of Lords. It was in keeping with Eve's snobbish destiny that in a dramatic flurry an hour or so later, Val's good friend, who had laid white flowers on his grave in France forty-five years previously, brought the world's press gawking to the hospital.

As Monty passed away that Thursday morning, Winston Churchill fell out of bed with a thud in the Hôtel de Paris and fractured his femur. Even while Eve mourned the still-warm body of her nonagenarian companion in a nearby room, her husband's obituarist, whose words were hung framed on Ian Fleming's wall, was wheeled on a trolley into the clinic and sedated with an injection. He woke to find his left leg in a huge plaster cast, with hordes of reporters outside the hospital, and roared, 'You monsters! You monsters! Leave me alone.'

LXII
THE SECRETS OF A MAN

'The nightmare of those last years'
ANN FLEMING

It had horrified Ian to watch the evisceration of Eve, the oppressive force who had trained him to be afraid of love. She was upheld in the eyes of the judge as the prosecution had sought to characterise her, 'evasive, opinionated, worldly, snobbish, and untruthful'. On 24 March 1961, Ian appeared in the same High Court to face his own charge of dishonesty, for 'an infringement of copyright'.

Ann told Waugh, 'Thunderbird's secretary and Mrs Crickmere were very excited and said he was to be arrested at the airport.' Ann knew where to point her finger. 'It all comes of keeping bad company.' Ian 'shouldn't know people like Bryce and McClory'.

Waugh vowed to pray 'for poor Thunderbird in prison'.

Ian was not, however, to repeat the fate of Waugh's scoundrel Captain Grimes. The judge refused McClory's application after lawyers for Ian and Cape argued that publicity for *Thunderball* was too far advanced, with 32,000 copies already distributed to 864 booksellers and the first reviews expected to appear that weekend.

Publication could proceed.

Ominously, McClory's lawyer promised to bring another action claiming damages. 'This novel owes a great deal to the film script.' For the next two years, Ian lived knowing he would have to appear again in the High Court to defend his reputation. 'It was pending for a long time,' said Ann, 'and it worried him very much.'

Ian summed up his experience to waiting reporters. 'Quite ghastly. I'm sure Bond never had to go through anything like this.' He had been cast as mendacious and dishonest, no better than the greedy delinquent in Ian's first edition of Henry Allan's 1869 'Prize essay on Kleptomania': 'an ambitious Kleptomaniac who copied word for word a book on chemistry, which had been lent him to read, and affirmed it to be entirely his own composition. "The result of great toil and research," said he.'

At Kemsley House, John Pearson observed his anguish. 'To be accused of plagiarising your own creation is pretty serious, especially to someone like Ian who put so much importance on reputation, appearance, keeping up a good face on everything. It was insufferable to have someone taking him to court and saying James Bond is not yours, it's mine.'

Soon after, *Thunderball* was reviewed in *The Times* as 'a highly polished performance, with an ingenious plot well documented and plenty of excitement'. But Ian's next appearance in *The Times*, on 22 April, was under the headline 'INVALIDS'. There was in fact only one: 'Mr. Ian Fleming, the novelist, is in the London Clinic, where, an official said yesterday, "he is very comfortable".'

The official failed to mention Ian's heart attack.

Waugh told Ann that on a visit to Ireland his daughter Margaret had overheard her host, Lord Mersey, say, 'Ian Fleming is dying.'

'In connection with the reference to the heart attack suffered by Ian Fleming shortly after the injunction proceedings in the Thunderball action, we wish to make it clear that Ian Fleming had for some time previously been suffering from ill-health.'

Kevin McClory's lawyers compelled Cape to insert this sticker in Pearson's biography after an 'incensed' McClory learned that Ann and Ivar Bryce had depicted him as being responsible for Ian's death. Ann never changed her mind on this. She inscribed in Ian's copy of *Diamonds are Forever* that she sold to the Lilly Library: 'the case undoubtedly caused Ian's coronary. A.F.'

'How frail men feel when they are sick,' Ian wrote in his Bond notes. Bond is always sick. ('He knelt down and was sick as a cat.') Another Bond note reads: 'You can tell most of the secrets of a man by the contents of his medicine cabinet.'

'One of the secrets of both Ian and Ann's lives is ill-health.' Fionn remembers the ashtray full of Turkish cigarette stubs in the top floor bathroom that she shared with Ian at Victoria Square. There was also his bumper bottle of Phensic tablets, a popular analgesic at the time, containing aspirin, caffeine and the later banned phenacetin. Ann was addicted to barbiturates and smoked and drank too much. 'Whisky is a food,' she claimed her doctor told her. Ian's doctor, Jack Beal, had treated Ian at his consulting room in Sloane Court West since their bachelor days in the Cercle, when they would dash off to Sandwich and Deauville. 'They were typical of their era,' says Beal's son, Richard. 'The amount of alcohol consumed by professional people was enormous. Not surprisingly, some of them became alcoholics.'

Ian's telegram to Ann in July 1962 suggests the couple's febrile state after a decade of marriage. 'PLEASE PLEASE CONCENTRATE ON YOUR HEALTH WHICH CONSIDERABLY EXPLAINS & EXCUSES THE LAST INCREASINGLY MISERABLE YEARS STOP'.

His health had been fragile for as long as Alaric Jacob had known him. 'He had strained his heart at Eton, as well as having his nose broken . . . His heart trouble made him always seem a bit delicate, a bit on the edge of things.' Cardiac disease ran in the family, says Kate Fleming. 'Ian would die at fifty-six, Peter at sixty-four, Richard at sixty-seven and my brother Nichol also at fifty-six – all from heart.'

Ian had hurt his back at Sandhurst in addition to suffering from 'hammer toes'. At Reuters, he had blood poisoning from a shaving cut. A year on, he had a tapeworm after eating infected caviar in Moscow. In June 1938, he was with Mary Pakenham at a Surrealist exhibition when he doubled up with pain from appendicitis. At the Admiralty, 'he used to have terrible colds,' said Ted Merrett. Headaches were a constant. He retired with a migraine the first time he invited Ann to Ebury Street, unable to speak for an hour. Maud Russell noticed how he twitched following the death of Muriel Wright.

Ian told Blanche Blackwell that he had suffered a minor stroke after the war. In 1946, he complained to a doctor in New York of 'a constricting pain in the heart' and admitted 'to smoking seventy cigarettes a day and drinking at least a quarter of a bottle of gin'. Dr Franz Groedel thought the tightness in his chest was the result of nicotine poisoning. However, Ian's 'rapid pulse' attacks on the golf course in 1948 and 1950 were consistent more with coronary disease – the speciality of Ian's great-grandfather. 'His arteries were clearly beginning to go,' said Jack Beal.

Then 'the screaming pain' of kidney stones. Beal gave him intravenous heroin after Ian had an attack while eating dinner at the Étoile with a lady who helped him back to his flat. In 1956, he collapsed on Ann's bedroom floor and lay writhing. He spent a week in the London Clinic and suffered another kidney attack in New York that summer. After a specialist gave him 'a shot', he reported that 'the Stone Age at least is passed & now to strangle La Dame Sciatica.'

A Bond note written at the time reflected his weakened state. 'Those saddest of phrases, "Mind the stairs. They're steep. You've had a hard day. Feel better now?"'

In Jamaica, a Dr Cooper diagnosed a bad case of fibrositis in Ian's hip muscles. In October 1957, Ian wrote to Ann from Tangier: 'I was ill for three days when I got here – conjunctivitis in one eye, a huge boil on my nose and then I stuck a fork through my lip having lunch with Ali [Forbes]! I fed on Aureomycine and things and am now only cold and exhausted.'

Weeks before McClory's court hearing in March 1961, Ian spent New Year with Ann and Caspar in the Engadine in the Swiss Alps. He felt too breathless to ski, Ann reported. 'The height has affected Thunderbird's blood pressure, and at night he has to be propped up with pillows because of panting.' He then went out in a blizzard without a coat and caught pneumonia. He arrived in Jamaica on 20 January, running a temperature of 103. Noël Coward found him 'scarlet and sweating in a sopping bed and in a hellish temper'.

By the time Ian took his place on the bench to contest McClory's charge of plagiarism, it concerned Ann that he was a powder keg primed to explode. 'I am certain it was the threat of a big lawsuit that brought on his heart attack.'

Ian had his coronary a fortnight after the court case, in Lord Kemsley's old office.

On Tuesday 12 April 1961, Ian attended the weekly morning editorial conference at the *Sunday Times* to hear plans for a 'new shiny magazine'. He had argued for this 'Glossy' for a decade, a colour supplement being merely one of his bids to inject modern American tastes and journalism into Kemsley's moribund newspaper chain. But following a dinner alone with Kemsley and his son Lionel, Ian wrote in despair to his chief ally in the office, Denis Hamilton, to say that he was 'more than ever aware that there is absolutely no hope of our revitalising the machine at the present time or altering its inevitable progress towards the edge of the abyss'.

Even though Ian had continued to oversee scoops like Richard Hughes's interview with Burgess and Maclean, he derived less and less pleasure from working at Kemsley House. 'If you have ever tried writing a weekly column,' he wrote to Cuneo, after Atticus had replaced Mercury in November 1953 as Kemsley's priority, 'you will realise what a ghastly chore this is going to be.' What in 1947 Ian had regarded as 'this great citadel of Freedom and Intellect' had become 'this grim building'. Barbara Skelton, now divorced from Cyril Connolly, noticed the effect on him of the slimming down of his foreign news service. 'Since doing the Atticus column, Ian seems to have become a very dried up and red-veined plain family man. Has lost any semblance of glamour or good looks, a bottlenecked figure with a large bum.'

'I just can't bear to get back to K. House.' Ian made the same complaint each time he girded himself to leave Goldeneye, but as he wrote to Ann, 'I must stop being inert about the whole thing, and either have a bash at the paper or get out. It's not much use having a bash with Gomer there. One only gets stomach ulcers to make him more rich.'

It was, therefore, a shock when, in 1959, without telling anyone, Gomer Kemsley decided to sell the *Sunday Times* to the Canadian Roy Thomson. Ian took this as his cue to step down as Foreign Manager, renting a fourth-floor, two-roomed office in Mitre Court off Fleet Street. But Thomson, 'a charming panda in pebble glasses', asked him to stay on the editorial board for £1,000 p.a. (approximately £27,000 today) with the backing of Hamilton, who in 1961 became the new editor.

One of Ian's duties was to continue attending the Tuesday editorial meetings. At 10.50 a.m. on 12 April, he walked with Leonard Russell up one flight of stairs to Kemsley's former plush office.

Given the exciting agenda, it was an insipid conference, recalled Russell. Ian hardly intervened, 'his usual flow of suggestion and expostulation and ironic and sometimes faintly savage laughter was missing.' Russell looked at him curiously once or twice. He seemed to be sweating slightly and staring continuously at the carpet.

Thomson was taking the conference when, just after noon, Ian suddenly stood up and muttered something to Denis Hamilton. Bryce wrote, 'he described to me the tightening pain, as the iron crab tightened his iron claw across the chest and consciousness was blotted agonisingly out.'

It was Hamilton, the no-nonsense ex-Brigadier, who saved him. 'I thought he was dying because he was a deathly white; I tried to get him out of the stuffy room, but he resisted. I said, "Come on, Ian, you'll bloody well do as I tell you! We'll go out, and I'll get you a doctor." I summoned a car to take him home and arranged for his doctor to be waiting there.' When the office car arrived at Victoria Square, Beal's green chauffeur-driven Daimler was parked outside.

Ian spent a month at the London Clinic and a fortnight at the Dudley Hotel on the beachfront at Brighton. 'He was so ill I wasn't allowed to visit him at first,' Hamilton wrote, 'but he'd smuggle out handwritten letters.' Not until early May was Ian supposed to receive visitors. Somerset Maugham was turned away, although not Blanche Blackwell, to Ann's distress. 'The fact that you saw her in the nursing home reveals your feelings for her, for you do not want to see many people.'

Leonard Russell was one other exception. Russell had only recently been a patient himself at the London Clinic for a heart attack. He found Ian sitting up in bed 'and looking like a rather fleshy Roman emperor in short-sleeved pyjamas'.

Russell asked if there was anything he could get him.

'Nothing, old boy, nothing – unless it's a game of golf.'

Ian's one regular visitor, wearing green-rimmed glasses, was his new secretary, Beryl Griffie-Williams, 'behaving like a hen bird', who slipped into his room to take dictation. 'I went in to see Mr Fleming on Friday evening against all the rules,' she told Admiral Godfrey, 'but he insisted on dealing with some letters. I was rather shocked by his appearance.'

Described by one of Ian's visitors as 'a nice lady with grey hair', 'Griffie' had worked for demanding employers including Rebecca West and Nancy Spain. She took charge of Ian's typewriter. 'They still refuse to let me do any writing,' Ian explained to Eve, who had sent him a red flamingo lily. He thanked Godfrey for his 'superfine' flowers and Ivar for his box of caviar, which became muddled up in the hospital fridge with that of 'poor old' Lord Dovercourt, who 'passed on in the next room last Saturday!' The bottle of sixteen-year-old Bourbon on Ian's mantelpiece was a gift from Ernie Cuneo, who claimed to be the originator of the phrase 'iron crab'. Ian hastened to assure Cuneo that he was alive. 'The iron crab made a quick snatch at me but missed by a whisker.'

Messages streamed in. 'Get well soon,' from Mr Baker at Scott's. From John Betjeman, 'Bung ho, ole man,' with suggestions of five Gothic revival windows they might visit in Brighton once Ian was better.

Ann's lover Hugh Gaitskell sent a book and some recommendations, following his own heart troubles. 'Please don't forget what I told you when we last met – that it's all perfectly all right so long as for 6 months or so you really *do* behave carefully. I hope you'll not resent this advice from one old heart case to another.'

Ian's early hero Selby Armitage arrived with the most unexpected gift: Ian's letters from Kitzbühel in the 1920s, full of ambitions for the kind of writer he had hoped to be, in the tradition of Mann and Joyce. Armitage had re-read the letters before returning them. He remarked to Ian 'it was a pity that he didn't stick to the idea of novel-writing he had expressed then, instead of taking the line he had. I don't suppose he liked me saying that.'

Forbidden to use a typewriter, Ian resorted to pen and paper. He declined Godfrey's proposal to take this time to embark on the admiral's biography. 'I am writing a children's book,' Ian told Michael Howard at Cape, 'so you will see that there is never a moment, even on the edge of the tomb, when I am not slaving for you.' Duff Dunbar had given Ian a copy of Beatrix Potter's *The Tale of Squirrel Nutkin* – 'which, apart from the illustrations, I thought was the most terrible bilge' – and suggested Ian write up the bedtime story that he used to tell Caspar, about Commander Pott and his magic car that flew. Ian wrote the three adventures of Chitty-Chitty-Bang-Bang in pencil, the only published work he ever wrote by hand.

In the Bahamas, Kevin McClory later owned a car that he drove into the sea, not telling his petrified passenger it was amphibious. Ian cast his present situation as though it were an automobile fantasy. He assured Stephenson that his 'mechanics', as he referred to his doctors, were satisfied that 'the engine, though less oiled than previously, is now running on at least eleven out of its twelve cylinders, and that the twelfth should start firing soon so long as I continue to obey their infuriating instructions, which are, broadly speaking, that I should do none of the things I want to do.' He smuggled a postcard to Amaryllis: 'Don't believe everything you read in the papers. I'm having a delicious rest surrounded by beautiful nurses and when in a few weeks I can "go for a drive" it will be to you. Being "ill" is heaven.' The postcard was of the rock crystal 'Aztec' skull in the British Museum.

'One knows one's own vintage car by now.' Stretched out on his back, he plotted how to resume life in the fast lane. He had written to Barbara Skelton, 'When can I come over and take you out in the Thunderbird? Don't answer; I will suddenly appear out of the setting sun.' He longed to be that person again.

Ian's specialist had advised that he would have 'to give up golf and all forms of physical exercise for a year or more', but he was permitted three ounces of hard liquor a day. Ready to rebel, Ian sought a second opinion from Godfrey's doctor, Dr Daley. 'Please ask Daley on the q.t. – how much weight he places on smoking and drinking & what he would cut me down to after 25 years of 50-70 cigs a day & about 1/3 bottle of spirits daily & what about eggs? & how soon golf?' The last was especially important. Ian had been appointed to the handicap committee at Royal St George's and he fretted for a foursome.

To extract another 'vital piece of information', he dictated a letter to Churchill's son-in-law, Christopher Soames, at the Ministry of Agriculture, Fisheries and Food, wanting to know 'which is the finest refined spirit, gin whisky or brandy on the market at any price.' The answer: 'Green Charteuse is the most alcoholic being 102 [degrees] proof.'

Like the car in his children's book, Ian was determined to defy the natural order and get airborne. He reached out to Jack Whittingham, yet another who had suffered a heart attack – while snorkelling in the Bahamas with McClory – to get in touch with Ian's lawyers to resolve their legal dispute amicably. 'A graceful composure of such differences as you and I may have between each other might be wisdom. However, as I say, this is all on the "Old Boy" wave and the main thing is that we should both be in good heart (!) again as soon as possible.'

Cars still on his mind, he wrote to Antony Terry in Berlin to ask for details of the new 220 Mercedes convertible coupé. 'I am making lightning progress and expect at least to be on all fours again very shortly.' But when Patrick Leigh Fermor saw Ian at Chatsworth a few days later, he was walking in slow steps with a stick like Monty Winchester, 'and rather un-James Bond-ish at the moment'.

Earlier, Ian had communicated from his hospital bed with Plomer about the Bond typescript that he had delivered before his coronary, *The Spy Who Loved Me*. He wanted Plomer to read it 'entirely privately – & then tell me what you think. You see, there is an excellent opportunity to kill off Bond, appropriately & gracefully, and though when it came to the point in the story I forebore, I feel, and have felt before this address, that the time has come.'

He was too late. Ian's whole life had been about galvanising the forces to create secret agent 007, who parks anywhere, glides free. All the cigarettes and liquor and scrambled eggs and women were the raw material of James Bond, who never has to pay the price because his Dorian Gray is in room 425 at the London Clinic. Ian's generative material and vitality was on the wane, but his vigorous fictional character was fuelled by his illness, from which he would emerge more real than his creator.

The reason was the film deal Ian signed shortly after leaving the hospital.

LXIII
'A REGULAR SKYSCRAPER'

'More than half the world's population has seen a James Bond film.'
'CUBBY' BROCCOLI

On 17 April 1961, his fifth day in the London Clinic, Ian learned that an American military force had landed in the Bay of Pigs.

It was exactly a month since the *Life* magazine article featuring *From Russia, with Love* on its list of 'Ten Kennedy favorites'. News that Ian had a fan in the Oval Office led to his name appearing in the *Times* for the third time in a month. 'President Kennedy is reported to enjoy, in his lighter moments, the improbable adventures of Mr. James Bond, the creation of Mr. Ian Fleming whose capacity for bearing physical torture is no less than his intimate knowledge of the Soviet underground or his attraction for handsome women. Mr. Bond has emerged as part of the Administration's answer to communist political warfare.' Few suspected how near to the actual situation this was.

Cuneo said, 'When Kennedy announced that Fleming was one of his favourite readings, it made Bond overnight.' Precisely as the Prime Minister's visit to Goldeneye had kick-started British interest in Bond, the presidential endorsement introduced a relatively unknown English author to an American audience of 13 million. This was the boost Ian's New York publishers needed. Ian's American sales took off like Chitty-Chitty-Bang-Bang.

It needs to be emphasised that there was no ready supply of James Bond titles in American bookshops at the time. *Casino Royale*, under the title *You Asked for It*, and *Moonraker*, renamed *Too Hot to Handle*, had performed unremarkably, and paperback sales of *From Russia, with Love* were 'not much beyond average', according to Truman 'Mac' Talley, editorial vice president at Ian's paperback house, New American Library. 'Ian Fleming's caviar aspects may have, thus far, put off short-order readers.' When Talley read Ian's latest manuscript, *The Spy Who Loved Me*, he felt it should not be published.

All changed that summer with the American publication of *Thunderball* when, as Ian's New York agent put it, 'the gusher burst'. Chosen as a Book of the Month Club title, the first for a Bond novel, the first printing sold out within a week. In July, Macmillan produced an omnibus hardback edition of Ian's first four novels, *Gilt-Edged Bond*s, with an introduction by Paul Gallico. In November, Talley relaunched in paperback, with new covers, the President's favourite, *From Russia, with Love*, and *Diamonds are Forever*, with *Casino Royale*, *Dr. No* and *Live and Let Die* set to follow in February.

'An increase in tension?' Beneath this strapline, a brochure sent to booksellers pictured a White House in the dark with a solitary light blazing. 'You can bet on it he's reading one of those Ian Fleming thrillers.' 1962 was the year when readers in huge numbers followed the President's example. Orders quadrupled. Each title had an initial print run of 200,000. Each went on to sell more than a million copies. Ian's high rise was assured. His novels were serialised in *Playboy*. *Sports Illustrated* carried his lengthy article, 'The Guns of James Bond'. *Life* profiled him, as did *Esquire*.

Months later, Evelyn Irons, the *Sunday Times* correspondent in New York, wrote to him, 'Can't find a magazine without an article by or about Ian Fleming, he's a regular skyscraper.' Ian savoured the moment when he went into Abercrombie & Fitch in New York to buy some golf clubs, and the girl assistant, echoing Jack Kennedy at their first meeting, said 'Not *the* Mr Fleming.'

JFK cannot claim all credit, though – nor his brother Robert, to whom Ian wrote wishing 'to thank Kennedys everywhere for the electric effect their commendation has had on my sales in America'. Ian's astronomical ascent would not have occurred without the help of the film industry. But it was President Kennedy's approval of Bond in America, together with the simultaneous plagiarism case against Ian in London, which combined to break the impasse that had stymied Ian's previous attempts to have a movie made.

*

The foundations for the deal that Harry Saltzman and 'Cubby' Broccoli signed with Ian in June 1961 – leading to what Broccoli called 'the most successful series of movies in motion-picture history' – had been laid six months previously, when Ian agreed to give Saltzman a six-month option as a safeguard against Kevin McClory.

'It is because of the McClory situation that Harry gets control,' says John Cork, 'and that happens because Fleming is desperate to tie up the rights.'

In December 1960, Saltzman's solicitor, Brian Lewis from Harbottle & Lewis, had been helping Ian to establish a valuation on his books. McClory was threatening to sue Ian and Bryce for not giving him the Bond project. Ian asked Lewis how he could protect himself.

There is no paper trail, only a lunch at Les Ambassadeurs. Even so, Cork's theory remains the most plausible until the producers of the Bond franchise open up their archives to independent researchers. 'I believe that Brian Lewis told Fleming, "McClory can't get rights from you that you don't own." I believe Lewis contacted Saltzman and said, "I have a valuable property for you, and it won't cost you anything to tie up." Saltzman wasn't a producer that Ian wanted to get into bed with, nor one who was chomping at the bit to option the Bond stories, but he was someone of whom Ian and his lawyers could say, "Nope, we don't have the film rights to James Bond. They are owned by this producer, Harry Saltzman." Saltzman, I believe, didn't pay a cent initially. Whatever agreement (verbal or written) that was put into place as a result of that December 1960 meeting, changed the fate of James Bond. And that was a meeting that did not involve MCA, Curtis Brown, or any other firm representing Ian Fleming's rights.'

Ian's improbable knight in armour was a corpulent forty-six-year-old London-based Canadian who had run away at seventeen to join the circus. Saltzman had produced 'Saturday Night and Sunday Morning' and 'Look Back in Anger', but his reputation as a major producer was declining along with the public's appetite for gritty industrial dramas. In short, Saltzman could not have afforded to pay the $50,000 (approximately $500,000 today) which was the sum due on the backend, apparently, for his option on all Bond titles, excluding *Casino Royale*.

Well-fed, with a supersalesman's talent 'to excite the room and lure the birds out of the trees', Saltzman was a colourful, volatile character, always rushing about. A presence at Europe's best eating places, Saltzman could never resist flaunting his credentials as a gourmet, as he once did to Ian in a fashionable restaurant in Istanbul, by sending the food back. 'He could be pretty rough,' says Ian's solicitor Matthew Farrer. 'I remember one breakfast at the Dorchester when he complained to the waiter that the kipper was cooked on one side better than the other.' It was said of Saltzman that had he been at the Last Supper he would have sent the food back.

He was poised to do the same with the rights to the Bond movies after discovering these had been hawked around for some time and none of the leading American or British producers had been tempted.

Saltzman's option had 'about thirty days' left to run when he received a call from the British screenwriter Wolf Mankowitz proposing that Saltzman meet with Albert 'Cubby' Broccoli.

Like Saltzman, Broccoli was a producer with nothing to produce after his last film 'The Trials of Oscar Wilde' had opened at the Paramount Theatre in Hollywood to an audience of fifteen; following this, he had dissolved his film company. The New York-born son of Calabrian immigrants, the fifty-one-year-old Broccoli had worked as a film agent in Hollywood, where he had sold hair driers and shampoos. According to his biographer, he was as warm, down-to-earth and self-effacing as Saltzman was not. 'Purveying Italianate affability, wrapped in Lacoste polo necks and hairy tweed jackets, he ruled with a ladle of iron.'

Len Deighton came to know Broccoli and Saltzman when working on the script of 'From Russia with Love'. 'It is important to remember that Cubby was a movie agent and remained so. Harry was a movie producer and remained so. That is how their partnership functioned.'

Farrer says, 'In the trade, they were known as Engine and Brake.'

Broccoli had first registered an interest in Bond three years earlier, but his then-business partner Irving Allen had 'a bad meeting' with Ian and his agent, at which the unpredictable Allen apparently told them: 'In my opinion, these books are not even good enough for television.'

Mankowitz was a friend of Broccoli's. After Broccoli disclosed to him in the late spring of 1961 that 'I've always had this urge to film Ian Fleming's

James Bond books,' Mankowitz, who knew that Saltzman owned the rights, arranged for Saltzman, whom Broccoli had not met, to come to Broccoli's Mayfair office.

'Saltzman made no attempt to hoodwink me,' Broccoli said. 'He said he had tried flogging James Bond all over town, but without any luck.' The time had come to send Bond back to the kitchen. 'The Fleming books are a bit of nonsense,' said Saltzman. He had another story he wanted to film, *Rapture in My Rags*. 'It's about a scarecrow.'

But Broccoli persisted. Saltzman yielded. Two days later, they flew to New York to meet United Artists.

The name Bond had a different ring to it now than in December. What Ian had struggled to achieve in nine years, Broccoli and Saltzman accomplished in thirty-five minutes. On 21 June, a deal was struck and a budget of $950,000 was settled upon (approximately $9.5 million today).

An old envelope in a New York desk was the single fly in the ointment. On the back of this, one year before, Ian had signed away his television rights to the producer recommended by Stephenson. Ann Marlow was at this moment trying to interest the president of a tobacco company to invest in 'the James Bond sausage'. Ian spent the last days of his convalescence frantic to retrieve the potentially deal-breaking scrap of paper.

Not until he had done so, on 7 July, was Ian free to share details with the quiet Canadian, currently living in Bermuda, who had introduced him to Marlow.

'Little Bill' Stephenson had long been a guiding presence in the background. He was Ian's sounding board for Intelligence and financial matters ('Should I now sink back into Caribbean Cement?'), and latterly the film business. Ten years earlier, Ian had been in touch with him over Eve's off-shore tax arrangements in the Bahamas. Since then, he had sought Stephenson's assistance to get Bond filmed there. The Canadian was a radio and television pioneer, and the former owner of Korda's London studio; few others had connections that stretched so far back into the broadcasting industry. Stephenson told Ian what he would like in return for all his advice. 'The least you can do is make me Bond's boss in your books and give me the vicarious thrill of watching a film of Bond endeavouring to put the blonde into a state of gravidation.'

Shortly after being discharged from the London Clinic, Ian was pleased to be the bearer of good news. He had sorted things out with 'the darling Marlow'. 'I sent her a small token from Cartier's to signal my love and appreciation . . . Briefly, a very big Bond film deal is in the offing, and it could not go through so long as she had the option on my television rights.'

He revealed the development with United Artists. 'The deal itself starts with a minimum payment of $150,000 [approximately $1.45 million today] amounting by $100,000 with each further film U.A. makes. There is no object in my arranging a Bermuda company for all these, as the film rights are owned by Caspar's Trust and therefore avoid all tax. But, in addition, I get 5% of the producer's gross, which is very carefully defined, and if this should look like getting too big, I would consult you again about a Bermudan gambit.'

Ian was not yet counting his chickens. There was a 'slight copyright problem which is being ironed out', he had informed Harry Saltzman in the contract they signed on 9 June. This was after Cuneo warned Ian and Bryce that while the *Thunderball* script remained the subject of a controversy 'no one will buy or finance it'. There was also the question of payment. Only after the first day of shooting did Ian stand to receive all the money for the first film. Still, after nearly a decade of persistence, he was on the cusp of earning a serious income from his writing.

He did not disclose one significant factor. The exorbitant sums Ann was lavishing on their new house in the country made it important the deal go through.

LXIV
ARCHAEOLOGICAL HEAP

'Who wouldn't rather play golf?'
THE DIAMOND SMUGGLERS

McClory's plagiarism case certainly played a role in Ian's heart attack, but Ian believed that his coronary was 'due to accumulating pressure from a number of directions'. A further source of stress was the home Ann was building seven miles north-east of Swindon; at present, a heap of ruins.

Ann had tired of spending weekends and holidays at White Cliffs near Dover. 'I had no friends in that district and detested the East wind.'

White Cliffs was not suited for the entertaining she had in mind. It had no privacy. A line of rooms led one into the other, with no corridor, and guests had to share a bathroom. There was a back courtyard and garages with nets to catch the lumps of chalk that fell 'like a crash of thunder' onto the roof.

A regular visitor was Ann's young nephew, Francis Grey, her sister Mary Rose's son. He says, 'When it was very windy and wet, we were not allowed out. I recall having our noses pressed against the window, and with Caspar watching the waves, and sometimes there came a big one, wallop, and it went over the house.'

Ann's dislike of finding seaweed in the drawing room and sand hoppers in her bedroom was shared by Loelia Westminster, whose father, a golf maniac, had bought a large house at the foot of these cliffs. 'How I hated it.' The depressing image of long roads of silent, shuttered houses had haunted Loelia. 'The boredom at St Margaret's Bay was indescribable.' On top of everything, it rained non-stop.

But Ian was like Loelia's father, a golfer who played whatever the weather. Ian loved being so close to St George's and the sea. He loved that White Cliffs was known as 'The First House in England', that Caesar had landed nearby, as had the French aviator Louis Blériot. He loved that on a clear day he could see the clock tower in Calais, and watch cricketers play out on Goodwin Sands at low tide. The chalk sands were constantly churning up wrecks of Tudor ships and World War Two bombers that carried Ian back to when he had paced the cliffs above, keeping his binoculars trained for a German *Schnellboot*.

The overriding attraction was the nearby golf course. Ian had been a Royal St George's member since 1948 and he worked his life around it. Ann said: 'His routine was to go to the golf club at 12.00, where I think he used to drink and talk to his friends, have an early lunch, play golf, have tea in the golf club and come home at about 6.00 or 6.30.' It pained her to have to admit that 'his golf-playing became much more exaggerated after we married.'

In few other surrounds did Ian feel more at ease than on these links or in the leather-backed wing chair on the left of the bay window, talking to buddies about the 'Pepper King' Garabed Bishirgian beneath the portrait of Dr William Purves, the club's Scottish founder. The warmth of his reception was a far cry from how Ann's Oxford professors treated him. 'Ian was a chap you were thrilled to see,' says Murray Lawrence, one of the same group who played golf with him for years. 'Your face lit up when you saw he was there that day. He definitely was a true life-enhancer, definitely, definitely, definitely.'

The other members were his type, an awful lot of them from Eton, the City and the Armed Forces, who Ian had known since schooldays, such as Hilary Bray, who had nominated him for membership. Ian donated his trophy of a silver chamber pot to the Old Etonian Golfing Society and was a popular non-playing captain at the Halford Hewitt public schools tournament, annually producing for the team a bottle of genuine Russian vodka and an enormous tin of caviar.

Ann had first met Ian at a golfing weekend in Le Touquet. 'He enjoyed the male society of the golf club. I'm certain he was happier there than anywhere else.' Ian's stepson Raymond says, 'the longest day I spent with him in male company was on the golf course.'

He had learned to play at prep school, then at Huntercombe with his grandmother Kate, captain of the Oxfordshire Ladies County Golf committee. What he had missed most in Kitzbühel was 'the thud of club against turf'. In Geneva, he played with Sir Eric Drummond at the Domaine de

Divonne Club, and at Reuters with Bernard Rickatson-Hatt at Swinley Forest Golf Club. In the Blitz, there was a reason why Britain became known by the Abwehr as 'Golfplatz' (golf course), and Bletchley by its inmates as 'the Golf and Chess Society'. During the tense days of the Norway campaign, Dunkirk and the V-bombs, Ian relied on golf to steady his nerves. In 1948, when Ann was giving birth to their baby girl, he advanced in blustery weather at St Andrew's to the fifth round of the Calcutta Cup, which may have been as far as he ever progressed.

At St George's, Ian was practically unique in never winning one of the countless competitions. Francis Grey recalls: 'He would ask "Do you think I'll win?" Caspar would always say "No."'

'He was not bloody interested,' says John Suckling, who sometimes caddied for him. 'Fifteen bob a round he'd pay me. Always eighteen holes. I think he was just Mr Average, enjoyed who he played with and to have a good old laugh, and it took him away from writing books.'

His handicap of nine was the same as Bond and Goldfinger. An enthusiastic but erratic player, Ian had a flat, scything swing that he called the 'Fleming flail' and was compared by a friend to 'a housemaid sweeping the floor'. Nevertheless, he managed to get a terrific kick out of the game; his talent was to make it an adventure.

William Weir was playing with Ian at the eighth hole when Ian said, 'If you promise not to tell anyone, I'll show you something.' A very rare, famous wild orchid was off to the left in the rough. Ian said, 'I hit such a horrific hook shot off the tee and I found this. I've never told anyone before.' It was a white lizard orchid smelling of goats.

'You didn't just play golf with Ian,' said Ralph Arnold. 'Everything in the game became dramatic, romantic. It was all a dream world, specially made for the maximum excitement' – like the method Ian devised for playing at dusk. On Sunday afternoons in winter, says Suckling, it got dark so quickly that Ian designed a luminous golf ball. 'When we came down the 18th, with lights on in the clubhouse, you could see it on the fairway, glowing. "We'll be all right."'

Golf offered a glorious rescue. Each shot was an isolated moment, an escape to the present. Each shot demanded that he take pleasure in the present and not dwell on the past. Each of his strokes had a goal, a surrounding narrative around it. Ian could be in the rough – it did not matter how he got there, this was irrelevant. Now he had a fantastic opportunity to salvage the situation.

A remark he treasured was the answer a Frenchman gave in Jamaica when Ian asked why, in a game of canasta, he had put everything on one hopeless hand. '*J'aime les sensations fortes.*' Plomer thought it 'would make just the right epigraph to your collected works!'

Ann said, 'He liked golf because it could give him this feeling. "Skill, concentration, focus," he used to say.'

To intensify his focus, he prefered to play for something unusual, a monogrammed pair of pyjamas, a new shirt; or else a lot of money. In 1963, he suggested playing with Bill Deedes and 'Jim' Swanton for £100. Deedes was aghast. '£100 in those days was worth something like £1,500. I was in Cabinet at the time on £5,000 a year and felt quite rich. Jim Swanton said coolly, "Why not a golf ball?" This struck Ian Fleming as an original idea. The difference in value between £100 and a golf ball was immaterial to him.'

Ian played golf the world over. With a diamond-smuggling expert at the Diplomatic Country Club in Tangier ('I was too often in the impenetrable rough, ablaze with iris and asphodel'). With Ivar Bryce in Vermont and the Bahamas ('We used to play with bare feet,' wrote Bryce, 'enjoying the feel of sunwarmed grass and sand'). When staying with Raymond in Ireland, at the Royal County Down or Royal Portrush. At 'the finest golf course in the East', the Royal Hong Kong Club, 'a few miles from the communist frontier where the rattle of Bren-guns at the ranges and the occasional passing of a tank are apt to disturb one's swing'.

Like ornithology, golf was an agreeable mask for other activities. The course was a venue where Ian could spy out the local ground and conduct business. He reminded Churchill's wartime publisher Desmond Flower of his promise, 'extracted, I admit, under the influence of the 19th hole at Muirfield' to compose for the *Sunday Times* 'a long article about Winston's writing techniques'. Ian negotiated his most important business deal on the green. It was while playing the eighteenth hole at Huntercombe in 1963 that he made his overture, three minutes before his last putt, to sell his company Glidrose, which owned the rights to Ian's books, to his Eton contemporary Jock Campbell. 'We were on the course and Ian suddenly said, "Would you like to buy me?"'

Among the Bond titles Campbell bought was *Goldfinger*.

A most treasured book in Ian's collection was *The Golfer's Manual* (1857), by 'A Keen Hand', the first account in English of the rules of the game. In 1947, Ian had it republished by the Dropmore Press. The third rule referred to 'changing the balls' and was a central motif in *Goldfinger*. 'The ball struck off from the tee must not be changed, touched or moved before the hole is played out . . .'.

Vital to Ian's plot, which contains one of fiction's most famous golfing scenes, was distracting the other player. A partner of Ian's, Bunny Roddick, had the 'trick of rattling coins in his pocket'. At Huntercombe,* Ian discussed with Stephen Potter the tennis trick he remembered from Kitzbühel – 'as the other man is about to serve, you suddenly say "go away!" to a crowd of imaginary people'. This worked with the dogs that were continually appearing on the course. 'The idea was to shoo the dog off, even when he was miles away, in the middle of another man's swing.'

It was John Suckling who told Ian the story, passed down from Suckling's father, a caddie, of the White's Club tournament held at St George's in the 1940s. 'The men were taking bets on the first tee. This guy had a caddie, a real tramp, Teddy O'Neill. They got to the eleventh, and the bloke smashed it out to the right, and the rough there in July time is very thick. They went to look, and couldn't find the ball. O'Neill had a hole in his trousers and went there with his trousers half mast, and one of the people watching saw him drop the ball, and of course he got reported straight away. My father Jack told me this.' It was how Goldfinger's caddie tried to help outwit Bond.

After beating Ian, and receiving a couple of golf balls as his prize, Bill Deedes estimated that 'Bond could hit the ball a lot further than Fleming, but then it is not unknown for authors to endow their characters with talents they themselves lack but long to possess.'

Ann had initiated the move away from the coast, Ian reminded her. 'When we were in St Margaret's you were always decrying it with that deadly

---

* In 1966, Peter suggested planting a yew tree in Ian's memory at Huntercombe Golf Course, with one proviso: 'There should be no reference to James Bond on the plaque.' The chosen words were: 'Presented by Peter Fleming in memory of his brother Ian. Author and golfer.'

"realism" you are so proud of.' With Caspar growing up, their beach-side house was no longer 'a nest': a family home was needed.

In a hurry in October 1957, Ian took the Old Palace at Bekesbourne near Canterbury, twenty miles away, in the grounds of the old palace lived in by Archbishop Cranmer: an eighteenth-century red-brick house with a crenellated parapet, black oak beams, six bedrooms and a nursery annexe. Cranmer's motto was carved into the stonework of the two-and-a-half-foot-thick walls. *Nosce teipsum et Deum*; Know thyself and God. It was close to the railway and said to be haunted – 'but damned if I could find the ghost,' says Francis Grey, 'or the tunnel from the dining room that led the whole way to Canterbury cathedral'.

Ann hated it from the start. 'An ugly house, in an ugly county,' she complained to Clarissa – after inviting the canon and his unmarried sisters to sherry and biscuits. The 'change of house has depressed me'.

Ian refused to be held responsible. 'We both agreed it was only a temporary measure to meet an emergency. And now you blame me and treat me like an enemy...'

They resumed motoring off at weekends to look for 'a modest house in which to spend our old age'. Ian had preferences from childhood – Dorset, the Scottish west coast ('I would love to live on Islay, for instance, but I know that's no good for you'), and latterly the Petworth area. 'I've always wanted to be at least within reach of the sea.' He repeated to Hilary Bray: 'I MUST be able to see the sea.'

Ian was adamant about where he did not want to live. 'The only reason I don't like Ox and Glos is because I don't like hunting or shooting and I was always miserably bored there . . . Couldn't we find somewhere that is a bit further away and a bit more adventurous? . . . If we could live mostly in the country I'm sure we would both be much happier and live a more leisurely, relaxed and civilised life and see far more of Caspar into the bargain.'

Caspar was their common ground. They had moved inland 'largely for his benefit'. Even so, Ian expressed concern to Ann about the expense of another new home. 'I'm frightened of ending up in some huge palace which we can't afford to heat or staff and where we have to dress for dinner every weekend. One cannot live by architecture alone . . . And I beg you to have a stream or a river in the grounds. I shall simply pine away if we go to live in the middle of a lot of plough with deadly little walks down lanes and dons every weekend. But anything, anything to make you smile again and find you somewhere where you will rest and not tear yourself to pieces. Honestly, all I get is the fag end of a person at the end of the day or at weekends.'

The toll of their incompatibility struck Maud Russell on meeting Ian after his move to Bekesbourne. 'He looked haggard, tired & much older as if Ann was in the process of destroying him. He never stood a chance with her though he thought he did. He seemed to me a sad sight. I asked him how his marriage was going. He said: "As well as I deserve" or some such melancholy answer . . . I thought he was very depressed. He talked about Goldeneye & what a wonderful present it had been & that he spent 2 months there every year.'

Ann wanted him to sell Goldeneye to pay for their new house.

They found Warneford Place in August 1959, eighteen months before Ian's coronary. It lay on a medieval site at the end of a long drive in a small valley enclosed by the Wiltshire countryside. The original building dated from the time of Richard I. It had been extended in the 1770s and then, less sympathetically, in 1902, by a director of the Great Western Railway. A conglomerate of clashing styles with different extensions added on over generations, it resembled nothing so much as a train station.

Ann had been tipped off by Robert 'Mad Boy' Heber-Percy, who lived nearby at Faringdon and wanted her as a neighbour.

Set in twenty-three acres, the dilapidated mansion overlooked a lawn on which stood two colossal Roman urns, which later bore bullet marks from Caspar's guns, and a stagnant lake reflecting herons that had escaped the nearby heronry in Buscot, Ian and Ann's bolt-hole in the war. The property had been left unoccupied since 1945, and was in an advanced state of decay. The clock on the 1734 clock tower had stopped, the weathercock was immobilised by rust, the hedges were overgrown, and the paths choked with duck droppings.

Ann had long wanted to live in Wiltshire or Gloucestershire, where she had grown up. She pictured herself entertaining here in the spectacular style of her grandmother at Stanway or her great-aunt Margot Asquith. But as she wrote to Waugh, 'alas there is a ballroom, billiard room and 40 bedrooms to be demolished.'

Ian outlined their plans to his solicitor. 'We intend to demolish a very large part of the present structure retaining only the right hand wing attached to which we will build a five or six-bedroom house in the appropriate style.'

In the 1930s, Eve had rebuilt Greys Court at preposterous expense, but even Ian's mother considered Warneford Place too large for a family of three. After he drove her to see it, she voiced her opinion that 'Ian must be out of his senses.' On the last day of his convalescence, he wrote to reassure her. 'Please don't worry too much about the house. I am not happy about it myself, but it's quite impossible being married unless you are prepared to compromise, and I shall just help Ann as much as I can with it and go fifty/fifty on the cost. At least, it will be a good solid base in the country.'

Once again, Caspar was a main consideration. 'One of the factors that decided us on Warneford was that he simply adores having a place to run about in, and it will be close by both for Summer Fields [Caspar's prep school in Oxford, twenty-five miles away] and Eton.' Ian explained to his solicitor: 'it is an ideal small property in which to teach my son to shoot.' Plus, it was a place 'where I can have a proper library which I've never had before'.*

The building work began in September 1960. The roof came off. Pipes and bits of broken brick lay strewn everywhere. When the lake was drained, at the cost of £2,000, Ann reported to Waugh: 'The lawn is covered with sludge and dead eels; in December, the house will be demolished, and the rubble spread upon the other lawns; but we are very optimistic if only we can pay the bills.' It would be another four years before they moved in.

Ian told Ann, 'I don't want to see the place again until it's ready to live in.' Temporarily without a bolt-hole, he took a lease on a spartan first-floor apartment close to Royal St George's. Ann listened to the shutters banging in the wind, as miserable in Flat 4, the Whitehall Building, Pegwell Bay, with its

---

* In 1940, Ian moved his collection to Eve's house in Oxfordshire. In vain, Eve asked the Bodleian Library in Oxford to look after what now amounted to over a thousand volumes ('They are in sacks, each book in a box'). Ann, early on, viewed Ian's first editions with the detachment that she later treated his Bond manuscripts: 'I have also thought about you selling your library', she wrote in 1948, 'if the money would help buy us a house!' Ian had since stored the collection at the Pantechnicon depository in London.

'dung-coloured wallpaper and curtains', as Ian was when he contemplated exchanging Kent for an unmanageable country house near Swindon. She wailed to Waugh: 'T[hunder]-B[ird] does not want to leave Sandwich, he is on the golf committee, and his only happiness is pink gin, golf clubs and men. So he wants to alter the plans and keep a flat here and build a rabbit hutch for me instead of a mansion.'

The expense of pulling down Warneford Place plunged Ian into 'such despair' that he forked out a further five guineas on a fortune teller. She scrutinised her crystal ball and 'told him that the house would cost more than he thought'.

He was very worried about money. He wrote to thank his mother for her cheque to help cover his costs at the London Clinic. 'It has taken a great weight off my mind as finances really are quite a problem.' The 'ravages of Sur-tax' – at a rate of ninety-one per cent – meant that 'I get my hands on very little money from all these books.'

The situation grew tenser after Ian left the hospital in June. Ann blithely informed Waugh: 'We are homeless until Christmas 1961.'

With nowhere else to go but Victoria Square, Ian made a bee-line back to the flat in Sandwich, having alerted one of his golf partners. 'All I need to put me absolutely right is a foursome with you and Bunny, and I look forward to this immensely.'

Out on the fairways of Royal St George's, he could escape the stresses that were plaguing him. Days later, Ian reported that he had played two rounds of golf, 'and the reduced hypertension and lower blood pressure have happily had a decelerating effect on my swing'.

His doctors had advised him to cut back on golf, cigarettes and alcohol, but he admitted to Stephenson, 'I am losing no time in loosening up on their counsels of moderation in all things.' Lisl afterwards blamed Jack Beal 'for not putting the fear of God into him after that first heart attack of his'. This was unfair to Beal. 'The trouble was that he didn't like accepting the fact that there were certain things he shouldn't do. He should have dropped golf. Instead, he went out of his way to do crazy things like continuing to play two rounds of golf in an icy wind at Sandwich.' The irony is that golf was probably not the problem. Modern medicine would have encouraged it, and warned instead against the cigarettes and alcohol.

It grieved Ann that 'after the heart attack in 1961 he would do nothing he was asked to'. For Ian, the issue was simple. 'I trust you with your friends such as Hugh [Gaitskell] & I enjoy your pleasure in them. You must trust me with such as Ivar & the golfsters & be happy that I find pleasure with them – incomprehensible as it may seem to you'.

Meanwhile, he was bullish that his health was returning. In mid August, he wrote to Stephenson, 'I am staying in London and Sandwich, where my more relaxed golf swing and an increased handicap (I happen to be on the handicapping Committee!) has confounded my enemies'.

From the summer of 1961 on, St George's became the focus of Ian's final ambition, which was to ascend to the highest level on the club's committee. In the meantime, he needed to pay for the Gatsbyesque house that was rising on the banks of its excavated lake in Wiltshire.

Ann had the bit between her teeth. Her son Raymond had recently rebuilt Shane's Castle. She desired the same for herself. Bond gave her the means.

'It's so exhausting spending Ian's trust money,' she wrote to Waugh. 'I squander £1,000 per afternoon and envy the poor'. Ian was funding his half of Warneford Place with a £40,000 mortgage taken out by Caspar's trust fund, 'which contained some £20,000 and which, by a film deal for my stories now in progress, stands to benefit by vastly greater sums'. But until the deal with United Artists was finalised, Ian warned grimly, 'we really will get into money troubles' if they were not careful. Without appearing to recognise her part in either, Ann reported on the 'combination of T[hunder]-B[irds]'s permanent angry misery and the terrible expenditure on this folly'.

Under Ann's uninhibited direction, costs continued to escalate at a furious rate. Dry rot had been discovered in one wing, acres of soil had to be imported to fill in the lake, the house needed to be linked to the water mains, a swimming pool built, and the long driveway mended. Ian wrote to his solicitor: 'the building of Warneford Place is proving far more expensive than we had anticipated'.

If Ian opened his heart, it was to Robert Harling who had found them Victoria Square. On his release from the London Clinic, 'convalesced', Ian drove Harling in his Thunderbird to inspect the 'archaeological heap', describing it as 'a semi-open prison for geriatrics, but not for me'. He told

Harling what he had told Maud and Noël Coward: Ann wanted him to sell Goldeneye to pay for the renovations. But he still loved Jamaica. Even though Stephenson, Bryce and Beaverbrook had sold up as the island hastened towards independence, Ian did not want to leave.

Harling judged the battle to rebuild Warneford Place 'the most depressing and destructive of the many discordant episodes in their marriage. Fleming undoubtedly regarded this as the most decisive of their conflicts, the defeat of defeats.'

Maud was shocked at Ian's altered state when she met him six months after his heart attack, at a bridge party in the diplomat Fred Warner's room in Albany. 'I hadn't seen him since he was ill in the spring & was saddened to see what a strange wreck he has become & how ill he still is.' He resembled the house he was pulling down. 'He seemed half derelict.'

Ann was physically different too. 'She is a hard-faced middle-aged woman & much heavier. Her beautiful eyes have changed & lost their dancing, winning charm; her expression, which was so lively, is now elderly . . . I suppose they had been wrangling . . . I felt relieved I had nothing to do with their lives.'

The Flemings' lives were all of a sudden centred around James Bond. At last, a film was in the offing. Three days before, on 3 November 1961, United Artists announced the name of the actor who had been chosen to play the lead.

LXV
HOWLS OF LAUGHTER

' "*I think we've got a bit of a hit here,*" *my solicitor said.*
"*This is going to run and run.*" '

MONTY NORMAN

Saltzman and Broccoli had planned to begin with the latest Bond book, *Thunderball*. But they opted instead for *Dr. No*, published in 1958 and the sixth novel in the series, wary of McClory's ongoing legal dispute. No studio wanted to buy trouble.

To make the film, they bought a fifty–fifty ownership of a shelf company (like Glidrose) which came with existing losses. It was called EON, which Harry liked to say stood for Everything Or Nothing.

'So they've decided on you to fuck up my work,' was how Ian greeted the producers' third-choice director, Terence Young, a man described by Len Deighton as 'rather superior and majestic'. An old Harrovian and former wartime officer in the Guards Armoured Division, Young was put off at first by Ian's manner. 'I thought he was a pompous son of a bitch, immensely arrogant. I said, "Well, let me put it this way, Ian, I don't think anything you've written is immortal as yet, whereas the last picture I made [*Black Tights*] won the [Special Golden Award] at Venice. Now let's start level." He said, "My, you're a prickly guy, aren't you?" and I said, "Yes, I am, now let's go and have dinner quietly," which we did. We left the party and went off and had dinner. We eventually became enormously good friends. Ian was an intensely shy person, which never showed.'

Ian avoided pre-production meetings. He told Simenon, 'They consult me, and I give them my ideas, perhaps at a lunch, but that's all.' Still, he was unable not to involve himself. After he was shown a draft screenplay, he supplied notes. There were no giant clams in the Caribbean. Bond wouldn't carry a visiting card. And 'cut out "old boy". I think we should always omit chumminess whenever it tends to creep in.'

He suggested the British-Ghanaian actor Paul Danquah for Quarrel, and Noël Coward to play Dr No. 'If you will, you'd suit the part,' he wrote to Coward – eliciting the famous response, 'NO NO NO NO NO.' Meanwhile, the screenwriters were exploring the idea of casting a spider monkey as the villain.

Ian's primary concern was who would play the lead.

Had the filming of 'Thunderball' gone smoothly ahead under the original direction of Kevin McClory, using Jack Whittingham's script, there is little likelihood that James Bond would still be remembered sixty-five years on. 'If you read the screenplay,' says Broccoli's stepson, Michael G. Wilson, 'it's almost a certainty that we would not be here today discussing Bond. One scene is so ridiculous. Bond is running about looking for a sun-hat in the Bahamas, and buys it off a guy with a donkey which has a hat on its head.' McClory's choice for 007 was no less awry: Sweden's new heavyweight boxing champion, Ingemar 'Ingo' Johansson. 'He is looking for an acting career,' McClory had written enthusiastically to Bryce. 'And my golly he would make a wonderful James Bond.' To date, an American had floundered in the role and after that a South African. The overwhelming probability is that McClory and 'Ingo' would have made a one-picture flop like Charles Feldman's *Casino Royale* (1967), an all-star satirical comedy with David Niven as Sir James Bond that was dismissed by the *New York Times* in one of the politer reviews as 'reckless, disconnected nonsense'.

Since the mid 1950s, many well-known actors had been approached. Gregory Ratoff had the arresting idea of having Bond played by a woman, Susan Hayward. Ian had entertained several possibilities, from Richard Burton ('I think that Richard Burton would be by far the best James Bond'), to James Stewart ('I wouldn't at all mind him as Bond if he can slightly anglicise his accent'), to James Mason ('We might have to settle for him'). Other actors who had entered the frame were Peter Finch, Cary Grant, Dirk Bogarde, Trevor Howard, Rex Harrison, Richard Todd, Michael Redgrave, Patrick McGoohan, Roger Moore and Richard Johnson. Robert Fenn was Ian's film agent in London. 'We tried twenty or thirty. No major actor would play the part for more than one picture, and we couldn't set up a deal with a distributor without commitment from a main actor.'

An idea which gained momentum was to give the part to a young actor no one had heard of. Ian wrote to Bryce, 'I do think the idea of creating our own James Bond from an unknown and for Xanadu [Bryce's production company] to sign him up for ten years and have a very valuable human property on their hands . . . is an excellent one.' Broccoli warmed to this suggestion. An unknown might work for not much money: the actor they chose was paid £6,000 (approximately £165,000 today).

'Who decided on Connery as Bond?' asked Sean Connery's biographer, Christopher Bray. 'The likelihood is we will never really know.' As with so much about Bond and Fleming, all those involved in the film have claimed some retrospective say. It is the same with the places Fleming stayed in, or where he shopped or ate or drank. Everyone that Ian had dealings with, everyone he met, is eager to share in his legend, and one of the effects of this has been to lend an element of fantasy to all he touched.

Bray has little doubt: 'It was Connery who made Bond' – as it was Bond who made Connery. 'There is no gainsaying the fact that had they not cast Connery in "Dr No" there would have been no later Bonds – and no subsequent series – to argue about.'

Since 1995, Michael G. Wilson has co-produced the Bond films with his half-sister, Broccoli's daughter Barbara. She says, 'Sean Connery was the right guy in the movie for the right time. If it hadn't been Sean, who knows? Would it have captured the attention of the whole world?'

'Oh, disaster, disaster, disaster.' Terence Young had worked with Connery and was categorical in believing he was *not* the right guy. Not only that, Connery had ignored his advice. Young had recommended Connery wear a suit, but he ambled into the EON office in 'a sort of lumber jacket'.

Saltzman remembered, 'Whenever he wanted to make a point, he'd bang his fist on the table, the desk or his thigh, and we knew this guy had something.'

Connery's background – naval boxer, lifeguard, art class model – was a marketable asset. He was brought up in a Scottish slum, like Ian's grandfather. His father was a truck driver, his mother a cleaning lady. Among choice biographical details: he had delivered milk to Bond's second school

Fettes, and acted at the Oxford Playhouse as an aristocratic diplomat in Pirandello's *Naked*. He afterwards maintained that 'portraying Bond is just as serious as playing Macbeth on stage'.

Connery's son Jason says, 'He had worked with Yat Malmgren, a teacher my mother introduced my dad to. He was very influential and had an acting technique, part of which was physical as well as emotional.' Malmgren had advised Connery to think about large jungle cats during the interview, because 'they are very loose'. Even as Connery strode out of 2 South Audley Street following the audition, both Saltzman and Broccoli, without discussing it, went over to the window to look at the way he walked. Michael G. Wilson, aside from co-producing the franchise, has appeared in cameo roles in Bond films. 'Walking is a fairly important thing for an actor, believe it or not. It's how you're going to appear on screen.'

Saltzman and Broccoli tracked Connery cross the road to his fiancée's Fiat. 'My dad was in the navy,' says Jason Connery, 'and tended to walk like a sailor, you know, rocking. He dodged through the traffic, round a couple of cars, and slipped through.'

'He's got balls,' Saltzman murmured.

Broccoli agreed. 'It was the sheer self-confidence he exuded ... He walked like the most arrogant son-of-a-gun, you've ever seen – as if he owned every bit of Jermyn Street from Regent Street to St James. "That's our Bond," I said.'

'But first Fleming had to meet him,' remembered Fenn, 'and of course was shocked because he couldn't speak the Queen's English. Fleming said, "He's not my idea of Bond at all, I just want an elegant man, not this roughneck."'

Connery soon heard the stories. How Ian Fleming had told somebody he was 'an over-developed stuntman'. How Fleming doubted that a working-class Scotsman had 'the social graces' to play his hero.

Ivar Bryce's cousin Janet Milford Haven says that she brought Ian around after he invited her to lunch with Connery in London. 'I'm a judge of people, on the magistrate's bench at Westminster, and every night at Annabel's. Ian was like an old father. He knew I had a lot of different boyfriends. "You've got rather good taste in men." I could choose the best man. A lot of actors he'd shown me were too good-looking, too glamorous.'

On the appointed day, Janet turned up at the Savoy.

'When you look at someone, you don't look at the face too much, but what's coming out of the eyes, the mouth, they way they move. Connery didn't talk to me. Ian was talking about London theatre. This is the first time Ian's met him without masses of others.

'After Connery left, Ian took me home with a chauffeur to my flat in Wilton Street, and walked me to the door. I said, "I think that fellow is divine. He's not too good-looking, he looks masculine, he looks like a proper man and one that would be used to that life. He looks like he is very clever, he looks like he would know how to do everything, who could kill." '

Ian wrote to Blanche a week before United Artists broke the news: 'the man they have chosen for Bond, Sean Connery, is a real charmer – fairly unknown but a good actor with the right looks and physique.' After viewing the rough cut of 'Dr. No', Ian became still more convinced. Connery was 'not quite the idea I had of Bond, but he would be if I wrote the books over again.' Just as Alec Guinness reshaped the character of Smiley for le Carré, Ian responded to Connery's cinematic Bond by putting some Scottish blood into him in his next novel, *On Her Majesty's Secret Service*.

With unconcealed relief, Ian wrote to Stephenson on 7 November 1961: 'The film deal with United Artists is going ahead and they are going to film "Dr No" in Jamaica in January and February.' Ian had pulled some strings so that the film-makers could shoot at Laughing Waters, a secluded beach belonging to a relation of Blanche's. Ann decided to join him at the last moment. 'I was very ambivalent about going,' she wrote to a friend, 'but finally the thought of Ian and the black woman seemed worse than the terror of flying.' 'Boofy' Gore warned her not to get over-excited. 'Have you ever watched a film being made? It is the most boring thing I know. Absolutely nothing happens.' To counter the boredom, she invited Peter Quennell and Stephen Spender.

The shoot did provide one memorable image: Ian ducking out of sight of his protagonist at the instant of his cinematic birth. On the day that Bond was going to be filmed meeting Honey Ryder, Ian took Quennell and Spender down to Laughing Waters. They wandered on to the beach, only to be screamed at by Young, 'Lie down, you bastards!' so he could film the sequence of the unknown Swiss actress, Ursula Andress, stepping ashore in her ivory bikini singing 'underneath the mango tree' and Connery on the beach answering her.

The composer Monty Norman had arrived in Jamaica to write the music and he watched Young shout at them – 'They were shooed off like little boys.' Ian and his friends were left lying behind a dune, forgotten, until someone remembered to release them half an hour later.

Not many images capture so succinctly Ian's relationship with his character. Concealed behind James Bond at every step, keeping his head low, smiling to himself, yet always there a few feet away, crouches his creator, as if half-expecting to be exposed at any moment. Ann added one contraceptive detail: 'The sand ridge was planted with French letters full of explosive – by magic mechanism they blew up the sand in little puffs.'

There were no outrageous hopes for the film. Ian's favourite newspaper, the *Gleaner*, reported, 'Dr No promises to be a slapdash and rather regrettable picture'. The actor who finally agreed to play Dr No, Joseph Wiseman, referred to the project as 'just another Grade-B Charlie Chan mystery'.

'It was going to be a low-budget flop,' says Blanche's son Chris who, thanks to Ian, although much to Ann's irritation, had secured a job as a location manager. 'It all changed when we watched the rushes of Ursula Andress emerging from the sea.'

Chris Blackwell was present on the evening in the Cove cinema in Ocho Rios when James Bond transformed from a B-movie character with not a lot of prospects into a cultural phenomenon. 'It was electrifying. We suddenly felt, "Gosh, we've got a movie." '

As vital to the film's success was Monty Norman's score. This inspired Simon Winder to consider the opening twenty seconds of 'Dr. No' as 'the most important in British cinema'.

Incredible to relate, the James Bond theme tune originated in a cast-off song that Norman had composed for an aborted Peter Brook musical based on V. S. Naipaul's 1961 novel *A House for Mr Biswas*.* Norman says, 'I wrote

---

* The future Nobel prize-winner attended the opening of 'Thunderball' in Kampala in 1966, apparently unaware that his novel had inspired the Bond theme tune. 'Inside, we were told, was the new President, whose army had recently been at work, with real guns, on a hostile civilian population.'

five or six numbers, basic quick first drafts, which I put in my bottom drawer. One of them was called "Bad Sign, Good Sign". It had an Asian feel. I quite liked it and thought I'd offer it for the Bond theme. I'm sitting at the piano in my flat in Cannon Hill with my wife. It was just an idea. "Let's see what it's like if I take a sweep and split the notes." I saw immediately – it had all the qualities of James Bond: mood, mystery, sexiness, it's all there. With a good start of eight bars, I couldn't believe it would be so different and lose the Asian qualities of the song. I got John Barry, a young orchestrator, to do the orchestration and then I played it to Harry and Cubby and they were just knocked out, as everyone was. I've now heard a million different orchestrations on it, and what I am amazed at is how it is still fresh after sixty years.'

'Dr. No' was edited quickly. On 2 August, four days before Jamaica gained independence, Terence Young invited the Flemings to a preview at the Travellers' Club. Ian wrote to Plomer, 'As you can imagine, I am longing for Annie's comments on the picture.' She did not disappoint.

'It was an abominable occasion,' Ann told Waugh. They had taken the Crickmeres, plus Caspar and his nanny. 'I feared Mrs Crickmere might give notice and no more coconut soup; luckily she found the film "quite gripping". I wish I had, for our fortune depends upon it. There were howls of laughter when the tarantula walks up James Bond's body.'

No one was sure how to interpret these howls. Terence Young was embarrassed and Broccoli had to reassure him. It was impossible to tell whether the reaction of this select audience boded well for the film's prospects, or the opposite.

Behind the scenes, the Fleming marriage teetered on the same knife-edge.

LXVI
CASPAR

'My favourite platitude is that no work of art is created
without a certain amount of dissatisfaction.'
CASPAR FLEMING, aged sixteen

'Their connubial situation is rocky,' Noël Coward reported.

Robert Harling had observed the gradual dissolution of the couple's early passion into a 'tragically querulous relationship' which had them arguing about everything. 'They couldn't live with each other or without each other.'

Their bickering drove Ernie Cuneo to quote Kierkegaard – *rather well-hanged than ill-wed.* 'There is evidence that Ann and Ian did not drift apart; they tore each other apart instead.'

Ann had left Goldeneye as 'Dr. No' was being filmed, two weeks earlier than planned, citing Blanche Blackwell; the first thing Ian had wanted to do on arrival was to ring her at Bolt. Ann afterwards wrote to him: 'I think you must try to realise how painful it has been to me that since Mrs Blackwell's hard buttocks, our sex life, such as it was, has ceased totally . . . though I hope you will be well enough to have sex again, it will certainly not be with me.'

Without mentioning her love affair with Gaitskell, Ann levelled this charge against Ian: 'I fear that since the rise of James Bond, you do not care for a personality that in any way can compete with yours, and no doubt there is more adulation to be had at Bolt, and you refuse to see that it is an impossible situation for me. If you were well and we were both younger, our marriage would be over, but I love you and want to look after you and grind my teeth when you smoke and am pleased when you refrain from the deadly gin after whisky.'

Ann repeated: 'your personality has greatly changed with success, Bond and bad health – this is a *general* opinion.'

Ian contested Ann's accusations. 'Everything is fogged up by your rage with me at having married me.' Their marriage was as toxic as an unripe akee. The only way 'out of this barbaric deadlock that is making us both sick to the stomach' was to 'settle down with each other's personalities and stop trying to change them'. Instead of doing this, Ann's letters had grown, as he told her, 'terrifyingly authoritarian' in tone. 'You seem to have built me up in your mind into a sort of nightmare figure who wants only the worst for you and Caspar.'

The thing that made Ian most anxious, he wrote, was Caspar; 'watching his character deteriorate under your *laissez-faire* depresses me beyond words because I see him not being casually spoiled now but spoiled when it comes to facing the world. You say I should impose my authority. I cannot when you abrogate the position of father as well as mother & when Nannie abets you.'

Unusually, Ann recognised that it was a problem for Caspar to live with 'three middle-aged people who doted on him'. But his behaviour had begun to concern her.

Caspar's first cousin Sara says, 'We all agreed he was not absolutely normal. There was something odd, a curious intensity about him, and a very fixed stare, I can see it now, when talking to me, even if only to say, "I'd rather have scones than toast." He was good-looking, solid, moved rather jerkily, and frightfully absent-minded. He thought in absolutely straight vertical lines. What was missing was the horizontal weave.'

After he threatened Sara's dog at White Cliffs, Sara's mother warned her, 'You've got to be very careful with Caspar. I told him not to fold the deck chair, and he said, "If you do that to me again, I'm going to break that terrier's neck." I think the child's a murderer.'

It was obvious to Fionn that her complex half-brother had not inherited the excitement about the natural world shared by his parents. 'Caspar liked the supernatural and the unnatural.'

Aged four, Caspar had wanted to call himself Mary. He next set his sights on playing Baby Jesus in the school nativity play, but Nanny Sillick discouraged this – rather to Ann's disappointment. 'I was enjoying him saying "Baby Jesus will soon put this stone in your eye."' Unable to be Christ, Caspar looked around for other roles.

He was not athletic, as Ian had been. 'Caspar was not physical in any way,' says his cousin Francis Grey. 'I shouldn't think he knew which end to hold a hockey stick.' Nor did Caspar share Ian's early love of poetry – 'just another field in which I have no aspirations whatever'. However, after Clarissa Eden's early gift of a penknife 'caused the maximum excitement', he took a precocious interest in weapons.

His shooting-mad uncle Peter, who was also his godfather, oversaw Caspar's graduation from penknives to shotguns. 'Dear Cracker,' Peter wrote to Ian in December 1960. 'I am *v.* keen to see Cas, about whom I have done nothing at all . . . What are or will be Caspar's tastes? If and when they include shooting, I can always help.' Following Ian's death, Peter arranged for Caspar's trustees to pay £115 for a 16-bore shotgun until he could handle his father's 1912 12-bores. 'By then, Caspar had a lot of weapons,' says Francis Grey. 'A Browning Mark Three semi-automatic rifle and a Luger that ended up for a time in Scotland Yard's Black Museum. He also had a Sten gun, a 9mm, a 22mm, a 32mm, a .455 Webley and a muzzle-loading 1861 Colt Navy used in the US civil war.' This unregistered armoury got Peter and Caspar into trouble later on.

Antiquities were another obsession. Caspar spent a disproportionate amount of his boyhood in furrowed fields sifting for flint arrowheads from the Mesolithic period. When Fionn later took him out from his Oxford prep school, all he wanted was to visit antique shops and bargain fiercely for pieces of Egyptiana to add to his collection. On holiday with Ann in Luxor, he returned triumphant 'with a bundle of fake scarabs and amulets'. These were not the usual interests of a boy his age. 'Caspar was never a child,' says his friend Randal Keynes. 'He was always an adult in a way.'

Digging things up, not fitting the box, breaking the rules with a frenetic sense of excitement. This was Ian's son in 1962, a man of nine years, who was known to Ann's friends as 'Old Caspar'. Few activities thrilled him more than to fire his catapult at helicopters landing golfers at Sandwich, or race down the dunes in a four-wheeled trolley, or dig in the sand for bones. 'He knows the Earl and Countess of Guilford were blown up in the vicinity during the war,' Ann wrote to Waugh.

Caspar's first girlfriend, Louise Allison, afterwards had the impression that his parents had been 'too tied up in their own selfish, social pastimes and ambitions to pay him enough attention, and he was left far too much alone to get on with his own solitary interests of flint/coin hunting. Ian and

Ann presumably loved him – hence *Chitty-Chitty-Bang-Bang* – but they either couldn't show it, or were too preoccupied with their own lives, to take the trouble of loving and giving a little boy what he needed. As a result, Caspar became more and more precocious, and relied on his intelligence to get their attention on their terms.'

Not even as a nine-year-old did Caspar go out of his way to charm his parents' friends. His godfather Noël Coward was overheard remonstrating, 'How *dare* you speak to me like that, you little *beast*.' Evelyn Waugh was thinking of letting his daughter Teresa go as Caspar's governess to Golden-eye before he turned against 'that delinquent Old Caspar'. Once, in the tea room of the Grand Hotel in Folkestone, Waugh made a face 'of such unbelievable malignity that the child shrieked with terror and fell to the floor' – prompting Ann to give Waugh a sharp slap, and later to seek revenge by accelerating him fast down a bumpy cart-track so that 'he swallowed half his cigar', although none of his prejudice. Waugh continued to consider Caspar 'a very obstreperous child, grossly pampered'.

Spoiling Caspar failed to improve his behaviour, though. Patrick Leigh Fermor described him as 'rather frail and slender and pale with a few scattered freckles and thick dark curls, rather like an angry and vulnerable faun' and 'giving a certain amount of hell to everyone but mainly to Ann'. Alexandra Henderson remembers how after lunch 'on dreaded walks, he would carry a flick-knife and flick it at Ann's ankles just as she moved her foot in time. A constant daring. And she would laugh about this quite dangerous thing.'

'Undoubtedly, he was on a self-destructive path,' says Francis Grey. 'Bipolar, perhaps – and Ian had an element of that.'

This is also Fionn's diagnosis. 'Caspar was bipolar.' At the time, the condition did not exist under that name. Ann later explained to Diana Cooper that 'the best of the "shrinks" described C.'s condition as "malignant depression".' Fionn says that her mother was also told that it was containable but not curable.

Society hostesses do not make good mothers. Peter Quennell's son Alexander remembers Ann as 'fairly ferocious' with children. 'I was eight when I asked, "What should I call you?" "I think Mrs Fleming will do, thank you."' Ann suspended any such formality with Caspar. 'Caspar calls me Granny,' she lamented to Waugh.

To Ian, Ann's doting was too reminiscent of how Eve had brought him up. He told Harling: 'Mothers can prove very influential in our early days, especially if they are dotty about success in their offspring.' Almost from the start, the frustrated intellectual in Ann pushed Caspar in directions he did not wish to go, repeatedly voicing her project for him to follow the example of Ann's uncle Terence O'Neill, who was Prime Minister of Northern Ireland for six years. 'I don't think it's worth having a son unless one directs him towards becoming Prime Minister.'

Caspar was resistant to her ambitions. 'At heart, he was a scholar,' says Rachel Toynbee, who became his girlfriend after Louise, 'but that wasn't what he was destined to be. His mother wanted him to belong to her world. She had a limited capacity for love in that she couldn't do the self-sacrificing part; the people she loved had to serve her purposes. Ian Fleming had to write Bond in order to keep up with Ann's friends and to afford what she wanted, and Caspar was trapped by the same thing. Loving someone is preferring their happiness to your own, and Ann was so beyond that. She saw him as an embellishment to her life, like her favourite famous people. She didn't ever think to ask, "What is my son actually like?"'

It distressed Bamber Gascoigne, Ann's nephew, to watch their curious interplay. 'She didn't understand children, and was so beastly to Caspar, and would make jokes about him and to him which as adults one realised were friendly jokes but as a teenager was incredibly embarrassing. I was aware that he must have been cringing.' The adult badinage of Ann's friends like Waugh, for whom 'the awful Caspar' became a standing joke, was not repartee that a sensitive child brushed off like an adult.

In his own way, Ian was just as fussy and overprotective as Ann. He had ensured that Caspar was buttoned to the chin in his pram so that the seagulls did not peck him, and refused to let him fly to Jamaica until Caspar was five. 'I really would be terrified if he was here, things are so sharp and the sun is so hot.'

Ian dazzled in an office environment with young people, but as a parent he was ineffectual. 'Daddy will *have* to leave the room if you go on being so naughty,' was his only effort at discipline when Caspar, still small, threw bread pellets at him. Caspar's response: 'If you take me out of the room now, you won't see me again this weekend.'

Abundantly clear to Ernie Cuneo was 'that Ian "loved" his son Caspar deeply, more deeply possibly than most fathers'. Maud noted in her diary: 'He talks about his child, whom he worships.' When Caspar went to Ann's choice of prep school in Oxford, Ian wrote to Eve with a pride he could not disguise: 'Caspar is getting on very well at Summer Fields and curiously enough being pushed rapidly up the school. He has even been made head of his dormitory, from which I can only guess that the other inhabitants must be the most appalling collection of little monsters. Anyway, he is looking wonderful.'

Francis Grey lived with them during this period. His reply, when asked to describe Ian's relationship with Caspar: 'Slightly distant.' He has vivid memories of Ian losing his temper. 'One rainy day, Caspar and I came across a green field and ran down it in the trolley, digging bits out of the grass and piling up stones to make a chicane. It was the fourth green at St George's. The only reason we were found out by the Club Secretary was that the last thing he did at the end of each day was to walk round the course, and he knew it was us. We got back and Ian was livid – it was shortly before he was made Captain. Ian made us stand to attention and bawled us out. On other occasions, we would open the window and fire stones from our catapult at a mark, and take it down an inch at a time until one or other of us broke the window. Ian used to go mental, it was terrifying. A real dressing down. "All weapons shall be removed for a week!"'

Not that Ian spared Caspar's mother. It enraged him when Ann took Caspar out from Summer Fields on her own for the weekend, without discussing it first with Ian. 'You seem to want to have only your own way about Caspar's upbringing.'

Already that summer of 1962, a furious argument over their son had caused Ian to flee back across the Atlantic to be soothed by Blanche Blackwell at Bolt. In a departure from routine, he flew to Goldeneye in July and arrived on 'this sudden trip to Jamaica' during the island's last month as a British colony. A letter he drafted to Ann from Sandwich conveys how near to the end of his tether he was:

Darling,

I'm sorry but I'm off.

I just can't stand the stress & strain anymore, and I must have some peace – at any rate a short while of it.

I have had this year. Too many doctors & lawyers & accountants & home troubles. I don't think I've deserved this avalanche. There's been too much bad news & there's not much prospect of anything better. So, for the first time in my life, instead of facing up to it all, I'm just going to escape it & run away.

This is nothing to do with 'love'. I love you & I'm not going to 'love' anyone else in Jamaica. I simply must have a rest . . .

I'm sorry, darling. But there it is.

I'll let you know as soon as I'm better. But please do remember that while you have too much pride, I have pride, too, as an individual.

'Am I a good husband? Are you a good wife?'

Above all – who is the better human being?

If you insist that you are, instead of calling it quits, we shall continue to be what Caspar calls 'uneasy'.

Shouldn't we try & be 'easy' at least for his sake.

I promise that I will be 'easy' – which means a kind of 'loving' – if you will bear with me, & with my kind of life, & my kind of friends.

Otherwise, life becomes such a burden, as it has become at this moment, that one simply has to fly away from it.

I'm sorry, my darling love. If, surrounded by your Oxford friends with me alone down here alone, you had rung up and told me about your days off with Casp, I would not have made this decision. But there it is. I tried to make up with my telephone call on Friday. But, when there was no loving counter-move, despondency & flight caught me by the heart.

And I mean 'heart'.

Ian

*

In another letter, posted from New York, he added: 'But for my love for you and Caspar, I would welcome the freedom that you threaten me with.'

Ian told a quite different story to Blanche, whom he was relieved to find in Jamaica. He had ended his previous novel, *On Her Majesty's Secret Service*, with the death of a marriage. In the opinion of John Cork, who interviewed Blanche in 2000, Ian was now ready to leave Ann to spend his life with Blanche. 'Of course, his moment of personal crisis is tied up with "Dr. No" having wrapped, with Ian moments away from serious new money, with his horror at what is happening at Sevenhampton, with his marriage having become sexless, with his knowledge about Gaitskell, with the critical failure of *The Spy Who Loved Me* in the London press and the *Thunderball* mess continuing . . .'

At Goldeneye, Blanche nursed Ian. 'He was sick and so miserable in his marriage. I looked after him. Jamaica and me: we could have kept him alive.' Their relationship had passed out of passion into 'TLC. Tender loving care treatment'. But she was not willing to accept a full-time life with him. She explained to Cork, 'I am not a lot like other people. I've lived a lot alone, I've had a lot of time to think, and I decided how I wanted to live, long ago.'

John Cork says, 'She could have kept him alive, but she told him she would only have an affair with him, that she would not be responsible for destroying his marriage to Ann, and that if he left Ann, she would likely never see him again. The consequence of that "no" was Ian's suicidal and self-loathing mood, and that's when he worked out his emotional turmoil on paper – at a point in time when he did not want to leave his bit of paradise, when he was going to have to return to Ann's side.'

For Ian to explore the outer reef, Blanche had given him a wooden coracle that he baptised 'Octopussy'. During these days at Goldeneye, the last before Bond 'exploded in a Vesuvius of popular consumption', in Cuneo's memorable phrase, Ian started writing his story: about the once-dashing Intelligence officer who had murdered the mentor of the young James Bond in Kitzbühel for a couple of gold bars, and has lived too long on the parings of his illicit bullion, and who, when poisoned by a scorpion fish and then grabbed at by an octopus, makes no attempt to save himself.

After a week, Ian received a cable from Ann – she was going into hospital for a dangerous medical operation, although Ann had not seemed ill to

Loelia Westminster when she came to stay on 15 July. 'Annie left rather bemoaning her lot,' was all Loelia wrote.

Ian suspected a melodramatic ruse, but Blanche persuaded him to return, saying he would not forgive himself if something happened. He nearly missed his flight. He informed his New York agent that he had to cut short his visit 'because Annie wasn't very well and owing to mechanical failure in aircraft at Montego Bay, I ended up having to run through Idlewild carrying my own bag last night to catch the Monarch to London.'

At the precise moment when his island sanctuary was breaking free, Ian, instead of leaving his wife, was scurrying back to her. 'He just gives up after that,' says John Cork. 'He is too weak to fight the move to Sevenhampton, too weak to stop the profligacy, too defeated to escape Ann, just as he had been too weak to escape Eve fully. And the next novel Ian writes just months later, *You Only Live Twice*, ends with James Bond on a small island living on the sea . . . with no memory of his past . . . until he gets a message on a piece of newsprint that sends him back into the world that we know will corrupt him . . . having to leave peaceful love behind.'

LXVII
BOND FEVER

'I am an insatiable Bondomane (what sensible man is not?)'
HERMAN LIEBERT to Ian Fleming

Despite Chris Blackwell's excitement on seeing the rushes, there was little outward sign that 'Dr. No' was poised to alter the course of cinematic history. After the film wrapped, Sean Connery at once accepted a part in Jean Giraudoux's *Judith* at Her Majesty's Theatre; his photograph did not even appear in the programme.

In America, 'Dr. No' was scheduled to open at an Oklahoma drive-in, and not in New York. Few critics predicted success for a movie with 'a Limey truck driver' playing the lead. A United Artists executive told Saltzman after a New York viewing, 'Well, all we can lose is $950,000.' The co-writer, Wolf Mankowitz, who had introduced Broccoli to Saltzman and set the Bond ball rolling, refused to have his name on the script. 'I don't want my name on a piece of crap, and that's a piece of crap.'

On Tuesday, 2 October, Len Deighton was having lunch at Pinewood with Saltzman, who had already engaged him to write the next Bond script, when a man came to their table and reported that people at the Press Showing had been laughing.

'With us?' Saltzman asked, obviously afraid the laughter was derisive.

The man said yes.

Saltzman nodded. 'That's all right,' and he started eating his soup.

Deighton says, 'Harry – always hands on – had pushed for an undertone of comedy, and this news justified his decision.' The film went on to gross sixty times its budget.

The first appearance of Bond at the London Pavilion, in the spectacular technicolour of Jamaica's tropical fruits, was an undeniable event. 'It was dazzling, like the arrival of a new galaxy,' wrote Ian's nephew James. 'Almost overnight, the whole paraphernalia of Fleming's imagination became visible: the guns, the girls, the villains, the gambling, the heroic escapes. Everything that had been denied to people by the hardships of World War II was there on the screen, to be gawped at and giggled over. There was no competition. As a result, his was no ordinary success; it was success on the grandest scale conceivable.'

As Broccoli had learned, 'the success and failure of a film often hangs on a question of timing.' 'Dr. No' opened in London on 5 October 1962, two days after Gaitskell addressed the Labour Party Conference as Britain's likely next Prime Minister. The Beatles released their debut single 'Love Me Do' on the same day. The Cuban missile crisis erupted two weeks later. President Kennedy ordered a naval blockade, demanding that Castro return the missiles already on the island to Russia. It felt like the plot of the film. The world was imitating Bond.

A hostile premature review in *Izvestia* confirmed how seriously the Soviet authorities regarded Fleming's influence on Kennedy and his former CIA chief Allen Dulles. The article, headlined 'Love and Horrors', had appeared as a spoiler three months earlier, in the main morning issue of 29 May, under the byline of Yuri Orlov from the Novosti Press Agency. It accused Ian – 'a retired spy who has turned mediocre writer' – of being an American propagandist for his 'best friend' Dulles, sacked architect of the 1961 Bay of Pigs calamity. James Fleming wrote in *Bond Behind the Iron Curtain*: 'Somewhere a decision had been made to ridicule Bond as a way of ridiculing the western way of life; in short, to take the offensive.' The attack against Bond in the official party newspaper was specific. 'Bond and the film of *Dr No* had somehow been identified as symptomatic of the decadence of the west and of its duplicity.'

In the West, by contrast, Bond acted as a shorthand for the individual freedom Kennedy represented. Ian's fictional character struck a responsive chord across every generation. *Time* magazine devoted half a page in its 'World Events' section to covering *Izvestia*'s attack. Ian then had the idea of using this to promote 'Dr. No' when it was released in the US in May 1963, with pre-written articles that could be placed in newspapers.

Following JFK's endorsement of Bond, Russia's condemnation, and the massive sales of books, nearing a million every two months in America, manufacturers thronged to have their products associated with 007. Ian was alert to the money to be made from what Griffie called 'the ghastly world of merchandising' ever since Floris sent him complimentary bath essence for having mentioned the brand in his novels. By the terms of his film contract with EON, an arrangement that lasted until 1989, Ian had retained half the merchandising rights for 'Dr. No'. He referred all enquiries about advertising to Robert Fenn. Acting quickly on the success of 'From Russia with Love' and 'Goldfinger', Fenn was soon operating in every country. 'I had 65 patent agents and 40 lawyers. It bought in hundreds of thousands.'

Applications poured into Fenn's Berkeley Street office to make James Bond ties, raincoats, socks, belts, pullovers, polo shirts, straw hats, attaché cases, cuff links, tie pins, money clips, key rings, jigsaw puzzles, vodka, bubble gum, batteries, cap-repeater pistols, cigarettes, razors. In America, Colgate-Palmolive offered a line of 007 toothpaste and shaving cream. In Australia, swimmers on Bondi beach could buy a '007 snorkel'. Not only the masculine market was targeted. In Paris's Galeries Lafayette, women could buy 'Become fit for James Bond' lingerie, a 'Margaret 007' bra, a hair dye with the guarantee '007 loves blondes', 'a good Bond for the lips' French lipstick, car rugs, bedspreads, and shoes with steel toe-caps. Meanwhile, children clamoured to wear pyjamas labelled '003½' and play, as Caspar did in the hall at Sevenhampton, with a gold Corgi diecast model of Bond's DB5 Aston Martin, the world's biggest-selling toy of 1965.

Book sales were boosted by 'Bond fever'. Cape reprinted the hardback edition of *Dr. No* twice, and Pan, Ian's paperback house, reported that they were selling 120,000 copies every week.

Ian owned the literary property through Glidrose. The screen version of Bond belonged to Saltzman and Broccoli, who overnight found themselves sitting on the rights to a 24-carat egg. Inevitably, the extraordinary reception of their film sharpened curiosity to know more about the man behind Bond. Who *was* this thriller writer?

Ian's talent for self-promotion led him to pose in a vintage Bentley with an Amherst Villiers supercharger – although Ian himself had never owned a

Bentley. He sat for Amherst Villiers to paint his portrait that Cape then used for publicity; he was photographed by Frank Herrmann talking on set to Sean Connery, by Horst Tappe smoking one of his signature Morlands out of a long holder, and by Loomis Dean staring down the barrel of a Beretta. He gave interviews to the *New Yorker* and *Playboy*. The autobiographical implication of the relationship advertised in the opening credits, 'Ian Fleming's James Bond', boosted his sales to record levels.

Just at the point when Ian had lost creative control of James Bond, he became inextricably associated with Bond in the popular imagination, an eye-catching *trompe l'oeil* like one of Dicky Chopping's covers, designed to deceive the public eye that he, Ian Fleming, *is* Bond.

Joan Bright's son, Richard Astley, was at Eton with Caspar when the first Bond films came out ('we used to enact scenes in our rooms'). One afternoon, he was summoned by his mother, whom he knew had worked with Ian and Peter in Intelligence. 'Ian Fleming wants you to come to tea.' Astley put on his best flannels and hurried with her to 16 Victoria Square, where he found Fleming with his cigarette holder standing beside the fire in the upstairs drawing room. 'He asked me to put a brick of smokeless fuel on the fire and got me to stoke it,' remembers Astley. 'Then he gave me a piece of paper he'd signed twenty times in two rows. "Sell 'em, sell 'em, you can make some money with this."'

'If only I'd held on to them,' regrets Astley. 'I wasn't very savvy. I probably gave them away.'

An early example of 'Bond fever' and 'how a name can carry something very light a long distance' was the James Bond Club of Oxford University.

On 8 February 1963, John Goodwin, a history undergraduate at Magdalen College, read a hostile review of recent crime books in the *Times Literary Supplement*, criticising Bond as 'a thoroughly detestable character'.

Stirred to reply, Goodwin defended Bond as 'perhaps the most extraordinary cultural phenomenon of our time', arguing that he was a force for good and civilisation. He ended his letter, which the *TLS* printed, with an announcement. 'It was with the intention of emulating his achievements in this field that I formed the James Bond Club in this university.' He styled himself 'President'.

Goodwin says, 'Having written this letter with what I now see is extraordinary rashness, I knew I quickly had to do it. I never expected it would be anything other than a dining club for a few. I ran around trying to find smart undergraduates – all who were interested in good nosh and a nice bottle of wine and pretending to play the game of being James Bond. The Bond association was amazingly provocative. "Dr. No" was already out, and the success of the film raised the level of consciousness considerably. The fuss my letter created was out of all proportion to the reality.'

The BBC's 'Tonight' programme invited Goodwin to appear on live television. He gave interviews to newspapers. Then on 19 February 1963, he hosted the first dinner of the James Bond Club in the Oscar Wilde Room at Magdalen College. The eight guests included the President of the Union; Mark Lennox-Boyd (son of Alan); Jonathan Aitken (great-nephew of Lord Beaverbrook); and Laurance Reed (grandson of the fashion retailer Austin Reed).

In his diary, Goodwin recorded how the club provoked a febrile reaction. 'Another member was kidnapped by SMERSH, the anti-Bond group [wrongly rumoured to be headed by Tariq Ali, then at Exeter College], and they sent me a telegram which was handed to me at dinner saying one of the people invited to dinner had been kidnapped by them. Somebody tried to fuse the lights, and then newspaper reporters tried to get into the dinner.' The ambushed member had been stuffed into a laundry basket and an attempt made to throw him into the River Cherwell.

Out of the blue, Goodwin received a letter from Ian thanking him for springing to his support in the *TLS*. Ian arranged for the club to watch a day's filming of 'From Russia with Love' at Pinewood and invited Goodwin to his office in Mitre Court, where he gave him a tie and inscribed a Japanese paperback edition of *Thunderball*: 'To the James Bond Club for advanced Study!'

Altogether, Goodwin met Ian three times. 'He had this reputation for being an absolute A1 shit, and clearly many aspects of him were rather that case, but he was capable of being unbelievably thoughtful and generous to people he didn't know or have to be kind to. It was a kind thing to do, to be bothered, frankly, with some little twerp showing off in Oxford.'

*

Maud Russell was reminded of Ian's better nature when she met him around this time for tea. 'He started a little stiffly and awkwardly but gradually became more natural, though it is difficult to pick up the threads after an interval of so many years with someone one had known so well. When I think of him, I remember him kindly & the good, fine, courageous and generous things in his character.'

Friends and acquaintances were falling right and left. When Hugh Gaitskell lay dying in January, Ann was the person he wanted to see. Ann had been tempted to cry wolf a second time so she would not have to travel to Goldeneye. 'Till the last moment I thought of inventing illness but I should have lost what little confidence Ian has in anybody forever.' Hugo Pitman died that summer. Ian wrote, 'I was similarly dunched by the death (I suspect suicide) of my friend Duff Dunbar'. Before that, Ann's alcoholic sister Mary Rose had been discovered dead by Francis Grey, her eleven-year-old-son, who then came to live with them. 'I was very conscious I was there to be a friend of Caspar.'

It was in terms of renewing an old friendship that Percy Muir asked if Ian would loan forty-four volumes to a landmark exhibition on 'Printing and the Mind of Man' that Muir was organising as part of an international trade fair at Earl's Court. This was the second attempt, after the curtailed 1940 Gutenberg exhibition in Cambridge, to stage an exhibition that illustrated 'the impact of print technology on the evolution of Western civilization during five centuries'.

Ian had not seen Muir 'for years' and was overjoyed to hear from him. 'Naturally I will do anything I can to help.' Largely unregarded since the war, Ian's collection was then stored in twenty large crates in a London warehouse, waiting to be installed in the dining room at Warneford Place in the shelves that had been prepared for them.

Muir wrote to Ian after inspecting the books in Motcomb Street: 'I was delighted to see so many of the old friends again and to realise how well we had done all those years ago when we got this collection together.'

Ian would be the next largest contributor after King's College, Cambridge. He had his forty-four titles valued at £2,368 (approximately £60,000 today). Impressed, he told Muir: 'You certainly invested quite brilliantly, and we were lucky to get into the market when we did and also when you were cruising round Europe so fruitfully. What fun it all was.' Together, they had made a mark. John Hayward, no great friend of Fleming, called the Fleming collection a 'pioneering achievement' and noted that Ian had pursued his aim 'largely on his own initiative with determined energy and zest'.

'Printing and the Mind of Man' opened on 16 July 1963 in the exhibition centre constructed by William Stephenson, and was an event of immense cultural and intellectual significance. John Carter, one of Ian's directors on the *Book Collector*, helped Muir with the catalogue, which later became a standard reference work, with editions being published in Japan, Germany and the US. Ian sent Muir a telegram that looked back with a sense of accomplishment and nostalgia to when they had rescued historic scientific texts from threatened booksellers in Berlin and Munich.

A THOUSAND CONGRATULATIONS ON YOUR WONDERFUL CATALOGUE AND PARTICULARLY ON HAVING ELEVATED OUR COLLECTION TO THOSE FANTASTICALLY PROUD HEIGHTS STOP I TRULY BLUSH WITH EMBARRASSED DELIGHT AND WARM WITH MEMORIES OF THOSE DAYS WHEN YOU TOOK ME BY THE HAND STOP GRUESS DICH GOTT [God bless you] – IAN.

Lovers of James Bond may yawn, but one reason his character appears so innovative is that Ian assembled him in the zestful spirit that he had formed his prestigious collection. Bond's pronounced lack of interest in books, save for three by Kennedy, Dulles and Tommy Armour (*How to Play Your Best Golf All the Time*), was a cover for his creator, who read Leo Perutz and Jacques Perret in their original languages. Further back, the fifty-five-year-old author of *On Her Majesty's Secret Service* had once been the twenty-year-old translator of Klaus Mann and Carl Jung, and at the same age 'just missed the job of translating' *All Quiet on the Western Front*.

In ecstatic terms, the head of Monotype Italia, Dr Massini, wrote to Muir that this 'wonderful exhibition' was 'a real review of the spiritual evolution of the human kind, in which each of us visitors could find the stages of our own education'. For bibliophiles like Massini, Ian's collection was of far greater importance than Bond, says James Fleming, on the grounds of the total originality of its ideas. 'What Ian and Percy Muir grasped, and at the time were alone in so doing, was that the value of a book did not lie in its edition, provenance or condition but in the ideas it contained and thus its importance to our civilisation. "Printing and the Mind of Man" represented the apogee of this great truth.' James Fleming, who today owns and edits the quarterly founded by his uncle, would add to that Ian's perseverance in funding its annual losses until his death, 'the *Book Collector* being the only serious magazine in the world for bibliophiles'.

Simultaneously with the arrival of the rest of Ian's collection from the Pantechnicon, the Flemings moved that summer into their new house at Sevenhampton. For Ian, the empty building stood at the end of its mile-long drive as a rebuke to the values being feted inside the Exhibition Centre: Ann complained of his books in their buckram boxes that 'it was impossible to fit them into any decorative scheme.'

Clarissa Eden was one of the first visitors. 'It was rather sad. The whole place a sea of mud, not much furniture, that obstreperous son, & nanny cooking the meals. Ann tired & depressed.'

Once the money from the Bond films and paperback sales began flowing, Ann drew ever more spontaneously on 'our pornography fund', as she had christened Caspar's trust money, to furnish and decorate the interior. She ignored Ian's advice to buy the beds from Heal's and paint all the doors white.

Ian confessed to being hurt when she toured the art galleries and auction rooms without him. 'At present, we even buy things separately – busts or pictures, although we both have to live with them.'

Ann behaved as if she were competing with Maud Russell's renovations at Mottisfont thirty years earlier. She bought an expensive Sidney Nolan of a giant baboon for £1,200 (approximately £30,500 today) to hang next to the Amherst Villiers portrait of Ian; an Augustus John drawing of Cyril Connolly for £300; and a huge polar bear rug to lay out on the black and white flagstones in the hall ('Ian's given many a scream when he put his foot in its mouth'). Apparent to Maud was that Ian had no power to restrain his wife. 'He has just bought Ann a chandelier costing £900 & a mink coat. He said their way of thinking did not meet on any point.'

Ian still felt a connection with Maud, Clare and Lisl, and most of all with

Blanche. Over that summer, she drove him on Thursday mornings to Henley and they had lunch in the Angel Hotel. Blanche then caught the train back to London and he took the car on to Sevenhampton.

Ann, now without a lover, haunted by Ian's affair with Blanche, resentful that Bond made her less relevant to Ian's daily existence, became more focused on what her husband's success with Bond could bring to her life, and less focused on how she could repair the damage in their marriage. When Ian told his British publishers to stop any further editions of *The Spy Who Loved Me*, after its bad reviews the previous year, Ann was put out. 'I am doing my best to reverse this foolish gesture because of the yellow silk for the drawing room walls.' Silk walls were not the limit of Ann's ambition. She brightly told Evelyn Waugh, 'I want to hire Italian plasterers to finish our home.' When Waugh was invited to Ann's housewarming party in October, he had to walk down a mud-ridden cart track after dark, having taken the wrong road. 'She has spent as much as the government has on the reconstruction of Downing Street, pulled down a large, commodious house and put up a cottage . . . the few bedrooms are tiny cubicles with paper thin walls through which every cough and sneeze is audible.' Waugh considered that her 'edifice' possessed 'almost every deficiency'. Not only that, but he calculated it had cost Ann more than twice the price demanded of the more beguiling houses in *Country Life*.

Robert Harling's estimate was nearer four.

Harling included Warneford Place, along with Ian's drinking and smoking, 'as among the definitive causes of Fleming's comparatively early death'. He placed Ian's move there as 'one of the more gruesome essays in sado-masochism I've encountered in this far-from cosy world'.

No single feature gave Ian the slightest pleasure. Ann had chosen a house without a golf course nearby and as far from Ian's Scottish mountains and the sea as possible. That was not all. In her project to turn it into an English Goldeneye, she invited Oxford dons like John Sparrow, Maurice Bowra and Isaiah Berlin for the weekend.

Not welcome were dogs. Ann was 'canine averse', according to her niece Sara, who recalls how Ian 'to his eternal credit was totally and completely on my side when Minimum, my white terrier, was a big cheat at croquet, with his nose pushing the ball, utterly brilliantly, the rest of the way into the hoop.

Isaiah Berlin and Roy Jenkins said I would not be allowed to play. Sitting on the steps, Ian said they were being childish to a degree. "Note this, these are some of the most eminent people behaving in a way which at your age would be considered contemptible." '

Ann had considered Warneford a gloomy name. She rechristened their new home Sevenhampton Place, after the village. Much later, when Arnold Goodman came into her life, aware of the aristocratic fondness for eliding names – thus Waugh's Beste-Chetwynde becomes Beast-Chained – he asked, 'Shall I call it Sunhaven?' Ian took to calling it 'the Towers', after Lord Ower's pile in Ian's story 'The Shameful Truth', while to neighbours like Susanna Johnston, it was 'Oh-Oh-Seven-hampton'.

'It has an air of lunatic fragility about it,' John Pearson decided after he came to see Ian at Sevenhampton. 'A Rex Whistler fantasy bought by Bond.' Ian clearly hated it. 'The septic tank had overflowed, which suddenly seemed to enrage his fastidious nature. It was the only time I saw him lose his cool. "Look at it. Shit. Everywhere." '

In the last autumn of his life, Ian recorded his feelings in 'The Gloom Book', as it was titled, 'compiled for Ann Fleming by her friends'.

Guests at Sevenhampton were invited to contribute the most melancholy quotation they could think of.

Peter Quennell, from Byron's *Don Juan*:

'You take things coolly, sir,' said Juan. 'Why,'
Replied the other, 'what can a man do?
There still are many rainbows in your sky,
But mine have vanished . . .'

Patrick Leigh Fermor, from Dante's *Inferno*:

'There is no greater sorrow/Than to be mindful of the happy time/In misery'

John Sparrow, from Dean Swift on seeing bonfires lit to celebrate his birthday: *'It is all folly, they had better let it alone.'*

Mark Bonham Carter, from Lord Salisbury's minute on a despatch: *'Nothing matters very much.'*

Ian's entry in blue biro took up the first page.

Solitude becomes a lover,
Loneliness a darling thing.
Says Ian.

What is arresting about these words is their timing. Even as Ian was scribbling them down in his large, slanting, angular hand, Ann was writing to her daughter in Brazil, 'the new Bond film has broken all records of any film ever made. I cannot understand why. Isaiah [Berlin] says it is a fairy tale, but I am still bewildered.'

LXVIII
ASHES

'James Bond gave with one hand, and took away with the other.'
ANN FLEMING

When Ian was at Eton, his headmaster set an essay on the topic 'Nothing fails like success'. Ian had never overcome his longing for the acclaim that his elder brother received early on. Yet like Colonel Fawcett in *Brazilian Adventure*, indeed like Peter himself, 'his quest had led him to No Lost City; even the mountains on which it was to have stood were missing.'

The need to succeed had been with Ian all the time. 'He wanted to get there,' says his nephew James. 'He doesn't know where "there" is, and when he gets there, he discovers that he doesn't want to be there, and is bitterly disappointed.' It was a repeat of his childhood letdown on a Cornish beach: the ambergris he had been determined to find was rancid butter.

In October 1963, Mary Pakenham saw Ian's name flashing outside the London Pavilion, advertising 'From Russia with Love'. She asked him how it felt and hoped he was enjoying the fame. In his last letter to her, Ian wrote back saying that she 'was vulgar to congratulate him on having his name in lights'.

But there seemed nowhere to escape the glare. He was the first proper celebrity writer, 'the oldest Beatle', Ann called him, at a time when this level of celebrity was unheard of and probably unfathomable to most of Ian's generation. When, not knowing where he lived, Enid Bagnold, widow of his former Reuters boss Sir Roderick Jones, wrote to 'Ian Fleming, c/o the Prime Minister, 10 Downing Street', the occupant of that address, Harold Macmillan, sent her letter on to him. A woman wrote a fan letter from Glasgow: 'It must be alarming to be responsible for so many people's fantasy lives.' In

Admiral Godfrey's opinion, 'Ian has achieved a unique worldwide acclaim and more publicity, I believe, than any other human being this century.'

Success, though, had failed to live up to the dream. When Ian's paperback publisher informed him that he had won a replica of a second-century BC statue of Pan plated with 18-carat gold, for having sold a million copies ('Poor man, you are now due to receive eight . . . and will be an all-time record holder'), it was as if Ian had become the girl in *Goldfinger*, coated with gold so that he could not breathe. Like Bond, 'he had asked, and it had been given . . . He had made his wish, and the wish had not only been granted, it had been stuffed down his throat.'

His niece Mary reflects, 'When Ian said his fame was ashes, just saying it brings tears to my eye. I know it's exactly how he felt.' Selby Armitage, someone he grew up with, who had known Ian all his life, met him not long before he died and they were talking under the lime trees at Nettlebed. 'Ian, what's it like, what's it really like to be famous? It's a thing you always wanted when you were young. Are you enjoying it now you've got it?' He looked very sorry for himself. 'It was all right for a bit . . . But now, my God. Ashes, old boy. Just ashes . . . I'd swap the whole damned thing for a healthy heart.'

At the premiere of 'Dr. No', Ian had tried to take his heart pills without anyone seeing, before Ann got him home and into bed. 'The premiere of the second Bond film, "From Russia with Love", also was not a happy occasion. Ian was awfully ill. It was a terrible ordeal for him to sign autographs, and for me to try to rescue him from the fans.' Ann had arranged for Dr Beal to be in the audience in case anything happened.

Ian enjoyed the limelight but hated crowds. 'The queues formed all day round and round Leicester Square,' he wrote to Amherst Villiers in California, keen for the artist to know that 'the whole of England was plastered with reproductions of your portrait and the doom-fraught eyes you gave me gazed out of practically every bookshop in the land'.

That fateful portrait was too near the bone. 'When the film was over,' Clarissa Eden observed, 'he got up like an old man, pale grey in the face, sweat beading his forehead, swallowing pills, & apparently in a daze. Ann was obviously worried to death and yet not daring to cross him in any way. She says he is worse.'

Following the screening on Thursday 10 October, Ian invited seventy guests home, including Loelia. 'Supper at Ann's consisting of £300 of caviar!!' Ian had won £300 at the Le Touquet casino where he and Loelia had gone gambling before the war. Ann said, 'in one of his James Bond gestures, he spent it all on caviar.' He had asked Nancy Mitford in Paris where to buy it and he had queued in the early morning.

That evening should have been his crowning success. Yet the something *wunderbar* he had wanted all his life had engulfed him like the avalanche he had caused to come tumbling down on his head in Kitzbühel. Seated at tables set out in the drawing room, Ian was surrounded by writers whose reputations he had envied – Evelyn Waugh, Cyril Connolly, Peter Quennell, Iris Murdoch, and his brother Peter. But he had more in common with Caspar, throwing stones through the drawing room window to get attention. Mary Pakenham could only speculate. 'He may have felt that *nobody* cared about anything except money and that the grown-ups had let him down again.'

Peter Fleming sat at a small round table on the landing with his daughter Kate, who remembers plates heaped with 'vast mounds of caviar', and Ian getting up and beginning the alpine ascent to bed. Peter murmured, 'Poor old Ian, he's had enough.'

Ian wrote to Plomer: 'Annie and the Dregs stayed up until 4.30 a.m., but I crept upstairs, beaten to the ground at about 1 a.m.' Jack Beal had had to warn him, 'Take it easy now, Ian, or you'll drop dead.'

On Beal's orders, Ian agreed to return to Enton Hall, the health farm near Godalming in Surrey that promoted fasting and osteopathy, to fortify himself for his next ordeal, the resumption of Kevin McClory's plagiarism trial. 'I, too, have become a casualty,' Ian wrote to a friend's daughter, who had been admitted to Guy's Hospital following a mental breakdown, 'and am retiring to one of those dreadful places in the country where you eat nuts and hot water.'

When talking to John Pearson about this time, Ann saw it as the point of no return. 'She seemed to think that the tragedy of his life was that everything came at once – the bestsellerdom, the films, the heart attack, the McClory lawsuit. And he never recovered.'

*

In November 1963, less than a month after the party in Victoria Square, Kevin McClory forced Ian back to the High Court. He had been threatening to do this ever since his failure to halt *Thunderball*'s publication in March 1961. It is improbable that McClory would have gone ahead with his suit for 'breach of copyright, breach of confidence, breach of contract, false representation of authorship and slander of title' had 'Dr. No' bombed like 'The Boy and the Bridge'.

'If it hadn't been a success,' says Jerry Juroe, a former EON executive who worked on fourteen Bond films, 'no one would have cared.'

The requirement to defend himself a second time in public upset Ian beyond measure. 'I'm now winding myself up like a toy soldier for this blasted case,' he confided to Plomer. 'I dare say a diet of TNT pills and gin will see me through but it's a bloody nuisance.' He merely commented, 'à la Khrushchev, "if you lie down with a dog, you must expect to get fleas".'

Even so, it gnawed. His solicitor Matthew Farrer says, 'I used to walk him over to see counsel from Lincoln's Inn to Chancery Lane and his heart was causing him trouble. "Could we stop a bit and have a rest?" Then he would say, "It's always the same. I always seem to stop opposite a shop selling rubber goods!"'

He was taking digoxin, Peritrate and quinidine. According to Dr Ottmar Mechow, a German specialist whom Ian consulted the following month, driving all the way to Bad Nauheim to see him, he 'feels contraction of the chest, stinging and pressure at the heart, especially in the morning after rising, but also during the day when walking the street and particularly when climbing the stairs'.

The plagiarism case started on 20 November. It reunited Ian for one of his last meaningful times with 'Burglar' Bryce: McClory and Jack Whittingham had summoned Bryce to be a co-defendant, along with Jonathan Cape Ltd.

Also involved in this 'damnable' humiliation were Ian's house contemporary at Eton and Washington wartime colleague, John Foster, QC, MP, acting as Bryce's lawyer; and Ernie Cuneo, supplier of the original outline for 'Thunderball', who 'came to London in our hour of need'.

His lawyers had insisted Ian was always in court. He sat upright and motionless on a hard-edged corner seat, looking tired while McClory was billed as a man 'on the way to the top – being one of the youngest producer-directors – until he became enmeshed in the events with which this case was concerned'.

Without Ian's knowledge, Ann and Ivar Bryce had arranged for a nurse to be sitting in the back at all times. This was after Bryce had consulted a heart specialist, who warned: 'Litigation is one of the worst things for a patient with heart problems.'

Ann attempted to pull a brave face, arguing to Waugh that the case did Ian 'a power of good, no smoking in court and one hour for a simple lunch'. Griffie described the true situation. 'The whole business caused him a terrible shock. He hated being accused of plagiarism.'

For two days, wrote Bryce in his unpublished account, 'McClory's toadies and dependents came and went through the witness box swearing unanimously to statements which were to me ridiculously impossible to believe. The whole surroundings were a dream removed from the hard facts of the real world.'

On the third day came news from Dallas. 'The whole world stunned,' was Loelia's diary entry for Friday, 22 November. 'Impossible to grasp the repercussions of this senseless deed . . . evening spent glued to television.' Next day: 'One can think of and talk about nothing but the assassination.' On Sunday: 'There is no end to the hideous drama of events. Now K's assassin has been shot dead leaving court. *What* a country!'

In Lee Oswald's boarding room were found two of the four James Bond paperbacks that Oswald had borrowed from the library; these included *From Russia, with Love*, featuring Donovan Grant, the prize assassin of SMERSH, whose international criminal ring of ex-members known as SPECTRE had been discussed in the High Court in London only the previous afternoon.*

Ian spent the weekend with Bryce and Cuneo at Moyns Park where it was decided to reject McClory's verbal offer of a deal. Foster was convinced they could win the case outright and 'pooh-poohed' Bryce's anxiety. Ian was

---

* William Donovan, whose name Ian borrowed for his assassin, had died of atrophy of the brain on 8 February 1959; he had reported spotting Russian troops marching into Manhattan across the Fifty-Ninth Street Bridge outside his Sutton Place window.

still processing the death of the American President, who more than any other individual had helped him arrive at this point. Kennedy's endorsement had propelled James Bond into the universally recognised character he now was, that McClory was effectively stealing. Not only that, but – if McClory was to be believed – improving upon. In court on the opening day, Ian had had to listen to McClory's claim for *Thunderball* – how 'some of the more observant critics had detected differences from the earlier novels. In particular, there were fewer excruciating episodes.'

'One can understand why Ian took it all so bitterly to heart,' John Pearson wrote in another unpublished account. 'For how could he explain to a High Court judge the emotional and psychological complexities of Bond, that, far from being a run-of-the-mill cooked-up character in a bestseller, James Bond was actually a romanticised version of himself, so how could he plagiarise himself, his psychological crutch, his precious alter ego . . . Bond belonged to Ian. Bond *was* Ian. And whatever the legal rights and wrongs might be, being his creation and his alter ego, Bond belonged immutably and emotionally to him, and McClory was stealing him . . . the mellifluous Irishman was suing the High Court to hi-jack an all-important part of Ian's persona.'

Both Foster and Ian's advocate, Sir Andrew Clark QC, remained confident of victory when, on the following Friday, Bryce 'took the fateful decision' to settle and pay costs and damages.

Bryce gave as his reason Ian's deteriorating health and 'fear of the physical danger to my friend'.* Robert Fenn, however, suspected a financial motive. 'Bryce pulled out because too much was being revealed of his tax deals.' A third factor was Bryce's wife, Jo.

At the preliminary trial in 1961, Ian had written to Cuneo: 'Jo thinks it would be vulgar for Ivar to go on to the witness stand!' On this occasion, Jo had stayed away in New York. For the first time, she was no longer prepared to bail out Ivar and his best friend. After two more weeks in court and with costs escalating, she had had enough. 'The reason I did not go to England for the trial was that I myself was fed up with this constant desire of Ivar's for

---

* In 1967, Jack Whittingham claimed Bryce had revealed to him that 'Fleming had two very bad heart attacks during the court case.'

wealth and luxurious living … I did not want to hear any more nagging remarks about money to be paid out to Ian and the lawyers and how poor it would leave him (Ivar).'

Under the conditions of the agreement hammered out in a packed Chancery Division chamber, Ian had to acknowledge that *Thunderball* was based on a screen treatment which was the joint work of himself, McClory and Whittingham. McClory received all film rights and £35,000 in compensation (approximately £890,000 today), and Bryce paid the costs of all parties, amounting to £80,000.

Bryce conceded: 'Ian did not himself agree at once, but consented to do what I decided as it was my money that was principally at stake.'

Ian was grievously disappointed. 'I won't budge one inch!' he had promised Matthew Farrer. Many, like Pearson, saw it as Bryce's final betrayal, 'the weak, rich man's sacrificing of someone who had become an embarrassment and so was threatening his own world'.

Ann was of this number. 'Ian thought he was dealing with a great friend,' she said. 'It was sad for him having to settle.' She had never liked or trusted Bryce. She now found herself in the unusual position of siding with Blanche Blackwell in feeling that 'Burglar' Bryce had lived up to his reputation in sacrificing Ian's. Ann vented her criticism in the frontispiece of Ian's copy of *Diamonds are Forever*: 'dedicated to "Ivar Bryce" who afterwards betrayed Ian in the law suit concerning "Thunderball"'.

No one knows what drove Bryce to make his unexpected move, but he lived on wretched terms with the consèquences, said Jo's daughter Nuala. 'He was frightfully upset. Really upset. It would cast a pall on everything – for several years. In fact, he really never got over that whole thing.'

One night in 1980, sixteen years after Ian's death, the Bryces were at a black-tie dinner in Nassau with a young banker, Manoli Olympitis. He says, 'As we left together with Ivar and Jo, a group including Kevin McClory – also in black tie – spilled out into the street from another dinner. It was then that Ivar spotted McClory and started shouting violently. Ivar was puce with fury, screaming at him. "*It's because of you Ian died! You sent him to his grave.*" Ivar had to be physically restrained by a couple of friends. McClory stood looking abashed and defensive.'

LXIX
THE FINAL GREEN

'The man was suddenly empty.'
IAN FLEMING'S 'BOOK OF GOLDEN WORDS'

His dismal experience in court led Ian to seek a buyer for Glidrose. He sensed that he had not much longer to live and wanted to shield his literary estate from future McClorys – and the taxman.

Ian negotiated the deal on his grandmother's local golf course where, since moving into 'the Towers', he had taken to driving 'almost every weekend' to play with Jock Campbell, chairman of the sugar company Booker Brothers McConnell.

Campbell remembered: 'He rang me the first day he was there and said, "Can I come over to Huntercombe with you to play golf?" I said, "Sure, come to lunch." And this was the start of what would become almost a routine.'

Philip Brownrigg, who worked with Ian on the *Sunday Times*, had re-introduced them, realising they had the West Indies in common: Campbell's business was underpinned by thirteen sugar plantations in British Guiana, as well as, since 1960, the Innswood estate in Jamaica.

Campbell had a dynamic memory, says his son John. 'He was telling a story to two Guianan women going up in the Booker Stores lift in Georgetown when they were interrupted. He met them ten years later and took up the story at the point he had got to.' The resumption of his relationship with Ian Fleming did not promise an outcome so favourable. On the last occasion he had seen Ian, when he was at Exeter College, Oxford, Campbell had dismissed him as 'an arrogant young shit'. They established better relations after Campbell visited Ian at Goldeneye.

As a trend-setting early capitalist supporter of Labour and later chairman of the *New Statesman*, Campbell's politics set him apart from their Eton contemporaries. The maverick part commended him to Ian, even if Ann increasingly perceived Campbell as a dangerous socialist. His favourite quotation was from *Dr Zhivago*, extolling 'an unprincipled heart . . . and the greatness of small actions'. A further appeal to Ian was his hard-driving attitude to sport.

A bald, stocky businessman with one shoulder lower than the other after contracting polio at school, Campbell was an abnormally competitive games player. His son John says, 'Games replaced social intimacy. He never socialized; he competed. He bet me £5 I would never beat him at anything before the age of 18.' He was determined to win at croquet, ping-pong, tennis, backgammon and golf.

Campbell was a four handicap at golf, which he liked to play at 8 a.m., dressed in brown tweed trousers and bright yellow socks knitted by his mother, and would whizz round, coming back for lunch at Crocker End, Campbell's weekend retreat near Nettlebed, to which, from that autumn onwards, he invited Ian.

Ian had broached the idea of selling himself when teeing up for the final hole. The significance of the eighteenth fairway, said Campbell, was that Ian was embarrassed by talking business. 'So he left raising the matter until the latest possible moment . . . the result was that none of the conversations ever lasted more than three minutes.'

In a snatched conversation, Ian told Campbell that he was coming late to considerable money from books, and going to die, and had no money for his family. He had to pay ninety-one per cent tax and didn't want to leave the country, as many people were doing. 'He felt he would have to sell to a friend because he dare not risk pressure to write more books.'

Although Campbell grew very fond of Ian and enjoyed playing golf with him, he had not read any of his books or seen the films. 'My colleagues and I at Booker simply didn't live in that world at all and knew nothing about it.' Campbell said he would mention it to them, 'but that I really didn't think it was on'.

His proposal to the board was 'an oddity which came out of the blue,' one colleague recalls, 'something he did because he knew Ian Fleming was in trouble, but it made no business sense.'

Even now, Campbell acted on the assumption that Ian was the lesser of the two literary Flemings. 'I play golf with Ian Fleming who is the brother of Peter Fleming; who owns all the land around me at Nettlebed.' His colleagues had to take Campbell's word that 'the "James Bond" success is as much a phenomenon in the publishing world as are the "Beatles" in the pop world'.

Still, the timing was not bad. Booker were seeking to diversify out of Guianese sugar because they knew that the Premier, Cheddi Jagan, would at some point nationalise the industry. The initial reaction of Campbell's board – 'it would look a zany thing for Booker to do' – yielded to a more businesslike attitude once they met Ian and examined Glidrose's accounts.

These were unexpectedly compelling. Gross profits on the books had risen from £8,000 in 1960, to £12,500 in 1962, to £35,000 following the film of 'Dr. No', and in the 10 months to 31 January 1964 to £115,000 (approximately £2.9 million today) 'and still climbing from 14 published works of which 3 are not yet released as paperbacks'. A lunch to solicit the views of West Indian writers to ascertain 'whether Ian was really anti-racial' clinched matters. 'They just laughed and all said that they enjoyed him.'

Campbell had been the architect of the 1951 Commonwealth Sugar Agreement, a significant arrangement which guaranteed the price and export quotas for all Commonwealth sugar-producers. He used his mercantile skills to agree with Ian's solicitor Matthew Farrer on a valuation for Ian's literary estate.

On 25 February 1964, Ian cabled from Goldeneye asking Farrer to finalise the deal. He thanked him for having negotiated 'excellently' on Ian's behalf the price of £100,000 that he received for selling his majority fifty-one per cent stake in Glidrose to Booker, excluding film and TV serial and comic-strip rights.

In what was to be a pioneering tax-reducing mechanism, Ian paid no capital gains tax on the capital sum. In addition, he received a reduction on tax paid for the business, paying thirty per cent on total income compared to ninety-one per cent; and on top of this, a substantial dividend.

Farrer says, 'I don't think anyone for a moment thought it would continue as long.' Encouraged by the success of the Glidrose contract, Booker went on to acquire interests in the literary estates of Agatha Christie, Georgette Heyer, Robert Bolt and Harold Pinter.

The deal done, Ian wrote to Griffie, 'I am rather relieved to be owned by a father figure . . .'

Meanwhile, Jock Campbell informed his board in a memo marked 'Most Confidential' that Booker would also receive twenty-five per cent of the income from 'advertising and gimmicry rights' for whatever other books Ian wrote – that is to say, 'while his health lasts' – with the caveat that 'the Chairman believed him to be a "bad risk".'

It grieved Campbell to have to flag that in all probability Ian Fleming was approaching the final green.

At a bridge evening in Boodle's in the autumn of 1963, Algy Cluff, then a young Grenadier Guards officer, sat next to Ian. 'He says to me how fatigued he is, exasperated, with his celebrity. It's not what he wanted. I said rather importunately, "What do you want in life?" and received the astonishing reply, "To be the Captain of the Royal St George's Golf Club."'

In October, Ian became chairman of the House Sub-Committee, responsible for the operation of the clubhouse. The appointment of the next captain was to take place in August. 'A lot of his buddies, Old Etonians especially, were past Captains,' says Ian's occasional caddie, John Suckling. 'Once you were in that swing, it was the icing on the cake. You'd be ambassador for the golf club, be there for events and prize-giving. To be Captain was a great honour.'

This was the summit Ian was aiming for in his last months. Ann said he seemed 'to attach more importance to this than to the success of his books'.

St George's fulfilled Ian's idea of the perfect course as laid out in *The Golfer's Manual*. 'The best site for a Golfing ground is by the sea shore.' Its members' aspirations were his. Ian's best friends were those 'hale old gentlemen' in the clubhouse who were invoked in the last paragraph of his favourite handbook: '*in our quiet pastime how keenly they enjoy themselves; how ruddy their cheek and bright their eye, when on the close of a bracing day in autumn, they come in from the enjoyment of their daily round. Golf, thou art a gentle spirit; we owe thee much!*'

In August 1963, shortly after moving into Sevenhampton Place, Ian had taken off in his low-slung black Avanti for Switzerland.

The ostensible purpose of the road trip was to interview one of his literary heroes, Georges Simenon, who lived outside Lausanne, for the *Sunday Times*. But Ian's tour had the characteristics of a man, said Blanche Blackwell, who 'knew he was dying'.

His wife, son, and Caspar's cousin Francis Grey, now part of the household, joined Ian for a fortnight on Lake Geneva at the Montreux Palace hotel. Once Ian had packed them back by train to England, he hoped to visit his first love Monique in Vich, then meet up in Zurich with his last love, Blanche, and drive her to Kitzbühel, the seat of so many of Ian's early romances.

Monique, now a divorcée, was again living at her family house near Geneva, but when Ian rang up and asked if he could come and see her, she refused. 'I suspect because it was painful for her,' says her son Charles de Mestral. 'And she also had not succeeded in marriage, except to produce me. She was capable of identifying remarkable men, but was unable to keep them.'

She had married George de Mestral, an electrical engineer and avid hunter who, with Monique's support, invented Velcro. He was inspired by the burrs in the high grass which had hooks that stuck to his socks and trousers. 'My father observed them on his dog while hunting, and had the idea of creating material that would model the burr.' They had divorced when Charles was five. 'What went wrong? I remember one story. My mother gave herself an Hermès scarf, and my father was totally red-faced because they were very low on money, all money should go into Velcro, and this was a terrible thing to do. Both were very strong characters who were going to run the show.'

Headstrong still, Monique felt reluctant to tear open old scars. Ian confessed to Blanche that 'she didn't want to see him'. Even so, when John Pearson visited Monique after Ian's death, he noticed 'a sort of Ian shrine' in which she kept her photographs of the twenty-three-year-old Ian and her visit to Joyce Grove in 1931.

Brushed off by the girl with blue-back hair whom Cuneo felt had been 'the cause of his deep wound', Ian stumbled on a place not far from Vich that gave him more unanticipated pleasure to write about in his last months than any other subject.

Ian's lively letter to Hilary Bray can be read as a fantastical pitch for the revolutions Ian hoped to introduce were he elected captain of his favourite golf club.

One bonus from this rather unrewarding holiday has been the providential discovery of the Nirvana among golf courses. I am referring of course to Aigle, which, as a golfer of international repute, you will know lies amidst the lush plain at the head of the lake. If you don't know, you soon will, because these links have certain features which will surely commend them to the golfing elite as soon as I can get my pen to the job.

First things first. The links are totally flat. The holes are slightly larger than is customary and the flag-sticks thinner . . . Everyone plays by him, or her, self which leads to an all-round improvement in scores and 90% of the players are nubile ladies wearing tight après-ski pants and even tighter sweaters. Apart from the natural charms God gave them, they could, and I hope will, make ideal opponents at the game of golf for they seem rarely to make contact with the ball. Their method consists (ah! if only we had such nymphets at Sandwich!) in rising on the toes of their expensive shoes and gently and with the utmost grace wafting the club OVER the ball. When, fortuitously, contact is made, it seems always to be off the toe or the heel of the club so that the ball shoots deep into the nearest bosque, where, supposing one had the privilege of playing with them, the game (haha!) could continue long into the sweet Swiss dusk . . .'

The welcoming of ladies as full members to St George's was but one of Ian's radical proposals. Another modernising idea – 'and it could easily be duplicated at Sandwich' – was for the introduction of mechanised golf-carts, like the machine an Italian caddie had driven towards Ian in an erratic bee-line at 20 m.p.h. – 'Do you play at him, over him, or round him?' Such exciting novelties were bound to give Ian's favourite sport 'a new dimension'.*

And none too soon, so far as I'm concerned. All you chaps at St George's are far too set in your ways . . . The game of golf can't stand still! There must be progress! Avanti! And Aigle leads the way! . . . Well, all this is just to show you what a dangerous thing it is to write a letter to an author. You get a book back! I must now prepare for an early night . . . Then off via Kitzbühel and Munich to Rotterdam and home.'

---

* Women were not admitted until 2015, after 128 years. In November 2022, John Suckling, who had caddied for Ian and was three times captain of Royal St George's permit-holders' club, was killed at the course in a golf buggy accident.

From the flat links to the peaks. In Kitzbühel, Ian hoped to climb the Kitzbühler Horn with Blanche, as he had ascended it first with Ernan Forbes Dennis, and after that with Lisl Popper and Cyril Connolly and Percy Muir and Adrian House and Edith Morpurgo and Muriel Wright and Ann, but his heart would not let him, and he had to go up in the ski-lift while Blanche climbed on her own. They met at the top for lunch. 'And then we walked down, he could walk down, but he couldn't walk up, and when we got to the very bottom, he said, "Well, that is the last walk I'll ever, ever do." '

The manner of his going was 'utterly tragic', wrote Admiral Godfrey in a private letter.

It started with a round of golf on Easter Sunday. Ann said, 'He would not cut down his golf, no matter what the weather.' On 29 March 1964, Ian woke up at Sevenhampton with a streaming cold and rain pouring down. Ann took his temperature. 'It was 100. I said, "You can't play golf today." And he said, "I couldn't possibly spend Sunday in the depths of the country with nothing to do." '

To her distress, he insisted on driving to Huntercombe, forty miles away, to play with Jock Campbell. He continued on in his wet clothes to London, where his cold developed into 'a small Messerschmidt virus', as he described it to Hilary Bray, 'and I have finally had to confine myself to barracks.' He had pleurisy. 'I thought only aunts got it.'

A fortnight on, Ian felt breathless from an atrial fibrillation. His lungs were full of fluid and he had swollen legs. Ann took him to King Edward VII's Hospital in Marylebone, known as 'Sister Agnes', where a blood clot was discovered on his left lung. He wanted Ann to take him home – the small room was too claustrophobic; it came as no surprise to learn that Harold Macmillan had resigned as Prime Minister the previous October in a room down the corridor. A young night nurse, Sister Bridget Forbes, had the patience to calm Ian down.

'Not yet up to correcting my stupid book.' Confined to his room in Sister Agnes, Ian set aside proofs of *The Man with the Golden Gun*, and picked up *Funeral in Berlin* by the young thriller-writer Len Deighton, with whom he had lunched at the White Tower the previous March after choosing *The Ipcress File* as his book of the year. Next, he raced through a study of the

Mafia, *The Honoured Society*, by Norman Lewis, whom he had sent to Cuba in 1958. Then *Diary of a Black Sheep*, by Richard Meinertzhagen, whom he had met at Mottisfont, seat of the Meinertzhagen family before Maud Russell bought it. 'Reading voraciously,' Ian reported to William Plomer, 'but I find I can now only read books which approximate to *truth*. Odd *stories* just aren't good enough. That's most of the reason I shy away from Bond.'

One of his Bond notes read: 'More important than *savoir vivre* is *savoir mourir*.' Ian's heart specialist reiterated the message that Jack Beal had tried to drum into him: no more golf. According to Griffie, Ian had taken this on board at last and 'was now resigned to leading a very different life'. As a golf substitute, he accepted an invitation on his release to go fishing with Selby Armitage, who offered him '£1 for every fish I catch, and I propose to take English country life by the throat and throttle it'.

Armitage was one of Ian's oldest friends, but even he had trouble recognising the person seen posing in newpapers and magazines and talking about himself on *Desert Island Discs*, and with his name flashing outside every cinema. That 'Ian Fleming' in lights was a comical decoy to anyone with knowledge of the author. Armitage unleashed his amusement after instructing Ian to get himself kitted out at an angler's establishment, the Hut, in preparation for their fishing trip. Ian told Hilary Bray how the Hut 'was apparently proud of my visit' when Selby appeared after Ian had made arrangements for the store to bill him for his modest purchases. 'Selby who has been doing this to me since I was about twelve, looked very dubious, "Of course I know him, but I'm afraid you've been had." "Here is the visitors' book, Sir." A sad shake of the head from Selby, "No, that's not his signature. There's a broken-down actor going around saying he is Ian Fleming. I should get your money quickly."'

He certainly felt like a ramshackle counterfeit. He told Sister Bridget when she checked on him, after it was decided she would accompany Ian home as his nurse companion, 'Oh, you've drawn the short straw.'

In the middle of June, Ian drove with her to the Dudley Hotel on the beachfront at Hove on the Sussex coast where he had recuperated following his first heart attack. Evelyn Waugh had heard from 'my consul Ann' how much Ian appreciated Sister Bridget rubbing his ' "sensitive areas" (hospitalese for bottom)'. Waugh could not resist Ann's suggestion of sending him a sought-after pack of toilet paper from America, like Ian had brought back in the war for Maud, in the spirit of adding an 'excessively rare' supplement to Ian's touted book collection. James Bond was bound to be familiar with the brand. 'I am sure that a man so fastidious & well descended would use only Bromo, now unprocurable. Here are some sheets of the genuine American product . . . The original edition, as you will remember, had a great deal of reading matter on the packet including the claim that it was a proved specific against "that distressing and well nigh universal complaint, the biles."'

Ian's 'darling' night nurse stayed with him in Hove. He wrote disconsolately to Hilary Bray, 'Thank God, Sister Agnes have loaned me a peeress among Sisters, Bridget Forbes, & she does my "smalls", washes my hair brush, & keeps my spirits up with her tiny adventures & tales of the denizens of the dining room. After the rich pabulum I am used to from Annie (who came down for lunch & put my pulse up to 120!) this is curiously restful.'

Ann was forced to admit that Ian 'found my anxiety trying and was best alone'. With Sister Bridget, by contrast, he enjoyed 'deliciously infantile conversations. "That is the West Pier. It is very pleasant to walk upon piers." "Yes, I will walk upon the West Pier this afternoon." "You might play bingo on the piers. It is an amusing game." "Yes, it would be fun to play bingo on the piers," etc., etc.'

He was still observing. He told Robert Fenn, 'You know Bob, until now, I'd never realised what a nurse thought about all day. Now I know.'

Yoked together in bottom-rubbing intimacy, Ian discovered all sorts of details about his chestnut-haired carer. Sister Bridget was twenty-seven, unmarried, brought up by cousins and aunts after her parents died when she was twelve, and had trained at the Radcliffe Infirmary. Her late father was a hotelier from Scotland, who had managed an inn near Oxford; her mother, the daughter of a gentleman farmer from Wootton; and her brother Ian, known as 'Tim', had been killed in a car accident two years before she was born. After Fleming died, she would nurse the novelist Nicholas Monsarrat, the actors Benny Hill and Kenneth More, and Carl Giles, the cartoonist. Professionally, she referred to her previous patients as 'Mister Monsarrat' or 'Mister Hill', but Ian Fleming was always 'Ian'. He and Sister Bridget got along so frictionlessly that it caused Ian to wonder whether she might be observing *him*. On one occasion, Ian went out to lunch with Ann in Brighton and they had such a row that he caught the bus back, a rare example of him taking public transport, and when he stepped off outside the hotel, he saw Sister Bridget standing there. 'I write spy novels,' he joked, 'but you're the biggest spy in the world.' He gave her a copy of *Thunderball*, signing it 'with gratitude and affection'.

What Ian yearned to play was not bingo but golf. He wrote to the Brays, 'Have booked in at the Guilford [his favourite hotel in Sandwich] for all August & the wild garlic & Nick [H. D. Nicholson, Club Secretary] & you both will certainly hoist me out of this stupid valley I have got into.'

Any human contact was draining. He had energy to see a select few only. Ann. Griffie. Blanche. William Plomer. The poet and editor Alan Ross – who took him to watch Ted Dexter make a brilliant century at the Sussex county cricket ground. Ian 'particularly enjoyed' having lunch with Cyril Connolly and sharing recollections of pre-war Kitzbühel, its dark pines, peat paths and white roads, up which the pair of them had walked in their prime. 'O Kitzbühler Horn, help me and save me,' Connolly wrote in *The Unquiet Grave*, a signed copy of which he now gave Ian, 'and ever present, as the bald peak of the Kitzbühler Horn, the unpunished pleasures of health; of mountain air, good food and natural living.' After Connolly had left, Ian sat smoking on a bench staring at the sea.

Like Evelyn Waugh at the end of his life, in the invalid chair that Ian bequeathed to him, a reclining wooden contraption upholstered in dull green velvet, with an arm extension to hold drinks or cigars, Ian gave the impression that he was suffering from 'a profound and cancerous unhappiness'.

This was how Admiral Godfrey discovered him a few days before Ian died. 'I saw at once that he was dreadfully ill & was greatly shocked . . . Of course, he wouldn't do what he was told, but there's much more to it than that. We walked very slowly along the front to a restaurant & he was exhausted & went to bed . . . I got the impression at Brighton that he'd lost interest in life . . . It's not a pleasant story.'

By an odd set of circumstances, Eve Fleming had ended up a mile away on the same beachfront. Ian had accompanied her back from Monte Carlo the previous spring and 'had to carry her jewel case (very heavy) and the X-rays of her gall bladder, also oversee fourteen cabin trunks'. He was too ill, though, to visit her in the Hotel Metropole in Brighton, where she died on

27 July, aged seventy-nine, of 'broncho-pneumonia, congestive heart failure, arterio-sclerotic heart disease, old age'.

Against his doctor's advice, Ian drove with Sister Bridget to attend his mother's funeral in Nettlebed. Passing by her coffin, Ian's nephew Valentine found it hard to square the long shadow that Eve Fleming had cast over the family with how 'so very small' she looked. Valentine wrote in his diary, 'Ian not looking well.'

Ian sat next to Amaryllis in St Bartholomew's church, gripping her hand. She said, 'He had always mocked the family in the past. Done his best to escape it. But now that he was ill, he got a sort of grim comfort from having them around.' Ann described the funeral – 'Operation Granite' – as 'tearless, musicless, and practically wreathless, they are a very Scottish family'.

His nephew James observed Peter's housekeeper go up to him at the reception afterwards.

'Mister Ian, what would you like to drink?'

'Gin and tonic,' in a severe voice.

'Mister Ian, you're not allowed.'

He said again, 'Gin. And. Tonic.' There was a redness in his face. To one friend, his strained complexion was 'the dry mauve of a paper flower'.

In the car back to Sevenhampton, Ian spoke to Ann of his mother's money. After waiting his entire life, he had inherited his share of Val's depleted trust, amounting to £142,355 (approximately £3.5 million today). 'What use is it to me now?' In her will, his mother left specific legacies to Peter, Amaryllis and Celia ('my Russian sable coat and hat'). Ian was singled out merely as one of Eve's four surviving children who were to receive a share of her Augustus John collection of the artist's portraits of her.

For fifty-six years, Ian's capricious mother had exerted considerable influence over his life and played a sizeable hand in determining his careers and relationships. 'She was Goldfinger's greed,' says John Cork, 'Blofeld's snobbery, Dr. No's icy heart, Rosa Klebb's sadism, the unspoken supernatural power of Baron Samedi, the imposing figure of Dr Shatterhand in her emotional armour in the impenetrable castle. No one else in Ian's life embodied so much of what Ian had James Bond fight against.' Free at last of her exasperating sway, Ian would outlive Eve by a mere sixteen days.

Caspar's school holidays had started. Ian wanted to see his son. He had hatched a plan to take Caspar and Ann to Scotland in August and show them Robert Fleming's origins. The American ambassador, David Bruce, had offered to put them up near Aviemore. 'When he heard we were going to Scotland, Ian said he would like particularly to come up with his family to stay with us, in order to revisit the scenes of his youth near the house we have taken.'

At Sevenhampton, Ian sat in the shade beside the lake, in the wooden invalid chair he had bought in Dover, avoiding the sun. 'This frightened me more than anything else,' said Ann, 'for sun and light had always been so vital to him.' At the same time, Ian cried out for 'Licht, mehr licht! Light, more light!' – recalling his youth when he had read Goethe's dying words in Kitzbühel. A superstitious streak resurfaced. He reacted to the number thirteen and hated anything black: the colour that Eve had painted Val's Scottish lodge in Arnisdale. He changed the black carpet in his downstairs bedroom to red. He ate and said less and less, 'but if he spoke, it was with a slight despairing impatience that he must get back to life or else'.

He called John Hayward ten days before his death, apologising for not attending the Annual General Meeting of the *Book Collector*. 'An awful year, dear boy.'

One of his last public acts had been to help Ann's niece Sara campaign for her thirty-one-year-old husband Charles Morrison, who was standing, very much the underdog, as a Conservative candidate for Parliament in the local Devizes by-election in May.

Sara says, 'I had a joke of asking Ian to deliver a message to his fellow Devizes constituents as though from James Bond. This was before social media. Ian said, "All right, what do you want me to say?" I can remember sitting on the edge of his chair while he wrote his little testimonial to say "You'd better vote Conservative," though Ian was almost as dicey a Conservative as I was.'

Sara's leaflet generated a lot of attention locally with its phrases like 'To Westminster with Love' and 'Charles Morrison – Licensed to Kill'. Labour had hoped to win the seat by 2,000 votes. To everyone's surprise, Morrison took it with a 1,600 majority.

Sara says, 'The last time I talked to Ian alone, he was leaning against the

682

mantelpiece at Sevenhampton. "Darling, I smell the undertaker's wind." I thought he was being melodramatic and all the things Peter Quennell saw in him, but all of a sudden I realised he wasn't being funny. I said to Charlie, "I'm terribly afraid that Ian has just said goodbye." '

One appointment Ian was determined not to miss. In early August, before going to Scotland, he insisted on taking Ann, Caspar, Francis, Nanny Sillick and Sister Bridget to the Guilford Hotel overlooking Royal St George's.

At 5.30 p.m. on Saturday, 8 August, Ian drove his Avanti to the clubhouse and walked into the smoking room. The outgoing captain, Eric Pemberton, was in the chair. Minutes later, the committee approved the first item on the agenda: 'The Captain's nomination of Ian L. Fleming to succeed him.'

The announcement was posted in the clubhouse immediately after the meeting. Ian Fleming had achieved his last ambition.

'You can learn something about the character of a man by where he chooses to die,' Bill Deedes wrote of Noël Coward, after visiting his grave in Jamaica, not far from Goldeneye. 'And you could say as much about Fleming.'

Evelyn Waugh had divined Ian's choice months earlier. 'Old Thunderbird wishes to end his life and is determined to have his final seizure on the golf course or at the card table.'

Denis Hamilton was standing on the quayside at Dieppe, where in the summer of 1944 he had lost more than 600 men, when he saw an English newspaper at a stall with the headline: 'Ian Fleming Dies on Golf Course'. This time, he had not been with him.

Ian did enjoy one whole day on the links as captain-designate, inhaling the scent of the wild garlic, but on the Monday he looked flushed and unsteady as he drove off.

He had a bad night at the Guilford, with a haemorrhage which he did not talk to Sister Bridget about. On Tuesday, he decided to stay in bed to save his strength for the following day, Caspar's birthday: his son was turning twelve, and Ian had resolved to tell him the facts of life. 'However, the nurse was not satisfied with his appearance,' according to what Griffie afterwards learned from her, 'so she called the doctor at lunchtime.' The local GP, Archibald MacPhail, prescribed an anti-coagulant.

Ann observed Ian staring from his bedroom window at the sea in total misery. 'Ian's life from now on hangs on a thread,' she wrote to her son-in-law. 'Poor Ian nags at me especially and then Caspar all the time. It ends all fun and is anguish to be with one one loves who is very mentally changed and fearfully unhappy. Poor old tiger.'

That evening, Ian and Ann had dinner in the Guilford with Michael and Pandora Astor, who lived nearby.

The last person Ian spoke to on the telephone after dinner was the American ambassador. Ann had contacted David Bruce to say that Ian would be too ill to travel to Scotland after all, and handed the receiver to Ian.

Bruce wrote in his diary the next day, Wednesday 12 August: 'As we concluded our conversation he remarked that "the nurse is just bringing me some whisky and cigarettes". He was taken to the hospital as an emergency case about ten o'clock and died about one o'clock this morning. This is a sad occurrence, although since stricken by repeated heart attacks, I think he had lost the will to live. Nevertheless, he remained a gay and amusing companion. I know of no recent instance of an author whose books enjoyed such popularity . . . He was a staunch friend, and I was devoted to him since I first met him in the early days of the war, when he worked so competently for Admiral John Godfrey in British Naval Intelligence.'

Two weeks later, Peter wrote to Godfrey: 'I know Ian owed a lot to you, but I like to think that he partly repaid the debt in loyal and resourceful service as your PA. He was a splendid & universal man. With less than a year between us, & with no father to keep the ring, we got very low marks for co-existence as small boys; but afterwards, we became very fond of each other, & I shall always miss him. He was a sort of warm-hearted Conquistador.'

Never consciously meaning to, Peter had done an enormous amount to transform his rebellious younger brother into that Conquistador. In reaction to Peter's impossible example, Ian had galloped away. Then, under Admiral Godfrey's bridle, he discovered how to re-harness his talents, win his spurs.

Peter wrote to another of Ian's friends: 'He was a splendid chap who got more than most people out of life & put more than most people into it . . . but there wasn't really anything ahead of him except a semi-invalid existence which was irking him terribly, so perhaps it was best to go out on the crest of the wave.'

Loelia Westminster heard the news in Salzburg. 'Ian Fleming died today, poor, poor Annie. How unhappy she'll be, for she really loved him. I suppose it happened at that nightmare Sandwich.' She marked his death by climbing a mountain. 'I walked halfway up the Gaisburg. *Exhausting*.'

Ann wrote to the last friend who had seen Ian alive, Michael Astor. 'I did love being with him when he would allow. He was a solitary, melancholic, and not illusioned by his strange success.' She had been concerned for their son. 'I was in despair that Caspar should see his father carried from the hotel.'

In the room that they shared at the Guilford, Caspar and Francis had slept through the arrival of the ambulance. They were looking forward to Caspar's birthday, Francis says. 'On our birthdays there was a tradition that we'd go first thing with Nanny Sillick, who would collect us in our pyjamas, and go to Aunt Ann and Ian's room, and whichever one of us had a birthday would receive a big present, and the other one would get a present too. On this day, August 12, Nanny came into our room.

'"Can you get dressed?"

'"Are we going to Ian and Ann's room?"

'"No, not today."

'So we got dressed and went downstairs to breakfast. We knew Ian was not well, but at that age we were more worried about what we were going to have for breakfast.

'"What's happening?"

'"There's a change of plan."

'A car came and collected us and we drove about twenty minutes to Hilary Bray's house, a big house with a grand frontage, with steps going up and Aunt Annie at the top of the steps in floods of tears. "Ian died last night in Canterbury Hospital."

'We were surprised. Nanny had covered it up very well.

'We were driven up to London later that day, to Victoria Square. There was a mass of press everywhere and we had to fight our way through. Nanny Sillick took us to a film.'

Hilary Bray settled the hotel bill at the Guilford and organised Ian's funeral three days later at St James's, Sevenhampton.

Fewer than twenty mourners were present in Ian's parish church on 15 August to experience his funeral start, and then start all over again from the beginning when Ann arrived late. 'I only really remember the horror of the vicar restarting the service,' says Elizabeth Fleming. 'It just seemed such a sad and lonely farewell for a fascinating man.'

Afterwards, Bray wrote to Mary Bond, who had visited Ian at Goldeneye with her ornithologist husband James: 'He was quite irreplaceable. And behind the gigantic cardboard image of the author was something much more valuable, as I am sure you perceived. He had a real affection, sympathy, and, when it was needed, compassion for people. So that one felt, as a result of his company, not only funnier and wiser (in some abstruse subject), but better too.'

The contrast could not have been greater to Ian's memorial service in London in September.

The Times did not have space to record every name, so many prominent men and women were packed into St Bartholomew the Great. All ranks were represented from a range of fields. There was a duchess (Loelia), a former Prime Minister's wife (Clarissa), the widow of an opposition leader (Dora Gaitskell), the French ambassador, an Air Chief Marshal, the Director of Naval Intelligence ('representing "36 Club"), editors of national newspapers (Denis Hamilton), publishers, book collectors (John Carter), bankers (Bernard Rickatson-Hatt), golfers, artists (Ben Nicholson, Dicky Chopping), film producers, philosophers (Isaiah Berlin), writers (Evelyn Waugh, Graham Greene, Cyril Connolly, John Betjeman), down to Mary and Edgar Crickmere.

Peter read the lesson in his tailcoat from Eton ('rather a snug fit'). Amaryllis played Bach's Sarabande in C Major on her cello from the organ gallery. William Plomer gave the address. He had edited all of Ian's books. Before that, he had worked alongside him for five and a half years in the war. Following Plomer's address, Peter was 'fairly certain that Ian would be grateful to you for all you have done to get his "image" in perspective. I'm bloody well certain that I am.'

Plomer began by saying how Ian had re-created in Bond 'a thoroughly romantic myth' for the modern age, a necessary escape valve for a post-war generation hammered by austerity. But Plomer emphasised to the congregation leaning forward in their seats to catch his words 'because it may not be fully understood even among those who knew him or thought they knew him' that Ian's enormous popular success was not his best claim to fame.

Instead, it was Ian's valuable wartime services long before he began to write his first book that deserved to be commemorated, and which established Ian, in a memorable phrase of Admiral Godfrey, as 'a war-*winner*', and it was Ian's work in the war and the work of those like him that 'made it possible for us to survive and to be here together indulging in reminiscence today'.

Nine months later, Peter wrote to Percy Muir: 'I still miss him very much.'

LXX
EPILOGUES

'It is not as if you can ever forget Ian – after all, he was (is) someone,
a personality whose views and feelings and possessions will continue to
reverberate many a long day.'
CYRIL CONNOLLY to Ann Fleming

ST JAMES'S CHURCH, SEVENHAMPTON. An American reporter
telephoned Griffie after Ian's memorial service to say that he had visited Ian's
grave and 'it was just a heap of mud'. Like his grandfather Robert Fleming,
who stipulated a funeral 'of the most simple and unostentatious description',
Ian had not conceived a grand burial for himself. He jokingly requested William Plomer to 'engrave for my headstone TIME WOUNDS EVERY
HEEL'. An oval slate on the four-sided obelisk designed by Ann carried a
line from Lucretius, *omnia perfunctus vitae praemia marces* (having enjoyed
all life's prizes, you now decay).*

Ian had always wanted to be active, whether at work or play. There is a
telling line in the obituary of Bond in *You Only Live Twice*: 'I shall not waste
my days in trying to prolong them. I will use my time.' Using his time could
mean anything from batting out two thousand words at speed to playing a
round of golf, planning a military operation or conducting a helter-skelter
affair, but it had to be done at pace, followed by another spurt of energetic
activity.

Peter's perception that his brother had led the fullest life possible was
echoed by the curator of the Lilly Library in Indiana, David Randall, who

---

* When the plaque was stolen in September 2021, Fionn believed it 'very likely' that the grave was
desecrated by someone who concluded that Fleming and his family were beneficiaries of the slave
trade simply 'because of Ian's home in Jamaica'.

had been negotiating with Ian since 1958 to buy his book collection. 'I know few people who got more fun out of life than he did,' Randall wrote to Percy Muir. Ian had died 'just when he was at the height of everything'.

'GOLDFINGER' premiered five weeks after Ian's death, becoming the highest-grossing film in the UK to date and enjoying a rapturous reception in France ('Goldfinger has hit Paris like a thunderbolt'), where Plon sold 480,000 copies of Ian's first four novels that summer.

'By now, the volcano of success was in permanent eruption,' wrote John Pearson. Bond's reach extended beyond the former Empire that he had been created to replace. According to *Time* magazine, there was 'no geographical limit to the appeal of sex, violence and snobbery with which Fleming endowed his British secret agent'. Ian's Armenian publisher said that Armenian children would not even read fairy tales in their traditional language, 'but they'll read Bond'. The first volume of Ian's children's book *Chitty-Chitty-Bang-Bang* was published posthumously in October 1964; the twelfth Bond novel, *The Man with the Golden Gun*, in April 1965. An estimated twenty-seven million Bond books sold that year in eighteen languages. Griffie marvelled, 'Everyone seems to be Bond-mad just now; even paper hats at Southsea are selling with the various Bond names on them! . . . they are even manufacturing a James Bond wigwam for children in Germany.'

Walking with his girlfriend, Rachel Toynbee, in the desert in southern Tunisia, Caspar looked into a dry ditch and saw a pink plastic gun marked '007'. That was in 1971. Fifty years on, in October 2021, EON Productions released the twenty-seventh Bond film 'No Time to Die' to a record number of 772 cinemas.

Its co-producer, Barbara Broccoli, attributes the endurance of the franchise to Ian's war work. 'Bond is a distillation of the heroism of Britain that Fleming saw at that time, Britain's finest hour. And we've extended Britain's finest hour over sixty years because of him.' Nor is 007 yet ready to hand in his licence. King Charles III has since succeeded Queen Elizabeth II, but James Bond is still there, still flourishing, still adapting. Broccoli says, 'There isn't a person you meet who doesn't have an idea about the next film – usually ending up with Goldfinger's daughter.' Take James Bond back to Ian Fleming's 1950s, says one. Make him a *her*, says the Leader of the Opposition. Keep him a *he*, says the Prime Minister. Why not a gay actor, says 'Q'? Or black? Or Asian? Or trans? 'Just give me a rest,' says Broccoli.

The film Bond may have drifted further and further away from the Bond of the novels, but Ian had created a character with central values that still hold appeal and are adaptable enough to be reinvented over decades. Broccoli's co-producer, Michael G. Wilson, served as a Bond double in the filming of the 1964 'Goldfinger'. He sums up their flexible recipe: 'Bond doesn't have any requirements to be anything.' Even so, one or two ingredients remain non-negotiable. 'He's not going to take bribes – Bond is incorruptible, he's patriotic, he's doing it for Queen and King and country, and by extension Commonwealth. And we have a thing he should be male. But that's about it.'

The sun may have set on colonialist misogynists, but not on Ian's addictive and unmistakeable conception of a patriotic British male, attractive to both sexes, who is impossible to pay off. As a signature of Britain, James Bond has proved impervious to time, to changing mores. Infinitely malleable, eternally refreshable, with his latest dialogue and behaviour contemporised by none other than Phoebe 'Fleabag' Waller-Bridge ('It was a big old Yes, please . . . this iconic character you've grown up with'), James Bond is the mythical hero who not only never dies – despite earlier heart-stopping intakes of alcohol and tobacco – but who goes on getting livelier. Over 100 million copies of Bond novels have been sold throughout the world. For Australian author Murray Bail, 'he encapsulates Englishness for the English and for the rest of the world in a way the English love, even though it's bullshit.'

Much in the same way, Bond's, and so Fleming's, influence on Britain's foreign Intelligence service has persisted. The former head of MI6, Richard Dearlove, concurs with one of his predecessors that the fictional spy has acted as 'the best recruiting sergeant'. Bond's impact on MI6 has 'definitely had a positive effect,' says Dearlove. 'It's made the Service the most famous Intelligence organisation in the world. There is no linking or reality at all, but that's not really the point. It's reputational, it's myth-building, it's contributed to the brand. In the most distant part of the world, everyone has heard of MI6. There are big espionage cases, not just walk-ins like Oleg Gordievsky and Vasily Mitrokhin, where people have gone to the British when it would be more logical to approach the Americans, and who particularly like the British because of the Bond culture.'

It indicates something about Ian's enduring impact on SIS that his intelligence-gathering unit has come out of retirement. Disbanded in 1945, 30AU was revived on 13 December 2010, in Plymouth, as the 30 Commando Information Exploitation Group, with 30AU's old motto *Attain by Surprise*.

The Ministry of Defence has continued to build on Bond and writers like Fleming, who were 'years ahead of their time in predicting the modern world around us, from the internet and mobile phones to the electric submarine and driverless cars'. In 2023, the Defence Science and Technology Laboratory revealed that it had commissioned novelists to provide 'useful fiction' as a means to foretell and imagine 'the future of conflict from a human perspective'. One scientist involved in the project points out, 'some of our bosses absorb stories better than facts.'

JAMES BOND had toyed with retiring to a chicken farm. In 1968, he was brought back by Kingsley Amis, writing as Robert Markham. *Colonel Sun* was the first of a 'continuation series', today exceeding forty-one titles, by established novelists including William Boyd, Sebastian Faulks and Anthony Horowitz. Initially, Ann was against the idea of a 'counterfeit Bond', recalling how Sax Rohmer's wife had once written to Ian 'asking if he'd continue Dr Fu Manchu' – and Ian's reply, 'that he did not think this could ever be done'. Ann wrote to Evelyn Waugh: 'No one understands why I am distressed; though I do not admire "Bond", he was Ian's creation and should not be commercialised to this extent. Is there a parallel in literature?' There was a precedent. Before Sapper died in 1937, he had handed on the Bulldog Drummond torch to Gerard Fairlie. Ann eventually agreed on condition that the Glidrose board of directors all read and approved the manuscript.

CASPAR FLEMING killed himself with an overdose on 2 October 1975, aged twenty-three. Not until after Ian's death were Caspar's 'bad manners', dramatic laugh and love of mayhem understood to have had an underlying pathology. His sad history says a huge amount about his parents, who both struggled themselves. In particular, he reveals Ian Fleming's fundamental weakness under all the flamboyance: one wounded child creating another.

The death of his father on his twelfth birthday had meant that Caspar was doomed to repeat Ian's pattern, a fatherless Little Boy Lost. He had blushed in the memorial service when Plomer said 'to whose future we hopefully look forward.' Conceived at the same instant as Bond, Caspar found it hard to be the son of a famous man. After Ian died, he inherited Goldeneye and £302,000 (approximately £7.5 million today), which was put in trust until he was twenty-one.

Weapons and antiquities remained his obsessions. 'At present Caspar's main occupation is playing with guns,' Griffie wrote to Admiral Godfrey in July 1965 – an enthralment Ann confirmed. '"Old Caspar" whose mind is better than his manners has won a high place at Eton and the science prize, an essay on explosives and vitriol.' When not teaching Ali Forbes's six-year-old son Peter how to make a Molotov cocktail, Caspar took pot shots at his cousin Francis Grey. 'We'd have shooting parties with our air rifles,' says Francis, 'starting at opposite ends of a field, and try and shoot each other in the back of the leg. You'd turn your face away so you didn't lose an eye.'

Caspar described Eton to a friend as a 'hothouse society – someplace between security & claustrophobia'. He also became friends with David Coke, son of Gerry, whose best man Ian should have been. 'Caspar was a bit of a skyrocket, clearly from a different planet, not like the rest of us, incredibly intelligent, and one of the nicer people of my generation. His perspective was infinitely wider and deeper. Our conversations by-passed those things that obsessed most of my friends. It was simply refreshing to talk with him, like going to sleep and having one of those beautiful dreams from which you wake up happier and more confident.' Caspar never spoke of his father, says Coke, and denied any connection if asked. 'In my presence, someone said to him, "Are you Ian Fleming's son?" "No." I didn't know until later that he was. He didn't want it to be known.'

Mark Blackett-Ord was in the same house, two years ahead of him. 'When Caspar arrived in 1965, the whole Bond thing was at its height. All the books had come out and were banished in the school for obscenity. He was rather spidery, very sharp of tongue, not popular, but not unpopular. He always had a whiff of slight danger about him, a feeling he might pull a knife on you and cheat at cards, both of which were true. I had to restrain him from taking a Turner watercolour he'd spotted hanging in an obscure corridor.'

Caspar purchased his first weapons at Eton. He was part of a group of amateur gun enthusiasts who met unofficially once a month in the gym changing-room and traded in handguns and explosives. The group included the future mercenary Simon Mann, and a boy called Nugent 'who wound up in the Belgian Congo and was never heard of again'. The masters had no idea what was going on, says Chris Seidler, another in the group. 'It was coming out of dad and grandpa's gunrooms, surplus stuff which had been brought back by parents from World War One and World War Two, and captured German stuff – SS and storm-trooper daggers for 30 bob. You needed a deep pocket for Sten guns.' Caspar had a deep pocket, says Blackett-Ord. 'A Sten gun cropped up, pinched from the Corps armoury, and Caspar bought it for £20. Caspar always had cash for that sort of thing. By that time, I was Captain of the House, and had powers which Mussolini would have envied, so under the floorboards in my room it was safe. We were mates. I was amused by his utter nefariousness. He had a taste for danger. The Sten gun thing was kicks. He liked kicks.'

Caspar wrote to Angela Bray, a girl he had met at a dance in Yorkshire and kissed, 'crime is the ultimate form of sensuality'.

Then, on 17 February 1969, as the sixteen-year-old Caspar prepared for his A-Levels, his housemaster found a loaded revolver in Caspar's room. The headmaster reported the discovery to the police, who were panicking about such weapons getting into the hands of the IRA. Caspar was interviewed with Peter Fleming present, his uncle acting *in loco parentis*. Caspar refused to reveal who had sold him the gun. The next morning he ran away. Ann wrote to Clarissa Eden: 'the world turned upside down when, ten days ago, your godson terminated his career at Eton and vanished for twelve unbearably long hours.'

Caspar's failure to return to school re-enacted his father's premature departure in 1926. 'He was never sacked,' Ann insisted. 'I merely telephoned the housemaster and said "Caspar has returned, and that will be that," banging down the receiver.'

Days later, Caspar wrote to Angela Bray: 'I have que dire? "dropped out" "rebelled against oppressive adult authority" – or even, maybe just run away . . . Hysteria has ensued. "What are you going to do now Caspar?" – "What indeed?" Because of the threat of this childish drama getting into the papers, have had (oh, woe!) to dispose of my prized possession of arms.'

Earlier, Peter had volunteered to take custody of Caspar's arsenal when it was likely that the police might turn up at Sevenhampton. Peter locked four automatic pistols and nineteen live rounds in a cupboard, but he had dropped Caspar's prize weapon, his Browning semi-automatic rifle, down the well next to the barn, and then rung up Ann to explain what he had done. He was unaware that the police were listening in on the line. They returned to interview him at Merrimoles. A Flying Squad officer with an electromagnet retrieved the Browning. At Henley magistrates' court, in a strangely embarrassing coda to his career, Peter was fined £10 on each of three charges of illegal possession.

In April, Caspar was fined £25 by the juvenile court. The story was kept out of the press thanks to Ann's newspaper contacts and the influence of her new companion and personal solicitor, Arnold (Lord) Goodman.* Caspar's barrister, appointed by Goodman, explained to Ann that 'if there is not a plan, he will probably be put on probation', but he 'knew of a school in Florence called the "Centro Linguistico Italiano" and it appears Caspar is pleased to go there on May 1.'

From Italy, Caspar wrote to Blackett-Ord in red felt-tip pen, 'Mark, dear heart, son of Horus, divine of Isis, how are you? Life here is all very idyllic. I buy antiquities & gulp antidepressants . . . acquisitions so far include an ornate Greek gold ring & a Greek gold & amber necklace – pas mal, pas mal . . . also, I have been doing some fairly serious archaeology study here.' He was thinking of going to Kabul and Kathmandu. Following a long talk with 'Stash' Balthus, son of the French artist, he had decided 'antiquity-wise, junk-wise, romance-wise, the East is for me'.

But Caspar never went East. On the Ponte Vecchio, he met a Scottish

* Ann boasted to Blackett-Ord, 'the press never trouble me because Arnold is the Chairman of the Observer Trust, I was married to the owner of the *Daily Mail*, and Ian was Foreign Manager of the *Sunday Times*.' When Caspar broke into Hailes Abbey months later and stole medieval tiles from a shed, the Wiltshire police came to interview him, but Francis Grey took the rap. 'I was fined £15 in Winchcombe magistrates' court and had a police record.'

girl, Louise Allison, eighteen months older, who was studying at the British Institute. She says, 'A friend I was with was going to see this boy who had swapped a 50cc motorbike for a Greek urn, which sounded interesting. I saw this young man coming towards us. I didn't know it was Caspar, and took one look and fell madly in love.' Two days later, Caspar persuaded her to go with him to Rome. With nowhere to stay, they broke into the Forum at dusk. 'He found a muddy, semi-underground place to hole up in, which he insisted was the Temple of the Vestal Virgins. He started excavating, scratching around in the dirt, and came up with a skull, small, dark in colour. There was no way of knowing if it was contemporary or ancient. At the same time, they were having a *Son et Lumière* in the Forum. We were in constant danger of being pin-pointed by search-lights.'

This was not his last attempt to scale a national monument. Summoned by Ann to join her at the British embassy in Athens, Caspar met the ambassador's seventeen-year-old daughter Lucretia Stewart, who had the idea of showing him the Acropolis after dinner. 'The gates into the Parthenon compound were locked, but we climbed over them. We wandered around the ruins for twenty minutes before the police arrived.' Returned to the embassy in a police car and exhilarated from their adventure, Caspar persuaded Lucretia to go to bed with him. His later girlfriend, Rachel Toynbee, wonders if 'Caspar's mad exploits were imitating James Bond'.

At a trattoria in Rome, days after meeting Louise, Caspar had asked her to marry him. She says, 'I didn't take it very seriously. He was sixteen, but it happened. I said yes, and next day he bought me a silver ring in the shape of a snake. I remember Ann commenting on it with a typical Ann chuckle and saying we were too young.' For the next two years they lived together in Oxford, in a wooden hut behind the Cotswold Lodge Hotel, while Caspar took his A-Levels at a crammer.

Caspar won a place to read English at New College. At his Oxford interview with John Bayley, another weekend guest at Sevenhampton, Caspar was asked about his mannered handwriting, and he replied that it was copied from the handwriting of Peter Quennell. He switched to read Egyptian and Assyrian studies, a postgraduate course at the Griffiths Institute. 'At Oxford, he worked fifteen hours a day and burned himself out,' says Francis Grey, who visited him in his room in New College. 'He was not eating. You'd go into his kitchen and it was the worst student mess you'd seen in your life. There were only four people studying Egyptology. Two Germans, a brilliant Chinese, and him. He had to teach himself German and Akkadian.'

It seemed to his friends like Blackett-Ord that Caspar had the fatal flaw of going home when everyone else wanted to escape. 'From the moment he arrived to the day he died, he went back to Sevenhampton every weekend. That was his pattern. It reflects how tied up he was with his mother. They were terribly entwined emotionally with each other, which was the tragedy.'

At Sevenhampton, Caspar kept his special treasures in a chest of drawers in his small bedroom upstairs, in a row of guest rooms. Randal Keynes had met him at Oxford and they had a shared interest in ancient stones. 'I can see the drawer now, and in it two objects. One was a fragment, a greenish stone carving of a foot with toes, Egyptian. The other object, quite as beautiful, was a Luger, World War Two, and very special because of the quality of the steel it was made out of. He showed it to me. He had a peculiar and interesting reason for loving certain things. I think that Luger was his favourite object.'

Caspar's obsession with weapons was causing concern. 'On one occasion,' says Raymond, 'my mother said there were too many rabbits on the lawn, and the next thing one heard was the sound of automatic gunfire, and that was a Sten gun which was being used to try and hit them.' Caspar tried to shoot Lucretia Stewart with a crossbow from an upstairs window as she climbed out of the swimming pool. He fired a gun at Louise Allison. 'One evening, I opened the door to go into Caspar's room, which I could see was completely dark. There was a flash and a bullet from a .22 went into the doorframe beside me.' In the most damaging incident, the Oxford historian Raymond Carr was sent to the cellar to replenish wine. 'Unfortunately, Ann's son Caspar flung an Army thunderflash into the confined space, injuring my eardrums. Since then, I have been deaf.'

His most self-destructive obsession was drugs. He got hooked while he was at Eton, says his half-brother Raymond O'Neill. 'I was told he couldn't sleep and he used to steal our mother's sleeping tablets, and then he overdid it, and it slowly caught up with him. And towards the end, he'd tried every sort of drug.' He took barbiturates off Ann, Benzedrine out of John Sparrow's medicine cabinet at All Souls, phenobarbitone from Lucretia Stewart, even stealing the painkillers that Patrick Leigh Fermor needed for his throat cancer. In this manic state, with one eye needing to master Akkadian and the other eye on the next fix, he abandoned his Oxford degree after two years. 'It was very, very, very sad,' says Rachel Toynbee, then an undergraduate at Somerville College, who had replaced Allison as his girlfriend. 'Once he left Oxford, that was it.'

All agreed: Caspar had a good eye. His tutor at the Griffiths Institute, Dr Jaromir Malek, considered him one of the best students reading Egyptology he had met. Caspar persuaded his trustees to set him up in the antiquities business in Chelsea, a ground-floor flat in Old Church Street with one room big enough to showcase his Byzantine marble capitals, Egyptian bronze ibis heads, Roman lamps and turquoise scarabs.

'If he had lived,' says Hume Shawcross, an antiquities dealer who knew him at Eton and had sheltered him when he ran away from the school, 'Caspar would have become one of the great eclectic collectors.' Except that he was on drugs. He seemed incapable of looking after himself. Fionn remembers him warming tins of baked beans in his bath and then eating them straight from the can.

In August 1973, Caspar turned twenty-one and was free to access his trust money. In addition, he inherited Goldeneye. He had not visited Jamaica since Ian's death, and he wanted to take friends there. 'Goldeneye was his great hope,' says Blackett-Ord. 'It represented a break from the past and rejoining a relationship with his dead father by getting away from what was going wrong.'

The following August, Caspar invited his cousin Frances Charteris with whom he was having a dangerous flirtation, and Blackett-Ord and his girlfriend, Lucy Neville-Rolfe.

At Goldeneye, Frances Charteris decided she was not romantically interested in Caspar, and Caspar was rather crushed. The other thing was the arrival of Blanche, who offered to show them Noël Coward's grave and the local area.

'She felt the need to talk to him,' says John Cork, who later spoke with Blanche about that summer. 'She was, in her way, trying to apologise for having sent Ian back to walk slowly and painfully into that early grave when she might have been able to prolong his life.'

Blackett-Ord witnessed the drama play out. 'It's the first time Blanche and Caspar had met since she taught him to swim. She tells him how Caspar's parents were a disaster, and Ian really loved her, and she made him happy, and how he came to Goldeneye to get away from Ann. Caspar is listening to this woman, whose name was unknown, not particularly nice nor particularly nasty, vivacious, and emphatically not a half caste, which Ann had called her. It fitted in with why Ann had said "Don't go to Goldeneye." She had built a picture. She had cut out the bad side of her marriage to Ian. Caspar was learning it as if for the first time.

'A day or so later, I'm playing chess with Lucy in the main room and he passes by. "I'm off." We think nothing of it, and he goes down to the beach below the house. He'd taken an overdose and swum out to sea. He was about to lose consciousness when luckily some black men in a boat caused him to swim back. He's on the beach in an unpleasant state of rigid semi-consciousness. We rang Blanche Blackwell. She got a helicopter to fly him to Kingston hospital.'

Caspar was flown back to a psychiatric hospital in London. His life came apart over the next year. The gallery was dismantled and sold. Rachel Toynbee was woken one night by an ambulance outside, and she saw Caspar being carried in. He had taken another overdose. He was in and out of the Bethlem Royal Hospital, the Maudsley and the Priory in Roehampton, where he was given electro-convulsive therapy. Ann wrote to a friend, 'I have been nowhere and seen nobody since C is a permanent problem . . . All the docs say C's glooms provoke handfuls of barbiturates but no one has come up with a cure.' Caspar unloaded his distress on Ann. When he struck her to the ground, and Nanny Sillick responded by slapping him as hard as she could, Ann dismissed her after thirty-five years of service. Fionn says, 'One of the side effects of the bipolar condition is that the sufferer turns against the person nearest to them, however loving. Before Caspar's condition worsened, Annie could make light of his saying that he hated her and wished to commit matricide.' This was no longer possible after his return from Jamaica, says Blackett-Ord. 'Goldeneye tipped him from being a person who could cope with drugs to being a junkie, hopelessly dependent.' Peter Fleming had died four years before. It fell to Caspar's remaining uncle Richard to bicycle in from Crosby Square every evening after work, despite his bad right leg caused by a shrapnel wound, to visit him in the Priory.

Rachel Toynbee says, 'Ann never came once, she couldn't face it,' although Fionn thinks it also possible that Caspar did not want to see her. Toynbee was teaching at a primary school and she called in after school. 'I would go for an hour, stop at the Army and Navy to buy a *mille-feuille* and take it to him and talk. I went every day to hospital and it wasn't enough and it was never going to be enough.'

During a remission in the summer of 1975, Caspar set out for a walk with Rachel on the Yorkshire moors to decide what to do next, and he told her he had been having an affair with a junkie.

Rachel told him, 'But that's completely destructive.'

'I know, I know, I know, but I can't resist it.'

She made a decision. 'I'm not going to see you till September because I don't think I can take it.'

His time had almost run out. At Sevenhampton, Fionn did not want her children to get into the swimming pool with Caspar 'because his body was covered with needle pricks'. The autopsy would record injection marks on his feet, thigh and elbow.

In September, Rachel was telephoned by the historian Philip Mansel, who had known Caspar at Eton and Oxford, and had let him use his flat in Prince of Wales Terrace, until Mansel's partner asked Caspar to leave because he was injecting himself.

'Come round and see Caspar,' said Philip. 'Please do.'

Rachel says, 'Caspar sat there. "If you don't come back to me, I will commit suicide." I said, "I can't do this." "Is there someone else?"

'"There is now."' Rachel had since met and fallen in love with the man she was to marry.

'Two weeks later, Caspar killed himself. Philip Mansel rang me. I was sitting marking books at the kitchen table when the telephone rang. I was deeply upset, but I didn't feel guilty. There was an inevitability about it.'

'Caspar's death was terrible for me,' says Fionn. 'He was my child as well as my brother. We spent so much time together, and we were much closer than I am to my real brother.'

When Caspar had visited Fionn the night before, he appeared to be in sparkling humour. He had been to stay in Northern Ireland with Raymond, who recalls how cheerful he was. 'He disappeared into the North Antrim hills looking for early axe-heads – if he'd survived he could have been a serious archaeologist – and we thought he was incredibly happy.'

After saying goodnight to Fionn, Caspar returned to the top-floor flat on Royal Hospital Road where he was sleeping in a room that Ann had secured for herself in London. Next morning, the cleaner discovered Caspar in bed, inert, and three empty pill bottles beside him. A flat-mate, Antoine Lafont, held a mirror to Caspar's face. Panicked, he telephoned Fionn, who came around and called the doctor after she found no sign of breathing. Folded in Caspar's pyjama pocket was a note: 'If it is not this time, it will be the next.' He had not addressed it to anyone.

Ann had to be sedated when told the news. Her sister Laura said 'Annie had so many false alarms that the real thing doesn't seem real to her.' Ann poured out her grief to Noel Annan. 'I shall miss him forever, until a year ago he was a marvellous companion and more recently one's heart was anguished for there was no help one could give.' Fionn says, 'In the last months, the image I have of my mother is of someone desperately holding out her hand to her child as he falls over a cliff.'

Only half a dozen of Caspar's friends attended his burial at Sevenhampton. Before she went into the church, Ann came up and seized Louise Allison's hand and said, 'Thank you for those years you had with Caspar, he was most happy with you.' Randal Keynes tossed a flint fossil into the grave. The line on Caspar's oval plaque was from Keats. 'To cease upon the midnight with no pain.'

Ann had wanted Caspar's close friends to have something of his. Thomas Heneage received Caspar's prehistoric flint implements. 'I organised his very good collection of Egyptian antiquities be given to the Ashmolean, and for ten years it had a special display, quite remarkable for a boy of twenty-three.'

GOLDENEYE was left to Caspar. Following Caspar's death, Blanche's son Chris paid £70,000 for the property in 1976 after Bob Marley bought it sight unseen and then pulled out. 'It was too posh for him, not anywhere he thought he could be comfortable.' In 1982, Violet wrote to Ivar Bryce, who had found Ian the original strip of bushland: 'I am always hoping to see you come back to Goldeneye. It is very nice now Mrs Blackwell has repaired it.

You would like it better. I am hoping you are well. I am not so well, but I am not in bed.' In 2011, the local Boscobel Aerodrome, where Ian had gone riding with Blanche, was renamed the Ian Fleming International Airport. Chris Blackwell continues to live in a cottage on the exclusive resort that he built on the property. 'When it's full, Goldeneye still seems empty, and you can spend a lot of time there without seeing anyone, as though the place is all for you . . . there is a world where you can wander over the footbridge that leads to the beachfront Bizot Bar and there's Elon Musk on his own having a drink, Ryan Gosling is on the phone to his agent at the end of the other bar, Sly and Robbie are coming out of the speakers, Jay-Z and Beyoncé are hidden in their villa on a romantic weekend, and in the ocean, Grace Jones is having a swim.'

TRAFALGAR SQUARE CHRISTMAS TREE. This is given each year by the city of Oslo 'to the people of London for their assistance during the years 1940–45'. The tradition was started by Ian one winter evening in 1942 in an episode recorded by Admiral Denning, penultimate Director of Naval Intelligence before the post was abolished in 1965. 'We had occasion to bring back from Norway a Norwegian agent operating there.' Ian organised a dinner at the Savoy, saying that after all the dangers Mons Urangsvåg had been exposed to it would be nice to give him 'a first class meal'; Ian even 'provided some of the fare for the Chef to cook'. Present at the dinner were Urangsvåg, Denning, Commander Eric Welsh RNVR, and Ian. After 'a convivial evening', they piled into a jeep 'only to discover that among the gear with the agent were two Christmas trees'. Urangsvåg had cut down these firs during a raid on the island of Hisøy and smuggled them over to Scotland at some discomfort, intending to present the trees to the Norwegian king, Haakon VII, then living in exile in Sunningdale. Denning wrote, 'It was Ian who suggested that it would be a nice gesture to put up one in Trafalgar Square.' The four men fastened the fir tree to a balustrade on the north side. 'There were no fairy lights, but one or two aircraft flares provided illumination.' They then toasted King George and King Haakon, the return of Urangsvåg and to the liberation of Norway with a bottle of aquavit that Urangsvåg had also brought back. 'Even on this occasion Ian showed his bon viveur attitude with the remark "I'm not complaining, but nevertheless I still maintain

Danish aquavit is the best and moreover this bottle has only travelled in a small ship from Norway to Scotland and not round the world as it should have done as real Norwegian aquavit." '

THE FLEMING COLLECTION – 'to include Ian's manuscripts as well as the collection of scientific books' – was sold by Ann in 1965 to the Lilly Library in Indiana for $150,000, of which $30,000 was allocated to the collection, and $120,000 to the James Bond novels. 'The value of '007's manuscripts is a gamble,' David Randall wrote to Percy Muir. 'As we said, he is no Sherlock Holmes; yet the more I think about it, the more I believe he may outlive his era. He represents senseless violence, technical knowledge, etc., etc., to a degree which may make him a symbol of our time.'

Waugh wrote to Nancy Mitford: 'Ian Fleming is being posthumously canonised by the intelligentsia. Very rum.'

Today, the James Bond manuscripts are, by far, the most frequently requested items in the Lilly Library with *Goldfinger* heading the list. The value of the first published editions has not stopped rising. A copy of *Live and Let Die* presented to Winston Churchill realised £190,000 at Sotheby's in 2020, the highest auction price paid for a published edition of Ian Fleming. Ian's nephew Fergus Fleming today runs the Queen Anne Press, the publishing house started by his uncle. 'The two authors that any antiquarian bookseller sells constantly are: Churchill and Fleming. There he is, alongside his hero in the world of books.'

His unpublished correspondence commands premium prices. In November 2008, Caroline Ponsonby sold four letters from Ian to her aunt, Loelia Westminster, for £33,650, 'and bought myself a Lexus'.

Still missing from Ian Fleming's complete oeuvre is his film adaptation of *Casino Royale*; an eighteen-page film treatment of his non-fiction work *The Diamond Smugglers*, and his 1928 volume of poems, *The Black Daffodil* ('Did he really consign every copy to the flames?' Donald McCormick wrote to Ivar Bryce. 'Is it possible that one copy or maybe two, exists somehow or other?'). He is also thought to have destroyed a short story, 'The True Tale of Captain Kidd's Treasure'.

Had Ian Fleming lived, what else might he have written? After his heart attack in 1961, he had considered setting Bond aside for a lighthearted book on golf. 'I have scraps of ideas for future books but nothing in the least firm . . . Laid low again, I am now thinking of a musical called "Fizz-an-Chips", but I haven't got further than the title.' In March 1964, he suggested to Michael Howard 'a cool, well-illustrated book on the "narcotic flora of the world" . . . You can't miss.' Two other ideas were 'a really stimulating travel guide to the Commonwealth and the remainder of our Colonies', and a biography of the French bordello-owner and politician, Marthe Richard (1889–1982), who had been a prostitute and spy in the First World War, and then, in 1946, closed down the brothels in France. Peter Quennell may have seeded the idea. 'He became very interested in what I told him about the brothel keepers of France running their own magazine called the *Tenancier*.'

Not that Ian had given up on thrillers. 'It is one of my ambitions to write a thriller based on big business,' he wrote shortly before his death. He dashed off a three-page outline with a theme that still feels contemporary. Entitled 'The Big Killing', his plot paid tribute to Ian's days as a Reuters reporter covering the Metropolitan-Vickers trial in Moscow. 'What I have in mind is the fight to obtain a £20,000,000 contract from the state of Astia by Magnum Electric, the great English operation. The contract would be for the supply of turbo-electric generators for the Central Astia Dam.' The English company would be up against America, Germany and Russia, the story proceeding with 'the gift of a Rolls Royce here, the promise of a big commission there', through sabotage at the demonstration, theft of the Magnum blue-prints, murder of the chief Magnum designer. 'All these goings on would be based, with much technical and business detail, on the true high skulduggery that surrounds – more particularly in the armament industry, perhaps – really big international business.'

Bond is not mentioned, but this does not mean that Ian had dispensed with his hero, perhaps keeping him for one further fling in a place he had never been. 'I have wonderful memories of Australia,' he wrote to a fan in New South Wales, 'and I hope one day I shall come back and bring James Bond and his Beretta with me in search of trouble and just that one final, fatal Australian blonde.'

Add to that a tantalising story that points to the existence of an unknown James Bond novel.

Caspar's friend, Thomas Heneage, founded one of the world's leading art bookshops and today is a renowned bibliographer. He was twenty-five when Caspar died. 'I had to go through Caspar's effects in his bedroom at Seven-hampton. There was an ottoman like we had at Eton. I found the first manuscript of *Chitty-Chitty-Bang-Bang*, which Ian had written for Caspar; and then, just under it, I came across a thick, four-and-a-half inch wodge of a one-sided typescript of a Bond book. I started reading. I got very excited. It was a new thing, a discovery, the beginning of a Bond story that I'd never seen or read and didn't know about. One could see the film coming out of it.

'I took it downstairs to show Ann. She was sitting on the edge of the sofa on the far side of the drawing room.

'"Look what I've found."

'"Oh," she said, "Ian's little booby," and chucked it on the fire.

'I was completely gobsmacked. I was utterly bowled over, seeing some-thing absolutely astonishing happening that you couldn't imagine happening. Talk about flabbergasting. I couldn't think of any explanation.'

LIST OF ILLUSTRATIONS

In northern France © Karen Recht; **William Donovan** Topfoto; . . . **Bill Marshall** From *The Secret Navies* by Hampshire, A. Cecil (Kimber, 1978); . . . **Ernan Forbes Dennis** . . . **Phyllis Bottome** © Frederica Freer; **Bernard Rickatson-Hatt** Reuters Archive; . . . **William Plomer** From *The Autobiography of William Plomer* by William Plomer (Taplinger Publishing Company, 1976); **Rear-Admiral John Godfrey** DNI 1942, from *Very Special Admiral: Biography of Admiral John Henry Godfrey* by Patrick Beesly (Hamish Hamilton, 1980); **Ernie Cuneo** © Jonathan Cuneo; . . . **Cyril Connolly** . . . **Peter Quennell** © Alexander Quennell; **Viscount Kemsley of Dropmore** Russell, L. mss., Lilly Library, Indiana University, Bloomington, Indiana; . . . **Una Trueblood** McKeown/Express/Getty Images; **At the *Sunday Times*** The Times / News Licensing; . . . **Kevin McClory** © Ivar Mountbatten; . . . **signing the contract for 'Dr. No'** DR. NO (1962). Courtesy of Eon Productions and Metro Goldwyn Mayer Studios. DR. NO © 1962 Danjaq, LLC and Metro-Goldwyn-Mayer Studios Inc. James Bond Trademarks, TM Danjaq. All Rights Reserved; **On set at Pinewood** © Frank Herrmann/www.pap-art.co.uk; **Ian with a pregnant Ann** Ian Fleming Images/Courtesy of Raymond Benson; **The Flemings at 16 Victoria Square** © Norman Parkinson/Iconic Images; **Caspar Fleming** Horst P. Horst, Horst Archive © Condé Nast; **Black Mount** Ian Fleming Images/© Fleming Family; **Joyce Grove** Ian Fleming Images; . . . **Goldeneye** Supplied by the author/Nicholas Shakespeare; . . . **Sevenhampton** Supplied by the author/Nicholas Shakespeare; **Fifty-year-old Ian Fleming** © Alexander Quennell; **Ian's monastic** © Louise Carr-Ellison; **Ian's last ambition** Ian Fleming Images/Copyright Ian Fleming Estate; **Peter Fleming's shrine** Ian Fleming Images

BIBLIOGRAPHY

BOOKS

Peter Alexander, *William Plomer*, OUP, 1989

Henry Allan, 'Prize Essay on Kleptomania', 1869

Eric Ambler, *The Dark Frontier*, Hodder and Stoughton, 1936

Kingsley Amis, *The James Bond Dossier*, Cape, 1965

Noel Annan, *Changing Enemies: The Defeat and Regeneration of Germany*, Harper-Collins, 1995

Ralph Arnold, *A Very Quiet War*, Macmillan, 1962

Joan Bright Astley, *The Inner Circle: A View of War at the Top*, Hutchinson, 1971

W. H. Auden and Christopher Isherwood, *Journey to a War*, Octagon, 1972

Roderick Bailey, *The Secret War of Louis Franck* (privately printed)

Sam Bassett, *Royal Marine*, Stein and Day, 1965

Alan Bath, *Tracking the Axis Enemy: The Triumph of Anglo-American Naval Intelligence*, Modern War Studies, 1998

Paul Baudouin, The *Private Diaries (March 1940 to January 1941)*, Eyre and Spottiswoode, 1948

Beverly Baxter, *Men, Martyrs and Mountebanks*, Hutchinson, 1940

Cecil Beaton, *Self-Portrait with Friends: Selected Diaries of Cecil Beaton*, Pimlico, 1991

Patrick Beesly, *Very Special Admiral*, Hamish Hamilton, 1980

J. G. Beevor, *SOE: Recollections and Reflections, 1940–45*, Bodley Head, 1981

Gill Bennett, *Churchill's Man of Mystery: Desmond Morton and the World of Intelligence*, Routledge, 2009

Tony Bennett and Janet Woollacott, *Bond and Beyond: The Political Career of a Popular Hero*, Routledge, 1987

Raymond Benson, *The James Bond Bedside Companion*, intro. Ernie Cuneo, Boxtree, 1984

William Berry, *William Camrose: Giant of Fleet Street*, Weidenfeld and Nicolson, 1992

Chris Blackwell, *The Islander: My Life in Music and Beyond*, Nine Eight Books, 2022

Mary Bond, *How 007 Got His Name*, Collins, 1966

Phyllis Bottome, *Danger Signal*, Little, Brown, 1939

—, *The Lifeline*, Faber, 1946

—, *Not in Our Stars*, Faber, 1955

—, *Alfred Adler: A Portrait from Life*, Vanguard Press, 1957

—, *The Goal*, Vanguard Press, 1962

Andrew Boyd, *British Naval Intelligence Through the Twentieth Century*, Seaforth, 2020

Christopher Bray, *Sean Connery*, Pegasus, 2012

Hilary Bray, *Toy Engine*, privately published, 1967

Hilary Bray: A Friend for all Seasons, ed. George Pike (privately published), 1982

Asa Briggs, *Secret Days*, Frontline, 2011

British Security Coordination: The Secret History of British Intelligence in the Americas, 1940–45, intro. Nigel West, Fromm International, 1999

Brian Brivati, *Hugh Gaitskell*, Metro, 1997

Cubby Broccoli, *When the Snow Melts*, Boxtree, 1998

David Bruce, *Ambassador to Sixties London*, Republic of Letters, Dordrecht, 2010

Ivar Bryce, *You Only Live Once: Memories of Ian Fleming*, Weidenfeld and Nicolson, 1975

Oliver Buckton, *The World is Not Enough: A Biography of Ian Fleming*, Rowman and Littlefield, 2021

Reader Bullard, *Inside Stalin's Russia*, 1930–34, Day Books, 2000

Cherie Burns, *Searching for Beauty: The Life of Millicent Rogers, the American Heiress Who Taught the World About Style*, St Martin's, 2012

Sheila Campbell, *Resident Alien*, Robert Hale, 1990

Truman Capote, *Too Brief a Treat; Letters of Truman Capote*, ed. Gerald Clarke, Random House, 2004

David Cannadine, *In Churchill's Shadow*, Penguin, 2003

Tim Card, *Eton Renewed*, John Murray, 1994

Anthony Cavendish, *Inside Intelligence*, Collins, 1990

Thelma Cazalet-Keir, *From the Wings*, Bodley Head, 1967

The Raymond Chandler Papers, ed. Tom Hiney and Frank MacShane, Grove, 2002

Henry 'Chips' Channon, *The Diaries 1918–38*, ed. Simon Heffer, Hutchinson, 2021

—, *The Diaries 1939–42*, ed. Simon Heffer, Hutchinson, 2021

—, *The Diaries 1943–57*, ed. Simon Heffer, Hutchinson, 2022

Hester Chapman, *Ever Thine*, Cape, 1951

James Chapman, *License to Thrill: A Cultural History of the James Bond Films*, Columbia University Press, 2001

Hugo Charteris, *The Coat*, Collins, 1966

Kenneth Clark, *Another Part of the Wood*, Harper and Row, 1974

Algy Cluff, *Get On With It: A Memoir*, Cluff and Sons, 2020

Nicholas Coleridge, *The Glossy Years: Magazines, Museums and Selective Memoirs*, Penguin, 2019

Ian Colvin, *Vansittart in Office*, Littlehampton, 1965

Jennet Conant, *The Irregular: Roald Dahl and the British Spy Ring in Wartime Washington*, Simon and Schuster, 2008

Cyril Connolly, *Enemies of Promise*, Routledge, 1938

—, *The Missing Diplomats*, intro. Peter Quennell, Queen Anne Press, 1952

—, *Previous Convictions: Selected Writings of a Decade*, Hamish Hamilton, 1963

Artemis Cooper, *Patrick Leigh Fermor: An Adventure*, John Murray, 2012

Diana Cooper, *Darling Monster: The Letters of Lady Diana Cooper to her son John Julius Norwich*, Chatto, 2013

Duff Cooper, *Operation Heartbreak*, Rupert Hart-Davis, 1950

Noël Coward, *Volcano*, 1956

—, *Pomp and Circumstance*, Heinemann, 1960

—, *Bon Voyage*, Doubleday, 1968

—, *The Noël Coward Diaries*, ed. Graham Payn and Sheridan Morley, Weidenfeld and Nicolson, 1982

—, *The Letters of Noël Coward*, ed. Barry Day, Methuen, 2008

—, *The Essential Noël Coward Compendium: The Very Best of His Work, Life and Times*, by Barry Day, Bloomsbury, 2009

Esmé Cromer, *From this Day Forward*, Thomas Harmsworth, 1991

A. J. Cummings, *The Moscow Trial*, Gollancz, 1933

Roald Dahl, *Love from Boy; Roald Dahl's Letters to his Mother*, ed. Donald Sturrock, John Murray, 2016

Edward P. Dallis-Comentale, Stephen Watt and Skip Willman, eds, *Ian Fleming and James Bond: The Cultural Politics of 007*, Indiana University Press, 2005

Patrick Dalzel-Job, *Arctic Snow to Dust of Normandy*, Pen and Sword, 2005

Alex Danchev, *Establishing the Anglo-American Alliance*, Potomac, 1990

François d'Astier de La Vigerie, *Le ciel n'était pas vide*, Julliard, 1952

Anne de Courcy, *The Viceroy's Daughters*, Weidenfeld and Nicolson, 2012

Len Deighton, *James Bond: My Long and Eventful Search for His Father*, Kindle

Sefton Delmer, *Black Boomerang*, Secker and Warburg, 1962

Deborah, Duchess of Devonshire and Patrick Leigh Fermor, *In Tearing Haste: Letters Between Deborah Devonshire and Patrick Leigh Fermor*, ed. Charlotte Mosley, John Murray, 2009

Jeremy Duns, *Duns on Bond: An Omnibus of Journalism on Ian Fleming and James Bond*, CreateSpace, 2014

Sybil and David Eccles, *By Safe Hand: Letters of Sybil and David Eccles 1939–42*, Bodley Head, 1983

Clarissa Eden, *Clarissa Eden: A Memoir – from Churchill to Eden*, ed. Kate Haste, Orion, 2007

Hugh Edwards, *All Night at Mrs Stanyhurst's*, Cape, 1933

Nicholas Elliott, *Never Judge a Man by His Umbrella*, Michael Russell, 1991

Julian Evans, *Semi-Invisible Man: The Life of Norman Lewis*, Cape, 2008

Duncan Fallowell, *How to Disappear: A Memoir for Misfits*, Ditto, 2011

Lara Feigel, *The Love Charm of Bombs*, Bloomsbury, 2013

[Fleming family], *Lyra Familiae*, Holywell Press, Oxford Ann Fleming, *The Letters of Ann Fleming*, ed. Mark Amory, Collins Harvill, 1985

J. Arnold Fleming, *Flemish Influence in Britain*, Jackson, Wylie and Co., 1930

Fergus Fleming, *Amaryllis Fleming*, Sinclair-Stevenson, 1993

—(ed.), *The Man with the Golden Typewriter: Ian Fleming's James Bond Letters*, Bloomsbury, 2015

—(ed.), *Talk of the Devil: Selected Journalism of Ian Fleming*, Queen Anne Press, 2008

Ian Fleming, *Casino Royale*, Cape, 1953

—, *Live and Let Die*, Cape, 1954

—, *Moonraker*, Cape, 1955

—, *Diamonds are Forever*, Cape, 1956

—, *From Russia, with Love*, Cape, 1957

—, *The Diamond Smugglers*, Cape, 1957

—, *Dr. No*, Cape, 1958

—, *Goldfinger*, Cape, 1959

—, *For Your Eyes Only*, Cape, 1960

—, *The Spy Who Loved Me*, Cape, 1960

—, *Thunderball*, Cape, 1961

—, *On Her Majesty's Secret Service*, Cape, 1963

—, *Thrilling Cities*, Cape, 1963

—, *You Only Live Twice*, Cape, 1964

—, *Chitty-Chitty-Bang-Bang: The Magical Car*, Cape, 1964

—, *The Man with the Golden Gun*, Cape, 1965

—, *Ian Fleming introduces Jamaica*, Deutsch, 1965

—, *Octopussy and The Living Daylights*, Cape, 1966

—, *Gilt-Edged Bonds*, intro. Paul Gallico, Macmillan, 1961

Ian Fleming and Antony Terry, *Yours Ever, Ian Fleming: Letters to and from Antony Terry*, ed. Judith Lenart, Nelson, New Zealand, 1994

James Fleming, *Bond Behind the Iron Curtain*, The Book Collector, 2021

John Fleming, *Looking Backwards for Seventy Years 1921–1851*, Aberdeen University Press, 1922

Kate Fleming, *Celia Johnson*, Weidenfeld and Nicolson, 1991

Peter Fleming, *Brazilian Adventure*, Cape, 1933

—, *One's Company*, Cape, 1934

—, *The Flying Visit*, Cape, 1941

—, *A Story to Tell*, Cape, 1942

—, *The Sixth Column*, Rupert Hart-Davis, 1951

—, *My Aunt's Rhinoceros*, Rupert Hart-Davis, 1956

Charles Fraser-Smith, *The Secret War of Charles Fraser-Smith*, Paternoster Press, 1991

Helen Fry, *The London Cage*, Yale, 2017

Sarah Gainham, *The Tiger Life*, Methuen, 1983

Richard Gant (Leslie Thomas), *Ian Fleming: The Man with the Golden Pen*, Mayflower-Dell, 1966

Leah Garrett, *X Troop: The Secret Jewish Commandos of World War II*, Chatto, 2021

Curt Gentry, *J. Edgar Hoover*, Norton, 2001

John Gielgud, *A Life in Letters*, Arcade, 2011

Jon Gilbert, *Ian Fleming: The Bibliography*, Queen Anne Press, 2017

Martin Gilbert, *The Churchill War Papers: At the Admiralty*, Norton, 1993

—, *Churchill and America*, Free Press, 2005

Frank Giles, *Sundry Times*, John Murray, 1986

Ian Gilmour, *Autobiography*, 2015

Sancho Glanville, *The Official History of 30AU*, compiled by Guy Allan Farrin, <https://www.30AU.co.uk>, 2007

Sandy Glen, *Target Danube*, Book Guild, 2002

J. H. Godfrey, *The Naval Memoirs of Admiral J. H. Godfrey*, 8 vols, Hailsham, 1964

The Golfer's Manual, by 'A Keen Hand', 1857

Michael Goodman, *Official History of the Joint Intelligence Committee*, vol. 1, Routledge, 2014

Arthur Gore, *Lord Arran Writes*, Hodder and Stoughton, 1964

Richard Greene, *Russian Roulette: The Life and Times of Graham Greene*, Little, Brown, 2020

Peter Grose, *Allen Dulles: Spymaster*, Deutsch, 2006

Lisa Rebecca Gubernick, *Squandered Fortune: The Life and Times of Huntington Hartford*, Putnam, 1991

Peter Haining, *The Mystery of Rommel's Gold*, Robson, 2004

Robert Harling, *Ian Fleming: A Personal Memoir*, Robson, 2015

Duff Hart-Davis, *Peter Fleming*, Cape, 1974

—, *The House the Berrys Built*, Hodder and Stoughton, 1990

—, *Man of War*, Century, 2012

Rupert Hart-Davis, *Arms of Time*, Hamish Hamilton, 1979

Denis Hamilton, *Editor-in-Chief: Fleet Street Memoirs*, Hamish Hamilton, 1979

Nigel Hamilton, *JFK: Reckless Youth*, Random House, 1992

A. Cecil Hampshire, *The Secret Navies*, Sphere, 1980

Selina Hastings, *Rosamond Lehmann: A Life*, Vintage, 2003

Donald Healey, *My World of Cars*, Patrick Stephens, 1989

Henry Hemming, *Our Man in New York*, Quercus, 2019

David Herbert, *Second Son*, Peter Owen, 1972

Gregg Herken, *The Georgetown Set: Friends and Rivals in Cold War Washington*, Knopf, 2014

John Higgs, *Love and Let Die: Bond, the Beatles and the British Psyche*, Weidenfeld and Nicolson, 2022

Pam Hirsch, *The Constant Liberal: The Life and Work of Phyllis Bottome*, Quartet, 2010

Philip Hoare, *Noël Coward*, Sinclair-Stevenson, 1995

Harold Hobson, Phillip Knightley and Leonard Russell, *The Pearl of Days: an Intimate Memoir of the Sunday Times 1822–1972*, Hamish Hamilton, 1972

John Hollingshead, *My Lifetime*, 1895

Diane Holloway and Lee Harvey Oswald, *The Mind of Oswald: Accused Assassin of President John F. Kennedy*, Trafford, 2006

Michael Holroyd, *Augustus John*, Chatto, 1996

Patrick Howarth, *Intelligence Chief Extraordinary*, Bodley Head, 1986

Richard Hughes, *Foreign Devil: Thirty Years of Reporting in the Far East*, Deutsch, 1972

Molly Huggins, *Too Much to Tell*, Heinemann, 1967

J. A. C. Hugill, *The Hazard Mesh*, Hurst and Blackett, 1946,

R. C. Hutchinson and Martyn Skinner, *Two Men of Letters*, Michael Joseph, 1979

H. Montgomery Hyde, *The Quiet Canadian*, Hamish Hamilton, 1962

Laurence Irving, *The Precarious Crust*, Chatto, 1971

—, *Great Interruption*, Airlife, 1983

Alaric Jacob, *Scenes from a Bourgeois Life*, Secker and Warburg, 1949

Robert Rhodes James, *Anthony Eden*, Papermac, 1987

Gladwyn Jebb, *The Memoirs of Lord Gladwyn*, Weidenfeld and Nicolson, 1972

Keth Jeffery, *MI6: The History of the Secret Intelligence Service, 1909–1949*, Bloomsbury, 2010

Christian Jennings, *The Third Reich is Listening: Inside German Codebreaking 1939–45*, Osprey, 2018

Roderick Jones, *A Life in Reuters*, Hodder and Stoughton, 1951

David Kahn, *Seizing the Enigma: The Race to Break the German U-Boat Codes 1933–45*, Frontline, 2012

Barbara Kaye, *The Company We Kept*, Werner Shaw, 1986

—, *Second Impression: Further Recollections of an Antiquarian Bookseller's Wife*, Oak Knoll Press, 1995

The Kemsley Manual of Journalism, 1950, Cassell Ludovic Kennedy, *On My Way to the Club*, Collins, 1989

Brian King, *Undiscovered Dundee*, Black and White, 2011

James Kirkup, *I of All People*, Littlehampton, 1988

Philip Larkin, *Required Writing, Miscelllaneous Pieces 1955–1982*, Faber, 1983

John le Carré, *Call for the Dead*, Penguin, 2011

—, *A Private Spy: The Letters of John le Carré*, ed. Tim Cornwell, Penguin Viking, 2022

Christopher Lee, *Tall, Dark and Gruesome*, Midnight Marquee Press, 2009

Rosamond Lehmann, *A Sea-Grape Tree*, Collins, 1976

Patrick Leigh Fermor, *The Traveller's Tree*, John Murray, 1950

—, *Dashing for the Post: The Letters of Patrick Leigh Fermor*, ed. Adam Sisman, John Murray, 2016

Judith Lenart, *Berlin to Bond and Beyond: The Story of a Fleming Man*, Athena, 2007

Cole Lesley, *The Life of Noël Coward*, Cape, 1976

Brian Lett, *Ian Fleming and SOE's Operation Postmaster: The Top Secret Story Behind 007*, Pen and Sword, 2012

Jeremy Lewis, *Cyril Connolly: A Life*, Cape, 1997

—, *David Astor*, Cape, 2016

Norman Lewis, *The World, The World*, Cape, 1996

Christoph Lindner, *The James Bond Phenomenon: A Critical Reader*, Manchester University, 2009

Elizabeth Longford, *The Pebbled Shore*, Weidenfeld and Nicolson, 1986

Andrew Lownie, *Stalin's Englishman: The Lives of Guy Burgess*, Hodder and Stoughton, 2015

Andrew Lycett, *Ian Fleming*, Weidenfeld and Nicolson, 1995

—, *From Diamond Sculls to Golden Handcuffs: A History of Rowe and Pitman*, Robert Hale, 1998

George Lyttelton and Rupert Hart-Davis, *The Lyttelton Hart-Davis Letters*, vols 1 and 2: *1955–1957*, John Murray, 1985

—, vols 3 and 4, *1958–1959*, John Murray, 1986

—, vol. 5, *1960*, John Murray, 1983

—, vol. 6, *1961–62*, John Murray, 1984

Earl of Lytton, *Antony*, Peter Davies, 1935

Bill Macdonald, *The True Intrepid*, Timberholme Books, 1998

—, *Intrepid's Last Secrets*, FriesenPress, 2019

David MacFadyen et al., *Eric Drummond and His Legacies*, Palgrave Macmillan, 2019

Ben Macintyre, *007: For Your Eyes Only*, Bloomsbury, 2008

—, *Operation Mincemeat*, Bloomsbury, 2010

Laura, Duchess of Marlborough, *Laughter from a Cloud*, Weidenfeld and Nicolson, 1980

Owen Matthews, *An Impeccable Spy: Richard Sorge, Stalin's Master Agent*, Bloomsbury, 2019

Donald McCormick, *17F: The Life of Ian Fleming*, Peter Owen, 1993

Donald McLachlan, *Room 39: Naval Intelligence in action 1939–45*, Weidenfeld and
Nicolson, 1968

Priscilla Johnson McMillan, *Marina and Lee*, Steerforth Press, 2013

S. P. B. Mais, *All the Days of My Life*, Hutchinson, 1937

Ivan Maisky, *The Maisky Diaries: Red Ambassador to the Court of St James's 1932–1943*,
ed. Gabriel Gorodetsky, Yale, 2015

Francis de Marneffe, *Last Boat from Bordeaux*, Coolidge Hill Press, 2005

Gabor Maté, *Scattered Minds: The Origins and Healing of Attention Deficit Disorder*,
Vermilion, 2019

Merlin Minshall, *Guilt-Edged*, Bachman and Turner, 1975

Elizabeth Montagu, *Honourable Rebel*, Montagu Ventures, 2003

Ewen Montagu, *Beyond Top Secret U*, Peter Davies, 1977

Alan Moorehead, *Eclipse*, Penguin, 2022

Frank Moorhouse, *Grand Days*, Pantheon, 1994

Malcolm Muggeridge: *Like It Was: The Diaries of Malcolm Muggeridge*, Harper-
Collins, 1981

Percy Muir, *Minding My Own Business*, Oak Knoll Press, 1991

Harold Nicolson, *Public Faces*, Penguin, 1945

David Nutting, *Attain by Surprise: Capturing Top Secret Intelligence in World War II*,
David Colver, 2003

Conrad O'Brien-ffrench, *Delicate Mission: Autobiography of a Secret Agent*, Skilton
and Shaw, 1979

Bernard O'Connor, *Blowing up Iberia: British, German and Italian Sabotage in Spain
and Portugal*, lulu.com, 2020

Alan Ogden, *Master of Deception: the Wartime Adventures of Peter Fleming*, Bloomsbury Academic, 2019

David O'Keefe, *One Day in August: Ian Fleming, Enigma, and the Deadly Raid on
Dieppe*, Icon Books, 2020

Joy Packer, *Deep as the Sea*, Eyre Methuen, 1975

Matthew Parker, *Goldeneye, Where Bond was Born: Ian Fleming's Jamaica*, Windmill,
2015

John Pearson, *The Life of Ian Fleming*, Cape, 1966

—, *Ian Fleming: The Notes*, Queen Anne Press, 2022

Thomas Pellatt, *Boys in the Making*, Methuen, 1936

Heinz Pellender, *Tambach*, Coburg, 1985

Joseph Persico, *Roosevelt's Secret War: FDR and World War II Espionage*, Random House, 2002

Leo Perutz, *Little Apple*, tr. John Brownjohn, Pushkin, 2016

William Plomer, *Turbott Wolfe*, Hogarth Press, 1926

—, *Address Given at the Memorial Service for Ian Fleming*, Westerham Press, 1964

James Pope-Hennessy, *A Lonely Business: A Self-Portrait of James Pope-Hennessy*, ed. Peter Quennell, Weidenfeld and Nicolson, 1981

Alan Pryce-Jones, *The Bonus of Laughter*, Hamish Hamilton, 1987

David Pryce-Jones, *Evelyn Waugh and his World*, Weidenfeld and Nicolson, 1973

—, *Cyril Connolly: Journal and Memoir*, Collins, 1983

Peter Quennell, *The Wanton Chase: An Autobiography from 1939*, Collins, 1980

Nicholas Rankin, *Ian Fleming's Commandos: The Story of the Legendary 30 Assault Unit*, OUP, 2011

—, *Defending the Rock*, Faber, 2017

Nicholas Reynolds, *Need to Know: World War II and the Rise of American Intelligence*, Mariner Books, 2022

Lee Richards, *Whispers of War: Underground Propaganda Rumour-Mongering in the Second World War*, lulu.com, 2010

Mark Riebling, *Wedge: From Pearl Harbor to 9/11*, Touchstone, 2002

J. P. Riley, *From Pole to Pole*, Bluntisham Books, 1989

Charles Ritchie, *Undiplomatic Diaries 1937–1971*, Emblem Editions, 2008

Cecil Roberts, *Pamela's Spring Song*, Hodder and Stoughton, 1929

—, *Spears Against Us*, Hutchinson, 1932

—, *The Bright Twenties*, Hodder and Stoughton, 1970

Robert Robinson, *Skip All That*, Century, 1996

Bruce A. Rosenberg and Ann Harleman Stewart, *Ian Fleming*, Twayne, 1989

Alan Ross, *Coastwise Lights*, Harvill, 1988

David F. Rudgers, *Creating the Secret State: The Origins of the Central Intelligence Agency 1943–1947*, University Press of Kansas, 2000

Maud Russell, *A Constant Heart: The War Diaries of Maud Russell 1938–1945*, ed. Emily Russell, Dovecote, 2017

Ian Sanders and Lorn Clark, *A Radiophone in Every Home: William Stephenson and the General Radio Company Ltd 1922–1928*, Loddon Valley Press, 2011

'Sapper', *Bulldog Drummond*, intro. Richard Usborne, Everyman, 1983

Robert Sellers, *The Battle for Bond*, Tomahawk Press, 2007

Mark Simmons, *Ian Fleming's War: The Inspiration for 007*, History Press, 2007

—, *Ian Fleming and Operation Golden Eye: Keeping Spain out of World War II*, Casemate Publishers, 2018

Adam Sisman, *John le Carré*, Bloomsbury, 2015

Barbara Skelton, *Tears Before Bedtime*, Faber, 2009

Bill Smith, *Robert Fleming 1945–1933*, Whittinghame House, 2000

Bradley Smith, *The Shadow Warriors: OSS and the Origins of the CIA*, Deutsch, 1983

Michael Smith, *Six: The Real James Bonds, 1909–1939*, Biteback, 2010

—, *The Secrets of Station X: How Bletchley Park Helped Win the War*, Biteback, 2011

—, *The Real Special Relationship: The True Story of How the British and US Secret Services Work Together*, Simon and Schuster, 2022

Peter Smithers, *Adventures of a Gardener*, Harvill, 1995

O. F. Snelling, *007 James Bond*, Panther, 1965

David Stafford, *Camp X*, Lester and Orpen Dennys, 1986

—, *The Silent Game: The Real World of Imaginary Spies*, University of Georgia, 1991

—, *American–British–Canadian Intelligence Relations, 1939–2000*, Routledge, 2000

—, *Roosevelt and Churchill: Men of Secrets*, Overlook Press, 2000

Humphrey Stone, *Reynolds Stone: A Memoir*, Dovecote Press, 2019

John Sutherland, *Curiosities of Literature*, Skyhorse Publishing, 2009

Will Swift, *The Kennedys Amidst the Gathering Storm: A Thousand Days in London, 1938–1940*, JR Books, 2008

A. J. P. Taylor, *A Personal History*, Atheneum, 1983

S. J. Taylor, *The Reluctant Press Lord: Esmond Rothermere and the Daily Mail*, Weidenfeld and Nicolson, 1998

Basil Thomson, *The Milliner's Hat Mystery*, Eldon Press, 1937

Jeremy Treglown, *Roald Dahl*, Farrar Straus and Giroux, 1994

Thomas F. Troy, *Donovan and the CIA: A History of the Establishment of the Central Intelligence Agency*, University Publications of America, 1981

—, *Wild Bill and Intrepid: Donovan, Stephenson and the Origin of CIA*, Yale, 1996

Alex von Tunzelmann, *Red Heat: Conspiracy, Murder, and the Cold War in the Caribbean*, Simon and Schuster, 2011

—, *Blood and Sand: Suez, Hungary and the Crisis that Shook the World*, Simon and Schuster, 2016

Richard Usborne, *Clubland Heroes*, Barrie and Jenkins, 1974

Hugo Vickers, *Cecil Beaton: The Authorized Biography*, Weidenfeld and Nicolson, 1985

Douglas Waller, *Wild Bill Donovan: The Spymaster Who Created the OSS and Modern American Espionage*, Free Press, 2011

Marina Warner, *Inventory of a Life Mislaid*, Collins, 2021

Alec Waugh, *Hot Countries*, Literary Guild, 1930

—, *The Sunlit Caribbean*, Camelot Press, 1948

—, *The Sugar Islands*, Cassell, 1958

Evelyn Waugh, *The Diaries of Evelyn Waugh*, ed. Michael Davie, Weidenfeld and Nicolson, 1976

—, *The Letters of Evelyn Waugh*, ed. Mark Amory, Weidenfeld and Nicolson, 1980

Evelyn Waugh and Diana Cooper, *Mr Wu and Mrs Stitch: The Letters of Evelyn Waugh and Diana Cooper*, ed. Artemis Cooper, Hodder and Stoughton, 1991

William Weaver, *Lives of Lucian Freud: Youth*, Bloomsbury, 2019

Tim Weiner, *Legacy of Ashes: The History of the CIA*, Allen Lane, 2007

Linton Wells, *Blood on the Moon*, Hamish Hamilton, 1937

Mary Wesley and Eric Siepmann, *Darling Pol, Letters of Mary Wesley and Eric Siepmann*, ed. Patrick Marnham, Harvill Secker, 2017

Loelia, Duchess of Westminster, *Grace and Favour*, Weidenfeld and Nicolson, 1961

—, *Cocktails and Laughter*, Hamish Hamilton, 1983

Philip Maynard Williams, *Hugh Gaitskell*, Cape, 1979

Tom Williams, *Raymond Chandler: A Life*, Quarto, 2012

Simon Winder, *The Man Who Saved Britain*, Picador, 2011

P. G. Wodehouse, *The Mating Season*, Herbert Jenkins, 1949

Jim Wright, *The Real James Bond: A True Story of Identity Theft, Avian Intrigue and Ian Fleming*, Schiffer, 2020

Henry A. Ziegler, *Ian Fleming: The Spy Who Came in with the Gold*, Popular Library, 1965

SELECTED ARTICLES AND INTERVIEWS

London Magazine, Dec. 1959, Ian Fleming, 'Notes on Raymond Chandler'

The Book Collector, 1959, Percy Muir, 'Reminiscences'

BBC, *Tuesday Talk*, 13/12/1960

Ian Fleming and William Plomer, 1962, 'The Writer Speaks', Durham University Archives; New American Library

CBS, *Eyewitness*, 9/3/1962

BBC, *Desert Island Discs*, 5/8/1963

CBC, 'Explorations', 17/8/1964

Redbook, June 1964, Ian Fleming and CIA chief Allen Dulles discuss spycraft, <https://www.mi6community.com/discussion/15014/ian-fleming-and-cia-chief-allen-dulles-discuss-spycraft>

Harper's Bazaar, 'The World of Bond and Maigret', Ian Fleming dialogue with Georges Simenon, Nov. 1964

Playboy, Ian Fleming interview with Ken Purdy, Dec. 1964

Oral History Interview, Allen Dulles, 5/12/1964, John F. Kennedy Presidential Library

Encounter, Jan. 1965, William Plomer's eulogy to Fleming: <https://bondfanevents.com/death-leaves-an-echo-plomers-memorial-service/>

The Book Collector, 1965, Percy Muir, 'Ian Fleming: A Personal Memoir'

Ladies' Home Journal, 'How James Bond Destroyed My Husband', Oct. 1966

Ann Fleming television interview with Pierre Berton, 1966, <https://www.ajb007.co.uk/discussion/47749/widow-to-a-legend-ann-fleming-speaks>

Global War Studies, 2015, David Kuhnen, 'Seizing German Naval Intelligence from the Archives of 1870–1975',

The Book Collector, 2017, 'Ian Fleming and Book Collecting',

Contemporary British History, Dec. 2018, Christopher Moran and Trevor McCrisken, 'The Secret Life of Ian Fleming: Spies, Lies and Social Ties'

Cryptologia, 2020, David Kenyon and Frode Weierud, 'Enigma G: The Counter Enigma'

ACKNOWLEDGEMENTS

This book owes a considerable debt to Ian Fleming's previous biographers, foremost among them John Pearson. By a strange set of coincidences, before he joined Fleming as his 'leg man' on Atticus, Pearson had shared a desk at the *Times Educational Supplement* with my father, who himself went on afterwards to perform a role more or less identical for Fleming's successor as Foreign Manager, Frank Giles, when he was Giles's assistant in Paris during the Algiers uprising.

Writers are superstitious. After I brought the two former colleagues together for lunch sixty-six years later, Pearson not only gave me encouragement to enter his biographical domain ('there really are quite a lot of mysteries still unsolved,' he wrote afterwards, 'and I'll do my best to help'), he also handed me a gift: his 'Fleming file'. That, and Pearson's notes from his original interviews (published in 2022 by the Queen Anne Press) have proved invaluable.

Ann Fleming's first choice had been James Pope-Hennessy, until Noël Coward stepped in – 'she will twist Pope H around her little finger' – and strongly advised him not to do it. Pearson's *Life of Ian Fleming* was designed to staunch further unauthorised biographies. Already out of the blocks in 1965 had been Henry Ziegler's *Ian Fleming: The Spy Who Came in with the Gold*, followed in April 1966 by *Ian Fleming: The Man With the Golden Pen*, by Richard Gant (aka Leslie Thomas, author of *The Virgin Soldiers*).

Written in a year ('I did it very quickly') and published in October 1966, Pearson's biography still has the strengths of readability and insider knowledge. Yet despite being authorised by Fleming's widow, family sensitivities prevented Pearson from including a lot of personal information ('she objected to quite a bit and asked me to remove it'); and little of Fleming's work in Naval Intelligence was known at the time. It took another three decades before Andrew Lycett filled in the gaps in his *Ian Fleming* (1995). It goes without saying that I have benefited from his exhaustive research, as must anyone wishing to retrace Fleming's steps, most recently, Oliver Buckton in his 2021 biography, *The World is Not Enough*.

There are other excellent, if partial accounts. Raymond Benson's *The James Bond Bedside Companion* (1984) concentrates on 'the world of 007'. Nicholas Rankin's *Ian Fleming's Commandos* (2011) provides a definitive history of the Intelligence-gathering unit that Fleming set up when at the Admiralty. Matthew Parker's *Goldeneye* (2014) achieves a comparable service for Fleming's post-war life in Jamaica. Further recent books include Robert Harling's memoir *Ian Fleming* (2015), Fergus Fleming's unusually revealing selection of Fleming's post-1952 letters, *The Man with the Golden Typewriter* (2015), and Jon Gilbert's encyclopaedic *Ian Fleming: A Bibliography* (2017). A first-rate overview commissioned to accompany a major exhibition of Fleming at the Imperial War Museum in 2008 – the IWM's most successful temporary exhibition ever – remains Ben Macintyre's *For Your Eyes Only* (2008).

Although this biography was authorised by the Fleming Estate, it was on condition that I be allowed to write what I found: the smallest suspicion that 'authorised' might also mean 'controlled' would not stand to benefit Fleming, his Estate, my publishers or me. That said, the family's support has been invaluable, facilitating access to the right people and to essential archives. For their support, I am grateful in particular to Peter Fleming's daughters, Kate and Lucy; to Richard Fleming's children, James, Fergus, Mary, Adam and Sandra; and to Michael Fleming's daughter Gilly. Nor could this book have been written without the unstinting assistance and generosity of Fleming's stepdaughter, Fionn Morgan, who, having grown up with him, is one of few who can recount lived memories.

A biography is the work of countless others in addition to the name on the cover. I am grateful to the following for reading early drafts and for their comments: John Cork, Peter Washington, David Robson, Michael Shelden, Murray Bail, Andrew Boyd, David Stafford, Nicholas Rankin, Michael Smith, Andrew Robinson, Michael Meredith, Tim Bowden, Tom Williams and Gillian Johnson. I cannot ask for a more supportive editor than Liz Foley or two more polymathic and painstaking copy-editors than Henry Howard in the UK and Roger Labrie in the US. I would also like to pay tribute to Nicholas Rankin for allowing me access to his papers, plus the loan of a box of rare Fleming-related books. He is confirmation of my experience that the most generous writers are also often the best. In the same spirit, Charles de Mestral, the son of Fleming's Swiss fiancée, loaned me the 1931 studio photograph that Fleming had given to Monique and which she treasured until the end of her life. Poker-faced, he has stared at me across my desk for four years, a man I now know well enough to know that there are cards still left to be played.

In Britain, for access to and permission to quote from the Fleming Archives, the James Bond Transcripts and the works of Ian and Peter Fleming, I am grateful to the Fleming Estate.

Extracts from the James Bond novels and *The Diamond Smugglers* reproduced with permission of Ian Fleming Publications Ltd, London © Ian Fleming Publications Ltd, www.ianfleming.com.

For access to and permission to quote from Ann Fleming's papers, I am grateful to Fionn Morgan.

For access to and permission to quote from his papers, I am grateful to Fergus Fleming.

For access to and permission to quote from her papers, I am grateful to Mary Fleming.

For access to and permission to quote from Valentine Fleming's diary, I am grateful to Elizabeth Fleming.

For access to and permission to quote from John Pearson's papers, I am grateful to Mark Pearson.

For access to and permission to quote from Maud Russell's diaries, I am grateful to Emily Russell and the Maud Russell Estate.

For access to and permission to quote from Lady Loelia Lindsay's diaries, I am grateful to Caroline Ponsonby and to Diana Roberts at Stansted Park House Archives for her uncomplaining assistance.

For access to and permission to quote from Mary Clive's papers, I am grateful to Alice Boyd and Charlotte Mitchell.

For access to and permission to quote from Robert Harling's papers, I am grateful to Amanda Harling.

For access to and permission to quote from Hilary Bray's papers, I am grateful to Andrew Joy and Sarah Tillard.

For access to and permission to quote from Beryl Griffie-Williams's papers, I am grateful to Louise Carr-Ellison.

For access to and permission to quote from Alan Hillgarth's papers, I am grateful to Justin and Tristan Hillgarth.

For access to and permission to quote from Ned Pleydell-Bouverie's papers, I am grateful to Robin Pleydell-Bouverie.

For access to and permission to quote from Nancy Caccia's papers, I am grateful to Clarissa Pryce-Jones.

For access to and permission to quote from the papers of Clarissa Eden and Cecil Beaton, I am grateful to Hugo Vickers.

For access to and permission to quote from John Godfrey's papers, I am grateful to Margy Kinmonth and the Godfrey Estate.

For access to and permission to quote from the diaries of Alice and Harry Hemming, I am grateful to John and Henry Hemming.

For access to and permission to quote from Edith Morpurgo's papers, I am grateful to Peter Harrington and Helmut Morpurgo.

For access to and permission to quote from his diary, I am grateful to John Goodwin.

For access to and permission to quote from the Cyril Connolly papers, I am grateful to Deirdre and Cressida Connolly.

For access to and permission to quote from James Pope-Hennessy's papers, I am grateful to Tom Roberts.

For access to and permission to quote from Jack Whittingham's papers, I am grateful to Sylvan Mason.

For access to and permission to quote from the papers of Judy Montagu and Milton Gendel, I am grateful to Anna Mathias.

For access to and permission to quote from Muriel Wright's papers, I am grateful to Nigel Wright and Victoria D'Avanzo.

For access to and permission to quote from Alaric Jacob's diary, I am grateful to Jasper Jacob.

For access to and permission to quote from her unpublished memoir, I am grateful to Lucretia Stewart.

For access to and permission to quote from Douglas Stott's papers, I am grateful to John Stott.

For access to and permission to quote from their papers, I am grateful to the following: Raymond Benson, Mark Blackett-Ord, Angela Bray, Tom Cull, Christopher Curtis, Brad Frank, Paul and Ralf Furse, Sir Claude Hankes, Thomas Heneage, Brian Lett, Sandy Malcolm, David Roberts, Mark Simmons, Michael Smith and Alan Tong.

For access to and permission to use photographs from his father's album, I am grateful to Alexander Quennell.

For access to the Royal St George's Golf Club and its archives, I am grateful to Algy Cluff and Tim Checketts.

For access to and permission to quote from the William Plomer Collection, I am grateful to Mike Harkness and the Durham University Library Archives and Special Collections.

For access to and permission to quote from the Churchill papers at the Churchill Archives Centre at Cambridge, I am grateful once more to Churchill College and Allen Packwood, and to Sophie Bridges and Madelin Evans.

For access to and permission to quote from Ivar Bryce's original manuscript of *You Only Live Once* and for use of photographs, I am grateful to Ivar Mountbatten.

For access to and permission to quote from his interview with Blanche Blackwell, I am grateful to Matthew Parker.

For access to and permission to quote from his interviews with Sandy Glen, Robert Harling, Peter Smithers and Joan Bright, I am grateful to Peter Liddell, Anne Wickes and the Second World War Experience Centre, Leeds.

For access to and permission to quote from the Eton College Archives, I am grateful to Michael Meredith, Stephie Coane, Georgina Robinson and Eleanor Hoare.

For access to and permission to quote from the Reuters News Archives, I am grateful to David Cutler, Rory Carruthers, and Reuters News Agency.

For permission to quote from the Beaverbook papers, I am grateful to Alexandra Fisher and the Parliamentary Archives.

For permission to quote from the Bletchley Park Collection, I am grateful to David Kenyon and Karen Lewis.

For permission to quote from the Sandhurst Collection, I am grateful to Anthony Morton.

For access to and permission to quote from Norman Denning's account of the Trafalgar Square Christmas Tree, I am grateful to Gareth Bellis and the National Maritime Museum, Greenwich.

In America, for access to and permission to quote from the Leonard Russell Collection, the John Pearson Collection and the William Plomer Collection, I am grateful to Joel Silver and the Lilly Library, University of Bloomington, Indiana.

For access to and permission to quote from his Bondiana Collection, I am grateful to Michael L. VanBlaricum and Pamela C. VanBlaricum and the University of Illinois at Urbana-Champaign.

For access to his transcripts and permission to quote from his taped interview with Nuala Pell and Blanche Blackwell, and for his insights and unstinting support, I am grateful to John Cork, who yields to no one as an authority on Fleming and his work.

For access to and permission to quote from the Ernie Cuneo papers, I am grateful to Jonathan Cuneo and the Franklin D. Roosevelt Presidential Library.

For access to and permission to quote from Stephen Potter's 'Bondmanship', I am grateful to Elizabeth L. Garver and the Harry Ransom Centre, University of Austin, Texas.

For permission to quote from the Kennedy papers, I am grateful to Abigail Malangone and the John F. Kennedy Presidential Library.

For access to and permission to quote from Mary Bond's diary, I am grateful to Jim Wright, Caitlin Goodman, and The Free Library of Philadelphia.

For access to and permission to quote from his taped interview with Robert Fenn, I am grateful to Steve Rubin.

In Canada, for access to and permission to quote from William Stephenson's papers, I am grateful to Elizabeth Seitz and the Archives and Special Collections, University of Regina.

In Australia, for access to and permission to quote from his interview with Richard Hughes, I am grateful to Tim Bowden.

For their hospitality and contributions, I would like to thank John Hatt, Nicholas Rankin, Lydia and Simon Lebus (in Cambridge), Michael Shelden (in Bloomington), Denny Lane (in Washington), Chris Blackwell and Butch Stewart (in Jamaica), Algy Cluff (in St Margaret's Bay), David Hands (in Morocco) and Peter and Didi Forster (in Kitzbühel). I would also like to thank Peter Forster for acting as my German translator, Stephen Ferguson for interrupting his legal duties to provide me with a four-year stream of Bond-themed media alerts, and my sons Max (Victor Ludorum when in the same house as Ian Fleming) and Ben (a second son like him) for their numerous welcome distractions and not only on the river bank. Once again, to their mother, my precious and beautiful wife Gillian, I owe my deepest thanks.

I would like to express my gratitude to the following: Clare Alexander, Victoria D'Avanzo, Alexis Albion, Louise Allison, Mark Amory, Mark Andrews (for tending to my eyesight), Elizabeth Archibald, Tommy Arran, Richard Astley, Michael Attenborough, Andrew Bailey, Christopher Balfour, Vivian Baring, Nicolas Barker, Richard Beal, Antony Beevor, Nigel Beevor, Gill Bennett, Raymond Benson, Mark Blackett-Ord, Chris Blackwell, Henry Blofeld, John Blofeld, Leslie Bonham-Carter, Alice Boyd, William Boyd, Tim Bowden, Angela Bray, Perina Braybrooke, Barbara Broccoli, Michael Brown, Amanda Brudenell, Janet Bruce, Mark Burgess, Justin Byam-Shaw, John Campbell, Lou Campbell, Louise Carr-Ellison, Cathryn Cawdor, Tim Checketts, Sue Clarke, Algy Cluff, Adam Clutterbuck, Stephanie Coane, David Coke, Cressida Connolly, Deirdre Connolly, Susan Cooper Cronyn, Ursula Corcoran, John Cork, David Cornwell, Spencer Cox-Freeman, Caroline Cranbook, Mary Crassweller, Harriet Crawley, Tom Cull, Jonathan Cuneo, Judith Curthoys, Christopher Curtis, Penelope Cuthbertson, Hunter Davies, Warren Davies, Richard Dearlove, Len Deighton, Michael Denison-Pender, Jack Deverell, Jasper Dick, Diana and Mark Dixon, Tamara Dorrien-Smith, Jane Duffy, Jeremy Duns, Charles Elliott, Julian Evans, Matthew Farrer, Ruth Fitzgibbons, Elizabeth Fleming, Mark Fleming, Robin and Vicky Fleming, Rachel Fletcher, Liz Foley, Freddie Fox, Eric Franck, Brad Frank, Antonia Fraser, Frederica Freer, Anders

Frejdh, Helen Fry, Nicky Gage, Elizabeth Garver, Bamber Gascoigne, Patrick Gifford, Jon Gilbert, Jamie Goldsmith, Michael Goodman, John Goodwin, Richard Greene, Francis Grey, Geirr Haarr, Graeme Hall, Nigel Hamilton, Sir Claude Hankes, Henry Hardy, Amanda Harling, Duff Hart-Davis, Selina Hastings, David Healey, Peter Healey, Simon Heffer, Henry Hemming, John Hemming, Thomas Heneage, Alan Henderson, Alexandra Henderson, Frank Herrmann, Seymour Hersh, Carol Hicks, Justin Hillgarth, Tristan Hillgarth, Pam Hirsch, Christopher Horne, Adrian House, Oliver House, Hugi Hreiðarsson, Charles Hue Williams, Fay Hughes, Larry Hughes, Anthony Hunter, Jaspar Jacob, Kenneth Jacob, Antony Jarvis, Philippa Jellicoe, Christian Jennings, Dan Johnson, Jon Johnson (for heart repair), Susanna Johnston, Andrew Joy, Alan Judd, Jerry Juroe, Barbara Kaufman, Christopher Kemp, David Kenyon, Randal Keynes, Mary Killen, Margy Kinmonth, Inga Kohn, David Kohnen, David Koppel, Denny and Naoko Lane, Josephine Lane, Murray Lawrence, Alexander Lebedev, Pauline Lee, Brian Lett, Karen Lewis, Lesley Lewis, Jean-Noël Liaut, Peter Liddle, Magnus Linklater, Angus Lloyd, Neill Lochery, Fredrik Logevall, Mikhail Lubimov, Bill Macdonald, David MacFadyen, Jonathan Macfarland, Ben Macintyre, Charles Maclean, James Magrane, Johann von Mallinckrodt, Sophie Mallinckrodt, Philip Mansel, David Marris, Francis de Marneffe, Rachael Marsay, Bill Marshall, Tom Maschler, Sylvan Mason, Anna Mathias, Daisy McNally, Paddy McNally, Victoria Mele, Diana Melly, Michael Meredith, Eleanor Michell, Janet Milford Haven, Peter Minshall, Charlotte Mitchell, Christopher Moran, Helmut Morpurgo, Sara Morrison, Anthony Morton, Anna Mosley, Harry Mount, Ivar Mountbatten, Lucy Neville-Rolfe, Gilly Newbery, Barry Newton, Monty Norman, Jacques Oberson, Columbus and Andrea O'Donnell, Alan Ogden, Manoli Olympitis, Raymond O'Neill, Heinrich Ortenburg, Thomas Pakenham, Matthew Parker, Mark Pearson, Dallas Pell, Jemima Pitman, Robin and Flickie Pleydell-Bouverie, Tim Pleydell-Bouverie, Lili Pohlman, Caroline Ponsonby, Clarissa and David Pryce-Jones, Alexander Quennell, David Ralli, Jonathan Ray, Karen Recht, Hugo Rittson-Thomas, David Roberts, Tom Roberts, Andrew Robson, Nick Rodger, Esmond Rothermere, Kevin Ruane, Steve Rubin, Ian Sayer, Cornelius Schregle, Richard Schuster, Chris Seidler, Mary Seymour, Hume Shawcross, Joel Silver, Mark Simmons, Richard Skaife, Anna

Slafer, Chris Smart, Bill Smith, Michael Smith, Amelia Smithers, Michael St John-McAlister, Tom Stacey, Irvin and Mary Jane Stefansson, Kristin Stefansson, Lucretia Stewart, Olivia Stewart, Humphrey Stone, Frances and Julia Stonor, John and Alison Stott, James Stourton, Margaret Ann Stuart, John Suckling, David Sulzberger, James Taylor, Jonathan Taylor, Sebastian Taylor, Christina Thistlethwayte, Lesley Thorne, Adam Thorpe, Sarah Tillard, Sibilla Tomacelli, Alan Tong, Frieda Toth, Una Trueblood, Corinne Turner, Mike VanBlaricum, Hugo Vickers, Jim Waddell, Sally (Marris) Wade-Gery, Peter Waelty, Simon Ward, Marina Warner, Christine Waterman, James Waugh, Septimus Waugh, Clara Weatherall, Marina Weir, Mark Whitcombe-Power, Luke Wilkinson (for saving my computer), Hugo Williams, Tom Williams, Skip Willman, Michael G. Wilson, Simon Winder, Susan Woolliams, Jim Wright and Nigel Wright.

SOURCE NOTES

PUBLIC ARCHIVES

Beinecke Rare Book and Manuscript Library; Churchill College, Cambridge, Churchill Archives Centre; Deutsche Nationalbibliothek – German National Library; Durham University, Archives and Special Collections (William Plomer papers); Eton College Archives; Franklin D. Roosevelt Presidential Library (Ernie Cuneo papers); Free Library of Philadelphia (Mary Bond papers); Harry Ransom Center, University of Austin, Texas; Imperial War Museum; John F. Kennedy Presidential Library; League of Nations Archives, Geneva; Lilly Library, University of Bloomington, Indiana (John Pearson Collection; Leonard Russell Collection; William Plomer Collection; Ian Fleming MSS); McMaster University, Ontario (Cookridge papers); Michael L. and Pamela C. VanBlaricum Ian Fleming and Bondiana Collection, University of Illinois at Urbana-Champaign (VanBlaricum Collection); National Archives, Kew; The National Archives and Records Administration (NARA); National Maritime Museum, Greenwich; Parliamentary Archive (Beaverbrook papers); Reuters News Agency, News Archives; Royal St George's Archives, Sandwich; The Sandhurst Collection; Second World War Experience Centre, Leeds (SWWEC); Special Collections, University of Reading (Peter Fleming Collection); University of Iowa, Special Collections and University Archives; University of Regina Archives and Special Collections (Willam Stephenson papers)

PRIVATE COLLECTIONS

Ian Fleming Archives (IFA); Raymond Benson papers; Mark Blackett-Ord papers; Tim Bowden papers; Angela Bray papers; Hilary Bray papers; Ivar Bryce papers; Gay Carr-Ellison papers; Mary (Pakenham) Clive papers; Cressida Connolly papers; John Cork papers; Tom Cull papers; Victoria D'Avanzo papers; Fergus Fleming papers; James Fleming papers; Mary Fleming papers; Valentine Fleming papers; Helen Fry papers; Paul Furse papers; John Godfrey papers; John Goodwin papers; Denis Hamilton papers; Sir Claude Hankes papers; Robert

Harling papers; Alice and Henry Hemming papers; Thomas Heneage papers; Alan Hillgarth papers; Alaric Jacob papers; Lady Loelia Lindsay papers; Sandy Malcolm papers; Sylvan (Whittingham) Mason papers; Judy Montagu papers; Fionn Morgan papers; Edith Morpurgo papers; Robert Murphy papers; Matthew Parker papers; John Pearson papers; Robin Pleydell-Bouverie papers; Caroline Ponsonby papers; James Pope-Hennessy papers; David Roberts papers; Steve Rubin papers; Maud Russell papers; Clarissa Pryce-Jones papers; Mark Simmons papers; Michael Smith papers; Lucretia Stewart papers; Douglas Stott papers; Alan Tong papers; Hugo Vickers papers; Nigel Wright papers

PRINCIPAL TEXTS AND ABBREVIATIONS

Mark Amory (ed.), *The Letters of Ann Fleming*, 1985; Raymond Benson, *The James Bond Bedside Companion*, intro. Ernie Cuneo, 1984; Ivar Bryce, *You Only Live Once*, 1975; Fergus Fleming (ed.), *The Man with the Golden Typewriter: Ian Fleming's James Bond Letters*, Bloomsbury, 2015 (*TMWTGT*); —, *Talk of the Devil, Selected Journalism of Ian Fleming*, Queen Anne Press, 2008 (*TOTD*); Ian Fleming, *Live and Let Die*, Cape, 1954 (*LALD*); —, *Diamonds are Forever*, Cape, 1956 (*DAF*); —, *From Russia, with Love*, Cape, 1957 (*FRWL*); —, *For Your Eyes Only*, Cape, 1960 (*FYEO*); —, *The Spy Who Loved Me*, Cape, 1960 (*TSWLM*); —, *On Her Majesty's Secret Service*, Cape, 1963 (*OHMSS*); —, *Thrilling Cities*, Cape, 1963; —, *You Only Live Twice*, Cape, 1964 (*YOLT*); —, *Chitty-Chitty-Bang-Bang: The Magical Car*, Cape, 1964 (*C-C-B-B*); —, *The Man with the Golden Gun*, Cape, 1965 (*TMWTGG*); Robert Harling, *Ian Fleming: A Personal Memoir*, 2015; George Lyttelton and Rupert Hart-Davis, *The Lyttelton Hart-Davis Letters*, 1978–86 (*LH-D Letters*); Andrew Lycett, *Ian Fleming*, 1995; Matthew Parker, *Goldeneye, Where Bond was Born: Ian Fleming's Jamaica*, 2015; John Pearson, *The Life of Ian Fleming*, 1966; —, *Ian Fleming: The Notes*, 2022 ('The Notes'); Nicholas Rankin, *Ian Fleming's Commandos: The Story of the Legendary 30 Assault Unit*, 2011; Emily Russell (ed.), *A Constant Heart: The War Diaries of Maud Russell 1938–1945*, 2017; The James Bond Transcripts, Ian Fleming Estate

NOTES

Conversion of currency to present-day values was done using <https://iamkate.com/data/uk-inflation/>. Information was correct as of April 2023.

EPIGRAPH
My name's Bond FYEO, 159

INTRODUCTION
Good evening Opening ceremony London Olympics, 27/7/2012; **Mr Fleming . . . Martini** John Pearson, *Ian Fleming: The Notes*, 266; **I was only** Gilly Newbery to NS, 14/7/2019; **sex, books and** Richard Greene, *Russian Roulette: The Life and Times of Graham Greene*, lxix; **moody, harsh** Cuneo papers, Franklin D. Roosevelt Presidential Library; **Darling, I think** James Bond Transcripts, Ian Fleming Archives (IFA); **flinging a squid** Peter Quennell, *The Wanton Chase*, 152; **As I looked** *The Notes*, 326; **brought colour** Robert Harling, *Sunday Times*, 16/8/1964; **I can see** Sara Morrison to NS, 9/1/2020; **He was rather** Raymond O'Neill to NS, 8/11/2019; **fateful** Robert Harling, *Ian Fleming* 355; **a high forehead** *TMWTGT*, 75; **The moulding** *The Notes*, 338; **Ian was the best . . . legs** Mary (Pakenham) Clive papers; **with rather large calves** EC interview with Raymond Benson, Benson papers; **Because of the image** Fionn Morgan to NS; **Ian moved as** Mary (Pakenham) Clive papers; **magnetic, electrically** *You Only Live Once* MS, Bryce papers; **Half of his** *The Notes*, 216; **All the things** ibid., 123; **the hilarious sessions** CB to Benson, 10/5/1982, Benson papers; **Mr Fleming was** Beryl Griffie-Williams to W. H. T. Fisher, n.d., IFA; **doom-fraught eyes** *TMWTGT*, 356; **an aged Dracula** IF to Mrs Coucill, 26/2/1963, IFA; **It was his innocence** CB to Benson, 10/5/1982, Benson papers; **After being with I[an]** *Constant Heart*, 277; **Sometimes I think** 17/10/1971, Maud Russell papers; **really he was** *The Notes*, 327; **A ladies' man** PS to Claude Hankes, 'Ian Fleming: Some Off the Cuff Reflections', 17/12/2001, Hankes papers; **The inimitable** *Sunday Times*, 16/8/1964; **The most generous** ibid.; **If he said** Matthew Farrer to NS, 23/4/2021; **Whatever you hear** Adam Fleming to NS, 3/12/2019; **to do good** RH interview, 1975, Bowden papers; **We were talking** John

Campbell to NS, 28/7/2022; **Like him?** Len Deighton to NS, 22/11/2019; **I like Peter** *The Notes*, 210; **It seems to me** Max Hastings to NS, 29/8/2022; **James Bond is** John Higgs, *Love and Let Die: Bond, the Beatles and the British Psyche*, 336; **You can't open** Tom Maschler to NS, 13/6/2019; **this Botoxed Bond** *Guardian*, 26/3/2022; **Let's face it** Dwight Macaulay, 'License to Intrigue', *Winnipeg Free Press*, 14/11/2020; **a product of his** Paul Gallico intro., *Gilt-Edged Bonds*, xv; **one of the most** *You Only Live Twice*, 79; **Almost any form** Peter Fleming, *The Sixth Column*, 28; **If you want** Richard Usborne, *Clubland Heroes*, 167; **There are parasite** Len Deighton to NS, 22/11/2019; **overtaken . . . disappeared** David O'Keefe, *One Day in August*, 30; **It took a Fleming** *Life*, 28/6/1964; **instinct with a** Philip Larkin, *Required Writing*, 270; **I spoke severely** IF to Cuneo, 3/12/1953, Cuneo papers; **all belly and** *The Notes*, 255; **I am already** IF to Cuneo, 23/5/1957, Cuneo papers; **the books of** EC notes on IF, March 1983, Cuneo papers; **Typical of** ibid.; **not a man** William Plomer, *Address Given at the Memorial service for Ian Fleming*; **a very private** Lycett, 325; **the whole gamut** Ann to IF, 1948, AF4a, Morgan papers; **highly heritable** <https://www.ncbi.nlm.nih.gov/pmc/articles/PMC3637882/>; **There was a** *The Notes*, 275; **interminable ruminations** CB to Benson, 21/8/1982, Benson papers; **Ian has** *more* 27/5/1952, Mary (Pakenham) Clive papers; **you never . . . the end** *The Notes*, 315–7; **He was good** *The Notes*, 167; **You never heard** ibid., 33; **Ian adored money** ibid., 238; **Money really wasn't** ibid., 149; **He was most** *Ladies' Home Journal*, Oct. 1966; **A real snob** Matthew Parker, *Goldeneye*, 274; **I never saw him** *The Notes*, 110; **When the Commander** ibid., 105; **He was completely** ibid., 194; **Nine out of ten** ibid., 313; **I always saw Bond** Raymond O'Neill to NS; **Ian hadn't the** 'Personal Assistant to DNI', 8/3/1965, Godfrey papers; **There's never** *The Notes*, 214; **'Ann,' he used** ibid., 78; **the least violent** ibid., 112; **A mystery remains** Mike VanBlaricum to NS, 24/3/2021; **Ian's basic complication** *The Notes*, 75; **how very little** J. H. Godfrey to E. L. Merrett etc., 11/3/1965, Godfrey papers; **I've never known** Pearson papers; **The mask reveals** EC to Bryce, 28/9/1983, Bryce papers; **I sometimes think** Hilary Bray, *Toy Engine*, 48; **central inaccessible** JHG to John Pearson, 22/4/1965, Godfrey papers

PART ONE

PROLOGUE
Will you be Goldfinger, 31; **He didn't say** Mary Fleming to NS, 7/11/2019; **I'm sorry to** Lycett, 443; **the many . . . value** W. H. T. Fisher to Hilary Bray 17/8/1964, Bray papers; **A terribly nice** 12/8/1964, Valentine Fleming papers; **not one of** Ann to Hugo Charteris, 25/6/1965, Morgan papers; **looking rather like . . . Ann was**

Elizabeth Fleming to NS, 2/12/2019; **Mrs Fleming with** *Wiltshire Gazette and Herald*, 20/8/1964; **A sad Service . . . cup of tea**, Valentine Fleming diary; **He'd never** Gilly Newbery to NS, 14/8/2019; **You read a lot** Susan Woolliams to NS, 13/1/2020

I 'LAIRN TO SAY NO, LADDIE'

Very strange people The Notes, 213; **Learned Engraver** Peter Fleming, *One's Company*, 151; **They become foolishly** Ian Fleming, 'State of Excitement', 86, IFA; **upon which were** John Fleming, *Looking Backwards for Seventy Years*, 79; **Alas, I am very** IF to Mary Murray, 30/9/1957, IFA; **I am no relation** IF to Dr Alan Barnsley, 21/4/1954, IFA; **We're not Scots** *The Notes*, 120; **To see them** Alaric Jacob, *Scenes from a Bourgeois Life*, 133; **the Flemings were** *The Notes*, 160; **for consorting with** Mary (Pakenham) Clive papers; **My grandfather's upbringing** *The Notes*, 183; **Men are . . . back to Scotland** EC notes on IF, March 1983, Cuneo papers; **to revisit the** David Bruce, *Ambassador to Sixties London*, 165; **You can't go back** Lycett, 263; **Talking about Dundee** Donald McCormick, *Life of Ian Fleming*, 206; **coddled him with** Ivar Bryce, *You Only Live Once*, 111; **I am Presbyterian** *Constant Heart*, 279; **Ian is determined** AF to Hugo Charteris, 25/9/1954, Morgan papers; **That's where I come** *OHMSS*, 184; **By 1928, he was** Adam Fleming to NS, 3/12/2019; **One probably did** Robin Fleming to NS, 4/11/2019; **some incredible . . . twenty times** CH to NS, 1/12/2019; **I come from** Mary Fleming to NS, 7/11/2019; **Ian was much** James Fleming to NS, 4/12/2019; **Forgetful of feeling** J. Arnold Fleming, *Flemish Influence in Britain*, vol. 2, 11; **I saw the** Gilly Newbery to NS, 14/7/2019; **The back of** Kate Grimond, *Celia Johnson*, 39; **If there is one** Bill Smith, *Robert Fleming*, 114; **at an average** Fleming, *Looking Backwards*, 15; **The emphasis . . . for you** JF to NS, 29/3/2020; **The real secret** JF to NS, 29/3/2020; **It was a wonder** JF to NS, 29/3/2020; **throughout his life** Bill Smith, 114; **the bestial drunkenness** Churchill, *Thoughts and Adventures*; **I always retain** Brian King, *Undiscovered Dundee*; **I had half** WSC to Clementine, 17/10/1909, in Queen's Hotel, Dundee; **seeing before me** Bill Smith, 14; **to make investments** RF to Jacob Schiff, 3/12/1918, James Fleming papers; **the scotch gift** *Looking Backwards*, 163; **he had not** Bill Smith, 49; **straight as a die** ibid., 114; **liking my train** IF to AF 1956, IF52a, Morgan papers; **I went in the** IF to AF 1954, IF3a, Morgan papers; **Fleming's theory** IF to AF 1948, IF5A, Morgan papers; **It is, I find** RF to J. G. Watson, 15/3/1893, James Fleming papers; **money made . . . believe it** Bill Smith, 67; **hereditary aversion** ibid., 2; **had one day** Fleming Family Newsletter, IFA; **He ran his** *Dr. No*, 6; **It gave Uncle Phil** Sandra Loder to NS, 7/11/2019; **In terms of day-to-day . . . a restaurant** former Flemings director to NS, 26/3/2023; **we're not mean** GN to NS, 14/7/2019; **unostentatious benevolence** Bill Smith, 115; **Only then I realised** Adam Fleming to NS; **how, after being** AV to

Zwart, 7/1/1966, Alan Tong papers; **Robert Fleming is . . . carry more weight** *New York Tribune* 23/2/1919; **often spoke with** *The Notes*, 171; **that most hazardous** Bill Smith, 63; **kind, very simple** Fergus Fleming, *Amaryllis Fleming*, 38; **my dear Robert . . . and won** Kate Fleming, 'Honeymoon Journals', 1881, Mary Fleming papers; **Generosity was not** Mary Fleming to NS; **an old rambling** 'Prince Curly or Stolen by Gipsies', Mary Fleming papers; **Scotland's Dick Whittington** at RF funeral service, St Michael's Cornhill; **a splendid building** *Honeymoon Journals*; **At great expense** *The Notes*, 304; **What a bloody awful** *Goldfinger*, 115; **rather like** Ziegler, 88; **chunk of rock** *Amaryllis Fleming*, 39; **She was a very** *The Notes*, 294; **You rich . . . a crofter** Adam Fleming to NS; **Much too young . . . quite spectacular** Peter Smithers, 2003, SWWEC, tape 1584; **On the bare back** 'Prince Curly or Stolen by Gipsies', Mary Fleming papers; **My father didn't talk** Robin Fleming to NS; **what a Sir Galahad** Mary (Pakenham) Clive, 'Two Jottings from a Notebook', Pearson Collection, Lilly; **We boys hardly** PF to WSC, April 1946, Churchill Archives Centre; **I have never been** Tom Pellatt to EF, 24/5/1917, IFA; **as if he was a sort of saint** *The Notes*, 162; **Robert came down** Fergus Fleming to NS, 5/3/2020; **one of the best** 7/11/1957, *LH-D Letters*, vol. 1 and 2, 384; **because he got . . . the war** *The Notes*, 181; **There was absolutely** Dorothy Fleming to Eve, May 1917, IFA; **the lurid bombshell** *Amaryllis Fleming*, 8

II EVE

Character would greatly From Russia, with Love, 62; **I've always** 'Book of Golden Words', IFA; **the book of golden** *Playboy*, Dec. 1964; **thoughts and comments** ibid.; **Never say 'no'** *C-C-B-B*; **you must never** PF to Celia, 14/3/1945, IFA; **You will understand** *The Notes*, 286; **Her expression was** 'My Life with the Flemings', Mary (Pakenham) Clive papers; **I am a good** EF to de László, n.d, IFA; **She gave me** Mary Fleming to NS, 7/11/2019; **He never met** IF to EF, 29/8/1950, Russell Collection, Lilly; **and married him** *The Notes*, 162; **Robert disapproved** ibid., 331; **half England** ibid., 160; **except in moments** P. G. Wodehouse, *The Mating Season*, 42; **a glorified jam** Hester Chapman, *Ever Thine*, 458; **Ian's dislike** *The Notes*, 162; **descended from** Bapsy Pavry telegram to IF 16/12/52, IFA; **learned their simple** John Hollingshead, *My Lifetime*, 54; **I think whatever** *The Notes*, 189; **the most capable** *The Sanitary Record*, 18/3/1898; **Why! You're virgo** John Sutherland, *Curiosities of Literature*, 66; **About five minutes** *Pall Mall Budget*, 22/4/1881; **so disreputable** 'My Life with the Flemings', Mary (Pakenham) Clive papers; **brought up . . . in living** *Times*, 22/7/1936; **because of . . . free spender** Christopher Lee, *Tall, Dark and Gruesome*, 40; **realised £1.15s** *Times*, 22/7/1936; **This is all** *Amaryllis Fleming*, 34; **we never met Ivor** Lee, 41; **to enable people** *Amaryllis Fleming*, 6; **A fortune once** Bill Smith, 67

III A STORMY CHILDHOOD

He was a complex RH to Clare Blanshard, 23/11/1964, Benson papers; **The four madmen** *Amaryllis Fleming*, 32; **no patter . . . bicycle** Stephen Potter, 'Bondsmanship', 1962, Harry Ransom Center, The University of Texas at Austin; **He said . . . childhood himself** 10/3/1942; 27/3/1942; *Constant Heart*, 153, 156; **the sense of deprivation** *The Notes*, 335; **He had everything** ibid., 344; **Now Master Ian** n.d., IFA; **He always made** *The Notes*, 186; **He always acted** ibid., 60; **Ian was a melancholic** *Ladies' Home Journal*, Oct. 1966; **My dear Baba** VF to IF, n.d., IFA; **a dotty red** Kenneth Clark, *Another Part of the Wood*, 89; **the tribal centre** Mary Fleming to NS; **for sporting holidays** *Amaryllis Fleming*, 8; **If you can** Bill Smith, 120–1; **Peter is flying** *LH-D Letters*, 20/9/1959, vol. 3 and 4., 310; **curiously muscle-bound . . . low** *Wanton Chase*, 153; **He used to** *The Notes*, 77; **Well, if it's all** ibid., 188; **Don't ask me** ibid., 291; **there are other** Sandra Loder to NS, 7/11/2019; **I don't like** IF to AF, IF90A, 1959, Morgan papers; **not greatly interested** *Thrilling Cities*, 195/6; **dangerous at both** *TC*, 196; **until you can** ibid.; **He never liked** *The Notes*, 181; **the empty hours . . . rain** 'State of Excitement', 106, IFA; **wet rhododendrons** Mary (Pakenham) Clive, Pearson Collection, Lilly; **dripping evergreens** *The Notes*, 74; **I spent some** Amory, 51; **Here we are** *Lyra Familiae*, 27; **For God's sake** *The Notes*, 227; **We were all wild** Sandra Loder to NS, 7/11/2019; **Her nephews and** Mary Fleming to NS; **To the exasperation** *Thrilling Cities*, 87; **absolutely free** Smith, 117; **a pathetic, dithery . . . shaking** *The Notes*, 304; *Essuyez*, **Robert!** *Lyra Familiae*, 19; **Kate, Ah'm naw** ibid., 12; **Rain was better** 'My Uncle Ian', *Book Collector*, Spring 2017; **We were absolutely** Mary Fleming to NS; **When Fleming meets** Kate Fleming to NS; **It wasn't recognised . . . Hotel** *The Notes*, 186; **We were going** 'The Diary of Mrs Valentine Fleming', Mary Fleming papers; **I once saw him** *The Notes*, 220; **Of course, we fought** ibid., 185

IV VAL

There is a tragedy 'Book of Golden Words', IFA; **The only areas** IF to AF, IF90A, 1959, Morgan papers; *Sunlight over* IFA; **the completely novel** *The Notes*, 321; **a most original** ibid., 186; **had to be torn** Chapman, 516; **Dear Mokie** IF to Val, n.d., IFA; **It is . . . unreverent** IF to Eve, n.d., IFA; **For some days** Pearson draft, *The Life of Ian Fleming*, Pearson Collection, Lilly; **Ian was basically** *The Notes*, 186; **Ian will be** TP to Robert Fleming 1/6/1917, IFA; **My Dear Jocky** Val to IF, n.d., IFA; **stupendous cataclysm** Pellatt, *Boys in the Making*, 271; **the casualty lists** *The Notes*, 324; **One dreads** TP to Robert Fleming 1/6/1917, IFA; **good swank lads** *Lyra Familiae*, 6; **It is indeed** RF to Jacob Schiff, 17/1/1918, IFA; **she had slapped** *The Notes*, 181; **a proper . . . seeing anyone** ibid., 183; **absolutely a non-politician** ibid., 181; **I believe if** HC Deb 13 March 1912, Hansard vol. 35 cc1185–227; **the lack of** HC Deb 01 November 1913, Hansard vol. 43 cc717–8W; **War was . . . seen them** 'Diary of

Mrs Valentine Fleming', 4/8/1914, IFA; **pulling out my** VF to EF, 7/10/15, IFA; **he wrote to me** EF to sons, 1933, IFA; **my sweet of sweets** VF to EF, n.d., IFA; **I hear women** *Diary of Mrs Valentine Fleming*, 14/11/1914, IFA; **this astounding conflict . . . *can't* do** VF to WSC, 10/11/1914, IFA; **A dish of scrambled** VF to EF, 30/4/1915, IFA; **they were quite** Bill Smith, 132; **You never saw . . . fat form** VF to EF, n.d., IFA; **Two of . . . the ball** W. G. S. to his father, NS papers; **I remember screaming** *The Notes*, 184; **I remember suggesting** PF to RF, May 1917, IFA; **he was hit** Franky Simons to Eve, May 1917, IFA; **It is almost** Arthur Villiers to Eve, 21/5/1917, IFA; **What held that** PF to RF, 22/5/1917, IFA; **as though . . . bellowing noise** Hart-Davis, *Peter Fleming*, 33; **How awful** *The Notes*, 324; **Poor fellow** Bill Smith, 133; **I cannot speak** ibid., 133; **I thought of him** ibid., 133; **It is in a ruined** WSC to Eve, 6/6/1917, IFA; **how upset** *The Notes*, 324; **In his four sons** WSC to Eve, 6/6/1917, IFA; **In my next** IF to PF, 1/8/1963, IFA

V DURNFORD

Don't *be downhearted* TP to EF, May 1917, IFA; **expressive grief . . . as I was** RF to EF, May 1917, IFA; **My wife is** TP to EF, May 1917, IFA; **Ian brought me** TP to EF, 17/6/1917; **The height holds** EF to her sons, winter 1933, IFA; **any sort of** *The Notes*, 303; **Auden and I** W. H. Auden and Christopher Isherwood, *Journey to a War*, 214; **At least he** R. Troughton to Tish Fleming, Oct. 1940, Gilly Newbery papers; **She will, of** Bill Smith, 134; **a bad will** Eve to her sons, winter 1933, IFA; **he was enormously** Adrian House to NS, 7/11/2019; **You're responsible** *The Notes*, 185; **He was a polished** Marina Warner, *Inventory of a Life Mislaid*; **part of the old** EC notes on IF, March 1983, Cuneo papers; **Let's go to** Bryce, *You Only Live Once*, 1; **The leaders were** ibid., 2; **There would be** *TOTD*, 292; **the painful grit** *OHMSS*, 2; **was as depressing** *Constant Heart*, 263; **the writing which** IF to BM, 6/6/1958 IFA; **the colour and** Laurence Irving, *The Precarious Crust*, 118; ***Dear Mr Pellatt*** *The Notes*, 323; **I was bullied** *TOTD*, 189; **I wouldn't say** *The Notes*, 186; **I had to write** *Thrilling Cities*, 254; **It was very** *The Notes*, 186; **Vespasian . . . gigantic pigeons** Irving, 121; **before which little** Peter Fleming, 'A Tent in Tibet,' *A Story to Tell*, 220; **a boy died** *The Notes*, 186; **My coff has** IF to EF, n.d., IFA; **Ian always chose** *The Notes*, 322; **an afternoon in** Chapman, 284; **registering pleasure** Peter Fleming, *Brazilian Adventure*, 41; **Kick, now** Irving, 132; **at the burial** Chapman, 516; **There's no bathing** ibid., 416; **Now the school** Irving, 196; **I have only** Chapman, 37; **Considerable prestige** Nicholas Elliott, *Never Judge a Man by His Umbrella*, 28; **I remember a rich** Chapman, 71; **Not one of Nell's** Irving, 121; **I am in an awfully** IF to EF, n.d., IFA; **a brilliantly . . . in life** Tom Pellatt, *Boys in the Making*, 226; **effortless assumption** Irving, *Great Interruption*, 67; **and there was** *The Notes*, 187; **It was difficult** ibid., 323; **My house is** IF to EF, n.d., IFA; **T.P.'s pi-jaw . . . good luck** Elliott,

28; **He had a passion** Mary (Pakenham) Clive archive; **the only woman** *The Notes*, 321; **his number Twenty-six** Chapman, 177; *A breathless kiss* IFA; **So you see** IF to Ann Rothermere, Jan. 1947, IF77A, Morgan papers; **I've only this** Chapman, 196; **to take the place** Humphrey Stone, *Reynolds Stone: A Memoir*, 20

VI ETON

English public schools TSWLM, 25; **first contact** IF to Leonard Russell, 14/5/1962, IFA; **You said the** Phyllis Bottome, *The Lifeline*, 41; **Ah yes, it even** *The Notes*, 230; **I was desperately** Robert Harling, *Ian Fleming: A Personal Memoir*, 225; **Oh, the colours** Jacob, 75; **At this moment** Amory, 294; **When the chips** intro., *James Bond Bedside Companion*, x; **Eton's strange faults** Bottome, *The Lifeline*, 42; **Lights out** Lycett, 362; **You can't grow** ibid., 298; **as deep and pervasive** Nicholas Coleridge, *Observer*, 29/9/2019; **the extent to . . . efficiency** Gladwyn Jebb, *The Memoirs of Lord Gladwyn*, 106; **an Old Boy** *Brazilian Adventure*, 17; **le sangfroid d'ancien** Peter Fleming, *News from Tartary*, 400; **We hoped devoutly** *Brazilian Adventure*, 107; **the only song . . . Mongolia** Peter Fleming, *One's Company*, 42; **the only Old** ibid., 52; **shaken about** Cyril Connolly, *Enemies of Promise*, 202; **The plopping of** ibid., 272; **I recognise** Arthur Gore, *Lord Arran Writes*, 47; **great brown** *Goldfinger*, 29; **One morning** Henry Blofeld to NS, 8/3/2020; **For at that** *The Notes*, 187; **Do draw** IF to EF, 9/3/1924, IFA; **The transfer** Elliott, 30; **a large, bald** Ludovic Kennedy, *On My Way to the Club*, 52–3; **I'm going to** *The Notes*, 109; **Ian hated** ibid., 228; **Ronnie considered** Phyllis Bottome, *Danger Signal*, 283; **Rather an inferior** 15/5/1957, *LH-D Letters*, vols 1 and 2, 300; **He had a thing** Andrew Robinson to NS, 5/6/2021; **sadist . . . his boyhood** Tim Card, *Eton Renewed*, 174; **unique pair . . . strong gesture** *Eton College Chronicle*, September 1933; **Slater would** *The Notes*, 245; **I am trying** IF to EF, 9/3/1924 **slightly flash** ibid., 188; **That hair oil** ibid., 342; **I did feel** ibid., 188; **Peter became the** ibid., 101; **He was** Mark Amory to NS, 5/6/2019; **Boys do not** *Enemies of Promise*, 228; **a great swell** Rupert Hart-Davis, *Arms of Time*, 136; **neat, black-haired** *The Notes*, 303; **even to his** Pearson, 23; **the great almighty** Earl of Lytton, *Antony*, 77; **the King of . . . too much** Hugo Charteris, *The Coat*, 25; **Bryce was his friend** *The Notes*, 129; **I decided that** Harling, 300; **a terribly good . . . a day** *The Notes*, 147; **the gooder Peter** ibid., 311; **I'm afraid I** IF, *Desert Island Discs*, 1963; **Mostly in Latin** YOLT, 109; **an ogre for** Jeremy Lewis, *Cyril Connolly: A Life*, 61; **for a black coffee** *The Notes*, 303; **I know I . . . nothing else** IF to EF, 9/3/1924, IFA; **walloped for** *The Notes*, 294; **Try and teach him** IF to AF, Feb. 1956, IF45; **It thrilled me** 21/2/1957, *LH-D Letters*, vols 1 and 2, 259; **an exceptionally . . . his years** Pearson Collection, Lilly; **I managed** IF to EF, 9/3/1924; **his shanks** Paul Gallico intro. *Gilt-Edged Bonds*, xii; **very sardonic man** <www.saxonlodge.net/getperson.php?personID=I0056andtree=Tatham>;

The achievement of *Eton College Chronicle*, 8/5/1924; **The strain over** Pearson papers; **The only man** Harling papers; **Ian was part** EC notes on IF, March 1983, Cuneo papers; **by bad luck** *The Notes*, 311; **Etonians fairly contently** Card, 170; **the Victor Ludorum** *The Notes*, 113; **being Victor Ludorum** ibid., 101; *Dear Ian won Lyra Familiae*, 19; **a feat unique** *Gilt-Edged Bonds*, xi; **we became** *You Only Live Once* MS, Bryce papers; **Do you think** IF to EF, 9/3/1924, IFA; **a shameless crib** IF to M. Howard, 28/3/1964, IFA; **absolutely ravishing** *Wyvern*, Eton College Archives; **a record sale** IF notebook, IFA; **both original . . . Philistines** Eton *Chronicle*, 25/6/1925; **couldn't tell** *Amaryllis Fleming*, 82; **reprehensible gossip** Michael Holroyd, *Augustus John*, vol. 2; **Oh, Addie** Adam Fleming to NS; **Mrs Val had** *The Notes*, 337; **She had no sense** ibid., 303; **It seems quite** *Amaryllis Fleming*, 34; **I remember** 13/1/1962, *LH-D Letters*, vol. 6, 151; **laughed for a** *Amaryllis Fleming*, 23; **Oh, she put** ibid., 117; **for being late . . . recovered** *Enemies of Promise*, 220, 252; **an autonomous . . . precision** *Times*, 25/10/1961; **I can't tell you** Earl of Lytton, 82; **after 1 hr 37 minutes** Eton Society records, 25/1/1926; **the most privileged** Lee, 57; **Having been in Pop** Jacob, 132; **7 successive . . . they deserved** Card, 179; **My dear boy** *Casino Royale*, 113; **The beatings were** *Enemies of Promise*, 197-8; **You nearly fainted** David Herbert, *Second Son*, 27; **the silken barbarity** Tom Hiney and Frank MacShane, *Raymond Chandler Papers*, 112; **came out in** Lewis, *Connolly*, 69; **part of the strange** *The Notes*, 164; **one day to** AW to EF, Russell Collection, Lilly; **Since m'tutor** IF to EF, n.d., IFA; **The Army Class** *The Notes*, 228; **the most terrible . . . headaches** ibid., 60; **several times** *The Notes*, 330; **towards the end** ibid., 185; **escapades . . . motor bike letters** Bryce papers; **His career at Eton** *YOLT*, 202; **a boy called** Charteris, 94; **I was bullied** *TOTD*, 189; **What the hell** *TSWLM*, 35; **after some trouble** Card, 179; **There is no Royalty** IF to Michael Howard, 12/10/1961, IFA; **sexuality (hetero-, homo-)** *Sunday Times*, 3/6/1962; **enormously sheltered** Bryce, 15; **absurdly innocent** Loelia Westminster, *Cocktails and Laughter*, 76; **in the end** Gore, 151; **not the sort** *Enemies of Promise*, 259; **occasionally intimated** Harling, 301; **I am afraid . . . Naughty Eric** Lewis, *Connolly*, 66; **My darling** IF, 14/3/1926, IFA; **It is entirely false** Cyril Alington to EF, 25/2/1927, IFA; **I've never come** Earl of Lytton, 84; **I didn't learn much** Jeremy Lewis, *David Astor*, 2016, 28; **His view of life** *The Notes*, 103; **in his best** Donald McCormick, *Life of Ian Fleming*, 75; **a mysterious affection** *Gilt-Edged Bonds*, xii; **secret initiation . . . adequately** Bottome, *The Lifeline*, 44; **No father** KF to NS, 22/3/2023

VII SANDHURST

He has the Pellatt to Sandhurst, n.d., Russell Collection, Lilly; **the despair of** Alan Pryce-Jones, *Bonus of Laughter*, 29; **We can neither** McCormick, 27; **exceptionally nice . . . literary ability** Pellatt to EF, 12/7/26, 12/10, 1926, Russell Collection,

Lilly; **He was really** *The Notes*, 336; **I shirked my work** Pam Hirsch, *The Constant Liberal: The Life and Work of Phyllis Bottome*, 156; **self-preserving insolence** *The Lifeline*, 123; **working him too** *The Notes*, 332; **the local Heidis** Lewis, *Connolly*, 297; **From day one . . . at Eton** General Sir Jack Deverell to NS, 18/6/2021; **Sandhurst wasn't** *The Notes*, 149; **and they never** ibid., 259; **senior officer** Rankin, 44; **There are only** John Pearson, James Bond Transcripts, IFA; **Capable . . . settle down** Lord Ailwyn, 27/7/1927, Russell Collection, Lilly; **general idleness** *The Notes*, 331; **tall in her** Lewis, 296; **Ian said that** *The Notes*, 100; **Uncle Phil used** ibid, 197; **she organised** Lycett, 28; **Ian tried to shoot** Mary (Pakenham) Clive papers; **What a brain** *The Notes*, 332; **a vastly discouraged** Forbes Dennis to JP, May 1965, Pearson Collection, Lilly; **I think that's** IF to EF, 9/3/1924, IFA; **so far at her** *The Notes*, 331; **He left Sandhurst** 1/12/1927, Russell Collection, Lilly; **that he had hammer** JP note, Pearson Collection, Lilly; **sent the commandant** *The Notes*, 191; **glorified garage . . . rumour** IF CV, IFA; **that the . . . thing** *Playboy*, Ken Purdy interview, Dec. 1964; **the British Army** Anthony Morton to NS, 13/1/2021; **All that happened** *The Notes*, 190; **saying that . . . decide** ibid., 333; **My infuriated mother** *Playboy*, Ken Purdy interview, Dec. 1964; **I go into** Lytton, 71

VIII KITZBÜHEL

I thought we OHMSS, 220; **There came to** William Plomer, *Turbott Wolfe*, 10; **already using** Plomer, *Address*; **he talked mostly** Lewis, 297; **that golden time** John Pearson, *Ian Fleming*, 48; **Ian with love . . . pleasure** Lycett, 440; **They were such** Frederica Freer to NS, 12/5/2021; **a face like** *The Notes*, 192; **the surgeon could** Hirsch, 97; **he took a few** IF to Leonard Russell, 14/5/1962, IFA; **The town, red** Cecil Roberts, *Pamela's Spring Song*, 68; **those young cabbages** Hirsch, 149; **Great Genius . . . her back** *Pamela's Spring Song*, 64; **the Valley of** Roberts, *Spears Against Us*, 73; **When Ian turned** *The Notes*, 190; **shouted on** Bottome, *The Goal*, 133; **There was . . . to him** EFD to JP, Pearson Collection, Lilly; **the long dull** EC to Bryce, 28/9/1983, Bryce papers; **He was immensely** *The Notes*, 100; **He used . . . quite did** ibid., 335; **endlessly inventing . . . drunk** ibid., 193; **What Austria had** ibid., 116; **indescribable squalor** ibid., 123; **a powerful weakness** *Thrilling Cities*, 192; **premarital laxity** *The Goal*, 135; **a plain-looking** Lycett, 36; **intelligent Jewesses** JP handwritten note, 3/4/1965, Pearson Collection, Lilly; **this extraordinarily** *The Notes*, 123; **he clings** Amory, 277; **He pointed out** Lycett, 340; **He was quite ruthless** *The Notes*, 123; **confident Adonis** Roberts, *The Bright Twenties*, 323; **a famous novelist . . . Europe** *Pamela's Spring Song*, 269; **cut away over** ibid., 81; **the confetti is** Amory, 221; **fluttered the** Roberts, *The Bright Twenties*, 323; **The flame of life . . . relationship** *Spears Against Us*, 115; **He was something** Conrad O'Brien-ffrench, *Delicate Mission*, 115; **as having . . . his friends** Hirsch, 329; **Ian** got one ibid., 397; **I see now . . . character** ibid., 157; **upside down** Bottome, *The Goal*, 136; **including Ian** *The Notes*, 333; **complete retraining** Bottome, *Alfred Adler: A Portrait from Life*, 221; **a rebel if** Hirsch, 170; **every neurosis** ibid., 169; **as a glossy racehorse** Frederica Freer to NS; **a person to . . . loved person** Pearson, 38; **Our boys** Bottome, *Adler*, 221; **I knew that what** Hirsch, 154; **strange hothouse** *The Notes*, 192; **the greatest child** Bottome, *Not in Our Stars*, 68; **one of the** ibid., 147; **the discovery of** Bottome, *Adler*, 31; **Ian played up** *The Notes*, 192; **a little pasty-faced** Bottome, *Not in Our Stars*, 225; **Ian Fleming had** *Times*, 4/3/1983; **I remember** *The Notes*, 120; **that Adler . . . ill afford** Mary (Pakenham) Clive papers; **Please do this** n.d., Lady Loelia Lindsay Papers; **Passing to** *TMWTGG*, 40; **Ian's qualities** EFD to EF, 27/2/1928, Russell Collection, Lilly; **but for someone** Pearson, 40; **on the idea** *The Notes*, 337; **thanks to the** Hirsch, 156; **if you'd really** IF to PF, April 1929, IFA; **We spent the** Percy Muir, 'Ian Fleming: A Personal Memoir', *Book Collector*, Spring 1965; **to advance £750** Percy Muir, 'Reminiscences', *Book Collector*, 1959, 276; **full of youthful** *The Notes*, 306; **my early hero** ibid., 305; **I've read** *Im Westen . . . too soon* IF to PF, April 1929, IFA; **which in my** *Playboy*, Dec. 1964; **Madame C.** Roberts, *Spears Against Us*, 326; **fairly fluent** Bryce, 7; **in bad Russian** *The Notes*, 126; **several well-known . . . fender** IF notebook, IFA; **I was delighted** IF to PB, 11/1/1962, IFA; **At the Tennerhof** *The Notes*, 337; **the Bluebeard** Connolly *The Evening Colonnade*, 388; **He was always** *The Notes*, 305; **In those days** ibid., 122; **aped Rupert Brooke** IF to Alan Ross, 2/5/1957, IFA; **I find a . . . its sway** IF notebook, IFA; **slim, dark . . . flames** Bryce, 7; **Looking back** IF to PB, 11/1/1962, IFA; **How lovely . . . his life** *TOTD*, 8-9; **Both Winston Churchill** *TMWTGT*, 201; **We helped him** EFD to JP, May 1965, Pearson Collection, Lilly; **I learned far** *Thrilling Cities*, 188; **He was a** *Octopussy*, 37; **She was such** IF to EFD, August 1963, IFA; **Kitzbühel was part** *The Notes*, 335; **To all of us** Popper to Godfrey, 30/5/1965, Godfrey papers; **a devoted . . . the world** *Thrilling Cities*, 188

IX MUNICH

Sixty-five million Bottome, *Not in Our Stars*, 224; **where I had spent** Richard Gant, *Ian Fleming: The Man With the Golden Pen*, 48; **all like Ian** Marita Mirbach to EF, 8/10/1928, Russell Collection, Lilly; **His command** *Book Collector*, Spring 1965; **Munich and Geneva** IF CV 1932, Reuters Archive; **was full of** *Cocktails and Laughter*, 136; **She was most . . . she went** Pearson, 58; **the only time** *Spears Against Us*, 82; **Mamma . . . on** him Hirsch, 42; **The boy . . . prestige thinking** Bottome, *Not in our Stars*, 12–14; **He should . . . like that** *The Notes*, 334; **Mrs Val was terrible** ibid., 303; **His mother was** ibid., 309; **I was terrified** Sandy Glen SWWEC; **With Mrs . . . them again** *Amaryllis Fleming*, 27; **One of those eating-up** *The*

Notes, 228; **They respected her** Fergus Fleming to NS; **I think Ian** *The Notes*, 161; **But darling** ibid., 68; **The City sounds** IF to PF, April 1929, IFA; **darling Mama . . . the world** IF to EF, summer 1929, IFA

X GENEVA

In Switzerland IF notebook, IFA; **happy-go-lucky** *Thrilling Cities*, 208; **holier-than-thou** ibid., 222; **in preparation for** author blurb, *TMWTGG*; **It was because . . . for long** *The Notes*, 337; **the banner of . . . inhabitants** IF notebooks, IFA; **This hero chap** *FRWL*, 107; **I'm glad you** C. Jung to IF, 29/11/1929, Russell Collection, Lilly; **I studied Social** *Thrilling Cities*, 226; **he read voraciously** *The Notes*, 265; **I have over** IF to Perutz, 14/1/1931, Deutsche Nationalbibliothek – German National Library; **a Swiss 'certificat'** IF to Roderick Jones, 1/10/1931, Reuters Archives; **into a pleasant** *TOTD*, 188; **atmosphere of . . . façade** *Thrilling Cities*, 226; **How many secrets . . . the world** Swiss notebook, IFA; **the curious long-haired** Basil Thomson, *The Milliner's Hat Mystery*, 87; **We were all** *The Notes*, 265; **complete lack of** <https://loomings-jay.blogspot.com/2013/06/gisela-von-stoltzenberg.html>; **If there's one subject** Pearson, 70; **The jokes about** Frank Moorhouse, *Grand Days*, 183; **greatest bag of** David MacFadyen, *Eric Drummond and His Legacies*, 101; **very bucked** *The Notes*, 337; **extraordinary soft way** *Sunday Times*, 24/4/1955; **Lockhart & his party** MacFadyen to NS, 7/7/2021; **Mine's Secretan** *Casino Royale* typescript, IFA; **I have just** IF to S. Pleeth, 29/6/1960, IFA; **and saw himself . . . James Bond** *FRWL*, 113; **as he has** 19/9/1930, file 1246, League of Nations Archives, Geneva; **Having worked** *Thrilling Cities*, 200; **alas! . . . at Geneva** *Spectator* competition 33, 1950; **I was once engaged** *Thrilling Cities*, 226; **One must consider** Mary (Pakenham) Clive papers; **of considerable . . . sincere** Charles de Mestral to NS, 19/7/2021; **after the animals** ibid.; **looked rather French** *LALD*, 89; **I'm longing to** PF to EF, 21/9/1931, IFA; **'Best love** PF to EF, n.d., IFA; **I would have** IF to WSM, 24/6/1954, IFA; **They were already . . . blankets** Charles de Mestral to NS; **usual diamond bracelet** Lycett, 48; **Mrs Val insulted . . . would** Mary (Pakenham) Clive papers; **The reason he** Mary Fleming to NS; **She did her** Lycett, 48; **She felt very** Charles de Mestral to NS; **so much as** *The Notes*, 325; **Mister Ian** Mary Fleming to NS; **It was a straight** *The Notes*, 130; **flung his hand** ibid., 314; **It ended with . . . asking for it** Mary (Pakenham) Clive papers; **This was an unheard** *The Notes*, 264; ***Kranzgeld*** information, Peter Waelty to NS, 19/7/2021; **The 'theory' . . . to do that** Charles de Mestral to NS; **Over the tiny valleys** IF Swiss notebook, IFA; **One day I shall** Amory, 52; **When you break . . . Bond** Charles de Mestral to NS; **In his mind's** *Goldfinger*, 152; **The feeling was** *The Notes*, 141; **often referred** Lycett, 68; **The breaking off** *The Notes*, 264; **one of the causes** BB, James Bond Transcripts, IFA; **The business over** *The Notes*, 130; **I always had**

EC to Michael VanBlaricum, 2/1/1987, VanBlaricum Collection; **but I couldn't** EC to Raymond Benson, n.d., Benson papers; **I knew him** FC notes on IF, March 1983, Cuneo papers; **I sensed there** EC intro., *James Bond Bedside Companion*, x

XI REUTERS

Some of my IF to David Chipp, 10/12/1957, IFA; **YOUR COPY . . . DONE** IF review of *A Life in Reuters*, *Sunday Times*, September 1951; **a bad knock** *The Notes*, 137; **no life** PF to MF, 22/10/1929, IFA; **rather a comedown** *The Notes*, 137; **really longing** IF to RJ, 1/10/1931, Reuters Archive; **no intention** Roderick Jones, *A Life in Reuters*, 227; **a terribly smart** *The Notes*, 138; **All I remember** Enid Bagnold, n.d. (1965), Russell Collection, Lilly; **I never spent** Jones, 349; **He always called . . . ideal cover** Anthony Hunter to NS, 21/11/2019; **the rimless eyeglass** *Moonraker*; **My mother** Anthony Hunter to NS, 21/11/2019; **a man with** July 1928, Reuters Archive; **Never tell** John Hatt to NS, 20/11/2019; **to lead his cohorts** IF review of *A Life in Reuters*; **to make Reuters** Robin Kinkead, 'Fleming in Moscow', May 1965, Russell Collection, Lilly; **the bemonocled** IF review of *A Life in Reuters*; **I was much . . . fine boys** BR-H to RJ, 7/10/1931, Reuters Archive; **I am so glad** EF to RJ, 20/10/1931, IFA; **an excellent impression** BR-H to RJ, 21/10/1931, Reuters Archive; **Wonderful! . . . enjoyable** 'Talk of the Town', *New Yorker*, April 1962; **The itinerant reporter** Jacob, 188; **To simplify without** *TOTD*, 118; **damned well** *Playboy*, Dec. 1964; **a lot about** *TSWLM*, 50; **That Reuters' . . . TV news journalist** *Playboy*, Dec. 1964; **too slow** BR-H to RJ, 29/10/1931, Reuters Archive; **My previous good** BR-H to RJ, 4/11/1931, Reuters Archive; **will help** C. Fleetwood-May to IF, 27/1/1932, Reuters Archive; **I understand . . . spirit** BR-H to IF, 19/4/1932, Reuters Archive; **Dear Fleming** BR-H to IF, 1/7/1932, Reuters Archive; **toasty warm** Peter Healey to NS, 21/2/2020; **a very nice man** David Healey to NS, 21/2/2020; **for some purpose** IF Reuters cable, *Times*, 28/7/32; **His only remedy** IF Reuters cable, *Times*, 29/7/32; **and in the climb** *Times*, 29/7/1932; **He spent the** David Healey to NS, 21/2/2020; **On many subsequent** Donald Healey, *My World of Cars*, 53; **with a broken** 'The Alpine Trial', *Motor Sports*, September 1932; **If there was one** *OHMSS*, 14; **Bond went at** *Goldfinger*, 14; **an adequate reply** BR-H to IF, 10/8/1932, Reuters Archive; **self-complacency** Arthur Watson to BR-H, 8/8/1932, Reuters Archive; **They were a** IF to BR-H, 12/8/1932, Reuters Archive; **I want you** BR-H to IF, 16/8/1932, Reuters Archive; **He is accurate** BR-H to RJ, 19/10/1932, Reuters Archive; **the superbly trim** IF review of *A Life in Reuters*; **I do feel . . . value** IF to RJ, 7/9/1932, Reuters Archive; **one of the** Robert White to RJ, October 1931, Reuters Archive; **The name of** IF to Jonathan Cape, 15/5/1953, IFA; **I am at** IF to BR-H, 9/2/1933, Reuters Archive; **I am quite sure** IF to BRH, 9/2/1933, Reuters Archive; **I am inclined** BR-H to RJ, 22/2/1933, Reuters Archive; **not to *mention*** RJ internal memo, 14/10/1932, Reuters Archive; **He is a**

great RJ to EF, n.d., Russell Collection, Lilly; **wearing a well-cut** Plomer, *Address*; **He was busy** Bryce, 26; **As a character . . . on him** Jacob, 132; **where he'd discovered** *The Notes*, 141; **he knew him** ibid., 143; **Miss Philby** *Goldfinger*, 59; **He looked like** Jacob, 132; **a striking young** Pearson Collection, Lilly; **an engine of** Harold Nicolson, *Public Faces*, 73; **in charge at** ibid., 234; **a masterpiece** ibid., 303; **published in the** ibid., 301

XII MOSCOW

His voice was FRWL, 46; **It supplies electrical** Reader Bullard, *Inside Stalin's Russia*, 58; **a tough Briton** Churchill, *Hinge of Fate*, 426; **He reckons** ibid., 166; **The government** ibid., 165; **This sort of thing** ibid., 167; **put through it** *Times*, 19/3/1933; **friendly conversation . . . story** IF to BR-H, 5/4/1933, Reuters Archive; **Since the blades** *Times*, 19/3/1933; **our facts** IF to BR-H, 5/4/1933, Reuters Archive; **no foreign journalist** Bullard, 207; **I spent about . . . the job** BR-H to RJ, 5/4/1933, Reuters Archive; **I AM SENDING** Lycett, 58; **I thought I might** Pearson, 69; **He had Fleming** Sylvan (Whittingham) Mason to NS, 7/1/2021; **Russia is . . . death** Leo Perutz, *Little Apple*, 102; **the implacable working** McCormick, 34; **a picture of** IF to M. Howard, 17/7/1956, IFA; **as depressing . . . moving** A. J. Cummings, *The Moscow Trial*, 53; **a dapper little** Linton Wells, *Blood on the Moon*, 341; **the most spectacular** Cummings, 21; **in a frenzy of frustration** A. T. Cholerton to L. Russell, 13/12/1965, Russell Collection, Lilly; **the man . . . that scene** *TOTD*, 115; **As the famous . . . Czarist days** *Times*, 12/4/1933; **a most perfidious** Cholerton to Russell, Russell Collection, Lilly; **England is humming** Bullard, 174; **startling and universal** Peter Fleming, *One's Company*, 25; **was of girls** Hilary Bray: *A Friend for all seasons*, 45; **and then discovered** *The Notes*, 142; **he got preferential** ibid., 325; **She wore a dainty** Cummings, 90; **extracted by OGPU**, *Times*, 12/4/1933; **Trial proceedings** taken from IF's Reuters cables to *Times*, *New York Times*, Bullard, Cholerton, Cummings, Kinkead; **MacD's 'confession'** Bullard, 175; **This created the** *New York Times*, 13/4/1933; **Standing upright . . . broke down** *Times*, 15/4/1933; **was that MacDonald** Bullard, 176; **by the usual** ibid.; **If you deny** Kinkead, 'Fleming in Moscow', Russell Collection, Lilly; **mechanically, in** *Times*, 15/4/1933; **It was pleasant** *YOLT*, 193; **a five-day . . . somewhere** *Times*, 17/4/1933; **There is one thing** Bullard, 169; **Listen, saboteurs** *Times*, 17/4/1933; **a number of . . . London** *Times*, 19/4/1933; **Fleming had ripped** Kinkead; **hatched a subtle** Cummings, 61; **possessed a news** Wells, 341; **in an envelope . . . tightly down** Cummings, 61; **The prisoners stood** *Times*, 19/4/1933; **The Central News** Kinkead; **One good thing** Bullard, 175; **Moscow was a** *The Notes*, 325; **he is now** BR-H to RJ, 25/10/1933, Reuters Archive; **harsh service messages** IF review of *A Life in Reuters*; **CENTRAL NEWS . . . OUR MONEY** 20/4/1933, Reuters Archive; **We here at** RJ to Linton Wells,

25/5/1933, Reuters Archive; **as a super-visa** Hart-Davis, *Peter Fleming*, 113; **he liked the** *The Notes*, 149; **to a number** Pearson, 88; **Such good judges** Henry Ziegler, *Ian Fleming*, 39; **with the help** *YOLT*, 203

XIII BERLIN
It's a beastly IF to BR-H, 23/10/1933, Reuters Archive; **Everyone adored** PF to EF, 10/6/1933, IFA; **It means I . . . more unreal** Kate Fleming, *Celia Johnson*, 44; IFA; QUITE HONESTLY PF to EF, 15/10/1933, IFA; **I am very ambitious** EF to sons, winter 1933, IFA; **You are still** IF to EF, n.d., IFA; **he wasn't getting enough** *The Notes*, 142; **That is the only** *OHMSS*, 252; **The financial prospects** IF CV, n.d., IFA; **to reinforce the** BR-H to RJ, 16/10/1933, Reuters Archive; **No salary mentioned** RJ to BR-H, 3/10/1933, Reuters Archive; **just a week** IF to BRH, 23/10/1933, Reuters Archive; **I knew him** *Constant Heart*, 213; **stupid and undignified** *The Notes*, 119; **Fleming confirmed** BR-H to RJ, 27/11/1933, Reuters Archive; **The idea of** IF to BR-H, 23/10/1933, Reuters Archive; **make enough . . . indefinitely** IF to EF, n.d., IFA; **very smitten . . . prim** 2/11/1933, Hemming papers; **This is rather . . . story** BR-H to RJ, 25/10/1933, Reuters Archive; **She popped . . . by God** 2/8/1933, Hemming papers; **Even the** *Times*, 13/11/1933; **strictly objective . . . of it** BR-H to RJ, 20/10/1933, Reuters Archive; **Fleming v. funny** 2/11/1933, Hemming papers; **very reluctantly** RJ to Christopher Chancellor, 29/11/1933, Reuters Archive; **I was pretty** IF to BR-H, 23/10/1933, Reuters Archive; **However much** *The Notes*, 318; **The fact is** BR-H to RJ, 27/11/1933, Reuters Archive; **He came to** BR-H to RJ, 18/12/1933, Reuters Archive; **Everyone has the** 'Book of Golden Words', IFA

XIV GLAMOUR BOY
They had leisure P. G. Wodehouse, *Psmith in the City*, 103; **When Ian** *The Notes*, 294; **In those days . . . skiing** *The Notes*, 102; **A City man** Bryce, 27; **I kept on popping** PF to Plomer, 27/5/1959, Durham University Archives; **a thorough materialist** *The Notes*, 345; **London has got** *The Notes*, 314; **He was merely** Mary (Pakenham) Clive papers; **he was very** *The Notes*, 196; **Everyone felt that** ibid., 139; **We saw hundreds** *Honeymoon Journals*; **You can have** PF to MF, 29/10/1929, IFA; **Anaconda's right** *Brazilian Adventure*, 247; **I could never** Ziegler, 57; **so much of** PF to EF, 8/1/1929, IFA; **He was the quiet** James Fleming, *Book Collector*, Spring 2017, 11; **Win as usual . . . Ian Fleming** Hemming papers; **ill-regarded** IF to Lord Bicester, 4/2/1943, Tom Cull papers; **We have admitted** 17/6/1935, Reuters Archive; **a long-term** Lycett, 72; **the doyen of** *The Naval Memoirs of Admiral J. H. Godfrey*, vol. 5, 106; **I always felt** Andrew Lycett, *From Diamond Sculls to Golden Handcuffs: A History of Rowe and Pitman*, 59; **with an eye** *The Notes*, 229; **He loved everyone** ibid., 120; **Everyone appreciated** ibid., 229; **This, after all** O'Brien-ffrench, 117; **a father/**

long-lost JP to Raymond Benson, 8/9/1982, Benson papers; **someone you . . . to France** Jemima Pitman to NS; **What do you think?** Mary (Pakenham) Clive papers; **would not cross** Lycett, *From Diamond Sculls*, 49; **because he couldn't** *The Notes*, 102; **in process of** IF to RJ, 27/11/1936, Reuters Archive; **by condensing . . . THINK** 15/12/1936, Reuters Archive; **It was fearfully** Mary (Pakenham) Clive papers; **risky stocks** Lycett, *From Diamond Sculls*, 102; **My brother Peter's** Pearson, 98; **sent shudders** Elizabeth Montagu, *Honourable Rebel*, 127; **I felt my commanding** GG to NS; 'The Evelyn Waugh Trilogy', BBC2, 1988; **throwing a fly** Harold Hobson, Phillip Knightley and Leonard Russell, *The Pearl of Days*, 257; **Envy has its ugly** *TOTD*, 185; **The thing which** Harling, SWWEC; **Peter Fleming goes** S. P. B. Mais, *All the Days of My Life*, 284; **the offhandedly** Duff Hart-Davis, 358; **Surely all who** 10/10/1956, *LH-D Letters*, vol. 1 and 2, 192; *Peter Fleming: sa place* Duff Hart-Davis, 357; **a Buchanish novel** RH-D to PF, n.d., 1939, IFA; **an investment out** *Book Collector*, Spring 1965

XV THE COLLECTOR

He's got some Moonraker, 184; **around two thousand** IF to David Randall, 6/11/1958, IFA; **one of the proudest** *Book Collector*, Spring 1965; **recovering from** *Playboy* transcript, VanBlaricum Collection; **started something** Barbara Kaye, *Second Impression*, 140; **milestones of progress . . . hypothesis** Percy Muir, *Minding My Own Business*, 204; **first editions . . . than that** *Book Collector*, Spring 1965; **The books themselves** *The Notes*, 28; **I think the** Nicolas Barker to NS, 17/5/2019; **so that no** IF to John Betjeman, 10/12/1963, IFA; **the cases cost** PM to David Randall, 12/1/1971, Lilly; **I couldn't believe** Bamber Gascoigne to NS, 13/1/2000; **Could you please** IF to PM, 16/12/1958 IFA; **if you will open** PM to IF, 17/12/1958, IFA; **I never saw him** Mary (Pakenham) Clive papers; **far enough away** McCormick, 41; **The Ebury Street** *The Notes*, 124; **Ebury Street was** ibid., 343; **a great business** ibid., 127; **Somewhere also . . . female friends** Mary (Pakenham) Clive papers; **a sure sign** William Weaver, *Lives of Lucian Freud: Youth*, 388; **be offered** Barbara Kaye, *Second Impression*, 320; **One I remember** Raymond O'Neill to NS; **He could crack up** *The Notes*, 316; **adept at cutting** IF to Harling, 14/2/1963, Harling papers; **no political prejudices** 18/4/1939, IFA; **I am not interested** IF to AF, Jan. 1946, IF55A, Morgan papers; **I am a totally** *Spectator*, October 1959; **Fascism in Britain** *Wyvern*, 31, Eton College Archives; **Marxist leanings** *The Notes*, 101; **a group of young** IF to JHG, 12/9/1940; David Kahn, *Seizing the Enigma*, 124; **with their intoxicating** Bryce, 104; **painful pre-war** *TOTD*, 53; **At meals we** Mary (Pakenham) Clive papers; **Pleasant creatures** Jacob, 132; **Ian's great attraction . . . her again** Mary (Pakenham) Clive papers; **a great reputation** *The Notes*, 30; **This was because** ibid., 244; **Dinner with Ian** Hemming papers; **I discovered he** JP to NS;

He had no Lycett, 69; He was always *The Notes*, 273; Myself and Byron! Harling, 296; He was known *The Notes*, 311; fanatical . . . master Norman Lewis, *The World, The World*, 154; If I can quote Len Deighton to NS; His forte was Mary (Pakenham) Clive papers; believes herself Rebecca West to Beryl Griffie-Williams, n.d., Gay Carr-Ellison papers; Ingenious excitement Mary (Pakenham) Clive papers; Apart from Harling, 299; You must treat Bryce, 101; Ian really knew *The Notes*, 128; If he had stayed ibid., 70; launched itself *TOTD*, 277; *She was like* Hugh Edwards, *All Night at Mrs Stanyhurst's*, 196; my sainted ibid., 65; as a sort of *The Notes*, 317; a humorous . . . solution Helmut Morpurgo to NS, 2/11/2020; His mistress Jacob, 132; thirtyish, Jewish Lycett, 178; I called it *The Notes*, 130; Esteemed baroness . . . hideous end IF to EM, private collection; She was very Joan Bright Astley, SWWEC; He was slightly Adrian House to NS, 7/11/2019; Her nieces looked Victoria D'Avanzo papers; Aunt Moo . . . horse-whip him Tamara Dorrien-Smith to NS, 7/3/2021; I was a clerk D. H. Lawrence, *Lady Chatterley's Lover*, 294; Within a couple Nigel Wright to NS, 26/2/2021; She broke away Cathryn Cawdor to NS, 20/10/2020; Until Mother *The Notes*, 162; His mother . . . mathematics Mary (Pakenham) Clive papers; I am miserable Hart-Davis, 187; not to be too *Celia Johnson*, 58; mixed up . . . his mind IF to EF, winter 1933, IFA; Even when she Mary (Pakenham) Clive papers

XVI A CHARACTER SKETCH
His reputation was Mary (Pakenham) Clive papers; To my amusement ibid.; the Renaissance ideal MP 29/9/1952 to John Pearson, Lilly; *If the creatures . . . so alive* MP portrait of IF, IFA; With Ian *The Notes*, 318

XVII 'M'
He said you Maud Russell diary, 1957, Russell papers; If his life *The Notes*, 295; At lugging ledgers P. G. Wodehouse, *Psmith in the City*, 147; If he did not Pryce-Jones, 234; His maitresse Mary (Pakenham) Clive papers; the age you IF to AF, n.d., IF65A, Morgan papers; I've an idea . . . Jewess *The Notes*, 58, 79; the most direct David Platzer, *British Art Journal*, vol. 18, no. 2, 2017, 89; a soft, gentle John Julius Norwich intro., *Constant Heart*, 7; Her strange mewing *A Lonely Business: A Self-Portrait of James Pope-Hennessy*, ed. Peter Quennell, 171; something a little *Constant Heart*, 24; I like the house 8/6/1949, Maud Russell papers; like some fair *Constant Heart*, 64; dumb with envy ibid., 53; He was surely . . . well of him Emily Russell to NS, 1/7/2019; Ian asked if *Constant Heart*, 276; He is a lonely ibid., 260; Really I. F. is 30/9/1938, Lady Loelia Lindsay papers; Interesting letter 25/8/1938, ibid.; *might* indulge IF to Loelia, August 1938; Caroline Ponsonby Papers; and he told *Constant Heart*, 45

No doubt his Bryce, 27; **on 1 June** 'Ian Fleming joined 1/6/39', NID Hist [C. Morgan], 1939–42, vol. 3, 17, ADM 223/297, The National Archives; **Balls. Of course** *The Notes*, 85; **was already in** ibid., 44; **ostensibly for** ibid., 143; **for Ian and Van . . . things** *Constant Heart*, 215; **extremely rare . . . for ever** *Times*, 28/9/1938; **master now** Ian Colvin, *Vansittart in Office*, 175; **spoke heatedly . . . whatsoever** *The Maisky Diaries*, ed. Gabriel Gorodetsky, 164; **through a sliding** *Times*, 24/3/1939; **Is that enough . . . industry** *The Notes*, 126; **a particularly close** IF to Nicholas Carroll, 3/1/1947, IFA; **wholly and completely** *Constant Heart*, 50; **It was enormous** IF to LW, n.d., Ponsonby papers; **Russia's strength . . . spawning-ground** 18/4/1939, IFA; **I think he** *Constant Heart*, 56; **Suddenly, I heard** *Playboy*, Dec. 1964; **One sat down** Patrick Beesly, *Very Special Admiral*, 246; **blinking and churning** Ruth Hotblack to Donald McLachlan, 4/5/1968, Churchill Archive Centre, GBR/0014/MLBE 6/3; **a corkscrew mind** Ben Macintyre, *Operation Mincemeat*, 51; **It had worked . . . imagination** *The Notes*, 84; **He said he** ibid.; **10.45 Adm Godfrey** <www.bankofengland.co.uk/archive/montagu-norman-diaries>; **I think we've** *The Notes*, 85; **high City authorities** *The Naval Memoirs of Admiral J. H. Godfrey* vol. 5, 106; **a couple of** *Playboy*, Dec. 1964; **I didn't really** *The Notes*, 85; **he was really** ibid., 74; **no doubt he was** *Naval Memoirs*, vol. 5, 199; **The dome of** Beesly, 251; **the legs of** ibid., 216; **the demonical relenting** Harling, 354; **by helping him** Susanna (Chancellor) Johnston to NS, 5/6/2020; **Having had** JHG to Donald McLachlan, 10/1/1967, Godfrey papers; **I quickly made** *Naval Memoirs*, vol. 5, 395; **With literally** ibid., 278; **when the balloon . . . work** ibid., 275; **Dinner HDH** JHG diary, Godfrey papers; **I spend much . . . Canyon?** IF to LW, n.d., Ponsonby papers; **the epitome** screenplay of 'The Fighting 69th', 1940; **sex and combat** Reynolds, 19; **dallying raised** Douglas Waller, *Wild Bill Donovan*, 113; **a sexy-seeming** Harling, 50; **He is going . . . the war** Lady Loelia Lindsay papers; **April 13, 1944** ibid.; **mingling beads** Loelia Westminster, *Grace and Favour*, 200; **Pleasant interlude** 18/7/1939, Lady Loelia Lindsay papers; **Bill Donovan suddenly** 11/7/1939, ibid.; **Now listen** IF to LW, n.d., Ponsonby papers; **never had a better** Will Swift, *The Kennedys Amidst the Gathering Storm: A Thousand Days in London, 1938–1940*, 174; **I have seen . . . my life** Channon, vol. 2, 594, 1039; 7/7/1939; 30/6/1941; **Blenheim was** *Constant Heart*, 60; **social period** *The Notes*, 208; **a surprising dalliance** 4/8/1939, Lady Loelia Lindsay papers; **Ian had already** *Minding My Own Business*, 196 and 217; **The wedding was** David Coke to NS

XIX ROOM 39

And with one Leo Perutz, *Little Apple*, 221; **All through** Mary Pakenham papers, 'Various Remarks', 29/9/1952; **Let old 'itler** *Naval Memoirs*; Ted Merrett recollection; **a round peg** IF to JHG, 2/12/1948, Godfrey papers; **I[an] was . . . skiing** *Constant Heart*, 67, 69; **The Admiralty is** JHG to Margaret Godfrey, 3/9/1939, Godfrey papers; **Everyone had . . . strokes** *Naval Memoirs*, vol. 5, 174; **Even I** WP to JHG, 14/1/1965, Godfrey papers; **a competent but** Ian Gilmour, *Autobiography*, 249; **all he commanded** Christopher Moran and Trevor McCrisken, 'The Secret Life of Ian Fleming'; **a secret trip** Ann O'Neill diary, 4/11/1940, Morgan papers; **lovely face . . . stopped him** *Constant Heart*, 96; **I can't imagine** Fionn Morgan to NS; **great care** Intelligent Assault Force Operations, August 1944, ADM 223/214, The National Archives; **it would have** Michael Smith to NS; **make an example** *TOTD*, 38-42; **missing, believed drowned** Nicholas Rankin, *Defending the Rock*, 201; **Fleming never uttered** EC notes on IF, March 1983, Cuneo papers; **we should all** Asa Briggs, *Secret Days*, 126; **you will not** Duff Hart-Davis, 347; **I shall be grateful** David Stafford, *Roosevelt and Churchill*, 131; **My work there** *Constant Heart*, 282; **They had these** Richard Dearlove to NS, 22/6/2021; **We burned a lot** Pauline (Burrough) Lee to NS, 25/11/2019; **the bulk of** Jack Beevor, *SOE*, 1981, 46; **everything burned** Thomas Troy, *Wild Bill and Intrepid*, 152; **I have spent** *The Notes*, 36; **contaminated by asbestos** Helen Fry, *The London Cage*, 218; **In the absence** Timothy Naftali, 'Intrepid's Last Deception', *Intelligence and Natonal Security*, vol. 8 (1993), 86; **I think (for me)** Duff Hart-Davis to NS, 24/2/2020; **nothing deceives** Henry Hemming, *Our Man in New York*, 22; **in the vital** David O'Keefe, *One Day in August*, 337; **as a matter** PS to Patrick Beesly, 5/2/1978, GBR/0014/MLBE 3/3, Churchill Archive Centre; **I am pestered** 2/2/1966, AF to CE, Morgan papers; **Am receiving** *TMWTGT*, 272; **to have got** Beesly to Harling, 17/6/1978, GBR/0014/MLBE 3/11, Churchill Archive Centre; **evade or gatecrash** draft letter JHG to JP, Godfrey papers; **You are the** WP to JHG, 14/1/1965, Godfrey papers; **Ian would have** JHG to DM, 30/3/1965, Godfrey papers; **Ian was so** JP to JHG, 1/6/1965, Godfrey papers; **I made a point** JHG to Denning, 11/1/1965, Godfrey papers; **The best . . . fog** JHG to JP, 22/4/1965, Godfrey papers; **Poor Pearson** JHG to DM, 30/3/1965, Godfrey papers; **It has taken** Michael Smith to NS, 11/11/2019; **It's impossible** Christopher Moran to NS, 7/1/2020; **and an equally** Pearson, 133; **He is beginning** *Constant Heart*, 143; **Ian always wanted** *The Notes*, 88; **This he could** Smithers, SWWEC, tape 1584; **having access to** 8/4/1940, HW 14-4; ADM 223/851, The National Archives; **Any ordinary CX** 25/2/1943, C. R. W. Lamplough to 'C'; ADM 223/851, The National Archives; **Ian, in spite** Peter Smithers, *Adventures of a Gardener*, 14; **kept the torch** JHG to Hillgarth, 16/10/1964, Hillgarth papers; **If you thought** David Kenyon to NS, 18/12/2019; **a war-*winner*** McLachlan, 10; **the country and** JHG to AF, 20/8/1964, Godfrey papers

A man who Naval Memoirs, 74; **Going to war** JHG to Margaret Godfrey, 3/9/1939, Godfrey papers; **indefatigable second** Beverley Baxter, *Men, Martyrs and Mountebanks*, 255; **How firmly Churchill** Geoffrey Shakespeare, private papers; **The wording . . . matter** Naval Memoirs, 46; **news agency gusto** McLachlan, 6; *Pray, could* CB to R Benson, 23/7/1982, Benson papers; **with Churchillian** Lycett, 200; **call no man 'Sir'** *FRWL*, 13; **Churchill the Immortal** Atticus, 3/11/1957; **I hope you** *TMWTGT*, 41–42; **In the higher** Winston Churchill, *Thoughts and Adventures*, 26; **all kinds of Munchausen** Prime Minister's Personal Minute, M.492/1, 30/4/1941, 20/36, Churchill Archive Centre; **strange sort** *The Notes*, 287; **to which ideas** JHG memorandum 1/6/1942, Naval Memoirs, 120; **You've simply** Sam Bassett, *Royal Marine*, 170; **Don't be afraid** Sara Morrison to NS; **dropping footballs . . . fresh one** Ben Macintyre, *Operation Mincemeat*, 51; **fully and convincingly** Naval Memoirs, 46; **somehow suited** PS to McLachlan 15/4/1978, GBR/0014/MLBE 3/3, Churchill Archive Centre; **almost as** Beesly, 112; **Godfrey needed somebody** Smithers, SWWEC; **the right place** Naval Memoirs, 74; **benevolent presence** Benson, 47; **He was quite** Eleanor Michell to NS, 11/1/2020; **He was the world's . . . a man** Andrew Boyd, *British Naval Intelligence Through the Twentieth Century*, 335; **brilliant, unconventional** Joy Packer, *Deep as the Sea*, 86; **the mind . . . his whimsy** IF to PS, 14/4/1942, IFA; **I'm sorry, James** 'Bond Strikes Camp', Cyril Connolly, *Previous Convictions: Selected Writings of a Decade*, 370; **Cyril was terribly** Deirdre Connolly to NS, 25/5/2019; **All his life** *The Notes*, 83; **It was really** ibid., 86; **Admiral Godfrey feels** McLachlan, 9; **They treated him** Smithers, SWWEC; **something very** Sandy Glen, SWWEC, tape 1609; **If we wanted** Smithers, SWWEC; **Hold Lieutenant** Smithers SWWEC, tape 1584; **Such are the** Smithers, 14; **somewhere in** Naval Memoirs, 288; **enchanting and beloved** Harling, 84; **Went to Admiralty** Diaries of Evelyn Waugh, 446; **a new kind . . . with Ian** Smithers, SWWEC; **He was Godfrey's** Andrew Boyd to NS, 18/10/2021; **Fleming's work and mine** Naval Memoirs, 273; **a paper specially** Nicholas Rankin, *Ian Fleming's Commandos*, 44; **Oddly enough** JHG to Menzies, 26/7/1942, ADM 223/851; **He has various** Constant Heart, 213; **Among other things** 7/3/1944, ibid., 238; **It was of** Smithers, SWWEC; **I once said** Naval Memoirs, 74; **Really, it was** *The Notes*, 281; **The expression 'phoney'** Naval Memoirs, 45; **so absorbed in** Constant Heart, 72; **the string-and-stickfast** *TOTD*, 249; **this remarkable man** IF to Conal Gannon, 11/5/1950, Russell Collection, Lilly; **There was only** Constant Heart, 69; **might have considerable** Fry, 92; **the most important . . . as possible** IF 28/9/1940, ADM 223/851, The National Archives; **MOST SECRET** 31/1/1941, ADM 223/851, The National Archives; **I am told that** Channon, 14/9/1940; **needed a diet**

Naval Memoirs, 326; **I was, though** Merlin Minshall, *Guilt-Edged*, 142; **just plain crazy** *The Notes*, 62; **and ignore** Boyd to NS

XXI 'THE MOST UNSCRUPULOUS MAN IN SPAIN'

I don't keep John Brooks, *New Yorker*, 28/3/1979 and 21/5/1979; **the most unscrupulous** Stafford, *Roosevelt and Churchill*, 89; **Hillgarth is pretty** ibid., 96; **strange and brilliant** Furse papers; **Mr March should** Brooks, *New Yorker*, 28/3/1979; **Franco can refuse** ibid.; **feasible, and very** Duff Hart-Davis, *Man of War*, 192; **It would be a mistake** Stafford, 89; **as some strange** Brooks, *New Yorker*, ibid.; **The Germans offered** Stafford, 88; **prodigious political** Brooks, *New Yorker*, ibid.; **a scoundrel** Stafford, 89; **There's absolutely** David Stafford to NS, 15/10/2021; **I should like . . . Spain** *Man of War*, 191; **If the Atlantic ports** McLachlan, 194; **On the whole** *Man of War*, 192; **The advantages . . . Ibiza** ibid.; **one of the strangest** Brooks, *New Yorker*, ibid.; **An account** GBR/0014/MLBE 3, Churchill Archive Centre; **to get briefs** McLachlan to JHG, 21/2/1967, GBR/0014/MLBE 6/3, Churchill Archive Centre; **traitorous and miserly** Brooks; **I think we** Rankin, 88; **A vague hint** Stafford, 90; **hideous old chap** Brooks, *New Yorker*, ibid.; **Dalton wanted** David Eccles, *By Safe Hand*, 15; **We couldn't fight** Stafford, 92; **never one to** Brooks, *New Yorker*, ibid.; **The Quislings** Eccles, 126; **In general, much** David Stafford to NS; **the Cavalry of St George** Stafford, 93; **it would never be found** Smithers, SWWEC; **It was fantastic** Furse papers; **that the Germans** JHG to McLachlan, GBR/0014/MLBE 6/3, Churchill Archive Centre; **I am very** Boyd to NS; **with the tide** Peter Loxley to DNI, 17/12/1943, ADM 223/851, The National Archives

XXII 'COMPLETELY OUTWITTED'

I gathered he Constant Heart, 172; **It was totally** Gladwyn Jebb, *Memoirs*, 98; **Norway was** Eccles, 107; **imperturbably** Joan Bright Astley, *The Inner Circle*, 96; **We were the first** Peter Fleming, *Report on Measures Taken at Namsos in connection with the landing of an Allied Expeditionary Force*, IFA; **We have been** 10/4/1940, *Churchill at the Admiralty*, 1001; **Admiralty in a state** 14/4/1940, ibid., 10063; **introduced with a** *The Notes*, 126; **I listened to Ian** *Constant Heart*, 89; **a Stockholm newspaper** *Nya Dagligt Allehanda*, 25/4/1940; **had a ghastly** Hart-Davis, *Peter Fleming*, 229; **many congratulations . . . Empire** PF diary, 27/4/1940, Special Collections, University of Reading; **in silk** Hart-Davis, *Peter Fleming*, 229; **splendid upheaval** A. J. P. Taylor, *A Personal History*, 153; **when, soon** Pearson, 145; **We were very** *Constant Heart*, 93; **War reads . . . at all** EC notes on IF, March 1983, Cuneo papers; **Well, I always** Kaye, *Second Impression*, 124; **to do snap** IF to Peter Smithers, 27/1/1942, IFA; **Ian was sitting** Raymond (Lord) O'Neill to NS; **A whole** battalion Kate Fleming, 79; **Throughout the whole** Ogden, 311; **He has a fracture** Eccles, 160; **He died in . . . him again** Gilly Newbery to NS, 14/7/2019; **This war has** Dick Troughton to Tish Fleming, Oct. 1940, Newbery papers; **Peter, poor Peter** *Amaryllis Fleming*, 53; **but had a . . . collapsing** *Constant Heart*, 97; **It was essential** *Naval Memoirs*, 275; **he meant to** ibid., 104; **a very substantial** Smithers, SWWEC; **The elegant fireplace** Montagu, 246; **a very vivid . . . route** *Naval Memoirs*, 275; **some of them** Montagu, 249; **a close colleague** IF to Mclachlan, 1947, VanBlaricum Collection; **even if it . . . Minister** François d'Astier de La Vigerie, *Le ciel n'était pas vide*; **one nation while** Paul Baudouin, *Private Diaries*, 116; **to come** *Naval Memoirs*, 118; **a twister** Beesly, 159; **He told me** Marina Weir to NS, 20/12/2020; ***Vous et les officiers*** 23/6/1940, Bletchley Park Trust; **some large and** Sellers, 23; **ran through** *Moonraker*, 29; **a vast ant** Montagu, 254; **one of which** Nurse Andrews's memoir, 'June 1940', Mark Simmons papers; **I love its colour** *Goldfinger*, 184; **overseeing the . . . *is located*** Roderick Bailey, *The Secret War of Louis Franck*, HS 8/214, The National Archives; **part of the gold bullion** Cookridge papers, McMaster University, Ontario; **I have very** Francis de Marneffe to NS, 10/11/2019; ***RECEIVED FROM*** Robin Pleydell-Bouverie papers; **Tomorrow, I'm** Gant, *Ian Fleming*, 14; **Ian thought . . . all sorts** Smithers, SWWEC; **They put them** Denny Lane to NS, 27/11/2019; **he didn't have** Francis de Marneffe, *Last Boat from Bordeaux*, 80; **He said, 'Well' . . . for Britain** Smithers, SWWEC; **Boarding this British** Marneffe, 78–83; **off his drunk** 1/6/1940, Lady Loelia Lindsay papers; **thinking of going** 26/40/1940, Lady Loelia Lindsay papers; **Commander Fleming . . . neutral country** Smithers, SWWEC

XXIII LITTLE BILL

I did more WS to Col. C. E. Ellis 18/9/1961, Churchill Archive Centre; **I think I see** Martin Gilbert, *Churchill and America*, 185; **the greatest intelligence** Stafford, *Roosevelt and Churchill*, 132; **the original . . . Secret Service** Troy, 127; **The suggestions** JHG to JP, 22/4/1965, Godfrey papers; **I had him** Denning to JHG, 25/2/1965, Godfrey papers; **might never have** David Stafford, *Camp X*, xvii; **We should abandon** Eccles, 312; **do all that** H. Montgomery Hyde, *The Quiet Canadian*, 28; **People often** *TOTD*, 59; **quick as a dash** Henry Hemming, *Our Man in New York*, 20; **Men of super** *TOTD*, 60; **He used to** Irvin Stefansson to NS, 1/12/2019; **He would talk** Hemming, 49; **the real thing . . . credentials** *TOTD*, 60; **Dr George Johnson** <www.intrepid-society.org/documents/Wpg_Real_Estate_News_22May 2009.pdf>; **he came back** Irvin Stefansson to NS; **a Canadian invention** advertisement; Bill Macdonald, *The True Intrepid*, 42; **in the dark** ibid., 46; **because he thought that** ibid., 47; **one of the great** *TOTD*, 62; **a brilliant scientist** *Daily Mail*, 27/12/1922; Ian Sanders and Lorn Clarke, *A Radiophone in Every Home*, 20; **There** was instant Troy, 185; **Winston and I** Macdonald, 64; **It was a fine** Montgomery Hyde, 30; **Your duty lies** *TOTD*, 62; **He became a** David Cornwell to NS, 3/11/2019; **the most powerful** *TOTD*, 62; **Much has been** Gill Bennett, *Churchill's Man of Mystery: Desmond Morton and the World of Intelligence*, 354; **with huge heaps** DS to NS, 14/1/2020; **Everyone did!** Macdonald, 246; **Bill's many chaps** 'A Man Called INTREPID' Transcripts of interviews [1972], 500.1-4, University of Regina Archives and Special Collections; **Had it not** *The True Intrepid*, 151; **When the full** ibid., 108; **All those who** Bill Macdonald, *Intrepid's Last Secrets*, 19; **Bill Stephenson taught** H. Montgomery-Hyde, 2

XXIV BIG BILL

We aren't as Waller, 23; **falling on their** Thomas F. Troy, *Wild Bill and Intrepid*, 60; **Anybody can start** from screenplay of 'The Fighting 69th'; **He has every** Thomas F. Troy, *Donovan and the CIA*, 25; **Donovan was like** Reynolds, 365; **certain aspects of** ibid., 21; **presently the** *strongest* Keith Jeffery, *M16*, 446; **all leading Government** Reynolds, 23; **got along famously** *Wild Bill and Intrepid*, 125; **Certainly you aided** McLachlan, 226; **It was Donovan . . . individual** O'Keefe, 318; **Give yourself** Jeffery, 443; **our intelligence services** *Roosevelt and Churchill*, xxii; **little more than** David Stafford, *The Silent Game: The Real World of Imaginary Spies*, 217; **the most important** Montgomery-Hyde, 44; **damn-me-Dykes** Reynolds, 45; **The one genuinely** Alex Danchev, *Establishing the Anglo-American Alliance*, 22; **a Fleming move** Harling, 27; **sat in on our** Sefton Delmer, *Black Boomerang*, 172; **It fell back** Ralph Arnold, *A Very Quiet War*, 53; **He could persuade** Joseph Persico, *Roosevelt's Secret War*, 94; **driving force** JIC paper, 25/6/1942, ADM 223/214, The National Archives; **complete fusion** McLachlan, 220; **a splendid American** Jennet Conant, *The Irregulars*, 91; **As he doesn't** Thelma Cazalet-Keir, *From the Wings*, 171; **attached to** *Constant Heart*, 125; **The plan to** *The Notes*, 349; **the whole . . . personalities** IF handwritten memo, 24/3/1941, ADM 223/490, The National Archives; **He is a brother** Danchev, 62; **They did drink** Janet, Lady Milford Haven to NS, 17/5/2019; **a prodigious amount** *Constant Heart*, 256; **I wondered what** Edward Merrett to JHG 8/3/1965, Godfrey papers; **the most explosive** Harling, 80; **a remarkable chap** IF to Smithers 13 /1/1944, IFA; **woken the town** Sally (Marris) Wade-Gery to NS, 15/7/2020; **a 20 foot V . . . done** IF to Smithers, 13/10/194, IFA

XXV RODNEY BOND

He set a very *London Gazette*, 1919; **I have total** Clarissa Pryce-Jones to NS, 1/7/2020; **his instant** Nancy Caccia to her parents, 4/5/1941, Pryce-Jones papers; **It is best to** Danchev, 60; **I think his** ibid., 58; **Fleming's Foot** Alan Ogden, *Master of*

Deception: *The Wartime Adventures of Peter Fleming*, 42; **sheer force of** Hart-Davis, *Peter Fleming*, 279; **do what I could** Ogden, 43; **the enemy . . . Tommy gun** ibid., 43; **'He is afraid . . . lost** 14/3/1941; 9/4/1941; 28/4/1941; *Constant Heart*, 125, 127, 128; **The Yaks . . . shivering** Nancy Caccia, 4/5/1941; **We were going . . . get us** Clarissa Pryce-Jones to NS, 1/7/2020; **I tell her about** Ogden, 52; *being attacked . . . rescuers* London Gazette, 16/1/1942; **He risked his . . . try Bond** Clarissa Pryce-Jones to NS, 1/7/2020; **If I were dictator** Anne de Courcy, *The Viceroy's Daughters*, 405; **Once my brother** IF to Smithers, 27/1/1942, IFA; **It's no place** PF to EF, 4/1/1942, IFA

XXVI 'SPECIAL SERVICES'

He founded the BB, James Bond Transcripts, IFA; **The war has** Eccles, 256; **intermediary . . . Americans** *Naval Memoirs*, vol. 5, 276; **Donovan would** *The Notes*, 278; **tired & never . . . fish** JHG to Margaret Godfrey 21/5/1941; 1/3/1943, Godfrey papers; **Lisbon was a cockpit** Paul Furse papers; **Madame A. cordially** Jack Beevor, *SOE*, 37; **crawling with . . . cleaned out** *TOTD*, 199; **the kernel of** ibid., 199; **he said that . . . lost** *The Notes*, 84; **Bermuda is** *Naval Memoirs*, 275; **Instead of** *The Notes*, 349; **a navy blue . . . leather** *New York Times*, 26/5/1941; **Our mission** Buckton, 123; **highly mechanised eyrie** *TOTD*, 63; **go up and** Conant, 293; **How much I admire** Hemming, 179; **to handle up to** *The Notes*, 280; **There were dozens** Benn Levy, 'A Man Called INTREPID'. Transcripts of interviews [1972], 500.1-4, University of Regina Archives and Special Collections; **just like dominoes** *The True Intrepid*, 279; **an amazingly quick** *The Notes*, 349; **chunky enigmatic** *TOTD*, 90; **rather creepy crawly** Persico, 89; **Collaboration hardly existed** *Naval Memoirs*, 133; **the only person** Beesly, 181; **At last I got** *Naval Memoirs*, 132; **to set up** Eccles, 283; **the pre-natal stages** ibid.; **to get the USA** ibid., 262; **and there on** ibid., 243; **I told the President** Hemming, 182; **handle troops** Reynolds, 56; **Donovan saw . . . efforts** *Wild Bill and Intrepid*, 130; **He offered . . . I do** Eccles, 303; **I spent some** IF to Col. Rex Applegate, March 1957, Troy, 127; **my memorandum** IF to Cornelius Ryan, 8/5/1962, Troy, 228; **locked in it** Bryce, 52; **You are my** Waller, 77; **This arrangement** Whitney H. Shepardson to IF 7/8/1942, RG226, Box 251, Folder 739, Relations with the British, 1944, NARA; **The information was** *The Notes*, 299; **I always made** Smithers, SWWEC; **One thing that** Michael Goodman to NS, 26/6/2020; **had no frontiers** *Naval Memoirs, vol. 5*; **I was a part** EC notes on IF, March 1983, Cuneo papers; **One of the leading** Harling, SWWEC; **You're not looking** Anna Slafer to NS, 2/6/2022; **to impart to** *Adventures of a Gardener*, 20; **We were not** Waller, 3; **energy and drive** Reynolds, 52; **His imagination . . . Tokyo** Tim Weiner, *Legacy of Ashes: The History of the CIA*, 5; **a remarkable mix** Reynolds, 70.; **Ian came over** Jemima Pitman to NS, 13/5/2020; **for having chosen** IF to Whitney H. Shepardson, 17/9/1942, RG226, Box 251, Folder 739, Relations with the British, 1944, NARA; **slightly travel stained** Hemming, 254; **See my . . . in order that** *TOTD*, 38; **President is very** IF to JHG 19/7/1941; Bennett, 257; **horrifying competition** Furse papers; **calamitous** *Donovan and the CIA*, 90; **Value of this** Bennett, 257; **will solve** IF notes, IFA; **One night** *The Notes*, 281; **Someone incited** Furse papers; **As far as I** Beesly, 181; **practically lived** Hemming, 236; **eighty-five per cent** ibid., 312; **most secret fact** *Wild Bill and Intrepid*, 132/3; **our present national** Stafford, *Roosevelt and Churchill*, 292; **You would have** ibid., 69; **He was reticent** Ann O'Neill diary, 20/8/1941, Morgan papers

XXVII 30AU

For such a novel JHG to JIC, 25/6/1942, ADM 223–214; **the quantities of** Barty Pleydell-Bouverie to Donovan 13/10/1942, Entry 210, Box 324, NARA; **who were later . . . information** *The Notes*, 279; **two or three times** IF interview with CBC, Feb. 1964; **When I was in** Smithers, SWWEC; **how to kill** Smithers to Claude Hankes, 17/12/2001; **Ian took extensive** *The Notes*, 278; **new uniforms** *Constant Heart*, 250; **Have you ever** Harling, 33; **A did not** Bill Marshall to NS, 11/12/2019; **Mention of** Intelligent Assault Force Operations, August 1944, ADM 223/214, The National Archives; **widely spread** I. G. Aylen, 'Recollections of Assault Unit No. 30 – I', *Naval Review*, vol. 65 (1977); **They work** Nicholas Rankin to NS, 27/2/2020; **a leading role . . . watch** McLachlan, 205; **the pink rat** Eccles, 202; **that the Straits** IF to Smithers, 27/1/1942, IFA; **the brand new** *FRWL*, 109; **He was a bit** Pauline (Burrough) Lee to NS; **I think the** Rankin, 66; **The idea was this** Smithers, SWWEC; **tough, bachelor** Charles Morgan, 'History of the Naval Intelligence and the Naval Intelligence Department 1939–42,' ADM 223/464, The National Archives; **risk of his** Smithers, 18; **My task was** Charles Fraser Smith, *The Secret War of Charles Fraser Smith*, 129; **He told me** Pearson Collection, Lilly; **Our little operation** IF to PS, 11/3/1941, IFA; **capture Intelligence material** IF draft memo 19/9/1942, ADM 223/500, The National Archives; **It was in** IF to Denning, 12/1/1961, IFA; **It was one** *The Notes*, 310; **30AU is . . . people** NR to NS; **Look! a** David Nutting, *Attain by Surprise*, 187; **one of the** Dalzel-Job to IF, 17/11/1957, IFA; **with a cannon** Tony Hugill diary, GBR/0014/HUGL 1-15, Churchill Archive Centre; **We would call** Nutting, 274; **just as a Polar** J. P. Riley, *From Pole to Pole*, 148; **something truly Elizabethan** J. A. C. Hugill, *The Hazard Mesh*, 12; **extraordinary charm** Hugill diary, GBR/0014/HUGL 1-15, Churchill Archive Centre; **For Christ's . . . language** O'Keefe, 383; **disdaining protocol** Nutting, 38; **I am right as** O'Keefe, 393; **Was Fleming . . . choice** AB to NS; **No raid** <www.rmhistorical-society.org/history/commandos-and-codes>; **a careful and** ADM 223/214; **the importance** O'Keefe, 284; **if possible, a** Leah Garrett, *X Troop*, 78; **to have any**

'History of SIGINT Operations Undertaken by 30 Commando/30AU', ADM 223/214, The National Archives; **what are you** JHG's daughter Eleanor Michell to NS, 11/1/2020; **extraordinary medley . . . guns** *TOTD*, 48–9; **with instructions . . . prize** 21/8/1942, IF to Marquis of Casa Maury, <https://www.facebook.com/photo /?fbid=10165077795665192&set=pcb.10165077796990192>; **a bloody gallant** *TOTD*, 57; **the most dreadful** *TMWTGT*, 177; **Even Ian who** Kate Fleming, 111; **I got a . . . useful** *Constant Heart*, 175; **Dieppe was** *TOTD*, 57; **while the question** ADM 223-214; Sancho Glanville, *Official History of 30AU*, 29; **this interesting . . . red tape** JHG 25/6/1942, ADM 223/214 ; **who should** IF minutes of meeting at COHQ, 22/7/1942, ADM 223/500; **this charming young** Nutting, 131; **for secur-ity . . . operation** Rushbrooke to Chief of Combined Operations', 6/7/1943, Rankin papers; **I myself know** Rankin, 312; **I was taught** Bill Marshall to NS; **should be encouraged** Rankin, 159; **to make out** *The Notes*, 103; **that boorish . . . paperback** Harling, 44; **I was astonished . . . so on** *The Notes*, 132; **The memories** Nutting, 28; **complete with . . . special plane** 13/11/42 telegram; Mavis Batey, August 2008, GBR/0014/BTEY 3/5, Churchill Archive Centre; **completely vindicated** Rankin, 158; **All the accumulated** *FRWL* manuscript, Lilly; **Your show, Peter!** A. Cecil Hampshire, *The Secret Navies*, 219-20; **a slightly damaged** Rankin, 179; **heard first . . . exuberant** *Constant Heart*, 222

XXVIII 'WHAT A NUISANCE SEX IS!'

Sometimes the EC notes on IF, March 1983, Cuneo papers; **Of course, he** *Daily Express*, 13/8/1989; **I relished the** Adam Sisman, *John le Carré*, 184; **he'd slept** *Constant Heart*, 290; **Everyone sleeping** Eccles, 332; **She told me** VG to NS, 28/2/21; **Trysts were** LD to NS, 22/11/2019; **Uniform suited** Barbara Kaye, *The Company We Kept*, 98; **With my twenty-six** <https://www.historyofinformation. com/detail.php?entryid=3429>; **owing to the** Brooke Crutchey to P. Muir, 20/5/1940, in Joel Silver, 'Books That Had Started Something', *Book Collector*, Spring 2017; **A terrific** Lady Loelia Lindsay papers; **like the enlarged** Lara Feigel, *The Love-Charm of Bombs*; **I hear that** PM to IF 11/10/1940, Russell Collection, Lilly; **London was flooded** Bill Marshall to NS; **his favourite for** *Constant Heart*, 111; **I liked the air-raids** Mary (Pakenham) Clive papers; **We were left** Gant, 47; **The story was told** *Constant Heart*, 114; **Could I please** Delmer, *Black Boomer-ang*, vol. 2, 24; **Darling Mama** IF to EF, 14/10/1940, IFA; **The place swayed** *Constant Heart*, 114; **a large block . . . existence** IF to Smithers, 13/1/1944, IFA; **a right swindler** Eric Maschwitz to Malcolm Muggeridge; 'The Two Bills', Shaun Herron interview with William Stephenson, April 1968, University of Regina Archives; **It will haunt him** Hemming, 170; **If you can** IF to PS, 23/7/1942, IFA; **If there is** IF to PS, 28/8/1941, IFA; **When I tell** IF to PS, 13/10/1941, IFA; **The** ordinary . . . go home Astley, SWWEC; **Pug Ismay** Channon, vol. 2, 1027; **A metallic . . . intriguer** ibid., 1026; **Sat next** 12/11/1941, Lady Loelia Lindsay papers; **private lives** JHG, 8/3/1965, 'Personal Assistant to DNI', Godfrey papers; **a mess . . . satisfaction** Peter Alexander, *William Plomer*, 245; **[Delmer] is a clever** Ann O'Neill diary, 22/10/1940, Morgan papers; **Nigel is** ibid., August 1941; **dazzling** *Constant Heart*, 145; **As midnight drew** Ann O'Neill diary, 31/12/1940, Morgan papers; **There was only** James Kirkup, *I, of All People*, 98; **Gay?** FM to NS, 19/1/2023; **a subtle bitch** Hugo Charteris to Mary Rose, 1956, Morgan papers; **I. and Oliver** *Constant Heart*, 236; **There was a** *The Notes*, 327; **I once said to** ibid., 318; **just like the** ibid., 106; **I loved him** ibid., 213; **Noël has always** Amory, 278; **I will not** FM to NS; **He's been very** *TMWTGT*, 170; **a herd of** *Goldfinger*, 314; **perhaps Bond's** *TMWTGT*, 185; **Bond's greatest success** 'Bondmanship' Stephen Potter papers, Harry Ransom Center, University of Texas at Austin; **with the recognition** *TMWTGG*, 101; **marriage and** *Moonraker*, 7; **sleep with a problem** McLachlan, 9; **Rather a deadpan** *The Notes*, 306; **I was pleased . . . as great** *Constant Heart*, 145, 234, 238, 204, 223; **JIC's BODYLINE subcommittee** Michael Goodman, *Official History of the Joint Intelligence Committee*, 77, 135, 166; **equivalent to** ibid., 135; **Don't just hold** Ann O'Neill to Duff Cooper, GBR/0014/DUFC 12/34, Churchill Archive Centre; **about the German** *Constant Heart*, 253; **If I had to** FM to NS, 19/1/2023; **the great inseparables** Channon, vol. 2, 1,042; **My father went off** Raymond O'Neill to NS; **A young man** Delmer, 74; **Ian must have** CB to Raymond Benson, 6/8/182, Benson papers; **We were friends** Harling, SWWEC; **a man called Harling** *TSWLM*, 48; **My dear** Nicholas Coleridge, *The Glossy Years*; **slim, dark-haired** Harling, 109; **Has Ian put** ibid., 111; **She was very** Antonia Fraser to NS, 24/3/2023; **I was terrified** KF to NS, 18/6/2021; **She was a** Sara Morrison to NS, 26/7/2022; **that at some** Harling, 117; **the rigmarole . . . into tears** S. J. Taylor, *The Reluctant Press Lord*, 14; **the desertion ticket** Channon, vol. 2, 603; **Esmond's fear . . . dead** Harling, 117; **the tragedy . . . her death** ibid., 218; **We'd been** SM to NS; **She was dotty** Harling, SWWEC; **and brought another** *Naval Memoirs*, 162; **Dispatch riders** IF to JHG, 26/8/1943, Godfrey papers; **I remember her** Tamara Dorrien-Smith to NS, 7/3/2021; **A large glossy** AH to NS, 7/11/2019; **the dream vision . . . parted** Delmer, 153; **Once her helmet** Harling, 53; **What is your** *Redbook*, June 1964; **Along with** Harling papers; **She demanded . . . difficulties** Ted Merrett, James Bond Transcripts, IFA; **JOKE ACHTUNG** IF to PS, 14/4/1942, IFA; **which of course . . . in between** 29/11/1943, Nigel Wright papers; **looking absolutely** Judith Foljahre, 16/7/1944, Wright papers; **He is worn** *Constant Heart*, 233; **We always came** Tamara Dorrien-Smith to NS; **A very noisy** *Constant Heart*, 239; *Dear Captain* Wright papers; **But your girl** *The Notes*, 212; **Ian was** Astley, SWWEC; **first time** *Constant Heart*, 241

They were small Rankin, 199; **hugely disinclined** Nutting, 243; **purely private . . . party spirit** Glanville, 241; ADM 223/214, The National Archives; **You can't** Rankin, 284; **to list enemy** Harling, 45; **a stupendous tabloid** Nutting, 244; **had worked out** *The Notes*, 134; **As I came** *Constant Heart*, 246; **V-1 'doodlebugs' started** ibid., 285; **We had a** ibid., 247; **Who is it?** Bill Marshall interview with NS, 11/12/2019; **The muscle that** NR to NS.; **for an airborne** IF to Charles Grey, 9/5/1945, IFA; **We were sending** Alan Schneider interview with John Cork, Cork papers; **Before we landed** Nutting, 171; **The Intelligence historian** Michael Smith to NS; **Irregular lumps** Hugill, 52; **blood flowing in** Rankin, 242; **after some rather** IF to Denning, 12/1/1961, IFA; **has made itself** letter from George O'Niell to Tully Shelley RG 313, Box 32, Folder A9/8, 18/8/1944, NARA; **I've 'ad three** Hugill diary, GBR/0014/HUGL 1-15, Churchill Archive Centre; **butterfly . . . breakfast egg** Patrick Dalzel-Job, *Arctic Snow to Dust of Normandy*, 123; **somewhat cold** ibid., 115; **the egregious Fleming** Nutting, 181; **We none of** Rankin, 247; **a pleasant talk . . . it's like** Hugill diary, GBR/0014/HUGL 1-15, Churchill Archive Centre; **As usual** *Constant Heart*, 251; **In pursuance of** Harling, 135; **I sent back** *The Notes*, 135; **a very beautiful** ibid., 341; **into believing** Hugill, 100; **the best of the** Hugill diary, GBR/0014/HUGL 1-15, Churchill Archive Centre; **It was like a blow** Rankin, 269; **a man so beloved** Nutting, 37; **In my memory** Dalzel-Job, 150

XXX GLOBETROTTER

In Ian CB to Benson, 6/8/1982, Benson papers; **Since the unit** *Official History of 30 Commando*, 226; **bored to . . . battles** *Constant Heart*, 258, 224, 223; **Poor I.** ibid., 264; **drinks with . . . Harbor** Jacob papers; **enquire into** IF Bletchley file card, 27/12/1944-3/1/1945, Michael Smith papers; **bitter wistfulness . . . buoy up** Simon Winder, *The Man Who Saved Britain*, 51; **He takes up masses** AH to Jean Colt, 23/12/1944, Hillgarth papers; **What could he** AB to NS, 18/10/2021; **the Head of ANDERSON** 5/3/1945, HW 8/35, NA; **a supreme discretion** AH, 14/6/1946, Benson papers; **Clare Blanshard was** Cuneo to Bryce, 28/9/1983, Bryce papers; **A beauteous** CB to Paul Blanshard, 22/1/1945, Benson papers; **a chuggish** CB notes, Pearson Collection, Lilly; **clearing the** Lycett, 155; **We went to** CB to Benson, 29/6/1982, Benson papers; **which he . . . he said** Pearson Collection, Lilly; **my ayah** IF to CB, 3/3/1945, IFA; **the Flying Midwife** CB to Benson, 25/4/1982, Benson papers; **in the breakers** IF to Harling, 3/8/1949, VanBlaricum Collection; **he felt as** *Constant Heart*, 276; **Ian appeared here** PF to Celia, 1/1/1945, IFA; **It was always** Astley, 96; **SEAC continues** Ogden, 160; **Burma was** ibid., 76; **You can't see** ibid., 150; **to create alarm** ibid., 237; **No indication** ibid., 232; **Not so our** ibid., 85; **all hell** ibid., 252; **at its best** ibid., 251; **I am bored** PF to EF, 31/7/1942, IFA; **It really is**

PF to EF, 30/3/1943, IFA; **it's about the** PF to EF, 28/2/1943, IFA; **this routine** PF to EF 31/7/1942, IFA; **the rubbish I've** Kate Fleming, 150; **I think you** PF to Celia, 5/4/1943, IFA; **the rather childish** Duff Hart-Davis, *Peter Fleming*, 301; **the old controversies** Kate Fleming, 150; **a partridge, two** Beesly, 249; **short visit to Delhi** 'Ian Fleming as PA to DNI', Godfrey papers; **Peter Fleming** JHG to Margaret Godfrey, 22/4/1943, Godfrey papers; **Admiral Godfrey** PF to EF, 30/3/1943, IFA; **I am well . . . clever operator**, GBR/0014/MLBE 3, Beesly – 'Very Special Admiral papers, 1940–1983', Churchill Archive Centre; **You are much** IF to JHG, 26/6/1943, Godfrey papers; **You will be** IF to JHG, 16/2/1944, Godfrey papers; **a first-rate companion** IF to Nicholas Carroll, 3/1/1947, IFA; **a very agile** *Naval Memoirs*, 102; **It's rather a** JHG to AH, 16/10/1964, Hillgarth papers; **somewhat overbearing** Goodman, 430; **I really asked** JHG to AH, 16/10/1964, Hillgarth papers

XXXI DRAX'S SECRETS

It is no exaggeration Cecil Hampshire, 301; **a mass of** *Thrilling Cities*, 82; **a typical Ian touch** Izzard to Pearson, 22/11/1965, Rankin papers; **We didn't know** IF to Ann Rothermere, Jan 1946, Morgan papers; **Atomic science!** Cecil Hampshire, 279; **They were hectic** Nutting, 240; **Tommy Atkins** ibid., 45; **It was a** Bill Marshall to NS; **Stott revealed** Douglas Stott papers; **Hitler is dead** Lady Loelia Lindsay papers; **a huge fish** Cecil Hampshire, 282; **spectacles on nose . . . blanket** Alan Moorehead, *Eclipse*, 329; **Unfortunately, his gases** Nutting, 253; **all secret papers and drawings** Glanville, 252; ADM 223/214, The National Archives; **it was with much** Nutting, 252; **with instructions to** 12/9/82, 'Reminiscences from John Brereton', David Roberts papers; **all secret documents** Nutting, 254; **Herr Oberst Quel** ibid., 251; **that nothing** ibid., 251; **A film . . . depth charges** ibid., 255; **the latest German** *Thunderball*, 188; **All in all . . . own work** Nutting, 256; **Bring two shovels** BM to NS, 11/12/2019; **The one thing** Christopher Curtis to NS, 24/2/2022

XXXII TAMBACH

We made a brief Nutting, 21; **plus two marines** Harling, 190; **he had arranged** ibid., 188; **A bas les Russes** IF to Charles Grey, 9/5/1945, IFA; *tatty lot heinie* David Kohnen, 'Seizing German Naval Intelligence from the Archives of 1870–1945', *Global War Studies*, vol. 12, no. 1, 2015, 161; II, RG 313, ComNavEu, Subject File, Box 10, Folder 53, NARA; **the most closely** Glanville, ADM 223/214, The National Archives; **logs of U-boats** Glanville, 257; **probably the most** ibid., 257; **all about his** *Constant Heart*, 284; **Rarely if ever** Rankin, 327; **one of the** Harling, 190; **his book collector's** Harling, 188; **one of the greatest** Kohnen, 171; **THE BEARER** ibid., 147; **believed to** ibid., 158; **were to be** Nutting, 19; **It was badly** ibid., 20; **The targets had** ibid., 273; **There were** ibid., 21; **one or two** Harling, 189; **formidable**

character Nutting, 261; **there would be** ibid., 261; **These people some** ibid., 260;
vast . . . and pigs Heinz Pellender, *Tambach*, 60; **an extremely . . . the joker!** Ralph
Izzard 'Answers to Questions Concerning NID', 22/1/1967, GBR/0014/MLBE 6/3,
Churchill Archive Centre; **a cart and oxen** Kohnen, 163; **a crateful of stuff** ibid.,
164; **failed to keep** Glanville, 267; **Cold. Dismal** Harling, 190; **shattered when**
ibid., 190; **to show posterity** ibid., 189; **quite a few** ibid., 191; **But, gentlemen** Heinrich, Graf zu Ortenburg and Johann von Mallinckrodt to NS, 17/12/2021; **swift**
rattling roar *Dr. No*, 92; **profoundly . . . next war** Cecil Hampshire, 299; **warmth**
of temperament Nutting, 268; **Alongside all** Curtis to Quill, 5/12/1947, ADM
223/214, 64, The National Archives; **weight of the** Kohnen, 165; **The situation in**
Rankin, 327; **Apart from stealing** IF to CB, 30/5/145, Benson papers; **to some**
extent Goodman, 163; **It's pretty significant** Richard Dearlove to NS, 22/6/2021;
the S.I.S . . . the next war IF draft to Bentinck, 24/4/1944, ADM 223/851, The
National Archives; **what DNI requires** IF to Rushbrooke, 6/2/1945; *Naval Memoirs*,
48-50; **We shall require** IF draft to Bentinck, 24/4/1944, ADM 223/851, The National
Archives; **Both centrally** Smithers, SWWEC; **Get the top** Izzard, GBR/0014/MLBE
6/3, Churchill Archive Centre; **to turn the** Goodman, 166; **the full integration**
Andrew Boyd, *British Naval Intelligence in the Twentieth Century*, 557

XXXIII THE COMPLETE MAN
My job in Playboy, Dec. 1964; **The saddest . . . evening** 4/11/1944, Lady Loelia
Lindsay papers; **I was at prep** Raymond O'Neill to NS; **I didn't know . . . salt** Fionn
Morgan to NS, 19/1/2023; **April 5 45 I** *Constant Heart*, 279; **Chaps used to** Harling,
SWWEC; **You're the one** *Constant Heart*, 16; **the sort of person** ibid., 244; **I**
thought her ibid., 289; **a failure and** ibid., 290; **The night before** Amory, 43; **I sup-**
pose because Harling, 223; **sole reason . . . wealth** Harling papers; **I went down**
Constant Heart, 290; **their lordships'** IF to JHG, 26/12/1948, Godfrey papers; **the**
extraordinary non-recognition Harling papers; **He had extracted** *Constant*
Heart, 287; **There was** ibid., 297; **the ordinary man . . . in him** Moorehead, 351–2

PART TWO

XXXIV A PUDDLE OF MUD
What did peace Usborne, 147; **It was the** *Constant Heart*, 293; **withering**
scorn . . . brass *Cocktails and Laughter*, 98; **to celebrate . . . all finished** *Wanton*
Chase, 75; **I couldn't resist** *Constant Heart*, 293; **Disastrously unexpected**
26/7/1945, Lady Loelia Lindsay papers; **Churchill never** Joan Astley, SWWEC;
All that seeming Evelyn Waugh, *When the Going Was Good*, 8; **We almost**

suffered *TMWTGT*, 76; **The war took** Fionn Morgan to NS, 19/1/2023/; **tension, excitement** *Constant Heart*, 232; **strange thought … gas** ibid., 296; **In 1945, none** Astley, SWWEC; **very tired and** *Constant Heart*, 285; **he thinks we** ibid., 223; **It was Peter** Elizabeth Longford, *The Pebbled Shore*, 247; **perhaps because** Hart-Davis, *Peter Fleming*, 302; **I'm always rather** Max Hastings to NS, 24/5/2021; **There is a doll's** Kate Fleming, 149; **just about the** ibid., 148; **I *have* made** Hart-Davis, *Peter Fleming*, 301; **signed off** ULTRA PF Bletchley file card, 13/10/1945, Michael Smith papers; **I don't think** Kate Fleming, 127; **smitten with the** ibid., 127; **very meagre portfolio** Pearson, 229; **thought at one** *The Notes*, 73; **whether to take** *Constant Heart*, 233; **that you would** Patrick Dalzel-Job to IF, 17/12/1957, IFA; **I would like** IF to EM, 1934, n.d., Morpurgo papers; **as his own special** Coward, *Volcano*; **Tahiti – or any** *Constant Heart*, 225, 227; **Ian came to** ibid., 235; **the kind of** Harling, 140; **likely to be offered** *Constant Heart*, 291; **He has refused** ibid., 294; **That life will** ibid., 297

XXXV SHAMELADY HALL

This really is *The Notes*, 17; **There was a big** ibid., 150; **a great house** ibid.; **the world's most** Bryce, 68; **We took the train** *The Notes*, 150; **mean little stink** Angus Calder, *The People's War*, 171; **toad-in-the-hole** Delmer, 103; **one of the oldest** *TMWTGG*, 45; **nothing but hills** David Pryce-Jones, *Cyril Connolly*, 83; **as good as** Alec Waugh, *The Sugar Islands*, 205; **How often** ibid., 215; **only be negotiated** Bryce, 70; **The evening was** 'Book of Golden Words', IFA; **the distant mirage** Bryce, 74; **really one** 16/1/1948, Lady Loelia Lindsay papers; **This was the hurricane** Bryce, 75; **She had on** Molly Huggins, *Too Much to Tell*, 93; **he spent some** Bryce, 75; *Jamaica's an island* *The Essential Noël Coward Compendium*, 37; **The spell was cast** Parker, 70; **which he reversed** Bryce, 70; **You know, Ivar** ibid., 72; **lush green beauty** *TOTD*, 290; **He said he** *The Notes*, 196; **violent addiction** Cuneo papers; **Ten acres or so** Bryce, 72; **I think I have** ibid., 36; **He used to take** *The Notes*, 281; **How many times** *Casino Royale*, 153; **This *must* be** Bottome, *Under the Skin*, 125; **We went down** *The Notes*, 151; **'Why Jamaica?** Harling, 140; **For the moment** 'Book of Golden Words', IFA; **Everything looked so** Huggins, 97; **paw paw with** *LALD*, 23; **completely different** Parker, 86; **He would obviously** KF to NS, 22/3/2023; **I never expected … warm sea** IF to Ann, 26/1/1947, IF99A, Morgan papers; **He would spend** *The Notes*, 152; **added a new** *TOTD*, 350; **I spent the … teeth** IF to Ann, early 1947, IF76A, Morgan papers; **like a small** *TOTD*, 257; **And if you** BB, James Bond Transcripts, IFA; **At last he was** JP note, Pearson Collection, Lilly; **They had neither** Alec Waugh, *The Sunlight Caribbean*, 34, 32; **than in any** Harling, 240; **How much I** Bryce, 140; **saying he had … *Shamelady*** *Constant Heart*, 299; **My budget** 31/3/1946, Maud Russell papers

XXXVI THE FOREIGN MANAGER

Only three things Pearson papers; **Then Ian came!** 26/3/1946, Lady Loelia Lindsay papers; **made it clear** Lycett, 167; **I am not going to** Astley, SWWEC; **the bust of** Hobson, Knightley and Russell, *The Pearl of Days*, 238; **latent tycoon instincts** *The Notes*, 232; **a newspaper . . . unconventional** *Pearl of Days*, 253; **I never knowingly** Pearson papers; **I'm a huge** Una Trueblood to NS, 23/9/2019; **with a conspiratorial . . . in Ian** *Times*, 10/2/2008; **that because Lord** Pearson papers; **more money** Denis Hamilton, *Editor-in-Chief: Fleet Street Memoirs*, 60; **lots of bridge** 23/7/1939, Lady Loelia Lindsay papers; **Kemsley believed** Bryce, 78; **He twisted old** *The Notes*, 206

XXXVII 'K'

Lady Ower and TOTD, 12; **whose very privies** Jacob, 134; **unopened books** Robert Robinson, *Skip All That*, 99; **as big as** *TOTD*, 30; **tasteless luxury . . . ostentation** Ann's notes on press barons, Morgan papers; **He'd do anything** Robinson, 103; **The vulgarity** Ann diary, June 1941, Morgan papers; **at once pompous** Frank Giles, *Sundry Times*, 150; **Lord K talked** Lady Loelia Lindsay papers; **if it had been** Lord Hartwell, *William Camrose, Giant of Fleet Street*, 275; **No place for** IF to CB 3/3/1945, Benson papers; **half-promised** *TOTD*, 14; **Crown Prince** Pearson, 209; **Rubens appearance** Channon, vol. 2, 309; **Everyone said . . . Bellyful** *TOTD*, 14; **I have the best** Hamilton, 58; **whose organs hung** Robinson, 109; **Lady Kemsley's in** Hamilton, 84; **What an intriguing** *Pearl of Days*, 280; **Now don't be** *The Notes*, 206; **THOSE ARE MY** Hamilton, 87; **He has deeply . . . history** Ann's notes on press barons, Morgan papers; **nothing in the** Robinson, 99; **Randolph [Churchill] reduced** 18/2/1942, Morgan papers; **Its feature page** Ann's notes on press barons, Morgan papers; **shut off from** Lewis, *David Astor*, 235; **the pall of genteel** *Pearl of Days*, 265; **weighed down with** IF to Kemsley, n.d. [c.1951], Russell Collection, Lilly; **In his debonair** Giles, 157; **secretly hoped** Buckton, 140; **as a rival to Reuters** Pearson papers; **after some exasperated** Bryce, 78; **a curious latter** Buckton, 141; **Would these books** *TOTD*, 350

XXXVIII MERCURY

Wasn't it just Moonraker, 142; **the dejected air** Robinson, 99; **lean loping gait** McLachlan, 9; **an outer office . . . No** Una Trueblood to NS, 23/9/2019; **Mrs Trueblood** IF to Wren Howard, 28/12/1956, IFA; **my invaluable secretary** IF to Anthony Berry, 8/4/1959, IFA; *Trueblood Dr. No*, 8; **would be useful** *The Notes*, 282; **an appalling thing** George Herken, *The Georgetown Set*, 82; **how Secret Service** *The Notes*, 256; **continually on the** *The True Intrepid*, 122; **preoccupied with the** ibid., 122; **to this day** *TV Guide*, 'A piece of cake in Tinseltown', 5/5/1975; **I nearly visited . . . fantasists** David Cornwell to NS, 10/11/2019; **I went up** JP to NS, 14/6/2019; **Ian was mildly** Tom Stacey to NS, 18/3/2022; **a fair old load** Lycett, 169; **It's very much** JP to NS; **the parallels between** McLachlan, 422; **amongst them** *Octopussy*, 69; **When Walter finished** Curt Gentry, *J. Edgar Hoover*, 218; **My father wrote** Jonathan Cuneo to NS, 11/10/2020; **like a country editor** Montgomery-Hyde, 168; **he and his** IF to PS, 27/1/1942, IFA; **I have started** IF to PS, 13/1/1944, IFA; **From what I** *Naval Memoirs*, vol. 5, 271; **an old-age** Buckton, 140; **something of the** *Pearl of Days*, 256; **Indeed, the Kemsley** Anthony Cavendish, *Inside Intelligence*, 77; **I remember** Una Trueblood to NS; **the ideal foreign** *Kemsley Manual of Journalism*, 244; **it looks like** Christopher Moran to NS, 7/1/2020; **He told me** KF to NS; **If Fleming was** Richard Dearlove to NS; **When I was . . . agenda** David Cornwell to NS, 4/1/2020; **They are most** Mary Wesley and Eric Siepmann, *Darling Pol*, 132; **They are providing** ibid., 131; **do nothing** ibid., 132; **a violent . . . war** ibid., 118; 116; **a good friend** 30/12/1963; *Yours Ever, Ian Fleming: Letters to and from Antony Terry*, 112; **the shit with** Judith Lenart, *Berlin to Bond and Beyond: The Story of a Fleming Man*, 27; **his double life** Sarah Gainham, *The Tiger Life*, 167; **had been expert** ibid., 90; **who has been** Terry, *Yours Ever*, 11; **to put into** Gainham, 324; **While my reports** Delmer, 33; **Tangier will be** IF to DM, 30/7/1946, IFA; **simple operations** *Casino Royale*, 5; **Your service continues** IF to DM, 19/9/1947, IFA; **to meet an** McCormick, 124; **We are at** *Kemsley Manual of Journalism*, 240; CYPHER CABLE IF to NC, 18/11/1946, IFA; **We badly need** IF to NC, 13/10/1947, IFA; **if ever . . . under-belly** IF to NC, 19/3/1947, IFA; **I would also** IF to NC, 13/10/1947, IFA; **I am sure . . . hospital** IF to NC, 1/9/1947, IFA; **The way you** *OHMSS*, 246; **I used to dabble** *Goldfinger*, 13; **He had little** Pearson, 237; **Perhaps Fleming didn't** Buckton, 159; **quite clear . . . pyramid** Norman Lewis, *The World, The World*, 153/4; **When Norman was** Lesley Lewis to NS, 22/7/2022; **Do you think** Julian Evans, *Norman Lewis*, 467; **I am leaving on** IF to Ted Merrett, Rankin papers; **of no immediate . . . activities** IF to Vladimir Wolfson, 4/7/1951, Russell Collection, Lilly; **my rather special** IF to VW, 9/11/1951, Russell Collection, Lilly; **As Foreign Manager** ibid.; **When imparting some** Philip Brownrigg to John Pearson, Russell Collection, Lilly; **Guests at these** Atticus on 36 Club, typescript, n.d., IFA; **the fraternity of** *TMWTGG*, 188; **the Cold War** Godfrey papers; **By emphasising that** Richard Greene to NS, 17/1/2022; **functions he attended** JHG to Ann, 20/8/1964, IFA; **S is finally** IF to WS, 11/10/1951, Russell Collection, Lilly; **there was a chance** *The Notes*, 283; HAVE **to dine** IF to Ann, n.d., Morgan papers; **In those days** Lycett, 169; **and looked like** ibid., 281; **I am afraid** IF to Denning, 12/1/1961, Russell Collection, Lilly

XXXIX THE MISSING DIPLOMATS

For this was FRWL, 100; **a giant Australian** *Thrilling Cities*, 3; **Some people, once** Sisman, 364; **He always . . . about you** RH interview with Tim Bowden, 1975, Bowden papers; **I have been into** McCormick, 134; **Demand that they** Lycett, 212;

He is the first John le Carré, 'To Russia, with Greetings', *Encounter*, May 1966; **the brilliant luxury-loving** Lycett, 313; **the man whom** ibid., 252; **It was as if** Owen Matthews, *An Impeccable Spy*, 24; **no one, ever** ibid., 34; **psychic twin . . . *undercoverus*** ibid., 17; **Ostentation is** ibid., 187; **If you . . . ever existed** RH interview with Tim Bowden, 1975; **been on the** *FRWL*, 41; **lies in the myth** ibid., 43; **members of the** Connolly, *The Missing Diplomats*, 15; **acted like a** Andrew Lownie, *Stalin's Englishman: The Lives of Guy Burgess*, 252; **Fleming was . . . heart-splitter** EC to Raymond Benson, n.d., Benson papers; **A myth is slowly** *Missing Diplomats*, 49; **Who is your best** 'Bond Strikes Camp', *Previous Convictions*, 367; **Inside every third** Lewis, *Connolly*, 451; **'Guy Burgess,' said** Lownie, 245; **The story hit** John Cork, intro. *Casino Royale*, xix; **one of the** Lownie, 262; **a mystery which** *Missing Diplomats*, 13; **and we all discussed** *Noël Coward Diaries*, 177; **He always believed** Connolly to JP, Russell Collection, Lilly; **It was a hot** RH interview with Tim Bowden, 1975; **Many first-class** Atticus, 25/9/1955; **Please don't mention** Amory, 161; **an Etonian radical** Ziegler, 71; **I think Khrushchev** Lycett 283; **in a filial cable** Richard Hughes, *Foreign Devil*, 123; **I told him** IF to Ann [1956], IF81B, Morgan papers; **buoyant . . . return** Hughes, 125; **a cup of . . . and Maclean** RH interview with Tim Bowden, 1975; **Summoned to phone** Ann to IF, 16/2/1956, Morgan papers

XL 'THE SHAMEFUL DREAM'

The essential leadership IF to Kemsley, 1951, Russell Collection, Lilly; **For the first** *The Notes*, 122; **Mainly, he sloped** Hunter Davies to NS, 18/10/2020; **I *did* care intensely** Hamilton, 107; **the superb way . . . shoulder** Brownrigg to Pearson, n.d. [1965], Russell Collection, Lilly; **the superficial, snide** McCormick, 17; **this Richard . . . overseas** ibid., 16; **an unsophisticated** Susan Cooper Cronyn to NS, 20/1/2022; **The mighty Kemsley** IF to Ann early 1946 IF55a, Morgan papers; **our small army** *Kemsley Manual of Journalism*, 244; **fantastically expensive** Lycett, 202; **My department is** IF to Ann 30/9/1948, IF89A, Morgan letters; **It is only by** *Yours Ever*, 33; **By hook . . . halved** ibid., 42; **already cost us** ibid., 45; **My Scottish blood** IF to Cuneo, 4/9/1953, Cuneo papers; **lack of . . . a vacuum** IF to Kemsley, n.d. [1950/1], Russell Collection, Lilly; **I felt rather** IF to Ann, n.d., Morgan papers; **run it as** McCormick, 131; **a small hurt** *Pearl of Days*, 256; **at the new . . . one moment** *TOTD*, 15; **Gradually, it** Pearson, 215; **I have always** *Kemsley Manual of Journalism*, vii; **As his close friend** Hamilton, 199; **deep distress** *TOTD*, 29; **something sacred** *TOTD*, 27; **tactless, a gaffeur** Channon, vol. 2, 993

XLI DROOPY

Droopy would never *Pomp and Circumstance*, 71; **They were . . . the stain** Esmond, Viscount Rothermere to NS, 18/5/2020; **deeply wounded by** Esmé Cromer, *From*

This Day Forward, 48; **There was an** S. J. Taylor, 40; **The image that** Vivian Baring to NS, 28/5/2020; **He had thinning** *Pomp and Circumstance*, 272; **as remote as** Ann to Hugo Charteris, 18/5/1950, Morgan papers; **If a joke suddenly** *Wanton Chase*, 106; **monosyllabic giant** S. J. Taylor, 46; **He is getting** 17/10/1943, Lady Loelia Lindsay papers; **She loves Esmond** Channon, vol. 2, 880; **about her sex** Mary (Pakenham) Clive papers; **and said, 'I always'** Amory, 104; **tempestuous childhood** Ann to Hugo, Dec. 1950, 4959, Morgan papers; **overwhelming** Ann's notes on press barons, Morgan papers; **excitable and worried** S. J. Taylor, 16; **a tiresome, common** Channon, vol. 1, 819; **He was a playboy** VB to NS; **My mother when** FM to NS; **Tennis in Monte Carlo** Ann's notes on press barons, Morgan papers; **It is a new** ibid.; **he has a goblin** ibid.; **the Dorchester Commandos** *Wanton Chase*, 59; **extremely vigorous** ibid., 108; **I had been scheming** Ann to Duff Cooper [1945], GBR/0014/DUFC 12/34, Churchill Archive Centre; **The** *Daily Mail* **was** Sara Morrison to NS, 9/1/2020; **If the strike gets** Ann to Duff Cooper [August 1948], GBR/0014/DUFC 12/34, Churchill Archive Centre; **penchant for solitude** Ann notes on press barons, Morgan papers; **He is alone** Amory, 93

XLII BUNNY

I've known him Pomp and Circumstance, 277; **I never showed** ibid., 41; **I threw it** IF to Ann, IF32A, Dec. 1946, Morgan papers; **I have been** IF to Ann IF55A, Jan. 1946, Morgan papers; **If Fleming turns** Cherie Burns, *Searching for Beauty*, 186; **miles of corridors** *Love from Boy; Roald Dahl's Letters to his Mother*, 263; **the finest and largest** Donald Sturrock, *Storyteller: The Life of Roald Dahl*, 235; **Yes, I'm fucking** Parker, 51; **the most sexually** Burns, 196; **right after I** Ziegler 74; **sweet, helpful . . . motor up** Burns, 188/9; **a dreamy little house** *New York Journal-American*, 8/2/1948; **She watched him** Rosamund Lehmann, *A Sea-Grape Tree*, 71; **the tall, slim** Burns, 189; **i have been** IF to Ann IF55A, January 1946, Morgan papers; **a damned inconvenient** Amory, 45; **old Gomer to** Lycett, 172; **Ian arrived . . . New York** ibid.; **You write sweet** IF to Ann, 1/2/1947, Morgan papers; **They were the** Ann to IF [1947], AF38a, Morgan papers; **They say 'The Dorset'** IF to Ann, n.d., IF20, Morgan papers; **We are both** IF to Ann, n.d., IF19a, Morgan papers; **Please write to** IF to Ann, n.d., IF58a, Morgan papers; **Darling, the misery** Ann to IF, 6/8/1947, AF26a, Morgan papers; **Esmond goes out** Ann to IF, n.d., AF41a, Morgan papers; **I would have** Ann to IF, n.d., AF9a, Morgan papers; **treating my letters** IF to Ann, n.d, 1F73a, Morgan papers; **I have said** IF to Ann, 1/10/1948, IF93a, Morgan papers; **his light-hearted** 8/1/1947, Maud Russell papers; **We both belong** IF to Ann, n.d., IF29a, Morgan papers; **holiday honeymoon** Ann to IF, 14/2/1948, AF17a, Morgan papers; **I remember seeing** Ruth Fitzgibbons to NS, 5/5/2020; **This has been** IF to Ann, Feb. 1949, IF61A; **He finds us** IF to Ann,

1948, IF66A; **I had happened** *Playboy*, Dec. 1964; **I was in on** CB notes, Pearson Collection, Lilly; **Alastair Forbes suggested** Amory, 62; **the nearest ear** Bryce, 80; **Ian's functional** 16/1/1948, Lady Loelia Lindsay papers; **I thought of Goldeneye** Harling, 240; **All you Flemings** Cole Lesley, *Life of Noël Coward*, 262; **all tasting of** ibid., 262; **the house is nearly** IF to Ann, 26/1/1947, Morgan papers; **just open spaces** EC 'Notes on Goldeneye', Jan. 1963, Benson papers; **up to one's** Harling, 242; **an overhanging fresco** Amory, 54; **It was incredibly** Raymond O'Neill to NS; **slept nervously** 17/1/1948, Lady Loelia Lindsay papers; **Ian said to me** Jemima Pitman to NS, 13/5/2020; **crouching gloomily** Coward, *Volcano*; **fantastically beautiful** Hirsch, 307; **We went out** 22/1/1948, Lady Loelia Lindsay papers; **After dinner** Amory, 62; **Only Ian could** ibid., 60; *There is no . . . hour away* IF to Olaf Hambro, 19/10/1951, Russell Collection, Lilly; **Couples have spent** *TOTD*, 350; **teaching me to** Richard Greene, *Graham Greene*, 459; **My darling, you** IF to Ann, Jan. 1947, IF76a, Morgan papers; **Suddenly nausea** Ann to IF, Feb. 1948, Morgan papers; **I hope your situation** S. J. Taylor, 40; **a lovely Easter** Ann to DC, 9/4/1947, GBR/0014/DUFC 12/34, Churchill Archive Centre; **an attack of** *The Notes*, 93; **I am sure you** Ann to IF [1948], AF28a, Morgan papers; **She is big** *Darling Monster: The Letters of Lady Diana Cooper to her Son John Julius Norwich*, 275; **rubbed oil** Ann to IF [1948], AF28a, Morgan papers; **He had an immense** 25/4/1948, Maud Russell papers; **Talked about** 19/8/1948, ibid.; **disastrous** 31/8/1948, Lady Loelia Lindsay papers; **poor Annie had** 21/8/1948, ibid.; **fighting every inch** 22/8/1948, ibid.; **It has left us** 24/8/1948, ibid.; **Annie may have** 25/8/1948, ibid.; **I just felt . . . more** IF to Ann, IF23a, Morgan papers; **I held my baby's** Amory, 101; **It is screaming** Ann to Hugo Charteris, 16/11/1951, Morgan papers; **the greatest . . . loves** Ann to Virginia Charteris, 31/10/1951, Morgan papers; **Darling Baby** IF to Ann, F21a, Morgan papers; **More horrors** 30/8/1948, Lady Loelia Lindsay papers; **There was morphia** Amory, 70; **They christened her** Ann to IF, AF3a, Morgan papers; **the hope that** Ann to IF, AF49a, Morgan papers; **my deep love** Amory, 101; **it mustn't happen** IF to Ann, IF66a, Morgan papers; **What does Esmond** FM to NS, 6/5/2022; **I feel I shouldn't** IF to Ann, IF26a, Morgan papers; **The trouble is** Amory, 80; **a hard . . . crack** ibid., 56; **Bad news from** IF to Ann, 1948, IF58a, Morgan papers; **a sort of Beau . . . hottest romance** *New York Journal-American*, 8/2/1948, Amory, 65; **I think C** Ann to IF, AF22a, Morgan papers; **How lucky** Amory, 65; **I fear that** IF to Ann, 24/2/1948, IF13a, Morgan papers; **tells me it** Ann to IF, AF43a, Morgan papers; **I wish, wish** Ann to IF, AF28a, Morgan papers; **most of the news** S. J. Taylor, 60; **If you want** *The Notes*, 319; **that particular chemical** *Pomp and Circumstance*, 146; **He was mad** ibid., 61; **I've known about** ibid., 275; **in all quarters** ibid., 217; **muddly affair** 19/5/1949, Maud Russell papers; **the status quo** Hugo Charteris to Mary Rose, n.d., Morgan papers; **I fear the situation** 18/3/1949, Lady

Loelia Lindsay papers; **sheer mischief making** Ann to IF, AF43a, Morgan papers; **He had no** Vivien Baring to NS; **an inner ferment** *Pomp and Circumstance*, 275; **poor affair . . . property** Harling, 261; **such an embarrassing . . . regularise their** Kaye, 238; **My Precious** Ann to IF, AF42a, Morgan papers; **tricoteuse** *FRWL*, 255; **back to her petit** *YOLT*, 188; **do you think** Ann to IF, AF24a, Morgan papers; **work out a** IF to Ann, IF24a, Morgan papers

XLIII 'QUITE A STEP'

Kissy wondered *YOLT*, 213; **Learned all sorts** John Goodwin diary, 16/12/1964; **Caspar was born** Mary (Pakenham) Clive papers; **would have to** FM to NS, 2/7/2020; **his supposedly carefree** Harling papers; **Jamaica is no** IF to Ann, 26/1/1947, IF99a, Morgan papers; **I never feel well** IF to Ann, IF76a, Morgan papers; **a wife who** Ann's notes on press barons, Morgan papers; **hopeless and like** IF to Ann, IF91a, Morgan papers; **The idea of the** Sara Morrison to NS; **He liked nothing** *The Notes*, 60; **I am going round** IF to Ann, IF65a, Morgan papers; **I wanted a home** *The Notes*, 59; **a lot of . . . freedom** IF to Ann, IF88a, Morgan papers; **It would be** IF to Ann, IF61a, Morgan papers; **rather like a** IF to Ann, IF66a, Morgan papers; **there was no** *The Notes*, 129; **because she found** Ivar Mountbatten to NS, 11/2/2023; **Dinner yesterday** IF to Ann, IF58a, Morgan papers; **There seems some** Amory, 66; **out of this dear** IF to Ann, IF95a, Morgan papers; **I'm afraid . . . too black** Amory, 78; **I don't believe** 19/10/1948, Maud Russell papers; **it has long** *Time*, 5/6/1950; **It is quite a** Amory, 103; **lack of courage** Ann to HC, 18/5/1950, Morgan papers; **Oh! God, oh!** Ann to IF, AF47a, Morgan papers; **I wish a fairy** Ann to IF, AF24d, Morgan papers; **carry on the** IF to Ann, IF76a, Morgan papers; **cream-puff fog** Amory, 82; **quite clearly** 8/1/1947, Maud Russell papers; **He never will** 8/6/1949, ibid.; **I cannot imagine** 25/1/1952, ibid.; **I had finished** *TOTD*, 133; **He used to say** John Pearson, James Bond Transcripts, IFA; **I know I've bashed** *Pomp and Circumstance*, 68; **You can't be** *Diamonds Are Forever*, 192; **divorce was such** *Cocktails and Laughter*, 46; **when Ann had** 21/9/1952, Maud Russell papers; **horrified at the** *The Notes*, 72; **He cabled Ian** ibid., 116; **I decided that** Amory, 102; **my bonnet** Ann to Noël Coward, 16/1/1952, IFA; **Aged 15** FM to NS, 2/7/2020; **will cause something** IF to Denis Hamilton, Hamilton papers; **Father was not** JP to NS; **It is my considered** *Pomp and Circumstance*, 214; **the moment the** ibid., 172; **He made a mistake** Pryce-Jones, 214; **Oh, it was** Glen, SWWEC; **Perhaps you will** Hirsch, 330; **a prospect which** Buckton, 141

XLIV WRITING BOND

For a moment he *FRWL*, 31; **My mental hands** Ian Fleming and Wlliam Plomer, 1962, 'The Writer Speaks', Durham University Archives; **If he were** *TMWTGT*, 70;

He would have McCormick, 18; **to the rank of Principal** *YOLT*, 201; **imaginatively pictured** Rankin, 313; **running the show** *Casino Royale*, 46; **the most hopeless** *Harper's Bazaar*, Nov. 1964.; **I think he** *The Notes*, 250; **Ian Fleming is a** Buckton, 277; ***On the floor*** Morgan papers; **Of course, my** *The Notes*, 142; **some pen pictures** IF to PS, 23/7/1942, IFA; **When I met Ian** *The Notes*, 102; **Of course, he** McCormick to Ivar Bryce, 1/1/1975, Bryce papers; **His favourite writer** *The Notes*, 124; **When I first** NL to NS, 4/5/1991; **About the time** *The Notes*, 205; **he always said** RL to Pearson, 26/5/1965, Pearson Collection, Lilly; **You beast** Ann to IF, AF35a, Morgan papers; **You might write** Ann to IF, AF28a, Morgan papers; **This is your** Ann to IF, AF16a, Morgan papers; **about five of** <https://debrief.commanderbond.net/topic/65378-widow-to-a-legend-ann-fleming-speaks/index.html>; **In due course** Harling, 97; **With a diffidence** Plomer, *Address*; **There would be** *The Notes*, 104; **Ian was the** ibid., 237; **Peter and Ian** Gilly Newbery to NS, 14/7/2019; **quite a lot . . . face** Naomi Burton to Benson, 1982, Benson papers; **non-thrilling . . . exist** Duff Hart-Davis, *Peter Fleming*, 327–8; **every gift, literary** ibid., 126; **as an antidote** Peter Fleming, *The Sixth Column*, 31; **They're twaddle** ibid., 36; **His secret was** ibid., 67; **He wrote because** Al Hart to Benson, 1/19/1982, Benson papers; **No Bulldog Drummond** *FRWL*, 237; **I don't believe** James Chapman, *Licence to Thrill*, 24; **thought he could** Una Trueblood to NS; **with more literary** Christoph Lindner, *The James Bond Phenomenon*, 47; **If a writer is** McCormick, 28; **This morning Ian** Amory, 108; **I had finished** Gant, 63; **battered Royal** blurb for *TSWLM*, 1962; **I was in a** 21/9/1952, Maud Russell papers; **a simple first-rate** Harling, 266; **the MO, Major** *Constant Heart*, 266; **brief, unromantic** IF to Mary Bond, 20/6/1961, IFA; **For pity's sake** IF to HB, 1963, Bray papers; **one of my bibles** IF to Mary Bond, 20/6/1961, IFA; **I thought, 'James Bond'** CBC interview, Feb. 1964; **What would you** Cuneo papers; **aiming to be** Pearson, 323; **who taught the** *TOTD*, 250; **On holiday this** *Sunday Times*, 26/4/1953; **there are times** Gant, 98; **All writers possessed** Kingsley Amis, *The Bond Dossier*, 115; **to admire the** IF to Olaf Hambro, 19/10/1951, Russell Collection, Lilly; **We all, when** 'The Writer Speaks', 1962; **Nothing on the** Amory, 361; **He said that** *The Notes*, 249; **You're just like** Weaver, 388; **served as a model** Cuneo papers; **A good fifty** *The Notes*, 239; **It's another nut** *TMWTGG*, 7; **Almost everyone** JP, James Bond Transcripts, IFA; **a large brownish** 'State of Excitement', 105, IFA; **two or three people** Usborne, 88; **All fictional characters** foreword to *Call for the Dead*, xiii; **In the end** Sisman, 75; **Well, yes, one** *TOTD*, 161; **Mostly expensive** *Casino Royale*, 14; **It's my experience** *Playboy*, Dec. 1964; **shenanigans . . . up in** CBC interview, Feb. 1964; **I think he** *The Notes*, 53; **his chronic sense** Pearson papers; **Is the following** EF to WSC, Churchill Archive Centre; **THANK YOU** WSC to EF, Churchill Archive Centre; **My brother Peter** IF to WSC, 27/5/1948, Churchill Archive Centre; **The truth, of course** Harling, 323; **Do you often . . . thirties** *Playboy*, Dec. 1964; **the Fleming/**

James Bond JC notes 3/11/1966, Carr-Ellison papers; **the next volume** Pearson, 432; **collected works** Bryce, 141; **I can say ninety** CBC interview, Feb. 1964; **he couldn't write** *The Notes*, 284; **Is Bond Fleming?** 'Bondmanship', Harry Ransom Center; **whole persona** Cubby Broccoli, *When the Snow Melts*, 159; **to counterbalance** JHG to Leonard Russell 7/4/1966, Godfrey papers; **He wasn't James** *The Notes*, 110; **I could not . . . reach** *Wanton Chase*, 146, 152–3; **no particular interest** blurb for *TSWLM*, 1962; **a wonderful machine** *Casino Royale*, 139; **Sometimes it came** Mary Seymour to NS, 1/10/2019; **There is only** *TOTD*, 191; **How *do* you do it?** *TMWTGT*, 215; **I believe you** ibid., 199; **Novels are very** interview with Brian Glanville, 1964; **Interesting statistics** *Darling Pol*, 125; **I work about** *Desert Island Discs*, 1963; **extraordinary life** Bryce, 96; **where you damned** *Playboy*, Dec. 1964; **A report should** 4/9/1942, Godfrey papers; **It holds up** interview with Brian Glanville; **not to be too** *Harper's Bazaar*, Nov. 1964; **I mustn't write** Amory, 82; **I'm beginning to** ibid., 173; **To me, epigrams** IF to Ann, 9/8/1954, IF14a, Morgan papers; **The reader's eyes** *TOTD*, 47; **an almost intolerable** Gant, 98; **used to frighten** *TOTD*, 127; **Maestro Ambler** IF to Leonard Russell, Russell Collection, Lilly; **There are not** Stafford, *Silent Game*, 180; **the squalor and** Buckton, 296; **a distinct feeling** *The Notes*, 143; **from all the** IF to EA, 13/7/1956, IFA; **the very reverse** IF to Mary Bond 20/6/1961, IFA; **a lantern-jawed . . . civilisation** Eric Ambler, *The Dark Frontier*, 38; **When one chapter** Ziegler, 84; **I went into writing** Gant, 63; **How could I** *TOTD*, 134; **If you interrupt** ibid., 201; **my formula** ibid.; **the great thing** McLachlan, 9; **start from the** IF to WS, 4/3/1961, Russell Collection, Lilly; **Never mind about** Bryce, 97; ***The scent and smoke*** *Casino Royale*, 1; **won some money** 7/8/1939, Lady Loelia Lindsay papers; **silence and economy** *Casino Royale*, 66, 86; **stark little** IF to Eileen M. Cond, 14/5/1953, VanBlaricum Collection

XLV A WEDDING

Precious Annie Amory, 200; **You could put** EF to IF, 18/12/1950, Russell Collection, Lilly; **a marvellous honeymoon** Amory, 106; **Ian didn't appreciate** *The Notes*, 154; **wicked Mrs Fleming** Amory, 362; **It is a hideous** ibid., 103; **Went to see** LW diary, 24/2/1956, Lady Loelia Lindsay papers; **I will bear in** IF to EF, 29/8/1950, Russell Collection, Lilly; **I thought that** *The Notes*, 56; **It was a stand-off** JF to NS; **someone along** Harling, 88; **seemed to lose** *The Notes*, 69; **marrying an old** IF to WS, 11/10/1951, Russell Collection, Lilly; **The flutter . . . least** *Times*, 1/11/1957; **We were informally** *Times*, 8/11/1957; **Old Winchester** 14/11/1957, *LH-D Letters*, vols 1 and 2, 387; **chronic impecuniosity** *Times*, 30/10/1958; **he is rather apt** *Times*, 9/11/1957; **No one could . . . works** *Times* 27/11/1957; **How pleased you** *Amaryllis Fleming*, 150; **I think, in fact** IF to WS, 11/10/1951, Russell Collection, Lilly; **We are** still *Amaryllis Fleming*, 150; **We are, of course** Amory, 106; **I've never heard** *The Notes*, 174; **as usual** ibid., 174; **surly, glowering** Cole Lesley, 320; **I shall wear** *The Letters of Noël Coward*, ed. Barry Day, 573; **I sensed that Annie** *Noël Coward Diaries*, 189; **doubts about their** ibid., 130; **Good misprint** IF to Plomer, 23/2/1961, Plomer Collection, Lilly; **She shook so** Philip Hoare, *Noël Coward*, 394; **surprisingly timorous . . . entirely** *The Notes*, 215; *Mongoose dig about* Laura, Duchess of Marlborough, *Laughter from a Cloud*, 121; **I have suffered** Amory, 106; **We need some** Ann to Clarissa, 20/2/1952, Hugo Vickers papers; **I am devoted** Ann to Beaverbrook, August 1952, Beaverbrook papers; **I looked at** Clarissa Eden to Duff Cooper, 26/8/1952, DUFC 12/3, Churchill Archive Centre; **I thought I had** *Ladies' Home Journal*, Oct. 1966

XLVI 'TELL ME THAT STORY AGAIN'

James and Tracy OHMSS, 184; **just on the . . . the picture** 5/2/1964, Mary Bond diary, 'Jamaica on-the-spot notes Oracabessa', the Free Library of Philadelphia; Mary Bond, *How 007 Got His Name*; Jim Wright, *The Real James Bond*; **a spare handsome** Amory, 337; **darling . . . prop** Mary Bond diary; **a magic catalyst** Ann to Jenny Bray 28/2/1963, Bray papers; **may even be** Pearson, 481; **the lovely . . . for you** Mary Bond diary; **that you had brazenly** *TMWTGT*, 279; **Yes, Bond's here** Mary Bond, *How 007 Got His Name*, 59; **I don't blame** Jim Wright, *The Real James Bond*, 17; **hysterical success** Amory, 336; **infernal** ibid., 338; **When am I** 27/2/1964, Bray papers; **Trying to preserve** *Ladies' Home Journal*, Oct. 1966; **aloof, polite** Mary Bond diary; **He smelled of** *TSWLM*, 171; **unlimited use** IF to Mary Bond, 20/6/1961, Russell Collection, Lilly; **when tentatively marking** HB to Mary Bond, 30/11/1964, Jim Wright papers; **He duly identified** Bryce, 93; **smashed to atoms** IF to HB, 27/2/1964, Bray papers; **Fleming's last erection** Hamilton, 201; **Alas, it was** Mary Bond diary; **Could you please** *Dr. No*, 136; **JB authenticus . . . appreciate Jim** Mary Bond diary; **a red letter day** Jim Wright, *The Real James Bond*, 18; **heavy pressure . . . command** Mary Bond diary; **Just** *don't let* MB to IF, 1/2/1961, Wright, 70; **the last hardcover** Philip Larkin, *Spectator*, 8/7/1966; **stuff we had pinched** Bill Marshall to NS; **I cannot help** Lenart, 77; **Major Smythe gave** *Octopussy*, 24; **worst winter weather** ibid., 30; **The tentacles snaked** ibid., 45; **How easy** *Spectator*, 8/7/1966; **Now he stay** *The Notes*, 23

XLVII TWO BIRTHS

I wrote 'Author' TOTD, 135; **Ian's martyrdom** Amory, 111; **Ian Fleming, tanned** Barbara Skelton, *Tears Before Bedtime*, 127; **Ian was excited** Mary (Pakenham) Clive papers; **inextinguishable extravagances** Harling, 274; **like a dozen** ibid., 261; **he had at last** Harling, 262; **William, if you** 'The Writer Speaks'; **so light that**

13/10/1956, *LH-D Letters*, vols 1 and 2, 195; **reached the stage** Amory, 117; **He wrote such** CB to Raymond Benson, 10/5/1982, Benson papers; **I went on my** *The Notes*, 124; **I came** *Cocktails and Laughter*, 98; **extracted it from me** *TMWTGT*, 16; **I read, I applauded** Plomer, *Encounter*, Jan 1965; **I sat up till 1.20** Daniel George to WP, 25/7/1952, Eton College Archives; **mesmeric readability** *Required Writing*, 266; **I bought six** David Bruce, *Ambassador to Sixties London*, 52; **hard & tightfisted** IF to Plomer, 23/2/1960, Russell Collection, Lilly; **against any form** *TMWTGT*, 27; **I thought its** Norman Lewis, *The World, The World*, 152; **I suppose we'll** Mary Fleming to NS; **you have done** *TMWTGT*, 16; **to say Annie** 9/8/1952, Lady Loelia Lindsay papers; **I didn't want . . . alarms** Amory, 120; **Please forgive me** Lycett, 229; **They decided to** Amory, 117; **Ann has had** 12/8/1952, Lady Loelia Lindsay papers; **He is the most** *TMWTGT*, 17; **I deserved an** IF to Clare Blanshard, 30/6/1952, Fergus Fleming papers; **This is only** *TMWTGT*, 16; **in a coma of** Ann to Beaverbrook, 8/9/1952, Beaverbrook papers; **Dearest Ann . . . granted** Amory, 121; **I think Adam** IF to Ann, n.d., IF7a, Morgan papers; **the child is** Clarissa Eden to Duff Cooper, 17/9/1952, Churchill Archive Centre; **I wonder what** Hugo Vickers, *Cecil Beaton*, 358; **considers himself** Amory, 119; **stout golf player** ibid., 119; **a splendid range** Ann to Beaverbrook, 8/9/1952, Beaverbrook papers; **The doctors have** Amory, 120; **very excited over** Mary Pakenham, 29/9/1952, Pearson Collection, Lilly; **paid him well** 21/9/1952, Maud Russell papers; **it's no good** Plomer, *Encounter*, 1965; **extreme self-confidence** Lewis, 152; **What I want is** Bryce, 103; **you'll be lucky** *The Notes*, 195; **I am only actuated** *TMWTGT*, 19; **Print them** Robert Fleming, 'Prince Curly', Mary Fleming papers; **to bulldoze Cape** Lewis, 155; **remorseless and hair-splitting** ibid., 152; **I toss your** *TMWTGT*, 19; **I think jackets** *Harper's Bazaar*, November 1964.; **I have designed** ibid., 22; **one of the first** Buckton, 279; **a far cry** *TMWTGT*, 371; **This thriller business** ibid., 35; **the foundations** Lewis, 155; **I am bludgeoning** IF to CB, 22/4/1953, VanBlaricum Collection; **I would not do** WSM to IF, Russell Collection, Lilly; **I started it last** WSM to IF, n.d. [April 1953], Russell Collection, Lilly; **Can I count** Ann to Beaverbrook, 29/3/1953, Beaverbrook papers; **didn't care** *The Notes*, 206; **My mother was** FM to NS, 6/5/2022; **My love, How** *TMWTGT*, 113; **Please be optimistic** IF to Ann, 9/8/1954, IF14a, Morgan papers; **was happy from** Gant, 63; **Had any rows** Skelton, 147; **For how long** ibid., 164–5; **came to lunch** Lady Loelia Lindsay papers; **by a piece** Ann to Beaverbrook, 17/6/1952, Beaverbook papers; **the fact was** *The Notes*, 58; **He said they** 21/9/1952, Maud Russell papers; **Childhood should** Harling, 271; **fashion tycoon** ibid., 272; **The 'Royale' in** *TMWTGT*, 18; **a truly fine** JG to NS; **My profits from** *TMWTGT*, 36; **My dear Thomas** Thomas Pakenham to NS, 15/12/2020; **Peter Cheyney . . . since Ambler** Lycett, 243; **these astonishingly** *TMWTGT*, 35; **if I am to** ibid., 34; **the new book** ibid., 37; **Daniel George and William** IF to Cape, 28/5/1953, IFA

What I endeavour TOTD, 94; **You must write** IF to Robert Ryder, 23/11/1953, IFA; **a bosomy spinster** Sara Morrison to NS, 26/7/2022; **Palms wave** Amory, 125; The first night Weaver, 389; **If it got lost** CB to Benson, 29/6/1982, Benson papers; The whole thing CB, Pearson Collection, Lilly; **Ian must have** CB to RB, 1/6/1982, Benson papers; **slightly angular . . . a tap** CB, Pearson Collection, Lilly; **I read it (them)** CB to RB, 10/5/1982, Benson papers; **Sometimes he altered** CB to RB, 29/6/1982, Benson papers; **His innocence was** CB to RB, 1/6/1982, Benson papers; **Would you please** IF to Michael Howard, n.d., IFA; **afraid to write** Benson papers; **I didn't care** CB to RB, 10/5/1982, Benson papers; **I did all** Benson papers; **I told him** Pearson Collection, Lilly; **to give it** IF to WP, 29/3/1960, Plomer Collection, Lilly; **From you** IF to WP, 30/4/1961, Plomer Collection, Lilly; **why write** WP to IF, 14/2/1960, Plomer Collection, Lilly; **M speaks 'drily'** WP to IF, 31/5/1954, Plomer Collection, Lilly; **the equivalent of** Gant, 97; **Fleming is constitutionally** Lycett, 421; **What's that** *Ladies' Home Journal*, Oct. 1966; **What is the** Gant, 13; **same book over** Pearson, 410; **a clever montage** Lindner, 47; **the thrilling story** MB to IF, 10/4/1955, Beaverbrook papers; **He is a tough** Gant, 152; **Bond must be** IF to IB, 23/10; Sellers, 56; **killed their men** Usborne, 5; They gave us ibid., 9; **the security of** *DAF*, 66; **the moral fibre** *YOLT*, 79; **It is one of** *TOTD*, 108; **there was only** *Goldfinger*, 221; **IF's recipe is** 5/11/1959, *LH-D Letters*, vols 3 and 4, 334; **But I cannot** 13/6/1957, *LH-D Letters*, vols 1 and 2, 314; **D'Artagnan and Don Juan** Richard Maibaum, 'James Bond and his girls', Special Collections and University Archives, University of Iowa; *But don't you* Sapper, *The Saving Clause*, 173; **A lot of Ian** Pearson papers; **He is the first** 'Bondmanship', Stephen Potter papers, Harry Ransom Center; **He had come** *TSWLM*, 176; **The conventional parabola** *Casino Royale*, 149; **I recognise in myself** V. S. Naipaul, *New Statesman*, 28/10/1966; **what pleases and** *TOTD*, 195; **Detail fascinated him** *TMWTGT*, 83; **a cross between** IF to Whitney Straight, 23/7/1957, Russell Collection, Lilly; **I don't think** Raymond O'Neill to NS, 18/11/2019; **He was monumentally** EC to RB, Jan. 1963, Benson papers; **who to go to** *The Notes*, 50; *the true basis* ADM 223/479; **I clearly missed** V. S. Naipaul, *New Statesman*, 28/10/1966; **adroit blend of realism** *TLS*, 5/6/1981; **that prince among** *OHMSS*, 17; **Felix Leiter bought** *MWGG*, 93; **please note** *TOTD*, 196; **I know the place** *Octopussy*, 61; **Not very clever** Usborne, 117; **he explained each** *TMWTGT*, 75; **Bond is a connoisseur** Sam Leith intro. *Octopussy* (2012); **the Edwardian Room** ibid., 120; **For the rest** Lindner, 52; **smashing success . . . know how** *Thrilling Cities*, 135, 139; **IF POSSIBLE GET** IF to CB, 1/1/1953, Russell Collection, Lilly; **The great nightmare** *Times*, 1/2/2023; **usually works to** Lindner, 40; **great disappointment** IF to Smithers, 13/10/1941, IFA; **I spent last** IF to WS, 15/10/1959, Russell Collection, Lilly; **So I had to give** Gant, 74; **that Piesporter** *TMWTGT*,

202; **Steradent is something** TD to IF, n.d., IFA; **a sheaf of acid** IF to G. Gibson, 23/6/1959, IFA; **People picked holes** Gant, 123; **I pride myself** IF to N. Lingeman, 18/1/ 1956, IFA; **Oh look** LF to NS, 13/3/2020; **He got a number** *The Notes*, 189; **This kind of** Pearson, 438; **I hate to** *TMWTGT*, 338; **I suppose until** ibid., 50; **I am afraid** IF to R. L. Sjostrom, 3/7/1963, IFA

XLIX 'BLOODY INTELLECTUALS'

The higher one Channon, vol. 2, 572; **Ian said he** RO'N to NS, 18/11/2019; **a happy escape** McCormick, 162; **the way to stay** IF to Ann, IF94a, n.d.; **I have an abiding** TP to NS, 15/12/2020; **I naturally turn** Ann to Hugo, 25/9/1954, Morgan papers; **Ian's in America** Amory, 143; **he was a cunt** Weaver, 388; **a kind of Sunday** ibid., 498; **Ian sends his** Amory, 103; **smoked trout . . . brulée** Judy Montagu papers; **a bouquet of** *Wanton Chase*, 106; **I remember the** *The Notes*, 31; **The noise in** Parker, *Goldeneye*, 168; **mixture of chuckle** IF to Hilary Bray, March 1964, Bray papers; **I don't think** Susanna Johnston to NS, 5/6/2020; **I am covered with** Ann to DC, GBR/0014/DUFC 12/34, Churchill Archive Centre; **Annie Fleming gave** Jo Alsop to Judy Montagu, 26/4/1963, Montagu papers; **her parties are . . . bed** *Self-Portrait with Friends: Selected Diaries of Cecil Beaton*, 274; **sitting beside** Amory, 133; **I was wagging** Margaret Anne Stuart to NS, 15/3/2020; **most strange to** *The Notes*, 31; **The geisha party** *YOLT*, 5; **masturbating his** Ann to James Pope-Hennessy, 11/6/1958, Pope-Hennessy papers; **First of all** Lycett, 235; **than all you lot** ibid., 251; **Annie is always** *The Notes*, 274; **a young and equally** IF Hamburg notebook, Eton College Archives; **I can't stand her** Harling, 312; **dismal conversational** Ziegler, 75; **In a scene** Randal Keynes to NS, 3/4/2021; **He suddenly became** Connolly to Pearson [1965], Russell Collection, Lilly; **'We had dinner** Clarissa Pryce-Jones to NS, 1/7/2020

L THE FAST CAR LIFE

In the books *The Notes*, 286; **great annual cowpat** IF to WP, June 1964, Plomer Collection, Lilly; **As they . . . at things** Pearson papers; **The darkness . . . smuggling** IF notebooks, IFA; **his custom-made** Benson, 55; **an expensive . . . success** *TMWTGT*, 173; **I think Ian was** Amory, 137; **the kilometres clicking** Pearson, 332; **Heaven is a place** Atticus, 'Personal Paradise', IFA; **Please see what** Terry, 37; **I have adventures** McCormick, 155; **You must . . . frightening** *The Notes*, 69; **To: James Bond** Alan Lennox-Boyd to IF, 11/5/1958, Russell Collection, Lilly; **My parents never** JC to NS, 11/10/2020; **The furniture is** IF to Ann, 9/8/1954, IF14a, Morgan papers; **I see deer** IF to Ann, 12/8/1957, IF42a, Morgan papers; **Lived here like** Buckton, 197; **He would always** *The Notes*, 155; **She did wonderful** Nuala Pell interview with John Cork, 2000, Cork papers; **Divorce her** Lycett,

259; **in filling him** Nuala Pell interview with John Cork; **Rich friends** Loelia Westminster, *Grace and Favour*, 39; **slender, always** JC to NS, 11/10/2020; **a bizarre but** IF to Alan Ross, 2/5/1957, Russell Collection, Lilly; **Bond summed him** *Thunderball*, 7; **No one else** EC to Bryce, 27/5/1984, Bryce papers; **some riotously . . . between us** ibid.; **He wrote to me** EC to Raymond Benson, n.d., Benson papers; **the world's richest** *The Notes*, 238; **Everything Ian Fleming** Cuneo papers; **'Bryce,' said Bond** *LALD*, 137; **Your name please** *Dr. No*, 136; **To the degree** EC to Bryce, 28/9/1983, Bryce papers; **It's a pity** Ann to Beaverbrook, 1955, Beaverbrook papers; **the wickedest man** Lycett, 208; **I *love* Ivar** Amory, 173; **Ivar and Ian** JMH to NS, 11/2/2023; **the Scylla and** ibid., 302; **some kind of a** EC to Raymond Benson, n.d., Benson papers; **Come home quickly** Ann to IF, AF34a, 1958, Morgan papers; **They used to take** JMH to NS, 17/5/2019; **For wealth on** *The Notes*, 239; **among the most . . . to read it** Lisa Rebecca Gubernick, *Squandered Fortune*, 178; **I had tried** JB to Pearson, 21/9/1966, Pearson Collection, Lilly; **At one point . . . I die** Columbus O'Donnell to NS, 13/5/2019; **None of us** JMH to NS, 17/5/2019; **acted as chaperone** JB to Pearson, Pearson Collection, Lilly; **slightly enchanted** ibid.; **rather greater than** *The Notes*, 240; **practically taking** IF to Stephenson 16/11/1951, Russell Collection, Lilly; **mustard tweed** IF to Ann, 1953, IF53a, Morgan papers; **Ian consistently . . . belief** JB to Pearson; **usual August visit** IF to Cuneo, 14/5/1956, Cuneo collection; **nearly defunct** *The Notes*, 232; **wire service . . . life** Bryce, 90; **Ian was by** *The Notes*, 174; **Robert is heaven** IF to Ann, Oct. 1954, 1F71a, Morgan papers; **I found it** *The Notes*, 231; **He spends all** EC to Bryce, 28/5/1984, Bryce Papers; **Apparently, he considers** IF to EC 30/9/1953, Cuneo papers; **Apparently, he** IF to EC, 9/10/1953, Cuneo papers; **Both he and Ernie** WS to IF, 15/10/1951, Russell Collection, Lilly; **Take a letter** *Thrilling Cities*, 10; **While you were** Bryce, 100; **wallowing and waffling** EC to Bryce, 28/5/1984, Bryce Papers; **I want an adult** IF to CB, 22/4/1953, VanBlaricum Collection; **Ernie is fed up** IF to Ann, 9/8/1954, IF14a, Morgan papers; **I was able** *The Notes*, 232

LI 'THAT ASS BOND'

My source material TMWTGT, 125; **He was getting** ibid., 91; **Call it what** *The Notes*, 251; **He has been** *TMWTGT*, 97; **I think we are** IF to MH, 20/9/1955, IFA; **wanted to take** UT to NS, 23/9/2019; **to more or less** *Playboy*, Dec. 1964; **Ian detected very** JP, James Bond Transcripts, IFA; **for the first** Tom Hiney and Frank MacShane, eds, *The Raymond Chandler Papers*, 194; **His great frustration** Tom Williams to NS, 28/4/2022; **Disaster** *The Notes*, 201; **the St John's Wood** *The Raymond Chandler Papers*, 211; **A word from you** *TMWTGT*, 224; **you are probably** ibid., 225; **It is the curse of** 'Notes on Raymond Chandler', *London Magazine*,

Dec. 1959; **I think you will** *TMWTGT*, 227; **Probably the fault** ibid., 228; **to their absolute** ibid., 231; **Anyone who writes** ibid., 229; **my own muse** ibid., 230; **I am still in** IF to JHG, 11/9/1956, Godfrey papers; **I have got so** IF to Ann, Feb 1956, IF96a, Morgan papers; **Bond pivoted slowly** *FRWL*, 259; **I seriously doubt** *TMWTGT*, 126

LII 'THE GREATEST FIASCO OF ALL TIME'

He was much Cuneo papers; **very urgent work** Hugh Foot to IF, 14/12/1956, Russell Collection, Lilly; **They say Eden** 10/12/1956, Lady Loelia Lindsay papers; **Diana Cooper says** Channon, vol. 3, 1079; **It has been the** ibid.; **He's attempted to** Hirsch, 324; **In the whole** Pearson, 422; **a monumental stroke** 'State of Excitement', chapter 2, IFA; **Anthony's toothy** Ann to Beaverbrook, 18/1/1956, Beaverbrook papers; **Jerk is a bad** Ann to IF, 24/2/1956, AF60a, Morgan papers; **the fatuous Eden** Channon, vol. 2, 865; **one of the most** ibid., vol. 2, 2; **I do not know** Charles Ritchie, *Undiplomatic Diaries, 1937–1971*, 90; **cold hatred** Alex von Tunzelmann, *Blood and Sand*, 90; **The whole affair** Chips Channon, vol. 2, 633; **I find only one** IF to JHG, 11/9/1956, Godfrey papers; **an act of disastrous** Philip Maynard Williams, *Hugh Gaitskell*, 286; **a few other . . . 'tiresome'** 19/11/1956, Maud Russell papers; **it was not the** Cuneo papers; **in constant need** von Tunzelmann, 116; **I think the** ibid., 251; **He is of the** *Noël Coward Diaries*, 337; **Anthony very depressed** von Tunzelmann, 360; **The doctors at** *Clarissa Eden: A Memoir*, 320; **that the PM** Channon, vol. 3, 1069–70; **When the sanctuary** *Pearl of Days*, 294; **Fleming's luxurious** Parker, 223; **Ian was a bit** Hamilton, 200; **Considering the fuss** *The Notes*, 217; **beloved brother-in-law** Channon, vol. 3, 1078; **so naturally . . . through it** Amory, 188/9; **It was all terribly** UT to NS, 23/9/2023; **the major decisions** *Pearl of Days*, 295; **It was very** Mary Crassweller to NS, 13/3/2022; **punching up** IF to Hugh Foot, 26/11/1956, Russell Collection, Lilly; **No, I obey** *The Notes*, 157; **for considerable publicity** Parker, 214; **I must be calm** *The Notes*, 23; **Violet's divine** ibid., 217; **He gossiped with** Ann to Beaverbrook, 25/1/1957, Beaverbrook papers; **the fairly well** Parker, 217; **They made such** *Playboy*, Dec. 1964; **We are blissfully . . . coral** Clarissa to Ann, 1/12/1956, Hugo Vickers papers; **that old rubber boat** IF to Al Hart, 17/12/1956, Russell Collection, Lilly; **I do not think** AE to IF, Russell Collection, Lilly; Lycett, 307; **The immediate reaction** Ann to Clarissa, 20/12/1956, Hugo Vickers papers; **even Hitler** Robert Rhodes James, *Anthony Eden*, 583; **my father became** Susanna Johnston to NS; **I saw in his eyes** Rhodes James, 594; **Anthony Eden has** 9/1/1957, Lady Loelia Lindsay papers; **The benefit of Jamaica** AE to WSC, 9/1/1957, Churchill Archive Centre; **We sold . . . Fredericton** Beaverbrook to IF, 21/3/1964; 31/3/1964; Beaverbrook papers; **I am quite** *TMWTGT*, 127

LIII LEADERKINS

I suppose I shall AF to Lord Beaverbrook, 30/6/1956, Beaverbrook papers; **Owing to my … beach** Amory, 192; **Apparently Annie** 5/2/1957, Lady Loelia Lindsay papers; **a v. nice** IB to Rowland Burdon-Muller, 9/9/1962, Henry Hardy papers; **it would be** Ann to IF, AF40a, 13/2/1948, Morgan papers; *This familiar face* Ann to IF, AF45a, Morgan papers; **had you put** Ann to IF, AF2a, n.d., Morgan papers; **slightly to the** Sara Morrison to NS, 9/1/2020; **proletarians … oligarchs … incorrect** Raymond Carr, *Saga*, April 2005; **and August holiday** Ann to Clarissa, n.d., Morgan papers; **If we have to** Brian Brivati, *Hugh Gaitskell*, 228; **reading aloud parties** Ann to Beaverbrook, n.d. Beaverbrook papers; **and swooping** Giles, 127; **As you know** HG to IF, n.d., Russell Collection, Lilly; **a 30-page letter** RH to Pearson, 27/1/1982, Pearson papers; **She was far** Harling papers; **He is a changed** Ann to Beaverbrook, 25/1/1957, Beaverbrook papers; **He had never** Amory, 189; **On Tuesday afternoons** Sara Morrison to NS; **gentle and loving** Parker, 209; **how much one** Ann to Judy Montagu, 25/2/1963, Montagu papers; **For many years** Parker, 209; **For six years** Ann to Hugo, n.d., Morgan papers; **I am profoundly** Ann to Diana Cooper, Jan 1963, AF57a, Morgan papers; **The ambiguity of** HG to IF, n.d., Russell Collection, Lilly; **Annie was … tradition** IF to RH, 14/2/1963, Harling papers; **behind a cactus** Ann to Clarissa [Feb 1960], Morgan papers; **horribly amused** Ann to Beaverbrook, 3/2/1960, Beaverbrook papers; **that ghastly grey** *Pomp and Circumstance*, 246; **Violet Cripps** IF to Ann, 1959, IF87a, Morgan papers; **I think Ian** FM to NS, 19/1/23; **That's my wife's** Lycett, 392; **His laughter about** EC to Bryce, 28/9/1983, Bryce papers; **I had to cut** John Pearson papers

LIV 'IAN'S BLACK WIFE'

Don't be tarred Ann to IF, AF34a, Morgan papers; **I do hope** Amory, 65; **little temptation** IF to Ann, 24/2/1948, IF13a, Morgan papers; **a gay** *sabreur* Channon, vol. 3, 740; **Writes terrible books** IFA; **a heavy sadist** *Guardian*, 15/1/2016; **I brought up** Nuala Pell interview with John Cork, 2000; **Ian, you know** Lycett, 312; **He wanted her** *Casino Royale*, 92; **a sexual twilight** ibid., 115; **We talked of** *Constant Heart*, 114; **Reputedly, he used** John Hatt to NS; **There was a cruel** Anthony Hunter to NS, 21/11/2019; **'Oh, men like'** Hugh Edwards, *All Night at Mr Stanyhurst's*, 47; **A little baggage** ibid., 24; **a shoe-horn** 'Bond Strikes Camp', *Previous Convictions*, 368; **She is writing** IF to Coward, 17/6/1958, Russell Collection, Lilly; **We've had** Deborah Devonshire and Patrick Leigh Fermor, *In Tearing Haste*, 100; **I do hope** IF to Ann, IF52a, 1956, Morgan papers; **whipped the surface** *TOTD*, 2; **whipped the action** *Casino Royale*, 51; **My love and** IF to Connolly, 4/1/1954, Russell Collection, Lilly; **I must whip** IF to Ann, IF34a, Morgan papers; **I have** absolutely **IF** to Beaverbrook, 21/11/1961, Beaverbrook papers; **I have lived** *TMWTGT*, 366; **Whacko!** ibid., 214; **I'll give you** *Thunderbird*, 8; **Honey, get** *Dr. No*, 142; **Come on Calamity** *Goldfinger*, 103; **He stopped smoking** AF to NS; **would be much** Amory, 62; **I remember a** Jean-Noël Liaut to NS, 21/7/2020; **all women love** *TSWLM*, 176; **Ann would talk** Rachel Toynbee to NS, 20/9/2022; **I want to leave** Amory, 42; **You have made** IF to Ann, IF77a, Morgan papers; **I must be** S. J. Taylor, 39; **10 on each** IF to Ann, 24/2/1948, F13a, Morgan papers; **It's terribly difficult** Fionn to NS, 19/1/23; **to alleviate the smart** Lycett, 243; **the spanky bit** Sara Morrison to NS, 9/1/2020; **Unfortunately, I couldn't** IF to Ann, 1/2/1947, Morgan papers; **It remains an** FM to NS, 19/1/23; **I see no prospect** IF to Ann, 1/2/1947, Morgan papers; **He really had** *The Notes*, 315; **in a drowsy** Lycett, 371; **same like film** *Thrilling Cities*, 34; **seizing my hand** ibid., 69; **She must have** *The Notes*, 157; **His last words . . . adored him** BB to RH, 13/12/1996, Harling papers; **I'm very strange!** Parker, 204; **A very rich** John Gielgud, *A Life in Letters*, 258; **an island between** IF to Ann, Feb 1956, IF81a, Morgan papers; **Don't use up** IF to Ann, IF92a, Morgan papers; **I pray that Enton's** Amory, 213; **He came up** BB, James Bond Transcripts, IFA; **like the sound** Parker, 48; **Her peals of** Bryce, 136; **He was so desperately** BB, James Bond Transcripts, IFA; **lively as a** Coward, *Volcano*; **The idea dropped** *Letters of Noël Coward*, 631; **she v helpful** IF to Ann, March 1956, IF97a, Morgan papers; **It was all built up** Parker, BB interview with notes; **She is a fine** Bryce, 136; **to go and swim** BB, James Bond Transcripts, IFA; **I used to come** Parker, 241; **He took me . . . to do** BB, James Bond Transcripts, IFA; **She imported me . . . everything** Christina (Herridge) Thistlethwayte to NS, 7/3/2021; **No other excitements** IF to Ann, IF81a, Morgan papers; **We didn't become** BB, James Bond Transcripts, IFA; **I said, Noel** Hoare, 423; **someone called** Parker, 224; **I can tell you** Hugh Foot to IF, 14/12/1956, Russell Collection, Lilly; **to wearing a hibiscus** Ann to Clarissa, n.d., Hugo Vickers papers; **really a member** *C-C-B-B*, 58; **I must say B** IF to Ann, 20/2/1957, IF10a, Morgan papers; **What was wonderful** BB, James Bond Transcripts, IFA; **stacks of . . . the book** IF to Ann, March 1957, IF92a, Morgan papers

LV A HIDEOUS ISLAND

I'm an Englishman *Dr. No*, 36; **It will amuse** IF to Hugh Foot, 20/12/1956, Russell Collection, Lilly; ESSENTIAL YOU *TOTD*, 266; **to put him . . . wayside** EC to Bryce, 28/5/1984, Bryce papers; **one of the greatest** *Sunday Times*, 15/4/1956; **flamingo tongues** *TOTD*, 270; **We must teach** IF to Ann, March 1956, IF97a, Morgan papers; **the rotten-egg** *TOTD*, 269; **and the last** ibid., 267; **where virtually** Robert Murphy, 'Notes on Inagua Island 1956', VanBlaricum Collection; **the original flame-throwing** Bryce, 113; **It is a hideous** *TOTD*, 267; **The rain had** Murphy,

'Notes'; **It has been** IF to Miss Caley, 8/4/1957, IFA; **The belt made** *Dr. No*, 79; **Ian was a little** Jean-Noël Liaut to NS, 21/7/2020; **Honeychile I regard** *TMWTGT*, 174; **If we were going** BB, James Bond Transcripts, IFA; **of the classical** Lycett, 345; **Of course, there** *The Notes*, 273; **There was something** FM to NS, 19/1/2023; **My mother was** Chris Blackwell to NS, 8/4/2019; **I was treated . . . end of it** BB, James Bond Transcripts, IFA; **Fleming had undoubtedly** Harling papers; **It was a romance** C[H]T to NS, 7/3/2021; **she was implacably** Noel Annan, memorial address, 20/11/1981; **Ann rather quarrelsome** *Like It Was: The Diaries of Malcolm Muggeridge*, 474; **apple of discord** Annan address; **Ann, that's an** Parker, 241; **If I went to . . . any** Parker, BB interview notes; **All your news** *TMWTGT*, 257; **There's no doubt** FM to NS, 19/1/2023

LVI 'CAVIAR FOR THE GENERAL'

I had a wonderful IF to Denise Simenon, Aug. 1963; **celebrification . . . borealis** Pearson papers; **far and away** *TMWTGT*, 126; **There is a danger** ibid., 132; **I. F. is too** 2/5/1957, *LH-D Letters*, vol. 1 and 2, 292; **He was engaged** *TOTD*, 190; **I have had** IF to JHG, 1/10/157, Godfrey papers; **I dare say** *TMWTGT*, 215; **when he became** *TOTD*, 191; **I think some** *TMWTGT*, 86; **not infrequently had** Cuneo to Bryce, 28/9/1983, Bryce papers; **i am the only** Amory, 51; **He never confused** Bryce, 97; **I regard my** *oeuvres* Harper's Bazaar, Nov. 1964; **a spare-time** *TMWTGT*, 64; **My dear fellow** Pearson papers; **Book still going** IF to Beryl Griffie-Williams, March 1964, Carr-Ellison papers; **Critics rarely remark** Bryce, Foreword; **was always such** *The Notes*, 144; **demi-giants** Kingsley Amis, *James Bond Dossier*, 132; **I think the** John Betjeman to IF, 7/12/1963, Russell Collection, Lilly; **I have always** SM to IF, Russell Collection, Lilly; **here's magnificent** Gant, 125; **As a writer** *The Notes*, 244; **as P. G. Wodehouse** Jan Morris intro., *Thrilling Cities* (2009); **I think it is** Anthony Burgess intro., *FRWL* (1988); **Bond was Fleming's** *New Statesman*, 28/10/1966; **so embarrassing** Jeremy Treglown, *Roald Dahl*, 230; **it would be** Lewis, 151; **appalling writer** Stafford, *Silent Game*, 167; **I'm quite fond** *Too Brief a Treat: Letters of Truman Capote*, ed. Gerald Clarke, 390; **Bond is very** Le Carré to NS, 3/3/2020, Germany Embassy, London; **Bond on his magic** *A Private Spy: The Letters of John le Carré*, 155; **I am sure he** *The Notes*, 215; **an extraordinary** Naomi Burton to Raymond Benson, 1982, Benson papers; **I have just** IF to HS Baker, 2/5/1962, IFA; **a unique experiment** IF to Florence Taylor, 18/4/1962, IFA; **He could have** *Ladies' Home Journal*, Oct. 1966; **I refuse to write** IF to Clare Blanshard, 1955, Fergus Fleming papers; **One felt that deep** DM to Bryce, 1/1/1975, Bryce papers; **If I really** *Playboy* transcript, VanBlaricum Collection; **I would like** *TOTD*, 397; **He read widely** *Sunday Times*, 16/8/1964; **wine or cigars** Russell to IF, 20/6/ 1962, Russell Collection, Lilly; **He knew his** Nicolas Barker to NS, 14/5/2019;

Mr Ian Fleming IF to WP, 12/1962, Plomer Collection, Lilly; **The most disgusting** Lycett, 244; **It is believed** James Fleming, 'My Uncle Ian', *The Book Collector*, Spring 2017; **What does P.F.** *LH-D Letters*, vol. 3 and 4, 334; **Peter is the soul** ibid., 336; **You must not** Mary (Pakenham) Clive papers; **which frankly** *The Notes*, 189; **'In the twilight'** Peter to Mary Fleming, 31/8/1963, Mary Fleming papers; **really gone off** *LH-D Letters*, vol. 3 and 4, 49; **The new Ian** *LH-D Letters*, vol. 6, 27; **There are some** IF to Tammy Miller, 9/1/1963; **The usual, Commander?** John Russell, *Spectator*, 23/12/1955; **James Bond is** Gant, 161; **Somebody once** Anon., 'to IF/and or his secretary', 14/2/1959, IFA; **Did you read** 9/4/1958 *LH-D Letters*, vol. 3 and 4, 49; **the nastiest . . . phenomenon** *New Statesman*, 5/4/1958; **I hear it said** *Playboy* transcript, VanBlaricum Collection; **this was a big** *Daily Express*, 12/5/1998; **Ian's fans** *raven* WP to Ann, 4/4/1957, AF7a, Morgan papers

LVII A DINNER

Ian had everything *The Note*s, 270; **What a mysterious** 24/10/1948, Lady Loelia Lindsay papers; **we never . . . one another** Leiter, James Bond Transcripts, IFA; **Jack, I've been** *The Notes*, 268; **He rang up . . . arrived** Leiter, James Bond Transcripts, IFA; **valorous efforts** *YOLT*, 202; **It was never** Alexis Albion to NS, 1/5/2022; **An American television** Amory, 292; **en masse** Atticus, 29/7/1956; **the resident** *The Notes*, 271; **Undoubtedly, Bond** ibid, 253; **Here is a book** Peter Grose, *Gentleman Spy*, 471; **the next two** Dulles, Oral History Interview, 5/12/1964, John F. Kennedy Presidential Library; **He is obsessed** Ann to Clarissa Eden, 16/2/1964, Morgan papers; **As you know** Robert Kennedy to IF, 1/6/1962, IFA; **the entire Kennedy** Henry Brandon to IF, 30/10/1961, IFA; **It was a late** Sibilla Tomacelli to NS, 6/6/2019; **I think Jack** Leiter, James Bond Transcripts, IFA; **the perfect candidate** Gregg Herken, *The Georgetown Set*, 247; **There would be** *The Notes*, 243; **people changed when** ibid., 231; **I's personality is** 25/4/1948, Maud Russell papers; **The rapport was** Leiter, James Bond Transcripts, IFA; **Jack was mesmerised** *The Notes*, 270; **must have been** ibid., 148; **a good deal** Nigel Hamilton, *Reckless Youth*, 129; **All that macho** ibid., 359; **men adored him** Seymour Hersh to NS, 9/3/2021; **a sort of family** *The Notes*, 294; **Durie Chevlin** 'Book of Golden Words', 30/12/1958, IFA; **in Spalding's apartment** Nigel Hamilton to NS, 15/1/2021; **a large file of** Skip Willman, 'The Kennedys, Fleming and Cuba', *Ian Fleming and James Bond, The Cultural Politics of 007*, 188; **best friend** *Izvestia*, 29/5/1962; **the man unwittingly** Grose, 492; **absolute discretion** ibid.; **the Kennedys did** IF to Geoffrey Bocca, 26/3/1963, IFA; **Cuba was just** *The Notes*, 269; **I wonder when** Val Fleming to Robert Fleming, 25/4/1915, IFA; **trouble was brewing** *TMWTGT*, 205; **Ian had some** Norman Lewis to NS, 4/5/1991; **to be the absolute** *TMWTGT*, 85; **Ann's friends did** *Cocktails and Laughter*, 99; **Ian began . . . Castro** *The Notes*, 269; **There have** been Lee Richards, *Whispers of War*, 95; **to attack Nazi** Peter Haining, *The Mystery of Rommel's Gold*, 28; **have short furry** Ogden, 209; **'Everyone roared'** *The Notes*, 269; **I want him murdered** David Stafford, *American–British–Canadian Intelligence Relations, 1939–2000*, 104; **Assassination may be** Grose, 501; **might get shot** Stafford, 124; **Just as Ian** JP, James Bond Transcripts, IFA; **half a dozen** Lycett, 418; **that my Agent** *TMWTGT*, 352; **We need some** *TSWLM*, 132; **We had quite** *Life*, 28/8/1964; **Celestial Dulles** inscription *YOLT*; **even attempted** *Izvestia*, 29/5/1962; **very interesting . . . discuss Cuba** Leiter, James Bond Transcripts, IFA; **the US's sole** Julian Evans, *Semi-Invisible Man: The Life of Norman Lewis*, 456; **JFK's fixation** Willman, 179; **Fleming's pillow-book** Skip Willman to NS, 23/6/2022; **fill the sky** Willman, 196; **There was a poison** Alex von Tunzelmann, *Red Heat: Conspiracy, Murder, and the Cold War in the Caribbean*, 286; **So you're our** Willman, 196; **Why can't you** ibid., 196; **loved James . . . laughingly** ibid., 197; **and 65 hours later** Bay of Pigs veterans to NS, 29/11/2014; **It was one of** von Tunzelmann, 111; **Why couldn't this** Willman, 194; **Yesterday, I heard** Evelyn Irons to IF, 30/11/1963, IFA; **like a bomb** James Bond Transcipts, IFA; **It's terrifying** IF to Tammy Miller, 9/1/1963; **adding and some** Diane Holloway and Lee Harvey Oswald, *The Mind of Oswald*, 198; **he spoke a lot** Jonathan McFarland to NS, 23/1/2023; **could be seen** Willman, 199; **may have been** Priscilla Johnson McMillan, *Marina and Lee*, 328; **He worked as** *Times*, 20/4/1971; **a failure at** Allen Dulles, Oral History Interview, John F. Kennedy Presidential Library; **the chief executioner** *FRWL*, 237; **He was a reader** <https://www.mediafire.com/file/mnqnbqtju8cx2u7/FBI-article-Oswald-BondWannabe.pdf>

LVIII THE DARK FRONTIER

I hate Bond *The Notes*, 163; **murdered Ian Fleming** 'The Curse of Bond', Pearson papers; **a woman in** 5/2/1964, Mary Bond diary; **In my memory** *Ladies' Home Journal*, Oct. 1966; **Gamblers just before** 'Book of Golden Words', IFA; **He'll never . . . monster** *Ladies' Home Journal*, Oct. 1966; **leg man** JP to Benson, 8/9/1982, Benson papers; **It was one . . . about him** Pearson papers; **I've just . . . Devil** MM to JP, 30/10/1966, Pearson papers; **the strange sick** Pearson papers; **He starts as Ian . . . he did** James Waugh to NS, 3/6/2020; **He did a fantastic** Septimus Waugh to NS, 3/6/2020; **Whatever his literary . . . enigma** Cuneo intro., *James Bond Bedside Companion*, x; **his son Caspar . . . enigma** Cuneo papers; **I have created** Jeremy Duns, *Need to Know*, 67; Jenkins to Pearson, 24/9/1965, Geoffrey Jenkins papers; **Like Hemingway** *Sunday Times*, 1966; **Fleming fell** *Eton College Chronicle*, 3/4/1926; **He pushed us** *The Notes*, 168; **Am terribly stuck** IF to WP, 23/2/1960, Plomer Collection, Lilly; **'I am feeling'** *TMWTGT*, 351; **Mask is a flop** IF to CB, n.d., Fergus Fleming papers; **My mind is** IF to Phyllis Jackson, 28/5/1963, IFA; **I said he would** Bryce, 123; **lawsuits, court cases** Sellers, 18

LIX 'MINK-COATED INCUBUS'

It does seem TMWTGT, 219; **That caller** Deighton, *James Bond: My Long and Eventful Search for his Father*, 5; **Harry Saltzman** Deighton to NS, 22/11/2019; **legalistic brew** Deighton, 113; **dickering** IF to Robert Fenn, 13/4/1959, IFA; **Will you please** IF to PF, 6/10/1958, IFA; **Gentlemen, I return** PF to Farrer and Co., 8/3/1962, IFA; **Everyone knows . . . fine** Peter Fleming, *A Story to Tell*, 42; **You would be** TMWTGT, 97; **This is a feather** Sellers, 20; '*The Boy and*' Sellers, 25; **this mink-coated** TMWTGT, 219; **dangerous and slippery** IF to Wren Howard, 27/4/1959, IFA; **I have an idea** Pearson, 376; **It's fun making** IF to Ann, IF3a, 1954, Morgan papers; **For films** *The Notes*, 144; **What sums** IF to J. M. Ruddy, 15/9/1952, IFA; **borrowed duplicate** IF to Cape, 20/10/1952, IFA; **here is a rip-snorter** Lycett, 233; **Isn't it wonderful** Leonard Russell, Russell Collection, Lilly; **Your book** Alexander Korda to IF, 1/1/1954, IFA; **I originally thought** IF to Joyce Briggs, 2/10/1956, IFA; **A film synopsis** AK to IF, 15/1/1954, IFA; **I can type . . . *undeniably blue*** IF script of 'Moonraker', IFA; **pilot film . . . matter** IF to Vallance Lodge, 12/6/1967, IFA; **on edge of** IF to Naomi Burton 12/6/1958, IFA; **innumerable legalistic . . . MCA** IF to Philip Brownrigg, 2/8/1962, IFA; **Everything about** Winder, 153

LX McCLORY

Ian was battered Len Deighton, *James Bond: My Long and Eventful Search for his Father*, 113; **a certain affluence** Coward, *Bon Voyage*, 44; **Really he wanted** Sellers, 14, 35; **saved the whale** ibid., 13; **He is of . . . the venture** unpublished chapter, *You Only Live Once*, Bryce papers; **practically had a flat . . . went** JMH to NS, 23/2/2023; **I thought that** Bryce, 123; **to make a full-length** Sellers, 18; **impressed with the** Bryce deposition 13/5/1963, 28/8/1962, IFA; **After seeing your** ibid., 19; **but not of . . . held** unpublished chapter, *You Only Live Once*, Bryce papers; **without raising his** Bryce deposition 13/5/1963, 28/8/1962, IFA; **While Ian was** Deighton foreword, Sellers; **Always travel . . . extravagance** Deighton, 137; **The meeting was** Peter Janson-Smith, James Bond Transcripts, IFA; **He owed me** LD to NS, 22/11/2019; **Ivar and Ian** JMH to NS, 11/2/2023; **Fleming's packet** John Cork to NS, 24/6/2019; **I have never** unpublished chapter, *You Only Live Once*, Bryce papers; **steeped in sadism** Sellers, 17; **Kevin had . . . rewritten** LD to NS, 22/11/2019; **A lot of these** PJ-S, James Bond Transcripts, IFA; **He never used to** *The Notes*, 38; **Thunderball I** *The Notes*, 261; **Ernest Cuneo wrote** 21/9/1966, Pearson Collection, Lilly; **He has a** Sellers, 54; **since James Bond** ibid., 24; **the 'Old Boy' wave** IF to Jack Whittingham, 10/5/1961, Sylvan Mason papers; **the rather airy** Sellers, 26; **This is an awkward** ibid., 25; **Ivar's film** IF to WS, 29/4/1959, Russell Collection, Lilly; **The frost-bitten right** Sellers, 63; **a contemptible individual** Bryce deposition 13/5/1963, 28/8/1962, IFA; **the riff-raff** unpublished chapter, *You*

Only Live Once, Bryce papers; **stream through** Sellers, 55; **I am driven mad** ibid., 50; **approximately £12,000** Bryce deposition, IFA; **I don't particularly** Sellers, 35; **Showbiz is** ibid., 63; **best of all** ibid., 34; **I know Hitchcock** ibid., 35; **Then Atropos** unpublished chapter, *You Only Live Once*, Bryce papers; **Bobo Sigrist** Ann to Judy Montagu, 2/10/1959, Montagu papers; **the first James** Bryce, 139; **I am now** *TMWTGT*, 220; **He urged me** IF to Robert Fenn, 15/3/1961, IFA; **It was McClory** *The Notes*, 302; **was excited by** Peek deposition, IFA; **There isn't** Cuneo to Brian Lewis, 2/6/1963, IFA; **All writers** Bruce Chatwin to NS, 1988; **writing a novel** Jeremy Duns, *Duns on Bond*, 21; **with the same** *The Notes*, 242; **All the McClory** JC to NS, 26/3/2023; **rich, middle-aged** ibid., 262; **in a bemused** IF to WS, 16/8/1961, Russell Collection, Lilly; **I need something** *The Notes*, 262; **To MCA . . . paper** IF to Fenn, 3/7/1961, IFA; **the films wouldn't** *The Notes*, 262; **99 per cent . . . old boy** Sellers, 75; **He came out** IF to Robert Fenn, 15/3/1961, IFA; **buckled at the** Sellers, 79; **Have given Kevin** ibid., 79; **clearly not . . . very British** ibid., 78; **They'd say** *The Notes*, 282; **nothing from Kevin . . . here** IB to IF, 13/9/1960, IFA; **unfair and unjust** KM to IB, 8/12/1960, IFA; **Ernie thinks that** IB to IF, 13/9/1060, IFA; **this copyright problem** Sellers, 91; **you have been . . . suckers** Cuneo to IB, 29/1/1960, IFA; **about a foot** James Bond Transcripts, IFA; **it was the face** Deighton foreword, *The Battle for Bond*; **Ian and I** unpublished chapter, Bryce papers; **in a state** IB to IF, 6/2/1961, IFA; **I had the** *The Notes*, 38; **It could only** Pearson, James Bond Transcripts, IFA

LXI THE BLACK CLOUD
There has never Marguerite Wenner-Gren to EF, 19/9/1953, IFA; **Everybody calls** BP to Winchester, n.d., IFA; **a trio for** Harling, 318; **How silly can** *LH-D Letters*, vols 1 and 2, 380; **she inclines to dress** Amory, 209; **the woman of steel'** Harling papers; **that Lord Winchester** *Times*, 7/11/1957; **pale and red-lipped** Duncan Fallowell, *How to Disappear: A Memoir for Misfits*, 43; **the Black Cloud** Bryce to Raymond Benson, 1984, Benson papers; **Bapsy's breathtaking** Fallowell, 56; **she never really** ibid., 54; **it would . . . head** ibid., 55; **was not a chaste** *Times*, 9/11/1957; **recognised for** *Times*, 2/11/1957; **That was sheer** *Times*, 6/11/1957; **a series of** ibid.; **That's how** *Times*, 9/11/1957; **Mrs. Fleming was** *Times*, 12/11/1957; **The garden is** *Times*, 8/11/1957; **as happy as** *Times*, 6/11/1957; **My darling Bapsy** Fallowell, 54; **all its former** *Times*, 27/11/1957; **It can't have** Fallowell, 50; **awful mistake** *Times*, 2/11/1957; **your mistress Fleming** BP to Lord Winchester, 6/4/1953, IFA; **Your title . . . I do** *Times*, 6/11/1957; **Everyone says** BP to Lord Winchester, n.d., IFA; **The world will** BP to Peter, Ian and Richard, 16/12/1953, IFA; **He said that** *Times*, 5/11/1957; **an overweight Indian** Bryce, 110; **I shall send** *Times*, 6/11/1957; *Elle ment et* Mary Fleming to NS; **The**

Judge had *Times*, 8/7/1958; **that small cell** IF to EF, 1/6/1961, Russell Collection, Lilly; **She enters his** *Times*, 30/10/1958; **low cruising speed** Christopher Balfour to NS, 13/3/2020; **You monsters!** <https://www.ncbi.nlm.nih.gov/pmc/articles/PMC6423520/>

LXII THE SECRETS OF A MAN

The nightmare of Ann to JP, Pearson papers; **evasive, opinionated** *Times*, 12/11/1957; **an infringement of** *Times*, 24/3/1961; **Thunderbird's secretary** Amory, 281; **shouldn't know people** Ann to Noël Coward, 26/1/1961, Morgan papers; **for poor Thunderbird** *Letters of Evelyn Waugh*, 562; **This novel owes** Sellers, 97; **It was pending** *Ladies' Home Journal*, Oct. 1966; **Quite ghastly** Sellers, 97; **an ambitious Kleptomaniac** Henry Allan, 'Prize essay on Kleptomania', 31; **To be accused of** Pearson papers; **Ian Fleming is** Amory, 291; *In connection . . . incensed* Russell Collection, Lilly; **He knelt down** *TMWTGG*, 156; **One of the secrets** FM to NS, 19/1/2023; **They were typical** Richard Beal to NS, 13/5/2021; **PLEASE PLEASE** IF to Ann, July 1962, Carr-Ellison papers; **He had strained** *The Notes*, 141; **Ian would die** KF to NS, 23/3/2023; **he used to have** ibid., 110; **a constricting . . . gin** *The Notes*, 92; **His arteries** ibid., 94; **the Stone Age** IF to Ann, July 1956, IF27a, Morgan papers; **Those saddest of** 'Book of Golden Words', IFA; **I was ill for** IF to Ann, Oct. 1957, IF98a, Morgan papers; **The height has** Amory, 277; **scarlet and sweating** 29/1/1961, *Noël Coward Diaries*, 463; **I am certain** *Ladies' Home Journal*, Oct. 1966; **new shiny magazine** IF to Denis Hamilton, 25/4/1961, Hamilton papers; **more than ever** *TMWTGT*, 112; **If you have ever** IF to EC, 19/10/1955, Cuneo papers; **this great citadel** IF to Ann 1947, IF62a, Morgan papers; **this grim building** IF to Maugham 6/5/1954, Russell Collection, Lilly; **Since doing the** Skelton, 177; **I just can't bear** IF to Ann, IF10a, 20/2/1957, Morgan papers; **I must stop** IF to Ann, IF97a, n.d., Morgan papers; **a charming . . . missing** Leonard Russell, Russell Collection, Lilly; **he described to** Bryce, 125; **I thought . . . letters** Hamilton, 201; **The fact that** Ann to IF, AF2a, 1962; **and looking . . . golf** Leonard Russell, Russell Collection, Lilly; **behaving like** BG-W to JHG, 15/5/1961, Godfrey papers; **I went in** BG-W to JHG, 17/4/1961, Godfrey papers; **a nice lady** Robin Kinkead, Russell Collection, Lilly; **They still refuse** IF to EF, 24/4/1961, Russell Collection, Lilly; **poor old . . . Saturday!** *TMWTGT*, 269; **The iron crab** IF to EC, 19/4/1961, Cuneo papers; **Bung ho, ole** JB to IF, 19/5/1961, Russell Collection, Lilly; **Please don't forget** HG to IF, 4/5/1961, Russell Collection, Lilly; **it was a pity** *The Notes*, 306; **I am writing** IF to MH, 24/4/1961, Russell Collection, Lilly; **which, apart from** Lycett, 384; **the engine, though** IF to WS, 16/8/1961, Russell Collection, Lilly; **Don't believe** *Amaryllis Fleming*, 211; **One knows one's** IF to Plomer, 20/5/1964, Plomer Collection, Lilly; **When can I come** IF to Barbara Skelton, 29/5/1956, Cressida Connolly papers; **Please ask Daley** IF to JHG, 6/5/1961, Godfrey papers; **vital piece of** *TMWTGT*, 269; **Green Charteuse is** Soames to IF, 13/5/1961, Russell Collection, Lilly; **A graceful composure** IF to JW, 10/5/1961, Sylvan (Whittingham) Mason papers; **I am making** 1/5/1961, Terry, 105; **and rather un-James** *Dashing for the Post: The Letters of Patrick Leigh Fermor*, ed. Adam Sisman, 198; **entirely privately** *TMWTGT*, 268

LXIII 'A REGULAR SKYSCRAPER'

More than Broccoli, xiii; **President Kennedy** *Times*, 25/4/1961; **When Kennedy announced** Cuneo to Benson, [1982,] Benson papers; **not much . . . readers** John Cork, *Book Collector*, Spring 2017; **the gusher burst** *The Notes*, 254; **An increase in** ibid., 175; **Can't find** EI to IF, 1/5/1963, IFA; **Not *the* Mr** *The Notes*, 11; **to thank Kennedys** *TMWTGT*, 330; **the most successful** Broccoli, ix; **It is because . . . rights** John Cork to NS, 18/6/2022; **to excite the** Michael G. Wilson to NS, 7/7/2022; **He could be** Matthew Farrer to NS, 23/4/2021; **about thirty days** Broccoli, 148; **Purveying Italianate** ibid., xvi; **It is important** Len Deighton to NS, 22/11/2019; **In the trade** Matthew Farrer to NS, 23/4/2012; **a bad . . . television** Broccoli, 126; **I've always** ibid., 147; **Saltzman made** Pearson notes, Pearson Collection, Lilly; **The Fleming books** Broccoli, 149; **the James Bond** Sellers, 24; **Should I now** IF to WS, 16/8/1961, Russell Collection, Lilly; **The least you** WS to IF, 22/10/1959, Russell Collection, Lilly; **the darling . . . gambit** IF to WS, 16/8/1961, Russell Collection, Lilly; **slight copyright'** IF lawyer to Saltzman, 9/6/1961, IFA; **no one will buy** Cuneo to Bryce, 29/1/60, IFA

LXIV ARCHAEOLOGICAL HEAP

Who wouldn't rather The Diamond Smugglers, 128; **due to accumulating** IF to Morris Cargill, 20/6/1961, IFA; **I had no friends** *The Notes*, 177; **like a crash** Ann to IF, 7/2/1956, AF37a, Morgan papers; **When it was** Francis Grey to NS, 25/7/2022; **How I hated** *Grace and Favour*, 76-8; **His routine was** *The Notes*, 199; **his golf-playing** ibid., 177; **Ian was a chap** Murray Lawrence to NS, 21/11/2019; **He enjoyed the** *Ladies' Home Journal*, Oct. 1966; **the longest day** R'ON to NS, 18/11/2019; **the thud of** IF to Peter Fleming, May 1929, IFA; **He would ask** Francis Grey to NS; **He was not** John Suckling to NS, 7/5/2020; **a housemaid** *Daily Telegraph*, 14/7/2011; **If you promise** William Weir to NS, 20/12/2020; **You didn't just** *The Notes*, 196; **would make just** *TMWTGT*, 116; **He liked golf** *The Notes*, 61; **£100 in those** Bill Deedes, *Golf Quarterly*, no. 1, Spring 2010; **I was too** *The Diamond Smugglers*, 54; **We used to** Bryce, 111; **the finest . . . swing** *Thrilling Cities*, 11, 48; **extracted, I admit** IF to Desmond Flower, 8/11/1967, IFA; **We were on** *The Notes*, 47; **The ball struck** *The Golfer's Manual*, 83; **trick of rattling** IF to Hilary Bray, June 1963, Bray papers; **Presented by Peter** J. Adams, Club Secretary, to Philip Mitford, 1/2/1983, IFA; **as the other . . . swing** *The Notes*, 351; **The men were** John Suckling to NS, 17/5/2020; **Bond could hit** Deedes, *Golf Quarterly;* **When we were** IF to Ann, 1959, IF85a, Morgan papers; **but damned** Francis Grey to NS, 25/7/2022; **An ugly house** Ann to Clarissa, 3/12/1960, Morgan papers; **We both agreed** IF to Ann, 1959, IF87a, Morgan papers; **a modest house** Amory, 161; **I would love** IF to Ann, 1959, IF90a, Morgan papers; **I've always** IF to Ann, Jan 1959, IF83a, Morgan papers; **I MUST be** IF to Hilary Bray, June 1963, Bray papers; **The only reason** IF to Ann, 1959, IF90a, Morgan papers; **largely for** IF to Leslie Farrer, 28/9/1959, IFA; **I'm frightened** IF to Ann, Jan 1959, IF83a, Morgan papers; **He looked haggard** 23/7/1958, Maud Russell papers; **alas, there** Amory, 237; **We intend to** IF to Hobbs and Chambers, 27/7/1960, IFA; **Ian must be** JP notes, Pearson Collection, Lilly; **Please don't . . . before** IF to EF, 1/6/1961, Russell Collection, Lilly; **it is an ideal** IF to Hobbs and Chambers, 22/10/1959, IFA; **They are in sacks** EF to Bodleian, 3/6/1941, Bodleian, RC 2009/487; **I have also thought** AF to IF, 1948, AF23, Morgan papers; **The lawn is** Amory, 266; **I don't want** *The Notes*, 67; **dung-coloured** Amory, 283; **T[hunder]-B[ird] does** ibid., 270; **such despair . . . thought** ibid., 275; **It has taken** Pearson, 482; **ravages of Sur-tax** Jock Campbell to Booker board, 21/2/1964, IFA; **I get my hands** IF to Eve Fleming, 1/6/1961, Russell Collection, Lilly; **We are homeless** Amory, 266; **All I need** IF to Lord Cohen, 24/4/1961, Russell Collection, Lilly; **and the reduced** IF to Philip Brownrigg, 2/8/1961, IFA; **I am losing** IF to WS, 7/11/1961, Russell Collection, Lilly; **for not putting** *The Notes*, 130; **The trouble was** ibid., 94; **after the heart** ibid., 111; **I trust you** IF to Ann, October 1959, IF37a, Morgan papers; **I am staying** *TM WTGT*, 289; **It's so exhausting** Amory, 326; **which contained some** IF to Leslie Farrer, 22/8/1961, IFA; **we really will** IF to Ann, 1959, IF90a, Morgan papers; **combination of T[hunder]-B[irds]'s** Ann to Waugh, Sept. 1963, Morgan papers; **the building of** IF to Michael Farrer, 5/9/1962, IFA; **convalesced . . . defeats** Harling, 328; **I hadn't . . . lives** 6/11/1961, Maud Russell papers

LXV HOWLS OF LAUGHTER
I think we've Monty Norman to NS, 8/1/2021; **So they've decided** Andrew Yule, *Sean Connery*, 58; **rather superior and** Len Deighton to NS, 22/11/2019; **They consult me** *Harper's Bazaar*, Nov 1964; **cut out 'old'** IF comments on 5th draft screenplay, 15/1/1962, IFA; **If you will** *Tall, Dark and Gruesome*, 331; **NO NO** *The Notes*, 215; **If you read** Michael G. Wilson to NS, 7/7/2022; **He is looking** Sellers, 54; **reckless, disconnected** *New York Times*, 29/4/1967; **I think that . . . for him** Sellers, 53; **I wouldn't at** ibid., 44; **We tried** Steve Rubin interview with Robert Fenn, 1977; **I do think** Sellers, 54; **Who decided** Christopher Bray, *Sean Connery*,

71; **It was Connery . . . about** ibid., 137; **Sean Connery was** Barbara Broccoli to NS, 7/7/2022; **Oh, disaster** Broccoli, 179; **a sort of . . . something** Bray, 73; **portraying Bond is** ibid., 127; **He had worked . . . slipped through** Jason Connery to NS, 19/11/2019; **they are very** Bray, 73; **Walking is a** Michael G. Wilson to NS; **He's got balls . . . said** Bray, 73-4; **But first Fleming** Steve Rubin interview with Robert Fenn, 1977; **an over-developed** Parker, 274; **I'm a judge . . . kill'** JMH to NS, 17/5/2019; **the man they** Buckton, 286; **The film deal** IF to WS, 7/11/1961, Russell Collection, Lilly; **I was very** Ann to Judy Montagu, 7/1962, Montagu papers; **Have you ever** Gore, 104; **Lie down, you** Parker, 280; **They were shooed** Monty Norman to NS; **The sand ridge** Amory, 297; **Dr No promises** Parker, 275; **just another Grade** Bray, 70; **It was going** Chris Blackwell to NS, 8/4/2019; **the most important** Winder, 188; **Inside, we were** V. S. Naipaul, 'A Rolls-Royce Job', *New Statesman*, 28/10/1966; **I wrote five** Monty Norman to NS; **As you can** IF to Plomer, 24/5/1962, Plomer Collection, Lilly; **It was an abominable** Amory, 315

LXVI CASPAR

My favourite platitude Caspar to Angela Bray, 1969; **Their connubial situation** 29/1/1961, *Noël Coward Diaries*, 463; **tragically querulous** Harling, xi; **They couldn't live** ibid., 296; **There is evidence** *James Bond Bedside Companion*, x; **I think . . . general opinion** Ann to IF, 1962, AF2a, Morgan papers; **Everything is . . . them** IF to Ann, 1959, IF87a, Morgan papers; **terrifyingly authoritarian . . . Caspar** IF to Ann, IF94a, Morgan papers; **watching his character** Amory, 296; **three middle-aged** *The Notes*, 200; **We all agreed . . . murderer** Sara Morrison to NS, 9/1/2020; **Caspar liked the** Fionn Morgan to NS, 19/1/2023; **I was enjoying** Ann to IF, 7/2/1956, AF37a, Morgan papers; **Caspar was . . . civil war** Francis Grey to NS; **just another field** Caspar to Angela Bray, n.d., 1969; **caused the maximum** Ann to Clarissa, n.d., Morgan papers; **Dear Cracker** PF to IF, Dec. 1960, Russell Collection, Lilly; **£115 for a 16-bore** Lycett, 449; **with a bundle** Amory, 367; **Caspar was never** Randal Keynes to NS, 7/10/2020; **He knows the** Amory, 264; **too tied up** Louise Allison to NS, 20/9/2022; **How *dare* you** JP note, Lilly, Pearson Collection; **that delinquent Old** Evelyn Waugh and Diana Cooper, *Mr Wu and Mrs Stitch*, 313; **of such unbelievable** David Pryce-Jones, *Evelyn Waugh and his World*, 237; **a very obstreperous** Amory, 158; **rather frail and** ibid., 408; **on dreaded walks** Alexandra Henderson to NS, 12/5/2020; **Undoubtedly, he was** FG to NS, 25/7/2022; **Caspar was bipolar** FM to NS, 5/9/2019; **the best of the 'shrinks'** Amory, 414; **fairly ferocious** Alexander Quennell to NS, 15/11/2019; **Caspar calls me** Ann to Waugh, Sept. 1963, Morgan papers; **Mothers can prove** Harling, 296; **I don't think** ibid., 236; **At heart, he** Rachel Toynbee to NS, 20/9/2022; **She didn't understand** Bamber Gascoigne to NS, 13/1/2020; **I really would** IF to Ann, 1956,

IF45, Morgan papers; **Daddy will** *have The Notes*, 108; **If you take me** ibid., 200; **that Ian 'loved'** Cuneo papers; **He talks about** 6/11/1961, Maud Russell papers; **Caspar is getting** IF to EF, 1/6/1961, Russell Collection, Lilly; **Slightly distant** FG to NS, 25/7/2022; **You seem to** IF to Ann, n.d., IF94a, Morgan papers; **this sudden . . . me with** IF to Ann, 1962, IF30a, Morgan papers; *Darling, I'm sorry* IF to Ann, June 1962, Carr-Ellison papers; **But for my love IF to AF**, July 1962, IF30a, Morgan papers; **Of course, his moment** JC to NS, 23/3/2023; **He was sick** Parker, 291; **TLC** 'Book of Golden Words', IFA; **I am not a lot** BB interview with with JC, 2000, Cork papers; **She could have** JC to NS, 23/3/2023; **exploded in a** *TMWTGT*, 91; **Annie left rather** 15/7/1962, Lady Loelia Lindsay papers; **because Annie wasn't** IF to Phyllis Jackson, 18/7/1962, IFA; **He just gives up** JC to NS, 23/3/2023

LXVII BOND FEVER

I am an insatiable TMWTGT, 300; **a Limey** Broccoli, 177; **Well, all we** Bray, 85; **I don't want** Broccoli, 163; **With us? . . . decision** LD to NS 22/11/2019; **It was dazzling** James Fleming, *Bond Behind the Iron Curtain*, 21–2; **the success and** Broccoli, 142; **a retired . . . best friend** James Fleming, 28–9; **Somewhere a decision** ibid., 32; **Bond and the** ibid., 30; **the ghastly world** BG–W to Richard Hughes, 11/8/1964, Carr-Ellison papers; **I had 65 patent** Rubin interview with Fenn, 1977; **we used to enact . . . away** RA to NS, 10/5/2019; **how a name** John Goodwin to NS, 25/9/2019; **a thoroughly detestable** *TLS*, 8/2/1963; **perhaps the . . . President** *TLS*, 22/2/1963; **Having written** JG to NS, 25/9/2019; **Another member** JG diary, 19/2/1963; **He had this reputation** JG to NS; **He started a** 22/5/1963, Maud Russell papers; **Till the last** AF to Hugo Charteris, Jan. 1963, Morgan papers; **I was similarly** IF to Harling, Feb. 1963, Harling papers; **I was very conscious** FG to NS, 25/7/2022; **the impact of print** John Carter and Percy Muir, *A Descriptive Catalogue Illustrating the Impact of Print on the Evolution of Western Civilization During Five Centuries*, 1967; **for years . . . help** *TMWTGT*, 334; **I was delighted . . . all was** ibid., 349; **pioneering achievement . . . zest** *Book Collector*, Winter 1964, 431; **A THOUSAND** PM to IF, 10/7/1963, IFA; **wonderful exhibition . . . own education** Dr A.M. Massini to Muir, 25/7/1963, James Fleming papers; **What Ian** JF to NS, 4/4/2023; **it was impossible** Barbara Kaye, *Second Impression*, 141; **It was rather** Clarissa to Beaton, 1963, Hugo Vickers papers; **our pornography** Amory, 314; **At present, we** IF to Ann, IF74a, n.d., Morgan papers; **Ian's given many** Ann to PLF, 16/2/1964, Morgan papers; **He has just** 22/5/1963, Maud Russell papers; **I am doing** Amory, 306; **I want to hire** ibid., 308; **She has spent** *Letters of Evelyn Waugh*, 614; **edifice . . . deficiency** ibid., 615; **as among the . . . world** Harling, 329; **canine averse . . . contemptible** Sara Morrison to NS, 26/7/2022; **Shall I call it . . . Oh-Oh-Seven-hampton** Susanna Johnston to NS, 5/6/2020; **It has an** Pearson papers; **The Gloom Book** Morgan papers; **the new Bond** Ann to FM, Morgan papers

John Campbell to NS, 28/7/2022; **So he left . . . was on** JC notes, 3/11/1966, Carr-Ellison papers; **an oddity which** Barry Newton to NS, 30/7/2022; **I play golf** 3/11/1966, Carr-Ellison papers; **the 'James . . . paperbacks** JC to Booker board, 21/2/1964, IFA; **it would look** 3/11/1966, Carr-Ellison papers; **whether Ian was** *The Notes*, 48; **I don't think** MF to NS, 23/4/2021; **I am rather** IF to GB-W, 29/2/1964, Carr-Ellison papers; **advertising . . . risk'** JC to Booker board, 21/2/1964, IFA; **He says to me** Algy Cluff to NS, 16/11/2019; **A lot of his** John Suckling to NS; **to attach more** Ann h/w to John Pearson, VanBlaricum Collection; **The best site . . .** *thee much!* *The Golfer's Manual*, 78; **knew he was** BB, James Bond Transcripts, IFA; **I suspect because . . . show** Charles de Mestral to NS, 19/7/2021; **she didn't want** BB, James Bond Transcripts, IFA; **a sort of Ian shrine** Mary (Pakenham) Clive papers; *One bonus from . . . home* IF to Hilary Bray, Aug. 1963, Bray papers; **And then we** BB, James Bond Transcripts, IFA; **utterly tragic** JHG, 8/3/1965, Godfrey papers; **He would not . . . to do** *Ladies' Home Journal*, Oct. 1966; **a small Messerschmidt** IF to Hilary Bray, 23/4/1964, Bray papers; **I thought . . . stupid book** *TMWTGT*, 369; **Reading voraciously** ibid., 373; **More important than** 'Book of Golden Words', IFA; **was now resigned** BG-W to JHG, 6/7/1964, Godfrey papers; **£1 for every . . . quickly** IF to Hilary Bray, 23/4/1964, Bray papers; **Oh, you've drawn** James Magrane to NS, 10/8/2022; **my consul . . . biles'** EW to IF, 12/7/1964, Russell Collection, Lilly; **Thank God, Sister** IF to Bray, n.d., Bray papers; **found my anxiety** Ann h/w to Pearson, VanBlaricum Collection; **deliciously infantile** IF to Plomer, June 1964, Plomer Collection, Lilly; **You know Bob** *The Notes*, 42; **I write spy** Magrane to NS; **Have booked in** IF to Bray, n.d., Bray papers; **particularly enjoyed** Lewis, *Connolly*, 515; **O Kitzbühler Horn** ibid., 297; **a profound and** R. C. Hutchinson, *Two Men of Letters*, 65; **I saw at once** JHG to Alan Hillgarth, 16/10/1964, Hillgarth papers; **had to carry** Amory, 324; **broncho-pneunomia** EF death certificate, 27/7/1964, IFA; **so very small** 30/7/1964, Valentine Fleming papers; **He had always** *The Notes*, 162; **Operation . . . family** Amory, 349; **Mister Ian** James Fleming to NS; **the dry mauve** Alan Ross, *Coastwise Lights*, 197; **What use is** Lycett, 441; **She was Goldfinger's** JC to NS, 26/3/2023; **When he heard** Bruce, 165; **This frightened . . . or else** Ann to JP, VanBlaricum Collection; **An awful year** *The Notes*, 30; **I had a . . . goodbye** Sara Morrison to NS, 26/7/2022; **The Captain's nomination** Royal St George's Archives, 8/8/1964; **You can learn** Deedes, *Golf Quarterly*; **Old Thunderbird** *TMWTGT*, 344; **However, the nurse** BG-W to JHG, 1/9/1964, Godfrey papers; **Ian's life from** Amory, 349; **As we concluded** Bruce, 165; **I know Ian** PF to JHG, 25/8/1964, Godfrey papers; **He was a** PF to John Carter, 16/8/1964, Eton College Archives; **Ian Fleming died** 12/8/1964, Lady Loelia Lindsay papers; **I did love . . . hotel** Amory 356; **On our birthdays . . . a film** FG to NS, 25/7/2022; **I only really** Elizabeth Fleming to NS; **He was quite**

HB to MB, 30/11/1964, Mary Bond papers, The Free Library of Philadelphia; **rather a snug** PF to Plomer, 25/8/1964, Durham University Archives; **fairly certain that** PF to Plomer, 21/12/1964, ibid; **a thoroughly romantic . . . today** Plomer, *Address*; **I still miss** PF to PM, 4/4/1965, Sandy Malcolm papers

LXX EPILOGUES

It is not as Amory, 358; **it was just** BG-W to JHG, 25/4/1966, Godfrey papers; **of the most** Smith, 142; **engrave for my** IF to WP, 5/5/1961, Plomer Collection, Lilly; **I shall not** *You Only Live Twice*, 203; **I know few** David Randall to Percy Muir, 19/8/1964; Joel Silver, *Book Collector*, Spring 2017; **Goldfinger has hit** *Licence to Thrill*, 91; **By now, the** Pearson papers; **no geographical** *Time*, June 1965; **but they'll read** Peter Janson-Smith, James Bond Transcripts, IFA; **Everyone seems** BG-W to JHG, 23/6/1965, 25/4/1966, Godfrey papers; **Bond is a . . . rest** Barbara Broccoli to NS, 7/7/2022; '**Bond doesn't have** Michael G. Wilson to NS, 7/7/2022; **It was a big** Phoebe Waller-Bridge, BBC R4 'Woman's Hour', 21/2/2020; **he encapsulates** Murray Bail to NS, 23/11/22; **the best recruiting** Moran and McCrisken, 'James Bond, Ian Fleming and Intelligence', *Intelligence and National Security*, vol. 33, No. 6, 2018, 807; **definitely had** Richard Dearlove to NS, 22/6/2021; **years ahead of** <https://www.gov.uk/government/publications/stories-from-the-future-exploring-new-technology-through-useful-fiction/>; **some of our bosses** Defence scientist at Porton Down to NS, 14/3/2023; **asking if he'd** *Ladies' Home Journal*, Oct. 1966; **No one understands** Amory, 372; **At present Caspar's** BG-W to JHG, 13/7/1965, God-frey papers; '**Old Caspar' whose** Ann to PLF, 26/7/1965, Morgan papers; **We'd have shooting** FG to NS, 25/7/2022; **hothouse society** Caspar to Angela Bray, n.d., 1969; **Caspar was a bit** David Coke to NS, 29/1/2021; **When Caspar arrived** Mark Blackett-Ord to NS, 20/9/2022; **who wound up . . . Sten guns** Chris Seidler to NS, 5/6/2019; **a Sten gun** MB-O to NS, 20/9/2022; **crime is the** Caspar to Angela Bray, March 1969, Bray papers; **the world . . . receiver** Amory 392; **I have que dire** Caspar to Angela Bray, March 1969, Bray papers; **the press never** MBO to NS, 20/9/2022; **I was fined** FG to NS, 25/7/2022; **if there is not** Ann to Milton Gendel, 11/4/1969, Montagu papers; **Mark, dear heart** Caspar to MB-O, n.d., Blackett-Ord papers; **A friend I was . . . too young** Louise Allison to NS, 20/9/2022; **The gates into** Lucretia Stewart, unpublished memoir; **Caspar's mad exploits** Rachel Toyn-bee to NS, 20/9/2022; **At Oxford, he** FG to NS, 25/7/2022; **From the moment** MB–O to NS, 20/9/2022; **I can see the** Randal Keynes to NS, 7/10/2020; **On one occasion** Raymond O'Neill to NS, 18/11/2019; **One evening, I opened** LA to NS, 20/9/2022; **Unfortunately, Ann's son** Raymond Carr, *Saga*, April 2005; **I was told** R'ON to NS, 18/11/2019; **It was very, very** RT to NS, 20/9/2022; **If he had** Hume Shawcross to NS, 18/9/2022; **Goldeneye was his** MB–O to NS, 20/9/2022; **She felt** the need JC to NS, 23/3/2023; **It's the first** MB–O to NS, 20/9/2022; **I have been** Ann to Milton Gendel, 4/2/1975, Montagu papers; **Goldeneye tipped him** MB–O to NS, 20/9/2022; **Ann never came** RT to NS, 20/9/2022; **because his body** FM to NS, 19/1/2023; **Caspar's death was** FM to NS, 2/7/2020; **He disappeared into** RO'N to NS, 18/11/2019; **Annie had so** Milton Gendel diary, 4/10/1975, Montagu papers; **I shall miss** Amory, 414; **In the last months** FM to NS, 6/5/2019; Thank you for LA to NS, 20/9/2022; **I organised his** Thomas Heneage to NS, 18/6/2020; **It was too** Chris Blackwell, *The Islander*, 388; **I am always** Violet to Bryce, 28/10/1982, Benson papers; **When it's full** Blackwell, 389; **We had occasion . . . aquavit** DEN/2/4, National Maritime Museum, Greenwich; **The value of** Randall to Muir, 7/5/1965, Silver, *Book Collector*; **Ian Fleming is** *TM WTGT*, 377; **The two authors** Fergus Fleming to NS; **and bought myself** Caroline Ponsonby to NS, 2/9/2021; **Did he really** McCormick to Bryce, 1/1/1975, Bryce papers; **I have scraps** *TM WTGT*, 278; **a cool, well-illustrated** ibid., 366; **a really stimulating** Lycett, 391; **He became very** *The Notes*, 106; **It is one of . . . business** IF synopsis of *The Big Killing* (1963), IFA; **I have wonderful** IF to Ian McKenzie, 20/10/1954, IFA; **I had to go** Thomas Heneage to NS, 18/6/2020

INDEX

Atlantic (ship), 15
atomic bomb, 331, 336, 358
Attlee, Clement, 358, 445
Auden, W. H., xxvi, 46
Australia, 324, 703
Ayer, A. J., 58
Aylen, Jan, 283, 312, 333–6

Bacon, Francis, 536
Bagnold, Enid, 125, 664
Bahamas, 467–8, 596–7
Bail, Murray, 690
Bainbridge, Peggy, 83–4, 88
Balcony House, Nassau, 467, 552,
    594, 596–7
Baldwin, Stanley, 283, 288, 321
Balfour, Arthur, 536n
Ball, Joseph, 188, 195
Bannister, Roger, 67
Baring, Vivian, 416, 418
Baring Brothers, 228
Barjot, Pierre, 238, 526
Barker, Nicolas, 169, 562
Barnes, J., 387
Barnes, Tracy, 580
Barry, John, 643
Barstow, Oliver, 264–5
Bassett, Sam, 216, 398
Batey, Mavis, 213, 293
Battle of Cassel (1940), 236
Battle of the Triangle (1944), 352
Battle of Ypres (1914), 40
Bax, Margaret, 312, 348
Baxter, Edward, 14
Bay of Pigs invasion, 577–80, 620
Bayley, John, 695
BBC (British Broadcasting
    Corporation), 139, 143, 156
Beal, Jack, 172, 523, 613–14, 634,
    665–6, 678
Beano, The, 13
Beatles, 654
Beaton, Cecil, 188, 430, 486, 506–7, 536
Beaverbrook, Lord, see Aitken,
    Maxwell, 1st Baron Beaverbrook
Bedson, Derek, 251

Beesly, Patrick, 228, 240, 329n
Beevor, Jack, 207, 270
Belgium, 241–3
Bellevue House, Jamaica, 362, 364–6
Benedictus, David, 76
Bennett, Gill, 253
Bentley, Walter, 130
Bentley's Complete Phrase Code, 388
Bergson, Henri, 114
Berlin, Germany, 152–7
Berlin, Irving, 272
Berlin, Isaiah, 534, 661–3
Bermuda, 270, 385–6, 624–5
Berry, Gomer, 1st Viscount Kemsley,
    159, 196–7, 235, 360, 491, 614–15
  Fleming and, 372–82
  Kemsley Manual of Journalism,
    The, 413, 448
  moral standards, 410–14, 437–8,
    443, 483
  Reuters and, 517–18
  see also Kemsley Newspapers
Berry, Lionel, 2nd Viscount
    Kemsley, 615
Berry, Michael, 404
Berry, Pamela, 404
Berry, William, 1st Viscount Camrose,
    360, 378
Bertrand, Gustave, 239–40
Besant, Jim, 342
Betjeman, John, xviii, 49, 560, 617
Beverly Hills Hotel, 83
Bierer, Joshua, 97, 107
'Big Killing, The' (ILF; novel
    outline), 703
Birch, Frank, 285
Birch, Nigel, 300
Birds of the West Indies (Bond),
    454, 473
Bishirgian, Garabed, 161
'Black Book', 312, 332, 340, 343
Black Daffodil, The (ILF), 103, 207, 702
Black Hole Hollow, Vermont,
    511–12, 516
Black Mount, Argyllshire, 30–33
black propaganda, 259, 575–6, 579

794

Blackett-Ord, Mark, 692–4, 696–8
Blackwell, Blanche, xxv, 4, 87, 122,
    174–5, 268, 370, 530, 543–9,
    649, 661, 671, 677
  Ann's jealousy, 557, 616, 644
  Ian's death and, 675, 697–8
  importance to Ian, 554–6, 651–2
Blackwell, Chris, 430, 642, 653,
    700–701
Blanshard, Clare, xvi–xvii, xxvi, 304,
    325–6, 388, 426, 483, 485,
    494–5, 519, 523, 587
Blenheim Palace, 200–201
Bletchley Park, Buckinghamshire, xxix,
    205–8, 212–13, 240, 285–6,
    293–4, 312, 456n, 628
Blofeld, Thomas Robert, 59–60
Blunt, Anthony, 404
Bodker, Victor, 155–6
Bogarde, Dirk, 638
Bolt, Jamaica, 547–8, 557, 644
Bolt, Robert, 673
Bond, James (character), xix–xxiii,
    44, 127, 150, 156–7, 200, 278,
    453, 455–6, 703
  '007' code name, 456n
  as a 'dark force', 583–7
  as a role model, 568–70
  Britishness and, xx–xxi,
    496–7, 689–90
  character, 496–500
  chauvinism, 498
  creation of, 445–6
  inspiration for, xxii–xxiii, 249,
    266–7, 453–4, 456–60
  Kitzbühel and, 87
  origin of name, 115–16, 453–4
  Russia and, xx, 446
  Scotland and, 9
  sex/sexuality, 302, 541–2
  strip cartoon, 533, 558
  United States and, xx, 620–21
Bond, James (naturalist), 454, 473–8
Bond, James Charles (SOE agent), 454
Bond, John, 35
Bond, Mary, 473–8, 583

Bond, Rodney, 266–7, 453–4
Bond Behind the Iron Curtain (James
    Fleming), 654
'Bond fever', 655–7, 689
Bond films, xxiii, 588–90,
    622–4, 689–90
  'Casino Royale', 702
  'Dr. No', 581, 637–8, 641–3, 653–4, 665
  'From Russia with Love', xxiii, 580,
    623, 655, 665
  'Goldfinger', 655, 689
  merchandising rights, 655
  'No Time to Die', 689
  theme music, 642–3
  'Thunderball', 516, 638
Bond novels, 445–7, 493–7, 520–21,
    558–9, 655, 690
  bans, 565
  Blofeld (character), 457, 681
  covers, 488, 656
  critics, 560–66
  Delacroix, Monique (character), 122
  details, 498–500, 502–3
  editing, 494–6
  errors and inconsistencies, 502–3
  film rights, 590, 602, 621–3
  heroines, 498
  killing off Bond, 493, 519–20, 551–2,
    583–4, 587, 619
  Leiter, Felix, (character), 340, 466
  'M' (character), 217–18, 221
  Moneypenny (character), 451, 542
  research, 498–9, 509
  Soviet reaction to, 654
  SPECTRE, 240
  spoofs, 564
  TV rights, 590, 601–2, 624–5
  typeface, 487
  US market, 620–21
  see also names of individual novels
Bond Strikes Camp (Connolly), 218,
    404, 541, 564
'Bondmanship' (Potter), 460, 498
Bonham Carter, Mark, 520–21, 662
Boodle's Club, 59–60, 370, 390,
    504, 674

Runyon, Damon, 235
Rushbrooke, Edmund, 217, 292,
  318, 323–4
Russell, Gilbert, 153, 161, 187–9, 191,
  194, 510
Russell, John, 564
Russell, Leonard, 373, 388, 521, 528,
  562, 615–16
Russell, Martin, 326
Russell, Maud, xvii, 28–9, 153, 187–91,
  194, 199–201, 204–7, 235, 294,
  298, 300–302, 308–10, 313,
  357–61, 658
  Ann Fleming and, 425, 431–2, 436, 442
  Goldeneye and, 370–71, 430–32
  NID and, 206, 221, 302, 323, 351
  Raymond and, 28, 303
Russell, Raymond, 28, 303
Russia, 137–50, 194, 275, 333–4,
  358, 393–4, 401–7, 423, 501–2,
  574, 654
Ryan, Cornelius, 274
Ryder, Robert, 289, 450, 493

Sackville-West, Vita, 69, 166
sadism, 540–44
Saint Phalle (stockbrokers), 129
Saltzman, Harry, 585n, 588, 622–5,
  637, 639–40, 643, 653–5
Samuel Montagu & Company, 241
Sandhurst Royal Military Academy,
  Camberley, 80–86
  exams, 74, 80
Sapper see McNeile, H. C.
Sargent, John Singer, 163, 188
Saunders, Joan, xxvii
Sayle, Murray, 402
Scaramanga, G. A. and T. A., 59
Scenes from a Bourgeois Life (Jacob),
  135, 450
Schiaparelli, Elsa, 270–71
Schiff, Jacob, 15
Schlick, Franz 'Graf', 91–2, 102–3
Schneider, Alan, 316
Schneider, Hannes, 479
School of Street Fighting, 281, 292

Scotland, 8–10, 30–32
Scott, Edward, 456n
Scottish American Trust, 14, 24
Sea-Grape Tree, A (Lehmann), 422
Secrétan, Charles, 115
Securities for Investment (company
  newsletter), 165
Seidler, Chris, 693
Seif, Leonard, 107
Selborne, Lord, see Palmer, Roundell,
  3rd Earl of Selborne
Selby, Derek, 394
Serocold, Claude, 162, 195–6
Sevenhampton Place, 5, 301, 477,
  585, 651–2, 660–62, 674, 677,
  682–3, 696
sexual promiscuity, 295–6, 299–302
Seychelles, 511
Seymour, Mary, 461
Shakespeare, Geoffrey, 214
Shakespeare, W. G., 41–2
Shakespeare, William, 559
'Shameful Dream, The' (ILF;
  unfinished), 378–9, 411–13
  Bone, Caffery (character), 411–12
Shamelady Hall, see Goldeneye, Jamaica
Shane's Castle, Ireland, 424, 635
Shaw, M. D., 387
Shawcross, Hume, 697
Shearer, Moira, 484–5
Shelley, Tully, 340
Shevlin, Durie, 572
sibling rivalry, 95–9, 165–6,
  198, 450–52, 572
Sicily, 294
Siepmann, Eric, 380, 389, 391–2, 411
Siepmann, Harry, 391
Siepmann, Phyllis, 391
Sigrist, 'Bobo', 589, 599
Sillick (nanny), 306, 493, 534, 549,
  645, 683, 685, 698
Sim, Pearl, 75–7
Simenon, Georges, 113, 462, 488, 675
Simon, John, 139
Simple Art of Murder, The
  (Chandler), 558

ABOUT THE AUTHOR

NICHOLAS SHAKESPEARE's books have been translated into twenty-two languages. They include *The Vision of Elena Silves*, winner of the Somerset Maugham Award, and *The Dancer Upstairs*, which was made into a film of the same name by John Malkovich and chosen by the American Library Association as the Best Novel of 1997. His nonfiction includes the critically acclaimed authorized biography of Bruce Chatwin, *In Tasmania*, and *Priscilla: The Hidden Life of an Englishwoman in Wartime France*. Shakespeare is married with two sons and lives in Wiltshire.